Families and the Law in Canada

in Canada

Cases and Commentary

MARY JANE MOSSMAN
Osgoode Hall Law School
York University

2004
EMOND MONTGOMERY PUBLICATIONS LIMITED
TORONTO, CANADA

Printed in Canada.

Edited, designed, and typeset by WordsWorth Communications, Toronto.

We acknowledge the financial support of the Government of Canada through the Book Publishing Industry Development Program (BPIDP) for our publishing activities.

Statistics Canada information is used with the permission of the Minister of Industry, as Minister responsible for Statistics Canada. Information on the availability of the wide range of data from Statistics Canada can be obtained from Statistics Canada's Regional Offices, its World Wide Web site at http://www.statcan.ca/, and its toll-free access number 1-800-263-1136.

Library and Archives Canada Cataloguing in Publication

Mossman, Mary Jane
   Families and the law in Canada : cases and commentary / Mary Jane Mossman.

ISBN 1-55239-083-7

   1. Domestic relations — Canada — Cases — Textbooks.   2. Domestic relations — Ontario — Cases — Textbooks.   I. Title.

KE538.5.M68 2004   346.7101′5   C2004-904779-5
KF505.ZA2M68 2004

For my students

Preface

This book provides an introduction to family law principles and critical reflections about them. In the past few decades in Canada, families and ideas about families have changed, often rapidly and quite dramatically; and family law has been the focus of reform initiatives in both the legislatures and the courts. In this context, family law teachers have faced significant challenges in presenting law school courses, and some of us have experienced difficulty in "keeping up" with the pace of change in family law and the need to guide students effectively in the family law context. In addition, the explosion of scholarly interest in families seems to require us to examine fundamental concepts about families in law in a comparative and critical context.

Over a number of years, I have been grappling with these challenges in annual revisions of my course materials and in thinking about family law within the overall law school curriculum. As this book demonstrates, I have increasingly focused on "families and the law" and the legal problems arising out of familial relationships. This approach is somewhat broader in scope than the law's traditional focus on "marriage and divorce," and even earlier approaches to "matrimonial causes." Yet, such a broader scope appears necessary to take account of legal recognition of relationships of cohabitation as well as marriage, both of which include opposite-sex and same-sex partners. In addition, this broader approach encourages exploration of legal principles concerning parent-child relationships, not just in relation to decisions about custody at divorce, but also in other contexts such as adoption, which offer excellent opportunities to examine fundamental assumptions about families and law.

In exploring families and the law in this way, moreover, I found it helpful to compare approaches to family law issues in different provinces across Canada. Although this book clearly does not purport to offer a comprehensive analysis of family law principles in all the provinces, it does examine different approaches to a variety of legal issues affecting families, particularly where there are useful comparisons of approach and interpretation in different parts of the country. Although much of family law in Canada remains the subject of provincial legislation, some federal initiatives have tended to increase the degree of uniformity across the country, especially in common law provinces but sometimes including civil law Quebec as well. Clearly, the laws of marriage and divorce are federal as a matter of the constitutional division of powers. In addition, however, the collaboration of the federal, provincial, and territorial governments to create child-support guidelines in relation to divorce and separation has encouraged more uniformity across Canada on these issues. Similarly, the Supreme Court's decisions on spousal support during the past two decades have arguably contributed to greater uniformity, even though there remains a lively debate about the appropriateness of the court's jurisprudence. Current reforms concerning reproductive technology and proposed reforms in relation to custody and access principles may similarly contribute to this trend to a "national" family law in Canada. Indeed, even in areas that are clearly within provincial jurisdiction, such as child protection, recent Supreme Court decisions have identified basic standards for state intervention in families. In such a context, while the primary focus of this book is Ontario, I have found it intriguing to consider national perspectives on family law matters, comparing initiatives and patterns in different provincial and territorial contexts.

Patterns of family law principles across Canada also suggest a need to rethink the fundamental approaches of family law. For example, new definitions of "families" have been recognized in Charter jurisprudence about same-sex couples, and the Charter has been applied in a number of other areas of family law as well. Clearly, assisted reproduction technologies have challenged traditional legal definitions of "parents" and "children." More subtly perhaps, legislative provisions and judicial decisions have engaged in redefining "families" to include the members of *former* families after divorce or separation—"the post-divorce families." All these developments have important consequences for families and governments in terms of their respective responsibilities for the economic dependency of individual family members—children, the disabled or unemployed, and poor elderly persons; in this way, family law principles are linked to important issues of public policy in Canada and elsewhere. Moreover, new developments in methods of dispute resolution have effected major changes in the practice of family law, at least for some clients, while issues about legal aid services have created serious problems with respect to legal representation for others. Although these developments may appear to affect practitioners primarily, they may also be factors in determining which issues reach the courts and how definitive legal principles are fashioned in specific factual contexts. In addition, issues about race, religion, ethnicity, and class, particularly in the context of family law problems, may shape the definition of legal issues and judicial responses to them.

In exploring these fundamental concerns about families and the law, this book examines legislative principles and judicial decisions, as well as some of the rich comparative and critical writing about family law. Particularly in assessing current patterns and proposed reforms, this comparative and critical material offers important insights that may assist students to understand the legal issues in a broader social, economic, and political context. The book makes references to relevant federal and provincial legislation, with a particular focus on Ontario, but it does not always include excerpts from legislative provisions; accordingly, it will be necessary for students to use a compilation of federal and provincial legislation in conjunction with this book (taking account of specific provincial jurisdictions). In addition, this book is intended to provide a basic introduction to issues about families and the law, and some (more) complex matters are not examined in detail; however, references to additional cases and materials throughout the book will assist those who wish to pursue these issues in more detail. Primarily, however, the book is intended to provide a critical introduction to issues about families and the law, using an Ontario focus but with references to other jurisdictions in Canada and elsewhere for comparisons of approach and interpretation.

This book has been a long time in the making. In my work as a family law teacher, I acknowledge the inspiration of colleagues and students at Osgoode and elsewhere who have shared their materials and ideas with me, and especially the good discussions about families and family policies with my colleague Jerry Ginsburg. Osgoode Hall Law School has supported this project in many ways, including the provision of annual funding for research assistance. In addition, the Foundation for Legal Research provided funding in 2002, support that was especially helpful in moving the project forward at an important point. Osgoode reference librarians and library staff have, as always, been helpful, patient and cheerful, especially in locating elusive materials. Several excellent research assistants made it possible to complete this project: Cindy L. Baldassi in 2003, and Leanna Bayliss, Wendy Greyling, Jonathan Hood, and Mary Paterson in 2004. At an earlier point, Onofrio Ferlisi, Jessica Ginsburg, and Karen Wenckebach provided research on particular aspects of the project; and I also want to acknowledge the inspiration and contributions of many students and research assistants in past years. Hazel Pollack at Osgoode, who coped with the preparation of the manuscript with her usual skill and good humour, made an inestimable contribution, and Nancy Ennis and other staff at Emond Montgomery remained calm and patient, as well as encouraging, as this project moved (much too slowly) to completion. Finally, it is necessary in this project more than in any others to thank my families, and especially Brian Bucknall.

Mary Jane Mossman
Toronto, June 2004

Acknowledgments

This book, like others of its nature, contains extracts from published materials. We have attempted to request permission from, and to acknowledge in the text, all sources of such material. We wish to make specific references here to the authors, publishers, journals, and institutions that have been generous in giving permission to reproduce in this text works already in print. If we have inadvertently overlooked an acknowledgment or failed to secure a permission, we offer our sincere apologies and undertake to rectify the omission in the next edition.

Alberta Law Review   Laura Shanner, "Pregnancy Intervention and Models of Maternal–Fetal Relationship: Philosophical Reflections in the Winnipeg CFS Dissent" (1998), 36:3 *Alberta Law Review* 751, at 764. Reprinted by permission.

Aspen Publishers Inc.   Pauline H. Tesler, "Collaborative Law: What It Is and Why Family Law Attorneys Need To Know About It" (1999), 13 *American Journal of Family Law* 215, at 216, 219. Reprinted by permission.

Martha Bailey   Martha Bailey, "Custody, Access and Religion: Comment on Young v. Young and D.P. v C.S." (1994), 11 *Canadian Family Law Quarterly* 317.

Martha Bailey and Nicholas Bala   Martha Bailey and Nicholas Bala, *Assessing Compliance with the UN Convention on the Rights of the Child* (unpublished presentation to CALT Family Section), 1988.

Patricia A. Baird   Patricia A. Baird, "Reproductive Technology and the Evolution of Family Law" (1997-98), 15 *Canadian Family Law Quarterly* 103, at 113.

Rhonda Bessner   Rhonda Bessner, "The Duty To Report Child Abuse" (2000), 17 *Canadian Family Law Quarterly* 278.

Blackwell Publishing Ltd.   Susan B. Boyd, "Legal Regulation of Families in Changing Societies," in Austin Sarat, ed., *The Blackwell Companion to Law and Society* (Oxford: Blackwell Publishing Ltd., 2004), 255, at 265.

Blackwell Publishing Ltd.   John Dewar, "The Normal Chaos of Family Law" (1998), 61 *Modern Law Review* 467, at 467-8, 470, 484.

Blackwell Publishing Ltd.   Katherine O'Donovan, "Legal Marriage—Who Needs It?" (1984), 47 *Modern Law Review* 111, at 116.

Blackwell Publishing Ltd.   Katherine O'Donovan, "Should All Maintenance of Spouses Be Abolished?" (1982), 45 *Modern Law Review* 424, at 430.

Blackwell Publishing Ltd.   Austin Sarat and William F. Felstiner, "Law and Social Relations: Vocabularies of Motive in Lawyer/Client Interaction" (1988), 22:4 *Law & Society Review* 737, at 764.

Blackwell Publishing Ltd.   Pamela Symes, "Property, Power and Dependence: Critical Family Law" (1987), 14 *Journal of Law and Society Review* 199, at 202-4, 206-7.

Susan B. Boyd   Susan B. Boyd, "Potentialities and Perils of the Primary Caregiver Presumption" (1990-91), 7 *Canadian Family Law Quarterly* 1, at 28.

Susan B. Boyd   Susan B. Boyd, "Teaching Policy Issues in Family Law" (1989-90), 8 *Canadian Journal of Family Law* 11, at 13-15.

Cambridge University Press   Carol Smart, "Wishful Thinking and Harmful Tinkering? Sociological Reflections on Family Policy" (1997), 26 *Journal of Social Policy* 301, at 301-21. Reprinted with the permission of Cambridge University Press.

Canadian Bar Association   Canadian Bar Association Task Force, *Touchstones for Change: Equality, Diversity and Accountability* (Ottawa: Canadian Bar Association, 1993), at 204. Reprinted by permission.

Canadian Community Law Journal   David Thompson, "A Consideration of the Mental Capacity Provisions of the Marriage Act in View of the Charter of Rights and Freedoms and Webb v. Webb" (1986), 9 *Canadian Community Law Journal* 101, at 106.

Canadian Journal of Law and Society   Shelley Gavigan, "Legal Forms, Family Forms, Gendered Norms: What Is a Spouse?" (1999), 14:1 *Canadian Journal of Law and Society* 127, at 156.

Canadian Journal of Law and Society   Paul Millar and Anne Gauthier, "What Were They Thinking? The Development of Child Support Guidelines in Canada" (2002), 17:1 *Canadian Journal of Law and Society* 139, at 157-58.

Canadian Journal of Women & the Law   Susan B. Boyd, "Child Custody, Relocation and the Post-Divorce Family Unit: Goertz v. Gordon at the Supreme Court of Canada" (1997), 9:2 *Canadian Journal of Women & the Law* 457.

Canadian Journal of Women & the Law   Jane Gordon, "Multiple Meanings Equality: A Case in Custody Litigation" (1989), 3 *Canadian Journal of Women and the Law* 256.

Canadian Journal of Women & the Law   Elizabeth Grace and Susan Vella, "Vesting Mothers with Power They Do Not Have: The Non-Offending Parent in Civil Sexual Assault Cases" (1994), 7:1 *Canadian Journal of Women and the Law* 184, at 186.

Canadian Journal of Women & the Law   Hester Lessard, "Mothers, Fathers and Naming: Reflections on the Law Equality Framework and Trociuk v. BC (Attorney General)" (2004), 16:1 *Canadian Journal of Women and the Law* 37-39.

Canadian Journal of Women & the Law   Margaret McCallum, "Caratun v. Caratun: It Seems That We Are Not All Realists Yet" (1994), 7 *Canadian Journal of Women and the Law* 197, at 206-7.

Canadian Review of Sociology and Anthropology   Ross Finnie, "Women, Men and the Economic Consequences of Divorce: Evidence from Canadian Longitudinal Data" (1993), 30:2 *Canadian Review of Sociology and Anthropology* 205, at 229.

Carswell   B. Hovius and T.G. Youdan, *The Law of Family Property* (Scarborough, ON: Carswell, 1991), 315, 574-75. Reprinted by permission of Carswell, a division of Thomson Canada Limited.

Carswell   Diana Majury, "Annotation of B v. A" (1990), 29 *R.F.L.* (3d), at 258. Reprinted by permission of Carswell, a division of Thomson Canada Limited.

Carswell   James G. McLeod, "Annotation to Chartier v. Chartier" (1998), 43 *R.F.L.* (4th) 1, at 3. Reprinted by permission of Carswell, a division of Thomson Canada Limited.

Carswell   James G. McLeod, "Annotation to Futia v. Futia" (1990), 27 *R.F.L.* (3d) 81, at 81-82. Reprinted by permission of Carswell, a division of Thomson Canada Limited.

Carswell   James G. McLeod, "Annotation to Nowell v. Town Estate" (1997), 30 *R.F.L.* (4th) 107, at 108-13. Reprinted by permission of Carswell, a division of Thomson Canada Limited.

Carswell   James G. McLeod, "Annotation to Shute v. Premier Trust Co." (1993), 50 *R.F.L.* (3d) 441, at 443-46. Reprinted by permission of Carswell, a division of Thomson Canada Limited.

Carswell   James G. McLeod, "Annotation to Sullivan v. Sullivan" (1999), 50 *R.F.L.* (4th) 326, at 326-28. Reprinted by permission of Carswell, a division of Thomson Canada Limited.

Carswell   James G. McLeod, "Case Comment: Moge v. Moge" (1993), 43 *R.F.L.* (3d) 455-64, at 459. Reprinted by permission of Carswell, a division of Thomson Canada Limited.

Carswell   Marcia Neave, "Three Approaches to Family Property Disputes: Intention/ Belief, Unjust Enrichment and Unconscionability," in T.G. Youdan, ed., *Equity, Fiduciaries and Trusts* (Scarborough, ON: Carswell, 1989), 247, at 251. Reprinted by permission of Carswell, a division of Thomson Canada Limited.

Brenda Cossman and Bruce Ryder   Brenda Cossman and Bruce Ryder, "What Is Marriage-Like Like? The Irrelevance of Conjugality" (2001), 18 *Canadian Journal of Family Law* 271, at 279-80, 296-97, 326.

Susan Crean   Susan Crean, *In the Name of the Fathers: The Story Behind Child Custody* (Toronto: Amanita Publications, 1988). Reprinted by permission.

Christine Davies   Christine Davies, "The Ever-Changing Picture of Support and Other Developments" (2002-3), 20 *Canadian Family Law Quarterly*, 213 at 233.

Ruth Deech   Ruth Deech, "The Case Against Legal Recognition of Cohabitation," in John Eekelaar and Sanford Katz, eds., *Marriage & Cohabitation in Contemporary Societies: Areas of Legal, Social and Ethical Change* (Toronto: Butterworths, 1980), 300, at 301-3.

Margrit Eichler   Margrit Eichler, "The Limits of Family Law Reform" (1990-91), 7 *Canadian Family Law Quarterly* 59, at 66-69, 81-83.

Stephen Grant   Stephen Grant, "Deductions Under the Family Law Act: The Sequel" (1990), 6 *Canadian Family Law Quarterly* 257, at 258.

Guilford Press   R. Emery, *Renegotiating Family Relationships: Divorce, Child Custody and Mediation* (New York: Guilford Press, 1994), 12-13.

Guilford Press   G. Kitson, with W. Holmes, *Portrait of Divorce: Adjustment to Marital Breakdown* (New York: Guilford Press, 1992), 3-4, 14-15.

H.R. Hahlo   H.R. Hahlo, *Nullity of Marriage in Canada* (Toronto: Butterworths, 1979), 1, at 1-2, 32.

Hart Publishing Ltd.   John Eekelaar, "Uncovering Social Obligations: Family Law and the Responsible Citizen," in Mavis Maclean, ed., *Making Law for Families* (Oxford and Portland, OR: Hart Publishing Ltd., 2000), 9, at 16.

Hart Publishing Ltd.   Mavis Maclean, "Introduction," in Mavis Maclean, ed., *Making Law for Families* (Oxford and Portland, OR: Hart Publishing Ltd., 2000), 1-2.

Harvard University Press   Eleanor Maccoby and Robert Mnookin, *Dividing the Child* (Cambridge, MA: Harvard University Press, 1992), 266.

Winifred Holland   Winifred Holland, "Intimate Relationships in the New Millennium: The Assimilation of Marriage and Cohabitation" (2000), 17 *Canadian Journal of Family Law* 114, at 151.

Irwin Law, Inc.   Simon Fodden, *Family Law* (Toronto: Irwin Law, Inc., 1999). Reprinted by permission of the publisher.

Kluwer Academic Publishers   Hilary Lim, "Messages from a Rarely Visited Island: Duress and Lack of Consent in Marriage" (1996), 4:2 *Feminist Legal Studies* 195, at 216-17, 219. Reprinted with kind permission from Springer Science and Business Media.

Law Society Gazette   A. Leonoff, "Joint Custody and Beyond" (1995), 29:1 *Law Society Gazette* 29, at 35-37.

Law Society of Upper Canada   Nicholas Bala, "The Best Interests of the Child in the Post-Modern Era," in Harold Niman and Gerald P. Sadvari, eds., *Family Law: Best Interests of the Child* (Toronto: Law Society of Upper Canada, 2001), 1, at 1-5.

LexisNexis   American Law Institute, *Principles of the Law of Family Dissolution: Analysts and Recommendations* (Washington, DC: Matthew Bender & Co., Ltd., 2002), 1, at 23-25, 95-96, 789.

John Lowman   John Lowman, "Child Saving, Legal Panaceas, and the Individualization of Family Problems: Some Comments on the Findings and Recommendations of the Badgley Report" (1985), 4 *Canadian Journal of Family Law* 508, at 511-12.

Lene Madsen   Lene Madsen, "Citizen, Worker, Mother: Canadian Women's Claims to Parental Leave and Childcare" (2002), 19 *Canadian Journal of Family Law* 11, at 53.

Diana Majury   Diana Majury, "Unconscionability in an Equality Context" (1991), 7 *Canadian Family Law Quarterly* 123.

Manitoba Law Reform Commission   *Report on Adult Protection and Elder Abuse* (Winnipeg: Manitoba Law Reform Commission, 1999), 2.

Anne McGillivray   Anne McGillivray, "Transracial Adoption and the Status Indian Child" (1985), 4 *Canadian Journal of Family Law* 437, at 449-50.

Mary Jane Mossman   Mary Jane Mossman, "'Running Hard To Stand Still': The Paradox of Family Law Reform" (1994), 17 *Dalhousie Law Journal* 5, at 24.

Robert Mnookin   Robert Mnookin, "Divorce Bargaining: The Limits on Private Ordering," in J.M. Eekelaar and S.N. Katz, eds., *The Resolution of Family Conflict: Comparative Legal Perspectives* (Toronto: Butterworths, 1984), 364.

Nelson Thomson Learning   Tania das Gupta, "Families of Native People, Immigrants and People of Colour," in N. Mandell and A. Duffy, eds., *Canadian Families: Diversity, Conflict, and Change*, 2d ed. (Toronto: Nelson Thomson Learning, 2000), 146, at 150.

Nelson Thomson Learning   Carol O'Brien and Aviva Goldberg, "Lesbians & Gay Men Inside and Outside Families," in N. Mandell and A. Duffy, eds., *Canadian Families: Diversity, Conflict, and Change*, 2d ed. (Toronto: Nelson Thomson Learning, 2000), 115, at 128, 133.

Ontario Law Reform Commission   *Report on Family Property Law* (Toronto: Queen's Printer for Ontario, 1993). Reprinted with permission.

Ontario Law Reform Commission   *Report on Human Artificial Reproduction and Related Matters* (Toronto: Queen's Printer for Ontario, 1985), 233-34. Reprinted with permission.

Ontario Law Reform Commission   *Report on Pensions as Family Property: Valuation and Division* (Toronto: Queen's Printer for Ontario, 1995). Reprinted with permission.

Ontario Legal Aid Review   Brenda Cossman and Carol Rogerson, "Case Study in the Provision of Legal Aid: Family Law," in *Report of the Ontario Legal Aid Review: A Blueprint for Publicly Funded Legal Services* (Toronto: Queen's Printer for Ontario, 1997), Volume 3, 773, at 785. Reprinted with permission.

Osgoode Hall Law Journal   Brenda Cossman, "Lesbians, Gay Men and the Canadian Charter of Rights and Freedoms" (2002), 40 *Osgoode Hall Law Journal* 233, at 247.

Oxford University Press   Susan B. Boyd, *Child Custody, Law and Women's Work* (Don Mills, ON: Oxford University Press Canada, 2003). Reprinted by permission of the publisher.

Oxford University Press   John Dewar, "Family Law and Theory" (1996), 16 *Oxford Journal of Legal Studies* 725. Reprinted by permission of Oxford University Press.

Oxford University Press   Sarah Wilson, "Identity, Genealogy and the Social Family: The Case of Donor Insemination" (1997), 11 *International Journal of Law, Policy and the Family* 270, at 281-82. Reprinted by permission of Oxford University Press.

Pluto Press   Katherine O'Donovan, *Family Law Matters* (London: Pluto Press, 1993), 18-20, 106.

Polity Press   Carol Smart, Bren Neale, and Amanda Wade, *The Changing Experience of Childhood: Families and Divorce* (Cambridge: Polity Press, 2001), 19, 69, 167, 173, 121-22. Used by permission of the publisher.

Public Works and Government Services Canada   Martha Bailey and Michelle Giroux, *Relocation of Custodial Parents* (Ottawa: Status of Women Canada, 1998). Her Majesty the Queen in Right of Canada. All rights reserved. ISBN 0-662-63445-5, Catalogue No.: SW21-25/1998. Reproduced with the permission of the Minister of Public Works and Government Services Canada, 2004.

Public Works and Government Services Canada   Law Commission of Canada, *Beyond Conjugality: Recognizing and Supporting Close Personal Relationships*, at xi-xvi. http://www.lcc.gc.ca/en/themes/pr/cpra/cpra_main.asp, Law Commission of Canada, Her Majesty the Queen in Right of Canada. Reproduced with the permission of the Minister of Public Works and Government Services Canada, 2004.

Public Works and Government Services Canada   Linda MacLeod, *Battered But Not Beaten ... Preventing Wife Battering in Canada* (Ottawa: Status of Women Canada, 1987), at 88-90. Her Majesty the Queen in Right of Canada. All rights reserved. ISBN 0-662-94289-2, Catalogue No.: LW31-27/1987E. Reproduced with the permission of the Minister of Public Works and Government Services Canada, 2004.

Public Works and Government Services Canada   Special Joint Committee on Child Custody and Access, *For the Sake of the Children* (Ottawa: Parliament of Canada, 1998), Her Majesty the Queen in Right of Canada. Reproduced with the permission of the Minister of Public Works and Government Services Canada, 2004.

Helen Rhoades   Helen Rhoades, "The Rise and Rise of Shared Parenting Laws: A Critical Reflection" (2002), 75 *Canadian Journal of Family Law* 75, at 90-91, 107.

Carol Rogerson   Carol Rogerson, "The Child Support Obligations of Step-Parents" (2001), 18:1 *Canadian Journal of Family Law* 9, at 152-53.

Carol Rogerson   Carol Rogerson, "Child Support Under the Guidelines of Cases of Split and Shared Custody" (1998), 15 *Canadian Journal of Family Law* 11, at 15, 94.

Carol Rogerson   Carol Rogerson, *Developing Spousal Support Guidelines in Canada: Beginning the Discussion* (Background Paper) (Ottawa: Department of Justice, 2002).

Carol J. Rogerson   Carol J. Rogerson, "The Causal Connection Test in Spousal Support Law" (1989), 8 *Canadian Journal of Family Law* 95, at 105, 106-18.

Carol J. Rogerson   Carol J. Rogerson, "Judicial Interpretation of the Spousal and Child Support Provisions of the Divorce Act, 1985" (1992), 7 *Canadian Family Law Quarterly* 155, at 161-63.

Carol J. Rogerson   Carol J. Rogerson, "Judicial Interpretation of the Spousal and Child Support Provisions of the Divorce Act, 1985 (Part II)" (1991), 7 *Canadian Family Law Quarterly* 271, at 274.

Carol J. Rogerson   Carol J. Rogerson, "Spousal Support After Moge" (1997), 14 *Canadian Family Law Quarterly* 281, at 385.

Carol J. Rogerson   Carol J. Rogerson, "Spousal Support Post-Bracklow: The Pendulum Swings Again?" (2001), 19 *Canadian Family Law Quarterly* 185.

D.A. Rollie Thompson   D.A. Rollie Thompson, "Who Wants To Avoid the Guidelines? Contracting Out and Around" (2001), 19 *Canadian Family Law Quarterly* 1, at 2-3, 20.

Routledge/Taylor & Francis Books, Inc.   Susan B. Boyd, "From Gender Specificity to Gender Neutrality: Ideologies in Canadian Child Custody Law," in Carol Smart and Selma Sevenhuijsen, eds., *Child Custody and the Politics of Gender* (London: Routledge/Taylor & Francis Books, Inc., 1989), at 126, 149-52. Reproduced by permission of Routledge and Kegan Paul/Taylor & Francis Books, Inc.

Routledge/Taylor & Francis Books, Inc.   Martha Fineman, *The Neutered Mother, the Sexual Family and Other Twentieth Century Tragedies* (New York: Routledge/Taylor & Francis Books, Inc., 1995), at 3, 5-6. Reproduced by permission of Routledge/ Taylor & Francis Books, Inc.

Routledge and Kegan Paul/Taylor & Francis Books, Inc.   Carol Smart, *The Ties That Bind: Law, Marriage and the Reproduction of Patriarchal Relations* (London: Routledge and Kegan Paul/Taylor & Francis Books, Inc., 1984), at 190-91. Reproduced by permission of Routledge and Kegan Paul/Taylor & Francis Books, Inc.

Sage Publications Ltd.   Carol Smart, "The 'New' Parenthood: Fathers and Mothers After Divorce," in Elizabeth Silva and Carol Smart, eds., *The New Family?* (London: Sage Publications Ltd., 1998), 100, at 113. Reprinted by permission of Sage Publications Ltd.

Sage Publications Ltd.   Carol Smart, "The 'New' Practices and Politics of Family Life," in Elizabeth Silva and Carol Smart, eds., *The New Family?* (London: Sage Publications Ltd., 1998), 1, at 9. Reprinted by permission of Sage Publications Ltd.

Saskatchewan Law Review   Julien D. Payne, "An Overview of Theory and Reality in the Judicial Disposition of Spousal Support Claims Under the Canadian Divorce Act" (2000), 63:2 *Saskatchewan Law Review* 403.

Martha Shaffer and Carol J. Rogerson   Martha Shaffer and Carol J. Rogerson, "Contracting Spousal Support: Thinking Through Miglin" (2003-4), 21 *Canadian Family Law Quarterly* 49, at 100.

Andrew Sheppard   Andrew Sheppard, "Rawluk v. Rawluk: What Are the Limits of the Remedial Constructive Trust?" (1990), 9 *Canadian Journal of Family Law* 152, at 161.

Colleen Sheppard   Colleen Sheppard, "Uncomfortable Victories and Unanswered Questions: Lessons from Moge" (1995), 12 *Canadian Journal of Family Law* 284, at 328.

Statistics Canada   "Distribution and Trend of Family Expenditures," adapted from the Statistics Canada publication *Family Expenditure in Canada,* 1996, catalogue no. 62-555, July 28, 1998.

Statistics Canada   "Statistics About Families in Canada," adapted from the Statistics Canada publication *Income of Canadian Families, Analysis series, 2001 Census*, catalogue no. 96F0030, May 13, 2003, pages 7-11.

John Syrtash   John Syrtash, *Religion and Culture in Canadian Family Law* (Toronto: Butterworths, 1992), 161. Reprinted by permission.

Thompson Educational Publishing, Inc.   James P. Felstiner, "Child Welfare Hearings from an Unfamiliar Perspective," in Joseph Hornick, Nicholas Bala, and Robin Vogl, eds., *Canadian Child Welfare Law: Children, Families and the State,* 1st ed. (Toronto: Thompson Educational Publishing, Inc., 1999).

George Thomson   George Thomson, "Judging Judiciously in Child Protection Cases," in Rosalie Abella and Claire L. Heureux-Dubé, eds., *Dimensions of Justice* (Toronto: Butterworths, 1983), 213.

Margaret Thornton   Hilary Astor, "The Weight of Silence: Talking About Violence in Family Mediation," in Margaret Thornton, ed., *Public and Private: Feminist Legal Debates* (Melbourne: Oxford University Press, 1995), 174 , at 184.

Tulane University Law School   Cheryl Meyer, "Legal, Psychological and Medical Considerations in Lesbian Parenting" (1992), 2 *Law & Sexuality* 237, at 239-41.

University of Michigan Press   June Carbone, "Child Support Comes of Age: An Introduction to the Law of Child Support," in J. Thomas Oldham and Marygold S. Melli, eds., *Child Support: The Next Frontier* (Ann Arbor, MI: University of Michigan Press, 2000), 3, at 11.

University of Toronto Press Inc.   M. J. Mossman and M. MacLean, "Family Law and Social Assistance Programs: Rethinking Equality," in P.M. Evans and G.R. Wekerie, eds., *Women and the Canadian Welfare State* (Toronto: University of Toronto Press Inc., 1997), 117. Reprinted by permission of University of Toronto Press Inc.

University of Toronto Press Inc.   Marcia Neave, "Resolving the Dilemma of Difference: A Critique of the Role of Private Ordering in Family Law" (1994), 44 *University of Toronto Law Journal* 97, at 105, 123-26. Reprinted by permission of University of Toronto Press Inc. (htpp://www.utpjournals.com/).

University of Windsor Faculty of Law   Shauna van Praagh, "Faith, Belonging and the Protection of Our Children" (1999), 17 *Windsor Yearbook of Access to Justice* 155.

Vanier Institute of the Family   Maureen Baker, "Thinking About Families: Trends and Policies," in Maureen Baker, ed., *Canada's Changing Families: Challenges to Public Policy* (Ottawa: Vanier Institute of the Family, 1994), 3-4.

Vanier Institute of the Family   *Profiling Canada's Families II* (Ottawa: Vanier Institute of the Family, 2000), iv-v.

Vanier Institute of the Family   Rix Rogers, "The Anguish of Child Abuse—Is Prevention Possible?" in *Transition* (Ottawa: Vanier Institute of the Family, 1995), 9.

Vanier Institute of the Family   Roger Sauvé, "Trends in Canadian Family Finances," in *Transition* (Ottawa: Vanier Institute of the Family, 1999), 10, at 13.

Jeffrey Wilson and Mary Tomlinson   Jeffrey Wilson and Mary Tomlinson, *Children and the Law*, 2d ed. (Toronto: Butterworths, 1986).

Faye L. Woodman   Faye L. Woodman, "Tax Aspects of the New Child Support Guidelines: One Year Later" (1998), 15 *Canadian Journal of Family Law* 221, at 226.

Zheng Wu   Zheng Wu, *Cohabitation: An Alternative Form of Family Living* (Toronto: Oxford University Press, 2000), at 154.

Yale University Press   Deborah Rhode and Martha Minow, "Reforming the Questions: Questioning the Reforms," in S.D. Sugarman and H.H. Kay, eds., *Divorce Reform at the Crossroads* (New Haven, CT: Yale University Press, 1990), 191, at 209, 210.

Bruce Ziff   Bruce Ziff, "Recent Developments in Canadian Law: Marriage and Divorce" (1986), 18 *Ottawa Law Review* 121, at 135-36, 140.

Summary Table of Contents

Detailed Table of Contents

Table of Cases

A page number in boldface type indicates that the text of the case or a portion thereof is reproduced. A page number in lightface type indicates that the case is merely quoted briefly or discussed. Cases mentioned within excerpts and footnotes are not listed.

CHAPTER ONE

Families and Family Law: Contexts and Themes

I. INTRODUCTION

Diversity, plurality, and individuality distinguish [Canadian] families of the 1990s. Today, multiple forms and structures—dual earner, never married, reconstituted, cohabiting, gay and lesbian—co-exist with more traditional units, making it almost impossible to talk about "the" family. Definitions of what constitutes a family have enlarged, focussing more on what families do than on what they look like. These more expansive family definitions reflect the experience of individuals and their intimate relationships, and acknowledge that families evolve and change.

> Nancy Mandell and Ann Duffy, eds.,
> *Canadian Families: Diversity, Conflict and Change*,
> 2d ed. (Toronto: Harcourt Canada, 2000), 1

Once upon a time, things were easy for family lawyers. Their object of study was clearly marked out (marriage, divorce and their consequences), while theoretical debate about the subject was rare or non-existent. Although it is difficult to locate this Garden of Eden in real time, most family lawyers would share the perception that things have become more complex of late. For one thing, it is no longer obvious where the boundaries of the subject lie. Recent events have shown that marriage is only one of a number of legally significant concepts implicated in the legal regulation of family life, with parenthood and cohabitation increasingly presenting themselves as alternatives. There has been a move away from exploring exclusively the role of law when "things go wrong" (divorce, for example) towards an interest in how law regulates the ongoing family. In addition, and allied to this, there has been an explosion of theoretical interest in law and the family.

> John Dewar, "Family, Law and Theory"
> (1996), 16 *Oxford Journal of Legal Studies* 725

These comments about families and family law emphasize how both are changing in complex ways. As the first comment suggests, definitions of families have increasingly focused on what families do rather than on what they look like, an approach that emphasizes the *functions* rather than the *form* of families. The second comment similarly identifies how family law has been expanding to take account of families defined by cohabitation or parenthood, in addition to those defined by traditional marriage; and to explore more complex relationships between law and families, for both intact and disintegrating units. Such an approach means that defining the "boundaries of the subject" of family law presents new challenges.

At the same time, issues about families and family law have become more visible during the past few decades, both in the work of legislatures across Canada and in decisions of the courts. For example, there have been new challenges to definitions of family in relation to the validity of same-sex marriage and entitlements to spousal benefits for same-sex cohabitees; and in the need to recognize parenthood in a variety of new situations involving assisted reproduction as well as adoption. There have also been challenges to traditional ideas about family responsibilities, including the amount of financial support owed to children after separation or divorce (and the respective responsibilities of biological and social parents for providing this support); and the appropriate basis for determining entitlement to spousal support at the end of an intimate relationship. Similarly, relationships between private families and the public sphere have been challenged by legal claims that require courts to balance individual autonomy with the need to protect vulnerable family members (particularly in the context of violence and abuse) in family decision making. Moreover, because governmental policies about immigration, taxation, and social security, for example, increasingly intersect with social expectations about families and their legal obligations, the nature and scope of family law present important challenges.

In providing an introduction to families and family law, this chapter begins with an overview of the contexts for families in Canada. At the outset, it presents some current demographic information about families in Canada as a way of exploring the concrete contexts of family lives, contexts that are both fluctuating and, paradoxically, also enduring. In addition, because family law principles often reflect the need for financial support, this material includes basic information about the current economic circumstances of Canadian families. In examining this information, it is important to explore how governmental and social policies, either explicitly or implicitly, may support or constrain the formation of families and the enjoyment of family relationships. Both historical and more recent examples reveal the complexity of relationships between families and law, with family law sometimes reflecting the social contexts of families, and at other times challenging social practices.

Second, this chapter provides an introduction to current themes about family law in Canada. In spite of the complexity of a shared constitutional authority for legislating on family law in Canada and the rapid pace of new judicial decisions on family law issues, many of the themes remain constant and remarkably similar in different parts of the country. Indeed, as a result of a number of decisions of the Supreme Court of Canada in the past decade, coupled with new national initiatives in matters such as child support guidelines, it is arguable that we are closer to achieving a national family law in Canada than ever before. Not only marriage and divorce, but also issues of spousal and child support, principles for custody and access, and the basic requirements for intervention in child protection proceedings are now being addressed as national issues of family law. As well, federal reform proposals concerning issues of assisted reproduction and parenting after divorce may create even more similarity on family law matters across the country. As a result, there is a need to examine Canadian family law in a broader perspective than in the past.

In this regard, the chapter provides an introduction to some of the theoretical frameworks that are often used to explain, and to justify, particular approaches in the family law context. In addition, it explores some of the basic themes of Canadian family law, including:

1. themes of equality, in relation to both families and family members, and the impact of the *Canadian Charter of Rights and Freedoms* on family law;

2. themes of individual and family autonomy, and their connections with ideas about the state's role in protecting and supporting families and individual family members; and

3. themes about the processes of family law disputes, including the balance between rules and discretion and the respective roles of legislatures and courts in defining family law principles; and issues about fact finding and problem solving, including the use of expert knowledge and trends away from adversarial processes in family law.

These themes will be explored in more detail, of course, in subsequent chapters focusing on particular family law issues.

Some Perspectives on Family Law

At the outset, it may be important to acknowledge that there are not always easy answers in family law. In examining the following comments, try to identify the kinds of concerns being expressed about family law issues and processes, and consider whether, or to what extent, the authors are identifying special kinds of problems for family law.

Katherine O'Donovan, *Family Law Matters*
(London: Pluto Press, 1993), 106

How are we to approach family law as told to us in various texts, in cases, statutes, textbooks? How are we to discern the messages, the values, the subtexts, that are immanent or embedded in what we read? How can we identify the values assumed in various manifestations of law? What are the stories told to us of family conflicts and disputes that go to law, and become the stuff of which the law is made? Do these stories represent what was told, or have they been transformed by lawyers, judges and others, by law's procedures and practices? And what of the stories untold in law because the silent cannot speak or lawyers cannot hear? To talk about these questions we must think about what family law was, is, and is about to be.

Susan B. Boyd, "Teaching Policy Issues in Family Law"
(1989-90), 8 *Canadian Journal of Family Law* 11, at 13-15

In order to become socially responsible lawyers, students must be introduced to a wider range of materials than traditional law sources or doctrinal expositions of the "evolution" of family law. These traditional sources have a tendency to lose sight of the forests for the trees. As legally trained people, we have a tendency to get lost in the technicalities of legal rules and the niceties of legal distinctions made by judges. This is especially true in a period when we have so much new legislation to be interpreted, as we now do. Yet, by the time many of the students to whom we teach these technical issues graduate into the "real world" to practise, these legal questions will be already resolved, or students will have forgotten the minutiae of legal debates.

This provides a strong argument for discussing with students the larger questions around the impact of law, the role of law in social change, so that they learn to take responsibility for their actions, legal or otherwise, in the real world of which law school is a part. The implications of our choices of particular issues in family law to illustrate the more micro-level technical questions must also be considered. Students need not be introduced to all of these technical questions, though clearly they must learn to do technical legal analysis, and examples might be chosen with a view to considering how wide the social significance of a particular issue is, rather than how attractive the issue is to the technical legal mind. ...

The above-mentioned themes ... can be used to encourage students to study the efficacy of legal change vis-à-vis the family in light of the wider social context. They can also be used to remind students that what legislation and judges say is not always an accurate description of reality, due to the sometimes false assumptions which our legal system contains about the family and family members. Students can learn to take a critical perspective on policy-oriented legal approaches which ignore the complex nature of social change, of which legal change is only one part.

Report of the Canadian Bar Association Task Force on Gender Equality in the Legal Profession, *Touchstones for Change: Equality, Diversity and Accountability*
(Ottawa: Canadian Bar Association, 1993), 204

As lawyer after lawyer and judge after judge raised the issue of status, it became progressively clearer that these expressions of concern were more than just reflections of personal discomfort. While it was true ... that many lawyers were hurt by, and troubled about, crass and insulting comments which were made about the area of law in which they worked, more serious problems were also exposed.

It is important for a good judge or lawyer to be able to use the legal system to achieve fair results. The ability to do this is essential if one hopes to have a successful and rewarding legal practice or a satisfying career as a judge. To develop that reputation for skill which enables one to have a growing practice one must be able to deliver "justice" to clients or litigants at reasonable cost and in a timely fashion.

Family law at present combines limited resources and unduly complex procedures with lack of respect and inadequate financial reward—and as a result the amount of "justice" which family lawyers can produce for their clients is severely limited. In family law this is a special problem as there are very few aspects of family law practice which permit the lawyer working alone to provide a complete service. In family law a high proportion of cases require dispute resolution or the achievement of what philosophers call distributive justice—a fair result which divides scarce assets fairly. In consequence, most clients of family law practitioners care profoundly about (and are deeply affected by) the scarcity of resources available to their lawyers. Scarcity of resources, in turn, occurs when those who allocate resources view certain needs as unimportant. In family law practice, as well as in family courts, the shortage of vital judicial and financial resources has reached a critical point in Canada. Those who submitted their views to the Task Force felt that this was a direct result of the low status attributed to family law in Canada.

SELECTED REFERENCES

John Dewar and Stephen Parker, eds., *Family Law: Processes, Practices, Pressures* (Oxford and Portland, OR: Hart Publishing, 2003).

John Eekelaar and Mavis Maclean, eds., *Family Law* (Oxford: Oxford University Press, 1994).

Christine Piper, "How Do You Define a Family Lawyer?" (1999), 19 *Legal Studies* 93.

II. CONTEXTS FOR FAMILIES IN CANADA

A. Definitions and Data

[If] we ask ourselves, or anybody else, who is their family, most people will be able to give a clear and unambiguous answer. For instance, they may say, "my family consists of my spouse, my children, my parents, and Aunt Sally." However, they may not list Uncle Herbert, because there is very little interaction with him.

> Margrit Eichler, *Families in Canada Today:*
> *Recent Changes and Their Policy Consequences*
> (Scarborough, ON: Gage Publishing, 1983), 4

As this comment reveals, people often define their families without taking account of law. At the same time, of course, individuals' perceptions about their families may not always match definitions of family relationships in Canadian law. Significantly, family law does not actually define family; instead, it defines particular kinds of relationships—for example, spouse, parent, or child. Moreover, family law defines these relationships in different ways for different legal purposes. Thus, the law's definition of parent for the purpose of consenting to the adoption of a child may be different for the purpose of determining obligations of child support—in the adoption context, biological parenthood may be necessary, while social parenthood alone may be a sufficient basis for ordering payment of child support. Further, legal definitions may, or may not, correspond to an individual's perception of being a spouse or a parent, particularly where such perceptions result from cultural or religious commitments that are widely accepted within a particular community, but not reflected in legal principles of general application. For example, some children may feel obligations to provide a home and personal care for their aging parents, even though no such duty to provide personal care is required by law. Thus, ideas about relationships of families, as well as obligations that bind members of families within their communities, may often diverge, sometimes quite significantly, from legal definitions and principles.

1. The Census Family

It is interesting that even official definitions may not match legal definitions of familial relationships. For example, the definition of a "census family" used by Statistics Canada may include some legally recognized relationships, but not others. Thus, according to Statistics Canada, a census family includes

> a now-married couple (with or without never-married sons and/or daughters of either or both spouses), a couple living common-law (again with or without never-married sons and/ or daughters of either or both partners), or a lone parent of any marital status, with at least one never-married son or daughter living in the same dwelling.

For the census of 2001, a new definition of common law couple was adopted:

> two people of the opposite sex or of the same sex who live together as a couple but who are not legally married to each other.

Thus, for the first time, data about same-sex couples was officially collected in the census figures. Because Statistics Canada data is used by policy makers to support initiatives relating to families, its definition is critical, even though it may not match legal definitions of family relationships nor capture all aspects of families in Canada.

2. Other Approaches to Defining Families

Some researchers have adopted other approaches to defining families in relation to their research goals. For example, the Vanier Institute of the Family considered the Statistics Canada definition too narrow for its purposes.

Vanier Institute of the Family, *Profiling Canada's Families II*
(Ottawa: Vanier Institute of the Family, 2000), iv-v

> Statistics Canada's definition ... concerns what can be objectively measured—who lives with whom and under what circumstances. It captures a central element of everyone's notion of a family—people living together in a long-term relationship. However, it does not deal with important matters such as the emotional bonds that continue to tie parents and children to one another, even after the children have left home. Nor does the definition of a "census family" reveal much about the relationships between siblings once they have left home or between grandparents, uncles, aunts and cousins. ...
>
> Knowing that there is more to family than meets the eye, and much more than what can be counted, the Vanier Institute of the Family defines families as:
>
>> ... any combination of two or more persons who are bound together over time by ties of mutual consent, birth and/or adoption or placement and who, together, assume responsibilities for variant combinations of some of the following:

- Physical maintenance and care of group members
- Addition of new members through procreation or adoption
- Socialization of children
- Social control of members
- Production, consumption, distribution of goods and services, and
- Affective nurturance—love

This definition directs attention toward the work and accomplishments of people who commit themselves to one another over time—to what people do as distinct from where they live and how they are related to each other. It is a definition that acknowledges and respects heterosexual and same-sex couples, lone-parent families, extended patterns of kinship, step-families and blended families, couples with children and those without, the commitments of siblings one to another and the obligations and affection that unite the young and the old as their lives weave together. People in families provide for and care for one another, they teach and discipline, they are financially, economically and psychologically dependent upon one another and they love one another.

Definitions like these, which provide more comprehensive descriptions of the range of family functions, are often derived from sociological research about what actually occurs in families. As will be apparent, of course, not all families function in the same ways.

Recent research about gay and lesbian relationships, for example, suggests that while there are many similarities between heterosexual and homosexual couples, there are also some interesting contrasts.

Carol-Anne O'Brien and Aviva Goldberg, "Lesbians and Gay Men Inside and Outside Families"
in Mandell and Duffy, eds., *Canadian Families: Diversity, Conflict and Change*, 115, at 128 and 133

The research literature shows that lesbian and gay relationships provide many contrasts to heterosexual relationships that are organized around inequality. Studies have found that lesbian and gay relationships are more egalitarian than heterosexual relationships; for example, finances and decision making are characterized by a high degree of equality and high levels of self-esteem.

Implicated in the greater degree of equality within lesbian and gay couples is the finding that in virtually all lesbian and gay-male relationships, both partners are wage earners and that gay men and lesbians are often characterized by a high level of "material self-sufficiency." ... Also relevant are the findings in the scant number of studies that have examined housework and the division of labour in gay and lesbian households. Unlike heterosexual relationships in which each gender is automatically given duties and rights, lesbian and gay couples most commonly negotiate a division of labour based upon skill, preference, and energy related to age and ability. ...

Lesbian- and gay-headed households may ... take a variety of family forms, but there is no valid reason for refusing to call them families. They fall under every conceivable sociological criterion for identifying families. They are groups of co-resident kin providing jointly through income-pooling for each other's survival needs of food and shelter. They socialize children, engage in emotional and physical support, and make up part of a larger kin network.

From the perspective of family law, differing approaches to defining families suggest a need to avoid making uninformed assumptions about what or who are families, or how individuals actually live together in families.

3. Statistics About Families in Canada

At the same time, while there are many different arrangements of families, most data about families in Canada is derived from the census figures collected by Statistics Canada,* using the census family definition. In this context, data released after the 2001 census reported that diversification among Canadian families was continuing. Some highlights of the report indicated that:

1. The proportion of traditional families—mom, dad, and the kids—continues to decline, while families with no children at home are on the increase:

   a. the proportion of married or common law couples with children under age 24 living at home was 44 percent of all census families in 2001, by contrast with 49 percent of all families in 1991 and 55 percent of all families in 1981; and

   b. the proportion of couples without children living at home was 41 percent of all census families in 2001, by contrast with 38 percent in 1991 and 34 percent in 1981.

2. An increasing proportion of couples are common law couples:

   a. the proportion of married-couple families was 70 percent in 2001, by contrast with 83 percent in 1981;

   b. the proportion of common law families increased from 5.6 percent in 1981 to 14 percent in 2001; and

   c. in Quebec, the proportion of common law couples represented 30 percent of all couple families in the province, a proportion that is greater than that of Norway, Finland, and France, and comparable to that of Sweden; the proportion of common law couples in Quebec is the major reason why the prevalence of common law couples is roughly twice as high in Canada as it is in the United States.

---

*   Statistics Canada, *Profile of Canadian Families and Households: Diversification Continues* (Ottawa: Statistics Canada 2001 Census Analysis Series, 2002), 3-8.

3. Lone-parent families represented 16 percent of all families. (It is interesting that, at the beginning of the 20th century, close to 14 percent of families were led by lone parents, 8 out of 10 of whom were widows or widowers. As such, lone-parent families were almost as common in 1901 as they were at the end of the century. The main difference is that, in 1901, more were caused by the death of one of the parents: see *Profiling Canada's Families II*, at 30.)

4. A total of 34,200 same-sex common law couples were counted in Canada in 2001, representing 0.5 percent of all couples:

   a. Ontario had the largest number of same-sex couples;

   b. male same-sex couples represented 55 percent of the total of same-sex couples; but more female same-sex couples had children living with them (15 percent of female same-sex couples had children living with them, by contrast with 3 percent of male same-sex couples); and

   c. 85 percent of male same-sex couples lived in metropolitan areas, compared with 76 percent of female same-sex couples.

5. The number of larger households declined; the proportion of households consisting of four or more people fell from one-third in 1981 to one-quarter in 2001. This decline results partly from lower fertility rates, and may have implications for housing in the future.

6. In 2001, 19 percent of Canadian children did not live with both parents; most of these children lived with a lone parent, the majority of whom were women. Grandparents lived in the same household as children in 3.3 percent of census families, but only 0.4 percent of children lived with grandparents in the absence of their parents.

7. "The percentage of individuals living in families with low income and little financial wealth remained virtually constant between 1984 and 1999. ... Although the financial wealth of other families rose substantially between 1984 and 1999, the median financial wealth of low-income families did not increase; therefore, the wealth gap between low-income families and other families rose during the period. Compared to their counterparts in the mid-1980s, the vast majority of low-income families at the end of the 1990s had no more savings with which to protect themselves against adverse events ... . Of all families, female lone-parent families were by far the most likely to suffer persistent low income." (See René Morisette, "On the Edge: Financially Vulnerable Families" (Winter 2002), no. 67 *Canadian Social Trends* 13, at 17.)

8. The median income of Canadian families was essentially unchanged between 1990 and 2000, after adjusting for inflation ($55,016 in 2000 and $54,560 in 1990). However, "incomes of families at the bottom half of the income distribution showed little or no improvement during the 1990s, [while the 10 percent] of Canadian families with the highest incomes experienced substantial gains" (representing 28 percent of total family income). The median income of lone-parent

families in 2000 was about $26,008, up from $21,797 in 1990; and child benefits were substantially redistributed to low-income families by 2000. However, half of children in low-income families lived in two-parent nuclear families; and one-third of children with recent immigrant parents lived in low-income families (see Statistics Canada, *2001 Census: Analysis Series: Income of Canadian Families* (Ottawa: Minister of Industry, 2003), 5-10).

9. Between 1984 and 1999, the wealth (defined as assets minus debts—that is, more than just income) of the top 40 percent of couples with children rose significantly (between 21 percent and 43 percent), while the wealth of the middle 20 percent of such couples with children rose only 3 percent. For the bottom 40 percent of couples with children, there was a significant decline in net wealth, so that the gap between the bottom and the top has widened. Such large differences in wealth among families may translate into huge gaps in opportunities for children, for example, in relation to the rising costs of post-secondary education or access to home ownership (see Canadian Council on Social Development, *The Progress of Canada's Children 2002* (Ottawa: Canadian Council on Social Development, 2002), 19).

10. In 2001, Statistics Canada compared the median income for census families in Canada (taking into account changes in the census family definition in 2001) with the median income for 1996.

	Median family income	
Census family type	2001	1996
All census families	$55,016	$55,352
Couples, with children (−18)	$65,962	$66,062
Couples, no children	$50,509	$50,300
Couples, children (18+) only	$80,545	$81,262
Lone parents, children (−18)	$26,008	$26,073
Lone parents, children (18+)	$43,187	$43,693

Statistics Canada also reported that the 10 percent of families with the highest incomes experienced the biggest income gains between 1990 and 2000: an increase of 14.6 percent. At the same time, families in the middle and bottom end of the income distribution experienced essentially stable income levels. Employment income remained the largest component of total family income in 2000, although lower-income families were more reliant on government transfers.

The same report indicated that:

a. one-half of the 1,245,700 children under 18 who were living in low-income (as defined by Statistics Canada) families were living in nuclear families with two parents;

b. low-income families with children were disproportionately lone-parent families; although only 14 percent of all children lived in lone-parent families in 2000, these children accounted for 39 percent of children in low-income families; and

    c. although low income for children with Canadian-born parents has declined, the low-income rate for children with immigrant parents (one or both of whom arrived in the 1990s) was 33 to 39 percent.

(See Statistics Canada, *2001 Census: Analysis Series: Income of Canadian Families*, released May 13, 2003, 7-11. For further analysis, see Roger Sauvé, *The Current State of Canadian Family Finances, 2002 Report* (Ottawa: Vanier Institute of the Family, 2003), especially at 11-13.)

Roger Sauvé, "Trends in Canadian Family Finances"
(1999), *Vanier Institute of the Family: Transition* 10, at 13

[In the following chart, the author demonstrated significant changes in spending and consumption patterns. Consider the effect of these changes on families at high- and low-income levels. According to Sauvé (at 14), "the near doubling of the miscellaneous category is due to greatly increased spending on games of chance."]

% Distribution and Trend of Family Expenditures

	1969	1978	1986	1996	change*
		% distribution			69-96
Food	18.8	16.8	14.3	12.2	−6.6
Shelter	14.8	15.6	15.4	16.5	1.7
Household operation	4.0	4.1	4.3	4.6	0.6
Furniture & equipment ...	4.8	4.6	3.7	2.7	−2.1
Clothing	8.3	7.0	6.4	4.4	−3.9
Transportation	13.1	13.0	13.6	12.6	−0.5
Medical & health care ...	3.4	1.9	1.8	2.0	−1.4
Personal care	2.2	1.6	1.9	1.7	−0.5
Recreation	3.4	5.0	5.1	5.5	2.1
Reading & education	1.5	1.2	1.4	1.7	0.2
Tobacco & alcohol	3.7	3.2	3.1	2.3	−1.4
Miscellaneous	1.6	2.4	2.6	2.9	1.3
Total consumption	79.5	76.3	73.7	69.1	−10.4
Personal taxes	13.6	17.1	18.9	22.4	8.8
Financial security	4.5	4.2	4.6	5.4	0.9
Gifts & contributions	2.4	2.3	2.8	3.1	0.7
Total expenditures	100.0	100.0	100.0	100.0	

* Change in percentage points.
  Source: People Patterns Consulting based on Statistics Canada, *Family Expenditure in Canada*.

Discussion Notes

Cohabitation and Families

How do the findings reported from the 2001 census correspond to popular definitions of families in Canada? What might be explanations for the increase in cohabiting relationships and the corresponding decrease in marriages, particularly in Quebec? For example, does this development signal an increasing interest in individual autonomy in arrangements for personal relationships or a decline in respect for the legal status of marriage; does it reflect the fact that many current cohabitees were themselves the children of divorce a generation ago; or does it suggest other factors? What are the consequences of large numbers of cohabiting relationships in Canada? Should family law provide the same benefits and obligations for cohabiting couples and married couples when their relationships end in separation? Why or why not? These issues were recently considered by the Supreme Court of Canada in *Nova Scotia v. Walsh*, [2002] SCC 83; (2002), 221 DLR (4th) 1; 32 RFL (5th) 81, discussed later in chapter 6.

Family Law and Financial Arrangements

How is data about the financial well-being of census families relevant to family law? What are the issues that need to be considered in understanding different levels of income for single-parent families by contrast with two-parent families? In the context of family breakdown, for example, one economist argued that decisions that are made in a family unit will often maximize the well-being of the unit as a whole; but if the family unit breaks up, some of these decisions may disproportionately disadvantage individual family members, requiring family law principles that adjust these economic relationships: see Jack L. Knetsch, "Some Economic Implications of Matrimonial Property Rules" (1984), 34 *University of Toronto Law Journal* 263. One response of Canadian courts has been to construct a post-divorce family unit—even though the parents have divorced to go their separate ways, financial family obligations may continue. These issues are discussed in more detail later in these materials.

4. "Families" in Law

> [There] exists within society a network of social norms which is formally independent of the legal system, but which is in constant interaction with it. Formal law sometimes seeks to strengthen the social norms. Sometimes it allows them to serve its purposes without the necessity of direct intervention; sometimes it tries to weaken or destroy them and sometimes it withdraws from enforcement, not in an attempt to subvert them, but because countervailing values make conflicts better resolved outside the legal arena.

(John Eekelaar, "Uncovering Social Obligations: Family Law and the Responsible Citizen," in Mavis Maclean, ed., *Making Law for Families* (Oxford and Portland, OR: Hart Publishing, 2000), 9, at 16.)

According to Eekelaar (at 9), it is critical to examine assumptions about the "significant relationship between the legal and the social ... which can explain certain features of contemporary family law." Similarly, an American family law scholar, Mary Ann Glendon, argued that it is necessary to be attentive to the relationships between legal and social norms in defining families:

> The law, torn between promoting modern ideals and attending to human needs, displays the same ambivalence that is deeply embedded in our culture and in the hearts of individuals. It is likely that most persons still entertain ideals of family solidarity and cooperation, and that these ideals guide a functioning family, more or less. It is also likely that these ways of imagining family relations will undergo revisions in times of stress. The lack of firm and fixed ideas about what family life is and should be is but an aspect of the anguish of modernity. And in this respect, the law seems only to reflect the fact that in modern society more and more is expected of personal relationships at the very time that social conditions have rendered them increasingly fragile.

(Mary Ann Glendon, *The Transformation of Family Law: State, Law, and Family in the United States and Western Europe* (Chicago and London: University of Chicago Press, 1989), 147.)

Consider these concerns about connections between legal and social ideas of family in the two cases that follow. To what extent is there a difference in the law's approach to defining families, by contrast with the views of individuals within "family" units?

Sefton Holdings v. Cairns, [1988] 2 FLR 109 (CA Civ. Div.)

In reflecting on the law's role in relation to social norms, consider the distinction drawn by a court in the United Kingdom in 1988 between "*being* a member of the family" and "living *as* a member of the family."

In *Sefton Holdings v. Cairns*, the applicant was a woman who had accepted the invitation of parents of her female friend to live with them. At the time when she moved into their home in 1941, the applicant was 23 years old, and her parents were dead; as well, her boyfriend had been killed in World War II. The parents of her friend treated the applicant as a daughter, and the applicant called them "Mom and Pop." Forty-five years later, after both her friend and her friend's parents had died, the applicant sought to establish that she was a member of the family in order to remain in the home under the protection of the *Rent Act, 1977*. According to the Court of Appeal (at 112), the applicant was not entitled to recognition as a member of the family; the court stated succinctly: "[T]o be a member of a family is different from being treated as a member of the family."

Is this distinction appropriate? Why, or why not? How significant is the context in which the claim is being asserted? Compare the approach in *Sefton* to the following Canadian decision: are they consistent in their approaches to ideas about families?

Baker v. Canada (Minister of Citizenship and Immigration)
(1999), 174 DLR (4th) 193 (SCC)

[A mother of four children, all born in Canada and Canadian citizens, was ordered deported after living in Canada for 11 years. She applied for exemption on humanitarian and compassionate grounds pursuant to the *Immigration Act*, RSC 1985, c. I-2. Her case primarily focused on issues of fairness in procedures for administrative decision making in relation to the *International Convention on the Rights of the Child*. In allowing her appeal, Justice L'Heureux-Dubé focused briefly on the family relationships in this situation.]

(a) The Objectives of the Act

[68] The objectives of the Act include, in s. 3(c):

> to facilitate the reunion in Canada of Canadian citizens and permanent residents with their close relatives from abroad;

Although the provision speaks of Parliament's objective of *reuniting* citizens and permanent residents with their close relatives from abroad, it is consistent, in my opinion, with a large and liberal interpretation of the values underlying this legislation and its purposes to presume that Parliament also placed a high value on keeping citizens and permanent residents together with their close relatives who are already in Canada. The obligation to take seriously and place important weight on keeping children in contact with both parents, if possible, and maintaining connections between close family members is suggested by the objective articulated in s. 3(c).

(b) International Law

[69] Another indicator of the importance of considering the interests of children when making a compassionate and humanitarian decision is the ratification by Canada of the *Convention on the Rights of the Child*, and the recognition of the importance of children's rights and the best interests of children in other international instruments ratified by Canada. International treaties and conventions are not part of Canadian law unless they have been implemented by statute. ... I agree with the respondent and the Court of Appeal that the Convention has not been implemented by Parliament. Its provisions therefore have no direct application with Canadian law.

[70] Nevertheless, the values reflected in international human rights law may help inform the contextual approach to statutory interpretation and judicial review. As stated in R. Sullivan, *Driedger on the Construction of Statutes* (3rd ed., 1994), at p. 330:

> [T]he legislature is presumed to respect the values and principles contained in international law, both customary and conventional. These constitute a part of the legal context in which legislation is enacted and read. *In so far as possible, therefore, interpretations that reflect these values and principles are preferred.* [Emphasis added.]

The important role of international human rights law as an aid in interpreting domestic law has also been emphasized in other common law countries. ...

[71] The values and principles of the Convention recognize the importance of being attentive to the rights and best interests of children when decisions are made that relate to and affect their future. In addition, the preamble, recalling the *Universal Declaration of Human Rights*, recognizes that "childhood is entitled to special care and assistance." A similar emphasis on the importance of placing considerable value on the protection of children and their needs and interests is also contained in other international instruments. The United Nations *Declaration of the Rights of the Child* (1959), in its preamble, states that the child "needs special safeguards and care." The principles of the Convention and other international instruments place special importance on protections for children and childhood, and on particular consideration of their interests, needs and rights. They help show the values that are central in determining whether this decision was a reasonable exercise of the [humanitarian and compassionate] power.

(c) The Ministerial Guidelines

[72] Third, the guidelines issued by the Minister to immigration officers recognize and reflect the values and approach discussed above and articulated in the Convention. As described above, immigration officers are expected to make the decision that a reasonable person would make, with special consideration of humanitarian values such as keeping connections between family members and avoiding hardship by sending people to places where they no longer have connections. The guidelines show what the Minister considers a humanitarian and compassionate decision, and they are of great assistance to the Court in determining whether the reasons of Officer Lorenz are supportable. They emphasize that the decision-maker should be alert to possible humanitarian grounds, should consider the hardship that a negative decision would impose upon the claimant or close family members, and should consider as an important factor the connections between family members. The guidelines are a useful indicator of what constitutes a reasonable interpretation of the power conferred by the section, and the fact that this decision was contrary to their directives is of great help in assessing whether the decision was an unreasonable exercise of the [humanitarian and compassionate] power.

[73] The above factors indicate that emphasis on the rights, interests, and needs of children and special attention to childhood are important values that should be considered in reasonably interpreting the "humanitarian" and "compassionate" considerations that guide the exercise of the discretion. I conclude that because the reasons for this decision do not indicate that it was made in a manner which was alive, attentive, or sensitive to the interests of Ms. Baker's children, and did not consider them as an important factor in making the decision, it was an unreasonable exercise of the power conferred by the legislation, and must, therefore, be overturned. In addition, the reasons for decision failed to give sufficient weight or consideration to the hardship that a return to Jamaica might cause Ms. Baker, given the fact that she had been in Canada for 12 years, was ill and might not be able to obtain treatment in Jamaica, and would necessarily be separated from at least some of her children.

Discussion Notes

Family Law Cases

To what extent does the relationship between legal and social norms explain the differing outcomes in *Sefton Holdings* and in *Baker*? What are the underlying concerns in each case? To what extent do the different contexts explain the different outcomes? Are these cases "family law" cases? Why or why not?

Families and Law Reform Policies

To what extent are social norms relevant to legal policy making? As you consider family law issues, and particularly proposals for reforming family law, consider the extent to which reform proposals take account of empirical studies and concrete data about families in Canada and their needs. In this context, consider Stephen Cretney's assessment of the 1969 divorce reform in the United Kingdom, which radically altered divorce law. Cretney reported that the public was advised that "the Law Commission was simply giving objective and disinterested advice on technical matters—a proposition which in retrospect seems so implausible that it is astonishing that it was ever taken seriously": see Stephen Cretney, *Law, Law Reform and the Family* (Oxford: Clarendon Press, 1998), 71. To what extent is it possible for family law reform to be technical?

SELECTED REFERENCES

CANADIAN FAMILIES

Sharryn Aiken and Sheena Scott, "Baker v. Canada (Minister of Citizenship and Immigration) and the Rights of Children" (2000), 15 *Journal of Law and Social Policy* 211.

Maureen Baker, ed., *Families: Changing Trends in Canada*, 4th ed. (Toronto: McGraw-Hill Ryerson, 2001).

Margrit Eichler, *Family Shifts: Families, Policies, and Gender Equality* (Don Mills, ON: Oxford University Press, 1996).

Nancy Mandell and Ann Duffy, eds., *Reconstructing the Canadian Family: Feminist Perspectives* (Toronto: Butterworths, 1988).

Zheng Wu, *Cohabitation: An Alternative Form of Family Living* (Toronto: Oxford University Press, 2000).

COMPARATIVE LITERATURE

A. Coote, H. Harman, and H. Hewitt, "Changing Patterns of Family Life," in John Eekelaar and Mavis Maclean, eds., *A Reader on Family Law* (Oxford: Oxford University Press, 1994), 29.

John Eekelaar and Thandabantu Nhlapo, eds., *The Changing Family: International Perspectives on the Family and Family Law* (Oxford: Hart Publishing, 1998).

Sheila B. Kamerman and Alfred J. Kahn, eds., *Family Change and Family Policies in Great Britain, Canada, New Zealand and the United States* (Oxford: Clarendon Press, 1997).

Carol Smart, Bren Neale, and Amanda Wade, *The Changing Experience of Childhood: Families and Divorce* (Cambridge, MA: Polity Press, 2001).

B. Families and Family Policies

Some countries, particularly in western Europe, have developed explicit family policies with governmental departments specifically charged with their implementation. By contrast, family policies in Canada (other than in Quebec) are generally more implicit and are sometimes not well-coordinated across the country. According to Maureen Baker, there are three categories of family policies. The first includes laws relating to family issues (for example, marriage, adoption, divorce, and child support); issues are the primary focus of these materials. A second category includes policies related to income support, including tax concessions for families with children and parental leaves and benefits. A third category involves the provision of direct services, such as child care and child protection services. (See Maureen Baker, *Canadian Family Policies: Cross-National Comparisons* (Toronto: University of Toronto Press, 1995), 5-9.) Although the latter two categories of family policies are not examined extensively in these materials, it is important to understand how family policies define the state's role in family life and the role of family law in implementing these policies.

1. The (Changing) Context of Family Policies

Family policies are often designed to respond to changing trends in family composition and functions. In reviewing data about Canadian families and changes that have occurred in the decades since World War II, for example, Maureen Baker identified five significant family trends since World War II and some of the challenges of policy making about families.

Maureen Baker, "Thinking About Families: Trends and Policies"
in Maureen Baker, ed., *Canada's Changing Families: Challenges to Public Policy*
(Ottawa: Vanier Institute of the Family, 1994), 3-4

[First, birth rates have been declining. According to Baker the birth rate in Canada, as in other industrialized countries, fell significantly in the 20th century. At the same time, birth rates for some populations within Canada have fallen more significantly than others. Second, there was a significant rise in the life expectancy for both males and females in Canada during the 20th century. Third, more people are living together outside marriage. Fourth, more mothers are working for pay. In 1941, about 4.1 percent of married women were working in the labour force, while by 1992, this figure had risen to 61.4 percent. Fifth, the percentage of lone-parent families has been rising, contributed to both by a rising rate of separation and divorce and a rise in births outside marriage.]

Policy makers often bring to their jobs assumptions about the way families live, and these ideas are not always representative of the broad range of lifestyles prevalent in modern society. Also, because their advisors have often come from similar gender, cultural and socioeconomic backgrounds and receive their training in specialized fields such as law or economics, they do not always reflect the thinking of everyday

people or even the wider range of the social sciences. These factors help to perpetuate the transmission of biases and myths in policy making. Although it was feminist
social scientists who first articulated their concerns about these biases, now most
researchers and some policy makers are trying to present a more balanced and realistic portrayal of family life. ...

The field of family policy is not without controversy. An attempt to create a more
explicit and cohesive family policy arises from two separate traditions. One tradition
is based on the realization that families are changing, with more two-income and
lone-parent families, that parents make an important contribution to society in having
children and that they increasingly need social support to combine more effectively
family life with earning a living. The other tradition assumes that "the family" is
deteriorating and attempts must be made to legislate supports to help the traditional
nuclear family maintain its position against the intrusion of alternative lifestyles. In
both cases, there has been a new emphasis placed on strengthening families. Yet those
who applaud new family forms are suspicious of the call for "a family policy" because
they fear that it could represent a conservative agenda opposing greater equality for
women, gays, and "families of choice." Creating social policies which bring together
these two opposing viewpoints and deal adequately with the multidimensional aspects
of family life is indeed a challenge.

2. Historical Examples of Family Policies in Canada

In exploring family policies in Canada, it is important to examine how governmental
policies historically prevented the creation of families or constrained the enjoyment of
family life for some groups in Canadian society. In reading the excerpt that follows,
consider whether these policies should be characterized as explicit or implicit family
policies. How might the use of these policies continue to affect families and family life in
Canada? What is the current role for family law in these contexts?

**Tania das Gupta, "Families of Native People, Immigrants, and
People of Colour"**
in Mandell and Duffy, eds., *Canadian Families: Diversity, Conflict
and Change*, 146, at 150ff.

Native People

Genocide of the Culture, Genocide of the Family

When Europeans landed on this continent, they encountered well-developed, highly
organized, and stable formations of Native societies, including family formations.
Families varied in lineage and locality, but they were extended, and women and men
related to each other with reciprocity and sharing. Such family structures were supported by an economic infrastructure that was itself based on reciprocity, sharing,
and production for subsistence of the community. The products of labour were appropriated not by one class or group of people, but by the community or band.

However, these arrangements were a hindrance to the European project of colonization and capitalism. In order to subjugate and disempower Native people, the mercantile colonizers embarked on a campaign to penetrate, exploit, and distort Native families, and finally to destroy them altogether.

Bourgeault talks about the experience of the Dene-Chipewyan people of the subarctic in the seventeenth century onwards, when the Hudson's Bay Company and the North West Company established fur-trading posts. The fur trade could not have been pursued without a suitable and sufficient pool of labour. Native women were appropriated by selective "enslavement." They were taught about mercantile trade and then used as conduits for mobilizing their own band members to work as labourers for the trade post. A male comprador class was thus created among the people, transforming Native egalitarian relations between men and women into hierarchical and dependent ones.

In the absence of white European women, white officials took "wives," often by force, initially from the Native community and later from the racially preferred Métis community. These women were used to transport goods, prepare furs, make shoes, knit, stitch, and "keep house" for white men. Native men became the hunters and trappers for the companies and also acted as middlemen in the fur trade. Women's labour was thus diverted from their own communities toward the maintenance of individual men and the colonial trading companies. Native men sometimes resorted to "several wives" in order to accomplish their middlemen roles. Bourgeault critiques the conclusion made by some that communal societies were polygamous by arguing that the existence of several wives was a creation of mercantile capitalism, imposed on egalitarian Native societies.

Initially, most Métis children were abandoned by their white fathers and grew up as Native people. Later, white fathers attempted to assimilate the children, particularly females, into European Christian culture with the assertion that Native culture was inferior.

As capitalism predominated and immigration from all over the world took hold, the labour of Native peoples, including the Métis, was not as crucial as it had been in the early years of capitalist development. Nor was Native peoples' labour as malleable as that of immigrants, since Natives retained the option of not assimilating into the predominant capitalist system. So the European colonialists, with the help of the Church, adopted a strategy of biological and cultural assimilation of Native peoples. At the centre of this approach lay an effort to destroy Native family formations, including by the destruction of Native children.

Two institutions that have played very key roles [in this process] are the schools and the child welfare agencies. ...

Residential schools provide the most dramatic examples of what education did to Native children and to families. York presents vivid documentation of the horror of missionary teachers and government officials threatening bodily harm or arrest to force Native parents to send their young children to residential schools. Residential schools were hostels where children were separated from their families, prevented from speaking their own languages and practising their own traditions, and made to practise a semi-militaristic lifestyle, including wearing uniforms and having their hair shaved off. They were brainwashed to believe in the "goodness" of the Bible and the "barbarism" of Native religions. All this happened with the aid of severe corporal punishment and, frequently, these children were sexually abused. Generations of depression, alcoholism, suicide, and family breakdown are the legacy of such traumatic experiences and are described as the "residential school syndrome" by Native peoples themselves. ...

Now, Native bands operate schools on reserves and some operate boards of education. This strategy has ended the abuse and the forced separation of Native children from their families and communities and is reversing the drop-out trends. Unfortunately, the federal government continues to cut back its commitment to fund Native education. There are still thousands of Native students who must attend provincial schools, where non-Native curricula, white teachers, and white officials dominate, and where they still face an alienated and colonial educational system that ignores the historical experience of Native peoples.

Just as the residential-school system was being phased out in the 1960s, the child-welfare system stepped into view in the form of Children's Aid Services, which removed Native children from their parents on the pretext that the parents were "inconsistent" or "abusive." This was a dominant phenomenon in most Native communities on- and off-reserve. ...

In 1979, a national report on adoption and welfare found that 20 percent of children in foster care were Native, while only 6 percent of the Canadian population were Native. In Manitoba, 60 percent of children in foster care were Native, while the overall Native population in the province was 12 percent of the total. In the 1970s, 80 percent of Native children in Kenora, Ontario, were in "care." This trend continued into the early 1980s. Most children were placed in non-Native homes, including homes outside Canada. ...

Immigrants and People of Colour

. . .

Chinese Families

In the absence of appropriate and adequate European immigration in the late 1800s, and because of the near genocide of Native peoples, about 15 000 Chinese men were admitted into Canada to work on the railways, despite protests from BC politicians and people at large. However, once the railway was completed in 1885, the *Chinese Immigration Act* was passed to restrict the entrance of the Chinese by imposing a $50 head tax, which rose to $500 per head by 1903.

The wives of Chinese labourers usually stayed behind in China, not always because they wanted to but often because they or their husbands could not afford the head taxes. Valerie Mah, a Toronto teacher and historian, called the Toronto Chinese community between 1878 and 1924 the "bachelor" society because of the absence of women. The head tax was a way of systemically excluding a group of people because of race, ethnicity, and sex. ...

South Asian Families

As in the case of Chinese immigrants, immigrants from the Indian subcontinent, re-ferred to as South Asians, were prevented from coming to Canada by systemic barri-ers. By an immigration stipulation of 1908, South Asians could land in Canada only by continuous journey. Yet the Canadian Pacific Railway, which operated the only continuous steamship passage on that route, was forbidden to sell any tickets. More-over, under the *Immigration Act* of 1910, each Asian immigrant had to possess $200 to enter Canada. These two rules effectively prevented the entry of South Asians. ...

South Asian women were banned from Canada, although, in 1910, the wives of two professional men entered. Immigration of South Asian women of all classes was decried by society at large, including white women's groups, for fear of encouraging the settlement of South Asians in Canada.

It was not until 1919 that South Asian women could enter Canada, and then only as wives. Repeated pressure from British colonial officials at the Imperial War Con-ferences, between 1917 and 1919, had the ban removed. Yet few women and children emigrated to Canada because they were formally required to be registered as legiti-mate "wives and children" in India, and few procedures facilitated marriage registra-tions there until 1924. Between 1921 and 1923, only eleven women and nine children entered. Older children could not emigrate to reunite with their parents, a rule that disregarded the fact that, unlike Canadian children, older children often lived with their parents up to the time of their marriage. ...

Japanese Families

Before 1908, evidence suggests that the Japanese in Canada were mainly a commu-nity of single males and that some may have sought solace with prostitutes. Most lived with other men in company shacks and bunkhouses near their workplaces, just like their Chinese and South Asian counterparts.

In 1907, self-regulation of immigration from Japan was negotiated in the form of a gentlemen's agreement, according to which the Japanese government voluntarily restricted the number of emigrants to Canada. Canada resorted to this approach to maintain diplomatic relations with Japan, an ally of Britain at the time. The agree-ment covered the immigration of domestic and agricultural workers; wives, children, and parents were allowed to arrive freely until 1928. The agreement came on the heels of a race riot in British Columbia aimed at Chinese and Japanese immigrants.

Adachi describes the period after 1908 as the "family building phase," when single men sought wives in several ways. Some visited Japan for arranged marriages; others sent for "picture brides" from a catalogue. ...

Anti-Japanese feelings reached a zenith in the war years with the bombing of Pearl Harbor. In the name of national security, mass evacuations of Japanese were begun in January 1942; all males between 18 and 45 had to be removed from the West Coast by April 1942. This resulted in the dismantling of families and the disruption of children's schooling. Most of the men were removed to work in road camps in other parts of Canada. Women and children were, initially, forced to reside in hastily converted public buildings, lacking complete privacy, before being moved to camps in the BC Interior, first to tents and then to shacks.

On June 24, 1942, the Canadian Security Commission decided to reunite married men in detention camps with their families, by transporting wives and children to the camps for the winter. As a result, the camps became extremely crowded and ill-equipped, and the movements of residents were closely monitored by security officials. Unmarried men in the camps were prevented from marrying lest they should try to stay with their wives. Even though the commission was supposed to provide the basic necessities of life, evacuees had to buy their own food with incomes between 22.5 and 40 cents an hour. The old and the infirm lived on provincial relief based on the number of family members. Japanese children were excluded from provincial schools, so that camp residents themselves had to build their own schools with their own finances and staff them with hastily trained Japanese teachers.

Familial authority and socialization processes were transformed in the semi-communal camp life. The authority that Issei (first generation) parents had over their children was weakened, which then weakened parents' abilities to transfer their indigenous language and culture.

The disruption of families continued in the postwar years, when all Japanese Canadians were encouraged to go back to Japan or to work on sugar beet farms, extremely strenuous work. Many young, single members of the Nisei (the second generation) chose to move to Ontario and other Eastern provinces, away from their parents.

Adachi writes about the difficulty of gauging the psychological effects of internment on individuals, families, and the community. However, it is notable that the Nisei and the Sansei (third generation) are quite often assimilated into dominant Anglo-Canadian culture. The Sansei have about a 59 percent rate of intermarriage, compared with the 99 percent rate of endogamy of the Issei. Could this be a way of shielding themselves from the ravages of state racism that their Japanese parents and grandparents experienced?

Black Caribbean Families

If we look at the history of white European immigrant women, we find a pattern of large numbers coming to Canada as poor, single, young domestic workers. White women had a choice of settling in Canada or returning to their home countries. Between 1900 and 1930, about 170 000 British women came under this category. In 1929, 1288 out of 1618 Finnish women arrived as domestics. Immigration policies differed for domestics who were women of colour. If they came as temporary or contract domestic workers, they could not alter this status in Canada. If they did not fulfil their contractual agreements, they were forced to go back to their home countries. ...

Women of colour who have been brought to Canada as contracted domestic workers have been predominantly black Caribbean and Filipina women. These women have been, and still are, admitted for limited contractual periods. They remain in Canada only in the job and with the employer with whom the contract exists. The periods during which these women could, in fact, use the domestic scheme to emigrate to Canada have been brief, so that few women have been able to take advantage of it. As a result of political lobbying by community organizations since 1981, domestic workers have been able to apply for immigration after two years of contracted work.

However, systemic barriers remain, since applicants have to fulfil certain conditions, such as maintaining stable employment, demonstrating financial-management skills, and demonstrating their involvement in the community. Just as in the case of Asian male immigrants in the early part of the twentieth century, it has been a policy of the government not to encourage the possibility of developing families among women of colour who came as domestic workers. Thus, their status as "single" and as "temporary" is deliberately organized by immigration policies. ...

The "singleness" of black domestic workers from the Caribbean was maintained in the second domestic scheme (1955-67), when a quota system was established for admitting as immigrants to Canada only unmarried women without children and not in common-law relationships. Proposed changes to immigration regulations in the early 1960s may have been what eventually prompted many of these women to apply to sponsor their close relatives, fiancés, and children. Not only was this very disappointing to Immigration officials, but they could not reconcile the fact that women breadwinners were sponsoring men as fiancés, a departure from traditional gender roles. ...

Immigrant Domestic Workers and White Families

One of the issues that has rarely been discussed is the contribution of domestic workers in reproducing white Canadian-born families in Canada. By definition, they "mother" white Canadian-born children by cooking, cleaning, washing, dusting, and even fulfilling sexual services under coercion. While their own families, including those with very young children, are forced by immigration laws and employment conditions to remain far away from their mothers, these women nurture, feed, dress, and nurse their employers' children. They enable mainly upper-class and middle-class white women to escape their traditional gender roles to develop lucrative careers or to enjoy leisure time. By the same token, the government can save on crucial day-care services, which are urgently needed by working women with preschool children. In this process, domestic workers are prevented from ever establishing their own families and communities.

Das Gupta focused on historical policies affecting Canadian families, particularly in the context of First Nations and non-white immigrant families. Feminist scholars have also assessed governmental policies in relation to women's roles in families. As Norene Pupo argued, relationships between women's lives within their families and the state have often been contradictory; they have regarded the state as both "a source of protection and justice and as the basis of inequality" because of its patriarchal bias: see Norene Pupo, "Preserving Patriarchy: Women, the Family, and the State," in Mandell and Duffy, eds., 207, at 229. Similarly, in an assessment of policy reforms concerning women, Dorothy Chunn argued for a critical examination of dominant liberal conceptions of the state, law, and family.

Dorothy E. Chunn, "Feminism, Law, and 'the Family':
Assessing the Reform Legacy"
in Elizabeth Comack, ed., *Locating Law: Race/Class/Gender Connections*
(Halifax: Fernwood Press, 1999), 236, at 255-56

Liberal conceptions of these institutions—the state as "umpire," law as the protector of equality rights, the family as nuclear and private—are taken as givens. They are viewed as homogeneous rather than differentiated and contradictory, timeless as opposed to historically and culturally bounded. ... [There is a need to analyze] the structural embeddedness of patriarchal relations in state, law, and family; the different forms and content of patriarchal relations in different types of social organization; or how differences generated by race, ethnicity, class, sexual orientation, and (dis)ability shape the social construction of gender.

3. Family Policies and the Role of Law

Mavis Maclean, "Introduction"
in Mavis Maclean, ed., *Making Law for Families*
(Oxford and Portland, OR: Hart Publishing, 2000), 1-2

My starting point is to set up a number of policy models for regulating the relationship between individual, family and the state, organised around the aim of the activity. These ideal types would include a residual model for family law, which would aim to keep law out of family life and do no more than protect personal safety. Such a function might be covered sufficiently by the criminal law, though even the strictest limits placed on legislative intervention within the family tend to favour a special role for child protection. The family is often conceptualised as a "Black Box," and in a residualist approach the walls of this box are both strong and opaque. The family is "trusted" by society with self-regulation—an approach that thrives in a cohesive and stable society with well understood norms and values, such as a traditional Catholic society, or where the state is committed to liberal non-intervention, as under the recent Thatcher administration in the UK. Such a model tends to favour the status quo and therefore to be unacceptable to reformers, including feminists, concerned to counter patriarchal hegemony. At the other extreme on the continuum lies the instrumentalist model of family law, where the walls of the Black Box are transparent and permeable. Here the state uses the law to direct family life in a particular direction—whether seeking to impose a religious regime as in Israel, or a political regime as in Central and Eastern Europe between the Second World War and 1990. Extreme communitarianism may lead to a similar approach, as, for example, in the close legal control over discipline for children in Scandinavia. A "third way" may be found in what I would describe as a facilitative rights-based model, which sits well with increasing experience of multiculturalism in a global society. Here the law aims to provide a framework within which individual choice is maximised, but within the constraints of protecting human rights. For example, different ways of raising children according to religious beliefs are acceptable only up to the point at which a child's health and safety might be put at risk.

_____

Although Maclean concluded that the third, facilitative rights-based model was the most useful model for an increasingly multicultural and global society, she also cautioned (at 5) that it presented some conceptual problems:

> [The] conceptualisation of human rights comes from concern about the relationship between the individual and the state. In family law, on the other hand, the requirement is to balance the obligations and rights of individual, family and state, and of the individual as a member of a family, not only now but in the future.

Which of Maclean's three models appears most appropriate for Canadian family policies? You may want to consider whether different models should apply in different legal contexts or in different geographical parts of Canada.

The Quebec government, for example, introduced an explicit family policy in 1987. Although the policy was wide-ranging in scope, an important aspect was the availability of cash payments to parents at the birth of a child, with substantially higher amounts payable on the birth of a third or subsequent child. Implementation of the policy was criticized because its main goal seemed to be an increase in the birthrate, and not primarily a support for children and families; as a result, it was characterized as not really a family policy but rather a pro-natal policy: see C. Le Bourdais and N. Marcil-Gratton (with D. Bélanger), "Quebec's Pro-Active Approach to Family Policy: 'Thinking and Acting Family,'" in Maureen Baker, ed., *Canada's Changing Families: Challenges to Public Policy* (Ottawa: Vanier Institute of the Family, 1994), 103. Do you agree that it was not appropriate to characterize a pro-natal policy as a family policy? Why might a provincial family policy be designed to encourage an increase in the number of births? How would you characterize this policy in relation to Maclean's three models? What would constitute an explicit national family policy in Canada?

Discussion Notes

Family Policies and Economic Interests: The Dionnes

To what extent do family policies promote economic interests of the state? In an analysis of two extraordinary cases in Ontario in the 1930s, Mariana Valverde argued that the boundaries between families and the economy were not fixed realms but categories in flux. One case concerned the Dionne quintuplets, who were separated from their parents and siblings and managed by the Ontario government; according to Valverde, the government intervened in the lives of the Dionne quintuplets, not pursuant to a child protection regime, but rather to manage the Quints as natural resources. For Valverde, the government's guardianship of the five girls was "an aspect of provincial economic policy," not unlike Niagara Falls. In the second case, the government failed to intervene successfully when an eccentric lawyer died, bequeathing a legacy to the Toronto woman giving birth to the largest number of children within a 10-year period. According to Valverde, these cases reveal how mothers and children "were managed and administered through processes normally associated with the regulation of the economy": see Mariana Valverde, "Families, Private Property, and the State: The Dionnes and the Toronto Stork Derby" (1994-95), 29 *Journal of Canadian Studies* 15, at 16. How do these cases affect ideas about the role of law and policy in relation to families?

Compensating for Harmful Family Policies

Reparations for harms caused by state policies that destroyed or dislocated families remain live issues in Canada. For example, compensation was paid by the federal government in the 1990s to descendants of Japanese Canadians who had been interned during World War II; in addition to separating families, the government had confiscated property owned by them. Claims for compensation on the part of First Nations people who were removed from their families and communities and segregated in residential schools are currently being negotiated. Recently, the Ontario Court of Appeal denied a claim for compensation for the head tax paid by Chinese male workers: see *Mack v. Canada (Attorney General)* (2002), 217 DLR (4th) 583; 60 OR (3d) 737 (CA).

Family Policies in the Welfare Context

Family policies are also embedded in other areas of the law. For example, the Ontario Court of Appeal held unconstitutional the provincial government's definition of spouse in relation to a male cohabitee's relationship to a single mother in receipt of welfare assistance: see *Falkiner v. Ontario (Director, Income Maintenance Branch, Ministry of Community and Social Services)* (2002), 212 DLR (4th) 633; 59 OR (3d) 481 (CA). How would you characterize the relationships between the state and families in the welfare context in terms of Maclean's models? This issue is addressed again later in these materials.

SELECTED REFERENCES

CANADIAN ASSESSMENTS

Susan B. Boyd, ed., *Challenging the Public/Private Divide: Feminism, Law, and Public Policy* (Toronto: University of Toronto Press, 1997).

————, "(Re)Placing the State: Family, Law and Oppression" (1994), 9 *Canadian Journal of Law and Society* 39.

Bettina Bradbury, "Social, Economic, and Cultural Origins of Contemporary Families," in Maureen Baker, ed., *Families: Changing Trends in Canada*, 4th ed. (Toronto: McGraw-Hill Ryerson, 2001), 69.

Marlene Brant Castellano, *Aboriginal Family Trends: Extended Families, Nuclear Families, Families of the Heart* (Ottawa: Vanier Institute of the Family, 2002).

Patricia M. Evans and Gerda R. Wekerle, eds., *Women and the Canadian Welfare State: Challenges and Change* (Toronto: University of Toronto Press, 1997).

Philip Girard, "Why Canada Has No Family Policy: Lessons from France and Italy" (1995), 32 *Osgoode Hall Law Journal* 579.

E. Jane Ursel, *Private Lives, Public Policy: 100 Years of State Intervention in the Family* (Toronto: Women's Press, 1992).

COMPARATIVE REFERENCES

Claire Archbold, "Family Law-Making and Human Rights in the United Kingdom," in Maclean, ed., *Making Law for Families* (Oxford and Portland, OR: Hart Publishing, 2000), at 185.

Alison Diduck and Felicity Kaganas, *Family Law, Gender and the State: Text, Cases and Materials* (Oxford: Hart Publishing, 1999).

John Eekelaar, *Family Law and Social Policy*, 2d ed. (London: Weidenfeld and Nicolson, 1984).

Lorraine Fox Harding, *Family, State and Social Policy* (London: Macmillan, 1996).

Katherine O'Donovan, *Family Law Matters* (London: Pluto Press, 1993).

III. THEORY AND THEMES IN FAMILY LAW

A. Theoretical Frameworks

It is time for the family to come out. … Is it true that families are little empires for the tyrannical and capricious exercise of power by some members over others, discreet centres of coercion conveniently shielded from public scrutiny? … Overstatement, distortion, partial truth or myth [?] … Which items appear on [our] agenda and how we approach them will very largely be determined by two things: our theory of human nature and probably, more importantly, our view of what we consider to be the appropriate concerns of the lawyer. Michael Freeman has reminded us that "lawyers who remain technicians cannot contribute to the … debate currently raging about the family."

> Pamela Symes, "Property, Power, and Dependence:
> Critical Family Law"
> (1987), 14 *Journal of Law and Society* 199, at 199

Although it is unclear whether family lawyers were ever merely technicians, there is no doubt about the liveliness of current theoretical debates about family law, revealed in case law, law reform proposals, and academic critique. Many of these theoretical approaches are examined in more detail in these materials in relation to particular family law issues, but it seems helpful at the outset to provide a brief introduction to current theories in the family law context.

Katherine O'Donovan, *Family Law Matters*
(London: Pluto Press, 1993), at 18-29

[In *Family Law Matters* (at 18-29), Katherine O'Donovan usefully outlined a variety of methods of thinking and writing about family and law, and demonstrated how different methods, theories, and writing styles can reveal different parts of the family law picture. As will be apparent, these different approaches may be applicable to different aspects of family law, and in relation to different kinds of legal analyses. In the brief summary that follows, consider what kinds of theoretical approaches would be useful to different family law contexts.

Positivism: Positivism is an assertion of what the law is, a system of rules deriving its authority from law. Lawyers are in control, and law both defines relevance and excludes alternative perspectives and claims. "Excluded are broader questions of law's provenance in non-formal legal sources, alternative ways of seeing and doing" (at 18).

Functionalism: Functionalism examines what families actually do, rather than what law states about them. Informal sources of law may be used in functional analysis, particularly in assessing how well laws actually achieve defined goals. However, functionalism may also be criticized for being too descriptive and static in relation to current family arrangements and for its inability to challenge and change current distributions of power among members of families.

Familialism: Familialism refers to ideologies modelled on family values or values taken to be associated with families—for example, the idealized "cornflakes family." Although there are several strands in this theoretical approach, including idealization of a mythical past, it opens up important questions about how idealized families (often patriarchal and heterosexual) are deeply embedded within social and legal policies; and it challenges the validity of assumptions that all family members share the identity of interests so often assumed by law and policy.

Public and private: This approach reflects the dichotomy within liberalism between the public world of state, market, and politics (generally a male world) and the private realm (generally a female world) associated with the family. Some critics have argued that the dichotomy is constructed rather than real, or that, if there is a dichotomy, it is fluid rather than static. Among feminist theorists, theories of public and private are most often criticized for creating a private sphere immune to legal intervention, particularly with respect to male violence against women and children.

Critical family law: This approach builds on critiques of familialism and theories about public and private. It rejects ideas about law's objectivity, asserting that law is political, part of the totality of social relations and institutions, and that there are inherent contradictions in family law between ideas of individualism and community.

Postmodernism: As in other disciplinary contexts, postmodern approaches to family law reject the possibility of attaining an overall theory, not subject to critique and qualifications. Instead, postmodernism focuses on small-scale and open accounts of experiences of the world, emphasizing form and style as well as content. Postmodernism provides opportunities to consider families and law from the perspectives of the excluded and the oppressed because it encourages various realities, various stories, various standpoints. Clearly, postmodern approaches present problems for a family law goal of defining (one) truth.

Autopoietic theory: According to this theory, law and society are not separate, so that the legal system engages in the reproduction of the overall social system, thereby participating in society's construction of reality. For those who regard legal discourse as autopoietic, law exists independently of the individuals who are involved in it; thus, by contrast with some other theoretical approaches, individual actors are products of the system of knowledge in which they operate, rather than independent actors. This theory also suggests that it will be difficult for actors to communicate effectively across disciplines because separate discourses cannot be bridged, an assertion that may explain, but also challenge, efforts to use different kinds of professionals in family law processes.]

Which of these theoretical approaches are likely to be found in legislation; in judicial decisions; in academic critiques? Which approaches may be most helpful in different kinds of family law disputes—for example, claims about child support, determining the validity of a marriage, or allegations of sexual abuse?

According to O'Donovan (at 18), these approaches reveal

> a variety of methods of thinking and writing about family and law. [They illustrate] the overlap between methods, theories and writing styles. It is not being claimed that there is one way or a "right" way. On the contrary, the discussion ... shows how different methods, theories and presentations can reveal various parts of the picture.

Consider the approaches identified by O'Donovan in two cases in the United Kingdom, discussed below, and the ways in which legal principles interact with social ideas about families. How would you characterize the theoretical approaches in the two decisions? In Smart's analysis of them? Do you agree with O'Donovan that there is no right way to resolve such disputes?

Carol Smart, "Wishful Thinking and Harmful Tinkering? Sociological Reflections on Family Policy"
(1997), 26 *Journal of Social Policy* 301, at 316-17

Below I outline two almost identical legal cases over contact/access issues which occurred only three years apart. In the first case the mother is seen to be a good mother, working in the interests of her child. In the second case the mother, who is behaving in exactly the same way, is seen as working to damage the welfare of her child. In the first case she was allowed to form a fresh relationship and to have a clean break; in the second she was not and the weight of state intervention was brought to bear on her such that her second relationship became unstable.

Re S.M. (A Minor) (Natural Father: Access), [1991] 2 FLR 333

In this case a woman had an illegitimate child by a man from whom she parted before the birth. He saw the child regularly for nearly two years. She then remarried her former husband and contact between the child and the "natural" father ceased. When the "natural" father applied for access (old Act) the magistrates granted it. The mother appealed. The case was heard by the President of the Family Division who ruled in favour of the mother who had argued that the child was now in a stable family unit and that to introduce the "natural" father would destabilise the unit and disturb the child who knew him as an uncle.

Re R. (A Minor) (Contact), [1993] 2 FLR 762

This involved a married couple but otherwise the facts are similar. That is to say, a married woman had a child by her husband, but she left him soon after the birth and went to live with another man who raised the child as his own. The child in this case had been brought up to believe that her mother's cohabitee was her father and she did not know her "natural" father who had not seen her for four years. [In the Court of Appeal,] the mother argued the same case as the mother in *Re SM* (namely that the child was now in a stable unit and should not be disrupted) but was unsuccessful. Butler-Sloss LJ argued that it was the right of a child to know the truth as to the identity of its "natural" father and that it was the right of a child to have a relationship with both "natural" parents. Thus, against the wishes of the mother, she ordered a child psychiatrist to work with the child to overcome the trauma of discovering the truth of her parentage and that a guardian *ad litem* should be appointed to advise the court on when contact could be resumed with the "natural" father.

In the first instance the mother is held to be doing the best for the child in providing a stable family and she is allowed her clean break, as is the child. In the second, a mere three years later, the mother is labelled implacably hostile and is seen as failing to recognise the true interests of her child. This mother is obliged to restart a relationship which will endure for as long as the child's natural father wishes. These cases reflect an important shift in the normative order governing divorce. In a remarkably short space of time the idea that one can turn over a new leaf and start again has been redefined as a form of selfish individualism generated by a combination of moral decline and feminist inspired self-interest. The disdain with which such an aspiration is now met obliterates completely the social history that gave rise to what was once a perfectly legitimate desire associated with divorce, namely the desire to separate from a spouse or former sexual partner.

To what extent can the differing outcomes in these cases be explained as legal change? As social change? What theories of family law are useful in explaining these changes?

Discussion Notes

Other Theoretical Approaches: Privatization and Family Law

In commenting on O'Donovan's book, John Dewar concluded that it revealed yet another theoretical approach—namely, a "constructivist" account of family law:

> the way legal discourse privileges certain family forms, individual behaviours or orientations, or more generally "constructs" sexuality, or our subjective sense of ourselves.

See John Dewar, "The Normal Chaos of Family Law" (1998), 61 *Modern Law Review* 467. Does a constructivist explanation assist in understanding the shift in assumptions in the two cases critiqued by Smart? What other theoretical approaches are revealed in these two cases?

As Dewar's comment about O'Donovan's book makes clear, theoretical approaches may overlap and connect with others in a variety of ways. In this context, for example, some theorists might argue with O'Donovan's decision to place Marxist theories within her discussion of familialism, rather than considering its critique of the public/private dichotomy, or identifying its emphasis on the political economy of families as an entirely different approach: for example, see Michele Barrett and Mary McIntosh, *The Anti-Social Family*, 2d ed. (London: Verso, 1991).

In the context of current privatization agendas in Canada, how would you characterize the theoretical approach in the following critique?

> As provinces ... shift responsibility for social assistance and child welfare to the private sphere, families and non-profit and for-profit organizations are expected to assume responsibility for certain aspects of that system. Invocations of community responsibility are prevalent, and rather than "community" assuming a public or collective meaning, in this context it is a tool of privatization. Given the high proportion of women in the ranks of those who perform volunteer, "community," and "family" work in Canadian society, it is they who will be expected to assume the lion's share of low-paid and unremunerated work as society is restructured in the interests of capital.

(Susan B. Boyd, "Challenging the Public/Private Divide: An Overview," in Boyd, ed., *Challenging the Public/Private Divide: Feminism, Law, and Public Policy* (Toronto: University of Toronto Press, 1997), 3, at 19.)

Family Law: "The New Legalism"?

Dewar argued that even O'Donovan's constructivist approach does not tell the whole story. Instead, he claimed that family law was necessarily incoherent and chaotic, because it engages with areas of social life and feeling that raise controversial "questions about rights, justice, autonomy, relationships and values." Although he acknowledged that family law is often not regarded as "real law," Dewar argued that family law is "a paradigm example of modern law, an exemplary case of what Marc Galanter calls the 'new legalism.'" According to Galanter, the new legalism "extensively incorporates materials or information from other disciplines," and it operates not with "brightline" rules but rather through "indirect symbolic controls" that "radiate messages." In this context, Dewar suggested that "far from straying from the true path of the law, family law may tell us a good deal about where mainstream legalism is headed": see Dewar at 467-68 and 470; and Marc Gallanter, "Law Abounding: Legalisation Around the North Atlantic" (1992), 55 *Modern Law Review* 1.

SELECTED REFERENCES

CANADIAN ASSESSMENTS

Susan B. Boyd, ed., *Challenging the Public/Private Divide: Feminism, Law, and Public Policy* (Toronto: University of Toronto Press, 1997).

Janine Brodie and Linda Trimble, eds., *Re-Inventing Canada: Politics of the 21st Century* (Toronto: Prentice Hall, 2003).

Elizabeth Comack, ed., *Locating Law: Race/Class/Gender Connections* (Halifax: Fernwood Press, 1999).

Brenda Cossman and Judy Fudge, eds., *Privatization, Law, and the Challenge to Feminism* (Toronto: University of Toronto Press, 2002).

COMPARATIVE REFERENCES

Alison Diduck and Felicity Kaganas, *Family Law, Gender and the State: Text, Cases and Materials* (Oxford: Hart Publishing, 1999).

Michael Freeman, ed., *The State, the Law, and the Family: Critical Perspectives* (New York: Tavistock Publications, 1984).

Katherine O'Donovan, *Family Law Matters* (London: Pluto Press, 1993).

Frances E. Olsen, "The Family and the Market: A Study of Ideology and Legal Reform" (1983), 96 *Harvard Law Review* 1497.

Jana Singer, "The Privatization of Family Law" (1992), *Wisconsin Law Review* 1443.

B. Themes in Family Law

1. The Charter and Equality for Families: Extending Spousal Status

Equality is a prominent theme in Canadian family law—equality for different kinds of families and also equality among individual family members. Reflecting the goals of both human rights legislation and s. 15 of the *Canadian Charter of Rights and Freedoms*, family law principles have increasingly extended benefits to opposite-sex and same-sex cohabitees that were once reserved only for married couples. In promoting equality for different kinds of families, judges have frequently compared the *functions* performed within cohabiting intimate relationships. Thus, for example, in a dissenting judgment in a case concerning entitlement of a gay man to "spousal" bereavement leave at the death of his partner's father, Justice L'Heureux-Dubé focused on what families "do."

Canada (Attorney General) v. Mossop
[1993] 1 SCR 554; (1993), 100 DLR (4th) 658, at 709ff.

To look beyond the specific forms a family might take is to ask what value one sees in the family and what lies at the base of society's desire to recognize and support families. In order to define "family status," it is no error to examine the underlying values of families so that, as Lisa R. Zimmer says in "Family, Marriage, and the Same-Sex Couple" (1990), 12 *Cardozo L Rev.* 681, at p. 699, "*actual* families, rather than theoretical stereotypes, may enjoy their protected status." ...

It was argued by the intervener Focus on the Family that one of the values of the family is its importance to society in fostering procreation, and that procreation requires families to be heterosexual. The argument is that procreation is somehow necessary to the concept of family, and that same-sex couples cannot be families as they are incapable of procreation. Though there is undeniable value in procreation, [it is not valid to suggest] that the capacity to procreate limits the boundaries of family. If this were so, childless couples and single parents would not constitute families. Further, this logic suggests that adoptive families are not as desirable as natural families. The flaws in this position must have been self-evident. Though procreation is an element in many families, placing the ability to procreate as the inalterable basis of family could result in an impoverished rather than enriched vision. ...

Given the range of human preferences and possibilities, it is not unreasonable to conclude that families may take many forms. It is important to recognize that there are differences which separate as well as commonalities which bind. The differences should not be ignored, but neither should they be used to de-legitimize those families that are thought to be different and as Audre Lorde puts it in "Age, Race, Class and Sex: Women Redefining Difference" in *Sister Outsider*, 114 at p. 122: "we must recognize differences among [people] who are our equals, neither inferior nor superior, and devise ways to use each other's differences to enrich our visions and our joint struggles."

The principles of equality were also used to extend spousal benefits under an insurance policy to an opposite-sex cohabitee in *Miron v. Trudel*, [1995] 2 SCR 418; (1995), 124 DLR (4th) 693. By contrast, in *Egan v. Canada*, [1995] 2 SCR 513; (1995), 124 DLR (4th) 609, a gay man applied for a spousal allowance when his partner in a relationship of 45 years became eligible for a pension under the *Old Age Security Act*. Five members of the court held that the denial of a spousal allowance to a same-sex partner in *Egan* represented discrimination pursuant to s. 15, but one of the five judges joined with the dissenting opinion, holding that the discrimination was saved under s. 1. Thus, according to *Egan*, same-sex cohabitees were not included as spouses in relation to old age security.

In spite of the negative outcome in *Egan*, however, subsequent court decisions concerning spousal benefits for same-sex couples were more successful, in part as a result of the Supreme Court's 1998 decision in *Vriend v. Alberta*, [1998] 1 SCR 493; (1998), 156 DLR (4th) 385, which narrowed the scope for upholding discriminatory legislation pursuant to s. 1. In this context, the federal government decided not to appeal a decision of the Ontario Court of Appeal in *Rosenberg v. Canada* (1998), 38 OR (3d) 577; (1998), 158 DLR (4th) 664 (CA), in which the court held that provisions of the *Income Tax Act*, which precluded registration of an employer pension plan that provided spousal survivor benefits for same-sex couples, were unconstitutional. In Quebec, the Superior Court (Civ. Div.) ruled that same-sex couples were cohabitees for purposes of surviving spousal rights in relation to rental accommodation: see *Québec (Commission des Droits de la Personne et des Droits de la Jeunesse) c. Québec (Procureur Général)*, [1998] AQ n° 3264 and *Le Journal de Barreau*, April 1, 1999. Following the Supreme Court's decision in *M. v. H.* (1999), 171 DLR (4th) 577 (SCC), which held that it was unconstitutional to exclude same-sex spouses from the spousal support provisions of Ontario's *Family Law Act*, a number of provinces amended their legislative schemes concerning spousal status and the federal government enacted the *Modernization of Benefits and Obligations Act*, SC 2000, c. 12.

In June 2003, moreover, the Ontario Court of Appeal held that same-sex partners were entitled to marry because there were no significant differences between same-sex relationships and married couples, so that the denial of entitlement to marry infringed s. 15 of the Charter: see *Halpern v. Canada (Attorney General)*, [2003] OJ no. 2268, discussed in further detail in chapter 2. What kinds of theoretical approaches are revealed in these analyses of same-sex couples?

By contrast with these developments, the Supreme Court of Canada upheld an appeal by the government of Nova Scotia concerning opposite-sex cohabitees in relation to the constitutionality of the provincial legislative regime for property sharing by spouses at separation. The court confirmed that it was not discriminatory for provincial legislation to establish a property-sharing regime for married couples, while excluding from its provisions the needs of cohabiting couples at the breakdown of their relationships: see *Nova Scotia v. Walsh*, [2002] SCC 83; (2002), 221 DLR (4th) 1; 32 RFL (5th) 81. This decision, discussed further in chapter 6, may reflect new concerns on the part of judges in the Supreme Court of Canada about using a functional approach in claims concerning equality for families.

There have been academic criticisms of judicial reasoning that employs a functional approach to achieve equality for different kinds of intimate relationships, especially for gays and lesbians. In this context, moreover, there have been criticisms of judicial reasoning that assumes functional equality for marriage and cohabiting relationships. In her review of the impact of the Charter's 20th anniversary, for example, Brenda Cossman expressed her concerns about treating opposite-sex and same-sex couples in the same way:

> The new legal subject is a familialized subject. The new lesbian and gay subject lives in a monogamous and respectable relationship with responsibilities of mutual care and commitment. It is a subject constituted in and through ideologically dominant discourses of familialism at the same time as this subject reshapes these discourses. Ideologically dominant discourses of family have emphasized the heterosexual nuclear family as the basic and natural site for social reproduction—for producing and raising children and caring for dependent members. With the rise of the neo-liberal state and its emphasis on reprivatization, there is rather less emphasis given to the composition of the family (who a family is) and rather more importance given to the functions that a family performs (what a family does). The incorporation of lesbian and gay subjects into these ideologically dominant discourses of family is illustrative of this new emphasis on function over form and suggests that the traditional heterosexuality of these discourses is being displaced.

(Brenda Cossman, "Lesbians, Gay Men, and the Canadian Charter of Rights and Freedoms" (2002), 40 *Osgoode Hall Law Journal* 223, at 247.)

For another critique, see Susan B. Boyd and Claire F.L. Young, " 'From Same-Sex to No Sex'? Trends Towards Recognition of (Same-Sex) Relationships in Canada" (2003), 1:3 *Seattle Journal for Social Justice* 757. The report of the Law Commission of Canada, *Beyond Conjugality: Recognizing and Supporting Close Personal Adult Relationships* (Ottawa: Minister of Public Works and Government Services, 2001), recommended a major change in the ways that the Canadian government and Canadian law pursue "important state objectives" by recognizing significant, non-conjugal, adult relationships. This report is considered in greater detail in chapter 2.

Discussion Notes

Equality for Family Members: The Impact of the Charter

Charter and human rights litigation has also been used to define equality among family members. For example, the Supreme Court of Canada held that provisions of BC's *Vital Statistics Act*, which permitted a mother to register the birth of a child without including the name of the child's father, contravened s. 15 of the Charter (as sex discrimination) and were not saved by s. 1. However, the court suspended its declaration of invalidity for a period of 12 months to permit British Columbia and other provinces to amend these provisions to meet the constitutional requirements. In addition, the Supreme Court expressly rejected the father's request that his particulars be included on the registration of birth and that the surnames of the children (triplets born in 1996) be changed to a hyphenated surname (including the mother's and father's names). Instead, the court directed the father to apply pursuant to provincial legislation for the recording of his particulars on the birth registration and for consideration of his request of the change of surname, both to be determined in accordance with the best interests of the children: see *Trociuk v. British Columbia (Attorney General)*, 2003 SCC 34, discussed in chapter 3.

The significance of relying on the equality guarantee in *Trociuk* was confirmed by its contrast with a similar case concerning the provisions of the *Vital Statistics Act* in Ontario, in which there was no Charter challenge; the Ontario Court of Appeal dismissed the father's application: see *Kreklewetz v. Scopel* (2002), 60 OR (3d) 187; 214 DLR (4th) 385. The equality principle has also been important in birth registration cases involving lesbian parents. A BC human rights tribunal held that lesbians who are co-parents of a child born to one of them with sperm from an anonymous donor may register as parents on the birth certificate, thus ensuring that lesbian parents were treated in the same way as heterosexual parents who conceive a child using sperm from an anonymous donor: see *Gill v. Murray*, [2001] BCHRTD no. 34 (Human Rights Tribunal) (QL).

In addition to Charter and human rights litigation concerning equality, ideas about equality are also evident in the interpretation of gender-neutral provisions of family law statutes, particularly in relation to spousal benefits and obligations. Yet, while equality litigation pursuant to the Charter and human rights legislation has most often sought to establish equal *benefits* for families, cases interpreting gender-neutral statutory language have frequently imposed familial *obligations* on the basis of equality. In this way, the theme of equality is closely linked to issues about relationships between families and the state.

SELECTED REFERENCES

CANADIAN ASSESSMENTS

Nicholas Bala, "The Charter of Rights and Family Law in Canada: A New Era" (February 2001), 18 *Canadian Family Law Quarterly* 373.

Tamara D. Barclay, "For Richer or for Poorer: A Comparison of Same-Sex Support and Benefit Rights in M. v. H. and Rosenberg v. Canada (Attorney General)" (1998-99), 16 *Canadian Family Law Quarterly* 213.

Susan B. Boyd, "From Outlaw to Inlaw: Bringing Lesbian and Gay Relationships into the Family System" (1999), 3 *Yearbook of New Zealand Jurisprudence* 31.

_____, "The Impact of the Charter of Rights and Freedoms on Canadian Law" (2000), 17 *Canadian Journal of Family Law* 283.

Hester Lessard, Bruce Ryder, David Schneiderman, and Margot Young, "Developments in Constitutional Law: The 1994-95 Term" (1996), 7 *Supreme Court Law Review* (2d) 81.

Claire L'Heureux-Dubé, "Making Equality Work in Family Law" (1997), 14 *Canadian Journal of Family Law* 103.

_____, "What a Difference a Decade Makes: The Canadian Constitution and the Family Since 1991" (2001), 27 *Queen's Law Journal* 361.

Martha A. McCarthy and Joanna L. Radbord, "Family Law for Same Sex Couples: Chart(er)ing the Course" (1998), 15 *Canadian Journal of Family Law* 101.

IMPACT OF HUMAN RIGHTS AND EQUALITY CLAIMS ON FAMILY LAW IN THE UNITED KINGDOM

Claire Archbold, "Family Law-Making and Human Rights in the United Kingdom," in Mavis Maclean, ed., *Making Law for Families* (Oxford: Hart Publishing, 2000), 185.

OTHER REFERENCES

Martha Minow, "All in the Family & in All Families: Membership, Loving, and Owing" (1992-93), 95 *West Virginia Law Review* 275.

_____, "Redefining Families: Who's In and Who's Out" (1991), 62 *University of Colorado Law Review* 269.

2. Individuals, Families, and the State: Autonomy and Dependence, Support and Protection

A second theme in family law is the complex relationship among individuals, families, and the state. On one hand, members of families value individual autonomy and opportunities to make choices about their private lives, including their family relationships. At the same time, most people experience dependency at some point in their lives. In this context, either families or the state (or a combination of both) provide financial and other kinds of support for individual dependency.

Pamela Symes, "Property, Power and Dependence: Critical Family Law"
(1987), 14 *Journal of Law and Society* 199, at 202-4 and 206-7

[According to Pamela Symes, there are a number of different categories of dependence, although they are all part of the human condition:

Unavoidable dependence: This is the form of dependence experienced by children, and often again in old age; as Symes argues, however, we increasingly regard children, in spite of their incapacities, as having rights.

Accidental dependence: This form of dependence arises for those who suffer a disabling condition; but as Symes notes, these persons are encouraged to develop independence to the extent of their abilities. Symes also included self-inflicted dependence in this category to take into account persons whose lack of independence is the result of addiction, for example.

Delayed dependence: This form of dependence arises from arrested or incomplete development, usually as a result of a psychological condition; although acknowledging that most human beings have some psychological interdependence as social beings, Symes suggests that delayed dependence represents more than the mutual support characterized by relationships of interdependence.

Enforced dependence: According to Symes, this category included, until recently, women because of their lack of full legal personality; however, she also asserts that vestiges of enforced dependence remain for women who are engaged in both career and motherhood.]

In addition to recognizing that dependency is part of human life, reflect on the extent to which individual autonomy may be compromised within families. That is, how can family decision making subtly reflect the views of those who hold, or who are perceived to hold, the greatest power? What principles are appropriate for defining the obligations of families, by contrast with the state, for dependency of individual family members?

Recall the census figures about family income and levels of poverty in families with children. Consider Symes's comments in relation to ideas about dependency and financial support and their relevance for family law:

[The] problems of the poor as a direct consequence of family life and the demands of raising children are not traditionally seen as coming within the ambit of family law. If families are poor, we have a system of social security to deal with that. Family lawyers do not ask *why* so many families are poor, nor do they see it as their concern to take on the poverty problem. ... [There] has been a remarkable reluctance to undertake any real analysis of the cost of raising children which would be the necessary prelude to formulating any family policy as such. The link has been made but to do anything about it would involve an invasion of that "private" territory.

In fact, Canadian courts have sometimes focused on these issues about the adequacy of financial resources, particularly in the context of family breakdown. Indeed, in *Moge v. Moge*, [1992] 3 SCR 813; (1992), 99 DLR (4th) 456, the Supreme Court of Canada took judicial notice of the phenomenon of the "feminization of poverty" for post-separation wives and children. At the same time, however, legal principles concerning the distribution of family resources have most often been decided in cases where there was sufficient family wealth to make extensive litigation possible. Yet, the same legal principles must also be applied in cases of ordinary Canadian families, families in which levels of wealth and income may be marginal indeed. Thus, data about the concrete financial circumstances of families may challenge theoretical legal ideas about autonomy and independence for individual family members.

Discussion Notes

Intervention and Non-Intervention by the State

Relations between individuals, families, and the state do not envisage a strong affirmative obligation on the part of the state to intervene in family life to ensure adequate levels of income support. However, the state does intervene in family autonomy to provide protection for vulnerable and dependent family members, particularly those who are at risk in relation to issues of violence or abuse. Often, protective intervention by the state is regarded as an option to be exercised only when all other possibilities have proved ineffective. However, scholars such as Frances Olsen have argued that the basic concepts of intervention and non-intervention are incoherent: "It is meaningless to talk about intervention and non-intervention, because the state constantly defines and redefines the family and adjusts and readjusts family roles." See Frances E. Olsen, "The Myth of State Intervention in the Family" (1985), 18 *University of Michigan Journal of Law Reform* 835, at 842.

In reflecting on the relationships between individuals, families, and the state, two American commentators proposed that the paradoxes of these relationships in family law principles must be revisioned:

> We believe that any adequate family law must be based on principles that take account of two paradoxical characteristics of family life and the family's relationship to the state. First, the individual must be seen simultaneously as a distinct individual and as a person fundamentally involved in relationships of dependence, care, and responsibility. ... Second, family law and political theory must take account of the additional paradox that family relationships are simultaneously outside of and yet shaped by the political order. ... The creation of a just family law requires reform not only of family law itself but also of the larger political and legal processes by which family law is created and applied.

(Martha Minow and Mary Lyndon Shanley, "Relational Rights and Responsibilities: Revisioning the Family in Liberal Political Theory and Law" (1996), 11 *Hypatia* 4, at 22-25.)

SELECTED REFERENCES

CANADIAN ASSESSMENTS

Mary Jane Mossman, "Individualism and Community: Family as a Mediating Concept," in Allan C. Hutchinson and Leslie J.M. Green, eds., *Law and the Community: The End of Individualism?* (Toronto: Carswell, 1989), 205.

Mary Jane Mossman and Morag MacLean, "Family Law and Social Welfare: Toward a New Equality?" (1986), 5 *Canadian Journal of Family Law* 79.

Hon. Bertha Wilson, "Women, the Family and the Constitutional Protection of Privacy" (1991), 23 *Ottawa Law Review* 431.

Zheng Wu, *Cohabitation: An Alternative Form of Family Living* (Toronto: Oxford University Press, 2000).

OTHER ASSESSMENTS

Martha Fineman, "Cracking the Foundational Myths: Independence, Autonomy, and Self-Sufficiency" (1999), 8 *Journal of Gender, Social Policy & the Law* 101.

Nancy Fraser and Linda Gordon, "A Genealogy of 'Dependency': Tracing a Keyword of the US Welfare State," in Nancy Fraser, *Justice Interruptus: Critical Reflections on the "Postsocialist" Condition* (New York: Routledge, 1997), 121.

Susan Moller Okin, *Justice, Gender and the Family* (New York: Basic Books, 1989).

Frances E. Olsen, "The Family and the Market: A Study of Ideology and Legal Reform" (1983), 96:7 *Harvard Law Review* 1497.

Nikolas Rose, "Beyond the Public/Private Division: Power and the Family" (1987), 14 *Journal of Law and Society* 61.

Carol Smart, *The Ties That Bind: Law, Marriage and the Reproduction of Patriarchal Relations* (London: Routledge & Kegan Paul, 1984).

3. Making Decisions: Processes and Practices

Family law decision making generally reflects processes for resolving civil disputes, with a determination of facts (if necessary, using the advice of experts), the selection of legislative principles or rules, and their interpretation and application in the courts. Lawyers provide advice and, in adversarial proceedings, legal representation. As with other forms of civil proceedings, many disputes have always been settled through negotiation, without resorting to the courts. In recent years, however, there has been increasing use of alternative methods of dispute resolution, including mediation, and in the family law context, new developments such as collaborative law.

At the same time, claims are frequently made that the practice of family law is not the same as other kinds of civil law practice. As noted earlier in this chapter, for example, the Task Force of the Canadian Bar Association expressed grave concern about the problems experienced by family law practitioners "struggling to provide justice to litigants in this area": see Canadian Bar Association, *Touchstones for Change: Equality, Diversity and Accountability* (Ottawa: Canadian Bar Association, 1993), 203. The report identified a lack of resources in courts and in legal aid funding, as well as problems of perception and support for family law across Canada. Although the Supreme Court of Canada decided that state-funded counsel was necessary, pursuant to s. 7 of the Charter, in child protection proceedings involving an indigent mother in New Brunswick in 1999 (*New Brunswick v. G.(J.)*, [1999] 3 SCR 46; (1999), 177 DLR (4th) 124), problems in access to legal aid funding in family law matters remain: see Report of the Canadian Bar Association, *Making the Case: The Right to Publicly Funded Legal Representation in Canada* (Ottawa: Canadian Bar Association, 2002).

In addition, issues about fact finding, the roles of legislatures and courts, and alternatives to the adversarial system in family law continue to challenge courts and policy makers. Although these issues will be considered in more detail later in these materials, it may be helpful at the outset to reflect on the following questions:

1. How should facts be determined in family law matters? In many cases, family law issues are both private and emotional, and in some cases, they involve children.

To what extent can parties to a family law dispute give reliable evidence? When, and how, should experts be used to "explain" the perspectives of the parties? Is there a danger that experts will decide matters that should be resolved by the parties? According to a British judge, for example, family law is different from other civil proceedings because the judge in a family law matter must make a decision "that belongs to the parties" about the family's future needs: see Judge Nigel Fricker, "Family Law Is Different" (1995), 33 *Family and Conciliation Courts Review* 403, at 404.

2. What is the appropriate balance between legislative rules and their discretionary application by courts in family law matters? Such a question requires an examination of the nature of legislative rules. For example, in relation to many matters concerning children, the statutory principle to be applied is the "best interests of the child," a principle frequently qualified by a list of factors to be taken into account, but without any direction as to which factors are most important. In such a situation, it is scarcely possible to argue that there is a rule to be applied. By contrast, John Dewar argued that there is currently a return to rules in family law, but only in some areas (for example, child support) so that lawyers and courts are involved in both the application of quite rigid rules and, at the same time, forced to exercise discretion in relation to other family law issues. As Dewar suggests:

   [Family law] becomes the context in which those contradictions or oppositions that cannot be resolved politically are worked through. I would argue that this is the case in family law: that in seeking legislatively to re-constitute a sense of organic or collective family values around the family and divorce, legislators have in fact created a set of inconsistent principles and commitments ... while at the same time using law to give the appearance of having created shared values; and then have off-loaded the detailed working out of those contradictions to the legal system.

   (John Dewar, "The Normal Chaos of Family Law" (1998), 61 *Modern Law Review* 467, at 484.)

3. When are adversarial processes appropriate for family law matters? How should alternative dispute resolution processes be used in family law? Critics of mediation, for example, have expressed concern about mandatory mediation programs in family law, even though most provincial governments in Canada have warmly embraced them, in many cases on the basis of expected cost savings:

   When mediation is imposed rather than voluntarily engaged in, its virtues are lost. More than lost: mediation becomes a wolf in sheep's clothing. It relies on force and disregards the context of the dispute, while masquerading as a gentler, more empowering alternative to adversarial litigation.

   (Trina Grillo, "The Mediation Alternative: Process Dangers for Women" (1991), 100 *Yale Law Journal* 1545, at 1610.)

A recent alternative that is gaining support in Canada and elsewhere is collaborative family law (a variant of collaborative law in other civil proceedings). Collaborative law is based on a settlement model, with lawyers who represent each client committed to creating an environment in which issues can be resolved without resort to litigation. (If the parties decide to litigate, each of them must seek other counsel.) Such a process requires lawyers and their clients to discuss issues openly with each other and within a new paradigm of seeking to achieve both the rights and also the interests of the parties: see Richard W. Shields, Judith P. Ryan, and Victoria L. Smith, *Collaborative Family Law: Another Way To Resolve Family Disputes* (Toronto: Carswell, 2003). Issues about dispute resolution are discussed in more detail in a number of the following chapters, particularly chapter 5.

SELECTED REFERENCES

Martha L. Fineman and Anne Opie, "The Uses of Social Science Data in Legal Policy Making: Custody Determinations at Divorce" (1987), *Wisconsin Law Review* 107.

Carrie Menkel-Meadow, "Lawyer Negotiations: Theories and Realities—What We Learn from Mediation" (1993), 56 *Modern Law Review* 361.

Christine Piper, "How Do You Define a Family Lawyer?" (1999), 19 *Legal Studies* 93.

Austin Sarat and William L.F. Felstiner, *Divorce Lawyers and Their Clients: Power and Meaning in the Legal Process* (New York: Oxford University Press, 1995).

Shelley Day Sclater and Christine Piper, eds., *Undercurrents of Divorce* (Aldershot, UK: Ashgate Dartmouth, 1999).

PROBLEM: "JOHN'S CASE"

John is 55 years old. He started paid employment in a large industrial factory at age 16, where he worked until he was laid off at age 48 (when his employer was involved in restructuring). At that time, six people were dependent on him for financial support and three others were benefiting from his subsidizing their rent. His support relationships changed a number of times over the course of his working life, although he was never involved in marriage or a cohabiting relationship, and he never became a biological father.

Nonetheless, John was involved in relationships of co-residence, economic pooling, and sharing within his own household and with others, and in caregiving and committed long-term emotional relationships with friends and children. At the same time, many of these commitments were not recognized formally—for example, he could not claim dependants for income tax purposes nor obtain family benefits for them in relation to his employment. If any of them fell ill, he had no entitlement to be consulted about medical decisions, and he would not have been entitled to leave from employment to attend any of their funerals. Although his life may seem extraordinary, parts of his story are common experiences for many people. In this way, his case is useful in assessing how and why law should recognize and support family relationships.

Here are some details of John's life:

Age 30: John bought a small house with his savings, and his friend Jane and her two children (Patricia aged five and Michael aged three) moved in with him. They lived together as friends for five years, with both John and Jane contributing equally to all household and childcare expenses and sharing the practical and emotional caregiving of the children.

Age 35: Jane moved to join her new lover, but John provided her with some money each month to help support the children, and Patricia and Michael visited John's house frequently. By this time, two other friends were sharing John's house—Peter and his son David, aged five, and Stephen. The three adults were not involved in spousal relationships, but they pooled their earnings and other money into a joint account and shared all the household tasks, including caring for David.

Age 40: Peter and Stephen both moved away after they were laid off at work. Although David moved with his father, he continued to come to John's house for a month every summer and he and John remained close through telephone and letters. By this time, John was sharing the house with a longtime friend, Tony, who was separated from his wife and had custody of his daughter Kathy, aged seven, for six months of each year. John and Tony shared household work and child care and contributed equally to expenses, but they kept separate accounts.

Age 45: John bought a new house that was located next door to the home owned by his elderly parents. He provided some care for them, often ate meals with them, and gave them financial support. He rented his former home to Jane and her partner, and they lived there with their new baby. By this time, John was paying an allowance to Michael for room and board while he attended community college, and the costs of rent and daycare for Patricia and her baby daughter Sarah. When David was accepted at university, John agreed to pay for his tuition and residence costs.

In thinking about issues about legal recognition of these people as John's family, consider the following:

- Should a person who is family for purposes of access to benefits *automatically* be subject to family obligations? For example, should the law make distinctions between someone who is family for purposes of obtaining medical information, but not for payment of child support? What are the arguments that favour recognition of family membership for all purposes, rather than just some? How can the complexity of family relationships be recognized in law?

- Should a person who undertakes support (either emotional or financial) on a *voluntary* basis be *required by law* to continue such support? If so, what criteria should be relevant to the creation of this legal obligation—for example, should a legal obligation be assumed after some years of voluntary contributions? If so, how many?

- Should entitlement to benefits and obligations of family status be mutual and reciprocal, or are there some cases where a person should have responsibility to someone else, but that person have no similar responsibility? Why might asymmetrical responsibilities be necessary in some cases? Is it possible to *enforce* such obligations by law?

- Now, consider that John was married to a woman, or involved in a long-term cohabiting same-sex relationship. Re-examine the above questions in relation to these family relationships. To what extent are there differences or similarities? And, to what extent should John's willingness to support children, particularly in relation to educational expenses, be recognized as a benefit to the state? If it should be recognized, what options are available to accomplish this purpose?

For further discussion, see Margrit Eichler, "Case History: The Story of John by Meg Luxton," in Margrit Eichler, ed., *Family Shifts: Families, Policies, and Gender Equality* (Toronto: Oxford University Press, 1997), 138ff. You may also wish to reconsider this problem, particularly in relation to married and cohabiting relationships, after reviewing the materials in chapter 2, and especially the report of the Law Commission of Canada, *Beyond Conjugality: Recognizing and Supporting Close Personal Relationships* (Ottawa: Minister of Public Works and Government Services, 2001).

CHAPTER REFERENCES

Aiken, Sharryn and Sheena Scott. "Baker v. Canada (Minister of Citizenship and Immigration) and the Rights of Children" (2000), 15 *Journal of Law and Social Policy* 211.

Baker, Maureen. *Canadian Family Policies: Cross-National Comparisons* (Toronto: University of Toronto Press, 1995).

_____. "Thinking About Families: Trends and Policies," in Maureen Baker, ed., *Canada's Changing Families: Challenges to Public Policy* (Ottawa: Vanier Institute of the Family, 1994).

Barrett, Michele and Mary McIntosh. *The Anti-Social Family*, 2d ed. (London: Verso, 1991).

Boyd, Susan B. and Claire F.L. Young. " 'From Same-Sex to No Sex'? Trends Towards Recognition of (Same-Sex) Relationships in Canada" (2003), 1:3 *Seattle Journal for Social Justice* 757.

_____. "Challenging the Public/Private Divide: An Overview," in Susan B. Boyd, ed., *Challenging the Public/Private Divide: Feminism, Law, and Public Policy* (Toronto: University of Toronto Press, 1997), 3.

_____. "Teaching Policy Issues in Family Law" (1989-90), 8 *Canadian Journal of Family Law* 11.

Canadian Bar Association. *Making the Case: The Right to Publicly Funded Legal Representation in Canada* (Ottawa: Canadian Bar Association, 2002).

_____. *Touchstones for Change: Equality, Diversity and Accountability* (Ottawa: Canadian Bar Association, 1993).

Canadian Council on Social Development. *The Progress of Canada's Children 2002* (Ottawa: Canadian Council on Social Development, 2002).

Chunn, Dorothy E. "Feminism, Law, and 'the Family': Assessing the Reform Legacy," in Elizabeth Comack, ed., *Locating Law: Race/Class/Gender Connections* (Halifax: Fernwood Press, 1999), 236.

Cossman, Brenda. "Lesbians, Gay Men, and the Canadian Charter of Rights and Freedoms" (2002), 40 *Osgoode Hall Law Journal* 223.

Cretney, Stephen. *Law, Law Reform and the Family* (Oxford: Clarendon Press, 1998).

Das Gupta, Tania. "Families of Native People, Immigrants, and People of Colour," in Nancy Mandell and Ann Duffy, eds., *Canadian Families: Diversity, Conflict and Change*, 2d ed. (Toronto: Harcourt Canada, 2000), 146.

Dewar, John. "Family, Law and Theory" (1996), 16 *Oxford Journal of Legal Studies* 725.

_____. "The Normal Chaos of Family Law" (1998), 61 *Modern Law Review* 467.

Eekelaar, John. "Uncovering Social Obligations: Family Law and the Responsible Citizen," in Mavis Maclean, ed., *Making Law for Families* (Oxford and Portland, OR: Hart Publishing, 2000).

Eichler, Margrit. *Families in Canada Today: Recent Changes and Their Policy Consequences* (Scarborough, ON: Gage Publications, 1983).

_____. "Case History: The Story of John by Meg Luxton," in Margrit Eichler, ed., *Family Shifts: Families, Policies, and Gender Equality* (Toronto: Oxford University Press, 1997), 138.

Fricker, Judge Nigel. "Family Law Is Different" (1995), 33 *Family and Conciliation Courts Review* 403.

Gallanter, Marc. "Law Abounding: Legalisation Around the North Atlantic" (1992), 55 *Modern Law Review* 1.

Glendon, Mary Ann. *The Transformation of Family Law: State, Law and Family in the United States and Western Europe* (Chicago and London: University of Chicago Press, 1989).

Grillo, Trina. "The Mediation Alternative: Process Dangers for Women" (1991), 100 *Yale Law Journal* 1545.

Knetsch, Jack L. "Some Economic Implications of Matrimonial Property Rules" (1984), 34 *University of Toronto Law Journal* 263.

Law Commission of Canada. *Beyond Conjugality: Recognizing and Supporting Close Personal Adult Relationships* (Ottawa: Minister of Public Works and Government Services, 2001).

Le Bourdais, C. and N. Marcil-Gratton (with D. Bélanger). "Quebec's Pro-Active Approach to Family Policy: 'Thinking and Acting Family,' " in Maureen Baker, ed., *Canada's Changing Families: Challenges to Public Policy* (Ottawa: Vanier Institute of the Family, 1994), 103.

Maclean, Mavis. "Introduction," in Mavis Maclean, ed., *Making Law for Families* (Oxford and Portland, OR: Hart Publishing, 2000), 1.

Mandell, Nancy and Ann Duffy, eds., *Canadian Families: Diversity, Conflict and Change*, 2d ed. (Toronto: Harcourt Canada, 2000).

Minow, Martha and Mary Lyndon Shanley, "Relational Rights and Responsibilities: Revisioning the Family in Liberal Political Theory and Law" (1996), 11 *Hypatia* 4.

Morisette, René. "On the Edge: Financially Vulnerable Families" (Winter 2002), 67 *Canadian Social Trends* 13.

O'Brien, Carol-Anne and Aviva Goldberg. "Lesbians and Gay Men Inside and Outside Families," in Nancy Mandell and Ann Duffy, eds., *Canadian Families: Diversity, Conflict and Change*, 2d ed. (Toronto: Harcourt Canada, 2000), 115.

O'Donovan, Katherine. *Family Law Matters* (London: Pluto Press, 1993).

Olsen, Frances E. "The Myth of State Intervention in the Family" (1985), 18 *University of Michigan Journal of Law Reform* 835.

Pupo, Norene. "Preserving Patriarchy: Women, the Family and the State," in Nancy Mandell and Ann Duffy, eds., *Canadian Families: Diversity, Conflict and Change*, 2d ed. (Toronto: Harcourt Canada, 2000), 207.

Sauvé, Roger. "The Current State of Canadian Family Finances, 2002 Report" (Ottawa: Vanier Institute of the Family, 2003).

_____. "Trends in Canadian Family Finances" (1999), *Vanier Institute of the Family: Transition* 10.

Shields, Richard W., Judith P. Ryan, and Victoria L. Smith. *Collaborative Family Law: Another Way To Resolve Family Disputes* (Toronto: Carswell, 2003).

Smart, Carol. "Wishful Thinking and Harmful Tinkering? Sociological Reflections on Family Policy" (1997), 26 *Journal of Social Policy* 301.

Statistics Canada. *Profile of Canadian Families and Households: Diversification Continues* (Ottawa: Statistics Canada 2001 Census Analysis Series, 2002).

_____. *2001 Census: Analysis Series: Income of Canadian Families* (Ottawa: Minister of Industry, 2003).

Symes, Pamela. "Property, Power and Dependence: Critical Family Law" (1987), 14 *Journal of Law and Society* 199.

Valverde, Mariana. "Families, Private Property, and the State: The Dionnes and the Toronto Stork Derby" (1994-95), 29 *Journal of Canadian Studies* 15.

Vanier Institute of the Family. *Profiling Canada's Families* (Ottawa: Vanier Institute of the Family, 1994).

_____. *Profiling Canada's Families II* (Ottawa: Vanier Institute of the Family, 2000).

CHAPTER TWO

Forming Families in Canada: Marriage in the Context of Cohabitation

I. INTRODUCTION

Marriage has been well said to be something more than a contract, either religious or civil—to be an Institution. It creates mutual rights and obligations, as all contracts do, but beyond that it confers a status.

> *Hyde v. Hyde and Woodmansee*, [1866] 1 LR 130
> (Div. & Mat. Causes), at 133

Marriage has been widely debated in recent years. Perhaps no single issue touches more people. Everyone—those who are married, those who have chosen not to marry or remarry and those who have not had the opportunity to choose—has an opinion. Their opinions are based on their own experiences and on the experiences of their parents, their children and families, friends and neighbours, as well as on their values and beliefs.

> Department of Justice Canada, *Marriage and Legal*
> *Recognition of Same-Sex Unions: A Discussion Paper*
> (Ottawa: Department of Justice, 2002)

This chapter and the one that follows focus on legal issues relating to family formation, either by marriage or by the creation of parent–child relationships. Traditionally, Canadian family law focused on the creation of families through marriage. As the English court described the marriage relationship in *Hyde* (just one year before Confederation in Canada), marriage was traditionally understood as both a contract and a legal status with prescribed rights and obligations. At the present time, however, the law of marriage in Canada is in flux, with a number of reform proposals under consideration, particularly as a result of Charter equality litigation that confirmed the availability of marriage for same-sex couples in mid-2003 in two provinces, Ontario and British Columbia, and in 2004 in Quebec. At the same time, the rate of marriage for opposite-sex couples has been declining in recent years as increasing numbers of couples have chosen to cohabit informally rather than enter into legal marriages. In this context, it is clear that there are a variety of different views about the significance of marriage as a legal and social institution in Canada.

From a family law perspective, marriage needs to be examined in relation to cohabitation (opposite-sex and same-sex), particularly to assess the implications of current reform proposals. In addition, the law of marriage reveals important relationships between legal norms and the ways that families actually live their lives. Although many people form families without regard to the legal rights and obligations that result, their lack of attention to law does not make it irrelevant, nor does it make their legal obligations unenforceable. More important, the law of marriage may create norms and ideals about families that operate to create social expectations for families. In this way, the law of marriage provides an opportunity to examine underlying assumptions about intimate relationships, and the legal rights and obligations that flow from them, and to explore the potential impact that these assumptions have on current reform proposals.

Thus, this chapter examines the formation of families through marriage. It begins by examining the background to the law of marriage in relation to two sets of issues: first, the relationship between marriage and cohabitation, including some information about the extension of the legal rights and obligations of marriage to cohabitees; and, second, the historical context of marriage in relation to the law of annulment and the constitutional division of powers in Canada. The material then explores some of the traditional legal principles about the validity of marriage, focusing on the historical requirements of English common law and of provincial statutes in Canada. This material provides the background for examining recent Charter challenges in relation to same-sex marriage in Canada, similar developments in other jurisdictions, and a variety of reform proposals currently under consideration. In this context, recent litigation challenges about marriage and transsexuals also provide an opportunity to examine underlying assumptions about the law of marriage.

II. CONTEXTS FOR LEGAL MARRIAGE

A. Marriage and Cohabitation

Today, there is very little difference between marriage and cohabitation. Marriage encompasses a range of relationships, some characterized by various forms of dependency, while others involve spouses who are quite independent, financially and otherwise. Marriage may or may not involve procreation. Cohabitation relationships are found along a similar spectrum. There is no reason to differentiate between the two based on the notion that cohabitation is different from a *traditional* marriage. When we compare cohabitation and modern-day marriage there are few distinctions.

> Winnifred Holland, "Intimate Relationships in the New
> Millennium: The Assimilation of Marriage and Cohabitation?"
> (2000), 17 *Canadian Journal of Family Law* 114, at 151

1. Statistical Trends

Holland's assertion provides a useful starting point for examining the law of marriage in Canada. As the data in chapter 1 illustrates, the percentage of married-couple families has been declining for several decades, at the same time as the numbers of cohabiting couples have been rising, sometimes quite dramatically. According to Statistics Canada, the rate of marriage in 1996 was 5.2 per 1,000 population, a rate that was lower than in previous decades, including during the Depression in the 1930s when the rate was 6.4 per 1,000 population (Vanier Institute of the Family, *Profiling Canada's Families II* (Ottawa: Vanier Institute of the Family, 2000) at 40-41). For 2000, the marriage rate was slightly lower at 5.1 per 1,000 population.

The average age of marriage has also been rising. For women who married in 2000, their average age was 31.7 years (up 2.7 years from 1990 and 5.8 years from 1980). The average age of men who married in 2000 was 34.3 years (also an increase of 2.7 years from 1990 and 5.8 years from 1980). For first time marriages in 2000, the average age for women was 28, and the average age for men was 30. About two-thirds of all marriages in 2000 were first time marriages (65.3 percent), by contrast with almost three-quarters in 1980 (73.5 percent). However, these figures also demonstrate an increasing proportion of subsequent marriages, a fact that suggests that marriage remains an important commitment for some Canadians: see Statistics Canada, *Marriages 2000*, online at http://www.statcan.ca/Daily/English/030602/d030602a.htm.

2. Form and Function in Marriage and Cohabiting Relationships

According to Holland, the features of *modern* marriage and cohabiting relationships are similar. In such a context, it may be that only the form of families is changing, not their fundamental nature. Recent studies of marriage and (opposite-sex) cohabitation have examined a number of explanations for the increase in cohabiting relationships. For example, Zheng Wu identified both economic and sociological explanations.

Zheng Wu, *Cohabitation: An Alternative Form of Family Living*
(Toronto: Oxford University Press, 2000), 154

[According to economic analyses, women's increased participation in the labour force has reduced women's economic dependence and weakened the sexual division of labour within the family, making marriage less necessary and cohabitation more attractive:]

Cohabitation implies less commitment while offering many of the advantages of marriage. It allows the couple to live in a family environment, provides the couple with the scale of economy, and, at the same time, offers them benefits of the single state. More important, it allows them to try out the relationship and see whether the relationship will work.

Sociological explanations also confirm the increasing attraction of cohabitation for opposite-sex couples. Identifying the significant ideological change in the Western family from family-oriented interests to more individualistic pursuits, sociological explanations focus on the rejection of traditional gender roles and increasing acceptance of sexual activity outside of marriage to conclude that changing social attitudes have weakened the attraction of marriage as a social institution (see Wu, at 155-56).

3. Legal Regulation of Cohabiting Relationships

From the perspective of family law, these changes in the rate of opposite-sex cohabitation and in social attitudes about it have created significant policy issues: to what extent should family law extend the benefits and the obligations of marriage to cohabiting couples? That is, should cohabiting couples be treated, for legal purposes, *as if* they were married; or should they be regarded as single persons, subject only to such obligations or entitled to such benefits as they may mutually agree on by contract? The view that cohabitation should not be subject to legal regulation was argued forcefully by Ruth Deech more than two decades ago.

> ### Ruth Deech, "The Case Against Legal Recognition of Cohabitation"
> in John Eekelaar and Sanford Katz, eds., *Marriage and Cohabitation in Contemporary Societies: Areas of Legal, Social, and Ethical Change* (Toronto: Butterworths, 1980), 300, at 301-3

[According to Deech, there are three reasons why cohabitation should not be treated as marriage by law:

1. *Different expectations:* Deech argued that married couples and cohabitees have different expectations, which should be met. For example, some cohabitees are seeking a trial period before deciding to marry; for those cohabitees who subsequently choose not to marry, there is no reason to penalize them by imposing the same obligations that would apply if they had been married. Thus, if a couple has decided that cohabitation is in their best interests, the law should not force them to take part in a legal relationship that they expressly chose not to enter.

2. *Rejection of legal incidents of marriage:* Some cohabitees reject the legal incidents of marriage, perhaps because traditional laws seem unsuitable or unattractive to them, and "there ought to be a corner of freedom for such couples to which they can escape and avoid family law" (at 302). For such cohabitees, contractual agreements may be more appropriate.

3. *Nature of the marriage commitment:* Deech suggested that the nature of the commitment of married couples is not necessarily shared by cohabitees, and that the law should respect individuals' freedom to create alternative relationships without the threat that they will be "converted" to marriage by law. As she argued, the law should recognize the importance of preserving "the freedom to try alternative forms of relationship, a freedom which is at present being eroded by the increased tendency of the law to impose on the formerly cohabiting couple the status and structure of traditional marriage" (at 302).]

Other Academic Assessments

Zheng Wu also acknowledged arguments for distinguishing marriage and cohabitation in law, including the preservation of choice for individuals in designing their families, as well as the need for the state, through its legal regulation, to provide incentives for individuals to marry. At the same time, Wu's assessment of existing patterns of cohabitation in Canada indicated a high degree of functional similarity between marriage and cohabitation, and he recommended legal recognition of the need to ensure protection for dependency when either marriage or cohabitation ends. Wu also cited the requirements of legal equality and the need to avoid public confusion about differing legal consequences for marriage and cohabitation as additional reasons for legal regulation of cohabitation (at 167):

> In recognition of the changing patterns of non-marital cohabitation, the rights and responsibilities imposed on matrimonial couples should be extended to cohabiting couples in all provinces provided that some permanence of the relationship is established [by cohabiting continuously for one year, by becoming the natural or adoptive parents of a child, or by registering as partners pursuant to provincial legislation]. In short, cohabiting individuals should have the same rights and obligations as married persons.

Similarly, Holland concluded (at 166) that law reform is needed to eliminate the remaining legal distinctions between marriage and cohabitation:

> The similarity between married and a long-term cohabitation should be recognized and there should be an extension of all rights and obligations, traditionally associated with marriage, to cohabitants [including both opposite- and same-sex].

According to Holland, cohabitees who wish to opt out of these rights and obligations would be required to contract out of them expressly. For her (at 167), "since there is little to distinguish marriage and long-term cohabitation, the assimilation of the two is appropriate."

Some studies have tried to ascertain what factors may encourage couples to cohabit rather than to marry. For example, Anne Millan examined data from the 2001 General Social Survey to determine the extent to which never-married and previously married people, who had never lived in a cohabiting relationship, would be willing to do so in future. Interestingly, 62 percent of men, but only 36 percent of women, said they would consider cohabitation, although the willingness to do so declined with age for both sexes. Higher levels of education and labour force participation were also factors more often associated with a willingness to consider cohabitation. The study confirmed that people in Quebec were more willing, by comparison with other parts of Canada, to cohabit; however, the proportion of people willing to consider cohabitation in Quebec was higher for persons whose home language was French (63 percent), by contrast with those whose home language was English (46 percent); and only 26 percent of those whose home language was other than English or French expressed willingness to consider cohabitation. Similarly, the willingness to cohabit was higher for Canadian-born individuals than for those born outside Canada. Frequent attendance at religious services was associated with less willingness to cohabit and greater interest in marriage. The study also suggested that childhood experiences of family breakup were somewhat related to a willingness to cohabit: for "[m]en and women who, at least up to the age of 15, lived with both their parents [were less willing to cohabit] than those whose parents had divorced, separated, or become widowed: 58% versus 45%": see Anne Millan, "Would You Live Common-Law?" (Autumn 2003), *Canadian Social Trends* 2, at 5. Consider this data, and the views expressed about marriage and cohabitation, above, in relation to legal rights and benefits for these families.

Judicial Views About Marriage and Cohabitation

To some extent, the recommendations of Wu and Holland reflect the current trend of legal regulation of cohabitation in Canada, where many of the same rights and obligations have increasingly been extended to both married couples and cohabitees. For example, obligations of spousal and child support currently apply to both married couples who divorce and to cohabitees (both opposite-sex and same-sex) who separate. However, only married persons are eligible to obtain a divorce, and the Supreme Court of Canada has upheld provincial property regimes that are applicable to married couples, but not to cohabitees, at separation: see *Nova Scotia v. Walsh*, 2002 SCC 83; (2002), 221 DLR (4th) 1; 32 RFL (5th) 81 (discussed in chapter 6). In this way, the rights and obligations of married couples and cohabitees currently remain somewhat different in Canadian law.

Moreover, as a result of judicial decisions permitting same-sex marriage in British Columbia, Ontario, and Quebec, it is arguable that these legal distinctions between marriage and cohabitation now apply to both opposite-sex and same-sex couples. Prior to the availability of same-sex marriage, of course, only opposite-sex couples had *choices* about whether to marry or cohabit. Thus, the extension of marriage to same-sex couples in these two provinces has now created choices of marriage or cohabitation for them as well. In this context, traditional legal principles of marriage must be assessed in the context of patterns of cohabitation, and in relation to underlying policies about the legal regulation of families in Canada.

B. Marriage, Law, and the Constitution

1. Constitutional Authority for Marriage Legislation

Current proposals to reform the law of marriage in Canada attest that reform is complicated by two factors: the constitutional authority for legislating about marriage and the common law history of marriage.

As Peter Hogg, *Constitutional Law of Canada* (Toronto: Carswell) (looseleaf), at s. 26:1, noted in relation to the constitutional context, s. 92(13) of the *Constitution Act, 1867* accords responsibility to provincial legislatures in relation to "property and civil rights," ensuring that much of family law falls within the jurisdiction of the provinces.

More specifically, in relation to marriage, however, s. 91(26) assigns authority to legislate with respect to "marriage and divorce" to the federal Parliament. At the same time, s. 92(12) provides that provincial legislatures may legislate with respect to "the solemnization of marriage in the province," a provision that clearly necessitates some division of responsibility in relation to marriage legislation, including any proposed reform legislation. The relationship between federal and provincial authority for legislating about marriage was considered by the Privy Council in *Reference re Marriage Legislation in Canada*, [1912] App. Cas. 880 (PC). The Privy Council gave a large and liberal interpretation to the provincial authority; it specifically concluded (at 886-87) that provincial legislatures could enact "conditions as to solemnization which may affect the validity of the contract."

Although the Privy Council decision thus confirmed that failure to comply with either federal or provincial requirements might result in the invalidity of a marriage, the precise scope of the provincial power to legislate with respect to "the solemnization of marriage," as an exception to the federal power to legislate with respect to "marriage," remained somewhat unclear. According to Hogg (at s. 26.3 (a)):

> Following the *Marriage Reference*, it is clear that a province has power to stipulate pre-ceremonial requirements such as, the issue of a licence or the publication of banns, and to stipulate the qualifications of the person performing the ceremony, even if breach of the stipulations renders the marriage a nullity. These are matters closely associated with the performance of the ceremony—the solemnization.

As Hogg noted, however, two subsequent decisions of the Supreme Court of Canada concluded that provincial authority also extended to legislating a requirement of parental consent as a condition of validity of the marriage. In *Kerr v. Kerr*, [1934] SCR 72, at 82-83 (citing *Sottomayor v. De Barros* (1877), 3 Prob. Div. 1, at 7), the court stated that "consent must be considered a part of the ceremony of marriage, and not a matter affecting the personal capacity of the parties to contract marriage." Commenting on this decision and *Attorney-General of Alberta v. Underwood*, [1934] SCR 635, Hogg suggested that these cases were decided on "the dubious ground that parental consent was a 'formality' of marriage rather than a matter governing the capacity of the parties." As is evident, the court equated authority to legislate in relation to "solemnization" with the idea of "formalities," arguably a broader category than ceremonial requirements. As a result, the scope of provincial authority with respect to marriage legislation was expanded. In relation to the requirements for a valid marriage, illustrated in the sections that follow, consider the extent to which they appear to reflect matters of capacity, or matters of solemnization or formalities. How do these constitutional provisions, as interpreted by the courts, affect the context of current proposals for reforming the law of marriage?

In addition to the complexities of federal and provincial constitutional authority for legislating with respect to marriage, the law of marriage in Canada is complicated by the fact that although the provinces have enacted statutes governing the requirements of solemnization, the federal Parliament has not enacted comprehensive marriage legislation. With a few exceptions, therefore, the federal law of marriage is based on common law requirements of capacity, frequently derived from 19th-century English cases interpreting provisions of the 1857 *Divorce and Matrimonial Causes Act*, 20 and 21 Vict., c. 85, cases that may not well reflect the needs of modern marriage in Canada. Thus, in the context of current reform proposals, some of these common law requirements may need to be reassessed, in whole or in part. At present, however, an understanding of the common law of marriage remains central to issues about the law of marriage: see Christine Davies, *Family Law in Canada* (Scarborough, ON: Carswell Legal Publications, 1984), at chapters 2 and 3.

2. The History of Marriage and the Law of Nullity

The common law of marriage is complicated by its history as a social and religious institution that was only later regulated by law. According to Martin Ingram, an indissoluble union could be created as early as the 12th century solely by the consent of the two parties expressed in words in the present tense (*per verba de praesenti*). Solemnization in church was not required, nor was the presence of witnesses; the emphasis was on individual freedom of consent. Eventually, concerns about evils arising from clandestine marriages, as well as confusion and uncertainty about marital status, resulted in the decree of the Council of Trent in 1563. The decree, which applied to Catholic Europe, invalidated marriages not performed in public before a parish priest; similar changes were adopted in some continental Protestant countries. However, it was not until 1753 that similar provisions were formally adopted by the English Parliament in *Lord Hardwicke's Act: An Act for the better preventing of clandestine marriages*, 26 Geo. II, c. 33. All the same, Ingram suggested that social and legal pressures encouraged public ceremonies of marriage even prior to 1753: see Martin Ingram, *Church Courts, Sex, and Marriage in England, 1570-1640* (Cambridge: Cambridge University Press, 1987), at 132-33 and 218.

In this context, ecclesiastical courts had responsibility for determining the validity of marriage, issuing decrees of nullity for marriages that failed to meet requirements based on social and religious practices, as well as a few established by Acts of Parliament. Some of these requirements remain in force still—for example, the consent of the parties remains an important requirement for a valid marriage, and public affirmation of consent by the couple is still part of the marriage ceremony. When the English *Matrimonial Causes Act* was enacted in 1857, however, it abolished the jurisdiction of ecclesiastical courts, assigning this jurisdiction to the regular system of courts in England. Interestingly, for some years, judges in Ontario asserted that Ontario courts did not have jurisdiction to grant decrees of nullity because no similar ecclesiastical court jurisdiction had ever existed in Ontario, and thus this jurisdiction had never been transferred to Ontario courts. As a result, federal legislation was enacted in 1930—the *Annulment of Marriages Act* (Ontario)—conferring on Ontario courts the jurisdiction to grant decrees of nullity: see RSC 1970, c. A-14. This legislation introduced into Ontario the law of nullity in England as of July 15, 1870. Ontario's current law of nullity is thus derived from principles adopted by the English ecclesiastical courts. In the four western provinces of Canada, the 1857 legislation remains the law of annulment, while some pre-1857 colonial statutes remain effective in the Maritimes: see Davies, at 35-39. Because of their common origin in canon law, moreover, these principles are similar to those in the Quebec *Civil Code*.

Before the advent of accessible divorce actions, nullity actions represented the only way for married couples to end their relationships legally. By contrast, because grounds for divorce can now be established generally by a period of one year of separation, actions for nullity are less common, although not unknown, particularly where one spouse wishes to avoid religious problems that may accompany divorce. Yet, although nullity and divorce both result in the end of a marriage, they are conceptually quite different.

H.R. Hahlo, *Nullity of Marriage in Canada: With a Sideways Glance at*
Concubinage and Its Legal Consequences
(Toronto: Butterworths, 1979), at 1-2

A decree of nullity is not a divorce by another name. Divorce presupposes a valid marriage. It is based on a post-nuptial event, and depending on the legal system, the event may be a serious matrimonial offence ... [or] ... marriage breakdown. ... [A divorce] dissolves the marriage *ex nunc*—as from the date of the decree. Nullity results from some defect or disability which exists at the time of the marriage ceremony ... and prevents an unassailable marriage from coming into existence. Where the ground of annulment is one which renders the marriage void *ab initio*, the decree of nullity declares that there never was a marriage; where the ground of annulment is one which renders the marriage voidable, the decree of nullity annuls it, at common law, with retroactive effect.

It is interesting that in spite of the differences between divorce and nullity, statutes may provide for the same rights and obligations—for example, see the definition of spouse in s. 1(1) of Ontario's *Family Law Act*, RSO 1990, c. F.3, which includes parties to a void or voidable marriage.

A void marriage is one that is non-existent, even if it has not been annulled formally by a court of law. By contrast, a voidable marriage is one that stands until it is annulled. In both cases, however, courts declare such marriages "void." The issue of what makes a marriage void or voidable is a matter of some complexity in English common law. For example, bigamy usually renders a marriage absolutely void, because there is a valid marriage in existence at the date of the second marriage. By contrast, parties who are underage may have a voidable marriage, but it may be validated if they choose to remain married after attaining the age of majority. Rules also restrict applications for annulment to the parties to the marriage if the marriage is void, while permitting other interested parties to bring such actions if the marriage is merely voidable. In the civil law of Quebec, the law of annulment also includes concepts of absolute and relative nullity. These distinctions are not addressed in detail here; for further discussion, see Hahlo, at 1-56.

Discussion Notes

Options for Reforming Marriage in Law

As these materials suggest, there are significant similarities between marriage and co-habitation relationships, and the legal principles applicable to marriage have been derived from developments in social and religious practices in England, often many centuries ago. Yet, although both these factors suggested a need for reform, governments did not generally engage in significant reform efforts until the success of recent litigation challenges concerning same-sex marriage. In this context, the Department of Justice Discussion Paper in 2002 suggested three alternatives: (1) the status quo; (2) the extension of marriage to same-sex couples; and (3) relinquishing legal authority for marriage altogether.

According to this third alternative, religious bodies would be entitled to continue to conduct marriage ceremonies in accordance with their beliefs, but such marriages would have no legal impact. Instead, there would be a registry for opposite-sex and same-sex couples, and provincial and territorial governments would be required to establish regimes governing the breakdown of these registered relationships. The law would not be retroactive, and divorce would still be available to those couples already married. Over time, however, "marriage" would again become a social and religious, but not a legal, institution, just as it was many centuries ago: see Department of Justice Canada, *Marriage and Legal Recognition of Same-Sex Unions: A Discussion Paper* (Ottawa: Department of Justice, 2002). What arguments support such an arrangement? Leaving aside the practical problems of federal–provincial cooperation that would be required to achieve this reform and other concerns about recognition of registered relationships outside Canada (large problems, of course), what are the advantages and disadvantages of removing marriage from legal regulation?

Marriage and Cohabitation: The Use of Contract

Some critics have suggested a need to create intimate relationships "outside" the law through the use of contracts: see, for example, Lenore J. Weitzman, *The Marriage Contract: Spouses, Lovers, and the Law* (New York: The Free Press, 1981) and Michael D.A. Freeman and Christina M. Lyon, *Cohabitation Without Marriage* (Aldershot, UK: Gower, 1983). In a review of the latter, Katherine O'Donovan noted the limits of the contractual approach in Freeman and Lyon:

> Freeman and Lyon are in a bind. On the one hand they object to the assimilation of cohabitation with marriage, partly because of the sexism of legal structures, and partly because of their own espousal of the values of individualism and autonomy. Yet they admit that the problem with express contracts is that their usefulness is limited to the articulate middle-classes; the problem with implied contracts is that their interpreters are likely to be imbued with the patriarchal attitudes so rightly deplored in relation to marriage.

(Katherine O'Donovan, "Legal Marriage—Who Needs It?" (1984), 47 *Modern Law Review* 111, at 116.)

Do you agree with this assessment? Contrast this contractual approach in Freeman and Lyon (contract as the basis for the formation of intimate relationships) with Holland's recommendation that legal regulation should apply in the same way to both marriage and cohabitation, subject to the right of couples (married and cohabiting) to contract out of legal rights and responsibilities (a contracting-out approach). Which role for contract is preferable? Why?

Common Law Marriage

It appears that common law marriage—that is, legal recognition of a marriage that does not conform to statutory requirements—may still exist in some US states. In Canada as well, a court in the Northwest Territories in *Re Noah Estate*, (1961) 32 DLR (2d) 185; 36 WWR 577 (NWT Terr. Ct.) recognized a marriage between aboriginal persons that was celebrated in accordance with Inuit custom, apparently recognizing it as a valid common law marriage: for a discussion of this case and others, see Bradford W. Morse, "Indian and Inuit Family Law and the Canadian Legal System" (1980-81), 8-9 *American Indian Law Review* 199.

Common law marriage was also examined in Ontario in *Dutch v. Dutch* (1977), 1 RFL (2d) 177 (Ont. Co. Ct.). A couple married in 1954 and divorced in 1971. Pursuant to the separation agreement, the former husband agreed to pay spousal support to his former wife "during her lifetime, and so long as she remains unmarried." The former wife commenced living with another man (G.) after the divorce decree, but she did not marry him. Her former husband ceased paying spousal support to her, arguing that there was a "marriage at common law" between his former wife and G., a form of marriage recognized in Ontario; and that since the only reason that his former wife had not married G. was to ensure continuation of the spousal support payments, the obligation to pay support was contrary to public policy and inequitable. The court rejected both arguments, holding that the former husband had an obligation to continue to pay spousal support. In doing so, the court reviewed the history of marriages in England and the reception of English marriage law in Canada at the time of Confederation.

The issue about the meaning of marriage at Confederation became significant more recently in the same-sex marriage challenge in British Columbia, where it was argued that the concept of marriage in s. 91(26) had a fixed meaning that could not accommodate same-sex marriages. In an analysis of these issues, Mark Walters argued that English common law acknowledged both ecclesiastical and natural law sources for marriage: "the classical natural law tradition that informed English and other European laws characterized matrimony as the moral precept upon which civil and political society depended." In addition, Walters suggested that the reception of English law by the colonies of Nova Scotia, New Brunswick, and Upper Canada (Ontario) accommodated distinctive approaches to marriage for French-Canadian and aboriginal communities, but that there were few other differences among the common law jurisdictions: see Mark D. Walters, "Incorporating Common Law into the Constitution of Canada: Egale v. Canada and the Status of Marriage" (2003), 41 *Osgoode Hall Law Journal* 75, at 94; and *Egale Canada Inc. v. Canada* (2001), 95 BCLR (3d) 122 (SC); 19 RFL (5th) 59; rev'd. 2003 BCCA 251.

SELECTED REFERENCES

Nicholas Bala and Marlène Cano, "Unmarried Cohabitants in Canada: Common Law and Civilian Approaches to Living Together" (1989), 4 *Canadian Family Law Quarterly* 147.

Alain Bélanger and Pierre Turcotte, "L'Influence des caractéristiques sociodémographiques sur le début de la vie conjugale des Québecoises" (1999), 28 *Cahiers Québecois de Démographie* 173.

Colin Chapman, *Ecclesiastical Courts, Their Officials, and Their Records* (Dursley, England: Lochin Publishing, 1992).

Shelley A.M. Gavigan, "Paradise Lost, Paradox Revisited: The Implications of Familial Ideology for Feminist, Lesbian, and Gay Engagement to Law" (1993), 31 *Osgoode Hall Law Journal* 589.

George Elliott Howard, *A History of Matrimonial Institutions*, 3 vols. (Chicago: University of Chicago Press, 1904).

Leslie Katz, "The Scope of the Federal Legislative Authority in Relation to Marriage" (1975), 7 *Ottawa Law Review* 384.

Judith Keene, "Domestic Contracts Between Cohabiting Spouses" (1978), 1 *Canadian Journal of Family Law* 477.

Évelyne LaPierre-Adamcyk, Céline Le Bourdais, and Nicole Marcil-Gratton, "Vivre en couple pour la première fois: La signification du choix de l'union libre au Québec et en Ontario" (1999), 28 *Cahiers Québecois de Démographie* 199.

Bruce Ziff, "Recent Developments in Canadian Law: Marriage and Divorce" (1986), 18 *Ottawa Law Review* 121.

III. THE VALIDITY OF MARRIAGE AND ACTIONS FOR NULLITY

Nullity occupies a strange place within the sphere of family governance. It is in one sense the most law-like part of family law, for it is ostensibly concerned with technical questions of contract law and decisions about nullity of marriage are often made within the higher echelons of the legal system with all their attendant regalia. On the other hand nullity of marriage ... is both bizarre and rare [and there is something in the narratives of nullity that constitutes "the baroque"].

> Hilary Lim, "Messages from a Rarely Visited Island: Duress and Lack of Consent in Marriage" (1996), IV *Feminist Legal Studies* 195, at 216-17

In accordance with the constitutional authority discussed above, the federal Parliament has authority to legislate with respect to marriage. Thus, it is responsible for defining elements of legal capacity to marry. With a few exceptions, however, Parliament has not legislated about capacity to marry, leaving these requirements as defined at common law. According to common law requirements, a valid marriage required that the parties

- be of opposite sexes (an issue that is addressed more fully in the next section, focusing on both same-sex marriage litigation challenges and the legal challenges faced by transsexuals in this context);
- have capacity to consent to the marriage—that is, have the capacity to understand and be free from duress and without taking account of reservations about or limited purposes of marriage;
- have capacity to consummate the marriage;
- not be within the prohibited grounds of consanguinity and affinity;
- not be a partner in an existing valid marriage; and
- have attained the age required for a valid marriage.

In addition to examining these matters of capacity, this section briefly reviews some of the provisions of provincial statutes concerning marriage, pursuant to the provincial legislatures' authority to legislate with respect to solemnization in s. 92(13) of the Constitution and formalities as defined by judicial decisions.

A. Capacity

1. Consent to Marriage

a. Mental Capacity to Consent

Durham v. Durham

In *Durham v. Durham* (1885), 10 PD 80, the Earl of Durham sued for a declaration of nullity of marriage by reason that, at the time of the celebration of the marriage in 1882, Lady Durham was of unsound mind and incapable of contracting marriage. At the time of the hearing, Lady Durham was described by the court as "hopelessly insane." However, the court held that the burden of showing that she was insane at the time of the marriage rested with the party asserting it; that the test was whether she was capable of understanding the nature of the contract and the duties and responsibilities created by it; and that she was free from any "morbid delusions" about it. In this case, the court held that Lady Durham was able to give her consent at the time of the marriage. As Sir John Hannen stated (at 82):

> [It] appears to me that the contract of marriage is a very simple one, which does not require a high degree of intelligence to comprehend. It is an engagement between a man and a woman to live together, and love one another as husband and wife, to the exclusion of all others.

Webb v. Webb and the Impact of Mental Illness

The requirement of consent focuses on whether a person has the mental capacity to give legal consent. In this context, the fact that a person has a mental illness is not, by itself, sufficient to invalidate a marriage—the issue is whether the person was able to give consent to the marriage. The test was considered in *Webb v. Webb* (1968), 3 RFL 129; (1968), 3 DLR 100 (NS Ct. Div. & Mat. Causes), a case in which two residents of a Nova Scotia psychiatric hospital married. The husband was 22 and had been diagnosed with chronic, progressive schizophrenia; the wife was a minor, also resident in the psychiatric hospital, and pregnant. Although four priests refused their request to marry, a judge agreed to perform the ceremony. Seven months later, the wife gave birth to a child, and less than a year after the child's birth, they separated permanently. The court held that the test for determining mental capacity was whether there was capacity to understand the nature of the contract and the duties and responsibilities it entailed. In this case, the court decided (at 144) that the husband "was mentally capable of appreciating the nature of the contract of marriage and that it involved the responsibilities normally attached to marriage." The court rejected evidence about the limits of the respondent's ability to consent to marriage:

> The witnesses who gave it as their opinion that the respondent was not capable of understanding the nature of the contract he was entering into and the responsibilities normally flowing from that contract seemed to me to be having regard more to the capacity and ability of the respondent to discharge the responsibilities rather than his capacity to appreciate the responsibilities which normally flow from the marriage contract.

As a result, the application for a decree of nullity was dismissed.

In commenting on the *Webb* case, David Thompson reviewed studies about marriages involving persons with mental disabilities and argued that such marriages should not be prohibited:

> There are studies that clearly indicate the success of mentally disabled individuals involved in marriages. In a 1973 study following forty marriages where one or both of the parties had been hospitalized: two had divorced, two separated and sixty percent indicated a satisfactory marriage. There were thirty-two children, two died, six had been removed from their parent's control and only three were retarded. A similar study conducted in 1975 of fifty-four couples showed only fifteen percent had divorced or separated, and only one case where the court had removed the child. The conclusion to the study indicated that at least fifty percent of the couples could sustain a marriage for at least several years with a reasonable degree of competence and that children did not, at least in the first few years, serve as a burden. Studies in 1975 and 1976 yielded the same type of results. It was obvious from these marriages that the majority worked on a complementary basis with one partner taking up the slack of the other; as couples they were able to cope and appeared to be more highly motivated to make the marriage work. Finally they were realistic about the challenges that marriage presents. There was either little or no correlation between the degree of handicap and success of the partnership in either subjective or objective terms and in nearly every instance the marriage had brought a substantial enrichment to the lives of those people studied.

(David Thompson, "A Consideration of the Mental Capacity Provisions of the Marriage Act in View of the Charter of Rights and Freedoms and Webb v. Webb" (1986), 9 *Canadian Community Law Journal* 101, at 106.)

Similarly, an Australian scholar suggested:

> Research has shown that the perceptions of intellectually disabled couples do not differ greatly from [those of] other couples. Interviews show that these couples understand the nature and effect of their marriages, describing their thoughts about their partners, homes and future plans in ways which reflect the views of society in general.

(Kay Maxwell, "Family Law and the Intellectually Disabled in Australia" (1993), 7 *Australian Journal of Family Law* 151, at 154.)

In addition, Thompson argued that the provisions of some provincial statutes in Canada may contravene the Charter rights of persons with mental disabilities, both because the statutory language is overinclusive and because of the disparity caused by variations among different provinces in Canada. Interestingly, there appears to be no impediment to cohabitation for persons with mental illnesses: see Thompson, at 108. Assuming that Thompson is correct in his assessment of the vulnerability of provincial legislation to Charter challenge, what factors may explain the absence to date of major challenges?

b. Duress in Relation to Consent

Scott v. Sebright, Cooper v. Crane, and Buckland v. Buckland

In *Scott v. Sebright* (1886), 12 PD 21, a woman requested a declaration of nullity in relation to her marriage a few months earlier to the respondent. As a 22-year-old woman with a significant fortune, she had been persuaded to lend funds, which then fell into substantial arrears, to the respondent, causing her serious concerns for her reputation. The respondent persuaded her that the only way to avoid declaring bankruptcy was to marry him; he also threatened to shoot her if she suggested that she was not acting with free will at the ceremony. The parties separated after the ceremony, and the marriage was not consummated. Justice Butt granted a declaration of nullity, stating (at 23-24):

> The Courts of law have always refused to recognize as binding contracts to which the consent of either party has been obtained by fraud or duress, and the validity of a contract of marriage must be tested and determined in precisely the same manner as that of any other contract. True it is that in contracts of marriage there is an interest involved above and beyond that of the immediate parties. Public policy requires that marriage should not be lightly set aside, and there is in some cases the strongest temptation to the parties more immediately interested to act in collusion in obtaining a dissolution of the marriage tie. These reasons necessitate great care and circumspection on the part of the tribunal, but they in no wise alter the principle or the grounds on which this, like any other contract, may be avoided. It has sometimes been said that in order to avoid a contract entered into through fear, the fear must be such as would impel a person of ordinary courage and resolution to yield to it. I do not think that is an accurate statement of the law. Wherever from natural weakness of intellect or from fear—whether reasonably entertained or not—either party is actually in a state of mental incompetence to resist pressure improperly brought to bear, there is no more consent than in the case of a person of stronger intellect and more robust courage yielding to a more serious danger. The difficulty consists not in any uncertainty of the law on the subject, but in its application to the facts of each individual case.

Scott v. Sebright was distinguished in *Cooper v. Crane* (1891), P 369. In *Cooper* the action for annulment was brought three years after a marriage ceremony took place between cousins—the woman was 24 and the man not yet 21, although he had obtained a licence for the marriage by falsely stating his age. The woman had rejected the man's proposal, but was persuaded to go through a ceremony of marriage at a church (previously arranged by the man) when he told her to come into the church and marry him or he would "blow [his] brains out and she would be responsible." After the ceremony, the parties returned to their own homes, and the woman did not mention the matter to her family or friends. The man subsequently discovered that the woman did not have money (as he had thought) and indicated that he was not interested in being married to her. However, the court refused to grant a declaration of annulment, stating that the facts were not sufficient to rebut the presumption of consent.

Although there was evidence that the woman was of weak character, "without much power of resistance and easily overpowered by a stronger influence" (at 372), the court concluded (at 376-78) that the evidence did not demonstrate that she did not understand what she was doing, or that her powers of volition were paralyzed. Is this result consistent with *Scott v. Sebright*? Are there differences of fact, or differences in the legal test applied, that explain the contrasting outcomes in the two cases? Compare these cases to *Buckland v. Buckland*, [1967] 2 All ER 300 (PDA Div.), involving a husband who claimed duress that vitiated his consent to a marriage. Justice Scarman granted a declaration of nullity at the request of the husband, a British police officer serving in Malta. The court concluded that the husband had agreed to marriage solely to avoid going to prison in relation to a charge of "corrupting a minor," a charge which Justice Scarman believed had been falsely laid against him by a Maltese family in relation to their pregnant daughter. In these circumstances, the court concluded (at 302) that the husband "agreed to his marriage because of his fears, and that his fears, which were reasonably entertained, arose from external circumstances for which he was in no way responsible." Is this test the same as the one applied in *Scott* and in *Cooper*? Consider the application of these precedents in *S.(A.) v. S.(A.)* (1988), 15 RFL (3d) 443; 65 OR (2d) 720 (UFC)—is the test for duress in Canada an objective or subjective test?

S.(A.) v. S.(A.)
(1988), 15 RFL (3d) 443; 65 OR (2d) 720 (UFC)

MENDES DA COSTA UFCJ: In this case, the applicant is A.S. and the respondent is A.S. The applicant seeks the annulment of her marriage to the respondent or, in the alternative, a divorce. The respondent did not file an answer or appear at the hearing. The applicant's testimony was the only evidence adduced to the court.

1. The Facts

The applicant was born on 9th April 1969. On 28th February 1986 she went through a form of marriage with the respondent, who had recently arrived in Canada. The marriage was celebrated at the city hall, Hamilton, and the certificate of marriage was filed as Ex. 2. At this date, the applicant was 16 years of age. Her parents had separated, and she was living with her mother and her stepfather. The consent of the mother to the marriage was contained in a certificate of consent filed as Ex. 3.

Paragraph 8 of the application contains the grounds for relief and comprises subparas. (a) to (e). Subparagraphs (b), (c) and (d) read as follows:

(b) The applicant married the respondent after considerable pressure being applied against her by her natural mother and step-father. The applicant did not know the respondent but was told that he would be ordered to leave Canada unless he married a Canadian citizen.

(c) The applicant's mother and step-father were to receive $500.00 for arranging to have the applicant marry the respondent. This was the motive for their participation. The applicant was particularly sensitive to the pressure because there was a history of sexual abuse by the step-father toward her. In fact, the applicant was removed from the home for a period of three years by the Children's Aid Society in Calgary, Alberta because of this abuse.

(d) The applicant never lived with the Respondent and she has never had sexual intercourse with him.

The applicant stated that she was first approached by her mother and her stepfather, who applied pressure to her to marry the respondent. The applicant was told that the respondent wished to marry because he wanted to live in Canada. She testified that her mother and stepfather told her that there was $2,000 involved and that they said that "we can have all this nice stuff that we didn't have before with all this money." The applicant said that she told her mother that she did not want to marry the respondent, that her mother "was talking to my step-father and then there was more pressure." The applicant further testified that she did not want to marry the respondent, that she did not live with him after the ceremony, that the parties never engaged in sexual intercourse, and that the respondent subsequently left Canada. The applicant, in her evidence, stated that a few years ago she had been made a ward of the Children's Aid Society in Alberta because she had been sexually abused by her stepfather, and that she had remained in care until she turned 16 years.

· · ·

4. Duress

It was submitted by Mr. Rogers that the applicant was pressured into marrying the respondent by her mother and stepfather and that, given the surrounding circumstances, she was not able to withstand that pressure. During argument, I questioned this submission.

The applicant made no allegation of the use of physical force, nor did she allege that the use of physical force had been threatened. Moreover, the conduct alleged as duress did not emanate from the respondent. The conduct contended by Mr. Rogers to constitute duress was pressure of a non-physical nature, which was directed at the applicant by the mother and stepfather, who sought to obtain financial benefit from the proposed marriage, be it $500, as stated in para. 8(b) of the application, or $2,000 as related by the applicant during her evidence.

There are relatively few reported cases dealing with annulment of marriage induced by duress, and the applicable principles seem to have emerged in a series of older decisions: *Field's Marriage Annulling Bill* (1848), 2 HL Cas. 48, 9 ER 1010, where there is a reference to early cases; *Scott v. Sebright* (1886), 12 PD 21; *Cooper v. Crane*, [1891] P369.

[Mendes da Costa J quoted the words of Butt J in *Scott v. Sebright*, above, and continued:]

The principles expounded by Butt J seem as sound today as they were when they were uttered in 1886. Public policy still requires that marriages "should not be lightly set aside." No doubt, also, there is in some cases the "strongest temptation to the parties more immediately interested to act in collusion." A court is, indeed, required to exercise care and circumspection to ensure that the ground alleged as duress has been established. However, since 1886 there has been a considerable change in the availability of divorce. Under the *Divorce Act, 1985*, SC 1986, c. 4, the ground for divorce is breakdown of marriage. Leaving aside adultery and cruelty, relief is available where, in general terms, the spouses have lived separate and apart for at least one year. As a more or less parallel development, the status of illegitimacy has been eradicated from the law of the province and, to some extent, "spouse" has received an expanded definition in the *Family Law Act, 1986*, SO 1986, c. 4. At this point in time, there seems no need for parties to turn to the law of nullity simply to obtain relief denied them by divorce law. I believe, therefore, that the courts should approach a proceeding for nullity in a manner no different from that of any other matrimonial cause.

The above passage from *Scott v. Sebright* was referred to in *Thompson v. Thompson*, 4 RFL 376, [1971] 4 WWR 383, 19 DLR (3d) 608 (Sask. QB). In this case, the plaintiff sought the annulment of her marriage to the defendant. The court found that the plaintiff had agreed to marry the defendant as a result of his persistent urging, at a time when her resistance was reduced by her state of depression arising from her rejection by another man. Once the wedding plans were underway, the plaintiff was not able to muster sufficient courage to cancel them, because of the social consequences insofar as her family was concerned. She believed that, if she did cancel the marriage plans, there would be a rift between herself and her family. The plaintiff's mother, the court concluded, had exerted influence on the plaintiff to continue with the plans. The marriage was consummated, albeit reluctantly on the part of the plaintiff. The court held that the plaintiff had not established a case that would fall within the principles enunciated in the authorities and dismissed the action. Annulment has also been refused in the following cases: *Singh v. Kaur* (1959), 29 WWR 95 (BCSC); *Parihar v. Bhatti* (1980), 17 RFL (2d) 289 (BCSC); *K. v. K.*, [1921] 1 WWR 1072, 57 DLR 746 (sub nom. *Korulak v. Korulak*) (Sask. KB); *Kawaluk v. Kawaluk*, [1927] 3 DLR 493 (Sask. KB); *Kecskemethy v. Magyar*, [1961] 2 FLR 437 (NSWSC); *Williams v. Williams*, [1966] VR 60 (SC).

In *Pascuzzi v. Pascuzzi*, [1955] OWN 853 (HC), the plaintiff sought an annulment of her marriage. The claim was unopposed. At the time of the marriage she was 15 years of age and the defendant was 19 years of age. Prior to the marriage, during a visit to Toronto, the parties engaged in sexual intercourse. The plaintiff being a juvenile, complaints were made to the police and both the plaintiff and the defendant were taken into custody, the plaintiff being detained on a charge of juvenile delinquency and the defendant being faced with a criminal charge. According to the evidence, it was intimated to the plaintiff that if she and the defendant were married no criminal charges would be laid. It was necessary to secure the consent of the plaintiff's mother to the marriage and, at first, she refused but, finally, after she had been called upon by a solicitor representing the defendant, she gave her consent. The plaintiff was not only reluctant to go through a form of marriage but, on more than one occasion, protested that she would not do so. As stated by Aylen J at p. 854:

> No doubt with the best intentions in the world, those to whom the plaintiff turned for advice all urged her so strongly to marry the defendant that it became practically an impossibility for a child of her age to continue to refuse, especially as her only home at the time was with the defendant's parents.

The ceremony was performed on 27th February 1954, and the plaintiff left the defendant on or about 31st December 1954. The court considered the delay in the plaintiff leaving the defendant understandable in the circumstances. Afer a reference to the law of duress, the court held that the marriage between the plaintiff and the defendant should be declared a nullity. Annulment has also been granted in the following cases: *H. v. H.*, [1954] P258, [1953] 3 WLR 849, [1953] 2 All ER 1229; *Buckland v. Buckland*, [1968] P296, [1967] 2 WLR 1506, [1967] 2 All ER 300. The last decision

I will mention is *Marriage of S.* (1980), 42 FLR 94 (Aust. Fam. Ct.). In this case, the court pointed out that the emphasis on terror or fear in some judgments seemed unnecessarily limiting. In granting a decree of nullity, Watson J, at p. 102, stated that it was "the effect of the oppression on his mind that should be the operative factor, not the form of such oppression." I turn now to state my understanding of the authorities.

A valid marriage is grounded upon the consent of each party. Oppression may vitiate consent and, if there is no consent, there is no valid marriage. Different people may respond to oppression in different ways, and conduct that may overmaster the mind of one person may not have this impact upon the mind of another. It matters not, therefore, whether the will of a person of reasonable fortitude would—or would not—have been overborne; the issue is, rather, the state of mind of the applicant. To constitute duress, it must be established that the applicant's mind was so overcome by oppression that there was an absence of free choice. The point that falls for decision is whether the consent given at the time of the ceremony was a real, understanding and voluntary consent. Oppression can take various forms; it may be generated by fear, or by persuasion or pressure. Essentially, the matter is one of degree, and this raises a question of fact for the court. The determination involves a consideration of all relevant circumstances, including the age of the applicant, the maturity of the applicant, the applicant's emotional state and vulnerability, the lapse of time between the conduct alleged as duress and the marriage ceremony, whether the marriage was consummated, whether the parties resided together as man and wife and the lapse of time between the marriage ceremony and the institution of the annulment proceeding. As long as the oppression affects the mind of the applicant in the fashion stated, physical force is not required and, no more so, is the threat of such force a necessary ingredient. Nor is the source of the conduct material. Where duress is alleged, the onus of proof is upon the party seeking annulment, and it is an onus that is not lightly discharged.

The principles of law relating to duress seem to be relatively clear and certain. However, as pointed out by Butt J in *Scott v. Sebright*, the difficulty consists in the application of the law to the facts of each individual case. I have given this matter my most anxious consideration and, upon reflection, I am satisfied that the applicant has discharged the onus of proof and is entitled to a declaration of nullity. It appears to have been the view that lack of consent rendered a marriage void. Curiously, however, it seems also to have been considered that a marriage, void for lack of consent, could be subsequently ratified when oppression was withdrawn. I prefer, however, to adopt the view of Taylor J, in the *Kawaluk* case, that consent obtained by duress renders a marriage voidable on the application of the aggrieved party.

[Mendes da Costa J granted a decree of annulment. In addition, he concluded that, if the applicant were not entitled to the decree of annulment, she would be able to establish grounds for divorce.]

Duress and Arranged Marriages: Hirani v. Hirani

The concept of duress has also been used by petitioners whose parents have required them to enter into "arranged marriages" in accordance with family and cultural traditions.

As David Bradley suggested in "Duress and Arranged Marriages" (1983), 46 *Modern Law Review* 499, in 1971 the English Court of Appeal distinguished economic, social, parental, or cultural pressures from the legal requirements of duress: "fear caused by threat of immediate danger ... to life, limb or liberty": see *Singh v. Singh*, [1971] P 226; 2 All ER 828 (CA) and *Szechter v. Szechter*, [1970] 3 All ER 905; [1971] P 286 (PDA Div.), in which petitions for annulment were rejected. Similarly, in *Singh v. Kaur* (1981), 11 FL 151 (Eng. CA), where the petitioner gave in to his Sikh parents' request to accept an arranged marriage in order to avoid disgracing his family and losing the opportunity to work in the family business, the court rejected his petition. Although the court recognized that the husband was in a sad position, the judgment indicated (at 152) that "he has to make up his mind, as an adult, whether to go through with the marriage or whether to withstand the pressure put upon him by his family."

By contrast, in *Hirani v. Hirani* (1982), 4 FLR 232, the English Court of Appeal granted a request for annulment to a young Hindu woman, aged 19. Although she wished to marry a Muslim man, her parents arranged for her to marry a Hindu man whom they had not previously met. The marriage was not consummated and the wife left her husband six weeks after the marriage. In granting the declaration of nullity, the court stated:

> The crucial question in these cases, particularly where a marriage is involved, is whether the threats, pressure, or whatever it is, is such as to destroy the reality of consent and overbears the will of the individual. It seems to me that this case, on the facts, is a classic case of a young girl, wholly dependent on her parents, being forced into a marriage with a man she has never seen and whom her parents have never seen in order to prevent her (reasonably, from her parents' point of view) continuing in an association with a Muslim which they would regard with abhorrence. But it is as clear a case as one could want of the overbearing of the will of the petitioner and thus invalidating or vitiating her consent.

Discussion Notes

Duress and Community Values: Multiculturalism

Do you agree with Bradley, who suggested that "the threat and fear of homelessness and ostracism in *Hirani* will be a distinguishing feature from cases where there is no external pressure but only cultural and parental expectations"? See Bradley, at 502. As Bradley suggested (at 504), the issues about consent in these cases of arranged marriages involve particular conflicts for second and subsequent generations of ethnic cultures:

> The diverse and sometimes conflicting interests involved in the arranged marriage system include those of the second and subsequent generations exposed to two cultures, the immediate family including siblings, the wider kinship network and the ethnic group as a whole. Inevitably these cannot all be accommodated in a family law in which the prevailing ethic is individualism.

In *Parihar v. Bhatti* (1980), 17 RFL (2d) 289, the BC Supreme Court dismissed an application to declare an arranged marriage invalid on the basis of duress. The court held (at 291):

There are many situations where families, or others, bring great persuasion upon a person to enter into marriage. However, the cases indicate that the duress sufficient to set aside the marriage must be of such a nature that her powers of volition were so affected that it really was no consent.

Similarly, in *Singh v. Singh*, [1980] OJ no. 2080 (UFC) (QL), the court dismissed an application for nullity on lack of consent. The plaintiff was induced to participate in the ceremony on the promise by the respondent's family to provide material benefits. The negotiations were conducted by the plaintiff's mother. The parties had not met before the marriage arrangements. The court held that the conduct of the family did not amount to duress.

Contrast this approach of the Canadian courts to an arranged marriage case in Australia: *In the Marriage of S.*, [1980] FLC 90-820 (Fam. Ct. Aust.),

> [A] young Egyptian woman had glumly participated in an arranged marriage. She had done so solely out of love and respect for her parents and to avoid any prejudice to the future marital opportunities of her younger sisters. There were no other tangible or intangible repercussions that would have flowed from a refusal to marry. In a thorough and well-reasoned judgment, Watson SJ held that duress creating a nullity should be broad enough to encompass non-violent but controlling parental coercion. In so holding, he emphasized the need to regard the coercive action from the subjective vantage point of the unwilling bride.

See Bruce Ziff, "Recent Developments in Canadian Law: Marriage and Divorce" (1986), 18 *Ottawa Law Review* 121, at 133-34. See also Andrea Cotter-Moroz, "Multiculturalism and the Law" (1992), 6 *Australian Journal of Family Law* 191 for a review and assessment of the Australian Law Reform Commission's Report on Multiculturalism relating to the family.

Which of these approaches is more appropriate in a multicultural community? For a review of cases that recognized aboriginal customary marriage practices in Canada, see *Casimel v. Insurance Corp. of BC* (1993), 82 BCLR (2d) 387 (BCCA) and Norman Zlotkin, "Judicial Recognition of Aboriginal Customary Law in Canada: Selected Marriage and Adoption Cases," [1984] 4 CNLR 1.

Duress and Gender

In an assessment of two recent decisions in England, Hilary Lim suggested that the cases on duress demonstrate the significance of gender in the application of legal principles to the facts: see Hilary Lim, "Messages from a Rarely Visited Island: Duress and Lack of Consent in Marriage" (1996), IV *Feminist Legal Studies* 195. Lim compared the reasoning in *Mahmood v. Mahmood*, [1993] SLT 589 (a young woman who was married by her parents' arrangement, had informed her future husband that she had no wish to marry him, and cohabited for about three months) with *Mahmud v. Mahmud*, [1994] SLT 599 (a man of 30, who had been cohabiting with another woman and was the father of her child, was married by his parents' arrangement to a woman in Pakistan—he had not met her before the ceremony and never saw her again after it was over). According to Lim, the language of the two judgments is different: the young woman in *Mahmood* was held to have entered into the marriage because she was dominated by a will stronger than her own, while the man in *Mahmud* was being challenged by competing demands on his conscience from his girlfriend and his family. Thus, Lim concluded (at 202) that while "he made a moral choice: she merely acted upon the dictates of her parents." According to Lim (at 219):

> The legal narratives of gendered otherness which dominate the caselaw on duress in marriage contain more than the vestiges of colonialist and liberalist discourses produced in this and earlier centuries. To petition successfully for a decree of nullity the wife must become a player in a story of negation, a mute penitent, devoid of sexual or emotional feelings and incapable of independent action ... . Evidence of any resistance to the "duress" ... must be ironed out. Only by transforming herself into the preferred object of the White Man's gaze will she obtain release from the unwanted marriage. And so the endless repetition of Exotic Otherness is pressed out.

Assuming that Lim is correct, what policy should be adopted by Canadian courts in relation to issues of duress and arranged marriages? Is there a need for reform?

c. Consent and Limited Purpose Marriage

Iantsis v. Papatheodorou

In a number of cases, courts have been asked to grant decrees of nullity where a marriage has taken place solely in order for a non-citizen to acquire immigration status in Canada. Although there were some cases in which such requests were granted, the Ontario Court of Appeal held in 1971 that where "all that is alleged is a mental reservation on the part of the defendant, ... that is not sufficient to derogate from the effect to be given to the solemn declaration of the spouses made in the course of the marriage ceremony": see *Iantsis v. Papatheodorou* (1970), 3 RFL 158, at 164; [1971] 1 OR 245 (CA). As was explained in *S.(A.) v. S.(A.)* (above), this principle means:

> The mere fact, therefore, that parties go through a form of marriage for a "limited" or "extraneous" purpose will not, of itself, render the marriage invalid. In this respect, no heed is paid to their mental reservations. Indeed, their motive would seem to support a finding of validity. Where parties seek, by marriage, to confer upon a respondent a right to reside in Canada, it would seem to follow that they do only what they intend: enter into a marriage relationship as the means of achieving the desired result.

In *Singla v. Singla* (1985), 46 RFL (2d) 235; 69 NSR (2d) 60 (SCTD), Nunn J considered the validity of a marriage that was arranged according to Hindu custom by the brothers of the plaintiff and defendant; the parties were married according to Hindu custom in India and the marriage was properly registered in India. The plaintiff alleged, however, that the marriage was fraudulently obtained by the defendant to facilitate his immigration to Canada. The plaintiff and defendant had never met until the date of the ceremony; they spent one week together in India after the ceremony (without marital relations); the defendant did not write much to the plaintiff after she returned to Canada, while he remained in India for 8 months. On the defendant's arrival in Canada, they lived together for 12 days and had marital relations once at the insistence of the plaintiff.

Nunn J concluded that the law of Nova Scotia was as stated by Schroeder JA in *Iantsis*: because there was no mistake about the nature of the ceremony or the identity of the parties, the marriage was valid. According to the judge (at 239):

> [T]o hold otherwise would be to open the floodgates for the dissolution of many marriages on the basis that one of the parties was deceived as to the intent of the other ... . I realize that in an individual case this policy may cause a particular hardship; however, it is necessary that the broad policy be accepted as the law of this province.

In an annotation of this case, James McLeod acknowledged that the decision was "correct" and in accordance with the principles enunciated in the Ontario Court of Appeal in *Iantsis*: see James McLeod, "Annotation of Singla v. Singla" (1985), 46 RFL (2d) 235. McLeod agreed that a general rule that courts should not delve into the subjective intention of the parties in the interests of certainty is appropriate. However, where a court is satisfied that no marriage was intended, he argued that it is hard to see what goal is served by validating the marriage. As he suggested (at 236):

> The purpose ... of the validity rules should be to ensure that "marriage" only arises when people with the appropriate capacity enter into a relationship which has at least a chance of functioning as a social unit.

Do you agree with this assessment?

Other Approaches

Contrast the approach of the Canadian courts with the approach of the American, French, and Scottish courts, as summarized by Hahlo:

> In *US v. Rubenstein*, Judge Learned Hand held that the consent required to establish a valid marriage was lacking:
>
> > [If] spouses agree to a marriage only for the sake of representing it as such to the outside world and with the understanding that they will put an end to it as soon as it has served its purpose to deceive, they have never really agreed to be married at all. They must assent to enter into the relation as it is ordinarily understood, and it is not ordinarily understood as merely a pretence, or cover, to deceive others.
>
> French and Scottish Courts have taken the same view. In France it is settled law that in order to create a valid marriage relationship, it is not sufficient that the parties express consent, but they must have the intention to establish a true marriage relationship: *une veritable intention conjugale*. In Scotland, likewise, immigration marriages have been annulled on the ground of lack of consent.

(H.R. Hahlo, at 32.)

2. Capacity To Consummate the Marriage

Like the need for consent for a valid marriage, the requirement of consummation derives from early marriage practices. The requirement of capacity to consummate was later recognized in the law of nullity by the ecclesiastical courts in England and continued as a common law requirement after the 1857 legislation. Thus, it is still a requirement for a valid marriage in Canada, although it has been abolished in some other jurisdictions such as Australia: see *Family Law Act 1975* (Cth) and *Marriage Act 1961* (Cth) and discussion in *Attorney-General for the Commonwealth v. Kevin* (2003), 30 Fam. LR 1.

Cases in which applicants seek an annulment on the grounds of incapacity to consummate inevitably require the presentation in public of evidence about the intimate relations of the parties. For this reason, the cases may appear to invade their privacy—the state is clearly intruding into "the bedrooms of the nation." Moreover, courts are often faced with conflicting accounts of the parties' efforts to consummate the marriage, so that issues of credibility must be determined. In choosing to accept the evidence of a husband or a wife (when their evidence conflicts), the decisions may sometimes reveal judges' ideas about what is "normal" or "reasonable" in heterosexual intimate relationships. In this context, it may also be important to consider why married spouses would ever seek an annulment on the grounds of incapacity to consummate. Does this requirement constitute an invasion of family privacy that is not appropriate as a matter of policy? Should this ground for nullity be abolished in Canada?

In this context, Hilary Lim reported that the largest number of annulments in England in 1994 were based on the ground of non-consummation, citing C. Barton, "Judicial Statistics" (1996), *Family Law* 53-54 and (London: HMSO, 1995), table 5.5. Moreover, there have been a number of decisions concerning the consummation requirement in Canada in recent years, a factor that suggests that some married spouses remain willing to assert this ground to obtain an annulment. As you review the case excerpts concerning the requirement of capacity to consummate, try to assess why the claims were presented on this ground and whether there were other remedies available to the applicants. To what extent do these cases reflect the law's view of what constitutes a "real" marriage?

Gajamugan v. Gajamugan
(1979), 10 RFL (2d) 280 (Ont. SC (HCJ))

CARRUTHERS J: This is an action for annulment. The parties went through a civil form of marriage on 23rd June 1978, followed by a religious ceremony on 24th June 1978. Following the religious ceremony on 24th June, in the evening, the parties retired to a room in a hotel and there slept together for the first time.

The plaintiff's evidence and the defendant's evidence consisted, in part, of an extremely detailed account of their respective memories of what occurred during the evening and night that they first slept together. The effect of the plaintiff's evidence is that he attempted to have sexual intercourse with the defendant but as soon as he touched her face with his hand he had a mental revulsion to the marks on her face. The effect of this reaction, so far as sexual intercourse is concerned, according to the plaintiff, was that his penis, which had become erect, became flaccid. He said that this occurred within a minute. There never was any penetration. Thereafter, the parties slept in the same bed, but, as the plaintiff said, "apart." This abortive attempt at sexual intercourse occurred about 10:30 or 11:00 p.m. on the evening of 24th June

1978. No further attempts were made over the course of that evening. The parties slept together again on the evening of 25th June 1978 and a further attempt was made at sexual intercourse and, according to the plaintiff, "the same thing happened." He was not able to proceed with intercourse. There was no penetration. He said in evidence that when he kissed and touched the defendant's face he "lost his erection." They again slept together, that is, in the same bed, but, as the plaintiff said, "apart." There were no further attempts made at sexual intercourse while the parties were together in Malaysia where they were married.

As planned the plaintiff left Malaysia to return to Canada on 27th June. The defendant was unable to accompany him because of difficulty with her visa. She arrived in Woodstock on 3rd January 1979. On the night of her arrival, the parties again attempted sexual intercourse. The plaintiff said again that he lost his erection because of "the same mind," due to a revulsion because of the marks on the defendant's face. He described it as being a repeat of what had happened on the previous attempts at intercourse. He said it was "in my mind" and it was caused by "touching." That night the plaintiff slept in a separate room. They never slept together again and no further attempts at sexual intercourse have ever been made.

The plaintiff said in evidence that he tried to overcome the problem by simply trying to forget it. He said he could not. The plaintiff denies that he had any problem of impotence, having had a child by his first marriage and, from his description, a reasonably active sexual life during the course of that marriage and on occasions thereafter, prior to his marriage to the defendant. He had no idea before his marriage to the defendant that he would have the problems he now describes as having had on the occasions when he attempted sexual intercourse with the defendant. His first knowledge was in the hotel where they first slept together on the evening of 24th June 1978.

The defendant remained with the plaintiff in his house in Woodstock for nine days after her arrival. He said that during that time he could not look at her face. He could not talk with the defendant and after three days he did not want to come home. He could not eat what she cooked.

He said that on no occasion was his problem due to the consumption of alcohol or a drug. On 12th January 1979 the plaintiff advised the defendant that, "This marriage isn't going to work out." He bought her a ticket to go home. He felt that it was best for her to go home because she had a sister there "to console her." He bought her a one-way ticket on Air France. He took her to the airport in Toronto and left her at security.

The defendant did not return home in January 1979. Apparently she passed out at the airport and eventually she was returned to Woodstock. The incident at the airport followed by five days an incident which occurred at the home in Woodstock when she drank a quantity of liquid bleach upon learning that the plaintiff was sending her back to Malaysia. She indicated that in Malaysia, girls can only marry once. She could not, if she returned to Malaysia, face people and, therefore, wished to remain in Woodstock, married to the plaintiff.

In her evidence she confirmed the evidence of the plaintiff as to the nights upon which they had slept together following their marriage. She denied, however, that the plaintiff had any other difficulty other than being "impatient" and his refusal to "push hard enough" in order to bring about penetration. Specifically she said that at no time was she aware of any problem that the plaintiff was having in maintaining an erection. She said that he never mentioned anything about the marks on her face. At the time of her first attempt to have intercourse with the plaintiff she was a virgin, never having had sexual intercourse previous to that date.

For the purposes of my decision, I am prepared to adopt an overview of the essential ingredients to be proved in an action of nullity because of impotence as outlined in an article by J. David Fine, "Annulment of Marriage for Impotence in the Common Law of Canada" (1973), 8 RFL 129. It reads as follows [at 129]:

> A good overview of the essential ingredients to be proved in an action for nullity because of impotence was provided by Laidlaw JA in the Ontario Court of Appeal in 1944: *Rae v. Rae*, [1944] OR 266, [1944] 2 DLR 604; summarized in *Hardick (Fox) v. Fox* (1970), 3 RFL 153 (Ont.); (1) Impotence must exist at the time of marriage: *Napier v. Napier*, [1915] P 184 at 190; (2) the incapacity pleaded must be such as to render intercourse impractical: *D. v. A.* (1845), 1 Rob. Ecc. 279, 163 ER 1039; (3) the incapacity may stem from "a physical or mental or moral disability": *H. v. P.(H.)* (1873), LR 3 P & D 126; and (4) the impotence must be incurable: *Welde (Aston) v. Welde* (1731), 2 Lee 580, 161 ER 446.

I am prepared to accept the evidence of the plaintiff, particularly where it conflicts with that of the defendant. When I consider her evidence in the light of her demeanour and attitude seen while she was in the witness-box, I conclude that what she had to say was influenced by her personal concern of having to return home not married.

I must confess that the decision I have reached in this matter was not reached without anxious consideration. My prime concern stems from the requirement that the disability, mental in this case, must be found to be incurable. No evidence was led specifically to deal with this point. Counsel for the plaintiff asks that the court infer, because the condition existed on two nights in June 1978 and again in January 1979, that it be deemed incurable, particularly when it is such a subjective matter and something about which medical evidence would be of little value in assisting the court to come to a conclusion. I am prepared to accept that position.

There will, therefore, be a declaration that the marriage in question is void.

At trial, the defendant's pleading was amended so as to claim relief for maintenance under the provisions of the *Family Law Reform Act, 1978* (Ont.), c. 2. Counsel for the plaintiff did not oppose that motion and the amendment was, therefore, allowed.

I think it reasonable that the plaintiff pay to the defendant, on account of her maintenance forthwith, the lump sum of $3,000, and that the plaintiff continue to pay the sum of $100 a week on the dates provided in the order of the Provincial Court now outstanding, and if no such dates are provided commencing as of 1st April 1979. The plaintiff is to continue to make those payments in this amount until such time as this court shall otherwise order, upon the application of either party. There shall be no costs of the action.

Declaration of nullity granted.

Juretic v. Ruiz
(1999), 49 RFL (4th) 299; 126 BCCA 196

Introduction

RYAN JA: This is an appeal and cross-appeal from a decision of Mr. Justice J.T. Edwards in the Supreme Court in Vancouver ordering the parties divorced, refusing Mr. Juretic's application for an order declaring the marriage to be null and void, and ordering spousal support and the division of family assets.

Mr. Juretic appeals the order refusing him a decree of nullity. Both parties challenge the manner in which the family assets were divided and the amount of spousal support awarded.

Factual Background

Following his retirement as a marine engineer, Mr. Juretic advertised for a bride in a Honduran newspaper. He was interested in finding a Spanish-speaking wife, a virgin, who wished to be a homemaker. Ms. Ruiz answered the advertisement.

In 1995 Mr. Juretic travelled to Honduras where he met Ms. Ruiz and spent two weeks visiting her family. Ms. Ruiz agreed, with her parents' approval, to come to Vancouver and if things worked out, to marry Mr. Juretic.

Ms. Ruiz arrived in Vancouver on July 28, 1996. Immediately on her arrival Ms. Ruiz moved into Mr. Juretic's apartment on West Broadway and began living with him.

Mr. Juretic and Ms. Ruiz were married on October 5, 1996. At the time of the marriage Mr. Juretic was 66 years of age, and Ms. Ruiz was 23.

Following the marriage ceremony and a reception at a local restaurant, the parties returned to Mr. Juretic's apartment where Mr. Juretic anticipated the consummation of the marriage. Ms. Ruiz rebuffed his affectionate embraces, she told him if he wanted sex she was his, but she did not want him to touch her. Mr. Juretic did not persist. Two days later when he made the same advances Ms. Ruiz told him again she would have sex with him, but that she did not wish to be touched. Mr. Juretic testified he never tried again. He told the trial judge that sex under those circumstances would be like rape. He gave up trying.

Mr. Juretic and Ms. Ruiz continued to sleep in the same bed from the date of their marriage to the date of separation in March 1997. They ate together, lived together and represented themselves as a couple to others within the community. Ms. Ruiz left the matrimonial home on March 12, 1997. At the same time, or shortly afterward, she became romantically involved with another man.

Annulment

To warrant a declaration of nullity for non-consummation, the applicant must demonstrate an incapacity of some kind. In *Heil v. Heil*, [1942] SCR 160 (SCC), Taschereau J said this for the majority at pp. 162-3:

[I]t is now settled that there must be an incapacity of some kind, which in certain cases is a structural defect, but which may also arise out of mental condition, with the resulting effect of creating in the mind of the woman an aversion to the physical act of consummation. ...

The latest pronouncement on the matter is a decision of the House of Lords in the case of *G. v. G.* [[1924] AC 349], where it was held that the conclusion to be drawn from the evidence was that the wife's refusal was due, not to obstinacy or caprice, but to an invincible repugnance to the act of consummation, resulting in a paralysis of the will which was consistent only with incapacity, and that the husband was entitled to a decree of nullity. The words of Lord Phillimore are as follows:

> The evidence here seems to me to prove "invincible repugnance," "invincible" in the full sense of an unconquerable, uncontrollable nervous condition which is physical and which creates nullity.

Counsel for Mr. Juretic, Mr. Mason, agreed that the trial judge properly articulated the test to apply. However, he disagreed with the way in which it was applied. The trial judge concluded that because Mr. Juretic was rebuffed on his wedding night, "he was unable on any later occasion to achieve an erection and have sex with Ms. Ruiz." Mr. Mason submitted that having made this finding the trial judge was obliged to find that the test was met.

In refusing to declare a nullity the trial judge said this:

> The law with respect to a declaration of nullity is that such declaration can only be made if a party has an "invincible aversion" to the act of sexual intercourse. A simple failure or refusal to consummate the marriage is not sufficient for a declaration of nullity. *Heil v. Heil*, [1942] SCR 160.
>
> In British Columbia there is a presumption of validity of marriage such that the plaintiff must prove that he has an invincible aversion to the sexual act to obtain a declaration of nullity. *Lehoux v. Woolward* (1994), 2 RFL (4th) 382.
>
> Mr. Juretic has not proven an "invincible aversion."
>
> The mere fact that he was unable to obtain an erection when he was with Ms. Ruiz does not reach the standard of invincible aversion referred to in *Heil*. Accordingly, his action for annulment is dismissed.

In this case Mr. Juretic was put off by the attitude of Ms. Ruiz. He was unable to pursue a cold sexual act which he found akin to rape. After two attempts at the beginning of his marriage he made no further attempts to have sexual relations with his wife. The trial judge was not persuaded that Mr. Juretic's response to his wife could be said to have reached the level of "invincible aversion." I cannot say he was wrong in his finding. Put another way, it could be said that Mr. Juretic's situation fell short of an "unconquerable repugnance." I would dismiss this ground of appeal.

[The court also reviewed the division of property and spousal support ordered by the trial judge, confirming his order apportioning the interests in family assets to reflect a 90 percent interest for Juretic and a 10 percent interest for Ruiz, and awarding Ruiz spousal support of $1250 per month for three years.]

Sangha v. Aujla
(2002), 32 RFL (5th) 445 (BCSC)

McEWAN J: The plaintiff seeks a declaration of nullity of her marriage to the defendant.

The parties were married February 16, 2002 in Vancouver, British Columbia. They ceased living together on April 4, 2002.

The marriage was arranged by the parties' families. They first met in about March of 2001 through a go-between and discussions followed among the parties' parents and an uncle and aunt of the defendant. The discussions included whether or not the defendant had any kind of criminal record. I accept the plaintiff's evidence that there was a direct and repeated representation that the defendant had nothing of the kind in his past. The parties themselves had virtually no opportunity to get to know each other before the marriage, the suitability of which was assessed almost entirely on the basis of the representations that passed between more senior family members.

Once the parties were married they lived in a basement suite in the home of the plaintiff's uncle and aunt. They were virtually never alone in that setting, and subsequently moved in with the plaintiff's parents.

The plaintiff says the marriage was never consummated. In the first few weeks after the wedding this was because the plaintiff felt she had had no opportunity to get to know the defendant and wanted some time. The defendant respected her wishes.

In the course of discussions during that time about who they were and what their experiences had been, the defendant had suggested that for a period of about four years he had "travelled." When he was more closely questioned, he acknowledged that this was untrue and that he had, in fact, been imprisoned in England for robbery.

This was too much for the plaintiff and a short while later the parties separated.

The defendant, by way of an improperly sworn but uncontroversial affidavit, agrees that the marriage was never consummated. He takes the position however, that the marriage should not be annulled, but that the plaintiff should simply ask for a divorce.

The plaintiff's position is that an annulment is preferable in her circumstances because a divorce significantly diminishes her reputation and prospects of marriage within her culture.

The plaintiff has offered two medical opinions to corroborate her evidence. The first, a letter from Dr. Arthur G. Willms, her family doctor, describes her condition as found on physical examination, and concludes as follows:

> I can state with a high degree of confidence that this woman has not had sexual intercourse with vaginal penetration. I would support her claim that she had not been sexually active in this marriage.

The second is an opinion from a Dr. Douglas A. Steane, Registered Psychologist. His conclusions were as follows:

> Sonia Sangha's marriage to Tarjinder Singh Aujla seems to have been a formal arrangement devoid of opportunities to develop a minimum amount of rapport or any psychological and emotional intimacy. While Tarjinder's point of view is not represented in this report, it is assumed that he is still motivated to make the marriage work and that

he is more emotionally involved in the relationship than his wife, since it is believed that he will object to any attempt to annul the marriage, but may not necessarily object to a divorce. However, Sonia's discovery that Tarjinder was deceitful with respect to his criminal record, before getting emotionally involved with him, would naturally create an emotional barrier and repugnance to consummating the marriage. For these reasons, it is important to emphasize that Ms. Sangha is not refusing to consummate the marriage. She is a responsible, emotionally well-adjusted, young woman who is not psychologically capable of consummating the marriage because, from her perception of experiences with her husband, he has not succeeded in connecting with her cognitively and emotionally. Expecting a mature woman to consummate a marriage with a man with whom she has not developed a positive emotional connection is not that psychologically different from asking her to prostitute herself.

I turn now to the law. ...

[The court reviewed a number of authorities, including *Heil v. Heil*, [1942] 1 DLR 657 (SCC), noting that the test for nullity on grounds of non-consummation was "rather high," and continued.]

More recently, in *Deo v. Kumar*, [1993] BCJ No. 2051 (BCSC), Lander J articulated the test in the following terms:

The test ... is a practical impossibility of consummation. It must be caused by physical or psychological defect. Wilful and persistent refusal amounting to caprice or obstinacy is not a ground for annulment. See *Heil v. Heil*, [1942] 1 DLR 657 (SCC).

The words "invincible repugnance" are commonly used to describe such a psychological defect. It has been held that such repugnance may be toward the particular spouse, and not the act of sexual intercourse generally, see *Orr v. Orr* (1956), 2 DLR (2d) 627 (NS), and *Greenlees v. Greenlees*, [1959] OR 419-423, as well as *Koelman v. Lansdaal* (1953), 9 WWR 381 (NS). I find that, due to Ms. Deo's discovery of Mr. Kumar's pre-marital sexual activities, compounded by his contraction of a sexually transmitted disease, she has developed an overpowering psychological abhorrence for him, rendering her incapable of even the contemplation of consummation. She psychologically required no more of her prospective mate than she demanded of herself: a completely disciplined abstinence from pre-marital sexual relations.

Here, the plaintiff is in the position that a clear precondition or premise upon which the marriage was founded did not exist, and had, in fact, been actively misrepresented. I think it quite understandable that this, and the fact that in this particular arrangement, the parties remained effectively strangers until after they were married, renders consummation a practical impossibility for the plaintiff. I do not think it necessary for the court to describe her normal, predictable reaction to the situation in pathological terms in order to grant the declaration sought. There can be no basis in public policy for promoting marriage to the extent of denying this application.

Accordingly, I declare the marriage of the plaintiff and defendant which took place February 16, 2002 and was registered in British Columbia under No. 2002-59-001294 (Certificate #66328767) annulled.

Discussion Notes

Judicial Reasoning About Consummation

What is the explanation for the decision to grant an annulment to the husband in *Gajamugan*, but to deny the decree of annulment in *Juretic*? To what extent do the judges in each situation rigorously apply the legal principles? Was the condition in *Gajamugan* incurable? Why was the application in *Juretic* denied, by contrast with the application in *Sangha*? Is gender relevant? To what extent is fault an issue?

In assessing the reasoning in these cases consider also the comments in *Falk v. Falk* (1999), 251 AR 135 (QB), where the parties married in June 1998 and separated in November 1998. The husband applied for an annulment on the ground that he was incapable of consummating the marriage and that it had not been consummated; the wife did not appear. After reviewing the case law, the court concluded (at paras. 32-34):

> There is a lack of evidence here as to the Plaintiff's "incapacity" to consummate. While there appears to be no medical reason behind the incapacity, there also does not appear to be any other reason behind the Plaintiff's refusal or inability to have sexual relations with his wife.
>
> The decision as to whether or not to grant an annulment is a serious one in law, in my opinion. It would be far too convenient, based on my review of the case law to grant an annulment simply on the basis of one's refusal or self-described inability to consummate the marriage.
>
> As such, the Plaintiff's existing request for an annulment is not granted at this time, however, the Plaintiff shall have leave to bring this matter back before me with further evidence as to his problems and reasons in not consummating his marriage.

Are the reasons for denying the husband's application for annulment in *Falk* more or less persuasive than in *Juretic*? Are there other reasons for the result in *Juretic*? Consider, for example, that the court awarded Ruiz an interest in *Juretic*'s property, an entitlement generally available to only married spouses.

Evidence and Credibility

Cases about capacity to consummate may be decided on the basis of issues of credibility. For example, in *Leung v. Liang* (2001), 206 DLR (4th) 380; aff'd. 2003 BCCA 313, a woman brought an action to annul her marriage. She gave evidence that she had never resided with her husband after their marriage, that he had rebuffed her suggestions of intimacy, and that he had claimed to be homosexual. Her husband, who had married her shortly after immigrating to Canada from China, testified that they had resided together and that they had engaged in sexual intercourse on 60 occasions, but there was no evidence corroborating his assertions, and he was unable to recall any distinguishing features of the woman's anatomy. The court granted the declaration of nullity, expressly accepting the woman's evidence rather than the man's.

In *S.S.C. v. G.K.C.*, 1999 ABQB 822, the parties married in India in 1996, but they did not consummate the marriage. The husband gave evidence that he wished to do so but that his wife had refused to engage in any kind of sexual activity and "steadfastly and cruelly resisted all his advances." The wife gave evidence that she was willing to engage in sexual intercourse and did everything she could to encourage him but that he was never able to achieve penetration. According to her, the husband's frustration and embarrassment resulted in him becoming mean and cruel to her. Eventually she left and filed for divorce in British Columbia, but the parties agreed to stay the divorce application pending the outcome of the husband's action for annulment in Alberta. In granting the annulment, the Alberta court stated (at paras. 22-23):

> I understand there is no advantage to either party in ending this marriage by way of a divorce rather than an annulment. Indeed I was given to understand that in their culture an annulment is less problematic to them than a divorce. In all the circumstances I think it best that the parties be put out of their matrimonial misery as expeditiously as possible.
>
> I will therefore conclude the matter by accepting as fact the only relevant evidence the parties could agree on, namely that they at no time ever engaged in any sexual activity. I find that was either the result of the defendant's invincible repugnance toward the sex act with the plaintiff, or the result of his impotence. I accept that whichever is the case, the condition is permanent as between this couple. On that basis I will grant the annulment.

Is this an appropriate solution to the issue of credibility?

See also *M. v. M.* (1984), 42 RFL (2d) 55 (PEISC (Fam. Div.)), in which a man obtained a declaration of annulment on the basis that his wife was psychologically unable to consummate the marriage, although no physical impediment existed; and *W. v. W.* (1987), 5 RFL (3d) 323 (PEISC (Fam. Div.)), where the court rejected a woman's application for nullity because there was no evidence of her "invincible repugnance" to sexual intercourse, but just an "inability to respond." Can these cases be reconciled? What underlying concerns are reflected in these decisions?

Annulment and the Ideology of Marriage

In *Norman v. Norman* (1979), 9 RFL (2d) 345 (Ont. UFC), the court denied an action for annulment of a marriage between a 64-year-old widow and a 65-year-old widower. The wife gave evidence that, based on her husband's inability to consummate the marriage, she did not expect to have a sexual relationship but just "companionship." The court denied the annulment, stating that it was not open to the woman, "having entered into what might be termed a platonic marriage, to complain of the absence of sexual intercourse." How should this case be characterized in relation to ideas about marriage as contract or status? To what extent may courts' decisions be based on implicit ideas about the extent to which parties should be able to "consent" to end their marriage? For example, consider whether the following comments, expressed in *Rae v. Rae*, [1944] OR 266 (Ont. CA), at 269, may have been relevant to the decision in *Norman*:

> A marriage ought not to be lightly interfered with, but on the contrary the Court ought to be fully satisfied that the grounds advanced by a petitioner are sufficient to justify the termination of the relationship of the parties. In my opinion it is not in the best interest of public morals and social welfare that the burden of proof necessary in law to end the solemn vows and undertakings of married persons should be discharged with any degree of ease.

Annulment, Divorce, and the Need for Reform

In *Chirayath v. Chirayath* (1980), 19 RFL (2d) 235, the Ontario Court of Appeal granted a divorce based on s. 4(1)(d) of the former *Divorce Act* of 1968 (non-consummation of the marriage). In this context, the court noted that the medical reports would have been insufficient to establish incapacity in an action for annulment, but that they were quite satisfactory to meet the requirements of the divorce statute: an inability "by reason of illness or disability to consummate the marriage." James McLeod approved this decision in an annotation of the case, suggesting that "with the availability of divorce at the present time, the doctrine of nullity should not be extended": see James McLeod, "Annotation" (1980), 19 RFL (2d) 235. Do the recent cases concerning annulment because of incapacity to consummate reflect McLeod's view? If not, what is the explanation for these decisions? Is the availability of divorce after separation for one year an adequate remedy in these cases?

In addition to these issues, it is obvious that current legal principles were developed in relation to heterosexual marriage. Is it appropriate to apply them to same-sex marriage? If it is not appropriate to do so, should this requirement for a valid marriage be abolished entirely? To what extent do you agree with Simon Fodden, who argued that "citizens do not wish this form of state interference with respect to sexual practices within marriage": Simon Fodden, *Family Law* (Toronto: Irwin Law, 1999), at 14-15. What arguments, if any, support the preservation of this ground of nullity?

3. Prohibited Degrees of Consanguinity and Affinity

Persons related too closely by consanguinity (relationships of blood) and affinity (relationships by marriage) are prohibited from marrying. The prohibited degrees of consanguinity and affinity at common law were set out in Archbishop Parker's Table of 1563, as reproduced in the *Book of Common Prayer* of the Church of England. This list of prohibited degrees was incorporated into Ontario law through the *Annulment of Marriages Act (Ontario)*: see *Divorce Act (Ontario) 1930*, SC 1930, c. 14 and *Annulment of Marriages Act*, RSC 1970, c. A-14. This list was amended by the *Marriage Act*, RSC 1970, c. M-5, ss. 2-3, removing the following prohibitions: wife's sister, wife's niece, husband's brother, and husband's nephew. The list of prohibited degrees was set out for convenience in Form 1 of Ontario's provincial *Marriage Act*.

Bruce Ziff discussed some of the rationales underlying the traditional prohibited degrees of consanguinity and affinity, in the context of Parliamentary amendments in the 1990s.

Bruce Ziff, "Recent Developments in Canadian Law: Marriage and Divorce"
(1986), 18 *Ottawa Law Review* 121, at 135-36

The traditional policies behind affinal restrictions, put succinctly, are the insulation of the nuclear or extended family from sexual meddling, the promotion of marriage outside of the family and the preservation of perceived societal norms or Judeo-Christian religious beliefs. Restrictions based on consanguinity have been supported on these grounds, but there is, as well, the additional concern that genetic and even eugenic defects are more common in the offspring of close blood relations. The amendments reflect an abandonment of the first cluster of reasons, presumably either because they no longer reflect public policy, or because marriage prohibitions are seen as ineffective vehicles with which to pursue these goals. A reduction in the restrictions based on consanguinity seems in accord with current scientific opinion that the physical dangers are not as significant as once was thought, particularly where the blood relationship between the parents is not close.

Principles concerning prohibited degrees of consanguinity and affinity are now contained in federal legislation: the *Marriage (Prohibited Degrees) Act*, SC 1990, c. 46, which came into force in 1991. The Hansard Report, June 7, 1990 (third reading in the Senate), provided the following statement about the intention of the new legislation:

> In the case of persons related by blood, Bill S-14 reaffirms the law that persons may not marry if they are related lineally or if they are brothers or sisters, but it otherwise relaxes the law to allow marriage between persons who are related as uncle and niece or as aunt and nephew. In the case of persons related by marriage, it clarifies the law by providing that a person whose marriage has been dissolved by divorce may marry the brother or sister, nephew or niece, or uncle or aunt of the divorced spouse; something that is not now permitted under the law. There would be no prohibition against marriages involving step-relationships.

An amendment to the Bill was included to treat the relationship of adopted persons within the family "as if they were natural relationships," an arrangement that is consistent with provincial adoption law and policy. In relation to degrees of affinity and the law of domicile, see *Canada (Min. Employment and Immigration) v. Narwal* (1990), 26 RFL (3d) 95; [1990] 2 FC 385 (CA).

4. No Prior Subsisting Marriage

Although it is possible to marry more than once, it is necessary to end the first marriage—by a decree of divorce or nullity or as a result of the death of the spouse—before marrying a second or subsequent time. Particularly where a first marriage ends in divorce, problems may arise in relation to legal issues concerning the recognition of foreign decrees. For example, in *Knight v. Knight* (1995), 16 RFL (4th) 48 (Ont. CJ (Gen. Div.)), a husband from Ontario obtained a divorce from his first wife in Mexico and then married his second wife in Pennsylvania. He gave evidence that he had decided to marry in Pennsylvania because Ontario did not recognize the validity of his Mexican divorce. When his second marriage ended, he argued that it was void because he was still validly married to his first wife at the time of the second marriage. However, the court decided (at 56) that it would be against public policy to permit the husband to succeed with this argument, and proceeded to determine issues of property and support in relation to the second marriage.

As James McLeod suggested, however, these issues require careful attention to conflict-of-law principles. In his annotation, he argued that the Mexican divorce would not have been recognized in Ontario because neither the husband nor his first wife was domiciled in Mexico. Thus, the second marriage was void because of the prior subsisting marriage: see James McLeod, "Annotation of Knight v. Knight" (1995), 16 RFL (4th) 48, at 50. In this context, how should the court have resolved the issues concerning property sharing and support at the end of the second "marriage"? Recall the definition of "spouse" in s. 1 of Ontario's *Family Law Act*.

Issues about marriage validity may also be affected by practices of polygamy. Section 290 of the Canadian *Criminal Code* makes it an offence for a person to have a marriage or conjugal union with more than one person at the same time; the offence is punishable by imprisonment for up to five years (s. 291). However, in relation to a fundamentalist Mormon sect who live in rural British Columbia and who practise polygamy, there have been no prosecutions to date, apparently because of concern that the Code provisions may contravene the Charter's protection for freedom of religion. A former wife in the community attempted to launch a class action against the Morman church in a BC court in November 2002, but the outcome of her legal action, if any, remains unclear: see Robert Matas, "Woman To Bring Suit Against Mormon Church," *Globe and Mail*, November 19, 2002.

Some provincial jurisdictions define "spouse" in their family law statutes to include persons who are parties to a polygamous marriage that was valid in the jurisdiction where the marriage took place: see, for example, Ontario's *Family Law Act*, s. 1(2). In this way, even if it is not possible to enter into a valid polygamous marriage in Ontario, the law may recognize such relationships for persons who reside in Ontario after entering into a valid polygamous marriage elsewhere in the world. Although similar provisions exist in English law, France changed its policy and outlawed polygamy in 1993, a situation that has created great hardship for persons who have lived for many years in polygamous relationships: see Jon Henley, "I Can't Say to a Wife of 20 Years She Has To Go," *The Guardian*, May 9, 2001.

5. Age and Validity of Marriage

The right to marry requires that the parties be "of age." As noted in section II, Contexts for Legal Marriage, the courts decided that issues of parental consent were matters of formality within the authority of provincial legislatures. In most cases, provincial statutes provide that the issuance of a licence to marry is restricted to persons who are at least 18, or at least 16 with parental consent. Such provisions appear very close to matters of capacity within the authority of the federal government. However, the federal government has not legislated with respect to age requirements, and thus it is common law provisions that define capacity in terms of age. Consider how those common law requirements were interpreted in the following case.

Legebokoff v. Legebokoff
(1982), 28 RFL (2d) 212 (BCSC)

[The wife petitioned for an order declaring that her marriage was invalid because she was only 15 at the time of the ceremony. The ceremony was conducted in accordance with the rites of the Doukhobor faith, the parties lived together for 16 years, and they had 3 children. The court held (at 215) that the marriage was valid.]

The Parliament of Canada has exclusive legislative authority in regard to the capacity of persons to marry, and it is silent on the minimum age. At common law, derived from ecclesiastical law, the marriage of a child of less than seven years is void. The marriage of a male older than seven years but younger than 14 years, or a female older than seven but younger than 12 years is voidable at the instance of the infant upon his or her attaining the requisite minimum age. Further, a marriage where either or both parties were under age becomes validated if they continue to cohabit as husband and wife after reaching the age of capacity: *Kerr v. Kerr*.

In rejecting the petitioner's request in *Legebokoff*, the court noted (at 215) the presumption of validity of a marriage, a presumption that reflected the law's "favourable attitude toward [marriage]." In reaching its conclusion, the court may have taken into account the long period of cohabitation after the plaintiff was "of age." Are there reasons why a person might choose not to challenge the validity of marriage until 16 years after attaining the requisite age for entering into a valid marriage? If so, how should this issue be reflected in legal principles? Is there a need for reform? How should the age requirement be reflected in reform legislation?

B. Solemnization and Formalities

The provinces have jurisdiction to legislate in relation to the formal validity of marriage—for example, banns, licences, and permits; the authority of marriage officers; parental consent; and the registration of marriages. Adherence to these formalities can be a condition of a valid marriage. Consider the significance of these requirements in the following case.

Alspector v. Alspector
[1957] OR 454; (1957), 9 DLR (2d) 679 (CA)

[In *Alspector*, the Ontario Court of Appeal considered the significance of s. 33 (now s. 31) of the Ontario *Marriage Act*: now RSO 1990, c. M.3. In this case, Mr. Alspector married Mrs. Noodleman in a marriage ceremony performed at the home of a cantor according to all of the requirements of the Jewish faith. However, the parties neglected to get a marriage licence. While Mr. Alspector had been told by his friends and by the cantor that a marriage licence was required, he did not believe that they needed one because they intended to live together in Israel. The couple lived together for seven years in Ontario. Then, Mr. Alspector had a stroke, and his family challenged the validity of the marriage. Mrs. Alspector brought an application for a declaration of the validity of the marriage. Mr. Alspector died before the trial.

The trial court took the view that the parties had intended to be married in accordance with both Jewish and Ontario law, and that s. 33 (now s. 31) of the *Marriage Act* applied. The Court of Appeal dismissed the appeal, stating (at 465-66):]

Even if the cantor's evidence be accepted that he told Mr. Alspector that because no licence had been issued the marriage would not be a civil marriage there is no evidence that that opinion was conveyed to the plaintiff. … Even if it should be held that she knew as a fact that a licence had not been issued, I think it fair to conclude on her evidence that she did not know that the absence of a licence in the circumstances of this case could affect the validity of her marriage; and that she intended that the marriage be in compliance with the law of the Province. As for Mr. Alspector, it is not unreasonable to conclude that although he knew that a licence had not been issued he proceeded in good faith believing that a licence was not necessary because of his intention shortly thereafter to go with the plaintiff to reside in Israel.

In *Alspector*, the plaintiff required a determination of the validity of her marriage in relation to succession issues. In addition, issues about the validity of marriages have arisen in relation to the definition of "spouse" under provincial statutes relating to family property and support at marriage breakdown. For example, in *Reaney v. Reaney* (1990), 28 RFL (3d) 52; 72 DLR (4th) 532, the Ontario Supreme Court held that the term "spouse" under Part I of the *Family Law Act* included a party to a void marriage only if the person claiming the relief went through the marriage in good faith. In *Reaney*, the marriage was void due to the prior existing marriage of the plaintiff. Because the plaintiff knew he was already married at the time of the second marriage, he did not enter the marriage in good faith and, therefore, was not a "spouse" under the *Family Law Act*. Accordingly, he was not entitled to an equalization of net family property as set out in the Act.

Debora v. Debora
(1999), 43 RFL (4th) 179; 167 DLR (4th) 759 (Ont. CA)

[In *Debora*, the parties were married in a religious ceremony that they both knew did not comply with the *Marriage Act*. Seven years later, they were married in a valid ceremony. When they separated, the trial judge relied on *Reaney* and held that equalization should be calculated from the date of the valid marriage. The Ontario Court of Appeal dismissed the appeal, stating (at 184-85):]

From a policy point of view, it is reasonable to argue for fairness in the interpretation of a statute such as the *Family Law Act*. However, it is my view that in this instance the stronger policy argument is for certainty of identification of the status of being married as the indicator for the distribution of assets. The appellant's reading of "good faith" [in s. 1(1)], as referring to the state of mind of the applicant as to the legality of the marriage, which was knowingly not conducted pursuant to the laws of Ontario, creates unlimited scope for uncertainty and inevitable conflicts in the evidence presented by parties whose interests are at stake over what would be, in the last analysis, a subjective assumption as to a legal status. …

Thus, reading "marriage" as meaning marriage under the *Marriage Act* gives purpose to the definition of spouse consistent with the *Family Law Act* and does not introduce the myriad of uncertainties that would flow from a broader interpretation.

In this case, the wife alleged, and the husband disputed, that she agreed to the absence of a marriage licence on the basis of representations from the husband that the effect of the marriage ceremony would be the same. Between the date of the religious ceremony and the *Marriage Act* ceremony, the husband acquired significant assets, which he did not have to include as family property to be shared with his wife as a result of the court's decision that the date of the marriage corresponded to the later ceremony.

How would you characterize the differences between *Debora* and *Alspector*? In relation to *Debora*, James McLeod criticized the Court of Appeal decision, suggesting that the fear of "floodgates" on such issues was unrealistic, and that it would be fairer to permit parties to access the property regime under the *Family Law Act* rather than rely on equitable principles. Contrasting judicial willingness to extend spousal rights to unmarried same-sex and opposite-sex couples, McLeod stated that this decision appeared inconsistent: see James McLeod, "Annotation of Debora v. Debora" (1999), 43 RFL (4th) 179, at 181. See also *Upadyhaha v. Sehgal*, noted in Norman MacInnes, "Money Advanced a Gift, Not a Loan," *The Lawyers Weekly*, October 6, 2000, at 10. You may wish to revisit these questions in relation to issues about property at marriage breakdown, discussed later in these materials.

SELECTED REFERENCES

H.R. Hahlo, "Nullity of Marriage," in D. Mendes da Costa, ed., *Studies in Canadian Family Law*, vol. 2 (Toronto: Butterworths, 1972), at 651, and *Supplement* 1977, at 250.

Leslie Katz, "The Scope of the Federal Legislative Authority in Relation to Marriage" (1975), 7 *Ottawa Law Review* 384.

Patrick Parkinson, "Taking Multiculturalism Seriously: Marriage Law and the Rights of Minorities" (1994), 16 *Sydney Law Review* 473.

IV. MARRIAGE AND EQUALITY: THE REFORM CONTEXT

A. Same-Sex Marriage

What then, is the nature of [marriage] as understood in Christendom? ... [What] are its essential elements and invariable features? ... I conceive that marriage, as understood in Christendom, may ... be defined as the voluntary union for life of one man and one woman, to the exclusion of all others.

Hyde v. Hyde (1866), PD 130, at 133

Same-sex relationships fit within the constitutional definition of marriage because same-sex marriage serves the same state interests as heterosexual marriage. ... Marriage is not simply a sacred institution. It has become a civil institution and, as a result, is a creature of the state. ... [Promotion] of homosexual monogamy serves a vital state interest. It establishes a method of weaving homosexuals into the quilt of society, rather than relegating them to a fringe status.

Lisa R. Zimmer, "Family, Marriage, and the Same-Sex Couple" (1990), 12 *Cardozo Law Review* 681, at 705-6

1. The Impact of Hyde v. Hyde

Hyde v. Hyde (1866), PD 130

In *Hyde v. Hyde*, where an English court stated that a valid marriage required "one man and one woman," Lord Penzance, the Judge Ordinary, reviewed a husband's petition for dissolution of his marriage on the ground of his wife's adultery. The parties were married in 1853 at Salt Lake City in Utah Territory by Brigham Young, president of the Mormon Church (both parties were Mormon) and also governor of the Territory. They cohabited and had children together. Three years later, the husband left Utah and renounced the Mormon faith, and a sentence of excommunication was pronounced against him in Utah; this sentence freed his wife to remarry. Although the parties communicated by letter, the wife elected to remain in Utah; she remarried in 1859 or 1860 and had children with her second husband. The petitioner, English by birth, returned to England in 1857 and became the minister of a dissenting chapel. Although both parties were single at the time of the marriage in Utah in 1853, the court expressed doubt about the jurisdiction of the English court to grant any remedy in relation to their marriage, because the parties had married in a jurisdiction that recognized polygamy. In this situation, the court decided that it was inappropriate to consider a petition for divorce on the ground of adultery, concluding (at 138), "as between each other [the petitioner and his wife] are not entitled to the remedies, the adjudication, or the relief of the matrimonial law of England."

As is apparent, the decision in *Hyde* more than a century ago focused primarily on the availability of divorce remedies in an English court in relation to a marriage entered into in a foreign jurisdiction in which polygamy was practised. In denying jurisdiction in respect of a petitioner who had himself married only once, the strength of the court's opposition to the recognition of polygamy is clearly evident. Yet, in spite of this context, the decision has been cited much more frequently to support the requirement of heterosexuality for a valid marriage, as stated by Lord Penzance, clearly a matter that was not at issue at all in *Hyde*.

2. Unsuccessful Same-Sex Marriage Challenges in Canada: From North v. Matheson to Re Layland and Beaulne and Ontario

In an early same-sex marriage case in Manitoba, *North v. Matheson* (1974), 20 RFL 112; 52 DLR (3d) 280 (Man. Co. Ct.), the court cited dictionary definitions of marriage as well as *Hyde*, and dismissed an application for registration of a marriage involving two men. Because both parties were the same sex, the purported marriage ceremony was a nullity. *North v. Matheson* was cited in an Ontario decision almost two decades later: *Re Layland and Beaulne and Ontario Ministry of Consumer and Commercial Relations* (1993), 14 OR (3d) 658; 104 DLR (4th) 214 (Gen. Div.). Although the Ontario Court of Appeal had decided in *Haig v. Canada* (1992), 9 OR (3d) 495; 94 DLR (4th) 1 that sexual orientation was an analogous ground of discrimination under s. 15 of the Charter, the majority of the court in *Layland* concluded that the equality guarantee in the Charter did not alter the requirement of "a man and a woman" in *Hyde*. As the court stated (OR, at 666-67):

> The personal difference involved in the case at bar is homosexuality, which is a matter of capacity. That characteristic is not irrelevant to the restriction of marriage at common law to

unions of persons of opposite sex [citing procreation as an important purpose of marriage]. ... The law does not prohibit marriage by homosexuals provided it takes place between persons of the opposite sex. ... The fact that many homosexuals do not choose to marry, because they do not want unions with persons of the opposite sex, is the result of their own preferences, not a requirement of the law. Unions of persons of the same sex are not "marriages," because of the definition of marriage. The applicants are, in effect, seeking to use s. 15 of the Charter to bring about a change in the definition of marriage. I do not think the Charter has that effect.

In a detailed dissenting judgment, Justice Greer examined the requirements of s. 15 in the light of *Haig* and asserted (at 675) that the denial of a marriage certificate to Layland and Beaulne was discriminatory: "The message they receive must surely give them the perception that they are inferior persons in our society." Moreover, the dissenting judgment recognized (at 677) an interest in the state in fostering "all family relationships, be they heterosexual or same-sex relationships." Significantly, however, Justice Greer relied on arguments that the common law must grow to meet society's expanding needs, that it need not be exactly the same "in all countries which have a common law system of law" (at 679), and that the law must recognize and support a variety of family forms (at 680):

> Surely the argument by the Attorney General that there is only one societal concept of marriage is flawed. One has only to examine how multiple marriages have become the norm in our North American society, how step-parents have become an integral part of children's lives in these marriages, how divorce has become widely recognized in society, and how "common law" relationships have become classified as marriages without the sanction of a marriage certificate but with most of the benefits conferred by one. There was even a time in history when a woman became the property of her husband. That concept of marriage became no longer valid. ... The common law and legislated law both change to meet a changing society.

Re Layland and Beaulne was decided in a context in which same-sex couples, both in Canada and in other jurisdictions, were increasingly challenging their exclusion from marriage, but also in relation to the legal benefits of spousal status. Although such benefits were denied in *Andrews v. Ontario Ministry of Health* (1988), 9 *Canadian Human Rights Reporter* D/5089, spousal status for same-sex couples was established in a variety of contexts: see *Leshner v. Ministry of the Attorney-General* (1992), 16 *Canadian Human Rights Reporter* D/184; *Rosenberg v. Canada* (1998), 38 OR (3d) 577 (CA); *OPSEU Pension Plan Trust Fund v. Ontario*, [1998] OJ no. 5075 (Gen. Div.); and *Québec (Commission des Droits de la Personne et des Droits de la Jeunesse) c. Québec (Procureur Géneral)*, [1998] AQ n° 3264 (Sup. Ct. (Civ. Div.)). Moreover, in 1999, the Supreme Court of Canada decided that the definition of spouse in Ontario's *Family Law Act*, in relation to entitlement to spousal support at the end of a relationship, discriminated against same-sex couples contrary to s. 15 of the Charter: see *M. v. H.*, [1999] 2 SCR 3; (1999), 171 DLR (4th) 577; 46 RFL (4th) 32 (SCC), discussed in chapter 7.

In this context, the issue of discrimination in the *Hyde* requirement of heterosexuality once again became the focus of litigation challenges pursuant to the Charter.

3. Judicial Recognition of Same-Sex Marriage

An Overview of the Litigation

In due course, challenges were launched in three provinces in relation to the restriction of marriage to opposite-sex couples. In 2001, a trial judge in British Columbia concluded that the definition of marriage could not be amended at common law but only by legislation; that the meaning of marriage in s. 92(26) of the Constitution was defined at Confederation and was thus not amenable to Charter scrutiny; and that if it was subject to the Charter, it infringed s. 15 equality but was saved by s. 1: see *EGALE Canada Inc. v. Canada (Attorney General)* (2001), 95 BCLR (3d) 122; 19 RFL (5th) 59 (SC). By contrast, the Ontario Divisional Court unanimously concluded in 2002 that the common law bar to marriage for same-sex couples contravened s. 15 of the Charter, and was not saved by s. 1. A majority of the judges suspended the effect of their decision for a period of 24 months to permit Parliament to legislate on the issue: see *Halpern v. Canada (Attorney General)* (2002), 215 DLR (4th) 223; 28 RFL (5th) 41 (Ont. Div. Ct.). Several weeks later, a decision of the Superior Court of Quebec adopted the reasoning and conclusions of the Ontario court: see *Hendricks v. Quebec (Attorney General)*, [2002] JQ no. 3816 (SC).

All these decisions were appealed. In May 2003, the British Columbia Court of Appeal allowed the appeal, expressly agreeing with the reasoning in the Divisional Court in *Halpern* in Ontario and suspending the effect of its decision to July 12, 2004 to correspond with the period of suspension in *Halpern*: see *EGALE Canada Inc. v. Canada (Attorney General)*, 2003 BCCA 251. However, on June 10, 2003, the Ontario Court of Appeal released its decision in *Halpern*, upholding the decision of the Divisional Court, but also eliminating the period of suspension: *Halpern v. Toronto (City)* (2003), 38 RFL (5th) 32. As the *per curiam* judgment explained (at para. 153):

> There is no evidence before this court that a declaration of invalidity without a period of suspension will pose any harm to the public, threaten the rule of law, or deny anyone the benefit of legal recognition of their marriage. We observe that there was no evidence before us that the reformulated definition of marriage will require the volume of legislative reform that followed the release of the Supreme Court of Canada's decision in *M v. H.* In our view, an immediate declaration will simply ensure that opposite-sex couples and same-sex couples immediately receive equal treatment in law in accordance with s. 15(1) of the Charter.

Following this decision, the federal government announced its decision not to appeal these decisions in Ontario and British Columbia. As a result, on July 8, 2003, the British Columbia Court of Appeal lifted the order suspending its decision, on consent by the Attorney General of Canada and the Attorney General of British Columbia, so that same-sex couples in British Columbia would be immediately entitled to marry, as in Ontario: see *EGALE Canada Inc. v. Canada (Attorney General)*, 2003 BCCA 406. Then, in March 2004, the Quebec Court of Appeal released its decision, unanimously upholding the lower court decision allowing gay marriages: see [2004] QJ no. 2593 (QL). The appellate court confirmed that article 365 of the Quebec *Civil Code* infringed the equality guarantee of the Charter. See Tu Thanh Ha, "Same-Sex Couples Win Right To Marry in Quebec," *Globe and Mail*, March 20, 2004.

Although the parties presented a wide a range of legal arguments in all of these cases, the appellate decisions were primarily based on the Charter's guarantee of equality in s. 15 and the lack of justification for discrimination pursuant to s. 1. From a family law perspective, however, it was the reasoning in the lower court in *Halpern* that revealed most clearly how differing conceptions of the nature and purpose of marriage in the 21st century had to be confronted in relation to this Charter analysis.

Halpern v. Canada
(2002), 60 OR (3d) 321 (Div. Ct.)

BLAIR RSJ:

I. Background and Overview

[1] Are same-sex couples entitled under Canadian law to marry?

[2] The question is deeply controversial in today's society. It touches the core values and beliefs of Canadians across a broad cultural, political, moral and religious spectrum; and it does so in most profound ways.

[3] In these proceedings the applicant Couples and the Metropolitan Community Church of Toronto seek Orders which, if granted, will require the Clerk of the City of Toronto to grant marriage licences to gay, lesbian and bisexual couples, and the Registrar General of Ontario to register "marriages" solemnized in a Church under the authority of the publication of banns of marriage. At the present time, only one country in the world—the Netherlands—permits such marriages. The issue raised by these proceedings is whether Canada is to become the second.

The Individual Applicants

[4] Each of the applicant Couples, and each of the two couples "married" under the banns, has long-term committed relationships. They love and care for each other dearly. They share their lives and live in a relationship that is "marriage-like" in everything but name. The depth of their covenants to each other, and of their desire to be accepted as full members of society, can be sensed from the following statements taken from the affidavits filed:

Dawn Onishenko

In our eyes we are married. Our relationship carries with it the privilege of love and fidelity as well as the obligation to be active contributors to society and to be responsible citizens. We would like to know that society takes our relationship as seriously as we do. ...

Finally, and above all, it is my love for Julie that brings me to seek legal recognition of our marriage. I am not seeking marriage for marriage's sake, but rather marriage contextualized. I love this person with all my heart and soul. I know that I will spend the rest of my life with her regardless of the obstacles we face together and as individuals. Julie is my family in the fullest sense of the word. She is the love of my life and the heart of my heart. I am a better person because she is in my life. I am a better daughter, sister, friend and citizen. I live my life more fully because of her. I care more deeply. I want to tell her and the world of this love. I want to manifest this commitment through marriage.

Gail Donnelly

I have faith that one day I will have the same opportunity to participate in legal marriage in the same manner as straight persons. I have faith that I will not have to prove that I am an intelligent, compassionate human being with the same wants and needs as everyone else. I have faith that society will stop judging people based on their sexual attraction and start looking at the values that we each cherish and believe. All I wish for is to be treated in the same fashion as my parents, siblings and friends. I am, after all, a human being with the same values and the same capacity to love as anyone.

Michael Leshner

I met Mike Stark on May 23, 1981, and we have cohabited since 1984. Mike and I are known as "the Michaels."

I will not explain our personal characteristics further in this Affidavit as I do not believe that the details of our lives and relationship are relevant. It should not be necessary for me to justify my application for a marriage licence and requiring me to do so would be discriminatory, humiliating, and upsetting. My love for Mike Stark *is* the same as the love of other marriage licence applicants.

Being denied a marriage licence suggests that Mike and I, while supposedly equal citizens of this great country, are deemed non-persons, because we are gay.

Other Views

[5] The opposing views respecting the recognition in marriage of same-sex relationships were presented principally through the Attorney General of Canada, the Interfaith Coalition of Marriage and Family, and the Association for Marriage and the Family in Ontario (the latter two as intervenors). The evidence put forward by these participants does not reflect the same personal poignancy as that of the applicants. It demonstrates, nonetheless, that what is at stake in these proceedings evokes strongly held views which run very deep in the history and traditions of this society and which are exceptionally important for many Canadians who do not share the beliefs and values of the applicants.

· · ·

[20] I have had the opportunity to read the thorough and well-reasoned decision of Justice La Forme in this matter and, with the exception of his opinion respecting the remedy to be applied, I concur with and adopt his conclusions as to the disposition of the proceedings.

[21] Justice La Forme determined,

    a) that there is no statutory impediment to the issuance of marriage licenses to same-sex couples who otherwise meet the requisite criteria, or to the registration of their church marriages pursuant to the publication of banns of marriage. ...

b) that there is a common law rule—as the common law presently stands—which is an impediment to same-sex marriages. ...

c) that the existing common law rule is inconsistent with constitutional values in modern Canadian society, and offends the equality rights of gays and lesbians under s. 15(1) of the Charter. ...

d) that the inconsistency and infringement of s. 15(1) cannot be demonstrably justified in a free and democratic society, and therefore cannot be saved by a s. 1 analysis under the Charter, to the extent that such an analysis may be necessary when dealing with a common law provision.

I agree, although I am more inclined than La Forme J to think that a s. 1 analysis is required in these circumstances.

e) that the existing common law rule does not infringe the s. 2(a), s. 2(b) or s. 7 Charter rights of the Applicant Couples or the MCCT. ...

f) and that the argument to the effect that any change in the word "marriage," as found in the division of powers in ss. 91 and 92 of the *Constitution Act, 1867* requires a constitutional amendment, cannot succeed. ...

[22]   Finally, La Forme J concluded that the appropriate remedy in the circumstances is for the court to reformulate the common law rule, itself. "Marriage," as currently defined in the common law, is the lawful and voluntary union of one man and one woman to the exclusion of all others: see, *Hyde v. Hyde and Woodmansee* (1866), LR 1 P & D 130, *per* Lord Penzance; *Layland v. Ontario (Minister of Consumer & Commercial Relations)* (1993), 14 OR (3d) 658 (Div. Ct.). La Forme J would redefine the common law rule respecting marriage by substituting the words "two persons" for the words "one man and one woman" in the foregoing definition.

[23]   Respectfully, I disagree. In my opinion, it is the primary responsibility of Parliament (and, where applicable, the Legislatures) to reformulate the definition of marriage, given the significance of the change involved and the uncertain ramifications flowing from it. They should be afforded the opportunity to do so.

[24]   I turn now to a consideration of marriage, the common law relating to it, and the *Charter of Rights and Freedoms.*

III. The Definition of Marriage, and Section 15 of the Charter

No Statutory Impediment

[25]   For the reasons articulated by La Forme J, I agree there is no statutory impediment to the relief claimed by the applicants.

[26]   It is the federal government that has the constitutional authority to define marriage, by virtue of the division of powers in ss. 91 and 92 of the *Constitution Act, 1867.* Section 91(26) gives Parliament authority over marriage and divorce. Parliament has not legislatively defined what is meant by "marriage," however.

[27] The closest Parliament has come to doing so is in section 1.1 of the *Modernization of Benefits and Obligations Act*, SC 2000, c. 12 ("the *MBOA*"). Section 1.1 is the "interpretation" clause in the legislation—which was an omnibus bill designed to amend a large number of federal statutes to comply with the law respecting gays and lesbians following the decision of the Supreme Court of Canada in *M. v. H.* It states that "the amendments made by this Act do not affect the meaning of the word 'marriage,' that is, the lawful union of one man and one woman to the exclusion of all others." While this statutory provision may provide a strong indication of Parliament's view on marriage, at the time of the enactment of the *MBOA*, it does not constitute a statutory definition of marriage that would feed the Ontario legislation governing the issuance of marriage licenses and registration of marriages performed under the authority of banns, and preclude the relief sought by the applicants, in my view.

[28] Even if the language of s. 1.1 of the *MBOA* were construed to constitute a statutory definition of marriage, however, it would be unconstitutional on the same Charter grounds that apply to the common law definition, to which I now turn.

The Common Law Impediment

[29] There is a common law impediment to the relief claimed by the applicants, as the common law presently stands.

[30] I accept that the common law in Ontario is currently governed by the 1993 decision of this Court in *Layland v. Ontario (Minister of Consumer & Commercial Relations)*, supra. The majority decision in that case remains the law in this province unless and until it is altered. "Marriage," as defined by the common law, is the lawful and voluntary union of one man and one woman to the exclusion of all others.

[31] The common law cannot isolate itself from the dictates and reality of modern society, however. It must evolve. Indeed, the essential characteristic of the common law over the centuries has been its ability to do just that. As Greer J noted, in her strong and articulate dissent in *Layland*, with which I agree (at p. 667):

> One of the questions the court was being asked to consider was whether there was a common law prohibition against same-sex marriages.
>
> The object of the common law is to solve difficulties and adjust relations in social and commercial life. It must meet, so far as it can, sets of fact abnormal as well as usual. *It must grow with the development of the nation. It must face and deal with changing or novel circumstances.* Unless it can do that it fails in its function and declines in its dignity and value. An expanding society demands an expanding common law.
>
> That the common law expands to meet social needs is not a new concept. The above words were written by McCardie J of the King's Bench Division in a 1924 sale of goods case, *Prager v. Blatspiel, Stamp & Heacock Ltd.*, [1924] 1 KB 566 at p. 570, [1924] All ER Rep. 524. *The common law does not remain static. Its very essence is that it is able to grow to meet the expanding needs of society.* (Emphasis added.)

[32] There is thus a short answer to the question posed by the applicants in these two proceedings. It is this: the constitutional and Charter-inspired values which

underlie Canadian society today dictate that the status and incidents inherent in the foundational institution of marriage must be open to same-sex couples who live in long-term, committed relationships—marriage-like in everything but name—just as they are to heterosexual couples. Each is entitled to full and equal recognition, and the law must therefore be adapted accordingly.

[33] While much has been written, and much more will undoubtedly be written by the courts on the journey to this destination, I am fully satisfied that in the end the law must arrive at that point. How that is to be accomplished, and through what sort of regime in law, are thorny issues to be grappled with, however. ...

Marriage and the Law Today

[59] What, then, of marriage today?

[60] If the courts are to examine the common law definition of marriage through the prism of Charter rights and values, it seems to me they must recognize and appreciate the changes that have occurred over the centuries, and more rapidly in recent years, in the attitudes of society towards the family, marriage and relationships, as outlined above. To do otherwise is to abandon the purpose of section 15—which is to promote equality and prevent discrimination arising from such ills as stereotyping, prejudice and historical wrongs—and to fail to consider the common law principle under review in a contextual fashion. As noted already, the courts are mandated to take a purposive and contextual approach to the analysis and interpretation of s. 15 equality rights: *Law v. Ontario (Minister of Employment and Immigration)* [[1991] 1 SCR 497; 170 DLR (4th) 1]. ...

[61] Given this background of dramatically shifting attitudes towards marriage and the family, I have a great deal of difficulty accepting that heterosexual procreation is such a compelling and central aspect of marriage in 21st century post-Charter Canadian society that it—and it alone—gives marriage its defining characteristic and justifies the exclusion of same-sex couples from that institution. It is, of course, the only characteristic with which such couples are unable to conform (and even that inability is changing).

[62] Yet that is the nub of the argument put forward by the respondents. They submit that the institution of marriage,

> is unique in its essence, that is, its opposite-sex nature. Through this essence, marriage embodies the complementarity of the two human sexes.

[63] Stripped to its essentials, this contention is based upon the notion that heterosexual procreation is the ultimate defining characteristic of marriage, which is thus inherently heterosexual in nature. This unique opposite-sex nature of marriage does not imply that the human dignity of those in other relationships is diminished, the respondents argue. The "definitional boundaries" of marriage, they say, do not violate the constitutional rights of equality of those whose unions have an essential difference—or, for that matter, their freedom of religion or of expression, or their right to security. In any event, if they do, preserving marriage's definitional uniqueness is both justifiable and in accordance with principles of fundamental justice, and s. 1 of the Charter applies to save the existing common law definition.

[64] If this understanding of marriage forms the starting point of the analysis, I agree [that] the argument that s. 15(1) is violated by the common law definition of marriage is harder to make. Viewed from this standpoint, same-sex couples are not excluded from the institution because of their sexual orientation; rather, they are simply ineligible because they fall outside of the "definitional boundaries of marriage." They are incapacitated from entering the institution, not precluded from doing so on the basis of their personal characteristics.

[65] On the other hand, if marriage is viewed through a looking glass with a broader focus—and not conceived as a social, cultural, religious and legal edifice built upon heterosexual procreation as its fundamental infrastructure—the s. 15(1) analysis is directly engaged. In this approach to marriage, same-sex couples are not precluded from participating by reason of its innate characteristic. They are precluded simply because of their sexual orientation. The evidence is clear: same-sex couples can and do live in long-term, caring, loving and conjugal relationships—including those involving the rearing of children (and, in a modern context, even the birth of children). In short, their relationships are characterized by all the indicia of marriage, as traditionally understood, save for classic heterosexual intercourse, and they live in unions that are marriage-like in everything but name.

[66] The underlying question, then, is whether the law in Canada today is sufficiently open and adaptable to recognize a broader rationale as the defining characteristic of marriage than heterosexual procreation and its surrounding religious paraphernalia. In my view, it is. Indeed, this is where the evolutionary nature of the common law comes in. To invoke the words of Greer J in *Layland*, *supra*, again:

> The common law does not remain static. Its very essence is that it is able to grow to meet the expanding needs of society.

[67] It may well be that historically marriage has almost universally been conceived as a union of a man and a woman. Undoubtedly, this historical fact has had much to do with the needs of procreation and with the necessity for society to provide a setting in which children could be born, raised and protected, and through which human life could be sustained and perpetuated. The "family" has long been perceived as the ideal unit for these purposes, and since procreation—until relatively recently, at least—has been the product of physical sexual intercourse between a man and a woman, the "family" has classically been considered to be founded on a heterosexual union.

[68] Cultures and social mores, however, as well as faiths and religions and laws and economies, all tend to be reflective of the physical, environmental, technological and scientific realities of the times. Those realities can and do shift. Indeed, since the early to mid-20th century, developed societies have been transformed in geometrically progressive fashion as a result of changes in technology, communications, transportation, applied sciences, social sciences, world economies, global mobility and—in Canada, particularly—multi-culturalism. We live in the "global village." Cultural and religious diversity are defining features of the Canadian mosaic. Former "realities" are not necessarily any longer current "realities."

[69] "Procreation"—the production of offspring naturally—is amongst the concepts affected by the evolution wrought by these changes. Scientific advances have

made it possible for children to be born to couples—heterosexual or homosexual—through artificial insemination, in vitro fertilization in its various forms, surrogate motherhood, et cetera. While it remains true—at least for now—as Justice Gonthier observed in *M. v. H.*, that birth in a same-sex union by necessity must involve a third person, procreation through heterosexual coupling, as the source of the "reality" of children being born into a family, and therefore as the characteristic giving marriage its principal rationale and unique heterosexual nature, is becoming an increasingly narrow and shaky footing for the institution of marriage.

[70] Too narrow, and too shaky, in my opinion, to be tenable as the legal base for such a foundational institution in society as marriage. To be sure, the production, care and raising of children is a principal purpose of marriage. But that purpose, as I have indicated, is presently attainable through means other than heterosexual intercourse. There is much more to marriage as a societal institution, in my view, than the act of heterosexual intercourse leading to the birth of children. Moreover, the authorities are clear that marriage is not dependent upon the presence of children; nor are incapacity or an unwillingness to have children a bar to marriage or a ground for divorce: see, *Layland, supra*, at p. 666; *M. v. H., supra*, per Gonthier J at p. 132.

[71] Marriage has a physical sexual component to it, of course. Marriage is more fully characterized in my opinion, however, by its pivotal child-rearing role, and by a long-term conjugal relationship between two individuals—with its attendant obligations and offerings of mutual care and support, of companionship and shared social activities, of intellectual and moral and faith-based stimulation as a couple, and of shared shelter and economic and psychological interdependence—and by love. These are the indicia of the purpose of marriage in modern Canadian society. As McLachlin J noted, in *Miron v. Trudel*, [1995] 2 SCR 418, at p. 500, para. 157, 124 DLR (4th) 693:

> To most in our society, marriage is a good thing; to many a sacred thing. There is nobility in the public commitment of two people to each other to the exclusion of all others.

[72] Indeed, in fairness to the respondents and the intervenors who support them, they do not argue that marriage is a one-dimensional institution. They recognize that marriage has companionship, support, shared-workload, shared-economies, and shelter aspects to it. They simply contend that its historical recognition as a different-sex union based upon the need for procreation is its ultimately defining characteristic.

[73] This viewpoint is the same as that expressed by the majority of the Divisional Court in *Layland*, and by the minority of the judges in the Supreme Court of Canada for whom Justices Gonthier and La Forest wrote in *Miron* and in *Egan*, respectively. It is well summarized by La Forest J in the following passage from his decision in *Egan v. Canada*, [1995] 2 SCR 513, at p. 536, 124 DLR (4th) 609:

> My colleague Gonthier J in *Miron v. Trudel* has been at pains to discuss the fundamental importance of marriage as a social institution, and I need not repeat his analysis at length or refer to the authorities he cites. Suffice it to say that marriage has from time immemorial been firmly grounded in our legal tradition, one that is itself a reflection of long-standing philosophical and religious traditions. *But its ultimate raison d'être transcends all of these and is firmly anchored in the biological and social realities that*

heterosexual couples have the unique ability to procreate, that most children are the product of these relationships, and that they are generally cared for and nurtured by those who live in that relationship. *In this sense, marriage is by nature heterosexual.* It would be possible to legally define marriage to include homosexual couples, but this would not change the biological and social realities that underlie the traditional marriage. (Emphasis added.) See also, *Layland v. Ontario, supra, per* Southey J at p. 666.

[74] It should be noted, however, that neither the decision of Gonthier J in *Miron* nor that of La Forest J in *Egan* represented the views of the majority of either court in those cases on this point. The majority of the members of the court did not find it necessary to base their decisions on an understanding of the fundamental meaning of marriage. Indeed, just as they had in *Egan, supra* (p. 583), Justices Cory and Iacobucci stressed in *M. v. H., supra* (pp. 48-49) that the question of whether same-sex couples could marry remained open. ...

[80] Whether one approaches "marriage" from the classical perspective based upon the narrow basis that heterosexual procreation is its fundamental underpinning and what makes it "unique in its essence, that is, its opposite sex nature," or whether one approaches it from a different perspective, is pivotal to the s. 15 analysis, however. If one accepts the former view as the starting premise, there is little debate, it seems to me. The institution of marriage is inherently and uniquely heterosexual in nature. Therefore, same-sex couples are not excluded from it on the basis of a personal characteristic giving rise to differential treatment founded upon a stereotypical difference. Same-sex couples are simply *incapable* of marriage because they cannot procreate through heterosexual intercourse. Thus it is a distinction created by the nature of the institution itself which precludes homosexuals from access to marriage, not a personal characteristic or stereotypic prejudice. The equality provisions of s. 15 are not violated, and even if they were, the same analysis would justify the law in preserving the institution for heterosexual couples and therefore save the classic definition of marriage on a s. 1 analysis.

[81] On the other hand, once it is accepted that same-sex unions can feature the same conjugal and other incidents of marriage, except for heterosexual intercourse, and if heterosexual procreation is no longer viewed as the central characteristic of marriage, giving it its inherently heterosexual uniqueness, the s. 15 argument must succeed. If heterosexual procreation is not essential to the nature of the institution, then the same-sex couples' sexual orientation is the only distinction differentiating heterosexual couples from homosexual couples in terms of access to the institution of marriage. For all of the reasons articulated by Justice La Forme, this differentiation is discriminatory of the same-sex couples' equality rights as set out in s. 15 of the Charter and cannot stand.

[82] First, the common law definition of marriage draws a formal distinction between the applicant couples and the couples "married" by the MCCT, on the one hand, and heterosexual couples, on the other hand, on the basis of their personal characteristics, i.e., their sexual orientation. Secondly, the claimants are subject to differential treatment on the basis of a ground of discrimination which has been held to be a ground analogous to those enumerated in s. 15, namely, sexual orientation.

Finally, the differential treatment of the claimants discriminates against them in a substantive sense, bringing into play the purpose of s. 15(1) of the Charter in remedying such ills as prejudice, stereotyping and historical disadvantage: see *Law v. Canada (Minister of Employment and Immigration)* ... , per Iacobucci J at p. 524, adopted by Cory J and Iacobucci J in *M. v. H., supra,* at pp. 46-47.

[83] The evidence supports a conclusion that "marriage" represents society's highest acceptance of the self-worth and the wholeness of a couple's relationship, and thus touches their sense of human dignity at its core.

[84] The equality provisions of s. 15(1) of the Charter are therefore violated. ...

[In assessing the appropriate remedy for this violation, Blair RSJ stated in part:]

[119] In my view ... "the question of how [the common law] ought to be extended in order to comply with the Constitution cannot be answered with a sufficient degree of precision on the basis of constitutional analysis," and "it is [Parliament's] role to fill in the gaps, not the Court's."

[120] The debate starts on the footing that the required change in the law is in sharp contrast to Parliament's present—and clearly expressed—choice regarding marriage. It is evident that Parliament's current approach to the institution is rooted in the common law definition: see the *Modernization of Benefits and Obligations Act, supra,* s. 1.1; the *Federal Law—Civil Law Harmonization Act, No. 1,* SC 2001, c. 4, ss. 5-7; Parliamentary Motion, *House of Commons Debates,* 1st sess., 36th Parl., vol. 135 at 15960-93, 16034-16036, and 16068-16069 (8 June 1999). I do not accept, however, that Parliament will not change its views in the face of the newly declared unconstitutionality of the common law rule, and will engage in what the applicants fear will be an approach of "remedial evasion." The *MBOA* is itself an indication of Parliament's willingness to legislate in response to required, albeit contentious, constitutional change. The fact that the change respecting the concept of marriage, required by this ruling, is in such contrast to Parliament's current views is a factor in favour of providing Parliament with an opportunity to craft its own solution to the problem, rather than a factor in favour of directly imposing a judge-made rule on Parliament, in my opinion.

[121] There are legislative offshoots of this constitutionally mandated change—actual and potential—which should be kept in mind as well. Although various pieces of omnibus legislation enacted by Parliament and the provinces in the wake of the Supreme Court of Canada's decision in *M. v. H.* have extended benefits and obligations to same-sex couples on the same basis as opposite-sex couples in a wide variety of situations—the *MBOA,* itself, amended 69 federal statutes—there remain areas where benefits and protections are still a function of male/female-spouse language. Differences in the treatment of same-sex and opposite-sex partners remain in such federal spheres as the way in which the testimony of spousal-like partners is dealt with under the *Canada Evidence Act* and the way in which sponsorship applications are handled under the *Immigration Act* and Regulations. As well, in Ontario at least, certain benefits continue to be enjoyed exclusively by opposite-sex married couples under the statutory regimes governing family law rights to property and equalization,

and the law of estates and succession. There may be considerations relating to the changes in these spheres consequent upon the inclusions of same-sex unions in the institution of marriage which need to be addressed simultaneously with a recognition of that inclusion, which the court cannot foresee and with which Parliament and the legislatures will be required to deal. This factor also militates towards legislative deference from the court in these circumstances, in my view.

[122] As I have suggested, the ramifications of the change required to bring the law into conformity with Charter rights and values are potentially extensive and, to some extent, uncertain. They will evoke robust socio-political, cultural, economic, religious and moral debate. In short, *democratic* debate will ensue. Parliament is the forum for that type of discussion and for the balancing of such conflicting societal interests. It should be accorded some flexibility in dealing with contentious and morally laden issues: see: *Rodriguez v. British Columbia (Attorney General)*, [1993] 3 SCR 519, at p. 614; *R v. Hess*, [1990] 2 SCR 906; *Vriend* [[1998] 1 SCR 493], p. 564. ...

[128] Although reformulating the concept of civil marriage to replace the union of "one man and one woman" with the union of "two persons" is obviously a leading alternative for consideration in bringing the law into line with Charter values, it is not the only option.

[129] The example most commonly put forward is the "registered domestic partnership" regime which has been implemented in various northern European countries, and in the State of Vermont, and the Province of Nova Scotia. Since the argument of these Applications—on June 7, 2002—the National Assembly of Quebec passed a "Civil Union" Bill. A registered partnership model allows same-sex partners (and in some cases, opposite-sex partners) to register their relationship with the state. Registration brings with it most of the rights and duties of marriage, but provides a "parallel" recognition of the relationship, leaving "marriage" to opposite-sex couples. There are variations between regimes. Some have restrictions with respect to adoption, filiation and biogenetic reproduction.

[130] Like Justice La Forme, I have some concerns about the adequacy of the registered domestic partnership regime to meet the requirements of the Charter. Equality of benefits and protection are not necessarily the same thing as full and equal recognition. Having said that, however, this court does not have before it a legislatively enacted registered partnership scheme for consideration and measurement against the requirements of the Constitution and the Charter. Accordingly, I do not think the court can, or should, effectively judge that question in advance and out of context.

[131] There is another option as well. The notion of civil marriage could be replaced altogether, and "marriages" left to be performed by the various religious institutions in accordance with their faith-based traditions and conscience. Instead of civil marriage, there might be a system of "legal civil unions" into which both opposite-sex and same-sex couples who take part in a form of religious marriage are required to enter. Such a civil union could also be open to couples who choose not to go through a religious marriage, but who wish to formalize their relationship in a state-sanctioned fashion that provides full and equal recognition to all.

[132] This option does not seem to have been considered to date in jurisdictions that have moved towards equal treatment for same-sex couples. Nonetheless, in a

discussion Paper released in December 2001, the Law Commission of Canada has thrown open just such a possibility—as well as others—for discussion. ...

[133] Thus, there *are* other alternatives that might be weighed in determining how marriage—or the institution in present-day Canadian society that will afford full and equal recognition to same-sex couples as marriage presently does to opposite-sex couples—is to be redefined, or reformulated.

[134] Even if opening up marriage to same-sex couples as the Dutch have done is the appropriate alternative, in order to comply with Charter dictates, legislatures and not courts are the proper venue for the crafting of that solution, in my opinion. Even the Dutch "marriage" maintains some distinctions between same-sex and opposite-sex marriages: same-sex marriage will have no consequences in relation to the law of filiation based on descent, meaning that a child born into a same-sex marriage will not have an automatic legal filiation link to both spouses; presumptions of paternity do not apply; in the context of a marriage between two men, a child born into the marriage by means of a surrogate mother will have to be recognized by the biological father (or have paternity judicially established), and be adopted by the other "parent" with the consent of the mother; in the context of a marriage between two women, only the biological mother would have a direct filiation link to the child and the other parent would have to adopt; a Dutch same-sex marriage will not likely be recognized abroad.

[135] Undoubtedly, issues similar to these will have to be addressed in Canada, together possibly with other questions arising in connection with the alternative birthing methods necessarily resorted to by same-sex couples. It strikes me that such matters are more effectively dealt with by legislatures rather than by the court simply "reformulating" the common law definition of marriage by reading out the words "one man and one woman" and reading in the words "two persons."

[136] For these reasons, I am satisfied the appropriate remedy in the circumstances of this case is to strike down the common law definition, but to suspend the operation of the declaration of invalidity for a period of time to afford Parliament and the legislatures an opportunity to resolve the problem before the declaration becomes effective.

Halpern v. Canada
(2003), 65 OR (3d) 161 (CA)

[The Ontario Court of Appeal focused on the principles established in *Law v. Canada*, [1999] 1 SCR 497 and held (at 181) that the claimants were the subject of differential treatment because the common law definition of marriage "creates a formal distinction between opposite-sex and same-sex couples on the basis of their sexual orientation." The court further held that the differential treatment was based on the analogous ground of sexual orientation. In addition, the court examined the differential treatment in relation to the tests for discrimination set out in *Law* and in *Gosselin v. Quebec v. Canada (Attorney General)*, 2002 SCC 84; 221 DLR (4th) 257 and the four contextual factors used to demonstrate that a law demeans a claimant's dignity, either in purpose or effect. In assessing the correspondence between the grounds and the claimant's actual needs, capacities, or circumstances, the Attorney General argued (at 185) that "marriage relates to the capacities, needs and circumstances of opposite-sex couples" and that "the concept of marriage—across time, societies and legal cultures—is that of an institution to facilitate, shelter and nurture the unique union of a man and woman who, together, have the possibility to bear children from their relationship and shelter them within it." Rejecting this argument, the court held (at 186-87):]

[It] is important to remember that the purpose and effects of the impugned law must at all times be viewed from the perspective of the claimant. The question to be asked is whether the law takes into account the actual needs, capacities and circumstances of same-sex couples, not whether the law takes into account the needs, capacities and circumstances of opposite-sex couples. In *Law* at p. 538 SCR, Iacobucci J cautioned that "[t]he fact that the impugned legislation may achieve a valid social purpose for one group of individuals cannot function to deny an equality claim where the effects of the legislation upon another person or group conflict with the purpose of the s. 15(1) guarantee. …

[A] law that prohibits same-sex couples from marrying does not accord with the needs, capacities and circumstances of same-sex couples. While it is true that, due to biological realities, only opposite-sex couples can "naturally" procreate, same-sex couples can choose to have children by other means, such as adoption, surrogacy and donor insemination. An increasing percentage of children are being conceived and raised by same-sex couples: *M v. H* at p. 75 SCR.

Importantly, no one, including the AGC, is suggesting that procreation and childrearing are the only purposes of marriage, or the only reasons why couples choose to marry. Intimacy, companionship, societal recognition, economic benefits, the blending of two families, to name a few, are other reasons that couples choose to marry. As recognized in *M v. H* at p. 50 SCR, same-sex couples are capable of forming "long, lasting, loving and intimate relationships." Denying same-sex couples the right to marry perpetuates the contrary view, namely, that same-sex couples are not capable of forming loving and lasting relationships, and thus same-sex relationships are not worthy of the same respect and recognition as opposite-sex relationships.

Accordingly, in our view, the common law requirement that marriage be between persons of the opposite sex does not accord with the needs, capacities and circumstances of same-sex couples.

The court concluded that there was an infringement of s. 15 of the Charter. In assessing whether the infringement was justifiable under s. 1, the court applied the test in *R v. Oakes*, [1986] 1 SCR 103; 26 DLR (4th) 200 and held (at 196) that the government had failed to show that the objectives of excluding same-sex couples from marriage were pressing and substantial, or that the means chosen to achieve the objectives were reasonable and justified in a free and democratic society. Thus, the court proceeded to reformulate the common law definition of marriage (at 199) as "the voluntary union for life of two persons to the exclusion of all others." The court declined to order a suspension of the declaration of invalidity or of the reformulated common law definition; it issued orders of mandamus, requiring the issuance of marriage licences to same-sex couples and requiring the Registrar General of the Province of Ontario to accept the marriage certificates of same-sex couples for registration. As noted above, the appellate courts in British Columbia and Quebec also confirmed the availability of marriage to same-sex couples.

Discussion Notes

Judicial Reasoning and Law Reform

Does the reasoning in the Divisional Court in *Halpern* in 2002 reveal different views about the fundamental nature of marriage, by contrast with *Re Layland and Beaulne* in 1993? How would you characterize the arguments in these two cases about the importance of procreation in marriage? How should legal and policy arguments about the importance of reproduction for society as a whole be balanced with respect for individual choice about bearing and/or raising children? Should courts take account of increasing opportunities for non-biological reproduction among opposite-sex or same-sex couples? Do your answers to these questions suggest that law should reflect social trends? Should it encourage them?

Blair RSJ clearly concluded that these were important issues to be considered by Parliament. As a result, his order created an opportunity for Parliamentary action within a two-year period, but he held that in the absence of such action by Parliament, the *Hyde* definition of marriage would be amended by replacing the words "one man and one woman" with the words "two persons." Although the other two judges in the Divisional Court agreed that the definition of marriage contravened s. 15 and was not saved by s. 1, they disagreed about the appropriate remedy. Smith ACJSC similarly suspended operation of the declaration of invalidity for two years, but left open the possibility of later applications if Parliament failed to act. La Forme J, relying on criticism expressed in the Supreme Court of Canada in *Vriend* about "incrementalism," concluded that the court should remedy the discrimination by immediately replacing the words "one man and one woman" with the words "two persons."

In the Ontario Court of Appeal, as noted above, the judges concluded that there were no significant legislative reforms required to extend marriage to same-sex couples and declared the *Hyde* definition unconstitutional. Yet, although legislation has extended spousal benefits and obligations for many cohabitees, including same-sex cohabitees, some issues remain uncertain with respect to same-sex marriage. For example, Canadian divorce legislation defines spouse for purposes of divorce proceedings as "either of a man or a woman," a provision that will likely also be amended judicially or by Parliament; otherwise, same-sex couples will have the right to marry, but not the right to divorce: see *M.M. v. J.H.*, an application for divorce filed by a woman in a same-sex marriage (Tracey Tyler, "Now It's Divorce, Same-Sex Style," *Toronto Star*, July 24, 2004) . In addition, because there is no residence requirement for marriage, persons who are resident in other provinces or other jurisdictions will now be able to marry in Ontario. However, there is a residency requirement for divorce (normally one year in the province in which the proceedings are commenced: see *Divorce Act 1985*, s. 3). It is also possible that there will be problems relating to recognition of same-sex marriages in other jurisdictions. Some issues concerning recognition were reviewed in Martha Bailey, "Hawaii's Same-Sex Marriage Initiatives: Implications for Canada" (1998), 15 *Canadian Journal of Family Law* 153, particularly with respect to trends in interpreting principles of conflict of laws. See also Christopher Marquis, "US Gays Who Marry in Canada Face Hurdles," *New York Times*, June 19, 2003.

The Impact of Same-Sex Marriage Cases: Parliament

As noted above, same-sex partners became entitled to marry in Ontario on June 10, 2003, in British Columbia on July 8, 2003, and in Quebec on March 19, 2004. Although the federal government had referred the issue to a Parliamentary committee after the lower court decisions, its discussion paper (November 2002) was largely overshadowed after the appellate court decisions. In September 2003, a coalition of conservative and religious groups vowed to hold prayer protests and to target federal MPs who had expressed approval for same-sex marriage: see Tonda MacCharles, "Gay-Marriage Foes Plan Prayer Protests," *Toronto Star*, September 3, 2003, at A17. The House of Commons also voted on a motion proposed by the Canadian Alliance, which called on Parliament to preserve the definition of marriage as "the union of one man and one woman, to the exclusion of all others." The motion was narrowly defeated, 137–132: see Kim Lunman and Drew Fagan, "Marriage Divides the House," *Globe and Mail*, September 17, 2003, at A1.

In this context, the federal government decided to refer the issue to the Supreme Court of Canada and to request the court to define the constitutionality of proposed federal legislation concerning gay marriage. The constitutional reference requested the court's opinion as to whether provisions respecting aspects of legal capacity for marriage for civil purposes were within the federal government's exclusive legislative authority, whether a provision extending capacity to marry to persons of the same sex was consistent with the Charter, and whether the Charter's guarantee of freedom of religion would protect religious officials from being compelled to perform same-sex marriage, contrary to the officials' beliefs. Although it was expected that the court would hear arguments in the reference in April 2004, the federal government (under the leadership of a new prime minister) referred an additional question to the court in January 2004, thus necessitating a delay in the judicial proceedings. The new question stated:

> Is the opposite-sex requirement for marriage for civil purposes, as established by the common law and set out for Quebec in s. 5 of the Federal Law—*Civil Law Harmonization Act, No. 1*, SC 2001, c. 4, consistent with the [Charter]?

In response to criticism, the minister of justice stated that the court's answer to the additional question was important for an informed debate on the proposed legislation in Parliament: see Valerie Lawton, "Ottawa Accused of Same-Sex Delay," *Toronto Star*, January 29, 2004, at A7.

Clearly, in the context of three unanimous appeal court decisions in Ontario, British Columbia, and Quebec, it seems likely that the Supreme Court's analysis of Charter guarantees will support same-sex marriage. Such a decision will provide some impetus for Parliamentary legislation, although it will by no means guarantee success, particularly if the composition of the House of Commons changes in the 2004 federal election. Undeniably, these developments confirm that issues about defining families in law are profoundly political.

The Impact of the Same-Sex Marriage Cases: Gays and Lesbians

The availability of marriage for same-sex couples was celebrated by many gay and lesbian couples. Between June 10, and August 30, 2003, a total of 590 gay and lesbian couples applied for marriage licences in Toronto, just over 10 percent of the 5,500 couples who received licences during that period. More than 100 of the gay couples were American. By contrast, others in the gay and lesbian community expressed concern about entering a relationship like marriage, fearing that it would undermine their unique sense of culture and the opportunity to foster social change; for these same-sex couples, marriage seemed likely to lead to "complacent ... gay and lesbian soccer moms": see Clifford Krauss, "Free To Marry, Canada's Gays Say, 'Do I'?" *New York Times*, August 31, 2003 and Mitchel Raphael, "Who Says All Gays Want To Marry?" *Globe and Mail*, April 7, 2004, at A19.

In addition to these issues, Claire Young had earlier argued that it is necessary to pay attention to specific contexts in determining whether legal recognition of same-sex couples constitutes real advantages or disadvantages. Comparing the tax implications for three same-sex couples (one in which both partners were taxed at the highest rate; one in which both were taxed at a low rate; and one in which one taxpayer was taxed at the highest rate, while the other had no taxable income), Young concluded that

> if the "advantage" of being included as spouse under the [*Income Tax*] *Act* is determined by reference to tax dollars saved, then it will be the lesbian or gay couple in a relationship in which one partner is economically dependent on the other who will benefit the most from being included as spouses under the Act. Conversely it will be the low income couple in which each partner earns approximately the same amount of income that will suffer the greatest disadvantage. ... [Moreover,] gender cannot be ignored when discussing the tax system ... [because] the tax system discriminates against women. ... [Thus,] gay men will, on average, benefit more than lesbians by being included as spouses under the Act.

(Claire Young, "Taxing Times for Lesbians and Gay Men: Equality at What Cost?" (1994), 17 *Dalhousie Law Journal* 534, at 547 and 555.)

To what extent should law reform proposals mandating equality for same-sex couples in marriage take account of issues of gender and economic class? For a different approach, see the *Report on the Rights and Responsibilities of Cohabitants Under the Family Law Act* (Toronto: Ontario Law Reform Commission, 1993), at 51-59, which recommended choice for gays and lesbians as to whether they wished to have their cohabiting relationships recognized in law. See also Patricia Le Febour, "Same-Sex Spousal Recognition in Ontario: Declarations and Denial: A Class Perspective" (1993), 9 *Journal of Law and Social Policy* 272; Brenda Cossman, "Lesbians, Gay Men and the Canadian Charter of Rights and Freedoms" (2003), 40 *Osgoode Hall Law Journal* 223; Didi Herman, "Are We Family? Lesbian Rights and Women's Liberation" (1990), 28 *Osgoode Hall Law Journal* 789; and Shelley A.M. Gavigan, "Legal Forms, Family Forms, Gendered Norms: What Is a Spouse?" (1999), 14 *Canadian Journal of Law and Society* 127.

Same-Sex Families and Benefits: Different Approaches in Canada

As noted earlier, the same-sex marriage cases occurred in the context of significant developments concerning benefits for same-sex spouses. Indeed, following the decision of the Supreme Court of Canada in *M. v. H.*, [1999] 2 SCR 3 (discussed in chapter 7), the federal government enacted the *Modernization of Benefits and Obligations Act* in 2000, a statute that extended spousal benefits and obligations in many federal statutes to same-sex couples. This statute also contained a declaration (s. 1.1) that the amendments did "not affect the meaning of the word 'marriage,' that is, the lawful union of one man and one woman to the exclusion of all others." (Prior to the introduction of this legislation, the federal government faced another litigation challenge: *Foundation for Equal Families v. Canada (Attorney General)*, [1999] OJ no. 3119 (Sup. Ct. J) (QL); [1999] OJ no. 2561 (Sup. Ct. J) (QL); and [2000] OJ no. 1995 (Div. Ct.) (QL).

Similarly, a number of provinces enacted legislation extending spousal benefits to same-sex couples. In Ontario, the government enacted its *Amendments Because of the Supreme Court of Canada Decision in M. v. H., 1999*, SO 1999, c. 6, extending benefits and obligations pursuant to 67 provincial statutes to same-sex couples. Earlier, the British Columbia legislature had amended a number of statutes to extend spousal benefits to same-sex couples: *Family Relations Amendment Act, 1997*, SBC 1997, c. 20; *Definition of Spouse Amendment Act, 1999*, SBC 1999, c. 29; and *Definition of Spouse Amendment Act, 2000*, SBC 2000, c. 24. Manitoba, New Brunswick, Newfoundland, and Saskatchewan also enacted legislation that extended some benefits to same-sex couples: see *An Act to Comply with the Supreme Court of Canada Decision in M. v. H.*, SM 2001, c. 37; *An Act to Amend the Family Services Act*, SNB 2000, c. 59; the *Family Law (Amendment) Act*, SN 2000, c. 29; and *An Act to Amend Certain Statutes Respecting Domestic Relations*, SS 2000, cc. 47 and 48, and SS 2001, cc. 50 and 51.

By contrast, Alberta enacted the *Domestic Relations Amendment Act, 1999*, SA 1999, c. 20, which defined "common law relationship" as an opposite-sex relationship and directly challenged the federal authority for defining capacity by enacting the *Marriage Amendment Act, 2000*, SA 2000, C.3, which confirmed that "'marriage' means a marriage between a man and a woman." To date, this legislation's constitutionality has not been reviewed. Other provinces have enacted legislation to permit opposite-sex and same-sex couples to register as "domestic partners" and thereby obtain most of the rights and obligations of married spouses. For example, Nova Scotia enacted domestic partnership legislation in 2000, and also amended other statutes to ensure that the definition of "common law partner" included both opposite-sex and same-sex couples who had cohabited for two years: see *Law Reform (2000) Act*, SNS 2000, c. 29. In 2002, Quebec enacted *An Act Instituting Civil Unions and Establishing New Rules of Filiation*, 2002 SQ, c. 6, a comprehensive set of amendments defining "civil union" relationships pursuant to the *Civil Code* and other statutes. Manitoba's legislation extended to common law partners all the benefits of spouses: see the *Common-Law Partners Property and Related Amendments Act*, SM 2002, c. 48.

Some commentators have suggested that the existence of "civil union" legislation shows respect for gays and also for marriage by legally recognizing same-sex partnerships while preserving marriage as a heterosexual institution involving the possibility of procreation: see Margaret Somerville, "Separate but Equal," *Ottawa Citizen*, September 3, 2003, at A13. By contrast, the United Church Moderator suggested that faithfulness to marriage may require change, asserting that the United Church's decision to welcome all those "willing to give themselves to transformation by love in the honourable estate [of marriage]" was the response of religious faithfulness: see Right Rev. Peter Short, "Let No One Be Turned Away," *Globe and Mail*, January 31, 2004, at A21.

For further reading, see also EGALE Canada Inc., "Division of Powers and Jurisdictional Issues Relating to Marriage" (Ottawa: Law Commission of Canada, 2000), at 64; Susan Blackwell, "Federal Same-Sex Benefits Legislation" (March 2000), *Money and Family Law* 21; Irène Demczuk, "Draft Bill on Civil Unions: Is the Quebec Government About To Create Separate Equality for Same-Sex Couples and Their Children?" (2002), 21:1 *Jurisfemme* 1; and Claudine Ouellet, "Brief Presented to the Standing Committee on Justice and Human Rights on Marriage and Recognition of Same-Sex Unions: A Question of Law and Nothing Else" (Quebec: Coalition Gaie et Lesbienne du Québec, 2003).

Same-Sex Marriage: Developments Outside Canada

Recent Charter litigation in Canada reflects similar challenges in a number of other western jurisdictions. Thus, just as *North v. Matheson* was unsuccessful in Manitoba in the 1970s, the decision of *Singer v. O'Hara*, 522 P2d 1187 (1974) in the Washington Court of Appeal confirmed that same-sex marriage was prohibited, relying on a narrow interpretation of the US constitution's guarantee of equal protection. Then, in 1993, the same year that the Ontario court decided *Re Layland and Beaulne*, the Hawaii Supreme Court ruled that a ban on same-sex marriage might well violate the state constitution's prohibition against sex discrimination, unless the state could show a "compelling" reason for it: *Baehr v. Lewin*, 852 P2d 44 (1993); affirmed as *Baehr v. Miike*, 910 P2d 112 (1996). The state was unsuccessful in demonstrating a compelling reason. In response, the Hawaii legislature enacted a bill to amend the state constitution, giving Hawaii the power to reserve marriage to opposite-sex couples, and this bill was ratified in the general election of 1998. Hawaii also adopted legislation in 1997, the *Act Relating to Unmarried Couples* (1997), now Rev. Stats Hawaii 2000, c. 572c, which defined the rights of "reciprocal beneficiaries."

In addition, in response to the judicial decisions in Hawaii, the Senate and House of Representatives of the United States enacted the *Defense of Marriage Act* (DOMA), Pub. L no. 104-199, 110 Stat. 2419 (1996), providing that states need not recognize same-sex marriages from other states. DOMA also amended chapter 1 of title 1 of the US Code, defining "marriage" and "spouse" in s. 7 as follows:

> In determining the meaning of any Act of Congress, or of any ruling, regulation, or interpretation of the various administrative bureaus and agencies of the United States, the word "marriage" means only a legal union between one man and one woman as husband and wife, and the word "spouse" refers only to a person of the opposite sex who is a husband or a wife.

Some commentators argued that this provision contravened the constitutional requirement to give "full faith and credit" to decisions of other states of the United States, although the issue has not been tested, because (until recently) no state had recognized same-sex marriage.

However, in response to a 1999 decision recognizing same-sex spouses, *Baker v. Vermont*, 744 A2d 864 (Vt. Sup. Ct. 1999), Vermont enacted civil union legislation (see now *Civil Unions*, Vt. Stat. Ann., tit. 15, ss. 1201-1207 (2003)), which extends (at s. 1204(a)) "all the same benefits, protections and responsibilities under law, whether they derive from statute, administrative or court rule, policy, common law or any other source of civil law, as are granted to spouses in a marriage." Moreover, according to Barbara Cox, 3500 cities and other organizations offered same-sex benefits and domestic partnership arrangements in 1999: see Barbara J. Cox, "'The Little Project': From Alternative Families to Domestic Partnerships to Same-Sex Marriage" (2000), 15 *Wisconsin Women's Law Journal* 77.

In June 2003, a New Jersey court dismissed a claim presented by seven gay and lesbian couples who were denied marriage licences, holding that the issue should be settled by the state legislature, not the courts: see Andrew Jacobs, "Judge in New Jersey Hears Arguments on Gay Marriage," *New York Times*, June 28, 2003. In January 2004, the New Jersey Senate passed legislation to recognize same-sex domestic partnerships: see Laura Mansnerus, "New Jersey to Recognize Gay Couples," *New York Times*, January 9, 2004. More dramatically, the Massachusetts Supreme Court declared in February 2004 that only marriage, not just civil unions for gay couples, would comply with the state's constitution; the court was responding to a question posed by the Senate as to whether legislation such as Vermont's civil union statute would meet constitutional requirements. As a result of the court's decision, same-sex marriages were performed in Massachusetts as of May 17, 2004, although there remains controversy about whether out-of-state gay and lesbian couples can marry in Massachusetts: see Pam Belluck and Katie Zezima, "Massachusetts Shifts a Bit on Gay Marriage," *New York Times*, May 5, 2004, at A24. In addition, the mayor of San Francisco, declaring that same-sex couples were entitled to be married on the ground that the constitution of California outlaws all forms of discrimination, asked the San Francisco County Clerk in February 2004 to begin issuing marriage licences on a non-discriminatory basis; the first same-sex marriage ceremony was performed for Phyllis Lyon, aged 79, and Del Martin, aged 83, women who had been together for a half-century: see David Stout, "San Francisco City Officials Perform Gay Marriages," *New York Times*, February 12, 2004. According to press reports, 3,700 same-sex couples were married in San Francisco before the California Supreme Court ordered the mayor to refrain from issuing licences to gay and lesbian couples: see "California's High Court Halts Gay Mariages," *National Post*, March 12, 2004.

Clearly, the issue of same-sex marriage remains controversial. For example, the Ohio legislature became the 38th state to prohibit recognition of same-sex unions when it enacted sweeping legislation in February 2004 to bar state agencies from giving benefits to both gay and heterosexual domestic partners. Legislators in several states, moreover, have begun to press for a federal constitutional amendment defining marriage as the union of one man and one woman. See Terence Neilan, "Gays Have Full Marriage Rights, Massachusetts Court Says," *New York Times*, February 4, 2004 and James Dao, "Ohio Legislature Votes To Ban Same-Sex Unions," *New York Times*, February 4, 2004. In this context, President Bush announced his intention in February 2004 to seek a constitutional amendment to confirm marriage as a union of a man and a woman.

Interestingly, the American government had earlier promoted marriage in relation to its welfare program, Temporary Assistance to Needy Families (TANF), in 2003 by allocating $300 million each year to promote marriage for TANF recipients; this funding was directed only to opposite-sex families: see Center on Fathers, Families, and Public Policy, 5:1 *National Policy Briefings* (January 2003), available online at http://www.cffpp.org/ briefings/; and Michael Tanner, "Wedded to Poverty," *New York Times*, July 29, 2003, at A27. For an overview of American developments, see David J. Garrow, "Toward a More Perfect Union," *New York Times Magazine*, May 9, 2004, at 52.

Developments beyond North America have been varied. For example, a New Zealand appellate court in Wellington in 1997 upheld a lower court decision that refused recognition for same-sex marriage: see *Quilter v. Attorney General*, [1998] 1 NZLR 523 (CA). In New South Wales, Australia, however, legislation was enacted in 1999 to recognize same-sex relationships in a wide variety of contexts (not including marriage) and, at the same time, created statutory rights for others in interdependent relationships, called "domestic relationships": see Reg Graycar and Jenni Millbank, "The Bride Wore Pink ... to the Property (Relationships) Legislation Amendment Act 1999: Relationships Law Reform in New South Wales" (2000), 17 *Canadian Journal of Family Law* 227. (The reference to "The Bride Wore Pink" is to a report prepared by the Gay and Lesbian Rights Group in 1994: see Jenni Millbank, "The Property (Relationships) Legislation Amendment Act 1999 (NSW) versus the De Facto Relationships Amendment Bill 1998 (NSW)" (2000), 9 *Australasian Gay and Lesbian Law Journal* 1.)

By 2004, same-sex marriage had been recognized in the Netherlands (2000) and Belgium (2003), and the newly elected prime minister of Spain announced in April 2004 that his government would legalize gay marriage: see *New York Times*, April 15, 2004. As well, a large number of European countries had introduced forms of domestic partnership legislation: Denmark (1989), Norway (1993), Sweden (1994), Iceland (1996), Catalonia (1998), and France (1999): see Caroline Forder, "European Models of Domestic Partnership Laws: The Field of Choice" (2000), 17 *Canadian Journal of Family Law* 371. In the United Kingdom, proposals to establish a "civil partnership scheme" to create rights and obligations for same-sex couples were introduced in mid-2003; they were not expected to become law for at least two years: see *The Guardian*, July 3, 2003; see also *Civil Partnership: A Framework for the Legal Recognition of Same-Sex Couples* (London: Women and Equality Unit, Department of Trade and Industry, 2003). Significantly, rights associated with same-sex marriage and/or domestic partnership have often been precisely defined in these legislative provisions. For example, the Danish Parliament did not permit stepchild adoption for registered partners until 1999; and the same-sex legislation in the Netherlands provided that a child born into such a unit would not automatically be the child of both spouses. For details, see Ingrid Lund-Andersen, "The Danish Registered Partnership Act, 1989: Has the Act Meant a Change in Attitudes?" (University of London: Conference on the Recognition of Same-Sex Partnerships, July 1999), at 6; and Kees Waaldijk, "Text of Dutch Law on the Opening Up of Marriage for Same-Sex Partners" (Universiteit Leiden, The Netherlands, 2001), online at http://athena.leidenuniv.nl/ rechten/meijers/index.php3?c=86.

Marriage as a Voluntary Union "for Life"

Although the *Hyde v. Hyde* definition of marriage has been cited frequently to deny same-sex marriage on the basis of its reference to "one man and one woman," it has seldom been invoked in relation to its requirement of a voluntary union "to the exclusion of all others for life." In the context of rising levels of divorce and remarriage, it is clear that marriage is not always enjoyed as "an exclusive union for life." In *Davis v. Davis* (2002), 35 RFL (5th) 48; [2002] OJ no. 4980 (Sup. Ct. J), the court considered the claim of an "uncontrolled philanderer" that his marriage became "an affair of simple carnal convenience" (para. 14) in 1985 so that his wife's claim for a half share in his pension had become statute-barred. Although the parties lived together on weekends in Midland, he had a separate long-term relationship with another woman during his working week in Toronto. The court accepted evidence of neighbours in Midland and family members to conclude that there was an ongoing marriage: see Christin Schmitz, "Marriage of 'Philanderer' Ruled Not a Mere 'Affair,' " *The Lawyers Weekly*, January 24, 2003, at 3.

In the United States, the death of Douglas Cone's wife and his marriage to his mistress of 27 years, Hillary Carlson, created similar controversy; it appears that Mr. Cone lived in a million-dollar home with his wife and their children on weekends, and with Ms Carlson and their two children during the week: see Christine Boyd, "Two Names, Two Wives, Two Families, But One Man," *Globe and Mail*, August 13, 2003, at S1. In the light of rates of divorce and remarriage in North America, where marriage is not always "for life," is it arguable that the *Hyde* definition is inappropriate for this reason as well? Does this mean that those who oppose the extension of marriage to same-sex couples should also oppose the availability of divorce? Why or why not?

SELECTED REFERENCES

CANADIAN ASSESSMENTS

Thomas G. Anderson, "Models of Registered Partnership and Their Rationale: The British Columbia Law Institute's Proposed Domestic Partner Act" (2000), 17 *Canadian Journal of Family Law* 89.

Nicholas Bala, "Alternatives for Extending Spousal Status in Canada" (2000), 17 *Canadian Journal of Family Law* 169.

John Boswell, *The Marriage of Likeness: Same-Sex Unions in Pre-Modern Europe* (London: Fontana Press, 1996).

Susan B. Boyd and Claire F.L. Young, " 'From Same-Sex to No-Sex'?: Trends Towards Recognition of (Same-Sex) Relationships in Canada" (2003), 1:3 *Seattle Journal for Social Justice* 757.

Kathryn Chapman, "Halpern v. Canada (AG), [2002] OJ no. 2714 (Ont. Div. Ct.)" (2002), 19 *Canadian Journal of Family Law* 423.

Brenda Cossman and Bruce Ryder, "The Legal Regulation of Adult Personal Relationships: Evaluating Policy Objectives and Legal Options in Federal Legislation" (Ottawa: Law Commission of Canada, 2000).

_____, "What Is Marriage-Like Like? The Irrelevance of Conjugality" (2001), 18 *Canadian Journal of Family Law* 271.

Christine Davies, "The Extension of Marital Rights and Obligations to the Unmarried: Registered Domestic Partnerships and Other Methods" (1999-2000), 17 *Canadian Family Law Quarterly* 247.

EGALE Canada, "Division of Powers and Jurisdictional Issues Relating to Marriage" (Ottawa: Law Commission of Canada, 2000).

Roderick A. Macdonald, "Perspectives on Personal Relationships" (Kingston, ON: Conference on Domestic Partnerships, 1999).

Mark D. Walters, "Incorporating Common Law into the Constitution of Canada: Egale v. Canada and the Status of Marriage" (2003), 41 *Osgoode Hall Law Journal* 75.

AMERICAN ASSESSMENTS

Jennifer Gerarda Brown, "Competitive Federalism and the Legislative Incentives to Recognize Same-Sex Marriage" (1995), 68 *Southern California Law Review* 745.

David Orgon Coolidge and William C. Duncan, "Definition or Discrimination? State Marriage Recognition Statutes in the 'Same-Sex Marriage' Debate" (1998), 32 *Creighton Law Review* 3.

Jill R. Green, "Comment: Will the Marriage of Dick and Jane Evolve into the Marriage of Jane and Jane? Same-Sex Marriage: A Viable Union in the 21st Century" (1999), 45 *Loyola Law Review* 313.

Michael T. Morley, Richard Albert, Jennie L. Kneedler, and Chrystiane Pereira, "Developments in Law and Policy: Emerging Issues in Family Law" (2003), 21 *Yale Law and Policy Review* 169.

EUROPEAN ASSESSMENTS

David Bradley, "Regulation of Unmarried Cohabitation in West-European Jurisdictions—Determinants of Legal Policy" (2001), 15 *International Journal of Law, Policy, and the Family* 22.

Claude Martin and Irène Théry, "The PACS and Marriage and Cohabitation in France" (2001), 15 *International Journal of Law, Policy, and the Family* 135.

B. Marriage and Transsexuals: Defining a "Man" and a "Woman"

I do not agree ... that a decision in favour of the applicants is ground-breaking. ... It is true that this judgment canvasses some interesting new medical evidence, and that the discussion of legal principle has been wide-ranging. While I have made findings about the medical evidence and offered a view about the underlying basis for such decisions as *Corbett*, the end result does not depend on acceptance of either of these matters. Ultimately, the basis for this judgment is very simple and mundane. It is that no good reasons have been shown why the ordinary legal meaning of the word "man," which includes post-operative female to male transsexuals, should not also apply to marriage. Because the words "man" and "woman" have their ordinary contemporary meaning, there is no formulaic solution to determining the sex of an individual for the purpose of the law of marriage.

> Chisholm J, in *Re Kevin: Validity of Marriage of Transsexual*
> (2001), 28 Fam. LR 158 (Fam. Ct. Aust.); upheld on appeal
> (2003), 30 Fam. LR 1 (Fam. Ct. Aust.)

1. Re Kevin and Legal Approaches to Defining Sex

The requirement for a valid marriage stated in *Hyde v. Hyde*, a union of a man and a woman, has also been addressed in cases involving transsexuals, persons born as one sex who have sought to change their sex at a later point in their lives, usually by means of hormonal treatment and surgical intervention. In the Australian context, where it is possible for post-operative transsexuals to obtain new identity papers (for example, drivers' licences and passports) confirming their post-operative sex, the court in *Re Kevin* concluded that there was no impediment to recognizing the applicant's post-operative sex for purposes of declaring the validity of his marriage as well. Thus, Kevin, who had been born female and had undergone sex reassignment surgery as an adult, was held to be validly married to a woman. In fact, Kevin and his wife had already been accepted as a heterosexual couple at an infertility clinic and, at the time of the court's decision, they were the parents of one child conceived using anonymous donor sperm; and Kevin's wife was pregnant with a second child. Because Australia does not currently recognize same-sex marriage, however, the validity of Kevin's marriage depended on legal recognition of his post-operative sex rather than his sex at birth.

Cases such as *Re Kevin* require a legal determination as to whether a person is a "man" or a "woman," a determination that is often important for a number of reasons, including the validity of marriage. In *Re Kevin*, the attorney general for the Commonwealth appealed Chisholm J's decision, but the appellate court dismissed the appeal. After quoting the report of the Law Commission of Canada, *Beyond Conjugality: Recognising and Supporting Close Personal Adult Relationships* (Ottawa: Law Commission of Canada, 2001), discussed later in this chapter, the appellate court stated (at 18 and 24):

> [We] think it plain that the social and legal institution of marriage as it pertains to Australia
> has undergone transformations that are referable to the environment and period in which the
> particular changes occurred. The concept of marriage therefore cannot, in our view, be
> correctly said to be one that is or ever was frozen in time. The relevance of this conclusion
> for the purposes of these reasons for judgment is that on the sources we have had to identify

for ourselves, there is no historical justification to support Mr. Burmester's contention that the meaning of marriage should be understood by reference to a particular point in time in the past, such as 1961. To the contrary, it lends support to the arguments of the respondents and the Human Rights and Equal Opportunity Commission as to statutory interpretation and the decision of the trial judge that the meaning of the term should be given its ordinary contemporary meaning in the context of the *Marriage Act*. ...

The real point of the Attorney-General's submission was to support an argument that procreation is one of the essential purposes of marriage. It was argued that it follows from this that the biological characteristics of a person are central to determining a person's status as a man or a woman. It was put that the historical importance of the sexual relationship in marriage remains and that it is because of this significance that the law continues to look to the physical attributes, and not the psychological or social attributes, of a person. It is therefore said that because of Kevin's biological inability to procreate, the marriage to Jennifer could not be a valid marriage.

Apart from the stated purpose of procreation relied upon by the Attorney-General, we accept, as did the trial judge, that marriage has a particular status. Like the trial judge, we reject the argument that one of the principal purposes of the marriage is procreation. Many people procreate outside marriage and many people who are married neither procreate, nor contemplate doing so. A significant number of married persons cannot procreate either at the time of the marriage or subsequently—an obvious example being a post-menopausal woman. Similarly, it is inappropriate and incorrect to suggest that consummation is in any way a requirement to the creation of a valid marriage. Subsequent to the passage of the *Marriage Act*, inability to consummate a marriage ceased to be a ground for making a declaration of nullity: see s. 51 of the *Family Law Act* and ss. 23, 23A and 23B of the *Marriage Act*.

2. Rethinking Corbett v. Corbett: The Human Rights Approach

As the quotation from the judgment of Chisholm J, above, noted, it was necessary for the Australian court to consider an earlier English decision, *Corbett v. Corbett*, [1970] 2 WLR 1306 (PDA), and to determine whether it should be followed in Australia. In *Corbett*, the issue was the validity of a marriage where the wife (April Corbett) had been born male and had subsequently undergone hormonal therapy and surgery to become female. After a relationship for some years with Arthur Corbett, she married him. Not long after the marriage, her husband sought to annul the marriage on the ground of "non-consummation." In a detailed judgment, the court determined that the marriage was void because April Corbett was legally a man. According to the court (at 1323):

[T]he biological sexual constitution of an individual is fixed at birth (at the latest), and cannot be changed, either by the natural development of organs of the opposite sex, or by medical and surgical means.

In reaching this conclusion, the court held that an individual has a "true sex" and that it cannot be altered by surgery. The *Corbett* case focused on biological criteria—chromosomes, gonads, and genitals—and concluded that if they were congruent, sex for purposes of marriage should be determined accordingly, ignoring any psychological discordance. In addition, however, the court in *Corbett* stated (at 1324-25) that since marriage has an "essentially heterosexual character," the test for an individual's sex must be biological,

because even extreme transsexualism or hormonal imbalance in a male could not reproduce "a person who is naturally capable of performing the essential role of a woman in
marriage." That is, although April Corbett had undergone surgery to remove testicles and
to fashion a vagina for purposes of sexual intercourse, she did not have the capacity to
conceive or bear a child. Although it is possible that the judge was partly influenced by
the facts in *Corbett* (the marriage was brief, unstable, and the husband was a transvestite),
the biological test established in *Corbett* created an important legal precedent.

Until recently, the decision in *Corbett* has been followed in a number of common law
jurisdictions. For example, a South African court refused to grant a divorce decree
(which requires a valid marriage) in a case involving a transsexual: see *W. v. W.*, [1976] 2
S Afr. LR 308 (WL Div.). A number of decisions in the United States have also agreed
that sex is determined at birth and cannot be altered legally thereafter: see *Anonymous v.
Weiner*, 270 NYS 2d 319 (Sup. Ct. 1966); *Anonymous v. Anonymous*, 325 NYS 2d 499
(NY Sup. Ct. 1971); *In re Gardiner*, 42 P3d 120 (Kansas Sup. Ct. 2002); and *Littleton v.
Prange*, 9 SW 3d 223 (Texas App. Ct. 1999). In *Littleton*, Christie Littleton was born a
male, but undertook sex reassignment surgery as well as psychological and psychiatric
treatment for four years to become a woman. She married a man, and after he died in
medical care, she sued for medical malpractice as his surviving spouse. In concluding
that Littleton was a man (and that her marriage was therefore a same-sex marriage and
invalid), the court stated (at paras. 59 and 61):

> We recognize that there are many fine metaphysical arguments lurking about here involving
> desire and being, the essence of life and the power of mind over physics. But courts are wise
> not to wander too far into the misty fields of sociological philosophy. Matters of the heart
> do not always fit neatly within the narrowly defined perimeters of statutes, or even existing
> social mores. ... There are some things we cannot will into being. They just are.

In *Littleton*, the court noted another US decision, which recognized a post-operative
transsexual's sex for legal purposes: *M.T. v. J.T.*, 140 NJ Super 77; 355 A2d 204 (1976).
In that case, the court held that the wife's marriage was valid, even though she had been
born a male, recognizing that sex reassignment surgery permitted her to function sexually
as a woman. As a result of the validity of the marriage, the husband was liable to provide
financial support to his wife when he left the marriage. However, as this decision was not
binding in Texas, the court in *Littleton* chose not to follow it. In a Florida case, the
appellate court overturned a lower court decision, denying legal recognition of a sex
change (female to male) by Michael Kantaras: see Jim Loney, "Transsexual Cannot
Marry Woman: Court," *National Post*, July 24, 2004.

Until recently, courts in the United Kingdom and in Europe have also followed
Corbett, holding that sex must be determined for legal purposes at birth. For examples,
see *Rees v. United Kingdom* (1986), 9 EHRR 56; *Van Oosterwijck v. Belgium* (1980), 3
EHRR 557; and *Cossey v. United Kingdom* (1991), 13 EHRR 622. In *Bellinger v.
Bellinger*, [2001] EWCA Civ 1140; [2002] 1 All ER 311; aff'd. [2003] UKHL 21; 2 All
ER 593, however, the Court of Appeal held that legal recognition of marriage was a
matter of status, involving questions of public policy, so that it was appropriate for
Parliament to legislate on the issue of recognition of the sex of a post-operative trans-
sexual (and the House of Lords agreed). Because the wife in *Bellinger* had been born a
man, the Court of Appeal concluded that her sex had been determined at birth, following

Corbett, and that her marriage was thus invalid. In addition, however, the majority of the court expressed dismay that the government had taken no action in relation to a report submitted in 2000 by a Working Group established to review the legal problems for transsexuals, stating (at para. 96) that this inaction represented "a failure to recognise the increasing concerns and changing attitudes across Western Europe ... which ... need to be addressed by the United Kingdom." Moreover, in a dissenting opinion, Justice Thorpe concluded (at para. 160) that it was no longer appropriate in 2001 to apply the reasoning in *Corbett*, because of both medical and social developments:

> The range of rights claimed by transsexuals falls across the divisions of our justice systems. The present claim lies most evidently in the territory of the family justice system. That system must always be sufficiently flexible to accommodate social change. It must also be humane and swift to recognise the right to human dignity and to freedom of choice in the individual's private life.

The European Court of Human Rights released two decisions in July 2002, both involving post-operative male to female transsexuals. In both cases, the court confirmed violations by the United Kingdom of the applicants' right to privacy and the right to marry pursuant to articles 8 and 12 of the European Convention on Human Rights: see *Goodwin v. United Kingdom*, [2002] ECHR 28957/95; and *I. v. United Kingdom*, [2002] ECHR 25680/94. In *Goodwin*, the court stated (at para. 103):

> While it is for the Contracting State to determine inter alia the conditions under which a person claiming legal recognition as a transsexual establishes that gender re-assignment has been properly effected or under which past marriages cease to be valid and the formalities applicable to future marriages (including, for example, the information to be furnished to intended spouses), the Court finds no justification for barring the transsexual from enjoying the right to marry under any circumstances.

These decisions are consistent with the Australian court's decision in *Re Kevin*, above. Moreover, following these decisions in the European Court of Human Rights, the UK government announced in mid-2003 that Parliamentary legislation will be introduced to permit post-operative transsexuals to marry: see Kamal Ahmed, "Transsexuals Win Right To Marry," *The Observer*, July 6, 2003.

3. Canadian Approaches to Defining Sex

In Canada, there have been few reported legal challenges on the part of transsexuals. In *C.(L.A.) v. C.(C.C.)*, [1986] BCJ no. 2817 (SC) (QL), the court considered an application for nullity on the grounds that the husband was a pre-operative transsexual, but the judge did not decide the matter, citing problems of evidence. However, in *C.(L.) v. C.(C.)* (1992), 10 OR (3d) 254 (Gen. Div.), when a woman applied for a declaration that her marriage was a nullity, the court granted the application. The applicant had married the respondent, who was also a woman, after the latter underwent hormonal treatment, a hysterectomy and surgery to remove her breasts. The respondent told the applicant that she also planned to have surgery to construct male genitals, but she never did so. The court held that the parties were both female at the time of the marriage, so that it was a nullity. See also *Canada v. Owen*, [1993] FCJ no. 1263; 70 FTR 308 (TD), where a "spouse" was held to be ineligible for benefits under the *Old Age Security Act* because although he had "held himself out to be" female, he was still a male person.

In another case, an Ontario court concluded that the applicant was not entitled to spousal support under the *Family Law Act* because, on the basis of her sex at birth, she was still a female, and her cohabitee was also female. (At the time, the *Family Law Act* had not yet been amended to permit same-sex partners to claim support at separation: see now SO 1999, c. 6.) Although the case involved a claim for "spousal" support rather than recognition of the validity of marriage, it is useful to examine its reasoning against the backdrop of cases such as *Re Kevin* and recent human rights decisions concerning transsexuals. Would this case be decided differently now? Why, or why not?

B. v. A.
(1990), 29 RFL (3d) 258; 1 OR (3d) 569 (Sup. Ct.)

MASTER CORK: The parties each bring motions before me, but these reasons are principally addressed to the motion by the applicant B. for support from the respondent A., under somewhat unique circumstances.

The issue before me, briefly, is whether the applicant B. is a "man" within the definition of "spouse" in s. 29 of the *Family Law Act, 1986*, so as to qualify B. as claimant of support from A.

Originally, both A. and B. were born female, A. then developing normally, eventually marrying and bearing children who are living today. There is no issue before me raised by any party that A. is not a woman, and I am proceeding on this understanding.

I am told that B., sometime after birth, while anatomically a female, developed discomfort and a recurrent desire to possess the body of the opposite sex, which has been defined as the syndrome "gender dysphoria." She states that she never has been able to identify with, or behave as, a woman, and she had behaved as a man throughout most of her life. However, she has married and bore a child from her husband, which child also is living today. Shortly after the birth of this child, B. and her husband separated, and her husband thereafter plays no part in the proceedings now before me.

B. and A. first met in October 1969, when A. states that B. was introduced to her as a woman separated and with a child. At that time it appears B. dressed as a woman, but shortly after the meeting, A. reports she learned that B. regarded herself as a man trapped inside a woman's body, and that she wanted to become a man.

At about the end of 1969, B. and her child moved into the basement apartment of the matrimonial home of A., A.'s husband and their four children. Thereafter, B. began appearing, at least within the home, in the clothes of a man, and I am told that B. then began "sex reassignment and gender reorientation therapy" at the Clarke Institute of Psychiatry in 1972. After counselling and tests, it appears that the Clarke Institute diagnosed B. as a transsexual, and after this process of assessment was under way, B. began taking testosterone hormone therapy in the latter part of 1972. I understand that the hormone injections, started in 1972, still continue, and presently B. administers one injection to herself each month. It would appear that this consistent injection of hormone is necessary to maintain B.'s present apparent physical appearances as a male, and should those injections cease, then B. will revert back to a female appearance.

After B. underwent testosterone therapy for some time, there was a redistribution of her body fat and an increased growth of facial and body hair. The ovarian function was suppressed, menstruation ceased and mammary tissues shrunk.

After taking testosterone therapy for over a year, B. then had the actual physical outward appearance of a male, and then she underwent a course of female to male transsexual surgery. On 22nd December 1973 B. had a bilateral mastectomy, with a subsequent reconstruction of a male chest contour, and nipple transplantation. On 4th November 1974 B. had a pan-hysterectomy with the removal of the fallopian tubes and ovaries.

It would appear that some time in the spring of 1971 A. and her husband separated, the husband leaving the matrimonial home, and some time thereafter a relationship was started between A. and B. This relationship then continued throughout all assessment, hormone therapy and surgery, and continued for some 20 odd years, until B. and A. separated in January 1990. After the early tentative changes by B. to a masculine role, and certainly after the hormone therapy was started, B. began appearing as a male, and has continued then to appear to be a male within the "family" with A. and their various children, and now grandchildren, to the date of separation. I gather that the original children were aware of the change of B. from her original form, although there is now some question as to whether the grandchildren are aware of this unusual history, their knowledge of B. being only after B. changed appearance to a male.

During the 20 odd years that B. and A. resided together as apparent man and wife, they collected assets which in time have grown quite valuable. At separation, the connection B. had with those assets was then cut by A., who apparently holds title or control of them, and hence now B. moves under the *Family Law Act* for interim support.

The *Family Law Act* states:

[s. 29]: "spouse" means a spouse as defined in subsection 1(1), and in addition includes either of a man and woman who are not married to each other and have cohabited,

(a) continuously for a period of not less than three years.

Section 1(1) of the *Family Law Act* states:

"Cohabit" means to live together in a conjugal relationship, whether within or outside marriage.

It would therefore appear that for B. to be entitled to support, B. must come under the definition of "man," and then have lived with A. in a conjugal relationship continuously for a period of not less than three years.

The issue therefore is whether B. is a "man" and if so, then did he and A. live together in a conjugal relationship outside marriage for the 21 years they lived together?

Turning to the primary issue, that of whether B. can now be defined as "man," I am given no direct, totally pertinent authority as to what precisely is the definition of a "man" under these circumstances.

I am obliged to both counsel for a most thorough supply of authorities as to prior decisions dealing with various problems relating generally to the issues at hand. Suffice to say, however, I do not believe that I have been referred to any case of particular specific similarity to the case at hand. I have had reference to decisions dealing with transsexual changes between parties to a marriage, which render the marriage void or voidable; homosexual marriages, or residing in circumstances resembling matrimony, and whether they attract rights of support one from the other under the then pertinent statutes; a transsexual who changed from male to female by way of sex reassignment surgery to harmonize her gender and genitalia, so that she became physically and psychologically unified and capable of sexual activity as a woman, and then subsequently married, the marriage then being not void and the husband having a legal obligation to support her as his wife; but I have had no reference to any decision dealing with the actual change of a female to a male.

Argument was also adduced from the applicant's side that the parties did live together in a conjugal relationship, outside of marriage, having cohabited within the definition of "spouse" under s. 29 of the *Family Law Act*. I think that indeed the parties had an appearance of living in a conjugal relationship, with their various children as being the presumed offspring of such relationship, but which was biologically impossible to achieve. The fact, however, that they appeared to the outside observer to be man and wife, I believe, does not necessarily mean what s. 29 refers to "either of a man and woman."

I have also been referred by the parties to the *Vital Statistics Act*, RSO 1980, c. 524, s. 32 … :

Changes Resulting From Transsexual Surgery

32(1) Where the anatomical sex structure of a person is changed to a sex other than that which appears on the registration of birth, the person may apply to the Registrar General to have the designation of sex on the registration of birth changed so that the designation will be consistent with the results of the transsexual surgery.

(2) An application made under subsection (1) shall be accompanied by:

(a) a certificate signed by a medical practitioner legally qualified to practise medicine in the jurisdiction in which the transsexual surgery was performed upon the applicant, certifying that,

(i) he performed transsexual surgery on the applicant, and

(ii) as a result of the transsexual surgery, the designation of sex of the applicant should be changed on the registration of birth of the applicant;

(b) a certificate of a medical practitioner who did not perform the transsexual surgery but who is qualified and licensed to practise medicine in Ontario certifying that,

(i) he has examined the applicant,

(ii) the results of the examination substantiate that transsexual surgery was performed upon the applicant, and

(iii) as a result of the transsexual surgery, the description of the sex of the applicant should be changed on the registration of birth of the applicant; and

(c) evidence satisfactory to the Registrar General as to the identity of the applicant.

The applicant has then shown me copies of the 1990 application made to the Office of the Registrar General for Ontario, with attendant certificates attached, so to amend the registration of birth of B. from female to male. The first medical certificate states that the doctor performed transsexual surgery on B. in December 1973 and that the result of that surgery now requires the designation of the sex of B. to be changed from female to male. The second certificate is from another physician that she examined the results of the transsexual surgery on 1st February 1990 and concludes again that the sex of B. should be changed on registration from female to male.

Section 32(1) of the *Vital Statistics Act* clearly assumes that the change of the anatomical sex structure of a person must be that done by way of transsexual surgery. It is to be noted here that the hormone treatment of B. must continue, and if such fails or is discontinued, then it is a given understanding that B. would then revert to his original female form, or appearance, at least to some degree. Such transitory changes are not contemplated by this section.

As mentioned earlier, the only surgery that has been done on B. is the hysterectomy, in which the internal reproductive organs were removed from B.'s body, and a double mastectomy, the removal of the breasts, with then attendant plastic surgery to the general form of chest and nipples. The genitalia of B., to my understanding, have in no way been touched surgically, and still exist presumably in the same apparent form as when B. was born, was married and produced her child.

I would think it probably common ground to assume that in this day of universal awareness of breast cancer, especially in women, a double mastectomy is not within itself an unusual event. Similarly, possibly for the same reasons, or other serious medical considerations, many females today undergo a hysterectomy. Indeed, I would anticipate we have many females who have had both surgical treatments, yet who continue completely as female.

It is my considered opinion that the purpose of s. 32 of the *Vital Statistics Act* has within it the intent that there be some radical and irreversible surgical intervention with all the fundamental reproductive organs, more than their simple removal, before the legislature anticipated the necessity of changing the initial birth documentation from female to male.

In my view, the intent of this section of the Act does not have within it any concept of psychological tendency or history of conjugal relationships, but deals strictly and only with the "anatomical sex structure of a person," which is to my view solely physical in definition.

If one considers the emotional aspects or the desire of a person to change sex, stemming from psychological pressures, howsoever gained or inherited, or historically apparent conjugal relationships with another person so as to fulfil those psychological pressures, then all these aspects surely must be beyond the definition of this particular section under the *Vital Statistics Act*.

Accordingly, I must differ with the medical reports mentioned, that transsexual surgery was performed sufficient to require the Office of the Registrar General of Ontario now to effectively have the initial birth records of B., now changed from female to male. What would happen if now B. ceased the intake of hormones? There would be then no effective surgical intervention at all, leaving B. in the position of legal male, whereas his body would be changed back to female, at least as to outward appearances, the genitalia continuing to be female in any event.

It is also interesting to note that I believe there to be some form of official or unofficial prohibition against homosexual marriages, or marriages between parties of the same gender. In the present case such could be achieved, if after hysterectomy or mastectomy, or perhaps only one of such, the one female partner to the proposed marriage changes the sexual designation under the *Vital Statistics Act*, and then applies with the other female partner, as male and female, for a marriage licence, which would then be required to be issued. Surely, this is well beyond the legislative intent of this amendment in the *Vital Statistics Act*.

While then I do agree that there can be a change in sex so as to create the legal basis of "cohabit" under s. 29 of the *Family Law Act*, I believe that such must be at least irrevocable, and independent of exterior continuing circumstances after the surgery is completed. Neither of these circumstances are available to B. in this present case.

It is also my opinion that the certificates of the doctors filed under the *Vital Statistics Act* are patently erroneous in their conclusion.

It is therefore my conclusion that the present applicant B. is not under the definition of "man" under s. 29 of Pt. 3 of the *Family Law Act* and therefore does not have the right to apply for interim support from the respondent.

Of course, this is in no way ... intended to impede any trust arguments that may be raised by B. against A. for the division of the assets that they amassed together during their time under the same roof, but certainly I am persuaded that B. cannot now qualify as a quasi "spouse" for the present purposes of a support claim.

Motion dismissed.

Diana Majury, "Annotation of B. v. A."
(1990), 29 RFL (3d) 258

While we may think that the categories of sex and gender are fairly fixed and certain, situations such as that of B. should lead us to question our assumptions about the meaning and significance of gender in our society and to question our ability to define female and male, woman and man. In the absence of any "direct totally pertinent authority" on the matter at issue in this motion, Master Cork had the opportunity to apply a somewhat open-ended definition of "man" and "woman" that would take into consideration a person's self-identification and lived experience. Instead, he chose to apply a narrow and outdated biological definition of sex that many doctors and scientists would describe as inadequate. His choice to apply irrevocability as an essential criterion in the determination of one's sex is not justified either in terms of logic or legislative purpose. To reduce the issue of spousal support to this level of inquiry— is this person "really" a woman or a man—misses the point at a number of levels. Such a limited and limiting approach seems contrary to the intention of the expanded definition of spouse for the purposes of support under the *Family Law Act*. ...

[Majury also critiqued this decision on the basis that the application of the test may mean that there is an infringement of sex equality guarantees. As she suggests, there are also some interesting examples of sexual stereotyping in the language used by Master Cork. In reading this critique, assess the extent to which you agree with her conclusion that the decision was motivated by a concern that a positive outcome of the plaintiff in *B. v. A.* might have permitted lesbian or gay couples to "take advantage" of the ruling in future cases.]

Nowhere does Master Cork address the question whether or not it is more difficult, or even impossible, for a woman to change her sex in the full, irrevocable biological terms that Master Cork requires than it is for a man to change his sex. It is also possible that, if a penis could be constructed much the same way that a vagina could be constructed, phallocentrism would mean that, while the constructed vagina would be accepted as proof of femaleness, the constructed penis would not be accepted as proof of maleness because it would not be seen as the real thing. If either of these scenarios is accurate, Master Cork would be applying a standard that, although apparently gender neutral on its face, would have a differentially negative impact on women and would therefore itself constitute a discriminatory standard.

This question takes on added significance in the context of this decision because of other indicators of discriminatory attitudes at work. The sexist underpinnings of this decision surface in the ways in which Master Cork refers to B. and his relationship with A. At one point he describes B. as changing to a "masculine role." This concept of a masculine role within a spousal relationship is a stereotype that has long had a very negative effect for women and is a concept that has been critiqued and rejected even to a large extent in the legislation which Master Cork is attempting to apply.

A little further on in his decision, Master Cork refers to the couple as appearing "to the outside observer to be man and wife." The appearance of marriage is not the pertinent factor for the purposes of spousal support; the issue would more appropriately be described as the appearance of heterosexual cohabitation. But, much more significantly, the reference to man and wife rather than to husband and wife is a very outdated and sexist way to refer to the partners to a marriage. It denotes the male partner as the person of importance in the relationship and the female partner as the appendage, described in terms of her relationship to the male partner. The use of this kind of language in a legal decision in Ontario in 1990 is surprising. It raises the question whether for Master Cork it would ever be possible for a woman to be seen as male, in this sense of being the person of primary importance, no matter what she does to her body in order to do so.

Along similar lines, it is worthy of note that Master Cork invokes what he believes to be "some form of official or unofficial prohibition against homosexual marriages, or marriages between parties of the same gender" to support his interpretation of the *Vital Statistics Act*, RSO 1980, c. 524, and the *Family Law Act*, SO 1986, c. 4. Master Cork's concern about opening the back door to gay and lesbian marriage would seem to stem more from homophobia and heterosexism than from anything to do with the actuality of the relationship under scrutiny. The way in which this couple presented themselves to the world and the extremely serious measures which B. undertook to make himself male would indicate that neither of the people involved in this relationship would in any way have considered themselves as being in a lesbian relationship. Master Cork's fear is that if he decides in B.'s favour, lesbians might then be able to undergo surgery ("hysterectomy or mastectomy, or perhaps only one of such" [at 267], change their sexual designation under the *Vital Statistics Act* and then apply, with their female partner, for a marriage licence. It is not a usual use of a floodgates argument to take it to its most extreme and then use this to preserve the status quo. This feared spectre of a possible back door route to lesbian and gay marriage reflects a remarkably stereotypic understanding of who and what lesbians are. Lesbians are not women who want to be men; they are women who love women as women.

Discussion Notes

Evidence of Sex

On what basis did the court conclude that it was not appropriate to alter the designation of sex for B., pursuant to the *Vital Statistics Act*? Is this a problem of evidence, or a problem of interpreting the evidence in relation to s. 19 or to sections of the *Family Law Act*? To what extent was it appropriate for the court to take into account the fact that the surgical intervention was not "irreversible"? Why was the judge concerned about "some form of official or unofficial prohibition against homosexual marriages"? (Note that same-sex partners now have responsibility for the provision of spousal support under Ontario's *Family Law Act*, a matter addressed more fully in chapter 7.)

According to a scientific report about sexuality, there are actually five sexes, not just the two that are recognized for legal purposes. In the light of *B. v. A.*, how should courts or legislatures respond to this context in terms of law reform measures? See Anne Fausto-Sterling, "The Five Sexes: Why Male and Female Are Not Enough," *The Sciences*, March/April 1993, at 20.

Legal Ethics and the Sex of Clients

If you were the lawyer consulted by B. (the potential plaintiff) in *B. v. A.*, and B. explained to you that he had lived for over 20 years as a man, but that he had been a woman prior to that time, how would you approach these facts in the context of the claim for spousal support? Are these facts relevant to such an application? Why or why not? Do you have an ethical duty to inform the court of these facts? Do you have any ethical duty to B. to inform him of the possible outcome of the case and the extent to which the court may not only deny spousal support, but may also deny B.'s longtime sexual identity? What kinds of ethical obligations do lawyers have in such cases? Do you have to help B. assess whether it is "worth" it to pursue this claim by taking account of these other factors?

Is *B. v. A.* consistent with the case discussed in relation to marriage validity above, *M. v. M.* (1984), 42 RFL (2d) 55 (PEI Sup. Ct.)? In that case, the court granted a husband's application for nullity on the basis of evidence that his wife had a "latent incapacity" for heterosexual intercourse, which became apparent only after several years of cohabitation and consummation of the marriage. According to the court, the wife was a "latent transsexual" and there was clear evidence of her intention to live as a man—she had changed her given name to one that was more masculine, registered in a land surveying school as a male, and commenced treatment (but had not undergone any surgery) at the Clarke Institute to assist her transition to a male lifestyle. Would this evidence have sufficed in *B. v. A.*? Is it relevant that the wife in *M. v. M.* did not appear and was not represented in the action?

Attorney General v. Otahuhu Family Court: Sex and Gender

In a New Zealand case, *Attorney General v. Otahuhu Family Court*, [1995] 1 NZLR 603 (HC), in which the court declined to follow *Corbett*, the court identified (at 614) the procedure for a female-to-male transition, and relied on evidence about the difficulties involved in surgical intervention, particularly for female-to-male transsexuals:

> There is a group of people who identify themselves as transsexuals, and who socially and psychologically operate in the sex of their choice (differing from the sex into which they were born) but who have not yet had surgical intervention. In these cases the question must be asked why it is necessary that a transsexual should have to go through a risky surgical procedure before he or she can be eligible to marry as a person of his or her chosen sex. Such procedures will no doubt also be expensive.
>
> This is particularly difficult in the case of female to male transsexuals. Hormone administration will produce secondary sexual characteristics, such as facial hair and a deeper voice. The breasts may be removed and a radical hysterectomy performed, but the construction of any kind of artificial penis involves difficult plastic surgery and requires the use of tissues from other parts of the body which means the surgery is more complicated and intrusive. Some female to male transsexuals will therefore choose not to undertake a phalloplasty.

How should these concerns be addressed in legal principles? In 2000, for example, the *Law Times* reported that the Ontario Human Rights Commission had adopted a policy to protect transgendered people from discrimination on the grounds of sex: see David Gambrill, "HR Policy Includes 'Transgendered,'" *Law Times*, July 24, 2000, at 2. As the report explained:

> The transgendered community is diverse, [including] cross-dressers; intersexed people (people with both male and female sex characteristics); transgenderists (people whose gender identity does not match their sexual characteristics, but who do not intend to have sex reassignment surgery); and female-to-male or male-to-female "pre-ops" or "post-ops" (designating a person's state before or after sex reassignment surgery).

To what extent should legal principles take account of the relative difficulty of achieving female-to-male transition, as suggested by the New Zealand court?

SELECTED REFERENCES

Anthony Bradney, "Transsexuals and the Law" (1987), 17 *Family Law* 350.

Julie A. Greenberg, "Defining Male & Female: Intersexuality and the Collision Between Law and Biology" (1999), 41 *Arizona Law Review* 205.

Laura Hermer, "Paradigms Revised: Intersex Children, Bioethics and the Law" (2002), 11 *Annals of Health Law* 195.

Lori Johnson, "The Legal Status of Post-Operative Transsexuals" (1994), 2 *Health Law Journal* 159.

Sir Roger Ormrod, "The Medico-Legal Aspects of Sex Determination" (1972), 40 *Medico-Legal Journal* 78.

Douglas K. Smith, "Transsexualism, Sex Reassignment Surgery, and the Law" (1971), 56 *Cornell Law Review* 963.

C. Reforming (Legal) Relationships

With the slow, steady and (hopefully) relentless recognition of both the rights and obligations of same-sex relationships, we are all called upon to raise our eyes from the realm of conventional heterosexual families to look over a vista of other relationships which have always been present but have seldom been named. ... Can we raise our eyes a little higher and see a whole range of relationships which the state should be fostering?

> Brian Bucknall, "A New Model for State-Approved Familial Partnerships," *Lawyers Weekly*, August 22, 1997

These comments were made shortly after the lower court's decision in *M. v. H.*, the decision that recognized that same-sex partners might have legal obligations of support at the end of their relationships: see (1996), 27 OR (3d) 593 (Gen Div.). Yet, *M. v. H.* also suggested a need to examine the nature of relationships beyond marriage, cohabitation, and same-sex partners. How should law structure benefits and obligations in relation to individuals and their families?

Law Commission of Canada, *Beyond Conjugality: Recognizing and Supporting Close Personal Adult Relationships*
(Ottawa: Law Commission of Canada, 2001), at xi-xix

[In its 2001 report, the Law Commission of Canada proposed (at ix) a "comprehensive and principled approach to the legal recognition and support of the full range of close personal relationships among adults." It defined three categories of these relationships:

- Conjugal relationships (including marriage and cohabitation, both opposite-sex and same-sex);
- Non-conjugal households and non-conjugal relationships ("economic families," such as adult siblings or non-relatives who live together); and
- Persons with disabilities and their caregivers (paid and non-paid).

In this context, the report suggested (at xi) that "recognizing and supporting personal adult relationships that involve caring and independence is an important state objective."

In the past, governments have provided this recognition and support for married couples, and have gradually extended them to cohabiting couples. According to the report, however, it is now time to move away from conjugality as the marker for recognition and support for close personal relationships among adults. That is, rather than advocating that the law cover an ever broader range of relationships, the report argued (at xix) that "it is time for governments to re-evaluate the way in which they regulate personal adult relationships."

In the excerpt that follows, consider how the proposed values and relevant questions would affect current arrangements for marriage and cohabitation. Some of these issues will also need to be addressed in relation to other aspects of family law later in these materials, but it is important to begin to address the role of marriage and cohabitation in structuring the law's relationship to families.]

Fundamental Values and Principles

Equality and autonomy are the two most important values that governments need to consider in framing policies that recognize and support personal adult relationships. State regulation of personal relationships should also seek to enhance other values: personal security, privacy and religious freedom, while pursuing legitimate government objectives in a coherent and efficient manner.

Governments must respect and promote two kinds of equality. *Relational equality* seeks to equalize the legal status among different types of relationships. Legislation like the federal government's *Modernization of Benefits and Obligations Act* largely eliminated distinctions between these two groups [conjugal and non-conjugal relationships]. However, by focusing only on conjugal couples, it entrenches unequal legal treatment of conjugal and non-conjugal relationships which may share the functional characteristics of emotional and financial interdependence. The principle of relational equality requires more than equal treatment of conjugal couples.

The concept of *equality within relationships* seeks to overcome unequal distributions of income, wealth and power, much of it based on historic inequality between men and women, or the lack of state support for persons with disabilities.

The value of *autonomy* requires that governments put in place the conditions in which people can freely choose their personal relationships. While governments should discourage the formation of abusive relationships, they should not create financial or other kinds of pressure to discourage relationships without reference to their qualitative attributes. The state should therefore remain neutral with regard to the form or status of relationships and not accord one form of relationship more benefits or legal support than others.

Personal security—whether physical, psychological or economic—enhances the ability of individuals to make healthy choices about entering or remaining in relationships. The state has a role to play in ensuring physical security within a relationship as well as economic security outside the relationship.

Healthy personal relationships are founded on candour and trust; they can flourish only if we are confident that our intimate thoughts and acts will not be discovered by or revealed to others. To promote the *privacy* that is necessary to such relationships, the state should avoid establishing legal rules that require intrusive examinations into, or forced disclosure of, the intimate details of personal adult relationships, unless the relationship involves violence or exploitation. Privacy rights must be balanced, however, and in some circumstances must give way to compelling objectives such as the state interest in prosecuting and preventing crime, including the commission of crimes involving domestic violence and abuse.

Contemporary Canadian understandings of *religious freedom* and equality require that the state not take sides in religious matters. The history of marriage regulation in Canada has thus been characterized by a progressive uncoupling of religious and legal requirements, reflecting a growing emphasis on the separation of church and state in a secular and pluralistic political community. Our current understanding of religious freedom requires that laws and policies, including those that regulate personal adult relationships, pursue objectives that can be defended in secular rather than religious terms. *Coherence* requires that laws have clear objectives, and that their legislative design corresponds with the achievement of those objectives. This would avoid reliance on marital status in a law whose objectives do not necessarily relate to marriage.

The *efficiency* of a law, policy or program may be measured by how effective it is, for example, in reaching its intended beneficiaries and whether it can be administered without undue costs or delays. Perfect coherence may not be achievable if the costs of administering a specifically targeted law are prohibitive.

A comprehensive approach to the recognition and support of personal adult relationships should be guided, first and foremost, by the values of equality and autonomy. In addition, state policies should protect and advance personal security, privacy and religious freedom, and they should seek to accomplish legitimate state objectives in a coherent and efficient manner. Proposed laws and the operation of existing laws should be carefully scrutinized to eliminate any detrimental effects on these values and principles.

Reconsidering the Relevance of Relationships

It is time to try to imagine a legislative regime that more effectively accomplishes its goals by relying less on whether people are living in particular kinds of relationships. The Law Commission proposes a new methodology for assessing any existing or proposed law that employs relational terms to accomplish its objectives. It consists of four questions.

First Question: Are the objectives of the law legitimate?
If not, should the law be repealed or fundamentally revised?

Second Question: Do relationships matter?
If the law's objectives are sound, are the relationships included in the law important or relevant to the law's objectives?

Third Question: If relationships matter, can individuals be permitted to designate the relevant relationships themselves?
Could the law allow individuals to choose which of their close personal relationships they want to be subject to the particular law?

Fourth Question: If relationships matter, and self-designation is not feasible or appropriate, is there a better way to include relationships?

If relationships do matter, and public policy requires that the law delineate the relevant relationships to which it applies, can the law be revised to more accurately capture the relevant range of relationships? This question applies where it is not possible to individualize rights and responsibilities, nor to allocate them on a basis of self-designation. Where the state must ascribe rights and responsibilities to achieve its objectives, it would be preferable to more carefully tailor laws to take into account the functional attributes of particular relationships. ...

The Report recommends that Parliament apply this four-step methodology in the development and implementation of all future law and programs. In Chapter Three, this methodology is applied to a variety of federal statutory provisions that rely on relational status. Examples are drawn from the *Marine Liability Act*, the *Canada Labour Code*, the *Immigration Act*, the *Canada Evidence Act*, the *Employment Insurance Act*, the *Bankruptcy and Insolvency Act*, the *Bank Act*, the *Income Tax Act*, the *Old Age Security Act* and the *Canada Pension Plan*.

The Report considers statutory provisions where the law makes presumptions based on relational status in order to achieve objects that are not necessarily or exclusively connected to the targeted relationships. For example, under the *Employment Insurance Act*, employees who are related to their employer must prove their employment was similar to an arm's length relationship in order to be eligible for employment insurance, a burden of proof that is difficult for them to satisfy in practice. If the purpose of the provision is to guard against sham employment contracts set up just to claim benefits, it should do that by examining the features of any employment contract, not just those among family members.

Fraudulent preference provisions in the *Bankruptcy and Insolvency Act* and conflict of interest provisions in the *Bank Act* target only family members. In so doing, they miss capturing all persons who may be receiving preferential treatment from a bankrupt person or a bank officer because of a personal relationship that is outside the family categories defined in those Acts. The Report recommends amending these provisions to reduce the emphasis on certain types of relationships. ...

Income Tax Act

Since income tax has been used extensively as an instrument for delivering government subsidies and transfer payments to individuals, the income tax legislation provides an excellent prism through which to examine the role of government in regulating close personal adult relationships. As a preliminary matter, the Report recommends retaining the individual as the basic unit for the calculation of income tax.

The Report goes on to look at some specific tax provisions that rely upon relational status. For example, in the area of dependent relative and spouse and common-law tax credits, the Report determines that the *Income Tax Act* could more accurately capture the range of relevant relationships. As a result, the Report recommends that Parliament replace the *Income Tax Act*'s spouse and common-law partner tax credit with enhanced or new programs that more carefully target caregivers and children for direct income support. The Report also recommends that Parliament extend the tax credits for dependent relatives so that they can be claimed by any taxpayer who has provided financial or caregiving support to a person who is dependent by reason of age, disability or illness, without reference to relationship status, and that it consider extending income assistance to caregivers by making dependants' credits refundable or by delivering direct grants outside of the tax system. It further recommends that Parliament consider providing income support, by way of direct grants or refundable tax credits, to disabled people to enable them to hire or purchase the supports they require.

As a second example, the Report concludes that, while the rollover rules for transfers of property between spouses and common-law partners serve valid objectives, the provisions should be extended to all persons living together in economically interdependent relationships. This would make the targeted relationships more relevant to the objectives of the provisions: reducing the intrusiveness of the tax system in the lives of those with close personal relationships and encouraging the redistribution of property.

Other legislative provisions examined through the lens of the Commission's four-step methodology include provisions setting out eligibility for compensation for the accidental death or injury of a family member in the air or at sea; entitlement to caregiver leave or bereavement leave under the *Canada Labour Code*; income security programs under the *Old Age Security Act*; survivors' benefits under the *Canada Pension Plan*; and family sponsorship under the *Immigration Act*. In each of these cases, comparison of the objectives of the legislation with the means used to achieve them reveals that the provisions could be better tailored to achieve their aims more coherently.

In considering how state regulation can recognize and support close personal relationships in a more principled and coherent manner, the first task is to clarify the objectives of laws that take relationships into account and determine whether they are valid. The next question is whether relationships are relevant to those objectives. If not, the law should eliminate reliance on relational considerations and individualize the rights and responsibilities in question.

In those areas where relationships are relevant to the legislative objectives, we analyzed whether it is possible to allow individuals rather than governments to choose the relevant relationships. In other contexts, we suggested that some limits be placed on these choices, restricting self-selection to a limited range of relationships.

Where self-selection is not workable, we considered alternative ways for governments to include relationships in legislation and provided examples where relational definitions could be redrawn to cover the full range of relevant relationships.

The Legal Organization of Personal Relationships

People want stability and certainty in their personal relationships, as in other aspects of their lives. The state must provide adequate legal structures to support the relationships that citizens develop, structures that respect the values of equality, autonomy and choice. Marriage has long been the main vehicle by which two people publicly expressed their commitment to each other and sought to ensure certainty and stability in their own and their family's relationship. But marriage is no longer a sufficient model, given the variety of relationships that exist in Canada today. What legal frameworks can the state offer to respond to the need of all its citizens for certainty and stability in their personal relationships?

Four legal modes can be used to regulate personal relationships: private law, ascription, registration and marriage. The *private law* model operates by default—when governments do not provide a legal framework, people are always at liberty to express their commitments through contracts. They can then turn to the courts when they feel that the other party has not fulfilled his or her contractual obligations. They may also rely on private law remedies, such as unjust enrichment or constructive trust. This mechanism is very burdensome. It can be costly, it favours the party with the greater resources or bargaining power and its after-the-fact remedies are uncertain.

Governments use *ascription* to prevent the risks of exploitation inherent in a contractual model by imposing (ascribing) a set of obligations on people in conjugal relationships that are presumed to correspond to the expectations of the majority of people involved in such relationships. While ascription may help to prevent exploitation, it is a blunt policy tool, treating all conjugal relationships alike. It infringes on autonomy, as people are not always aware they may opt out of certain provisions. While appropriate for conjugal relationships in some instances, it would be inappropriate for non-conjugal relationships.

Recently, there has been a move toward the creation of a new status, often called registered partnership. Its objective is to provide an alternative way for the state to recognize and support close personal relationships. When people register their relationships, a range of rights and responsibilities are then open to them. *Registrations* provide an orderly framework in which people can express their commitment to each other, receive public recognition and support, and voluntarily assume a range of legal rights and obligations. These regimes may also provide for an orderly and equitable resolution of the registrants' affairs if their relationship breaks down.

Registration schemes merit consideration because they provide a vehicle for recognizing a broader range of caring and supportive relationships, both conjugal and non-conjugal. They affirm the autonomy and choices of Canadians in their close personal relationships, offering the opportunity for public declarations of commitment that will be respected by government. Registration also does not compromise privacy within a relationship in the way that ascription often does.

Discussion Notes

Legal Models for Defining Family Relationships

Consider the report's suggestions about the use of private law, ascription, and registration in relation to the materials at the beginning of this chapter: which model would be preferred by Ruth Deech; by Zheng Wu; or by Winnifred Holland? Are there concerns that these authors identified that are not addressed in this brief summary of the LCC report? What kinds of criteria should be considered in choosing regimes for different kinds of family benefits and obligations?

In Australia, legislation has included non-conjugal relationships for some legal purposes for a few years. For example, the *Domestic Relationships Act 1994* (ACT), A1994-28, which defines a legislative property division scheme, is applicable to same-sex couples, but also to persons in a "domestic relationship," defined as

> a personal relationship (other than a legal marriage) between two adults in which one provides personal or financial commitment and support of a domestic nature for the material benefit of the other, and includes a de facto marriage.

The definition specifies (at s. 3(2)(a)) that a "personal relationship may exist between persons even if they are not members of the same household." For further details about the government's objectives, see *A Proposal for Domestic Relationship Legislation in the ACT: Discussion Paper* (Canberra: Attorney General's Department, 1993). In 1999, New South Wales enacted the *Property (Relationships) Legislation Amendment Act*, which extended protections for opposite-sex cohabitees to same-sex cohabitees, and also introduced the concept of "domestic relationship" (at s. 5(1)(b)):

> a close personal relationship (other than a marriage or de facto relationship) between two adult persons, whether or not related by family, who are living together, one or each of whom provides the other with domestic support and personal care (s. 5(1)(b)).

For further information, see Reg Graycar and Jenni Millbank, "The Bride Wore Pink … to the Property (Relationships) Legislation Amendment Act 1999: Relationships Law Reform in New South Wales" (2000), 17 *Canadian Journal of Family Law* 227, at 245-50. The Australian legislation reveals that governments in other jurisdictions are also seeking to provide recognition and support for non-conjugal relationships, although the LCC report may be more comprehensive in its scope.

Reforming Marriage: The Impact of the LCC Report

In its paper *Marriage and Legal Recognition of Same-Sex Unions: A Discussion Paper* (Ottawa: Department of Justice, 2002), the Department of Justice acknowledged the work of the Law Commission of Canada. However, the paper suggested (at note 4) that:

> Federal law currently includes family and other adult non-conjugal relationships only in some circumstances. But further study would be needed before Parliament can decide whether it is appropriate to treat non-conjugal relationships in the same way as spouses or common-law partners in all federal laws, and so these suggestions are beyond the scope of this paper.

Thus, it appeared that the government's reform proposals were more narrowly focused on the issue of same-sex marriage, and subsequent developments in the appeal courts in Ontario, British Columbia, and Quebec have further intensified this focus. What factors might assist in broadening the scope of reform with respect to the benefits and obligations of families that are defined other than by marriage or cohabitation? Should these proposals have been drawn to the attention of the Ontario Court of Appeal before it concluded that there were no significant consequences if same-sex marriage were recognized immediately?

SELECTED REFERENCES

Brenda Cossman and Bruce Ryder, "The Legal Regulation of Adult Personal Relationships: Evaluating Policy Objectives and Legal Options in Federal Legislation" (Ottawa: Law Commission of Canada, 2000).

Caroline Forder, "European Models of Domestic Partnership Laws: The Field of Choice" (2000), 17 *Canadian Journal of Family Law* 371.

Roderick A. Macdonald, "Perspectives on Personal Relationships" (Kingston, ON: Conference on Domestic Partnerships, 1999).

PROBLEM: DRAFTING NEW MARRIAGE LEGISLATION

The federal government is seeking legal advice with respect to the enactment of a comprehensive marriage statute in Canada. There are three challenges:

1. The issue of how to take account of same-sex marriage in accordance with the rulings of the three appellate courts in British Columbia, Quebec, and Ontario. This issue requires careful attention to Charter reasoning in these cases; it may be clarified as a result of the federal government's reference to the Supreme Court of Canada.

2. Whether, and if so how, to codify current common law requirements for a valid marriage. This issue requires a precise understanding of traditional legal precedents. What criteria should be used to determine whether all the existing requirements should be included? How should the statute be drafted? In addressing this question, consider whether there are any current requirements in the law that are no longer needed, and why.

   In relation to this issue, consider the current federal law of Australia with respect to marriage. Does this statutory language adequately reflect the current law in Canada? Is it still appropriate? Which provisions might require further changes to reflect current practices and/or aspirations about marriage in Canada in the 21st century?

Family Law Act 1975 (Cth.), No. 53

51(1) An application under this Act for a decree of nullity of marriage shall be based on the ground that the marriage is void.

(2) A marriage that takes place after the commencement of this Act is void where—

(a) either of the parties is, at the time of the marriage, lawfully married to some other person;

(b) the parties are within a prohibited relationship;

(c) the marriage is not a valid marriage under the law of the place where the marriage takes place, by reason of a failure to comply with the requirements of the law of that place with respect to the form of solemnization of marriages;

(d) the consent thereto of either of the parties is not a real consent because—

(i) it was obtained by duress or fraud;

(ii) that party is mistaken as to the identity of the other party or as to the nature of the ceremony performed; or

(iii) that party is mentally incapable of understanding the nature and effect of the marriage ceremony; or

(e) either of the parties is not of marriageable age,

and not otherwise.

(3) Marriages that are within a prohibited relationship are marriages—

(a) between a person and an ancestor or descendant of the person; or

(b) between a brother and a sister (whether of the whole blood or the half-blood).

(4) Any relationship specified in sub-section (3) includes a relationship traced through, or to, a person who is or was an adopted child, and, for that purpose, the relationship between an adopted child and his adoptive parent, or each of his adoptive parents, shall be deemed to be or to have been the natural relationship of child and parent.

3. Whether, or to what extent, a reform of the law of marriage in Canada should address the conclusions and recommendations of the Law Commission of Canada. Do you agree with the views expressed in the Department of Justice *Discussion Paper* that these issues fall outside the current urgency to legislate with respect to same-sex marriage? Why, or why not?

Consider how to formulate legal advice for the federal government with respect to issues concerning marriage reform in Canada.

CHAPTER REFERENCES

Ahmed, Kamal. "Transsexuals Win Right To Marry," *The Observer*, July 6, 2003.

Bailey, Martha. "Hawaii's Same-Sex Marriage Initiatives: Implications for Canada" (1998), 15 *Canadian Journal of Family Law* 153.

Barton, C. "Judicial Statistics" (1996), *Family Law* 53-54 (UK) (London: HMSO, 1995).

Belluck, Pam and Katie Zezima. "Massachusetts Shifts a Bit on Gay Marriage," *New York Times*, May 5, 2004.

Blackwell, Susan. "Federal Same-Sex Benefits Legislation" (March 2000), *Money and Family Law* 21.

Boyd, Christine. "Two Names, Two Wives, Two Families, But One Man," *Globe and Mail*, August 13, 2003.

Bradley, David. "Duress and Arranged Marriages" (1983), 46 *Modern Law Review* 499.

Bucknall, Brian. "A New Model for State-Approved Familial Partnerships," *The Lawyers Weekly*, August 22, 1997.

"California's High Court Halts Gay Marriages," *National Post*, March 12, 2004.

Center on Fathers, Families, and Public Policy. (2003), 5:1 *National Policy Briefing* [Madison, Wisconsin], available online at http://www.cffpp.org/briefings/.

Civil Partnership: A Framework for the Legal Recognition of Same-Sex Couples (London: Women and Equality Unit, Department of Trade and Industry, 2003).

Cotter-Moroz, Andrea. "Multiculturalism and the Law" (1992), 6 *Australian Journal of Family Law* 191.

Cossman, Brenda. "Lesbians, Gay Men and the Canadian Charter of Rights and Freedoms" (2003), 40 *Osgoode Hall Law Journal* 223.

Cox, Barbara J. " 'The Little Project': From Alternative Families to Domestic Partner-ships to Same-Sex Marriage" (2000), 15 *Wisconsin Women's Law Journal* 77.

Dao, James. "Ohio Legislature Votes to Ban Same-Sex Unions," *New York Times*, February 4, 2004.

Davies, Christine. *Family Law in Canada* (Scarborough, ON: Carswell Legal Publications, 1984).

Deech, Ruth. "The Case Against Legal Recognition of Cohabitation," in John Eekelaar and Sanford Katz, eds., *Marriage and Cohabitation in Contemporary Societies: Areas of Legal, Social, and Ethical Change* (Toronto: Butterworths, 1980), 300.

Demczuk, Irène. "Draft Bill on Civil Unions: Is the Quebec Government about To Create Separate Equality for Same-Sex Couples and Their Children?" (2002), 21:1 *Jurisfemme* 1.

Department of Justice Canada. *Marriage and Legal Recognition of Same-Sex Unions: A Discussion Paper* (Ottawa: Department of Justice, 2002).

EGALE Canada Inc. "Division of Powers and Jurisdictional Issues Relating to Marriage" (Ottawa: Law Commission of Canada, 2000).

Fausto-Sterling, Anne. "The Five Sexes: Why Male and Female Are Not Enough," *The Sciences*, March/April 1993, 20.

Fodden, Simon. *Family Law* (Toronto: Irwin Law, 1999).

Forder, Caroline. "European Models of Domestic Partnership Laws: The Field of Choice" (2000), 17 *Canadian Journal of Family Law* 371.

Freeman, Michael D.A. and Christina M. Lyon. *Cohabitation Without Marriage* (Aldershot, UK: Gower, 1983).

Gambrill, David. "HR Policy Includes 'Transgendered,' " *Law Times*, July 24, 2000.

Gavigan, Shelley A.M. "Legal Forms, Family Forms, Gendered Norms: What Is a Spouse?" (1999), 14 *Canadian Journal of Law and Society* 127.

Graycar, Reg and Jenni Millbank. "The Bride Wore Pink ... to the Property (Relationships) Legislation Amendment Act 1999: Relationships Law Reform in New South Wales" (2000), 17 *Canadian Journal of Family Law* 227.

Ha, Tu Thanh. "Same-Sex Couples Win Right To Marry in Quebec," *Globe and Mail*, March 20, 2004.

Hahlo, H.R. *Nullity of Marriage in Canada: With a Sideways Glance at Concubinage and Its Legal Consequences* (Toronto: Butterworths, 1979).

Henley, Jon. "I Can't Say to a Wife of 20 Years She Has To Go," *The Guardian*, May 9, 2001.

Herman, Didi. "Are We Family? Lesbian Rights and Women's Liberation" (1990), 28 *Osgoode Hall Law Journal* 789.

Hogg, Peter. *Constitutional Law of Canada* (Toronto: Carswell) (looseleaf).

Holland, Winnifred. "Intimate Relationships in the New Millennium: The Assimilation of Marriage and Cohabitation?" (2000), 17 *Canadian Journal of Family Law* 114.

Ingram, Martin. *Church Courts, Sex, and Marriage in England, 1570-1640* (Cambridge: Cambridge University Press, 1987).

Jacobs, Andrew. "Judge in New Jersey Hears Arguments on Gay Marriage," *New York Times*, June 28, 2003.

Krauss, Clifford. "Free To Marry, Canada's Gays Say, 'Do I'?" *New York Times*, August 31, 2003.

Law Commission of Canada. *Beyond Conjugality: Recognizing and Supporting Close Personal Adult Relationships* (Ottawa: Law Commission of Canada, 2001).

Lawton, Valerie. "Ottawa Accused of Same-Sex Delay," *Toronto Star*, January 29, 2004.

Le Febour, Patricia. "Same-Sex Spousal Recognition in Ontario: Declarations and Denial: A Class Perspective" (1993), 9 *Journal of Law and Social Policy* 272.

Lim, Hilary. "Messages from a Rarely Visited Island: Duress and Lack of Consent in Marriage" (1996), IV *Feminist Legal Studies* 195.

Loney, Jim. "Transsexual Cannot Marry Woman: Court," *National Post*, July 24, 2004.

Lund-Andersen, Ingrid. "The Danish Registered Partnership Act, 1989: Has the Act Meant a Change in Attitudes?" (University of London: Conference on the Recognition of Same-Sex Partnerships, July 1999).

Lunman, Kim and Drew Fagan. "Marriage Divides the House," *Globe and Mail*, September 17, 2003.

MacCharles, Tonda. "Gay-Marriage Foes Plan Prayer Protests," *Toronto Star*, September 3, 2003.

MacInnes, Norman. "Money Advanced a Gift, Not a Loan," *The Lawyers Weekly*, October 6, 2000.

Majury, Diana. "Annotation of B. v. A." (1990), 29 RFL (3d) 258.

Mansnerus, Laura. "New Jersey To Recognize Gay Couples," *New York Times*, January 9, 2004.

Marquis, Christopher. "US Gays Who Marry in Canada Face Hurdles," *New York Times*, June 19, 2003.

Matas, Robert. "Woman To Bring Suit Against Mormon Church," *Globe and Mail*, November 19, 2002.

Maxwell, Kay. "Family Law and the Intellectually Disabled in Australia" (1993), 7 *Australian Journal of Family Law* 151.

McLeod, James. "Annotation of Chirayath v. Chirayath" (1980), 19 RFL (2d) 235.

_____. "Annotation of Singla v. Singla" (1985), 46 RFL (2d) 235.

_____. "Annotation of Knight v. Knight" (1995), 16 RFL (4th) 48.

_____. "Annotation of Debora v. Debora" (1999), 43 RFL (4th) 179.

Millan, Anne. "Would You Live Common-Law?" (Autumn 2003), *Canadian Social Trends* 2.

Millbank, Jenni. "The Property (Relationships) Legislation Amendment Act 1999 (NSW) versus the De Facto Relationships Amendment Bill 1998 (NSW)" (2000), 9 *Australasian Gay and Lesbian Law Journal* 1.

Morse, Bradford W. "Indian and Inuit Family Law and the Canadian Legal System" (1980-81), 8-9 *American Indian Law Review* 199.

Neilan, Terence. "Gays Have Full Marriage Rights, Massachusetts Court Says," *New York Times*, February 4, 2004.

O'Donovan, Katherine. "Legal Marriage—Who Needs It?" (1984), 47 *Modern Law Review* 111.

Ontario Law Reform Commission. *Report on the Rights and Responsibilities of Cohabi- tants Under the Family Law Act* (Toronto: Ontario Law Reform Commission, 1993).

Ouellet, Claudine. "Brief Presented to the Standing Committee on Justice and Human Rights on Marriage and Recognition of Same-Sex Unions: A Question of Law and Nothing Else" (Quebec: Coalition Gaie et Lesbienne du Québec, 2003).

A Proposal for Domestic Relationship Legislation in the ACT: Discussion Paper (Canberra: Attorney General's Department, 1993).

Raphael, Mitchel. "Who Says All Gays Want To Marry?" *Globe and Mail*, April 7, 2004.

Schmitz, Christin. "Marriage of 'Philanderer' Ruled Not a Mere 'Affair,'" *The Lawyers Weekly*, January 24, 2003.

Short, Peter. "Let No One Be Turned Away," *Globe and Mail*, January 31, 2004.

Somerville, Margaret. "Separate but Equal," *Ottawa Citizen*, September 3, 2003.

Statistics Canada. *Marriages 2000*, online at http://www.statcan.ca/Daily/English/030602/ d030602a.htm.

Stout, David. "San Francisco City Officials Perform Gay Marriages," *New York Times*, February 12, 2004.

Tanner, Michael. "Wedded to Poverty," *New York Times*, July 29, 2003.

Thompson, David. "A Consideration of the Mental Capacity Provisions of the Marriage Act in View of the Charter of Rights and Freedoms and Webb v. Webb" (1986), 9 *Canadian Community Law Journal* 101.

Tyler, Tracey. "Now It's Divorce, Same-Sex Style," *Toronto Star*, July 24, 2004.

Vanier Institute of the Family. *Profiling Canada's Families II* (Ottawa: Vanier Institute of the Family, 2000).

Waaldijk, Kees. "Text of Dutch Law on the Opening Up of Marriage for Same-Sex Partners" (Universiteit Leiden, The Netherlands, 2001), online at http://athena.leidenuniv.nl/ rechten/meijers/index.php3?c=86).

Walters, Mark D. "Incorporating Common Law into the Constitution of Canada: Egale v. Canada and the Status of Marriage" (2003), 41 *Osgoode Hall Law Journal* 75.

Weitzman, Lenore J. *The Marriage Contract: Spouses, Lovers and the Law* (New York: The Free Press, 1981).

Wu, Zheng. *Cohabitation: An Alternative Form of Family Living* (Toronto: Oxford University Press, 2000).

Young, Claire. "Taxing Times for Lesbians and Gay Men: Equality at What Cost?" (1994), 17 *Dalhousie Law Journal* 534.

Ziff, Bruce. "Recent Developments in Canadian Law: Marriage and Divorce" (1986), 18 *Ottawa Law Review* 121.

Zimmer, Lisa R. "Family, Marriage and the Same-Sex Couple" (1990), 12 *Cardozo Law Review* 681.

Zlotkin, Norman. "Judicial Recognition of Aboriginal Customary Law in Canada: Select- ed Marriage and Adoption Cases" (1984), 4 CNLR 1.

CHAPTER THREE

Forming Families in Canada: Relationships of Parent and Child

I. INTRODUCTION

Marriage is a relationship easily terminated. Parent–child ties, by contrast, tend to last—they are not as fragile in our contemporary society.

> Martha Fineman, *The Neutered Mother, the Sexual Family*
> *and Other Twentieth Century Tragedies*
> (New York: Routledge, 1995), 3

On the one hand, marriage has become increasingly freely interchangeable, terminable at will, and non-exclusive. On the other hand, biological parenthood is being increasingly emphasized as an unchangeable, continuing relationship, that is not generally terminable at will, and is indeed regarded as exclusive. This is so, despite the fact that the consequences of changes in marital law have been an increasing complexity of relationships between (social and biological) parents and children.

> Rosalind Edwards, Val Gillies, and Jane Ribbens McCarthy,
> "Biological Parents and Social Families: Legal Discourses
> and Everyday Understandings of the Position of
> Step-Parents" (1999), 13 *International Journal of Law,*
> *Policy, and the Family* 78, at 79

As these comments suggest, "families" are formed by parent–child relationships as well as by marriage. Moreover, the scope of rights and responsibilities for parents and children, as defined by legal principles, often appear to be less flexible than those defined by marriage. In this way, while individuals may choose to end a marriage or a cohabiting relationship, there may be less opportunity for individual choice about the scope and the duration of parental responsibilities, on the basis that "parenthood is forever."

At the same time, legal definitions of who is a "parent" and who is a "child" do not always conform to everyday notions about parent–child relationships, and the legal definitions themselves vary in different contexts. For example, the definition of parent for purposes of consenting to adoption may differ from the definition of parent in relation to obligations to pay child support. As a result, the legal context in which families are formed by parent–child relationships requires careful attention to how such relationships, and their rights and responsibilities, are defined.

Mother–Child as a Core Family Relationship?

In thinking about families and law, Martha Fineman, an American scholar, suggested that the mother–child relationship should replace marriage as the core family unit for purposes of legal policies. According to Fineman, the effort to fit more and more intimate unions into the category of marriage, as a way of organizing legal rights and responsibilities, is less appropriate than focusing on mother–child relationships as families; she recommended instead the mother–child relationship: "a vertical rather than horizontal tie; a biological rather than a sexual affiliation, an intergenerational organization of intimacy."

> **Martha A. Fineman,** *The Neutered Mother, the Sexual Family and*
> *Other Twentieth Century Tragedies*
> (New York: Routledge, 1995), at 5-6

[In] defining a core family unit what has happened is the creation of a norm, a baseline. It does not mean that other adult family characters are excluded: fathers, or nonprimary caretakers who have sexual affiliation to the primary caretaker, are certainly free, under my model, to develop and maintain significant connections with their sexual partner and her children if she agrees to such affiliation. The mother may also wish to forge ties and relationships with nonsexual affiliates.

Under my intimacy scheme, however, single mothers and their children, indeed all "extended" families transcending generations, would not be the "deviant" and forgotten or chastised forms that they are considered to be today because they do not include a male head of household. Family and sexuality would not be confluent; rather, the mother–child formation would be the "natural" or core family unit—it would be the base entity around which social policy and legal rules are fashioned. The intergenerational, nonsexual organization of intimacy is what would be protected and privileged in law and policy.

Fineman's proposal for defining families in terms of mother–child relationships presents one alternative to the recommendations of the Law Commission of Canada, discussed in chapter 2. In examining the issues in this chapter about parent–child relationships, consider whether, or to what extent, Fineman's recommendations offer advantages, by contrast with proposals to redefine marriage. What kinds of legal issues need to be addressed in relation to her proposals?

This chapter focuses on selected issues concerning the definition of parent–child relationships. Although such relationships exist routinely as a result of biological reproduction, of course, claims have been litigated about the respective rights of mothers and fathers, and the extent to which legal principles permit them to exercise choices about their responsibilities as parents. In addition to biological reproduction, moreover, processes for the adoption of children reflect important ideas about relationships between biological and social parents. Introduced in many common law jurisdictions in the late 19th and early 20th centuries, adoption laws were designed to create new legal relationships between adoptive parents and an adoptee and to terminate the legal status of the adoptee's biological parents. The efficacy of these principles has been challenged in recent years in cases concerning the recognition of customary adoption practices, interracial adoption, and adoption processes for gay and lesbian families. In these contexts, principles of adoption reveal important, sometimes hidden, assumptions about what families should look like and how their members should be defined.

In addition, recent medical developments with respect to processes of assisted reproduction have also challenged norms about parent–child relationships. In the context of donated eggs and sperm and the use of gestational carriers, for example, it is now possible for "intentional" parents to have no genetic or biological connection to "their" child. In these circumstances, definitions of who is a "parent" and who is a "child," pursuant to statutory provisions that reflect traditional biological reproductive relationships, may fail to provide appropriate legal solutions for these families.

Discussion Notes

Changing Pictures of Families

According to Carol Smart, researchers interested in issues about families have typically asked respondents to draw maps of their families. Originally, the results were intended to measure social integration and family relationships. Thus, according to Smart, "the adult who placed friends closer than kin might be defined as having some kind of pathology, and the child who drew more than one family would certainly be seen as incipiently problematic." However, such drawings now elicit different responses. For example, Smart suggested that identification of "friends" as "family" is now more often regarded as

> a reflection of how the subjective meaning of family is changing and how individuals may be shifting their locus of intimacy and support away from kin towards other people. In some instances the maps which are produced are a long way from the idealized picture of mother, father and two siblings, and even where the standard stock of kin appear within the circles, others now may find a place, disrupting the taken-for-grantedness of primacy of blood and marital relationships.

(Elizabeth B. Silva and Carol Smart, "The 'New' Practices and Politics of Family Life," in Elizabeth B. Silva and Carol Smart, eds., *The New Family?* (London: Sage Publications, 1999), 1, at 9.)

To what extent does this comment reflect the data about families in Canada generally, or your family in particular? Is this view consistent with Fineman's proposal to eliminate marriage as the core unit, replacing it with the mother–child relationship? Why, or why not?

SELECTED REFERENCES

Roberta Hamilton, "Women, Wives, and Mothers," in Nancy Mandell and Ann Duffy, eds., *Reconstructing the Canadian Family: Feminist Perspectives* (Toronto: Butterworths, 1988), 3.

Nancy Mandell, "The Child Question: Links Between Women and Children in the Family," in Mandell and Duffy, eds., 49.

Carol Smart, Bren Neale, and Amanda Wade, *The Changing Experience of Childhood: Families and Divorce* (Cambridge: Polity Press, 2001).

Robert A. Stebbins, "Men, Husbands, and Fathers: Beyond Patriarchal Relations," in Mandell and Duffy, eds., 27.

II. BIOLOGICAL REPRODUCTION: FATHERS AND MOTHERS

The question of what constitutes "good (enough) fathering" is one which has, throughout the 1990s, assumed a central importance within a range of conversations taking place around the legal regulation of family practices across western societies. ... [A] concern with fatherhood can be seen to be central to contemporary cultural representations *of* and political debates *about* the parameters of "the family" and understandings of "family life."

> Richard Collier, "In Search of the 'Good Father': Law, Family
> Practices, and the Normative Reconstruction of Parenthood"
> (2001), 22 *Studies in Law, Politics, and Society* 133, at 133-34

A. Birth Registration and the Naming of Children

As Collier noted, issues about the nature of fatherhood have increasingly been raised in relation to issues of parenting and biological reproduction, both in marriage and in relationships of opposite-sex cohabitation. In Canada, litigation concerning fathers and mothers, and their relationships at the birth of children, have focused on rights concerning the registration and naming of children pursuant to provincial and territorial vital statistics legislation.

Details of these statutes vary considerably across Canada. In Alberta, Prince Edward Island, and both the Northwest Territories and Nunavut, the mother has primary responsibility for registering a child's birth, although the director may also accept a father's registration in Alberta: see *Vital Statistics Act*, RSA 2000, c. V-4, s. 3(2)(a) and (b); *Vital Statistics Act*, RSNWT 1988, c. V-3, s. 2(2)(a), also applicable to Nunavut; and *Vital Statistics Act*, RSPEI 1988, c. V-4, s. 4(1)(a). In Quebec, art. 113 of the *Civil Code* provides that only a parent can declare filiation to himself or herself; but art. 114 permits married parents to make such a declaration for their spouse. Nova Scotia permits either parent to register a "legitimate" child, but only the mother can register an "illegitimate" child: see *Vital Statistics Act*, RSNS 1989, c. 494, s. 4(2)(a) and (b). Only Manitoba's legislation appears to expressly address registration of a child if the birth is the result of artificial insemination: see *Vital Statistics Act*, CCSM, c. V60, s. 3(6).

In three provinces, British Columbia, Saskatchewan, and Ontario, both parents may register a child's birth, but the mother is permitted to register alone "if the father is incapable or is unacknowledged by or unknown to the mother": see *Vital Statistics Act*, RSBC 1996, c. 479, s. 3(1)(b); *Vital Statistics Act*, RSS 1995, c. V-7.1, s. 5(2)(b), and *Vital Statistics Act*, RSO 1990, c. V.4; s. 9(3)(b). (As explained below, the legislation in British Columbia was amended in May 2004: see SBC 2004, c. 55.) Provisions in the statutes of Newfoundland and Labrador, New Brunswick, and Yukon also address situations in which a father is unknown or unacknowledged, or unwilling to register the birth of a child: see *Vital Statistics Act*, RSNL 1990, c. V-6, s. 10(3); *Vital Statistics Act*, SNB, c. V3, s. 7(5)(b); and *Vital Statistics Act*, RSY 2002, c. 225, s. 4(2).

How should the phrase "unacknowledged by or unknown to the mother" be interpreted? Two recent cases in Ontario and British Columbia addressed this question, although only the BC case focused on the constitutionality of the legislative provision. In examining the following excerpts from the two cases, consider the factors used by the courts in these differing legal contexts.

Kreklewetz v. Scopel
(2001), 52 OR (3d) 172; 13 RFL (5th) 408 (Sup. Ct. J);
aff'd. (2002), 60 OR (3d) 187; 214 DLR (4th) 385 (CA);
leave to appeal to SCC denied (2003), 62 OR (3d)

[The biological father of a child appealed from a lower court decision that had interpreted the Ontario *Vital Statistics Act* to deny an unmarried father's request to be named on the birth registration form and to give his surname to his son. The mother and father had engaged in an "on again off again" relationship that ended shortly after their son was born. The mother gave evidence that she had initially acceded to the father's request to register the child's birth, using both their surnames. However, she also stated that she had agreed to this arrangement as a result of being pressured by the father to do so and on the understanding that the three of them would become a "family." Some months after the child's birth, the mother realized that the father had lied about his intentions, and that he had vacationed with other women on several occasions during the time that he and the mother were together. The father married another woman.

The Ontario Court of Appeal upheld the decision of Greer J, who had interpreted the statute so as to permit the child's mother to register the birth without acknowledging the father and to give the child her own surname. In interpreting sections 9(3)(b) and 10(3) of the statute, which provided authority for the mother to register the child's birth by herself and give the child her own surname if the father was "unacknowledged by or unknown to" her, the court held that the mother was not required to acknowledge the father for purposes of the birth registration and surname, even though she knew his identity and had acknowledged him as the child's father for purposes of access and child support. According to the appellate court (at 200-3):]

[35] If the Act is interpreted in the manner advocated by the appellant [father], having acknowledged the father for one purpose, the mother would be obliged to acknowledge him in her certifying statement. It would only be in circumstances where the mother has been able to successfully avoid identifying the father for any purpose, that she would also be able to avoid acknowledging him under the Act.

[36] In my view, in structuring the provisions as it did, the legislature made a policy decision to allow the mother to have the ultimate ability to determine the surname of the child in recognition of the fact that there will be circumstances where a mother will have the ongoing responsibility for the child, and should not be forced to have the child linked by name with the biological father. ...

[38] In the British Columbia Court of Appeal decision in *Trociuk*, all three judges agreed that the father could be unacknowledged by the mother even if he was not

unknown to her. Having made that finding the majority concluded that the provisions did not contravene s. 15 of the Charter, while Prowse JA, in dissent, concluded that they did.

[39] In her reasons, Madam Justice Southin, one of the judges speaking for the majority, at para. 65 dismissed the argument of the father that "he had a right to complete the birth registration because he is not 'unacknowledged by or unknown to the mother' within s. 3(1)(b) of the Act." Although she found the submission attractive because it would preserve a right of husbands and give the same right to fathers of children born out of wedlock to have their names on the birth certificates of their children, she could not accept it. Her interpretation of the section as a whole, was that it gives the mother the choice of whether the father's name is on the birth certificate, and that the mother is under no obligation to either acknowledge paternity or give her child the father's surname. ...

[42] I agree with the conclusion reached by the British Columbia Court of Appeal. In my view, the only interpretation which gives an effective meaning to the phrase "unacknowledged by" as distinct from "unknown to" in s. 10(3) of the Act, is the one which allows the mother to know the identity of the father, to acknowledge him as the father for other purposes, but not to acknowledge him for the purpose of registration of the birth of a child under the Act. This is the only interpretation which gives effect to the plain meaning in the context of the section as a whole.

[43] I am satisfied that it is also the appropriate interpretation on the criteria endorsed in the *Teck* case [*Teck Corp. v. Ontario (Minister of Finance)* (1999), 124 OAC 58 (CA)]. It satisfies the requirements of plausibility, efficacy and acceptability as a legislative choice for accomplishing the purposes of the Act. Furthermore, for the appellant, as a father of a child born out of wedlock, the Act does not remove any right to be included in the register or to have the child bear his surname, as he never had such rights under prior legislation or at common law. There was no Charter challenge of the provision in this case. The issue of infringement of a father's rights will be dealt with by the Supreme Court of Canada in the *Trociuk* appeal.

In reaching its conclusions, the Ontario Court of Appeal also noted that *Kreklewetz v. Scopel* did not require the court to assess the validity of the statute pursuant to the Charter. However, the court expressed its agreement with the majority of the BC Court of Appeal in *Trociuk v. British Columbia (Attorney General)* (2001), 90 BCLR (3d) 1; 200 DLR (4th) 685 (CA); aff'g. (1999), 67 BCLR (3d) 389; 47 RFL (4th) 79 (SC), which held that a birth mother was entitled to register and name her children without acknowledging their father; and that these legislative provisions did not contravene the equality guarantee in the Charter. Consider *Kreklewetz* in the light of the subsequent decision of the Supreme Court of Canada in *Trociuk*. What is the impact of the SCC decision on *Kreklewetz*?

Trociuk v. British Columbia (Attorney General)
[2003] 1 SCR 835

[Wayne Trociuk and Reni Ernst were the parents of triplets born in 1996. The children's mother registered their birth on her own and marked the father as "unacknowledged by the mother"; she also chose and registered the children's surname as hers alone. Her actions were authorized by ss. 3(1)(b) and 4(1)(a) of the BC *Vital Statistics Act*, RSBC 1996, c. 479; s. 3(6)(b) precluded the father from altering the registration. The parents became estranged after the birth of the triplets, although the father obtained an order for court-supervised access and the mother was later granted an order for custody, child support, and paternity testing (which resulted in Trociuk being declared father of the children). Trociuk petitioned for an order of mandamus to compel the director of Vital Statistics to register his name on the forms and to change the surname of the children to Ernst-Trociuk; he also asked the court to exercise its inherent *parens patriae* jurisdiction to order that the children bear the hyphenated surname. In addition, Trociuk also claimed a declaration that s. 3(1) of the *Vital Statistics Act* infringed s. 15 of the Charter on the grounds of sex discrimination.

The Supreme Court of Canada unanimously allowed the appeal from the judgment of the BC Court of Appeal. Applying the test for s. 15 of the Charter set out in *Law v. Canada (Minister of Employment and Immigration)*, [1999] 1 SCR 497; (1999), 170 DLR (4th) 1, the court concluded that ss. 3(1)(b) and 3(6)(b) were invalid because they infringed s. 15 and were not saved by s. 1. The court suspended its declaration of invalidity for one year to permit the provincial legislature to revise the statute in accordance with constitutional requirements. In doing so, the court directed the legislature to account for the variety of interests involved in registering and naming children, including the legitimate interests of the mother, the right of the father not to be discriminated against on the basis of sex, and the best interests of the child. The court's decision suggested that Trociuk could apply, pursuant to amendments enacted in October 2002, to have his particulars included on the birth registration: see *Health Planning Statutes Amendment Act*, SBC 2002, c. 15. However, the court expressly declined to make an order with respect to the surname of the children; since the children were already seven years old, the court indicated that their best interests would have to be considered in assessing this request.

In assessing the significance of the father's interests, pursuant to *Law*, the court stated (at paras. 16-17):]

Including one's particulars on a birth registration is an important means of participating in the life of a child. A birth registration is not only an instrument of prompt recording. It evidences the biological ties between parent and child, and including one's particulars on the registration is a means of affirming these ties. Such ties do not exhaustively define the parent–child relationship. However, they are a significant feature of that relationship for many in our society, and affirming them is a significant means by which some parents participate in a child's life. The significance of this affirmation is not only subjectively perceived. The legislature of British Columbia has attached important consequences to the presence of a father's particulars on his child's birth registration. It has decided that where a father's particulars are included on the birth registration, his consent is always required for his child's adoption. However, where his particulars are not included, a father must fulfill at least one of an alternative set of conditions. ...

Contribution to the process of determining a child's surname is another significant mode of participation in the life of a child. For many in our society, the act of naming a child holds great significance. As Prowse JA notes, naming is often the occasion for celebration and the surname itself symbolizes, for many, familial bonds across generations.

In the context of this reasoning, how should provincial legislation be drafted to meet the concerns identified in *Trociuk*? Is there a need to revise legislative provisions in other provincial statutes? In May 2004, the British Columbia legislature enacted the *Vital Statistics Amendment Act*, SBC 2004, c. 55: see s. 4.

In a comment on *Trociuk*, Hester Lessard argued that the Supreme Court's decision recognized genetic relationship as a sole basis for establishing parental (fathers') rights with respect to the registration and naming of children. Such a focus on genetic relationships for defining parenthood appears problematic in the context of developments with respect to assisted reproduction, discussed later in this chapter. In addition, recent developments in family law principles have considerably broadened definitions of "spouse" and "parent" to include a wide range of relationships other than those that are based on genetic ties. In thinking about the Supreme Court's decision in *Trociuk*, consider Lessard's examination of the facts in the case and whether they should have been more carefully considered in the Supreme Court's reasoning.

Hester Lessard, "Mothers, Fathers, and Naming: Reflections on the Law Equality Framework and Trociuk v. British Columbia (Attorney General)"
(2004), 16:1 *Canadian Journal of Women and the Law*, at 37-39

Trociuk's relationship to the triplets was something more than simply genetic although something less than what the case law would call parental. To begin with, Ernst's relationship with Trociuk itself does not fit easily into existing legal categories. It was not a casual short lived relationship. ... Trociuk and Ernst had lived together for a little more than a year at one time but then lived separately while maintaining a sexual relationship. However, the length of their cohabitation was too short for Ernst and Trociuk to meet the statutory criteria for imposing interspousal obligations on unmarried cohabitants. Furthermore, the triplets were conceived over a year after Trociuk and Ernst ceased cohabitation, with the result that legislative provisions that typically provide for a presumption of paternity based on cohabitation or marriage with the mother at time of conception or birth did not apply. ...

[Trociuk did, however, provide some emotional support during Ernst's risky pregnancy. Ernst was in hospital for a month after the birth; she then stayed with Trociuk for about six weeks before moving in with her foster daughter at the time when two of the triplets were first released from hospital. Although Trociuk sought and was granted access to the triplets, it seems that access was exercised infrequently.]

Nothing in terms of Trociuk's interactions with Ernst and then with the triplets in the pre- and post-natal periods qualifies Trociuk as what the jurisprudence calls a "social parent." Thus, in law, Trociuk's claims are based solely on his contribution of genetic material for the conception of the children. The story of Ernst and Trociuk's relationship might support an argument that we need to complicate the legal discourse of fatherhood to recognize persons whose contributions to children's existence fall short of "social fatherhood" but are more than casual. Deschamps J's analysis goes in the opposite direction, reducing fatherhood to genetic paternity while at the same time according genetic fathers the full panoply of constitutionalized parental rights.

According to Lessard, the Supreme Court decision stripped away the factual context in its application of the *Law* principles in a way that

cements into place as a background feature to these competing constitutional interests, a naturalized version of the traditional family, organized around a heterosexual conjugal unit which reflects the biological "truths" of human procreation.

Lessard's comment is important for its questioning of underlying assumptions about what creates the parent–child bond and the ways in which constitutional equality principles must examine these relationships in *substance*, not just *form*. In addition, she raises questions about the state's interest in registration and naming practices and the implicit assumptions of provincial vital statistics legislation. Some of these issues are considered again later in this chapter in relation to children born as a result of the use of reproductive technology.

B. Genetic Fathers and Access

In addition to claims about the registration and naming of children, fathers have litigated to obtain access to their children. Although such claims most often occur in the context of the breakdown of marriage or of a cohabiting relationship, such a claim was considered as a result of an arrangement between a man and a woman to produce a child together in the case that follows. In reviewing this case, consider the court's treatment of the agreement alleged by the mother and the reasons for concluding that the father's access to the child was in the child's best interests.

Johnson-Steeves v. Lee
(1997), 29 RFL (4th) 126; 203 AR 192 (QB); aff'd. (1997), 33 RFL (4th) 278; 209 AR 292 (CA)

[This case concerned a four-and-a-half-year-old boy, Nigel Lee Johnson-Steeves. He lived with his mother and her two young sons from her previous marriage; Nigel's biological father was Dr. Lee, who lived in Toronto. Ms Johnson-Steeves was receiving social assistance as well as child support from her former husband and, in relation to Nigel, from Dr. Lee.]

...

The Positions of the Parties

Ms. Johnson-Steeves brings this application before the Court pursuant to the *Domestic Relations Act*, RSA 1980, c. D-37 seeking permanent custody of Nigel, an order that Dr. Lee be denied access to Nigel, and an order for child support in an amount that the Court considers appropriate.

Dr. Lee defends the claim for "no access" and submits that it is in the best interests of Nigel that he be granted access. He is also prepared to continue to pay support for Nigel, which he has been doing since prior to Nigel's birth. He leaves it to the Court to determine the appropriate amount of support on an ongoing basis.

The issues raised by the parties in this case are extremely interesting. Ms. Johnson-Steeves asserts that the parties entered into a paternity agreement which she submits is a binding contract and should be upheld by this court. That contract provided that Dr. Lee would act as a sperm donor so that Ms. Johnson-Steeves could conceive another child, that he would financially support the child, and that he would not interfere with issues concerning the health and welfare of the child. In the alternative, Ms. Johnson-Steeves says that if the court finds there is no contract, then the court must distinguish between a biological father who is not entitled to access as of right and a social father who would have rights of access. She avers that Dr. Lee is only a biological father and, given the circumstances surrounding the conception and birth of Nigel, is not entitled to access. She says that to grant access would be to impose on her a family relationship which she specifically did not want, hence the agreement.

Dr. Lee argues there is no such paternity agreement as defined by the mother. Rather, he readily concedes that he agreed to father a child with Ms. Johnson-Steeves and did so. He agreed to financially support the child which he has been doing, and further he agreed not to interfere with health and welfare issues with respect to the child. He says there was no specific discussion with respect to access and never any intention that Nigel would grow up not knowing his dad. He submits Nigel has a right to know his father and that it is in Nigel's best interest that Dr. Lee be granted access to him.

Facts

[The court reviewed how Lee and Johnson-Steeves had met in Ontario in the early 1980s; they then lost contact for some time. After Johnson-Steeves's marriage and separation, however, she contacted Lee in 1991 to invite him to visit her in Calgary during his ski holiday in Whistler, and he agreed. Before the visit, however, Johnson-Steeves suggested that they go to Las Vegas for three days; she explained that she needed a break from her ongoing difficulties arising out of her divorce and custody battles with her former husband.]

···

What Dr. Lee did not know until he arrived in Las Vegas was that this trip was contrived by Ms. Johnson-Steeves for the purpose of asking Dr. Lee to help her conceive a child. In her testimony Ms. Johnson-Steeves said that she always wanted another child, especially a girl as she already had two boys. She had also had long and extremely difficult pregnancies and deliveries with her first two children which she attributed to the size of her husband who was 6'3" tall. She felt like a failure because she was not able to have natural births and therefore wanted another child so that she could prove to herself that she could, to use her very words at the trial, "do it right." She denies wanting to have another child just to stay on social assistance. Dr. Lee testified, however, that one of the reasons she gave him as to why she wanted another child was that her oldest child had some medical problems and she wanted to spend more time with him. If she was pregnant, social services would give her another two years grace before making her go back to work.

When asked why she chose Dr. Lee to help her conceive a child, Ms. Johnson-Steeves said there were four reasons. First of all he was of much smaller stature than her husband with "small hands and feet." These features would increase her chances of carrying a smaller child which would allow for an easier delivery. He was also academically extremely bright. The second reason was that he "fit the financial mould." She did not want this child to be part of the welfare system. She knew she needed financial support and Dr. Lee had the financial means to care for the child. She even went so far as to enquire as to his income to satisfy herself that he had sufficient financial resources. The third reason for choosing Dr. Lee was that the child would be of mixed heritage and this would be "a nice way to bring the world together." Dr. Lee is of Chinese heritage while Ms. Johnson-Steeves is part Caucasian and part Jamaican. The fourth reason was that he was not a stranger. Through their letter writing, she had checked out his personal life and determined that he was still single. It was important to her that he be free of other responsibilities.

There were of course other options available to Ms. Johnson-Steeves to have a child; however, she discounted them. When asked about using a sperm bank, she responded that there was a cost of $500 for each attempt and she did not have the money. With this option she would also have the financial responsibility of raising the child and she knew that she could not do so without financial support. She also found the sperm bank too impersonal. She wanted Nigel to know and be aware of his origins.

Adoption was also not an alternative to her. Were she to adopt, she again would be solely financially responsible for the child and again she knew she did not have the financial ability to support another child. Adoption would also deprive her of the opportunity to carry and deliver a child naturally which she needed to do to prove to herself that she could.

[The court then reviewed the discussion between the parties in the room that they shared in Las Vegas. There was some discussion about Lee becoming a "sperm donor" but he advised Johnson-Steeves that transporting sperm from Toronto to Calgary would require medical intervention. Thus, although she explained that she was reluctant to do so, the parties had sexual intercourse. They did so again during Lee's visit to Calgary the following month. Before engaging in sexual intercourse, they discussed certain conditions.]

… The first was that Dr. Lee would either donate sperm or father a child. In my view the term used is not determinative of the issue and therefore there is no need for me to prefer one version over the other. The second condition was that Dr. Lee would be a financial provider. Ms. Johnson-Steeves said that she had to have a way of ensuring her own financial security. The third condition was that Dr. Lee would not interfere in the health and welfare issues of the child. Specifically she says she wanted to raise the child her way and did not want interference from him on issues such as schooling, breast feeding and immunization.

Dr. Lee agrees in substance that these were the matters discussed. I find that these were the conditions discussed by the parties.

Ms. Johnson-Steeves says that they did not discuss "access" at all. She says she told Dr. Lee that he could see the child whenever he was passing through. Dr. Lee says that they specifically discussed the fact that he wanted to see the child and that her response was that of course he could see the child and that she would never deny kids the right to see their dad. I find that there was no discussion about specific terms of access at all or what role Dr. Lee would play in the child's life but rather both parties understood that Dr. Lee would see the child from time to time. In hindsight it appears that they had very different views as to what that contact would be but it was obviously not a significant concern at the time particularly to Ms. Johnson-Steeves. She was the one setting out the conditions and I am satisfied she would have certainly incorporated access had it been an issue with her. …

[Although the parties remained in contact with each other, their relationship had deteriorated by the time that Nigel was born. Lee had provided Johnson-Steeves with about $3,500 before Nigel's birth, and he was thrilled to become a father. Johnson-Steeves did not register Lee as the child's father, but Lee travelled to Calgary to visit Nigel and made a formal agreement to pay $300 per month for his support. In addition, Lee provided Johnson-Steeves with $3,000 in the months after Nigel's birth. Although the latter sum was paid directly to Johnson-Steeves, the monthly payments of $300 were required to be paid to the welfare department and were deducted from her social assistance payments. Eventually, Johnson-Steeves decided that Lee could no longer visit Nigel and Lee then commenced an action for access to Nigel.]

… When asked why she did not want Dr. Lee to have any access to Nigel, Ms. Johnson-Steeves said that she had given it a lot of thought and did not want Nigel to go through the same thing that her other two boys had to go through which was the requirement to see their dad every week. She found this stressful given the difficult legal proceedings involved with her divorce. She would rather that they did not have to go to visit their dad but knew that it could not be helped as there is a court order in place. She says it upsets Nigel to be without his brothers when they visit with their dad. Although it appears that Ms. Johnson-Steeves' ex-husband has offered to take Nigel with them, she does not want Nigel to go with him as, in her view, he is not a good role model.

Ms. Johnson-Steeves believes that Nigel has a family and to set up visitation with Dr. Lee would break up her family. She feels Nigel lacks nothing, has plenty of role models in his life, has extended family in the area and has the family *she* chose for him. In her view, Dr. Lee can add nothing to Nigel's life and in fact the visitation would simply disrupt her life and Nigel's life. She does not want Nigel put in the same situation as her own children being moved back and forth between their parents. She is worried that she would lose control over him and be unable to protect him.

I heard evidence from Ms. Johnson-Steeves' parents and other friends and relatives. They all appear to be wonderful and supportive people. Her parents in particular are very involved in Ms. Johnson-Steeves' life and that of her children, their grand-children. In fact, it appears that they provide a great deal of not only emotional support but also substantial financial support to the family.

Ms. Johnson-Steeves is of the view that Dr. Lee has a temper, a reason which renders him unsuitable as a parent to Nigel. Dr. McElheran, who I qualified as an expert in the area of personality assessments, conducted an assessment on Dr. Lee. He found Dr. Lee to be organized, controlled, very intelligent, practical and with high ego strength, moral values and loyalty. He showed no aggressive drive or hostility. There was nothing in the testing that concerned Dr. McElheran at all with respect to the issues at this trial. I accept his evidence in that regard.

I heard many complaints by Ms. Johnson-Steeves about Dr. Lee's behaviour and I heard his explanation about their disagreements. On the whole of the evidence in this area, I find their disagreements to be no different than those most of the population engage in and certainly nothing that would concern this Court. The difficulty is that Ms. Johnson-Steeves wants complete control over all aspects of her life and if some-one disagrees with her she considers that they are simply trying to make her life difficult. She appears to take no responsibility for any of the difficulties in her life.

Dr. Kneier also gave evidence at this trial. He was qualified as an expert in the area of child psychology. Dr. Kneier had never met either of the parties or Nigel. The purpose of his testimony was to provide information to the Court about access issues in general and how they might apply to a case such as this. He opined that fathers are good for children and having a father is "good news not bad news." This was in response to Ms. Johnson-Steeves' concern that for Nigel to meet his father after all this time would cause him psychological trauma. It should be noted that the reason Dr. Lee has not seen the child since he was 10 months old has nothing to do with his lack of effort, but rather the refusal of Ms. Johnson-Steeves to allow him access, resulting in these proceedings.

It is Dr. Kneier's view that although children can, and often do, achieve a healthy development without a father, provided they have a good relationship with their mother and reasonable socioeconomic circumstances, it is better for children to have a relationship with their father than not to have one. He says even a limited relation-ship is better than none at all. The only time no relationship is better is when there is a "bad or damaging or inadequate father."

Dr. Kneier opined that a good relationship by a boy with his father helps to develop intelligence and drive, improves academic achievement and helps develop independence, empathy and social adequacy with peers. His view on the timing of any reintroduction is "the sooner, the better." He sees no benefit from delay. Where conflict exists, as appears to be the case here, Dr. Kneier believes that there are mechanisms available to address those conflicts as long as the parents focus on the child.

In a nutshell, I took from Dr. Kneier's evidence that it is in children's best interests to have the influence of a "good or adequate" father than not to have that relationship at all. Although a child can develop normally in a one-parent household, they do better with the influence of both parents. Dr. Kneier says fathers are important to young boys, they yearn for a father and a child may wonder why he has no father when other people do. A child would be happy, curious, and interested to know the man who was their dad. As he said, "It's good news to have a dad."

Issues and Decision

I now turn to the issues before me.

1) Is there a paternity agreement between the parties respecting the child Nigel?

I find on the evidence before me that there was no paternity contract with respect to the conception of the child. What I do find, however, is that there was a discussion between Ms. Johnson-Steeves and Dr. Lee about conceiving a child. Ms. Johnson-Steeves wanted another child and Dr. Lee was prepared to play a role in that conception. It is clear from the evidence that they each had their own reasons for participating in this plan. Ms. Johnson-Steeves attached certain conditions to the conception. I find those conditions to be that Dr. Lee would assist Ms. Johnson-Steeves in conceiving a child, that he would provide financial support for that child and that he would not interfere in health and welfare decisions affecting the child. I find that there was no specific discussion with respect to access to the child nor what Dr. Lee's role would be in the life of the child. It is clear, however, that they both were aware, at the time of this discussion, that Dr. Lee would be seeing the child. The form of that visitation was not discussed and it appears now that they each had very different perceptions as to how that would take place.

These are two people who intended to and did in fact conceive a child through sexual intercourse. There were discussions about certain things that Ms. Johnson-Steeves wanted in this arrangement. Dr. Lee agreed with some of those requests. That arrangement in my view does not constitute a legally binding paternity agreement.

2) In the event that I find no contract, as I have found, I am then asked by Ms.
   Johnson-Steeves to distinguish between a biological father and a social father.

She says that biological fathers do not have an entitlement to access but that social fathers do. In making this argument Ms. Johnson-Steeves says that there are many cases where the Courts have allowed an application by a non-biological father to be declared a father. This may arise, for example, in situations of artificial insemination or where a man has developed a relationship with the child. I agree that social fathers are sometimes declared to be fathers of children even if they are not the biological father. That has no bearing on this situation, however, as Ms. Johnson-Steeves acknowledges that Dr. Lee is the biological father of the child. I find he is also the parent to this child. Under the *Parentage and Maintenance Act*, a father is defined as the biological father of the child. "Parent" under that same statute means a mother or father. A parent may enter into an agreement that provides for maintenance for the child. Dr. Lee and Ms. Johnson-Steeves entered into such an agreement.

Under the *Domestic Relations Act*, a mother or father may apply to the court for an order regarding the custody of the child and the right of access to the child of either parent. That is the application the parties have brought herein. Dr. Lee is clearly the father and, I find, a parent to this child. Ms. Johnson-Steeves says, however, that that alone is not enough to entitle him to access to the child. I agree. I must determine whether or not it is in Nigel's best interest to have access with his father, Dr. Lee.

Ms. Johnson-Steeves submits that the parties had an agreement that Dr. Lee would not be a social father to Nigel and that where there is not a relationship between the parties and no intended relationship between the parties then it is not in the child's best interest to create a social father from a biological father. She says that she intended that Nigel would not have a father parent, and has created her "family" with this in mind. In Ms. Johnson-Steeves' perception, Dr. Lee is simply a sperm donor, Nigel has no "father," Nigel's family consists of she as mother and her two children only and Dr. Lee has no role to play in their "family." By allowing access, Ms. Johnson-Steeves says that this court would be forcing on her a family structure that she did not choose.

All of the above focuses on Ms. Johnson-Steeves and what *she* wants. It was clear throughout the trial of this matter that she was annoyed at all of the legal proceedings she was involved in with her ex-husband and the stress and turmoil that it caused her. She also finds it frustrating that she now must continue to deal with her ex-husband who has access to their children and a person for whom she clearly has no respect. This is one of the reasons that she chose to proceed the way that she did with respect to the conception of Nigel. She wanted another child but did not want the father around to disrupt her life. What struck me throughout the trial was how little was said about what would be in Nigel's best interest and how much was said about the lifestyle Ms. Johnson-Steeves wanted for herself and her children. I find that her attitude was totally selfish. Her primary concern was herself rather than the true subject of these proceedings, Nigel. That is exemplified by her desire to have all of the advantages of Dr. Lee and none of the corresponding disadvantages. ...

Ms. Johnson-Steeves also raises constitutional issues for this court to consider. Section 7 of the Charter grants the right not to be deprived of life, liberty or security of the person except in accordance with the principles of fundamental justice. She argues that deciding that a child will not have a father and will be raised in a single-parent family is a liberty interest projected by the Charter. If this court grants access, it will infringe on Ms. Johnson-Steeves' right to liberty. I do not accept this argument.

The duty of this court is to determine what is in Nigel's best interest. Although he was conceived under circumstances that many would consider unusual and perhaps distasteful, he was conceived and delivered with the intent of bringing him into this world. He lives with his mother and two brothers in Calgary with a large extended family and network of friends. He has a father who chose to have him, who provided financial support for his mother during her pregnancy, who came to visit him regularly after the birth, who has since continuously provided financial support for him and who has expressed by his words and his deeds an overwhelming desire to be a part of this child's life. Ms. Johnson-Steeves asks this Court to redefine the term "family." She says the notion that a family consists of a mother, father and children, as long defined by our law, is antiquated and does not reflect current realities. Ms. Johnson-Steeves says that Dr. Lee is only a sperm donor and not a father. It was her choice to create a family unit without a father and she did so. She argues any access will create a family that was not intended and will violate Nigel's understanding of his family unit. This, she says, is not in Nigel's best interests. She intends to tell Nigel that Dr. Lee is a special friend who contributed the genetic material to create him. ...

I am of the view ... that society and biology have not yet reached the point where we have dispensed with fathers or mothers completely. They form an integral part of each child's life whether or not they reside with their children.

Nigel has a father and Ms. Johnson-Steeves' desire that it not be so, does not make it so. Ms. Johnson-Steeves' interest in arranging her world as she would like to see it does not mean that it is also in Nigel's best interest. Nigel knows or will come to know that he has a father and mother as all children do. It is Nigel's right of access to his father and not his mother's right to bargain away. At this stage, it does not matter to Nigel whether he was conceived by artificial insemination, during a one night stand, or during a long-term relationship or marriage. What he does know is that he has a father and a mother. The fact that his father does not live with Nigel does not make Dr. Lee any less a father.

I have heard evidence about Dr. Lee's background and extended family. In my view he has the desire and ability to contribute positively to Nigel's well-being and development. Dr. Lee has no intention at this time of interfering with the day-to-day rearing of Nigel or the health and welfare issues surrounding Nigel. What he does want is access so that he can contribute as only he can to Nigel's life. I find that it is in Nigel's best interest for Dr. Lee to have access to him. This in no way detracts from the mother's primary role in Nigel's life or the roles played by so many other members of the extended family. What it does do is recognize that a good and decent parent, and without hesitation I so categorize Dr. Lee, can enhance this child's life. Indeed, to the extent that only such a father could do. ...

[The court then ordered access, but subject to arrangements appropriate to reintroducing Nigel to his father. The court also agreed to hear further arguments on the amount of child support to be paid by Lee.]

Johnson-Steeves v. Lee
(1997), 33 RFL (4th) 278 (Alta. CA)

[In concluding that the trial judge had reached the correct conclusions, the appeal court stated (at 282ff.):]

This is not a sperm donor case. This Court will decide on the law relating to custody and access issues in sperm donation cases if and when it has such a case before it. This case must be decided on the evidence presented at trial and the factual findings of the Trial Judge, who correctly decided that the respondent was a parent of the child.

The child, Nigel, was conceived in the course of a short-term intimate relationship between his biological parents, both of whom wished to have a child. Nigel has two parents, a mother and a father, both of whom wish to be involved in Nigel's life. The respondent agreed to and has contributed financially to the support of the child, and wishes to be involved in Nigel's life. The respondent is not an anonymous faceless figure who has donated sperm by whatever means and shown no other interest in the child. While the respondent agreed not to interfere with the appellant's decisions in health and other issues relating to the child, the respondent did not agree that he would have no role to play in his child's life. On the facts of this case, the most glaring inconsistency with simple sperm donation is the respondent's agreement to financially support the child. The suggestion that the respondent agreed to provide financial support for the child without having any opportunity to develop a relationship with the child is incomprehensible to us. ... No evidence, other than that of the appellant, was adduced during the trial which demonstrates that it would not be in Nigel's best interest to have a relationship with the respondent. The Trial Judge's finding is supported by the evidence and we agree with it. In fact, it is difficult to imagine circumstances in which the Court would deny a right of access to a biological father of good character, who is able to make a positive contribution, financially and emotionally, to the child's life, and who wishes to maintain a relationship with the child. It is even more difficult to imagine why any court would deprive the child of the benefits of such a relationship.

The learned Trial Judge found that the parties did not make any agreement limiting or denying access to the respondent. ... The issue of access, left undefined by the parties, was determined by the Trial Judge. We need not and do not decide the public policy implications of any such agreement between parents of a child, and whether such an agreement would be enforced by Alberta courts. ...

[Assuming] without deciding that s. 7 applies to such actions, we reject the suggestion that s. 7 creates a right for the custodial parent to decide on a family model which excludes the other parent from the life of their child, especially where such a model is inconsistent with the best interests of the child, as found by the Trial Judge in this case. If s. 7 protects the rights of parents, it protects the rights of both parents.

... The appellant urges upon us a theory recognizing a distinction between a purely biological parent and a social parent, and rights to be accorded to each. We need not consider whether such a distinction should be adopted in this province. As found by the Trial Judge, the respondent cannot be described as a mere biological parent or "sperm donor." At all times before and after the birth of the child, the respondent maintained an interest in the child, and exhibited a willingness to fulfil his financial and other obligations to the child. If he and the child have not had the opportunity to establish the type of emotional attachment often found in child–parent relationships, that is through no fault of his. The appellant prevented him from seeing the child.

Do you agree that this is not a "sperm donor" case? If it were such a case, should different factors be used to determine the legal relationships among the father, mother, and child? Why, or why not? Do you agree that agreements between adults (such as that alleged by the mother) should always be unenforceable? What about agreements on the part of "intentional parents" to use the services of a gestational mother to bear a child? Should these agreements be regarded differently? Why, or why not? Is it relevant that the agreement in *Johnson-Steeves* was oral, and that neither party was legally represented? If Ms Johnson-Steeves had requested a lawyer to produce a written agreement in these circumstances, would it have been possible to include provisions that enhanced its enforceability? What kinds of problems are created for lawyers in relation to the drafting of such contracts? You may want to consider these questions again after reviewing the materials about assisted reproduction later in this chapter.

Discussion Notes

Recognizing Fathers

In *Johnson-Steeves v. Lee*, the mother did not include the father's name on the birth registration forms. In the light of the decisions in *Kreklewetz v. Scopel* and *Trociuk v. British Columbia*, would Dr. Lee be entitled to be registered as Nigel's father? What factors were significant to the court's decision in *Trociuk*? What factors should be relevant to determine legal recognition of a child's father in relation to birth registration forms: financial support; an interest in visiting the child; concerns about biological ties; or the need for a male person in a child's life? Are these the same factors that are relevant to issues about access? Do these cases suggest that courts are becoming more responsive to the significance of fatherhood?

In this context, Richard Collier argued (at 145) that there remains a "gap between the rhetoric and the reality of family life," at least with respect to the law's recognition of fathers' rights. In Britain, where contact between children and both of their parents (after separation) is encouraged by statute, Collier suggested (at 148) that even though the welfare of the child is supposed to be paramount, there is almost a legal presumption in favour of contact or shared parenting, a presumption that may run counter to the wishes of children themselves in relation to their fathers. Did the court in *Johnson-Steeves* respond to Nigel's best interests or to Dr. Lee's? Were their interests different? What factors were most significant for the court in assessing Dr. Lee's potential contribution to Nigel's life? What factors might have altered the court's views with respect to Nigel's best interests in relation to Dr. Lee's request for access?

Equality for Fathers and Mothers

In the Supreme Court's decision in *Trociuk*, the judgment identified reforms in the Quebec *Civil Code* in the 1970s that extended to mothers the ability to transmit their surnames to their children. Such a reform reveals how law may reflect changing conceptions about equality with respect to paternity and maternity. Do these cases about the rights and responsibilities of fathers and mothers in relation to birth registration, children's names, and parental access signal other changes in ideas about parenthood, families, or biological reproduction in Canada? Are the positions of fathers and mothers the same in relation to biological reproduction? Was the court's decision in *Trociuk* based on ideas about formal or substantive equality? Note that one newspaper account of the Supreme Court's decision in *Trociuk* reported that it was the first decision to recognize men as a "historically disadvantaged group" in Canadian society: see *Globe and Mail*, June 7, 2003, at A3. You may want to reconsider these issues in the next section, in relation to definitions of mothers and fathers for purposes of consenting to adoption.

Family Policies and Legal Principles

Looking at these questions from a larger historical and policy context, particularly in relation to fathers' rights to contact with children post-divorce, Carol Smart argued:

> The focus on the welfare of the child and the concern to attach men to their children are both policies which have developed as correctives to what have been seen as past errors in family law policy. But because the scope of this policy is limited to the field of private law, this method of achieving "progress" may only exacerbate other problems which are outside the remit of family law. ... The active pursuit—by family law—of equal, joint parenting *after* divorce combined with welfare and employment policies which make equal, joint parenting *during* marriage virtually impossible for the majority, gives rise to a form of disenfranchisement of motherhood rather than a new beginning for parenthood. Rather than increasing the quantum of care that children receive through the more active involvement of fathers *after* divorce, this policy may make it increasingly "rational" for mothers to behave more like fathers *during* marriage in order to ameliorate the future deficit to their status as citizens in the context of a modern welfare state which increasingly values paid work and independence over unpaid care and commensurate dependence. Under such a scenario the "new" parenthood may seem less desirable than once imagined.

(Carol Smart, "The 'New' Parenthood: Fathers and Mothers After Divorce," in Silva and Smart, eds., 100, at 113.)

Do Smart's comments shed light on these cases about parenthood in relation to biological reproduction? Note, for example, that there was no evidence that any of the fathers in the above cases wished to have day-to-day custody and care of the children; all of them appeared content to leave these responsibilities to the children's mothers. How should the rights and responsibilities of parents in relation to issues of recognition (registration, naming, and access) be balanced with issues about responsibility (caring for children on a daily basis)?

SELECTED REFERENCES

Chris Barton and Gillian Douglas, *Law and Parenthood* (London: Butterworths, 1995).
Susan B. Boyd, *Child Custody, Law, and Women's Work* (Toronto: Oxford University Press, 2003).
Roxanne Mykitiuk, "Beyond Conception: Legal Determinations of Filiation in the Context of Assisted Reproductive Technologies" (2001), 39 *Osgoode Hall Law Journal* 771.
Carol Smart and Bren Neale, *Family Fragments?* (Malden, MA: Polity Press, 1999).
Alison Harvison Young, "Reconceiving the Family: Challenging the Paradigm of the Exclusive Family" (1998), 6 *American University Journal of Gender and the Law* 505.

C. Legal Regulation of Women's Sexuality

Abortion and Sterilization

It must also be noted that law regulates parenthood with respect to issues about abortion and sterilization. Until 1988, abortion was regulated pursuant to s. 251 of the *Criminal Code*, RSC 1985, c. C-46. In that year, however, the Supreme Court of Canada struck down this section of the *Criminal Code* in its entirety in *R v. Morgentaler*, [1988] 1 SCR 30; (1988), 44 DLR (4th) 385. Chief Justice Dickson (Lamer J concurring) held that the law constituted state interference with bodily and psychological integrity violating s. 7 of the Charter. Further, the regulatory framework governing abortion was unconstitutional because its exculpatory provisions created unfair procedural irregularities. Mr. Justice Beetz (Estey J concurring) held that the procedural requirements of s. 251(4) delayed legal procurement and unjustifiably risked a mother's health. Madam Justice Wilson alone found that the law violated a substantive liberty interest and that it also infringed upon freedom of conscience under s. 2(a) of the Charter. Dissenting, Mr. Justice McIntyre (La Forest J concurring) held that s. 7 did not protect a woman's right to procure an abortion.

There were a number of different provincial reactions to the *Morgentaler* decision, including a number of problems with access and funding. In Nova Scotia, for example, legislation was enacted to prevent abortions being performed outside a hospital; at the time, Dr. Morgentaler had indicated publicly his intent to establish an abortion clinic in Halifax. In the fall of 1989, Dr. Morgentaler was charged under the *Medical Services Act* of Nova Scotia for performing abortions outside a hospital. At the trial level, the court granted the province an injunction against the clinic on the basis of the public interest in seeing that laws are not openly flouted: *Nova Scotia (Attorney General) v. Morgentaler* (1989), 93 NSR (2d) 202; 64 DLR (4th) 297 (SCTD). An appeal in March 1990 was dismissed: (1990), 96 NSR (2d) 54; 69 DLR (4th) 559 (SCAD). The court held that no substantial injustice had been done and that at the interlocutory stage, no court can fully explore all the merits of a case. Leave to appeal from this decision to the Supreme Court of Canada was refused. In October 1990, the provincial court acquitted Dr. Morgentaler of the charge, however, holding that the *Medical Services Act* was, in pith and substance, criminal law made primarily to control and restrict abortion in the province and therefore beyond the province's constitutional authority: *R v. Morgentaler* (1990), 99 NSR (2d) 293 (Prov. Ct.). In September 1993, the Supreme Court agreed: [1993] 3 SCR 463; (1993), 107 DLR (4th) 537.

Meanwhile, in May 1990, the House of Commons passed Bill C-43, *An Act Respecting Abortion*. It sought, according to the government, "to balance the constitutional rights of the woman with society's interest in the protection of the foetus." It was regarded as an unhappy compromise by many Canadians, and in an unusual step, the Senate defeated the bill in a tie vote in January 1991. Apparently, the government has no plans to enact new legislation.

During these years, there were also legal challenges by women's partners in relation to their decisions to have abortions. In Ontario, O'Driscoll J issued an order, on the application of Gregory Murphy, enjoining his partner Barbara Dodd (then a 22-year-old mother of two children) from having an abortion. Ms Dodd was not present and subsequently sought a motion to set aside the order. Gray J set aside the order, concluding that Mr. Murphy had perpetrated a fraud on the court under rule 59.06 by holding himself out as the father when, in fact, he might not have been. The judge also found that Mr. Murphy had misrepresented to the court the state of Ms Dodd's health. Although O'Driscoll J's order was the first time an injunction had been granted against a woman to prevent her from having an abortion, Gray J specifically declined to rule on the substantive issues in the case (*Murphy v. Dodd* (1989), 63 DLR (4th) 515; 70 OR (2d) 681 (HCJ)).

In Quebec, Jean-Guy Tremblay brought an application for a provisional injunction restraining his former fiancée Chantall Daigle from having an abortion. The application was granted, and Daigle's appeal to the Quebec Court of Appeal was dismissed. Leave was granted for an appeal to the Supreme Court of Canada in an unusual summer sitting and before all nine justices. The appeal was decided despite the fact that Ms Daigle had had an abortion in Massachusetts.

The Supreme Court held that there were no substantive rights upon which the injunction to restrain the abortion could be founded; the *Civil Code of Lower Canada* did not recognize the fetus as a human being with a juridical personality and, further, a father had no legal right based on his interest in a fetus to support an injunction to restrain an abortion (*Tremblay v. Daigle*, [1989] 2 SCR 530; (1989), 62 DLR (4th) 634).

There have also been cases in which courts have reviewed applications for non-therapeutic operations, particularly in relation to reproductive capacity. In a number of cases, parents have brought applications to courts to obtain consent for hysterectomy operations for a mentally disabled daughter. For example, see *Re K.*, [1985] 4 WWR 724; (1985), 19 DLR (4th) 255 (BCCA); and *Re Eve*, [1986] 2 SCR 388; (1986), 31 DLR (4th) 1. For an excellent analysis of the decision in *Re Eve*, see Patricia Peppin, "Justice and Care: Mental Disability and Sterilization Decisions" (1989/90), 6 *Canadian Human Rights Yearbook* 65. In the 1990s, Leilani Muir sued the Alberta government for sterilizing her under the province's *Sexual Sterilization Act*. She was one of 2,844 people sterilized in Alberta between 1928 and 1972 under this law, apparently created to prevent the "feeble minded" from having children who might inherit disabilities. Although Alberta and British Columbia were the only Canadian provinces to pass sterilization laws, it is believed that operations may also have been carried out in other provinces, including Ontario. In January 1996, Justice Joanne Veit of the Alberta Court of Queens Bench found the province's treatment of Muir "unlawful, offensive and outrageous," and ordered damages of $740,000: see *Toronto Star*, June 12, 1995 and June 30, 1996.

SELECTED REFERENCES

S.I. Bushnell, "The Welfare of Children and the Jurisdiction of the Court Under Parens Patriae," in Katherine Connell-Thouez and Bartha Knoppers, eds., *Contemporary Trends in Family Law: A National Perspective* (Scarborough, ON: Carswell, 1984), 223.

Claire Farid, "Access to Abortion in Ontario: From Morgentaler 1988 to the Savings and Restructuring Act" (1997), 5 *Health Law Journal* 119.

III. ADOPTION: BIOLOGICAL PARENTS, ADOPTIVE PARENTS, AND CHILDREN

[Are] the assumptions implicit in our adoption laws ... valid in our changing society? Do we still wish to continue premising our laws upon a concept of relinquishment? ... [By contrast, we might decide] that changing attitudes about family and the definition of a parent dictate an examination of other options different from our present one which envisages a permanent severing of the "old" family bond and a permanent new reconstituting. In any such examination, the customary attitudes of Native people towards adoption would be instructive.

> Kerry J. Daly and Michael P. Sobol, *Adoption in Canada: Final Report* (Guelph, ON: National Adoption Study for Health and Welfare Canada, 1993), 99

A. Changes in Adoption Practices and Policies

In their study of adoption law and practices in Canada, Daly and Sobol reviewed (at 67) the history of adoption in common law provinces. Although Britain did not enact adoption legislation until after World War I, New Brunswick passed an adoption statute as early as 1873, based on the model in existence in Massachusetts; Nova Scotia similarly enacted adoption legislation in 1896, and adoption statutes were passed in most other common law provinces in Canada between 1920 and 1930.

The early legislation was enacted in a context in which pregnant unmarried women placed their babies for adoption to avoid the stigma of "illegitimacy," and childless couples adopted them to avoid the problems of "incompleteness" in their families. These twin goals required secrecy in the adoption process so that the adoptive parents could be regarded "as if" they were the biological parents of a child. Provisions for altering the child's birth certificate to show the adoptive parents as "birth parents" and for extinguishing the child's relationships to the biological parents and their families confirmed the existence of new families. In recent decades, adoption orders have been required to meet the test of the "best interests of the child," a test which Daly and Sobol suggest has tended to promote more openness in adoption processes. One result of openness about adoption may be the continuing presence of a biological parent in the life of a child who, at the same time, has two legally recognized parents. How should the biological parent be viewed, in terms of legal rights and responsibilities, in this context?

In a longitudinal survey of children in 1994-95, Statistics Canada identified that 1.2 percent of all children under the age of 12 had been adopted. Of these 57,300 children, 60 percent had 2 adoptive parents, while 40 percent had just 1; some of the children in the latter group were adopted by a new spouse after divorce and the creation of a blended family: see Vanier Institute of the Family, *Profiling Canada's Families II* (Ottawa: Vanier Institute of the Family, 2000), at 64-67. According to Daly and Sobol (at 7), moreover, the number of children born in Canada and subsequently placed in adoptive homes has declined steadily, with 5,376 children adopted in 1981 but only 2,836 so placed in 1990, a drop of 47.3 percent. Both the numbers and proportions of public, by contrast with private (and international), adoptions decreased.

Analysis of the data demonstrated, however, that the decline in adoptions was not connected to increased access to abortion, but rather to a significant increase in the percentage of pregnancies that resulted in the birth mother or a non-adopting surrogate raising the infant. Thus, Daly and Sobol reported (at 9-10) that in 1981, 46.1 percent of single young women chose to raise their infant, but that this figure had risen to 59.9 percent by 1989. By contrast with abortion, however, adoption was seen as a good alternative to raising the child (Daly and Sobol, at 20):

> Unlike abortion, adoption was believed to be a fairly good alternative, at least in theory. ...
> In general, it was seen as an altruistic act on the part of the mother because it would serve the best interests of the child. ... On the other hand, the physical commitment to carry the child to term and the ensuing emotional attachment to it were major barriers to choosing this option.

Changing societal views about children born "outside marriage" and single parenting were reflected in some controversial adoption cases: for example, see *Martin v. Duffell*, [1950] SCR 737; (1950), 4 DLR 1 and *Re Mugford*, [1970] 1 OR 601; (1970), 9 DLR (3d) 113 (Ont. CA); aff'd. [1970] SCR 261. In reviewing some of the materials about adoption that follow, consider the extent to which legal policies may affect individual decision making about adoption, as well as the ways in which social expectations about parenting are reflected in legal principles.

B. Birth-Parent Consent and Its Consequences

1. Who Is a "Parent"?

> When a law alters the history and the dynamics of a relationship in such a fundamental way, there must be safeguards against misunderstanding or abuse. The most important of these is consent.
>
> Daly and Sobol, at 68

Provincial adoption statutes generally require parental consent before the placement of children or orders for adoption and the resulting change of the child's legal status. However, there are a variety of different provisions with respect to who is entitled to consent, whether there are any limits on giving consent immediately after a child's birth or only after a "cooling off" period, whether and how consents may be withdrawn, and the extent to which informed consent is ensured by way of counselling or legal advice: for example, see Ontario's *Child and Family Services Act*, RSO c. C.11, ss. 137-139 and provincial comparisons in Daly and Sobol, at 68-71 and appendix A. Significantly, Ontario's *Child and Family Services Act*, s. 137, which lists a number of categories of persons whose consent may be required, expressly includes "the child's mother"; however, the consent of the child's father is required only if he falls within one of the categories described in s. 137, especially that of a "presumed" father pursuant to s. 8(1) of the *Children's Law Reform Act*, RSO 1990, c. C.12.

Pursuant to s. 8(1), for example, a man who is married to the child's mother at the time of birth is presumed to be the child's father, although this presumption can be rebutted with evidence, on the balance of probabilities, that he is not the father. This differential treatment of mothers and fathers was challenged by the father of a child whose mother had consented to the child's adoption. Because the father did not qualify within any of the categories of s. 8(1) of the *Children's Law Reform Act*, he claimed that the differential treatment of mothers and fathers under s. 137 for purposes of consenting to a child's adoption contravened the provisions of s. 15 of the Charter on the basis of sex discrimination.

Re Attorney General of Ontario and Nevins
(1988), 64 OR (2d) 311; 13 RFL (3d) 113 (HCJ)

[Pursuant to adoption proceedings under the *Child and Family Services Act*, the biological mother had executed the required consent and sworn by affidavit that the biological father was a non-parent under the provisions of the *Child and Family Services Act*, now s. 137(1). The trial judge raised a constitutional question of the validity of s. 137(1), which includes all biological mothers within the definition of "parent," but excludes biological fathers unless they have married or cohabited with the mother, or acknowledged parenthood or demonstrated responsibility for the child.

The trial judge held that the definition of parent violated s. 15(1) of the Charter because it discriminated on the basis of sex. The Attorney General applied for judicial review of the decision, for a ruling on the constitutionality of s. 137(1) and an order of mandamus requiring the trial judge to proceed with the adoption.

The Divisional Court held (at 316) that s. 137 did not violate s. 15 of the Charter:]

[O]ur reading of the sections as a whole lead us to the view that the only natural father who is not by definition a "parent" whose consent is required by [s. 137(1)] of the Act, is a male person who by an act of casual sexual intercourse impregnates a woman and demonstrates no sense of responsibility for the natural consequences of the act of sexual intercourse. It is a man who shows no sense of responsibility to the woman he has made pregnant nor to the life that he has helped to procreate.

[With regard to the differential treatment between biological mothers and biological fathers, the court held (at 316-17) that the two groups were not similarly situated.]

... The mother because of physical necessity has shown responsibility to the child. She carried and gave birth to it. The casual fornicator who has not demonstrated any interest in whether he did cause a pregnancy or demonstrate even the minimum responsibility to the child required by [s. 137] cannot be said to be similarly situated to the mother. The statute recognizes as a parent, a father who demonstrates the minimum interest in the consequences of his sexual activity. Most fathers are defined as parents. Only those who do not demonstrate some responsibility to the child are not.

[Moreover, in assessing the claim in relation to s. 1 of the Charter, the court held (at 318-19):]

… [T]he obvious objective of this legislation is to ensure that children whose parents are unwilling or unable to care for them receive early placement in a permanent home where they will have the opportunity to be reared as members of a family.

[Noting that there was overwhelming evidence that delay in placement might result in serious risks of long-term behavioural, emotional, or psychological harm for the child, the court stated:]

… [T]he legislative measure by which the consent of the irresponsible casual fornicator is dispensed with is obviously fair and cannot be said to be arbitrary.

The court further noted (at 319) that because "there is little realistic possibility that the right of the casual fornicator would be accepted and exercised by him," the court ought to be cautious "before letting the protection of that right obstruct the fulfilment of an important government objective." Thus, if s. 137(1) violated the equality guarantee, it was nevertheless justified pursuant to s. 1 of the Charter.

Cases in Other Provinces

The constitutionality of BC's adoption legislation was challenged in *Re F.L.; N.M. v. Superintendent of Family and Child Services and Ministry of Human Resources*, [1987] 3 WWR 176 (BCSC). At issue was s. 8(1)(b) of the *Adoption Act*, RSBC 1979, c. 4, which required only the mother's consent if the mother and father of a prospective adoptee had never been married. In *Re F.L.*, the father of the child alleged that s. 8(1)(b) violated his Charter rights by discriminating against him and other unwed fathers on the basis of sex and marital status. The court held that s. 8(1)(b) discriminated against unmarried fathers, first, because it treated unmarried fathers differently and less preferentially than unmarried mothers, and, second, because it treated unmarried fathers less preferentially than their married counterparts. Because neither sex nor marital status are necessarily relevant considerations in the ability or willingness to parent, such distinctions were held unreasonable.

According to the court, the legitimate aim of the Act was to provide for children whose biological parents were unable or unwilling to care for them. Concerns about fathers who cannot be found to give consent were adequately addressed by a subsequent subsection permitting the court to dispense with consent in appropriate cases. Thus, the court declared the section in violation of the rights of unwed fathers and therefore of no force or effect. A number of later decisions also recognized the right to consent on the part of biological fathers who had demonstrated an interest in the child: for example, see *M.(C.G.) v. W.(C.)* (1989), 63 DLR (4th) 216 (BCCA) and *Waddell v. Halley* (1993), 48 RFL (3d) 203 (BCSC).

A few years later, in *Re T. and Children's Aid Society and Family Services of Colchester County* (1992), 91 DLR (4th) 230, the NS Supreme Court exercised its *parens patriae* jurisdiction to permit the father of a child to make an application for custody. The child had been born to a woman whom the father had briefly dated; he did not know, until after the child's birth and placement for adoption, that a child had been born and that the mother had made arrangements for and consented to the adoption of the child. The court held that the failure to give notice to the father in these circumstances was consistent with the legislative requirements and that the legislation did not constitute discrimination under s. 15 of the Charter. However, relying on its *parens patriae* jurisdiction, the court concluded that it was in the best interests of the child for the court to hear the father's application for custody.

On appeal, the NS Court of Appeal reversed this decision, concluding that there was no *parens patriae* jurisdiction in the court where the legislature had clearly decided to exclude the need for a father's consent as in this case: see (1992), 92 DLR (4th) 289.

Is there a need to review these decisions, distinguishing the rights to consent of mothers and fathers, in the light of the Supreme Court of Canada's decision in *Trociuk v. British Columbia (Attorney General)*, discussed in the previous section. Can these cases be distinguished because *Trociuk* involved the inclusion of information about the biological father on the birth registration form and the right to name a child, while these cases concern the right to consent to the adoption of a biological child? Why, or why not? Should the decision in *Trociuk* be explained in terms of more enlightened views about the importance of fathers in the lives of their children? What are the practical consequences for mothers in such cases?

2. The Consequences of Adoption

> [In adoption,] the woman who gave birth to [the child] is deemed to not have had a child and to not be the mother; a different woman is then deemed to have had the child and to be the mother. Leaving aside the issue of what exactly makes a mother ... why is the law so intent on erasing the motherhood of one of these women?
>
> Katrysha Bracco, "Patriarchy and the Law of
> Adoption: Beneath the Best Interests of the Child"
> (1997), 35 *Alberta Law Review* 1035

Access by Birth Parents

An order for adoption results in a child becoming in law the child of an adoptive parent and ceasing to be the child of a birth parent. For example, Ontario's *Child and Family Services Act*, s. 158 states that an adopted child is, as of the date of an adoption order, the child of an adoptive parent "as if the adopted child had been born to the adoptive parent." As a result, provincial legislation often terminates the birth parent's access to an adopted child, although some cases have recognized exceptions for family adoptions (where the birth parent and adoptive parents are related) and in similar situations, usually subject to the child's best interest: see *Catholic Children's Aid Society v. T.S.* (1989), 20 RFL (3d) 337; 69 OR (2d) 189 (CA); *Nouveau-Brunswick (Ministre de la Santé & des Services Communautaires) c. L.(M.),* [1998] 2 SCR 534; (1998), 165 DLR (4th) 58 (SCC); *Re S.(D.M.)* (1992), 98 Sask. R 226 (QB); and *R.(S.) v. R.(M.)* (1998), 43 RFL (4th) 116 (Ont. CA) and Annotation.

Sometimes, it seems that access may be denied even if it is in a child's best interests. In *Re British Columbia Birth Registration no. 86-09-038808* (1990), 26 RFL (3d) 203 (BCSC), the court concluded that access by a birth father to his daughter was in the child's best interests. Nonetheless, the court denied access because the child's mother and her husband (who was seeking to adopt the child) found visits by the child's father emotionally difficult. Thus the court granted the adoption and denied the biological father's continuing access to the girl, aged three-and-a-half. Although critical of the attitudes of the adoptive father and the child's mother, the court accepted that their emotions were understandable.

Issues about the best interests of the child test were also considered in a case involving a request for access by a young boy to his sister. Both had been permitted to immigrate to Canada to be adopted, but their adoptive mother later decided to raise only one child and placed the boy in foster care: see *P.(M.A.R.) v. V.(A.)* (1997), 33 RFL (4th) 124 (Ont. Ct. J (Prov. Div.)) and (1998), 40 RFL (4th) 411 (Ont. Ct. J (Gen. Div.)). Although access was eventually arranged for the siblings, the adoptive mother thwarted the boy's access efforts and he was raised on his own in a series of foster homes. His tragic circumstances some years later, when he was facing deportation, were reported in Margaret Philp, "A One-Way Ticket Out of Only Nation He Knows," *Globe and Mail*, July 15, 2003, at A1.

Records and Disclosure

Because the transfer of legal status of an adopted child, from a birth parent to an adoptive parent, has traditionally occurred in a closed hearing for which the records have been sealed, issues about adoption disclosure have frequently arisen. In *R.J.L. v. Children's Aid Society of Metropolitan Toronto*, [1976] OJ no. 138 (HCJ) (QL), the court (at paras. 9-10) characterized the competing concerns about disclosure this way:

> There can surely be no doubt but that any child, knowing he has been adopted, will be curious about his origins. ... [T]here is more than mere curiosity but a basic, if sometimes unexpressed, need for a child, who knows he has been adopted, to get in touch with his natural parents. This need becomes most apparent during early adolescence. To know who his *real parents* are gives a child a sense of identity, an assurance of belonging, and an awareness that he has not come from nowhere, but has his own place in history as the child of *known parents.* ...
>
> On the other hand, the sense of security of the child in his new home ought not to be disturbed readily. He must continue to know that this is indeed his home, that he is entitled to demand the loyalty of his *new parents* and that he is obliged to give them his loyalty in return. That sense of security, and loyalty, would be diminished if the *adopting parents* felt that a *natural parent* could interfere with the affection of the child, or their authority over him. They might feel that they were *mere custodians* of the child, with less than *ordinary*

parental rights and responsibilities. Another factor, of general public policy, which I think is almost conclusive with children's aid societies, is that prospective adopting parents would be more difficult to find if they were generally aware that natural parents might be permitted to regain contact with adopted children. [Emphasis added.]

As the emphasized words indicate, issues about adoption disclosure reflect fundamental ideas about who is a (real) parent. Moreover, generous opportunities for disclosure of adoption information generally reveal a paradigm of continued connections between birth parents and adoptees, by contrast with earlier notions of a new start for adoptees and their adoptive parents, a "rebirth, through which all ties with the biological family would be severed and an illusion created that an adoptee was born into the adoptive family": D. Marianne Brower Blair, "The Impact of Family Paradigms, Domestic Constitutions, and International Conventions on Disclosure of an Adopted Person's Identities and Heritage: A Comparative Examination" (2001), 22 *Michigan Journal of International Law* 587, at 595.

In recent years, reforms have tended to emphasize continued connections among birth parents, adoptees, and adoptive parents, even though statistics about disclosure requests suggest that some birth parents and adult adoptees may prefer not to have these connections. According to Brower Blair, for example, there were over 7,000 applications for records between November 1996 and March 2000, of which 21 percent were from birth mothers, 2 percent from birth fathers, and 77 percent from adult adoptees. In the same period, however, just over 3,000 disclosure vetoes were filed, 75 percent of which were from birth mothers, 3 percent were from birth fathers, and 23 percent were from adoptees; in addition two-thirds of about 300 no-contact declarations were filed by birth mothers: see Brower Blair, at 605. Thus, while there is evidence that some birth parents (many more mothers than fathers) and adoptees wish to obtain information and to make contact with each other, other birth parents and adoptees may not be interested in doing so; and some may be actively opposed to such contact. In this context, the legislative challenge is to determine what is the "default" position, and the extent to which contact should depend on an applicant making a positive request—or registering a positive rejection.

There are two kinds of information that may be of use to participants in the adoption process—identifying information and non-identifying information. Identifying information includes data that could permit an adopted child to identify his or her biological parents, or vice versa. By contrast, non-identifying information provides background and medical information about adopted children and biological parents; its disclosure may often be provided with the consent of the adoptive parents until the child is no longer a minor. The balancing of different interests in relation to adoption disclosure has resulted in differing arrangements across Canada with respect to the release of identifying information (with opportunities for the parties to exercise a veto power) and non-identifying information.

Many recent reform efforts concerning the release of identifying information have resulted from lobbying by birth parents and adult adoptees. For example, Marilyn Churley, a birth parent and MPP in Ontario, introduced a bill to provide access to birth and adoption records to adult adoptees and birth parents upon demand; her proposal would also establish arrangements to implement a no-contact notice and make counselling available on request: see Bill 16, *An Act To Amend the Vital Statistics Act and the Child and Family Services Act in Respect of Adoption Disclosure*, 1st reading May 5, 2003, 2d reading May 15, 2003. In other provinces, including Alberta, Manitoba, Saskatchewan, and British Columbia, as well as the Northwest Territories and Nunavut, legislation permits "release of identifying information to adult adoptees and birth parents upon request, subject to a disclosure veto or a contact veto, either of which the subject of the information can choose to file": see Brower Blair, at 627-28.

Discussion Notes

Law Reform and Adoption Policies

To what extent are the differing arrangements for consent and disclosure pursuant to provincial statutes justifiable? Are considerations about who is a parent for purposes of consent or the circumstances in which information about adoption can be disclosed matters that reflect fundamental values in different parts of Canada? Are there more advantages to uniformity or diversity in this context? According to Daly and Sobol (at 98-100), there are good arguments in favour of diversity in matters of adoption, and they thus recommended a national record-keeping protocol and a national database, but not a national system of adoption. For an overview of the underlying values, see Ralph Garber, *Disclosure of Adoption Information* (Toronto: Ministry of Community and Social Services, 1985). In two reported cases in Ontario, courts denied applications by birth mothers for identifying information in relation to their adopted children, pursuant to Ontario's statutory provisions: see *Ferguson v. Director of Child Welfare* (1984), 36 RFL (2d) 405; 44 OR (2d) 405 (Ont. CA) and *Tyler v. District Court of Ontario* (1986), 1 RFL (3d) 139 (Dist. Ct.).

In 1998, the Canadian Bar Association—Ontario made recommendations about open adoption, distinguishing the concept of access after adoption from their proposal for post-adoption contact: see Marvin Bernstein, Diane Caldwell, G. Bruce Clark, and Roselyn Zisman, "Adoption with Access or 'Open Adoption'" (1991-92), 8 *Canadian Family Law Quarterly* 283. Similarly, Daly and Sobol (at 107) recommended more openness in adoption law and practices. How do such recommendations change current definitions of families? To what extent is this a matter of choice for individuals? How should different viewpoints be taken into account in the adoption context? Are adoptive families different from families related "by blood"? In the United States, a birth mother, whose child located her many years after she had placed the child for adoption, sued the private investigator who located the birth mother, claiming invasion of privacy and mental distress: see *Toronto Star*, November 6, 1998. How should this claim be resolved?

Ideas About "Natural" Families

Although adoption has not attracted a large amount of theoretical scholarship to date, issues about legal arrangements for consent and disclosure mask significant ideologies about "natural" families and social conceptions about mothering. The fact that birth mothers in particular are prepared to relinquish their children calls into question accepted notions about the primacy of natural mother–child bonds; the adoptive mother may similarly be seen as not a "real" mother by reason of the lack of biological connection with an adopted child. As Josephine Reeves argued (at 412), "discourses that have informed the socio-legal progression of adoption through the twentieth century have, increasingly, shaped the construction of women's sexuality."

Interestingly, as Reeves also noted (at 424), current trends toward openness in adoption appear inconsistent with efforts to ensure confidentiality for sperm donors in the context of assisted reproduction: "why should an open adoption policy be so important to the welfare of the child when the child born from gamete or embryo donation is allowed no access to genetic records?" See Josephine Reeves, "The Deviant Mother and Child: The Development of Adoption as an Instrument of Social Control" (1993), 20 *Journal of Law and Society* 412. In this context, Katrysha Bracco argued that adoption practices in Canada perpetuate the nuclear family, a patriarchal family model, and asked (at 1045) "Who would be harmed by a family having more or less than two parents?" See Katrysha Bracco, "Patriarchy and the Law of Adoption: Beneath the Best Interests of the Child" (1997), 35 *Alberta Law Review* 1035. To what extent are the views of Reeves and Bracco similar? You may want to reconsider these ideas after reviewing the materials about assisted reproduction later in this chapter.

Rethinking Identity

Issues about adoption records, anonymous sperm donors, and other kinds of assisted reproduction all focus on ideas about individual and familial identity. In an assessment of legal models for disclosure of information in these cases, and in relation to "the disappeared" in Argentina, for example, Sarah Wilson defined identity as narrative rather than fixed, dynamic rather than static, and influenced by community, as well as personal values:

> In my view, a helpful way of approaching the idea of identity is as an agglomeration or tapestry of different threads of narratives which people use to represent and to reflect on their lives. Identity is tied up with the process of self-discovery and self-development through reflecting on, interpreting and reinterpreting these narratives of their different experiences.
>
> The use of the term self-development and not only self-discovery is intended to indicate that identity should not be considered in static terms, but as fluid in response to a person's (social) environment and experiences. In other words, this is not identity in the sense of constructing a "psychological whole" but rather [in the sense] of a reflection of processes of re-evaluation and reinterpretation based on new information or experiences. This notion of identity would seem similar to Giddens' description of "self-identity" as "[t]he reflective project of the self, which consists in the sustaining of coherent, yet continuously revised biographical narrative." [A. Giddens, *Modernity and Self-Identity: Self and Society in the Late Modern Age* (London: Polity Press, 1991), 5.]
>
> Further, the process of construction of identity is not only a passive but can also be a creative process. Although a person is very much influenced by her or his social environment she or he is not determined by it and retains the possibility of agency. Examples of this process are provided by the responses of people in marginalized or less well socially accepted positions to their situation. The creation of identity can be a way of coping with difference or to feeling socially prejudiced in a certain way. A strong identification with a

cultural or other group may often be expressive of resentment at past or present mistreatment of that group.

A radical distinction between individual and collective influences on identity is therefore not possible. People are very much influenced by the views of those around them. A person's identity is greatly influenced by her or his interaction and relationships with others. "The narrative of any one life is part of an interlocking set of narratives." Some of the most important interactions when one is young are generally those with the social family or community in which one was brought up. Further, the meaning say of historical events to an individual will be influenced by those views held by many in that community or society. As argued above however, this does not mean that a person's views will be determined by those around her or him.

This influence of those around us on feelings of identity may also help to explain the significance of the past to many people's feeling of identity. Part of the relationship with the people with whom one grows up often involves asking them questions about one's own or their past, or their community's past. Answering the question "who am I?" [also] seems to require some reference to "background" or family history. Important influences on a person's sense of identity that one cannot remember or never experienced may then extend from the past.

In this section therefore I have tried to articulate a notion of identity to contrast with a notion of fixed identity. "Narrative identity" sits more comfortably with ideas of social construction and aspirations to social reform. It is also more compatible with the importance of social family.

See Sarah Wilson, "Identity, Genealogy, and the Social Family: The Case of Donor Insemination" (1997), 11 *International Journal of Law, Policy, and the Family* 270, at 281-82. What consequences follow from this characterization of narrative identity in relation to adoption policies and practices?

SELECTED REFERENCES

Cindy L. Baldassi, "The Quest To Access Closed Adoption Files in Canada: A Review of Legal Resistance to Change" (2003) (unpublished).

Naomi Cahn, "Birthing Relationships" (2002), 17 *Wisconsin Women's Law Journal* 163.

Jeannie House, "The Changing Face of Adoption: The Challenge of Open and Custom Adoption" (1997), 13 *Canadian Family Law Quarterly* 333.

Heather Katarynych, "Adoption," in Nicholas Bala, Joseph Hornick, and Robin Vogl, eds., *Canadian Child Welfare Law: Children, Families, and the State* (Scarborough, ON: Thompson Educational Publishing, 1991), 133.

Paul Sachdev, *Unlocking the Adoption Files* (Lexington, MA: Lexington Books, 1989).

Elizabeth J. Samuels, "The Idea of Adoption: An Inquiry into the History of Adult Adoptee Access to Birth Records" (2001), 53 *Rutgers Law Review* 367.

Shirley K. Senoff, "Open Adoptions in Ontario and the Need for Legislative Reform" (1998), 15 *Canadian Journal of Family Law* 183.

C. Custom Adoption

For many aboriginal people, customary aboriginal adoption is preferable to statutory adoption schemes as it permits the natural parents to know where their child has been placed, and it emphasizes and recognizes the importance of maintaining the child's cultural ties.

> Judge Murray Sinclair, Donna Phillips, and Nicholas Bala, "Aboriginal Child Welfare in Canada," in Nicholas Bala, Joseph Hornick, and Robyn Vogl, eds., *Canadian Child Welfare Law: Children, Families, and the State* (Scarborough, ON: Thompson Educational Publishing, 1991), 171, at 180

Issues about custom adoption practices and their recognition reveal how some First Nations' conceptions of family relationships differ from those pursuant to statutory law. Specifically, although arrangements were often made for children to be raised by adults other than their biological parents, these traditional arrangements were not secret, and children's relationships generally continued with their biological parents. Although the term "custom adoption" is used widely, the actual arrangements vary among different First Nations groups, and their similarity to statutory adoption arrangements are not always exact. Particularly as a result of increasing interest in open adoption, however, concepts of custom adoption have been embraced in Canadian courts, and the 1984 decision in *Re Tagornak*, [1984] 1 CNLR 185; (1983), 50 AR 237 (NWTSC) confirmed recognition and protection for custom adoption under s. 35 of the Constitution.

In 1993, the BC Court of Appeal allowed an appeal in a case relating to a claim for insurance benefits by the "dependent parents" of an aboriginal man who died in an accident; the benefits were claimed by his grandparents on the basis that they qualified as "dependent parents" because of their relationship to the deceased in accordance with the traditions of custom adoption. In allowing the appeal, the BC Court of Appeal described the relationships in the family and set out the principles as follows.

Casimel v. Insurance Corp. of BC
(1993), 82 BCLR (2d) 387; 106 DLR (4th) 720 (CA)

Louise Casimel is now 79 years old and has been blind for some years. Francis Casimel is 99 years old. They have been married to each other for many years. They are members of the Stellaquo Band of the Carrier People. Until recently they maintained their family home on the Stellaquo Reserve near Burns Lake. There they raised their family, including their two daughters, Mary Casimel and Charlotte Casimel.

In 1960, Mary Casimel bore a son, Ernest Casimel. Ernest's father was unknown. Mary took no interest in her son and from the beginning he was looked after by Mary's mother and father, Louise and Francis, the present plaintiffs, with the help of Mary's sister, Charlotte. Three or four years later Mary left home to marry. She moved to Vancouver with her husband and lived there for several years. She then returned to live on the Stellaquo Reserve but not with her parents. Charlotte also married and left home. The remaining family unit then consisted of Louise, Francis and Ernest. Ernest was raised by Louise and Francis and he was treated in all respects as their own son.

He referred to them as "Mom" and "Dad," and they referred to him as their "son." Charlotte referred to Ernest as her brother and she treated him as her brother. Ernest did not maintain any significant relationship with his biological mother and rarely saw her, even after she returned to the reserve. When he did speak of her he called her "Mary."

As Ernest grew up and Louise and Francis became older, instead of Louise and Francis looking after Ernest, Ernest started looking after them. In due course he became eligible to have a house of his own on the Reserve but he never applied for one. He lived with Louise and Francis and he looked after them. In the words of the trial Judge, Mr. Justice Wong: "Ernest washed the clothes, chopped wood for heat and took Louise and Francis shopping since neither of them was able to drive. Ernest did the cooking, washed the dishes and used his money to buy groceries for the whole household. As far as Charlotte can recall, Louise, Francis and Ernest did not have bank accounts and they would simply pool their money together for household expenses. Ernest would cash their cheques and look after the household money. Ernest worked from time to time and when he was not working he received social assistance or unemployment insurance benefits."

Shortly before his death, at age 28, Ernest was elected Chief of the Stellaquo Band. After his death he was succeeded as Chief by Robert Michell who, in an affidavit, said: "The late Ernest Joseph Casimel was raised and cared for by Louise and Francis Casimel and Louise and Francis Casimel were considered by the Stellaquo Band to be his parents."

II

The plaintiffs filed a Statement of Claim seeking "no fault" death benefits under ss. 92, 93 and 94 of Part VII of the *Insurance (Motor Vehicle) Regulations* as "dependent parents" of Ernest Casimel. ...

Mr. Justice Wong dismissed the action. He decided that the customary adoption under the customs of the Stellaquo Band of the Carrier People gave rise to moral rights and obligations but not to legal rights and obligations, and that for that reason the plaintiffs were not entitled to be treated as parents under the *Insurance (Motor Vehicle) Regulations.* ...

III

In the course of his reasons Mr. Justice Wong stated the issue in this way:

At issue is whether the meaning of the words "dependent parent" in the Regulation includes a dependant customary adoption parent.

Mr. Justice Wong also described the plaintiffs as "biological grandparents and customary adoptive parents of [Ernest Casimel]."

I consider therefore that Mr. Justice Wong has found as a fact that a customary adoption in accordance with the customs of the Stellaquo Band of the Carrier People had taken place and that in accordance with those customs Ernest was treated by other band members as the son of Louise and Francis, and Louise and Francis, in turn, were treated by other band members as the parents of Ernest. Both parties to this appeal conceded that such a customary adoption had taken place. In view of Mr. Justice Wong's finding and in view of that concession, I propose to regard Ernest as having been adopted as their son by Louise and Francis in accordance with the customs of the Stellaquo Band of the Carrier People. I also propose to assume that under those customs not only were Francis and Louise regarded as the parents of Ernest, but that Mary was no longer regarded as a parent of Ernest and ceased to have any of the rights or obligations of a parent. The assumption is entirely consistent with the evidence though the precise nature of the customary adoption, which both parties agreed had occurred, was not explored in the evidence. Since the fact of the customary adoption had been agreed, there was no need to explore it.

I consider also that Mr. Justice Wong has found as a fact that Louise and Francis were dependent on Ernest within the meaning of "dependant parent," which is defined in s. 1(1) of the *Insurance (Motor Vehicle) Regulations*, in this way:

> "dependant parent" means a surviving parent of an insured who, at the date of an accident for which a claim is made, resides with the insured and receives most of his financial support from the insured. ...

V

That brings me to the decisive issue in this appeal, namely: the consequences under the general law of the province of a customary adoption brought about in the exercise of aboriginal rights.

. . .

In *Re Katie* (1961), 32 DLR (2d) 686; 38 WWR 100 (NWT Terr. Ct.) Mr. Justice Sissons decided that an Inuit customary adoption conferred the status of parent and child on the respective parties to the adoption. Mr. Justice Sissons decided that the *Northwest Territories Act*, the *Adoption Ordinance* and the *Child Welfare Ordinance* did not end customary adoptions by Inuit custom.

In *Re Beaulieu* (1969), 3 DLR (3d) 479 (NWT Terr. Ct.) Mr. Justice Morrow followed *Re Katie* and decided that a Dogrib Indian customary adoption should be recognized.

In *Re Deborah E4-789* (1972), 27 DLR (3d) 225 (NWTSC) an Inuit customary adoption was challenged by the natural parents. Mr. Justice Morrow recognized the Inuit customary adoption and the status it conferred and he rejected the challenge of the natural parents. Mr. Justice Morrow's decision was appealed to the Northwest Territories Court of Appeal. Mr. Justice Johnson, for the court, upheld Mr. Justice Morrow's decision. See (1972), 28 DLR (3d) 483 (NWTCA). At p. 488, Mr. Justice Johnson set out the legal foundation for the recognition by the common law of adoption by aboriginal custom in this way:

> Custom has always been recognized by the common law and while at an earlier date proof of the existence of a custom from time immemorial was required, Tindal CJ in *Bastard v. Smith* (1837), 2 M & Rob. 129 at 136, 174 ER 238, points out that such evidence is no longer possible or necessary and that evidence extending "... as far back

as living memory goes, of a continuous, peaceable, and uninterrupted user of the custom" is all that is now required. Such proof was offered and accepted in this case.

In *Re Wah-Shee* (1975), 57 DLR (3d) 743 and in *Re Tagornak* (1983), 50 AR 237 the Supreme Court of the Northwest Territories declared adoption by aboriginal custom to be valid, notwithstanding that in each case one of the adopting parents was Caucasian.

I conclude that there is a well-established body of authority in Canada for the proposition that the status conferred by aboriginal customary adoption will be recognized by the courts for the purposes of application of the principles of the common law and the provisions of statute law to the persons whose status is established by the customary adoption. ...

VII

In my opinion, by the customs of the Stellaquo Band of the Carrier People, Ernest Casimel became the son of Louise Casimel and Francis Casimel, and Louise and Francis Casimel became the parents of Ernest Casimel. Such a customary adoption was an integral part of the distinctive culture of the Stellaquo Band of the Carrier People (though, of course, other societies may well have shared the same custom or variations of that custom), and as such, gave rise to aboriginal status rights that became recognized, affirmed and protected by the common law and under s. 35 of the *Constitution Act, 1982*.

The status of parent, recognized by the common law and by the constitution of Canada, is sufficient to bring Louise Casimel and Francis Casimel within the definition of "dependent parent" in Part VII of the *Insurance (Motor Vehicle) Regulations* and so they are both entitled to the "no-fault" death benefits provided under ss. 92, 93 and 94 of those Regulations.

I would allow the appeal and give judgment for the plaintiffs accordingly.

Discussion Notes

Recognizing Custom Adoption

A comment about this case identified its potential significance for aboriginal self-government: "By affirming the legitimacy of one aspect of Aboriginal customary law, *Casimel* acknowledged the constitutional protection of customary rights": see Caryl Silver, "Case Comment" (1995), 3 CNLR 8. By contrast with this assessment, to what extent is it appropriate to assess the ways in which the appellate court accepted this family group because it was similar to adoptive families pursuant to provincial statutes? That is, does recognition by Canadian law of aboriginal customary adoption depend on the extent to which the customary practices are recognizable according to typical family arrangements under Canadian law? For example, would aboriginal customary practices with respect to the adoption of adults be so easily recognized? For a non-aboriginal case that refused to recognize a foreign adoption involving adults who lived as man and wife, see *Wende v. Victoria (County) Official Administrator* (1998), 37 RFL (4th) 172 (BCSC).

To what extent do aboriginal custom adoption practices offer a useful model for provincial adoption legislation, particularly in relation to open-adoption reform proposals? In reviewing a variety of custom adoption practices among the Mi'kmaq people in Nova Scotia, for example, Jeannie House reported (at 362) that practices varied from band to band, and that they revealed the "flexible, ambiguous nature" of custom adoption practices in Canada and elsewhere. Thus:

> The flexible nature of a custom adoption model is problematic for those trained in and used to the precise formulations of the formal Canadian legal framework. [Lawyers want] to know the exact definition and factors for a custom adoption. This is hard to provide in view of the changeable nature of such a model. In dealing with custom and open adoptions, guidelines rather than rules will need to be used to determine the parameters of the adoption in question.

(Jeannie House, "The Changing Face of Adoption: The Challenge of Open and Custom Adoption" (1997), 13 *Canadian Family Law Quarterly* 333, at 362.)

What kinds of guidelines might be drafted to assist in this process?

In his memoirs, Sissons J, who decided *Re Katie's Adoption* (discussed in *Casimel*) in 1961, described the problems created by the statutory requirements for adoption in the NWT. He explained that, because of these problems, when he went on circuit to the Eastern Arctic in 1965, he registered as many "custom adoptions" as possible: in Frobisher Bay (now Iqaluit), he issued more than 200 declarations: see J. Sissons, *Judge of the Far North* (Toronto: McClelland & Stewart, 1968), 142-45. A carving by Alec Banksland depicting Katie's adoption (two couples meeting to exchange a baby) is on display in the Yellowknife courthouse: see Dorothy Harley Eber, *Images of Justice: A Legal History of the Northwest Territories as Traced Through the Yellowknife Courthouse Collection of Inuit Sculpture* (Montreal and Kingston: McGill-Queen's University Press, 1997), 108. In 1994, the NWT legislature enacted the *Aboriginal Custom Adoption Recognition Act*, SNWT 1994, c. 26. For a case interpreting its application in relation to an application for child support against the biological father, see *S.K.K. v. J.S.*, [1999] NWTJ no. 94 (SC).

SELECTED REFERENCES

Bill Lomax, "Hlugwit'y, Hluuxw'y—My Family, My Child: The Survival of Customary Adoption in British Columbia" (1997), 14 *Canadian Journal of Family Law* 197.

Maev O'Collins, "The Influence of Western Adoption Laws on Customary Adoption in the Third World," in Philip Bean, ed., *Adoption: Essays in Social Policy, Law, and Sociology* (London: Tavistock Publications, 1984), 288.

Report of the Aboriginal Justice Inquiry of Manitoba: The Justice System and Aboriginal People (Manitoba: Queen's Printer, 1991).

Norman Zlotkin, "Judicial Recognition of Aboriginal Customary Law in Canada: Selected Marriage and Adoption Cases" (1984), 4 CNLR 1.

D. Adoption and Issues of Race and Culture

The study of transracial adoption is a study of values in conflict. Adoption outside racial lines is an affirmation of ideals of racial integration; conversely, it is a blow to goals of racial autonomy. The two views are apparently irreconcilable.

> Anne McGillivray, "Transracial Adoption and the Status Indian
> Child" (1985), 4 *Canadian Journal of Family Law* 437, at 450

The Context of Interracial Adoption

Issues of race and culture are reflected in adoption law and policies. As McGillivray explained (at 449-50), the decline in babies available for adoption in the 1960s and 1970s coincided with a rise in social consciousness during those decades that made transracial adoption attractive, but parental motives were mixed:

> Some wanted a white child and settled for one of "mixed or other" race. Some were emotionally caught by agency advertising of available minority-race children. Others, moved by the so-called "rescue fantasy," adopted in order to "save" an imperilled child. A significant number found in transracial adoption a means of realizing their belief in racial integration, and viewed the child's racial and cultural heritage as a valuable contribution to the family.

Statistics on transracial adoption are not easily available, but it appears that children from some racial groups fare better than others. For example, a 1993 study identified an "adoption breakdown" rate of about 10 percent for African-American and mixed-race (black-white and Asian-white) adoptions. By contrast, a study of Native Canadian adoption breakdowns in the same year reported that, by the age of 17, nearly half of these children had broken with their adoptive families; as a result, the study concluded that "native children, as members of a cultural group, should not be adopted outside their communities." A similar study in 1996 of Vietnamese, Korean, and Native Canadian adoptees found that a much smaller percentage of adoptees who were Native Canadians had developed successful attachments to their adoptive parents: see Marie Adams, *Our Son, a Stranger: Adoption Breakdown and Its Effects on Parents* (Montreal and Kingston, ON: McGill-Queen's University Press, 2002), xxiv-vii.

According to Adams, Native adoptees have a double burden: they absorb the negative stereotypes of Native Canadians within Canadian society at the same time as they are isolated from all the positive aspects of aboriginal culture and values. In the context of communities disabled by the residential school system and other policies of assimilation, moreover, Native Canadian children experience particular challenges in white society. As a brief from several native organizations to the minister of community and social services in Ontario stated in 1983:

> Even under the best of conditions, Native children do not, generally speaking, become successfully "integrated" or "acculturated" or "adjusted" within the dominant societal frame-work, as a result of being placed in non-Native settings, either family or institution. ... In simple words—it doesn't work.

(Ontario Native Women's Association et al., quoted in Adams, at 188-89.)

Although some research has suggested better integration for black children, some black adoptees have also claimed, as adults, a sense of loss and sadness, even though their white parents were full of good intentions: see Bill Taylor, "Shades of Gray," *Toronto Star*, May 18, 1995 and Ghislaine Routhier, "Black Children, White Parents" (1988), *Intercultural Horizons* 10.

In this context, legislative provisions requiring courts to assess a child's best interests in adoption cases reveal how underlying values about appropriate families and parent–child relationships must necessarily be addressed. In examining the decision of the Supreme Court of Canada that follows, consider the options available and the choices adopted at different points in the case.

A.N.R. and S.C.R. v. L.J.W.
(1983), 36 RFL (2d) 1; [1983] 2 SCR 173

WILSON J: This appeal [from 32 RFL (2d) 153; [1983] 2 CNLR 157; 19 Man. R (2d) 186 (CA)] emphasizes once more, this time in an inter-racial context, that the law no longer treats children as the property of those who gave them birth but focuses on what is in their best interests.

L.G.W. ("L.") was born at Portage la Prairie, Manitoba, on 4th September 1976 to L.W., an Indian who was at the time the wife of L.W. L.W. was not the father of the child and divorce proceedings were underway when L. was born. There are two children of the W. marriage, J., aged 9, and L., aged 8. Mrs. W. on her own admission had a serious alcohol problem and was unable to care for L. First her brother and then her sister took the infant. The older children, J. and L., stayed with their father.

On 20th October 1976, when she was six weeks old, L. was apprehended by the Children's Aid Society of Central Manitoba pursuant to the protection sections of the *Child Welfare Act, 1974* (Man.), c. 30 (also CCSM, c. C80) ("the Act"), and placed in a foster home. In February 1977 Kimelman Prov. J, with her mother's consent, made her a ward of the society for a one-year period which was subsequently extended for a further six months. On 11th February 1977 L. was placed in the foster home of S.R. (later R.) and her husband L.R. The R.s separated in the summer of 1977 and in September of that year S. started to cohabit with A.R. whom she subsequently married. L. remained in their home with the sanction of the Children's Aid Society until the wardship order expired in March 1978. Arrangements were then made by the society to return her to her mother who was living in Brandon with her other two children. The R.s co-operated fully in this transfer which took place on 4th May 1978.

Mrs. W. had made no effort to contact L. during the period of the wardship but had suggested to the society early in 1978 that her sister might adopt her. The sister apparently had reservations about this and nothing came of it. The R.s by this time had, of course, developed an attachment to the child and were concerned as to whether she was being properly cared for. They therefore took up Mrs. W.'s invitation to pay her a visit. In fact they paid two visits to see L. and on the second visit in May 1978, with Mrs. W.'s consent, took L. home with them. The evidence as to Mrs. W.'s intention to [relinquish] custody of L. to the R.s is conflicting. She says they were to have L. "just for a while" until she came for her in a couple of weeks' time. The R.s believed that she had surrendered the child to them on a permanent basis. She had confided to them that she was having difficulties with L.W. with whom she was periodically cohabiting and she appeared to be aware herself that she was in a state of emotional instability. Consistent with the R.s' understanding that they were now to have L. on a permanent basis they got in touch with the Children's Aid Society about the possibility of adopting her. Mrs. W. by this time had returned to the reserve with L.W. The society advised the R.s that it no longer had responsibility for the child and that if they wished to adopt her they should retain legal counsel. They followed this advice and on 5th October 1978 filed a notice of receiving a child for private adoption under s. 102(1) [re-enacted 1979, c. 22, s. 72] of the Act.

The R.s heard nothing from Mrs. W. until October 1978 when she arrived at their home announcing that she had left L.W. because he was abusing her, that she was on her way to Regina and wanted her sister to have L. The R.s refused to give her up. They heard no further word from Mrs. W. until January 1982 when she launched an application for habeas corpus. On 24th February 1982 the R.s applied for an order of de facto adoption.

It is apparent from the evidence that Mrs. W. from January 1978 on was attempting with varying degrees of success to rehabilitate herself. She wanted to rid herself of her alcohol problem, to free herself of her association with L.W., and to engage in a program of self-improvement. However, none of this was easy and periods of achievement when she underwent treatment for alcoholism and attended classes to upgrade her education would be followed by periods of backsliding. It took her five years and the support of friends, relatives and her extended family on the reserve to accomplish her objective. By the time she did L. was 5 or 6 years old and an established part of the R. family. They had brought her up as if she were their own. The evidence discloses that they are a very fine couple, active and respected in their community, and excellent parents. They have two other children, M., aged 4 and 2-year-old J.

L. is apparently a well-adjusted child of average intelligence, attractive and healthy, does well in school, attends Sunday School and was baptized in the church the R. family attends. She knows that S.R. is not her natural mother, and Mrs. W. is her natural mother, and that she is a native Indian. She knows that A.R. is not her natural father and that he is a Metis. This has all been explained to her by the R.s who have encouraged her to be proud of her Indian culture and heritage. None of this seems to have presented any problem for her thus far. She is now 7 years old and the expert witnesses agree that the R.s are her "psychological parents."

An unfortunate incident occurred on 3rd February 1982. When the court proceedings brought by Mrs. W. in January 1982 were adjourned for the preparation of home study reports, she decided to take things into her own hands and with the assistance of friends attempted to abduct L. first from her school and then from the R. home. Fortunately, the child was not in the home at the time. The RCMP had to be called. The R.s obtained an ex parte order granting them interim custody and enjoining Mrs. W. from further attempts at abduction. Mrs. W. moved to vary the order and was granted supervised access. On her first exercise of access she arranged for a reporter and a photographer from the Winnipeg Free Press to be present. The story was given considerable prominence in the newspaper with a photograph of Mrs. W. and L. The child was upset by the notoriety.

The R.s' application for adoption and Mrs. W.'s application for custody were heard by Krindle Co. Ct. J in a trial lasting eight days. The application for custody was dismissed and the adoption order granted. Mrs. W. appealed to the Manitoba Court of Appeal which overturned the adoption order, made L. a ward of the Court of Appeal, granted custody to the R.s and left it open to Mrs. W. to apply subsequently for access or custody. The Court of Appeal subsequently on a motion for directions referred Mrs. W.'s application for access to Huband JA. Huband JA, on being advised that an application was being made for leave to appeal to the Supreme Court of Canada, held the application for access in abeyance. This court gave the R.s leave to appeal on 17th May 1983 and ordered a stay of proceedings. L. continued to reside with the R.s and Mrs. W. has had no access since Krindle Co. Ct. J's order of adoption on 12th May 1982. Mrs. W. cross-appealed in this court on the ground that the Manitoba Court of Appeal erred in not restoring legal custody to her when they set aside the order of adoption in favour of the R.s.

The R.s' application for adoption was made under s. 103 [as amended 1982, c. 45, s. 22] of the Act, i.e., a de facto adoption based on the fact that L. had been cared for and maintained by them for a period of three consecutive years. Section 103(2) states that in the case of such an adoption the consent of the parents or guardian is not required. Krindle Co. Ct. J found that the R.s had cared for and maintained L. for the required three-year period and indeed had rescued her as an infant from an intolerable situation, given her an excellent home, been devoted parents, were fully sensitive to the special problems of raising a native Indian child in a predominantly white environment and were coping with those problems in mature and responsible fashion. She concluded that the R.s were well able to cope with any identity crisis L. might face as a teenager. Moreover, as a Metis A.R. was no stranger to the hurt racial prejudice could inflict on a sensitive soul and, in the view of the learned trial judge, was a model for L. of how to survive as a member of a much maligned minority. As to Mrs. W., Krindle Co. Ct. J expressed respect and admiration for her courage and determination and the degree of success she had achieved in rehabilitating herself. At the same time, however, she expressed some concern as to whether she was going to be able to maintain her progress. She saw danger signals in "the venom of her anti-white feelings" and wondered what effect "her visible hatred for all things white" would have on her child. She also wondered whether Mrs. W.'s concern was for the child as a person or as a political issue. The media incident, in Krindle Co. Ct. J's view, manifested an incredible indifference to the effect such an incident might have on her child. It made L., a very private little girl, into a "cause célèbre" in her school and community. Krindle Co. Ct. J concluded that it was in the child's best interests that she remain with the R.s.

In addition to finding that it was in L.'s best interests to remain with the R.s, Krindle Co. Ct. J also made a finding that Mrs. W. had abandoned L. between October 1978 and January 1982. She made this finding because of her concern as to whether s. 103(2) had the effect of dispensing with parental rights in the case of a de facto adoption. If it did have that effect, then the sole issue was the best interests of the child. However, if it did not, then under the common law a natural mother could lose custody of her child to a stranger in blood only by abandoning it or so misconducting herself that in the opinion of the court it would be improper to leave the child with her: See *Martin v. Duffell*, [1950] SCR 737, 4 DLR 1; *Hepton v. Maat*, [1957] SCR 606, 10 DLR (2d) 1; *McNeilly v. Agar*, [1958] SCR 52, 11 DLR (2d) 721.

Having made her findings as to abandonment and the child's best interests, Krindle Co. Ct. J made the adoption order in favour of the R.s and dismissed Mrs. W.'s application for custody.

As already mentioned, the Court of Appeal overturned the adoption order. Each of the panel of three judges gave separate reasons. Hall JA would have affirmed the adoption order but, because his two colleagues were for overturning it, he yielded to the majority and then went on to align himself with the alternate course advanced by O'Sullivan JA rather than that advanced by Matas JA.

O'Sullivan JA decided that the best course to follow was to make L. a ward of the court with custody in the R.s, leaving it open to Mrs. W. at some future time to apply for access. Matas JA, on the other hand, did not think making the child a ward of the court was a workable alternative. He favoured a new trial as to custody (as opposed to adoption) with interim custody in the R.s in the meantime and such access to Mrs. W. as might be agreed upon or as might be ordered by the court.

On what grounds then did the Court of Appeal upset the judgment of the learned trial judge? Hall JA identified the basis on which in his view it should have been affirmed. He pointed out that the trial judge had the tremendous advantage of seeing and hearing the parties and their witnesses and that she had accepted the evidence of some experts in preference to that of others. She had the benefit also of home study reports and reflected in her reasons the concern expressed in them about the consequences of moving the child from the only permanent home she had ever known and separating her from the de facto parents to whom she was now psychologically bonded. He referred to the strong statement made by the trial judge after a review of the whole of the evidence [32 RFL (2d), at 157]:

> I have absolutely no doubt whatsoever that the circumstances of this case demand the granting of an order of adoption of L. to the R.s.

He found that the findings and conclusions reached by the trial judge were fully supported by the evidence. He pointed out that the trial judge was well aware of the importance of L.'s cultural background and heritage and the potential difficulties involved in an inter-racial adoption. She gave particular attention to the evidence of the expert who suggested that L. could face a major identity crisis in her teenage years as a result of being reared in a predominantly white environment. She concluded that the R.s would be well able to deal with such a crisis if it arose.

Matas and O'Sullivan JJA had certain concerns in common about the judgment of the learned trial judge. ...

[Wilson J reviewed these issues and concluded.]

It is apparent that Matas and O'Sullivan JJA put an entirely different interpretation on the evidence from that put upon it by the learned trial judge and I agree with the appellant that it is not the function of an appellate court to re-interpret the evidence. …

Accordingly, even if a finding of abandonment was a prerequisite for an adoption order under s. 103, I am of the view that the evidence was there to support Krindle Co. Ct. J's finding.

Nor do I accept the submission of counsel that the trial judge was precluded from finding abandonment by Mrs. W. on the basis of some kind of estoppel operating against the R.s. The R.s' refusal to return the child to Mrs. W. in October 1978 when she suddenly appeared at their home at a late hour in the evening and intimated that she had left L.W., was moving to Regina and wanted to pass L. on to her sister was in my view a perfectly responsible act on the part of the R.s. I do not think they were, as Matas JA suggests, setting themselves up as a court to decide the ultimate fate of the child. They had had the care of L. since she was an infant except for a brief period in May 1978 following the expiry of the wardship order and had become very attached to her. I believe their conduct was prompted by concern for the child. No doubt they were of the view that if Mrs. W.'s intention in taking L. from them was to pass her on to her sister rather than to look after her herself, she might well be better off with them—at least until a proper authority had looked into the kind of home she would have with the sister. It must be recalled that the R.s thought that Mrs. W. had given L. permanently into their care in May and were planning to adopt her. They had heard nothing from her from May until her sudden appearance in October and, indeed, heard nothing further from her until the writ of habeas corpus in January 1982. With all due respect to the majority of the Court of Appeal, I think it is quite inappropriate to characterize the conduct of the R.s as some kind of illegal assertion of title! We are dealing with a child who had been brought up in their home after being apprehended by the Children's Aid Society. It was for the court to decide whether the R.s' conduct in refusing to give up L. in October 1978 was reasonable in the circumstances and whether it really prevented Mrs. W. from pursuing her legal right to custody. The trial judge obviously concluded that it did not. She could have proceeded immediately with her habeas corpus application and not waited three years to do so. Matas JA, in holding the R.s estopped from alleging abandonment by their refusal to give up the child in October 1978, states [at 178-79]:

> In my view, Mr. and Mrs. R. cannot now rely on a claim that Mrs. W. abandoned her child when they deliberately refused to return the child to Mrs. W. in 1978 and embarked on a three-year waiting period to simplify the legal procedures to be followed in adopting L. And it is impossible for us to say now what may have been the result if an application for adoption had been made properly in 1978. At least the court would not have been faced with the argument of the particularly long lapse of time.

With respect, I see nothing "improper" about the R.s proceeding by way of de facto adoption. The statute contemplates it. Moreover, in my view the crucial question is not what a court would have done with an adoption application made in 1978 but what it would have done with a habeas corpus application. Mrs. W. might have succeeded on such an application in 1978 had she proceeded with it. Her failure to do so permitted her child to develop a dependency on the R.s as her psychological parents. It seems to me that Mrs. W. had a responsibility when her rights were challenged to pursue them in the court if necessary and not to wait until her child was bonded to the R.s with all the problems for the child that the disruption of that bond was likely to create.

I frankly cannot see this as a situation for the application of the doctrine of estoppel. I believe there was evidence before the learned trial judge on which she could make her finding of abandonment between October 1978 and January 1982 although I feel impelled to say that I myself would probably not have made that finding. I believe that the significance of a person's conduct must be assessed in the context of that person's circumstances. Acts performed by one may constitute abandonment when the same acts performed by another may not. I think I would have been disposed to take a more charitable view of Mrs. W.'s failure to contact her child given her circumstances than that taken by the learned trial judge.

Be that as it may, I do not think a finding of abandonment was necessary to the trial judge's decision. I think the statute is clear and that s. 103(2) dispenses with parental consent in the case of a de facto adoption. This does not mean, of course, that the child's tie with its natural parent is irrelevant in the making of an order under the section. It is obviously very relevant in a determination as to what is in the child's best interests. But it is the parental tie as a meaningful and positive force in the life of the child and not in the life of the parent that the court has to be concerned about. As has been emphasized many times in custody cases, a child is not a chattel in which its parents have a proprietary interest; it is a human being to whom they owe serious obligations. In giving the court power to dispense with the consent of the parent on a de facto adoption the legislature has recognized an aspect of the human condition— that our own self interest sometimes clouds our perception of what is best for those for whom we are responsible. It takes a very high degree of selflessness and maturity, for most of us probably an unattainable degree, for a parent to acknowledge that it might be better for his or her child to be brought up by someone else. The legislature in its wisdom has protected the child against this human frailty in a case where others have stepped into the breach and provided a happy and secure home for the child for a minimum period of three consecutive years. In effect, these persons have assumed the obligations of the natural parents and taken their place. The natural parents' consent in these circumstances is no longer required. ...

I turn now to the crucial issue on the appeal. Did the learned trial judge err in holding that L.'s best interests lay with the R.s? The majority of the Court of Appeal thought she did. They appear to share a concern about the finality of an adoption order in terms of cutting L. off both from her natural mother and from her Indian heritage and culture. Matas JA said [at 179-80]:

> As part of his submission, counsel for Mrs. W. argued that a transracial adoption results in the loss of contact by the child with his heritage and culture and that this would not be in the best interests of the child. I would reject this argument if counsel meant that no transracial adoption order should ever be granted by the courts in this province. The legislation is not restrictive. In an appropriate case, the court may grant a transracial order of adoption. However, I agree that a child's culture and heritage should be considered by the court as one of the factors to be weighed as part of the circumstances

envisaged by s. 89 of the Act. Depending on the circumstances, it is a factor which, could have greater or lesser influence in the court's final decision. In the case at bar, the evidence supports the view that the factor is an important one.

Hall JA did not underestimate the importance of the fact that the child was an Indian. However, he adopted the conclusion the trial judge drew from the expert evidence before her as to the R.s' sensitivity to the inter-racial aspect and their appreciation of the need to encourage and develop in L. a sense of her own worth and dignity and the worth and dignity of her people. The trial judge found that they had amply displayed their ability to guide L. through any identity crisis she might face in her teenage years. Hall JA also accepted the trial judge's finding based on the psychiatric evidence that to risk the removal of L. from the R.s' home at this stage could cause her permanent psychological damage. This was the only home she had ever known and she was securely bonded to the R.s. Hall JA concluded that, important a factor as her Indian heritage and culture might be, the duration and strength of her attachment to the R.s was more important.

The majority of the Court of Appeal obviously saw in their alternate courses a means of keeping the door open for access to the natural mother. If the child were a ward of the court the court could grant her access while maintaining custody in the R.s if this seemed appropriate. Similarly, if a new trial were ordered as to custody, access rights could be claimed in those proceedings. The majority were loath to close the door on access by the finality of an adoption order. With respect, I think this overlooks something—something adverted to by Hall JA when he said [at 156]:

> In my opinion, it is quite unlikely that a solution to the problem will be found in either of the ways proposed by my colleagues. Rather, my forecast is lengthy, bitter and costly litigation which in itself would not serve the best interests of L. A difficult choice has to be made. Either the order of adoption should stand or she should be returned to Mrs. W. The record is as complete as it is ever likely to be.

I agree with Hall JA that this child should not be allowed to become a battleground, in the courts or in the media, and I believe that there is a very real risk of this if the court refuses to "bite the bullet." In my view, when the test to be met is the best interests of the child, the significance of cultural background and heritage as opposed to bonding abates over time. The closer the bond that develops with the prospective adoptive parents the less important the racial element becomes. As the witness, Dr. McCrae, expressed it [at 159-60]:

> I think this whole business of racial and Indian and whatever you want to call it all has to do with a parameter of time and if we had gone back to day one and L.W. is now being relinquished by her mother in terms of priorities at that time, we would have said—supported a hundred times over "let's place the child with its cultural background." That would be a very—would have been very reasonable. But if that is not done and time goes by, that priority drops down. The priority is no longer there, the priority of ethnic and cultural background. That drops and now must go way down because now it's the mother–child relationship. It doesn't matter if S.R. was Indian and the child was white and L.W. was white. This same argument would hold. It has nothing

to do with race, absolutely nothing to do with culture, it has nothing to do with ethnic background. It's two women and a little girl, and one of them doesn't know her. It's as simple as that; all the rest of it is extra and of no consequence, except to the people involved, of course.

I think the learned trial judge recognized that reality, considered all the factors which were relevant to the determination of what was in the child's best interests including the fact that she was of Indian parentage, and weighed them in the balance. I cannot find that she erred in carrying out this rather difficult process.

Much was made in this case of the inter-racial aspect of the adoption. I believe that inter-racial adoption, like inter-racial marriage, is now an accepted phenomenon in our pluralist society. The implications of it may have been overly dramatized by the respondent in this case. The real issue is the cutting of the child's legal tie with her natural mother. This is always a serious step and clearly one which ought not to be taken lightly. However, adoption, given that the adoptive home is the right one and the trial judge has so found in this case, gives the child secure status as the child of two loving parents. While the court can feel great compassion for the respondent, and respect for her determined efforts to overcome her adversities, it has an obligation to ensure that any order it makes will promote the best interests of her child. This and this alone is our task.

I would allow the appeal and reinstate the order of adoption made by the trial judge. I would dismiss the cross-appeal. I would make no order as to costs.

Appeal allowed; adoption order reinstated.

Identify the differing perspectives of Mrs. W. and the R.s in relation to the facts in this case. Is it possible to argue that Mrs. W. thought that she was arranging a custom adoption for her child? Why, or why not? By the time that the case reached the Supreme Court of Canada, was there anything that Mrs. W. could have done to obtain a different outcome in this case? Is a child's bonding with adoptive parents always more important than other considerations—that is, is a degree of bonding always "in a child's best interest"?

Discussion Notes

H. v. M., [1999] 1 SCR 328

In a subsequent case, *H. v. M.*, an American couple adopted two Native Canadian girls as children and raised them to adulthood. One of the girls had a child; apparently, the father was African-American, but he did not acknowledge paternity and made no claim to the child. Shortly after her son's birth, the mother discovered her biological parents in Vancouver. She went to visit her father, leaving her son in the care of her adoptive parents for eight months. After returning for a visit with her adoptive parents, she secretly travelled back to Vancouver, taking her son with her, and moved into the home occupied by her biological father and other members of his family. The family was poor and in receipt of social assistance. The child lived in this home for about two years.

After discovering the mother's whereabouts, the adoptive parents initiated action to obtain custody of the child. Although the child's mother did not wish to assert custody, she supported a claim launched by her biological father, who was awarded interim custody. At the trial, however, the adoptive parents were awarded custody with reasonable access to the child's mother. The BC Court of Appeal reversed this decision and granted custody to the mother's biological father, expressly acknowledging the legislative trend to keep aboriginal children in aboriginal families. By the time that the case reached the Supreme Court of Canada, the child was nearly four years old and he had moved with his aboriginal grandfather to the grandfather's reserve north of Manitoba. The Supreme Court of Canada allowed the appeal on the basis that there was no error in the decision of the trial judge. Consider what factors were relevant to the Supreme Court's decision to award custody to the adoptive parents in this case: how should factors such as race and bonding be interpreted here? Does this case affect the legal principles set out in *A.N.R. and S.C.R. v. L.J.W.*? In a recent Ontario case, the court held that Native children do not have an absolute right to be placed with Native families: see Joseph Brean, "Native Upbringing Not a Right, Judge Rules," *National Post*, May 1, 2004 and *Algonquins of Pikwokanagon First Nation v. Children's Aid Society of Toronto*, [2004] OJ no. 174 (Sup. Ct. J) (QL).

The Role of First Nations Communities in Adoption Proceedings

In *H. v. M.*, the biological father requested a rehearing to permit his First Nation to make arguments, but the Supreme Court dismissed his application on the ground that his counsel had already made arguments in support of the views of his First Nation: [1999] 1 SCR 761. In a number of other cases, aboriginal bands have participated in decisions about custody and adoption of aboriginal children: for example, see *S.(S.M.) v. A.(J.)* (1992), 89 DLR (4th) 204; 38 RFL (3d) 113 (BCCA) and *Sturgeon First Nations v. Alberta* (1999), 47 RFL (4th) 199 (Alta. CA). In the United States, the *Indian Child Welfare Act*, 25 USCS 1911(c), 1912(a) (1994) applies to state court proceedings and operates to prevent Indian children from being placed with non-Indian parents without possible tribal intervention to protect the child's cultural roots: see Keri B. Lazarus, "Adoption of Native American and First Nations Children: Are the United States and Canada Recognizing the Best Interests of the Children?" (1997), 14:1 *Arizona Journal of International and Comparative Law* 255.

In *C.(J.M.N.) v. Winnipeg Child and Family Services* (1998), 33 RFL (4th) 175; Man. R (2d) 81 (QB), the applicants were non-Native foster parents of a 5-year-old Native child for whom they sought guardianship; the child had been in their care for 22 months at the time of the trial. Although the child's biological parents were not involved in the trial, the Awasis Agency of Northern Manitoba intervened in the matter and sought that the child be transferred to their care by the Winnipeg CAS. The court ruled that it was in the best interests of the child to grant the applicants' request for guardianship of the child.

In response to the intervenor's arguments that cultural heritage is more important for aboriginal children than constancy, the court noted that the child had not lived in a culturally appropriate residence for half of his life. The court also noted that the female applicant had the best guardianship qualifications it had ever encountered and was better qualified than the social worker in the case—she had specialized in early childhood education, qualified as a professional caregiver, and had done postgraduate work on emotional and mental health of children. The court also noted that the applicants were deeply committed to the child and his future, and that the experts who placed greater importance on culture and linguistic heritage than attachment and bonding had never observed or interviewed the child or the applicant parents. How would you characterize the respective values of bonding and race in this case?

Re British Columbia Birth Registration no. 030279 and Asian Heritage

Race and culture have also been considered with respect to adoption applications involving Asian-Canadian children. In *Re British Columbia Birth Registration no. 030279* (1990), 24 RFL (3d) 437 (BCSC), the application by a birth mother to revoke her consent to the adoption of her child was refused. At the time of her application, she was 29 years old and a Korean-born business woman. She had become pregnant during her engagement to a Korean diplomat, but the marriage was eventually called off. According to the court, the mother found herself in "an impossible position" because in the Korean culture, it was a matter of great shame to be pregnant without being married. At the same time, she did not want to have an abortion and could not imagine raising the child on her own. She had little or no support from close members of her family; indeed, some of her family were estranged from her because of the shame and disgrace that she had brought to their family as a result of her pregnancy.

Although ambivalent about doing so, the mother eventually decided that the child would be better off in a two-parent family and signed the papers for the child to be adopted. She acknowledged that she had signed the consent forms voluntarily and with full knowledge of the contents. She signed the papers about two months after the child's birth, concerned about her ability to care for the child properly in the light of her need to work long hours in the family grocery store. The child was placed for adoption, but, about four months later, the mother decided that she had made a mistake and wanted to revoke her consent. The court considered her request to revoke her consent on the basis that both the mother and the adoptive parents were well qualified to care for the child.

The court decided to deny the mother's application, having regard to the best interests of the child, and stating that the scales were weighted in favour of the adoptive parents, totally apart from the burden of proof:

> In my view, the stability of the adoptive family, both in terms of their immediate family, and in terms of the family-oriented neighbourhood where they have lived for many years, is an important factor which weighs in the best interests of the child. The natural mother has stated that she wishes to move to another neighbourhood should this decision be in her favour, and, although I have no doubt that she would choose a proper home for the child, she is not in a settled arrangement at the present time. Although she has the ability to call upon her sister for support, she will have to set up a network of other supportive relationships in her new location. Again, that is not an insurmountable task, but it is a factor to consider.
>
> It is also a matter of some concern to me that both the natural mother and her sister allowed their pride to stand in the way of working out their problems in the past. Although I am satisfied that the natural mother has learned the folly of placing pride before more

important concerns, it was not clear to me that her sister is flexible enough to offer her assistance unconditionally in the future. The natural mother would unquestionably need unconditional support in order to cope with the stresses of single parenthood.

Another factor to consider is that the natural mother is embarking on a new job within the next month or so which will also place demands on her at precisely the time she would be attempting to settle into a relationship with her child. That job will involve her travelling to Los Angeles for a week in March 1990, and will also involve her travelling to Korea at least once a year, and to locations in the United States from time to time, depending on how well the business does. In other words, there are other changes taking place in the life of the natural mother at the present time, aside from the prospect of having to cope with motherhood for the first time.

Of all of the factors which I have mentioned which weigh in favour of leaving the child with the adoptive parents, the most compelling is the fact that the child is safe, secure, happy and healthy in his present environment. He does not know the grief which his mother has suffered, for he has not suffered at all. Nor is there any evidence to suggest that he will suffer as a result of his adoptive status in the future. The adoptive parents impressed me as being well able to deal with any uncertainties which may arise in the future when the child comes to the realization that he is adopted.

The question of how the factor of blood ties should be weighed in the balance in this case was present in my mind throughout the trial. I have given it serious consideration, bearing in mind the fact that some of the benefits that flow to a child from blood ties are intangible, and not readily put into words. Having struggled with the issue, I am drawn to the conclusion that the factor of the blood tie in this case, even when combined with the other factors favouring the natural mother, does not satisfy me that the consent of the natural mother to adoption should be set aside. The best interests of the child dictate otherwise.

In closing, I know that there are no words which I can say that will relieve the anguish which the natural mother will experience as a result of this decision. I trust that others will do their best to give her solace.

What factors were significant in the court's decision to deny the application to withdraw consent to the adoption? How would you characterize the relevance of race and bonding in this case?

In *C.(D.H.) v. S.(R.)* (1990), 26 RFL (3d) 301; 106 AR 196 (QB), an Alberta court considered an application for adoption of a two-year-old child who was one-quarter Japanese. The natural parents had consented to adoption but the grandmother requested guardianship of the child. The expert evidence provided in the case was in conflict as to the effect of changing the primary caregivers, the importance of raising a child in the ethnic background of the natural parents, and the merits of inter-familial and extra-familial child rearing. The court granted the adoption on the basis of the best interests of the child because of the risk of stress and development impairment of a removal from the adoptive home in Alberta to the grandmother in California. Do you agree that this decision was "in the best interests of the child"? Why, or why not?

International Adoptions

To what extent do interracial adoption cases reveal underlying values about how families should "look"? Are these cases that reinforce or challenge critiques about ideas of families and parenthood? How important are societal values and perspectives to the "success" of non-traditional family arrangements? Are these decisions consistent with current ideas and practices in relation to international adoption? For example, statistics suggest that Canadians have adopted between 1,800 and 2,200 children from other countries in each year between 1995 and 2002, with the highest numbers of adoptions in recent years from China: see Adoption Council of Canada, "International Adoptions Steady: 1,891 in 2002" (Ottawa, May 6, 2003), online at www.adoption.ca/news/030506stats02.htm.

The same report acknowledged that although 20,000 Canadian children remain in care, only about 2,000 are placed annually, so that the numbers of international and domestic adoptions remain similar. According to another report, Canadians have adopted 7,000 Chinese children in the past 13 years; although there are positive perceptions about these adoptions, research is not yet fully available: see Sue Ferguson, "A New Community Comes of Age," *Maclean's*, February 24, 2003, at 47. According to other reports, the average cost of international adoptions is about $20,000, including fees payable to a licensed international adoption agency, a social work study, travel, hotel, fees to foreign governments, and immigration papers in Canada; these figures were cited in relation to a request to abolish provincial fees for international adoptions of $925 per child: see "Scrap Adoption Tax, Ontario Urged," *Toronto Star*, April 1, 2000, at A6. For lawyers, there may be special issues about fees for international adoptions: see *Re K.*, [1998] AJ no. 1373 (QB) (QL).

In the context of declining rates of birth in the western nations of the world, international adoption practices also raise issues about economic and political power more generally. Gillian Pascall has referred to these issues with respect to the ways in which political economy and feminist analysis have characterized these problems:

> For "underdeveloped" countries it is the relationship to the western capitalist world which produces the drain on resources and the inability to support children. The children themselves then become an export. While this explains the patterns of adoption on an international scale it also has relevance within countries. "For it is only the developed countries that have this century been able to care for their own children—and then only for the children of the groups that form part of the capitalist world, not for the children of the satellite groups within the developed countries." ... The "solution" of adoption works well for those children who find new homes, but the impoverishment and family dislocation produced in this way makes a different story for countless other children.

See Gillian Pascall, "Adoption: Perspectives in Social Policy," in Philip Bean, ed., *Adoption: Essays in Social Policy, Law, and Sociology* (London: Tavistock, 1984), 19, at 19-20, citing M.K. Benet, *The Character of Adoption* (London: Jonathan Cape, 1976). For other issues concerning international adoption, see William Duncan, "Regulating Intercountry Adoption—An International Perspective," in Andrew Bainham and David Pearl, eds., *Frontiers of Family Law* (London: Chancery Law Publishing, 1993), 46 and

International Convention on Protection of Children and Co-operation in Respect of Intercountry Adoption (May 29, 1993), 32 ILM 1134.

SELECTED REFERENCES

Vaughan Black, "GATT for Kids: New Rules for Intercountry Adoption of Children" (1994), 11 *Canadian Family Law Quarterly* 253.

Jennifer Craven-Griffiths, "Race and Substitute Families" (1990), 134:12 *Solicitors Journal* 326.

Verlyn F. Francis, "In the Application of the 'Best Interests of the Child' Test in Adoption, There Must Be a Place for the Consideration of Race" (Ottawa: National Association of Women and the Law, 1994).

Suzanne Hoelgaard, "Cultural Determinants of Adoption Policy: A Columbian Case Study" (1998), 12 *International Journal of Law, Policy, and the Family* 202.

Angela T. McCormick, "Transracial Adoption: A Critical View of the Courts' Present Standards" (1989-90), 28 *Journal of Family Law* 303.

Tshepo L. Mosikatsana, "Sawan v. Tearoe" (1994), 11 *Canadian Family Law Quarterly* 89.

Twila L. Perry, "Race and Child Placement: The Best-Interests Test and the Cost of Discretion" (1990-91), 29 *Journal of Family Law* 51.

L. Schwartz, "Religious Matching for Adoption: Unravelling the Interests Behind the 'Best Interests' Standard" (1991), 25 *Family Law Quarterly* 183.

E. Adoption and Gay and Lesbian Parents

The most striking feature of the research on lesbian mothers, gay fathers, and their children is the absence of pathological findings. The second most striking feature is how similar the groups of gay and lesbian parents and their children are to the heterosexual parents and their children.

> Jeffrey Loomis, "An Alternative Placement for Children in Adoption Law: Allowing Homosexuals the Right To Adopt" (1992), 18 *Ohio Northern University Law Review* 631, at 663

Issues about the eligibility of gays and lesbians to adopt children similarly reveal fundamental ideas about the nature of families and parents. Although these issues have been litigated infrequently, a number of reported decisions have recognized that lesbians and gays are excellent parents. In Ontario, this issue was addressed in the context of an application by the "spousal" partners of four lesbian mothers who wished to become the adoptive parents of their partners' children. Although the *Child and Family Services Act*, RSO 1990, c. C.11, s. 146 permitted a spouse of the child's parent to apply for an adoption order, the definition of "spouse" (pursuant to the *Human Rights Code*, RSO 1990, c. H.19, in accordance with s. 136) was limited to opposite-sex cohabitees. The claimants successfully challenged the definition in s. 136 and its heterosexual limitation.

Re K.
(1995), 15 RFL (4th) 129; 125 DLR (4th) 653 (Ont. Ct. J (Prov. Div.))

NEVINS PROV. J: Four homosexual couples have presented a series of seven joint applications for adoption to this court. Three of these lesbian couples each wish to apply for adoption of two children, the fourth couple seeks to apply to adopt one child. In each case, one of the partners is the birth mother of the children. Since the adoption legislation only permits joint applications by spouses and defines spouses as persons of the opposite sex, the constitutional validity of this legislation has been challenged.

Because the preliminary constitutional question raised by each of these applications is identical, the cases were brought on to be heard at the same time to resolve this issue, with the arguments and evidence presented to be applied to all the cases. Once this threshold issue is resolved, the applications will then be considered individually on their merits. ...

I. The Issue

Part VII of the Act permits the presentation of an application for adoption of a child either by one individual, or jointly, by two individuals who are "spouses" of one another. The Act also provides that, upon the making of an adoption order, the biological or "birth parent" "ceases to be the parent of the adopted child." An exception to this rule terminating birth parent rights is provided for those situations in which the birth parent is the "spouse" of the adoptive parent. In those instances, the birth parent still retains his or her parental rights to the child if an adoption order is granted in favour of the birth parent's spouse.

The definition of "spouse" in subs. 136(1) of the Act incorporates the definition of "spouse" as found in the *Human Rights Code*, and provides that "spouses," whether married or unmarried, are persons of the opposite sex. And so, by operation of that definition and other provisions in Pt. VII, the Act as it stands now does not permit the presentation of a joint application for adoption by the couples in these cases, since they are of the same sex, nor does it permit the presentation of an individual application by the partner of the mother of the child, if the mother wishes to retain her parental rights to the child after the adoption.

The preliminary issue raised is whether this definition of "spouse" is constitutionally valid, in that it is alleged to be a denial of the equality rights protected in subs. 15(1) of the Charter. More precisely, at issue in these cases is whether these homosexual couples, living in a conjugal or "marriage-like" relationship, should be allowed the right to apply jointly for the adoption of these children, so that the question of whether the requested adoptions would be in the best interests of the particular children could be determined, on the merits of each case, by a court.

From the outset, it is important to appreciate that the issue in these cases is not whether homosexual persons in general may apply to adopt children. At present, there is no legal prohibition either in the Act or any other statute against a lesbian or gay person from applying to adopt a child and obtaining an adoption order if it is seen to be in the best interest of the child. In fact, since 1984, except for some precautionary provisions regarding applicants under the age of eighteen, any person who is over the age of sixteen has the right to apply for the adoption of a child, with no restrictions as to sex or sexual orientation.

Rather, the question is whether there is a constitutionally valid reason why an application for adoption by a homosexual couple, living in a conjugal relationship, one of whom is the biological mother of the child, should not be accepted by the court and decided on the basis of what is in the best interests of the child.

2. The Adjudicative Facts

All of the applicants are lesbian couples who have been living together in committed relationships for varying lengths of time. From the evidence that I have before me, I have no hesitation in finding as a fact that, in all respects, these relationships might be termed "conjugal," in that they have all the characteristics of a relationship formalized by marriage. Each of the couples have cohabited together continuously and exclusively for lengthy periods, ranging from six to thirteen years; their financial affairs are interconnected; they share household expenses, have joint bank accounts and in some cases, they own property together in joint tenancy; they share the housekeeping burdens to the extent that they are able in light of their respective careers and employments; the individual partners share a committed sexual relationship. Most importantly, they all share equally the joys and burdens of child rearing.

All of the children who are the subject of these applications were conceived through artificial insemination and were born during the currency of the respective existing relationships to one of the partners. In all cases, the decision to have children was a joint decision of the respective couples, and since the birth of the children, who range in age from approximately one year to ten years, all of the couples have shared in, and committed themselves equally to, the care of the children. Although the extended families of all the couples are supportive of their relationships and their roles as parents, all of the children involved have known only the respective applicants as their parents for their entire lives. All of the couples, in my opinion, clearly fall within the definition of "parent," both in Pts. III and VII of the Act and subs. 1(1) of the *Family Law Act*, RSO 1990, c. F.3. In this respect, although it is certainly not an issue before me but is a relevant consideration, I am equally of the opinion that each of these applicants would be prima facie liable to contribute financially to the support of the respective children under the *Family Law Act*, they being persons who, to use the wording of subs. 1(1) of that Act, have clearly "demonstrated a settled intention to treat the children involved as children of her family." In one case, the couple have obtained an order for joint custody.

From these facts, therefore, these relationships appear to exhibit all the indicia of a "spousal" relationship except that the couples are of the same sex, and it is this circumstance that brings a constitutional consideration of the cases before the court. ...

[The court then considered the legislative context of the *Child and Family Services Act* and the *Human Rights Code* and continued.]

4. Acceptable Standard of Child Care

An essential prerequisite to the resolution of the equality issue before me is an appreciation of the level of child care that·our society, through its laws, demands of parents. To this end, I believe it is appropriate to examine the *Child and Family Services Act* further and to consider the standard of child care concept that is imposed by the law and the courts in child protection cases under Pt. III of that Act.

Generally, Pt. III of the Act establishes the acceptable standard for the level of care that children receive at the hands of their parents. The presumption in the statute and the case law is that the preferable environment for the child in which to be raised is a stable, caring home, with natural parents, free to raise their children in a manner that they see fit. It is only when the level of care provided the children in that home falls below that which is seen to be acceptable by the community that the children are seen to be "in need of protection" and the state is authorized, and in fact compelled, to intervene in the best interests of the children.

In these "protection" cases, the law is clear that the state should not, and has no authority to, require of all parents that they provide the best possible care for their children, failing which the state will encroach upon the autonomy of the family unit. Our society does not demand perfection of parents, nor does it demand that parents produce assembly-line children, all reaching their full potential, free of any imperfections or defects. The expectation, rather, is that parents provide an adequate level of care for their children. And so long as the parents are providing such care, then the family and the parent–child relationship should remain inviolable, free from state intervention or intrusion. It is only when the care given to children is at a level that is seen to be unacceptable by community standards that the state, fastidiously monitored by the courts, is permitted to intervene.

Because of this philosophy, the Act sets out in subs. 37(2) certain categories of child care that are in and of themselves deemed to be inadequate, unacceptable by our community standards and that, if proven to exist, justify the ultimate violation of civil rights, involuntary intervention by the state in the family.

I have adopted and modified the same general approach to the parenting ability issue in the present cases. What does the available research reveal as to the ability of homosexual people to parent children in a manner that is considered "adequate" or acceptable by community standards? What evidence is there to indicate that children raised in a family structure in which both parents are homosexual persons, and particularly lesbian couples, exhibit symptoms or indicia of inadequate care significantly more often than one would see in the general population? Is there evidence that the fact of being raised and cared for by homosexual parents would likely lead to physical, emotional, sexual, psychological or social problems in children to a significantly greater degree or frequency than is present in children in the general population, raised by heterosexual parents? The answer to these questions is, in my opinion, fundamental to the resolution of the issues raised in these cases, for if the evidence does indicate the fact of having homosexual parents is likely, on a balance of probabilities, to produce any combination of the symptoms described above to a significantly greater degree or frequency than one would normally expect to see in the general population of children raised in "traditional" family structures, then the homosexuality of the parents might be seen, in and of itself, to be a level of care below that which is acceptable in our community.

5. *Evidence of the Adequacy and Effects of Homosexual Parenting*

In the course of the hearing on this constitutional issue, I have been presented with a considerable amount of evidence on the ability of homosexual persons to parent, individually or as couples, and the effects of homosexual parenting on children. This evidence was presented principally through the extensive affidavits from Dr. Margrit Eichler, Dr. Rosemary Barnes, and Dr. Susan Bradley. These documents and the research papers accompanying them as exhibits, reviewed in considerable detail the scientific literature and research that has accumulated in this area over the last fifty years, and in particular since the mid-1970s. In addition to this affidavit evidence, I had the benefit of hearing viva voce evidence from Dr. Bradley. ...

Having considered the evidence received through these sources, I come to the following factual conclusions:

The traditional family model of two, middle class, heterosexual parents in which the woman is a full-time housewife and the man has full-time paid employment outside the home, which has long been assumed to be the structure most favourable to healthy child development, is now a minority and several varieties of non-traditional families appear in our society, including families in which gay fathers and lesbian mothers are the primary care-givers. The sexual orientation of the parents is considered along with race, ethnicity, household composition and maternal employment as one of a number of ways in which families vary from the traditional model.

During this century, families in highly industrialized countries have been undergoing drastic changes, not just in the nature of their composition but in gender roles within the family. These changes have precipitated research into the dimensions of family interactions and the result of this research indicates a wide variety in the nature and degree of interaction between family members. Moreover, studies by various researchers have convincingly demonstrated that the same internal variations exist between same-sex couples and opposite-sex couples and that both groups demonstrate the full range of dimensions indicative of family structure. As Dr. Eichler pointed out:

> Overall, the differences among opposite-sex couples and among same-sex couples are greater than the differences *between* these two groups. [Emphasis added.]

Recent studies on the effects of the non-traditional family structure on the development of children suggests that there is no reason to conclude that alteration of the family structure itself is detrimental to child development. The prevailing opinion of researchers in this area seems to be that the traditional family structure is no longer considered as the only framework within which adequate child care can be given. Rather, child development researchers have "highlighted the multiplicity of pathways through which healthy psychological development can take place and the diversity of home environments which can support such development."

Progressively more rigorous empirical research in the area of child development has produced the notion that *the most important element in the healthy development of a child is a stable, consistent, warm, and responsive relationship between a child and his or her care-giver*. Factors that appear to have a significant effect on the healthy emotional and psychological development of a child are more related to conflicts in spousal relations than family type or structure. A parent's capacity to support and be emotionally available to a child is enhanced in the context of a supportive relationship, especially if there is good communication, effective problem solving, and sharing of family responsibilities.

Research on the effects of gay and lesbian parenting on child development has focussed on various stereotypical beliefs regarding homosexual persons and couples. ...

In summarizing the results of the various studies and research on the effects of homosexual parenting on children, Dr. Barnes had this to say:

What is crucial to the children of lesbians and gay men, as to the children of heterosexual men and women, is loving, stable parenting. The opportunity for a lesbian or gay male parent to adopt a biologically unrelated child whom they parent provides a socially and legally recognized structure for an emotional relationship of great importance to the child. Such a structure recognizes the role and authority of the non-biological parent both in ordinary activities such as school enrolment and doctor's appointments and in times of transition or crises such as illness, disability and death. Such a structure also helps to ensure arrangements which fully recognize parenting relationships of importance to the child in the event of relationship breakdown and/or separation. Although many lesbian and gay male parents are able to make fair and orderly decisions about issues of child support and custody in the absence of a legal framework, the emotions associated with relationship breakdown can make this process difficult if not impossible for some. Where a child has been legally adopted by a non-biological parent, this structure may assist in clarifying the needs of the child and parental responsibilities.

Now Dr. Bradley candidly acknowledged that the studies to date in this area are not exhaustive, in that "most were done on white, well-educated samples." She did add, however, that:

[T]here is no reason to believe that future research will not confirm these findings as there has been reasonable consensus across samples and the findings are consistent with what we know about development generally.

In her conclusion, Dr. Bradley made the following comments:

Based on my academic and clinical work in this area of child psychiatry, it is my opinion that same sex couples should generally be treated in the same manner as are opposite sex common law couples with regard to the issue of adoption of children. Having regard to matters related to healthy child development, it is my view that sexual orientation of a person should not, in itself, be grounds for excluding a person from consideration as an adoptive parent.

This conclusion is based on my knowledge of child development and the aspects of parenting which are essential to healthy child development, as well as the literature which does not demonstrate a deleterious impact on children raised by gay or lesbian parents. In fact, all studies conducted to date show remarkable similarity in child development patterns of children whose parents are gay or lesbian compared to children whose parents are heterosexual.

... [I]t is reasonable to conclude that children raised by gay or lesbian parents should not be expected to differ substantively in any aspect of their development. Therefore, it is my opinion that gay and lesbian persons have the same capacity to care for children as do heterosexual persons.

[In part VI, Nevins Prov. J reviewed the provisions of the Charter and the analysis of ss. 15 and 1 in recent cases, including *Andrews v. Law Society (British Columbia)*, [1989] 1 SCR 143], and concluded that s. 136(1) contravened s. 15 and could not be saved by s. 1 of the Charter. As part of the analysis (at 160), he focused on ideas about the family.]

... What may be questioned at this point is the nature of the "family" contemplated by the provisions and philosophy of the Act. Although there has been no clear judicial pronouncement on this topic, it is obvious that the Act recognizes the fact of non-traditional families and affords them the same rights and protections as the more traditional form. By removing the requirement of marriage in the definition of spouse, unmarried or "common law" partners are given the right to apply for adoption, and by analogy, are given financial, custodial and property rights in other statutes. As discussed earlier, single persons are permitted to apply for adoption, without any restriction other than the best interests of the child. And so, the legislation accepts and respects the fact of single-parent families. As well, the concept of "parent" is no longer restricted to the biological parent but now includes any person, married or unmarried, an obvious reflection in the Act of the fact that non-traditional families are a fact of life in our society. ...

[The court held that s. 136 of the *Child and Family Services Act* was of no force or effect, and "read in" language to include same-sex relationships.]

Similar decisions were reached by courts in other provinces: see *Re A.* (1999), 181 DLR (4th) 300; 2 RFL (5th) 358 (Alta. QB). To what extent are these decisions reflective of a new idea about families and parenthood? In an earlier study of the bases for accepting applications for adoption, researchers reported that 84 percent of adoption agencies would reject an unmarried female applicant in a stable homosexual relationship: see Benjamin Freedman, P.J. Taylor, Thomas Wonnacott, and Katherine Hill, "Criteria for Parenting in Canada: A Comparative Survey of Adoption and Artificial Insemination Practices" (1988), 3 *Canadian Family Law Quarterly* 35, at 43 (table I). Thus, there is some evidence of changing patterns with respect to gay and lesbian households. These issues also need to be addressed in relation to the next section concerning assisted reproduction.

Discussion Note

Gay and Lesbian Adoption: Families and Ideology

Re K. was litigated in Ontario after the defeat of Bill 167 in the Ontario legislature. Bill 167 would have redefined spouse to include persons in same-sex relationships in all provincial legislation. It was a highly controversial bill, and when it appeared destined for defeat, the attorney general attempted to save it by introducing an amendment to restrict the definition of spouse in relation to adoption: the amended proposal would have ensured that gay and lesbian couples would not be able to adopt children. Bill 167 was nonetheless defeated.

It was in this context that four lesbian couples sought to adopt the children they were parenting. In *Re K.*, they succeeded in their quest. However, in doing so, the applicants were required to demonstrate that they "fit" the required legal form. As Shelley Gavigan argued:

> As profound as the challenge of the lesbian adoptions is, it is clear that striking down of the opposite sex requirement alone does not, cannot, address the constraints and assumptions that are embedded in the adoption legislation in Ontario. Under this legislation, it is not enough for the lesbian social parents to be "parents." In order to make a joint application, and thereby preserve the biological mother's tie to the child(ren), they must also be spouses in Ontario, and indeed in every province other than British Columbia. In order for the lesbian parents to be full parents, they have to be spouses, same-sex spouses to be sure, but spouses nonetheless. The spousal requirement for joint adoptions and preservation of children's ties to their biological parents is not amenable to constitutional challenge. The legal form of spouse coupled with its foundational place as a social form triumphs as it shapes and constrains the nature of the challenges that can succeed.

(See Shelley A.M. Gavigan, "Legal Forms, Family Forms, Gendered Norms: What Is a Spouse?" (1999), 14:1 *Canadian Journal of Law and Society* 127, at 156.)

In reflecting on this comment, consider what interests are served by ensuring that same-sex parents must also be spouses. What are the underlying assumptions of parent–child relationships in the law?

SELECTED REFERENCES

J. Ewall, "Sexual Orientation and Adoptive Matching" (1991), 25 *Family Law Quarterly* 347.

Shelley Gavigan, "A Parent(ly) Knot: Can Heather Have Two Mommies?," in Julia J. Bartkowiak and Uma Narayan, eds., *Having and Raising Children: Unconventional Families, Hard Choices and the Social Good* (Pittsburgh, PA: Pennsylvania State University Press, 1999), 87.

Nancy D. Polikoff, "This Child Does Have Two Mothers: Redefining Parenthood To Meet the Needs of Children in Lesbian-Mother and Other Non-Traditional Families" (1990), 78 *Georgetown Law Journal* 459.

Mary Lyndon Shanley, *Making Babies, Making Families* (Boston: Beacon Press, 2001).

Susan Ursel, "Bill 167 and Full Human Rights," in Katherine Arnup, ed., *Lesbian Parenting: Living with Pride and Prejudice* (Charlottetown, PEI: Gynergy, 1995), 341.

IV. ASSISTED REPRODUCTION AND PARENTHOOD

A. New Questions for Family Law?

Family law has new questions to answer. Reproductive technologies have a wide range of consequences, with implications for family law that it has never been called on to deal with before. In some cases there may be no existing law which applies to the specific situation, while in other cases existing law may be based on assumptions which are no longer valid because of the use of assisted conception procedures. Therefore, there is a need to re-examine and to develop new legal principles to deal with some questions, and to rethink some underlying assumptions for others. ... In the absence of legislation explicitly dealing with these situations, the courts are going to be in the position of having to determine the rights and obligations, if any, of each of these parties, so that the best interests of the child are protected. ... It cannot possibly be in the best interests of a child to have issues such as these settled, case-by-case, in the courtrooms of our nation. Well thought out social policy goals are needed in this area, and the law needs to be amended in the attainment of these goals.

> Patricia A. Baird, "Reproductive Technology and the Evolution of Family Law" (1997-98), 15 *Canadian Family Law Quarterly* 103, at 103 and 113

Despite the fact that pregnancy and childbirth are biological events, reproduction is more of a social than a biological process. ... Reproduction is also a political process.

> Susan A. McDaniel, "Women's Roles, Reproduction, and the New Reproductive Technologies: A New Stork Rising," in Nancy Mandell and Ann Duffy, eds., *Reconstructing the Canadian Family: Feminist Perspectives* (Toronto: Butterworths, 1988), 175, at 176-77

As both these comments suggest, issues about assisted reproduction, including reproductive technologies, have created new legal challenges within the social and political context in Canada. Although there have been a number of reform efforts, many of these issues have been considered to date on a case-by-case basis. This section provides an overview of some of the issues that have been raised, in conjunction with reform proposals and developments in other jurisdictions.

1. Assisted Reproduction and Adoption: The Same or Different?

In reviewing these materials, it may be useful to compare the legal regulation of parent–child relationships in the context of assisted reproduction with the principles developed in relation to adoption. Are these situations comparable, in fact or in law? In both contexts, for example, it may be necessary to define who is a "parent" in law. As well, in both situations, issues are frequently raised about disclosure of biological connections.

In a study of workers at adoption agencies and Children's Aid Societies (who were involved in choosing adoptive parents) and directors of infertility clinics (who were involved in selecting parents for artificial insemination by donor), researchers attempted to compare the significance of criteria for decision making about adoption and assisted reproduction. Even though artificial insemination by donor results in the *creation* of a child, while adoption involves the *placement* of a child, both can be contrasted with biological reproduction. The results of the study revealed a large amount of discretionary decision making in relation to both assisted reproduction and adoption, with different processes for determining "acceptable" parents and different degrees of reliance on factors deemed relevant to the decisions.

However, there were also some discernable differences between adoption agencies and fertility clinics. Both groups agreed that adoption should be more restrictive than artificial insemination: adoption respondents pointed to the challenges of accepting a child that was not "biologically your own." By contrast, physicians in fertility clinics appeared to be simply "aiding the natural reproductive process," and these decisions were generally characterized as medical rather than social. In addition, the results suggested that adoption agencies were much more concerned with the probable stability of the relationship in the family unit, while fertility clinics proceeded on the basis that "our society does not require a person to satisfy some test to be licensed to parent." See Benjamin Freedman, P.J. Taylor, Thomas Wonnacott, and Katherine Hill, "Criteria for Parenting in Canada: A Comparative Survey of Adoption and Artificial Insemination Practices" (1988), 3 *Canadian Family Law Quarterly* 35, at 50.

Should legal issues about assisted reproduction be framed as an analogy to adoption? Are there similarities or differences that need to be taken into account in designing legal principles with respect to assisted reproduction? For example, issues about disclosure, as with adoption, have been raised in relation to the identity of sperm donors. Even though sperm donors have traditionally provided sperm on condition of anonymity, newspaper reports have documented increasing interest on the part of children, now grown to adulthood, in locating "their" sperm donors: for example, see Paul McKeague, "Seeking the Mystery of Birth," *Ottawa Citizen*, September 27, 1999 and "I Just Want To Know Who My Father Is," *Ottawa Citizen*, September 28, 1999; and Madeleine Bunting, "Donor Insemination Raises Big Questions About Children's Rights To Know Their Biological Fathers," *The Guardian*, July 2, 2001.

These issues concerning sperm donation may also surface with respect to egg or embryo donation. According to the *Globe and Mail*, July 9, 1998, elite universities (including the University of Toronto, Harvard, and Princeton) are among a number of universities where advertisements seeking women students as egg donors are common; according to this report, the fees for such donations may be as high as $US 35,000. Often, the advertisements specify IQ levels as well as features such as skin, hair, and eye colour; see also Barbara Vobejda, "Egg Donation Develops into a Fertile Business," *Toronto Star*, April 11, 1999, at B1. In 2002, moreover, the *Globe and Mail* reported on the "adoption" of an embryo belonging to a Canadian couple, which resulted in the birth of a daughter to an American couple: see Lisa Priest, "Special Delivery," *Globe and Mail*, August 31, 2002, at F1. What kinds of legal problems arise in these situations? How should law respond?

2. The Assisted Human Reproduction Act

The Canadian federal government has responded by introducing Bill C-6 (formerly Bill C-13), the *Assisted Human Reproduction Act*, SC 2004, c. 2. The act identifies as

"prohibited activities" the "purchase, offer to purchase or [advertisement] for the purchase of sperm or ova from a donor or a person acting on behalf of a donor" (s. 7(1)).
Among "controlled activities," the act states that, except in accordance with regulations
and a licence, "no person shall ... obtain, store, transfer, destroy, import or export ... an
in vitro embryo" (s. 10(3)(b)). How will these provisions affect the arrangements for
sperm, egg, or embryo donation described above?

SELECTED REFERENCES

Ruth Macklin, "Artificial Means of Reproduction and Our Understanding of the Family"
    (Jan/Feb 1991), *Hastings Center Report*, at 5.
Rebecca Mead, "Eggs for Sale" (August 1999), *New Yorker* 56.
Sarah Wilson, "Identity, Genealogy, and the Social Family: The Case of Donor Insemina-
    tion" (1997), 11 *International Journal of Law, Policy, and the Family* 270.
Alison Harvison Young and Angela Wasunna, "Wrestling with the Limits of Law: Regu-
    lating New Reproductive Technologies" (1998), 6 *Health Law Journal* 239.

B. Surrogacy Arrangements and Parenthood: Private Agreements and Public Policies

> The different viewpoints about whether it is liberatory or oppressive to women to be free to
> make contracts and to be paid for this use of their bodies are reflected in arguments over what
> to call a commissioned pregnancy. Proponents tend to use the term "surrogate motherhood,"
> while those with reservations resist calling a woman who bears a child a "surrogate" mother.
>
>   Mary Lyndon Shanley, *Making Babies, Making Families*
>   (Boston: Beacon Press, 2001), 104

1. Surrogacy and a Child's Best Interests

Surrogacy arrangements have been used to permit an infertile couple to obtain a child
who is biologically connected to one or both of them, using the gestational services of
another woman. Shanley used the term "complete surrogacy" to define a situation in
which a woman becomes pregnant as a result of insemination, either with anonymously
donated sperm or with sperm of the male intentional father. In this context, the gestational mother's egg is used for conception. By contrast, in "gestational surrogacy," the
gestational mother has implanted in her uterus an embryo created in vitro from the egg
and sperm of the couple or of anonymous donors. As is evident, there may be as many as
five persons involved in the birth of the child—the intentional mother and father, the
donors of the egg and sperm, and the gestational mother.

Legal responses to surrogacy arrangements have grappled with the tension between
their private contractual nature and the implications for public policy in relation to the
birth of children—what kind of legal principles are needed to ensure the best interests of
children in this context? For example, the new *Assisted Human Reproduction Act* prohibits
payment to a woman for surrogacy services; it also prohibits acceptance of consideration

for arranging for the services of a surrogate mother and payment of such consideration. In addition, no one may counsel or induce, or provide medical assistance to, a female person under 21 years of age to provide surrogacy services (s. 6(1) to 6(4)). However, controversial debates continue to exist with respect to surrogacy arrangements and the wisdom of prohibiting it for commercial purposes. Thus, this section provides a brief overview of these issues in the context of defining parenthood in law. The case that follows illustrates many of the competing concerns in relation to surrogacy arrangements.

In the Matter of Baby M.
537 A2d 1227; 109 NJ 396 (Sup. Ct. 1988)

[A New Jersey appellate court reviewed a surrogacy contract entered into by William Stern and Mary Beth Whitehead. The contract recited the infertility of Stern's wife, Elizabeth, and provided for the artificial insemination of Whitehead with Stern's own sperm. Whitehead agreed to carry a child to term, bear it, deliver it to the Sterns, and do what was necessary to enable Elizabeth Stern to adopt the child. She agreed to terminate her own legal rights to the child. Whitehead's husband was also a party to the contract, and he also agreed to renounce rights to the child, including affirmatively providing evidence to rebut any presumption of paternity arising out of his marriage to the gestational mother. In return for her work, Stern agreed to pay Whitehead $10,000; he also contracted separately to pay $7,500 to the infertility centre that brought the parties together and assisted in their contractual arrangements.

The facts also indicated that most of Stern's family had died in the Holocaust during World War II, so that a biological connection to a child was of special significance to him. In addition, it appears that Elizabeth Stern feared pregnancy because of potential health problems arising from a diagnosis of multiple sclerosis; although the court viewed the risks as minor, it was clear that her fears were real. The Sterns met as PhD students and Elizabeth had pursued a medical degree.

Whitehead became pregnant in accordance with the contract, and Baby M. was born in March 1986. However, Whitehead realized, almost immediately, that she could not part with the child. Nonetheless, she initially handed over the child; three days later, she went to the Sterns' home in despair and requested an opportunity to have the baby for a week. Concerned for her well-being, the Sterns agreed, but Whitehead and her husband fled to Florida with the child, where they were constantly on the move in an effort to avoid the Sterns' claim to the child. Eventually, legal action launched by the Sterns resulted in the police forcibly removing Baby M. from Whitehead; a custody order in favour of the Sterns was renewed, with limited visitation rights for Whitehead.

In due course, the Sterns initiated an action to enforce the contract. At trial, the court held that the contract was valid, terminated Whitehead's parental rights, granted custody to Stern, and ordered that Elizabeth Stern be permitted to adopt Baby M. immediately. According to the appellate court, the lower court's decision recognizing the validity of the contract was entirely consistent with the child's best interests; however, no specific performance was possible unless it was in Baby M.'s best interests.

Nonetheless, the appeal court decided that the contract was invalid, because it conflicted with state statutes and because it was not consistent with the state's public policies.]

B. Public Policy Considerations

The surrogacy contract's invalidity, resulting from its direct conflict with the above statutory provisions, is further underlined when its goals and means are measured against New Jersey's public policy. The contract's basic premise, that the natural parents can decide in advance of birth which one is to have custody of the child, bears no relationship to the settled law that the child's best interests shall determine custody. ... The fact that the trial court remedied that aspect of the contract through the "best interests" phrase does not make the contractual provision any less offensive to the public policy of this State.

The surrogacy contract guarantees permanent separation of the child from one of its natural parents. Our policy, however, has long been that to the extent possible, children should remain with and be brought up by both of their natural parents. ... This is not simply some theoretical ideal that in practice has no meaning. The impact of failure to follow that policy is nowhere better shown than in the results of this surrogacy contract. A child, instead of starting off its life with as much peace and security as possible, finds itself immediately in a tug-of-war between contending mother and father.

The surrogacy contract violates the policy of this State that the rights of natural parents are equal concerning their child, the father's right no greater than the mother's. "The parent and child relationship extends equally to every child and to every parent, regardless of the marital status of the parents." *NJSA* 9:17-40. As the Assembly Judiciary Committee noted in its statement to the bill, this section establishes "the principle that regardless of the marital status of the parents, all children *and all parents* have equal rights with respect to each other." ... The whole purpose and effect of the surrogacy contract was to give the father the exclusive right to the child by destroying the rights of the mother.

The policies expressed in our comprehensive laws governing consent to the surrender of a child, ... stand in stark contrast to the surrogacy contract and what it implies. Here there is no counselling, independent or otherwise, of the natural mother, no evaluation, no warning.

The only legal advice Mary Beth Whitehead received regarding the surrogacy contract was provided in connection with the contract that she previously entered into with another couple. Mrs. Whitehead's lawyer was referred to her by the Infertility Center, with which he had an agreement to act as counsel for surrogate candidates. His services consisted of spending one hour going through the contract with the Whiteheads, section by section, and answering their questions. Mrs. Whitehead received no further legal advice prior to signing the contract with the Sterns.

Mrs. Whitehead was examined and psychologically evaluated, but if it was for her benefit, the record does not disclose that fact. The Sterns regarded the evaluation as important, particularly in connection with the question of whether she would change her mind. Yet they never asked to see it, and were content with the assumption that the Infertility Center had made an evaluation and had concluded that there was no danger that the surrogate mother would change her mind. From Mrs. Whitehead's point of view, all that she learned from the evaluation was that "she had passed." It is apparent that the profit motive got the better of the Infertility Center. Although the evaluation was made, it was not put to any use, and understandably so, for the psychologist warned that Mrs. Whitehead demonstrated certain traits that might make surrender of the child difficult and that there should be further inquiry into this issue in connection with her surrogacy. To inquire further, however, might have jeopardized the Infertility Center's fee. The record indicates that neither Mrs. Whitehead nor the Sterns were ever told of this fact, a fact that might have ended their surrogacy arrangement.

Under the contract, the natural mother is irrevocably committed before she knows the strength of her bond with her child. She never makes a totally voluntary, informed decision, for quite clearly any decision prior to the baby's birth is, in the most important sense, uninformed, and any decision after that, compelled by a pre-existing contractual commitment, the threat of a lawsuit, and the inducement of a $10,000 payment, is less than totally voluntary. Her interests are of little concern to those who controlled this transaction.

Although the interest of the natural father and adoptive mother is certainly the predominant interest, realistically the *only* interest served, even they are left with less than what public policy requires. They know little about the natural mother, her genetic makeup, and her psychological and medical history. Moreover, not even a superficial attempt is made to determine their awareness of their responsibilities as parents.

Worst of all, however, is the contract's total disregard of the best interests of the child. There is not the slightest suggestion that any inquiry will be made at any time to determine the fitness of the Sterns as custodial parents, of Mrs. Stern as an adoptive parent, their superiority to Mrs. Whitehead, or the effect of the child of not living with her natural mother.

This is the sale of a child, or, at the very least, the sale of a mother's right to her child, the only mitigating factor being that one of the purchasers is the father. Almost every evil that prompted the prohibition on the payment of money in connection with adoptions exists here. ...

[The court noted the differences between an adoption and a surrogacy contract, including the fact that surrogacy is unlikely without payment; the payment of money in surrogacy arrangements is what creates the problem; and payment may lead to decisions to turn over children to the "highest bidders." In addition, however, the court noted that consent in the adoption context is revocable. The court also noted that surrogacy may be used for the benefit of the rich at the expense of the poor, and indicated that the net assets of the Whiteheads were probably negative, while Mr. Stern was a biochemist and Mrs. Stern a medical doctor. Then the court considered the argument that Mrs. Whitehead had agreed to this contract.]

The point is made that Mrs. Whitehead *agreed* to the surrogacy arrangement, supposedly fully understanding the consequences. Putting aside the issue of how compelling her need for money may have been, and how significant her understanding of the consequences, we suggest that her consent is irrelevant. There are, in a civilized society, some things that money cannot buy. In America, we decided long ago that merely because conduct purchased by money was "voluntary" did not mean that it was good or beyond regulation and prohibition. ... Employers can no longer buy labor at the lowest price they can bargain for, even though that labor is "voluntary," 29 *USC* §206 (1982), or buy women's labor for less money than paid to men for the same job, 29 *USC* §206(d), or purchase the agreement of children to perform oppressive labor, 29 *USC* §212, or purchase the agreement of workers to subject themselves to unsafe or unhealthful working conditions, 29 *USC* §§651 to 678. (Occupational Safety and Health Act of 1970.) There are, in short, values that society deems more important than granting to wealth whatever it can buy, be it labor, love, or life. Whether this principle recommends prohibition of surrogacy, which presumably sometimes results in great satisfaction to all of the parties, is not for us to say. We note here only that, under existing law, the fact that Mrs. Whitehead "agreed" to the arrangement is not dispositive.

The long-term effects of surrogacy contracts are not known, but feared—the impact on the child who learns her life was bought, that she is the offspring of someone who gave birth to her only to obtain money; the impact on the natural mother as the full weight of her isolation is felt along with the full reality of the sale of her body and her child; the impact on the natural father and adoptive mother once they realize the consequences of their conduct. Literature in related areas suggests these are substantial considerations, although, given the newness of surrogacy, there is little information. ...

The surrogacy contract is based on principles that are directly contrary to the objectives of our laws. It guarantees the separation of a child from its mother; it looks to adoption regardless of suitability; it totally ignores the child; it takes the child from the mother regardless of her wishes and her maternal fitness; and it does all of this, it accomplishes all of its goals, through the use of money.

Beyond that is the potential degradation of some women that may result from this arrangement. In many cases, of course, surrogacy may bring satisfaction, not only to the infertile couple, but to the surrogate mother herself. The fact, however, that many women may not perceive surrogacy negatively but rather see it as an opportunity does not diminish its potential for devastation to other women.

In sum, the harmful consequences of this surrogacy arrangement appear to us all too palpable. In New Jersey the surrogate mother's agreement to sell her child is void. Its irrevocability infects the entire contract, as it does the money that purports to buy it. ...

[The court also considered constitutional arguments about privacy and the right to procreate, pursuant to the US Constitution, and then turned to the custody claims.]

Having decided that the surrogacy contract is illegal and unenforceable, we now must decide the custody question without regard to the provisions of the surrogacy contract that would give Mr. Stern sole and permanent custody. (That does not mean that the existence of the contract and the circumstances under which it was entered may not be considered to the extent deemed relevant to the child's best interests.) With the surrogacy contract disposed of, the legal framework becomes a dispute between two couples over the custody of a child produced by the artificial insemination of one couple's wife by the other's husband. ...

Our custody conclusion is based on strongly persuasive testimony contrasting both the family life of the Whiteheads and the Sterns and the personalities and characters of the individuals. The stability of the Whitehead family life was doubtful at the time of trial. Their finances were in serious trouble (foreclosure by Mrs. Whitehead's sister on a second mortgage was in process). Mr. Whitehead's employment, though relatively steady, was always at risk because of his alcoholism, a condition that he seems not to have been able to confront effectively. Mrs. Whitehead had not worked for quite some time, her last two employments having been part-time. One of the Whiteheads' positive attributes was their ability to bring up two children, and apparently well, even in so vulnerable a household. Yet substantial question was raised even about that aspect of their home life. The expert testimony contained criticism of Mrs. Whitehead's handling of her son's educational difficulties. Certain of the experts noted that Mrs. Whitehead perceived herself as omnipotent and omniscient concerning her children. She knew what they were thinking, what they wanted, and she spoke for them. As to Melissa, Mrs. Whitehead expressed the view that she alone knew what that child's cries and sounds meant. Her inconsistent stories about various things engendered grave doubts about her ability to explain honestly and sensitively to Baby M.—and at the right time—the nature of her origin. Although faith in professional counselling is not a *sine qua non* of parenting, several experts believed that Mrs. Whitehead's contempt for professional help, especially professional psychological help, coincided with her feelings of omnipotence in a way that could be devastating to a child who most likely will need such help. In short, while love and affection there would be, Baby M.'s life with the Whiteheads promised to be too closely controlled by Mrs. Whitehead. The prospects for wholesome, independent psychological growth and development would be at serious risk.

The Sterns have no other children, but all indications are that their household and their personalities promise a much more likely foundation for Melissa to grow and thrive. There *is* a track record of sorts—during the one-and-a-half years of custody Baby M. has done very well, and the relationship between both Mr. and Mrs. Stern and the baby has become very strong. The household is stable, and likely to remain so. Their finances are more than adequate, their circle of friends supportive, and their marriage happy. Most important, they are loving, giving, nurturing, and open-minded people. They have demonstrated the wish and ability to nurture and protect Melissa, yet at the same time to encourage her independence. Their lack of experience is more than made up for by a willingness to learn and to listen, a willingness that is enhanced by their professional training, especially Mrs. Stern's experience as a pediatrician. They are honest; they can recognize error, deal with it, and learn from it. They will try to determine rationally the best way to cope with problems in their relationship with Melissa. When the time comes to tell her about her origins, they will probably have found a means of doing so that accords with the best interests of Baby M. All in all, Melissa's future appears solid, happy, and promising with them.

Based on all of this we have concluded, independent of the trial court's identical conclusion, that Melissa's best interests call for custody in the Sterns. ...

It seems to us that given her predicament, Mrs. Whitehead was rather harshly judged—both by the trial court and by some of the experts. She was guilty of a breach of contract, and indeed, she did break a very important promise, but we think it is expecting something well beyond normal human capabilities to suggest that this mother should have parted with her newly born infant without a struggle. Other than survival, what stronger force is there? We do not know of, and cannot conceive of, any other case where a perfectly fit mother was expected to surrender her newly born infant, perhaps forever, and was then told she was a bad mother because she did not. We know of no authority suggesting that the moral quality of her act in those circumstances should be judged by referring to a contract made before she became pregnant. We do not countenance, and would never countenance, violating a court order as Mrs. Whitehead did, even a court order that is wrong; but her resistance to an order that she surrender her infant, possibly forever, merits a measure of understanding. We do not find it so clear that her efforts to keep her infant, when measured against the Sterns' efforts to take her away, make one, rather than the other, the wrongdoer. The Sterns suffered, but so did she. And if we go beyond suffering to an evaluation of the human stakes involved in the struggle, how much weight should be given to her nine months of pregnancy, the labor of child-birth, the risk of her life, compared to the payment of money, the anticipation of a child and the donation of sperm?

There has emerged a portrait of Mrs. Whitehead, exposing her children to the media, engaging in negotiations to sell a book, granting interviews that seemed helpful to her, whether hurtful to Baby M. or not, that suggests a selfish, grasping woman ready to sacrifice the interests of Baby M. and her other children for fame and wealth. That portrait is a half-truth, for while it may accurately reflect what ultimately occurred, its implication, that this is what Mary Beth Whitehead wanted, is totally inaccurate, at least insofar as the record before us is concerned. There is not one word in that record to support a claim that had she been allowed to continue her possession of her newly born infant, Mrs. Whitehead would have ever been heard of again; not one word in the record suggests that her change of mind and her subsequent fight for her child was motivated by anything other than love—whatever complex underlying psychological motivations may have existed.

We have a further concern regarding the trial court's emphasis on the Sterns' interest in Melissa's education as compared to the Whiteheads'. That this difference is a legitimate factor to be considered we have no doubt. But it should not be overlooked that a best-interests test is designed to create not a new member of the intelligentsia but rather a well-integrated person who might reasonably be expected to be happy with life. "Best interests" does not contain within it any idealized lifestyle; the question boils down to a judgment, consisting of many factors, about the likely future happiness of a human being. *Fantony v. Fantony* [21 NJ 525; 122 A2d 593 (Sup. Ct. 1956)]. Stability, love, family happiness, tolerance, and, ultimately, support of independence—all rank much higher in predicting future happiness than the likelihood of a college education. We do not mean to suggest that the trial court would disagree. We simply want to dispel any possible misunderstanding on the issue.

Even allowing for these differences, the facts, the experts' opinions, and the trial court's analysis of both argue strongly in favor of custody in the Sterns. Mary Beth

Whitehead's family life, into which Baby M. would be placed, was anything but secure—the quality Melissa needs most. And today it may be even less so. Furthermore, the evidence and expert opinion based on it reveal personality characteristics, mentioned above, that might threaten the child's best development. The Sterns promise a secure home, with an understanding relationship that allows nurturing and independent growth to develop together. Although there is no substitute for reading the entire record, including the review of every word of each experts' testimony and reports, a summary of their conclusions is revealing. Six experts testified for Mrs. Whitehead: one favored joint custody, clearly unwarranted in this case; one simply rebutted an opposing expert's claim that Mary Beth Whitehead had a recognized personality disorder; one testified to the adverse impact of separation on *Mrs. Whitehead*; one testified about the evils of adoption and, to him, the probable analogous evils of surrogacy; one spoke only on the question of whether Mrs. Whitehead's consent in the surrogacy agreement was "informed consent"; and one spelled out the strong bond between mother and child. None of them unequivocally stated, or even necessarily implied, an opinion that custody in the Whiteheads was in the best interests of Melissa—the ultimate issue. The Sterns' experts, both well qualified—as were the Whiteheads'—concluded that the best interests of Melissa required custody in Mr. Stern. Most convincingly, the three experts chosen by the court-appointed guardian *ad litem* of Baby M., each clearly free of all bias and interest, unanimously and persuasively recommended custody in the Sterns.

Discussion Note

Surrogacy Cases in the United Kingdom and Canada

Surrogacy arrangements have also been reviewed in the United Kingdom in relation to an application for adoption by a couple who had arranged for another woman to bear a child conceived as a result of sexual intercourse with the husband of the adoptive couple. The gestational mother agreed to provide her services for the sum of £10,000, an arrangement permitted pursuant to English law (which prohibited commercial surrogacy agencies, but did not preclude individuals from acting as surrogate mothers and being paid). In a comment on this and a related case, it was suggested that there was a need for more comprehensive guidelines and greater supervision to safeguard the best interests of the child: see S.P. de Cruz, "Adoption—Whether Permissible Following Commercial Surrogacy Arrangement" (1987), *Journal of Social Welfare Law* 314 and (1987), 2 All ER 826.

In Canada, there are few reported decisions about surrogacy arrangements, although the court in *Re Ontario Birth Registration #88-05-045846*, [1990] OJ no. 608 (Prov. Ct. (Fam. Div.)) (QL) reviewed a situation in which a daughter apparently gestated a child for her mother, having been artificially inseminated with sperm from her mother's second husband. The mother had undergone a hysterectomy, and some months after the baby's birth, the mother and her husband applied to adopt the child. The court assessed the arrangements and concluded that it was in the child's best interests to grant the requested order for adoption.

Newspaper accounts also confirm surrogacy arrangements in Canada: for example, see Debra Black, "Surrogate Motherhood 'Expression of Love,'" *Toronto Star*, December

31, 1999, providing an account of an agreement by a York Region police officer to gestate a child for her long-time friend living in California; the gestational mother was implanted with the intentional mother's egg and fertilized by the sperm of the intentional father. See also Nancy J. White, "Offering an 'Incredible Gift,' Surrogate Mother Carries Baby for Her Friend," *Toronto Star*, December 11, 1999, at N1. Although the federal government expressed its concerns and attempted to attain a voluntary moratorium on surrogacy arrangements, news reports have indicated that it is a growing phenomenon, with gestational carriers becoming pregnant under contract for payments of $10,000 to $20,000: see Dennis Bucckert, "Surrogate Motherhood Flourishing," *Toronto Star*, May 31, 1999, at A3. Lawyers have expressed satisfaction with the work of negotiating surrogacy contracts: see Peter Bakogeorge, "Helping Clients 'Build' Families," *Law Times*, July 8, 2002, at 15.

2. Birth Registration: (Re) Defining Parents

J.R. v. L.H.
[2002] OTC 764; OJ no. 3998 (Sup. Ct. J)

KITELEY J:

Background

This is a good news case. It involves two families who shared a common goal. The applicants and respondents are not adverse. Indeed, they have collaborated in their gestational carriage agreement and this application is simply the legal outcome of a wonderful arrangement.

This is an application for a declaration that the applicants are the biological mother (J.R.) and father (J.K.) of twins; for an order awarding custody of the twins to the applicants; for a declaration that the respondent G.H. is not the father of the twins; and for an order directing the Registrar General to register a Statement of Birth consistent with the foregoing declaration.

The twins were born on February 9, 2002. This application was issued on March 1, 2002. The matter originally came on before me on March 5, 2002. There were difficulties with the affidavits and consequently the matter was adjourned to March 21, 2002. On that date, I received another application record and I heard further submissions from counsel.

Section 9 of the *Vital Statistics Act* requires the mother and father to make and certify a statement of the child's birth within thirty days of the birth. Section 9(12) provides that on receiving a certified copy of an order with respect to the child's parentage, the Registrar General shall amend the particulars of the child's parents shown on the registration. The Statement of Birth had not been contained in the affidavits. On March 21, 2002, I asked Ms. Blom to obtain it on the basis that I needed to see the existing Statement of Birth which had been filed to ascertain the amendments which the Registrar General should be required to make. Having heard submissions, I directed counsel to file supplementary evidence as to the Statement of Birth for each child.

Ms. Blom reported on April 8, 2002 that she was having difficulty obtaining the record due to the labour disruption. Ms. Blom filed a supplementary affidavit in early May. In that supplementary affidavit of a law clerk in Ms. Blom's office, I was given a copy of the "Proof and/or Time of Birth Statement" for each child. This appears to be the statement required to be provided pursuant to section 8 of the *Vital Statistics Act* by the medical practitioner who attends at the birth. In this supplementary affidavit, Ms. Deacon reported that the Statements of Birth required by section 9(2) had not been filed by the applicants. They had decided to await the outcome of this application before submitting the requisite form. Consequently, section 9(12) of the *Vital Statistics Act* does not apply because the Registrar General cannot be expected to amend a record which has not yet been filed. It may be that since May, a Statement of Birth has been filed. In view of the lengthy time between May 7th and the release of these reasons, I elected not to seek clarification from Ms. Blom. In the order below, I have tried to anticipate the procedural options.

The applicants are common law spouses. J.R. is unable to have children. J.R. and J.K. investigated the possibilities of gestational carriage. They were accepted as candidates for the in vitro fertilization program at a Toronto hospital. They signed the consent form required to participate in the program. The respondent L.H. is the woman who is the gestational carrier. She and her husband G.H. also signed the consent form. The applicants and respondents signed a gestational carriage agreement. On February 9th, 2002 the twins were born. On February 11th, J.R. and J.K. provided blood samples for the purpose of determining the biological parentage of the children. The results of the DNA testing established that J.R. and J.K. are the biological mother and father of the twins. The children have lived with the applicants since the birth.

The application was served on the respondents. In their affidavits filed by Ms. Blom, they support the application. They have signed a consent to a draft judgment which is consistent with the relief sought.

There is no issue as to the enforceability of the gestational carriage agreement.

Declarations with Respect to Parentage

Section 4 of the *Children's Law Reform Act* is as follows:

(1) Any person having an interest may apply to a court for a declaration that a male person is recognized in law to be the father of a child or that a female person is the mother of a child.

(2) Where the court finds that a presumption of paternity exists under section 8 and unless it is established, on the balance of probabilities, that the presumed father is not the father of the child, the court shall make a declaratory order confirming that the paternity is recognized in law.

(3) Where the court finds on the balance of probabilities that the relationship of mother and child has been established, the court may make a declaratory order to that effect.

Section 97 of the *Courts of Justice Act* is as follows:

The Court of Appeal and the Superior Court of Justice, exclusive of the Small Claims Court, may make binding declarations of right, whether or not any consequential relief is or could be claimed.

I will first address the relief with respect to the applicants. The blood tests indicate that the probability that J.R. and J.K. are the mother and father respectively is greater than 99.99%. I find that on a balance of probabilities, they are the genetic parents of the twins. Pursuant to section 4(1), J.K. is entitled to be "recognized in law" as the father of the children and J.R. is entitled to be "recognized in law" to be the mother of the children.

I turn next to the respondents. G.H. did not contribute genetic material. He is not the biological father. He is involved because he is the husband of the woman who is the gestational carrier and, pursuant to section 8(1) of the *Children's Law Reform Act*, he is presumed to be the father of the children. The presumption has been rebutted.

Section 4(1) and (2) provide that the court may make positive declarations. But the *Children's Law Reform Act* is silent as to whether the court may make negative declarations. The *Courts of Justice Act* makes no such distinction. I agree with Potts J that the right to know whether or not one is a parent of a child is of such significance that the issue may be the subject of a declaratory order pursuant to s. 97 of the *Courts of Justice Act* (*Raft v. Shortt* (1986), 2 RFL (3d) 243). The applicants have established that a declaration that G.H. is not the father ought to be made.

In the application there is no request for declaratory relief with respect to L.H. However, at paragraph 39 of the factum, there is a request for a declaration that L.H. is not the mother of the children. If the application had been opposed, the omission from the application may have been problematic. However, it has not been opposed. Furthermore, L.H. supports the requests contained in the application. In her affidavit, L.H. described the circumstances of the gestational carriage agreement and the birth of the children and she specifically deposed that she is not the "mother" of the children. In the draft judgment contained in the second application record, she has consented to a judgment in those terms.

Even with the consent of all concerned, the issue with respect to L.H. has different dimensions from the others. In section 1 of the *Vital Statistics Act*, "birth" is defined as "the complete expulsion or extraction from its mother of a fetus that did any time after being completely expelled or extracted from the mother breathe or show any other sign of life ... ." L.H. is clearly the birth mother.

In *Chapman and Linto v. Her Majesty the Queen in Right of the Province of Manitoba and the Department of Vital Statistics*, [2000] MJ no. 482 (October 20, 2000), the genetic parents, the birth mother and her spouse all applied before the birth of the child for a declaration compelling the Local Hospital Authority and staff attending the birth to complete documentation showing that the genetic parents were the natural and legal parents. The application was opposed. That case differs from this in that the application was brought before the birth. But it is similar to this case in that the potential parents were all in agreement. The court declined to grant a declaration primarily because the woman who was the gestational carrier would be giving "birth" within the meaning of their legislation and accordingly, the "birth" had to be so recorded. But the court pointed out that a declaration of parentage could be made after that preliminary step.

In some cases, there is a conflict between the genetic parents and the woman who is the gestational carrier. For example, in *A.J. v. M.C.* (1992), 286 Cal. Rptr. 369, the woman who was the gestational carrier of an egg and sperm of the genetic parents sought to be declared the birth mother in addition to the genetic mother. The Court of Appeals agreed with the trial judge that the genetic parents were the "natural and legal parents of the child" and the woman who was the gestational carrier was not entitled to a declaration of her parenthood.

If such a conflict existed, I would have to consider whether s. 4(1) enables a declaration that there is more than one mother, as Benotto J raised but did not determine in *Buist v. Greaves*, [1997] OJ no. 2646 (1997), Carswell Ont 2243. However, the disposition in this case is facilitated because the birth mother agrees with the genetic parents that she ought to be declared not to be a parent.

The *Children's Law Reform Act* does not apply. But it is appropriate to make the declaration pursuant to section 97 of the *Courts of Justice Act*.

In the few relevant cases, there is no suggestion that the "best interests of the children" ought to be considered in cases in which declaratory relief is sought. Whether or not it is a criterion which I must consider, I have no hesitation in finding that these declarations are in the best interests of the children. The affidavits describe thoughtful, responsible persons who entered into this arrangement with the sole objective of bringing children into the world who would be well-cared for. That objective has been achieved.

Custody

Section 20 of the *Children's Law Reform Act* provides that the father and the mother are equally entitled to custody of the children. Pursuant to section 21, a parent may apply for an order respecting custody of the children. Any such order must be made in the best interests of the children.

Immediately after the birth, the twins began to live with J.R. and J.K. L.H. is not only content but enthusiastic about the care which the children will receive from the applicants. G.H. supports his wife in asserting that they believe that it will be in the best interests of the twins to remain in the care and custody of the applicants. The evidence amply supports such a finding.

Amendment of Registrations

As indicated above, it appears that as of the end of April, 2002 the Statement of Birth had not been filed within the 30 days specified in section 9(2) of the *Vital Statistics Act*. If that is the case, then the Registrar General need not make any amendment to the records. It may be that the Statement has subsequently been submitted, in which case section 9(12) would apply. As the supplementary affidavit indicates, the physician did comply with section 8 by submitting the Proof and/or Time of Birth form for each child in which the mother was identified as L.H. It may be that the Registrar

General has registered the birth of the twins based on the physician's form. Given the declaratory relief to be granted, it is logical that whatever order is required to enable the registrations consistent with the declarations ought to be made.

Sealing the Court File

[In response to a request to seal the court files, pursuant to s. 137(2) of the *Courts of Justice Act*, the court concluded.]

... In the absence of any evidence to justify the request, I am not prepared to speculate or infer what factors would be weighed on the part of the applicants. I have only the presumption of openness which I must apply.

The rules provide a less secretive remedy, namely the use of pseudonyms or initials [see rule 14.08]. This issue of gestational carriage agreements (and indeed traditional surrogacy agreements) is an emerging matter of public policy. Ms. Blom could not provide me with any cases in which orders such as this have been made. Undoubtedly there have been some, indeed many. A roadmap is necessary so that the genetic parents and the "birth mother" and her spouse if there is one, know what to expect in the conclusion of the legal process. It is in the public interest that the roadmap be available for those considering such a procedure. It is equally as important that the public have the opportunity to know and understand how these issues are resolved. But it does not mean that the identity of the members of the two families need to be publicized. Without evidence from any of the parties, the balance between those issues is found in the use of pseudonyms. I am prepared to find that these parties would consider it a significant intrusion on their privacy if their identities were made public. Their privacy can be protected while the fundamental value of openness is observed if the participants are identified with initials.

It will be necessary for Ms. Blom to prepare a copy of the order with the full names of the adults and the children in order that it be sent to the Registrar General. She may forward a copy of that order to me for signing.

Order To Go as Follows

1. Pursuant to s. 4(1) of the *Children's Law Reform Act*, I declare that J.K. is the father of the children J.N.K. and M.C.K., both born February 9, 2002 and that he shall be recognized in law to be their father.

2. Pursuant to s. 4(1) of the *Children's Law Reform Act*, I declare that J.R. is the mother of the children J.N.K. and M.C.K., both born February 9, 2002 and that she shall be recognized in law to be their mother.

3. Pursuant to section 97 of the *Courts of Justice Act*, I declare that G.H. is not the father of the children J.N.K. and M.C.K., both born February 9, 2002.

4. Pursuant to section 97 of the *Courts of Justice Act*, I declare that L.H. is not the mother of the children J.N.K. and M.C.K., both born February 9, 2002.

5. If a Statement of Birth has been filed pursuant to section 9(2) of the *Vital Statistics Act* for the children, or if the Registrar General has registered the parentage of the children based upon the "Proof and/or time of Birth Statement," on receiving a certified copy of an order consistent with the endorsement, the Registrar General shall amend the particulars of the parents of the children J.N.K. and M.C.K., both born February 9, 2002.

6. If a Statement of Birth has not been filed pursuant to section 9(2) of the *Vital Statistics Act* for the children, the applicants are authorized to submit a Statement of Birth for the children J.N.K. and M.C.K., both born February 9, 2002 which is consistent with the declarations contained above.

7. Pursuant to s. 21 of the *Children's Law Reform Act*, the applicants shall have custody of the children J.N.K. and M.C.K., both born February 9, 2002.

8. The request for an order pursuant to s. 137(2) of the *Courts of Justice Act* is refused.

9. The title of proceedings shall be changed for all purposes except item 6 above to reflect [this order]. ...

And the Registrar of the Superior Court of Justice is directed to amend the records accordingly.

Discussion Notes

J.C. v. Manitoba and Rypkema v. British Columbia

In *J.R. v. L.H.*, above, the court referred to a Manitoba decision, *J.C. v. Manitoba* (2000), 12 RFL (5th) 274; (2002), 151 Man. R (2d) 268 (QB), in which the gestational mother and her husband joined in an application, prior to the birth of a child, by the intentional parents for a declaration that the hospital file documentation of the child's birth should show the intentional parents as the "natural and legal parents" of the child to be delivered by the gestational mother. The intentional parents supplied the egg and sperm that were placed in the womb of the man's sister, the gestational mother. The court considered the statutory provisions and concluded that only the person who gives birth (with "birth" as described in the *Vital Statistics Act*, RSM 1987, c. V60, s. 1: as "the complete expulsion or extraction from its mother") may be recorded as the child's mother. By contrast, a declaration of paternity was available pursuant to Manitoba legislation prior to the birth of the child. In denying the application, the court stated (at paras. 9-10):

> Without going into any potential ramifications if the application were allowed, suffice it to say that the Department of Vital Statistics is set up to record just that, vital statistics, one of which is birth or the extraction from its mother of a product of conception. S.J.L. is the individual who will be giving birth to this unborn child, and the records of the Department of Vital Statistics should reflect that fact. It is interesting to note that in the application the applicants themselves refer to S.J.L. as the "birth mother." A declaration of parentage can follow the recording of this fact.

I would be prepared to give a declaration of paternity in favour of J.C. at this point, but the applicants do not want J.C. named as father on the same birth registration that shows his sister as the birth mother. This is completely understandable. Therefore, rather than making that declaration of paternity, and not being prepared to make a declaration of maternity before a child is born and before the registration of birth shows the birth mother as S.J.L., the application for relief will be dismissed.

According to a subsequent newspaper account of this case, the intentional parents were required to "adopt their own child": see Mike McIntyre, "Parents Forced To Adopt Own Baby," *Winnipeg Free Press*, October 28, 2000, at A1.

In addition, in *Rypkema v. British Columbia*, [2003] BCJ no. 2721 (SC) (QL), the genetic parents of a child born to a gestational mother were declared to be the child's parents for purposes of the birth registration process maintained by the provincial government. In *Rypkema*, the petitioners were both genetic and social parents of the child, and the gestational mother supported the application. The court cited the Supreme Court's decision in *Trociuk*, discussed earlier in this chapter, and its recognition of the significance of birth registration in establishing parent–child relationships. The court also stated that the vital statistics legislation had not kept pace with reproductive technologies: see Gary Oakes, "Genetic Parents in Surrogate Birth Win Registration Right" (January 16, 2004), *The Lawyers Weekly* 7. Clearly, the cooperation of the gestational mothers was significant in both *Rypkema* and *J.R. v. L.H.* By contrast, in *A.H.W. v. G.H.B.* 339 NJ Super 495 (2000), biological parents of an unborn child were not entitled to place their names on the child's birth certificate immediately, but were required to wait until the gestational mother relinquished her rights.

Models for Regulating Surrogacy

What is the appropriate relationship between issues of contract (and the contract's enforcement) and concerns to ensure the best interests of the child? These issues have been assessed by a number of scholars.

For example, Rosemarie Tong assessed four kinds of models for regulating surrogacy: (1) making contracts unenforceable; (2) criminalizing such arrangements; (3) using contracts to enforce surrogacy arrangements; and (4) assimilating surrogacy arrangements to adoption. After considering these models, Tong concluded that it was not appropriate to ban surrogacy altogether, but that it was necessary to protect gestational and contracting mothers. She suggested that it is necessary to adopt a model that encourages social recognition of women's willingness to bear children. On this basis, she concluded that the adoption model was preferable:

> Women as a *whole* will benefit from an approach that stresses their right, not their duty, to be mothers (and not simply baby machines). The adoption approach, with its change of heart clause, replaces what strikes me as the *heartless* contract approach. A deal is not always a deal—at least not when one is trading in some of the deepest emotions human beings can ever feel. Any approach that *binds* women to reproductive decisions—as does the contract approach—must be regarded with deep suspicion.

(Rosemarie Tong, "Feminist Perspectives and Gestational Motherhood: The Search for a Unified Legal Focus," in Joan C. Callahan, ed., *Reproduction, Ethics, and the Law: Feminist Perspectives* (Bloomington and Indianapolis, IN: Indiana University Press, 1995), 55, at 75.)

Diana Majury reached similar conclusions in Canada: see Majury, "Pre-Conception Contracts: Giving the Mother the Option," in Simon Rosenblum and Peter Findlay, eds., *Debating Canada's Future: Views from the Left* (Toronto: J. Lorimer & Co., 1991), 197.

By contrast, the Ontario Law Reform Commission's report in 1985 recommended the use of contract for surrogacy arrangements, but suggested that courts should ensure their validity:

> It is our view that, given the nature of surrogate motherhood arrangements, regulation should take the form of intervention before any aspect of the agreement is implemented and, in particular, before artificial conception technology is employed to achieve a pregnancy. We believe that mandatory minimum standards to which these arrangements must conform should be established unambiguously by statute. Each prospective surrogate motherhood arrangement should be scrutinized to ascertain whether it complies with the enunciated standards. In our opinion, the institutions best suited to undertake this crucial supervisory responsibility are the courts concerned exclusively with family law issues, that is, the Provincial Court (Family Division) and the Unified Family Court.
>
> Accordingly, we recommend that, before an artificial conception procedure may be employed in furtherance of a surrogate motherhood arrangement, the approval of the Provincial Court (Family Division) or the Unified Family Court, as the case may be, should be obtained in accordance with the proposals that we shall make in the balance of this chapter. In order for a court to evaluate the acceptability of a surrogate motherhood arrangement in accordance with legislative standards, we recommend that the terms of the agreement should be in writing. The court should be required to approve the terms and to ensure that they adequately protect the child and the parties and are not inequitable or unconscionable.

(Ontario Law Reform Commission, *Report on Human Artificial Reproduction and Related Matters* (Toronto: Ministry of the Attorney General, 1985), at 233-34.)

This recommendation was not implemented. Nor were the recommendations of the Royal Commission on New Reproductive Technologies to criminalize commercial surrogacy arrangements and to identify the gestational mother as the "mother" for legal purposes at birth: see Royal Commission on New Reproductive Technologies, *Proceed with Care* (Ottawa: Queen's Printer, 1993); for a review and critique, see Diana Majury, "Is Care Enough?" (1994), 17 *Dalhousie Law Journal* 279. Proposed legislation was introduced in the federal Parliament after the Royal Commission report. For an assessment, see Alison Harvison Young and Angela Wasunna, "Wrestling with the Limits of Law: Regulating New Reproductive Technologies" (1998), 6 *Health Law Journal* 239. After this proposed legislation died on the order paper, new legislation was introduced: Bill C-13, the *Assisted Human Reproduction Act*, and it was enacted in 2004: see SC 2004, c. 2. Recall that this legislation will prohibit commercial surrogacy and regulate the use of reproductive materials. How does this statute help to define Canadian public policy with respect to assisted reproduction?

SELECTED REFERENCES

Lori Andrews, *Between Strangers: Surrogate Mothers, Expectant Fathers, and Brave New Babies* (New York: Harper & Row, 1989).

Rachel Cook and Shelley Day Slater, with Felicity Kaganas, eds., *Surrogate Motherhood: International Perspectives* (Oxford and Portland, OR: Hart Publishing, 2003).

Martha Field, *Surrogate Motherhood: The Legal and Human Issues* (Cambridge, MA: Harvard University Press, 1990).

Caroline Forder, "Human Rights Aspects of Assisted Procreation: A European Perspective" (1999), 1 *Journal of Women's Health and Law* 69.

Adam Marshall, "Choices for a Child: An Ethical and Legal Analysis of a Failed Surrogate Birth Contract" (1996), 30 *University of Richmond Law Review* 275.

Derek Morgan, "Undoing What Comes Naturally—Regulating Medically Assisted Families," in Andrew Bainham and David Pearl, eds., *Frontiers of Family Law* (London: Chancery Law Publishers, 1993), 94.

Carl E. Schneider, "Surrogate Motherhood from the Perspective of Family Law" (1990), 13 *Harvard Journal of Law and Public Policy* 125.

Mary Lyndon Shanley, " 'Surrogate' Motherhood: The Limits of Contractual Freedom," in Shanley, *Making Babies, Making Families* (Boston: Beacon Press, 2001), 102.

Pamela Laufer-Ukeles, "Approaching Surrogate Motherhood: Reconsidering Difference" (2002), 26 *Vermont Law Review* 407.

C. New Challenges: More Than Two Parents?

The definition of parenthood has again been challenged by lesbians and gays, in relation to the recognition of a parent–child relationship in the absence of any biological connection. In 2003, an Ontario court reviewed an application for a declaration that the same-sex partner of a biological mother was also the "mother" of a child. In examining the reasoning in this case, consider whether there were alternative approaches available.

A.A. v. B.B. and C.C.
[2003] OJ no. 1215 (QL); (2003), 225 DLR (4th) 371 (Sup. Ct. J (Fam. Div.))

[The applicant requested a declaration that she was a "parent," specifically a "mother" of a two-year-old child, D.D. The respondents B.B. and C.C. were the biological parents of D.D., and they both consented to the order sought by A.A.

The applicant and C.C. established a cohabiting same-sex relationship in 1990; in 1992, they participated in a public ceremony to confirm their commitment as lifelong partners. They eventually wished to have a child and they agreed that C.C. would be the biological mother. The couple's long-time friend B.B. agreed to assist them; the three adults made a commitment whereby A.A. and C.C. would be the primary custodial and decision-making parents, but B.B. would have an active and participatory role in the child's upbringing. After the birth of the child, A.A. and C.C. were both actively involved in decision making and day-to-day care of the child, who referred to both of them as "momma." B.B. was also regularly involved with the child, sometimes in the company of his cohabiting partner and his other children. Aston J stated that he was prepared to make the declaration sought by A.A. if there was jurisdiction to do so.

Aston J noted that s. 1 of the *Children's Law Reform Act* established B.B. and C.C. as the parents of D.D. He also compared the broader definitions of parent in the *Family Law Act*, and noted the limitations of an adoption order pursuant to the *Child and Family Services Act*; or an order for custody, access, and guardianship, pursuant to the *Children's Law Reform Act*. Aston J also noted that the applicant was not seeking Charter relief, but rather an interpretation of the *Children's Law Reform Act* that would enable her to obtain a declaration that she too was a "parent."]

Recognition of parentage under the *Children's Law Reform Act* does not depend upon marital status. Subsection 1(14) provides that "any distinction at common law between the status of children born in wedlock and born out of wedlock is abolished." The inability of A.A. to legally marry C.C. does not provide any impediment to her present application.

[Note that, although marriage became legally available to A.A. and C.C. in June 2003, this legal change did not affect their "parental" rights.]

With this background context, I now turn to the specific provisions of Part II of the *Children's Law Reform Act* upon which this application is founded.

Subsections 4(1) and 4(3) read as follows ... :

4(1) Any person having an interest may apply to a court for a declaration that a male person is recognized in law to be the father of a child or that a female person is the mother of a child. ...

(3) Where the court finds on the balance of probabilities that the relationship of mother and child has been established, the court may make a declaratory order to that effect.

In *Buist v. Greaves* (1997), 72 ACWS (3d) 301, 11 OFLR 3, [1997] OJ no. 2646, 1997 Carswell Ont 2243 (Ont. Gen. Div.), the court was asked to declare the applicant a "mother" of a child in the context of a custody and access dispute between two same-sex partners. Justice Mary Lou Benotto was of the opinion that the use of the definite article "the" in subsection 4(1) of the Act indicated the drafters of the legislation did not consider that more than one person could be a "mother" of a child. However, she stopped short of actually determining the question under subsection 4(1), instead finding that the applicant had not met the test set out in subsection 4(3) in the case before her. The learned judge concluded (paragraph [35]):

Even if I had the jurisdiction to declare that a child could have two mothers under section 4, I would not, on the facts of this case, exercise my discretion to do so. Ms. Buist has not, on balance of probabilities established the relationship of mother and child.

Justice Benotto did not dismiss the application on the basis that both parties were female but because of the evidence at trial concerning the nature of the parent–child relationship.

Modern technology challenges traditional concepts. The issue of whether a child may have more than two "natural" mothers may be more complex than one might imagine. In *J.R. and J.K. v. L.H. and G.H.* (2002), 117 ACWS (3d) 276, [2002] OJ no. 3998, 2002 Carswell Ont 3445 (Ont. Sup. Ct.), the parties entered into a gestational carriage agreement. The female applicant provided the genetic material but the female respondent carried the child and became the "birth" mother as defined in the *Vital Statistics Act*, RSO 1990, c. V.4 [as amended 1998, c. 18], thereby giving the respondent the legal right to register the child as her own. The two women agreed the applicant ought to be recognized in law as the only mother of the child so it was not necessary for the court to decide whether both could be recognized in law as mothers. Justice Frances P. Kiteley was content to allude to the potential problem without deciding it. She held that:

> If there had been a conflict between the genetic parents and the woman who is the gestational carrier, I would have to consider whether section 4(1) [of the *Children's Law Reform Act*] enables a declaration that there is more than one mother, as Benotto J raised but did not determine in *Buist v. Greaves*, [1997] OJ no. 2646, 1997 Carswell Ont 2243 (Ont. Gen. Div.). However, the disposition in this case is facilitated because the birth mother agrees with the genetic parents that she ought to be declared not to be a parent.

The case *Low v. Low* (1994), 114 DLR (4th) 709, 4 RFL (4th) 103, 1 LWR 573, [1994] OJ no. 896, 1994 Carswell Ont 398 (Ont. Gen. Div.), stands for the proposition that it is not necessary for a child to be the "natural" (or biological) child of a person for a declaration to be granted under section 4 of the *Children's Law Reform Act*. That case dealt with an application by a father rather than a mother. At paragraph [18], Justice Lee K. Ferrier concluded:

> [T]he declaration authorized in section 4(1) is not that a male person is the "natural father," rather that he is "recognized in law to be the father" of the child. This also suggests an intention of a meaning broader than merely the "biological" father.

I adopt the reasoning and the conclusion at paragraph [21] in that case, that "[n]owhere in s. 5 is there any suggestion that the 'relationship of father and child' must have a biological or genetic character." Adapted to the facts of this case, subsection 4(3) of the *Children's Law Reform Act* does not require that "the relationship of mother and child" must have a biological or genetic character. Mothers and fathers are to be treated on an equal footing.

In every case brought to my attention, the court has chosen between potential mothers or potential fathers, deciding that one or the other of them is recognized in law to be the mother or the father. As previously noted, adoption orders could grant legal recognition of two mothers or two fathers for a particular child. But, even in that context, the adoption order extinguishes any other parental relationship so the number of parents has always been limited to two, even if they share a common gender.

As an exercise in statutory interpretation, it all comes down to this: Does section 4 of the *Children's Law Reform Act* allow the court to declare more than two persons to be parents of a child? ...

[Aston J focused on principles of statutory interpretation, citing the Supreme Court's approval of Driedger's "modern principle" for statutory interpretation:]

> Today there is only one principle or approach, namely, the words of an Act are to be read in their entire context and in their grammatical and ordinary sense harmoniously with the scheme of the Act, the object of the Act, and the intention of Parliament. ...

Children's Law Reform Act, Part II—Establishment of Parentage

Section 4 of the *Children's Law Reform Act* (quoted above) uses the definite article "the" in both subsection (1) and subsection (3). I start with Justice Benotto's suggestion in *Buist v. Greaves*, supra, that this connotes a singular person or relationship.

In the 4th edition of Sullivan and Driedger on the *Construction of Statutes* (Toronto: Butterworths, 2002) at pages 22-23, Professor Ruth Sullivan wrote:

> Although judges regularly establish the ordinary meaning of words by looking them up in dictionaries, in fact the definitions found in dictionaries say very little about the meaning of a word as used in a particular context. Since the purpose of a dictionary is to reveal the full range of senses a word may have or the different ways it may be used, dictionary entries focus in effect on the ambiguity of language.

At pages 26-31 of her text Professor Sullivan explained at greater length why dictionary definitions are a poor tool to use for statutory interpretation.

[The court concluded that the dictionary reference failed to create contextual ambiguity and that legislation is presumed to be accurate and well crafted.]

. . .

When the legislation uses a word such as "the," it is presumed to do so precisely and for a purpose. It represents a choice of the definite article over the indefinite article. Considerable weight must be given to its clear and ordinary meaning.

A conclusion that Part II of the *Children's Law Reform Act* contemplates a single mother and a single father (outside the adoption exception already noted) is reinforced by its consistency with another provision in the Act. Subsection 8(1) provides a list of certain rebuttable presumptions whereby a male person "shall be recognized in law to be the father of a child." For example, a person who is married to the mother of the child at the time of the child's birth, or within 300 days before the child's birth, or who cohabited with the mother within that time is presumed to be the father. The presumption also arises if the person has "certified" the child's birth as provided in the *Vital Statistic Act* or if the person marries the child's mother after the child's birth and "acknowledges" that he is the natural father. Significantly, subsection 8(3) provides:

> Where circumstances exist that give rise to a presumption or presumptions of paternity by more than one father under subsection (1), no presumption shall be made as to paternity and no person is recognized in law to be the father.

The legislator could have left open the possibility of more than one father but, instead, made an express opposite choice. There is no logical reason to suppose the legislator would choose to limit the number of fathers to one while allowing for more than one mother.

This conclusion is also consistent with other legislation, namely the adoption provision in the *Child and Family Services Act*, whereby no more than two persons can apply for an adoption order and the order extinguishes other parental status. Adoption thus limits the number of parents to a maximum of two.

Therefore, the plain and ordinary meaning of the word "the" is unambiguous, consistent with other expression of legislative intent and not inconsistent with any Charter or common law principle.

In my view, part II of the *Children's Law Reform Act* does not afford authority for the court to grant this application.

Inherent Jurisdiction of the Court

The alternative submission of the parties is that the court can grant the application by exercising its parens patriae authority to fill a legislative gap. Courts are generally reluctant to fill gaps in legislation. One reason is that a "gap" may be deliberate. Perceived gaps from provisions that seem under-inclusive effectively require the court to legislate. In my view that is the case here. There is no legislative gap.

The granting of the application could certainly be perceived to reflect the best interests of this particular child. That is not reason enough to resort to the court's parens patriae jurisdiction. As Justice Cheryl J. Robertson stated in *Lennox and Addington Family and Children's Services v. T.S., D.M., C.M. and R.M.* (2000), 6 RFL (5th) 331, [2000] OTC 267, [2000] OJ no. 1420, 2000 Carswell Ont 1352 (Ont. Fam. Ct.), at paragraph [20]:

> [20] The court is unable to repair any legislative shortcoming through parens patriae. As a court of superior jurisdiction, parens patriae authorizes the court through its inherent jurisdiction to intervene and rescue a child in danger. It can sometimes be used to bridge a legislative gap. It does not confer supplemental jurisdiction so as to rewrite legislation and procedure.

Furthermore, the court also must be concerned about the best interests of other children not before the court. For example, if this application is granted, it seems to me the door is wide open to stepparents, extended family and others to claim parental status in less harmonious circumstances. If a child can have three parents, why not four or six or a dozen? What about all the adults in a commune or a religious organization or sect? Quite apart from social policy implications, the potential to create or exacerbate custody and access litigation should not be ignored.

Polarized views exist concerning the definition of the modern family. Court decisions may sometimes necessarily impact on that debate, particularly where Charter considerations are engaged. However, when it comes to creating or shaping social policy, political considerations belong to the legislature.

The parties do not challenge the *Children's Law Reform Act* as constitutionally flawed. It would be wrong effectively to amend the Act using the indirect route of reliance upon an inherent jurisdiction of the court.

The application must, therefore, be dismissed. As stated in paragraph [12] above, this case is not about gender, sexual orientation or the definition of marriage. The result would be the same if A.A. and C.C. were husband and wife.

Discussion Notes

The Charter and Human Rights Equality: Gill v. Murray

If the court is correct, and the statutory provision allows only one mother, does this provision constitute an infringement of the equality guarantee in s. 15 of the Charter? Why was it hard for this applicant to make a claim that the statute should recognize that a child may have two parents who are both women? In this context, consider *Gill v. Murray*, [2001] BCHRTD no. 34 (QL). Two complaints were filed with the BC Human Rights Commission by the same-sex partners of birth mothers, alleging that their treatment by the Vital Statistics Agency constituted sex and sexual orientation discrimination. They alleged that the agency refused to permit them to be registered as parents, thus requiring them to obtain orders for adoption.

In this context, they demonstrated that the agency routinely permitted males in opposite-sex relationships to be registered as parents, without inquiring as to whether the males were biologically related to the child whose birth was being registered. The Commission's decision stated in part (at paras. 79-84):

> When the partner of the mother is not a biological parent of the child, Vital Statistics will only register that parent if an adoption order under the provisions of the *Adoption Act*, RSBC 1996, c. 5 has been obtained. Although this is theoretically the case whether the partner is the same or the opposite sex as the mother, in practice only same-sex partners of mothers are questioned as to their biological relationship with the child. Opposite sex partners of women giving birth are not similarly questioned.
>
> Furthermore, women who give birth to a child born using a donor egg are registered as mothers without question. Similarly, men who self-identify as fathers are able to register themselves as such on the Birth Registration forms. Neither parent is required to adopt, or resort to the Court, to establish the parent–child relationship.
>
> With the advent of various forms of reproductive technology, it is possible for a child to have legal social parents, biological parents, and a birth mother who is neither a legal social or biological mother. It is evident that the Birth Registration regime established by Vital Statistics has not kept up with reproductive technologies. The same-sex partner of the biological mother of a child is denied the presumptive proof of her relationship to the child, including the right to register her child in school, to obtain airline tickets and passports for her child, as well as denying her the ability to assert her child's rights with respect to a myriad of other laws, from the *BC Benefits (Child Care) Act* to the *Young Offenders Act*, unless and until she resorts to the adoption process.
>
> In my view, Vital Statistics has denied same-sex couples the right to register a birth in the same way that opposite sex couples do, based on the Director's definition of "father," as well as its practice of allowing males to register as fathers without any inquiry into a biological relationship with a child. The process of registering births, upon which birth certificates are based, is based solely on a heterosexual view of the family. Because the

Complainants are women living in same sex relationships who have a child together, they can only establish families through the adoption process. This differential treatment to access to a process that confers a benefit offends the principles of equality on the bases of sexual orientation, family status and sex.

I conclude that Vital Statistics has denied the Complainants access to the benefit of verification and documentation of parent/child relationships available to others without the necessity of the adoption procedure, and has thus contravened s. 8 of the Code. I find that Vital Statistics has discriminated against Ms. Gill and Ms. Popoff on the basis of sex, sexual orientation and family status. I also find that Vital Statistics has discriminated against Ms. Maher and Ms. Murray on the basis of sex, sexual orientation and family status. Had Ms. Maher and Ms. Murray been male, they would not have been questioned as to their sex or biological connection to their child, nor would they have been directed to take steps to adopt their child.

Further, I find that Vital Statistics has discriminated against the infant children on the basis of sex, sexual orientation and their family status by denying them the right to have their parents named on the birth registration, and birth certificate, even though both parents acknowledge and fulfil the parental role. In that respect, the infant Complainants are treated differently than children of opposite sex parents.

Is the reasoning in this case useful in rethinking *A.A. v. B.B. and C.C.?* Why, or why not? See also *Re P.(N.)* (2000), 193 DLR (4th) 706), where the Quebec Court of Appeal declined to make a declaration that a same-sex partner was a "parent" of the biological child of her partner. To what extent is *Gill v. Murray* consistent with the Supreme Court of Canada decision in *Trociuk v. British Columbia (Attorney General)*, discussed earlier in this chapter in relation to registration of genetic relationships and the right to name children pursuant to vital statistics legislation? How should provincial legislation be drafted to conform to the decisions in *Trociuk* and *Gill v. Murray*? What fundamental issues preclude the recognition in law of more than two parents?

In *Doe v. Canada (Attorney General)*, [2003] OJ no. 5430 (Sup. Ct. J), the court declared moot a Charter challenge to semen regulations under the *Food and Drug Act* when the lesbian applicant gave birth after self-insemination using the semen of a donor she had selected. Doe wanted to challenge provisions in the regulations that created barriers to her using the sperm of a donor of choice. Since she had become pregnant by self-insemination, using sperm from her donor of choice, the court declared the challenge moot; however, the judge stated that a woman seeking assisted conception from a fertility clinic must be treated in the same way, whether she is lesbian or heterosexual.

Reproductive Technology and Family Relationships

Issues about definitions of "parents" in relation to reproductive technology have also addressed problems about inheritance: for example, see *In re the Estate of K* (1996), no. M25/1996 (Tasmania). In the United States, a number of cases have considered the legal relationships created by reproductive technologies: for example, see *Johnson v. Calvert*, 4 Cal. Rptr. (2d) 170; 822 P2d 1317 (CA 1992) and *Re Marriage of Buzzanca*, 61 Cal. App. 4th 1410; 77 ALR (5th) 775 (CA 1998). In *Buzzanca*, an anonymous embryo donation was implanted into a gestational surrogate, pursuant to a contract with the Buzzancas. However, a month before the child's birth, the father petitioned for dissolution of the marriage, asserting that he was not accepting any responsibility for the child. The gestational mother disclaimed any assertion that she was the child's parent, but Mrs. Buzzanca was not related to the child genetically or gestationally. Eventually, the appellate court ruled that the Buzzancas were the legal parents of the child. By that time, the child was three years old.

There are also some cases relating to the potential rights to fatherhood status for a male who has donated sperm to enable a lesbian woman to have a child. In *Thomas S. v. Robin Y.*, 599 NYS 2d 377 (Fam. Ct. 1993) and 209 AD 2d 298; 618 NYS 2d 356 (Ct. App. 1994), the parties had agreed that the sperm donor would not have any parental rights or obligations, but the Court of Appeals overturned the lower court decision that had confirmed this agreement. A majority of the appellate court ruled it was appropriate to make an order of filiation in favour of the sperm donor, and that the oral agreement between the parties could not be enforced. The court was obviously concerned about cutting off the parental rights of the biological father. For a critique of this case, see Katherine Arnup and S. Boyd, "Familial Disputes? Sperm Donors, Lesbian Mothers, and Legal Parenthood," in Didi Herman and Carl Stychin, eds., *Legal Inversions* (Philadelphia: Temple University Press, 1995), 77. See also Katherine Arnup, "Finding Fathers: Artificial Insemination, Lesbians, and the Law" (1994), 7 *Canadian Journal of Women and the Law* 97. Is it possible to distinguish contracts between sperm donors and their recipients on one hand from contracts with gestational mothers and intentional parents on the other? Why, or why not? Recall *Johnson-Steeves v. Lee*, discussed earlier in this chapter—is it consistent with *Thomas S. v. Robin Y.*? Why, or why not?

SELECTED REFERENCES

Mary Ann Glendon, *Abortion and Divorce in Western Law* (Cambridge, MA: Harvard University Press, 1987).

Michael T. Morley, Richard Albert, Jennie L. Kneedler, and Chrystiane Pereira, "Developments in Law and Policy: Emerging Issues in Family Law" (2003), 21 *Yale Law and Policy Review* 169.

Roxanne Mykitiuk, "Beyond Conception: Legal Determinations of Filiation in the Context of Assisted Reproductive Technologies" (2001), 39 *Osgoode Hall Law Journal* 771.

Jo Shaw, "The Right to Posthumous Use of Sperm and the Free Movement of Persons Under European Community Law" (1997), 19:4 *Journal of Social Welfare and Family Law* 507.

Richard Storrow, "Parenthood by Pure Intention: Assisted Reproduction and the Functional Approach to Parentage" (2002), 53 *Hastings Law Journal* 597.

PROBLEM: LEGAL RECOGNITION OF PARENT–CHILD RELATIONSHIPS

In relation to the parent–child issues in this chapter, consider whether and to what extent the "rights" of parents are different for genetic parents (mothers and fathers); adoptive or biological parents who both wish to remain involved in a child's life; or parents (genetic, gestational, or social) who are interested in having a relationship with a child who was created using assisted reproductive technologies. Are these situations of parent–child relationships sufficiently different to warrant the use of different legal principles? To what extent is it possible to develop more consistent legal principles concerning parent–child relationships and their rights and responsibilities? Is there a need to recognize additional kinds of relationships between "parents" and "children"? Should all such relationships result in similar rights and obligations? To what extent should law grant priority to biological relationships? Why? If biological relationships are especially important in law, how should the respective rights of mothers and fathers be recognized?

In this context, reconsider Martha Fineman's suggestion that the mother–child relationship should be the primary legal relationship, not marriage or other intimate relationships among adults. Which category of parents (biological, adoptive, social) did she have in mind in making her suggestion? Is her proposal easily applicable in all of these different circumstances of parent–child relationships? In balancing recognition for mothers and fathers, are there other principles that could be adopted more effectively?

CHAPTER REFERENCES

Abraham, Carolyn. "We Bought It … It's Ours," *Globe and Mail*, September 11, 1999, at D1.

Adams, Marie. *Our Son, a Stranger: Adoption Breakdown and Its Effects on Parents* (Montreal and Kingston, ON: McGill-Queen's University Press, 2002).

Adoption Council of Canada. "International Adoptions Steady: 1,891 in 2002" (Ottawa, May 6, 2003), online at www.adoption.ca/news/030506stats02.htm.

Arnup, Katherine. "Finding Fathers: Artificial Insemination, Lesbians, and the Law" (1994), 7 *Canadian Journal of Women and the Law* 97.

Arnup, Katherine and Susan Boyd. "Familial Disputes? Sperm Donors, Lesbian Mothers, and Legal Parenthood," in Didi Herman and Carl Stychin, eds., *Legal Inversions* (Philadelphia: Temple University Press, 1995).

Bainham, Andrew and David Pearl, eds., *Frontiers of Family Law* (London: Chancery Law Publishing, 1993).

Baird, Patricia A. "Reproductive Technology and the Evolution of Family Law" (1997-98), 15 *Canadian Family Law Quarterly* 103.

Bakogeorge, Peter. "Helping Clients 'Build' Families," *Law Times*, July 8, 2002, 15.

Bala, Nicholas, Joseph Hornick, and Robin Vogl, eds., *Canadian Child Welfare Law: Children, Families, and the State* (Scarborough, ON: Thompson Educational Publishing, 1991).

Bean, Philip, ed. *Adoption: Essays in Social Policy, Law, and Sociology* (London: Tavistock, 1984).

Benet, M.K. *The Character of Adoption* (London: Jonathan Cape, 1976).

Bernstein, Marvin, Diane Caldwell, G. Bruce Clark, and Roselyn Zisman. "Adoption with Access or 'Open Adoption'" (1991-92), 8 *Canadian Family Law Quarterly* 283.

Black, Debra. "Surrogate Motherhood 'Expression of Love,'" *Toronto Star*, December 31, 1999, A3.

Bracco, Katrysha. "Patriarchy and the Law of Adoption: Beneath the Best Interests of the Child" (1997), 35 *Alberta Law Review* 1035.

Bream, Joseph. "Native Upbringing Not a Right, Judge Rules," *National Post*, May 1, 2004.

Brower Blair, D. Marianne. "The Impact of Family Paradigms, Domestic Constitutions, and International Conventions on Disclosure of an Adopted Person's Identities and Heritage: A Comparative Examination" (2001), 22 *Michigan Journal of International Law* 587.

Bueckert, Dennis. "Surrogate Motherhool Flourishing," *Toronto Star*, May 31, 1999, A3.

Bunting, Madeleine. "Donor Insemination Raises Big Questions About Children's Rights To Know Their Biological Fathers," *The Guardian*, July 2, 2001.

Callahan, Joan C., ed. *Reproduction, Ethics, and the Law: Feminist Perspectives* (Bloomington and Indianapolis, IN: Indiana University Press, 1995).

Collier, Richard. "In Search of the 'Good Father': Law, Family Practices, and the Normative Reconstruction of Parenthood" (2001), 22 *Studies in Law, Politics, and Society* 133.

Daly, Kerry J. and Michael P. Sobol. *Adoption in Canada: Final Report* (Guelph, ON: National Adoption Study for Health and Welfare Canada, 1993).

de Cruz, S.P. "Adoption—Whether Permissible Following Commercial Surrogacy Arrangement," [1987] *Journal of Social Welfare Law* 314.

Duncan, William. "Regulating Intercountry Adoption—An International Perspective," in Andrew Bainham and David Pearl, eds., *Frontiers of Family Law* (London: Chancery Law Publishing, 1993), 46.

Edwards, Rosalind, Val Gillies, and Jane Ribbens McCarthy. "Biological Parents and Social Families: Legal Discourses and Everyday Understandings of the Position of Step-Parents" (1999), 13 *International Journal of Law, Policy, and the Family* 78.

Ferguson, Sue. "A New Community Comes of Age," *Maclean's*, February 24, 2003, 47.

Fineman, Martha. *The Neutered Mother, the Sexual Family and Other Twentieth Century Tragedies* (New York: Routledge, 1995).

Freedman, Benjamin, P.J. Taylor, Thomas Wonnacott, and Katherine Hill. "Criteria for Parenting in Canada: A Comparative Survey of Adoption and Artificial Insemination Practices" (1988), 3 *Canadian Family Law Quarterly* 35.

Garber, Ralph. *Disclosure of Adoption Information* (Toronto: Ministry of Community and Social Services, 1985).

Gavigan, Shelley A.M. "Legal Forms, Family Forms, Gendered Norms: What Is a 'Spouse'?" (1999), 14:1 *Canadian Journal of Law and Society* 127.

Harley Eber, Dorothy. *Images of Justice: A Legal History of the Northwest Territories as Traced Through the Yellowknife Courthouse Collection of Inuit Sculpture* (Montreal and Kingston: McGill-Queen's University Press, 1997).

Harvison Young, Alison and Angela Wasunna. "Wrestling with the Limits of Law: Regulating New Reproductive Technologies" (1998), 6 *Health Law Journal* 239.

Herman, Didi and Carl Stychin, eds., *Legal Inversions* (Philadelphia: Temple University Press, 1995).

House, Jeannie. "The Changing Face of Adoption: The Challenge of Open and Custom Adoption" (1997), 13 *Canadian Family Law Quarterly* 333.

International Convention on Protection of Children and Co-operation in Respect of Intercountry Adoption (May 29, 1993), 32 ILM 1134.

Lazarus, Keri B. "Adoption of Native American and First Nations Children: Are the United States and Canada Recognizing the Best Interests of the Children?" (1997), 14:1 *Arizona Journal of International and Comparative Law* 255.

Lessard, Hester. "Mothers, Fathers, and Naming: Reflections on the Law Equality Framework and Trociuk v. British Columbia (Attorney General)" (2004), *Canadian Journal of Women and the Law* (forthcoming).

Loomis, Jeffrey. "An Alternative Placement for Children in Adoption Law: Allowing Homosexuals the Right To Adopt" (1992), 18 *Ohio Northern University Law Review* 631.

Majury, Diana. "Is Care Enough?" (1994), 17 *Dalhousie Law Journal* 279.

_____. "Pre-Conception Contracts: Giving the Mother the Option," in Simon Rosenblum and Peter Findlay, eds., *Debating Canada's Future: Views from the Left* (Toronto: J. Lorimer & Co., 1991), 197.

Mandell, Nancy and Ann Duffy, eds. *Reconstructing the Canadian Family: Feminist Perspectives* (Toronto: Butterworths, 1988).

McDaniel, Susan A. "Women's Roles, Reproduction and the New Reproductive Technologies: A New Stork Rising," in Nancy Mandell and Ann Duffy, eds., *Reconstructing the Canadian Family: Feminist Perspectives* (Toronto: Butterworths, 1988), 175.

McGillivray, Anne. "Transracial Adoption and the Status Indian Child" (1985), 4 *Canadian Journal of Family Law* 437.

McIntyre, Mike. "Parents Forced To Adopt Own Baby," *Winnipeg Free Press*, October 28, 2000, A1.

McKeague, Paul. "I Just Want To Know Who My Father Is," *Ottawa Citizen*, September 28, 1999.

_____. "Seeking the Mystery of Birth," *Ottawa Citizen*, September 27, 1999.

Oakes, Gary. "Genetic Parents in Surrogate Birth Win Registration Right" (January 16, 2004), *The Lawyers Weekly*.

Ontario Law Reform Commission. *Report on Human Artificial Reproduction and Related Matters* (Toronto: Ministry of the Attorney General, 1985).

Pascall, Gillian. "Adoption: Perspectives in Social Policy," in Philip Bean, ed., *Adoption: Essays in Social Policy, Law, and Sociology* (London: Tavistock, 1984), 19.

Peppin, Patricia. "Justice and Care: Mental Disability and Sterilization Decisions" (1989-90), 6 *Canadian Human Rights Yearbook* 65.

Philp, Margaret. "A One-Way Ticket Out of Only Nation He Knows," *Globe and Mail*, July 15, 2003, A1.

Priest, Lisa. "Special Delivery," *Globe and Mail*, August 31, 2002, F1.

Reeves, Josephine. "The Deviant Mother and Child: The Development of Adoption as an Instrument of Social Control" (1993), 20 *Journal of Law and Society* 412.

Rosenblum, Simon and Peter Findlay, eds., *Debating Canada's Future: Views from the Left* (Toronto: J. Lorimer & Co., 1991), 197.

Routhier, Ghislaine. "Black Children, White Parents" (1988), *Intercultural Horizons* 10.

Royal Commission on New Reproductive Technologies. *Proceed with Care* (Ottawa: Queen's Printer, 1993).

Shanley, Mary Lyndon. *Making Babies, Making Families* (Boston: Beacon Press, 2001).

Silva, Elizabeth B. and Carol Smart. "The 'New' Practices and Politics of Family Life," in Elizabeth B. Silva and Carol Smart, eds., *The New Family?* (London: Sage Publications, 1999).

Silver, Caryl. "Case Comment" (1995), 3 CNLR 8.

Sinclair, Murray J., Donna Phillips, and Nicholas Bala. "Aboriginal Child Welfare in Canada," in Nicholas Bala, Joseph Hornick, and Robyn Vogl, eds., *Canadian Child Welfare Law: Children, Families, and the State* (Scarborough, ON: Thompson Educational Publishing, 1991), 180.

Sissons, Jack. *Judge of the Far North* (Toronto: McClelland & Stewart, 1968).

Smart, Carol. "The 'New' Parenthood: Fathers and Mothers After Divorce," in Elizabeth B. Silva and Carol Smart, eds., *The New Family?* (London: Sage Publications, 1999), 100.

Taylor, Bill. "Shades of Gray," *Toronto Star*, May 18, 1995.

Tong, Rosemarie. "Feminist Perspectives and Gestational Motherhood: The Search for a Unified Legal Focus," in Joan C. Callahan, ed., *Reproduction, Ethics, and the Law: Feminist Perspectives* (Bloomington and Indianapolis, IN: Indiana University Press, 1995), 55.

Vanier Institute of the Family. *Profiling Canada's Families II* (Ottawa: Vanier Institute of the Family, 2000).

Vobejda, Barbara. "Egg Donation Develops into a Fertile Business," *Toronto Star*, April 11, 1999, B1.

White, Nancy J. "Offering an 'Incredible Gift,' Surrogate Mother Carries Baby for Her Friend," *Toronto Star*, December 11, 1999, N1.

Wilson, Sarah. "Identity, Genealogy, and the Social Family: The Case of Donor Insemination" (1997), 11 *International Journal of Law, Policy, and the Family* 270.

CHAPTER FOUR

Families in the Shadow of the State: Responsibilities of Care and Protection

I. INTRODUCTION

The state clearly has a direct interest in the functioning of the family as a means of distribution of resources to children and ... their carers. Failure of that system has immediate impact on the community. It has always been at times when such failures have been perceived as constituting a serious threat to the community that the law has intervened, attempting to force families to behave as ideology says they should. ... [It] is also true that increased sensitivity to the interests of individual family members leads to more intrusive intervention, as in the case of child sexual abuse. ... The only way this can be tolerated within current political ideology is by sanctioning such intervention through elaborate procedural devices, which provide some *legitimation* for intrusion.

> John Eekelaar and Mavis Maclean, "Introduction,"
> in John Eekelaar and Mavis Maclean, eds., *A Reader on Family Law*
> (Oxford: Oxford University Press, 1994), 1, at 18 and 21

Traditionally, family law focused on issues about the formation of families (marriage) and family breakdown (divorce). In this context, the law's regulation of "intact" families was not considered family law; issues about child protection, for example, were often included in law school courses about children's law and thus quite separate from traditional family law principles concerning the creation and dissolution of heterosexual adult relationships. More recently, the law's increasing recognition of violence in intimate relationships and child sexual abuse within families has required analysis of the impact of these problems on the legal rights and relationships of individuals within families—legal principles must balance a need to protect vulnerable family members with continued support for the intact family unit as a whole. In so doing, legal principles reflect complex tensions between the state's interest in ensuring the protection of vulnerable individuals who are members of families, while also providing support for families themselves as units of society entitled to autonomy, privacy, and respect.

Thus, as the title of this chapter makes clear, intact families exist within the shadow of the state, particularly with respect to obligations of protection for vulnerable family members. Therefore, the scope of family law needs to take some account of relationships between families and the state. Although these issues are clearly revealed when the state intervenes to protect individual family members, law has also been used to implement a range of governmental policies that affect both the forms of families and the nature of their legal obligations as individuals and as family units. In this way, policy assumptions about families are "hidden" within the interstices of many other areas of law—for example, tax law, property and inheritance law, criminal law, and labour law.

Moreover, not only positive statutory provisions, but also the *absence* of legal regulation may define relationships between state and family responsibilities for vulnerable individuals. In this respect, the absence of legal regulation, which reflects state policies of non-intervention in family life, may clearly assign responsibilities for these matters to families. As Nikolas Rose explained in relation to the state's choices not to intervene in some "private" matters:

> Designating [some matters] personal, private and subjective makes them appear to be outside the scope of the law as a fact of nature, whereas in fact non-intervention is a socially constructed, historically variable and inevitably political decision. The state defines as "private" those aspects of life into which it will not intervene, and then, paradoxically, uses this privacy as the justification for its non-intervention.

(Nikolas Rose, "Beyond the Public/Private Division: Law, Power and the Family" (1987), 14 *Journal of Law and Society* 61, at 64-65.)

This chapter explores selected legal issues relating to intact families and their relationships to the state, focusing particularly on issues about care and protection for vulnerable family members. It begins with a brief examination of legal regulation of child care, an example of limited intervention on the part of the state and thus a significant private responsibility for families with young children. The chapter then examines some issues relating to child protection, where more complex legal regimes have been established in an effort to balance state interests in protecting children with state goals of supporting family integrity. The materials look at some legal aspects of child sexual abuse, a phenomenon that has attracted considerable legal intervention in recent decades; they also provide an overview of issues about violence in intimate relationships and the ways that legal policies have attempted to balance the need to provide protection for vulnerable adults while also supporting an ongoing family unit. In this context, the chapter briefly identifies some emerging issues of abuse of elderly persons in families and in family-like settings.

II. FAMILIES AND THE STATE: RESPONSIBILITIES OF CARING FOR CHILDREN

Our crazy quilt of child care policy has evolved during a period in which employment for mothers with young children has become the norm rather than the exception. [In 1967, 1 in 6 mothers with preschool children was in the labour force, but by 2002, the figure was 7 in 10 mothers.] This represents a sea change in the way we raise children, yet public policy and private industry do not seem to have reacted. By and large, working mothers are left on their own to make child care arrangements. ... [And, in spite of a series of promises,] the federal government has yet to launch a significant child care initiative.

> Michael Krashinsky, " 'Are We There Yet?': The Evolving
> Face of Child Care Policy in Canada" (2001-2), *Transition*
> (Vanier Institute of the Family) 3, at 3-4

As this comment suggests, there have been significant changes in the rate of women's participation in paid work in recent decades. Moreover, the rate of participation of mothers of preschool-aged children has also increased sharply. Yet, in spite of a number of studies that have recommended the adoption of national standards and funding for child care, the care of young children remains substantially a matter of (private) familial responsibility, with only minimal state intervention. The following excerpt focuses on Canadian child-care (and parental-leave) policies; it reveals how these policies represent choices of non-intervention on the part of the state, thus assigning primary responsibility for child care to individual families. As the comment suggests, Canada's non-intervention in this area contrasts sharply with different choices in other jurisdictions, particularly in western Europe, and has important consequences for parents, particularly women, in the paid workforce.

Lene Madsen, "Citizen, Worker, Mother: Canadian Women's Claims to Parental Leave and Childcare"
(2002), 19 *Canadian Journal of Family Law* 11, at 53ff.

Canadian law and policy makers have engaged, on paper at least, with the issue of childcare for upwards of twenty years. Successive commission and task forces have produced reports and recommendations, which, although with variation in emphasis, agree in their findings that affordable quality childcare would benefit Canadian children, support the Canadian economy, reduce child poverty, and contribute to gender equality. In 1986, the federally funded *Task Force on Child Care* appointed by the Liberals in 1984 recommended the establishment of a fully funded childcare system; in 1987, the *Special Committee on Child Care* appointed by the Conservatives in 1985 recommended an expansion of tax measures, coupled with a new federal spending program to address childcare needs; in 1987, the Conservative government introduced the *National Strategy on Child Care*, followed in 1988 by the *Canada Child Care Bill* (sharply criticized at the time, but nevertheless an attempt to deal with childcare as a pressing social need), which died on the order paper, was not reintroduced after the election, and was formally abandoned in 1992; in 1993, the Liberals included a commitment to childcare in their "Red Book"; and in 1995 the report of the *Social Security Review* recognized the importance of childcare. Yet, in 2001, despite the thousands of pages written which document the need for and potential advantages of a comprehensive national childcare system, and despite clear evidence that most Canadian families consider childcare to be a pressing priority, childcare is presently poorly organized, haphazardly regulated, under-funded, of variable quality, and insufficiently available to the majority of families requiring services. As noted in a recent commentary in the *Globe and Mail*:

> [F]or all the political rhetoric about an agenda for children, for all the millions of dollars invested in research and pilot projects probing the precious first few years of life, most children are standing in the same spot they were a decade ago. ...

The State of Canadian Childcare

At present, the available childcare mix includes a small number of regulated daycare centre spaces, a limited number of regulated family/home care spaces, and unregulated care, which may include care by relatives, care by friends and or neighbours, or paid-for but unlicensed care by others in the community. A very recent report estimated that while there are approximately 3.2 million Canadian children in need of childcare, a mere 360,000 regulated spaces are available to address this need. The vast majority of children are thus cared for in unregulated settings while their parents work outside the home. Given the consistent evidence that the quality of care in regulated settings is in general superior to that available in unregulated settings, assessments of the adequacy of Canadian childcare options focus on the former.

Childcare advocates and scholars typically assess regulated daycare options in Canada with respect to their accessibility, affordability, and quality, and have with alarming agreement found the situation on all three fronts to be sorely lacking. Assessing the state of *regulated* care, they have found that Canada's childcare provisions fall well behind those of European countries, and do not come close to meeting the needs of working parents. Says Maureen Baker, "Canada's child care system ranks well below those of most of the countries studied in terms of level of funding, availability of spaces, cost to parents, and quality of care."

Accessibility concerns the extent to which parents are able to find an age appropriate space for their child(ren); in a reasonably proximate location; with opening hours that match the needs of the parents; and which is sensitive to cultural, physical, social and developmental needs. Studies show and the numbers above indicate that only a fraction of the needed regulated spaces are available, thus compelling many parents to use unregulated care even when they would prefer a regulated setting. Opening hours are also a significant obstacle for many parents—while most care is provided on the basis of a "standard workweek," roughly corresponding to a 9-5 workday, many parents are in need of services during evenings, nights, and weekends. Indeed, over 40% of the Canadian workforce does not work a "standard" schedule. While home-based care is in general more flexible than centre-based care, there is still a serious shortage of care during "off-hours." Serious issues of accessibility also arise with respect to children with special needs. Most "regular" daycare centres are not open to children with disabilities, either due to physical barriers or staffing limitations. Although there is some funding to assist some parents, "a very significant number of children with special needs are not receiving childcare services." Maureen Baker summarizes the current situation with respect to accessibility:

> Parents with able-bodied children between three and five, who live in cities, and who can afford to pay higher fees, have the most options from which to choose.

Affordability concerns the extent to which parents who require care are able to purchase regulated spaces for their children. While there are important variations amongst the provinces, there is no question that childcare claims a significant portion of the after tax income of families requiring paid care. Indeed, one study indicated that childcare for *one* preschooler, for a family with an average income living in a medium-sized Ontario city, represented fully 15% of after-tax earnings. Maureen Baker has noted that the cost of daycare can "more than double the annual cost of raising young children and is usually the greatest single child-related expense the family incurs." Childcare is primarily funded through parent fees, which in some cases are reduced by subsidies. However, as will be discussed below, this mechanism is insufficient to alleviate the burden on many families requiring childcare. Studies consistently show that childcare is a significant financial burden for all but the wealthy, and that many parents who would prefer regulated care options for their children simply are not able to afford them.

"Quality" childcare has been identified as an important tool to enhance the healthy development of children, which assists in fostering their physical, intellectual, social, and emotional development, while ensuring that children are "school-ready" by age six. Indicators of quality include but are not limited to the training of staff as well as the staff–child ratio. The fact that fully 90% of childcare is presently unregulated is thus cause for serious concern. This issue will be discussed more fully below.

Childcare Without the State

The sorry state of Canadian childcare can largely be attributed to the fact that at present, childcare in Canada is considered a private concern, to be addressed by individual families through the family or the market place. ... [Childcare] in Canada ... is a state concern "only when the market or family fails, and this is presumed to apply to a small share or residual of the population." It is conceived of in many respects as an "anti-poverty program" for lower income groups, rather than as an entitlement *per se*. At present, government involvement in childcare is limited to essentially three areas: the extension of two tax measures; the provision of subsidies to narrowly specified "target groups"; and the regulation of some childcare spaces. Since the early 1990s, and particularly since the adoption of the CHST [Canada Health and Social Transfer], government involvement in childcare has been steadily decreasing.

The primary method of funding childcare in Canada is the *Child Care Expense Deduction*, provided for in section 63 of the *Income Tax Act*, which allows families to deduct from the taxable income of the lower earning spouse the cost of childcare, up to a maximum of $7,000 per year for children under 7 and $4,000 for children between

8 and 16. The deduction can be claimed only for childcare expenses incurred to allow the parent to work outside the home or to study; and expenses must not exceed two thirds of the "earned income" of the lowest earning parent. The limitations of section 63 are numerous: it does not reflect the actual cost of childcare, which can be considerably more expensive; being structured as a deduction, this mechanism is regressive, delivering the greatest potential benefit to those in higher tax brackets; the value of the deduction is limited by the fact that it must be claimed by the lower earning spouse; the limits placed on what constitutes "earned income" for the purpose of claiming the deduction constrains the ability of women to utilize the deduction if the bulk of their income is spousal support; and the requirement of actually *filing* receipts limits the deduction of expenses where care is given in the informal sector, as it often is. In addition, it cannot be used by parents who care for their own children in their own home.

A second tax measure is the *Canada Child Tax Benefit*, a refundable tax credit targeted at working families earning less than $29,590 (in the year 2000). The basic amount of the benefit is $1,020 for the first child, with supplementary amount of $955 for each child where no childcare expenses are deducted under Section 63 (above). The benefit is paid in monthly increments to the primary caregiver of the child, which under the ITA is rebuttably presumed to be the female parent. Like section 63, this tax measure also evidences numerous problems. First, as it is targeted at the working poor, it does not address the needs of even poorer families receiving social assistance. The structure of the benefit does not recognize that many women in particular "cannot 'afford' to participate in the paid labour force" due to their lack of childcare. Secondly, the benefit is not indexed to inflation of less than three percent, meaning that the real value of the benefit has been steadily eroding since its creation in 1997.

In addition to tax measures, the government engages in childcare through the provision of a small number of subsidized childcare spaces, intended to assist lower income parents to remain in the labour force. Subsidies may range from being "full subsidies" covering all or most of the costs associated with childcare, to small partial subsidies. Subsidies are generally administered by provinces, although in Alberta and Ontario municipalities are involved.

Although subsidies could potentially be an important source of relief for parents paying for childcare, there are numerous limitations. First, they are available to a fraction of the many families who would require this assistance. Tyyskä, for example, indicates that in Ontario a mere 7%-15% of families technically eligible (estimated to be 72% of parents in need of childcare) actually receive subsidies. As funds disbursed to provinces have decreased under the CHST, so too provincial funds to municipalities, particularly in provinces with conservative governments, have been cut. Second, the threshold to receive assistance is extremely low in most provinces, in general targeting only the very poorest working families. Many modest and middle-income families, for whom childcare also represents an onerous expense, are not eligible. Doherty et al. indicate, for example, that in 1993, the average combined income of two-parent families receiving subsidies was $26,000, with a range between $17,820 and $34,460. According to their calculations, families with average family incomes are effectively shut out of subsidies, and only those at or close to the poverty level are eligible. Thirdly, due to the absence of any federal oversight, there is a great degree of variation across provinces, territories, and municipalities, both in terms of the level of subsidization available and priorities for eligibility. In some Ontario municipalities, for example, the priority may be teenaged parents who are returning to school after the birth of a child, while in another it may be the working poor. Finally, subsidies are currently jeopardized by restructuring, both in terms of size and coverage, due to the diminished transfer payments to the provinces under the CHST. Tyyskä reports that in Ontario, for example, between 1996 and 1998, allocations for daycare were reduced from $520 million to $432 million, with clear implications for the ability to maintain subsidy levels. With reference to childcare, she says, "The CHST opened a new door to a reduction in spending in an area particularly vulnerable to changes in economic or political climate."

Governments also engage in childcare policy through the regulation of some childcare spaces. This regulation is intended primarily to assure the basic safety of children, and to a much lesser degree, to ensure [that] certain minimum standards of quality are maintained. Provinces and in some cases municipalities will regulate daycare centres, for which standards are set regarding the training of staff and the staff–child ratio for example, as well as some home-based care providers.

There are two fundamental concerns with the current approach to regulation. The first is that there are simply not enough regulated spaces. Doherty et al. report that, in 1993, a mere 4.9% of spaces were regulated in Newfoundland, with a "high" of 16.9% of spaces in Alberta, and that the gap between available regulated care and need has increased in the last decade. This is clearly insufficient to ensure that children are in care facilities of an adequate standard. The second concern is that the level of regulation may simply not be high enough to ensure that children in these spaces are receiving a quality of care which would support their development. Indeed, there are indications that with home-based care in particular, regulation is concerned more with simple safety issues than with ensuring that children are being cared for in a manner that will support their physical, intellectual, and social development. Although, as mentioned, studies have shown that in general, quality is higher in regulated than in non-regulated care, researchers have found that many provincial regulatory standards are "significantly below levels found by research to be necessary for a high quality program."

Governmental engagement with childcare—through tax measures, subsidies, and regulations—thus essentially leaves the provision of childcare to the private realm of the family and the market. By choosing such a level of involvement, the federal government has effectively relinquished the opportunity to "shape the quality, availability, or affordability of childcare services." This approach also fails to recognize what has been identified as the critical link between childcare and other social issues, including the overall well-being of children, the need for a skilled and efficient workforce, and equality-based concerns. Further, the few chosen policy measures, while they may provide limited relief to some families and ensure a baseline level of care in some services, do not contribute in any way to increasing the supply of regulated care, nor do they contribute to improving the quality of childcare overall. According to the Childcare Resource and Research Unit (CRRU):

Canada has not taken a pro-active or even facilitative approach to developing a system of high quality childcare services. Rather, childcare has developed in a haphazard manner driven by market forces … . The current childcare situation does not meet the needs of children, families, or women.

Impacts of the Childcare Deficit on Women

Many researchers have identified a connection between affordable childcare services and gender equality in the labour market.

There are essentially three possible effects of the failure to provide adequate childcare options on the "choices" of women. First, some women may simply choose not to return to work after their children are born. As seen, this is a choice confined largely to women in two-parent families where the spouse or partner has a sufficiently large income to financially support the family. Where regulated care is unavailable, too expensive (as it will often be if the family has more than one child), or inaccessible due to scheduling constraints or the need for special needs care, women may decide to stay home rather than turn to unregulated care or other solutions. According to Judith Frankel, "many women are simply not able to work when such services (childcare) are not available."

Second, women may choose to work part time, in a position with more flexible hours, in order to be available when childcare is not. Doherty et al. indicate that due to the persistent wage gap, when families consider which parent should or could consider part time work in order to care for children, it will usually be the woman who reduces her labour market participation to accommodate family caregiving obligations. This echoes findings discussed above with respect to parental leave choices. Both of these solutions, as seen above, have serious and long-term implications for women's economic independence and position. According to Freiler and Cerny, "[T]ime spent outside the labour force looking after young children is a major contributor to labour market poverty … . It is well documented that women continue to be at an economic disadvantage even after re-entry into the labour market." Meg Luxton similarly emphasizes that

> if women are out of the paid labour force for significant periods of time to provide caregiving for children and others, then those women are permanently disadvantaged, at risk of living in poverty for extended periods, and in need of a variety of protections, training, and reentry assistance when they rejoin the labour force. Policy initiatives that facilitate women's labour force participation and their work in social reproduction, such as a national, high quality, comprehensive daycare system, will in the long run be less disruptive and less costly.

Finally, women may "choose" either for professional or financial reasons to maintain full participation in the labour force despite the difficulties of securing care. Doing this may require the use of unregulated care, care by a relative, or sibling care if there are older children in the family. Where this approach is chosen in the current childcare milieu, it is likely to lead to a high degree of stress and anxiety, in addition to reduced work productivity for both parents, but particularly mothers, as they strive to meet the demands of both their full-time employment and family obligations. This is particularly so given the lack of parental leave in Canada for the purpose of tending to sick children or other family responsibilities. Again, this has implications for women's labour market status.

As with maternity and parental leave, the policy choices made with respect to the provision of daycare profoundly affect women's ability to engage in the labour force and hence their overall equality interests. According to Martha Friendly:

> Without the availability of affordable, reliable childcare, women (single parents or those in two-parent families) may be compelled to remain out of the labour force, to work at poorly paid employment, or not to take advancement; some are forced into dependence on public assistance and poverty.

The current lack of a systematic approach to the provision of regulated care, and the confinement of care "choices" to the private realm, impact and limit women's ability to participate in the paid labour force to the full extent of their qualifications and abilities. Unlike the case of maternity and parental leave however, where differential impacts of the extension of benefits is evident, there seems to be near universal agreement among childcare advocates that a comprehensive national approach to daycare would benefit most if not all women. ...

Conclusion: Contemporary Leave and Childcare Entitlements— The Erosion of Social Citizenship

...

The present state of parental leave policy and the childcare context can be understood within the context of economic and ideological restructuring underway in Canada at present, and illustrates the erosion of social citizenship which has accompanied the effective demise of the welfare state. From an economic perspective, both the extension of parental leave and the retrenchments in childcare testify to a continued and accelerating privatization of the care of children, and an aversion on the part of the state to viewing such care as a public investment. The extension of parental leave, while potentially incurring some costs for the government, will likely be of limited financial consequence given the eligibility limits discussed above (and will be offset by the gains achieved on the ideological front regarding the privatization of care). In reality, as the quality of employment declines in the context of restructuring, and as women increasingly find themselves in part-time, contract, or "flexible" labour, many women (and men) will not be able to "afford" to take the [parental] leave, even if eligible. The continued failure to act on childcare, and indeed the contraction of spending in this field in the wake of the CHST, reflect the current fiscal climate, focused as it is on spending reductions and a general withdrawal of the state from areas of formerly public provision. Present policy choices with respect to daycare, for example, are consistent with the approach of short-term cost-cutting rather than longer-term social investments and a market-based rather than public approach to social infrastructure. ...

From an ideological perspective, policy choices with respect to parental leave and childcare are also quite consistent. As discussed above, the increased focus on "individual responsibility" and "self-reliance" has permeated contemporary political discourse, limiting the range of what can "legitimately" be claimed from the state. The care of children, whether in infancy or as they grow older has increasingly been defined as a "private responsibility." Parents are expected to identify private solutions to childcare needs, in line with their general obligation to "take care of themselves." Extending parental leave fits neatly into this thinking: parents, in the guise of being given a "benefit" are confirmed in their role as the primary source of childcare. They are given the "choice" to take more "individual responsibility" for their children. Similarly, the failure to act on childcare issues, and the steady erosion of the already limited state involvement in this area confirms the ideological prioritization given to parents making private arrangements, whether through the market or through the family, for the care of their children.

Underpinning this renewed individualism has been the increased glorification of the family, and particularly of the "traditional" family. ... As state supports are eroded and increasingly the provision of caring functions is downloaded onto the family, the "new moral order," as described by Janine Brodie, legitimates and justifies the increasing burdens on the family. Despite the clear costs of parental leave in terms of labour market position for those who avail themselves of this benefit, these costs are hidden by the emergence of the expectation that families *should* provide infant care at home. Similarly, the policy failures with respect to daycare are justified by a rhetoric that implies that family care of children is the best care.

Rendered invisible by the ideological veil are the very real consequences of parental leave and daycare policy for women's caregiving responsibilities and capacity to engage in the paid labour force. The downloading of care is perceived as being onto the "family," not onto women *per se*, and families then "choose" how to share the increased burdens. The role of fiscal realities and gendered expectations is hidden as women "choose" to leave or reduce their participation in the paid workforce, or are compelled to reduce their labour market aspirations in order to accommodate family responsibilities. ... This combination of fiscal and ideological restructuring illustrates ... that not only do gender relations underpin and shape social provision, but policy choices in turn shape gender relations. In the case of parental leave and childcare, in downloading the responsibilities for childcare onto the family, policymakers are acting, consciously or subconsciously, on assumptions that women will provide the care not offered by the state; and, in making this assumption, they are reinforcing and in fact continually recreating the household and market divisions of labour, which effectively consign women to continued inequality.

Discussion Notes

Child Care and Tax Policy: Symes v. Canada

Tax policies have frequently been challenged in relation to their impact on families. For example, in *Symes v. Canada*, [1993] 4 SCR 695; (1993), 94 DTC 6001, a practising lawyer appealed from assessments of income tax in relation to payments to her full-time nanny, who had cared for Symes's two preschool-aged children during the tax years 1982-1985. Symes claimed deductions, as "business expenses," for the full amounts paid to the nanny each year (ranging from about $10,000 to $13,300 in each of the four years). The minister of national revenue disallowed these amounts and permitted her to claim only the amounts allowed by s. 63 of the *Income Tax Act* as deductions for child care ($1,000-$4,000 for each of the four years). In doing so, the minister claimed that the amounts were not expended for the purpose of gaining or producing income from business, but were "personal or living expenses."

In the Federal Court Trial Division, Cullen J upheld Symes's claim, suggesting that women workers' entry to the paid workforce required a modern interpretation of the idea of business expenses. His conclusion relied on expert evidence presented by Dr. Patricia Armstrong about changes in women's paid work. Cullen J also held that the *Income Tax Act* violated s. 15 of the Charter in relation to the plaintiff's claim. In the Federal Court of Appeal, an appeal was allowed.

In a further appeal to the Supreme Court of Canada, the majority dismissed the appeal, with Justices L'Heureux-Dubé and McLachlin dissenting. Although there was disagreement in the Supreme Court of Canada about the "discriminatory" nature of the provisions of the *Income Tax Act*, the case ultimately determined that Symes was not entitled to the deductions as "business expenses." The case was controversial because a successful outcome would have affected only women who, as self-employed women, were entitled to claim "business expenses," but it would not have changed the statutory limits for employed women at all. For additional comments and analysis of *Symes*, see Rebecca Johnson, *Taxing Choices: The Intersection of Class, Gender, Parenthood, and the Law* (Vancouver: UBC Press, 2002); Lorna Turnbull, *Double Jeopardy: Motherwork and the Law* (Toronto: Sumach Press, 2001); and Audrey Macklin, "Symes v. MNR: Where Sex Meets Class" (1992), 5 *Canadian Journal of Women and the Law* 498.

Child Care and Domestic Workers: Between Public and Private

Issues about the role of the state and families in relation to child care must also focus on the legal regulation of domestic workers, particularly foreign domestic workers, a complex intersection of issues in immigration and employment law in relation to families. According to Sedef Arat-Koc (at 39), domestic workers are "*in* the family, but not *of* it, ... involved in the work of a *house*, but not the pleasures and intimacies of a *home*." Neither a family member nor a worker with corresponding rights and privileges, domestic workers are "squeezed between the private and public spheres." Although some aspects of the work of domestic workers has been regulated, their situation is often precariously at the margins of regulation: see Sedef Arat-Koc, "In the Privacy of Our Own Home: Foreign Domestic Workers as Solution to the Crisis in the Domestic Sphere in Canada" (1989), 28 *Studies in Political Economy* 33 and Irene J. Kyle, "Family Child Care in Canada" (Winter 2001-2), *Transition* (Vanier Institute of the Family) 10.

Child Care: Families and the Workplace

Connections between work and family life in relation to child care were explored in a human rights case concerning a woman's right to breast feed her child at work, on her own time, in a private space. Although the British Columbia Council of Human Rights concluded that the case did not involve sex discrimination, the BC Supreme Court set aside this decision and remitted the matter to the Council for consideration of the claim of sex discrimination: see *Poirier v. BC (Council of Human Rights)*, [1996] BCJ no. 1795 (SC) (QL). In relation to child care, are there different issues to be addressed in regulating care at home and care provided in a workplace? What kinds of policies are likely to best accomplish support for families?

In this context, note that claims have also been litigated with respect to equal parental leave at the time of the birth or adoption of children, pursuant to employment insurance legislation: see *Schachter v. Canada*, [1992] 2 SCR 679; (1992), 93 DLR (4th) 1 and *Schafer v. Canada* (1997), 149 DLR (4th) 705; 3 OR (3d) 1 (CA); leave to appeal dismissed, [1997] 2 SCCA no. 516. In addition, some women have challenged the provisions of the *Employment Insurance Act*, SC 1996, c. 23 on the basis of sex discrimination, particularly because of the statute's impact on part-time or "secondary" earners, who are most often women with child-care responsibilities: see *Canada (Attorney General) v. Lesiuk* (2003), 299 NR 307 (FCA) and Kerri A. Froc, "Commentary on Canada (Attorney General) v. Lesiuk" (2003), 22:3 *Jurisfemme* 6.

Family Policies and the State: Models and Approaches

As Madsen noted (at 21), policies concerning child care in Canada suggest the adoption of a "liberal model," according to the typology developed by Gösta Esping-Andersen, a comparative scholar of late 20th-century capitalism. Esping-Andersen identified three models of welfare capitalism: a social democratic model, characterized by universalism of social rights, evident in Scandinavia; a conservative-corporate model, in which "the family" is the cornerstone of social policy, with state provision available when family resources are inadequate or unavailable, evident in such countries as Italy, France, and Germany; and a liberal model, characterized by the predominance of the market and the "liberal work ethic," and evident in the United States and the United Kingdom as well as in Canada: see G. Esping-Andersen, "The Three Political Economies of the Welfare State" (1989), 26:1 *Canadian Review of Sociology and Anthropology* 10.

In a detailed analysis of comparative family policy in eight countries, including Canada, Kathy O'Hara concluded that Canadian policy incorporated values of self-reliance, individualism, and family privacy. Overall, O'Hara argued that Canadian policy exhibited ambivalence about the state's role in family matters:

> This has meant that although the role of the state in the family has increased steadily in Canada, as in other countries, governments in Canada (with the exception of the provincial government in Quebec) have avoided major interventions and steering policies of the kind developed in some European countries. Canadian policy has instead taken a minimalist approach to the need to adapt to changing demographic and labour market realities.

See Kathy O'Hara, *Comparative Family Policy: Eight Countries' Stories* (Ottawa: Canadian Policy Research Networks, 1998), 7-8. Significantly, in her review of the impact of recent changes in tax policies, Lisa Philipps argued that these changes have not resulted in less intervention, but rather in a changing regulatory role: "[The state] is engaged in redefining the boundaries of public and private in a manner that shifts political and economic resources away from social reproduction and towards accumulation": see Lisa Philipps, "Tax Law and Social Reproduction: The Gender of Fiscal Policy in an Age of Privatization," in Brenda Cossman and Judy Fudge, eds., *Privatization, Law, and the Challenge to Feminism* (Toronto: University of Toronto Press, 2002), 41, at 45.

In 1997, Quebec implemented its Early Childhood and Child Care Strategy. One part of the strategy involved early childhood agencies, which are expected to deliver child care at daycare centres and as regulated family daycare for a fee of five dollars a day. The program is intended to be universally accessible, and the number of regulated child-care spaces grew from about 72,000 in 1997 to 135,000 by 2002. According to Jocelyne Tougas, this initiative demonstrated a turning point: "a time when, for a number of cultural, political and societal reasons, the government and the people in Quebec have agreed that children and families are indeed a priority and that bettering their lives calls for substantial social investments": see Jocelyn Tougas, "Quebec's Child Care Model: Making Family a Priority" (Winter 2001-2), *Transition* (Vanier Institute of the Family) 13.

In another example, the mayor of the small town of Torredonjimeno, Spain announced in July 2003 that men would be fined by local police if they were found in bars in the town on Thursday evenings between 9 p.m. and 2 a.m. (the hours when men traditionally gather in local bars). The mayor explained that he expected men to remain at home on Thursdays (one night per week) to look after children and do the washing up, so that women could have a night out, and that he hoped to turn the town into "an international reference point" for sex equality. Money from fines was to be directed to groups dealing with domestic violence and sex equality: see Giles Tremlett, "Spanish Mayor Bans Men from Bars," *The Guardian*, July 21, 2003.

Child-Care Policies: The Impact at Separation or Divorce

In the context of the statistics and analysis outlined by Madsen, consider the economic consequences for families at separation or divorce. To what extent do current child-care policies ensure that men and women are equally situated to provide for themselves financially? How should the inequalities identified by Madsen be resolved? To what extent would more extensive governmental support for child care alleviate problems of poverty for children in both intact and separated families? You may wish to reconsider these questions in relation to discussion of divorce and corollary relief in subsequent chapters.

SELECTED REFERENCES

Carol T. Baines, Patricia M. Evans, and Sheila M. Neysmith, eds., *Women's Caring: Feminist Perspectives on Social Welfare*, 2d ed. (Toronto: Oxford University Press, 1998).

Maureen Baker, *Canadian Family Policies: Cross-National Comparisons* (Toronto: University of Toronto Press, 1995).

P.M. Evans, "Divided Citizenship? Gender, Income Security, and the Welfare State," in P.M. Evans and G. Wekerle, eds., *Women and the Canadian Welfare State: Challenges and Change* (Toronto: University of Toronto Press, 1997), 91.

Susan A. McDaniel and Martha Friendly, "Child Care Policy in Canada: Putting the
Pieces Together" (1996), 27 *Journal of Comparative Family Studies* 576.

Ministry of Women's Equality, *Women and Men in the Workplace: A Discussion of
Workplace Supports for Workers with Family Responsibilities* (Victoria, BC: Province
of British Columbia, 1993).

Sheila Neysmith, *Restructuring Caring Labour: Discourse, State Practice, and Everyday
Life* (Toronto: Oxford University Press, 2000).

Norene Pupo, "Preserving Patriarchy: Women, the Family, and the State," in Nancy
Mandell and Ann Duffy, eds., *Reconstructing the Canadian Family: Feminist Perspectives* (Toronto: Butterworths, 1988), 207.

Kathy Teghtsoonian, "Who Pays for Caring for Children: Public Policy and the Devaluation of Women's Work," in Susan B. Boyd, ed., *Challenging the Public/Private Divide:
Feminism, Law, and Public Policy* (Toronto: University of Toronto Press, 1997), 113.

Annis May Timpson, *Driven Apart: Women's Employment Equality and Child Care in
Canadian Public Policy* (Vancouver: UBC Press, 2001).

Lorna Turnbull, *Double Jeopardy: Motherwork and the Law* (Toronto: Sumach Press, 2001).

III. PROTECTING CHILDREN: RESPONSIBILITIES OF FAMILIES AND THE STATE

A. Defining "Children in Need of Protection" in Families

The suffering of children at the hands of the family is the hard case for law. The primacy of
the family as the locus of childrearing and the foundational social unit is recognized in all
societies. Respect may be expressed in protection of paternal or parental authority through
doctrines of privacy which discourage scrutiny of parenting practices, confound development of coherent state–child relations and children's rights theory, render child abuse
invisible and remove it from the ambit of "grown up" or principled law.

> Anne McGillivray, "Reconstructing Child Abuse: Western Definition and
> Non-Western Experience," in Michael Freeman and Philip Veerman, eds.,
> *The Ideologies of Children's Rights* (Dordrecht, Netherlands: Martinus
> Nijhoff Publishers, 1992), 213, at 230

1. The Context: Governmental Inquiries and Child Protection

As McGillivray suggested, the protection of children within the family is a "hard case"
for law. The challenge of balancing the tension between children's individual well-being
and the autonomy of families has often been revealed in high-profile cases about harm or
neglect of children in families, cases that have also fuelled demands for changes in
legislation and in child-protection arrangements.

For example, the Gove Inquiry into Child Protection in British Columbia concluded
that a child had died as a result of too little emphasis on the part of child protection
workers on the needs of the *child* within the *family* context. At the time of his death,
Matthew Vaudreuil was severely underweight, his body revealed many bruises, and he

had a fractured arm and 11 fractured ribs; the autopsy report concluded (at 127-28) that the injuries "show all the hallmarks of child abuse." As the Inquiry report stated:

> In spite of their mandate to make child safety and well-being their paramount concern, many social workers seem to consider family unity to be paramount, even to the detriment of the child. For example, one social worker testified that "the ministry's policy was families first and apprehension only as a last resort. ... When dealing with Matthew, that was always my concern, ... to keep him in the home ... to ensure that the integrity of the family was maintained."

(Gove Inquiry into Child Protection (BC), *Report of the Gove Inquiry into Child Protection in British Columbia*, vol. 1 (Vancouver: Ministry of Social Services, 1995), 136.)

The Inquiry's report made a series of recommendations to improve child protection in British Columbia. However, even before the inquiry's report, amending legislation was introduced that declared as its guiding principle that "in the administration and interpretation of this Act the safety and well-being of a child shall be the paramount considerations": see *Child, Family and Community Service Act*, SBC 1994, c. 27, s. 2; and *Report of the Gove Inquiry*, vol. 2, 207ff. As a subsequent report on the implementation of the Gove Inquiry recommendations noted, the new "paramountcy test" was included in the legislation as well as in the policy manual: see Ombudsman, Province of British Columbia, *Getting There: A Review of the Implementation of the Report of the Gove Inquiry into Child Protection* (Public Report no. 36 to the Legislative Assembly of British Columbia, March 1998), 2.

Similarly, as a result of the deaths of children in Ontario who were receiving child welfare services, the government established a panel of experts in late 1997 to review existing legislation and make recommendations for change. The resulting report, submitted in March 1998, concluded that "the legislative principles regarding the least restrictive or disruptive course of action and the autonomy and integrity of the family have been emphasized to the detriment of the child's safety, protection and well-being": see Panel of Experts on Child Protection (Ontario), *Protecting Vulnerable Children: Report of the Panel of Experts on Child Protection* (Toronto: Ministry of Community and Social Services, 1998), 7. The Ontario report recommended (at 17) that the standard for intervention, "substantial risk," was too high and that "likelihood of risk" would provide more protection for children.

In addition, there were recommendations (at 37ff.) for child-protection workers to have greater access to information about past parenting practices and for information sharing through systematic computerized databases. Moreover, the report also recommended (at 18-19) that neglect be included as a basis for state intervention in families. Amendments to Ontario's *Child and Family Services Act*, SO 1999, c. 2 were introduced to implement these recommendations. In spite of these reforms, however, there was extensive national coverage of another tragic story of an Ontario child who died after being abused by adult family members: see Christie Blatchford, "Randy Dooley: The Life and Death of an 'Outside Child,'" *National Post*, April 17, 2002, A14-17.

Generally, the focus for implementing these protection policies in provincial legislation is the definition of "child in need of protection." For example, s. 37(2) of Ontario's amended legislation now defines "in need of protection" to include not only physical, emotional, and sexual abuse, but also neglect of a child in relation to "caring for, providing for, supervising or protecting the child." However, interpreting the definition of "child in need of protection," as Nicholas Bala argued (at 147), requires "professional judgment and sometimes very difficult individualized decision-making": see Nicholas Bala, "Reforming Ontario's Child and Family Services Act: Is the Pendulum Swinging Back Too Far?" (1999), 17 *Canadian Family Law Quarterly* 121. Moreover, this decision making occurs within an overall context of scarce community resources. Thus, while the scope of the legal definition has arguably been enlarged in Ontario, its implementation in relation to governmental policy goals is dependent on professional and financial resources. In his assessment of these recent Ontario amendments, Bala pointed out (at 172) that, beyond legislative reforms, there is a need for "resources, training and morale in the child welfare and justice systems." Such resources may be more difficult to achieve than "inexpensive legislative reform."

2. Child-Protection Resources: Supporting Families or Removing Children?

Resources may be needed both to support families with children and to provide for children who are removed from their homes. Like other provincial statutes, Ontario's *Child and Family Services Act* provides that, in addition to the paramount purpose of promoting the best interests, protection, and well-being of children, there are additional purposes, including support for the autonomy and integrity of families and use of the "least disruptive course of action" to assist a child (see s. 1(2)). However, issues about how the state should intervene may also require an assessment of resources. In an annotation to a 1990 Manitoba decision, for example, James McLeod posed the questions bluntly:

> In times of budgetary restraint, the hard question facing a court is: How much of a tight budget should the society be forced to devote to one family? Does there come a point where all concerned must "bite the bullet" and accept that the amount of money necessary to turn the parents/family into a marginally functioning unit does not justify the overall cost to the agency and other clients of the agency and permanent wardship or guardianship should be ordered? Should the court only look at the particular family in question or must it look to overall realities?

(James McLeod, "Annotation re Winnipeg South Child and Family Services Agency v. S.(D.D.)" (1990), 24 RFL (3d) 290, at 290-91.)

On the other hand, intervention decisions may also need to take account of the consequences of removal of children, particularly if lengthy court proceedings are required. According to one study, for example, children who were temporarily removed from their parental homes lived in an average of 4 homes before the age of 16, while those removed permanently lived in an average of 8 homes before they reached 16: see Jeffery Wilson and Mary Tomlinson, *Children and the Law*, 2d ed. (Toronto: Butterworths, 1986), 65. Thus, issues about state intervention pursuant to legislative policies concerning child protection may require complex assessments of legal principles, but they may also involve difficult questions about community resources and their allocation. Consider these issues in relation to the case that follows: do you agree that the court achieved the goal of balancing child protection and family autonomy? Why or why not?

Winnipeg South Child and Family Services Agency v. S.(D.D.)
(1990), 24 RFL (3d) 290 (Man. QB (Fam. Div.))

[The agency, which was requesting permanent guardianship of a child, had apprehended the child on a number of occasions since his birth. During the eight-day trial, a large number of professionals gave evidence about the assistance that had been provided to the father and mother in an effort to support the family together: there were a number of social workers, two homemakers, an experienced counsellor, a public health nurse, a pediatrician at the hospital, a family support worker, a clinical psychologist, and two psychiatrists, all of whom had been involved with the parents and the child. The professionals also gave evidence about the (in)abilities of the parents to meet the needs of the child. The judge described (at 301) the child's parents and the relevant legal principles.]

The mother, who is 30 years of age, gave evidence and admitted that she is a compulsive liar, that she was wrong and made mistakes in caring for the child, but wants to start all over again. She said the father told her the previous night that all he wanted was to have them together with the child. With respect to the balance of her evidence, I observed her carefully while giving her evidence and regret that she is a sad, pathetic, simple woman whom I cannot believe. Without a doubt, she is not, and could not be, capable of caring for the child for a lengthy period, if ever. The risk of abuse would be extremely high.

The father, who is 34 years of age, and who has been unemployed since shortly after the child's birth, also gave evidence. He admits to having lost his temper and pushed and slapped his wife to the extent that the police were called on four occasions, but no charges were laid. He said that prior to the birth of the child, he was afraid the child would not be physically normal because of his problems with alcohol and drugs. He said he "wasn't sure what was what for the first two or three months," but his wife was not able to care for the child. He said he is guilty of not showing the child the love and support he should and he was blind to the way this emotionally affected the child. He said the child should not come home now because both he and the wife were not ready. If the child did, he would be gone in a month. He said the foster parents were the best thing for the child now. He said he has lost his bond with the child. He said that a child should not have to wait for him to get help to parent the child. He said he is leaving his wife and either getting a separation or a divorce. He also said he would like the child placed in his care. On cross-examination he said he agreed that he had absolutely no plans for care of the child and that he does not think he can give the child everything he needs. He said he is not sure what is best, that the only reason the child should be with him is because he is his biological father. He said he does not know if he can care for the child, that he may be selfish, and that he may not be ready to be a father. He said he does not want to make the decision and he thinks that the agency is more aware of the needs and wants of the child.

This is a case that requires one to consider the totality of the evidence. ... Counsel for the father, during the course of the trial, pointed out that the court should not compare the foster home situation to the parents' home. I am mindful of the decision in *Re H.(R.M.)* (1984), 40 RFL (2d) 100, 53 AR 375 (CA), to the effect that permanent wardship is not to be ordered solely on the basis that the foster home is providing the child with better living conditions than those provided by the natural parents. The conditions in the foster home, although significantly better, were not a factor in my decision.

I have also considered the decision in *CAS, Winnipeg v. M.* (1980), 15 RFL (2d) 185, at 188 (Man. CA), wherein Freedman CJM stated:

> The right of a natural parent to the care and control of a child is basic. It is a right not easily displaced. Nothing less than cogent evidence of danger to the child's life or health is required before the court will deprive a parent of such care and control.

I have also considered the decision in *Dauphin v. Dir. of Pub. Welfare* (1956), 64 Man. R 142, 19 WWR 97, 24 CR 238, 117 CCC 45, 5 DLR (2d) 275 (CA), for the proposition that the court should never be called upon to wait until physical injuries have been received and minds unhinged. It is sufficient if there be a reasonable apprehension that such things will happen, and the court should interfere before they have happened if that be possible. ...

I must, on the totality of the evidence before me, find that the child, J.D.S., born 25th May 1988, has been and is in need of protection as the parents have been and are obviously unable to provide adequate care, supervision or control of the child and are unlikely to be able to do so for a lengthy period of time, if ever. ...

Application granted.

Do you agree with McLeod's suggestion, above, that there was a necessity in this case to "bite the bullet"? Was the tension between child protection and family autonomy resolved satisfactorily in this case?

Consider also the position of the professionals who testified about the parents—how should parents relate to agency professionals who have a responsibility to provide assistance to parents and families, but who may subsequently be required to give evidence about deficiencies in parental caregiving? Although the parents in this case clearly lacked some basic skills, were they completely unrealistic in failing to trust agency personnel and others who were providing assistance to them? What kind of processes might be useful to resolve this dilemma? What factors may affect decision making about child protection?

How should judges and lawyers define their roles as professionals in child-protection proceedings? In thinking about these questions, consider the comments of a judge who took the role of a parent in a mock hearing, and then explained how he experienced a sense of exclusion and powerlessness, just as parents may feel in such cases.

Judge James P. Felstiner, "Child Welfare Hearings from an Unfamiliar Perspective"
in Nicholas Bala, Joseph P. Hornick, and Robin Vogl, eds., *Canadian Child Welfare Law: Children, Families, and the State*
(Scarborough, ON: Thompson Educational Publishing, 1991), 306, at 306-7

[My] lawyer made a number of statements without consulting me. I knew that he and I had prepared for the pre-trial for over an hour the day before, with my telling him about my situation. But I was not prepared for his ad-libbing as new or different slants came up, and sometimes he was not very accurate. He couldn't be; he had never been in my house and had never seen me with my kid.

My frustration with my lawyer not talking to me was small compared to my anger as I listened to the agency's lawyer misrepresent facts as I knew them. The agency's lawyer also attacked my character and belittled my strengths. ... [My] lawyer only told me to let him handle the case and that I was not to interrupt. ... By the end of this play-acting, I, the mother, felt powerless and helpless. ... No one represented exactly what I wanted to say. Many of the statements did not match my perception of the situation which had led to my child being grabbed by the police.

In a context in which legislation requires that the child's interests take priority over family autonomy, is there any solution to the problems identified by Felstiner J? See also Jennifer A. Blishen, Susan G. Himel, and Judge Mary Jane Hatton, "The Lawyer's Role," in Bala, Hornick, and Vogl, eds., 195. (See also Nicholas Bala, Michael Kim Zapf, R. James Williams, Robin Vogl, and Joseph P. Hornick, eds., *Canadian Child Welfare Law: Children, Families, and the State*, 2d ed. (Toronto: Thompson Educational Publishing, 2004).)

Discussion Note

Child-Protection Procedures and the Charter

Procedures in child-protection statutes have been increasingly scrutinized pursuant to the Charter. In *Winnipeg Child and Family Services (Central Area) v. W.(K.L.)* (2000), 191 DLR (4th) 1; [2000] 2 SCR 519, the Supreme Court of Canada dismissed the appeal of a woman whose child was apprehended without a warrant pursuant to s. 21 of the *Child and Family Services Act*, SM 1985-86, c. 8. Although the court agreed that the apprehension of a child without a warrant created a grave risk of intervention in family life, a majority of the court held that the legislative requirement of an *ex post facto* hearing satisfied the principles of fundamental justice in s. 7 of the Charter. For the majority (at para. 131), the balance between the state's responsibility for the well-being and safety of children and parental rights and family autonomy was satisfied by the legislative requirement of a hearing after a warrantless apprehension:

> The apprehension of children constitutes a significant state intrusion into the family. Less disruptive means of dealing with parenting issues are to be preferred as a matter of policy

whenever possible. ... [However,] provided that the threshold for apprehension is, at a minimum, that of a risk of serious harm to the child, the need for swift and preventive state action to protect a child's life or health in such situations dictates that a fair and prompt post-apprehension hearing is the minimum procedural protection mandated by the principles of fundamental justice in the child protection context.

Two members of the court dissented, arguing that a warrantless apprehension in non-emergency situations did not meet the requirements of fundamental justice in s. 7. Indeed, several other provinces require warrants in such cases, usually on an *ex parte* basis: for example, see Ontario's *Child and Family Services Act*, s. 40. To what extent do these views reflect similarities or differences between family law and criminal law proceedings?

3. "In Need of Protection" and Community Standards

The legal definition of "child in need of protection" has often been considered in relation to "community standards"—that is, the extent to which standards in a particular community should be considered in assessing whether parental conduct is inappropriate. In an early case, *Re Brown* (1975), 9 OR (2d) 185, at 189; 21 RFL 315 (Co. Ct.), for example, the court stated that

> the community ought not to interfere merely because our institutions may be able to offer a greater opportunity to the children to achieve their potential. Society's interference in the natural family is only justified when the level of care of the children falls below that which no child in this country should be subjected to.

Is this an objective or subjective standard? Was the same standard applied in *Children's Aid Society of Ottawa-Carleton v. Steven W. and Monica W.*, [1988] WDFL 458; [1987] OJ no. 1896 (Prov. Ct. (Fam. Div.)), where children were found in need of protection because their father used corporal punishment, and the court made a supervision order? Apparently, the father was a minister of a small congregation that advocated the use of corporal punishment. To what extent did the court adhere to "community standards" in its application of the legal standard in this case?

The issue of corporal punishment in relation to s. 43 of the *Criminal Code* (which permits the use of reasonable force by parents and others in disciplining children) was considered by the Supreme Court of Canada in *Canadian Foundation for Children, Youth and the Law v. Canada (Attorney General)*, 2004 SCC 4. The court dismissed the appeal (6:3) from the decision of the Ontario Court of Appeal, confirming that s. 43 did not infringe children's rights under the Charter; at the same time, the court commented on the kinds of physical force acceptable in such cases. In doing so, the court tried to balance the responsibilities of parents and the need to prevent criminalization of their actions. According to Chief Justice McLachlin (at para. 68):

> I am satisfied that a reasonable person acting on behalf of a child, apprised of the harms of criminalization that s. 43 avoids, the presence of other governmental initiatives to reduce the use of corporal punishment, and the fact that abusive and harmful conduct is still prohibited by the criminal law, would not conclude that the child's dignity has been offended in the manner contemplated by s. 15(1). Children often feel a sense of disempowerment and

vulnerability; this reality must be considered when assessing the impact of s. 43 on a child's sense of dignity. Yet, as emphasized, the force permitted is limited and must be set against the reality of a child's mother or father being charged and pulled into the criminal justice system, with its attendant rupture of the family setting, or a teacher being detained pending bail, with the inevitable harm to the child's crucial educative setting. Section 43 is not arbitrarily demeaning. It does not discriminate. Rather, it is firmly grounded in the actual needs and circumstances of children. I conclude that s. 43 does not offend s. 15(1) of the *Charter*.

Does this reasoning adhere to community standards?

"Community standards" have sometimes been invoked in protection cases involving aboriginal children. For example, in assessing whether a child was "in need of protection" in *Re E.C.D.M.* (1980), 17 RFL (2d) 274, at 275; [1982] 2 CNLR 53 (Sask. Prov. Ct.), the court stated:

> In my view, in order for a child to be found in need of protection there must be a significant departure from a standard of child care that one would generally expect for a child of the age of the child in question. Furthermore, while there is a minimum parental standard for all society, a secondary standard must be established for parents of the age of the parent in question and for the type of community in which the parent resides. A teen-aged parent cannot live up to the standard expected for a middle-aged parent. Similarly, different standards of parenting apply to parents of Cree ancestry who reside in a small rural community in Northern Saskatchewan than would apply to white middle-class parents living, for example, in Regina. What is an acceptable standard for the former might be unacceptable to the latter.

Is this standard objective or subjective? Interestingly, in *Re E.C.D.M.*, the court concluded that, even using appropriate "community standards," the child's mother had failed to provide care of a sufficient level.

In a number of provinces, legislation provides for aboriginal child welfare services on reserves, in an effort to ensure that decision making reflects community values and the authority of aboriginal communities with respect to their children. For an overview of some early initiatives, see Anna Pellatt, *An International Review of Child Welfare Policy and Practice in Relation to Aboriginal People* (Calgary: Canadian Research Institute for Law and the Family, 1991). More recently, Manitoba enacted new child welfare legislation, a joint initiative of the provincial government and First Nations and Metis agencies, to provide culturally appropriate child welfare services for aboriginal children and families off-reserve: see *Child and Family Services Authorities Act*, SM 2002, c. 35 and Deana Driver, "New Manitoba Child Welfare Law Said 'Unprecedented in Canada,'" *The Lawyers Weekly*, January 9, 2004.

4. Decision Making About Child Protection

To what extent do the definitions of "child in need of protection" limit or guide judicial discretion? According to Wilson and Tomlinson, above at 61ff., judicial decision making in this context is complicated:

The judge in a child welfare proceeding must make a ... difficult assessment of whether the quality of parenting has fallen below a nebulous community standard such that the child would be better off in the foster parent/group home stream, which is a potentially devastating stream in itself. Consciously or unconsciously, the judge reacts to political, sociological, psychological and/or psychoanalytic theories and values of the role and standard of parenting within the context of his own particular background and diverse community.

Consider this comment in relation to the following excerpt.

George Thomson, "Judging Judiciously in Child Protection Cases"
in Rosalie Abella and Claire L'Heureux-Dubé, eds., *Dimensions of Justice*
(Toronto: Butterworths, 1983), 213, at 230-31

In most jurisdictions the issue of child abuse is not only receiving major attention generally, but is the subject of extensive media coverage. Further, the results of a decision not to intervene in a family tend to be much more visible than the results of one that brings the child into care. Or at least the causal connection between the decision and the results is more tenuous in the latter situation, given the fact that responsibility for decisions on behalf of the child is usually spread amongst a number of people. When these two factors are combined, it is easily recognized that the environment within which decisions are made is having a clear impact upon what is recommended. Appropriate risk-taking in this world of fallible decision-making becomes very difficult when one's whole career may be destroyed by a single decision to return a child to his or her home, if that child is then subjected to further abuse. This is particularly so when, conversely, the decision to take the child out of the home normally passes responsibility on to someone else. As a judge, it can be very difficult to assess whether, at least subconsciously, possible proposals to the court are not being made because of the environment in which they would be carried out. And it is only logical to ask whether this also affects the judge, who must feel a sense of personal responsibility for the results when a child is returned to his or her home. This is perhaps less likely to be present when the child is removed and placed in the care of the state. ...

It is also possible to illustrate how the narrower environment of the court complicates decision-making. The easiest illustration is the artificial environment within which the hearing itself takes place, subject to rules and procedures that are often unintelligible to family and child, and in which one observes persons who, in the midst of the worst crisis of their lives, are functioning in ways that may only vaguely resemble their normal behaviour. ...

A final point should be made, even though it is not strictly part of the discussion: what is presented to the judge may, of course, bear little relationship to what anyone might characterize as a full presentation of the information relevant to the issues at hand. The reasons for this may be both obvious and many in number: not all parties are represented; representation is inadequate on one or both sides; lawyers are demonstrating the role confusion that is the norm in these matters; much of the information discussed earlier in this paper is not known by those presenting the case to the court; much of it either is not seen as relevant, or is clearly inadmissible; only one expert is available and he or she has firm views on the issue of causation or risk of further abuse; insufficient time is available for the matter because of the pressure of court dockets; the factual data presented to the court are both imprecise and incomplete; and so on.

Child-protection cases raise challenging problems in relation to evidence and legal representation. To some extent, these problems reflect the tensions about state and family responsibilities for the protection of children. For example, as noted above, when lawyers for state agencies present evidence, they frequently rely on expert evidence from professionals who were earlier involved in assisting parents and their children, a situation which may create tensions in relation to future relationships of trust between these professionals and the family. Joanne Wildgoose suggested, for example, that *parents* may need to be represented at all stages of protection negotiations because of the power imbalance between them and agency professionals, particularly because parents involved in protection cases tend to be "the least educated, least articulate, poorest segments of our society": see Joanne Wildgoose, "Alternative Dispute Resolution of Child Protection Cases" (1987), 6 *Canadian Journal of Family Law* 61, at 65.

In addition, *children* may also be represented in these proceedings, but the precise role for counsel for a child remains contested. For example, the responsibility of counsel for a child to act "in the child's best interests" rather than on the child's instructions was confirmed in an Alberta decision: *Re A., C. and S.* (1990), 23 RFL (3d) 121; 103 AR 241 (Prov. Ct. (Youth Div.)). According to the court (at 123), it was incumbent on counsel "to form their own opinion as to what is in the best interests of the children, even though that position may be different from the views of the clients, the children." A somewhat different view was expressed for the role of counsel for a child in Ontario: see *Catholic Children's Aid Society of Metropolitan Toronto v. M.(C.)* (1991), 37 RFL (3d) 202 (Ont. Ct. J. (Prov. Div.)). See also James McLeod, "Annotation" (1991), 37 RFL (3d) 302. The Quebec Bar Committee also reviewed these issues in the preparation of a consultation paper on the representation of children: see Quebec Bar Committee, "The Legal Representation of Children: A Consultation Paper Prepared by the Quebec Bar Committee" (1996), 13 *Canadian Journal of Family Law* 49. To what extent do differing views about representation reflect different perspectives on relationships among families, their individual members (especially children), and the state?

Legal representation for parents in child-protection proceedings also raises important access issues. Because many of these parents are poor, their representation may necessitate access to provincial legal aid services. In the decision of the Supreme Court of Canada in *New Brunswick (Minister of Health and Community Services) v. G.(J.)*, [1999] 3 SCR 46; (1999), 50 RFL (4th) 63, the court held that state-funded legal counsel should have been provided for a mother in New Brunswick who faced the loss of her children in child-protection proceedings. The court unanimously relied on s. 7 of the Charter, concluding that the failure to provide state-funded counsel constituted an infringement of the mother's "security of the person." As a result, the court held that state-funded counsel was required in child-protection proceedings, having regard to the "seriousness of the interests at stake, the complexity of the proceedings, and the capacities of the [party]":

see also Rollie Thompson, "Annotation" (1999), 50 RFL (4th) 74 and M.J. Mossman, "New Brunswick (Minister of Health and Community Services) v. G.(J.): Constitutional Requirements for Legal Representation in Child Protection Matters" (2000), 12 *Canadian Journal of Women and the Law* 490. In *T.L.J. v. CAS of the United Counties of Stormont, Dundas and Glengarry*, [2002] OJ no. 3944 (Sup. Ct. J.) (QL), the judge expressed grave concerns about lack of representation for parents in child-protection proceedings. For a decision in which an Ontario court permitted an "unpaid, non-lawyer, agent-friend" to appear for a parent in a child-protection hearing, see *Children's Aid Society (Niagara Region) v. P.(D.)* (2002), 62 OR (3d) 668 (Sup. Ct. J.)—to what extent might this decision be connected to the (lack of) availability of legal aid services?

Child and Family Services of Western Manitoba v. R.A.Y. and S.D.M.
(1990), 29 RFL (3d) 330; 74 DLR (4th) 749 (Man. CA)

[Problems for lawyers, in terms of issues of representation and roles, were clearly illustrated in this Manitoba case. In the course of its review of a trial judge's decision, the Manitoba Court of Appeal considered the appropriateness of counsel's role in an application by the agency for permanent custody of a nine-month-old child. The parents were mentally handicapped. The mother was the primary caregiver; the father participated in caregiving, but was not always available. The agency had acknowledged their concerns about the parents' abilities from the time of the child's birth.

At the hearing of the agency's application, the mother was not represented and the matter was adjourned. It was subsequently understood that the father's lawyer would act for her as well and that she was content with this arrangement. After her agreement, however, she asked for legal aid, but it was refused to her and legal aid authorized the father's lawyer to act for her. When the agency was granted permanent custody, the parents appealed and the mother asserted that she had not been properly represented. A majority of the Court of Appeal held that the lawyer for the father had taken instructions from both parents and had advanced their joint interests; there was no denial of rights or miscarriage of justice. However, O'Sullivan JA dissented:]

O'SULLIVAN JA (dissenting): Giesbrecht Prov. J has found that the child, M.M., was and is in need of protection. This finding is amply justified by the evidence presented. I am concerned, however, that the mother was not called to give her side of the story and perhaps explain some of the criticisms directed against her. I am concerned also that the court did not hear from Linda Winter, a parents' aid who attended at the M. home up to five times a week and who had daily contact with the home during the time when it is alleged the child was in need of protection. Indeed, it is difficult to understand how the child could have been in need of protection when the child was being looked after not only by his parents, but also by the parents' aid, a mental retardation worker, a Child and Family Services worker, income security officers, a public health nurse and a student public health nurse, as well as doctors and a child development clinic.

At the trial, counsel appeared and said he was representing the mother, R.A.Y. Yet he told the court he did not think his client was capable of looking after her child. He submitted it was the father who could look after the child and who should be given custody. He led evidence that R.A.Y. had admitted she was not able to look after her child. ...

In argument before us, Mr. Kernaghan said he had never been retained by R.A.Y. for the purpose of her being represented at the hearing. I cannot understand how it could be in the best interest of R.A.Y. or her child for her to have a case presented based on her incompetency to look after the child.

In these circumstances, I would prefer to have a new trial which I understand can be arranged quickly. It is important that justice be done and be seen to be done.

How should the issues of representation in such a case be determined after the Supreme Court's decision in *New Brunswick v. G.*? To what extent are views about the need for representation of parents in child-protection proceedings relevant to public policies concerning relationships between state and family responsibilities for the protection of children?

5. Risk of Future Harm

Many provincial child-protection statutes identify evidence of both past harm and risk of future harm as the basis for a determination that a child is in need of protection. How should courts assess the risk of future harm? How will evidence of risk of future harm differ from evidence of harm that has already occurred? Consider what kind of evidence was used to determine risk of future harm in the case that follows.

Family and Children's Services of London and Middlesex v. G.(D.)
(1989), 20 RFL (3d) 429 (Ont. Prov. Ct. (Fam. Div.))

[In this case, the court decided that there was substantial risk to the child's health and safety and that the child's well-being could not be achieved in her mother's care, with or without supervision. In concluding that the agency's evidence had satisfied the legal test, the court stated (at 430-31):]

There is no doubt that the mother's consort, R., has been assaultive in the past towards, at the least, the mother. He has been incarcerated for that transgression. Nonetheless, she is adamant that she continue to live with him and has even given up the custody of another child in order to continue her relationship. While it is sought to characterize this as an example of her candid admission of the child's best interests, in my view it is just an example of the extent to which she is in his thrall.

It may be true that R. has not hurt or abused *this* child, but that is not the burden which the legislature has imposed on the society to prove. The society must simply show reasonable and probable grounds to believe that substantial risk exists: see *CCAS, Metropolitan Toronto v. L.(P.)*, [1986] WDFL 1746 (Ont. Dist. Ct.), per Hawkins DCJ.

I think these grounds have been clearly made out. The multitude of stories told by the mother in explaining the physical abuse of the first small child are telling evidence against her and cannot be explained away as simply convenient fabrications to stop the society workers badgering her.

In addition, the assessment report of Drs. Leschied and Sudermann is not optimistic and quite clearly sets out the fear that a reuniting of the living unit of the mother and R., when coupled with the demands of the child, would lead to a situation where more abuse would ensue, from which the mother (from her past history) would be unable to disassociate herself and the child.

I do not accept the proposition that the many planned interventions in the life of the mother by various social agencies would remove the risk to the child. Even daily visits would not do so.

Is this test for risk of future harm appropriate? See also *Regional Dir. of Child Welfare v. R.(R.)* (1989), 23 RFL (3d) 68; 99 AR 67 (QB), where a court decided that Alberta's legislation also contemplated emotional injury in the future as a basis for intervention.

Discussion Notes

Evolution of the Welfare Principle

In *The Welfare of the Child: The Principle and the Law* (Aldershot, UK: Ashgate, 1999), Kerry O'Halloran traced principles concerning the welfare of children in feudalism and early common law; then in relation to the Poor Laws, the ecclesiastical courts, and equitable jurisdiction; and, finally, in modern legislation in the United Kingdom. In considering the future of the "welfare principle," O'Halloran suggested that "[t]he legislative emphasis on promoting the welfare interests of children in the care of the state is perhaps more aspirational than realisable in the short-term but also indicates an awareness of a need to improve rather than to just monitor existing rudimentary care standards." Do these comments reflect the current status of child-protection statutes in Canada?

Harm for Families and Communities: B.(R.) v. CAS of Metropolitan Toronto

In *B.(R.) v. Children's Aid Society of Metropolitan Toronto*, [1995] 1 SCR 315; (1995), 9 RFL (4th) 157, the Supreme Court of Canada examined the definition of "child in need of protection" under the former Ontario legislation (the *Child Welfare Act*, RSO 1980, c. 66), and dismissed an appeal from the Ontario Court of Appeal. In particular, the court was asked to rule on whether the parents had been denied the right to choose medical treatment for a child contrary to s. 7 of the Charter and whether the parents' freedom of religion under s. 2(a) of the Charter had also been infringed.

The child had suffered from a number of serious illnesses and doctors in Toronto concluded that surgery was necessary, thereby also necessitating a blood transfusion. When the parents refused to consent to the proposed surgery (on the basis of religious belief), a 72-hour temporary wardship was obtained and then extended twice. The operation and transfusion took place during the course of the temporary wardship. In the Court of Appeal, it was held that s. 7 of the Charter did not guarantee a right to family autonomy and that the parents' right to freedom of religion and their right to choose medical treatment for their child according to their religious beliefs were protected by s. 2(a) only so long as their beliefs did not impede the overriding state concern for the health and life of a child. Any violation of the parents' s. 2(a) rights were saved by s. 1.

In the Supreme Court of Canada, there were several different judgments, but all nine justices agreed that the Charter's provisions did not preclude the actions taken by the Children's Aid Society in this case. Four justices (La Forest, L'Heureux-Dubé, Gonthier, and McLachlin JJ) concluded that although the statutory provisions deprived the parents of their right to decide what medical treatment should be administered to their child, they did so in accordance with the principles of fundamental justice in s. 7 of the Charter. Three justices (Cory, Iacobucci, and Major JJ) decided that because parental duties must be exercised according to the "best interests of the child" test, there is no room in s. 7 for parents to override the child's right to life and security of the person. For Lamer CJ, there was no infringement of s. 7 because that section does not protect the right of parents to choose or refuse medical treatment without undue interference from the state. Sopinka J declined to decide whether there was an infringement of s. 7 because the threshold requirement of a breach of the principles of fundamental justice had not been met. For further analysis of the reasoning in *B.(R.)*, see D.A. Rollie Thompson, "Case Comment" (1995), 9 RFL (4th) 345.

In examining a similar American case about medical intervention, Martha Minow suggested that the views that people hold about the appropriateness of state intervention in the family are determined by differing views about families and family law. According to Minow, one view of the family is that it is a place of love and affection, a private haven where authority can be trusted, property is shared, and sex is a consequence of love. In this context, state intervention appears frequently unjustified, and poses grave risks to family life. By contrast, another view characterizes the family as oppressive, violent, and brutal, an arena in which the state is seen to have a major responsibility to protect the economically and socially less powerful members. Yet, Minow argued, in the end, "the state always intervenes because it allocates power over the ... decision, whether it carves out a sphere of parental autonomy or instead permits strangers or state officials to challenge and supplant parental decisions": see Martha Minow, "Beyond State Intervention in the Family: For Baby Jane Doe" (1985), 18 *University of Michigan Journal of Law Reform* 933, at 951.

In addition, Shauna Van Praagh argued that state intervention in family life may also challenge children's sense of identity and community affiliation: see Shauna Van Praagh, "Faith, Belonging, and the Protection of 'Our' Children" (1999), 17 *Windsor Yearbook of Access to Justice* 154. Focusing on the decision of the Supreme Court of Canada in *B.(R.)*, Van Praagh argued (at 202-3) that state action in such cases may have an impact on community identities as well as parental authority, and that it is important to recognize children's identities within communities based on race, religion, ethnicity, language, and heritage as shaping and being shaped by diversity:

> Perhaps the most important conclusion to be drawn from the analysis offered here is that decision-makers in law have an active role to play in defining "multifaithism" and "multiculturalism" in Canada. That is, judges cannot simply look to our constitution or any

piece of legislation for a definition of multiculturalism and what it dictates. Rather, we are all engaged in an ongoing process of defining the notion and its reality and decisions by judges (along with legislators, child protection agencies and workers, schools, parents) are pieces in the puzzle. We can only figure out the meaning of diversity in a country like Canada through a myriad of tiny actions, decisions, forms of intervention and instances of cooperation, all of which have an impact on individuals and their many communities.

A plural society, then, is not simply one with parallel co-existing communities operating to the exclusion of each other. Rather, individuals—and children, in particular—are members of multiple communities. Importantly, this fact of membership does not submerge the individual. Instead, individuals remain at the centre of any analysis of law's role, where they are understood to develop in context from childhood on, and to display complex internal perspectives on the meaning of their faith and identity. When community members tell their stories of affiliation, when those stories change shape as they mingle with those of other communities and their members, when they are listened to, absorbed and retold by the state, then the law truly grapples with the multiple identities and shifting definitions of integrity that exist for its subjects. If the space provided by the "principles of fundamental justice" and a "free and democratic society" can incorporate these features, then those aspects of our constitution may truly reflect the complexities of our lives and connections.

To what extent do you agree that community identity may be relevant to these issues?

Consider Van Praagh's arguments in relation to the following decision. In *H.(T.) v. Children's Aid Society of Metropolitan Toronto* (1996), 138 DLR (4th) 144 (Ont. Ct. (Gen. Div.)), a 13-year-old girl and her mother both refused permission for blood products on religious grounds. The Children's Aid Society obtained an order for temporary wardship to ensure treatment; the court concluded that the girl was not a "mature minor," capable of making treatment decisions, and that her condition required this treatment to save her life. In a later hearing to determine whether the court's order violated the girl's own constitutional rights under ss. 2(a) and 7 of the Charter, the court held that the principles of fundamental justice in s. 7 had been met; and that any infringement of the girl's freedom of religion under s. 2(a) was justified pursuant to s. 1. In assessing the justification pursuant to s. 1, the court stated (at 175):

> Although T.'s right to freedom of religious practices was infringed by the wardship order, I conclude that the infringement was justified by section 1. As a society, we encourage and nurture our children to develop moral and religious values. We encourage our children to grow, be independent and learn to think for themselves. The maturation process from child to adult is a gradual and, at times, subtle one. A child's religious faith, where possible, should be respected. However, T. was in a life-threatening situation. The medical evidence was unequivocal. Without treatment with blood products, T. was risking death. She did not have sufficient maturity or judgment to weigh and balance the reasonably foreseeable consequences of the decision not to accept blood products. In these circumstances, the ability of the state to protect children requiring medical treatment who are not capable of making a treatment decision is a reasonable limit to T.'s freedom of religion that is demonstrably justified in a free and democratic society. The balancing of the rights of the individual must yield to the ability of the state to protect its children.

To what extent is the court's decision attentive to issues of religious community as proposed by Van Praagh? How might courts take account of "harm" to a child's sense of community as part of a Charter analysis? For earlier cases, see *Re S.D.* (1983), 34 RFL (2d) 34; 145 DLR (3d) 610 (BCCA) and *Re L.D.K.: Children's Aid Society of Metro Toronto v. K. and K.* (1986), 48 RFL (2d) 164; 23 CRR 337 (Ont. Prov. Ct. (Fam. Div.)).

SELECTED REFERENCES

CANADIAN ASSESSMENTS

Nicholas Bala, "Child and Family Policies for the 1990s," in Laura C. Johnson and Richard Barnhorst, eds., *Children, Families, and Public Policy in the 90s* (Scarborough, ON: Thompson Educational Publishing, 1991), 105.

Marion Bernstein, "Child Protection Mediation: Its Time Has Arrived" (1998-99), 16 *Canadian Family Law Quarterly* 73.

Canadian Bar Association, *Making the Case: The Right to Publicly Funded Legal Representation in Canada* (Ottawa: Canadian Bar Association, 2002).

Xiaobei Chen, "Is It All Neo-Liberal? Some Reflections on Child Protection Policy and Neo-Conservatism in Ontario" (2000), 45-46 *Canadian Review of Social Policy* 237.

Brenda Cossman and Carol Rogerson, "Case Study in the Provision of Legal Aid: Family Law," in Ontario Legal Aid Review, *Report of the Ontario Legal Aid Review: A Blueprint for Publicly Funded Legal Services*, vol. 3 (Toronto: Government of Ontario, 1996), 773.

M.I. Hall, "A Ministry for Children: Abandoning the Interventionist Debate in British Columbia" (1998), 12 *International Journal of Law, Policy, and the Family* 121.

Karen Swift, "Contradictions in Child Welfare: Neglect and Responsibility," in Carol T. Baines, Patricia M. Evans, and Sheila M. Naysmith, eds., *Women's Caring: Feminist Perspectives on Social Welfare* (Toronto: Oxford University Press, 1998), 160.

Bernd Walter, Janine Alison Isenegger, and Nicholas Bala, " 'Best Interests' in Child Protection Proceedings: Implications and Alternatives" (1995), 12 *Canadian Journal of Family Law* 367.

Philip Zylberberg, "Minimum Constitutional Guarantees in Child Protection Cases" (1992), 10 *Canadian Journal of Family Law* 257.

COMPARATIVE LITERATURE

Robert Dingwall, John Eekelaar, and Topsy Murray, *The Protection of Children*, 2d ed. (Aldershot, UK: Avebury, 1995).

Caroline Sawyer, "Conflicting Rights for Children: Implementing Welfare, Autonomy, and Justice Within Family Proceedings" (1999), 21:2 *Journal of Social Welfare and Family Law* 99.

B. A Case Study: Protection Issues and Fetal Apprehension

Neither the majority nor the minority in *DFG* assess state interference in the reproductive
lives of women in a manner fully compatible with women's equality and participation in
Canadian life. Nor do they place this incidence of juridical intervention within a history of
legal involvement with women's reproductive capacity, of which this is only the most recent
example.

> Sanda Rodgers, "Winnipeg Child and Family Services v. D.F.G.:
> Juridical Interference with Pregnant Women in the Alleged
> Interest of the Fetus" (1998), 36 *Alberta Law Review* 711, at 720

Rodgers's comments focused on the 1997 decision of the Supreme Court of Canada in
which a majority of the court concluded that there was no authority for the state to
"apprehend" a fetus, either pursuant to tort law or on the basis of the court's inherent
parens patriae jurisdiction. In reaching this conclusion, the majority recognized that it
was not possible to apprehend the fetus without also apprehending a pregnant woman. By
contrast, the dissenting judgment asserted a need to reconsider the "born alive" rule in
tort law in the light of new medical developments and an expansive view of the court's
parens patriae jurisdiction. In assessing the arguments of the majority and dissenting
judgments, consider their relationship to state and family responsibilities for protecting
children. Is this a case about family integrity or individual rights? How do the judgments
reflect different viewpoints about the respective roles for the state and for families and
their individual members? Is gender significant to these relationships? Why, or why not?

Winnipeg Child & Family Services (Northwest Area) v. G.(D.F.)
[1997] 3 SCR 925; (1997), 31 RFL (4th) 165

McLACHLIN J (Lamer CJC, La Forest, L'Heureux-Dubé, Gonthier, Cory, and
Iacobucci JJ concurring): In August 1996, a judge of the Manitoba Court of Queen's
Bench ordered that the respondent, five months pregnant with her fourth child, be
placed in the custody of the Director of Child and Family Services and detained at the
Health Sciences Centre until the birth of her child, there to follow a course of treatment prescribed by the Director. The purpose of the order was to protect the
respondent's unborn child. The respondent was addicted to glue-sniffing which may
damage the nervous system of the developing fetus.

The order was stayed two days later and ultimately set aside on appeal. The
respondent voluntarily remained at the Health Sciences Centre until discharged
August 14. She stopped sniffing glue and in December gave birth to an apparently
normal child, which she is now raising.

While the problem that gave rise to these proceedings has been resolved, the legal
issues it raised have not. Hence this appeal. Winnipeg Child and Family Services
("the agency") asks this Court to overturn the order of the Manitoba Court of Appeal
striking down the original order for detention. The respondent argues that the courts
have no power to order a mother into custody against her will for the purpose of

protecting her unborn child, and that such a radical departure from the existing law is best made, if it is to be made at all, by the legislature.

I would dismiss the appeal on the ground that an order detaining a pregnant woman for the purpose of protecting her fetus would require changes to the law which cannot properly be made by the courts and should be left to the legislature. ...

[McLachlin J outlined the history of the proceedings and the agency's assertion that two of the respondent's three children had been injured by her glue-sniffing addiction, thereby justifying its decision to intervene. She noted as well that the respondent had sought treatment at an earlier point, but had been turned away because of a lack of facilities; the respondent had agreed to take treatment eventually; and she had remained at the hospital until she was discharged.]

This is not a story of heros and villains. It is the more prosaic but all too common story of people struggling to do their best in the face of inadequate facilities and the ravages of addiction. This said, the legal question remains: assuming evidence that a mother is acting in a way which may harm her unborn child, does a judge, at the behest of the state, have the power to order the mother to be taken into custody for the purpose of rectifying her conduct? It is on this footing that I approach the case. ...

[McLachlin reviewed the lower court decisions, including the decision of Schulman J to make an order for detention on two grounds: that the respondent was suffering from a mental disorder within the meaning of the Manitoba *Mental Health Act*, RSM 1987, c. M110; and on the basis of the court's *parens patriae* jurisdiction—that is, "the power of the court to act in the stead of a parent for the protection of a child." As McLachlin noted, Schulman J acknowledged that the courts have never exercised this power on behalf of an unborn child, but he saw no reason why the power should not be extended to the protection of the child before birth. The Court of Appeal held that the evidence did not establish incompetency under the *Mental Health Act*. Nor, in the view of the court, could the order be supported on the ground of an extension of the court's *parens patriae* jurisdiction to protect the child or as an injunction to restrain tortious conduct.]

Having concluded that the existing law of judicial *parens patriae* powers and tort did not support the order, the Court of Appeal asked whether it could or should extend the law. Citing a host of difficulties, it concluded that it could not. Any restraint would involve moral choices and difficult conflicts between the rights of the mother and the interests of the unborn child. Extending the power of the courts to make this sort of order could have adverse effects; for example expectant mothers fearing state intervention might avoid detection by not seeking desirable prenatal care. The difficulty of enforcement and incompleteness of the remedy presented obstacles. Given the difficulty and complexity entailed in extension of the law, the task was more appropriate for the legislature than the courts. For these reasons, the Court of Appeal set aside the order for detention. ...

[According to McLachlin J, the case raised two issues. One related to the scope of tort law; the other related to the scope of the *parens patriae* jurisdiction of the court. In a lengthy review of the tort law context, she reviewed existing legal principles concerning the lack of legal status of a fetus.]

I turn to the general proposition that the law of Canada does not recognize the unborn child as a legal or juridical person. Once a child is born, alive and viable, the law may recognize that its existence began before birth for certain limited purposes. But the only right recognized is that of the born person. This is a general proposition, applicable to all aspects of the law, including the law of torts.

By way of preamble, two points may be made. First, we are concerned with the common law, not statute. If Parliament or the legislatures wish to legislate legal rights for unborn children or other protective measures, that is open to them, subject to any limitations imposed by the Constitution of Canada. Further, the fact that particular statutes may touch on the interests of the unborn need not concern us. Second, the issue is not one of biological status, nor indeed spiritual status, but of legal status. As this Court put it in *Tremblay c. Daigle*, [1989] 2 SCR 530, at p. 553:

> The task of properly classifying a foetus in law and in science are different pursuits. Ascribing personhood to a foetus in law is a fundamentally normative task. It results in the recognition of rights and duties—a matter which falls outside the concerns of scientific classification. In short, this Court's task is a legal one. Decisions based upon broad social, political, moral and economic choices are more appropriately left to the legislature.

What then is the status of the fetus at common law? In *Tremblay c. Daigle*, the father of a fetus sought an injunction to prevent the mother from terminating the pregnancy. He argued that a fetus was a "human being" entitled to the "enjoyment of life" under s. 1 of the *Charter of Human Rights and Freedoms*, RSQ, c. C-12. This Court unanimously rejected that contention on the ground that neither the Quebec civil law nor the common law of England and Canada recognize the fetus as a juridical person. While injury to a fetus due to the negligence of third parties is actionable, the right to sue does not arise until the infant is born. ...

[After reviewing a number of other decisions, McLachlin J concluded.]

The position is clear. Neither the common law nor the civil law of Quebec recognizes the unborn child as a legal person possessing rights. This principle applies generally, whether the case falls under the rubric of family law, succession law or tort. Any right or interest the fetus may have remains inchoate and incomplete until the birth of the child.

It follows that under the law as it presently stands, the fetus on whose behalf the agency purported to act in seeking the order for the respondent's detention was not a legal person and possessed no legal rights. If it was not a legal person and possessed no legal rights at the time of the application, then there was no legal person in whose interests the agency could act or in whose interests a court order could be made.

Putting the matter in terms of tort, there was no right to sue, whether for an injunction or damages, until the child was born alive and viable. The law of tort as it presently stands might permit an action for injury to the fetus to be brought in the child's name *after its birth*. But there is no power in the courts to entertain such an action before the child's birth. The action at issue was commenced and the injunctive relief sought before the child's birth. It follows that under the law as it presently stands, it must fail. ...

[McLachlin J then considered arguments about the appropriateness of extending the law of tort to cover this situation and concluded that they were "not the sort of changes which common law courts can or should make." In her view, they should be addressed by legislatures because they constitute major changes, affect other areas of tort law, and involve moral choices.

McLachlin J examined the issues relating to a judicial extension of these principles, reviewing the right of a fetus to sue and, particularly, the right to exercise control over "lifestyle" choices on the part of the mother. She concluded that before a court could impose a new duty of care, it would be necessary to demonstrate (1) a sufficiently close relationship between the parties to give rise to such a duty; and (2) the absence of considerations that should negate the duty, the class of persons to whom it is owed, or the damages to which a breach would give rise. Although she acknowledged the existence of a sufficiently close relationship between a pregnant woman and a fetus, McLachlin J was not satisfied that the second requirement had been met. In particular, she rejected the agency's argument that the duty of care should be defined to preclude a pregnant woman from engaging in activities that have "no substantial value" to her well-being and right of self-determination and that have potential to cause irreparable harm to "the child's life, health and ability to function after birth."]

The problem with this test lies in the terms "substantial value" and "well-being or right of self-determination." They are vague and broad and may not be adequate by themselves to narrowly confine the duty of care. What does substantial value to a woman's well-being mean? What does a woman's well-being include? What is involved in a woman's right of self-determination—all her choices, or merely some of them? And if some only, what is the criterion of distinction? Although it may be easy to determine that abusing solvents does not add substantial value to a pregnant woman's well-being and may not be the type of self-determination that deserves protection, other behaviours are not as easily classified. At what point does consumption of alcohol fail to add substantial value to a pregnant woman's well-being? Or cigarette smoking? Or strenuous exercise? No bright lines emerge to distinguish tortious behaviour from non-tortious once the door is opened to suing a pregnant mother for lifestyle choices adversely affecting the fetus. ...

These difficulties would be complicated by the fact that determining what will cause grave and irreparable harm to a fetus—the threshold for injunctive relief—is a difficult endeavour with which medical researchers continually struggle. The difference between confinement and freedom, between damages and non-liability, may depend on a grasp of the latest research and its implications. The pregnant women most likely to be affected by such a "knowledge" requirement would be those in lower socio-economic groups. Minority women, illiterate women, and women of limited education will be the most likely to fall afoul of the law and the new duty it imposes and to suffer the consequences of injunctive relief and potential damage awards.

A further problem arises from the fact that lifestyle "choices" like alcohol consumption, drug abuse, and poor nutrition may be the products of circumstance and illness rather than free choice capable of effective deterrence by the legal sanction of tort. ... While the law may properly impose responsibility for the consequences of addictive behaviour, like drunkenness, the policy question remains of whether extending a duty of care in tort in this particular situation as the remedy for redressing problems which are caused by addiction is a wise option. Given the lack of control pregnant women have over many of these harmful behaviours, it is doubtful whether recognizing a duty of care to refrain from them will significantly affect their choices. As a result, the general deterrent value of the proposed new duty of care is questionable. ...

I conclude that the order for detention cannot be upheld as an application of tort law. ...

Alternatively, the appellant seeks to sustain the order for the detention of the respondent by an extension of the court's *parens patriae* jurisdiction to permit protection of unborn children. Courts have the power to step into the shoes of the parent and make orders in the best interests of the child; *E. (Mrs.) v. Eve*, [1986] 2 SCR 388. The agency argues that this power should be extended to orders on behalf of unborn children.

I would reject this submission for reasons similar to those enunciated in connection with the submission that the law of tort should be extended to the unborn. The submission requires a major change to the law of *parens patriae*. The ramifications of the change would be significant and complex. The change involves conflicts of fundamental rights and interests and difficult policy issues. Not surprisingly these difficulties have led all appellate courts that have considered the extension to reject it. I share their view.

The law as it stands is clear: the courts do not have *parens patriae* or wardship jurisdiction over unborn children. This is the law in the European Community, Great Britain and Canada. In Canada, all courts which have considered the issue, save for the trial judge in this case, appear to have rejected the proposition that the *parens patriae* jurisdiction of the court extends to unborn children. In *A., Re* (1990), 28 RFL (3d) 288 (Ont. UFC), the Children's Aid Society of Hamilton-Wentworth brought an action for a supervision order to ensure that a pregnant woman seek appropriate prenatal care deemed necessary for the welfare of the fetus. Steinberg UFCJ, having concluded that there was no jurisdiction to make the order under the *Child and Family Services Act*, SO 1984, c. 55, considered whether the *parens patriae* jurisdiction was broad enough to force the confinement of a pregnant woman to protect her fetus. He held it was not broad enough. At p. 298, he concluded:

> The essence of the parens patriae power is that the court is empowered to take steps to protect the child or the fetus *in the place of the parent*. But here the child is actually inside of the mother. It is, therefore, impossible in this case to take steps to protect the child without ultimately forcing the mother, under restraint if necessary, to undergo medical treatment and other processes against her will. I believe that the parens patriae

jurisdiction is just not broad enough to envisage the forceable confinement of a parent as a necessary incident of its exercise. Even if it were, however, the court should be very wary about using its powers in such instances, as its routine exercise could possibly lead to some abuse of pregnant mothers. [Emphasis in original.]

Similarly, the New Brunswick Court of Queen's Bench has also held that the *parens patriae* jurisdiction does not extend to protection of the unborn: *New Brunswick (Minister of Health & Community Services) v. Hickey* (November 4, 1996) (NBQB), unreported, *per* Young J.

The English Court of Appeal has taken the same view: *F. (in utero), Re*, ... [[1988] 2 All ER 193 (Eng. CA)]. The local authority sought a wardship over the unborn child of a severely mentally disabled woman given to roaming and periodic disappearance. In separate judgments, all members of the court agreed that the wardship power could not be used in the manner requested. May LJ emphasized the effect such an order would have on the liberty of the pregnant woman and the incompatibility of a wardship order with those interests (at p. 194):

In wardship proceedings the court is exercising a parental jurisdiction in which the paramount consideration is the child's welfare. But in the case of an unborn child the only orders to protect him or her which the court could make would be with regard to the mother herself. Thus in the first place there would have to be an order authorising the local authority to find the mother. Then perhaps an order that she should live in a certain place and probably attend a certain hospital. All of these would be restrictive of the mother's liberty. Further, there could well be medical problems which would have to be solved: the mother might wish one course of action to be taken; it might be in the interests of the child that an alternative procedure should be followed. Until the child is actually born there must necessarily be an inherent incompatibility between any projected exercise of wardship jurisdiction and the rights and welfare of the mother.

May LJ gave four reasons for limiting the court's jurisdiction to born children. First, a fetus does not attain legal personhood until birth and therefore, the order would be contrary to that principle. ... Second, applying the principle that the interests of the child are to be predominant would create conflict between the existing legal interests of the mother and those of the unborn child. Third, there could be difficulties in enforcing against the mother any order in respect of an unborn child. And finally, he held that under the *Supreme Court Act 1981* only "minors" could be made wards of the court and that in light of the *Family Law Reform Act 1969*, a "minor" could only be a person, in the sense that he or she had been born.

Balcombe LJ also emphasized the incompatibility between wardship of the unborn and the pregnant woman's freedom. He pointed out that (as in Canada) the *Mental Health Acts* regulate and limit when a person may be confined against her will. If a pregnant woman was to be subject to controls for the benefit of her unborn child, Parliament should so legislate, as it had in the case of mentally incompetent persons. ... Staughton LJ, in rejecting the authority's application, emphasized the inseparability of the fetus from the mother, citing the European Commission on Human Rights ... in *Paton v. UK* (1980), 3 EHRR 408, at 415 (para. 19): "The 'life' of the foetus is intimately connected with, and cannot be regarded in isolation from, the life of the pregnant woman."

As the English Court of Appeal's reasons eloquently attest, the same problems encountered in relation to extending tort jurisdiction to the unborn, surface in relation to extending the *parens patriae* jurisdiction of the court. The law sees birth as the necessary condition of legal personhood. The pregnant woman and her unborn child are one. Finally, to make orders protecting fetuses would radically impinge on the fundamental liberties of the pregnant woman, both as to lifestyle choices and how and as to where she chooses to live and be.

It is argued that the *parens patriae* jurisdiction over children necessarily involves overriding the liberty of parents, and that there is nothing new in this. This argument overlooks the fact that the invasion of liberty involved in making court orders affecting the unborn child, is of a different order than the invasion of liberty involved in court orders relating to born children. The *parens patriae* power over born children permits the courts to override the liberty of the parents to make decisions on behalf of their children where a parental choice may result in harm to a child: *B.(R.) v. Children's Aid Society of Metropolitan Toronto* (1994), [1995] 1 SCR 315. The only liberty interest affected is the parent's interest in making decisions for *his or her child*. By contrast, extension of the *parens patriae* jurisdiction of the court to unborn children has the potential to affect a much broader range of liberty interests. The court cannot make decisions for the unborn child without inevitably making decisions for the mother herself. The intrusion is therefore far greater than simply limiting the mother's choices concerning her child. Any choice concerning her child inevitably affects her. For example, to sustain the order requested in the case at bar would interfere with the pregnant woman's ability to choose where to live and what medical treatment to undergo. The *parens patriae* jurisdiction has never been used to permit a court to make such decisions for competent women, whether pregnant or not. Such a change would not be an incremental change ... but a generic change of major impact and consequence. It would seriously intrude on the rights of women. If anything is to be done, the legislature is in a much better position to weigh the competing interests and arrive at a solution that is principled and minimally intrusive to pregnant women.

I conclude that the law of *parens patriae* does not support the order for the detention of the respondent. ...

[McLachlin J also indicated that her conclusions meant that it was unnecessary to address arguments about the constitutionality of the order, raised by some intervenors.]

I conclude that the common law does not clothe the courts with power to order the detention of a pregnant woman for the purpose of preventing harm to her unborn child. Nor, given the magnitude of the changes and their potential ramifications, would it be appropriate for the courts to extend their power to make such an order. The changes to the law sought on this appeal are best left to the wisdom of the elected legislature. I would dismiss the appeal. ...

MAJOR J (dissenting) (Sopinka J concurring): I respectfully disagree with the conclusion of McLachlin J that an order detaining a pregnant woman addicted to glue sniffing for which she has rejected abortion and/or medical treatment and decided to carry her child to term, would require a change to the law which cannot be properly made other than by legislation.

To the extent that a change in the law in the circumstances of this case is required, the much admired flexibility of the common law has proven adaptable enough over centuries to meet exigent circumstances as they arise. That flexibility is surely needed in the appeal.

Under existing Canadian law the expectant respondent at her sole discretion could have chosen an abortion. Instead she chose to continue her pregnancy and to continue her glue sniffing which in the past had resulted in two serious and permanently handicapped children being born who are now permanent wards of the state.

There are three questions that arise in this appeal. What are the rights of the pregnant woman? Does the unborn foetus have independent rights? Does the state also have a separate right to intervene to prescribe proper medical treatment in the hope of achieving the birth of a healthy child as opposed to standing idly by and watching the birth of a permanently and seriously handicapped child who has no future other than as a permanent ward of the state?

… The respondent, on becoming pregnant for the fourth time, made the decision not to have an abortion. She chose to remain pregnant, deliver the child, and continue her substance abuse.

In my opinion, the state has an enforceable interest in ensuring, to the extent practicable, the well-being of the unborn child and the appeal should be allowed.

Historically, it was thought that damage suffered by a foetus could only be assigned if the child was born alive. It was reasoned that it was only at that time that damages to the live child could be identified. The logic for that rule has disappeared with modern medical progress. Today by the use of ultrasound and other advanced techniques, the sex and health of a foetus can be determined and monitored from a short time after conception. The sophisticated surgical procedures performed on the foetus before birth further belies the need for the "born alive" principle. …

[Major J then listed the material submitted by intervenors on the prevalence of mental and physical disabilities in children as a result of substance abuse by their mothers while pregnant. For example, Southeast Child and Family Services and West Region Child and Family Services, both of them aboriginal child and family service agencies delivering services to 18 First Nation communities in Manitoba, urged the court to create a legal remedy. These intervenors submitted that "such a remedy would be consistent with the aboriginal world view, and that the common law should be expanded to help alleviate what is particularly an aboriginal problem." Major J continued in relation to the court's *parens patriae* jurisdiction.]

The law of this country is consistent with the grant of a remedy in this case. The *parens patriae* jurisdiction of the superior courts is of undefined and undefinable breadth. This Court's decision in *Eve, Re*, [1986] 2 SCR 388, indicates that inherent power resides in the provincial superior courts to act on behalf of those who cannot act to protect themselves. A foetus suffering from its mother's abusive behaviour is particularly within this class and deserves protection.

It has been submitted, however, that a foetus acquires no actionable rights in our law until it is born alive. In my view, the "born alive" rule, as it is known, is a common law evidentiary presumption rooted in rudimentary medical knowledge that has long since been overtaken by modern science and should be set aside for purpose of this appeal.

This means that a superior court, on proper motion, should be able to exercise its *parens patriae* jurisdiction to restrain a mother's conduct when there is a reasonable probability of that conduct causing serious and irreparable harm to the foetus within her. While the granting of this type of remedy may interfere with the mother's liberty interests, in my view, those interests must bend when faced with a situation where devastating harm and a life of suffering can so easily be prevented. In any event, this interference is always subject to the mother's right to end it by deciding to have an abortion.

The arguments against state intervention are that it improperly interferes with the rights of the mother, that there are innumerable hazards to safe pregnancies, and that the state should not impose health standards on adults without consent. Those arguments are answerable.

Once the mother decides to bear the child the state has an interest in trying to ensure the child's health. What circumstances permit state intervention? The "slippery slope" argument was raised that permitting state intervention here would impose a standard of behaviour on all pregnant women. Questions were raised about women who smoke, who lived with a smoker, who ate unhealthy diets, etc. In response to the query of where a reasonable line should be drawn it was submitted that the pen should not even be lifted. This approach would entail the state to stand idly by while a reckless and/or addicted mother inflicts serious and permanent harm on to a child she had decided to bring into the world.

There can be no general formula and each case must be decided on its own facts. However, as a minimum to justify intervention the following thresholds have to be met:

(1) The woman must have decided to carry the child to term.

(2) Proof must be presented to a civil standard that the abusive activity will cause serious and irreparable harm to the foetus.

(3) The remedy must be the least intrusive option.

(4) The process must be procedurally fair. ...

[In discussing the *parens patriae* jurisdiction of the court, Major J stated:]

In *Eve, supra,* this Court faced a different issue, a mother's request for a court order authorizing the sterilization of her mentally incompetent daughter. In determining this question La Forest J examined the history and scope of the *parens patriae* jurisdiction. His reasons explain the undefined and undefinable breadth of the power of the court in this area. ...

In summarizing his opinion on the *parens patriae* jurisdiction he stated, at pp. 425-27:

From the earliest time, the sovereign, as *parens patriae*, was vested with the care of the mentally incompetent. This right and duty, as Lord Eldon noted in *Wellesley v. Duke of Beaufort* ... [(1827), 2 Russ. 1; 38 ER 236 (Ch. D)], at 2 Russ., at p. 20, 38 ER, at p. 243 is founded on the obvious necessity that the law should place somewhere the care of persons who are not able to take care of themselves. In early England, the *parens patriae* jurisdiction was confined to mental incompetents, but its *rationale* is obviously applicable to children and, following the transfer of that jurisdiction to the Lord Chancellor in the seventeenth century, he extended it to children under wardship, and it is in this context that the bulk of the modern cases on the subject arise. The *parens patriae* jurisdiction was later vested in the provincial superior courts of this country, and in particular, those of Prince Edward Island.

The *parens patriae* jurisdiction is, as I have said, founded on necessity, namely the need to act for the protection of those who cannot care for themselves. The courts have frequently stated that it is to be exercised in the "best interest" of the protected person or, again, for his or her "benefit" or "welfare."

The situations under which it can be exercised are legion; the jurisdiction cannot be defined in that sense. As Lord MacDermott put it in *J. v. C.*, [1970] AC 668, at p. 703, the authorities are not consistent and there are many twists and turns, but they have inexorably "moved towards a broader discretion, under the impact of changing social conditions and the weight of opinion. ..." In other words, the categories under which the jurisdiction can be exercised are never closed. Thus I agree with Latey J in [*Re X. (a minor)*, [1975] 1 All ER 697 (Fam. Div.)], at p. 699, that the jurisdiction is of a very broad nature, and that it can be invoked in such matters as custody, protection of property, health problems, religious upbringing and protection against harmful associations. This list, as he notes, is not exhaustive.

What is more, as the passage from *Chambers* cited by Latey J underlines, a court may act not only on the ground that injury to person or property has occurred, but also on the ground that such injury is apprehended. I might add that the jurisdiction is a carefully guarded one. The courts will not readily assume that it has been removed by legislation where a necessity arises to protect a person who cannot protect himself.

I have no doubt that the jurisdiction may be used to authorize the performance of a surgical operation that is necessary to the health of a person, as indeed it already has been in Great Britain and this country. And by health, I mean mental as well as physical health. In the United States, the courts have used the *parens patriae* jurisdiction on behalf of a mentally incompetent to authorize chemotherapy and amputation, and I have little doubt that in a proper case our courts should do the same. Many of these instances are related in *Strunk v. Strunk*, 445 SW 2d 145 (Ky. 1969), where the court went to the length of permitting a kidney transplant between brothers. Whether the courts in this country should go that far, or as in *Quinlan* permit the removal of life-sustaining equipment, I leave to later disposition.

Though the scope or sphere of operation of the *parens patriae* jurisdiction may be unlimited, it by no means follows that the discretion to exercise it is unlimited. It must be exercised in accordance with its underlying principle. Simply put, the discretion is to do what is necessary for the protection of the person for whose benefit it is exercised; see the passages from the reasons of Sir John Pennycuick in *Re X.*, at pp. 706-07,

and Heilbron J in [*Re D. (a minor)*, [1976] 1 All ER 326 (Fam. Div.)], at p. 332 ... .
The discretion is to be exercised for the benefit of that person, not for that of others. It
is a discretion, too, that must at all times be exercised with great caution, a caution that
must be redoubled as the seriousness of the matter increases. This is particularly so in
cases where a court might be tempted to act because failure to do so would risk imposing an obviously heavy burden on some other individual.

While the breadth of the jurisdiction available under *parens patriae* is apparent from
La Forest J's reasons in *Eve*, what is unclear is whether the jurisdiction to act in the
best interests of a *child* can also include the power to act in the best interests of a *foetus*.

It has been held to the contrary both in the Manitoba Court of Appeal's ruling in
this case, and in the English Court of Appeal in *F. (in utero), Re*, [1988] 2 All ER 193
(Eng. CA). Both decisions relied on the common law "born alive" rule. This rule
requires that a foetus achieve personhood before it can acquire actionable rights. The
child must be born alive before any rights can accrue or remedies can be sought. In
my view, the reliance on this rule was misplaced. The rule is a legal anachronism
based on rudimentary medical knowledge and should no longer be followed, at least
for the purposes of this appeal.

If a foetus is a "person" for purposes of the *parens patriae* jurisdiction, he or she is
in a particularly vulnerable position. A foetus, absent outside assistance, has no means
of escape from toxins ingested by its mother. The *parens patriae* jurisdiction exists
for the stated purpose of doing what is necessary to protect the interests of those who
are unable to protect themselves. Society does not simply sit by and allow a mother
to abuse her child after birth. How then should serious abuse be allowed to occur
before the child is born? ...

[Major J then considered the born-alive rule in the context of its genesis and purpose,
and with respect to new medical technology, and concluded that it should not apply.]

Present medical technology renders the "born alive" rule outdated and indefen-
sible. We no longer need to cling to an evidentiary presumption to the contrary when
technologies like real time ultrasound, fetal heart monitors and fetoscopy can clearly
show us that a foetus is alive and has been or will be injured by conduct of another.
We can gauge fetal development with much more certainty than the common law
presumed. How can the sophisticated micro-surgery that is now being performed on
foetuses *in utero* be compatible with the "born alive" rule? ...

The "born alive" rule should be abandoned, for the purposes of this case, as it is
medically out-of-date. It may be that the rule has continuing utility in the context of
other cases with their own particular facts. The common law boasts that it is adaptable. If so, there is no need to cling for the sake of clinging to notions rooted in
rudimentary medical and scientific knowledge of the past. A foetus should be considered within the class of persons whose interests can be protected through the exercise
of the *parens patriae* jurisdiction.

In my opinion, it is a modest expansion on La Forest J's statements in *Eve, supra*,
to include a foetus within the class of persons who can be protected by the exercise of

the *parens patriae* jurisdiction. However, clearly, the only person by law able to choose between an abortion or carrying to term is the mother. She too has the right to decide her lifestyle whether pregnant or not. The court's ability to intervene must therefore be limited. *It will only be in extreme cases, where the conduct of the mother has a reasonable probability of causing serious irreparable harm to the unborn child, that a court should assume jurisdiction to intervene.* [Emphasis in original.] ...

I do not believe our system, whether legislative or judicial, has become so paralysed that it will ignore a situation where the imposition required in order to prevent terrible harm is so slight. It may be preferable that the legislature act but its failure to do so is not an excuse for the judiciary to follow the same course of inaction. Failure of the court to act should occur where there is no jurisdiction for the court to proceed. Outdated medical assumptions should not provide any licence to permit the damage to continue. Where the harm is so great and the temporary remedy so slight, the law is compelled to act.

Discussion Notes

Roles for Courts and Legislatures: Re A.

The differing views in the majority and dissenting judgments in the Supreme Court of Canada reveal different perceptions about the respective roles of legislatures and courts in relation to the legal status of a fetus. In addition, however, they appear to reflect different perceptions about the respective rights to make decisions on the part of the state and families. To what extent do the dissenting views reflect an emphasis on state responsibilities for children with health problems? To what extent do the majority views reflect an emphasis on the autonomy of the pregnant woman? How should the law balance these concerns for potential state responsibilities and the autonomy of individual pregnant women with the protection and well-being of children? Whose interests are protected by the absence of legislation? For some consideration of these issues, see T. Brettel Dawson, "Re Baby R.: A Comment on Fetal Apprehension" (1990), 4 *Canadian Journal of Women and the Law* 265. In a report on an inquest into the suicide of an aboriginal teenager in Manitoba, Judge Linda Giesbrecht reviewed problems experienced by children with fetal alcohol syndrome, and made a number of recommendations about training and services to respond to these problems. She also noted that it might be necessary for legislators to tackle this difficult problem, while suggesting that the absence of legislation necessitated the implementation of policies of prevention, education, and early diagnosis: see Deana Driver, "Judge Recommends Legislation To Protect Fetuses from Effects of Mother's Substance Abuse," *The Lawyers Weekly*, February 28, 2003, 8.

At the time of the trial court's decision in Manitoba, there was a precedent in Ontario, which had reached a different conclusion. In *Re A.* (1990), 28 RFL (3d) 288; 75 OR (2d) 82 (UFC), the parents of an unborn child had four other children who were all Crown wards; at the time of the motion, there was an application before the court to terminate the parents' access to them. The mother had toxemia and there was a possibility that she might develop eclampsia, which would put her life, and the life of the unborn child, at risk. However, the mother failed to continue appropriate medical treatment, and would not tell the CAS who the treating doctor was. There was evidence that the father was violent and had an "antisocial personality disorder." There was also a history of poor attention to proper sanitary conditions for the couple's children.

The CAS brought an *ex parte* motion respecting the unborn child. Specifically, the CAS sought an order that the mother attend regularly with a qualified medical doctor for prenatal care, the name of the doctor be provided to the CAS, and the mother make immediate plans to attend at a hospital until the child's birth where she would undergo all necessary medical procedures for the well-being of the unborn child.

The court dismissed the motion and held that there was no jurisdiction under Ontario's *Child and Family Services Act* to grant protection-related relief in respect of an unborn child. In reaching its decision, the court considered three cases relied on by the CAS: *CAS (Belleville) v. T.(L.)* (1987), 59 OR (2d) 204 (Prov. Ct. (Fam. Div.)); *Supt. of Fam. & Child Service v. M.(B.)* (1982), 135 DLR (3d) 330 (BCSC); and *Re Brown*, supra.

The court concluded that these decisions could not be applied to the situation at bar, as each of them related to children who had been already born at the time the respective actions had been commenced.

In reaching its decision, the court noted that neither the definition of "child" in the Act nor the declaration of principles in s. 1 of the Act accorded an unborn fetus any status as a person, or any right to protection under the Act. The court stated that the essence of the *parens patriae* jurisdiction empowers a court to take steps to protect a child or fetus in the place of a parent; it does not envisage forced confinement of a parent as a necessary incident of its exercise. As it was impossible to protect the fetus without forcing the mother to undergo medical treatment against her will, there was no jurisdiction to grant the CAS's requested relief. Could the Manitoba trial court in *G.(D.F.)* have used this Ontario decision as a non-binding but useful precedent? Were there factual differences between the two cases that should have been taken into account? Why, or why not?

Intervention in the Maternal–Fetal Relationship

Why is it appropriate, as a case study about child protection, to examine a case concerning fetal protection? How does this Supreme Court decision assist in defining the principles concerning protection of children? To what extent is the decision significant for defining the relationship between individuals, families, and the state?

In a critique of the Supreme Court's decision, Laura Shanner examined the approach of the dissenting judges, arguing that it failed to take into account the broader context of pregnancy.

Laura Shanner, "Pregnancy Intervention and Models of Maternal–Fetal Relationship: Philosophical Reflections in the Winnipeg CFS Dissent"
(1998), 36:3 *Alberta Law Review* 751, at 764-66

An important problem is the distinction between implied consent and explicit consent. Is declining to have an abortion truly equivalent to deciding to carry the child to term, as Major J claims? The psychological, philosophical and legal distinctions between assent and consent (and other variations) are compelling. Note, for example, how much trouble was generated by "negative marketing" undertaken by the Rogers cable television company in 1997, when new channels were automatically provided and billed to customers unless the customer took steps to prevent the addition. Failing to take active steps to avoid an outcome is clearly not always equivalent to embracing that outcome as a positive commitment.

A related problem is the conflation of two different, albeit related, decisions. A common but unpersuasive anti-abortion argument is that women who did not want to get pregnant ought not have had sex; clearly, having sex and having babies are not identical propositions, and agreement for one does not necessarily entail agreement for the other. Similarly, one might reject abortion (perhaps on religious grounds) but not positively commit to continued pregnancy.

Any discussion about reproductive decisions must take account of the socio-political context of abortion in North America. Abortion was decriminalized only 25 years ago in the US, and only 10 years ago in Canada. Although abortion is legally available, it is not always practically available: women living in poverty, and especially in rural or remote communities, may have little or no access to abortion providers. North American medical schools are increasingly making abortion procedures an elective rather than standard component of obstetrics/gynaecology education, which means that finding qualified abortion providers will become increasingly difficult. The continued social and political strife surrounding abortion—including protests and harassment at abortion clinics, bombing of clinics and violence against abortion providers—indicates clearly that abortion is not considered to be equally attractive or acceptable as continuing pregnancy. Thus, while abortion is a legally available choice, the social attitudes and behaviors surrounding abortion in our communities undermine genuinely informed and voluntary consent to continue pregnancy rather than terminate it. Some women are denied access to abortion, while for others the choice not to abort a pregnancy may be nothing more than a choice to avoid harassment.

The gendered inequality of commitments or moral responsibility for pregnancy despite shared causal responsibility presents a larger frame of reference on the social context of pregnancy. While it would be a good thing to reward women for their active commitments and efforts in continuing pregnancies, will men shoulder their fair share of moral responsibility for healthy pregnancy continuation? This challenge is not intended to castigate men, but to call attention to larger systemic issues of gender inequality, economic disparities, the lack of adequate day care and parenting assistance, minimal maternity leave and job security after pregnancy, etc. While women bear the physical and moral responsibility for pregnancy continuation, women cannot, by themselves, change the social and economic contexts in which pregnancies occur; men must also take active responsibility for creating conditions that make the continuation of pregnancy—as well as the termination of pregnancy—equally possible and attractive commitments if we are to adopt Major J's framework.

Aspects of individual human psychology that affect reproductive decisions must also be considered. An important element of choice involves a person's locus of control, which is the subjective placing of oneself on a gradient from fully autonomous to fully coerced. People with an internal locus of control feel themselves to be autonomous and capable of making choices that lead to anticipated outcomes, and thus they feel responsible for their choices, successes and failures. Those with an external locus of control either feel unable to make choices at all, or perceive that the outcomes of their choices are determined by fate, God, or people other than themselves. A person's locus of control frequently changes throughout his/her life and may vary at a given time in reference to different situations. We should note that stereotypical gender roles define different appropriate loci of control for men and women: men are expected to be autonomous and in control, while women are more likely to be depicted as dependent and irrational. Indeed, it is common for women who actively take control of aspects of their lives to be chastised as unfeminine and aggressive.

There is evidence that an internal locus of control is correlated with more reliable and effective contraceptive use, and thus that women with an external locus of control are more likely to have unintended pregnancies. Why ought we to believe that unexpectedly becoming pregnant would suddenly shift a woman's locus of control inward, such that she would actively choose to abort or choose to remain pregnant rather than merely muddle through the pregnancy? It seems far more plausible that women with an external locus of control are not only more likely to experience unintended pregnancies, but also to feel stuck with them rather than capable of altering their own fate. Locus of control problems may be especially acute for women who suffer abuse, who are in marginalized economic or ethnic groups, or who (like D.G.) are influenced by substance addiction.

To what extent do you think that gender is relevant to the majority and the dissenting views in this fetal-apprehension case? How should these concerns be taken into account? Is this a matter for the courts or for legislatures?

SELECTED REFERENCES

S.I. Bushnell, "The Welfare of Children and the Jurisdiction of the Court under *Parens Patriae*," in Katherine Connell-Thouez and Bartha Knoppers, eds., *Contemporary Trends in Family Law: A National Perspective* (Scarborough, ON: Carswell, 1984), 223.

Thelma McCormack, "Fetal Syndromes and the Charter: The Winnipeg Glue Sniffing Case" (1999), 14 *Canadian Journal of Law and Society* 77.

Laura Shanner, "Pregnancy Intervention and Models of Maternal–Fetal Relationship: Philosophical Reflections on the Winnipeg CFS Dissent" (1998), 36 *Alberta Law Review* 751.

C. State Intervention and Sexual Abuse of Children: Families as Sites of Harm

Reports made to authorities indicate that female children are sexually abused in greater numbers than male children, and that adult males are the majority of offenders. This picture is changing rapidly, however, as more First Nations adults who attended residential schools in Canada as children are speaking out. Also, there are increased reports from males [in church schools and other church settings, and in junior hockey clubs]. ... There remains considerable resistance from some professionals and the public to accept the prevalence of child sexual abuse. Moreover, individuals in authority positions who hold with a more conventional approach to the victimization of children have difficulty acknowledging that such abuse arises out of the social legitimation of unequal power relations within families.

> Betty Joyce Carter, *Who's To Blame?*
> *Child Sexual Abuse and Non-Offending Mothers*
> (Toronto: University of Toronto Press, 1999), 175

1. Recognition of the Problem: Government Reports

Legal recognition of child sexual abuse in recent decades has resulted in increased state intervention, including the use of criminal sanctions, to protect children from abusers who are often members of their own families. Governmental inquiries and reports have regularly identified the problem of child sexual abuse and proposed a variety of different kinds of legal responses. For example, the 1984 Badgley Report reported on the prevalence of child sexual abuse, stating that "at some time during their lives, about one in two females and one in three males have been victims of one or more unwanted sexual acts": see Committee on Sexual Offences Against Children and Youths (Badgley Committee), *Sexual Offences Against Children: The Badgley Report* (Ottawa: Minister of Supply and Services Canada, 1984), at 175. The recommendations of the Badgley Report focused mainly on changes in the administration of criminal justice. According to John Lowman, the potential impact of the report was limited by the narrowness of its focus on criminal law measures. Partly as a result of this narrow focus, Lowman argued that the report failed to recognize important features of the problem of child sexual abuse.

John Lowman, "Child Saving, Legal Panaceas, and the Individualization of Family Problems: Some Comments on the Findings and Recommendations of the Badgley Report"
(1985), 4 *Canadian Journal of Family Law* 508, at 511-12

One of the main findings emerging from the Committee's research was that a large proportion of offences against children occurred in the home, and that many offenders were closely related to the victim. Despite the importance of these findings the report offers virtually no analysis of power relationships within the family.

More problematically the Committee makes virtually nothing of the overwhelmingly obvious character of what some observers consider to be its most important research finding. As Clark points out, the significance of the sex of offenders is passed by almost without comment. An overwhelming 99.2% of sexual offences against females and 96.9% of offences against boys were committed by males. The Committee ignores the nature of the social reproduction of male sexuality and implicitly portrays the sexual abuse of children as being independent of the social system in which it occurs.

As Lowman noted, the Badgley Committee's recommendations were lauded for being child-centred and for recognizing that children can tell the truth in court. At the same time, the report failed to take seriously the data collected from child prostitutes, many of whom stated that they had left home because of abuse suffered there and therefore preferred to live on the street rather than to return home. Thus, Lowman concluded (at 512) that the report had failed to analyze "power structures in the family." As he argued (at 513), "[there is a need for] discussion of the marginal position of the juvenile in the labour force, the extensive problem of youth unemployment, and the accentuation of these difficulties for young women. All these structural issues are avoided [in the report]." Other studies have also confirmed that child prostitutes are more likely than other children to have been the target of sexual abuse in their own homes: see Christopher Earls and Hélène David, "Early Family and Sexual Experiences of Male and Female Prostitutes" (1990), 38:4 *Canada's Mental Health* 7. Thus, while changes in the administration of criminal justice may be necessary, the issues appear to require other responses as well.

2. Sexual Abuse and Children in Need of Protection

In the family law context, issues about the sexual abuse of children may be considered in relation to the definition of children in need of protection. In examining the following case, consider the problems of evidence and proof, as well as the relationships between the parents and children. How would you describe the principles about state intervention in the family in relation to this case?

Minister of Social Services for Saskatchewan v. A.J. and C.J.
(1987), 10 RFL (3d) 69; 42 DLR (4th) 150 (Sask. CA)

SHERSTOBITOFF JA (Vancise JA concurring): The Minister of Social Services appeals an order [sub nom. *Re T.J.*, [1986] WDFL 568] of Dickson J, sitting as a judge of the Unified Family Court, made under the *Family Services Act*, RSS 1978, c. F-7, returning sexually abused children to their parents, under the supervision of the Department of Social Services, for a period of one year.

   The issue is whether or not the judge was in error in making such an order when, after having found the children to be sexually abused and having committed them to the minister for a fixed period, the parents continued to refuse to admit any sexual abuse and thereby made it impossible for the counselling services made available by the minister to work with them in an attempt to ameliorate conditions in the home for the children.

   The children in question are H., born 14th June 1982; M., born 24th July 1980; B., born 24th March 1979; and T., born 10th November 1976. The school at which B. and T. attended showed a film on sexual abuse. Their reaction caused the school authorities to call the Department of Social Services. An officer of the department, along with a police officer, interviewed B. and T. B. told them that her father would take her pants down and "tickle her pussy" and that her father would have her "tickle his dooey" to the extent that he would obtain an erection. T. told them that his mother would make him take down his pants and that she would "pull his dooey." Further investigation disclosed a neighbour who had had a conversation with the mother of the children in which the mother had expressed concern about her husband becoming sexually stimulated by having H., the 3-year-old, in bed with him.

All of the children were apprehended immediately after the interview, on 13th June 1985.

At a hearing before Dickson J, the parents denied any sexual abuse. They said that the family sometimes bathed together because a shortage of water required the family to share the same bath water. The mother admitted that she had twice grabbed T. by the penis as a form of discipline when he had refused to put his clothes on after having a bath.

On 16th January 1986 Dickson J found the children to have been sexually abused, in need of protection, and committed them to the minister for a temporary period ending 30th June 1986.

The children were put into the care of their paternal aunt. They have had a supportive, warm and loving relationship with their aunt and other members of her family and adjusted well and quickly to their new home and environment. They have had regular supervised visits with their parents.

In making the order of 16th January 1986, the judge noted that the parents refused to talk to the social worker unless their lawyer was present and rebuffed any invitation to participate in family therapy.

After the order of 16th January 1986, nothing changed and, as a result, as the period of temporary wardship neared expiry, the Department applied for an order for permanent wardship on the basis that the continued denial of inappropriate sexual activity with the children on the part of their parents and their resultant inability to confront the problem made it in the best interests of the children that they be committed to the minister.

At the second hearing before Dickson J, the parents again gave evidence denying any sexual abuse. They claimed to be willing to undergo any counselling suggested by the Department, but the MacNeil Clinic would not see them because it could not help in the absence of an admission of sexual abuse. The parents were seeing a psychiatrist for treatment to assist them in coping with the stress of losing their children.

Dickson J, in making the order of 17th October 1986 that the children be returned to the parents, but under the supervision of the Department for a period of one year, agonized over a difficult decision. He said, in part, as follows:

> As I mentioned, during argument, I am quite convinced that they are in need of further protection and I am convinced of that because of the parents' position, their steadfast denial of inappropriate sexual activity with their children, which I believe happened. There is no new evidence before me to make me less certain of that conclusion than I was when I made the original finding.
>
> The only question then I must address further is what is the appropriate order in view of my continuing conviction that these children were subjected to inappropriate sexual activity. Now I have the same difficulty today as I had in September in knowing exactly what was this inappropriate sexual activity. Was it the mindless action of vulgar personalities unknowing of the dreadful impact that such vulgarity and coarseness can

have on the sensitive minds of young people or was it an attempt by the parents them-selves to obtain sexual gratification? I do not know. ...

Can I, being convinced, that their parents have done something reprehensible return them to their parents or shall I keep them away from their parents' home for another temporary period hoping that their parents will come to their senses? I do not think I can say to these parents: All right, because you have not yet admitted these accusations I am going to give you more time to do so. I am going to hold your children away from you until you come clean. I do not think that is the approach that I should take. I think I have to accept the fact that they have refused to acknowledge the accusations and deal with it that way; deal with it in a way that I think will further the maturing process of these children; in such a way that will not place them at greater risk.

I do not think keeping the children out of the home for any further temporary period is going to advance their cause. I think they should go home. ...

I am mindful of the risk I am taking. It is not only the fear that these parents will touch the private parts of their children. I do not think that as long as they do not do that everything will be okay in the home. I do not believe that sexual abuse is that simple. Parents who do these things worry me. Their fitness to care for children is brought into question, particularly if they do what they do for their own gratification. ...

When there is no proof before me that the activity of the parents was anything other than mindless vulgarity then I think I must given them the benefit of the doubt, and I must give the children the benefit of the doubt. I must give the children the opportunity of continuing their association with their parents, as mindful as I am of the risk.

Now I think that risk is somewhat lessened by the vigilance of the Minister's agents, by their power of supervision. ...

But I believe that in the circumstances of this case it is better for these children to be returned home under the supervision of the minister for a period of one year and I so order.

The Department launched an appeal from the order. On 5th December 1986 the Department and the parents entered into an agreement. ...

[The agreement specified counselling for the parents and expert recommendations concerning the duration and nature of parental visits with the children and conditions under which the children could be returned to their family home; in addition, the parents were given responsibility for arranging appointments with the counsellor, Dr. Wollert, a registered psychologist.]

An affidavit of Dr. Wollert was filed. After meetings with the parents and with B. and T., he concluded that sexual abuse had in fact occurred and that the parents should be involved in psychotherapy directed towards (a) validating the disclosures of abuse by B. and T. and (b) clarifying the breach of parental responsibility that has occurred. He was convinced that the parents had discouraged the children from talking about the sexual abuse and was against unsupervised visits or the return of the children to their parents. Not only was there danger of re-occurrence of the sexual abuse but the children then would have firm grounds for believing that no agency or person could advocate for them in the event that they were re-abused and there was thus no use in making any self-protective efforts of disclosure. He thought B. and T. were highly motivated for working towards appropriate goals but that the parents remained adamantly opposed. He saw the parents as preoccupied with their own welfare and as having lack of concern for the wishes of the children.

An affidavit filed in reply by the mother and concurred in by the father termed the sessions with Dr. Wollert to be upsetting and unproductive. Dr. Wollert insisted that they admit to sexual abuse and the parents refused to do so. They characterized [Dr.] Wollert as being inflexible and manifestly hostile. They indicated a willingness to continue with individual and family counselling with any therapist with the exception of Dr. Wollert.

In the outline of evidence, there has been reference to affidavits dealing with events which occurred after the date of the order appealed from. That evidence was accepted and considered by reason of the broad power to receive such fresh evidence conferred by s. 36 of the *Family Services Act*. ... The scope of review under s. 36 of the *Family Services Act* is very broad.

The predominant purpose of the Act is to protect children against neglect or abuse. Parental rights must, of necessity, be subordinated to that purpose. ...

The authority of the court of first instance is found in s. 29 of the Act which provides as follows:

29. Where on a hearing the judge finds that the child is in need of protection he may:
    (a) subject to such conditions as he considers advisable, order that the child remain with, or be returned to, his parent under departmental supervision for a period not to exceed one year;
    (b) order that the child be committed to the minister for such specified temporary period not exceeding one year as in the circumstances the judge considers necessary; or
    (c) order that the child be committed to the minister. ...

The *Family Services Act* does not specify what is expected or required of the parents of the children or of the Department of Social Services when children have been placed in the temporary custody of the minister. Under s. 29 of the Act, the judge may impose conditions when he orders that the children remain with, or be returned to, the parents under departmental supervision, but there is no authority to impose such conditions either on the parents or the minister when the children are committed to the minister. A committal to the minister makes the minister the legal guardian of the child (s. 43) but does not confer upon the minister any power to require the parents to do anything.

However, the following is self-evident. Where, as here, children have been placed into the temporary custody of the minister, and the parents wish to have the children returned to them, they must make efforts to improve or remove the conditions or circumstances in the home which have resulted in the children being taken from the parents. Furthermore, there is a responsibility on the minister, as the legal guardian of the children, to ensure, before consent to return of the children to the parents, that conditions have changed to a degree that the children are no longer in need of protection within the meaning of s. 15 of the Act. In order to achieve this end, the Department should give directions to the parents in order to assist them in achieving conditions which would permit return of their children, and to let the parents know what is expected of them.

These are the things which the judge must look at when reviewing an order under s. 29. Since the directions given by the minister do not have legal force, non-compliance with them does not necessarily mean that the court will conclude that the parents have made no effort to improve their situation. The court must look at all of the circumstances giving rise to the temporary committal order and determine what is required in the best interests of the children at the time of review.

In this case, the parents and the minister reached an immediate stalemate. The only direction given by the minister was that the parents take counselling at the MacNeil Clinic in respect of the sexual abuse. The parents maintained that no sexual abuse had occurred. The MacNeil Clinic declined to see the parents in the absence of any admission of sexual abuse because, in its view, counselling in those circumstances was impossible. The parents have maintained their position throughout and their sense of grievance and persecution is almost palpable. The situation was characterized at the hearing of the appeal as an omnipotent, all-pervasive government saying to the helpless parents, "admit the guilt that you continue to deny or you will never have your children back." This plays upon the inherent aversion that any person trained in law has to any form of governmental pressure upon a person to incriminate himself. However, this overlooks that there has been, in this case, a finding by the court of sexual abuse by the parents after two separate hearings.

The finding of sexual abuse is, upon review of all of the evidence, supportable. Indeed, there has been no appeal taken against the finding of sexual abuse. No fault can therefore be found with the stance of the minister. It is reasonable for him to insist upon counselling and satisfactory results from the counselling before consent to the return of the children to their parents. If such counselling requires, as a condition precedent, that the parents admit the validity of their children's complaints, the court must accept that, no matter how difficult it may be for the parents. (There is no suggestion here that counselling may be successfully carried out while the parents continue to deny that they did anything wrong.) The decisive factor must be the health and welfare of the child—that overrides any parental right to continue as before.

Given the finding that sexual abuse has occurred, continued denial of it by the parents, whether because they see nothing wrong with their conduct or whether because they think denial will permit them to escape the consequences, leads to the irresistible conclusion that the sexual abuse or related serious problems will probably recur if the children are returned to their parents. It must be remembered that the problem goes beyond actual sexual abuse. There are the problems which gave rise to the abuse. There are the problems consequent upon the abuse. There are also the problems flowing from the fact that the children informed the authorities of the abuse and, as a result, were in the custody of the minister. The parents and children will have to deal with these things. In the present circumstances, the risk of further abuse or other emotional harm to the children, if they are returned to their parents, is not less than it was prior to the order of temporary committal. If it was proper to commit them in the first place, it is proper to commit them now, since there has been no change except the intervention of the Department.

The evidence indicates, and common sense tells us, that Departmental supervision would not, by itself, prevent further abuse or continuing serious problems within the family. The children, having been returned to their parents, would be in no position to defend themselves against further abuse or to report it. Acceptance of responsibility and appropriate counselling is the only solution. Accordingly, the judge erred in ordering the children returned to their parents. His own findings of fact make it clear that they are still in need of protection to the extent that their custody must remain in the hands of the minister.

Another aspect of the evidence is relevant to this conclusion. The evidence given by the parents during both hearings, and their affidavit evidence filed in response to Dr. Wollert's affidavit, clearly shows a good deal of stress, anguish, and a sense of grievance on the parts of the parents, but it is all directed at their own feelings of hurt, consequent upon deprivation of their children. There is a marked absence of any concern throughout their own evidence for the welfare of their children. They blame everyone but themselves. They had one social worker removed from the case. They now refuse to deal with Dr. Wollert. This indicates an inability or refusal to deal with the problem.

The judge below also erred when he considered the motivation of the parents in the actions which constituted the sexual abuse to be relevant. He found himself unable to decide whether it was "the mindless action of vulgar personalities" or an attempt to obtain sexual gratification. The motivation is irrelevant because the effect on the children, in the circumstances of this case, is clearly the same in either case. The result of returning the children to the care of their parents would also be the same. The fundamental concern must be the health and emotional welfare of the children rather than the motivation behind the conduct of the parents.

The appropriate order is a further committal to the minister for a temporary period of one year. The children have a good home with their aunt. The parents and the minister will have an opportunity to work toward the return of the children to the family home. This judgment should bring the parents to realize that full cooperation in counselling and therapy is their last and only hope for reunion of the family. The result will be, it is hoped, a home that will provide a proper upbringing for the children and the normal benefits of parenthood for the parents.

The appeal is accordingly allowed. There will be an order under s. 29 of the *Family Services Act* that the children be committed to the minister for a temporary period of one year.

Appeal allowed; temporary guardianship continued.

Discussion Notes

Process Issues: Evidence and Burden of Proof

How would you describe the standard of proof required in this case? In *D. v. Children's Aid Society of Kent* (1981), 18 RFL (2d) 223, at 227 (Ont. Co. Ct.), the court described the standard of proof in child-protection proceedings in this way:

> The standard of proof, therefore, is not that of the balance of probabilities per se; nor is it a
> test akin to the onus in criminal matters. No magic formula need be devised other than the

heavy onus on the director of the children's aid society to satisfy the court [that] the allegations necessary to intervene are met and clearly met without reference or deference to the second issue after a finding is made, i.e., the finding that the child is in need of protection, as to the appropriate placement under s. 30 of the Act.

According to this statement, the test is one of a "heavy onus." In some provinces, moreover, the court is directed to determine first whether a child is in need of protection and only after making this finding can the court proceed to consider the placement issue: for example, see Ontario's *Child and Family Services Act*, RSO 1990, c. C.11, s. 57. What is the purpose of such a provision?

In *Director of Child Welfare v. R.(T.)* (1990), 26 RFL (3d) 329; 106 AR 173 (QB), the court decided to remove two children from the home of their foster mother (who was also their aunt) because the children had experienced sexual abuse and, thus, they had special needs that the foster mother could not meet. In part, the court's conclusion that the aunt did not have the skills to meet the needs of the children seemed to be based on the fact that the foster mother had herself experienced sexual abuse as a child and had not really come to terms with it. What are the underlying assumptions in such a decision with respect to the placement issue?

Reaching for Solutions: Recommendations for Change

In *Reaching for Solutions: The Report of the Special Advisor to the Minister of Health and Welfare on Child Sexual Abuse in Canada* (Ottawa: Minister of Supply and Services Canada, 1990), the difficulties of prosecuting child sexual abuse allegations were noted (at 58):

Because of the difficulties in proving abuse, especially when the victims are very young, it must be appreciated that there will be cases where, although investigators are satisfied that abuse has occurred, they will not be prosecuted because there may be insufficient evidence. There may also be cases where, even with appropriate support services and such protective devices as closed-circuit television, there is a strong apprehension that the child will be unduly traumatized by the court process. In such situations, the Crown Attorney, acting in consultation with other professionals and non-offending parents, may decide that the case should not proceed.

The report recommended (at 96) special programs in Canadian law schools on issues of child sexual abuse and the relationships among professionals, including lawyers, in dealing with these issues. See also Special Advisor to the Minister of National Health and Welfare on Child Sexual Abuse in Canada, *Status Report on the Federal Response to Reaching for Solutions: Report of the Special Advisor on Child Sexual Abuse* (Ottawa: Minister of Supply and Services, 1993).

According to Rix Rogers, the author of *Reaching for Solutions*, the idea of preventing child sexual abuse is applied in three different ways:

- education for children about safety, including sexual safety, in schools;
- processes for stopping recurring patterns of abuse after one or more incidents; and

- fostering a "changed society" over the long term—the idea that we must move from being concerned about our own children to being concerned about the well-being of all children.

See Rix Rogers, "The Anguish of Child Abuse—Is Prevention Possible?" (September 1995), *Transition* (Vanier Institute of the Family) 9ff.

Gender and Sexual Abuse

Although statistics in both the Badgley Report and *Reaching for Solutions* suggested that the vast majority of perpetrators of sexual abuse were men, there is some evidence of women engaging in such abuse as well. According to Myriam S. Denov, "A Culture of Denial: Exploring Professional Perspectives on Female Sex Offending" (2001), 43 *Canadian Journal of Criminology* 303, there is a tendency among police officers and psychiatric professionals to downplay such actions by women. Thus, she argued (at 324):

> The culture of denial within the organizational context may not only exonerate the female sex offender, depreciate the seriousness of harm inflicted on the victim, or affect sentencing patterns. It is also likely to have an impact on the official recognition of female sex offending. As such, the low rates of female sex offending in official sources need to be understood within this context. Nonetheless, there is no substantive evidence to refute the common assumption that males represent the vast majority of child sexual abuse perpetrators. ... [However,] it is through an examination of all types of child sexual abuse that we may increase our awareness and understanding of a complex issue.

How should courts and the legal system respond to these recommendations?

3. Reporting Requirements

Another strategy for dealing with child sexual abuse is the use of legislative reporting requirements. Thus, provincial legislation may establish mandatory reporting for professionals, including physicians and teachers, for example, with penalties for failure to comply. Although legislators continue to espouse such reporting requirements as an important response to the problem of child abuse, especially sexual abuse, it appears that the statutory provisions have not been effective—there has been both a lack of reporting and a failure to impose penalties in these cases. In particular, doctors have failed to report abuse, particularly in cases where they believe that the problem may be better solved without legal intervention that might be detrimental to the family: see, for example, James McLeod, "R v. Cook: Annotation" (1985), 46 RFL (2d) 174. What conclusions should be drawn in these circumstances?

Consider the following analysis, particularly its suggestion about making the failure to report a criminal offence. What are the merits and disadvantages of this suggestion in the context of child sexual abuse?

Ronda Bessner, "The Duty To Report Child Abuse"
(2000), 17 *Canadian Family Law Quarterly* 278

Imposing a legal duty to report cases of physical and sexual child abuse constituted a significant departure from the common law, which regards individuals as independent and self-reliant. As stated in the *Report of the Committee on Sexual Offences Against Children and Youth*, known as the Badgley Report, our legal system tends to eschew laws that create a positive duty for one person to assist another. Under the common law, members of society are not obliged to come to the aid of others or to contact the government or the police to protect persons in danger. The sole inducement for individuals to assist others in need of protection is a moral rather than a legal duty.

Thirty to thirty-five years ago, this common law principle was questioned in [the] context of children at risk of acts of abuse. Legislators in different areas of North America began to subscribe to the view that "leaving these decisions exclusively in the realm of personal conscience provides little protection to the youngest and most vulnerable members of society." All ten provinces and the territories in Canada as well as the fifty American states enacted provisions addressed to the reporting of abused children.

The duty to report acts of child abuse is considered to be a fundamental component of the child protection system. As stated in the 1998 Ontario *Report of the Panel of Experts on Child Protection*, preventing child abuse "begins with timely reporting of abuse"; "it continues through investigation and cooperative sharing of information." There are several reasons why the duty to report suspected acts of abuse is regarded as essential to the healthy, sexual, physical, and emotional development of children. Child abuse often occurs in situations in which there are no witnesses. Infants and young children, in particular, have limited visibility with persons outside the home and do not have the linguistic ability to communicate that they have been subjected to abusive acts. To exacerbate the problem, many children do not comprehend the "injustice" of acts of abuse. In cases of long-term sexual abuse, for example, the child may not understand that the acts are inappropriate, immoral and illegal. Furthermore, caregivers and persons acting in parental roles who commit abusive acts have a great deal of control over the child. The child victim may also have strong emotional feelings toward the abuser and for that reason be incapable of disclosing the abusive acts to third parties. Children may also conceal the abuse for other reasons: the perpetrator may have threatened to harm the non-abusing parent, siblings, the family pet, or other significant persons in a child's life if the acts are revealed. Many children are fearful that if others learn of the acts of physical punishment, sexual abuse, or neglect, a breakdown of their family will occur.

The fundamental purposes of child-reporting legislation are to halt and to prevent acts of abuse from being perpetrated on children. It is a critical first step in identifying a child in peril. The philosophy underlying such statutory provisions is that children can only be protected if concerned individuals recognize the danger and then report it to designated government authorities. ... The child welfare statutes generally place the degree of suspicion required for reporting at a low level in order to encourage individuals to notify government authorities that a child may be in need of protection. ...

Lawsuits Initiated for Failing To Report

An examination of the case law rendered pursuant to the reporting provisions in provincial and territorial statutes reveals that few lawsuits have been initiated against persons for failing to report acts of child abuse. Of the cases that have been prosecuted, many occurred in the 1980s and the majority of those charged were acquitted. A brief review of some of these cases is provided.

In *R v. Cook* [(1985), 46 RFL (2d) 174 (Ont. CA)], a family physician was charged with failing to promptly report a suspected case of child abuse to a children's aid society in violation of the Ontario *Child Welfare Act*, the predecessor statute to the *Child and Family Services Act*. In this case, a 15-year-old girl informed her mother on February 7, 1983 that her stepfather had fondled her. The next day this information was disclosed to Dr. Cook at a medical appointment. The physician suggested that the mother confront her husband and return with him for counselling. On February 16, the mother informed Dr. Cook that the "touching" had stopped. The stepfather did not attend for counselling and Dr. Cook did not report the acts of sexual molestation to the children's aid society.

The doctor was acquitted because of the language of the criminal charge. The charge alleged that the family physician had reasonable grounds to suspect that the child "is" suffering from abuse. The case may have succeeded had the charge been drafted to state that the child in the past "had" suffered possible abuse.

In *R v. Strachula* [(1984), 40 RFL (2d) 184 (Ont. Prov. Ct.)], a family physician who had provided care to a family for over ten years was charged with failing to report in breach of the Ontario *Child Welfare Act*. In August 1983, a mother and 14-year-old daughter revealed to the physician that sexual relations had taken place between the 16-year-old brother and 14-year-old sister. There was a concern that the sister was pregnant. After this was confirmed, Dr. Strachula arranged for an abortion, which was performed at a hospital in Toronto.

Several months later, in December 1983, Dr. Strachula notified the Metropolitan Toronto Catholic Children's Aid Society of what had transpired. Dr. Strachula was subsequently charged under the Ontario reporting legislation. The case failed for two reasons. In attempting to prove that the family physician had reasonable grounds to suspect abuse, an expert, whose speciality was pediatrics with a subspeciality in child abuse, was called to give evidence. The court held that the standard of care applicable to pediatricians with expertise in child abuse was not the standard of care applicable to family physicians. Main J stated:

> The words "every person who ... in the course of *the person's* professional or official duties" carry with them the implication that there is a distinction which must be made between the various classes of such professionals and that there is no universal standard of care applicable to all such persons, but rather a standard of care particularly to the class in question. If the legislature had intended but one standard to apply to all professionals dealing with children, the subsection could have easily reflected that policy. In the alternative, a comprehensive and easily understood definition of the term "abuse" could have been provided and made applicable to all professionals dealing with children regardless of their class or qualifications.

> The standard of care applicable to paediatricians skilled in child abuse should not be the standard of care applicable to family practitioners or to others such as public health nurses, school teachers, family services workers or child care workers, to name but a few. The relevant standard must vary in accordance with the professional capacity of the person or persons involved in the particular case. In fulfilling its onus under s. 49(2), the Crown must lead evidence of the standard of care expected of the class of persons represented by the defendant before the court, and it has failed to do so.

A further reason for Dr. Strachula's acquittal was that the Crown did not lead evidence that the brother had "charge" of his 14-year-old sister in accordance with the language of the reporting statute. A similar situation occurred in *R v. R.(M.)* [(January 19, 1995), Doc. Sarnia 315/94 (Ont. Gen. Div.)]. In a prosecution against a doctor, the Crown was not able to establish beyond reasonable doubt that the alleged perpetrator had temporary charge of the child.

In *R v. Shubat* [(March 29, 1996), Doc. Goderich (Ont. Prov. Div.), Gale J; rev'd. (June 27, 1996) (Ont. Prov. Div.), Hunter J], an 8-month-old infant was brought to an emergency ward of a hospital. The father disclosed to the physician that he had repeatedly struck the child on the head. Another hospital at which the child was examined reported the abusive act to the local Children's Aid Society. The doctor who had the first contact with the patient was acquitted of failing to report. The court held that a physician has the authority to delegate his reporting duty.

Two unreported decisions rendered in Ontario in 1987 found physicians and an operator of a day care nursery guilty of failing to report a case of suspected child abuse. In *R v. Kates* [(August 21, 1987), Doc. 510-86 (Ont. Dist. Ct.)], a conviction was registered against the day-care nursery operator for not reporting to the Children's Aid Society acts of abuse known to have been committed on a child. In *R v. Lee and Hipwell* [(April 22, 1987) (Ont. Prov. Ct.), Coulson J], a family doctor and a physician in an emergency department of a local hospital were also found guilty of failing to report an act of suspected child abuse.

Discussions that took place in the consultation process confirmed that few prosecutions have been initiated for failing to report, and that the cases that have been launched have generally been unsuccessful. Several reasons were proffered for the lack of enforcement of the provincial and territorial legislation. It is often difficult to establish beyond reasonable doubt the elements of the offence in these quasi-criminal cases. In addition, limitation periods are sometimes obstacles to prosecutions under the reporting statutes. Another reason for the reluctance to prosecute individuals is that the reporter's co-operation may be necessary to establish the offence against the perpetrator of the child abuse. A further explanation is largely philosophical: an otherwise law-abiding citizen should not be subject to such a lawsuit.

In Ottawa recently, a teacher, a social worker and a principal were charged with failing to report a suspected case of child abuse allegedly perpetrated by a teacher. The school conducted an internal investigation of the matter, questioned the child, and in the opinion of the lawyers involved, tainted the evidence of the child. As a result, criminal charges were withdrawn against the alleged perpetrator. One of the reasons charges were also withdrawn against professionals at the school for failing to report was that it was unfair to prosecute school staff in a situation in which criminal charges were not being pursued against the alleged child abuser.

An Executive Director of a Children's Aid Society agreed that professionals are often not prosecuted for failing to report, or for not promptly reporting suspected cases of child abuse. In his organization, "reminding letters" are sent to professionals who do not discharge their statutory obligation. ...

Conclusion

The importance of reporting suspected and known cases of child abuse and neglect should not be underestimated. Children require the assistance of adults to convey to government authorities that they are in need of protection.

It was the view of several participants in the consultation process that a significant number of Canadians are not fulfilling their statutory duty to report. Fear of reprisals from the abuser, concern regarding the breach of a confidential relationship, lack of an understanding of the civil reporting laws, and a belief that government intervention will not enhance the position of the child were some of the reasons put forth for the failure to report. A 1999 federal government publication, entitled *Family Violence in Canada: A Statistical Profile*, stated that despite the existence of mandatory reporting laws in the provinces and territories, as many as 90 percent of the cases may not be reported to child welfare agencies. According to those consulted, the number of persons prosecuted for failing to report is minimal. Short limitation periods; belief that such lawsuits will not be successful; inadequate collaboration between the Crown, police, and child welfare agencies; and lack of familiarity of Crown counsel regarding the constituent elements of the civil reporting offences were cited as reasons for the paucity of legal actions initiated against those who do not report acts of child abuse.

Other problems that became apparent are related to child abuse investigations and information sharing. A number of reports of suspected child abuse do not result in investigations. This was also a finding of the Gove Inquiry, which stated that approximately one third of reports in British Columbia are not investigated. Failure to develop appropriate protocols, inconsistent application of protocols, and lack of resources of both child welfare and law enforcement agencies may be the reasons for this situation. It also became clear that files collected on the family's history as well as information acquired during the course of the investigation are not always shared between and among child welfare and law enforcement officials. Police officers often do not have access to child welfare files or to child abuse registries and child welfare agencies are not permitted to obtain information recorded on [police data systems]. Child welfare agencies are obstructed from securing information on the family's history from other agencies, and police officials encounter similar problems accessing information on occurrence reports from other law enforcement agencies. Difficulties exist within and between the provinces and territories.

Many of the concerns raised by the Badgley Report in 1984 remain unresolved. The committee concluded that a sizeable number of members of society—the non-offending parent, professionals, and lay persons—do not report child abuse. It stated that "the process of referral envisaged by provincial legislators and relied upon by child protection services is operating randomly and inefficiently." It further found that a significant number of cases are not recorded on child abuse registers and that child-protection workers only consult the register for one in every five cases. The committee also concluded that "the policies of various provinces concerning inter-jurisdictional information sharing are inconsistent and lack formal structure." As the Badgley Report stated, "this system cannot be construed as one that is particularly helpful in affording protection" to abused children.

Enacting a *Criminal Code* provision or a duty to report may rectify some of the problems raised in the consultation process. A criminal offence may serve as an incentive for professionals and lay persons to report child abuse: it will provide a national standard for reporting; police and the justice system may be involved earlier in the process; serious penalties can be imposed; and a hybrid offence will obviate limitation problems.

It is important to note, however, the concerns of those who oppose enacting such an offence. The provision may deter people from reporting, as members of society are generally reluctant to become involved with the criminal system; the onerous burden of proof on the Crown may result in many unsuccessful prosecutions; and child victims will once again be obliged to testify and be subjected to cross-examination by defence lawyers. Many were also philosophically opposed to imposing penal sanctions on law-abiding persons.

It is fundamental that empirical research be conducted on a national scale on the issues raised in this article respecting child abuse reporting. Information must be acquired on the magnitude of the problem and on the issues that require the attention of legislators and policy makers. It is of the utmost importance that the various provincial–territorial and federal ministries that deal with children's issues—social services, health, education, solicitor general, justice—work in unison to ensure that Canada's young and vulnerable members of society are properly protected.

4. Sexual Abuse and Fiduciary Obligations

Sexual abuse issues have also been assessed according to principles applicable to fiduciary relationships. Fiduciary relationships have been held to exist between parents and their children and also, for children residing in institutional settings, between administrators or teachers and these children.

J.(L.A.) v. J.(H.) (1993), 102 DLR (4th) 177; 13 OR (3d) 306 (Gen. Div.)

In this case, a young woman brought a civil action against her mother and stepfather after her stepfather was convicted of sexually assaulting her and imprisoned. The successful civil action resulted in damages based in tort and breach of fiduciary duty. In relation to the mother's liability for breach of a fiduciary duty, the court held that the mother knew of the sexual assaults and failed to protect her daughter from harm. The evidence suggested that the mother had observed an assault on one occasion, but had (inappropriately) accepted her husband's promise that it would never happen again; that she was aware of lavish gifts to the daughter from her husband; and that she had discovered condoms under the daughter's bed. In addition, she had deflected inquiries from a social worker from the Children's Aid Society during a short period of time when she had fled to a shelter with her daughter; she had subsequently returned home. Thus, applying the principles concerning parental duties to care for and protect children set out in *M.(K.) v. M.(H.)*, [1992] 3 SCR 6, the court stated (at 185-86):

> In the circumstances of this case, recognizing that the defendant mother was of limited means and education, it was still well within her ability and, therefore, her discretion, to take her daughter away from the abusive situation which she was well aware of or report the situation to the authorities with the probable result of the abuser being removed from the situation. The defendant mother had relatives in the area who could have helped but she sought no help. There are social agencies which could have helped as well, but she sought no help and actively ensured that the Children's Aid Society was turned away from its legitimate inquiries. Instead of pursuing means that were open to her to protect her daughter from the injurious circumstances of which she was aware, the defendant mother put her own interests above those of her daughter. She wanted to keep her husband and her daughter with her but at the expense of her daughter's well-being.
>
> Some may think it harsh to hold a mother to a standard by which she must, in certain circumstances, choose to take action which is destructive to her family unit. However, where serious sexual abuse of a child within a family unit must be weighed against the destruction of that unit, there can be no doubt how the balance must tip. The consequences of serious child abuse are so clear, both for the immediate development of the victim as well as in terms of the sins of parents being repeated in subsequent generations, that the risks inherent in the fracturing of a family unit in order to separate a child from abuse are infinitely preferable to the risk of the consequences, both immediate and long-term, of leaving an abusive situation to continue to its natural conclusion.

Family Relationships and Fiduciary Duties

The evidence in *J.(L.A.) v. J.(H.)* suggested that the daughter had suffered serious and long-term harm. Nonetheless, the court's decision to recognize liability on the part of the mother has been questioned, both in relation to the dynamics within the family and with respect to the broader community context. For example, in relation to the husband's promise that his sexual relationship with the daughter would not recur, it has been suggested that

> [h]indsight is likely to be telescopic in such cases because the consequences of [mistakes] are so tragic, but the answer may not seem so obvious judged at the time and from inside the family. In some cases, a woman may be convinced that her spouse's drinking is the source of the problem and put her efforts into trying to change this, or that the stress of unemployment explains his behaviour and focus on supporting his search for work. At what stage is it fair to say that a woman should have realized that trying to change her spouse would not work, that dealing with the causes of the abusive behaviour was beyond her ken? The experts may know that expert intervention is advisable in these situations, but should we attribute such knowledge to the reasonable person?

(Denise Réaume and Shauna Van Praagh, "Family Matters: Mothers as Secondary Defendants in Child Sexual Abuse Actions" (2002), 17 *Supreme Court Law Review* 179, at 211-12.)

In another comment on this case, it was suggested that

> [t]he propriety of imposing liability on mothers must be considered in light of the gender inequality that permeates our social, economic, and political structures (including families), as well as the lack of publicly-funded shelters and treatment facilities for victims of sexual and physical abuse. ... It may be too late and, indeed, undesirable to turn back the clock on recent advances in the law pertaining to sexual assault that have imposed private law duties of care and fiduciary obligations on persons and institutions in positions of power and trust. However, there is a sad, if predictable, irony to these developments being used against one of the weakest links in the chain of child sexual abuse—namely, non-offending mothers. Unquestionably, mothers owe both a duty of care and a fiduciary duty to their children. The issue to be considered is whether, so long as they are denied viable choices and the power to prevent abuse, mothers should be held to have breached their legal obligations.

(Elizabeth Grace and Susan Vella, "Vesting Mothers with Power They Do Not Have: The Non-Offending Parent in Civil Sexual Assault Cases: J.(L.A.) v. J.(H.) and J.(J.)" (1994), 7 *Canadian Journal of Women and the Law* 184, at 186.)

To what extent do these comments suggest different views about the goals and means of the state with respect to intervention in families to prevent and to define liability for child sexual abuse? Consider also *M.(M.) v. F.(R.)* (1997), 52 BCLR (3d) 127 (CA), where the British Columbia Court of Appeal absolved a foster mother of liability for failure to detect sexual abuse on the part of her adult son against her foster daughter, using a more subjective standard of care than the court adopted in *J.(L.A.)*. Is this approach preferable? Why, or why not?

In *Flachs v. Flachs*, [2002] OJ no. 1350; 2003 Carswell Ont 755 (CA), a court awarded damages of $125,000 to a wife and $75,000 to a daughter of a husband/father as personal injury damages in a case in which the husband/father had engaged in violent and abusive behaviour against both women over a period of 38 years. The court also awarded to each plaintiff aggravated damages of $25,000 and punitive damages of $25,000. The husband/father had previously received light sentences for criminal convictions in rela-tion to his actions.

Fiduciary Obligations and Institutional Abuse

Claims relating to institutional abuse have also made use of the concept of fiduciary obligation in actions for redress: for example, see *A. v. C.* (1998), 42 RFL (4th) 427; 166 DLR (4th) 475 (BCCA) and *Bonaparte v. Canada (Attorney General)* (2003), 64 OR (3d) 1; [2003] 2 CNLR 43 (Ont. CA). In relation to such claims, the Law Commission of Canada reported in 2000 on the different kinds of needs of survivors of child abuse in institutions, including the need for a historical record and remembrance, acknowledgment, apology, accountability, access to therapy or counselling, access to education or training, financial compensation, and prevention/public awareness: see Law Commission of

Canada, *Restoring Dignity—Responding to Child Abuse in Canadian Institutions* (Ottawa: Law Commission of Canada, 2000), 74. These claims arise in a context in which children, particularly First Nations children, were removed from their families to live in institutional settings. Thus, in addition to the abuse they may have suffered, they also experienced the loss of family life. In *Bonaparte*, above, the claim included the loss of cultural traditions for the children of those institutionalized, since the latter were unable to pass on their heritage as a result of their removal as children. Should such losses be characterized as child abuse? Why, or why not? Issues about institutional abuse were considered in three cases in the Supreme Court of Canada in 2003: *K.L.B. v. British Columbia*, [2003] SCJ 51; *E.D.G. v. Hammer*, [2003] SCJ no. 52; and *M.B. v. British Columbia*, [2003] SCJ no. 53. Two cases involved abuse on the part of foster parents in which the plaintiffs were also suing the Crown; the third involved an assault by a school janitor in which a school board was named defendant. See also Loretta P. Merritt, "Trilogy of Abuse Cases Examined 6 Issues," *The Lawyers Weekly*, December 5, 2003, 6.

SELECTED REFERENCES

Kathy Au Coin, "Violence and Abuse Against Children and Youth by Family Members," in Canadian Centre for Justice Statistics, *Family Violence in Canada: A Statistical Profile 2003* (Ottawa: National Clearinghouse on Family Violence, Health Canada, 2003), 33.

Martha Bailey, "The Failure of Physicians To Report Child Abuse" (1982), 40 *University of Toronto Faculty of Law Review* 49.

Marvin M. Bernstein, "Child Protection Mediation: Its Time Has Arrived" (1998-99), 16 *Canadian Family Law Quarterly* 73.

Betty Joyce Carter, *Who's To Blame? Child Sexual Abuse and Non-Offending Mothers* (Toronto: University of Toronto Press, 1999).

Howard A. Davidson, "Child Abuse and Domestic Violence: Legal Connections and Controversies" (1995), 29:2 *Family Law Quarterly* 357.

Myriam S. Denov, "A Culture of Denial: Exploring Professional Perspectives on Female Sex Offending" (2001), 43 *Canadian Journal of Criminology* 303.

Bruce Feldthusen, "The Civil Action for Sexual Battery: Therapeutic Jurisprudence?" (1993), 25 *Ottawa Law Review* 203.

Margaret Isabel Hall, " 'Intuitive Fiduciaries': The Equitable Structure of Family Life" (2002), 19 *Canadian Journal of Family Law* 345.

Rix Rogers, "The Anguish of Child Abuse—Is Prevention Possible?" (September 1995), *Transition* (Vanier Institute of the Family) 9.

B. Wharf, ed., *Rethinking Child Welfare in Canada* (Toronto: McClelland & Stewart, 1993).

IV. PROTECTING WOMEN: RESPONSIBILITIES OF
FAMILIES AND THE STATE

Criminal justice services are only one part of a wide constellation of service options which should be available to battered women. Battered women share with all of us a human urge to hope. ... As a result, some battered women may reject what they see as short-term solutions which may dash their long-term hopes. Therefore, the arrest option and reliance on the criminal justice system is, to *some* women, a very unpalatable solution because they perceive that the intervention of the law will increase the chances of the marriage ending. In addition, the law gives her no assurance that the violence will end. Most battered women want help which will give them long-term hope.

> Linda MacLeod, *Battered but Not Beaten ... Preventing Wife Battering in Canada* (Ottawa: Canadian Advisory Council on the Status of Women, 1987), 89-90

We have had to face the fact that making women's equality a reality, whether within the family or outside it, poses complex issues incapable of a simple doctrinal resolution.

> Honourable Bertha Wilson, "Women, the Family, and the Constitutional Protection of Privacy" (1991), 23 *Ottawa Law Review* 431, at 441

A. Statistics on Spousal Violence Against Women

Statistics Canada figures indicate that one-quarter of all violent crimes reported to police services in 2001 involved family violence; two-thirds of these cases involved spousal violence (or violence committed by an ex-spouse); and 85 percent of the victims were women. In addition, more than 100,000 women and dependent children were admitted to shelters across Canada in 2001-2: see Julienne Patterson, "Spousal Violence," in Canadian Centre for Justice Statistics, *Family Violence in Canada: A Statistical Profile 2003* (Ottawa: National Clearinghouse on Family Violence, Health Canada, 2003), at 4, and "Highlights," at 1-2. As this report on spousal violence noted, "spousal violence in Canada is an important social issue with consequences for victims, their families and society."

While these figures suggest that women in families are at risk of violence, many feel ambivalent about legal intervention in their families to deal with this problem. Thus, like child abuse, violence against women in families may necessitate the balancing of state interests in protecting vulnerable family members with individuals' interests in maintaining family autonomy.

B. A Case Study: Violence at Separation

Violence may be an issue in families in a variety of different circumstances. However, some research suggests that the level of violence may escalate in circumstances where a woman attempts to bring an end to an intimate relationship (including marriage and cohabitation). "There is little doubt that separation and divorce are especially risky times": see Felicity Kaganas and Christine Piper, "Divorce and Domestic Violence," in Shelley Day Sclater and Christine Piper, eds., *Undercurrents of Divorce* (Aldershot, UK:

Ashgate Dartmouth, 1999), 183, at 188. The following case focuses on the situation of a woman who decided to petition for divorce and consequential relief. In reviewing the case, consider whether there is evidence that the woman's decision to divorce her husband was a factor in the escalation of violence in their relationship.

Behrendt v. Behrendt
Ottawa, March 6, 1990 (unreported)

[In February 1990, Pamella Behrendt filed a petition for divorce from her husband, Stefan Behrendt. The petition recited (at 4) that the parties had lived separate and apart under the same roof since January 1989 and, in addition, that the respondent had treated the petitioner with cruelty. Specifically, the petition stated:]

> The Respondent refuses to communicate and interact with the Petitioner. The Respondent locks himself into his son's bedroom which has two locks on the door and avoids contact with the wife and the parties' two daughters. The Respondent remains in his pyjamas most of the day and does not maintain his personal hygiene. The respondent's behaviour has caused extreme tension in the household which affects the Petitioner and the parties' daughters.

[The petition also stated (at 9) that the husband had been on a psychiatric disability pension for six years and that the wife had assumed responsibility for the family's financial support; she worked as a registered nurse. The wife also claimed exclusive possession of the matrimonial home, stating (at 10) that it was in the best interests of the two daughters to remain there to complete their schooling and that it was financially possible for the wife to maintain the (mortgage-free) family home while supporting the two children.

In addition to these claims relating to the divorce, the wife applied for an interim order (pending the hearing of the divorce petition) for exclusive possession of the home pursuant to Ontario's *Family Law Act*, RSO 1990, c. F.3, s. 24. This provision states that, in considering such an application, the court must take into account "the best interests of the children affected" and "any violence committed by a spouse against the other spouse or the children." In this context, the wife's petition for exclusive possession of the matrimonial home stated:]

> The husband has acted violently towards one of the children. The father's behaviour towards the Petitioner and towards the children is adversely affecting the children. The children's performance at school is suffering and the children are ashamed to bring friends into their home because of their father's behaviour.

[In her petition for exclusive possession of the home, filed in early March 1990, the wife stated that she earned about $37,000 per year as a nurse; she stated as well that her husband (who had a PhD in chemistry) received a pension in the amount of $14,000 per year from Carleton University, where he had been employed as a technician in the chemistry lab until 1984. Her affidavit also detailed the husband's abusive behaviour to the daughters and the tension it was creating for the wife and daughters.

In response, the husband filed an application for spousal support and occupation rent. He also denied the allegations of abusive behaviour. The parties' 22-year-old son, who lived away from home while attending university, filed an affidavit in support of his father's statements, including denying the allegations of any abusive behaviour by him. He explained the locks on his door as necessary to prevent one of his sisters from damaging his expensive computer equipment in the room.

The two motions were heard on March 5, 1990; a brief decision was released the following day, dismissing both. In relation to the wife's motion for interim exclusive possession, Justice Charron stated:]

> Undoubtedly it has become very difficult for the parties to live under the same roof. Nevertheless, the material presented on this motion does not, in my view, warrant granting exclusive possession of the matrimonial home to the applicant. The Court should only exercise its power to make such an Order with great care. The nature of the allegations, the contradictory view presented by one of the children and the age of the children living in the home all militate against the granting of the order. The motion is dismissed [with each party to bear his or her own costs].

In the context of an application for interim relief and the possibility of reviewing the situation again at the time of the divorce hearing, the court's decision that there was no immediate need to exclude the husband from the matrimonial home may seem reasonable, particularly since the husband had sworn that he had no other place to live. Unfortunately, however, the case ended tragically in June 1990 (three months after the motion was dismissed), when the husband used a chainsaw to murder his wife and then committed suicide at the matrimonial home: see Charles Lewis and Mike Blanchfield, "Man Kills Wife, Then Takes Own Life," *Ottawa Citizen*, June 12, 1990.

As a result, representatives of several Ottawa-based shelters forwarded a public letter to Ontario's Attorney General (November 18, 1990), identifying three aspects of the case that required further assessment: (1) concern that the absence of overt physical violence may have resulted in the allegations being seen as less serious: (2) the weight given to the contradictory affidavit of one child, even though he was not living in the home at the time; and (3) the fact that the decision seemed to indicate that, as teenagers, the two daughters were less at risk than younger children in an environment of violence. Challenging the validity of these assumptions, the letter stated (at 2):

> We feel that these same assumptions are held by other members of the judiciary and are woven throughout the decisions that on a daily basis, deny families access to violence-free homes. Such assumptions are not justified.

In thinking about the *Behrendt* case, consider the following description of the "silencing" of violence in families.

**Hilary Astor, "The Weight of Silence: Talking About Violence in
Family Mediation"**
in Margaret Thornton, ed., *Public and Private: Feminist Legal Debates*
(Melbourne: Oxford University Press, 1995), 174, at 184 ff.

Silence and the Nature of Violence

When a woman separates from a violent man, temporarily or permanently, she is
likely to become involved with the law. She may need to seek legal advice, apply for
protective orders, resolve disputes about property, support, custody and access. If she
is to achieve resolution of the disputes attendant upon separation, she must speak to
others—police officers, lawyers, magistrates, judges, mediators—about her relationship. If these disputes are to be resolved in a manner that protects her and her children,
and achieves a just result, she needs to be able to speak of the violence she has been
subjected to, and which is likely to have a powerful effect on her present situation
and behaviour. Women who have been the targets of violence by their male partners
in the home, however, have many reasons for keeping silent about the violence. Violence against women involves actions on the part of the perpetrator that exert control
over the target of violence. Enforcing silence about the violence is a part of that control. The silence of the woman who has been a target of violence may be ensured by
direct threats and warnings not to reveal the occurrence of the violence to others.
Further violence or harassment may be threatened or, typically, where there are disputes attendant upon separation and divorce that the perpetrator will litigate, delays
may be created, or challenges made to the woman's custody of the children. Women
who are the targets of violence, and those who work with them, are familiar with the
phenomenon of "car park violence," where the perpetrator writes the script for the
mediation (the court appearance, the interview with the lawyer or counsellor, and so
on) by threats or beatings in the car park. The instruction not to tell the mediator
about the violence is part of the violence. A woman who departs from the script by
saying anything that is disapproved of by the perpetrator in a mediation session may
be subjected to violence after the session to ensure her future compliance. One woman
who attended multiple counselling sessions, throughout which she remained silent
about her husband's violence, explained her silence:

> I wasn't going to walk around ... breaking out in prickles as we came back down the
> stairs going over what I'd said. Had I said anything? How is he going to take it? What is
> he going to remember out of what was said? I was very frightened—there was no way
> the truth was going to come out.

The silencing may not be the result of contemporaneous threats or violence. Many
women who have been the targets of violence will have become accustomed to an-
ticipating the wishes of the perpetrators and complying with them in the hope that
this will prevent further violence. ...

Women are expected to be able to speak about the violence perpetrated against
them when the main way in which our society deals with violence is by silence.
Violence against women is something that is actively concealed, not only by the

targets of that violence, but by its perpetrators, by family members, by agencies that deal with those individuals and by society as a whole. ...

Discussion Notes

Legal Responses to Violence: An Individual or Systemic Problem?

Were there any factors in the Behrendt file that identified (in March 1990) the husband's potential for murdering his wife and taking his own life? To what extent did factors such as the absence of physical violence, the husband's illness, the contrary assertions in the affidavits, the income available to the family, or other factors affect the judge's assessment? Who had the burden of proof in this case? To what extent is it difficult for counsel to overcome an assumption that both husband and wife should be entitled to live in the matrimonial home?

As the excerpt from Astor's work suggests, courts and mediation processes may need to take account of the impact of violence in an intimate relationship. In assessing Astor's view of the ways in which violence in a relationship may affect the willingness of women to confront a perpetrator of violence, consider the following critiques about the ability of the legal system to address domestic violence: to what extent do they accord with the views expressed by Astor?

> In the past there has been collusion on the part of all our social institutions to minimize or deny the level of violence that occurs within families. Within the family, everyone is supposed to be happy. Intervention is seen as an attack on the unity of the family.

(British Columbia Task Force on Family Violence, *Is Anyone Listening?* (Victoria, BC: Minister of Women's Equality, 1992), 48.)

> The legal system has been committed to a patriarchal ideology. It is this that must be challenged if violence against women is to diminish and ultimately to cease.

(Michael D.A. Freeman, "Legal Ideologies, Patriarchal Precedents, and Domestic Violence," in Michael D.A. Freeman, *State, Law, and the Family: Critical Perspectives* (London: Tavistock, 1984), 51, at 72.)

Assuming the need for institutional and systemic change, as advocated by these views, how should decision making in cases about exclusive possession of the matrimonial home (discussed further in chapter 6) take them into account? Were there any signals, however subtle, in the facts of the *Behrendt* case, that were ignored or not given sufficient weight by the judge?

State intervention in relation to violence against women in families has increasingly emphasized that such violence constitutes criminal behaviour. A national report in 2003 concluded that the justice system should respond to spousal violence with three key objectives in mind: "criminalizing spousal abuse, promoting the safety and security of the victim, and maintaining confidence in the administration of justice": *Final Report of the Ad Hoc Federal–Provincial–Territorial Working Group Reviewing Spousal Abuse Policies and Legislation* (April 2003), cited in *Family Violence in Canada: A Statistical Profile*

2003, at 12. According to this report, the cornerstone of the criminal justice response to spousal violence in Canada is the existence of "pro-charging" police policies (mandating charging of abusers), which were implemented in all jurisdictions by the mid-1980s.

Accompanying this strategy are policies in favour of prosecution (even against the victim's wishes), specialized domestic violence courts, systems for coordinating data on offenders, services for victims, and treatment for offenders. For example, Ontario announced an expansion of its domestic violence courts in May 2003, which "stream" offenders into first-time and repeat offenders: first-time offenders must complete a counselling program, while specialized procedures for evidence and prosecution are provided for cases involving repeat offenders. The court program also provides assistance for victims. These initiatives may respond to some of the ongoing challenges identified by Linda MacLeod, such as: ongoing training for judges, prosecutors, and police; better coordination in relation to these policies; and systematic data collection procedures.

There remains, however, the challenge of providing adequate protection for women who report abuse to the police. As MacLeod cautioned:

> Even though different governments are attempting to make more effective use of peace bonds and restraining orders, which instruct batterers to stay away from their wives, battered women and shelter workers spoke of the fear of retribution many women experience if they report the battering to the police.

(Linda MacLeod, *Battered but Not Beaten ... Preventing Wife Battering in Canada* (Ottawa: Canadian Advisory Council on the Status of Women, 1987), at 88.)

Moreover, there are some criticisms of pro-charging and pro-prosecution policies. As Laureen Snider argued:

> [T]here is no reason to conclude that arresting and charging more suspects is helpful to the women involved, or even that it represents the option she would have preferred. As always, the men arrested are not a representative sample of abusers—they are the abusers with the fewest resources and the least ability to resist. It is abundantly clear from self-report studies and other sources that poor men and natives are not the only, or even the most serious offenders against women. Mobilizing class bias (and probably racism as well) in the name of justice, *and of feminism*, is not a clever strategy. [Emphasis in original.]

(Laureen Snider, "Feminism, Punishment, and the Potential of Empowerment" (1994), 9 *Canadian Journal of Law and Society* 75, at 86-87.)

How should governmental strategies respond to these criticisms?

Domestic Violence Statutes

Related to these criminal justice initiatives are recently enacted civil actions that respond to problems of violence against women. For example, legislation has been enacted to provide for relief from violence in Saskatchewan, Prince Edward Island, Yukon, Alberta, and Manitoba; legislation was enacted in Ontario, but has not yet been proclaimed in force: see *Victims of Domestic Violence Act*, SS 1994, c. V-6.02; *Victims of Family Violence Act*, SPEI 1996, c. 47; *Family Violence Prevention Act*, SY 1997, c. 12; *Protection Against Family Violence Act*, SA 1998, c. P-19.2; *Domestic Violence and Stalking*

Prevention, Protection and Compensation Act, SM 1998, c. 41; and *Domestic Violence Protection Act*, SO 2000, c. 33. Why might women choose to take advantage of civil actions in relation to experiences of violence in families? What are the advantages and disadvantages of such approaches?

Violence in Context: Aboriginal Women

Recent literature on domestic violence reflects a need to examine different contexts in which women may experience violence in intimate relationships. For example, a national study of violence against women in Canada focused on differences for older women, women living in poverty, women with disabilities, rural women, lesbians, women of official language minorities, women of colour, young women, immigrant and refugee women, and domestic workers. In addition, the study looked at the situation of Inuit and aboriginal women: see Canadian Panel on Violence Against Women, *Changing the Landscape: Ending Violence—Achieving Equality: Final Report* (Ottawa: Minister of Supply and Services, 1993), 59-192.

Concerns about violence in relation to aboriginal women have been documented in a number of studies, many of which link the issues of violence to broader community issues and aboriginal conceptions of (extended) families. For example, in a report on family violence in aboriginal communities, Sharlene Frank concluded:

> The extended family, a holistic approach, the cultural and other diversities of communities, and First Nations' aboriginal and treaty rights means that family violence issues are generally approached or viewed from a different base than that of mainstream society.

(Sharlene Frank, *Family Violence in Aboriginal Communities: A First Nations Report* (Victoria, BC: Minister of Women's Equality, 1992), 9.)

How should legal policies concerning violence be formulated in relation to women in these differing situations?

In a recent report in Ontario, for example, it was recommended that "government ministries may need to change their funding programs and structures to be more flexible, creative, and responsive in how support is provided to Northern communities [including aboriginal communities]": see Joint Committee on Domestic Violence, *Working Toward a Seamless Community and Justice Response to Domestic Violence: A Five-Year Plan for Ontario* (Toronto: Ministry of the Attorney General, 1999), recommendation no. 2. The Joint Committee was formed to respond to recommendations arising from the inquest into the death of Arlene May by her estranged boyfriend Randy Iles, who then killed himself. According to the report (at iv), the concept of "seamlessness" was central to the inquest recommendations—that is, "that individual domestic violence initiatives must be coordinated and integrated into a unified plan, and that each sector of the response system must work in concert with the others."

Battered-Woman Syndrome: R v. Lavallee

In *R v. Lavallee*, [1990] 1 SCR 852; 4 WWR 1, the Supreme Court of Canada reviewed the admissibility of evidence of the battered-woman syndrome in relation to a woman charged with the murder of her cohabiting male partner. As Wilson J concluded (at paras. 871-73), expert evidence of the syndrome was essential to assessing the woman's culpability in criminal law:

> Expert evidence on the psychological effect of battering on wives and common law partners must, it seems to me, be both relevant and necessary in the context of the present case. How can the mental state of the appellant be appreciated without it? The average member of the public (or of the jury) can be forgiven for asking: Why would a woman put up with this kind of treatment? Why should she continue to live with such a man? How could she love a partner who beat her to the point of requiring hospitalization? We would expect the woman to pack her bags and go. Where is her self-respect? Why does she not cut loose and make a new life for herself? Such is the reaction of the average person confronted with the so-called "battered wife syndrome." We need help to understand it and help is available from trained professionals.
>
> The gravity, indeed, the tragedy of domestic violence can hardly be overstated. Greater media attention to this phenomenon in recent years has revealed both its prevalence and its horrific impact on women from all walks of life. Far from protecting women from it the law historically sanctioned the abuse of women within marriage as an aspect of the husband's ownership of his wife and his "right" to chastise her. One need only recall the centuries old law that a man is entitled to beat his wife with a stick "no thicker than his thumb."
>
> Laws do not spring out of a social vacuum. The notion that a man has a right to "discipline" his wife is deeply rooted in the history of our society. The woman's duty was to serve her husband and to stay in the marriage at all costs "till death do us part" and to accept as her due any "punishment" that was meted out for failing to please her husband. One consequence of this attitude was that "wife battering" was rarely spoken of, rarely reported, rarely prosecuted, and even more rarely punished. Long after society abandoned its formal approval of spousal abuse, tolerance of it continued and continues in some circles to this day.
>
> Fortunately, there has been a growing awareness in recent years that no man has a right to abuse any woman under any circumstances. Legislative initiatives designed to educate police, judicial officers and the public, as well as more aggressive investigation and charging policies all signal a concerted effort by the criminal justice system to take spousal abuse seriously. However, a woman who comes before a judge or jury with the claim that she has been battered and suggests that this may be a relevant factor in evaluating her subsequent actions still faces the prospect of being condemned by popular mythology about domestic violence.

In a subsequent decision, *R v. Lalonde* (1995), 22 OR (3d) 275; 37 CR (4th) 97 (Gen. Div.), a court concluded that it was not necessary, in the circumstances of that case, to lead expert evidence. The accused was represented by legal aid in relation to a charge of welfare fraud. He had cohabited with her during a period in her life when she was fearful of his violence and vulnerable if he were named as the recipient of family-based welfare payments. The court held that although Lalonde had lived with her cohabitee off and on for 10 years, "for much of that time he was there simply because she did not know how to extricate him from the situation."

In *R v. Malott*, [1998] 1 SCR 123; (1998), 155 DLR (4th) 513, the Supreme Court of Canada again reviewed the battered-woman syndrome; Justices L'Heureux-Dubé and McLachlin concurred with the reasoning of the majority, but expressly noted the need to avoid stereotyping women in such relationships. In *R v. J.V.* (1998), 77 OTC 379; 20 CR (5th) 102 (Ct. J (Gen. Div.)), although an expert testified that a male child suffered from child abuse syndrome in his relationship with his mother, the court convicted him of manslaughter after he murdered her.

How should evidence of family relationships, especially when they appear to be dysfunctional, be used in criminal proceedings? What is the relationship between family autonomy and state intervention in this context? In relation to family law, what kinds of processes may need to take account of the presence of violence in family relationships?

SELECTED REFERENCES

Nicholas Bala, "Spousal Abuse and Children of Divorce: A Differentiated Approach" (1996), 13 *Canadian Journal of Family Law* 215.

Ellen Faulkner, "Lesbian Abuse: The Social and Legal Realities" (1991), 16 *Queen's Law Journal* 261.

Susan Harris and Deborah Sinclair, "Holding the Big Picture: Working in the Best Interests of Children Exposed to Woman Abuse: Some Thoughts on Furthering Child Welfare and VAW Collaboration" (Winter 2002-3), 12:1&2 *Education Wife Assault Newsletter* 1.

Rosanna Langer, "Male Domestic Abuse: The Continuing Contrast Between Women's Experiences and Juridical Responses" (1995), 10:1 *Canadian Journal of Law and Society* 65.

Anne McGillivray and Brenda Comaskey, *Black Eyes All of the Time: Intimate Violence, Aboriginal Women, and the Justice System* (Toronto: University of Toronto Press, 1999).

Ruthann Robson, "Lavender Bruises: Intra-Lesbian Violence, Law, and Lesbian Legal Theory" (1990), 20 *Golden Gate University Law Review* 567.

E. Schollenberg and B. Gibbons, "Domestic Violence Protection Orders: A Comparative Review" (1992), 10 *Canadian Journal of Family Law* 191.

Martha Shaffer, "The Battered-Woman Syndrome Revisited: Some Complicating Thoughts Five Years After R v. Lavallee" (1997), 47 *University of Toronto Law Journal* 1.

"Stopping Family Violence: Steps Along the Road" (September 1995), *Transition* (Vanier Institute of the Family).

Leslie Timmins, ed., *Listening to the Thunder* (Vancouver: Women's Research Centre, 1995).

Roberta L. Valente, "Addressing Domestic Violence: The Role of the Family Law Practitioner" (1995), 29:1 *Family Law Quarterly* 187.

V. ELDER PROTECTION: RESPONSIBILITIES OF FAMILIES AND THE STATE

That older adults may have special needs and special claims on society is undeniable. However, elder abuse legislation may reinforce social stereotypes of older persons as frail, vulnerable, and less worthy because of social, legal, physical, or cognitive incompetence. This mistaken view may invite predation and contribute to an environment conducive to abuse and exploitation. Negative stereotyping, in other words, creates disrespect and disrespect contributes to the dynamics of abuse and exploitation.

> Manitoba Law Reform Commission, *Adult Protection and Elder Abuse* (Winnipeg: Manitoba Law Reform Commission, 1999), 2

Judith A. Wahl, *Elder Abuse: The Hidden Crime*
(Toronto: Advocacy Centre for the Elderly and Community Legal Education Ontario, 1991), at 2-3

Elder abuse has been defined as any harm done to an older person that is violent or abusive, and that is caused by a person who has control or influence over the older person. Elder abuse includes:

- [p]hysical abuse (physical assault, sexual assault, forced confinement);
- [f]inancial abuse (forced sales, stealing possessions or money, fraud, forgery, extortion, and the wrongful use of a Power of Attorney);
- [n]eglect (abandonment or withholding of food or health services, failing to give a dependent person what they need); and
- [m]ental abuse (humiliation, insults, threats, or "treating an older person like a child").

According to Wahl (at 6-7), "most elder abuse is caused by a family member," but elderly people may also be abused by health care or social service providers, both in the community and in care facilities. Although it is important to remember that not all elderly persons are vulnerable adults, increasing age is a factor: see also Report of the Review of Advocacy for Vulnerable Adults, *You've Got a Friend: A Review of Advocacy in Ontario* (Toronto: Queen's Printer, 1987), 52-57.

Manitoba Law Reform Commission, *Adult Protection and Elder Abuse*
(Winnipeg: Manitoba Law Reform Commission, 1999)

[According to the report of the Manitoba Law Reform Commission (at 7), recognition of elder abuse emerged in the late 1970s, after recognition of child abuse and wife battering. The report identified the negative image of aging and older persons, and its entrenchment in societal values and institutions. It also described (at 9) how elder abuse is connected with multiple factors on four levels of interaction: personal factors (including perceptions of dependency on the part of the elderly); interpersonal factors (including unresolved past conflicts and power struggles); situational factors (including the overburdening of middle-aged caregivers); and sociocultural factors (including ideologies of the elderly as non-contributing members of society).

In a small-scale study in Winnipeg, the report identified 75 cases of psychological abuse, 50 of financial abuse, 47 of physical abuse, and 13 of neglect. Significantly, a majority of the perpetrators of abuse involved males, but there were a large number of daughters who were abusers. As the study concluded, there is a need for more assessment of this phenomenon: "Daughters abusing mothers may be doing so for very different reasons than husbands abusing wives, and sons abusing parents": see Manitoba Law Reform Commission, at 13, citing R.M. Gordon and S.N. Verdun-Jones, *Adult Guardianship Law in Canada* (1992), at 51-52.]

In 1989, a national survey was conducted, which included over 2,000 older Canadians. Four percent of all seniors living in private dwellings indicated that they recently experienced some form of mistreatment. The most prevalent form of abuse was material: victims were persuaded to give away their money, to sign over title to their homes or relinquish control over their finances, or were subjected to undue influence or threats in making their wills. Physical violence was less frequent (0.5 percent). Among those in the category of "high risk" were people over 75 years old, those who depended on someone else for daily care, seniors who were isolated, and those with behaviours that included aggression, wandering, or incontinence: see "Education the Key To Stop Elder Abuse" (September 1995), *Transition* (Vanier Institute of the Family), 12, at 12-13.

Discussion Note

Mandatory Reporting of Elder Abuse

In making recommendations, the Manitoba Law Reform Commission addressed the issue of mandatory reporting, recognizing this requirement as a significant factor in relation to issues of child abuse. However, rather than extending the general requirements for public reporting, the commission recommended "that professional and care-providing organizations develop mandatory reporting standards for members as a matter of professional organization": see the commission's report, recommendation 24.

Why might it be appropriate to have reporting requirements for elder abuse and child abuse, but not for wife abuse? Is it appropriate to have requirements of public reporting for child abuse, but not for elder abuse? Why, or why not? For another review of these arguments, see Advocacy Centre for the Elderly, "Mandatory Reporting of Elder Abuse" (Fall 1989), 1 *ACE Newsletter* 5-6.

SELECTED REFERENCES

Denise Avard, "A Lifetime of Caring" (July 1999), *Families and Health: Vanier Institute of the Family* 1.

Stephen G. Coughlan, et al., "Mandatory Reporting of Suspected Elder Abuse and Neglect: A Practical and Ethical Evaluation" (1996), 19 *Dalhousie Law Journal* 45.

Brian K. Payne, *Crime and Elder Abuse: An Integrated Perspective* (Springfield, IL: Charles C. Thomas, 2000).

PROBLEM: CARING AND PROTECTING

Caregiving can mean everything from assistance with everyday activities, such as transportation, home maintenance, bathing and dressing, to providing sophisticated forms of medical care for someone recuperating after surgery. ... In Canada, about 80 per cent of care is provided informally by family and friends.

> Denise Avard, "A Lifetime of Caring" (July 1999), *Transition* (Vanier Institute of the Family) 2

Children under the age of 18 represent 21% of the population and were victims in over 60% of all sexual offences and 20% of all physical assaults reported to the police. ... One-quarter of all violent crimes reported to a sample of police services in 2001 involved cases of family violence. ... Spousal homicides involving victims aged 65 and older tend to be characterized by the suicide of the accused. ... Nearly half (47%) of the accused in spousal homicides of older women took their own life.

> Statistics Canada, *Family Violence in Canada: A Statistical Profile 2003* (Ottawa: Canadian Centre for Justice Statistics, 2003), 1-2

This chapter has explored the role of families and the state in relation to care and protection. In assessing these different contexts in relation to different kinds of vulnerability within families, consider what kinds of reforms may be appropriate: what is the role for legislatures and courts? What is the role for lawyers? For one example of an initiative designed to explore violence issues in relation to education in law and medicine, see A. Tan, S. Eastabrook, E. Edmonds, W. Pentland, and N. Bala, *A Multi-Disciplinary Team Approach to Domestic Violence Education for Students in Diverse Professions of Health Sciences and Law* (Kingston, ON: Queen's University, Faculty of Health Sciences and Faculty of Law).

CHAPTER REFERENCES

Advocacy Centre for the Elderly. "Mandatory Reporting of Elder Abuse" (Fall 1989), 1 *ACE Newsletter*.

Arat-Koc, Sedef. "In the Privacy of Our Own Home: Foreign Domestic Workers as Solution to the Crisis in the Domestic Sphere in Canada" (1989), 28 *Studies in Political Economy* 33.

Astor, Hilary. "The Weight of Silence: Talking About Violence in Family Mediation," in Margaret Thornton, ed., *Public and Private: Feminist Legal Debates* (Melbourne: Oxford University Press, 1995), 174.

Avard, Denise. "A Lifetime of Caring" (July 1999), *Transition* (Vanier Institute of the Family) 2.

Bala, Nicholas. "Reforming Ontario's Child and Family Services Act: Is the Pendulum Swinging Back Too Far?" (1999), 17 *Canadian Family Law Quarterly* 121.

Bessner, Ronda. "The Duty To Report Child Abuse" (2000), 17 *Canadian Family Law Quarterly* 278.

Blatchford, Christie. "Randy Dooley: The Life and Death of an 'Outside Child,'" *National Post*, April 17, 2002, A14-17.

Blishen, Jennifer A., Susan G. Himel, and Judge Mary Jane Hatton. "The Lawyer's Role," in Nicholas Bala, Joseph P. Hornick, and Robin Vogl, eds., *Canadian Child Welfare Law: Children, Families, and the State* (Scarborough, ON: Thompson Educational Publishing, 1991), 155.

British Columbia Task Force on Family Violence. *Is Anyone Listening?* (Victoria, BC: Minister of Women's Equality, 1992).

Canadian Panel on Violence Against Women. *Changing the Landscape: Ending Violence— Achieving Equality: Final Report* (Ottawa: Minister of Supply and Services, 1993).

Carter, Betty Joyce. *Who's To Blame? Child Sexual Abuse and Non-Offending Mothers* (Toronto: University of Toronto Press, 1999).

Committee on Sexual Offences Against Children and Youths (Badgley Committee). *Sexual Offences Against Children: The Badgley Report* (Ottawa: Minister of Supply and Services Canada, 1984).

Dawson, T. Brettel. "Re Baby R.: A Comment on Fetal Apprehension" (1990), 4 *Canadian Journal of Women and the Law* 265.

Denov, Myriam S. "A Culture of Denial: Exploring Professional Perspectives on Female Sex Offending" (2001), 43 *Canadian Journal of Criminology* 303.

Driver, Deana. "Judge Recommends Legislation To Protect Fetuses from Effects of Mother's Substance Abuse," *The Lawyers Weekly*, February 28, 2003, 8.

_____. "New Manitoba Child Welfare Law Said 'Unprecedented in Canada.'" *The Lawyers Weekly*, January 9, 2004.

Earls, Christopher and Hélène David. "Early Family and Sexual Experiences of Male and Female Prostitutes" (1990), 38:4 *Canada's Mental Health* 7.

"Education the Key To Stop Elder Abuse" (September 1995), *Transition* (Vanier Institute of the Family) 12.

Eekelaar, John and Mavis Maclean, eds., *A Reader on Family Law* (Oxford: Oxford University Press, 1994).

Esping-Andersen, G. "The Three Political Economies of the Welfare State" (1989), 26:1 *Canadian Review of Sociology and Anthropology* 10.

Felstiner, Judge James P. "Child Welfare Hearings from an Unfamiliar Perspective," in Nicholas Bala, Joseph P. Hornick, and Robin Vogl, eds., *Canadian Child Welfare Law: Children, Families, and the State* (Scarborough, ON: Thompson Educational Publishing, 1991), 306.

Final Report of the Ad Hoc Federal–Provincial–Territorial Working Group Reviewing Spousal Abuse Policies and Legislation (2003). Cited in Statistics Canada, Centre for Justice Statistics, *Family Violence in Canada: A Statistical Profile 2003* (Ottawa: National Clearinghouse on Family Violence, Health Canada, 2003), 12.

Frank, Sharlene. *Family Violence in Aboriginal Communities: A First Nations Report* (Victoria, BC: Minister of Women's Equality, 1992).

Freeman, Michael D.A. "Legal Ideologies, Patriarchal Precedents, and Domestic Violence," in Freeman, *State, Law, and the Family: Critical Perspectives* (London: Tavistock, 1984), 51.

Froc, Kerri A. "Commentary on Canada (Attorney General) v. Lesiuk" (2003), 22:3 *Jurisfemme* 6.

Genereux, Anne. "The Protection Hearing," in Nicholas Bala, Joseph P. Hornick, and Robin Vogl, eds., *Canadian Child Welfare Law: Children, Families, and the State* (Scarborough, ON: Thompson Educational Publishing, 1991), 55.

Gove Inquiry into Child Protection (BC). *Report of the Gove Inquiry into Child Protection in British Columbia* (Victoria, BC: Ministry of Social Services, 1995).

Grace, Elizabeth and Susan Vella. "Vesting Mothers with Power They Do Not Have: The Non-Offending Parent in Civil Sexual Assault Cases: J.(L.A.) v. J.(H.) and J.(J.)" (1994), 7 *Canadian Journal of Women and the Law* 184.

"Highlights" in Statistics Canada, Canadian Centre for Justice Statistics. *Family Violence in Canada: A Statistical Profile 2003* (Ottawa: National Clearinghouse on Family Violence, Health Canada, 2003), 1.

Johnston, Rebecca. *Taxing Choices: The Intersection of Class, Gender, Parenthood, and the Law* (Vancouver: UBC Press, 2002).

Joint Committee on Domestic Violence. *Working Toward a Seamless Community and Justice Response to Domestic Violence: A Five-Year Plan for Ontario* (Toronto: Ministry of the Attorney General, 1999).

Kaganas, Felicity and Christine Piper. "Divorce and Domestic Violence," in Shelley Day Sclater and Christine Piper, eds., *Undercurrents of Divorce* (Aldershot, UK: Ashgate Dartmouth, 1999), 183.

Krashinsky, Michael. " 'Are We There Yet?': The Evolving Face of Child Care Policy in Canada" (2001-2), *Transition* (Vanier Institute of the Family) 3.

Kyle, Irene J. "Family Child Care in Canada" (Winter 2001-2), *Transition* (Vanier Institute of the Family) 10.

Law Commission of Canada. *Restoring Dignity—Responding to Child Abuse in Canadian Institutions* (Ottawa: Law Commission of Canada, 2000).

Lewis, Charles and Mike Blanchfield. "Man Kills Wife, Then Takes Own Life," *Ottawa Citizen*, June 12, 1990.

Lowman, John. "Child Saving, Legal Panaceas, and the Individualization of Family Problems: Some Comments on the Findings and Recommendations of the Badgley Report" (1985), 4 *Canadian Journal of Family Law* 508.

Macklin, Audrey. "Symes v. MNR: Where Sex Meets Class" (1992), 5 *Canadian Journal of Women and the Law* 498.

MacLeod, Linda. *Battered but Not Beaten ... Preventing Wife Battering in Canada* (Ottawa: Canadian Advisory Council on the Status of Women, 1987).

Madsen, Lene. "Citizen, Worker, Mother: Canadian Women's Claims to Parental Leave and Childcare" (2002), 19 *Canadian Journal of Family Law* 11.

Manitoba Law Reform Commission. *Adult Protection and Elder Abuse* (Winnipeg: Manitoba Law Reform Commission, 1999).

McGillivray, Anne. "Reconstructing Child Abuse: Western Definition and Non-Western Experience," in Michael Freeman and Philip Veerman, eds., *The Ideologies of Children's Rights* (Dordrecht, Netherlands: Martinus Nijhoff Publishers, 1992), 213.

McLeod, James. "Annotation: Catholic Children's Aid Society of Metropolitan Toronto v. M.(C.)" (1991), 37 RFL (3d) 202.

_____. "Annotation re Winnipeg South Child and Family Services Agency v. S.(D.D.)" (1990), 24 RFL (3d) 290.

_____. "R v. Cook: Annotation" (1985), 46 RFL (2d) 174.

Merritt, Loretta P. "Trilogy of Abuse Cases Examined 6 Issues," *The Lawyers Weekly*, December 5, 2003.

Minow, Martha. "Beyond State Intervention in the Family: For Baby Jane Doe" (1985), 18 *University of Michigan Journal of Law Reform* 933.

Mossman, M.J. "New Brunswick (Minister of Health and Community Services) v. G.(J.): Constitutional Requirements for Legal Representation in Child Protection Matters" (2000), 12 *Canadian Journal of Women and the Law* 490.

O'Halloran, Kerry. *The Welfare of the Child: The Principle and the Law* (Aldershot, UK: Ashgate, 1999).

O'Hara, Kathy. "Comparative Family Policy: Eight Countries' Stories" (Ottawa: Canadian Policy Research Networks, 1998).

Ombudsman, Province of British Columbia. *Getting There: A Review of the Implementation of the Report of the Gove Inquiry into Child Protection* (Public Report no. 36 to the Legislative Assembly of British Columbia, March 1998).

Patterson, Julienne. "Spousal Violence," in Canadian Centre for Justice Statistics, *Family Violence in Canada: A Statistical Profile 2003* (Ottawa: National Clearinghouse on Family Violence, Health Canada, 2003).

Pellatt, Anna. *An International Review of Child Welfare Policy and Practice in Relation to Aboriginal People* (Calgary: Canadian Research Institute for Law and the Family, 1991).

Philipps, Lisa. "Tax Law and Social Reproduction: The Gender of Fiscal Policy in an Age of Privatization," in Brenda Cossman and Judy Fudge, eds., *Privatization, Law, and the Challenge to Feminism* (Toronto: University of Toronto Press, 2002), 41.

Quebec Bar Committee. "Legal Representation of Children: A Consultation Paper Prepared by the Quebec Bar Committee" (1996), 13 *Canadian Journal of Family Law* 49.

Réaume, Denise and Shauna Van Praagh. "Family Matters: Mothers as Secondary Defendants in Child Sexual Abuse Actions" (2002), 17 *Supreme Court Law Review* 179.

Report of the Panel of Experts on Child Protection (Ontario). *Protecting Vulnerable Children: Report of the Panel of Experts on Child Protection* (Toronto: Ministry of Community and Social Services, 1998),

Report of the Review of Advocacy for Vulnerable Adults. *You've Got a Friend: A Review of Advocacy in Ontario* (Toronto: Queen's Printer, 1987).

Rodgers, Sanda. "Winnipeg Child and Family Services v. D.F.G.: Juridical Interference with Pregnant Women in the Alleged Interest of the Fetus" (1998), 36 *Alberta Law Review* 711.

Rogers, Rix. "The Anguish of Child Abuse—Is Prevention Possible?" (September 1995), *Transition* (Vanier Institute of the Family).

Rose, Nikolas. "Beyond the Public/Private Division: Law, Power and the Family" (1987), 14 *Journal of Law and Society* 61.

Shanner, Laura. "Pregnancy Intervention and Models of Maternal–Fetal Relationship: Philosophical Reflections in the Winnipeg CFS Dissent" (1998), 36:3 *Alberta Law Review* 751.

Snider, Laureen. "Feminism, Punishment, and the Potential of Empowerment" (1994), 9 *Canadian Journal of Law and Society* 75.

Special Advisor to the Minister of National Health and Welfare on Child Sexual Abuse in Canada. *Reaching for Solutions: The Report of the Special Advisor to the Minister of Health and Welfare on Child Sexual Abuse in Canada* (Ottawa: Minister of Supply and Services, 1990).

_____. *Status Report on the Federal Response to Reaching for Solutions: Report of the Special Advisor on Child Sexual Abuse* (Ottawa: Minister of Supply and Services, 1993).

Statistics Canada, Canadian Centre for Justice Statistics. *Family Violence: A Statistical Profile 2003* (Ottawa: National Clearinghouse on Family Violence, Health Canada, 2003).

Tan, A., S. Eastabrook, E. Edmonds, W. Pentland, and N. Bala. *A Multi-Disciplinary Team Approach to Domestic Violence Education for Students in Diverse Professions of Health Sciences and Law* (Kingston, ON: Queen's University, Faculty of Health Sciences and Faculty of Law).

Status Report on the Federal Response to Reaching for Solutions: Report of the Special Advisor on Child Sexual Abuse (Ottawa: Minister of Supply and Services, 1993).

Thompson, D.A. Rollie. "Annotation" (1999), 50 RFL (4th) 74.

_____. "Case Comment: B.R." (1995), 9 RFL (4th) 345.

Thomson, George. "Judging Judiciously in Child Protection Cases," in Rosalie Abella and Claire L'Heureux-Dubé, eds., *Dimensions of Justice* (Toronto: Butterworths, 1983), 213.

Tougas, Jocelyne. "Quebec's Child-Care Model: Making Family a Priority" (Winter 2001-2), *Transition* (Vanier Institute of the Family) 13.

Tremlett, Giles. "Spanish Mayor Bans Men from Bars," *The Guardian*, July 21, 2003.

Turnbull, Lorna. *Double Jeopardy: Motherwork and the Law* (Toronto: Sumach Press, 2001).

Van Praagh, Shauna. "Faith, Belonging, and the Protection of 'Our' Children" (1999), 17 *Windsor Yearbook of Access to Justice* 154.

Wahl, Judith A. *Elder Abuse: The Hidden Crime* (Toronto: Advocacy Centre for the Elderly and Community Legal Education Ontario, 1991).

Wildgoose, Joanne. "Alternative Dispute Resolution of Child Protection Cases" (1987), 6 *Canadian Journal of Family Law* 61.

Wilson, Hon. Bertha. "Women, the Family, and the Constitutional Protection of Privacy" (1991), 23 *Ottawa Law Review* 431.

Wilson, Jeffery and Mary Tomlinson. *Children and the Law*, 2d ed. (Toronto: Butterworths, 1986).

CHAPTER FIVE

Divorce: Contexts and Processes for Creating Post-Divorce Families

I. INTRODUCTION

Our so-called divorcing society has been held to be responsible for a whole range of social ills, and many feel "the family" to be under threat. Anxieties about a whole range of broader social changes commonly touch base at the level of "family," which provides a convenient ideological location to address those wider concerns. In this context, it is perhaps unsurprising that a reform of the divorce law should seek to provide support for marriage. Arguably, however, the new law goes further than that; there is a sense in which it addresses concerns about the "decline of the family" by providing for the emergence of a new post-divorce family.

> Shelley Day Sclater and Christine Piper, "The Family Law
> Act 1996 in Context," in Day Sclater and Piper, eds.,
> *Undercurrents of Divorce* (Aldershot, UK: Ashgate
> Dartmouth, 1999), 3, at 6

Although this comment referred specifically to statutory reforms in the United Kingdom, it reflects similar concerns about divorce in Canada. As in other western countries, legal reforms in Canada reveal tensions between supporting marriage and families on the one hand and providing effective access to divorce on the other. In addition, increasing recognition of post-divorce responsibilities for former family members, particularly in relation to financial support, means that legal principles in Canada have similarly created post-divorce families.

A. Divorce Statistics and the Meaning of Family Breakdown

According to the Vanier Institute of the Family, "the rate of divorce in Canada has risen throughout the last quarter of the 20th century, with peak years following changes to the Divorce Act": Vanier Institute of the Family, *Profiling Canada's Families II* (Ottawa: Vanier Institute of the Family, 2000), 48. The rate of divorce was highest in 1987 following the statutory reform that made a one-year separation the primary basis for obtaining a divorce order (no-fault divorce). The duration of marriages that end in divorce has also fluctuated—in 1968, a marriage that ended in divorce lasted an average of 15 years, but this figure plunged to 9.1 years in 1986, then rose again to 12.7 years at the end of the century: see *Profiling Canada's Families II*, at 52. The rate of divorce has now been declining gradually for several years, however, mirroring the decline in marriage and the increasing prevalence of cohabitation. Because only married partners may divorce, the rate of divorce does not fully capture the rate of family dissolution; it does not include those who separate after cohabitation, nor those married persons who separate but do not seek a divorce. Moreover, while many of those who divorce choose to marry again, the rate of remarriage also began to fall in the 1990s, apparently because of decisions to cohabit instead: see *Profiling Canada's Families II*, at 50-51.

The role of divorce in society thus needs to be understood in relation to marriage. In this context, relationships between the rate of divorce and liberalizing reforms is frequently contested. In assessing some of the arguments about these connections, a Department of Justice study argued:

> The assumption is that the easier it is to divorce, the more likely divorce will occur. In one sense, this is of course true: if divorce is forbidden in a society, the divorce rate will be zero. But, the historical record shows that where State and/or Church have attempted to do just this, people found other ways to circumvent the law and have, generally, shown great resilience to such attempts to intervene into family matters. Thus, as our own history shows, prior to the introduction of uniform legislation in Canada, couples separated and men often deserted their wives. Simply, the divorce rate and the rate of marriage breakdown may be quite separate matters; actually seeking a divorce may often be to formalize, legally, what for some time was a fait accompli.

(Department of Justice Canada, *Evaluation of the Divorce Act, Phase II: Monitoring and Evaluation* (Ottawa: Department of Justice Canada, 1990), at 35-36.)

As the study also suggested, explanations for the rate of divorce must take account of structural factors, including the greater participation rate of women in the labour force (which may make divorce more feasible economically), the growing secularization and increasing emphasis on individualism in most western societies, and general transformations in concepts of the family. According to the study (at 36), "[these] are the tides of change which, in our view, cannot either be dammed through more repressive legislation or accelerated through liberal reform."

B. The Divorce Context

Gay C. Kitson, with William M. Holmes, *Portrait of Divorce:*
Adjustment to Marital Breakdown
(New York: Guilford Press, 1992), 3-4 and 14-15

[This American study of divorce examined links between legal principles and marriage dissolution. It suggested that increasing rates of divorce were connected to changes in social expectations about marriage in the late 20th century, with individuals expecting more from marriage, in terms of fostering affection, empathy, understanding and companionship, than ever before. Yet, because divorce occurs in a social context that includes more traditional ideas about the sanctity and inviolability of the marriage contract, the divorce process may create tensions for married partners as well as their families and communities.]

Even if there has been a change in attitudes about the reasons for maintaining a marriage, these long-standing and often negative societal attitudes continue to play a role in how others view the divorced and how the divorced view themselves. ... [Public] concern signifies the importance and fragility of the institutions of marriage and the family in our society. After all, if marriages were less important and more easily maintained, there would not be a need for so many legal and social safeguards against their disintegration. ...

[In an overview of the relationship between marriage and divorce, Kitson explored how divorce was once characterized in terms of "pathology and deviance," but by the 1990s, it was more often understood as "failure and loss."]

Being married is an important piece of a person's identity. Thus, in the eyes of others—and, more importantly, in one's own eyes—divorce is often a failure in a major role. To have chosen so badly, to have been so unaware of what one was getting into, or to have stayed so long in a relationship after it turned out to be bad, is perceived at best as a sign of bad judgment. ... To have a relationship that is entered into with such high hopes end, whether with a bang or a whimper, is not easy.

As these comments suggest, divorce is a legal process, but it is also closely connected to social ideas about marriage and family. In addition, divorce may have significant economic implications, with legal principles establishing ongoing responsibilities for the post-divorce family.

In this context, this chapter begins an examination of divorce by focusing on three sets of issues—the legal regime that establishes grounds for divorce in Canada; some aspects of the processes of divorce cases; and some policy concerns relating to the economic consequences of divorce. The following chapters then focus on issues of "corollary relief" in divorce cases—property rights and the matrimonial home; spousal support in the context of separation agreements; and problems concerning ongoing care and financial support of children. Although this chapter includes a brief overview of the history of divorce legislation, the materials focus primarily on the *Divorce Act, 1985* and related provincial statutes. In addition, there are brief references to Bill C-22, introduced into the federal Parliament in December 2002; however, since Bill C-22 focuses primarily on issues about children, it is discussed in more detail in chapter 8.

Discussion Notes

Divorce: Changing Conceptions of Harm

According to *Profiling Canada's Families II*, at 48, more than 50,000 Canadian children experienced the divorce of their parents in 1995. Other children, whose parents were cohabiting, found themselves in a period of family transition and uncertainty. As such statistics demonstrate, divorce frequently affects children in families, even though it is the parents whose marriage is ended by divorce. The impact of divorce on children varies; according to the Vanier Institute (at 48):

> For some children, the divorce of their parents meant an escape from a violent and abusive home life. For others, it was a time of grief and often separation from a parent.

According to British researchers, however, children's experiences of their parents' divorce have increasingly been characterized as harmful. In this context, the researchers cautioned that "harmism," a tendency to see *only* harm, may fail to capture the complexity of children's reactions to divorce:

> "Harm-ism" insists that the greatest harm to children is their parents' divorce; it pushes out or minimizes considerations of poverty, domestic violence, poor housing, inadequate financial provision and the possibility that an ongoing marriage might be worse for children than a divorce. [Harmism] has developed an independent existence and is resistant to any evidence which might modify the harm thesis. It has ... become a climate of opinion.

(Carol Smart, Bren Neale, and Amanda Wade, *The Changing Experience of Childhood: Families and Divorce* (Cambridge: Polity Press, 2001), at 37-38.)

Although these issues will be addressed further in chapter 8, it is important at the outset to be alert to these and other assumptions about the *impact* of divorce. To what extent should the legal regime of divorce coincide with societal views about marriage and divorce? Is the neutrality of the law desirable or possible? How should children's needs and interests be defined and taken into account in decision making by their parents or the courts at the time of divorce?

In the Canadian context, Julien Payne identified relationships between legal and social divorce by focusing on three crises of marriage breakdown—the emotional crisis, the economic crisis, and the parenting crisis. He suggested that the responses of lawyers and legal processes have often failed to take sufficient account of them:

> The dynamics of marriage breakdown, which are multi-faceted, cannot be addressed in isolation.

(See Julien Payne, "The Dichotomy Between Family Law and Family Crises on Marriage Breakdown" (1989), 20 *Revue Générale de Droit* 109, at 110.)

In reviewing these materials about divorce, consider whether and how lawyers and courts should respond to these three kinds of crises.

From a slightly different perspective, Shelley Day Sclater suggested that divorce involves coming to terms with "loss," but she argued that it is also a "positive process of the reconstruction of identity, and the pursuit of autonomy as a new and valued goal": Shelley Day Sclater, *Divorce: A Psychosocial Study* (Aldershot, UK: Ashgate, 1999), 2. In this process, she suggested, divorcing people commonly adopt "survival strategies" that need to be understood in assessing current and proposed legal principles concerning divorce. In examining the materials in this chapter, consider how legal principles may affect individuals who are coping with negative feelings of loss as well as more positive feelings of autonomy.

Divorce and Same-Sex Marriage   – *out of date* - *July 2005.*

The current *Divorce Act* permits a "spouse" to apply for divorce. Section 2(1) defines "spouse" as "either of a man or woman who are married to each other." Clearly, this definition precludes applications from a "spouse" in a couple who are cohabiting, but not married to each other. However, the current definition also appears to preclude same-sex couples who have married pursuant to the decisions of the courts in Ontario and British Columbia in 2003 and Quebec in 2004 (see chapter 2). It seems obvious that this problem must be rectified, but the federal government's reference to the Supreme Court of Canada does not appear to address the issue: see Canada, Department of Justice, "Reference to the Supreme Court of Canada," available online at http://canada.justice.gc.ca/en/news/nr/2003/doc_30946.html. Presumably, a court challenge to extend the provisions of the *Divorce Act* to same-sex married couples would succeed, using the constitutional arguments that permitted these couples to marry, although it also seems onerous for them to have to pursue another declaration of invalidity. Recall that the Ontario Court of Appeal's decision to implement its declaration immediately proceeded on the basis that there were no significant implications for other legislation—in this context, how should this gap in access to divorce be remedied? In July 2004, an application for divorce was filed by a same-sex spouse: see *M.M. v. J.H.* and Tracey Tyler, "Now It's Divorce, Same-Sex Style," *Toronto Star*, July 24, 2004.

SELECTED REFERENCES

Anne-Marie Ambert, "Divorce: Facts, Causes, and Consequences" (Ottawa: Vanier Institute of the Family, 2002).

Elaine Carey, "Divorce Breeds Divorce, Study Finds," *Toronto Star*, June 10, 1999, A20.

Wendy J. Owen and J.M. Bumstead, "Canadian Divorce Before Reform: The Case of Prince Edward Island, 1946-67" (1993), 8:1 *Canadian Journal of Law and Society* 1.

R. Phillips, *Putting Asunder: A History of Divorce in Western Society* (Cambridge: Cambridge University Press, 1988).

Shelley Day Sclater, "Narratives of Divorce" (1997), 19:4 *Journal of Social Welfare and Family Law* 423.

Carol Smart and Bren Neale, *Family Fragments?* (Cambridge: Polity Press, 1999).

J.G. Snell, *In the Shadow of the Law: Divorce in Canada 1900-1939* (Toronto: University of Toronto Press, 1991).

Zheng Wu, *Cohabitation: An Alternative Form of Family Living* (Toronto: Oxford University Press, 2000).

//

II. THE LEGAL REGIME FOR DIVORCE

[The 1986 *Divorce Act*] introduced the possibility of true no-fault divorce, and, together with the reduction of the waiting time, made something very like divorce on demand a reality. Moreover, where an application is uncontested, it is possible for parties to obtain a divorce simply by filing the necessary documents and affidavits; and, although it is still necessary for a court to judge that the grounds in fact exist, this can be done in chambers, and a personal appearance by the parties in an uncontested divorce is not required. ... [Yet, even] when the parties are in agreement as to what they want, a court must decide that the grounds for it exist. And the parties must provide the court with the evidence necessary for the making of that judgment.

Simon Fodden, *Family Law* (Toronto: Irwin Law, 1999), at 165

As this comment explains, divorce is available in Canada virtually on demand, but it continues to require a judicial decision, even when the parties are in agreement. In this way, divorce is not simply a private, consensual decision between two people who no longer wish to be married; the law remains involved in this decision, as in decisions to marry in the first place.

Before 1968, when the first comprehensive federal legislation on divorce was enacted in Canada, arrangements for divorce varied in different provinces; in both Quebec and Newfoundland, for example, divorce required the enactment of a private statute by the federal Parliament. In other provinces, arrangements for judicial divorce were substantially similar to English legislation enacted in 1857, the *Divorce and Matrimonial Causes Act*. This statute transferred authority to a new Court for Divorce and Matrimonial Causes in England, replacing the jurisdiction of the ecclesiastical courts, and it also introduced divorce into English law for the first time. However, the situation across Canada remained variable until the 1968 *Divorce Act*, SC 1968, c. 24, which provided for the first time a "Canada-wide law of divorce exclusively located in one statute"; it was hailed as a great improvement in the divorce law of Canada: see Christine Davies, *Family Law in Canada* (Scarborough, ON: Carswell, 1984), 325-30.

A. Legislative Authority for Divorce Proceedings

Federal legislation concerning divorce was required because the authority for legislating with respect to divorce is contained in s. 91(26) of the Constitution—pursuant to this section, the federal government has authority to legislate with respect to "marriage and divorce." In this context, the constitutional validity of legislation relating to divorce is clear.

However, as Peter Hogg explained, provisions in federal divorce legislation that dealt with corollary relief were more controversial because they had been generally regarded as within the competence of provincial legislatures before 1968. Thus, for example, because issues concerning property at marriage breakdown appear to fall within provincial authority to legislate concerning "property and civil rights" (s. 92(13)), it is difficult for federal divorce legislation to include provisions concerning property entitlement at divorce. As Hogg noted, "the federal Parliament probably could not enact a comprehensive regime of family property"; however, corollary relief provisions authorizing the transfer of property from one spouse to another at divorce would probably be constitutional: see Peter W. Hogg, *Constitutional Law of Canada* (Toronto: Thomson Carswell, 2003), 26:9 (looseleaf). In the absence of federal action, provincial legislation governs property entitlement at marriage breakdown, and thus property rights may vary across Canada.

By contrast with these arrangements for property, authority with respect to issues of support (for spouses and for children) and custody of children has been held to be within federal jurisdiction if they are related to divorce, but within provincial jurisdiction in other cases. In *Papp v. Papp* (1969), 1 OR 331, the Ontario Court of Appeal considered the validity of provisions of the 1968 *Divorce Act* concerning custody and concluded that they were valid because they had a "rational, functional connection" with divorce; this decision has been followed in relation to interim and final orders and to applications for variation of these orders, as long as they are connected to divorce proceedings. Similarly, interim and final orders, and applications for variation, in relation to spousal and child support have been held to be within federal authority, so long as they are connected to divorce proceedings; thus, the provisions of the federal *Divorce Act* relating to spousal and child support and to custody of children are valid in relation to divorce proceedings: see Hogg, at 26:5-8.

At the same time, however, courts have held that provincial legislation governing spousal and child support and custody, as well as property, is valid in so far as it relates to applications that do not involve divorce. Thus, for example, arrangements for support and custody at the end of a cohabiting relationship must be considered in relation to provincial legislation, because no divorce application is possible in the absence of marriage. In addition, however, some spouses who are married may separate without making any decision about whether to divorce; in the absence of divorce proceedings, their claims to support and custody will also be considered pursuant to provincial legislation: see *Re Adoption Reference*, [1938] SCR 402 and Hogg, at 26:9-14. In this way, issues about support and custody may fall within either federal or provincial legislative authority, depending on the circumstances.

Interestingly, however, there appear to be few examples of significant differences between the outcomes of such cases in different parts of Canada, even though the precise language of each provincial statute is often different, and also different from the corollary relief provisions of the *Divorce Act*. In part, this uniformity of outcomes has been created by decisions of the Supreme Court of Canada that have identified guiding principles on issues such as spousal support and child custody. In addition, the enactment of child-support guidelines through collective action on the part of the federal, provincial, and territorial governments has tended to create expectations of greater uniformity, although some differences remain in practice. As with Charter decisions in family law, these developments suggest that a national system of family law is now emerging. To what extent is this desirable? Are there issues relating to support and custody or property that should reflect provincial, rather than national, standards in Canada?

However, even though there may be increasing uniformity between federal and provincial family law regimes, the existence of two sets of legislative provisions may create conflicts for parties at separation. Hogg has suggested (at 26:9) that the possibility of conflict between federal and provincial statutes in relation to family law orders should be determined according to the doctrine of paramountcy, but he also noted that family law courts have "often disregarded the doctrine of paramountcy and have produced a remarkably inconsistent patchwork of decisions." Sometimes, for example, courts have tended to decide disputes pursuant to conflict-of-laws rather than constitutional principles: see *McKee v. McKee*, [1951] 2 DLR 657. However, because an order of a divorce court in any province has effect throughout Canada (see *Divorce Act*, s. 13) and is not an order of a foreign court but rather one pursuant to the federal divorce power, the doctrine of paramountcy should determine the priority between such an order and any order made according to provincial legislative authority.

The interesting question is when does inconsistency between a federal and provincial order in the family law context arise? Using the express-contradiction test, there is no doubt that there would be inconsistency between an order for custody and access made pursuant to the federal divorce power and a different one made pursuant to a provincial statute. It may be more difficult to apply these principles in the case of support. For example, Hogg suggested (at 26:10-11) that a federal order to pay $500 per month and a provincial order to pay $600 per month in respect of spousal support are not necessarily inconsistent; both can be honoured by paying $1,100 per month. Generally, however, courts have held that there is an express contradiction in such a case, although this result is not required by the test.

Issues of conflict also arise in relation to applications for variation of an order for corollary relief. In a case where a divorce court has issued an order for corollary relief at the time of a divorce order, the question is whether it is possible for a subsequent court to make a different (and inconsistent) order pursuant to provincial legislation at a later point in time. The case law has been somewhat inconsistent on this issue: see *Emerson v. Emerson*, [1972] 3 OR 5 (HCJ); *Ramsay v. Ramsay* (1976), 70 DLR (3d) 415 (Ont. CA); and *Hall v. Hall* (1976), 70 DLR (3d) 493 (BCCA). According to *Hall*, there is no such authority in the later court, acting pursuant to provincial legislation, and Hogg concluded that this authority is probably correct. However, if there has been no order for corollary relief at the time of the divorce order, Hogg suggested (at 26:13-14) that the express-contradiction test would validate any order pursuant to provincial legislation, made either before or after the divorce order. However, if an order for corollary relief is made after the divorce order, there will then be an express contradiction and the competing provincial order will be invalid. Finally, in a situation where there is a valid order pursuant to provincial law, and then an order for divorce is made, any order for corollary relief made by the divorce court that is inconsistent with the earlier order will be paramount to the provincial legislation.

An example of the application of these principles is *Spiers v. Spiers* (1996), 18 RFL (4th) 246 (BCSC). In that case, the parties divorced and the mother was granted sole custody and guardianship of the children. The divorce order referred to both the *Divorce Act* and the *Family Relations Act* of British Columbia, but did not specify under which Act the custody order was made. The father subsequently applied for an order for access in the Provincial Court, but the court refused to hear the application, holding that it had no jurisdiction following the previous ruling by the BC Supreme Court. The father petitioned for mandamus ordering the Provincial Court to hear the application, but the Supreme Court held that once an order for custody is made under the *Divorce Act*, the Provincial Court loses jurisdiction over the issue of access due to the doctrine of paramountcy. As this case reveals, issues about legislative authority are intertwined with issues about jurisdiction for courts, an issue that is addressed in section III below.

Discussion Note

Brooks v. Brooks: Orders in Different Provinces

The existence of shared jurisdiction in relation to corollary relief in divorce proceedings may create opportunities for protracted litigation. In *Brooks v. Brooks* (1998), 41 OR (3d) 191, the Ontario Court of Appeal reviewed the relationship between an order in a Manitoba court, granting interim custody to the father pursuant to the *Divorce Act*, and custody proceedings pursuant to provincial legislation in Ontario, which granted custody to the mother. Although the litigation was complicated by a number of additional factors, the appellate court concluded that the *Divorce Act* proceedings in Manitoba superseded the Ontario order.

In considering the situation, the court also interpreted s. 27 of the Ontario *Children's Law Reform Act*, RSO 1990, c. C.12. This section requires that a proceeding pursuant to provincial legislation be stayed if an application for divorce is filed. Although the section is clearly designed to avoid the necessity of applying the paramountcy doctrine, by preventing the existence of two inconsistent orders, it may also provide opportunities to use litigation strategies in family law proceedings. Consider also s. 36 of Ontario's *Family Law Act*, RSO 1990, c. F.3 in relation to issues of spousal support. How should these provisions be interpreted to prevent abuse? For another example, see *Willenbrecht v. Willenbrecht* (1999), 47 RFL (4th) 200 (Ont. CA).

SELECTED REFERENCES

Canada, Parliament, Special Committee of the Senate and House of Commons, *Report of the Special Joint Committee of the Senate and the House of Commons on Divorce* (Ottawa: Queen's Printer, 1967).
Christine Davies, *Family Law in Canada* (Scarborough, ON: Carswell, 1984).
Frederick Jordan, "The Federal Divorce Act (1968) and the Constitution" (1968), 14 *McGill Law Journal* 209.

B. Grounds for Divorce

1. The Role of Grounds for Divorce: Fault and No-Fault

According to Bruce Ziff, the grounds for divorce were once the source of "tempestuous debate and a wealth of jurisprudence," but now arouse only "diminishing interest" from commentators and the courts. At the same time, Ziff argued that the grounds for divorce retain some significance.

Bruce Ziff, "Recent Developments in Canadian Law: Marriage and Divorce"
(1986), 18 *Ottawa Law Review* 121, at 140

Successfully proving a ground will remain a necessary step in obtaining permanent corollary relief under the *Divorce Act* and the existence of such a ground provides the respective parties with bargaining endowments in the negotiation of corollary issues. Allegations of matrimonial misconduct in a petition may reduce settlement possibilities where the assertions offend the sensitivities of the respondent and precipitate the dropping of the gauntlet. Conversely, it is possible that the ability of the parties to vent their anger through such allegations serves a cathartic function and, absent this outlet, the tendency to use corollary relief proceedings as a vehicle for recrimination may be heightened.

As these comments suggest, the grounds for divorce must be understood in terms of both the legal regime and the social divorce. In reviewing the interpretation of the grounds for divorce in the materials that follow, consider the extent to which you agree with Ziff's assessment.

Although the 1968 *Divorce Act* contained 15 grounds for divorce, with both fault-based (s. 3) and marriage-breakdown (s. 4) grounds, the current statute provides that "marriage breakdown" is the *only* ground for divorce in Canada: see *Divorce Act*, s. 8. However, s. 8(2) in the current statute provides that the breakdown of a marriage may be established on the basis that the parties have lived "separate and apart" for one year (s. 8(2)(a)), or that the respondent in a divorce application has committed adultery or treated the applicant with physical or mental cruelty (s. 8(2)(b)). As Ziff noted (at 141-42), the vast majority of divorces granted under the 1968 statute were based on these three grounds (separation, adultery, and physical and mental cruelty), with only a few cases relying on the other grounds available under that legislation. In this way, the current statute establishes no-fault divorce in Canada without necessarily changing established practices for claiming divorce. Moreover, because the period of separation is now only one year (rather than the three or five years under the 1968 statute), more people may now rely on a period of separation to demonstrate marriage breakdown.

In keeping with the new ground of marriage breakdown, parties may also apply jointly for divorce if they are relying on the one-year period of separation to establish marriage breakdown (see s. 8(1)). In this way, assuming that they prepare the appropriate paper work, it is arguable that spouses may now end a marriage "on consent," after a one-year period of separation, *and* with the approval of the court—the "divorce on demand."

In assessing the brief excerpts that follow, which examine the interpretation of the requirements for divorce, consider the extent to which you agree with Fodden's characterization of divorce, above. Are there hidden barriers that affect entitlement to a divorce or corollary relief? To what extent is Canadian divorce law effectively a no-fault regime? In this context, note also that many of the precedents relating to divorce are based on the 1968 statute and, sometimes, on earlier legislation. What conclusions should be drawn from the fact that there is little current litigation about the grounds for divorce?

2. Living Separate and Apart

The language of s. 8(2)(a) defines precisely how the one-year period must be calculated to meet the requirement of living separate and apart. In addition, s. 8(3) defines the circumstances in which spouses may be deemed to be living separate and apart; note that only one spouse needs to have the requisite intention. In addition, s. 8(3)(b) provides that spouses who resume cohabitation for a total period of not more than 90 days, "with reconciliation as its primary purpose," may nonetheless meet the test of living separate and apart.

However, the statute is silent as to whether spouses who continue to live in the same home may be able to meet the test of living separate and apart. Why might spouses who wish to separate and divorce continue to live in the same home? As a matter of policy, how should courts treat applications for divorce in such cases? Consider these questions in relation to the following cases.

Rushton v. Rushton
(1968), 66 WWR 764 (BCSC)

McINTYRE J: The parties were married in 1936. By 1960 they had come upon difficulties and had begun to live separate lives, although they continued to reside in the same suite in an apartment building. In February, 1965, and probably from an earlier date, sexual intercourse ceased entirely. The petitioner lived in one room of the suite, the respondent in another; there was almost no contact between them. The wife performed no domestic services for the husband. She shopped and cooked only for herself. He bought his own food, did his own cooking, his own laundry and received no services from his wife. He paid her a sum monthly for maintenance. While it is true that they lived in the same suite of rooms, they followed separate and individual lives.

The petitioner continued to live in the suite because she and her husband were the joint caretakers of the apartment building in which the suite was situate, and to keep the position it was necessary to be, or to appear to be, husband and wife and to reside in the caretaker's suite.

In August, 1968, they became responsible for another apartment building where no such requirement exists. They now maintain separate suites in the same building.

I am of the opinion that in the case at bar the parties have been living separate and apart for three years within the meaning of [the relevant section of the *Divorce Act*, 1968]. The words "separate and apart" are disjunctive. They mean, in my view, that there must be a withdrawal from the matrimonial obligation with the intent of destroying the matrimonial consortium, as well as physical separation. The two conditions must be met. I hold that they are met here. The mere fact that the parties are under one roof does not mean that they are not living separate and apart within the meaning of the Act. There can be, and I hold that there has been, a physical separation within the one suite of rooms. To hold otherwise would be to deprive the petitioner here of any remedy under the new *Divorce Act* simply because she is precluded, or was for a period of time precluded, by economic circumstances from acquiring a different suite in which to live.

Dupere v. Dupere
(1974), 19 RFL 270 (NBSC (QB))

STEVENSON J: The petitioner by his petition dated 18th October 1973 and presented to the Court on 1st November 1973 sought a divorce on the alternative grounds of adultery or permanent marriage breakdown by reason of the spouses having lived separate and apart for a period of not less than three years.

By her answer the respondent disputes the grounds alleged by the petitioner and counter-petitions for a divorce alleging permanent marriage breakdown by reason that the spouses "have been living under the same roof but separate and apart for a period of almost five years." ... At the opening of the trial counsel for the petitioner abandoned the allegation of adultery.

Only the parties testified. In any case where the parties continue to live under the same roof the court must carefully consider the evidence in determining whether the spouses have been "living separate and apart" resulting in "a permanent breakdown of their marriage." ... Particular care is called for where, as here, both spouses seek a divorce on that ground alone.

The parties were married on 27th February 1960. The petitioner was 26 and the respondent 18. She had borne a child, Randle, of which the petitioner was the father, on 13th July 1958. There are two other children of the marriage—Heather, born 30th November 1960, and Jacqueline, born 9th February 1965.

Difficulties between the parties apparently developed in 1965 and they separated in 1966. A written separation agreement (Ex. R-1) was entered into on 12th July 1966. The respondent was to have custody of the children and the petitioner assumed financial obligations which were not clearly defined. The respondent took an apartment. When she was unable to pay the rent she rented a small house without toilet facilities for $30 per month. She and her two daughters resided there. Randle stayed with his maternal grandmother. The petitioner provided some financial support on a rather irregular basis.

In the fall of 1968, the petitioner moved in with the respondent and normal marital relations were resumed for about a month. However in December of that year the parties began to occupy separate bedrooms and both testify there has been no sexual intercourse between them since that time. They subsequently moved twice and had lived together at 72 Pauline Street in East Saint John from March 1970 until a week before the trial when the respondent moved to another address, taking the children with her.

The petitioner says he and the respondent stayed in the same house "for the sake of the kids." While I suspect the respondent may have stayed as a matter of economic necessity the evidence does not justify such a finding. The petitioner has supported the home, has clothed his wife and family and has given the respondent a $20 weekly allowance. The respondent says she was just a maid. It is not a situation where there was no communication between the parties and apparently where the children were concerned there was often mutual discussion and agreement. For instance the parties were able to jointly decide on how much should be spent on the children at Christmas and they "always made a big thing of Christmas." As between the parties discord continued and on only two occasions in the past five years did they go out together. The respondent has been friendly with another man with the knowledge and at least tacit consent of the petitioner.

The situation is not unlike that described by Holland J in *Cooper v. Cooper* (1972), 10 RFL 184 (Ont.) [at 186]:

> The parties obviously cannot get along and clearly there is considerable bad feeling between them. At the same time there is clearly good feeling towards the children, the children are being well looked after and are receiving all necessary care and attention from their parents, in spite of the fact that the attitude of the parents toward each other must be upsetting for each of them.

The petitioner, though lacking in formal education, has been successful in his occupation as a crane operator and now earns about $16,000 annually. Occasionally his work takes him away for periods of several months but he anticipates his present work will keep him in Saint John for four or five years. He is presently working 12-hour shifts, alternating between day and night shifts every two weeks.

While the petitioner seeks a divorce it is not clear what he intended for the future with respect to his wife. In response to questioning by the Court he quite candidly admitted that he would have been content to have the same living conditions continue. At the date of the trial he had not finalized any plans for a new home or for the employment of a housekeeper.

The landlord of the parties had given them notice to quit at the end of February. The petitioner has entered into an agreement to purchase a home at South Bay but financing has not been finalized. The respondent, not being able to get satisfactory answers from the petitioner as to what accommodation and arrangements were to be provided after the end of February, rented an apartment on her own and, as already mentioned, moved there with the children a week prior to the date on which this action was to be tried.

The respondent has been employed since December 1973 and presently is earning a net of $66 weekly.

I have read most, if not all, of the decisions reported since the advent of the *Divorce Act* dealing with cases where marriage breakdown is alleged on the ground of separation even though the spouses continue to live under the same roof. ...

The cases of *Cooper v. Cooper*, supra, and *Lachman v. Lachman*, 2 RFL 207, [1970] 3 OR 29, 12 DLR (3d) 221 (CA), while not involving the particular issue, are also helpful.

I think the following general statements can be extracted as representing the weight of judicial opinion:

(1) Great care must be exercised in considering the evidence and each case determined on its own circumstances.

(2) There can be a physical separation within a single dwelling unit.

(3) A case is not taken out of the statute just because a spouse remains in the same house for reasons of economic necessity.

(4) To meet the statute there must be both (a) physical separation and (b) a withdrawal by one or both spouses from the matrimonial obligation with the intent of destroying the matrimonial consortium.

(5) Cessation of sexual intercourse is not conclusive but is only one factor to be considered in determining the issue.

(6) There may be an atmosphere of severe incompatibility but remain one household and one home—a distinction may be drawn between an unhappy household and a separated one.

The remarks of Denning LJ (as he then was) in *Hopes v. Hopes*, [1949] P227, [1948] 2 All ER 920, a desertion case, are also, I think, applicable by analogy. At pp. 235-36 he said:

It is most important to draw a clear line between desertion, which is a ground for divorce, and gross neglect or chronic discord, which is not. That line is drawn at the point where the parties are living separate and apart. In cases where they are living under the same roof, that point is reached when they cease to be one household and become two households, or, in other words, when they are no longer residing with one another.

In *Cooper v. Cooper*, supra, Holland J pointed out that generally a finding that spouses were living separate and apart was made where the following circumstances were present [at 187]:

 (i) Spouses occupying separate bedrooms.
 (ii) Absence of sexual relations.
 (iii) Little, if any, communication between spouses.
 (iv) Wife providing no domestic services for her husband.
 (v) Eating meals separately.
 (vi) No social activities together.

It is probably not necessary to establish all six elements in each case and each case must stand or fall on its own merits. I refrain from commenting on the wisdom of incompatible spouses remaining together "for the sake of the children" but I do not think it was the intention of Parliament that a spouse who does so, under the circumstances in this case, can at his or her option at any time after such circumstances have continued for three years or more elect to opt out of the marriage and claim a divorce on the ground of permanent marriage breakdown. A mutual opting out in such circumstances would be little more than divorce by consent, something Parliament has not yet provided for.

The evidence does not satisfy me that for three years or more prior to presentation of the petition in this action the parties were living separate and apart within the meaning of the Act or that there was an intention on the part of either spouse to destroy the matrimonial consortium. Accordingly both the petition and the counter-petition will be dismissed.

Discussion Notes

The Requirement To Live Separate and Apart

How should courts deal with the criteria used in *Rushton* and *Dupere*? For example, what criteria are relevant to a determination that the spouses are living separate and apart when the husband regularly works away from home: see *Fotheringham v. Fotheringham* (1999), 1 RFL (5th) 50 (Nfld. CA)? What if the parties are living in separate accommodation but they engage in "isolated or occasional" acts of sexual intercourse: see *Deslippe v. Deslippe* (1974), 16 RFL 38? In another case, a wife objected to her husband's application for divorce on the basis of her religious commitments; nonetheless, the court granted the divorce: see *Ash v. Ash* (1994), 8 RFL (4th) 461 (BCCA); leave to appeal to the SCC refused (1995), 17 RFL (4th) 234. Do these cases reflect the idea of "divorce on demand"? What kinds of criteria are most significant?

Mental Capacity and Intention

Section 8(3) of the *Divorce Act* addresses the issue of mental capacity to form the intention to live separate and apart and to divorce. In *Calvert v. Calvert* (1997), 32 OR (3d) 281 (Gen. Div.); 37 OR (3d) 221 (CA), the court held that the wife, who was suffering from Alzheimer's disease and who was represented by a litigation guardian, had the capacity necessary to form an intent to separate from her husband and to seek a divorce. According to the evidence at trial, the wife had started to show some early signs of Alzheimer's in 1993. In early 1994, she went to visit her daughter in Calgary and never returned to Ontario. While in Calgary, she expressed the desire to divorce her husband and sought counsel from a family lawyer. The lawyer testified that he had no doubt that the wife had the capacity to give instructions to commence divorce proceedings. A medical doctor who examined the wife while she was in Calgary also testified that she had the capacity to separate from and divorce her husband.

The court granted the wife's petition, stating that there were three levels of capacity relevant to the action—the capacity to separate; the capacity to divorce; and the capacity to instruct counsel. The court noted that separation is the simplest, requiring the lowest understanding; divorce, while simple, requires more understanding, because it is the undoing of the contract of marriage. Based on the evidence, the court found that the wife had all levels of capacity required to proceed. When the husband appealed, the court rejected his argument that to support a finding of divorce, the court had to make a distinct finding with respect to the wife's mental capacity to intend to live separate and apart at the time of the petition for divorce and for the one-year period prior to the granting of the divorce. The court held that to require further proof or findings as to the wife's mental capacity and intention at each relevant point and for each relevant period would defeat the purpose of s. 8(3)(b)(i) of the *Divorce Act*. The Court of Appeal also rejected the husband's argument that the trial judge erred in awarding equalization of property. Leave to appeal to the SCC was dismissed, without reasons, on May 7, 1998, [1998] SCCA no. 161; see also (1998), 36 RFL (4th) 169 (Ont. CA); and (1998), 42 RFL (4th) 313 (Ont. CA). To what extent does the reasoning in *Calvert* resemble divorce on demand?

3. Adultery and Cruelty

The definitions of adultery and cruelty pursuant to s. 8(2)(b) of the *Divorce Act* are also frequently derived from cases decided some years ago. It is interesting that only the "innocent" spouse may apply for divorce on the basis of adultery or cruelty, even though adultery and cruelty are no longer grounds for divorce, but serve merely to establish marriage breakdown.

Adultery and Burbage v. Burbage

Consider the approach in *Burbage v. Burbage* (1985), 46 RFL (2d) 33 (Ont. SC (HCJ)), where the court considered a husband's counterpetition for divorce on the ground of adultery. The evidence showed that the wife, before separation, had developed a relationship with another man with whom she had spent a lot of time. It was admitted that on two occasions she had spent the night at the other man's apartment, but they both asserted that no sexual intercourse had taken place because the man was impotent. The co-respondent asserted that his impotence was due to back surgery some years earlier and to his own bad marriage, which had terminated the previous year. No evidence was called to confirm the back surgery because the surgeon had died.

The court held that there was (1) evidence of opportunity and (2) evidence of inclination (although the wife flatly denied that sexual intercourse had taken place), and continued (at 37-38):

> In the result the court is left on the one hand with at least a prima facie case of adultery because of the proven elements of opportunity and intimacy, and on the other hand with a bald-faced denial that any adultery occurred.
>
> In my view, once opportunity and intimacy are established on a balance of probabilities, there is a burden on the alleged adulterers to call evidence in rebuttal sufficient to dislodge the preponderant evidence. Despite the death of the back surgeon, the co-respondent could have submitted himself to a medical examination and either called the medical practitioner as a witness or submitted a medical report pursuant to the rules. This was not done and no sufficient explanation for the failure put forward. These facts may support an adverse inference. Furthermore, the testimony of the ex-wife could have been presented viva voce or by affidavit. Again, an adverse inference may be raised. I realize, of course, that psychic impotence may not be universal but may be directed or limited to a particular person, but the absence of evidence is not helpful in this case.
>
> On a balance of probabilities, therefore, I find that the allegation of adultery has been established. There will be a decree nisi granted to the husband.

Recall Ziff's comments about the continuing usefulness of grounds for divorce in relation to negotiations between the spouses—to what extent do his comments assist in understanding the wife's arguments in *Burbage*?

Cruelty, Knoll v. Knoll, and Subsequent Cases

Mental and physical cruelty has also been retained as a basis for establishing marriage breakdown. In *Knoll v. Knoll* (1970), 1 RFL 141, the Ontario Court of Appeal made these comments about the definition of "cruelty" in divorce proceedings:

> Over the years the Courts have steadfastly refrained from attempting to formulate a general definition of cruelty. As used in ordinary parlance "cruelty" signifies a disposition to inflict suffering; to delight in or exhibit indifference to the pain or misery of others; mercilessness or hard-heartedness as exhibited in action. If in the marriage relationship one spouse by his conduct causes wanton, malicious or unnecessary infliction of pain or suffering upon the body, the feelings or emotions of the other, his conduct may well constitute cruelty which will entitle a petitioner to dissolution of the marriage if, in the Court's opinion, it amounts to physical or mental cruelty "of such a kind as to render intolerable the continued cohabitation of the spouses."
>
> Care must be exercised in applying the standard set forth in [s. 8(2)(b)(ii)] that conduct relied upon to establish cruelty is not a trivial act, but one of a "grave and weighty" nature,

and not merely conduct which can be characterized as little more than a manifestation of incompatibility of temperament, between the spouses. The whole matrimonial relations must be considered, especially if the cruelty consists of reproaches, complaints, accusations or constant carping criticism. A question most relevant for consideration is the effect of the conduct complained of upon the mind of the affected spouses. The determination of what constitutes cruelty in a given case must, in the final analysis, depend upon the circumstances of the particular case having due regard to the physical and mental condition of the parties, their character and their attitude towards the marriage relationship.

While *Knoll* was decided under the *Divorce Act*, 1968, the language of that statute has been incorporated into the current legislation, although courts have continued to assert that each case must be decided on its own facts. In *Chouinard v. Chouinard* (1969), 10 DLR (3d) 263, for example, the New Brunswick Court of Appeal reiterated the approach in *Knoll*, indicating (at 264) that "behaviour which may constitute cruelty in one case may not constitute cruelty in another." The court also noted that there are both objective and subjective elements involved. In *Barron v. Bull* (1987), 5 RFL (3d) 427 (Alta. QB), the court rejected a husband's petition for divorce on the basis of s. 8(2)(b)(ii) because the alleged conduct of the wife, although displeasing to the petitioner, did not in fact cause him to suffer, stating (at 432):

> Realizing that the test for cruelty is largely subjective, I am unable to find that the petitioner has established the respondent's cruelty toward him could be characterized to be of such a kind as to render intolerable their continued cohabitation.

Discussion Notes

Fault Grounds for Divorce

As Davies noted, it has been suggested that the advent of no-fault divorce has altered the concept of marriage (at 336):

> Now it is a union dissoluble without misconduct at the will of one or both of the parties [if they have lived separate and apart]. Thus, it is said, it is in the public interest that a marriage which has irrevocably failed ought to be dissolved. It is submitted, however, that, although the grounds for divorce have been extended, the court will continue to guard against its own deception and will continue to insist that adultery be proven to its satisfaction regardless of whether the parties themselves desire a divorce and the marriage has broken down.

Do you agree that the above cases illustrate differing approaches to divorce applications based on living separate and apart, by contrast with adultery (and cruelty)? Should the courts approach these applications differently? Why, or why not?

B.(Y.) v. B.(J.): Homosexuality and "Cruelty"

In *B.(Y.) v. B.(J.)* (1989), 20 RFL (3d) 154 (Alta. QB), the wife applied for divorce on the grounds of adultery and mental cruelty. The petition was presented on affidavit evidence only without an appearance in court. In relation to "particulars of mental cruelty," the wife's affidavit stated that "the respondent has admitted to me and to my eldest daughter S. that he is a practising homosexual." The petition for divorce was refused on the basis (at 156) that "something in addition to homosexual practices" must be submitted in evidence "as constituting the grave conduct necessary to ground a divorce judgment." As the court stated (at 156):

> Moreover, as our Court of Appeal has held in *Anderson v. Anderson*, [1972] 6 WWR 53, 8 RFL 299, 29 DLR (3d) 587, there is an element of wilfulness in mental cruelty; being a homosexual is not equivalent to treating your spouse with cruelty. Cruelty implies callousness or indifference as referred to in that judgment. ...
>
> The fact that Parliament has also authorized divorce judgments to be issued in the absence of appearances in court does not mean that the standards of cruelty have been relaxed. The fact that the husband does not contest his wife's petition does not relieve the wife from the test which Parliament has established.
>
> In addition, the conduct relied upon to establish cruelty must be intolerable to the petitioner. There are no particulars in the supplementary affidavit of the subjective aspect of the grounds invoked.

What is the remedy for the wife in this case?

No-Fault Divorce: Perceptions of Lawyers and Clients

In his assessment of the *Divorce Act*, Bruce Ziff suggested that the new legislation of 1986 was "woefully unimaginative and unambitious," particularly because it retained "vestiges of matrimonial conduct": see Ziff, at 208. Although divorce proceedings based on adultery and cruelty are now less frequent than those based on one year of living separate and apart, are there reasons to retain these fault-based grounds? To what extent is it possible to attain no-fault divorce in the context of marriage breakdown?

In examining the interactions of divorce lawyers and their clients in the United States, two researchers identified contrasting approaches to divorce for lawyers and clients— lawyers tended to focus on "legal" no-fault divorce, but their clients were often seeking vindication by blaming their spouses:

> The vocabularies of motive used by clients in divorce cases excuse and justify their conduct and place blame for the failure of their marriage, as well as for problems in the legal process of divorce, squarely on their spouses. ... This emphasis poses an awkward choice for lawyers. ... Thus, most of the time lawyers remain silent in the face of client attacks on their spouses. They refuse to explore the past and to participate in the construction of a shared version of the social history of the marriage. When they do interpret behaviour they limit themselves to conduct that is directly relevant to the legal process of divorce ... . In this way they deflect what is, for many clients, a strong desire to achieve some moral vindication, even in a no-fault world.

(Austin Sarat and William F. Felstiner, "Law and Social Relations: Vocabularies of Motive in Lawyer/Client Interaction" (1988), 22:4 *Law & Society Review* 737, at 764.)

According to Sarat and Felstiner (at 765), lawyers' unwillingness to engage with client efforts "to give meaning to the past" may result in clients feeling dissatisfied with their lawyers because of a failure to empathize with them. In addition, it may create difficulties for the settlement process.

Interestingly, a report in 2000 indicated that "emotion-charged family law cases" were the biggest source of complaints about judges to the Canadian Judicial Council, with family law disputes representing 84 out of 177 complaints filed: see Cristin Schmitz, "Family Law Cases Main Source of Complaints Against Judges," *The Lawyers Weekly*, November 17, 2000, at 20.

How should these concerns be addressed in divorce law reforms? Is the abolition of fault-based grounds desirable as a goal of legal or social divorce processes?

4. Bars to Divorce

Traditional Bars to Divorce

The current *Divorce Act* retains, as bars to the granting of a divorce, collusion (ss. 11(1)(a) and 11(4)) and connivance and condonation in relation to applications based on allegations of adultery and cruelty (s. 11(1)(c)). Collusion appears to be an absolute bar; however, even though there is evidence of connivance or condonation, a court may exercise its discretion in the public interest to grant a divorce. These traditional bars relate primarily to fault-based grounds for divorce, although collusion has been considered in some recent cases in the context of "immigration marriages": for example, see *Johnson v. Ahmed* (1981), 22 RFL (2d) 141 (Alta. QB). (Note that Bill C-22 alters the wording in the definition of collusion in s. 11(4), but only with respect to proposed arrangements for parenting.)

Connivance traditionally related to a spouse who promoted or encouraged, even passively, the commission of adultery by the other spouse: see *Fleet v. Fleet*, [1972] 2 OR 530 (Ont. CA). Condonation referred to the resumption of cohabitation of a "guilty" spouse after being forgiven by the innocent spouse, after an act of adultery: see *Leaderhouse v. Leaderhouse*, [1971] 2 WWR 180 (Sask. QB) and s. 11(3).

Reasonable Arrangements for Children

In addition to these traditional bars, the *Divorce Act* requires a court to satisfy itself that there have been reasonable arrangements for the support of children of the marriage and, if necessary, to stay the granting of the divorce until such arrangements have been made (s. 11(1)(b)). Before the enactment of child-support guidelines, this provision was interpreted in a number of cases, including *F.(R.D.) v. F.(S.L.)* (1987), 6 RFL (3d) 413 (BCSC) and *Money v. Money* (1987), 5 RFL (3d) 375 (Man. CA).

In *Harper v. Harper* (1991), 78 DLR (4th) 548 (Ont. Ct. (Gen. Div.)), an Ontario court reviewed these and other decisions and identified criteria for assessing the arrangements for the support of children in divorce proceedings. In doing so, the court examined the relationship between child support and social assistance payments; the extent to which any agreement between the parents should be respected; and the need to take account of income tax implications, indexing, and the availability of medical coverage. *Harper* clearly revealed the court's concerns to implement s. 11(1)(b) effectively.

However, factors such as income tax implications have now become substantially redundant as a result of the introduction of child-support guidelines, which themselves have often been used in interpreting this section of the *Divorce Act*. Yet, it is important to note that the failure to make appropriate arrangements for the support of children may operate *independently* to prevent the granting of a divorce application: see *Orellana v. Merino* (1998), 40 RFL (4th) 129 (Ont. Ct. (Gen. Div.)); and *Ninhan v. Ninhan* (1997), 29 RFL (4th) 41 (Ont. Ct. (Gen. Div.)). See also James McLeod, "Annotation: Orellana v. Merino" (1998), 40 RFL (4th) 129.

Religious Bars

In addition to these bars, s. 21.1 of the *Divorce Act* permits a court to take action in a context where one spouse refuses to remove religious barriers to the remarriage of the other spouse as part of their divorce negotiations. Pursuant to s. 21.1(3)(c) and (d), the court may dismiss any application filed by the recalcitrant spouse and strike out their pleadings and affidavits.

John Syrtash, *Religion and Culture in Canadian Family Law*
(Toronto: Butterworths, 1992), 161ff.

[According to John Syrtash, these provisions of the statute do not infringe the Charter guarantee of freedom of religion because s. 21.1(4) permits the recalcitrant spouse to file an affidavit indicating "genuine grounds of a religious nature or conscientious nature" for refusing to remove such barriers to remarriage. Syrtash also discussed *G. v. G.*, August 7, 1991, file no. ND 155927/88 (Ont. Ct. (Gen. Div.)), an unreported decision interpreting these provisions.]

[The] court ruled that unless there was a removal of the barriers to the wife's religious remarriage within 15 days after service of a copy of the order by mail upon the husband, the wife could move without notice to the husband to strike all of his pleadings and affidavits. The wife could presumably move for judgment for an amount in child support which is considerably higher than what might have been ordered if the husband would have been in a position to defend his case. Without his pleadings, affidavit and financial statement before the court, it would be difficult to defend himself when his wife alleged what his real income and expenses might be.

   The decision in *G. v. G.* suggests that the recalcitrant spouse must meet a significant test in order to convince the court that he has genuine grounds. Mrs. G.'s counsel provided evidence to the effect that Mr. G. was married by an orthodox Jewish rabbi in a religious ceremony and that presumably he could not consent to marry within the Jewish faith and then object to being divorced within the same faith on "religious grounds." Although Master McBride made no mention of counsel's argument, it is clear that he did not accept the husband's evidence as being sufficient. At the very least, McBride's decision makes it clear that the onus to prove "genuine grounds" is on the spouse who is refusing to consent to removing the impediments, and not on the spouse who requires that the impediments be removed.

Although these provisions were adopted in relation to the Jewish *get*, the language is general and may thus affect other religious practices. In relation to the *get*, it has been suggested that some rabbis in New York have criticized similar legislation in that state on the basis that it might render the *get* less than voluntary, thereby affecting the requirements of Jewish law: see Edwin A. Flak, " 'Get' Law May Promote Invalid Marriage" (May 7, 1993), *The Lawyers Weekly*. In this context, Syrtash suggested (at 5) that it may be prudent for lawyers to consult a rabbi or other expert on Jewish law to ensure that any civil proceedings pursuant to the *Divorce Act* meet these religious requirements.

Some provinces have enacted similar provisions—for example, see Ontario's *Family Law Act*, ss. 56(5), (6), and (7).

The Possibility of Reconciliation

In addition to the above bars to divorce, ss. 9 and 10 of the *Divorce Act* require both lawyers and judges in divorce proceedings to discuss the possibility of reconciliation with the parties; lawyers must also explore possibilities for negotiation or mediation and certify compliance with this requirement before commencing a divorce proceeding. There are some additional amendments to these sections in Bill C-22, some of which are considered in the next section.

Discussion Notes

Section 11(1)(b) and Child Support Guidelines

In circumstances where spouses are not able to agree on the appropriate amount of child support, is the fact that they have agreed to permit a court to decide this issue sufficient to meet the test of "reasonable arrangements for the children" in s. 11(1)(b)? According to *Marinovic v. Marinovic* (1989), 20 RFL (3d) 404 (Ont. SC), the parties have complied with the requirements of s. 11(1)(b): see also James McLeod, "Annotation: Marinovic v. Marinovic" (1989), 20 RFL (3d) 404. A later case reached the opposite conclusion: see *MacLellan v. MacLellan*, [1996] OJ no. 3606 (Ont. Ct. (Gen. Div.)) (QL) and Fodden, at 175. To what extent should the criteria for determining child support pursuant to the guidelines be applied to s. 11(1)(b) in relation to the granting of the divorce application? Is this a matter for discretion on the facts of each case, or should there be a general guideline? You may want to reconsider these issues after considering child support in chapter 8.

Law Reform and Religious Communities

In a comment on Syrtash's arguments in relation to religion and culture for families, especially in relation to children, Shauna Van Praagh addressed the dynamic relationships between families, freedom of religion, and multicultural values in Canada, suggesting that it is important to understand that Orthodox Jewish women are not simply waiting for courts to grant the relief they need; they are also

> [undertaking] political activism within their communities and exerting pressure on not only their ex-husbands but also on the leaders and rabbis who might in turn influence an eventual change in the Jewish norms and practices themselves. The complex interaction between the legal system of the state and that of a community within the state, in the form of carefully researched and worded legislation, will not resolve the problem of the *get* for Jewish women. It may provide a serious signal, however, in addition to the women's voices themselves, that substantive change is required in Jewish law.

(Shauna Van Praagh, "Review" (1993), 38 *McGill Law Journal* 233, at 248-49.)

Does this comment suggest a need for greater connections between communities and law reformers? How should these connections be fostered? Is it appropriate to draft this kind of legislation in neutral (religious and/or gendered) terms? What are the advantages and disadvantages of doing so?

SELECTED REFERENCES

CANADIAN LITERATURE

Christine Davies, *Family Law in Canada* (Scarborough, ON: Carswell, 1984).

Simon Fodden, *Family Law* (Toronto: Irwin Law, 1999).

James MacDonald and Ann Wilton, *The 1999 Annotated Divorce Act* (Scarborough, ON: Carswell, 1998).

D. McKie, B. Prentice, and P. Reed, *Divorce: Law and the Family in Canada* (Ottawa: Statistics Canada, 1983).

J.D. Payne, *Payne on Divorce*, 4th ed. ((Scarborough, ON: Carswell, 1996).

COMPARATIVE LITERATURE

John Eekelaar, *Family Law and Social Policy*, 2d ed. (London: Weidenfeld and Nicolson, 1984).

Austin Sarat and William F. Felstiner, *Divorce Lawyers and Their Clients: Power and Meaning in the Legal Process* (New York: Oxford University Press, 1995).

Shelley Day Sclater and Christine Piper, *Undercurrents of Divorce* (Aldershot, UK: Ashgate Dartmouth, 1999).

Carol Smart, *The Ties That Bind: Law, Marriage, and the Reproduction of Patriarchal Relations* (London: Routledge & Kegan Paul, 1984).

III. THE PROCESSES OF DIVORCE: COURTS, LAWYERS, AND FAMILY LAW BARGAINING

There are many methods for resolving conflict. Some methods are distinguished by their non-adversarial nature. Clients may be involved with more than one method.

> B. Landau, M. Bartoletti, and R. Mesbur, *Family Mediation*
> *Handbook* (Toronto: Butterworths, 1997), 19

Although parties must satisfy the legal requirements in the *Divorce Act* to obtain an order for divorce, and it is necessary to have a court order, it is not necessary to have a trial. Instead, as the above authors noted, the parties may resolve issues relating to their divorce and corollary matters using a variety of processes, including adversarial and non-adversarial methods of dispute resolution. According to these authors, adversarial methods include both litigation and negotiation; by contrast, counselling, conciliation, mediation, and arbitration are characterized as non-adversarial methods of resolving disputes. Although the authors do not include collaborative law processes in their discussion, this new development has been embraced recently by lawyers, in both family law matters and other legal proceedings, as a further option for resolving conflict at divorce.

Yet, in spite of a wide range of processes for decision making, most family law clients choose, if they can, to be represented by lawyers; however, not all family law clients can afford legal services, and legal aid is not always available in family law matters. Whether or not the parties are represented by a lawyer, however, all divorce applications require the approval of a judge, although the current *Divorce Act* permits "desktop" divorces in some uncontested cases. In this way, all divorce processes need to be understood in relation to courts and lawyers, and the ways in which they interact in family law matters.

It appears that well over 90 percent of divorce cases are resolved without a trial. Thus, it is clear that parties must engage in bargaining, and often compromise, to reach a settlement. Moreover, because some corollary issues are ongoing, it may well be necessary for the parties to continue to interact for some years after an order for divorce—thus creating the post-divorce family. In relation to these issues, this section examines arrangements for courts; the role of lawyers and legal aid; and some alternatives to traditional processes of adjudication and negotiation, including an overview of issues concerning family bargaining.

A. Divorce and the Role of Courts

1. Unified Family Courts

One problem for divorce clients is the jurisdiction of courts to hear matters of divorce and corollary relief. The constitution requires that matters of divorce and property be heard by superior courts in the provinces; matters of corollary relief in a divorce action may also be heard by superior courts. However, in the absence of divorce, issues of custody and support are often presented to provincial courts: see Hogg, at 26:15-18. Some of these jurisdictional problems have been alleviated by the creation of Unified Family Courts in a number of Canadian provinces, which have jurisdiction to hear all family matters; the federal government has promised to increase the number of judges in

Unified Family Courts, starting in 2005, as part of its family justice strategy pursuant to Bill C-22: see s. 60. In examining these materials about divorce, and especially corollary relief, consider the advantages of Unified Family Courts for these cases. Are there advantages to specialized courts beyond issues of jurisdiction? Are there any disadvantages of specialized "family courts"?

2. Issues of Reconciliation and Privacy

Pursuant to the *Divorce Act*, judges must inquire (in most cases) about the possibility of reconciliation of the parties: see s. 10. This obligation was first established in the 1968 legislation, although it appears that it is usually satisfied in practice by a rather perfunctory inquiry, a situation that was criticized early on in *Rushton v. Rushton* (1969), 1 RFL 357, at 362-63 (NSSC (TD)): "Most petitioners will simply state that no possibility of reconciliation exists, else why would they be proceeding with the action?"

More controversially, family courts have increasingly had to respond to applications to preserve individual privacy in divorce proceedings, even though there is a general principle of openness of court proceedings: see *Edmonton Journal v. Alberta (AG)*, [1989] 2 SCR 1326. For example, the BC Supreme Court decided, as of September 2002, to modify its practice of posting all family law decisions on its Web site, opting instead to exercise discretion to post only those cases with precedential value and to "de-identify" personal factors not essential to the legal reasons: see Gary Oakes, "BCSC Modifies Plan To Ban Family Law Decisions on Website," *The Lawyers Weekly*, July 19, 2002, at 9, and Cristin Schmitz, "Courts Struggle with Issue of Private Divorces in Public Courts," *The Lawyers Weekly*, March 7, 2003, at 9. What are the arguments in favour of, and against, treating family law proceedings as just the same as other civil matters? Is the solution adopted in British Columbia appropriate? Why, or why not?

3. Efficient Processes and Client Education

As in other kinds of civil actions, family law courts have increasingly attempted to attain efficiency by adopting case management procedures. Both the current *Divorce Act, 1985* and the proposals in Bill C-22 provide for the use of mediation in divorce proceedings; indeed, Bill C-22 clearly evidences a preference for the use of mediation. These proposals confirm the governmental interest in encouraging the settlement of issues in divorce proceedings. In addition, in some provinces, parties have been required to attend educational programs about the divorce process. For example, rule 69.05.1 (*Rules of Civil Procedure*) in Ontario has required (with a few exceptions) that all parties in divorce actions attend mandatory information programs within 45 days after commencing their proceedings; additional steps in their proceedings are precluded until both parties have filed certificates of (separate) attendance at the programs. Similar programs in the United States have focused on improving parenting behaviour and stressed the need for divorcing parents to reduce the impact of conflict on their children. As Eileen D. Biondi reported in the mid-1990s, courts seeking to remedy the effect of divorce on children have benefited from state legislation mandating parental attendance at parent education programs prior to divorce: see Eileen D. Biondi, "Legal Implementation of Parent Education Programs for Divorcing and Separating Parents" (1996), 34:1 *Family and Conciliation Courts Review* 82, at 90.

Such parental education programs are not without controversy. In *Schulp v. Mackoff*, WL 525526 (Illinois Cir. 1994), for example, a court rule mandating such programs for *all* divorcing parents was struck down because it exceeded the legislative provision (permitting such court rules), which required judges to exercise discretion to order such attendance if it was found to be in the best interests of children. Significantly, a study of the content of divorce education programs in the United States revealed that the most intense coverage focused on the needs of children and the impact of parental behaviour on children: see Sanford L. Braver, Peter Salem, Jessica Pearson, and Stephanie R. DeLusé, "The Content of Divorce Education Programs: Results of a Survey" (1996), 34:1 *Family and Conciliation Courts Review* 41, at 52. The authors also reported (at 52-54) that there was moderate coverage of skills and information for parents; according to their research, the least intensive coverage applied to legal issues concerning divorce. As well, they noted that "issues concerning domestic violence receive[d] limited coverage."

Another study focused on the nature of parental education programs at divorce and concluded that skill-based programs, which focus on learning new skills and changing parental behaviours, may be more effective than information-based programs: see Kevin M. Kramer, Jack Arbuthnot, Donald A. Gordon, Nicholas J. Rousis, and Joann Hoza, "Effects of Skill-Based Versus Information-Based Divorce Education Programs on Domestic Violence and Parental Communication" (1998), 36:1 *Family and Conciliation Courts Review* 9. In addition, the authors acknowledged that the impact of divorce education programs on domestic violence was not known. What are the underlying assumptions about these educational programs for parents who are divorcing? What are the goals of such programs? In the study by Kramer and others, for example, the researchers reported that parents who attended such programs litigated less than half as often as non-attending spouses in a two-year period following divorce. How should such results be interpreted? Is it always appropriate to create such access barriers to family courts for clients in divorce actions?

In a study in the United Kingdom, Helen Reece examined the underlying policies of part II of the *Family Law Act, 1996*, legislation that abolished fault-based divorce: see Helen Reece, *Divorcing Responsibly* (Oxford and Portland, OR: Hart Publishing, 2003). In its place, spouses were required to attend information meetings about divorce, to engage in reflection for a period of months (extended for spouses with children), and to consider reconciliation. According to Reece (at 11-12), part II of the Act reflected "the use of divorce law and procedure to ensure that divorcing couples were made to honour their responsibilities to each other." Ultimately, however, Reece reported (at 197) that the government decided not to implement part II, following a trial period, because

> while divorcing couples agreed that they needed educating, they chose different lessons from the ones that the Government was recommending, opting for legal advice rather than mediation or marriage counselling. This was interpreted by the Government as a generalised failure to learn the moral lessons of divorce.

According to Reece (at 237), therefore, part II essentially treated information provision to divorcing parties "as a means of directing rather than informing people's decisions," a coercive governmental role that was rejected by parties seeking divorce.

Consider Reece's comments concerning UK developments in relation to the materials that follow concerning lawyers' roles at divorce and arrangements for divorce bargaining in Canada. How are the "costs of divorce"—for the parties and for governments—linked to issues about legal and other processes for dispute resolution in family law?

B. Lawyers and Legal Representation in Divorce Matters

1. Perceptions of Lawyers and Their Clients

Issues about lawyers in divorce proceedings reflect some of the tensions identified in Reece's study in the United Kingdom. According to Sarat and Felstiner, who observed lawyers and their divorce clients, the lawyers' role often included, for example, "teaching" their clients about the potential and limits of divorce law, particularly in the negotiation of settlements:

> [Lawyers] use and communicate their knowledge of the law and their understanding of the legal process as a resource in educating clients about what is "realistic" in the legal process of divorce. They use this knowledge strategically to move clients toward positions they deem to be reasonable and appropriate.

(Austin Sarat and William L.F. Felstiner, *Divorce Lawyers and Their Clients: Power and Meaning in the Legal Process* (New York: Oxford University Press, 1995), 145.)

Similarly, in a study in the United Kingdom, Christine Piper concluded that family lawyers were largely engaged in an "exercise to create and transfer particular values to the soon to be separated-but-continuing family": see Christine Piper, "How Do You Define a Family Lawyer?" (1999), 19 *Legal Studies* 93, at 106. Such comments reveal how lawyers' interactions with their clients are often crucial to defining issues and resolving disputes.

Moreover, while the image of adversarial litigation remains prominent, the processing of divorce actions more often involves negotiation and compromise within the context of statutory rules and legal principles in reported cases; as two American scholars suggested, divorcing spouses "bargain in the shadow of the law": see R.H. Mnookin and L. Kornhauser, "Bargaining in the Shadow of the Law: The Case of Divorce" (1979), 88 *Yale Law Journal* 950. In fact, as Sarat and Felstiner noted (at 150), there may also be considerable negotiation between lawyers and their own clients (rather than just in relation to the opposing party). Indeed, Sarat and Felstiner argued that the "fit between the legal categories through which lawyers see the world of divorce and the social and personal meanings that divorce holds for most clients is rarely very good." Interestingly, recent empirical studies in the United Kingdom of lawyers' relationships with divorce clients have also identified some differences in client expectation, at least with respect to arrangements for children: see Carol Smart and Bren Neale, *Family Fragments?* (Cambridge: Polity Press, 1999), at 158ff. Thus, the role of lawyers in divorce matters may involve tensions between ideas about divorce as a legal process and its social meaning for their divorcing clients.

2. Mediation and Other Decision-Making Processes

Legislation has increasingly emphasized the importance of achieving settlement for divorcing parents, particularly through the use of mediation. For example, the *Divorce Act, 1985* in Canada, which continued to require lawyers to investigate the possibility of reconciliation of the parties, introduced a new responsibility for lawyers: the obligation to discuss with clients the appropriateness of mediation services (s. 9). This provision of the *Divorce Act* raised expressly the possibility of alternatives to litigation and more traditional processes of negotiation for divorce matters. Moreover, as noted above, Bill C-22 expressly encourages mediation in divorce proceedings.

In recent decades, mediation services have become more widely available, with a range of professionals, including lawyers, involved. In a survey of 500 family mediators in Canada, for example, Edward Kruk reported on practice issues, strategies, and models and concluded that mediation services have become much more diversified in the past decade, moving beyond ideas about structured negotiation and neutrality: see Edward Kruk, "Practice Issues, Strategies, and Models: The Current State of the Art of Family Mediation" (1998), 36:1 *Family and Conciliation Courts Review* 195, at 214-15. In addition, the status of mediation has been enhanced by its recognition in some statutory provisions—for example, Ontario statutes expressly authorize court-ordered mediation in some circumstances: see Ontario's *Children's Law Reform Act*, s. 31(1) and *Family Law Act*, s. 3. As Landau, Bartoletti, and Mesbur argued (at 20-22), mediation offers four advantages to a divorcing couple: it ensures that the decision-making process remains within the clients' control; it avoids the trauma of the trial process; it produces settlements that work better for the parties than court-ordered results; and it assists clients to achieve long-term working relationships, especially with respect to their children.

By contrast, other commentators have pointed to the problems of mediation in family law matters, particularly divorce proceedings. For example, Martha Bailey argued that mediators have frequently failed to provide legal safeguards for clients and, although litigation may be harmful, the delivery of a child into the custody of an abusive parent (as a result of mediation) may be even worse: see Martha Bailey, "Unpacking the 'Rational Alternative': A Critical Review of Family Mediation Movement Claims" (1989), 8 *Canadian Journal of Family Law* 61 and the response by lawyer-mediator Barbara Landau, "Mediation Article Elicits Response" (1990), 9 *Canadian Journal of Family Law* 193. Other critics have argued specifically that mediation is inappropriate where there is evidence of violence or abuse in the family: see Hilary Astor, "Mediation and Violence Against Women" (Canberra: National Committee on Violence Against Women, 1991) and N.Z. Hilton, "Mediating Wife Assault: Battered Women and the 'New Family'" (1991), 9 *Canadian Journal of Family Law* 29. As Astor concluded in her study (at 29), a decision about the usefulness of mediation for clients whose relationships have involved violence is not easy because it involves "complex issues of gender roles in society, of the interrelationship of litigation and alternative methods, of criminal and civil law, of public policy and strategy."

In addition to such concerns, some critics of mediation in divorce proceedings have drawn attention to the propensity of mediation proponents to contrast mediation with litigation. For these critics, the more appropriate comparison is between mediation and traditional negotiation, because the latter process has traditionally been used to settle more than 90 percent of divorce cases; by contrast, only a small percentage have gone to trial. Thus, for example, a study funded by Status of Women Canada adopted the view that "[lawyer-assisted] negotiated agreements are the real comparator for mediated agreements, not litigated outcomes imposed by judges": see Sandra A. Goundry, Yvonne Peters, Rosalind Currie, and National Association of Women and the Law, *Family Mediation in Canada: Implications for Women's Equality* (Ottawa: Status of Women Canada, 1998), 6.

According to this study (at 16-18), the range of dispute resolution methods in divorce proceedings has included litigation, custody and access assessments, negotiation, "kitchen-table negotiations," counselling and therapy, conciliation, arbitration, and mediation. Moreover, the study suggested (at 18) that traditional methods of negotiation might be preferable to mediation because they ensure that bargaining occurs within "the shadow of the law": there are legal parameters for the negotiation and lawyers assist clients in the bargaining process. Particularly in relation to proposals for mandatory mediation (by contrast with voluntary mediation alternatives), the study emphasized (at 67) how the lack of data about private mediation services created problems of empirical assessment and cautioned that support for mediation alternatives should not result in any less support for reforming the family justice system:

> [By] implementing family mediation services, policy-makers and service providers are not relieved of their corresponding responsibility to improve the family justice system for women. ... [There] is a real danger that the current rush to embrace mediation as a panacea will result only in the entrenchment of the same problems that currently plague the court-based family justice system.

3. The Cost of Legal Services: Problems and Panaceas

To some extent, issues about mediation have become intertwined with concerns about the cost of legal services, particularly legal aid services. That is, to the extent that some proponents of mediation have asserted its cost-effectiveness, by contrast with litigation, some government policy makers have expressed enthusiasm for the use of mediators and other non-adversarial processes to reduce funding pressures in relation to courts and legal aid services. Once again, such an approach tends to focus on the efficacy of mediation as an alternative to litigation, rather than by comparison with negotiation, even though the latter is much more usual for the resolution of divorce matters.

As Cossman and Rogerson pointed out in their case study of legal services in family law matters, governmental policies have increasingly focused on negotiation and settlement, as well as mediation, reserving litigation as a process of last resort:

> [There] are ongoing efforts in family law to structure the process so as to promote settlement rather than litigation in recognition of both the inability of the majority of family law clients to bear the high costs of litigation and the higher levels of satisfaction that are likely with a negotiated outcome tailored to the parties' individual circumstances rather than one imposed by a court. The efforts to promote settlement include resort to alternative dispute resolution techniques, such as mediation, and the introduction of systems of case management, including settlement conferences and pre-trials, into family law litigation.

(Brenda Cossman and Carol Rogerson, "Case Study in the Provision of Legal Aid: Family Law," in Ontario Legal Aid Review, *Report of the Ontario Legal Aid Review: A Blueprint for Publicly-Funded Legal Services*, vol. 3 (Toronto: Ontario Legal Aid Review, 1997), 773, at 785.)

In addition to these issues about mediation, concerns have also begun to focus on the use of arbitration tribunals pursuant to Ontario's *Arbitration Act*, SO 1991, c. 17, which authorizes parties to resolve disputes outside the traditional court system. Although Jewish communities have used such arbitration procedures to create *Beis Din*, arbitration tribunals that use Jewish law to resolve civil disputes, a proposal to establish such tribunals within the Muslim community, applying *sharia* law, has attracted concern about both the principles to be applied and the degree of free consent that is available to women in the Muslim community. In June 2004, the Ontario government announced that it will review plans to use Islamic law to settle family disputes: see Caroline Mallan, "Islamic Law Proposal To Undergo Review," *Toronto Star*, June 11, 2004. For additional commentary, see Lynne Cohen, "Inside the Beis Din," *Canadian Lawyer*, May 2000, 27, and Pascale Fournier, "The Erasure of Islamic Difference in Canadian and American Family Law Adjudication" (2001), 10 *Journal of Law and Policy* 51.

Significantly, Cossman and Rogerson also noted (at 785) that many of the systems introduced to promote settlement in family law, such as case management, were also "heavily reliant on the involvement of lawyers to encourage settlement between court appearances." Family law clients typically need legal assistance in reaching settlements; their lawyers are involved in providing advice, preparing documents, and obtaining interim relief, as well as in negotiations to achieve settlement.

At the same time, funding pressures in the 1990s significantly reduced the availability of legal aid services in family law matters in many provinces across Canada and courts and court services were often severely stretched as well. As the Canadian Bar Association's report in 1993 concluded, the lack of resources for family lawyers and their clients in the justice system in Canada caused "real and insoluble problems for family lawyers and their clients": see Canadian Bar Association Task Force on Gender Equality in the Legal Profession, *Touchstones for Change: Equality, Diversity, and Accountability* (Ottawa: Canadian Bar Association, 1993), 208. Noting especially problems of the lack of legal aid resources and of judicial resources, the report asserted (at 203):

> In reviewing the evidence about the practice of family law in Canada, the Task Force found that the reality fell far short of our aspirations and our ideals. Lawyers struggling to provide justice to litigants in this area received little support despite verbal assurances from many levels of government. In the cynical words of one female lawyer, governments provide "all possible aid short of actual help."

In these circumstances, it seems that significant numbers of family law litigants have been unrepresented, a situation that has created difficulties for judges and opposing counsel as well as for the clients: for example, see *Fowler v. Fowler* (1997), 32 RFL (4th) 426 (Ont. Ct. (Gen. Div.)) and Cossman and Rogerson, at 823-27. Several articles recently addressed the problems for lawyers and courts of increasing numbers of self-represented litigants (those who choose not to hire a lawyer) and unrepresented litigants: see D.A. Rollie Thompson, "A Practising Lawyer's Fieldguide to the Self-Represented"

(2001-2), 19 *Canadian Family Law Quarterly* 529 and D.A. Rollie Thompson and Lynn Reierson, "No Lawyer: Institutional Coping with the Self-Represented" (in the same volume), at 455. See also Margaret Trussler, "A Judicial View on Self-Represented Litigants" (in the same volume), at 547.

A number of scholars have argued that the Supreme Court of Canada's decision in *New Brunswick v. G.(J.)*, [1999] 3 SCR 46, which unanimously concluded that the province was constitutionally obliged to provide state-funded counsel for an indigent mother in child-protection proceedings, may provide the basis for extending the right to legal aid services in family law and other proceedings: see Canadian Bar Association, *Report of the Canadian Bar Association, Making the Case: The Right to Publicly-Funded Legal Representation in Canada* (Ottawa: Canadian Bar Association, 2002). In this context, issues about costs in family law proceedings and representation by paralegals have also surfaced: see Cristin Schmitz, "Judge Blasts 'Outrageous' Overcharging in Family Law Cases," *The Lawyers Weekly*, February 28, 2003, at 3, and Cristin Schmitz, "Ontario Judge Clamps Down on Divorce Paralegals," *The Lawyers Weekly*, October 19, 2001, at 9; issues of costs were also reviewed in *Gold v. Gold* (1993), 49 RFL (3d) 56 (BCCA); leave to appeal to the SCC refused.

A number of recent innovations in family law proceedings have tried to respond to such concerns. For example, Alberta established specialized legal aid offices for family law clients, with staff lawyers mandated to provide innovative services that address "the special needs of these clients": see Nicky Brink, "Alberta Launches 4-Year Test of Family-Law Legal Aid Offices," *The Lawyers Weekly*, April 20, 2001, at 20. At about the same time, Ontario introduced new documentary requirements in family proceedings, but they initially created further delays for both lawyers and litigants, especially for unrepresented litigants: see David Gambrill, "New Family Law Forms Not Making Life Simpler," *Law Times*, January 22, 2001, at 1-2.

4. Collaborative Law Processes

On the other hand, where litigants are able to be represented by lawyers, some family lawyers have begun to engage in collaborative law processes. Emerging in the early 1990s as a way of overcoming the problems of adversarial negotiations, collaborative law processes require lawyers and their clients to work together to achieve "an efficient, fair, comprehensive settlement" in relation to divorce: see Pauline H. Tesler, "Collaborative Law: What It Is and Why Family Law Attorneys Need To Know About It" (1999), 13 *American Journal of Family Law* 215, at 219. According to Tesler (at 219), collaborative law represents a new paradigm:

> Collaborative law consists of two clients and two attorneys, working together. ... Each party selects independent collaborative counsel. Each lawyer's retainer agreement specifies that the lawyer is retained solely to assist the client in reaching a fair settlement and that under no circumstances will the lawyer represent the client if the matter goes to court. If the process fails to reach agreement, ... both collaborative attorneys are disqualified from further representation. ... Experts are brought into the collaborative process as needed, but only as neutrals, jointly retained by both parties [and they are also disqualified from

assisting either party if court action is initiated]. The process involves binding commitments to disclose voluntarily all relevant information, to proceed respectfully and in good faith, and to refrain from any threat of litigation during the collaborative process.

According to some reports, collaborative law is most attractive to senior family lawyers who have experienced the problems of traditional family law negotiations for many years: see Peter Bakogeorge, "Collaborative Law Gives 'Huge' Job Satisfaction" (March 17, 2003), *Law Times*, at 12. Although special training is required for lawyers who wish to engage in collaborative law processes, there are increasing numbers of lawyers qualified to work in this way. At the same time, not all family law cases are suitable for collaborative law processes—"if a case is precedent-setting, or if the clients are at risk of harm, a traditional process will likely be preferable": see Barbara Landau, "Collaborative Family Law: An Oxymoron or a Stroke of Genius?" (March 2001), *ADR Forum* 1, at 3. Some of these issues for collaborative law are also relevant to the discussion of family law bargaining in the next section.

Discussion Notes

Legal Challenges for Family Law

As these different developments in the roles of family lawyers reveal, there are significant challenges in providing legal representation in family law proceedings. These include legal aid funding, the scope for mediation services, tensions in traditional negotiation relationships, and the need for training to engage in collaborative law processes. As Cossman and Rogerson (at 843-44) concluded, legal representation in family law matters (both in court proceedings and in other contexts) is complex:

> Family law needs are complex, multidimensional, and extremely widespread. There is no way to finesse the fact that family law problems are legal problems and need legal assistance [but] there is no magical solution or blueprint to this complex set of social problems.

Recall the comments at the beginning of this chapter about the state's role in divorce decisions—to what extent would "delegalizing" divorce (that is, allowing couples to divorce "on consent") reduce the need for legal representation? Would it alter the need for a range of different methods of dispute resolution? In this context, consider as well the issues about family law bargaining in the next section.

New Brunswick v. G.(J.)

In *New Brunswick v. G.(J.)*, above, the Supreme Court formulated the test for provision of state-funded counsel for an indigent mother in child-protection proceedings; according to the court, state-funded counsel was required, having regard to (1) the seriousness of the interests at stake, (2) the complexity of the proceedings, and (3) the capacities of the litigant. The court concluded that there was an infringement of "security of the person" pursuant to s. 7 of the Charter and that fundamental justice required the provision of state-funded counsel. Significantly, the majority judgment declared that this remedy was necessary in the "unusual circumstances" of this case; by contrast, the concurring judgment suggested (at para. 125) that "trial judges should not ... consider the issue from the starting point that counsel will be necessary to ensure a fair hearing only in rare cases." In thinking about the test in relation to family law proceedings, other than child-protection matters, consider the suggestion that "security of the person" may be affected by any disparity of power between the parties, whether because the state is one party (as in *G.(J.)*) or because of different levels of access to resources (for example, by husbands and wives): see David Dyzenhaus, "Normative Justifications for the Provision of Legal Aid," in Ontario Legal Aid Review, *Report of the Ontario Legal Aid Review: A Blueprint for Publicly-Funded Legal Services*, vol. 2 (Toronto: Ontario Legal Aid Review, 1997), at 475.

Family Lawyering and Specialized Skills

To what extent do family law judges and lawyers require specialized education? According to Pauline Tesler (at 216), for example, most legal professionals have studied contracts and civil procedure as well as family law; some may have had courses in negotiation and mediation. But few have studied "the psychodynamics of the divorce process and of family breakdown and restructuring." As a result, lawyers may not understand how to incorporate the reality of divorce experiences into the legal process. Assuming that this criticism is appropriate, how should this problem be addressed in legal education?

SELECTED REFERENCES

Hilary Astor, "The Weight of Silence: Talking About Violence in Family Mediation," in Margaret Thornton, ed., *Public and Private: Feminist Legal Debates* (Melbourne: Oxford University Press, 1995).

Anne Bottomley, "What Is Happening to Family Law? A Feminist Critique of Conciliation," in Julia Brophy and Carol Smart, eds., *Women in Law: Explorations in Law, Family, and Sexuality* (London: Routledge & Kegan Paul, 1985).

Trina Grillo, "The Mediation Alternative: Process Dangers for Women" (1991), 100 *Yale Law Journal* 217.

Carla Hotel and Joan Brockman, "The Conciliatory-Adversarial Continuum in Family Law Practice" (1994), 12 *Canadian Journal of Family Law* 11.

Joan B. Kelly, "A Decade of Divorce Mediation Research" (1996), 34:3 *Family and Conciliation Courts Review* 373.

Rosanna Langer, "The Juridification and Technicisation of Alternative Dispute Resolution Practices" (1998), 13 *Canadian Journal of Law and Society* 169.

James McLeod, ed., *Family Dispute Resolution: Litigation and Its Alternatives* (Scarborough, ON: Carswell, 1987).

M.J. Mossman, "Gender, Equality, and Legal Aid Services" (1993), 15 *Sydney Law Review* 30.

_____, "Gender Equality, Family Law, and Access to Justice" (1994), *International Journal of Law and the Family* 357.

Forrest S. Mosten, "Emerging Roles of the Family Lawyer" (1995), 33:2 *Family and Conciliation Courts Review* 213.

Ruth Phegan, "The Family Mediation System: An Art of Distributions" (1995), 40 *McGill Law Journal* 365.

Austin Sarat and William F. Felstiner, "Law and Strategy in the Divorce Lawyer's Office" (1986), 20 *Law & Society Review* 93.

Rick Shields, Judith Ryan, and Victoria L. Smith, *Collaborative Family Law: Another Way To Resolve Family Disputes* (Toronto: Thomson Carswell, 2003).

Pauline H. Tesler, *Collaborative Law: Achieving Effective Resolution in Divorce Without Litigation* (Chicago: ABA Publications, 2001).

C. Family Bargaining at Separation or Divorce

> Students of negotiation seem to have begun to realize that negotiation processes were more complex than just mastering a number of simple strategies. The negotiator's objectives could be to "win" or to satisfy the underlying interests of the parties, or to achieve the most efficient or most just solution. And depending on what the objectives were, behaviour might have to be modified to achieve the outcome desired.
>
> > Carrie Menkel-Meadow, "Legal Negotiation: A Study of Strategies in Search of a Theory" (1983), *American Bar Foundation Research Journal* 905, at 936

In the family law context, negotiations frequently involve diverse and complicated objectives. Yet, many more divorce matters are settled by negotiation than at trial, and negotiation skills are at the heart of other processes such as mediation and collaborative law. As a result, the bargaining process is fundamental to proceedings about divorce, perhaps especially in relation to matters of corollary relief. This section briefly examines some issues of family law bargaining in relation to the creation of negotiated agreements between married spouses or cohabitees. Further issues about variation of these agreements are considered in chapter 7, because these issues have most often arisen in conjunction with claims about spousal support.

1. The History of Spousal Contracts

Although equitable settlements were often drafted by wealthy fathers in the 18th and 19th centuries, prior to *Married Women's Property Acts*, these settlements were not regarded as marriage contracts at common law. Moreover, contracts between spouses respecting marriage breakdown were traditionally regarded as contrary to public policy and unenforceable. Thus, for example, in *Balfour v. Balfour*, [1919] 2 KB 571 (Eng. CA), when a wife sought to enforce an agreement in which her husband had agreed to provide her with £30 per week in maintenance, Lord Atkin stated (at 578-79):

> To my mind those agreements, or many of them, do not result in contracts at all ... [They] are not contracts because the parties did not intend that they should be attended by legal consequences. ... [The] Courts of this country would have to be multiplied one-hundredfold if these arrangements were held to result in legal obligations. They are not sued upon, not because the parties are reluctant to enforce their legal rights when the agreement is broken, but because the parties, in the inception of the arrangements, never intended that they

should be sued upon. Agreements such as these are outside the realm of contracts altogether. The common law does not regulate the form of agreements between spouses.

In spite of these traditional views, provincial family law reform statutes enacted after the *Divorce Act* of 1968 provided for the enforceability of "domestic contracts" between married and opposite-sex spouses: for example, see Ontario's *Family Law Act*, part IV. Moreover, as a result of the Supreme Court of Canada's decision in *M. v. H.*, [1999] 2 SCR 3, the benefit of these provisions was extended to same-sex cohabitees as well: see *Amendments Because of the Supreme Court of Canada Decision in M. v. H. Act*, SO 1999, c. 6. Section 2(10) of the *Family Law Act* provides that "a domestic contract dealing with a matter that is also dealt with in this Act prevails unless this Act provides otherwise." In this way, the negotiated agreements of spouses, married or cohabiting, have been accorded substantial authority under provincial statutory regimes.

2. Contracts Relating to Marriage and Cohabitation

Although it may seem ironic to discuss marriage contracts (or cohabitation agreements) in the context of divorce (or separation), it seems that the validity or enforceability of these contracts has often arisen in practice at the time of marriage breakdown or separation. More specifically, a spouse may seek to set aside or vary the terms of such an agreement as part of the negotiation of issues about corollary relief at divorce. What principles should apply to determine the enforceability of marriage contracts?

Hartshorne v. Hartshorne
(2004), 236 DLR (4th) 193 (SCC)

[The parties began to live together in 1985; their first child was born in July 1987. They married in March 1989; their second child was born in November 1989. They separated in 1998 after nine years of marriage. The wife claimed entitlement to property and spousal support pursuant to BC's *Family Relations Act*, RSBC 1996, c. 128, while the husband argued that the pre-nuptial agreement, signed by the parties on their wedding day and by which the wife's potential claims were expressly limited, prevented the application of the provincial legislative regime. At the time of the marriage, the husband had significant assets while the wife had few assets and some significant debts.

The marriage was a second marriage for both parties. The husband gave evidence that his willingness to marry a second time depended on the parties' agreeing to a contract; in the event of marriage breakdown, he did not want to have to share his assets, as he had been required to do in his earlier divorce proceedings. Both the husband and the wife were lawyers; the wife had obtained independent legal advice about the proposed contract. In part, the legal advice suggested that the agreement was "grossly unfair" and advised the wife not to sign it. Nonetheless, both parties signed the agreement, which included an acknowledgment that the wife was doing so at the insistence of the husband and not voluntarily. Although the wife remained out of the workforce from 1987 to 1998, the parties maintained separate financial accounts, with the husband providing a monthly amount to the wife to meet her needs. Based on the husband's income, the parties enjoyed a generous lifestyle.

The wife's claims included custody of the children, spousal and child support, and a share of the husband's property, contrary to the terms of the agreement. After reviewing the circumstances of the signing of the agreement, which occurred between the wedding ceremony and the celebratory dinner, the trial judge concluded, at para. 46, that the evidence did not establish that the agreement was unconscionable or that it was entered into under duress, coercion, or undue influence, even though there was evidence that the wife was visibly upset at the time that she signed it. However, the trial judge concluded that the wife was entitled to share property owned by the husband because the pre-nuptial agreement was unfair according to the terms of s. 65 of the *Family Relations Act*: [1999] BCJ no. 2861 (SC) (QL) and additional reasons at (2001), 89 BCLR (3d) 110 (SC).

Section 65 expressly authorizes a court to reapportion property where a marriage agreement "would be unfair" having regard to a number of factors. According to the trial judge (at para. 57), several factors were relevant; these included the duration of the marriage, the fact that most of the husband's property had been acquired prior to this marriage, the needs of the wife to become economically independent and self-sufficient, and the impact of her role in home and child-care responsibilities in permitting the husband to concentrate on improving his law practice. Overall, the trial judge concluded (at para. 59) that the agreement was unfair and thus exercised the authority in s. 65 to reapportion some assets. According to the Supreme Court of Canada, the result of reapportionment meant that the wife received about 46 percent of the family assets; by contrast, she would have received about 20 percent pursuant to the agreement: 2004 SCC 22, at para. 25. A majority of the BC Court of Appeal, Thackray JA dissenting, dismissed the appeal: (2002), 6 BCLR (4th) 250; 2002 BCCA 587.

The Supreme Court of Canada released its decision in *Hartshorne*, with respect to marriage agreements, after its earlier consideration of the principles applicable to separation agreements in *Miglin v. Miglin*, [2003] 1 SCR 303; 2003 SCC 24. In both cases, the Supreme Court addressed the balancing of parties' interests in finality and autonomy with the need to promote goals of fairness for the spouses at divorce or separation. *Miglin* is reviewed in more detail in chapter 7 (in relation to spousal support and separation agreements). However, some comments in *Hartshorne* about bargaining in the family context provide a useful introduction to these issues here. Note, in particular, the range of provincial statutory tests for judicial intervention in private agreements—in relation to the court's conclusion that there was no basis for intervention pursuant to the BC statute, consider whether there is any role for judicial intervention in other provinces.

Three judges dissented (Le Bel, Deschamps, and Binnie JJ) from the majority judgment of Bastarache J. Consider their views with respect to the applicability of contractual principles and norms to the context of family bargaining.]

BASTARACHE J: ... Domestic contracts are explicitly permitted by the matrimonial property regime in British Columbia. They allow spouses to substitute a consensual regime for the statutory regime that would otherwise be imposed on them. Domestic contracts are, however, like the statutory regime itself, subject to judicial intervention when provisions for the division of property which they contain are found to be unfair at the time of distribution, after considering the various factors enumerated in s. 65 of the *Family Relations Act.* ...

At issue in this appeal is whether a marriage agreement respecting the division of property, entered into after receiving independent legal advice, without duress, coercion or undue influence, can later be found to be unfair and set aside on the basis that it failed "to provide anything for the respondent's sacrifice in giving up her law practice and postponing her career development," notwithstanding that the parties' agreement preserved the right to spousal support. The parties in this appeal also raised the issues of whether an agreement entered into prior to or at the time of marriage should be subject to the same review on appeal as a separation agreement, and whether, where provisions for the division of property in a marriage agreement are found to be unfair at the time of distribution, the whole agreement should simply be ignored. ...

The authorities generally agree that courts should respect private arrangements that spouses make for the division of their property on the breakdown of their relationship. This is particularly so where the agreement in question was negotiated with independent legal advice. The difficulty of course is in determining the proper approach to deciding, at the time of distribution, what is fair under the terms of s. 65 of the FRA. A domestic contract constituting a derogation from the statutory regime, it is obvious that its fairness cannot be determined simply on the basis of its consist–ency with the said regime. In fact, s. 65(1) also provides for judicial reapportionment on the basis of fairness in the case of the statutory regime in s. 56(2). The appellant in these proceedings argues that the majority of the Court of Appeal effectively found the Agreement to be unfair on the basis that it derogated from the statutory regime. After reviewing the provisions of the FRA as well as the Agreement, it is my opinion that said Agreement operated fairly at the time of distribution. ...

Most of the provinces provide for judicial oversight of marriage agreements. For example, s. 56(4) of Ontario's *Family Law Act*, RSO 1990, c. F3, permits a court to set aside a domestic contract or a provision thereof if a party failed to disclose significant assets or liabilities, if a party did not understand the nature or consequences of the contract, or otherwise, in accordance with the law of contract. See also *Family Law Act*, RSNL 1990, c. F-2, s. 66(4); *Family Law Act*, SPEI 1995, c. 12, s. 55(4), for this language. The threshold in Nova Scotia is a finding that any term is "unconscionable, unduly harsh on one party or fraudulent": see *Matrimonial Property Act*, RSNS 1989, c. 275, s. 29. Saskatchewan allows a court to redistribute property where an interspousal contract was unconscionable or grossly unfair at the time it was entered into: see *Family Property Act*, SS 1997, c. F-6.3, s. 24(2). New Brunswick permits a court to disregard a provision of a domestic contract where a spouse did not receive independent legal advice and application of the provision would be inequitable: see *Marital Property Act*, SNB 1980, c. M-1.1, s. 41. By contrast, in British Columbia, as earlier noted, a court may reapportion assets upon finding that to divide the property as provided for in the agreement or the FRA would be "unfair." Clearly, the statutory scheme in British Columbia sets a lower threshold for judicial intervention than do the schemes in other provinces. ...

[Bastarache J reviewed the purpose of the *Family Relations Act*, concluding that the primary policy objective in relation to division of property was fairness, and continued:]

To give effect to legislative intention, courts must encourage parties to enter into marriage agreements that are fair, and to respond to the changing circumstances of their marriage by reviewing and revising their own contracts for fairness when necessary. Conversely, in a framework within which private parties are permitted to take personal responsibility for their financial well-being upon the dissolution of marriage, courts should be reluctant to second-guess the arrangement on which they reasonably expected to rely. Individuals may choose to structure their affairs in a number of different ways, and it is their prerogative to do so: see generally *Nova Scotia (Attorney General) v. Walsh*, [2002] 4 SCR 325, 2002 SCC 83. ...

Marriage Agreements Versus Separation Agreements

Marital cases must reconcile respect for the parties' intent, on the one hand, and the assurance of an equitable result, on the other. The parties here adopted opposite views as to the degree of deference to be afforded marriage agreements; the appellant submitted that more and the respondent submitted that less deference should be paid to marriage agreements than to separation agreements.

This Court has not established, and in my opinion should not establish, a "hard and fast" rule regarding the deference to be afforded to marriage agreements as compared to separation agreements. In some cases, marriage agreements ought to be accorded a greater degree of deference than separation agreements. Marriage agreements define the parties' expectations from the outset, usually before any rights are vested and before any entitlement arises. Often, perhaps most often, a desire to protect pre-acquired assets or an anticipated inheritance for children of a previous marriage will be the impetus for such an agreement. Separation agreements, by contrast, purport to deal with existing or vested rights and obligations, with the aggrieved party claiming he or she had given up something to which he or she was already entitled with an unfair result. In other cases, however, marriage agreements may be accorded less deference than separation agreements. The reason for this is that marriage agreements are anticipatory and may not fairly take into account the financial means, needs or other circumstances of the parties at the time of marriage breakdown. ...

Miglin v. Miglin and the Issue of Deference

In addressing the issue of deference, this Court may apply *Miglin v. Miglin*, [2003] 1 SCR 303, 2003 SCC 24, for its general legal proposition that some weight should be given to marriage agreements. ...

[Bastarache J reviewed the decision in *Miglin*, and the two-stage approach it adopted. He looked first to the circumstances of the negotiation to determine whether one party took advantage of the other's vulnerability or if the substance of the agreement failed to comply with the goals of the *Divorce Act*. He next sought to determine whether the agreement, viewed from the time of the application to review, still reflected the intentions of the parties and was still in compliance with the objectives of the Act. After considering *Miglin*, however, Bastarache J concluded that the court in this case was required to follow the structure provided by the BC statute. Thus, in interpreting s. 65, he held (at para. 43):]

The court must determine whether the marriage agreement is substantively fair when the application for reapportionment is made. The essence of this inquiry is whether the circumstances of the parties at the time of separation were within the reasonable contemplation of the parties at the time the agreement was formed, and, if so, whether at that time the parties made adequate arrangements in response to these anticipated circumstances. ...

Thus, the determination that a marriage agreement operates fairly or unfairly at the time of distribution cannot be made without regard to the parties' perspectives. A contract governing the distribution of property between spouses reflects what the parties believed to be fair at the time the contract was formed (presuming the absence of duress, coercion, and undue influence). The parties would usually not be expected to deal with their present situation without any consideration of how they expect their situation will evolve over time. If the parties' lives unfold in precisely the manner they had contemplated at the time of contract formation, then a finding that the contract operates unfairly at the time of distribution constitutes, in essence, a substitution of the parties' notion of fairness with the court's notion of fairness, providing that nothing else would suggest that the parties did not really consider the impact of their decision in a rational and comprehensive way. Thus, central to any analysis under s. 65(1) of the FRA is consideration of how accurately the parties predicted, at the time of contract formation, their actual circumstances at the time of distribution, whether they truly considered the impact of their decision and whether they adjusted their agreement during the marriage to meet the demands of a situation different from the one expected, either because the circumstances were different or simply because implications were inadequately addressed or proved to be unrealistic.

... At the time of the triggering event, both the financial and domestic arrangements between the appellant and the respondent were unfolding just as the parties had expected. With respect to their financial arrangement, they were living out their intention to "remain completely independent of the other with regard to their own property, both real and personal." There was no commingling of funds, there were no joint accounts of significant value, and the assets that the appellant brought into the marriage remained in his name. On a personal level, as planned, the appellant and respondent had a second child and, as decided by the respondent, she did not resume her position at the law firm but remained at home to raise their two children.

Where, as in the present case, the parties have anticipated with accuracy their personal and financial circumstances at the time of distribution, and where they have truly considered the impact of their choices, then, without more, a finding that their Agreement operates unfairly should not be made lightly. This does not mean that no attention should be given to the possible deficit in the assets and future income of the spouse who chose to stay at home and facilitate the professional development of the other spouse, compared to what they would realistically have been otherwise. Section 65 mandates as much. A fair distribution of assets must of course take into account sacrifices made and their impact, the situation of the parties at the time of distribution, their age, education and true capacity to reintegrate into the work force and achieve economic independence in particular. But this must be done in light of the personal choices made and of the overall situation considering all property rights under the marriage agreement and other entitlements. In the present case, the main feature of the Agreement was the desire that each spouse retain the assets earned before the marriage, sharing equitably assets acquired afterwards being the rule. This will be fair on dissolution of the marriage if Mrs. Hartshorne is not left without means and facing true hardship in reclaiming her professional status and income, in light also of her parental obligations. Consideration must be given to the actual situation as it unfolded. ...

The ultimate point then is this: in determining whether a marriage agreement operates unfairly, a court must first apply the agreement. In particular, the court must assess and award those financial entitlements provided to each spouse under the agreement, and other entitlements from all other sources, including spousal and child support. The court must then, in consideration of those factors listed in s. 65(1) of the FRA, make a determination as to whether the contract operates unfairly. At this second stage, consideration must be given to the parties' personal and financial circumstances, and in particular to the manner in which these circumstances evolved over time. Where the current circumstances were within the contemplation of the parties at the time the Agreement was formed, and where their Agreement and circumstances surrounding it reflect consideration and response to these circumstances, then the plaintiff's burden to establish unfairness is heavier. Thus, consideration of the factors listed in s. 65(1) of the FRA, taken together, would have to reveal that the economic consequences of the marriage breakdown were not shared equitably in all of the circumstances. This approach, in my view, accords with the underlying principle of the FRA, striking an appropriate balance between deference to the parties' intentions, on the one hand, and assurance of an equitable result, on the other. ...

[Bastarache J then considered the factors in s. 65 and the relationship between the wife's entitlement to spousal support pursuant to the agreement and its potential to enable her to become independent and self-sufficient. He concluded (at para. 57) that spousal support was sufficient to meet these needs and that it would "continue the financial arrangement they lived out during the relationship." After examining the factors in s. 65, he stated (at para. 58):]

It is highly significant that the Agreement explicitly preserves a right to spousal support and that ... the appellant has a healthy and continuous flow of income. In looking at the division of property under the Agreement, Beames J should have assessed fairness in light of the preservation of a right to spousal support. Only after determining that the factors of self-sufficiency and need could not be met through an order of spousal support, should the trial judge have concluded that the Agreement operated unfairly.

[Bastarache J also examined (at paras. 60ff.) the role of independent legal advice provided to the wife prior to her signing the agreement:]

Independent legal advice at the time of negotiation is an important means of ensuring an informed decision to enter an agreement. In the case at bar, the respondent's lawyer prepared a written legal opinion for her. In that opinion letter, the lawyer: (1) confirmed that the respondent was in agreement with the principle that the appellant would retain ownership of the assets which he acquired prior to the relationship, but that she wished that any agreement be fair to both parties and to any children born of the marriage; (2) concluded that the Agreement proposed by the appellant was "grossly unfair"; (3) advised the respondent that, in the event that the marriage broke down, under the FRA she would have a *prima facie* right to an undivided one-half interest in all family assets, which would include any matrimonial home, furnishings, vehicles, savings and pensions; (4) informed the respondent that the Agreement was such that she would not "earn" even close to a one-half interest in the matrimonial home unless the marriage continued for approximately 20 years; (5) advised the respondent that "a Court would easily find such provision to be unfair and would intervene to redistribute the property on a more equitable basis"; (6) strongly recommended that the respondent not execute the Agreement "in its present form"; (7) recommended that in order to achieve a more fair result and yet still satisfy the desires of the appellant to retain the majority of his property separately, that the following assets remain the appellant's separate property—(a) bank deposits or securities, (b) the apartment at Osoyoos, (c) the Oroville lot, (d) interest in law firm and management company, (e) the 1969 Mercedes, (f) the boat, and (g) the motorcycle; and (8) strongly recommended that any agreement which the respondent executes makes it clear that there is nothing to bar any claim for maintenance or support for herself or for any children of the marriage.

It is clear from the detail in this opinion letter that the respondent was forewarned of the Agreement's "shortcomings." Indeed, the respondent made a few changes to the Agreement in response to her lawyer's advice, including the inclusion of the preservation of spousal support clause. The respondent was advised that the Agreement was "grossly unfair" and that a court would "easily find" the provision relating to interest in the matrimonial home to be unfair and would redistribute the property on a more equitable basis. Despite this advice, or because of it, as expressed by counsel for the respondent during the hearing before our Court, the respondent signed the Agreement. The respondent cannot now rely on her lawyer's opinion to support her allegation that because she thought the Agreement was unfair from its inception, for all intents and purposes, she never intended to live up to her end of the bargain. It is trite that a party could never be allowed to avoid his or her contractual obligations on the basis that he or she believed, from the moment of its formation, that the contract was void or unenforceable. ...

[Bastarache J reviewed the substantial assets brought into the marriage by the husband and the debts of the wife at that time, and then decided that the agreement was fair in accordance with s. 65 of the *Family Relations Act*:]

[By] signing the Agreement, the appellant and the respondent entered their marriage with certain expectations on which they were reasonably entitled to rely. If the respondent truly believed that the Agreement was unacceptable at that time, she should not have signed it. In this case, the intention of the parties, as expressed in the Agreement, was to leave with each party that which he or she had before the marriage. The question is not whether there is something fundamentally unfair about that, but whether the operation of the Agreement will prove to be unfair in the circumstances present at the time of distribution. In light of the provisions of the FRA, and after examining all of the provisions of the Agreement as well as the circumstances of the parties at the time of separation, it is my opinion that the Agreement was fair at the time of the triggering event. The trial judge erred in finding otherwise. The Agreement should be left intact. ...

Once an agreement has been reached, albeit a marriage agreement, the parties thereto are expected to fulfill the obligations that they have undertaken. A party cannot simply later state that he or she did not intend to live up to his or her end of the bargain. It is true that, in some cases, agreements that appear to be fair at the time of execution may become unfair at the time of the triggering event, depending on how the lives of the parties have unfolded. It is also clear that the FRA permits a court, upon application, to find that an agreement or the statutory regime is unfair and to reapportion the assets. However, in a framework within which private parties are permitted to take personal responsibility for their financial well-being upon the dissolution of marriage, courts should be reluctant to second-guess their initiative and arrangement, particularly where independent legal advice has been obtained. They should not conclude that unfairness is proven simply by demonstrating that the marriage agreement deviates from the statutory matrimonial property regime. Fairness must first take into account what was within the realistic contemplation of the parties, what attention they gave to changes in circumstances or unrealized implications, then what are their true circumstances, and whether the discrepancy is such, given the s. 65 factors, that a different apportionment should be made. ...

DESCHAMPS J (dissenting): Contrary to what was argued before us by the appellant, this appeal is *not* about whether two people can enter into a prenuptial arrangement which will determine, or even influence, the division of family assets upon their separation. Rather, this case is about giving effect to the explicit legislative intention that only fair agreements be upheld. Furthermore, to construe the issue in the way suggested by the majority presupposes that even unfair agreements will be given weight. With respect, I have reached a different conclusion.

The primary policy objective guiding the courts' role in division of assets on marital breakdown in British Columbia is fairness, regardless of whether the presumptive entitlement arises statutorily or through contract. The *Family Relations Act* ... does permit couples to sign marriage agreements on division of assets. However, to be enforceable, any such agreement must be fair; if it is not, it will be judicially reapportioned to achieve a fair division. To give effect to legislative intention, courts ought to encourage parties to enter into marriage agreements that are fair, and to respond to the changing circumstances of their marriage by reviewing and revising their own contracts for fairness over time. Telling parties that their unfair apportionment will nonetheless be given weight as a factor in reapportionment would defeat this objective.

[Deschamps J reviewed the obligation of appellate courts to defer to the trier of fact; he also reviewed the extensive litigation involved in this case over a period of years. In the end, she concluded that the husband should not be required to share his interest in his law practice, even though it was a family asset, but that in other respects, the decisions of the lower courts were appropriate. She also reviewed *Miglin* and the legislation in other provinces to argue (at paras. 74ff.) that the BC statute recognized a lower threshold for judicial intervention and was therefore appropriate for the court to order reapportionment in this case pursuant to s. 65:]

Many other jurisdictions provide for judicial oversight of the provisions of marriage agreements. The standard of review applicable in British Columbia can be better understood when compared with the schemes of other Canadian provinces. As recognized in *Property Rights on Marriage Breakdown*, Law Reform Commission of British Columbia's Working Paper No. 63 (1989), at p. 34, fn. 1:

> All Canadian common law provinces provide the courts with jurisdiction to depart from equal sharing, but British Columbia is the only province to define that jurisdiction by use of a general term with no fixed legal meaning. All other Canadian common law provinces use technical terms which indicate that the level of unfairness must be significant.

British Columbia's legislative choice to provide for a different, less restrictive, standard ought to be recognized by the courts.

The threshold in Nova Scotia is a finding that any term is *"unconscionable*, unduly harsh on one party or fraudulent"* (emphasis added): see *Matrimonial Property Act*, RSNS 1989, c. 275, s. 29. In New Brunswick a court may disregard a provision of a domestic contract where a spouse did not receive independent legal advice *and* application of the provision would be inequitable: see *Marital Property Act*, SNB 1980, c. M-1.1, s. 41. In Saskatchewan a court may reapportion property where a marriage contract was *unconscionable* or *grossly unfair* at the time it was entered into: see *Family Property Act*, SS 1997, c. F-6.3, s. 24(2). Ontario's *Family Law Act*, RSO 1990, c. F.3, allows a court, on application, to set aside a domestic contract or a provision if a party failed to disclose significant assets or liabilities, if a party did not understand the nature or consequences of the contract, or otherwise in accordance with the law of contract (s. 56(4)). Such restrictive language is also found in Newfoundland's *Family Law Act*, RSN 1990, c. F-2, s. 66(4), and in Prince Edward Island's *Family Law Act*, SPEI 1995, c. 12, s. 55(4). In contrast, British Columbia courts have been explicitly empowered to reapportion assets upon finding that the division of property in the agreement is "unfair." This is clearly a less deferential standard than what is required in other jurisdictions, and it should not mechanically be assimilated to a more exacting standard, such as unconscionability.

Courts must defer to this legislative choice and respect the lower threshold, as is now well established in British Columbia. ...

[Thus, according to Deschamps J (at para. 77):]

I believe that the deciding inquiry under s. 65(1) of the FRA is whether or not the agreement is *substantively fair at the time of application to the court* [emphasis in DLR]. ... Thus, under the FRA, the judge must review the fairness of the marriage agreement at the time of application to the court, considering the parties' rights, entitlements and obligations at that very moment, in light of the s. 65(1) factors. The legislation, both in its specific wording and taken as a whole, does not indicate otherwise. It is also clear from the nature of marriage agreements that their fairness only genuinely matters when they are invoked before a court. Finally, a judge can only review the fairness of such a prenuptial arrangement by considering it alongside the other conditions of separation covered by the FRA. These include custody as well as potential maintenance and support orders. This will only be feasible after an application has been made to the court.

What does fairness at the time of application to the court entail? Although the statutory regime provides for equal sharing, it is only a starting point, just as it is for marriage agreements. Fairness will not always be synonymous with equal division. In some marriages, the contributions of each spouse will not be equal. For example, one party may come into the marriage substantially wealthier, in an economic sense, than the other; the marriage may be very brief, indicating that an equal partnership never really came into being; or, a party may have transferred ownership of valuable personal assets. The various factors set out in s. 65(1) of the FRA reflect this reality. I believe the proper approach to determining whether a division of family assets under a marriage agreement is fair is for a judge to assess the division in light of the s. 65(1) factors. The original intention of the parties is relevant insofar as it points the court towards how the parties chose to address the requirements of fairness. If the parties fairly addressed the enumerated factors through other provisions in the agreement, that should be taken into account. That being said, the parties' original intention is not determinative at this stage. Fairness is a concept that is independent of any agreement. If a court establishes that a marriage agreement is fair in light of the s. 65(1) factors, it will stand. If it is not, the court will redress it. For greater certainty, a judge redressing the unfairness resulting from a marriage agreement may want to test the result of his or her s. 65(1) reapportionment by comparing it to the division the judge would have established had there been no agreement. Since the criteria are the same, the share apportioned to each spouse should be similar whether there is a contract or not. ...

Unlike s. 15.2(4)(c) of the *Divorce Act*, which was in issue in *Miglin, supra*, which requires courts to take into consideration "any order, agreement or arrangement relating to support of either spouse," s. 65(1) makes no mention of the agreement in the list of factors for courts to consider when assessing the *substantive* fairness of a division of assets. Consideration of the marriage agreement is not even implicitly alluded to. This is not surprising given that what is under review is the agreement itself. It would be a useless exercise if the fairness test were to be based on an unfair agreement. Thus, in British Columbia, spouses may not seek to rely on unfair provisions for the division of assets on marital breakdown. Those are the bounds of meaningful choice for spouses in that province.

Public policy supports this conclusion. The approach favoured by the majority would fail to encourage spouses to make genuine efforts to conclude fair agreements (and to update them for fairness as circumstances change), if a potentially intransigent party could tell himself or herself: "This may turn out to be unfair, but at least a court would still take it into account." In this case, the appellant testified that, on being informed that the respondent's lawyer considered the agreement "grossly unfair," he considered it "interesting," but refused to make substantive changes to render the agreement fair. Parties have many fair options about how to arrange their affairs and protect particular assets, and they need an incentive to consider them and take them seriously.

Moreover, with regard to assessing fairness, the original intentions of the parties may be particularly problematic in the case of premarital agreements, often executed years prior to separation. Most people enter into a marriage hoping that it will succeed, and their cost–benefit analysis before execution may be based on the assumption that the risk of the provisions ever coming into effect is low. Fairness must be established based on a contemporaneous evaluation of the factors set out in the FRA. As acknowledged by the majority of the British Columbia Court of Appeal in this case: "What the parties view as fair at the time of executing the agreement may become unfair as the relationship evolves, and as circumstances change" (para. 61). This is exactly what the judge ought to evaluate under s. 65(1). ...

The majority states that by choosing to execute the agreement despite having noticed that it might be unfair, the respondent signalled that she was not concerned. This analysis, in my view, is not acceptable and confuses fairness with unconscionability. While it is true that the agreement's shortcomings were apparent to some degree at the time of execution, foreseeability (or simply "signing" the agreement) does not cure its substantive unfairness. Although it may constitute a bar to setting the agreement aside on the ground of unconscionability, independent legal advice prior to execution does not render it fair nor does it leave the trial judge powerless. ...

There are indications that the respondent was in a vulnerable position in negotiation—not enough for the agreement to be unconscionable, but enough to suggest that the trial judge should be alive to the possibility that the agreement was unfair. The respondent had already been out of the workforce and dependent on the appellant for almost two years and had only ever worked as a lawyer (and before that, an articling student) in the appellant's firm. The agreement was concluded under pressure with the wedding fast approaching. The respondent sought changes to the agreement before execution but was unable to persuade the appellant to agree, except with respect to minor changes, such as the insertion of a clause to the effect that her signature was not voluntary and was at his insistence. These circumstances illustrate the appellant's position of power within the relationship, as well as the respondent's correlative dependence. That she remained at home for the rest of the marriage relationship to take care of the couple's children further illustrates the power dynamics at play. Taken as a whole, these circumstances justify reviewing the agreement with increased scrutiny. ...

Marriage is a "joint endeavour," a socio-economic partnership. ... On the one hand, married spouses are entitled to the full protection of their matrimonial regime. On the other, they must fully assume the responsibilities flowing from their decision to get married. By choosing to marry the respondent, to have children, and to support *and benefit* from his wife's work in the private sphere, Mr. Hartshorne agreed to bear all the consequences of the legislative regime regulating his decisions, including judicial review under s. 65 of the FRA. He cannot have his cake and eat it too.

[In the end, the majority of the Supreme Court ordered (at para. 65) that the marriage contract be enforced, and noted (at para. 64) that any economic disadvantage could be compensated through a spousal support order.]

Discussion Notes

Goals of Autonomy and Fairness in Family Bargaining

Are the reasons in the majority and dissenting judgments in *Hartshorne* in agreement with respect to the applicable principles? To what extent does each of these judgments encourage parties to negotiate fair agreements? What are the factors that made this agreement fair according to the majority? Why is it desirable to enforce the terms of a private agreement signed before marriage; during marriage? The balancing of goals of autonomy and fairness in family bargaining was considered by the Supreme Court in two other recent cases: *Walsh v. Bona*, [2002] 4 SCR 325, reviewed in chapter 6, and *Miglin v. Miglin*, [2003] 1 SCR 303, reviewed in chapter 7. These ideas are also explored at the end of this section after discussion of some aspects of separation agreements, another form of family bargaining.

Kaddoura v. Kaddoura

In *Kaddoura v. Kaddoura* (1998), 44 RFL (4th) 228 (Ont. Ct. J (Gen. Div.)), the court accepted an argument that the *Mahr*, a traditional payment included in a Muslim marriage agreement, was an unenforceable obligation pursuant to Ontario law. The court cited *Hermann v. Charlesworth*, [1905] 2 KB 123 (CA), in which a monetary element was regarded as an "unacceptable taint" in marriage, and continued (at paras. 24-28):

> While there may be much to some if not all of the contract and marriage contract law arguments raised by Mr. Snipper, I have concluded that the obligation sought to be enforced here is one which should not be adjudicated in the civil courts.
>
> The Mahr and the extent to which it obligates a husband to make payment to his wife is essentially and fundamentally an Islamic religious matter. Because Mahr is a religious matter, the resolution of any dispute relating to it or the consequences of failing to honour the obligation are also religious in their content and context. While not, perhaps, an ideal comparison, I cannot help but think that the obligation of the Mahr is unsuitable for adjudication in the civil courts as is an obligation in a Christian religious marriage, such as to love, honour and cherish, or to remain faithful, or to maintain the marriage in sickness or other adversity so long as both parties live, or to raise children according to specified

religious doctrine. Many such promises go well beyond the basic legal commitment to marriage required by our civil law, and are essentially matters of chosen religion and morality. They are derived from and are dependent upon doctrine and faith. They bind the conscience as a matter of religious principle but not necessarily as a matter of enforceable civil law. ...

Where, ... as seems to be the case here, the issue must be determined with reference to religious doctrine and principle, the civil court is, in my view, at least lacking in expertise and ... constitutionally beyond its proper territory. If in Canada, the line demarcating the proper territory for the civil courts in matters relating to religious issues is not a constitutional one, it will be a matter of public policy. See also: *Baxter v. Baxter* (1983), 45 OR (2d) 348 (Ont. HC).

Mr. Shaikh urged this Court to rely on the Islamic religious principles as expounded by Dr. Gamal and Mufti Khan and enforce the wife's right to the Mahr. I don't think, even if I have received clear and complete Islamic doctrine from these experts, that I could, as if applying foreign law, apply such religious doctrine to a civil resolution of this dispute. In any case, the matter isn't that easy. Mufti Khan in particular, said that only an Islamic religious authority could resolve such a dispute and a proper resolution involved a number of factors and a proper application of principles derived from the Holy Qur'an, the words of the Prophet and from the religious jurisprudence.

In my view, to determine what the rights and obligations of Sam and Manira are in relation to the undertaking of Mahr in their Islamic marriage ceremony would necessarily lead the Court into the "religious thicket," a place that the courts cannot safely and should not go.

Is there a difference between the arguments in *Kaddoura* and those of Lord Atkin in *Balfour*? Why, or why not? Are the principles established in *Hartshorne* relevant to the situation in *Kaddoura*? Why, or why not? Compare the reasoning in *Kaddoura* with decisions in British Columbia. For example, in *N.M.M. v. N.S.M.*, [2004] BCJ no. 642 (SC) (QL), the BC Supreme Court held the *Mahr* enforceable as a valid marriage agreement. See also *Nathoo v. Nathoo*, [1996] BCJ no. 2720 (SC) (QL) and *Amlani v. Hiram*, [2000] BCJ no. 2357 (SC) (QL).

3. Separation Agreements: Validity and Setting Aside

Consider again the goals of autonomy and fairness discussed in *Hartshorne* in relation to marriage agreements. To what extent are they relevant to family bargaining that occurs at the end of a relationship? Are there factors that may influence bargaining in a marriage agreement that are different from those that affect bargaining at the end of a relationship?

As indicated in the judgments of both the majority and the dissenting judges, legislative choices in the provinces are not exactly the same with respect to the balancing of goals of autonomy and fairness. Indeed, as Bastarache J pointed out, the threshold for judicial intervention is relatively lower in BC's *Family Relations Act* by comparison with other provincial statutes. In addition, some courts have held terms of a separation agreement unenforceable for reasons of public policy: for example, see *Buisey v. Buisey* (1999), 47 RFL (4th) 1, where the Newfoundland Court of Appeal refused to enforce a term in a separation agreement (relating to liability for tax) because it was contrary to public policy.

The provisions concerning domestic contracts (marriage, cohabitation, and separation agreements) in Ontario are found in part IV of the *Family Law Act*. Examine these provisions in the light of *Hartshorne*—to what extent should the principles established by the Supreme Court's decision apply?

Section 56(1) of Ontario's *Family Law Act* provides that a court may disregard any provision of a domestic contract respecting the education, moral training, or custody of or access to a child where it is in the child's best interests to do so. In addition, ss. 56(2) and (3) provide for the interpretation of clauses in a separation agreement respecting continued chastity. In addition, s. 56(4) defines three bases for setting aside agreements or any provisions in them:

1. where there was a failure to disclose significant assets, debts, or liabilities that existed when the contract was made;

2. where the party did not understand the nature or consequences of the contract; or

3. otherwise, in accordance with the law of contract.

Failure To Disclose Significant Assets or Debts

This provision was clearly designed to ensure that parties negotiate separation agreements with full information. In *Simon v. Simon* (1999), 47 RFL (4th) 60 (Ont. Sup. Ct. J), for example, the court set aside several clauses of a separation agreement because of the husband's failure to disclose fully "a change in his employment" and a material change in his income and assets. However, in *Dochuk v. Dochuk* (1999), 44 RFL (4th) 97 (Ont. Ct. J (Gen. Div.)), the court declined to set aside provisions in a contract where there was evidence that the husband had wilfully failed to disclose relevant information because it would not have affected the wife's decision to sign the contract. The court identified a number of factors to be considered in exercising discretion pursuant to s. 56(4) (at paras. 17-18):

In *Demchuk* ... , Clarke LJSC observed that how the Court will exercise its discretion whether to set aside a separation agreement pivots on the facts of each case. His Honour set out the factors that he took into account. These included:

(a) whether there had been concealment of the asset or material misrepresentation;
(b) whether there had been duress, or unconscionable circumstances;
(c) whether the petitioning party neglected to pursue full legal disclosures;
(d) whether he/she moved expeditiously to have the agreement set aside;
(e) whether he/she received substantial benefits under the agreement;
(f) whether the other party had fulfilled his/her obligations under the agreement. ...

In *Rosen* ... , the Ontario Court of Appeal re-affirmed the approach that Courts should take, in general, toward the validity of separation agreements. It is desirable that parties should settle their own affairs if possible. In doing so parties should know that the terms of such settlement will be binding and will be recognized. The Court of Appeal was clear that this approach is not applicable to contracts that are unconscionable. I conclude that where there are vitiating factors and a Court is being asked to exercise its discretion, the approach must be taken into consideration.

Not Understanding the Nature or Consequences of the Contract

By contrast with provinces like Alberta, where an enforceable contract requires that the parties must have received independent legal advice in relation to it (see *Matrimonial Property Act*, RSA 1980, c. M-9, s. 38(2)), independent legal advice is not required in Ontario. Yet, provisions of the contract may be set aside if either of the parties did not understand the nature and consequences of the agreement. In this context, the absence of independent legal advice may be a significant factor in assessing whether a party understood the nature and consequences of the agreement: see *Best v. Best* (1990), 30 RFL (3d) 279 (Ont. Ct. J (Gen. Div.)). However, where parties have deliberately declined to seek legal advice, courts have refused to set aside provisions. In *Rosen v. Rosen* (1995), 18 OR (3d) 641, for example, the Supreme Court of Canada dismissed an application for leave to appeal in relation to a decision of the Ontario Court of Appeal, which concluded that the wife had acted voluntarily in deciding not to obtain legal advice before signing a separation agreement; the Court of Appeal had also determined that there was no inequality in terms of bargaining power between the parties.

Otherwise in Accordance with the Law of Contract

As Nicholas Bala explained, this provision means that courts may consider unconscionability, duress, undue influence, fraud, misrepresentation, and mistake: see Nicholas Bala, "Domestic Contracts in Ontario and the Supreme Court Trilogy: A Deal Is a Deal" (1988), 13 *Queen's Law Journal* 1. Bala described the case of *Puopolo v. Puopolo* (1986), 2 RFL (3d) 73 (Ont. SC (HCJ)), in which a husband and wife signed a separation agreement relating to their property; the husband had title to the matrimonial home and the wife owned an apartment building. Initially, the husband requested 100 percent of both properties and, eventually, after her husband threatened her, the wife agreed to sell the apartment building and divide the proceeds equally with her husband; he kept the matrimonial home. Before signing the agreement, the wife obtained legal advice, which included a suggestion that she might be able to set aside the agreement in future. While expressing some concern about this legal advice, the court held that the wife was not under duress when she signed the agreement, that she wanted to "buy peace" with her husband, and that there was no basis for setting aside the contract.

In *Saul v. Himel* (1995), 9 RFL (4th) 419 (Ont. Ct. J (Gen. Div.)), another court upheld a separation agreement even though the husband claimed misrepresentation (as well as non-disclosure) in relation to provisions for supporting a child of whom he was not the biological father. However, the court decided that he had been aware, at the time of negotiating the agreement, that he might not be the biological father and that the wife had no duty to disclose these facts. Thus, it seems that Ontario courts have expressed reluctance to set aside provisions of a separation agreement, especially if the parties received legal advice. Recall that the trial judge in *Hartshorne* expressly concluded that there were no contractual grounds for setting aside the marriage contract in that case, but intervened on the ground that the agreement was unfair pursuant to s. 65 of the BC *Family Relations Act*—is the situation in Ontario comparable? Why, or why not?

Discussion Note

Family Law Bargaining, Judicial Intervention, and Social Assistance

Reconsider the facts in *Hartshorne* and the provisions of the BC *Family Relations Act* at issue in that case, in contrast with the provisions of Ontario's *Family Law Act*? What limits, if any, exist with respect to the autonomy of individuals to arrange their own affairs?

In Ontario, pursuant to the *Family Law Act*, s. 33(4), a court *may* set aside a provision for support or a waiver of support in a domestic contract if it results in unconscionable circumstances or if the result is that a party to the contract thereby qualifies for social assistance. This provision was considered in *Salonen v. Salonen* (1986), 2 RFL (3d) 273 (Ont. UFC); the court declined to set aside the agreement, even though it meant that the wife and children would require social assistance. The husband and wife negotiated a separation agreement after the wife decided to live with another man; the wife received legal advice before signing the agreement. The separation agreement required the husband to take responsibility for all of the couple's debts, a situation which left him unable to pay much child or spousal support. When her new relationship ended, the wife sought to set aside the contract in order to claim spousal and child support. In deciding to uphold the agreement, the court stated (at 286):

> [In] the case at bar, Mrs. Salonen not only had advice, but she retained her own lawyer who negotiated with Mr. Salonen's lawyer from September 1984 to December and he (on her behalf) drew the agreement and advised her away from the visible presence of her husband prior to signing. She had ample opportunity to consider its long- and short-term effects. She had Mr. Menente in tow when she attended her lawyer's office. She was observed by Mr. Arrell to be in no distress; she was anxious to sign the agreement and indicated she was going to live with Mr. Menente.
>
> Agreements of this kind should be upheld as a matter of public policy, ... else parties will be less motivated to seriously bargain and conclude such contracts. Parties in circumstances of marital distress should be encouraged to settle by bargain rather than litigation. This view was well stated in *Dal Santo v. Dal Santo* (1975), 21 RFL 117 at 120 (BCSC), where Anderson J said:
>
> > It is of great importance not only to the parties but to the community as a whole that contracts of this kind should not be lightly disturbed. Lawyers must be able to advise their clients in respect of their future rights and obligations with some degree of certainty. Clients must be able to rely on these agreements and know with some degree of assurance that once a separation agreement is executed their affairs have been settled on a permanent basis. The courts must encourage parties to settle their differences without recourse to litigation. The modern approach to family law is to mediate and conciliate so as to enable the parties to make a fresh start in life on a

secure basis. If separation agreements can be varied at will, it will become much
more difficult to persuade the parties to enter into such agreements.

The court held that it was not appropriate to set aside the agreement even though the
statute permitted the court to disregard an agreement if the result was that a party became
entitled to social assistance. Does the court's statement of policy explain the outcome of
many of the cases in which spouses have sought to set aside provisions of domestic
contracts? Is it consistent with the Supreme Court's interpretation in *Hartshorne*? To
what extent is the policy of encouraging private agreements appropriate for family law
disputes? Does a policy of encouraging settlement of divorce proceedings meet the needs
of public policies about the use of judicial and other resources as well as private interests
in defining family agreements? Some of these questions are addressed in the commentary
that follows.

4. Critiques of Family Bargaining: Problems of Private Ordering

Even though there are good public policy reasons for judicial support for privately
negotiated agreements, the literature on family law bargaining suggests that spouses may
be required to make their agreements at a time when they are least able to rationalize
their interests and determine priorities for the future. In a critique of private ordering in
family law, for example, Marcia Neave pointedly defined how family law bargaining
may be different from other contexts.

Marcia Neave, "Resolving the Dilemma of Difference: A Critique of 'The Role of Private Ordering in Family Law'"
(1994), 44 *University of Toronto Law Journal* 97, at 105ff.

I am sceptical of reasoning which assumes that couples deciding to marry or to separate calculate the costs and benefits with the degree of precision attributed to owners
of widget factories who enter into fire insurance policies.

[Neave's comments were made in the context of a critique of a proposal for "private
ordering" reforms to rules governing property and support after divorce: the reform
proposals were detailed in Michael J. Trebilcock and Rosemin Keshvani, "The Role
of Private Ordering in Family Law: A Law and Economics Perspective" (1991), 41
University of Toronto Law Journal 533. Neave compared the Trebilcock and Keshvani
proposals and the recommendations of the Institute of Family Studies in Australia:
see P. McDonald, ed., *Settling Up: Property and Income Distribution on Divorce in
Australia* (Sydney: Prentice Hall, 1986) and K. Funder, M. Harrison, and R. Weston,
Settling Down: Pathway of Parents After Divorce (Melbourne: Australian Institute of
Family Studies, 1993).

Neave identified (at 105) the need to question the impact of legal rules on the
behaviour of couples, but also recognized (at 123-26) how perceptions about individuals' bargaining positions may affect entitlements:]

Unfortunately there is little empirical evidence on the extent to which changes to rules regulating the financial consequences of divorce actually affect marriage and divorce behaviour. Many questions remain unanswered. Do rules improving the situation of women in traditional dependent relationships encourage them to remain full-time homemakers? Do such rules discourage men from marrying? Do they make men more prepared to share in the work of child-rearing? Alternatively, do rules which disadvantage "home-makers" discourage women from marrying or from becoming dependent on their husbands? To what extent is the decision of a person to leave an unhappy marriage affected by rules governing property and support entitlements?

It seems likely that the decisions which couples and individuals make about marrying, divorcing, and dividing labour during marriage are affected by a broad range of emotional and social factors which cannot be reduced to simple computations of costs and benefits. Like other law and economics scholars Trebilcock and Keshvani assume that legal entitlements have a significant impact on marriage and divorce behaviour. But, as La Forest J recognized in *Richardson v. Richardson*, "Lawyers and judges alike are prone to exaggerate the influence legal rules ... have on people's behaviour."

In the absence of clear evidence of the effects of particular reforms on the behaviour of men and women within marriage the best that can be done may be to design rules which rectify injustice in the short term, whilst ensuring that these rules can be rapidly modified if their long-term effects prove undesirable. ...

A recent article by Professor Carol Rose uses insights from game theory to explore the reasons why women in bargaining situations may end up worse off than men and, in some cases, worse off than they themselves would have been if they had not entered into such agreements. Rose examines the outcomes of employment contracts and domestic agreements on the assumption that (a) women tend to have a greater taste for cooperation than men (Gilligan's theory) or (b) men believe women to have a greater taste for cooperation, whether or not this is actually the case.

Although it is difficult to do justice to Rose's sophisticated analysis, I will attempt to describe it briefly. If the first assumption is correct Rose shows that in a zero-sum game a person with a greater taste for cooperation will inevitably end up worse off because he or she will be prepared to pay a higher price to induce the less cooperative party to enter into the agreement or to abide by its terms. For instance, suppose that wives, in general, tend to place a higher value on the maintenance of an amicable relationship with their former spouse and his relatives than husbands, in general, place on maintaining a continuing relationship with their wives. In this situation wives will be more likely than husbands to "trade off" matrimonial property or spouse maintenance in order to achieve this goal and will tend to do less well financially as a result. Some support for this hypothesis is supported by Lenore Weitzman's findings. Weitzman found that women generally had a lower tolerance for conflict and were more risk averse than men. Moreover, "women saw 'giving in' on monetary issues as a means of maintaining a relationship with their former husbands, or with his family, or between him and his children."

Even more interestingly, Rose argues that the same result may follow *even* if the propensity to behave cooperatively is equally distributed between men and women, *but* it is generally believed that women place a higher value than men on cooperative behaviour. Again the argument can be illustrated in the context of marital separation. Suppose that most men assume that women will usually take a smaller share of matrimonial property in order to avoid conflict, or in return for retaining custody of the children. Wives who challenge this assumption will be perceived as acting unreasonably (in comparison with other women) by their husbands, who may take a tougher bargaining position as a result. They may also be perceived as acting unreasonably by their own legal advisers, who will be influenced by their perception of the "normal" women's conduct.

Rather than singlehandedly challenging assumptions about the approach which women generally take in these situations, a particular woman may feel pressured to accept a smaller share of the matrimonial property, thus reinforcing the belief that all women are prepared to make such trade-offs. In other words, the effect of the assumption that women are more cooperative than men may be to make them behave more cooperatively.

Rose's discussion of game theory seeks to explain why women as a group do less well than men when negotiating agreements in the paid labour market and in the domestic context. However, she also attempts to explain why some women make agreements under which they are worse off in *absolute terms*. Women are more likely than men to be responsible for caring for children and other family members. Gilligan's work suggests they place a high priority on protecting those in positions of vulnerability and dependence. Rose argues that women may enter agreements under which they are worse off financially in order to protect third parties who can be used as "hostages" in the bargaining process. Although it is not possible to obtain reliable figures on the extent of domestic violence, women are physically abused in a relatively high proportion of marriages. Violence sometimes continues even after separation and divorce. Women who fear violence from their husbands may bargain away their financial rights in order to protect themselves and their children. It is doubtful whether contractual doctrines dealing with duress can provide practical protection in these circumstances, for women in this situation are often too frightened and powerless to seek to have agreements set aside.

If Neave's arguments are correct, how should family law (and family lawyers) respond to private ordering? For example, issues about the use of mediation for family disputes in which there is a history of violence have attracted concerns from both mediators and lawyers. In this context, Joan Kelly suggested that there may be some circumstances (involving past violence) in which mediation may be more appropriate than adversarial processes: see Joan B. Kelly, "A Decade of Divorce Mediation Research: Some Answers and Questions" (1996), 34:3 *Family and Conciliation Courts Review* 373, at 381, and Desmond Ellis, *Family Mediation Pilot Project, Hamilton Unified Family Court* (Toronto: York University, 1995). In the United States, the rise of mandatory mediation programs has generated a great deal of criticism, particularly in relationships of unequal power for women: for example, see Trina Grillo, "The Mediation Alternative: Process Dangers for Women" (1991), 100 *Yale Law Journal* 1545.

Robert Mnookin, "Divorce Bargaining: The Limits on Private Ordering"
in (1985), 18:4 *University of Michigan Journal of Law Reform* 1015

[Robert Mnookin has also identified advantages and disadvantages of resolving family disputes through contractual bargaining. Among the advantages, he finds that the enforcement of private agreements

1. gives expression to human individuality and individual rights;

   ADV. of K bargaining

2. is usually more efficient because parties themselves know best what is important to them and what they may be prepared to compromise about; and

3. is less costly, both for the individuals involved and also for the society; it is also likely to be less painful.

   Mnookin examined three problems of private ordering—those of capacity, inequality of bargaining power, and third-party effects (externalities). In relation to capacity, *DISADV.* Mnookin suggested that the idea of private ordering assumes that rational parties are involved in the bargaining process. However, those who are involved in divorce bargaining may often be subject to great stress and psychological turmoil that may make deliberate and well-informed judgments unlikely. He identified different phases for individuals involved in marriage breakdown over a two- or three-year period, and argued that "an otherwise competent person may at times have seriously impaired judgment," so that it may be the worst possible time to make permanent decisions.

   Mnookin also identified five elements of "bargaining power" that may be unequal between the parties, with the result that the bargaining may result in unfairness: legal endowments—that is, what each party is entitled to by law; the respective preferences of the parties; the parties' respective capacities to accept risk and uncertainty; differential abilities to withstand "transaction costs"; and strategic behavioural differences. Finally, in relation to "third party effects," Mnookin suggested that the spouses may make decisions that have consequences for third parties, which, if taken into account, would suggest that some other settlement might be more socially desirable. For example, the state's fiscal interests can be affected if the "economic terms of the bargain between the two spouses ... [affect] the odds that a custodial parent will later require public transfer payments." More significant, perhaps, the spouses' bargain may affect children in a way that reflects parental preferences, but does not adequately reflect children's needs and wishes. Thus, according to Mnookin (at 1032-33):]

[A] father may threaten a custody fight over the child, not because he wants custody, but because he wants to push his wife into accepting less support, even though this will have a detrimental effect on the child. A custodial parent, eager to escape an unhappy marriage, may offer to settle for a small amount in order to sever relations soon.

Some of these concerns suggest that problems of inequality may arise in bargaining and separation agreements, just as was noted in the mediation context above. Yet, as one study of family mediation suggested, lawyer-assisted negotiation provides safeguards that may be absent in mediation—there is knowledge of the legal parameters within which negotiations take place, and parties have the benefit of lawyers to assist them: see Goundry, Peters, Currie, et al., at 18. These assumptions may not always be valid, of course, especially if the parties are unrepresented as a result of the absence of legal aid funding. Moreover, for family law clients who have experienced violence or abuse within the family, inequality of bargaining power may be a significant problem even with lawyer assistance.

In this context, Diana Majury explored some of the features of lawyer-assisted negotiation for vulnerable women clients. Consider her analysis and suggestions in the context of Mnookin's concerns and the cases about the validity of separation agreements.

Diana Majury, "Unconscionability in an Equality Context"
(1991), 7 *Canadian Family Law Quarterly* 123

[In assessing contract unconscionability and the courts' authority to set aside an agreement on the basis of statutory provisions (and in variation applications), Majury argued that courts must pay more attention to the individual characteristics of the parties (which may affect their relative bargaining power), while also taking account of the broader issue of systemic gender inequality. Focusing on issues of gender inequality in family law bargaining, Majury argued (at 127) that even women who are "strong and self-sufficient" nonetheless operate "within a society in which women's agency is circumscribed by stereotypes, restricted opportunities, devaluation, violence (both overt and covert), hostility, and subordination." As a result, in assessing contract unconscionability and the inequality of bargaining power, she argued (at 133-48):]

The two essential ingredients—an unfair bargain and inequality of bargaining power—although obviously connected, are determined independently. The inequality of bargaining power is assessed on an individual basis. The cases are replete with references to impaired judgement, infirmity, weakness, ignorance, gullibility, vulnerability, dire need, domination and victimization, and such like. In order to obtain relief, the "victim" needs to be depicted as helpless and hopeless, someone incapable of standing up for herself and therefore in need of the court's benevolent protection.

By and large the contractual doctrine of unconscionability is one of paternalism. It therefore does not accord very well with the current presumed equality model of family law. Wives are no longer to be viewed as victims of the marriage, as helpless, dependent creatures unable to take care of themselves. The contract doctrine of unconscionability therefore provides relief in only the most extreme situations of individualized inequality.

There are, however, glimmerings in some contract cases of a more systemic understanding of inequality of bargaining power. Legislatures and courts have recognized that structural situations of inequality exist not because of some weakness inherent in the individual, but because of a weaker position imposed on or ascribed to certain groups of people in our society. Consumer, employment, and landlord/tenant relationships are perhaps the most commonly recognized as relationships of structural inequality. Legislation has been enacted to protect the structurally weaker party in these relationships.

An understanding of structurally induced inequality of bargaining power would provide the basis for a more sophisticated assessment of contractual unconscionability. In a situation of structural inequality, as with any other unconscionability case, the inequality of bargaining power alone would not be sufficient to overturn the contract; it would need to be coupled with an unfair bargain. However, if the courts were willing to recognize systemic inequality of bargaining power, one would not, in the relevant situations, need to portray the individual as incompetent or inadequate in order to obtain relief. The two-fold unconscionability test would in these circumstances consist of an unfair bargain, coupled with a systemically induced inequality of bargaining power presumed to have given rise to that unfair bargain. ...

An Inequality-Based Approach

A gender-based approach to unconscionability in the context of domestic contracts would involve the same two components required by unconscionability generally—an unfair contract, coupled with inequality of bargaining power. The applicant would need to convince the court that the agreement is unfair, that is, that the applicant is seriously disadvantaged by the terms of the agreement. The gendered analysis would be brought to bear on the question of inequality of bargaining power. Where the party raising unconscionability is a woman, the finding that an agreement is unfair would give rise to a presumption of inequality of bargaining position. This presumption of inequality flows from the fact of women's systemically subordinated position in our society. This presumption would replace the need for a determination of the dominant and subordinated positions of the individual parties with respect to the making of this specific agreement; that is, was this woman, because of some personal incapacity, bargaining from a lesser position and did this man take advantage of this situation to extract an agreement that favoured him. In the face of the presumption, the onus would be on the man to prove that individualized factors existed with respect to this specific couple sufficient to offset the systemic gender inequality. Basically he would be required to justify what, on the face of it, is an agreement that significantly advantages him at the expense of his former partner. ...

Inequality of Bargaining Power

An imbalanced domestic contract favouring the male spouse would not be overridden on the basis of unfairness alone; inequality of bargaining power would still be a necessary ingredient. However, the focus of the inquiry on the issue of equality of bargaining power would be shifted. Instead of having to prove individualized inequality in the face of an agreement disadvantaging the woman, systemic gender inequality would be presumed to have placed the individuals in unequal bargaining positions in the absence of evidence to the contrary.

A male applicant would be in the same position except that the presumption of inequality of bargaining power would not apply because there is no systemic basis for such a presumption. Having proven that the agreement is unfair, a male applicant would then have to prove that he was in an unequal bargaining position with respect to his former spouse. Although systemic power imbalances place men as a group in our society in a dominant bargaining position vis-à-vis women as a group, it is possible for an individual woman to be in a superior bargaining position vis-à-vis an individual man. It is this individualized dominance that a male applicant would have to prove but which would be presumed with respect to a female applicant subject to rebuttal by her former spouse. ...

The Role of Independent Legal Advice

Independent legal advice is often put forward as a key factor in the defence against an allegation of unconscionability. The implication is either that the agreement cannot be considered unfair if the lawyer did not advise against it and/or that the provision of independent legal advice is in and of itself sufficient to negate any inequality of bargaining power. Independent legal advice is thus set up as a safeguard against unconscionable domestic contracts. It is, however, inadequate as a safeguard; the burden it places on lawyers is too onerous and unrealistic. ...

The assistance of a lawyer giving advice and negotiating on a client's behalf may, in most circumstances, mitigate inequality of bargaining power. However, a lawyer is limited by the information to which she or he has access, an issue which is particularly relevant in situations of violence or threatened violence. Ultimately, a lawyer must either take instructions from the client or refuse to act for the client. Lawyers do negotiate contracts, on the instructions of their client, that according to the lawyer is contrary to the client's interests. The fact that the female party to the contract was represented throughout by a lawyer should be given some weight in assessing the contract, but it should certainly not be considered determinative of either the question of the fairness of the agreement or of the equality of the bargaining power.

As distinct from a lawyer who negotiates for her or his client throughout the contract process, a lawyer who merely provides independent legal advice with respect to the ramifications of an agreement provides little in the way of protection against unconscionability. Accordingly, this lawyer's role should be accorded little weight in an unconscionability determination. While a lawyer may legitimately be able to attest to his or her belief that the client fully understands the consequences of the agreement, such a belief on the part of the lawyer in no way addresses issues relating to inequality of bargaining power or even necessarily the issue of fairness.

Discussion Notes

Private Ordering and Fairness Principles

Does Majury's proposal balance the need to respect private ordering with an interest in ensuring fairness and equality in family law bargaining? To what extent would her proposal alter the outcomes of the cases referred to above? Consider also *Clayton v. Clayton* (1998), 40 OR (3d) 24 (Gen. Div.), where the parties separated after 23 years of marriage, having prepared and signed a separation agreement without legal assistance. Pursuant to the agreement, the wife received about $88,000 less than her entitlement in the equalization of the property. She later requested to have the agreement set aside on the grounds of lack of independent legal advice, duress, and unconscionability. How would Majury's proposal apply on these facts—who would have the onus of proof?

In *Clayton*, the court refused the wife's application, finding that she was quite capable of seeking legal advice, she had refused to do so, and there was no evidence of duress. Is it possible that Mrs. Clayton's capacity was impaired, as suggested by Mnookin? Compare this case to *Bossenberry v. Bossenberry* (1994), 6 RFL (4th) 47 (Ont. Ct. J (Gen. Div.)), where a court refused a husband's request to set aside a separation agreement on the basis that he had signed the final agreement in a depressed and emotional state and without legal advice. The court held that the final agreement was not significantly different from a draft agreement for which he had received legal advice. Is it possible that the court placed too much reliance on the fact that the husband had received independent legal advice? How would Majury's proposals affect this case? How should issues in cases like *Clayton* and *Bossenberry* be resolved?

The negotiation of separation agreements, with or without the assistance of lawyers, occurs in private, by contrast with reported decisions of cases that are adjudicated in public in the courts. Although it is assumed that parties "bargain in the shadow of the law," there is little detailed empirical research about the content of separation agreements, unless they are subsequently incorporated into corollary relief orders at the time of an order for divorce. For one study that examined actual provisions in separation agreements in New Brunswick, see Donald Poirier and Michelle Boudreau, "Formal Versus Real Equality in Separation Agreements in New Brunswick" (1992), 10 *Canadian Journal of Family Law* 239. In an effort to assist lawyers in negotiating separation agreements effectively, the Law Society of Upper Canada released a model separation agreement in 2002: see Philip M. Epstein, Stephen M. Grant, and Gerald P. Sadvari, *Separation Agreement Annotated* (Toronto: Law Society of Upper Canada, 2002).

Validity and Variation

Both the federal *Divorce Act* and provincial statutes contain provisions for the "variation" of agreements, an issue that is quite different from questions of validity and setting aside of contracts. Issues about the variation of agreements are considered in chapters 7 and 8 in relation to issues of spousal support and children. These cases often involve issues about changes in circumstances arising after (sometimes many years after) an agreement has been signed, and they are particularly controversial when one term of the agreement is that there will be no future variation. For an example where a court permitted a variation, even though the separation agreement stated that no variation was possible in the absence of "a catastrophic change, for the worse, in either party's circumstances," see *Bradley v. Bradley* (1997), 29 RFL (4th) 151 (Ont. Ct. J (Gen. Div.)).

Collaborative Law

In collaborative law processes, lawyers are engaged in negotiation, but their negotiation is bound by an agreement, *signed prior to commencing negotiations*, which defines the context for the collaborative law negotiation. Specifically, this agreement makes clear that if the parties and their collaborative lawyers are unable to reach agreement, the parties will have to engage other lawyers to litigate the matter. According to Tesler, at 221, this context changes the negotiation situation fundamentally:

> In a collaborative representation involving difficult issues, there is often a distinct trans- forming moment when everyone around the table recognizes that either the four of them must devise a solution or the process ends and someone else will do the deciding. At that point, instead of the oppositional negotiations that characterize litigation-dominated settle- ment conferences, it often happens that both parties and both lawyers enter a creative problem-solving mode in which all build on the ideas emerging around the table. In that situation, surprising solutions can emerge that would have been unimaginable in a conven- tional negotiation. ... None of these effects is impossible to achieve in a traditional settle- ment negotiation, but nothing about the traditional lawyer–client relationship fosters these effects as collaborative law does.

To what extent is collaborative law another method of private ordering in family law matters? Consider these issues in relation to the materials about corollary relief in the following chapters—to what extent are more imaginative solutions possible in collabora- tive law processes, by contrast with litigation and traditional negotiation? Even if there are more imaginative solutions, are there systemic problems that need to be addressed beyond issues of process in family law bargaining?

SELECTED REFERENCES

Martha Bailey, "Pelech, Caron, and Richardson" (1989-90), 3 *Canadian Journal of Women and the Law* 615.

Susan Boyd, ed., *Challenging the Public/Private Divide: Feminism, Law, and Public Policy* (Toronto: University of Toronto Press, 1997).

Brenda Cossman, "Family Feuds: Neo-Liberal and Neo-Conservative Visions of the Reprivatization Project," in Brenda Cossman and Judy Fudge, eds., *Privatization, Law, and the Challenge to Feminism* (Toronto: University of Toronto Press, 2002).

Elizabeth Jollimore, "Hartshorne, Miglin, the Variability of Domestic Agreements and the Supreme Court of Canada" (June 2004), 288 *Canadian Family Law Matters* 1.

Susan McDonald, with Pamela Cross, "Women's Voices Being Heard: Responsive Law- yering" (2001), 16 *Journal of Law and Social Policy* 207.

Carol Rose, "Bargaining and Gender" (1995), 18 *Harvard Journal of Law and Public Policy* 547.

Dana G. Stewart, "Single Custodial Females and Their Families: Housing and Coping Strategies After Divorce" (1991), 5 *International Journal of Law and the Family* 296.

IV. POST-DIVORCE FAMILIES AND THE STATE: THE ECONOMIC CONSEQUENCES OF DIVORCE (AND SEPARATION)

In its current form, the standard neoclassical model of the family postulates that men and women meet, make joint decisions, specialize, share, and stay together forever. It would seem that this should be extended to explicitly consider divorce. How can the economic consequences of divorce be interpreted within the neoclassical framework? How would the possibility of divorce affect the human capital investment, labour market participation, and earnings profiles of men and women? ... About 40 percent of Canadian marriages end in divorce (50 percent in the United States), with great consequences (on average) when it happens. It thus seems that our basic economic model of the family should be adapted to take divorce explicitly into account.

> Ross Finnie, "Women, Men, and the Economic Consequences of Divorce: Evidence from Canadian Longitudinal Data" (1993), 30:2 *Canadian Review of Sociology and Anthropology* 205, at 229

A. Data on the Economic Consequences of Divorce and Separation

Finnie's longitudinal study of the economic circumstances of men and women in marriages prior to separation, in the year of their separation, and in the few years immediately following separation (based on Canadian tax files in the 1980s) revealed the significant financial impact of divorce for both men and women. In addition, however, his statistics demonstrated disparity in the economic position of women, by contrast with men, in the year of separation and the years immediately thereafter. Finnie's findings indicated that women's family income dropped by one-half, and men's by one-quarter, in the first year of separation, while his calculations of income-to-needs ratios showed a small rise in men's economic well-being and a 40 percent drop for women.

A later study of married couples who separated between 1987 and 1993 similarly concluded that women experienced a decrease in adjusted family income after separation, while men showed a slight increase; in part, these results were explained because women more often had custody of children post-separation: see Diane Galarneau and Jim Sturrock, "Family Income After Separation" (1997), 9:2 *Perspectives on Labour and Income* 18, at 25, and Diane Galarneau, "Income After Separation—People Without Children" (1998), 10:2 *Perspectives on Labour and Income* 32. (As Galarneau and Sturrock explained, their results were somewhat lower than Finnie's, but the two studies were not readily comparable because of the different groups involved and different methodologies: see Galarneau and Sturrock, note 11.)

Figures frequently quoted in the United States reveal an even greater disparity between men's and women's financial circumstances after divorce: Lenore Weitzman reported in research in the 1970s that women's households suffered a 73 percent drop in their standard of living after divorce, while men's households had a 42 percent rise. These figures were recently challenged by Richard Peterson, who reanalyzed Weitzman's data and found that women's standard of living dropped by only 27 percent, while men had a 10 percent rise. According to the *New York Times*, Weitzman accepted responsibility for the mistake in her computer calculations, even though her original figures had already been cited in 348 social science articles, 250 law review articles, and 24 appellate cases

in the United States: see R.R. Peterson, "A Re-Evaluation of the Economic Consequences of Divorce" (1996), 61 *American Sociological Review* 61 and L.J. Weitzman,
*The Divorce Revolution: The Unexpected Social and Economic Consequences for Women
and Children in America* (New York: Free Press, 1985).

Yet, while issues about the validity of data and its interpretation remain, there appears
to be general consensus that divorce has an economic impact on families and that there is
likely to be some disparity in its impact on former wives, by contrast with former
husbands. In Canada, the introduction of child-support guidelines in 1997 may have
altered the situation to some extent, but it is nonetheless important to recognize that the
creation of two households post-divorce generally requires greater financial resources to
sustain them, in addition to the costs of the divorce process itself. These issues are
generally addressed by statutory principles concerning property entitlements at divorce,
and by arrangements for payment of spousal and child support, all issues of corollary relief.

B. Models for Meeting Dependency: Individuals, Families, and the State

Before examining how legislatures and courts have addressed these issues in the chapters
that follow, it is important to explore how issues of dependency within post-divorce
families are conceptualized by law—to what extent is individual dependency characterized as a responsibility of the post-divorce family or a matter that requires state intervention and support. In her assessment of post-divorce poverty for women and children, for
example, Margrit Eichler concluded that middle-class women are "only one man away
from welfare." Consider this assertion in relation to the excerpt that follows, which
identifies underlying policies for different models of economic relationships in families,
including post-divorce families.

Margrit Eichler, "The Limits of Family Law Reform"
(1990-91), 7 *Canadian Family Law Quarterly* 59, at 66-69 and 81-83

Models of the family that underlie policy analyses and proposals are rarely spelled
out explicitly. If we wish to uncover underlying models, we therefore need to ask
ourselves: What is the model of the family with which the policy under consideration
would be consistent?

Elsewhere, I have argued that we are currently experiencing a shift from a patriarchal model of the family to the individual responsibility model of the family. ...

The Patriarchal Model of the Family

The patriarchal model of the family is characterized by the following eight characteristics:

1. the household and family are treated as being identical;

2. as a consequence, a husband is equated with a father, and a wife is equated
   with a mother;

3. the family is treated, administratively, as a unit;

4. the father and/or husband is seen as responsible for the economic well-being of the family;

5. the wife-mother is seen as responsible for the household and personal care of family members, especially childcare;

6. conversely, the father and/or husband is *not* seen as responsible for the household and personal care of family members, especially childcare;

7. the wife and/or mother is *not* seen as responsible for the economic well-being of the family; and

8. society may give support to the man who supports his dependents (wife and/or children), but is not responsible for the economic well-being of the family where there is a husband (father) present, and is not responsible for the household and personal care of family members, especially childcare, where there is a wife (mother). ...

The Individual Responsibility Model of the Family

The individual responsibility model of the family shares the first three characteristics with the patriarchal family, but then diverges:

1. the household and family are treated as being identical;

2. as a consequence, a husband is equated with a father, and a wife is equated with a mother;

3. the family is treated, administratively, as a unit;

4. both husband and wife are seen as responsible for their own support as well as that of the other;

5. both father and mother are seen as responsible for the household and personal care of family members, especially children; and

6. society may give support to families, but, in principle, is not responsible for either the economic well-being of the family nor for the personal care of family members, especially childcare, when there is either a husband (father) or wife (mother) present.

Part of the attraction of the individual responsibility model is that it is ideologically premised on the notion of sex equality. However, the great problem with it is that it actually allows for a *decrease* in societal contributions to families. Where before the state would have replaced the financial contributions of the husband and/or father in case he cannot or does not make them, it will not do so if an individual responsibility model of the family is used, and likewise with the service contributions of the wife and/or mother. In such a case, the expectation on the lone-parent family will suddenly double—all in the name of equality.

This is clearly an absurd situation. It is intimately linked to Weitzman's (and other people's) charge that to treat people equally when they are not equal will increase inequality rather than reduce it.

At this point then, there are theoretically two directions one can choose to go. Given that women, as a group, do not have the same economic power as men, and given that in the vast majority of cases women have the major (and often sole) responsibility for dependent children, we can, through judicial fiat, put some of the economic burden back on to the men who fathered the children and used to be married to the women.

Alternatively, we can redefine societal obligations towards the raising of children, try to move towards equalizing the economic position of women with that of men, or move towards a third model of the family, the social responsibility model of the family. ...

The Social Responsibility Model of the Family

The social responsibility model of the family is characterized by only three assumptions:

1. Every adult is considered responsible for his or her own economic well-being. Where this is impossible, the support obligation shifts to the state, not to a family member.

2. For an adult in need of care, whether because of a permanent or temporary illness or handicap, it is the responsibility of the state (not of a family member) to pay for the cost of such care.

3. The cost of raising children is shared by the father, the mother, and the state, irrespective of the marital status of the parents.

Even if we were to move immediately towards the social responsibility model of the family, *in the absence of preceding economic changes* there would still be problems with respect to an equitable division of property between women and men, due to the weaker position of women in the economy. Nevertheless, such a move would go a far distance in solving some of the problems Weitzman has so well described.

In reality, it is a matter of how to place emphases, rather than what absolute choices to make at this moment in history. The problem I have with some (not all) of Weitzman's proposed solutions is that they point us towards the individual responsibility model of the family, which although ideologically premised on the notion of sex equality shares with the patriarchal model of the family the view that the economic status of wives and children is the individual responsibility of the spouses and parents (in fact, often of the man). Furthermore, these proposals are likely to be taken as a *substitute* for a move towards a social responsibility model of the family, rather than as a stop-gap measure.

Let us, then, consider into which direction the proposed solutions would lead us. At the heart of the proposals are three principles: first, to consider children as participants in their own merit when dividing property; second, to treat the family home as something more than property worth money, namely as a residence, a home, a means of providing social and emotional stability to its inhabitants; and third, to treat marriage under all circumstances as an economic union of equals, totally and unnegotiably.

Of these three principles, I full-heartedly endorse the first and second. It is the third principle with which I have problems.

Postulating an unnegotiable tight economic union between ex-husbands and ex-wives ties the economic status of the wife to that of the husband. To the degree that children are (in practice and in theory) rolled into that equation, we have reaffirmed the centrepiece of a patriarchal notion of the family—namely, that the economic status of the wife (and the children) is—and should be!—dependent on the economic status of the husband/father.

This approach can be characterized as neo-conservative, in so far as it points backwards rather than forwards, although in a different guise than we have had in the past. ...

The Limitations of the Individual Responsibility Model

As we have seen, even if we could solve all the problems that would come along with an even tighter economic union between ex-husbands and ex-wives and the compulsory sharing of the family home, and if we could somehow come up with an equitable formula for solving the competing claims of first and second families, we would only have addressed the problem of poverty for a small fraction of poor women and children.

Let us play this briefly through with the example of support. With the proclamation of the *Family Orders and Agreements Enforcement Assistance Act*, we will improve the enforcement of court-ordered support payments. That is a very important step forward.

However, the alternative to support payments for poor women and children is social assistance. Unfortunately, social assistance is likely to be cut exactly by the amount of the court-ordered support payment. Unless the support payment is higher than the amount paid by welfare (not likely in the majority of cases) the women and children are therefore *not* better off than they were on welfare. It is arguable whether it is harder to be dependent on support payments or social assistance payments. Better enforcement of support payments will therefore save the state money (we have seen this in Manitoba) but it will improve the situation of poor women and children only marginally, if at all.

In principle, family law is incapable of solving the problem of poverty of women and children. If, then, further reform of the family law is proposed as a solution to the problem of female and child poverty, we must ask ourselves what this *avoids* doing: namely asking for a comprehensive reform of the income security system, and of the overall economic structure such that poverty in general (whether subsequent to a divorce or not) is eradicated.

We need to break away from the idea that the economic status of wives and children is and should be a function of the economic status of the husband—a quintessentially patriarchal idea.

Arguing for a societal recognition of shared responsibility towards children between the father, mother and society, and for sex equality in the economy (which, of course, presupposes an excellent system of childcare, a wide network of services for families, etc., none of which are in place in Canada at the present time) does not mean that we should tolerate unfairness in the division of family property. It simply puts it into its proper place—something that is of social importance, that should be striven for, but that must not be burdened with expectations that it cannot, in principle, ever fulfil.

Discussion Notes

Family Law and Poverty

Eichler's recommendations focus on the problem of widespread economic inequality within and among families in Canada; her proposed solutions identify a limited role for family law reform in overcoming post-divorce poverty for women and children. It is important to note the relationships between the definition of problems and proposed solutions, of course. For example, in another Canadian study published in 1999, the author identified the poverty of women and children post-divorce and suggested that it was caused by no-fault divorce. In this context, Douglas Allen recommended the introduction of mutual-consent divorce to replace no-fault divorce. He argued that a mutual-consent requirement would mean that neither partner could leave a marriage without the other spouse's written consent; this requirement would restore the bargaining power of the unwilling party and ensure that benefits would flow to the couple's children. According to Allen, his proposal would prevent husbands from unilaterally deciding to leave the family and retaining the bulk of family assets: see Douglas W. Allen, "No-Fault Divorce and the Divorce Rate: Its History, Effect, and Implications," in Douglas W. Allen and John Richards, eds., *It Takes Two: The Family in Law and Finance* (Toronto: C.D. Howe Institute, 1999). Consider how this proposed solution has been designed to remedy the problem as defined by Allen—how would his proposal work if a woman who was being physically abused by her husband wished to leave a marriage?

Like Eichler, two American legal scholars have also argued that family law may not be sufficient, by itself, to provide solutions to the economic problems of divorce:

> Our central premise is that the legal issues surrounding divorce have been conceived too narrowly. Reform initiatives have too often treated divorce as a largely private dispute and have not adequately addressed its public dimensions. ... In our view, the most pressing problems stem from the inadequacy of public commitments both to equality between the sexes and to the quality of life, especially for children, following divorce. Addressing those concerns will require more fundamental reforms, not just in divorce law but in the broader family, work, and welfare policies with which it intersects.

(Deborah Rhode and Martha Minow, "Reforming the Questions: Questioning the Reforms," in S.D. Sugarman and H.H. Kay, eds., *Divorce Reform at the Crossroads* (New Haven, CT: Yale University Press, 1990), 191, at 191.)

The authors recommended continued opportunities for private ordering by individuals, but subject to principles of fairness and judicial safeguards against abuse. They also identified the need to ensure that sharing behaviour during marriage or cohabitation should be rewarded by principles of sharing economic assets at divorce. Moreover, in recognizing that these principles affected intact as well as post-divorce families, the authors conceded (at 210) that it was "not a modest agenda" for reform: "If we are serious about promoting gender equality in this generation and ensuring a decent start in life for the next, we need to translate our rhetorical commitments into social priorities." In examining the arguments concerning corollary relief in the following chapters, consider the extent to which judges assume that the economic consequences of divorce represent a problem for the post-divorce family or the state. What factors are relevant to defining the problem and the solution?

Families and the State

As Eichler suggested, a social-responsibility model of family assumes the active involvement of the state in supporting families and children. In this way, there is a link between the family as an economic unit and the wider social safety network. In the family law context, decisions that preclude dependants from receiving financial support may result in their entitlement to social assistance. Conversely, if a member of a post-divorce family is required to provide financial support to other members of the family, it is likely that the recipients will not be disentitled to social assistance. In this way, there is a relationship between private family support on marriage breakdown and entitlement to public assistance. However, the principles of family law and social assistance are not always congruent: for one analysis, see M.J. Mossman and M. MacLean, "Family Law and Social Assistance Programs: Rethinking Equality," in Patricia A. Evans and Gerda R. Wekerle, eds., *Women and the Canadian Welfare State: Challenges and Change* (Toronto: University of Toronto Press, 1997), 117.

In *Falkiner v. Ontario* (2002), 59 OR (3d) 481, the Ontario Court of Appeal reviewed a revised legislative definition of spouse in relation to social assistance entitlement, which did not correspond to the definition of spouse in family law legislation. As a result, some women who were not entitled to familial support from their cohabiting male partners were also not entitled to receive social assistance as single mothers. The court held that the definition discriminated against single mothers on the basis of sex and marital status, as well as on the analogous ground of "receipt of social assistance." However, the Charter analysis in *Falkiner* must be reconsidered in the light of the decision of the Supreme Court of Canada in *Gosselin v. Quebec (Attorney General)*, 2002 SCC 84.

These social assistance cases are further considered in chapter 7 with regard to corollary relief. At this point, however, it is important to be aware of the larger context within which issues about property, support, and custody must operate. Consider the extent of your agreement with this statement:

> With increasing numbers of sequential marriages, solutions to the financial crisis of marriage breakdown must be sought not only within the parameters of family law but also in social and economic policies that promote the financial viability of all persons in need, including the economic victims of marriage breakdown. The war on the feminization of poverty must be won by innovative and coherent socioeconomic policies.

(Julien Payne, "Family Law in Canada," in Maureen Baker, ed., *Canada's Changing Families: Challenges to Public Policy* (Ottawa: Vanier Institute of the Family, 1994), 13.)

For a fuller analysis of the kinds of policies that may be required, see Susan Moller Okin, *Justice, Gender, and the Family* (New York: Basic Books, 1989).

SELECTED REFERENCES

Arthur B. Cornell, "When Two Become One, and Then Come Undone: An Organizational Approach to Marriage and Its Implications for Divorce Law" (1992), 26 *Family Law Quarterly* 103.

M. Fineman, *The Illusion of Equality* (Chicago: University of Chicago Press, 1991).

Carolyne A. Gorlick, "Divorce: Options Available, Constraints Forced, and Pathways Taken," in Nancy Mandell and Ann Duffy, eds., *Canadian Families, Diversity, Conflict, Change*, 2d ed. (Toronto: Harcourt Canada, 2000), 260.

M. McCall, J. Hornick, and J. Wallace, "The Process and Economic Consequences of Marriage Breakdown" (Calgary: Canadian Research Institute for Law and the Family, 1988).

Mary Morton, "Dividing the Wealth, Sharing the Poverty: The (Re)Formation of 'Family' in Law in Ontario" (1988), 25 *Canadian Review of Sociology and Anthropology* 254.

M.J. Mossman, " 'Running Hard To Stand Still': The Paradox of Family Law Reform" (1994), 17:1 *Dalhousie Law Journal* 5.

PROBLEM

As this chapter demonstrates, divorce in Canada is based on the sole ground of marriage breakdown, but it continues to require state approval—it is not a matter of consent of the parties. Is this statement of the legal situation appropriate? Does it reflect the patterns of separation and divorce in Canada?

Consider the law of divorce in relation to the law of marriage. What are the implications of marriage law reforms for the law of divorce? If private ordering is desirable, how can potential reforms meet current criticisms of these processes? If divorce produces (at least some) economic vulnerability, how can potential reforms overcome this problem? You may also wish to take into account the principles of corollary relief, discussed in the following chapters, in formulating appropriate responses.

CHAPTER REFERENCES

Allen, Douglas W. "No-Fault Divorce and the Divorce Rate: Its History, Effect, and Implications," in Douglas W. Allen and John Richards, eds., *It Takes Two: The Family in Law and Finance* (Toronto: C.D. Howe Institute, 1999).

Astor, Hilary. "Mediation and Violence Against Women" (Canberra: National Committee on Violence Against Women, 1991).

Bailey, Martha. "Unpacking the 'Rational Alternative': A Critical Review of Family Mediation Movement Claims" (1989), 8 *Canadian Journal of Family Law* 61.

Bakogeorge, Peter. "Collaborative Law Gives 'Huge' Job Satisfaction," *Law Times*, March 17, 2003.

Bala, Nicholas. "Domestic Contracts in Ontario and the Supreme Court Trilogy: A Deal Is a Deal" (1988), 13 *Queen's Law Journal* 1.

Biondi, Eileen D. "Legal Implementation of Parent Education Programs for Divorcing and Separating Parents" (1996), 34:1 *Family and Conciliation Courts Review* 82.

Braver, Sandford L., Peter Salem, Jessica Pearson, and Stephanie R. DeLusé. "The Content of Divorce Education Programs: Results of a Survey" (1996), 34:1 *Family and Conciliation Courts Review* 41.

Brink, Nicky. "Alberta Launches 4-Year Test of Family-Law Legal Aid Offices," *The Lawyers Weekly*, April 20, 2001.

Canadian Bar Association. Report of the Canadian Bar Association, *Making the Case: The Right to Publicly-Funded Legal Representation in Canada* (Ottawa: Canadian Bar Association, 2002).

_____. Report of the Task Force on Gender Equality, *Touchstones for Change: Equality, Diversity, and Accountability* (Ottawa: Canadian Bar Association, 1993).

Cohen, Lynne. "Inside the Beis Din," *Canadian Lawyer* May 2000, 27.

Cossman, Brenda and Carol Rogerson. "Case Study in the Provision of Legal Aid: Family Law," in Ontario Legal Aid Review, *Report of the Ontario Legal Aid Review: A Blueprint for Publicly-Funded Legal Services*, vol. 3 (Toronto: Ontario Legal Aid Review, 1997), 773.

Davies, Christine. *Family Law in Canada* (Toronto: Carswell, 1984).

Day Sclater, Shelley. *Divorce: A Psychosocial Study* (Aldershot, UK: Ashgate, 1999).

Day Sclater, Shelley and Christine Piper. "The Family Law Act 1996 in Context," in Day Sclater and Piper, eds., *Undercurrents of Divorce* (Aldershot, UK: Ashgate Dartmouth, 1999), 3.

Department of Justice Canada. *Evaluation of the Divorce Act, Phase II: Monitoring and Evaluation* (Ottawa: Department of Justice Canada, 1990).

Dyzenhaus, David. "Normative Justifications for the Provision of Legal Aid," in Ontario Legal Aid Review, *Ontario Legal Aid Review: A Blueprint for Publicly-Funded Legal Services*, vol. 2 (Toronto: Ontario Legal Aid Review, 1997), 475.

Eichler, Margrit. "The Limits of Family Law Reform" (1990-91), 7 *Canadian Family Law Quarterly* 59.

Ellis, Desmond. *Family Mediation Pilot Project, Hamilton Unified Family Court* (Toronto: York University, 1995).

Epstein, Philip M., Stephen M. Grant, and Gerald P. Sadvari. *Separation Agreement Annotated* (Toronto: Law Society of Upper Canada, 2002).

Finnie, Ross. "Women, Men, and the Economic Consequences of Divorce: Evidence from Canadian Longitudinal Data" (1993), 30:2 *Canadian Review of Sociology and Anthropology* 205.

Flak, Edwin A. " 'Get' Law May Promote Invalid Marriage," *The Lawyers Weekly*, May 7, 1993.

Fodden, Simon. *Family Law* (Toronto: Irwin Law, 1999).

Fournier, Pascale. "The Erasure of Islamic Difference in Canadian and American Family Law Adjudication" (2001), 10 *Journal of Law & Policy* 59.

Funder, K., M. Harrison, and R. Weston. *Settling Down: Pathway of Parents After Divorce* (Melbourne: Australian Institute of Family Studies, 1993).

Galarneau, Diane. "Income After Separation—People Without Children" (1998), 10:2 *Perspectives on Income and Labour* 32.

Galarneau, Diane and Jim Sturrock. "Family Income After Separation" (1997), 9:2 *Perspectives on Income and Labour* 18.

Gambrill, David. "New Family Law Forms Not Making Life Simpler," *Law Times*, January 22, 2001.

Goundry, Sandra A., Yvonne Peters, Rosalind Currie, and National Association of Women and the Law. *Family Mediation in Canada: Implications for Women's Equality* (Ottawa: Status of Women Canada, 1998).

Grillo, Trina. "The Mediation Alternative: Process Dangers for Women" (1991), 100 *Yale Law Journal* 1545.

Hilton, N.Z. "Mediating Wife Assault: Battered Women and the 'New Family'" (1991), 9 *Canadian Journal of Family Law* 29.

Hogg, Peter. *Constitutional Law of Canada*, 3d ed. (Toronto: Carswell) (looseleaf).

Kelly, Joan B. "A Decade of Divorce Mediation Research: Some Answers and Questions" (1996), 34:3 *Family and Conciliation Courts Review* 373.

Kitson, Gay C., with William M. Holmes. *Portrait of Divorce: Adjustment to Marital Breakdown* (New York: Guilford Press, 1992).

Kramer, Kevin M., Jack Arbuthnot, Donald A. Gordon, Nicholas J. Rousis, and Joann Hoza. "Effects of Skill-Based Versus Information-Based Divorce Education Programs on Domestic Violence and Parental Communication" (1998), 36:1 *Family and Conciliation Courts Review* 9.

Kruk, Edward. "Practice Issues, Strategies, and Models: The Current State of the Art of Family Mediation" (1998), 36:1 *Family and Conciliation Courts Review* 195.

Landau, Barbara. "Collaborative Family Law: An Oxymoron or a Stroke of Genius?" (March 2001), *ADR Forum* 1.

————. "Mediation Article Elicits Response" (1990), 9 *Canadian Journal of Family Law* 193.

Landau, B., M. Bartoletti, and R. Mesbur. *Family Mediation Handbook* (Toronto: Butterworths, 1997).

Majury, Diana. "Unconscionability in an Equality Context" (1991), 7 *Canadian Family Law Quarterly* 123.

Mallan, Caroline. "Islamic Law Proposal To Undergo Review," *Toronto Star*, June 11, 2004.

McDonald, P., ed. *Settling Up: Property and Income Distribution on Divorce in Australia* (Sydney: Prentice Hall, 1986).

McLeod, James G. "Annotation: Marinovic v. Marinovic" (1989), 20 RFL (3d) 404.

————. "Annotation: Orellana v. Merino" (1998), 40 RFL (4th) 129.

Menkel-Meadow, Carrie. "Legal Negotiation: A Study of Strategies in Search of a Theory" (1983), *American Bar Foundation Research Journal* 905.

Mnookin, Robert. "Divorce Bargaining: The Limits on Private Ordering," in J.M. Eekelaar and S.N. Katz, eds., *The Resolution of Family Conflict: Comparative Legal Perspectives* (Toronto: Butterworths, 1984), 364.

Mnookin, R.H. and L. Kornhauser. "Bargaining in the Shadow of the Law: The Case of Divorce" (1979), 88 *Yale Law Journal* 950.

Moller Okin, Susan. *Justice, Gender, and the Family* (New York: Basic Books, 1989).

Mossman, M.J. and M. MacLean. "Family Law and Social Assistance Programs: Rethinking Equality," in Patricia A. Evans and Gerda R. Wekerle, eds., *Women and the*

Canadian Welfare State: Challenges and Change (Toronto: University of Toronto Press, 1997), 117.

Neave, Marcia. "Resolving the Dilemma of Difference: A Critique of 'The Role of Private Ordering in Family Law'" (1994), 44 *University of Toronto Law Journal* 97.

Oakes, Gary. "BCSC Modifies Plan To Ban Family Law Decisions on Website," *The Lawyers Weekly*, July 19, 2002, 9.

Ontario Legal Aid Review. *Report of the Ontario Legal Aid Review: A Blueprint for Publicly-Funded Legal Services* (Toronto: Ontario Legal Aid Review, 1997).

Payne, Julien. "The Dichotomy Between Family Law and Family Crises on Marriage Breakdown" (1989), 20 *Revue Générale de Droit* 109.

_____. "Family Law in Canada," in Maureen Baker, ed., *Canada's Changing Families: Challenges to Public Policy* (Ottawa: Vanier Institute of the Family, 1994), 13.

Peterson, R.R. "A Re-Evaluation of the Economic Consequences of Divorce" (1996), 61 *American Sociological Review* 61.

Piper, Christine. "How Do You Define a Family Lawyer?" (1999), 19 *Legal Studies* 93, at 106.

Poirier, Donald and Michelle Boudreau. "Formal Versus Real Equality in Separation Agreements in New Brunswick" (1992), 10 *Canadian Journal of Family Law* 239.

Reece, Helen. *Divorcing Responsibility* (Oxford and Portland, OR: Hart Publishing, 2003).

Rhode, Deborah and Martha Minow. "Reforming the Questions: Questioning the Reforms," in Sugarman and Kay, eds., *Divorce Reform at the Crossroads* (New Haven, CT: Yale University Press, 1990).

Sarat, Austin and William L.F. Felstiner. *Divorce Lawyers and Their Clients: Power and Meaning in the Legal Process* (New York: Oxford University Press, 1995).

_____. "Law and Social Relations: Vocabularies of Motive in Lawyer/Client Interaction" (1988), 22:4 *Law & Society Review* 737.

Schmitz, Cristin. "Courts Struggle with Issue of Private Divorces in Public Courts," *The Lawyers Weekly*, March 7, 2003.

_____. "Family Law Cases Main Source of Complaints Against Judges," *The Lawyers Weekly*, November 17, 2000.

_____. "Judge Blasts 'Outrageous' Overcharging in Family Law Cases," *The Lawyers Weekly*, February 28, 2003.

_____. "Ontario Judge Clamps Down on Divorce Paralegals, *The Lawyers Weekly*, October 19, 2001.

Smart, Carol and Bren Neale. *Family Fragments?* (Cambridge: Polity Press, 1999).

Smart, Carol, Bren Neale, and Amanda Wade. *The Changing Experience of Childhood: Families and Divorce* (Cambridge: Polity Press, 2001).

Syrtash, John. *Religion and Culture in Canadian Family Law* (Toronto: Butterworths, 1992).

Tesler, Pauline H. "Collaborative Law: What It Is and Why Family Law Attorneys Need To Know About It" (1999), 13 *American Journal of Family Law* 215.

Thompson, D.A. Rollie. "No Lawyer: Institutional Coping with the Self-Represented" (2002), 19 *Canadian Family Law Quarterly* 455.

Thompson, D.A. Rollie and Lynn Reierson. "A Practising Lawyer's Fieldguide to the Self-Represented" (2002), 19 *Canadian Family Law Quarterly* 529.

Trussler, Margaret. "A Judicial View of Self-Represented Litigants" (2002), 19 *Canadian Family Law Quarterly* 547.

Trebilcock, Michael J. and Rosemin Keshvani. "The Role of Private Ordering in Family Law: A Law and Economics Perspective" (1991), 41 *University of Toronto Law Journal* 533.

Tyler, Tracey. "Now It's Divorce, Same-Sex Style," *Toronto Star*, July 24, 2004.

Vanier Institute of the Family. *Profiling Canada's Families II* (Ottawa: Vanier Institute of the Family, 2000).

Van Praagh, Shauna. "Review" (1993), 38 *McGill Law Review* 234.

Weitzman, L.J. *The Divorce Revolution: The Unexpected Social and Economic Consequences for Women and Children in America* (New York: Free Press, 1985).

Ziff, Bruce. "Recent Developments in Canadian Law: Marriage and Divorce" (1986), 18 *Ottawa Law Review* 121.

CHAPTER SIX

Families, Property, and Family Property: Principles of Equality and Equity

I. INTRODUCTION

There is a sense in which the law of matrimonial property is concerned, not with property at all, but with human relations and ideologies in respect of property. ... The law regulating the spouses' property relations is fundamentally an index of social relations between the sexes, and ... affords a peculiar wealth of commentary on such matters as the prevailing ideology of marriage, the cultural definition of the marital roles, the social status of the married woman, and the role of the state *vis-à-vis* the family. ... In terms of the model of matrimonial partnership, ... husband and wife are seen as equal partners in co-operative labour, both making ... an essential contribution towards the economic viability of the family unit, and hence, towards the accumulation of matrimonial property. Whatever property is acquired by them during marriage is therefore acquired by reason of the partnership effort.

Kevin J. Gray, *Reallocation of Property on Divorce*
(Oxford: Professional Books, 1977), 1 and 24

In his comparative study of matrimonial property regimes in 1977, Gray argued (at 23) that this concept of matrimonial partnership, while distinct from commercial partnership, was intended to recognize "the unique community of life and purpose" in the marriage relationship. At the time of his study, many common law jurisdictions (including Canada) were just beginning to grapple with the *economic* consequences of more accessible divorce and to fashion new principles for sharing family property at marriage breakdown.

In the decades since Gray's study, the economic aspects of divorce proceedings have assumed more and more importance. For most spouses, concerns about property and spousal support, as well as custody and child support if there are children of the marriage, constitute the main issues in their negotiations. In this way, matters of corollary relief are more significant, as *practical* issues, than the divorce itself. At the same time, as the previous chapter explained, the divorce process may constitute an emotional crisis for either or both of the parties involved in it, with the result that they must negotiate complicated matters of corollary relief at a difficult time in their lives. In the context of examining issues of corollary relief in this chapter and those that follow, it is important not to lose sight of these tensions.

A. The Legal and Social Context of Family Property

Three background issues need to be addressed at the outset. First, family property constitutes just one aspect of economic readjustment at divorce; in addition, corollary relief includes separate legal categories of spousal support and care arrangements and ongoing financial support for children. These legal categories have different histories that are sometimes important to their legal interpretation. Thus, for example, spousal support was historically characterized as "alimony" or "maintenance" (pursuant to the English *Divorce and Matrimonial Causes Act* of 1857, 20 & 21 Vict., c. 85); some legislation in Canada also characterized it as maintenance, and the federal *Divorce Act* and provincial legislation now generally define it as spousal support: see *Divorce Act*, s. 15.2. Although the purposes of spousal support are identified in both federal and provincial statutes, these provisions (and their interpretation) sometimes reveal a variety of objectives, including traditional ideas that reflect the long history of this concept. By contrast, entitlement to family property at divorce is a much more recent development in common law provinces in Canada, all of which enacted legislation in the late 1970s in response to rising rates of divorce pursuant to the new federal legislation enacted in 1968. Guidelines for child support are even more recent, having been negotiated by the federal, provincial, and territorial governments only in the late 1990s.

Yet, in spite of such different origins, these legal categories of corollary relief together create an overall economic readjustment package at marriage breakdown. Moreover, for many post-divorce families, the overall package may be more significant than the individual legal categories. For post-divorce families, judicial concerns about characterization—that is, whether a source of family wealth should be regarded as property or support, or whether payment of a large sum for child support represents hidden spousal support—may appear unimportant. Thus, while these chapters are organized to reflect the significance of current legal categories, it is also important to understand how they constitute an overall economic package for family members at divorce or separation.

Relationships among different categories of corollary relief are sometimes important to legal principles as well. One example is the contrast between property and spousal support in terms of issues of finality. Provincial legislative regimes generally provide for a division of property, or its value, at one point in time, with no possibility of variation thereafter. In this way, property decisions are final. By contrast, judicial views about whether, to what extent, and in what circumstances it is appropriate to vary decisions about spousal support have differed greatly over the past two decades. Although the Supreme Court of Canada again addressed this issue in 2003 in *Miglin v. Miglin*, [2003] 1 SCR 303, its decision was not unanimous. *Miglin* is included for discussion in the following chapter, but it is important to highlight the difference between property and spousal support at this point. Clearly, if property decisions are not variable, while decisions about spousal support may be later revised, these differences may influence the substance and process of negotiations at marriage dissolution.

A second background issue is the tension between traditional property principles and the impact of recent social changes in families. Although family relationships and property principles have historically been linked very closely, demands for recognition of women's roles in the accumulation of family property (including their contributions to household work and child care) in recent decades have challenged fundamental legal principles of property law, not only with respect to legislative reforms but also in judicial decisions concerning the law of trusts. In this way, the interpretation of legal principles about family property often reveals some tension between adherence to traditional principles as they have always been applied and a need to recognize new understandings of property in the family law context. In relation to equitable property interests for cohabiting couples, for example, Marcia Neave argued that it was essential to identify the *purpose* of reallocating family property at the dissolution of the relationship:

> Rather than discussing whether a claim by an unmarried partner can be fitted within an existing category or whether the category can be extended to achieve this result, we should first attempt to determine whether equitable intervention is justified. If we can pinpoint the *purpose* of that intervention it may assist in identifying a method of analysis which is consistent with that purpose.

(Marcia Neave, "Three Approaches to Family Property Disputes: Intention/Belief, Unjust Enrichment and Unconscionability," in T.G. Youdan, ed., *Equity, Fiduciaries and Trusts* (Scarborough, ON: Carswell, 1989), 247, at 251.)

In the context of accessible divorce, legal arrangements for sharing family property require the application of traditional property principles to the new context and purposes of family law reforms, a significant challenge for both lawyers and courts.

The third background issue concerning property also relates to the reform context. Clearly, for couples who have accumulated little family property, this aspect of corollary relief will be of no significance. In fact, as the economic data in chapter 1 explained, there will be many cases in which couples have little or no property to share between them. In this respect, as Martha Fineman claimed, the law reform processes of the 1970s may have reflected the interests of middle-class families, particularly women, more than others: see Martha Fineman, "Implementing Equality: Ideology, Contradiction and Social Change: A Study of Rhetoric and Results in the Regulation of the Consequences of Divorce," [1983] *Wisconsin Law Review* 789. In addition, however, provincial legislative reforms concerning family property in Canada were restricted to married couples; cohabiting couples were excluded from these legislative regimes. The exclusion of cohabiting couples eventually resulted in judicial recognition of claims to family property in appropriate cases, using principles of unjust enrichment and constructive trust.

B. Murdoch v. Murdoch: A Reform Catalyst

The reform context is important to an understanding of the distinctive legal principles applicable to married couples (now including same-sex married couples) at separation or divorce, by contrast with cohabiting couples (opposite-sex and same-sex) at separation. Interestingly, it was a claim by a married woman for a declaration of trust that eventually resulted in the current availability of trust doctrines in cases of cohabitation. In *Murdoch v. Murdoch* (1973), 41 DLR (3d) 367 (SCC), Mrs. Murdoch left her husband in 1968, after 25 years of marriage. At separation, she filed claims for (among other things) financial support, and a declaration that her husband was trustee for her of an undivided one-half interest in property owned by him and in relation to which she claimed that they were equal partners. During the years of their marriage, Mrs. Murdoch had worked exten-sively in maintaining their large rural properties in Alberta, and the couple had acquired a number of such properties as a result of their successful work; however, title to all the properties was in the name of Mr. Murdoch alone. At trial, the judge concluded that there was no evidence of partnership and denied Mrs. Murdoch's claim to share in the property; he awarded her $200 per month by way of spousal support: (1971), 95 AR 119 (SC (TD). The Alberta Court of Appeal dismissed her appeal: (1972), 95 AR 118 (SC (AD)).

In the Supreme Court of Canada, Mrs. Murdoch argued that she was entitled to share in the property on the basis of the doctrine of resulting trust, a doctrine then subject to numerous and sometimes conflicting judgments in Canada and in the United Kingdom. For example, in an earlier case before the Supreme Court of Canada in 1960 (*Thompson v. Thompson* (1960), 26 DLR (2d) 1), the court had stated its conclusion firmly that, unless there was evidence to show that a wife had made a *financial* contribution to the acquisition of property held in her husband's name, she was not entitled to a declaration of resulting trust—that is, a wife's labour was not, by itself, sufficient to establish entitlement to a resulting trust. As the court in *Thompson* stated (at 9):

> [No] case has yet held that, in the absence of some financial contribution, the wife is entitled to a proprietary interest from the mere fact of marriage and cohabitation and the fact the property in question is the matrimonial home.

Similarly, in *Murdoch*, the court noted that although Mrs. Murdoch had worked, along with her husband, on their large properties, she had made no financial contribution that would sustain a declaration of resulting trust. Indeed, the majority judgment in the Supreme Court of Canada (at 376) reiterated the trial judge's conclusion that the work done by Mrs. Murdoch during the 25 years of her marriage was merely "work done by any ranch wife." By contrast, the dissenting judgment of Laskin J concluded (at 379) that the facts justified a declaration of constructive trust, recognizing the wife's significant "contribution of physical labour beyond ordinary housekeeping duties."

Ironically, it was the majority judgment, and particularly the judicial comment about ranch work that was expected of wives, that provided the catalyst for legal reform. Newspaper editorials suggested that the recommendation of the 1970 *Royal Commission on the Status of Women in Canada* for legislation recognizing the concept of equal partnership in marriage should be adopted: see Royal Commission on the Status of Women in Canada, *Report of the Royal Commission on the Status of Women in Canada* (Ottawa: Queen's Printer, 1970), 246. In addition, provincial and federal law reform commissions recommended changes to protect the interests of wives like Mrs. Murdoch. The federal report stated:

> The need for some fundamental reorganization of the existing property laws ... regulating the rights and obligations of family members was underlined in the recent decision of the Supreme Court of Canada in *Murdoch v. Murdoch*. The public reaction to that decision clearly indicates that the existing laws discriminate to the prejudice of the married woman and are no longer acceptable in contemporary society. A property regime must be devised that will promote equality of the sexes before the law.

(Law Reform Commission of Canada, *Studies on Family Property* Law (Ottawa: Infor-mation Canada, 1975), 3.)

Both public opinion and law reformers were in agreement about the need for reform after *Murdoch*. As a result, statutes concerning property entitlement at marriage break-down were enacted in all the common law provinces within a few years, beginning in 1978. In that year as well, the Supreme Court of Canada decided *Rathwell v. Rathwell*, [1978] 2 SCR 436, a decision that recognized the appropriateness of the constructive trust doctrine in the divorce context. In the face of widespread enthusiasm for the new statutory reforms, however, the availability of the constructive trust was not regarded as generally significant for married couples at divorce.

However, trust doctrines, particularly those relating to the constructive trust, were eventually extended to partners in cohabiting relationships at the time of separation. Because only married couples were entitled to the benefit of statutory regimes for defining spouses' property entitlement at separation or divorce, claims based on trust principles were necessary for cohabiting couples. This clear categorization of differing claims for married and cohabiting couples was, however, later complicated by the decision of the Supreme Court of Canada in *Rawluk v. Rawluk* (1990), 28 RFL (3d) 337, which held that married couples (at least in Ontario) were entitled to use trust doctrines, *in addition to* the statutory schemes, in resolving their property entitlements at marriage breakdown. *Rawluk* is included later in this chapter.

In the context of other litigation challenges to legislative definitions of spouse in the 1990s, moreover, a woman in a cohabiting relationship in Nova Scotia, whose relationship ended after 10 years, claimed that her exclusion from the provincial statutory regime constituted an infringement of the s. 15 equality guarantee in the Charter. The Nova Scotia Court of Appeal unanimously upheld her claim: *Walsh v. Bona* (2000), 183 NSR (2d) 74; 5 RFL (5th) 188. However, in December 2002, a majority of the Supreme Court of Canada held that the distinction between married and cohabiting couples in the provincial legislation did not contravene the Charter, thus upholding the distinction: see *Nova Scotia v. Walsh*, [2002] SCC 83; (2002), 221 DLR (4th) 1; 32 RFL (5th) 81. Thus, a majority of the Supreme Court concluded that the exclusion of cohabitees from the application of Nova Scotia's legislation did not contravene the equality guarantee in s. 15 of the Charter.

In this context, this chapter begins by examining the Supreme Court's decision in *Nova Scotia v. Walsh*, and its rationale for maintaining the availability of provincial statutory regimes exclusively for married couples. The chapter then explores aspects of provincial statutory regimes, including special issues concerning the matrimonial home, as well as the use of trust principles to define family-property entitlements for cohabiting couples. Because property is a matter within provincial constitutional authority, there are some important differences across Canada in the details of the statutory schemes. Although the material focuses primarily on the Ontario regime, it also provides some attention to the perspectives and legislative choices in other parts of Canada. As in other areas of provincial constitutional authority, it is interesting to consider whether local differences or national uniformity are more appropriate goals for family law policies about property arrangements at separation and divorce.

Discussion Note

The History of Property in Marriage

The history of property in marriage provides important insights about these social relationships. Before 19th-century statutory reforms, married women were generally unable to hold interests in property in accordance with the common law doctrine of coverture. According to Blackstone's classic statement of this doctrine, "by marriage, the husband and wife are one person in law": see William Morrison, ed., *Blackstone's Commentaries on the Laws of England*, vol. 1 (London: Cavendish, 2001), at 442. As a result, on marriage, a woman's property (subject to a few exceptions for personal property) became her husband's. Although a number of rationales were frequently suggested to justify this common law doctrine, an American scholar argued that none of them fully accounted for the common law system: see J. Johnston Jr., "Sex and Property: The Common Law Tradition, the Law School Curriculum, and Developments Toward Equality" (1972), 47 *New York University Law Review* 1033, at 1051.

Other scholars have examined the impetus for statutory reforms in common law jurisdictions in the latter part of the 19th century, generally concluding that married women's property legislation was enacted to preserve husbands' property from seizure by creditors, not to enhance the property rights of married women: for examples, see Norma Basch, *In the Eyes of the Law: Women, Marriage and Property in Nineteenth-Century New York* (Ithaca, NY: Cornell University Press, 1982) and Lee Holcombe, *Wives and Property* (Toronto: University of Toronto Press, 1983).

In Canada, the first legislation to reform married women's property was enacted in New Brunswick in 1851: *An Act To Secure to Married Women Real and Personal Property Held in Their Own Right*, SNB 1851, c. 24. Several statutes were enacted in Ontario, beginning in 1859: see Lori Chambers, *Married Women and Property Law in Victorian Ontario* (Toronto: Osgoode Society for Canadian Legal History, 1997) and Karen Pearlston, "Book Review of Married Women and Property Law in Victorian Ontario by Lori Chambers" (2000), 12 *Canadian Journal of Women and the Law* 247. In western provinces, issues about married women's property were concerned with dower interests: see Margaret McCallum, "Prairie Women and the Struggle for a Dower Law, 1905-1920," in Tina Loo and Lorna McLean, eds., *Historical Perspectives on Law and Society in Canada* (Toronto: Copp Clark Longman, 1994), 306.

All these reforms essentially permitted women to hold interests in property; however, as was evident in Mrs. Murdoch's situation, social conventions frequently resulted in husbands, rather than wives, being the owners of family property at the end of a marriage. In this context, consider the extent to which entitlement to family property at marriage breakdown represents a matter for legal or social reform. If wives and women in cohabiting relationships ensured that title to property was in their names, or their joint names with their partners, would family property regimes be necessary? Why, or why not? What factors might make legal reform, rather than social reform, more effective?

SELECTED REFERENCES

CANADIAN LITERATURE

Constance Backhouse, "Married Women's Property Law in Nineteenth-Century Canada" (1988), 6 *Law and History Review* 211.

Philip Girard and Rebecca Veinott, "Married Women's Property Law in Nova Scotia, 1850-1910," in Janet Guildford and Suzanne Morton, eds., *Separate Spheres: Women's Worlds in the 19th-Century Maritimes* (Fredericton, NB: Acadiensis Press, 1994), 67.

Nicholas Kasirer and Jean-Maurice Brisson, "The Married Woman in Ascendance, the Mother Country in Retreat: From Legal Colonialism to Legal Nationalism in Quebec Matrimonial Law Reform (1866-1991)," in *University of Manitoba Canadian Legal History Project*, Working Paper Series (Winnipeg: University of Manitoba, Faculty of Law, 1993).

Margaret McCaughan, *The Legal Status of Women in Canada* (Scarborough, ON: Carswell, 1977).

M.J. Mossman, " 'Running Hard To Stand Still': The Paradox of Family Law Reform" (1994), 17:1 *Dalhousie Law Journal* 5.

COMPARATIVE LITERATURE

Maeve Doggett, *Marriage, Wife-Beating, and the Law in Victorian England* (London: Weidenfeld and Nicolson, 1992).

Judith Freedman, Elizabeth Hammond, Judith Masson, and Nick Morris, *Property and Marriage: An Integrated Approach* (London: Institute for Fiscal Studies, 1988).

II. DEFINING A SPOUSE FOR FAMILY PROPERTY ENTITLEMENT: RATIONALES FOR MARRIAGE AND COHABITING RELATIONSHIPS

Ontario Law Reform Commission Recommendations

Many relationships formed by unmarried heterosexual couples resemble marriages. Common-law spouses pool their resources and make joint economic plans, they provide each other financial and emotional support, and they raise children. Society values the performance of these functions. To the extent that [provincial legislation] provides an effective legal regime to deal with the economic consequences of marriage, it should apply equally to unmarried heterosexual couples in functionally similar relationships.

> Ontario Law Reform Commission (OLRC), *Report on the Rights and Responsibilities of Cohabitants Under the Family Law Act* (Toronto: OLRC, 1993), 27

As is evident, the OLRC concluded in 1993 that it was appropriate to include opposite-sex cohabiting couples in functionally similar relationships to married couples within the statutory regime for defining property entitlement applicable to married couples at the end of their relationships. The commission's recommendation, based on analysis of existing human rights and Charter equality jurisprudence, identified four policy rationales for its recommendation: (1) functional similarities between married couples and opposite-sex cohabiting couples; (2) reasonable expectations of family members; (3) the need to compensate economic contributions to family well-being; and (4) relationships between family law and social assistance law. Although cohabiting couples would be entitled, similar to married couples, to contract out of the provisions of the statutory regime, the commission concluded that the preferred approach was to extend the legislative regime to cohabiting couples, requiring those who wished to avoid the legislative regime to opt out—that is, an opting-out regime for cohabiting couples, as for married couples.

In relation to same-sex cohabiting couples, the commission concluded that it had insufficient information to recommend automatic spousal status for property sharing for these couples at separation; it thus recommended (at 56-58) that only those same-sex couples who had registered their partnership (in accordance with defined procedures) should be subject to the legislation.

These recommendations are interesting for the ways in which they balance issues of individual choice and public policy. Recall the discussion in chapter 2, where Holland considered these policy alternatives and recommended ascription, subject to contracting out, as the basic policy for family law. That is, she argued that legal principles should apply to all those within marriage and cohabiting relationships, unless they have expressly contracted out of the obligations (as permitted); Holland rejected the option of requiring people to opt in to a legal regime.

These issues about the relationship between the basic legal regime and the extent to which individuals retain choices either to opt out or in were at issue in *Nova Scotia v. Walsh* in the Supreme Court of Canada. In reviewing the reasoning of the majority (eight judges) and of the dissent (L'Heureux-Dubé J), identify the factors that explained their differing approaches. How would you characterize the decision of the Supreme Court in relation to the OLRC's 1993 recommendations or to Holland's analysis in chapter 2? What are the economic consequences of the majority's decision for cohabiting couples in Canada?

Nova Scotia (Attorney General) v. Walsh
[2002] SCC 83; (2002), 221 DLR (4th) 1; 32 RFL (5th) 81

I. Introduction

BASTARACHE J: [1]   This case involves a Charter challenge to the Nova Scotia *Matrimonial Property Act*, RSNS 1989, c. 275 (MPA), and asks whether its failure to include unmarried cohabiting opposite sex couples from its ambit violates s. 15(1). The challenge revolves around the definition of "spouse" in s. 2(g) of the MPA, which is limited to a man and a woman who are married to each other.

[2]   The question before this Court, then, is whether the exclusion from the MPA of unmarried cohabiting persons of the opposite sex is discriminatory. In my view, it is not. The distinction chosen by the legislature does not affect the dignity of unmarried persons who have formed relationships of some permanence and does not deny them access to a benefit or advantage available to married persons. It is, therefore, not discriminatory within the meaning of s. 15(1).

II. Factual Background

[3] Susan Walsh and Wayne Bona lived together in a cohabiting relationship for a period of 10 years, ending in 1995. Two children were born out of this relationship, in 1988 and 1990 respectively. Walsh and Bona owned a home as joint tenants, in which Bona continued to reside after the separation, assuming the debts and expenses associated with the property. In 1983, Bona received as a gift from his father a cottage property which was sold after separation for $20,000. Approximately $10,000 was used to pay off the respondents' debts. Bona also retained 13 acres of surrounding woodland in his own name, valued at $6,500. The total value of assets retained by Bona at the date of separation including the house, cottage, lot, vehicle, pensions and RRSPs, was $116,000, less "matrimonial" debts of $50,000, for a net value of $66,000.

[4] The respondent Walsh claimed support for herself and the two children. She further sought a declaration that the Nova Scotia MPA was unconstitutional in failing to furnish her with the presumption, applicable to married spouses, of an equal division of matrimonial property. Her claim for a declaration was rejected by the chambers judge, whose decision was [unanimously] reversed on appeal. ...

VI. Analysis

A. Does the Matrimonial Property Act Discriminate?

[Bastarache J reviewed the principles established in *Law v. Canada*, [1999] 1 SCR 497 for determining whether a statutory provision violated the equality guarantee, citing the requirements set out at 548-49, and held that there was little debate that the *Matrimonial Property Act* provided differential treatment for married and cohabiting couples, and that marital status had been accepted as an analogous ground in *Miron v. Trudel*, [1995] 2 SCR 418; the appellant conceded both these arguments. Bastarache J continued:]

[33] It is with respect to the third broad inquiry that the appellant argues the Court of Appeal erred. In *Law*, *supra*, Iacobucci J set out four non-exhaustive factors for consideration of whether impugned legislation violates a claimant's human dignity:

(a) pre-existing disadvantage, stereotyping or vulnerability of the claimant;

(b) correspondence between the claim and the actual need or circumstances of the claimant;

(c) the ameliorative purpose or effect of the impugned law on other groups in society; and

(d) the nature and scope of the interest affected.

[34] In considering the four contextual factors, the Court of Appeal held pre-existing disadvantage and the nature of the interest affected to be most relevant. The appellant argues that the Court of Appeal failed to fully consider the nature of the

relationships involved before determining that Walsh's dignity was infringed. It points out that the court did not make any finding with regard to whether the parties had, upon entering into or during their relationship, any intention to contribute to one another's property acquisition or whether they deliberately avoided marriage and the consequences that flow from it. That is to say, the appellant argues that there is no evidence on which to conclude that the respondent considered herself disadvantaged by the non-marriage. Moreover, the appellant argues that it would in fact be unfair to make assumptions about all relationships and to impose a matrimonial property regime on persons who have chosen not to marry. It urges this Court to consider the exclusion of unmarried persons from the MPA as arising out of respect for the autonomy and self-determination of those who choose not to marry.

[35] I agree with the appellant that the examination of pre-existing disadvantage and the nature of the interest affected is dependent on the proper characterization of the relationships involved. In my view, the most important aspect of this question is not whether the situation in which Walsh and Bona found themselves at the time of trial was similar to that of married persons, but whether persons entering into a conjugal relationship without marrying are in fact entering into a relationship on the same terms as persons who marry. On the one hand, we have persons who choose to marry and thereby indicate their intention to assume all of the legal rights and responsibilities that the MPA attributes to persons who have that status. On the other, we have persons who cannot be presumed to have accepted all of the obligations of marriage. This is a significant aspect of the context in which the respondent's claim of discrimination arises. ...

[Bastarache J considered the argument presented by Walsh that the exclusion of unmarried spouses from the *Matrimonial Property Act* served to "perpetuate the view that unmarried couples are less deserving of recognition and respect in Canadian society." However, Bastarache J disagreed and held that it was not reasonable to conclude that exclusion from the provisions of the *Matrimonial Property Act* had the effect of demeaning personal dignity.]

[39] As this Court has stated on numerous occasions, the equality guarantee is a comparative concept. It requires the location of an appropriate comparator group from which to assess the discrimination claim. The two comparator groups in this case are married heterosexual cohabitants, to which the MPA applies, and unmarried heterosexual cohabitants, to which the MPA does not apply. Although in some cases certain functional similarities between these two groups may be substantial, in this case it would be wrong to ignore the significant heterogeneity that exists within the claimant's comparator group. The contextual analysis of the respondent's claim reveals that reliance solely on certain "functional similarities" between the two groups does not adequately address the full range of traits, history, and circumstances of the comparator group of which the claimant is a member.

[40] It is indeed clear from the evidence that some cohabitants have specifically chosen not to marry and not to take on the obligations ascribed to persons who choose that status (see: Z. Wu, *Cohabitation: An Alternative Form of Family Living* (2000),

at pp. 105-6, 116, 120-21; and University of Alberta Law Research and Reform Institute, *Survey of Adult Living Arrangements: A Technical Report* (1984), at pp. 64-72). In his study of alternative family forms, Professor Wu makes several conclusions, which include: (1) that common law relationships tend to be of much shorter duration than married relationships; (2) that cohabitation can be a "trial marriage"; (3) that cohabitation can be a deliberate substitute for legal marriage; (4) that persons who do not marry tend to have less conventional attitudes toward marriage and family and reject the institution of marriage on the basis of personal choice. These findings are indicative not only of the differences between married couples and cohabiting couples, but also of the many differences among unmarried cohabitants with regard to the manner in which people choose to structure their relationships. ...

[Bastarache J acknowledged that the court had recognized the historical disadvantage suffered by unmarried cohabiting couples and their recent social acceptance. Specifically, he referred to a number of legislative initiatives that followed the court's decision in *Miron* that extended a range of benefits available to married couples to unmarried cohabitants. Nonetheless, he acknowledged (at para. 42) that "social prejudices directed at unmarried partners may still linger, despite these significant reforms," and that the situation was not reducible to a simple matter of choice, quoting L'Heureux-Dubé J in *Miron*. However, he continued:]

[43] Where the legislation has the effect of dramatically altering the legal obligations of partners, as between themselves, choice must be paramount. The decision to marry or not is intensely personal and engages a complex interplay of social, political, religious, and financial considerations by the individual. While it remains true that unmarried spouses have suffered from historical disadvantage and stereotyping, it simultaneously cannot be ignored that many persons in circumstances similar to those of the parties, that is, opposite sex individuals in conjugal relationships of some permanence, have chosen to avoid the institution of marriage and the legal consequences that flow from it. As M. Eichler posited:

> Treating all common-law relationships like legal marriages in terms of support obligations and property division ignores the very different circumstances under which people may enter a common-law union. If they choose to marry, they make a positive choice to live under one type of regime. If they have chosen not to marry, is it the state's task to impose a marriage-like regime on them retroactively? (M. Eichler, *Family Shifts: Families, Policies, and Gender Equality* (1997), at p. 96.)

To ignore these differences among cohabiting couples presumes a commonality of intention and understanding that simply does not exist. This effectively nullifies the individual's freedom to choose alternative family forms and to have that choice respected and legitimated by the state. ...

[Bastarache J examined the history and purposes of the *Matrimonial Property Act* in Nova Scotia. In this context, he noted that the legislation provides additional significant benefits, but also imposes significant obligations on married spouses. By contrast,

Bastarache J concluded (at para. 49) that unmarried cohabitants "maintain their respective proprietary rights and interests throughout the duration of their relationship."
As he noted, unmarried cohabitants "are free to marry, enter into domestic contracts,
[or] own property jointly," and if they so choose, they would access all of the benefits
extended to married couples under the *Matrimonial Property Act*. Although
Bastarache J noted (at para. 52) Walsh's argument that there may be factors that preclude some individuals from marrying, thus denying them the benefits of the legislation, he was not persuaded that such arrangements resulted in "less recognition and
respect" for opposite-sex cohabitants. Moreover, Bastarache J distinguished the Supreme Court of Canada's decision in *Miron v. Trudel*:]

[53] In *Miron, supra*, this Court held the denial of insurance benefits to unmarried spouses to be discriminatory within the meaning of s. 15(1). In that case, the
impugned legislation denied automobile insurance benefits to persons in circumstances similar to married persons. Short of agreeing to marry, the cohabitants had no
ability to control the availability to each other of the benefits. Moreover, the extension or denial of these benefits had no impact on the rights and obligations of the
spouses *vis-à-vis* each other. The discriminatory distinction at issue in *Miron, supra*,
concerned the relationship of the couple as a unit, to third parties. The marital status
of the couple should have had no bearing on the availability of the benefit.

[54] In the present case, however, the MPA is primarily directed at regulating the
relationship between the parties to the marriage itself; parties who, by marrying, must
be presumed to have a mutual intention to enter into an economic partnership. Unmarried cohabitants, however, have not undertaken a similar unequivocal act. I cannot
accept that the decision to live together, without more, is sufficient to indicate a positive intention to contribute to and share in each other's assets and liabilities. It may
very well be true that some, if not many, unmarried cohabitants have agreed as
between themselves to live as economic partners for the duration of their relationship. Indeed, the factual circumstances of the parties' relationship bear this out. It
does not necessarily follow, however, that these same persons would agree to restrict
their ability to deal with their own property during the relationship or to share in all
of the other's assets and liabilities following the end of the relationship. As Eichler,
supra, points out, at pp. 95-96:

> There is a distinct difference between a young couple living together, having a child
> together, and then splitting up, and an older couple living together after they have raised
> children generated with another partner. If a middle-aged couple decide to move in
> together at the age of fifty-five and to split at age sixty, and if both of them have chil-
> dren in their thirties, the partners may wish to protect their assets for themselves and
> for their children—with whom they have had a close relationship for over thirty years—
> rather than with a partner with whom they were associated for five years.

[55] In my view, people who marry can be said to freely accept mutual rights and
obligations. A decision not to marry should be respected because it also stems from a
conscious choice of the parties. It is true that the benefits that one can be deprived of
under a s. 15(1) analysis must not be read restrictively and can encompass the benefit

of a process or procedure, as recognized in *M. v. H.* ... [[1999] 2 SCR 3; (1999), 46 RFL (4th) 32]. It has not been established, however, that there is a discriminatory denial of a benefit in this case because those who do not marry are free to take steps to deal with their personal property in such a way as to create an equal partnership between them. If there is need for a uniform and universal protective regime independent of choice of matrimonial status, this is not a s. 15(1) issue. The MPA only protects persons who have demonstrated their intention to be bound by it and have exercised their right to choose.

[56] The respondent Walsh argues that the choice to marry, to enter into a domestic contract or to register a partnership under the LRA still does not address her situation, nor does it address the circumstances of those individuals whose unmarried partner either refuses to marry or to register their domestic partnership. For these persons, as Walsh argues, the decision is not entirely within their control. Similarly, she argues that maintaining the proprietary *status quo* in unmarried cohabiting relationships unduly disadvantages both the non-title holding partner, who have historically been women, as well as the children of the relationship. The respondent argues that protection of women and children from the potentially dire economic consequences of marriage breakdown is one of the main purposes of the MPA. Excluding unmarried cohabitants, then, constitutes a denial of equal protection of women in conjugal relationships and the children of those relationships, the persons whom the legislation was specifically designed to protect.

[57] On this basis, the respondent submits that the only constitutionally acceptable formula is to extend the ambit of the MPA to all unmarried cohabitants, while providing consenting couples the opportunity to opt out, as the current MPA does with regard to married couples. The problem with that proposition, in my view, is that it eliminates an individual's freedom to decide whether to make such a commitment in the first place. Even if the freedom to marry is sometimes illusory, does it warrant setting aside an individual's freedom of choice and imposing on her a regime that was designed for persons who have made an unequivocal commitment encompassing the equal partnership described in the MPA? While there is no denying that inequities may exist in certain unmarried cohabiting relationships and that those inequities may result in unfairness between the parties on relationship breakdown, there is no constitutional requirement that the state extend the protections of the MPA to those persons. The issue here is whether making a meaningful choice matters, and whether unmarried persons are prevented from taking advantage of the benefits of the MPA in an unconstitutional way.

[58] Persons unwilling or unable to marry have alternative choices and remedies available to them. The couple may choose to own property jointly and/or to enter into a domestic contract that may be enforced pursuant to the *Maintenance and Custody Act*, RSNS 1989, c. 160, s. 52(1) and the *Maintenance Enforcement Act*, SNS 1994-95, c. 6, s. 2(e). These couples are also capable of accessing all of the benefits of the MPA through the joint registration of a domestic partnership under the LRA.

[59] It is true that certain unmarried couples may also choose to organize their relationship as an economic partnership for the period of their cohabitation. Similarly, some couples, without making a public and legally binding commitment, may

simply live out their lives together in a manner akin to marriage. In these cases, the law has evolved to protect those persons who may be unfairly disadvantaged as a result of the termination of their relationship. ...

[Bastarache J identified legislative provisions enabling cohabitants to apply for financial support, as well as the availability of constructive trust principles, stating:]

[61] Those situations where the fact of economic interdependence of the couple arises over time are best addressed through the remedies like constructive trust as they are tailored to the parties' specific situation and grievances. In my view, where the multiplicity of benefits and protections are tailored to the particular needs and circumstances of the individuals, the essential human dignity of unmarried persons is not violated.

[62] All of these factors support the conclusion that the extension of the MPA to married persons only is not discriminatory in this case as the distinction reflects and corresponds to the differences between those relationships and as it respects the fundamental personal autonomy and dignity of the individual. In this context, the dignity of common law spouses cannot be said to be affected adversely. There is no deprivation of a benefit based on stereotype or presumed characteristics perpetuating the idea that unmarried couples are less worthy of respect or valued as members of Canadian society. All cohabitants are deemed to have the liberty to make fundamental choices in their lives. The object of s. 15(1) is respected.

[63] Finally, it is important to note that the discriminatory aspect of the legislative distinction must be determined in light of Charter values. One of those essential values is liberty, basically defined as the absence of coercion and the ability to make fundamental choices with regard to one's life: *R v. Big M Drug Mart Ltd.*, [1985] 1 SCR 295, at p. 336; *R v. Oakes*, [1986] 1 SCR 103; *New Brunswick (Minister of Health and Community Services) v. G.(J.)*, [1999] 3 SCR 46, at para. 117. Limitations imposed by this Court that serve to restrict this freedom of choice among persons in conjugal relationships would be contrary to our notions of liberty. ...

[Not having found an infringement of s. 15 of the Charter, Bastarache J did not proceed to analyze s. 1.]

[In her dissenting opinion, L'Heureux-Dubé J concluded that the exclusion of heterosexual unmarried cohabitants from the definition of spouse in the *Matrimonial Property Act* constituted discrimination that was not justified pursuant to s. 1 of the Charter. After providing an overview of the Supreme Court of Canada's decision in *Law v. Canada*, she stated:]

[84] I conclude these preliminary remarks by observing that this Court is required, when conducting the above analysis, to review the claim from the perspective of a reasonable, dispassionate person, fully apprised of the circumstances, and possessing similar attributes to those of the claimant: *Law, supra*, at para. 60, referring to my comments in *Egan v. Canada*, [1995] 2 SCR 513, at para. 56. This subjective–

objective appraisal is necessary in order to recognize the reality of the claimant's situation while situating that claimant in the proper comparator group. The fact that the respondent Walsh has gone to the trouble of initiating this litigation and carrying it through this far suggests that, subjectively, she regards the definition of "spouse" as constituting a violation of her inherent human dignity. The question, however, is whether a person reflecting objectively on the claimant's situation would regard the exclusion of all heterosexual unmarried cohabitants as being a violation of the claimant's dignity. The objective element of the test also enables the Court to conduct the full contextual appraisal I noted earlier, evaluating in particular the individual's or group's "traits, history and circumstances": *Law*, *supra*. No analysis would be complete without this broad evaluation. ...

[L'Heureux-Dubé J considered in detail the steps required by *Law*: differential treatment, enumerated or analogous grounds, and substantive discrimination. In relation to the latter issue, she noted that the Supreme Court had recognized a degree of vulnerability and disadvantage for unmarried cohabitants in *Miron v. Trudel*. She also noted that the Nova Scotia legislation failed to take into account the actual needs, capacity, and circumstances of Ms Walsh. In addition, L'Heureux-Dubé J considered the ameliorative purpose or effects of the *Matrimonial Property Act* and the nature of the interests affected.]

(e) Recognizing Contributions to Non-Marital Relationships: The Purpose of the Matrimonial Property Act

[105] In para. 35 of his reasons, my colleague stresses the importance of distinguishing between the intentions of married persons and heterosexual unmarried cohabitants upon entering into their respective relationships. ... In effect, the appellant's position was that it was constitutionally justified in treating two different relationships differently, most notably by giving effect to the intentions of those entering into the two types of conjugal relationships involved. The Court of Appeal instead chose to focus on whether the complete non-recognition of the contributions made by heterosexual unmarried cohabitants to their relationship constituted discrimination. Given the purpose of the MPA, I believe that the Court of Appeal's focus on this crucial point was sound. In this section, I will deal with the purpose of the MPA and the non-recognition of contributions made by non-married persons. In doing so, I am mindful of McLachlin J's comments in *Miron*, *supra*, at para. 134, that the goal under s. 15(1) is to examine the actual impact of the distinction on the members of the targeted group (in this case, heterosexual unmarried cohabitants). In section (f), I will focus on the notion of intention in the formation of relationships.

[L'Heureux-Dubé J reviewed the history of married women's property, including the common law principles arising out of coverture; the statutory reforms; the recommendations of law reform commissions and others after the enactment of the *Divorce Act* in 1968; and the court's decision in *Murdoch*. She then examined the preamble of the Nova Scotia legislation and concluded:]

[112] In stark and simple terms, the preamble depicts a desire to recognize the contribution made by each spouse to the relationship and to the family, such contribution taking on the form of childcare, household management, and financial support. These three facets are acknowledged to be the joint responsibility of each spouse. In recognition of this joint responsibility and its discharge, the legislation presumes an equal entitlement to the matrimonial assets. The central theme, clearly, is the recognition of all contributions made by both spouses to the care and support of the family, it being stated that the family is central to society. ...

[Referring to the Supreme Court of Canada decision in *Clarke v. Clarke*, [1990] 2 SCR 795, L'Heureux-Dubé J agreed that the *Matrimonial Property Act* must be given "a broad and liberal construction" to achieve its remedial purpose. She also noted other cases in which the court had expressed such views (including *Moge v. Moge* and *M. v. H.*) and the similarity between the goals of the Nova Scotia legislation and Ontario's *Family Law Act*, and continued:]

[114] Both [statutes] are designed to recognize a need, namely the need for an equitable resolution to the dissolution of the relationship and the need to ensure that the public does not needlessly pay the costs associated with this breakdown. Both recognize this need through different means. In the case of the MPA, this is through a presumption of equal property sharing while in Ontario, the statute covers spousal support, child support, and the division of property. The consistent message from this Court is that family legislation of this type is remedial in that it recognizes a need and provides for its relief.

[115] This remedial interpretation is further supported by reference to the fact that the presumption of equal sharing only arises when the relationship comes to an end. ...

[116] This need is further illustrated by the desire to avoid diverting funds from the public purse in order to support separated individuals. It is no secret that divorce increases the likelihood that one of the divorced spouses will fall below the poverty line. This problem is no different for heterosexual unmarried cohabitants who experience the end of their relationship. In a report released in 1992, one author noted that

> ... the end of a marriage or *common-law relationship* increased the likelihood of poverty substantially. For those who were married and had children, the risk of poverty rose from 3.1 percent to 37.6 percent after divorce or separation. ... In 1982-86, the family income of women (adjusted for changes in family size) dropped by an average of about 30 percent in the year after their marriage ended. [Emphasis added.]

(T. Lempriere, "A New Look at Poverty" (1992), 16 *Perceptions* 18, at pp. 19-20, cited in M.J. Mossman, "'Running Hard To Stand Still': The Paradox of Family Law Reform" (1994), 17 *Dal. LJ* 5, at p. 6.)

[117] The goal of matrimonial property regimes, and indeed the goal of family law generally, is a redistribution of economic resources on the breakdown of the family. While the relationship is a going concern, this redistribution is presumed to occur automatically. Family law only steps in on dissolution to distribute resources and alleviate economic burdens. ... The preamble, this Court's previous statements concerning the goals of matrimonial property and similar legislation, the prevention

of poverty, and the use of public funds all point to one purpose for the MPA, that of recognizing the problems that erupt at the end of the relationship and redistributing wealth to ensure that these problems are resolved. Infused in this interpretation is the notion that both parties have contributed to the relationship and that, in recognition of this contribution, wealth will be presumed to be distributed to each party equally.

(ii) The Needs of Heterosexual Unmarried Cohabitants

[118] This brings me to the central theme of this factor. I hold that heterosexual unmarried cohabitants experience similar needs as their married counterparts when the relationship comes to an end. In this sense, the relationships are functionally equivalent. Since the purpose of the MPA is to recognize this need and to alleviate it, limiting the recognition to married cohabitants implies that the needs of heterosexual unmarried cohabitants are not worthy of the same recognition solely because the people in need have not married. Further, the MPA equal presumption is based on the recognition of the contribution made by both spouses to the family. Functionally, spouses contribute to various types of families. Failing to recognize the contribution made by heterosexual unmarried cohabitants is a failure to accord them the respect they deserve. This failure diminishes their status in their own eyes and in those of society as a whole by suggesting that they are less worthy of respect and consideration. Their dignity is thereby assaulted: they are the victims of discrimination. ...

[L'Heureux-Dubé J reviewed the statistics demonstrating the growth in numbers of unmarried cohabitants and stated (at para. 122): "The growth in the number of people living in non-marital relationships does not appear to be diminishing. If anything, this statistic signals an increased trend away from marriage towards unmarried cohabitation relationships." Based on the increasing numbers of unmarried cohabiting couples, she focused (at para. 125) on recommendations for redefining family. In particular, she identified Zheng Wu's conclusion that "cohabitation is slowly but surely becoming a substitute for legal marriage as a social institution where children are born, raised, and socialized to become members of our society."]

[126] The increased incidence of heterosexual unmarried cohabitation as a means by which children are raised and socialized and as a form of economic, emotional and social interdependence dictates some form of recognition of the functional equality displayed by both heterosexual married and unmarried cohabitants. The family is no longer an institution reserved for married persons. In essence, the family is a matrix of relationships through which values are transmitted, members are socialized, and children are raised. Disregarding the matrix because two of its members are unmarried fails to take into account the social reality that the same incidents of interdependence are faced by both the married and the unmarried living together in these relationships. ...

[L'Heureux-Dubé J reviewed other cases in which the court had recognized the functions of families, including *Pettkus v. Becker*, [1980] 2 SCR 834 and *Mossop*, [1993] SCR 554. She continued (at para. 131):]

In light of all this, it is interesting to note that, in some ways, the debate about family presents society with a false choice. It is possible to be pro-family without rejecting less traditional family forms. It is not anti-family to support protection for non-traditional families. The traditional family is not the only family form, and non-traditional family forms may equally advance true family values.

[132] By denying functionally equal relationships benefits based on a status wholly unrelated to their needs, the MPA ends up drawing an inappropriate distinction. ...

[133] The equivalency of functions described above gives rise to identical needs upon the breakdown of the family relationship. As both marital and non-marital co-habitation can be characterized by emotional, social, and economic inter-dependence, it follows that the termination of these relationships generates similar problems. ...

[135] These facts have not been lost on law reformers as well. In Nova Scotia, the Law Reform Commission released its report in 1997 dealing with proposed changes to the MPA that would allow individuals, including heterosexual unmarried cohabi-tants, to claim similar benefits to their married counterparts. The Commission's con-clusions regarding the nature of unmarried relationships are aptly set out at page 21 of their Final Report:

> ... [T]he Commission has reached the view that most cohabitation relationships are functionally similar to marital relationships, and deserve to be treated similarly by the law. Human beings seek out long-term relationships for a variety of reasons, including companionship, love, emotional support, sexual intimacy, procreation, economic need and social expectation. Such relationships, especially but not exclusively where there are children, often generate patterns of economic dependency. These patterns, which may not be apparent during the relationship, are exposed on its termination. ... The reason for the law to impose property division in marriage and cohabitation relation-ships is to respond to the economic interdependence which arises in such relationships, and to ensure that the dependent partner is not punished for the role which he or she has played during the relationship.

(Law Reform Commission of Nova Scotia, *Final Report: Reform of the Law Dealing with Matrimonial Property in Nova Scotia* (1997).) ...

[L'Heureux-Dubé J also noted the report of the OLRC, specifically addressing (at paras. 137ff.) the argument that relationships of marriage and cohabitation should be treated differently in law because cohabiting relationships were often shorter in dura-tion. Citing provisions in the statute that permitted courts to change legislative prin-ciples in relation to short marriages, she concluded:]

[140] It is no excuse to deny the benefit of equal sharing to all heterosexual un-married cohabitants simply because some members of the group do not seem to deserve nor want this equal division. The legislature is in the best position to craft legislation that takes into account the difficulties associated with extending the bene-fit. It is clear, though, based on the purpose of the MPA and the functional equiva-lency of the two types of relationships relative to that purpose, that extending the benefit of the equal presumption solely to married cohabitants constitutes a serious

attack upon the dignity of the claimant and all heterosexual unmarried cohabitants. It sends the message that, although the need for a simple means of dividing the assets on dissolution exists, only certain people are entitled to the benefit because of a status wholly unrelated to that need. In short, it demeans the dignity of an equal to treat him or her with less respect than his or her functional equals. Like the Court of Appeal, I agree that the MPA fails to recognize the contributions made by parties to a non-marital relationship and that such non-recognition has the effect of demeaning them as human beings.

(f) Choosing To Marry and Choosing To Cohabit: Effect on Dignity

[L'Heureux-Dubé J also addressed (at para. 141) the government's argument that marriage, unlike cohabitation, involved a "considered choice to enter into a relation-ship." … Rejecting this argument, she argued (at para. 142) that "the MPA has nothing to do with consensus and everything to do with recognizing the needs of the spouses."]

[143] I believe it to be highly problematic to conceive of marriage as a type of arrangement people enter into with the legal consequences of its demise taken into account. In the first place, most people are not lawyers. They are often not aware of the state of the law. Worse, many maintain positive misconceptions as to what obliga-tions and rights exist in association with marriage and other relationships. …

[144] Even assuming that people contemplating marriage are, as a whole, fully aware of their legal rights and obligations as married people, it is a mistake to base the obligations imposed by the MPA on the partners' perceived consensus to be bound by these obligations through marriage. …

[145] Couples do not think of their relationship in contract terms. The observa-tions of one author on this point are particularly poignant:

> Now, the confusion in the law arises from the fact that while marriages (and domestic partnerships) are quite obviously more like friendships than hamburgers, they also give rise to legally enforceable obligations, which lead some people to forget the obvious and think they are like hamburgers after all. The error apparently arises from the mis-taken assumption that the legal obligations arising from marriage must have their source in a bargained-for exchange. The mistake is probably facilitated by the fact that the reciprocal nature of a successful marriage gives it a superficial resemblance to a bargained-for exchange, which is, after all, the source of so many legal obligations. But we must remain clear about the difference. Lunch with my friend may leave me with a sense of social debt that is real, but non-specific. … Friendship involves communicating interest in and concern for one another's welfare over a longer time horizon; opportuni-ties to reciprocate may not present themselves in a convenient sequence for turn-taking. The debt to the restaurant, by contrast, involves paying $23.37 now.

(I.M. Ellman, " 'Contract Thinking' Was Marvin's Fatal Flaw" (2001), 76 *Notre Dame L Rev.* 1365, at pp. 1373-74.)

[146] In other words, the fact that marriage gives rise to legal obligations does not, by itself, signal that the source of those obligations is some bargained-for

exchange or the product of a consensus. While the price of a hair cut is known in advance and can be contracted for (with a higher price for perms than for brushcuts), the same cannot be said about marriage. The marital relationship changes over time. Houses and other assets are bought and sold, one of the partners is promoted or loses their job, children are born, accidents occur, or a member of the family becomes ill. These and other events are rarely anticipated at the outset and appropriately bargained for. Further, neither spouse can anticipate who will contribute what to the marriage. As a consequence, even the most intelligent of adults lacks the capacity to evaluate the commitments involved in any agreement dealing with the consequences of a dissolution that will only come after great change occurs in the relationship. ... [Moreover,] I consider it somewhat facetious for the appellant to argue that the MPA is designed to give effect to the choices made by married and heterosexual unmarried cohabitants when the legislation expressly applies to people who married at a time prior to the enactment of the MPA or its predecessor.

[148] If I am incorrect in concluding that the source of the obligations in the MPA is not based on the choice of marriage, it does not follow that heterosexual unmarried cohabitants enter into their relationships specifically to avoid those legal obligations. In other words, the choice argument fails from both sides: many unmarried partners do not choose to cohabit or remain unmarried so as to avoid the legal consequences of marriage.

[149] The reasons why people choose to cohabit are numerous. Some people have attempted to catalogue these potential reasons. ...

[150] It is impossible to pin any one of these reasons on all people who choose not to marry. In her study of heterosexual unmarried cohabitants living in Britain, C. Smart concluded that:

> The majority of the men and women in our study did not cohabit because they were selfish and immoral, or because they rejected the ideological/patriarchal basis of marriage. Cohabitation was not necessarily a self-centred nor a progressive form of union. On the contrary, some of these cohabiting unions seemed be [sic] very similar to an ideal type of marriage with its emphasis on companionship, shared interests, commitment to children and shared economic resources. Other cohabiting unions however seemed to reproduce some of the worst aspects of traditional heterosexual marriage such as domestic violence, a rigid sexual division of labour and financial insecurity for mothers. Only about a quarter of those interviewed saw themselves as taking a stand against marriage as an institution or saw marriage as an irrelevance in the light of a superior form of private commitment. Many of the women we interviewed actually wanted to get married (albeit to a better person that they had yet to meet). Equally, some of the men went on to marry other women with whom they formed relationships later on. We cannot, therefore, simply describe these trends as "progressive" or "regressive"—the choices people make have different meanings in different contexts and we need to be constantly in tune with these complexities rather than oversimplifying and over-generalising.

(C. Smart, "Stories of Family Life: Cohabitation, Marriage, and Social Change" (2000), 17 *Can. J Fam. L* 20, at p. 50.). ...

[151] Some commentators go even further by suggesting that personal autonomy and choice are very rarely involved in the choice to cohabit. In "Marriage and Co-habitation—Has the Time Come To Bridge the Gap?" in *Special Lectures of the Law Society of Upper Canada, 1993 Family Law: Roles, Fairness and Equality …* [(Scarborough, ON: Carswell, 1994)], 369, at p. 379, W.H. Holland espouses this view in the following words:

> … [I]n many cases, there is little planning and the parties cohabit without having given very careful thought to where the relationship is heading. In fact, it is doubtful whether many couples are aware of the differences in the legal consequences of marriage and cohabitation and that cohabitation is chosen to avoid the legal consequences of marriage. …

[152] I agree with this interpretation. It also reflects the fact that the existence of many heterosexual non-marital relationships are rarely the product of choice in the sense that the choice not to marry is not a matter belonging to each individual alone. The ability to marry is inhibited whenever one of the two partners wishes to marry and the other does not. In this situation, it can hardly be said that the person who wishes to marry but must cohabit in order to obey the wishes of his or her partner chooses to cohabit. This results in a situation where one of the parties to the cohabitation relationship preserves his or her autonomy at the expense of the other: "[t]he flip side of one person's autonomy is often another's exploitation" ([Holland, supra], … at p. 380). Under these circumstances, stating that both members of the relationship chose to avoid the legal consequences of marriage is patently absurd. …

[153] The argument that cohabitation is mainly the result of a considered choice was also rejected by the Court in *Miron, supra* [at para. 153]:

> In theory, the individual is free to choose whether to marry or not to marry. In practice, however, the reality may be otherwise. The sanction of the union by the state through civil marriage cannot always be obtained. The law; the reluctance of one's partner to marry; financial, religious or social constraints—these factors and others commonly function to prevent partners who otherwise operate as a family unit from formally marrying. *In short, marital status often lies beyond the individual's effective control.* [Emphasis added.]

I made the same observations at paras. 95-97, concluding that "[i]t is small consolation, indeed, to be told that one has been denied equal protection under the Charter by virtue of the fact that one's partner had a choice." Nothing has changed since *Miron* was decided to indicate that these statements are incorrect. They apply with equal vigour to the Charter challenge in the present case.

[L'Heureux-Dubé J then reviewed the findings of a number of studies, which she found to be ambivalent in their conclusions, and continued:]

[157] Based on the above comments, it is my view that the argument that the claimant's dignity was not violated by legislation enacted to respect her choice (and the choice of all heterosexual unmarried cohabitants) fails. This argument fails to

account for the fact that the MPA rights are not based on choice or consensus. More-over, it is incorrect to paint each unmarried cohabitant with the same brush as regards the "choice" to cohabit. For many, choice is not an option. For those where choice is in fact an option, few structure their lives by marrying or not marrying to take advan-tage or avoid particular legal obligations. The MPA does not therefore promote the dignity of the claimant. In fact, its failure to appreciate the absence of choice many cohabitants face with its concomitant exploitative features demeans the dignity of heterosexual unmarried cohabitants. ...

[Finally, L'Heureux-Dubé J considered legislative reforms and the equitable rem-edies available to cohabiting couples, concluding that the refusal to acknowledge contributions in cohabiting relationships suggested that, by virtue of marital status alone, such relationships were less worthy of respect, recognition, and value.]

[171] Members of this group feel the loss of dignity by this lack of acknowledg-ment. Moreover, their dignity is further attacked by claims that the MPA is designed to give effect to the intentions of married and unmarried persons at the outset of their relationships. Such claims ignore the express purpose of the MPA to remedy ills as-sociated with the termination of these relationships. The right to a presumption of equal contribution, after all, only arises when the relationship comes to an end. Initial intentions are, therefore, of little consequence. In fact, few people realistically believe that any significant number of human beings enter into relationships of love, affec-tion, and companionship in order to produce a particular legal outcome. If anything, some people are unaware or positively mistaken about their legal rights as married or unmarried cohabitants. Worse still, many heterosexual unmarried cohabitants cohabit not out of choice but out of necessity. For many, choice is denied them by virtue of the wishes of the other partner. To deny them a remedy because the other partner chose to avoid certain consequences creates a situation of exploitation. It certainly does not enhance the dignity of those who could not "choose" to cohabit.

[172] Recognition of the value of unmarried cohabitation by courts and by legis-latures also bolsters the view that historic non-recognition was unjust. Attempts to remedy this injustice confirm the existence of the injustice in not providing a remedy. Finally, it cannot be said that the MPA survives s. 15(1) scrutiny because of the avail-ability of alternative remedies. These remedies are inadequate relative to those accord-ed spouses under the MPA. They were not good enough for married people in 1980. That has not changed for their unmarried counterparts. I conclude that the purposes of s. 15(1) are not furthered by the unamended MPA. As such, the claimant has suc-cessfully shown a violation of her dignity.

[173] Given my conclusions on the first three steps, it follows that the MPA vio-lates s. 15(1) of the Charter and is, therefore, *prima facie* unconstitutional.

[In addition, L'Heureux-Dubé J concluded that the infringement of s. 15 was not jus-tified in accordance with s. 1. Gonthier J also delivered separate reasons, concurring with the reasons of Bastarache J.]

Discussion Notes

Recommendations of the American Law Institute

The contrasting views expressed in the majority and dissenting reasons in *Nova Scotia v. Walsh* reveal fundamental differences in approaches to cohabitation and to the role of family law principles at the end of a cohabiting relationship. In its analysis of domestic partners in the United States, the American Law Institute suggested that the rising rate of cohabitation (which is lower in the United States than in Canada: see chapter 1) meant that it was "increasingly implausible to attribute special significance to the parties' failure to marry." After identifying reasons for parties' failure to marry, the institute concluded:

> In all of these cases, the absence of formal marriage may have little or no bearing on the intentions of the parties, the character of the parties' domestic relationship, or the equitable considerations that underlie claims between lawful spouses at the dissolution of a marriage.

(American Law Institute, *Principles of the Law of Family Dissolution: Analysis and Recommendations* (Washington, DC: Matthew Bender, 2002), 33.)

More significantly, the institute suggested (at 34) that the use of contract law to define the rights and obligations of non-marital cohabitants was unsatisfactory and that ordinary principles applicable to marriage dissolution should replace concepts of contract in defining the rights and obligations of cohabiting partners at the end of their relationships:

> American contractual treatment of nonmarital cohabitation is unusual in that no other country approaches cohabitation solely as a matter of contract law. Other countries primarily ask the question: Does this nonmarital family look like a marital family? If so, they apply some or all of their family law to the dissolution of the nonmarital family. In other words, other countries look to the character of the relationship as it developed over time, and not just to the statements the parties may have made, or not made, to one another at its inception. ... [In its recommendations, the institute] draws inspiration from Canada, and also from Australia and New Zealand.

The institute recommended use of the same principles for dividing marital and domestic-partnership property: recommendation no. 6.05. In doing so, it expressly noted the relative absence of social security for dependent individuals in the United States, by contrast with some other countries; as a result, principles that allocate more responsibility to family members, by contrast with the state, appeared particularly attractive in the United States.

In relation to the majority reasons in *Nova Scotia v. Walsh* (which concluded that Walsh was not entitled to share in property at the dissolution of her cohabiting relationship with Bona), what is the practical result in terms of responsibilities of the family and the state to provide for dependency? To what extent did the majority address the issues in *Nova Scotia v. Walsh* from the perspective of economic support for post-separation dependency?

Empirical Data and Choice

What concepts of liberty and freedom of choice are reflected in the majority judgment, by contrast with the dissenting opinion? To what extent do these views rely on empirical evidence about cohabiting relationships generally or on the facts in this case? Should it make a difference whether cohabiting partners have discussed their intentions or not? As Thompson explained in his annotation of the decision, the choice issue became significant only late in the litigation process, so that there was no evidence in the record as to why Walsh and Bona had never married. Moreover, he argued that the use of Zheng Wu's data (see chapter 2) by the majority judgment was ironic since Wu recommended that married and cohabiting couples be treated the same in relation to issues at dissolution: see Zheng Wu, *Cohabitation: An Alternative Form of Family Living* (Oxford: Oxford University Press, 2000), 161-67. According to Thompson, however, while it was ideology, rather than data, that drove the analysis, the real issue was "not whether common-law couples are heterogeneous, but whether that heterogeneity makes their total exclusion from the MPA discriminatory": see D.A. Rollie Thompson, "Annotation of Walsh v. Bona" (2003), 32 RFL (5th) 87, at 90. For another analysis of cohabitation rights and obligations, see Law Reform Commission of Nova Scotia, *Discussion Paper on Matrimonial Property in Nova Scotia: Suggestions for a New Family Law Act* (Halifax: Law Reform Commission of Nova Scotia, 1996).

Marriage-Like Relationships: Grigg v. Berg

In *Grigg v. Berg Estate* (2000), 31 ETR (2d) 214 (BCSC), a cohabiting partner claimed that s. 2 of the BC *Wills Variation Act*, RSBC 1996, c. 490 infringed s. 15 of the Charter because it provided that relief could be claimed only by a husband, wife, or child, but not by a person in a marriage-like relationship, in relation to the will of the deceased person. How should this case have been decided? In fact, the court held that the provision of the statute was discriminatory pursuant to the Charter—how is this case different, in terms of family property issues, to *Nova Scotia v. Walsh*? Is it justifiable to treat cohabitees differently in relation to the dissolution of a relationship at separation, by contrast with dissolution by death?

Negotiating About Family Property: Legislative Policies

Thompson also argued (at 92) that the majority judgment failed to take account of the interests of Walsh's and Bona's two children as well as "imbalances of power between partners, and other harsh realities of the breakdown of relationships." He also noted (at 87) that Walsh and Bona had settled Walsh's claim after the decision of the Nova Scotia Court of Appeal, which held that Walsh was entitled to share equally in the property accumulated during the cohabiting relationship. In this context, the Court of Appeal's decision clearly affected the balance of power between Walsh and Bona in relation to their negotiations, and it may have alleviated some of the economic impact of the dissolution of their relationship. Although there is no available evidence about why Bona and Walsh (and their legal advisors) decided to settle after the Court of Appeal decision, its unanimous judgment was very likely a factor influencing their decision. In the Supreme Court of Canada, it was the Nova Scotia government that argued in favour of allowing the appeal—what factors may have influenced the government's decision to argue that cohabiting couples should not be entitled to use the provincial statutory regime at separation?

In addition to launching this appeal, the Nova Scotia government enacted the *Law Reform (2000) Act*, SNS 2000, c. 29 and SNS 2001, cc. 5 and 45, legislation that permitted registration of domestic-partner declarations. Both same-sex and opposite-sex couples were permitted to register these declarations, thereby becoming entitled to rights and obligations as spouses, including rights pursuant to the *Matrimonial Property Act*. Although the Supreme Court of Canada examined the issues in *Nova Scotia v. Walsh* without reliance on this statutory arrangement, how might its existence have influenced the judgments and reasoning? To what extent does it reflect an opting-in or an opting-out arrangement? Is it possible that the legislative choice to create an opting-in system affected arguments about the spouses' choice in the majority decision?

Consider the Nova Scotia legislation from a policy perspective—is it appropriate for married and cohabiting couples to have *exactly* the same rights and obligations? What are the fundamental issues for governments in making this legislative choice? To what extent are there links, in terms of public policy, between the issues in *Nova Scotia v. Walsh* and the same-sex marriage jurisprudence in chapter 2?

Cohabiting Relationships and the Use of Trust Principles

The exclusion of cohabiting couples from access to legislative regimes at dissolution of their relationships, pursuant to the majority decision of the Supreme Court of Canada, did not mean that they had no recourse at law. In addition to the legislation enacted in Nova Scotia (above), and in some other provinces, cohabiting couples (opposite-sex and same-sex) may claim property interests using the principles of constructive and resulting trusts. In reviewing the material that follows in relation to (1) the statutory regimes and (2) the use of trust doctrines, try to determine why it was important to Walsh to gain access to the statutory regime in this case. You may want to reconsider the reasoning of the majority and dissenting judgments in *Nova Scotia v. Walsh* again at the end of this chapter.

SELECTED REFERENCES

Nicholas Bala and Marlène Cano, "Unmarried Cohabitation in Canada: Common Law and Civilian Approaches to Living Together" (1989), 4 *Canadian Family Law Quarterly* 147.

Michael D.A. Freeman and Christine M. Lyon, *Cohabitation Without Marriage: An Essay in Law and Social Policy* (Aldershot, UK: Gower, 1983).

Mary Ann Glendon, *The New Family and the New Property* (Toronto: Butterworths, 1983).

Winnifred Holland, "Intimate Relationships in the New Millennium: The Assimilation of Marriage and Cohabitation?" (2000), 17 *Canadian Journal of Family Law* 114.

Don MacDougall, "Policy and Social Factors Affecting the Legal Recognition of Cohabitation Without Formal Marriage," in John M. Eekelaar and Sanford Katz, eds., *Marriage and Cohabitation in Contemporary Societies: Areas of Legal, Social, and Ethical Change* (Toronto: Butterworths, 1980), 313.

III. LEGISLATIVE REGIMES AT THE DISSOLUTION OF MARRIAGE: PARTNERSHIP AND PROPERTY PRINCIPLES

A. Basic Principles and Approaches

People enter family relationships to satisfy many human needs: social, sexual, and economic. When two people enter into a relationship they make joint economic decisions for the benefit of the family unit. Their decisions about what contributions each partner makes to the economic relationship and how the assets of that relationship are divided may be made because of cultural assumptions about the proper role of each partner or because of economic advantages that they will enjoy together. If a relationship breaks down, family members face the difficult task of extricating themselves from the economic arrangements they have made together. ... Simply leaving family property in the name of the partner who had legal title to it during the relationship may be grossly unfair.

OLRC, *Report on Family Property Law*
(Toronto: OLRC, 1993), 1

1. Issues for Legislative Policies

The principle that family property should be shared at the end of a marital partnership is relatively straightforward. Its implementation in practice, however, is often much more complex. Three issues dominate the policy choices of provincial legislation in Canada:

1. What is the underlying rationale for sharing family property at the dissolution of the relationship? Is it a consequence of the marital relationship itself, a presumption of equal contributions by the partners to the acquisition and maintenance of family assets, or a reflection of actual contributions by the partners? If marriage itself provides the rationale, should there be any differences between long-term and short-term marriages? If equality of contribution is to be presumed, should such presumptions be rebuttable, and if so, who should bear the onus of proof? If contributions are to be assessed, what factors are relevant?

2. What property is to be shared? In terms of property owned by each spouse at the breakdown of their relationship, should they be permitted to exclude property that was a gift, or property that was acquired before the marriage? In other words, is property that was jointly accumulated to be shared, or all property owned by each of them, regardless of how or when title was acquired? Related to this question is the issue whether all property or just family assets should be shared—for example, if one spouse owns a business and the other spouse has contributed nothing to it, should it be shared at breakdown or excluded as a non-family asset? In addition, there may be special issues about the matrimonial home; at breakdown, should the spouse who will provide primary care and custody for children have any right to stay in the home, even if it means postponing the division of family assets?

3. What should be the basic unit of entitlement? Should there be a presumption that each spouse is entitled to one-half of the family property or its value? If so, what factors are relevant to rebutting this presumption of equal shares and who has the

onus of proof? Or, should courts have discretion to allocate property or interests in property in accordance with legislative criteria designed to achieve equity and fairness (which may be different from equality) in certain circumstances? In other words, should there be fixed shares or discretionary decision making by courts? And how are these questions related to goals of certainty in terms of legal principles and efficacy in their implementation?

In addition to these three issues, provincial legislative schemes differ according to whether they divide property interests, or just the value of these interests, between the spouses. Some provincial regimes adjust property rights between the spouses, while others adjust the economic balance between them by determining the value of their respective interests and providing for an equalizing payment. As a paper prepared for the BC Law Reform Commission explained, recognition of property interests for non-owning spouses may create problems for third-party creditors that are, at least to some extent, avoided by a regime that provides for an equalizing payment but does not otherwise affect property interests. Moreover, the commission concluded that equally satisfactory measures could be adopted to protect the interests of the non-owning spouse, without a need to create property interests for them: see Law Reform Commission of British Columbia, *Working Paper on Property Rights on Marriage Breakdown* (Victoria: Ministry of the Attorney General, 1989), 110-13 and appendix E.

Although provincial regimes in the common law provinces across Canada reveal differing approaches to some of the above questions, there appears to be general agreement with respect to the fundamental rationale for family property regimes—marriage *per se* creates entitlement to a one-half share of family property for each spouse, subject to a limited number of exceptions (which may vary to some extent in different provinces in terms of specific circumstances). This basic principle has often been defined in terms of a presumption that, in marriage, the contributions of the spouses are equal. In this way, marriage provides the entitlement to an equal share of family property, or its value, on the basis of a *legal presumption* that spousal contributions were equal. In Ontario, this legal presumption is stated in s. 5(7) of the *Family Law Act*, RSO 1990, c. F.3:

> The purpose of this section is to recognize that child care, household management and financial provision are the joint responsibilities of the spouses and that inherent in the marital relationship there is equal contribution, whether financial or otherwise, by the spouses to the assumption of these responsibilities, entitling each spouse to the equalization of the net family properties, subject only to the equitable considerations set out in subsection (6).

Pursuant to this section, the spouses are presumed to have made equal contributions entitling them to equal shares in the value of family property. (Although this presumption can be rebutted, it is necessary to show that the inequality of contributions was extreme; the test is "unconscionability": see s. 5(6) and further discussion below.)

2. Comparing Legislative Approaches: Two Examples

While there is general agreement among the common law provinces with respect to the fundamental basis for equal sharing of family property at marriage breakdown, there are different approaches to the questions of what property is to be divided, the role and extent of judicial discretion to adjust basic entitlements, and whether a property interest or an equalizing payment is more appropriate. For example, provincial legislation in British Columbia and Ontario offer some contrasting approaches to these questions.

a. Family Property in British Columbia

Pursuant to s. 56 of the BC *Family Relations Act*, RSBC 1996, c. 128, each spouse is entitled to an interest in each family asset. Family assets are defined in ss. 58 and 59 of the Act; in addition to assets specifically identified, s. 58(2) provides that property owned by one or both spouses and "ordinarily used by a spouse or a minor child of either spouse for a family purpose" is a family asset. Included within this definition is any property that meets this test, whether it was acquired before or during the marriage by either spouse.

The BC statute also reflects the interest-in-property approach to family property division—s. 56(2) provides that each spouse is entitled (at the moment defined by the statute in relation to their separation) to a one-half interest in all family assets as a tenant-in-common. Clearly, this means that a non-owning spouse acquires a proprietary interest in family property owned by the other.

In addition to this statutory presumption of equal division, s. 65 provides for judicial discretion to make a reapportionment "on the basis of fairness," in accordance with a list of factors.

Thus, overall, BC's legislation provides for equal interests in family property, defined in terms of family usage, and for the exercise of discretion by a court in order to achieve fairness between the spouses.

An Example: Martin v. Martin

Interestingly, one factor to be considered in the exercise of judicial discretion on the basis of fairness pursuant to s. 65 of the BC statute is "the needs of each spouse to become or remain economically independent and self sufficient": see s. 65(1)(e). In *Martin v. Martin*, [1992] 67 BCLR (2d) 219, the BC Court of Appeal considered this provision in relation to the dissolution of a second marriage. At the date of marriage, the spouses were in their late 50s and early 60s, and their marriage lasted less than five years. Although the husband owned a home and a number of investments at the date of marriage, the wife had only a mobile home (sold for $28,000), a car, and savings of about $1,000. During the marriage, she contributed $7,000 from the proceeds of sale of the mobile home to renovate the husband's home; she also became disabled and retired from employment in receipt of a monthly pension until she turned 65 and began to receive old age security.

The trial judge decided that, instead of apportioning family assets, it was appropriate to award the wife a lump-sum judgment of $85,000. This decision left most of the assets in the husband's name, and he received more than half the total value of the assets. This outcome was justified on the basis that the husband had most of the assets at the time of the marriage, which was of short duration, and because approximately $9,000 was a gift from his father. The husband appealed the findings that some assets constituted family assets and the award of a lump-sum judgment of $85,000 to the wife.

In assessing the fairness of the outcome, the Court of Appeal stated (at paras. 29-32):

> Before the marriage the wife was employed, independent and able to look after herself. To accommodate the marriage she gave up her residence, possibly at a sacrifice price, and contributed $7,000 towards renovations. With respect, I agree with the conclusions ... in *Heinz v. Heinz* (unreported) January 26, 1990 (SCBC). ... In that case, as in this one, the elderly wife gave up her residence and would not be able "... to achieve any form of economic independence and self-sufficiency." Fairness, which is the test prescribed by [s. 65], requires that the wife in this case now receive enough to return her approximately to the position she was in before the marriage, so that both the family assets and the burden of the marriage failure may be distributed equitably between the spouses. ... [In relation to the award to the wife and the husband's retention of the matrimonial home and other assets,] I cannot say that an award of $85,000 is unfair to either the husband or the wife. There are unfortunate tax consequences to the husband consequent upon the liquidation of assets both to meet the judgment, and for his ongoing expenses, but he could, if he wishes, sell the home.

As a result, the court concluded that there was no unfairness in the "approximately equal distribution of family assets."

b. Family Property in Ontario

By contrast, Ontario's *Family Law Act* defines "property" to be shared by spouses very broadly in s. 4, but the legislative definition permits the exclusion or deduction of the value of property that does not represent property accumulated by the spouses during the marriage—for example, property owned at the date of marriage generally may be deducted, and gifts and inheritances received by one spouse from a third party during the marriage are excluded: see ss. 4(1) and (2). (To preserve the matrimonial home for sharing by the spouses, however, it cannot be deducted as pre-marriage property, nor can it be excluded as a gift or inheritance, an issue described in more detail later in this chapter.) Moreover, although a court may allocate more or less than one-half the value of family property to a spouse, the list of factors to be considered is quite narrow and the basic test for judicial intervention is high—that equalization would be unconscionable: s. 5(6). In this way, the Ontario legislation represents a more non-discretionary fixed shares approach, by contrast with BC's statutory regime.

In addition, although earlier Ontario legislation (the *Family Law Reform Act*, SO 1978, c. 2) adopted a family-assets approach relating to the use of property during the marriage, the current Ontario legislation uses an equalization-payment approach. Thus, without changing any entitlement to property owned by each spouse at the relevant date, the *value* of all property is calculated (each spouse's net family property (NFP)); the spouse with the higher NFP value must make an equalizing payment to the other spouse: see s. 5(1). The result is that each spouse shares equally in the economic wealth of the marriage at breakdown, without any change in property ownership. Consider the following excerpt from a case decided shortly after the adoption of this statutory scheme in Ontario as an example of the process of determining the equalizing payment.

Skrlj v. Skrlj
(1986), 2 RFL (3d) 305 (Ont. SC (HCJ))

[In this case, one of the first to be decided under the *Family Law Act, 1986*, Galligan J explained the approach to be used in relation to the new legislation and then provided (at 309) a step-by-step assessment of the value of the property owned by each spouse to determine the equalization amount required under s. 5(1) and the overall interpretation of ss. 4 and 5.]

Before dealing with the property issues, I want to make a very brief observation about the new regime of family law in Ontario. As I read the *Family Law Act, 1986*, it leaves the court with no discretion to decide spouses' affairs in accordance with a particular court's sense of fairness. Subject to a discretion if it finds unconscionability, under s. 5(6), the courts must decide the rights of separating spouses in strict compliance with the terms of the Act, even if, in an individual case, a judge may feel that the result does not appear fair according to that particular judge's sense of fairness. I think the legislature has clearly expressed its intent to remove judicial discretion from property disputes between separating spouses.

In this case certain suggestions were put to the court about how this dispute could be resolved by transferring assets to discharge corresponding liabilities. In my view, that is the stuff of settlement. Separating spouses can settle their differences as they see fit but if they do not settle them and decide to come to trial, they are entitled to, and should expect to get, adjudication, not mediation. I think that any remnants of "Palm Tree Justice" have now disappeared from Ontario.

I intend to decide this case, and other cases, strictly according to the *Family Law Act*, as I interpret it. The chips will fall where they may.

The scheme of the Act, insofar as it relates to property, is to determine the value of each spouse's net family property as at the valuation date as defined in the Act. (In this case it has been agreed that the valuation date is 18th June 1981.) Once the value of each spouse's net family property is determined, the spouse with the lesser value is entitled to one half of the difference, subject to any adjustment if unconscionability, as set out in s. 5(6) of the Act, is proved.

The first step is to determine what was owned by each spouse on the valuation date. The next is the deduction of debts and the value of assets owned by each spouse at the time of marriage. Property falling within s. 4(2) of the Act is of course excluded from a spouse's net family property.

In this case the assets are not extensive. I will discuss each of them briefly. The matrimonial home is owned jointly and has a present value of $75,000. There are no encumbrances. No estimate has been given of the value of the property on valuation day [V-day]. Since the property is owned jointly, in my opinion it is not necessary to be particularly concerned with its value on valuation day, because each spouse's property will have an identical amount attributed to it. I credit each spouse's property with one half of the appraised value, or $37,500. ...

[Galligan J then identified a joint account at Canada Trust with a total value of $10,200. Thus, each spouse was credited with $5,100. There was also a Canada Trust account in the husband's name with a value of $23,300. Galligan J ignored accounts opened after valuation day, as well as an account held by the wife for the benefit of her children. The wife's account with a value of $758 was included in her NFP, along with an RRSP owned by the husband on V-day.]

Once the value of the property owned by each spouse has been determined, there must be deducted from those amounts each spouse's debts or liabilities and the value of property owned by each at the date of marriage. I accept the wife's evidence that she had property at the time of marriage worth $1,000 and that her husband had a car with an equity worth approximately $300. I also accept her evidence that she had debts of $1,130 on valuation day. The husband had no debts or liabilities. The appropriate deductions will be made.

I have done a handwritten schedule and passed copies to counsel showing my calculations as follows:

	Wife	Husband
Property		
Matrimonial home	$37,500	$37,500
Canada Trust (Ex. 3)	5,100	5,100
Canada Trust (Ex. 4)		23,300
Canada Trust (Ex. 16)	758	
RRSP		2,000
Total Property	$43,358	$67,900
Deductions		
Property at time of marriage	$ 1,000	$ 300
Debts or liabilities	1,130	
Net family property	$41,228	$67,900

The result is that on valuation day she had net family property valued at $41,228. He had net family property of $67,900.

[It appears that the court made an arithmetical mistake—it failed to deduct Mr. Skrlj's pre-marriage property; the figure of $67,900 should have been $67,600.]

The difference is $26,672. She is *prima facie* entitled to payment of one half of that amount, of $13,336.

In the circumstances of this case, I think, however, that she is entitled to be awarded an amount greater than one half of the difference, because I find in this case that equalizing net family properties would be unconscionable. I do not intend to go into any lengthy discussion of the circumstances giving rise to the unconscionability. It will suffice to say that after valuation day each party took money out of the joint account Ex. 3 without permission of the other. The husband took $6,330 more than she did. In my opinion, it would have been unconscionable within s. 5(6)(h) of the Act for him to have that money and for her to have attributed to her property one half of the amount of the account on valuation day. One half of the amount of $6,330

($3,165) will be added to her equalizing payment. She will therefore have an order for payment, that is, judgment against her husband, for $16,501.

Discussion Notes

Comparing Approaches to Family Property

As the OLRC's report noted, the Ontario legislation was designed "to operate as a mechanical scheme with little scope for judicial discretion," reflecting the recommendations of the commission's earlier report in 1974: see OLRC, *Report on Family Property Law* (Toronto: OLRC, 1993), at 59, and *Report on Family Law: Part IV: Family Property Law* (Toronto: OLRC, 1974), 93. Significantly, both reports appear to assume that the achievement of equality between the spouses, in terms of their entitlement to family property at marriage breakdown, is the appropriate goal. Are there any factors that might undermine the appropriateness of this assumption in practice?

For example, Jack Knetsch argued that spouses often make decisions, while the family unit is intact, that benefit the unit as a whole; however, some of these decisions may mean that one spouse, frequently the wife, may be less well-positioned at marriage breakdown in terms of future financial well-being: see Jack Knetsch, "Some Economic Implications of Matrimonial Property Rules" (1984), 34 *University of Toronto Law Journal* 263. Does this argument suggest that achieving equality in relation to family property at divorce may not address broader, systemic economic inequalities for spouses in their situations post-divorce?

Compare the reasoning in *Martin v. Martin* in the BC court and the Ontario decision in *Skrlj v. Skrlj*—is the reasoning in *Martin* more discretionary than in the Ontario example, above? Is it appropriate to characterize the BC approach as palm-tree justice? Re-examine the outcome in *Skrlj v. Skrlj*—to what extent does it meet the post-divorce needs of the spouses in relation to property? Identify the advantages and disadvantages of these differing approaches—which is preferable? Why?

The Goal of Equality: Theory and Practice

In considering the question of equality more systemically, Martha Fineman argued that the problem of presumptions of equality in family property statutes arises out of the statutory conception of equality as "formal" rather than "substantive":

> The ideal of equality between spouses is at the centre of our current views of marriage and therefore exerts a powerful and symbolic influence on our process of fashioning rules to govern distribution of marital assets. ... This approach of using equality as the organizational concept in assessing appropriate rules for property division creates dilemmas. In its simplest form, equality demands sameness of treatment, and differentiation in any sphere may be considered a concession of inferiority or "unequalness."
>
> The ramifications of symbolic adherence to equality may be significant. Contribution is an equalizing concept, while need demands an acknowledgment and evaluation of differences. As such, a commitment to equality initially encourages its proponents to minimize or deny differences between the individuals.

(Martha Fineman, *The Illusion of Equality* (Chicago: University of Chicago Press, 1991), 46.)

Fineman's argument is that a goal of equality in property allocations will not meet the needs of many women post-divorce. At the same time, others have argued that there are limits on the role of property-adjustment rules at divorce, which may not address more fundamental, systemic problems of inequality in marriage. For example, the American Law Institute concluded (at 734) that a presumption of equality provides a "rough compromise" between competing claims of contribution and need: "The equal division rule typically provides [a] spouse more than he or she contributed financially, but less than a need-based rule might provide." In addition, the institute suggested that the equal-division rule requires little justification if one accepts, in principle, that spouses are entitled to share family property. At the same time, however, the institute argued that "the appeal of the equality rule is enhanced by the difficulties presented by its alternatives." Is this answer to Professor Fineman's argument entirely satisfactory? Is there a better solution available?

In an analysis of a small number of divorce files containing separation agreements of business couples in New Brunswick in the early 1990s, Donald Poirier and Lynne Castonguay concluded that married women frequently did not receive recognition for their contributions to business assets (assets excluded from sharing in the absence of proof of actual contribution by the non-owning spouse): "Our exploratory research ... corroborates writings on the distance between legal equality formally recognized in the marital property laws and real equality which can be ascertained in separation agreements." According to their study, one-third of the separation agreements did not respect the formal legal equality of New Brunswick's marital property law: see Donald Poirier and Lynne Castonguay, "Formal Versus Real Equality in Property Division on Marriage Breakdown of Business Couples: An Empirical Study" (1994), 11 *Canadian Family Law Quarterly* 71, at 85; see also D. Poirier, "Les Femmes Collaboratrices et la Loi sur les Biens Matrimoniaux du Nouveau-Brunswick" (1990), 39 *University of New Brunswick Law Journal* 23 and D. Poirier and M. Boudreau, "Formal Versus Real Equality in Separation Agreements in New Brunswick" (1992), 10 *Canadian Journal of Family Law* 239.

In addition to concerns about sharing business assets, interests in family farms often create special difficulties at marriage breakdown. In an appeal from Saskatchewan to the Supreme Court of Canada, the court rejected a proposal for valuing farmland differently from other family property: for an analysis of the court's decision in *Farr v. Farr*, [1984] 1 SCR 252 and suggestions for structuring methods of sharing such property, see Joseph Kary, "Farmland, Free Markets and Marital Breakdown" (1992), 11 *Canadian Journal of Family Law* 41.

B. The Process of Equalization in Ontario

Ontario legislation seems to provide a straightforward method of dividing entitlement to family property which, for the most part, does not depend upon judicial discretion or litigation.

> Law Reform Commission of British Columbia, *Working Paper on Property Rights on Marriage Breakdown* (Victoria: Ministry of the Attorney General, 1989), 109

To assist in examining the property provisions of Ontario's *Family Law Act* in more detail, the following list explains the steps required to determine the equalization payment pursuant to ss. 4 and 5 of the legislation. Because the statute defines the norm of equalization in s. 5(7), these steps are necessary to determine the *value* of property interests held by each spouse ("the net family property") and to calculate the amount of the equalization payment. In reviewing these steps and the explanatory materials that follow, consider the extent to which you agree that it is appropriate to characterize the Ontario statutory scheme as straightforward and not generally dependent on judicial discretion.

Introduction: Steps for Calculating the Equalization Payment

Step 1:   Determine the valuation date (s. 4).

Step 2:   Determine what property was owned by each spouse on V-day (s. 4).

Step 3:   Determine whether any property constitutes excluded property (s. 4(2)), note tracing (ss. 4(2) and (5)), and exclude such property.

Step 4:   Assign values to property.

Step 5:   Determine the value of deductions (s. 4):
Debts and liabilities at V-day;
Pre-marriage property (value at marriage less debts and liabilities at marriage).

Step 6:   Calculate each spouse's NFP and determine one-half the difference between the greater and the lesser (s. 5(1)).
This amount represents a debt owing, not an entitlement to property.

Note: Any claim for entitlement to more than one-half the difference (s. 5(6)); and

Note also: Special treatment of the matrimonial home (defined in s. 18) in relation to deductions and exclusions.

These legislative provisions establish the default regime in Ontario for spouses with respect to property at the dissolution of a marriage. However, spouses may contract out of this legislative regime, pursuant to s. 2(10) of the *Family Law Act*. In some cases, spouses may sign a marriage contract before or during the marriage, which limits the applicability of this legislative regime. Recall the Supreme Court of Canada decision in *Hartshorne v. Hartshorne*, 2004 SCC 22; (2004), 47 RFL (5th) 5, discussed in chapter 5, which focused on the fairness goals of s. 65 of the BC *Family Relations Act* in assessing whether to enforce the terms of a marriage contract. How should the *Hartshorne* decision be applied in relation to the Ontario statute? Pursuant to s. 2(10), spouses in Ontario may also negotiate a separation agreement defining their property rights. However, as s. 2(10) indicates, there are some limits on contractual rights—for example, any agreement in a marriage contract that limits possessory rights to the matrimonial home is unenforceable: s. 52(2).

It appears that family property provisions cannot generally be avoided by transfers prior to death. In *Stone v. Stone* (1999), 46 OR (3d) 31 (Sup. Ct. J), a wealthy husband who knew that he was fatally ill transferred business assets worth $1.3 million (more than half his net worth of about $2 million) to his children, fully realizing that the property would otherwise be subject to equalization if he died. After his death, his widow successfully challenged the transfers as contrary to the *Fraudulent Conveyances Act*, RSO 1990, c. F.29. In upholding the widow's challenge, the court stated that the Ontario *Family Law Act* created "a creditor–debtor relationship which takes the form of an open or running account which becomes a settled account on separation or death"; and that this concept was consistent with the goal of spouses sharing their net accretion in wealth during the marriage.

For similar analyses of the *Family Law Act*'s approach to sharing the *value* of family property, see *Webster v. Webster* (1997), 32 OR (3d) 679; 37 RFL (4th) 347 (Sup. Ct. (Gen. Div.)) and *Berdette v. Berdette* (1991), 3 OR (3d) 513; 33 RFL (3d) 113 (CA). In relation to issues about representation of spouses in matters of estate planning in such cases, see Maurice Cullity, "Ethical Issues in Estate Practice," in *Special Lectures of the Law Society of Upper Canada* (Scarborough, ON: Carswell, 1996), 425.

1. Determining the Valuation Date

The valuation date is defined in s. 4 of the *Family Law Act* as the earliest of five dates:

1. "the date the spouses separate and there is no reasonable prospect that they will resume cohabitation";

2. the date of a divorce order;

3. the date of an order of nullity;

4. the date when one spouse commences an action for improvident depletion of assets (s. 5(3)) that is subsequently granted; and

5. the date prior to the date of death of one spouse, leaving the other a surviving spouse.

In most cases of divorce, the valuation date is the date when the spouses permanently separate.

However, in spite of the clear wording of s. 4 in the Ontario statutes, the dissolution of a marriage may not occur at one point in time. Some spouses do not separate on one, clearly defined date; instead, the breakdown of their marriage may occur over a period of days, weeks, or even months. Thus, in determining the valuation date, the first step in calculating the equalization payment, courts may have to exercise some discretion. For example, in *Oswell v. Oswell* (1992), 43 RFL (3d) 180 (Ont. CA), where evidence showed that the marriage had been deteriorating between September 1987 and March 1988, the trial judge held that the valuation date should be January 1988; the Ontario Court of Appeal declined to interfere with the trial judge's determination.

In *Caratun v. Caratun* (1987), 9 RFL (3d) 337 (Ont. HCJ), the court also had to determine whether the date of separation could be the date when one of the spouses, although not the other, had decided to leave with no prospect of resuming cohabitation. The wife argued that the date of separation should be the point at which *both* parties accepted that there would be no reconciliation. In *Caratun*, the husband left his wife for another woman just as he obtained his qualifications in dentistry. The wife gave evidence that she had maintained a hope that he would return to the marriage—it was more advantageous, in relation to her claim for equalization, to have a valuation date that was three years after the date when her husband left their home. In determining that the date of separation was the date when the husband left the marriage, the trial judge held that the date of separation should be the date when there was no reasonable prospect of resumption of cohabitation. The court decided that the wife's continued expectation of reconciliation was not reasonable. In the result, it appears that the valuation date is the date when one spouse separates with no prospect of resuming marital cohabitation; it is not necessary for both spouses to hold this view. (*Caratun* is considered in more detail below.)

Although these cases reveal that courts may sometimes exercise discretion in defining the valuation date pursuant to the Ontario statute, particularly when the factual context is unclear, the *Family Law Act* does not permit a court to exercise discretion to change a valuation date to ensure fairness between the spouses. In *Russell v. Russell* (1999), 1 RFL (5th) 235, the Saskatchewan Court of Appeal provided a comprehensive review of provincial statutes and their differing approaches to the definition of valuation date. The court noted (at 251) that the Ontario statute "dictates an inflexible valuation date," and examined approaches to judicial discretion under other provincial statutes.

The lack of scope for discretion in the Ontario statute was confirmed by the Supreme Court of Canada in *Rawluk v. Rawluk* (1990), 28 RFL (3d) 86. In *Rawluk*, the wife left the matrimonial home in 1984; the value of the property owned by her husband increased dramatically in the next few years. Clearly, it was in the wife's interest to have the property valued at a later date than the date of separation. Although there were differing views in the Supreme Court about the availability of a remedy for the wife in these circumstances, all members of the court accepted that it was not open to the court to alter the valuation date pursuant to s. 4 of the *Family Law Act*; they did not express a view about whether such increases in value might constitute "unconscionability" pursuant to s. 5(6). (*Rawluk* is also considered in more detail below.)

By contrast with the Ontario statute, legislation in other provinces and territories often expressly permits the use of judicial discretion in defining the date of separation. For example, the trial judge in *Bartolozzi v. Bartolozzi*, [1992] NWTR 347 (Terr. Ct.) exercised discretion pursuant to the statute to value the matrimonial home at the date of trial, rather than the date of separation, so that both parties would share in the increase in value between the date of separation and the date of trial. For other examples, see *Pisiak v. Pisiak* (2000), 1 RFL (5th) 419 (Sask. QB); *Caldwell v. Caldwell* (1999), 1 RFL (5th) 284 (BCCA); *Thornett v. Thornett* (1999), 1 RFL (5th) 171 (BCCA); and *Reardon v. Smith* (1999), 1 RFL (5th) 83 (NSCA).

Discussion Notes

Law Reform Proposals

As the report of the OLRC explained, most provincial statutes provide for valuation of family property at the date of trial or permit courts to exercise discretion to ensure that spouses share post-separation changes in the value of family property: see *Report on Family Property Law* (Ontario), at 51-59. The report noted the problems of an inflexible date in the Ontario statute, but also drew attention to the problems of uncertainty created by the exercise of judicial discretion pursuant to the BC legislation. It also referred to the recommendations of the BC Law Reform Commission: see Law Reform Commission of

British Columbia, *Report on the Property Rights on Marriage Breakdown* (Victoria: Queen's Printer for British Columbia, 1990) and draft legislation, *Working Paper on Property Rights on Marriage Breakdown* (Victoria: Queen's Printer for British Columbia, 1989), 118-26. In addition, the Ontario report suggested that courts should have discretion to vary an equalization payment on the grounds of unconscionability; it also suggested that one factor relevant to unconscionability should be any significant change in value of assets between the valuation date and the date of trial.

In terms of goals of fairness and certainty, are these recommendations appropriate? In considering this question, identify the reasons why values may increase or decrease— should there be any difference in the exercise of judicial discretion if the reason for an increase or decrease in value relates to a spouse's work or neglect, by contrast with changes in market values? Can these differences be quantified easily?

The *Report on Family Property Law* (Ontario) summarized (at 56-57) the problems of valuation dates as follows:

> The different models for determining a valuation date adopted in common law provinces represent varied attempts to resolve the tension between the need to achieve consistency and predictability, and the desire to ensure that individuals receive fair treatment. In British Columbia, the great flexibility [under the statute, not in relation to the OLRC's recommendations] adopted by the courts has generated criticism of the inconsistencies that have resulted. In Ontario the rigidity of the valuation date appears to have redirected litigation into the factual question of when separation occurs, or into trust claims. This has the disadvantage of embroiling the courts in complicated factual and legal issues which may bear little relation to the real problem faced by the parties—a substantial fluctuation in the value of assets accumulated during the relationship.

Responding to these problems, the OLRC reviewed a number of suggested solutions. For example, one solution might be to delay the date of valuation until the date of trial, but the report concluded that this change might have an unwelcome impact on litigation tactics, with the spouse negatively affected by falling or rising markets seeking to delay the trial. Another solution would permit courts to exercise discretion to choose an appropriate valuation date, taking into account whether the change in value reflected market valuations or efforts on the part of a spouse. However, the report rejected this option because it would require courts to determine, with some precision, the cause of changes in valuation.

In the end, the report concluded (at 59) that none of these options was viable, and thus recommended no change to the definition of "valuation date" in s. 4; instead, the report suggested that these problems be addressed by other means, specifically by amendments to s. 5(6) to extend the court's discretion to make unequal equalization payments: at 68-69. Do you agree that amendments to the statutory definition of valuation date are not appropriate? Why, or why not?

Fleming v. Fleming

In reflecting on the recommendations of the OLRC, consider the husband's argument in *Fleming v. Fleming* (2001), 19 RFL (5th) 274 (Ont. Sup. Ct. J) that the date of separation would have occurred much earlier if he had known of his wife's extramarital affairs; he alleged that she had engaged in these affairs between 1986 and their separation in 1999. The court rejected the husband's argument, holding that there was no discretion to alter the valuation date pursuant to s. 4. In addition, the court held that the wife had no legal duty to disclose extramarital affairs during the marriage and that her failure to do so was not tortious. In addition to cases such as *Fleming*, there is anecdotal information suggesting that a spouse who has already formed an intention to separate may sometimes choose a date to leave on the basis of the rising and falling of the stock or real estate markets, depending on whether the separating spouse is the owner or non-owner of such assets. To what extent do these issues strengthen the concerns identified by the OLRC? How will the commission's recommendations respond to such problems?

SELECTED REFERENCES

American Law Institute, *Principles of the Law of Family Dissolution: Analysis and Recommendations* (Washington, DC: Matthew Bender, 2002).

Berend Hovius and Timothy G. Youdan, *The Law of Family Property* (Scarborough, ON: Carswell, 1991).

V. Jennifer MacKinnon, "Property Valuation Issues in the Common Law Provinces: Common Law?" (1989), 17 RFL (3d) 255.

James MacLeod, "Annotation of Caratun v. Caratun" (1987), 9 RFL (3d) 338.

2. Defining Property

As demonstrated in *Skrlj v. Skrlj*, the scheme of the *Family Law Act* requires that the property owned by each of the husband and wife be listed and valued as at the valuation date. In many divorce situations, such a process is not overly complex because the parties do not own much property; indeed, for many divorcing couples, the extent of their indebtedness may equal the value of property owned by them. In these cases, few issues about the definition of property in s. 4 of the *Family Law Act* will arise.

However, the definition of property in s. 4 is broad in scope—"any interest, present or future, vested or contingent, in real or personal property"—and includes three specific forms of property interests. Because of the breadth of the definition of property in s. 4, litigation has considered whether certain "things of value" were to be included within this definition. Three issues in particular have been considered. First, there were some early cases about professional degrees and whether they should be considered property and valued pursuant to the *Family Law Act* calculation. Related to this question was one concerning property capable of producing a "future stream of income," including income from trust funds. Second, there was a question about whether the definition of property includes beneficial ownership as well as legal title, and the extent to which trust doctrines (used with increasing frequency by separating cohabitees after *Murdoch*) continued to be available to married couples, in addition to their entitlements under the statutory regime. Third, issues about pensions as property must also be considered. These issues are briefly reviewed here. In exploring how these issues have been addressed, consider why spouses might want to make such claims about property. To what extent does recognition of such claims promote the statute's presumption of spousal equality in s. 5(7)?

a. Professional Degrees and Future-Income Streams

In *Caratun v. Caratun* (1992), 42 RFL (3d) 113, the Ontario Court of Appeal held that a professional licence (in this case, in dentistry) or a right to practise does not constitute property within the meaning of s. 4 of the *Family Law Act*. Thus, the value of the husband's dental licence and his right to practise as a dentist in Ontario were not valued and included in his net family property for purposes of calculating the equalization payment to his former spouse. The Court of Appeal's decision clarified the legal principles to be used in such cases after a number of lower court decisions had adopted different approaches to this issue.

Different Approaches Concerning Property and Professional Degrees

Briefly, there were three different approaches in the case law prior to the Court of Appeal decision in *Caratun*. On the one hand, in an early case decided in the Ontario Unified Family Court, *Corless v. Corless* (1987), 5 RFL (3d) 256, the court held that the husband's law degree was property within the meaning of s. 4; however, the court also decided that this property had no value because it could not be exchanged or transferred, being personal only to the holder. The court did award spousal support to the wife, taking into account that she had postponed her own career plans in order to assist her husband in his legal career.

By contrast, in the trial decision of *Caratun v. Caratun* (1987), 9 RFL (3d) 337 (Ont. HCJ), the court engaged in a detailed analysis of "new property"; it thoroughly canvassed the Act's provisions to determine how best to reward the wife's contribution to the husband's acquisition of his professional qualifications. The facts in *Caratun* suggested that the husband had taken advantage of his wife's generosity and unquestioning commitment in order to immigrate to Canada and acquire a professional degree; he then abandoned her for a new relationship just a few days after obtaining his qualifications. In the result, the trial court held that the licence and right to practise were property; however, after canvassing the possible approaches to implementing the Act, the judge decided to segregate this part of the property from the equalization accounting and assessed it in terms of principles of trust. On this basis, the wife was awarded a lump sum of $30,000 for her contribution to the acquisition of the husband's licence; she also obtained an order for child support in relation to the couple's child. On appeal, however, the Ontario Court of Appeal held that the licence and right to practise did not constitute property under the *Family Law Act*. Thus, for the Court of Appeal, a professional licence did not constitute property at all.

According to this third approach, one spouse's contributions to the acquisition of a professional degree by the other spouse should not be characterized as a property interest; instead, such a contribution should be compensated using the support provisions of the *Divorce Act* (now s. 15.2(7)) or similar provisions of the *Family Law Act*, particularly ss. 33(9)(j) and (l)(ii). Two earlier Ontario decisions had adopted this support-based approach: *Keast v. Keast* (1986), 1 RFL (3d) 401 (Ont. Dist. Ct.) (concerning the acquisition of a medical degree by the husband) and *Linton v. Linton* (1988), 11 RFL (3d) 444 (Ont. SC (HCJ)) (concerning the acquisition of a PhD by the husband). In considering the issue of whether the PhD was property in *Linton*, the court identified a number of reasons for rejecting such an approach (at 455):

There is a larger and broader reason why professional licences or degrees should not be treated as property. If the courts hold that the lawyer's right to practise, or the doctor's or dentist's licence, is property, where are the limits for such a holding within the framework of the employment patterns of our community? These professional qualifications do nothing more nor less than enable their possessors to work in a particular occupation and earn an income. How, then, can the law draw any rational and logical dividing lines between occupations when deciding which kind of job qualification will attract property assessment under [the *Family Law Act*]? In other words, if the so-called professional person is to be caught ... , why not any other person who is engaged in gainful employment? One student at university elects to go to law school and the next elects to go into a master's program in business administration. Each later gets a job and earns a substantial income. Equally, where is the difference in substance between the position of the lawyer and that of an electrician or welder or plumber? All of these latter tradesmen are required to go through lengthy apprenticeship or training programs, with their spouses being required to make the same sacrifices as the professional's spouse along the way, and most of these tradesmen will remain as lucratively paid employees for the rest of their lives.

If a right to practise as a professional person is property, then, logically, a right to work or, ultimately, any and every job must be considered as property. There is, I submit, no evidence in the [Act] that this was the intention of the legislature. To me, the legislature intended the courts, in interpreting and applying [the Act], to apply the existing common law criteria for property in identifying the net family properties of spouses. It should be remembered here that the ... equalization formula applies not only when a marriage has broken down but also when a spouse dies.

Linton was appealed to the Ontario Court of Appeal, and the support-based approach was confirmed there: see (1990), 30 RFL (3d) 1. Thus, the appellate court's decision in *Caratun* confirmed its preference to exclude professional degrees from the category of property pursuant to the *Family Law Act* and to provide compensatory spousal support instead. In examining the court's reasoning, consider whether an award of compensatory support achieved the objectives of equality pursuant to the *Family Law Act*.

Caratun v. Caratun
(1992), 42 RFL (3d) 113; 10 OR (3d) 385 (CA)

Contribution Toward the Obtaining of Appellant's Dental Licence

The reasons of the trial judge make it quite clear that Dr. Caratun's primary objective in marrying Mrs. Caratun and fathering their child was to assist him in immigrating to North America to practise dentistry. Mrs. Caratun worked extremely hard over a number of years in Israel and in Canada to assist Dr. Caratun in attaining his ultimate objective. Two days after attaining that objective, he rejected Mrs. Caratun as his wife, at a time when family assets were next to non-existent but his future income-earning ability was substantial.

Facts such as these raise difficult legal questions, given the purpose of the [*Family Law Act*], on the one hand, and its specific provisions, on the other. The combining of spousal efforts over a number of years to provide for the education and professional qualification of one spouse is not unusual in our society. The inevitable result, if there is a separation on attaining the joint objective, is that one family member is left with no assets and often very little in the way of educational or professional qualifications with which to sustain herself or himself in the future. The extreme unfairness of the situation is patent, but the possibility of a legal remedy is far from settled law.

Dental Licence as Property

Mrs. Caratun's position at trial, which was accepted by the trial judge, was that Dr. Caratun's dental licence is property within the meaning of that word as defined in s. 4(1). ...

That definition is broadly framed, and includes all conceivable types of property in the traditional common law sense. However, it does not, by its terms, extend the meaning of property beyond those limits. The contrary argument is that in construing that definition one must keep in mind the [Act's] policy of marriage partnership, which requires, on final separation, the equal division of wealth accumulated during the marriage; and that a licence to practise a particular profession constitutes wealth in the matrimonial context. ...

[The court reviewed the lower court decisions on this issue in *Keast* and *Caratun*, as well as a number of American authorities, and stated (at 121):]

In determining the issue of whether a professional licence constitutes "property," the cases and the numerous articles written on the subject concentrate primarily on two aspects of the problem: first, the nature or characterization of a licence, and, second, the difficulty of valuing a licence in the family property context.

(i) Characterization of Licence

The broad definition of property in the [Act] clearly encompasses many forms of intangibles—a classification into which a licence must fall if it is to be considered property. The common law has never had any difficulty in dealing with property evidenced by pieces of paper representing bundles of rights—such as a share certificate with its attendant rights to dividends, voting privileges, and distribution of assets on corporate dissolution. If a licence to practise a profession is property, what are its attendant rights? Apart from possible benefits, such as the right to join professional groups and clubs—which are not relevant in this context—the only real right conferred on the holder of the licence is a right to work in a particular profession. That right, assuming it is held at the time of separation, is a present right to work in the future, and it will continue for as long as the holder of the right is professionally and personally able to perform the activity involved. It is the nature of the right given by the licence which, in my view, causes insurmountable difficulties in treating such a licence as property for matrimonial purposes. Those difficulties arise, first, because it is not a right which is transferable; second, because it requires the personal efforts of the holder in order to be of any value in the future; and, third, because the only differ-ence between such a licence and any other right to work is in its exclusivity. ...

[The court considered each of these three difficulties. In relation to the issue of trans-ferability, the court distinguished a licence from a professional practice created by the holder of a licence, stating (at 121) that "[t]he practice itself is clearly capable of transfer for value, although the market is limited to other licensees." On this basis, the court concluded that rights or things that are inherently non-transferable do not constitute property in any traditional sense. In examining the requirement of personal efforts of the licensee, the court suggested (at 122) that it was not possible to include in net family property "work to be performed by either spouse in the future"; instead, such efforts were to be compensated by support awards.]

The policy of the FLA emphasizes principles of partnership during marriage, and self-sufficiency following its termination. When the marriage ends, the partnership ends. Placing a value on future labours of either spouse for purposes of the equaliza-tion payment would frustrate those policy objectives.

[The court also identified the problem that recognition of a licence as property would require the assessment of other kinds of work as well, noting that skilled workers such as plumbers, carpenters, and electricians must also spend time in apprentice-ships and that salespeople must spend time, for example, developing clientele. The court concluded (at 123) that it was clearly inappropriate to consider all of these attainments as property for purposes of determining equalization payments pursuant to the *Family Law Act*. The court then addressed (at 123) concerns about valuation of the licence.]

It is clear from the considerations referred to above that there are substantial diffi-culties, both practical and conceptual, in treating licences as "property." In addition, the valuation of such a right would be unfairly speculative in the matrimonial con-text. A myriad of contingencies, including inclination, probability of success in prac-tice of the profession, length of physical and mental capability to perform the duties of the profession, competition within the profession, and many others, all render a fair valuation of the licence unusually difficult. But a further potential inequity arises: support orders may be varied if circumstances change, but no amendment of an equal-ization payment is possible regardless of changed circumstances. ...

[After reviewing the trial judge's approach to valuing the licence and other possible methods of valuation in such cases, the court held (at 124):]

In the matrimonial context, the fallacy lies in treating a licence as property on valuation date, when most of its value depends on the personal labour of the licensed spouse after the termination of the relationship. That future labour does not constitute anything earned or existing at the valuation date.

For all of the above reasons, it is my view that a professional licence does not constitute property within the meaning of [s. 4 of the *Family Law Act*].

Constructive Trust

The trial judge decided that the appellant's dental licence was property within the meaning of [the Act]. However, she did not include the value of the licence in the appellant's net family property, but rather decided that the licence would be held by the appellant subject to a constructive trust in favour of the respondent in the amount of $30,000—that amount representing the value of the respondent's contribution to the acquisition of the licence. Given a finding that the licence constituted property, it is my view that the court had no discretion as to whether or not to include its value in net family property under s. 5(1) of the Act.

The finding of constructive trust was based on cases involving circumstances substantially different than those in this case. The two decisions of the Supreme Court of Canada in *Rathwell v. Rathwell*, [1978] 2 SCR 436, 1 RFL (2d) 1, [1978] 2 WWR 101, 1 ETR 307, 83 DLR (3d) 289, and *Becker v. Pettkus*, [1980] 2 SCR 834, 19 RFL (2d) 165, 8 ETR 143, 117 DLR (3d) 257, 34 NR 384, were decided at a time when the relevant statutes of Saskatchewan and of Ontario would not have permitted appropriate recovery to the spouses. Both cases involved real property and other tangible assets which would clearly come within the definition of "property" under the Ontario FLA. Since the enactment of the [*Family Law Act*], cases have applied the constructive trust doctrine for the purpose of allowing a spouse, in appropriate circumstances, to share in the increased value of property from the valuation date until the time of trial. But, again, those cases involve tangible physical assets. The three British Columbia decisions referred to by the trial judge—*Piters v. Piters* (1980), 19 RFL (2d) 217, [1981] 1 WWR 285, 3 Fam. L Rev. 123, 20 BCLR 393 (SC); *Underhill v. Underhill*, 34 RFL (2d) 419, [1983] 5 WWR 481, 45 BCLR 244 (CA); and *Jackh v. Jackh* (1980), 18 RFL (2d) 310, [1981] 1 WWR 481, 22 BCLR 182, 113 DLR (3d) 267 (SC)—are all cases dealing with the issue of a proprietary interest in a *professional practice*, as contrasted with the claimed proprietary interest in a *licence to practise*.

The trial judge stated that she did not see "any reason in principle why a professional licence cannot be subject to a similar proprietary interest in the form of a constructive trust" [at 355 RFL]. I agree that if the licence constituted "property," then there is no reason why, in a proper case, that property could not be subject to a constructive trust. However, if the licence does not constitute property, then there is nothing to which the constructive trust could attach. None of the cases relied on by the trial judge in this case assist in establishing that a licence is property to which a constructive trust can attach.

[The court also considered s. 5(6) and the possibility of awarding an unequal equalization payment. However, s. 5(6) applies only where there is property; thus it was not available to Mrs. Caratun. In the end, the court awarded compensatory support in the amount of $30,000, the sum determined by the trial judge to reflect Mrs. Caratun's contribution to the attaining of a dental licence on the part of her former husband.]

Margaret McCallum, "Caratun v. Caratun: It Seems That We Are Not All Realists Yet"

(1994), 7 *Canadian Journal of Women and the Law* 197, at 206-7

The definition of property in the Act is of little help in determining whether a career asset is property, since it suffers from the "horrible circularity" of most definitions of property. Mr. Justice Killeen, when faced with a similar problem in *Linton v. Linton*, said that the court cannot "torture basic personal property concepts" or jettison out of hand the "so-called 'traditional' forms of real and personal property, as established in the common law decisions and earlier statutes" in order to permit a spouse to claim a share in the value of a career asset of the other spouse. Mr. Justice Killeen noted that the definition of property in the *Family Law Act* is indeed broad, but argued that the specific examples of what was included in this definition showed the legislature's intention to "keep manageable and particularized limits on the concept of property. If the legislature had wished to go into *terra incognita*, or invite the courts to go there, surely the language could and would have been different."

In coming to this conclusion, Mr. Justice Killeen accepted the direction in the *Interpretation Act* to read the *Family Law Act* purposively and with the large and liberal construction necessary to give effect to its obvious remedial purpose. But in his view, a limited reading of the meaning of the word property was appropriate given that the *Family Law Act* did not create a full economic partnership, but only a form of partnership, in which the equalization payment permitted "a narrow and deferred sharing of accretions in value to defined spousal properties." Thus, the argument based on statutory interpretation is itself circular.

An alternative approach would recognize that the meaning of property cannot be found in lists of the resources, tangible or intangible, that have been recognized as property in the past. Property is not things or rights, but relationships. Saying "this is my book" describes my relationship not to the book but to other people who might want to use the book, and who will be able to do so only with my permission. So the court, in deciding whether Mr. Caratun's career asset is property, could inquire about the appropriate relationship envisioned by the *Family Law Act* between him and his former wife with respect to sharing in the benefits of his right to practise dentistry, a right that he acquired with her help, although only he could exercise it. ...

Could the court in *Caratun* have found any guidance in the handling of similar problems when a business partnership ends? The *Partnerships Act* defines partnership property as "all property and rights and interests in property originally brought into the partnership stock or acquired, whether by purchase or otherwise, on account of the firm, or for the purposes and in the course of the partnership business." On dissolution of a business partnership, the Act provides for distribution of the partnership property, after payment of the firm's debts, in accordance with each partner's share in the partnership. In addition, where one partner pays a premium to another on entering the partnership and the partnership is dissolved before the expiration of its term, the court may order repayment of all or some of the premium, unless, *inter alia*, the dissolution is wholly or chiefly due to the misconduct of the partner who paid the premium. If a partnership agreement is rescinded on the ground of fraud or misrepresentation, the party entitled to rescind may claim a lien on or retain the surplus of the partnership assets to recover any sum paid to purchase a share in the partnership and any capital contributed, and may also claim indemnification for all the debts and liabilities of the firm.

It does not require much imagination to put Mrs. Caratun in the place of the wronged partner, who paid a premium to join the partnership, expecting to share in the future profits, but finds out that she has been the victim of fraud and misrepresentation. The *Partnership Act* remedies, however, do not provide for a situation where the premium paid has been in kind rather than in money, and the assets are future profits. Yet courts could interpret the Act as giving one partner a lien on future profits of the other, given that its purpose is to provide a remedy for individuals whose investment plans go awry because they have chosen an untrustworthy partner.

Business partnerships raise similar issues to those in *Caratun* in another context, too: courts have to determine the value of the firm's goodwill in determining who has to pay whom when a partner withdraws or is expelled from the partnership. Goodwill as an asset on a firm's balance sheet is intangible property, and is usually of value only while the firm is an ongoing concern. Often in professional firms, the goodwill comes from the reputations of individual firm members, not from that of the firm itself. A recent article reviewing American case law on the value of professional partnership goodwill concludes that courts value goodwill differently for different purposes. Recognizing that goodwill is really the human capital owned by the partners individually, courts will value it highly if the spouse of a partner, in an action for property division on marriage breakdown, is claiming part of the value of his or her spouse's share in the professional partnership. If the partnership owns few assets, placing a high value on goodwill may be the only way to ensure that the partner's spouse is compensated for a contribution to the partner's ability to earn a good living. If courts can thus adopt a purposive approach to valuing goodwill, why not adopt a similar purposive approach to defining property? Surely such flexibility is within the means of a legal system that accepted a fee simple estate in time-shared condominium resorts, giving absolute ownership of a freehold estate but only for certain weeks every year. ...

Among the many meanings that one can draw from the result in *Caratun*, one stands out: a woman who sacrifices her own career opportunities in order to improve those of her husband is making a bad investment, unless she is able to obtain the benefits of her husband's career during the marriage. The wave of family law reform following the decision of the Supreme Court of Canada in *Murdoch v. Murdoch* profoundly altered the rights and obligations of spouses within marriage, and enhanced women's property and support rights on marriage breakdown. But the legislation works best for women who least need it, those who have resisted the idea that marriage is a partnership and have provided for themselves.

Discussion Notes

Property: Technical Meanings and Policy Goals

The debate in Ontario courts about the meaning of property in s. 4 of the Act is interesting both as a technical matter and in terms of the overall policies of family law. At the
technical level, the issue about whether to characterize professional degrees as property
or to provide compensation by way of support reflects the difference between economic
concepts of capital and income, concepts that frequently challenge legal arrangements of
many kinds, particularly in the law of taxation. The fact that the *Family Law Act* assumes
a distinction between property and support thus reflects a familiar legal concept. In
Corless, for example, the court reviewed meanings of property in a number of other legal
contexts before reaching its conclusion that property in the *Family Law Act* included
professional degrees. To what extent should the meaning of property in other legal
contexts affect its meaning for family property?

In addition, litigation about professional licences and the definition of property at
marriage breakdown reflect a real struggle for post-divorce resources. Having regard to
the statistical data in chapter 5 about the financial circumstances of men and women after
divorce, the issue of sharing the value of professional degrees (and incomes flowing
therefrom) is much more than a merely technical question. Moreover, if Jack Knetsch
was correct when he argued that family units make decisions to augment the well-being
of the unit as a whole, so that some individual members of the unit—that is, those with
the qualifications for which other family members made sacrifices or contributions—will
be unjustly enhanced when the unit dissolves, it seems clear that there is a need to provide
compensation: Knetsch, at 263. Thus, the question is whether compensation should be
provided by recognizing a property interest or by awarding compensatory support.

Why might the plaintiffs in these cases have wanted to establish a right to property, rather
than merely spousal support? You may want to consider this question again after reviewing
the material about spousal support in the next chapter; the material reveals that at the time
of litigation about professional degrees as property, the levels and duration of spousal
support awards were relatively insignificant. Are there any other advantages to attaining
a right to property, by contrast with entitlement to ongoing payments of spousal support?

According to Hovius and Youdan, claims to treat professional degrees as property
arise as "an argument for justice": Berend Hovius and Timothy G. Youdan, *The Law of
Family Property* (Scarborough, ON: Carswell, 1991), 176. In addition, citing Lenore
Weitzman's work, they suggest (at 277) that a spouse's earning capacity may be more
valuable than the spouse's assets at marriage breakdown. However, in addition to those
cited by the court, they identified arguments to support the decision of the court in
Caratun. In particular, they argued that the drafting of the legislation, which included
specific references to some forms of non-traditional property, but not to professional
degrees, suggested that professional degrees were not to be included. Moreover, in the
context of a rigid equalization process, they argued (at 279) that it was not appropriate to
include as property an asset about which a court would have to exercise discretion:

> It is one thing to characterize degrees, etc., as property so that they are included in the pool
> of assets over which a court may exercise a discretionary jurisdiction. It is another thing to
> include them as property in a system, like the *Family Law Act*, where the value of relevant

property is put into a formula that produces an entitlement subject only to a very limited judicial discretion.

Do these arguments focus on the fundamental purposes of equalization or the means of accomplishing them?

Family Property and Professional Licences in US Cases

As Hovius and Youdan indicate (at 269-71), these issues about property and professional degrees were also litigated in the United States. In an early case, for example, a trial court ordered a husband (whose wife had fully supported him through college and law school) to support her attendance at medical school after the marriage dissolved: the equivalent-opportunity option. However, the appellate court overturned this decision: see *Morgan v. Morgan*, 366 NYS 2d 977 (Sup. Ct. 1975); 383 NYS 2d 343 (Sup. Ct. (AD) 1976).

Although claims that professional degrees constitute marital property have been rejected by most state courts that have considered them, NY courts have included the value of professional licences as marital property pursuant to legislation that requires equitable distribution of such property: see *O'Brien v. O'Brien*, 66 NY 2d 576; 489 NE 2d 712; 498 NYS 2d 743 (CA 1985). In that case, the husband commenced his action for divorce two months after acquiring a medical degree; his wife had provided considerable financial support during his studies. In holding that the degree's value should be included, in accordance with a formula designed by the court, Simons J stated (at 717):

> That a professional degree has no market value is irrelevant. Obviously, a license may not be alienated as may other property and for that reason the working spouse's interest in it is limited. The Legislature has recognized that limitation, however, and has provided for an award in lieu of its actual distribution.

The principles established in *O'Brien* were applied in *McSparron v. McSparron*, 87 NY 2d 275; 662 NE 2d 745; 639 NYS 2d 265 (CA 1995), where the husband had acquired a law degree early in the marriage and the wife a medical degree shortly before the divorce action, and in *Grunfeld v. Grunfeld*, 94 NY 2d 696; 731 NE 2d 142; 709 NYS 2d 486 (CA 2000), where the husband had acquired a law degree. In the latter case, the court also reviewed principles for ensuring that the value of the degree included in the equitable-distribution award was not "double-counted" in the court's award of maintenance. In recognizing the problems of valuation of professional degrees as marital property, the court in *McSparron* stated (87 NY 2d 275, at 286):

> The existence of these complications ... is not a sound reason to introduce nettlesome legal fictions or to excise an asset to which the nontitled spouse has contributed from the marital estate. As we stated in *O'Brien*, the complexity of calculating the present value of a partially exploited professional license is no more difficult than the problem of computing wrongful death damages or the loss of earning potential that is occasioned by a particular injury. ... Nor does it lead to significantly more speculation than is involved in the now-routine task of valuing a professional practice for the purpose of making a distributive award.

Obviously, these NY courts are interpreting a different legislative regime than Ontario's *Family Law Act*; the requirement in the NY legislation to make an equitable-distribution award of marital property provides much greater scope for including the value of professional degrees. To what extent does this mean that the equality regime in Ontario may be less successful in accomplishing the purposes of family property goals than an equitable-distribution scheme, such as the one in New York? Assuming that compensatory support is the preferred method of accomplishing this objective in Ontario, how should such awards be structured and valued? To what extent does the elimination of professional degrees as property affect the negotiation of property and support issues as part of the overall package of economic readjustment at divorce?

By contrast with the decisions in New York, a Connecticut court reviewed claims concerning degrees as family property in *Simmons v. Simmons*, 708 A2d 949 (Conn. Sup. Ct. 1998) and concluded that the claims had been rejected in all but one other state court (from a total of 35 states); in Oregon, the legislature initially enacted a statutory amendment based on the *O'Brien* case in New York, but it was repealed a few years later: see 1999 Oregon Laws Ch 23, HB 2555. As the American Law Institute noted, moreover, even lower court decisions in New York have often struggled with the principles established by the Court of Appeals in *O'Brien*, *McSparron*, and *Grunfeld*. The institute recommended that educational degrees should not be considered marital property, but instead should be taken into account in relation to compensatory support. In exploring the rationale for this conclusion, the institute stated (at 697-98):

> [These] observations relate to a broader theme from which the differences between property and alimony [spousal support] emerge. The law has treated alimony as appropriate in only a subset of divorces in which there are circumstances, sometimes temporary, that justify equitable adjustments in post-marriage income between former spouses. In contrast, marital property claims are normally viewed as property entitlements created by the marriage alone, even if subject to equitable adjustment. The principle underlying this difference is that marriage creates property entitlements to certain *things* acquired during it, but does not create property entitlements against the *person* of the other spouse. ... [The recommendation] therefore reflects the longstanding distinction between claims on things and claims on another's personal attributes.

Is this rationale persuasive? Is the distinction between entitlements to *things* and entitlements against the *person* of the other spouse helpful in defining property in the *Family Law Act*? To what extent does it respond to the critiques of Knetsch and Fineman, above, with respect to equality goals at family breakdown?

Family Assets and Professional Degrees in British Columbia

Recall that the BC *Family Relations Act* adopted a concept of family assets: ordinary use for a family purpose. Thus, litigation in British Columbia focuses on this definition, not on the definition of property as in Ontario. Recall also that the BC legislation permits more judicial discretion in the reallocation of family assets. Nonetheless, in a number of cases, BC courts have held that a degree was not a family asset: for example, see *Johnson v. Johnson* (1988), 16 RFL (3d) 113 (BCCA). By contrast, in *Seymour v. Seymour* (1992), 71 BCLR (2d) 218 (BCSC), a commercial fishing licence was included as a family asset because it was not linked to knowledge or ability unique to its holder. Similarly, in *Jiwa v. Jiwa* (1992), 42 RFL (3d) 388 (BCCA), insurance proceeds were also held to be included. What factors explain these differing approaches?

Family Property and Future-Income Streams

In *Brinkos v. Brinkos* (1989), 20 RFL (3d) 445, the Ontario Court of Appeal allowed an appeal in relation to the issue of whether income from trust funds constituted property pursuant to s. 4 of the *Family Law Act*. The spouses married in 1965, at which time the wife had a bank account, originally established by her father in trust for her when she was a child; at the date of marriage it was valued at $224,475. A few years later, in 1972, the wife settled the trust by transferring into it all the funds from the account and appointing her mother and brother as trustees. Pursuant to the trust, the wife was entitled to an inalienable life interest in the net income from the trust property, which then totalled $305,175. The trust was created with the husband's knowledge, but it was agreed that it would not form part of the family property. The spouses separated in 1982; the trust was then valued at $609,933, including an additional gift from the wife's father during the marriage. In proceedings under the *Family Law Act*, the trial judge held that the wife's interest pursuant to the trust was not property and thus not included in her net family property.

The Ontario Court of Appeal allowed the husband's appeal, and held that the right to a future-income stream was property under the Act. In doing so, the court stated that not all rights to income, particularly if they were dependent on personal services, constituted property. Clearly aware of the lower court decisions concerning professional degrees as property, the court focused on the issue of non-transferability of degrees in relation to the inalienability clause in the trust agreement in *Brinkos*. As Hovius and Youdan explained (at 259), the court

> properly drew a distinction between the case where the interest in question is of a type which is incapable of transfer and the case where the interest is of a type which is capable of transfer but in the particular case has been made untransferable.

Is this distinction satisfactory in the context of the goals and purposes of family property? Although the court held that the present value of the future-income stream should be valued and included in the wife's net family property, she was permitted to deduct the value of her interest at marriage (see *Family Law Act*, s. 4: "deductions") and to exclude the portion of income stream that related to the gift to the fund from her father during the marriage (see *Family Law Act*, s. 4(2): "exclusions"). Such matters clearly involved some difficulties of valuation for the court, but they did not prevent the inclusion of the trust income as family property.

SELECTED REFERENCES

American Law Institute, *Principles of the Law of Family Dissolution: Analysis and Recommendations* (Washington, DC: Matthew Bender, 2002), 4:03.

Nicholas Bala, "Recognizing Spousal Contributions to the Acquisition of Degrees, Licenses, and Other Career Assets: Toward Compensatory Support" (1989), 8 *Canadian Journal of Family Law* 23.

Alicia Brokars Kelly, "Sharing a Piece of the Future Post-Divorce: Toward a More Equitable Distribution of Professional Goodwill" (1998-99), 51 *Rutgers Law Review* 569.

James McLeod, "Annotation of Brinkos v. Brinkos" (1989), 20 RFL (3d) 445.

_____, "Annotation of Caratun v. Caratun" (1992), 42 RFL (3d) 113.

Lenore Weitzman, *The Divorce Revolution: The Unexpected Social and Economic Consequences for Women and Children in America* (New York: The Free Press, 1985).

Scott E. Willoughby, "Professional Licenses as Marital Property: Responses to Some of O'Brien's Unanswered Questions" (1987), 73 *Cornell Law Review* 13.

b. Beneficial Interests as Family Property

Recall that the Supreme Court of Canada considered the claim for a declaration of trust by Mrs. Murdoch in *Murdoch v. Murdoch* after her marriage of 25 years ended. In that case, the court declined to grant the declaration, although the dissenting judgment indicated that Mrs. Murdoch was entitled to a constructive trust on the basis of unjust enrichment as a result of her significant work on the ranch properties owned by her husband. In 1978, the Supreme Court granted a declaration of constructive trust in *Rathwell v. Rathwell* in relation to a similar claim by a former spouse at divorce. As a result, it was clear after 1978 that a former spouse could seek such a declaration in circumstances of unjust enrichment.

However, in the late 1970s, all the common law provinces began to enact statutory family property regimes. In many cases, the statutory regimes provided greater certainty and efficiency for married couples at divorce, so that the *Rathwell* decision was not often invoked by married spouses. By contrast, this remedy was increasingly used by cohabiting couples, who were excluded from the statutory regimes in relation to family property matters: see part IV, below, for a review of these issues concerning cohabitees.

Here, however, it is necessary to examine the reasoning in *Rawluk v. Rawluk* (1990), 23 RFL (3d) 337, in which the Supreme Court of Canada addressed the question whether property pursuant to the *Family Law Act* included not only legal interests but also equitable or beneficial interests arising from constructive trusts. In reading the decision, examine the reasoning of the majority and the dissent with respect to the issue of whether the statutory regime precluded the *additional* use of trust doctrines by married couples.

Rawluk v. Rawluk
[1990] 1 SCR 70; 23 RFL (3d) 337

[The Rawluks were married for 29 years until 1984. During the marriage, they worked together in two businesses, including a farm machinery (sales and service) and a cash-crop and livestock farming business. According to the Supreme Court of Canada, Mrs. Rawluk had devoted herself to the couple's children and to farm chores in the first few years of the marriage, but in the late 1960s, she began to play a large role in the farm machinery business by performing all the bookkeeping functions, including most of the invoicing and banking, and by operating the parts department. As well, she took a large role in the farm operation, with responsibility for the "birthings, needling and feeding of the animals, ... the employee payroll and bookkeeping, ... augering wheat and [helping] to transport employees and crops at harvest." Over these years, the couple also acquired a number of other properties, and legal title to all of them was in the name of Harry Rawluk, except for a cottage property that was registered in

Jacqueline Rawluk's name for tax purposes. The couple also conducted their financial affairs from a single bank account, virtually always maintained in the husband's name; for a period of one year, the account was a joint account when Mrs. Rawluk placed an inheritance from her mother ($7,000) in this account. However, for daily needs, the parties used cash stored in a teapot in a china cabinet in their home, both dipping into it as needed; this teapot was a source of some strife in the home, Mr. Rawluk claiming that his wife was a spendthrift and his wife claiming that he was miserly.

In the early 1970s Mrs. Rawluk went to night school and qualified as a registered nursing assistant. In 1974, she worked full time in a Newmarket hospital; according to the court, she then changed her work arrangements because of complaints from her husband, and from 1975 to the date of separation, she worked part time, mostly evenings, so that she could also continue her previous work in the farming and farm machinery businesses. The parties initially separated when Mr. Rawluk left the matrimonial home in 1982, but they were reconciled; they then separated again as of June 1, 1984.

Although some proceedings had commenced under the former legislation, the *Family Law Act* was in effect by the time the parties came to trial in 1986. As of the valuation date (June 1, 1984), the Newmarket farm and machinery lot had been valued at $400,000 and another property at $139,000. However, the value of the property had increased dramatically by the time of the trial in 1986. Thus, "in order to share in one-half of the increase in value, Mrs. Rawluk claimed by way of a remedial constructive trust a beneficial one-half interest in the home farm and machinery lot and the other property." The husband's lawyer agreed that Mrs. Rawluk's work entitled her to have her proprietary interests recognized, but claimed that the *Family Law Act* had abolished the remedy of constructive trust. In the Supreme Court of Canada, four judges (Cory J, Dickson CJ, and Wilson and L'Heureux-Dubé JJ) upheld Mrs. Rawluk's claim (McLachlin, La Forest, and Sopinka JJ dissenting).]

CORY J: ...

The Judgments Below

... At trial [(1986), 55 OR (2d) 704; 3 RFL (3d) 113; 23 ETR 199; 29 DLR (4th) 754], Walsh J held that a remedial constructive trust could be imposed by the court to determine the ownership of assets of married spouses under the *Family Law Act, 1986*. He determined that the *Family Law Act, 1986* requires a court to decide issues of ownership prior to equalizing net family property. He held that in determining ownership a court must look to both legal and beneficial interests, including an interest arising by means of constructive trust. He observed that it was unlikely that the Ontario legislature would deny married spouses a remedy that they would have had if unmarried. Having decided that the constructive trust doctrine survived the enactment of the *Family Law Act, 1986*, he found that the facts supported a declaration of constructive trust with regard to the Newmarket home farm and machinery lot and awarded Mrs. Rawluk a one-half interest in the contested property. ...

The Court of Appeal [(1987), 61 OR (2d) 637; 10 RFL (3d) 113; 28 ETR 158; 43 DLR (4th) 764] affirmed Walsh J's decision. It decided that the provisions of the *Family Law Act, 1986*, far from superseding the constructive trust, appear to incorporate that doctrine into the process of determining ownership and equalizing net family property. The Act's provisions, it was said, clearly direct a court to determine ownership prior to ordering equalization. Accordingly, the constructive trust remedy should be applied as a part of the first step of ownership determination. The court reviewed several provisions of the Act in order to demonstrate that to deny the constructive trust remedy to married spouses in Ontario would create inconsistencies and inequalities. The court declined to decide whether a constructive trust can be forced upon a beneficiary to require that person to share in a decline in the value of property following valuation date. It simply noted that s. 5(6) of the Act might be used in such a situation to award an amount that differs from the standard equalization payment.

Position of the Appellant

The appellant contended, however, that the equalization provisions of the *Family Law Act, 1986* supersede and implicitly abolish the remedy of constructive trust as it applies to the division of matrimonial property held by married persons in Ontario.

The Historical Background

The issue presented by this appeal arises from a unique convergence of common law and statutory provisions, both of which are of relatively recent origin. The Canadian law of trusts with regard to matrimonial property was only in its infancy when the OLRC first proposed a matrimonial property regime of deferred equal sharing in its 1974 *Report on Family Law* (Ontario Law Reform Commission, *Report on Family Law*, Pt. IV (1974), p. 55). The Ontario legislature used that report as a model for the provisions of the *Family Law Act, 1986*, but declined to expressly clarify the relationship between the provisions of the Act and the doctrine of constructive trust, as it had evolved during the late 1970s and early 1980s.

(a) The Doctrine of Constructive Trust and Its Application in Matrimonial Cases

The evolution of the remedial constructive trust doctrine in Canada and its application to the division of marital property can be traced through a series of well-known decisions of this court beginning with the dissenting reasons of Laskin J (as he then was) in *Murdoch v. Murdoch*, [1975] 1 SCR 423, 13 RFL 185, [1974] 1 WWR 361, 41 DLR (3d) 367 [Alta.], and culminating in Dickson CJC's decision for an unanimous court in *Sorochan v. Sorochan*, [1986] 2 SCR 38, 2 RFL (3d) 225, [1986] 5 WWR 289, 46 Alta. LR (2d) 97, 23 ETR 143, 29 DLR (4th) 1, [1986] RDI 448, [1986] RDF 501, 74 AR 67, 69 NR 81. The doctrine developed when it appeared that the traditional approach to resolving property disputes was inappropriate and inequitable when applied to situations of marital breakdown. ...

[Cory J then reviewed the idea of "contribution" and "intent" and the Canadian and English decisions on the doctrine of constructive trust. He also considered the jurisprudence in the United States where "the constructive trust had long been recognized not as an institution, but as a broad restitutionary device that could be invoked in a wide variety of situations to compel the transfer of property to a claimant by the defendant in order to prevent unjust enrichment to the title holder." He then reviewed the Supreme Court's decisions in *Murdoch*, *Pettkus v. Becker*, and *Sorochan* and concluded (at 360):]

These cases show that in Canada the doctrine of remedial constructive trust has been accepted for almost a decade as an important remedial device whose prime function is to remedy situations of unjust enrichment. It is clear that at the time that the *Family Law Act, 1986* was enacted, the constructive trust was widely recognized as the pre-eminent common law remedy for ensuring the equitable division of matrimonial property. The validity and importance of the remedy designed, as it is, to achieve a measure of fairness between married persons and those in a marital relationship, must have been well known to the framers of the legislation. It would seem unlikely that they would, without a precise and specific reference, deprive parties of access to such an equitable remedy. ...

[Turning then to statutory reforms, Cory J reviewed the prior legislation in Ontario, the *Family Law Reform Act*, and relevant decisions pursuant to it. He then considered the *Family Law Act* provisions (at 362):]

The Family Law Act, 1986

In 1986, the *Family Law Reform Act* was replaced by the *Family Law Act, 1986*. In contrast to s. 8 of the *Family Law Reform Act*, the provisions of the *Family Law Act, 1986* did not attempt to duplicate the constructive trust remedy. Instead, the statute provided that all property should be equalized upon separation through the transfer of money from the title-holding or owning to the non-owning spouse.

Prior to this case the trial courts in Ontario have followed one of two approaches in deciding whether these equalization provisions implicitly abolish the use of the constructive trust in the matrimonial property context. The majority of the decisions followed the reasoning of Walsh J in the case at bar even before it was affirmed by the Ontario Court of Appeal: see *Seed v. Seed* (1986), 5 RFL (3d) 120, 25 ETR 315 (Ont. HC); *Leslie v. Leslie* (1987), 9 RFL (3d) 82, 27 ETR 247 (Ont. HC); *Cowan v. Cowan* (1987), 9 RFL (3d) 401 (Ont. HC); and *Corless v. Corless* (1987), 58 OR (2d) 19, 5 RFL (3d) 256, 34 DLR (4th) 594 (UFC). This approach was rejected, however, in two lower court decisions: *Benke v. Benke* (1986), 4 RFL (3d) 58, 25 ETR 124 (Ont. Dist. Ct.), and *Leonard v. Leonard*, [1987] OJ 1488 (unreported).

The reasoning set forth in the *Benke* decision was adopted by the appellant. In that case, the wife had claimed an interest in her husband's farm on resulting or constructive trust principles. The trial judge denied her claim, holding that the constructive trust could not be applied in the context of the *Family Law Act, 1986* and that the facts did not support a finding of resulting trust. In his opinion, the *Family Law Act, 1986* fully addressed the question of unjust enrichment between spouses by providing for monetary equalization based on the value of property at the time of separation. As he stated at p. 78:

What Laskin J (in *Murdoch*) declared to be "the better way" is now in place. The less adequate way was the doctrine of constructive trusts, and that less adequate way should no longer be available to, in effect, change the date of valuation whenever, either because of deflation or inflation, it suits the interests of one of the spouses to seek to advance it. If, in the total scheme of things, some injustice continues, it will be an injustice that arises from the application of an act of the legislature, and it will be for the legislature to correct it.

This position has been criticized. As Professor James McLeod comments in his annotation to *Benke v. Benke*, at p. 60:

In the end, cases such as *Benke v. Benke* ... reflect an unwillingness on the part of the judiciary to investigate the realities of a relationship. It is easier to strictly apply an equal division in all cases than to determine whether such division is fair to the particular parties. It is easier, but is it fair?

I prefer the approach taken by Walsh J and the Ontario Court of Appeal. In my view, far from abolishing the constructive trust doctrine, the *Family Law Act, 1986* incorporates the constructive trust remedy as an integral part of the process of ownership determination and equalization established by that Act.

Provisions of the Family Law Act, 1986 That Indicate That the Constructive Trust Doctrine Should Continue To Play a Role in Determining the Assets of Spouses and Their Division

It is trite but true to state that as a general rule a legislature is presumed not to depart from prevailing law "without expressing its intentions to do so with irresistible clearness" (*Goodyear Tire & Rubber Co. v. T. Eaton Co.*, [1956] SCR 610 at 614, 56 DTC 1060, 4 DLR (2d) 1). But even aside from this presumption, when the structure of the *Family Law Act, 1986* is examined and the ramifications of a number of its provisions are studied, it becomes apparent that the Act recognizes and accommodates the remedial constructive trust.

At the outset, the Act's preamble recognizes not only the need for the "orderly and equitable settlement of the affairs of the spouses," but also "the equal position of spouses as individuals within marriage" and the fact that marriage is a "form of partnership." These fundamental objectives are furthered by the use of the constructive trust remedy in appropriate circumstances. It provides a measure of individualized justice and fairness which is essential for the protection of marriage as a partnership of equals. Thus the preamble itself is sufficient to warrant the retention and application of this remedy.

In addition, various provisions of the Act lead to the same conclusion.

(a) Sections 4 and 5

Sections 4 and 5 of the *Family Law Act, 1986* create a two-step property division process that emphasizes the distinction between the determination of legal and equitable ownership and the equalization of net family property. These sections require a court first to determine individual "ownership piles" and then to equalize the spouses' assets by ordering the spouse with the larger ownership pile to pay money to the spouse with the smaller pile.

Before property can be equalized under s. 5 of the *Family Law Act, 1986*, a court is required by s. 4 to determine the "net family property" of each spouse. Under s. 4(1) this is defined as "the value of all property ... that a spouse owns on the valuation date." "Property" is defined in the same subsection as "any interest, present or future, vested or contingent, in real or personal property." This all-encompassing definition is wide enough to include not only legal but beneficial ownership. The appellant has conceded that "property" as defined under s. 4(1) includes a beneficial interest arising from an express or resulting trust. I see no reason why the remedial constructive trust should not be included in the list of equitable principles or remedies that may be used to calculate the beneficial ownership of net family property.

It is important in this respect to keep in mind that a property interest arising under a constructive trust can be recognized as having come into existence not when the trust is judicially declared but from the time when the unjust enrichment first arose. As Professors Oosterhoff and Gillese state, "the date at which a constructive trust arises ... is now generally accepted to be the date upon which a duty to make restitution occurs." ... It would seem that there is no foundation whatever for the notion that a constructive trust does not arise until it is decreed by a court. It arises when the duty to make restitution arises, not when that duty is subsequently enforced. ...

It must be emphasized that the constructive trust is remedial in nature. If the court is asked to grant such a remedy and determines that a declaration of constructive trust is warranted, then the proprietary interest awarded pursuant to that remedy will be deemed to have arisen at the time when the unjust enrichment first occurred. But, as Professor Scott makes clear, the fact that the proprietary interest is deemed to have arisen before the remedy was granted is not inconsistent with the remedial characteristics of the doctrine.

The distinction between a share in ownership and a share in property value through an equalizing transfer of money is more than an exercise in judicial formalism. This distinction not only follows the two-step structure of the *Family Law Act, 1986*, but reflects conceptual and practical differences between ownership and equalization. Ownership encompasses far more than a mere share in the value of property. It includes additional legal rights, elements of control and increased legal responsibilities. In addition, it may well provide psychological benefits derived from pride of ownership. Where the property at issue is one to which only one spouse has contributed, it is appropriate that the other spouse receive only an equalizing transfer of money. But where both spouses have contributed to the acquisition or maintenance of the property, the spouse who does not hold legal title should be able to claim an interest in that property by way of a constructive trust and realize the benefits that ownership may provide. The imposition of a constructive trust recognizes that the titled spouse is holding property that has been acquired, at least in part, through the money or effort of another. The non-titled spouse's constructive trust interest in this property is distinct from the right to an equalizing share of property value that is derived not from an independent property right but from the status as a married person.

(b) Section 5(6)

Section 5(6) of the *Family Law Act, 1986* allows a court to "award a spouse an amount that is more or less than half the difference between the net family properties if the court is of the opinion that equalizing the net family properties would be unconscionable." The Court of Appeal observed that if a post-valuation date increase or decrease in property values is significant enough to render a simple equalization unconscionable, a court might utilize s. 5(6) to remedy the resultant inequities. I need not and do not express any opinion as to whether s. 5(6) could be used in that way or whether the Court of Appeal's observation is correct. I have assumed solely for the purposes of argument that s. 5(6) might be available in some cases as an alternative remedy for dealing with post-valuation date changes in value. Even so, the section does not have the effect of supplanting the constructive trust remedy. The constructive trust is used in the matrimonial property context to allocate proprietary interests, a function that is totally distinct from the process of determining how the value of matrimonial property should be distributed under the equalization process.

Under the Act a court is, as a first step, required to determine the ownership interests of the spouses. It is at that stage that the court must deal with and determine the constructive trust claims. The second step that must be taken is to perform the equalization calculations. Once this is done, a court must assess whether, given the facts of the particular case, equalization is unconscionable. The s. 5(6) analysis, even if it could be considered, would be a third step—a last avenue of judicial discretion which might be used in order to bring a measure of flexibility to the equalization process. This step in the process, if it could be used, would have to be kept distinct from the preliminary determinations of ownership. ...

[Cory J also reviewed the impact of s. 10, which permits a spouse to apply to the court to determine a question of ownership or possession prior to equalization, and stated (at 367):]

The creation under s. 10 of a proprietary remedy that can be commenced during cohabitation provides further evidence that the Ontario legislature could not have intended the provisions of the *Family Law Act, 1986* to completely supersede the remedial constructive trust. Section 10 enables non-titled spouses to assert control over matrimonial property during cohabitation to the extent that their beneficial interests entitle them to do so. Even if the appellant's argument that the *Family Law Act, 1986* equalization provisions replace the constructive trust remedy were to be accepted, this would not prevent a deserving spouse from obtaining a declaration of constructive trust in his or her spouse's property during cohabitation pursuant to s. 10. Certainly such an application will not necessarily be followed by separation and equalization of property.

Since the spouse can thus obtain a constructive trust remedy prior to separation, it would be inconsistent to deny a spouse the same remedy when it is sought after a separation. To take such a position would encourage spouses to apply for a constructive trust interest early in a marriage, perhaps thereby creating unnecessary marital stress, fostering costly litigation and penalizing those spouses who waited until separation to enforce their common law rights. It is unlikely that the legislature intended a spouse's rights to depend on whether or not a constructive trust had been declared before or after the separation. ...

[Cory J also examined s. 14, which refers expressly to the resulting trust doctrine, and rejected the appellant's argument that this express reference to resulting trust meant that the doctrine of constructive trust had been abolished, concluding:]

I cannot accept that contention. Section 14 is, I believe, intended not to specifically preserve but rather to modify the resulting trust doctrine as it applies in the context of the *Family Law Act, 1986*. If anything, the combination of these modifying provisions and the legislature's silence on the subject of remedial constructive trust supports the view that the constructive trust is maintained in an unmodified form. ...

[Cory J then addressed s. 64(2), which equalizes the legal rights of married men and married women, but also declares that married persons have the same legal capacities as unmarried persons. Referring to the court's recognition of constructive trust doctrines in relation to issues of family property for cohabiting couples, Cory J suggested (at 368):]

It would not only be inequitable, but would also contravene the provisions of s. 64(2), if married persons were precluded by the *Family Law Act, 1986* from utilizing the doctrine of remedial constructive trust which is available to unmarried persons.

Conclusion

The review of the cases decided by this court from *Murdoch v. Murdoch, supra*, to *Sorochan v. Sorochan, supra*, demonstrates the importance that has been attached to the use of the remedy of constructive trust to achieve a division of property that is as just and equitable as possible. A marital relationship is founded on love and trust. It brings together two people who strive and sacrifice to attain common goals for the benefit of both partners. When it is terminated and acquired assets are to be divided, then in this of all relationships the concept of fairness should predominate in making decisions as to ownership. This was the fundamental equitable principle underlying the application of the constructive trust remedy to matrimonial cases. Where the application of the principle would achieve the goal of fairness it should not be discarded unless the pertinent legislation makes it clear that the principle is to be disregarded.

The *Family Law Act, 1986* does not constitute an exclusive code for determining the ownership of matrimonial property. The legislators must have been aware of the existence and effect of the constructive trust remedy in matrimonial cases when the Act was proposed. Yet neither by direct reference nor by necessary implication does the Act prohibit the use of the constructive trust remedy. Indeed, the foregoing review of the provisions of the Act supports the view that the constructive trust remedy is to be maintained. The Act's two-step structure and its individual provisions indicate that the constructive trust remedy still has an important role to play in the determination of matrimonial property disputes in Ontario. The application of the remedy in the context of the *Family Law Act, 1986* can achieve a fair and just result. It enables the courts to bring that treasured and essential measure of individualized justice and fairness to the more generalized process of equalization provided by the Act. That vital fairness is achieved by means of a constructive trust remedy and recognition of ownership.

In this case fairness requires that the dedication and hard work of Jacqueline Rawluk in acquiring and maintaining the properties in issue be recognized. The equitable remedy of constructive trust was properly applied.

I would therefore dismiss the appeal with costs.

[McLACHLIN J (on behalf of La Forest and Sopinka JJ), dissenting, asserted two principles (at 371):]

1. The doctrine of constructive trust, as it has developed in Canada, is not a property right but a proprietary remedy for unjust enrichment; as such, the availability of other remedies for the unjust enrichment must be considered before declaring a constructive trust.

2. The doctrine of constructive trust should not be applied in this case because the *Family Law Act, 1986* provides a remedy for the unjust enrichment of the husband to the detriment of the wife.

[McLachlin J approached the issues in *Rawluk* by examining the history of principles concerning unjust enrichment and constructive trust. She suggested that there were two different views in English jurisprudence: a traditional view, which characterized the constructive trust as an obligation attaching to property in defined situations, and a new model, chiefly developed by Lord Denning, of the constructive trust as a general remedy for unjust enrichment. According to McLachlin J, Canada had tended to move toward the American view of the constructive trust as an equitable remedy for unjust enrichment. In this way, the constructive trust represents a discretionary remedy, dependent on the inadequacy of other remedies for unjust enrichment. McLachlin J summarized her view (at 375):]

These passages establish the fundamentals of the Canadian approach to constructive trust in relation to unjust enrichment. First, the doctrine has as its purpose the remedying of unjust enrichment. Second, it is remedial rather than substantive. Finally, the remedy of constructive trust is but one of many remedies that may be available to correct unjust enrichment. Before applying it, the court must consider whether, given other available remedies, the remedy of constructive trust remains necessary and appropriate in the case before it.

This brings us to the issue raised in this case. Given that the doctrine of constructive trust, as it has developed in Canada, is remedial, what is the relationship of the remedy of constructive trust to other remedies for unjust enrichment? While Dickson CJC alludes to this issue in *Sorochan v. Sorochan*, little Canadian jurisprudence exists on the question. In these circumstances, it may be useful to have regard to the American experience. ...

The American law on constructive trusts, as set out in the Restatement of Restitution, recognizes the panoply of remedies for unjust enrichment and the need for the court, in considering a claim for constructive trust, to select among them. As a general rule, the remedies which operate *in personam* must be brought first, for example, actions for money had and received, *quantum meruit* and account [citing Donovan Waters, *Law of Trusts in Canada*, 2d ed. (Scarborough, ON: Carswell, 1984), 393]. ...

Thus I arrive at this point. Without denying the importance of the remedy of constructive trust, it must be remembered that it may be only one of several remedies for unjust enrichment. It must also be remembered that as a proprietary remedy, its imposition may interfere with the operation of other doctrines and the exercise by others, including third parties, of the rights attendant on their interests in the property made subject to the trust. For these reasons, it may be wise to insist that a plaintiff has exhausted his or her personal remedies before imposing the remedy of constructive trust.

Against this background, I return to the first of the two questions I posed at the outset. Is the doctrine of constructive trust as it has developed in Canada a substantive doctrine of trust, automatically conferring a property interest where the basic criteria for the trust are made out? Or is it a remedy, to be applied where necessary to remedy unjust enrichment?

The answer must be that in Canada, constructive trust, at least in the context of unjust enrichment, is not a doctrine of substantive property law, but a remedy. It follows that a constructive trust cannot be regarded as arising automatically when the three conditions set out in *Pettkus v. Becker* are established. Rather, the court must go on to consider what other remedies are available to remedy the unjust enrichment in question and whether the proprietary remedy of constructive trust is appropriate.

Neither of the courts below approached the matter in this way. Both the trial judge and the Court of Appeal assumed that the doctrine of constructive trust gave the wife a beneficial half interest in the property, the only question then being whether the statute took that right away. My colleague Cory J takes a similar approach, stating that the *Family Law Act, 1986* incorporates the constructive trust remedy "as an integral part of the process of ownership determination." ...

I cannot share this approach. In my opinion, the doctrine of constructive trust does not permit the court to retrospectively confer a property interest solely on the basis of contribution of one spouse and enrichment of the other. A further inquiry must be made, namely, whether, given the presence of another remedy, the remedy of constructive trust is necessary or appropriate. I now turn to that question. ...

This case poses the question of whether the doctrine of constructive trust should be applied where there exists a comprehensive statutory scheme providing a remedy for the situation where one spouse holds exclusive title to property to which the other spouse has contributed.

The *Family Law Act, 1986* sets up a comprehensive statutory scheme which recognizes the contributions of both spouses to the acquisition, preservation, maintenance or improvement of property during the marriage. It addresses the question of unjust enrichment between spouses by providing for a monetary equalization payment based on the value of the "net family property" at the valuation date, i.e., the time of separation (s. 5(1)).

The Act defines "property" broadly as including "any interest present or future, vested or contingent, in real or personal property ..." (s. 4). "Net family property" is defined as meaning "the value of all the property ... that a spouse owns on the valuation date" after deducting debts and the value of the property at the time of marriage (s. 4). The Act specifically requires the judge to apply the doctrine of resulting trust (s. 14), but makes no mention of constructive trust. The Act permits the judge to depart from the principle of equal distribution and adjust the award in a variety of circumstances, including "any other circumstance relating to the acquisition, disposition, preservation, maintenance or improvement of property" (s. 5(6)(h)).

The question may be put thus: given that there was an unjust enrichment arising from the fact that the property to which the wife contributed was in the husband's name, does the *Family Law Act, 1986* provide a remedy, which makes it unnecessary to resort to the doctrine of constructive trust? In my opinion, the answer to this question must be affirmative.

Both the statutory remedy and the remedy of constructive trust are, on the facts of this case, directed to the same end. The purpose of a constructive trust, as already discussed, is to permit a party without title to receive compensation for his or her contribution to the acquisition and maintenance of property standing in the other's name. The purpose of the *Family Law Act, 1986* is the same: it sets up a scheme to equalize the property holdings of each party to a marriage, regardless of who holds legal title. The only difference for the purposes of this case is that the *Family Law Act, 1986* provides for the equalization to be accomplished by a payment of money based on the value of the property at the time of the separation (a remedy *in personam*), while the doctrine of constructive trust would give a beneficial interest in the land which persists to the date of trial (a proprietary remedy).

If the doctrine of unjust enrichment is to be applied in this case, it is not for the purpose of rewarding the wife for her contribution to the property held in the husband's name, but for the purpose of permitting her to share in the increase in value of the property after separation. But this cannot support a claim for a constructive trust for two reasons.

First, the Act contemplates the problem that assets may increase or diminish in value between the date of separation and trial; s. 5(6)(h) permits the trial judge to vary the equal division of property as at separation, on the basis of circumstances relating to the disposition or improvement of the property. I agree with Cory J that this step of the process is distinct from the preliminary determinations of ownership.

Second, it would appear that the elements necessary to establish a constructive trust are not present where the enrichment occurs as a result of appreciation of the market value of the land after separation. Under the statute, the wife already receives a payment sufficient to give her 50 per cent of the family property, valued at the date of separation. There is no unjust enrichment there. What then of the fact that because of delays in obtaining judgment, the value of the property held in the hands of the husband increases pending trial? True, this is an enrichment of the husband. But there is no corresponding deprivation to the wife giving rise to an injustice. The husband is not being enriched at her expense or because of her efforts. In these circumstances, the first two requirements of a constructive trust posited in *Pettkus v. Becker*—unjust enrichment of one party and corresponding deprivation of the other—are absent.

In the final analysis, the *Family Law Act, 1986* provides complete compensation for the wife's contribution to the date of separation. Any disproportionate enrichment must occur because of the increase in value due to changing market conditions after that date. But that does not constitute an unjust enrichment under the principles set forth in *Pettkus v. Becker*, given that the wife made no contribution after that date. As a matter of legal principle, the legislature having provided a remedy for the unjust enrichment which would otherwise have occurred in this case, it is not for this court to impose an additional equitable remedy aimed at correcting the same wrong.

I add that application of the remedy of constructive trust to the statutory scheme may pose practical problems. The scheme under the Act is relatively clear and simple; the basic rule is equality between the spouses, an equality effected by an equalization payment from one spouse to the other, based on the value of the property at the valuation date, usually the date of separation. In most cases the parties can ascertain without difficulty what payment must be made, thereby settling their affairs without lengthy litigation. Grafting the remedy of constructive trust on to this scheme would add uncertainty and promote litigation featuring detailed inquiries into how much each party contributed to the acquisition, preservation, maintenance and improvement of the property to the end of having the court declare a constructive trust in one of the parties. Moreover, property rights which third parties have acquired in the interval may be adversely affected. One returns to Professor Waters' warning that to employ constructive trust where personal remedies suffice threatens to upset the operation of other doctrines.

One must also consider the converse situation to that of this case—the situation where instead of increasing in value after separation, the property loses value. Is the amount recoverable by the spouse lacking title to be diminished accordingly? One judge has said yes, imposing a beneficial constructive interest in the property on the wife as at separation, against her wishes and at the behest of the husband: *McDonald v. McDonald* (1988), 11 RFL (3d) 321, 28 ETR 81 (Ont. HC). So we arrive at the anomaly of the equitable remedy of constructive trust being applied against the wishes of the party found to have been unfairly treated, at the behest of the party who has been unjustly enriched. What does this leave of the maxim that he who seeks the aid of equity must come with clean hands? The fallacy at the root of such an approach is that of treating the *remedy* of constructive trust as though it were a *property interest*, which for the sake of consistency must be imposed regardless of the circumstances or of other remedies.

It is suggested that the position of the wife should not be worse than it would have been had the parties not married. The answer to this submission is that the legislature, acting within the proper scope of its authority, has chosen to confine the Act to married persons. Some Acts governing distribution of marital property apply to unmarried couples. While it may be a ground for criticism of the legislation, the fact that a person covered by legislation may be treated less generously than someone not under the statute cannot give rise to a claim for unjust enrichment; the doctrine of unjust enrichment does not go as far as that. ...

[McLachlin J also rejected the views of Cory J in relation to s. 10 of the Act, stating in part (at 381):]

It may seem anomalous that a married person might be able to obtain a declaration of constructive trust before but not after separation. It must be remembered, however, that the equalization provisions of the Act provide an alternative remedy to which the spouse becomes entitled upon separation. The fact that that remedy may not be as advantageous in some cases as the remedy of constructive trust does not justify the court in altering the doctrine of constructive trust.

I cannot leave this question without alluding to the quite different provisions found in Acts regulating the division of marital property in provinces other than Ontario. As Cory J points out, the relationship between the constructive trust doctrine and its "statutory equivalents" has been variously treated in different jurisdictions. While it is interesting to consider dispositions in other jurisdictions, it should be noted that the legislative provisions from province to province are not truly equivalent. In particular, none of the provincial statutes governing the division of marital property, save that of Ontario, appears to have a statutorily fixed and inflexible valuation date, the feature of the Act which gives rise to the wife's grievance in this case. There can be no simple or universally applicable answer to the question of whether the doctrine of constructive trust will apply in a statutory context: in each case, the circumstances of the case and the efficacy of alternative remedies conferred by the applicable legislation must be examined to ascertain whether, in that situation, a declaration of constructive trust should be declared.

In this case, I conclude that the remedy of constructive trust is neither necessary nor appropriate, given the remedies available under the *Family Law Act, 1986*. ...

Appeal dismissed.

Andrew Sheppard, "Rawluk v. Rawluk: What Are the Limits of the Remedial Constructive Trust?"
(1990), 9 *Canadian Jounal of Family Law* 152, at 161

What is the effect of a statutory remedy on an equitable remedy? As the two judgments show, the question is a difficult one. Cory J took the view that the enactment of the statutory regime for marital property did not affect the availability of the remedial constructive trust. He seemed to say that courts should grant a remedial constructive trust to any spouse who applies for and is entitled to it, because it is more just and equitable than the statutory scheme. On the other hand, McLachlin J went to the opposite extreme; in her view, a court should never grant a remedial constructive trust over a family asset to a spouse who also has a remedy by way of an equalization payment under the Act. The courts should keep the remedial constructive trust only for a party who is not entitled to an equalization payment.

Another approach may be worth considering, because it reconciles the two views, and is consistent with the result in *Rawluk v. Rawluk* and with other authorities. According to this view, the statutory equalization payment is the rule of general application, and a claimant should be entitled to it as of right. The remedial constructive trust is an equitable remedy, which means that before granting it, the court should decide two questions: (1) Is the equalization payment an inadequate remedy in the circumstances? and (2) Since equitable remedies are discretionary, should the court exercise its discretion to grant the decree, after weighing the equitable considerations? If the answer to either question is negative, the court should refuse the declaration of constructive trust, leaving the claimant to the statutory equalization payment. It is respectfully suggested that this principle will eventually emerge as the ratio of *Rawluk v. Rawluk*. These two principles are fundamental to equity jurisdiction. They also meet the concerns expressed in the majority and dissenting reasons for judgment in the *Rawluk* case. ...

In the *Rawluk* case, Cory J went too far in stating that the enactment of the *Family Law Act, 1986* imposes no limitation on the availability of the remedial constructive trust. Similarly, McLachlin J went to the opposite extreme by suggesting that a spouse who is entitled to an equalization is necessarily disentitled to a decree of constructive trust. Instead of taking the view that either the remedial constructive trust or the statutory equalization payment must reign over the division of marital property, the courts should allow both remedies to co-exist and to flourish: peaceful co-existence between the remedies is preferable to domination by either. It is respectfully suggested that, before being awarded a declaration of trust, the claimant should be required to demonstrate to the court that the equalization payment is, or may be, inadequate. On the facts of *Rawluk v. Rawluk*, it was not established that an equalization payment would deprive Mrs. Rawluk of a share in the post-separation real estate boom. However, there is authority to support that view. A genuine doubt about the adequacy of the legal remedy is sufficient to allow the court of equity to intervene. The imposition of a constructive trust without any determination of the inadequacy of the equalization payment may have been an error in principle, but it did not lead to an erroneous result: Mrs. Rawluk could have shown that the equalization payment was only a partial remedy in the circumstances.

To what extent do you agree with this suggested resolution of the differing views in *Rawluk*? Does it accord with the underlying goals of family property legislation? The issue about the relationship between a finding of unjust enrichment and the remedy of constructive trust was examined again by the Supreme Court of Canada in *Peter v. Beblow* (1993), 44 RFL (3d) 329, a case concerning a cohabiting, not a married, couple. In *Peter v. Beblow*, McLachlin and Cory JJ again wrote different judgments, but they were in agreement about the outcome in the case: see the next section for further discussion. The issues have also been addressed in a number of other cases: see *Bigelow v. Bigelow* (1995), 15 RFL (4th) 12 (Ont. Ct. J (Gen. Div.)); *Close v. Close* (1997), 33 RFL (4th) 210 (Ont. Ct. J (Gen. Div.)); *Franken v. Franken* (1997), 33 RFL (4th) 264 (Ont. Ct. J (Gen. Div.)); and *Roach v. Roach* (1997), 33 RFL (4th) 157 (Ont. CA).

Discussion Notes

Reform Proposals

The OLRC's *Report on Family Property Law* reviewed the *Rawluk* decision in some detail. Conceding that a spouse might well prefer to have a property interest, by contrast with just a monetary amount, in relation to significant family assets, the report also noted the lack of precision in decisions about spousal contributions to property in the family context. In addition, it expressed concern about the impact of this remedy on third-party creditors, and examined in detail (at 46-50) the implications of using this remedy in the context of bankruptcy and tax law. Overall, the report concluded (at 140):

> Without doubt, the remedial constructive trust continues to offer some benefits to spouses covered by Part I of the *Family Law Act*, but the problems in applying the common law to spousal relationships raise a question as to the advisability of preserving access to this remedy. The Ontario family property scheme, as conceived by this Commission and implemented by the Legislature, maintains separate ownership and creates a debt obligation. This approach balances the equitable sharing of spousal wealth with the need to preserve the ability of spouses to deal freely with their assets. Any apparent unfairness in restricting the ability of spouses to obtain an ownership interest must be considered in the light of this balance.

The report considered the advantages and disadvantages of either maintaining access to these remedies or abolishing such access entirely, particularly having regard to recommendations for reforming other sections of part I of the *Family Law Act* more generally; a number of these recommendations are considered later in this section. Overall, the report concluded that there should be limited access to the constructive trust and that access to the resulting trust should also be limited. Thus, recommendation no. 30 stated:

> Part I of the *Family Law Act* should be amended to preclude a spouse from applying as follows:
>
> a) for a declaration of a remedial constructive trust with respect to property owned by his or her spouse, as restitution for his or her contribution, either direct or indirect, to the acquisition, preservation, or enhancement of that property.
>
> b) for a declaration of resulting trust with respect to property owned by his or her spouse, based on the common or presumed intention of the spouses regarding his or her contribution, either direct or indirect, to the acquisition, preservation, or enhancement of that property.

To what extent do these recommendations differ from the suggestion proposed by Sheppard, above? Do you agree that the goal of equality pursuant to the statutory scheme is preferable to the exercise of equitable jurisdiction of the courts? What goals are thereby enhanced? To what extent are these problems concerning trust remedies connected to the issue of an inflexible valuation date? Recall the OLRC recommendations concerning the valuation date—do you agree with the resolution of these issues, taken together?

Trusts for Married Couples and Cohabitees

You may also wish to reconsider these questions after reviewing the material concerning resulting and constructive trust remedies for cohabiting couples—to what extent is it more or less advantageous to be married or in a cohabiting relationship with respect to property issues at family breakdown?

Interestingly, according to an empirical study undertaken by Poirier and Castonguay, cohabiting spouses appeared to obtain a better division of business assets in New Brunswick, by contrast with married spouses. Poirier and Castonguay recommend (at 87) that the principles in *Rawluk* might assist married spouses by permitting them to obtain an equal division of family assets and a share of business assets pursuant to the principles of unjust enrichment and the remedial constructive trust. However, they also noted that lawyers and judges appeared not to recognize the application of the *Rawluk* decision in divorce negotiations in New Brunswick. In the context of a property-division regime, by contrast with an equalization scheme, are there any arguments that might preclude the application of *Rawluk*? In a recent decision, the Ontario Court of Appeal upheld the availability of beneficial ownership for married couples who are entitled to equalization pursuant to the *Family Law Act*, although the court concluded that it was not applicable on the facts: see *Roseneck v. Gowling* (2002), 62 OR (3d) 789 (CA), examined in the problem at the end of this chapter.

c. Pensions and Family Property: A Brief Overview

There is little doubt that pensions may be included as family property pursuant to statutory regimes in a number of provinces. In some cases, pensions are expressly included—for example, Ontario's legislation includes pensions that have vested in the definition of property in s. 4(1). Similarly, s. 58(3) of BC's *Family Relations Act* includes "a right of a spouse under ... a pension, home ownership or retirement savings plan" as a "family asset." Even in circumstances where the legislation is silent, as in Nova Scotia, the Supreme Court of Canada concluded that a pension constituted matrimonial property: see *Clarke v. Clarke* (1990), 28 RFL (3d) 113, at 128-29, where the court asserted that "in the case of many Canadian families a pension is their only substantial asset."

At the same time, however, the legislative regimes do not always provide detailed guidelines for taking pensions into account as family property. For example, although the BC legislation contains, in part 6, quite specific provisions, the Ontario legislation provides no real guidance about how to take account of the value of pensions for purposes of equalization. Moreover, because there are different kinds of pension plans (based on defined benefits or defined contributions), and each plan is subject to its own terms as well as requirements of provincial regulatory legislation, it is difficult to derive generally applicable principles.

In addition, the legislative regimes are sometimes unclear about the scope of pensions as family property—for example, are sick-leave benefits, severance pay, or similar kinds of entitlements to be included? Because these issues have to be addressed in the context of each provincial family property statute, there is little uniformity across the country. For example, in *Inverarity v. Inverarity* (1993), 50 RFL (3d) 251 (Alta. QB), an Alberta court concluded that a disability pension should be included in family property under the Alberta legislation. The same court held that workers' compensation benefits were not exempt, but should be characterized as shareable assets: see *Rohl v. Rohl* (1993), 48 RFL (3d) 220 (Alta. QB). The Ontario Court of Justice held that a disability pension, received after health problems rendered the husband unable to work, formed part of his net family property for purposes of calculating the equalization payment; the pension was paid in respect of work done by the husband, not as compensation for disability and so was not exempt under s. 4(2): see *McTaggart v. McTaggart* (1993), 50 RFL (3d) 110 (Ont. Ct. J (Gen. Div.)). There is legislative authority for splitting entitlement to pension credits pursuant to the Canada Pension Plan at divorce, but it is necessary to make an application: see *Pension Benefits Division Act*, SC 1992, c. 46, Sch. 11, ss. 4(1) and 2(a). However, there is no right to credit splitting for those who divorced before January 1, 1978: see *Murray v. Canada* (1998), 42 RFL (4th) 204 (FCA). In *Swan v. Canada* (1998), 47 RFL (4th) 282 (FCA), the court reviewed the relationship between the federal *Pension Benefits Division Act* and the *Family Relations Act*.

In addition to these problems, there are complicated issues about how to value a pension for purposes of equalization in Ontario. A number of cases have explored the use of a termination method of valuation—that is, the pension is valued *as if* the pension holder's employment had terminated on the valuation date—and a retirement method (in which the value to the employee on retirement must be determined). Some courts have preferred to adopt a termination method, in part to avoid the complex calculations and assumptions required by the retirement method. However, both methods generally require expert accounting or actuarial advice, and the legal terminology has been critiqued: see J.B. Patterson, "Confusion Created in Pension Valuation for Family Breakdown Case Law by the Use of Expressions 'Termination Method' and 'Retirement Method' " (1998-99), 16 *Canadian Family Law Quarterly* 249.

In *Best v. Best* (1999), 49 RFL (4th) 1, the Supreme Court of Canada reviewed approaches to the valuation of a teacher's pension. Noting that the parties had agreed in this case on use of the termination method, Major J suggested in *obiter* that a retirement method might be more appropriate in some cases: see also G. Edmond Burrows and Penny E. Hebert, "The Supreme Court of Canada and Best v. Best" (2000), 17 *Canadian Family Law Quarterly* 263. The characterization of pensions as family property is arguably less complex in jurisdictions with an approach that involves "equitable distribution of family assets," such as in British Columbia.

Recently, the issue of payment of ongoing spousal support by a pension holder, after retirement, was addressed by the Supreme Court of Canada in *Boston v. Boston*, [2001] 2 SCR 413, an issue that reveals the intersection of issues of property and spousal support. In this case, the husband argued that the value of his pension had been taken into account in the equalization process so that it was not appropriate for him to have to pay spousal support, after his retirement, out of pension benefits: see Thomas J. Walker, "Double-Dipping: Can a Pension Be Both Property and Income?" (1994), 10 *Canadian Family Law Quarterly* 315. This issue is further addressed in chapter 7.

Discussion Note

Reform Proposals

The OLRC reviewed the issue of pensions and family property and made recommendations for significant reform, both in relation to issues of valuation and with respect to special options for dealing with pensions and the equalization process. These recommendations have not been implemented, even though the report stated that the existing situation was complicated and unsatisfactory. In making its recommendations for change, the commission identified (at 4) a series of guiding principles, while conceding that the principles "did not always point in the same policy direction":

- Family property should be divided fairly and equally with due regard being given to the unique nature of pension assets.
- The overall regime for dealing with pensions should be flexible enough to accommodate the different needs and circumstances of the parties involved.
- Given that the overall purpose of pensions, from both an individual and a societal perspective, is to provide income security on retirement, the regime should encourage the payment of pension benefits at retirement to both parties.
- Costs to the parties should be minimized and the need for recourse to the courts reduced.
- To the greatest extent possible, the process for pension division at source should be streamlined and should not place an undue financial burden on pension plan administrators.

See OLRC, *Report on Pensions as Family Property: Valuation and Division* (Toronto: OLRC, 1995), 4-5. Although the commission's recommendations are not reviewed in detail here, they provide a useful analysis of the issues of pensions as family property.

SELECTED REFERENCES

Berend Hovius and Timothy G. Youdan, *The Law of Family Property* (Toronto: Carswell, 1991).

Law Reform Commission of British Columbia, *Report on the Division of Pensions on Marriage Breakdown* (Victoria: Ministry of the Attorney General, 1992).

Diane Pask and Cheryl Hass, "Division of Pensions: The Impact of Family Law on Pensions and Pension Plan Administrators" (1992-93), 9 *Canadian Family Law Quarterly* 133.

Diane Pask, Cheryl Hass, and Keith L. McComb, *Division of Pensions* (Toronto: Carswell, 1990).

3. Excluding Property: Section 4(2)

After defining all the property owned by each spouse on the valuation date, it is necessary to determine whether any property may be excluded pursuant to s. 4(2). There are a number of specific kinds of property that may be excluded—for example, gifts or inheritances received by one spouse from a third party after the date of the marriage.

Silverberg v. Silverberg
(1990), 25 RFL (3d) 141 (Ont. SC (HCJ))

[One issue in *Silverberg v. Silverberg* was the characterization of some jewellery given to Mrs. Silverberg by her employer. Unbeknownst to her husband at the time of the gift, Mrs. Silverberg was involved in an affair with her employer with whom she subsequently decided to live. In discussing whether the jewellery was excluded property under the Act, the court stated (at 149):]

The parties agreed that the value of Mrs. Silverberg's jewellery on valuation date was $22,884. Mrs. Silverberg submits that jewellery having a value of $10,584 should be excluded from her net family property pursuant to s. 4(2) of the *Family Law Act* as such jewellery was a gift from Mr. Greenberg. While Mrs. Silverberg was working for Mr. Greenberg and living with her husband, Mr. Greenberg gave her a number of pieces of expensive jewellery. The jewellery was given to Mrs. Silverberg at Christmas and on her birthday. According to Mr. Silverberg, his wife told him that the jewellery was given to her in lieu of a monetary bonus. I am sure that Mrs. Silverberg made such statements to her former husband in order to wear the jewellery without Mr. Silverberg being suspicious that she was having an affair with Mr. Greenberg. If the jewellery was earned by Mrs. Silverberg, it must be included in her net family property. ...

I am sure that part of the reason for Mr. Greenberg giving Mrs. Silverberg the jewellery resulted from their relationship and accordingly part of the value represents a gift. I am also sure that part of the value of the jewellery represents a bonus or payment for Mrs. Silverberg's work within Mr. Greenberg's law practice. Accordingly, part of the value of the jewellery should be excluded property but, as I am unable to determine on the evidence which part is represented by a gift and therefore excluded, the plaintiff has failed to satisfy the onus of determining the property to be excluded as required by s. 4(3) of the FLA.

Exclusions and Onus of Proof: Section 4(3)

Note that, pursuant to s. 4(3) of the statute, the onus of proving entitlement to exclude property is on the person claiming that the value of property should be excluded; thus any doubt is resolved in favour of inclusion for purposes of calculating the equalization claim. For other examples, see *Spence v. Michell* (1997), 33 RFL (4th) 147 (Ont. CA) and *Chambers v. Chambers* (1997), 34 RFL (4th) 86 (Ont. Ct. J (Gen. Div.)).

In *Flatters v. Brown* (1999), 48 RFL (4th) 292 (Ont. Sup. Ct. J), the court reviewed a number of claims to exclude the value of property from the calculation of the equalization payment. In reiterating that the onus of proving entitlement to exclude property rested on the spouse making the claim, the court stated (at 295):

Equal possibility does not meet the burden of proof. It must be found to be more likely than not to tip the balance of probability.

Damages: *Vanderaa v. Vanderaa*

Section 4(2) also permits the exclusion of some damages awards. In *Vanderaa v. Vanderaa* (1996), 18 RFL (4th) 393 (Ont. Ct. J (Gen. Div.)), the spouses settled their action for damages after they separated in relation to a motor vehicle accident that had occurred before the date of separation. The husband, being unable to return to gainful employment, had received a settlement amount, including an amount for general damages; a disability benefits award; and a wage loss award. The husband applied to have all these moneys excluded from the calculation of his net family property pursuant to s. 4(2). The court granted the application in part; the funds relating to the wage loss accrued prior to the separation were included in the net family property, but the funds that replaced his wages after the separation were excluded, as were the disability benefits. For another discussion of the exclusion of an award of damages and/or disability benefits, see *Nesbitt v. Nesbitt* (1997), 31 RFL (4th) 297 (Sask. QB).

Tracing

According to s. 4(2), the value of property that can be traced to such exclusions may also be excluded. For example, in *McDougall v. McDougall* (1989), 23 RFL (3d) 320 (Ont. Dist. Ct.), the court considered a claim by the husband to exclude funds forgiven as a result of a bona fide tax-avoidance transaction with his parents. In holding that these amounts were not gifts, and thereby exclusions under s. 4(2), the court stated that it was not possible to recharacterize the transaction. In *Lefevre v. Lefevre* (1992), 40 RFL (3d) 372 (Ont. Ct. J (Gen. Div.)), the court traced funds from an inheritance and from a personal injury settlement, both received by the husband, to the matrimonial home at the valuation date; as a result, the husband was not entitled to an exclusion under s. 4(2).

The Matrimonial Home

As *Lefevre* indicates, the matrimonial home cannot be excluded pursuant to s. 4(2), a policy choice on the part of the legislature to ensure that the value of this family property always forms part of a spouse's net family property for purposes of calculating the equalization claim. Thus, even if the home was a gift from a third party after the date of the marriage, it must nonetheless be included. For example, the court in *DaCosta v. DaCosta* (1990), 29 RFL (3d) 422 (Ont. Ct. J (Gen. Div.)) considered the husband's claim to exclude the value of a home, purchased with funds from an inheritance, which he argued was not a matrimonial home as defined by s. 18. In analyzing the husband's claim (at 441), the court examined the language of s. 18, focusing on whether it was ordinarily occupied by the husband and his spouse as their family residence at the time of separation:

> There can be no doubt that [at] any given time spouses may have more than one matrimonial home, i.e., cottage, hobby farm or condominium. In this case it was the intention of the spouses to use Cedar Dee Farm as a weekend retreat. It had a beautiful house, swimming pool and stables for riding horses. The issue is whether it was ever "ordinarily occupied" by Mr. and Mrs. DaCosta as a matrimonial home. ... [The] evidence of Mrs. DaCosta is less than satisfactory. She claims to have cooked meals and moved furniture at Cedar Dee. I do

not believe her on this aspect of the case. Prior to the closing of the purchase of Cedar Dee, Mrs. DaCosta attended at the farm on two occasions. After the closing she attended at the farm on no more than three occasions. They did not stay overnight at the farm nor did they do any cooking at the farm. Mrs. DaCosta did not attend at the farm after the end of October 1986. It was after this date that the furniture which would allow the farm to be used as a matrimonial home was delivered from the garage at 291 Oriole Parkway. After the furniture was delivered to the farm, Mr. DaCosta spent considerable time at the farm. I find it impossible to reconcile Mrs. DaCosta's position that Cedar Dee Farm was ordinarily used as a matrimonial home and her failure to attend at the farm between 1st November 1986 and 27th March 1987. Surely, if it was being used as a matrimonial home, she would have attended at the farm. In my view, because of the stress in the marriage, Mrs. DaCosta by her own choice never used Cedar Dee Farm as a matrimonial home. In order to be a matrimonial home, it must be ordinarily occupied by the spouses at the time of separation. In this case it was never occupied as a matrimonial home. They may have intended to occupy it as a matrimonial home but they never carried out their intention, notwithstanding that they had an opportunity to carry out such an intention. Accordingly, Mr. DaCosta is entitled to exclude from the value of Cedar Dee Farm as of valuation day the sum of $149,613 which he inherited from his mother, grandmother and great aunt after his marriage to Mrs. DaCosta: s. 4(2) and 5 of the FLA.

The Ontario Court of Appeal confirmed the trial decision: (1992), 40 RFL (3d) 216. For another example, see *Kraft v. Kraft* (1999), 48 RFL (4th) 132 (Ont. CA).

Discussion Note

Reform Proposals and Rationales

According to the OLRC's *Report on Family Property Law* (at 78-81), this special treatment of the matrimonial home with respect to excluded property may create unfairness, permitting manipulation of the rules by a knowledgeable spouse to disadvantage a spouse who is not aware of their implications. In addition, the special treatment of the matrimonial home in relation to exclusions may affect decision making about the use of funds received as a gift or inheritance:

> As an example, if a spouse chooses to pay off the mortgage on the matrimonial home using an inheritance, she may not exclude that sum from her net family property. If she invested her inheritance in a guaranteed investment certificate or another instrument held in her own name, she would be able to exclude this asset from her net family property. ... [T]hese rules will catch only the unwary. Their impact, for those who are aware of them, is to discourage a spouse from applying capital in what might otherwise be the most advantageous manner.

See *Report on Family Property Law*, at 80.

Similar problems may also arise with respect to the special treatment of the matrimonial home in relation to deductions. Although these issues are addressed later in this chapter in relation to the matrimonial home, they also raise more fundamental concerns about underlying rationales of family property. Consider the following analysis, which addresses issues concerning both exclusions and deductions—to what extent does it support the legislative choices in s. 4(2) of the *Family Law Act*?

A property regime such as that established by Part I of the *Family Law Act* is based on the premise that both spouses make an essential and basically equal contribution to the economic viability of the family unit and hence to the acquisition of wealth by the unit. The total financial product of the marriage as an economic partnership is, therefore, generally shared equally when the relationship ends. It follows that the norm of equal sharing should be applied only to the net value of those property rights which constitute the economic product of the constructive collaboration of husband and wife, not to the gross value of all property held by the spouses at the end of the relationship. While this principle may be readily accepted, actual identification of the shareable financial product presents difficulty and may lead to reasonable differences of opinion. Least controversial is the treatment that should be accorded to the debts and liabilities of the spouses at the end of their relationship. In order to determine the financial product of their marriage relationship, the debts and liabilities of the spouses should generally be deducted from the value of their property. Similarly, account must be taken of pre-marital property since its existence cannot normally be attributed to the partnership effort. However, there are a number of issues relating to pre-marital property that have caused considerable debate. Should a spouse be given credit for pre-marital property that has decreased in value or been used to purchase consumables during the marriage? Should the increase in value of any pre-marital property be considered part of the product of the relationship? Finally, property may be acquired during the marriage in such a way, for example, by inheritance, that its value does not originate in the joint efforts of the spouses. Should it, nevertheless, form part of the financial product of the marriage? If some credit is to be given for acquisition of property in this way, should it be for the value at the date of acquisition or its value at the end of the relationship?

See Berend Hovius and Timothy G. Youdan, *The Law of Family Property* (Scarborough, ON: Carswell, 1991), 315.

4. Valuation

Fair Value

After determining all the property owned by each spouse, excluding property pursuant to s. 4(2), at the valuation date, it is necessary to assign values to each item of property. However, the *Family Law Act* provides little direction about valuation principles, and different views have been suggested about how to value such property. For example, Stephen Cole and Andrew Freedman argued that principles of fair value, rather than fair market value were more just and equitable and also consistent with the objectives of the statute. In criticizing the use of fair market value for *Family Law Act* valuations, they suggested:

> There may be nothing at all fair about the value that is derived by adopting the fair market value definition of value. It is important to note that "fair" modifies the word "market" and not the word "value" ... . Assigning a fair market value to shares that are closely held or to a trust interest (see *Brinkos*) or to a pension interest ... is particularly inequitable.
>
> The fair market value approach to property valuation has been used in matrimonial disputes only because it is a convenient, familiar standard. It is grafted on from income tax and estate tax legislation and litigation. More progressive securities legislation ... [etc.] has rejected it in favour of fair value.

See Stephen Cole and Andrew Freedman, "Recent Financial Issues in Family Law" (1990), 6 *Canadian Family Law Quarterly* 101, at 104.

Oswell v. Oswell
(1990), 28 RFL (3d) 10, at 20-22; 74 OR (2d) 15 (SC (HCJ))

[Examine the reasoning in *Oswell v. Oswell*. How would you describe this judge's approach to issues of valuation of Mrs. Oswell's property? Does it reflect a fair value or fair market value approach, or some other principle?]

The expert evidence as to the value of Mrs. Oswell's jewellery and furs was not satisfactory from either party. Mr. Shore testified that he is a gemologist and that he had valued certain items of Mrs. Oswell's jewellery. Two diamonds were valued at $11,000 on the basis of being sold back to the trade. A higher return might be realized if the jewellery was sold at auction. Mr. Shore valued the gold jewellery he was shown by Mrs. Oswell as scrap jewellery and not on an estate basis, as he said that many of the pieces were worn. He placed this value at $2,900. There was no list of the pieces which were brought to Mr. Shore to value. Mrs. Oswell's evidence is that all of the pieces with the exception of a watch were brought to him.

Mr. Robert Low, a consultant and evaluator with the firm of Campbell Valuation Partners, an expert in asset and business valuation with no personal expertise in valuing jewellery and furs, testified that the approach he had used for valuation was the appraised value of the item for insurance purposes less 50 per cent. The 50 per cent factor was reached after a conversation with a person he considered to be knowledgeable about such matters at Birks. The jewellery was not examined individually.

The valuations of Mr. Low are based on appraised value for insurance purposes, which was said to be replacement value as opposed to actual value. The 50 per cent reduction was an attempt to arrive at actual value, but it was admitted that the factor could vary. No account was taken of the price of gold when the jewellery was bought or the decline in the price of gold since 1977. Using this approach, Mrs. Oswell's jewellery was valued at $7,900 as at the date of marriage, $28,000 in 1984 and $32,400 in 1987 and 1988. Between 1977 and 1984 jewellery acquired by Mrs. Oswell cost $7,000. After that date Mr. Oswell did not purchase any other jewellery for his wife.

The parties would not agree to have the jewellery valued by a single independent appraiser whose values would be binding. In part this was because it was felt that, since Mr. Oswell had agreed to the method of valuation used by Campbell, the same method of valuation should be applied to Mrs. Oswell's assets. Despite the unsatisfactory evidence, the court must therefore do the best it can.

I am of the opinion that, with respect to the gold jewellery owned by Mrs. Oswell prior to marriage, any increase in value has been offset by the decline in the price of gold since 1977 and by normal wear. I find that Mrs. Oswell's net family property should show a net increase after marriage in the amount of $7,000 for jewellery. This figure assumes wear and tear is offset by any increase in the value of gem stones owned by Mrs. Oswell.

Mrs. Oswell testified that her father had been in the fur business and that she knew something about furs. A wild mink coat, which was purchased at a cost of $12,000, was indicated by her to be worth about $5,000 or $6,000 in 1984. I accept this value. According to a letter obtained by Mrs. Oswell from her furrier, this coat has a present value of $2,000. This is after a substantial decline in the price of furs in 1988. Given these parameters, I am of the opinion that the value to be assigned to this coat should be $4,000 in 1988. The value of the fox fur coat is also in dispute. It was purchased in late 1986 by Mr. Oswell for $7,500. It is indicated to have a value in 1990 of $1,500. In early 1988 I find that the value of this coat is $4,000.

According to Mrs. Oswell, the furs she owned at the date of marriage were worth $2,000 and are now practically worthless. I accept this. Mrs. Oswell's net family property statement should reflect her furs as a net increase of $6,000 after marriage.

Negative Values

In some cases, it is necessary to value intangible property: for example, see *Belman v. Belman* (1997), 32 RFL (4th) 453 (Ont. Ct. J (Gen. Div.)) and *Burnett v. Burnett* (1998), 33 RFL (4th) 356 (Ont. Ct. J (Gen. Div.)). In *Montague v. Montague* (1997), 23 RFL (4th) 62, the Ontario Court of Appeal agreed with the trial judge that land owned by the husband had no value at all—because the land was extremely polluted, the cost of cleanup exceeded the value of the land. Thus, the trial judge had concluded that the land had no value for purposes of the *Family Law Act*; the Ontario Court of Appeal held that the value of land is the highest price obtainable in an open market between informed and prudent parties acting at arm's length. Because an informed and prudent purchaser would take into account the cleanup costs in determining the price to pay for the land, the trial judge's valuation was appropriate.

Pensions and Valuation

As noted above, the Supreme Court of Canada reviewed issues of pension valuation in *Best v. Best* (1999), 49 RFL (4th) 1. Other cases have also grappled with the problems of pensions and valuation: see *Smiley v. Ontario (Pension Board)* (1994), 4 RFL (4th) 275 (Ont. Ct. J (Gen. Div.)) and *Monger v. Monger* (1994), 8 RFL (4th) 157 (Ont. Ct. J (Gen. Div.)). In *Huisman v. Huisman* (1994), 8 RFL (4th) 145 (Ont. UFC), the parties had separated and settled their affairs pursuant to the *Family Law Reform Act* (the legislation in effect in Ontario before 1986). The parties then reconciled and again separated after the *Family Law Act* had been enacted. Because the husband's pension was a non-family asset under the prior legislation, it had not been included in the earlier settlement. The wife's claim to equalization under the FLA including the pension was upheld by the court. For a comprehensive analysis of problems with the current statute and recommendations for reform, see OLRC, *Report on Pensions as Family Property: Valuation and Division* (Toronto: OLRC, 1995), at 84-106.

Discussion Note

Reform Proposals

Consider the following critique of current methods of valuing pensions under the *Family Law Act*. To what extent might these problems affect negotiation of a separation agreement?

> Since the *Family Law Act* contains no special provisions for valuing pension plans, considerable time is spent by the parties and their legal advisors in negotiating these issues. Actuarial assistance is necessary, and typically each spouse engages his or her own actuary. Failure to reach an agreement on actuarial issues often results in lengthy and expensive judicial proceedings.
>
> In order to provide greater certainty with respect to the valuation of pensions, the Commission has developed standard procedures for the valuation of pensions, and recommends that they be prescribed by regulation. It is hoped that the expense, delay, and litigation produced by disputes in this area under present law would be minimized by these reforms.
>
> The Commission drew much assistance in this task from the Standard of Practice for the Computation of the Capitalized Value of Pension Entitlements on Marriage Breakdown for Purposes of Lump-Sum Equalization Payments developed by the Canadian Institute of Actuaries (September 1, 1993) (hereafter referred to as the "CIA Standard of Practice"). These standards, while mandatory for actuaries, are not currently mandatory for the purposes of pension valuation under the *Family Law Act*. The CIA Standard of Practice deals with the economic and demographic assumptions to be used in the valuation of defined benefit plans on marriage breakdown for the purposes of lump-sum equalization payments under provincial *Family Law Acts* or similar statutes. The standards stipulate the assumptions and methods that may be employed for such valuations, as well as the content of actuarial reports.
>
> The CIA Standard of Practice addresses several major issues that were previously problematic in the valuation process. These include interest rates used to discount future payments; salary increase assumptions made under the retirement method of valuation; the mortality assumption; and the retirement ages for which values are to be reported. To ensure that the CIA Standard of Practice forms the basis for pension valuation in family matters in Ontario, the Commission has recommended that regulations to this effect be promulgated under the *Family Law Act*. The regulations would be based on the CIA Standard of Practice and would be mandatory for all pension valuations covered by the Act. ...
>
> In addition to the valuation problems addressed above, parties to a marriage breakdown may experience considerable difficulty in making appropriate arrangements to satisfy an equalization payment where there is a large pension asset. In this situation, the current law only allows spouses to divide the pension asset through "if and when" orders and agreements. This device has proved unsatisfactory for various reasons. Accordingly, in order to provide a more effective means of settlement where there is a pension asset, the Commission has made a number of recommendations for reform.
>
> Under the Commission's proposals, the non-member spouse will have two additional options for satisfying an equalization payment. The first is a transfer of a portion of the commuted value of the pension at the time of marriage breakdown. The second is a benefit split which creates, in effect, a separate pension for the non-member spouse.

See *Report on Pensions as Family Property*, at 2-5. Is there a need as well to reform principles of valuation for other forms of family property? No such recommendations were included in the OLRC's *Report on Family Property Law*.

5. Deductions

In calculating each spouse's net family property, it is necessary to deduct the value of debts at the valuation date, and also the net amount of pre-marriage property, other than a matrimonial home. The determination of appropriate deductions has also presented some difficulties, particularly because spouses may not have kept clear records, especially during a long-term marriage.

Stephen Grant, "Deductions Under the Family Law Act: The Sequel"
(1990), 6 *Canadian Family Law Quarterly* 257, at 258

This is reasonably easy to consider; it is historical. Bearing in mind that the onus of proving a deduction lies on the spouse claiming it, the exercise becomes one of dredging up old bank statements, deeds, bills of sale and the like to show ownership and value of property 5, 10 or 20 years ago. Obviously that oversimplifies a situation that for most separated spouses is a hassle and often more effort than it seems to be worth. Clients now marrying will be well advised to keep at least an inventory of their assets and liabilities on the date of marriage. Marriage, for the unwary, may well turn out to be an exercise in bookkeeping, whatever else it is.

There are, however, a few useful points to review. A matrimonial home which was owned by one of the spouses on the date of marriage but which was subsequently sold and replaced by a new residence, whether owned or rented, becomes just another piece of property for purposes of calculation of a spouse's NFP. In *Folga v. Folga*, Gravely LJSC found that:

> The status of a matrimonial home is not immutable and a spouse may lose the protection [given] by the matrimonial home status and ... a spousal owner may regain the right to deduct under s. 4(1)(b).
>
> Here it appears that although [the property in issue] was once the matrimonial home it is no longer so under ss. 4(1) or 18 since the parties were not ordinarily resident in it at the date of separation. Not being a matrimonial home, it now qualifies for deduction under s. 4(1)(b).

If the home is owned on both the date of marriage and the valuation date, the owner receives no deduction for the value of the home on the earlier date.

The Matrimonial Home

The application of these principles was reviewed in *Nahatchewitz v. Nahatchewitz* (1999), 1 RFL (5th) 395 (Ont. CA), where the husband sold the house (he held title) while his wife was away (in connection with requirements of obtaining her Canadian citizenship). A few years later, the parties separated. The Ontario Court of Appeal permitted the husband to deduct the value of this house because it was not ordinarily occupied by the parties as their family residence at the time of separation. The court expressly followed *Folga v. Folga* (1986), 2 RFL (3d) 358 (Ont. SC (HCJ)) and declined to follow *Miller v. Miller* (1987), 8 RFL (3d) 113 (Ont. Dist. Ct.). See also *Mazzarello v. Mazzarello* (1999), 44 RFL (4th) 142 (Ont. CA). For other examples concerning deductions under the *Family Law Act*, see *McDonald v. McDonald* (1997), 33 RFL (4th) 3 (Ont. CA) and *Wamsley v. Wamsley* (1998), 41 RFL (4th) 454 (Ont. Ct. J (Gen. Div.)).

Costs of Disposition

A particularly difficult problem for the calculation of deductions has related to notional tax and disposition costs for assets held by a spouse on the valuation date. Conflicting decisions in *McPherson v. McPherson* (1988), 63 OR (2d) 641 (CA) (a decision under the former *Family Law Reform Act* prohibiting such deductions in the absence of evidence about the plan for such disposition and income tax implications) and *Heon v. Heon* (1989), 22 RFL (3d) 273 (Ont. SC (HCJ)) (recognizing the validity of such deductions regardless of intent to dispose of them) were resolved in *Starkman v. Starkman* (1990), 28 RFL (3d) 208; the Ontario Court of Appeal affirmed the approach in *McPherson*. In *Sengmueller v. Sengmuller* (1993), 17 OR (3d) 208, the Ontario Court of Appeal identified (at 241) the appropriate approach:

> (a) [a]pply the overriding principle of fairness, i.e., that costs of disposition as well as benefits should be shared equally;
>
> (b) [d]eal with each case on its own facts, considering the nature of the assets involved, evidence as to the probable timing of their disposition, and the probable tax and other costs of disposition at that time, discounted as of valuation date; and
>
> (c) [d]educt disposition costs before arriving at the equalization payment, except in the situation where "it is not clear when, if ever, there will be a realization of the property."

See Melanie Manchee, "Family Law Update," Canadian Bar Association Ontario, September 1994.

Negative Values

In calculating the equalization claim, s. 4(5) provides that if a spouse's net famiiy property, calculated in accordance with the required principles, results in a negative value, it will be deemed to be zero. However, the statute is silent with respect to negative values in the calculation of deductions—that is, a negative value in pre-marriage property, where the value of the spouse's debts exceeded the value of his or her assets at the time of marriage. Consider these facts, for example:

Value of spouse's assets at V-Day: $50,000
Value of spouse's pre-marriage assets (assets minus debts) . . . . . −$10,000

In this context, a spouse who entered the marriage with $10,000 in debts must increase the value of his or her assets by *$60,000* in order to have assets of *$50,000* at the valuation date. In mathematical terms, the calculation will also result in a net family property value of $60,000, having regard to the deduction of a negative value.

Hovius and Youdan expressly agreed with this result, citing *Menage v. Hedges* (1987), 8 RFL (3d) 225, at 229 (Ont. Dist. Ct.):

> Although s. 4(1)(b) of the Act refers to "the value of property ... after deducting the ... debts," I am satisfied that this language can encompass a negative balance. Section 4(5) specifically contemplates that net family property balances could be less than zero and provides a remedy where this occurs at the conclusion of the calculation. It would have been simple for the legislator to insert a similar provision with respect to "property owned on the date of marriage" had this been the intention. Since the intention of the Act is to provide for equal sharing of values acquired after marriage, it seems logical that, where one spouse enters into the relationship with a negative balance, this negative balance be included in his or her "pile" for purposes of calculating the equalization claim.

6. Calculating the Equalization Claim

After calculating the value of each spouse's net family property, s. 5 of the *Family Law Act* requires that the spouse with the greater net family property pay to the other spouse one-half the difference between them. Recall that the onus of proving a claim for an exclusion or deduction is on the person asserting it: for example, see *Dubauskas v. Dubauskas* (1995), 14 RFL (4th) 160 (Ont. Ct. J (Gen. Div.)).

By contrast, the BC legislation provides that a person who claims that an item is *not* a family asset has the onus of establishing the claim: see *Family Relations Act*, RSBC 1996, c. 128, s. 60. Are these provisions consistent? Why, or why not? What goals do they promote in relation to family property?

7. Unequal Shares Under the Family Law Act

Sullivan v. Sullivan
(1986), 5 RFL (3d) 28 (Ont. UFC)

[After the parties married in 1966, the husband decided to undertake a BA degree at York University. He completed a first degree, and then pursued an MA. Completion of his education required more than seven years, during which time the wife worked full-time, supported her husband, financed his education, managed the family financial affairs, and cared for the couple's child. At the time of separation, the wife owned a corporation that operated a catering business; the trial judge concluded that the value of the wife's interest in this corporation should not be included in computing her net family property, stating (at 36-38):]

Mrs. Sullivan chose J=Systems Inc. as her vehicle for carriage of the business from which she derives most of her earnings. This vehicle was conceived by Mrs. Sullivan, brought into existence by her, managed by her and maintained by her without any contribution from Mr. Sullivan whatsoever. Over and above that management, Mrs. Sullivan, by all accounts of both parties, totally managed all family financial affairs, again without any help whatsoever from her spouse and it was from her earnings, leaving aside the financial management she provided, that the family was able to live for a continuous period of seven to eight years during which time Mr. Sullivan upgraded his education and very substantially so. And during that period, did Mr. Sullivan provide extensive assistance in the area of child care or household management that might offset his deficiencies in the areas of support or financial management that otherwise would usually be provided from a non-working spouse? The answer to that question is a clear "no" as Mrs. Sullivan had the day-to-day responsibilities of housekeeping and child raising while her husband studied, firstly, at York University in Toronto and then in Ottawa for post-graduate studies while his wife and child remained in Toronto. I find as a fact that the contribution made to the family unit during these several years was staggeringly uneven in all three major areas of contribution to family, i.e., child care, household management and financial provision.

Furthermore, one must examine the contribution of the parties once Mr. Sullivan had returned to the work force. The evidence of Mrs. Sullivan (and it is uncontroverted by Mr. Sullivan) is that once he had gainful full-time employment as a psychologist around 1980 and forward, gross earnings that ranged from $21,000 to $29,600 during the years 1981-1984, he offered her, firstly, the sum of $600 per month as his total contribution to the family welfare. He paid this to her and she was charged with the responsibility of managing all expenses, of maintaining their home and as well the day-to-day living expenses for all three. This he opted to reduce to $550 per month after nine months or so and eventually to $400 per month and apparently on some occasions he contributed nothing. All the while, Mrs. Sullivan managed J=Systems Inc. along with all her other family responsibilities including an obviously much greater financial contribution to the family's day-to-day needs. I might venture the view that but for this lady's wise management of family finances, along with her unarguable energies in earning wages (through two jobs on one occasion), Mr. Sullivan, whatever else he might have been doing vocationally, would today most certainly lack his present educational level that enables him to be presently employed as Senior Psychologist at Chedoke McMaster.

For these reasons, I propose simply to order that the shares of and equity in J=Systems Inc. are the exclusive property of Mrs. Sullivan. The note from this corporation due and owing at some time in the future to Mrs. Sullivan, if indeed the corporation's future ability to discharge this liability to Mrs. Sullivan germinates, is also an asset that should belong exclusively to Mrs. Sullivan.

I believe the legislative intent expressed in s. 5(6)(h) of the Act enables me to reach this conclusion for the extensive reasons already stated. This conclusion is, I believe, further strengthened by s. 5(7) (the purpose subsection) as it embraces the following concepts:

(a) that *child care, household management and financial provision* are joint responsibilities;

(b) that the assumption of these responsibilities is inherently equal by the terms of a marital contract;

(c) that equalization of net family property is subject to the *equitable* considerations of s. 5(6).

Much has and will be written on what the legislature intended in s. 5(6) in its use of the word "unconscionable." The Concise Oxford Dictionary defines the word as follows: "having no conscience; contrary to the dictates of conscience; not right or reasonable; unreasonably excessive." Webster's New Collegiate Dictionary defines it thusly: "not guided or controlled by conscience; excessive; unreasonable; shockingly unfair or unjust." I view the usage of this word by the legislature as creating a threshold whereby unequal division may be ordered where to do otherwise would be patently unfair or inordinately inequitable. The test is a subjective test and one that must be applied to all the facts that involve the three ingredients contained in s. 5(7) and the six factors in s. 5(6), i.e., (a) to (h) inclusive.

In the instant case I have concluded that it would be patently and grossly unfair to award Mr. Sullivan any part of either the equity in this corporation or in the nebulous value of the note due to shareholder that emanates from this corporation when his contribution to the three areas of marriage (child care, household management and financial provision), so important to the spirit of this new legislation, has been collectively so disproportionately at variance from that of Mrs. Sullivan.

In a material sense, it can be readily said that his benefits have been enormous while his contributions have been quite dismal.

Waters v. Waters
File no. 1024/86 (Ont. Dist. Ct.) [unreported]

[The husband and wife, both in their 50s, separated after 30 years of marriage. They had no children and both worked in factories, the wife earning about $35,000 and the husband about $21,000 at the time of trial. The wife claimed an unequal division of net family property because the husband was an alcoholic; because the husband had not been responsible with money (claiming that his mother had managed it for him before his marriage, his wife had done so during the marriage, and his sister had taken over this responsibility since the separation); and, finally, because she had performed a greater share of the household duties both inside and outside the home. The husband did not deny any of the allegations, admitting that he was an alcoholic and that his wife was a workaholic.

The court concluded that it was not unconscionable to award equal shares in this case. The judge stated that, on a global assessment of the respective contributions of the parties, it was clear that the wife had made a greater contribution. However, the court further concluded that the Act required the assessment to be made, not on a global basis, but on the basis of the provisions of ss. 5(6) and (7), stating (at para. 6):]

McNEELY DCJ: Subsection (7) does not say that inherent in the marital relationship there should be equal contribution; it says inherent in the marital relationship "there is equal contribution." The rationale is hardly self-evident. Spouses differ in earning capacity, education, intelligence, physical and emotional health, affection for children, interest or ability in child raising, spending habits and a host of other attributes. These attributes will determine to a large extent what contribution they make to the marital relationship. To say that it is inherent in the relationship that the contributions are equal is to say something that is patently untrue. Section 5(7) unless it is to be regarded as an affront to common sense must mean that as a matter of public policy the contributions are deemed equal (even when they are not) and that this deemed equality of contribution is the rationale of the equal division of family property provided for in Section 5(1).

The evidence in the present case therefore that the actual contribution to the marital relationship of the plaintiff in terms of performance of household duties, financial contribution, responsible emotional commitment, and general responsibility exceeded that of the husband does not in itself justify a departure from equality. It would not justify departure even if, on a global assessment of their contributions, it could be said that the wife's contributions so greatly exceeded the husband's that an equal sharing of assets would be unconscionable.

The Court is authorized to order an unequal division of the family property only pursuant to Section 5(6) and only in those cases where an equal sharing would be unconscionable having regard to the specific factors named in clauses (a) to (h). ...

The fact that these listed factors do not include factors such as child care, performance of household duties, financial contribution which are important factors of family contribution in the normal case is a clear indication that Section 5(6) was not intended as a means of departing from the rule of equal sharing by an attack on the legal fiction of equal contribution embodied in Section 5(7). While Section 5(h) is wide in its terminology it must receive an interpretation which is consistent with the scheme of the Act and with the legal presumption embodied in Section 5(7) rather than a wider interpretation which would subvert the scheme of the Act and make redundant and unnecessary most of the preceding clauses of subsection (6).

There are compelling public policy reasons which support the view that departures from equality should be uncommon. Most spouses cannot afford costly adversarial litigation which under the guise of searching for an ideal of fairness and equity would often leave both spouses despoiled of their assets. Moreover Section 5(1) by making the death of a spouse the legal equivalent of divorce, nullity or separation as far as its consequences are concerned has changed the law of succession.

Discussion Notes

Unequal Shares in the Supreme Court of Canada: Leblanc v. Leblanc

How should the different outcomes in *Sullivan* and *Waters* be explained? Compare these cases pursuant to the equalization regime in Ontario with a more discretionary legislative regime in New Brunswick. In *Leblanc v. Leblanc*, [1988] 1 SCR 217; 12 RFL (3d) 225, the Supreme Court of Canada considered the New Brunswick legislation in the context of spouses' unequal contributions to the marriage. In *Leblanc*, seven children were born to the couple in the first eight years of their marriage. The husband suffered from alcoholism, worked for only four years at the beginning of the marriage, and took no part in child-rearing responsibilities. After living for some years on welfare, the wife began to work as a waitress and then took out a loan and bought the restaurant. The husband did deliveries and assisted in contractual arrangements for buying delivery vehicles. The wife eventually bought a house in her own name and, although each spouse contributed $1,000 to the down payment, the regular mortgage payments were made out of the proceeds of the restaurant. Later on, the wife bought land and built a cottage and the husband supervised some of the construction work and did landscaping.

The trial judge concluded that the husband had made no contribution to child care, household management, or financial obligations of the family. He received recognition for his contribution to the down payment on the house of $1,000 and also for an amount of $6,000 representing his contribution to the business: see (1984), 54 NBR (2d) 388 (QB Fam. Div.). The New Brunswick Court of Appeal overturned this decision and concluded that the property should be divided between the husband and wife equally: (1986), 68 NBR (2d) 325; 1 RFL (3d) 159 (CA). On appeal to the Supreme Court of Canada, the trial decision was restored. La Forest J stated (at SCR 222):

> While a court should, in the words of Galligan J in *Silverstein v. Silverstein* (1978), 20 OR (2d) 185 at 200, 1 RFL (2d) 239, 87 DLR (3d) 116 (HC) [a decision under Ontario's *Family Law Reform Act*], "be loath to depart from [the] basic rule [of equal division]," it should nonetheless, as he indicates, exercise its power to do so "in clear cases where inequity would result, having regard to one or more of the statutory criteria set out in cls. (a) to (f)." This does not, as previously indicated, mean that a court should put itself in the position of making fine distinctions regarding the respective contributions of the spouses during a marriage. Nonetheless, where the property has been acquired exclusively or almost wholly through the efforts of one spouse and there has been no, or a negligible, contribution to child care, household management or financial provision by the other, then, in my view, there are circumstances relating to the acquisition, maintenance and improvement of property that entitle a court to exercise its discretion under s. 7(f).
>
> This is such a case. While the trial judge found that the husband did contribute $1,000 as part of the down payment of the matrimonial home, and was from time to time of some assistance in the operation of the wife's business, his overall findings are sufficient to warrant the exercise of his discretion. Without entering into details, he found the husband's drinking was "to say the least excessive, continuous and persistent." All the assets were in the wife's name, and these had been "earned entirely by her labour, with a great deal of assistance from her children when they were old enough to enter the labor force"; "the husband made no contribution to child care ... to household management, and in fact he made no financial contribution to the family in any way, shape or form."

See also *Williams v. Williams* (1989), 19 RFL (3d) 452 (NBQB), where property was divided unequally in favour of the husband in New Brunswick. The parties, married for only 29 months when they were both in their 70s, made very unequal financial and other contributions to the marriage. Do these cases suggest a need to reform Ontario's *Family Law Act*?

Discretion Under Ontario's Family Law Act

In some cases, courts have exercised considerable discretion in assessing the equality of contributions of the spouses. For example, in *Merklinger v. Merklinger* (1992), 43 RFL

(3d) 109 (Ont. Ct. J (Gen. Div.)), the parties were married for 18 years; they separated, with two children remaining with the husband and one with the wife. Both parties worked after separation, and the husband did not contribute support for the wife or the child who lived with her; as well he sold assets contrary to a preservation order. There were also some complicated financial transactions involving the wife's agreement to place a further mortgage on the matrimonial home (registered in her name) in order to discharge outstanding debts of the husband. As well, the husband permitted a mortgage on the cottage owned in the wife's name to go into default and then arranged to incorporate a company to purchase it for $650,000, when the debt owing was $800,000 and the cottage was valued at $1,000,000. The husband suggested that the court ignore the cottage in calculating the equalization entitlement. The wife requested that the net family property be distributed in her favour and that the husband be held in contempt.

The court ordered no equalization payment to the husband and held him in contempt. However, because he may not have appreciated the seriousness of his actions, the court refrained from ordering a jail term. The court held that the considerations in s. 5(6) permitted a judge to take into account post-separation conduct (such as the abandonment of the wife and child after separation) and that the conduct in this case broke the bargain implicit in s. 5(7). Thus, by not requiring the wife to make an equalization payment to the husband, she received more than half the difference between the parties' net family properties.

Does this case reflect the view that judicial discretion is limited in relation to the application of s. 5(6)? As *Waters* demonstrated, the presumption of equal contributions is very strong. In *Zabiegalowski v. Zabiegalowski* (1992), 40 RFL (3d) 321 (Ont. UFC), the parties separated after about three years of marriage, and the court denied both spouses' claims to an unequal share of family property. According to the court, the onus of establishing an entitlement under s. 5(6) was a heavy one and neither party had discharged it.

In *Warne v. Warne* (1992), 39 RFL (3d) 392 (Ont. Ct. J (Gen. Div.)), the court also held that a post-separation decline in value of property did not meet the test of s. 5(6) for unequal shares. In *Fillipponi v. Fillipponi* (1992), 40 RFL (3d) 296 (Ont. Ct. J (Gen. Div.)), however, Charron J awarded the wife an unequal share by reason of her husband's reckless depletion of assets, which "shocked the court." See also *Abaza v. Abaza* (2000), 16 RFL (5th) 1 (Ont. Sup. Ct. J), where the court concluded that it was appropriate, pursuant to s. 5(6) to order an unequal share of the spouses' net family properties. In this case, the husband had created significant debts in relation to his use of escort services. In the result, the amount of $16,000 of the husband's debts was disallowed, so that the wife received an equalization payment that was $8,000 more than she would otherwise have obtained. In addition, the court held that it was unreasonable to expect the wife to be able to provide precise evidence to prove her claim; instead, the court calculated the husband's debts on the basis of his credit card statements.

Equality Versus Equity: Hines v. Hines

In *Hines v. Hines* (1988), 23 RFL (3d) 261 (Ont. SC (HCJ)), the court considered property and spousal support entitlements together. It was a second marriage for both husband and wife, who were both in their late 60s. Their only income was old age and other pensions.

In assessing the husband's claim for equalization, Walsh J stated (at 263):

The husband, at the date of marriage, was an unemployed, divorced man who brought into the marriage a used car, a few items of furniture, and several thousand dollars worth of debts, together with a liability of $150 per month in support payments for his former spouse.

The wife was a widow who owned a fully furnished small bungalow in Scarborough and had some $16,000 of the proceeds of her late husband's life insurance in a premium savings account in the Toronto Dominion Bank, where she was also employed as a supervisor.

The spouses, throughout the marriage, maintained a joint savings account into which they contributed their earnings when they were employed, and out of which they paid all of their household and other expenses, including the payments on a new car every two years and a $5,000 investment the husband made, which was a complete loss. If there were insufficient moneys in their joint pot, the wife topped it up with moneys from her savings account.

The spouses separated some 13 days after the *Family Law Act* came into force in 1986. The husband departed, driving off in the car, which was at that time only some five months old. The wife continued to remain in her home. There were no moneys left at all in the spouses' joint account, nor in the wife's own premium savings account. The husband some two months later commenced this action, seeking the sale of the wife's home and an equal division of the proceeds of such sale.

I accept and prefer the evidence of the wife. Exhibit 8, the wife's net family property statement, shows the value of her home at $120,000 and, after adjustment of and allowance for a few other items, results in an equalization payment due to the husband of some $48,000. The wife has no means of satisfying this payment, other than by selling this little bungalow, which has been her home for the past 33 years. A mortgage would be clearly impossible for her to arrange or to carry on her minimal income.

The wife here seeks lump sum support from her husband to enable her to meet the imposition of the obligations cast upon her by Pt. I of the Act.

In my view this Act, the *Family Law Act*, must be read as a whole. It is an integrated Act, all parts working in concert, not [in] isolation from each other, to result in an orderly and equitable settlement of their affairs upon breakdown, as required by the preamble to the Act. Section 33(8)(d) of Pt. III requires the court to relieve financial hardship, and subs. (9)(f) to have regard to the accustomed standard of living while the parties resided together.

The circumstances of this case clearly require a lump sum award of $38,000 support to the wife. With that sum applied towards her obligation under Pt. I of the Act, the wife should then, over a period of time, be able to, even with her minimal resources, satisfy her obligation under Pt. I of the Act. To avoid the obvious hardship this payment will result in, s. 9(1)(c) provides that a payment may be delayed for a period not exceeding 10 years.

In the result, therefore, the plaintiff husband shall have judgment for the sum of $10,000, payable without interest of any kind, neither prejudgment or post-judgment, by the defendant wife to him on or before 15th September 1998.

In an annotation to *Hines*, James McLeod suggested that the reasons for the decision in *Hines* may be inconsistent with the *Family Law Act* and with the line of decisions that have interpreted it: see James McLeod, "Annotation of Hines v. Hines" (1988), 23 RFL (3d) 261. In particular, McLeod was critical of the way that Walsh J improperly used the support power "to effect a redistribution on the facts." Do you agree? Why, or why not?

Length of Cohabitation

Some earlier decisions had concluded that the length of cohabitation in s. 5(6)(e) in-cluded only cohabitation during marriage: see, for example, *Stewart v. Stewart* (1991), 39 RFL (3d) 88) (Ont. Ct. J (Gen. Div.)). However, the Ontario Court of Appeal concluded in *MacNeill v. Pope* (1999), 43 RFL (4th) 209 that "cohabitation" in s. 5(6)(e) includes pre-marital as well as marital cohabitation. In this case, the parties had cohabited for many years before marriage, so that even though they lived together after marriage for less than five years, s. 5(6)(e) did not apply. Is this decision consistent with the goals of the statute? Why, or why not?

In addition, a spouse has sometimes claimed that there should be an unequal equaliza-tion payment because of the short length of the marriage, where the other spouse has asserted that the reason for the short length of the marriage was abusive or violent behaviour on the part of the spouse claiming the unequal share. For example, in *Futia v. Futia* (1990), 27 RFL (3d) 81 (Ont. SC (HCJ)), the parties were married for less than two years and the wife alleged physical and mental cruelty in her petition for divorce. The petitioner and respondent were of different ages and religious persuasions (the petitioner was a Jehovah's Witness and the respondent a Roman Catholic). There was also friction in the marriage because the respondent's mother lived with the spouses, expressing hostility to the petitioner on many occasions. The major family asset at the valuation date was the matrimonial home, purchased and owned by the respondent. It had substantially increased in value, and the court decided that an unequal share in favour of the respond-ent was appropriate pursuant to s. 5(6)(e), even though the petitioner argued that the respondent's cruelty was the reason for the short duration of the marriage. In assessing the petitioner's claim, the court stated (at 85):

> While conduct may in some limited circumstances be relevant to the division of family property I am not persuaded that it is relevant to the issue in this case and accordingly I reject that argument. I reject the argument that the court should consider conduct of the respondent and disregard the shortness of cohabitation. In my view it would indeed be unconscionable for the petitioner to receive an equal division when she had contributed virtually nothing to the acquisition of the matrimonial home whose value increased substan-tially between the date of purchase and the date of separation.

> The question then becomes how much less than 50 per cent should the petitioner receive. The petitioner contends that if an amount less than 50 per cent is considered it should be not less than 40 per cent. The respondent proposes the division be fixed at 30 per cent.

> Having regard to the length of cohabitation which was one year and nine months and relating that period to the contemplated norm of five years, I accept the submission of counsel for the petitioner and find that she is entitled to receive 40 per cent of the net equity of the matrimonial home or $33,600. There is already $10,000 standing in court to the credit of this action. The petitioner is entitled to this amount and the amount payable to her by the respondent will be reduced to $23,600. The petitioner is also entitled to accrued interest on the funds in court.

In an annotation to this case, James McLeod raised the question whether the *reasons* for a short-term marriage should ever be relevant to an inquiry under s. 5(6):

The cases have made it clear that matrimonial misconduct, per se, is not relevant to proceedings for the distribution of matrimonial property. Accordingly, the wife should not be entitled to an increased share because her husband was abusive. However, this is not the same as saying the husband's conduct is irrelevant. Most courts have acknowledged that the economic effects of a spouse's conduct may be taken into account. No spouse should be expected to tolerate abusive behaviour. Thus, it does not seem unreasonable to adopt the *Firestone* [(1979), 11 RFL (2d) 150 (Ont. HC)] analysis and refuse to allow a spouse to allege the short duration of cohabitation if the spouse has caused the separation by unreasonable or unacceptable behaviour. The problem is that this analysis introduces the law of desertion into property law. However, it is difficult to see how the court can assess the importance of the termination of cohabitation without examining the reason for the separation.

See James McLeod, "Annotation of Futia v. Futia" (1990), 27 RFL (3d) 81, at 81-82.

Reform Proposals

In its *Report on Family Property Law*, the OLRC reviewed the statutory language and judicial interpretation of s. 5(6). As the report noted (at 65), the intent of this section is clear:

Courts have acknowledged the policy of the Act to enforce an equal sharing of the value of assets at the end of a marriage, unless that equalization shocks the conscience of the court.

The high threshold for invervention required by the test of unconscionability in s. 5(6) has generally restricted judicial discretion to award unequal equalization payments to spouses, although (as demonstrated in cases such as *Hines* above) some judges have exercised considerable ingenuity in order to achieve a fair result.

According to the commission, however, there was a demonstrated need to amend the statute to permit judicial discretion in a number of additional circumstances. For example, the commission recommended (at 144) that courts should have discretion to vary an equalization payment "to recognize a substantial post-valuation date change in value of an asset if necessary to ensure an equitable result, having regard to the cause of the fluctuation." According to the commission (at 69), such an amendment would remove the incentive for spouses to seek a remedial constructive trust, and it would also offer more flexibility than altering the valuation date. Recognizing that this recommendation might increase the costs and complexity of litigation, the commission also suggested (at 70):

The [amendment] should direct courts to consider both the cause of a change in value and the amount of that change. Such a provision will not end litigation on this point but will redirect it to the real issue, rather than to the requirements for a common law remedy, which may not be relevant to the cause of a fluctuation in value or to the determination of who should bear it.

Consider this proposal in relation to the facts in *Rawluk*, above. How would this proposal affect the outcome in that case? Is this outcome preferable? Why, or why not?

In addition to this proposal, the commission's report also included recommendations to permit courts to consider post-separation events, including conduct that is relevant to the factors in s. 5(6). As well, the commission recommended amendments to confirm the right to prejudgment interest in relation to equalization payments and to permit courts to order unequal equalization payments where the spouses' net family property amounts are equal: see *Report on Family Property Law*, at 68-72 and 144.

C. The Matrimonial Home

1. Equalization: Special Treatment

But the matrimonial home is more than a valuable asset. It is the place around which family life revolves. As a result, the spouses often develop deep emotional attachment to it. This may be especially true for a spouse who has functioned as a full-time homemaker during the relationship. Moreover, the right to occupy the matrimonial home satisfies one of the basic needs of individuals in our society—namely, the need for accommodation. In her critical analysis of American law dealing with the economic consequences of divorce, Lenore Weitzman notes that an equal division of marital property, however defined, frequently results in the forced sale of the couple's family residence. This compounds the financial dislocation and impoverishment of women and children generated by divorce. Where the spouses' only significant tangible asset is the matrimonial home and it is sold on the breakdown of the relationship so that the proceeds can be shared equally, often the custodial parent's share will be insufficient to acquire suitable accommodation. While this problem might be remedied by more generous support payments, the loss of the matrimonial home will invariably necessitate a move to new accommodation. This may well disrupt a child's schooling or neighbourhood and friendship ties, thereby creating additional stress and dislocation at the very time when the child most needs continuity and stability. For these reasons, Part II of the *Family Law Act* recognizes that the right to occupy the matrimonial home is important and that it cannot be governed by reference to ownership alone.

Hovius and Youdan, at 574-75

These comments reflect concerns about the matrimonial home as an asset that is qualitatively different from other family property. Such concerns resulted in the exceptions in ss. 4(1) and (2) of the *Family Law Act* with respect to deductions and exclusions. Because a matrimonial home, as defined in s. 18, cannot be deducted or excluded, its value must always be included in the net family property of the title holder(s). In this way, it is clear that a spouse with a valuable asset may be able to deduct it if it was pre-marriage property or exclude it if it was a gift from a third party during the marriage. However, if the asset is the matrimonial home at V-day, it cannot be either deducted or excluded. As explained earlier, the different treatment of the matrimonial home may be experienced as unfair to a title-holding spouse in some circumstances.

Clearly, the current legislative regime attempts to balance the interests of a title-holder and a non-title-holder at marriage breakdown. The current arrangements were reviewed by the OLRC's *Report on Family Property Law*, which recommended abolition of this special treatment of the matrimonial home. Examine the reasoning of the OLRC report, at 84-85: to what extent do you agree with its statement of the problem and its proposals for reform? Is it sufficient to confine principles about the matrimonial home within part II of the *Family Law Act*? Is the underlying purpose of equalization in part I better achieved by treating all property, including the matrimonial home, in the same way?

A more radical reform, but one in keeping with the central principle of Part I of the Act, would be to end special treatment of the matrimonial home under Part I. This would have the advantage of allowing owner spouses to take advantage of statutory deductions and exclusions. It would also allow spouses to continue to allocate ownership of the matrimonial home to protect it from creditors, as they are able to do with other assets. If a spouse has debts and liabilities at the valuation date, these may be set off against the full equity in the house. The need to protect the interest of a non-owner spouse in the preservation of an asset which provides shelter and is often the family property of the greatest value, would continue to be guaranteed by the provisions in Part II of the Act. A spouse without title would continue to have possessory rights in the home and the rights of the titleholder to encumber or dispose of the home would remain severely restricted.

The disadvantage to this approach is that a non-owner spouse will not share in the benefits of ownership, both psychological and practical, although in many cases both spouses may regard the property as "our home" and each may have contributed to its acquisition and maintenance. In most of those cases, however, the value of the home will continue to be shared because it will be included in the net family property of the titleholder, although subject to any deductions, debts or liabilities of that spouse.

It would be inequitable in a long-term relationship in which the home is the sole or major asset to deny a non-owning spouse a share in the capital growth in the value of the home. This would occur under existing law which provides that capital growth in the value of an excluded asset is not included in the net family property of the owner. If the Legislature amends the statute to allow the inclusion of changes in capital value of an excluded asset in the net family property of an owner, however, as we recommend above, this problem will not arise. If the Legislature does not introduce this amendment, it should introduce a more limited amendment to ensure that all changes in capital value of a home are included in the net family property of the owner. This would recognize the special contribution to the preservation and maintenance of a shared family residence made by many non-titled spouses.

In our view, the potential disadvantages of ending special treatment of the home in Part I are outweighed by the advantages. This amendment would prevent disparities in the treatment of similarly situated parties and accord with the rationale that spouses should share only wealth generated by the marital partnership. At the same time the provisions in Part II of the Act will continue to recognize the special nature of the home.

The Commission recommends that paragraph (b) of the definition of "net family property" in section 4(1), and section 4(2) of the *Family Law Act* should be amended to delete the special treatment of the family home [matrimonial home] for the purposes of Part I of the Act.

Spouses should continue to share in any capital gains or losses in the value of a home during the relationship. If the Legislature implements the Commission's recommendation to include all capital gains and losses in the value of excluded assets in the net family property of an owner, all spouses will share in the change in value of a house during a relationship. If the Legislature does not implement that recommendation, the Commission recommends that it should implement this reform with respect to the family home [matrimonial home] alone.

Assess the extent to which these recommendations would solve the problems identified by the OLRC in relation to special treatment of the family home for purposes of equalization.

What alternative reforms can you suggest? In this context, consider again the issues concerning discretion versus fixed shares in relation to family property. Is there a need for more discretion to achieve fairness in these situations?

2. Possessory Rights in the Matrimonial Home

Possessory rights in the matrimonial home are defined in part II of the *Family Law Act*. In this part of the statute, there are provisions to ensure that both spouses have rights to possession of the matrimonial home, regardless of the legal ownership arrangements— for example, title in one spouse only or joint tenancy. Essentially, the statute creates rights to possession of the matrimonial home that would not otherwise exist for a non-titled spouse. Moreover, in some cases, a non-owning spouse may be entitled to an order of exclusive possession, thereby evicting the titled spouse from possession: see s. 24. In examining the cases that follow, consider how courts have interpreted these possessory rights in different kinds of fact situations—do these cases reflect an appropriate balance between the rights of the title-holder and the non-owning spouse?

Rosenthal v. Rosenthal

(1986), 3 RFL (3d) 126 (Ont. SC (HCJ))

[In this case, the court considered an application by the wife for exclusive possession of the matrimonial home, a claim that was denied, essentially for economic reasons; the court stated (at 135):]

The matrimonial home is located as I have indicated at 1905 Labelle Street, in the city of Windsor. By agreement of counsel, its estimated value is $130,000 with a present mortgage of $85,000 to $86,000.

The three sons are residing with the petitioner in this home. Michael is in attendance at St. Clair College, and pursuant to the minutes of settlement that were formulated into the decree nisi, the respondent is paying $300 a month toward the support and maintenance of Michael. Jeffrey and Mark, although not working, are in receipt of income, one through Unemployment Insurance, and the other as a result of a work related injury. Both of these young men are paying to their mother the sum of $30 per week; however, in her financial statement, the petitioner has indicated that the cost of groceries is $175 per week. It is quite clear that the amount being paid for room and board does not even cover the individual cost of groceries to each of these young people.

They are accordingly being subsidized by their parents. The shelter costs, as indicated by the material filed, would include the monthly mortgage payment, the taxes, the utilities, the insurance, and annual repairs. On a monthly basis, this results in a cost of some $1,541.40. ...

[The court reviewed s. 24(3) and continued:]

Certainly, Mark and Jeffrey cannot be considered to be children affected by this application. As I have indicated by agreement, the respondent is already paying the sum of $300 for the support of Michael so that he might continue his education.

Paragraphs (b), (d), (e) and (f) in my view have no application to support the claim for exclusive possession by the wife.

The respondent is presently residing in a one-bedroom apartment, paying rent in the amount of $600 per month.

There is no question that Mrs. Rosenthal finds herself to be the aggrieved party in this unfortunate situation. The evidence of her doctor, heard by the court as a result of an application for an adjournment, clearly identifies the emotional stress that the petitioner is suffering as a result of the marital breakdown. However, the court must be bound by the provisions of the statute.

Mrs. Rosenthal in her evidence stated quite clearly that in her view, her choice of living standards should not in any way be affected by her husband's situation. This, of course, is an entirely unrealistic view of the result of a marital breakdown.

It is axiomatic that two people can live cheaper together than they can apart and this is something that Mrs. Rosenthal unfortunately must face. Her attempts to maintain the standard at which she was living prior to the marital breakdown must be viewed in the light of the moneys that are available to maintain that standard. Even during cohabitation, it is apparent that these two parties were living beyond their means, despite the relatively large joint income enjoyed by them. When one considers the financial statements filed by both parties, it becomes readily apparent that there are not sufficient funds to continue the occupation of the marital home.

Pursuant to the provisions of the statute, each party is entitled to a one-half interest in the matrimonial home. In order to have the court set aside that statutory right of the respondent, Mrs. Rosenthal must establish on the balance of probabilities that she falls within the provisions of s. 24(3). On the totality of the evidence, she has failed to satisfy the court that she has met this requirement. Unfortunate as it may be, it is the view of the court that the present situation cannot continue and it is in the best interest of both parties that the matrimonial home be sold for the best available price and that the excess moneys would, in accordance with the statute, be divided between them and form a portion of each net family property.

This will, of course, require Mrs. Rosenthal to acquire other accommodations, be it an apartment or a less expensive dwelling, either by rental or ownership. It is, of course, laudable that Mrs. Rosenthal might wish to have the three sons continue to reside with her. If that is their choice, then of course the sons, who are in receipt of income, would be required to pay their fair share of maintaining such accommodation.

The court is cognizant of the adverse effect that this determination will have upon Mrs. Rosenthal; however, as I have indicated, the court is bound by the provisions of the statute. There is no legal obligation upon this respondent to maintain Mark and Jeffrey in a style to which they have been accustomed. It is, for example, noted that each of the three boys owns and operates their own motor vehicle, as does Mrs. Rosenthal. To require Mr. Rosenthal to pay for the continuing occupation of the family unit in the matrimonial home would in effect be requiring him to support and maintain both Mark and Jeffrey under the present circumstances. Even apart from that, I am satisfied after review of the financial statements filed by both parties, that Mr. Rosenthal is entirely incapable of paying the amount that would be required to continue their occupancy of the matrimonial home at the price that I have indicated.

The application for exclusive possession of the matrimonial home is therefore dismissed and it is ordered that the matrimonial home be sold, hopefully through the cooperation of both parties, which will be to the benefit of both parties.

Pifer v. Pifer
(1986), 3 RFL (3d) 167 (Ont. Dist. Ct.)

[In this case, the court reviewed interim decisions regarding custody of children and exclusive possession of the matrimonial home. In considering the provisions of the *Family Law Act*, the court expressly noted the changes in the Act regarding entitlement to exclusive possession of the matrimonial home, by contrast with provisions in the *Family Law Reform Act*, the previous legislation. In particular, the court noted the reluctance of judges to remove a spouse from the matrimonial home, under the previous statute, unless there was serious and weighty evidence of physical and emotional harm to the children. By contrast, the court stated (at 170):]

The new legislation not only expands the criteria, it also is framed differently. It is significant to note that the question of violence committed by one spouse against the other spouse or children is a separate factor from the question of "the best interests of the children affected." Nor do I think that what constitutes "the best interests of a child" in subs. (4) is to be restricted solely to the two questions in that subsection, i.e., the disruptive effects of a move to other accommodation or the child's views and preferences. In my view, what amounts to the best interests of the child may include many other factors such as the psychological stresses and strains to a child arising out of the daily friction between parents.

Turning now to the material before me, the parties were married on 11th December 1976 in Milwaukee, Wisconsin. They have two young daughters, Laura, aged 6, and Jennifer, aged 4. The plaintiff is a nurse and the defendant an accountant. Apparently, they enjoyed a relatively comfortable lifestyle until the defendant decided to go into business for himself and purchased a Go-Camping franchise which involved rental and sales of motor homes and travel trailers. Unfortunately, the business lasted only a few months and the defendant found himself unemployed. To assist in the family finances, the plaintiff decided to seek employment first in February 1984 in a doughnut shop and later in May 1984 as a nurse at the K-W Hospital where she remains today. The defendant sought and obtained work in the accounting department of a law office and later with a chartered accountant. Since February 1986 he has attempted to establish his own accounting business.

The material indicates that until the plaintiff began to work, she assumed most of the responsibility for looking after the children. After she began work, the parties shared that responsibility with the defendant taking an active role particularly when the plaintiff was working shift work at the hospital. In April it was decided to hire a babysitter, Linda Gregoire, so that the defendant could devote more time to his new business.

The main allegation of the plaintiff is that the defendant has, over the last four months, started to drink heavily at home starting in the afternoon around 4:00 p.m. until he passes out around 10:00 p.m. There is also an allegation that he smokes heavily, leaving live cigarettes in the ashtrays, and leaves on a propane heater after he has gone to bed. She also says that the arguments between them have increased in frequency since he began to drink heavily and this affects the children and frightens the babysitter. The allegations of excessive drinking are supported by the babysitter in her affidavit. Although the defendant concedes drinking alcohol, he denies that it is to excess and also denies that he is endangering his family by the use of cigarettes or the propane heater.

The balance of all of the material indicates to me that there is a great deal of stress and strain in this household which is obviously affecting the children. There is no doubt in my mind that it would be in the best interests of the children if they were relieved of that stress by the separation of their parents. If it were not for the serious allegations of drinking and bizarre conduct by the defendant, as supported by the affidavit of Linda Gregoire, I might have considered granting him interim interim exclusive possession and custody because of the fact that he has more time to devote to looking after the children. However, because of those allegations, I am of the view that it would be in the best interests of the children that the plaintiff have custody of them and exclusive possession of the matrimonial home.

Insofar as access is concerned, the defendant will have liberal and generous access to his daughters subject to the condition that he not consume any alcohol while exercising access.

Hill v. Hill
(1987), 10 RFL (3d) 225 (Ont. Dist. Ct.)

FITZGERALD DCJ: The parties to this proceeding are the applicant wife and the respondent husband. Under the *Family Law Act* the wife, aged 69, seeks interim relief from her husband of the same age by way of exclusive possession of the matrimonial house, support and costs. There is no lack of money available in the short term to either party but it is apparent that the husband's business is the major asset and income producer in a marriage which lasted some 40 years. Within two years of marriage in August 1947, the wife gave up her employment as a clerk and has since devoted herself to running the matrimonial house and raising two sons born in 1951 and 1954.

The husband formed his own business firm in 1950. At first the wife assisted in that business but after the birth of the second child ceased to be active in the firm. The business has prospered. The parties enjoyed a generous lifestyle but their interests diverged. Mrs. Hill devoted her energies to the house while Mr. Hill devoted his to the business. Eventually Mrs. Hill indicated that she would seek a separation.

The response to this was delivery to Mrs. Hill by one of her sons of a handwritten statement of what would happen if she proceeded with her intention. These included:

We will evict you from house and cottage

You will have no money for 2 or 3 years until support awarded

You will die penniless and be buried in an indigent grave …

You will be up against … best lawyers—money no object—we are going to drag this out

No more medical payments by G.O. Hill

We will take car away

How are you going to pay litigation costs?

It is apparent that "we" refers to Mr. Hill and at least one of his sons. The effect of this document was intimidating in the extreme and constitutes harassment of a particularly invidious character.

In addition on this application two affidavits were sworn by friends of Mrs. Hill who, since the separation was contemplated, received anonymous notes identified by a handwriting expert as being written by Mr. Hill. These vindictive missives are of some relevance in support of Mrs. Hill's contention that her husband has undertaken a deliberate campaign of what I regard as psychological warfare against her and her friends in the hope of undermining her resolve to obtain a fair settlement on separation. Mr. Cyr sought to exclude these affidavits. While they must be received with caution I deem them relevant to the evaluation of Mr. Hill's conduct toward others as an indication of the veracity of Mrs. Hill's allegation of his conduct toward her.

Giving further credence to her allegations of intimidating conduct on his part is the actual conduct of the litigation to date.

The initial motion for interim relief in this matter resulted in an interim order made on 25th June 1987. This order, in light of the threats of legal and other consequences to arise from taking the application, led to the issue of an order of mutual non-harassment. There was also an order that neither party deplete assets and an order that Mrs. Hill be permitted to continue to use the Buick automobile she customarily used. The application was adjourned *sine die* to be brought back on seven days' notice by either party.

Delay now becomes apparent. Despite efforts to expedite the matter, no financial statement was delivered by the husband. This forced the wife to commence an action by delivery of a statement of claim dated 26th July 1987, including the wife's financial statement and income tax return [and] a notice to Mr. Hill to file a financial statement.

On 13th August 1987, not having received such statement, Mrs. Hill's solicitors wrote advising that, if none was forthcoming by 19th August 1987, a motion to compel production would be brought. That motion was brought returnable 20th August 1987. The statement of financial information was filed on the date the notice of motion was to be heard, 20th August 1987.

This statement turned out to be inaccurate. It did not disclose certain assets and certain transfers of funds.

While there was an invitation subsequently to consult with Mr. Hill's accountant, a revised statement was not received until 5th October 1987. Mr. Hill has not been available for cross-examination thereon prior to return of this motion on 8th October 1987.

Meanwhile the wife alleges that she continues to be harassed by the husband and that his conduct and attitude have driven her to seek psychiatric help. This harassment has been subtle. It consisted of changing the pattern of delivery of money for household and personal expenses as well as the delay in coming to grips with the legal proceedings.

On the other hand Mr. Hill did pay all the usual household expenses and did continue to supply Mrs. Hill with money. He spent only part of his time in the matrimonial home preferring to spend his time at the family cottage. He did use the home for his noon hour siesta and slept there some week nights. She reports that he frequently tells her such things as "the judge and the lawyers say you are crazy to leave me" and "[t]he judge is going to send you to an asylum [sic] where you will be locked up for several months and observed through a one-way mirror." As a result of such actions and his underhanded communications with her friends, the wife has begun to fear what her husband may do next and has begun absenting herself from home when he is there. Now that winter is approaching he will probably spend more time at home.

The report of Dr. Sheppard indicates that anxiety over the domestic situation, while not a cause of her neck pain, is a contributing factor. He says: "I believe that the continued co-habitation of Mrs. Hill and her husband is having a detrimental effect on her psychological state" and "since her decision to separate ... the symptoms have been worse."

While the doctor feels that emotionally she can handle a move out of the home he is far from enthusiastic. He puts it that "she would find some way of coping with moving out of the home" as she is "generally able to cope with a considerable amount of adversity."

As to the husband's effect on her he states:

> With regards to the issue of physical violence this does not seem to have been a feature of the marital relationship. ... [T]he symptoms to which Mrs. Hill is prone are symptoms of anxiety which are similar to symptoms of fear although the stimulus provoking these symptoms is different. I believe she finds the behaviour of her husband toward her to be of a "mentally abusive" nature. *It is this behaviour which in my opinion is largely responsible for the exacerbation of the severity of her anxiety symptoms.* [Emphasis added.]

Apart from filing a statement of defence and finally a corrected financial statement Mr. Hill has not responded to his wife's allegations. She has been extensively cross-examined on her affidavits. Mr. Hill has not yet made himself available for cross-examination on his financial statements.

On cross-examination, p. 52, Mrs. Hill admits that, if she had to, she could cope with leaving her home on the basis that anyone having any backbone "can manage to cope with anything." She reaffirms, however, the time and effort she has put into the home, the money of her own she had spent on it and that "the house is me" and "it would be more than traumatic" (to leave it). She goes on to say "I have given up the camp which was ... dreadful ... as I love the camp almost as much as I love the house."

From the wife's perspective the key issue is whether exclusive possession of the matrimonial home should be ordered.

The husband relies on statements made by the wife at pp. 40-42 which describe Mr. Hill on a typical day leaving the house at 8 a.m., coming home for lunch, lying down for a couple of hours and returning to work about 2 p.m. He would arrive home at 5 p.m. or later. He would spend Tuesday nights and weekends at the camp and would spend holidays there until Thanksgiving. I conclude that the husband uses the home primarily for his daily nap and, of course, resides there when he cannot be at the camp. There is no evidence that he has any emotional attachment to the home. The order for non-harassment of Mrs. Hill has been ignored.

In the short term both parties have the financial resources to find alternate accommodation. I find it is *not* feasible for the two of them to occupy the same dwelling having regard to the psychological warfare being waged by the husband against the wife and its effect upon her. Which of them should give up the house?

The *Family Law Act* provides in s. 24(3) that I shall consider:

> (c) the financial position of both spouses;
>
> (e) the availability of other suitable and affordable accommodation; and
>
> (f) any violence committed by a spouse against the other spouse or the children.

As to para. (c), the husband is worth at least $2¾ million and has available cash exceeding $150,000. The wife is worth $275,000 including cash of $39,000. If she is to maintain her lifestyle and finance an action involving the valuations necessary to a successful prosecution of her claim she can least afford to move.

As to para. (e) there is no evidence whatever from either party except that the respondent husband's two sons have physical room for his accommodation.

Paragraph (f) refers to "violence." In my view the violence in this context must be such that it makes continuation of joint cohabitation in the matrimonial dwelling impractical. Violence in my view includes psychological assault upon the sensibilities of the other spouse to a degree which renders continued sharing of the matrimonial dwelling impractical. Where, as here, the conduct of the husband in written and spoken communication to the wife is calculated to produce and does in fact produce an anxiety state which puts the wife in fear of her husband's behaviour and impinges on her mental and physical health, violence has been done to her emotional equilibrium as surely as if she had been struck by a physical blow.

Black's Law Dictionary includes in the definition of violence, "acting with or exerting great force on the mind."

Webster includes the definition, "the unjust use of force or power, as in a deprivation of rights" and "to do violence to ... to injure; as, he does violence to his own opinions."

In my view the sense and purpose of the *Family Law Act*, which is a remedial statute and hence to be liberally construed, must surely include in the meaning of violence that violence causing injury to a spouse which can be achieved by words and deeds and is not restricted to the violence which can be achieved solely by physical abuse.

I am required to consider the above criteria but I am not confined to these alone. As Nasmith Prov. J so carefully decided in *Miller v. Miller* (1978), 2 RFL (2d) 239, at 144 (Ont. Prov. Ct.), there is a duty to exercise the power to order exclusive possession with great care. The court, however, as stated in *Steward v. Steward* [[1948] 1 KB 507; [1947] 2 All ER 813 (CA)], adopted by Nasmith Prov. J at pp. 143-44, "It must always be a question for the exercise of the discretion of the judge, on all the facts before him in all the circumstances."

In my view it is the conduct of Mr. Hill which has rendered the matrimonial home incapable of being shared. His is the lesser emotional attachment to the home. He will be the least inconvenienced by finding alternate accommodation. His are the greater resources to do so.

Mr. Cyr suggests that having to move from the home will prejudice the husband's ability to attend to his business and that he has not the time to look for alternatives. Having in mind the time he spent at his camp at leisure I reject this argument. His daily siesta can be taken anywhere quiet.

For all the foregoing reasons it is "an equitable settlement of the affairs of the spouses" (preamble to the Act) that Mrs. Hill have interim exclusive possession of the matrimonial home and contents and I so order.

The respondent shall have the weekend next following the date of this order to remove his personal effects. I suggest that this not be regarded an abandonment of title to anything not removed at that time, this being an interim disposition only.

Having decided on the matter of exclusive possession there remains the question of the proper amount for interim support.

Discussion Notes

Evidentiary Requirements and Section 24(3)

In relation to these examples, which subsections of s. 24(3) appear to be most influential in relation to claims for exclusive possession of the matrimonial home? Recall the case of Pamela Berendt in chapter 4, in which she sought an order for exclusive possession unsuccessfully and some months later was murdered by her husband, who then committed suicide. In that case, the court held that it was appropriate to maintain a high standard of evidence before making such an order. Is *Hill* consistent with the *Berendt* case? Do the cases reflect different standards in relation to evidence and onus of proof, or are there other factors that are relevant?

In relation to issues of violence in families with fewer financial resources than the Hills, consider *Wilson v. Wilson* (1989), 19 RFL (3d) 259 (Ont. Dist. Ct.), at 260, in which the court found that the husband had a serious drinking problem and that he had committed acts of violence against his wife, resulting in criminal convictions; at the time of the wife's application for exclusive possession of the matrimonial home, the spouses were occupying separate households within the matrimonial home. According to the court (at 261):

> The husband is employed with Petro Canada Ltd. as a service station operator and earns an annual income of $17,034.80 which converts to approximately $1,400 per month. He shows actual expenses of approximately $1,600 which figure covers all household expenses including the expenses of himself, the wife and the three children, while residing in the home. ...
>
> The wife shows her monthly needs for herself and the three children while occupying the home as being approximately $1,000 per month, due mainly to the low monthly mortgage payment of $227 per month.
>
> It is acknowledged that there simply is not alternative affordable housing for the mother and the children. The wife who is unemployed receives approximately $100 per month by

way of family assistance and is capable of supplementing this income by performing babysitting services.

Maintaining two separate households on the basis of the husband's current income is a most difficult endeavour. The parties have sustained themselves financially by living together while apart. The wife should not have imposed upon her the continuation of such an arrangement because of the husband's limited means and realizes that she will have to accommodate her needs beyond the husband's ability to pay.

It would be in the best interests of the children bearing in mind that the wife has been a full-time mother and will continue to be so if interim custody, care and control of the children were granted to the wife with generous access to the husband.

The husband's behaviour including assault tendencies, and uncontrolled drinking, is a factor in granting interim exclusive possession of the matrimonial home to the wife. Furthermore, this would also be in the best interests of the children who would remain in familiar surroundings. The economic circumstances and the lack of alternative affordable accommodations make exclusive possession of the home to the wife necessary.

The husband has the means to pay to the wife for interim spouse and child support the sum of $550 per month commencing 1st February 1989. The wife is expected to pay the household expenses including the mortgage payment.

Is this decision consistent with *Hill* and/or *Berendt*? Which factors in s. 24(3) appear to be most significant for awards of exclusive possession? For another example, see *Re Luyks and Luyks* (1998), 39 OR (3d) 469 (Gen. Div.).

Possessory Rights for Aboriginal Spouses on Reserve Lands

Similar issues about possession of the matrimonial home have arisen in relation to aboriginal lands in Canada. In 1986, the Supreme Court of Canada considered the application of provincial family law legislation to native women living on reserves. In *Derrickson v. Derrickson*, [1986] 1 SCR 285, the court decided that the BC *Family Relations Act* was not applicable to lands on Indian reserves on the basis that "Indians and lands reserved for Indians" was a matter within federal legislative authority pursuant to the Constitution. In *Paul v. Paul*, [1986] 1 SCR 306, the court similarly decided that the provisions of the BC legislation could not be used to grant occupancy rights in a matrimonial home located on a reserve to the wife: see M.J. Mossman, "Developments in Property Law: The 1985-86 Term" (1987), 9 *Supreme Court Law Review* 419, at 430ff.

The Supreme Court of Canada decision in *Paul* was distinguished in *Wynn v. Wynn* (1989), 14 ACWS (3d) 107 (Ont. Dist. Ct.), where a wife sought interim exclusive possession of the matrimonial home, situated on an Indian reserve. Wright DCJ acknowledged that the court could not grant an order for exclusive possession of a matrimonial home that is located on a reserve; instead, he made an *in personam* order, without reference to the property, restraining the husband from interfering with the wife's possession of the matrimonial home. Interestingly, in *George v. George* (1997), 139 DLR (4th) 53, the BC Court of Appeal affirmed the trial judge's decision to award the wife a compensation order pursuant to s. 52(2)(c) of the *Family Relations Act*, even though the appellate court confirmed the absence of any jurisdiction to grant the wife an interest in the matrimonial home, located on reserve land. In *Kwakseestahla v. Kwakseestahla*, [1998] BCJ no. 283 (SC), however, where the parties had agreed on a consent order granting the wife a life interest in the matrimonial home on reserve land, the court rejected the husband's claim that there was no jurisdiction to enforce the order: the court held that it was enforcing the parties' contract, not making an order pursuant to provincial legislation. For a cogent analysis of the decisions in *Derrickson* and *Paul* and the problems of violence for First Nations women, see Mary Ellen Turpel, "Home/Land" (1991), 10 *Canadian Journal of Family Law* 17.

Possessory Rights and Cohabiting Couples

Pursuant to the *Family Law Act*, the provisions of part II do not generally apply to cohabiting couples. For a critique and recommendations, see Alva Orlando, "Exclusive Possession of the Matrimonial Home: The Plight of Battered Cohabitees" (1987), 45 *University of Toronto Faculty of Law Review* 153. Although these possessory rights in the matrimonial home were not expressly considered by the Supreme Court of Canada in *Nova Scotia v. Walsh* (2002), 221 DLR (4th) 1, the court's analysis appears to confirm the need for legislative reform if possessory rights are to be extended to cohabiting couples. As noted earlier, the OLRC recommended such an extension of all the provisions of parts I and II of the *Family Law Act* to cohabiting couples: see *Report on the Rights and Responsibilities of Cohabitants Under the Family Law Act*.

3. Family Property and the Rights of Third Parties

Transfers Without Consent and Section 21(1)

Section 21(1) of the *Family Law Act* offers some protection for a non-titled spouse in circumstances where the owning spouse attempts to transfer title to a third party. In *First City Trust Co. v. McDonough* (1993), 50 RFL (3d) 197 (Ont. Ct. J (Gen. Div.)), the spouses owned the matrimonial home as joint tenants; the husband had borrowed money under a demand promissory note from the plaintiff trust company without his wife's knowledge or consent. The husband defaulted on the note and the sheriff requested directions about the enforcement of the plaintiff company's writ of sale of the husband's interest in the home. The court held that the sale could proceed because the unsecured loan from the plaintiff to the husband was not a transaction that "disposed of or encumbered" his interest in the home. In *McDonough*, the court distinguished an earlier decision, *Bank of Montreal v. Bray* (1993), 12 OR (3d) 545 (Gen. Div.), stating (at 202):

> In my view, s. 21(1)(a) of the Act has no application to the facts of this case. The legislation prohibits a spouse from disposing of or encumbering his or her interest in the matrimonial home unless the other spouse "joins in the instrument or consents to the transaction." The "instrument" referred to in s. 21(1)(a) is the document by which the spouse effects the disposition or encumbrance of his or her interest in the matrimonial home, and the "transaction" referred to in the sub-section is the actual disposition or encumbrance. For example, if the spouse conveys his or her interest, the other spouse must either join in the deed or

transfer, or expressly consent to it. In this case Mr. McDonough's interest in the matrimonial home consists of the undivided one-half interest in it, which he owns jointly with Mrs. McDonough. The only transaction into which he entered was the borrowing of money from the judgment creditor as evidenced by a promissory note. This was an unsecured transaction. The question is whether this loan transaction constitutes a disposition or an encumbrance of Mr. McDonough's interest in the matrimonial home which required the consent of his wife or her joinder in the loan. The writ of seizure and sale which the judgment creditor wishes to enforce arose by operation of law as a result of the judgment obtained against Mr. McDonough, and is not a transaction into which he entered by which he encumbered his interest in the matrimonial home.

See also *Fulton v. Fulton* (1993), 17 OR (3d) 641 (CA) and *Robinson v. Royal Bank of Canada* (1995), 26 OR (3d) 627 (Gen. Div.). Note that *Bank of Montreal v. Bray* was overturned on appeal to the Ontario Court of Appeal: see (1997), 36 OR (3d) 99. How do such decisions affect the rights of a non-titled spouse to family property?

Notice

There have also been problems of interpretation relating to notice under part II. In *Stoimenov v. Stoimenov* (1985), 44 RFL (2d) 14 (Ont. CA), the court considered provisions of the *Family Law Reform Act* that are similar to those in part II of the *Family Law Act*. In *Stoimenov*, a husband, shortly after separating from his wife, mortgaged the matrimonial home and swore false affidavits (that the property was not a matrimonial home and that he was not married). Then, having obtained the mortgage funds, he promptly moved to Yugoslavia, leaving his wife in the matrimonial home. She applied to have the mortgages set aside. The issue was whether the mortgagee had the requisite notice, triggering the statutory provisions.

Under the *Family Law Reform Act*, the concepts of notice and actual notice were relevant; by contrast, only notice is relevant under the *Family Law Act*. The case remains significant for lawyers by reason of the discussion of notice and the fact that both the mortgagee, Greymac, and the lawyer for the transaction had actual notice to the contrary of the assertions in the husband's affidavit. On this basis, the wife was successful in her application.

In *Shute v. Premier Trust Co.* (1993), 50 RFL (3d) 441 (Ont. Ct. J (Gen. Div.)), the court reviewed the concept of notice pursuant to the *Family Law Act*. The spouses owned the matrimonial home as joint tenants; the wife obtained a line of credit and later a mortgage with the trust company by forging the husband's signature. The wife disappeared for a period of time and the husband discovered the forgery. The lawyer for the trust company had dealt only with the wife and had never contacted the husband; he witnessed and swore the wife's signature on the documents. Each time, the wife explained that her husband was out of the country and the lawyer permitted her to take the documents home for his signature; the lawyer made no effort to contact the husband to confirm the signatures.

In the result, the property was vested in the husband subject to an earlier encumbrance, the mortgage was set aside, and the trust company was given judgment against the lawyer. As James McLeod's "Annotation of Shute v. Premier Trust Co." (1993), 50 RFL (3d) 441 suggested (at 445-46):

In the end, Jenkins J's lack of concern for Premier Trust could have been because of the recovery against the lawyer. Although the lawyer had expert evidence that he was not negligent, the litigation could have been avoided if he had met or spoken with the husband. As Jenkins J correctly points out, lawyers who act on both sides of a real estate deal may be in a conflict of interest. A lawyer requires the consent of all the parties to continue to act. The Rules of Professional Conduct are clear. The lawyer violated rules 5 and 23, and losses were incurred by Premier Trust. Although the rules may relate to ethics only, the court is justified in using them to assess negligence. Ultimately, the liability is imposed on the person who could have best prevented it—the lawyer acting on the deal. Lawyers must be careful in accepting signatures not signed in front of them. They should be particularly conscientious where they represent both sides in a transaction and the matrimonial home is the subject of the encumbrance. The problem with *Shute* is not the result of the court's failure to address the restitution problems raised on the facts. At the very least, Jenkins J's reasons should prompt counsel to review their rules of professional conduct!

Partition Applications

There have also been a number of cases about the relationship of the *Family Law Act* to other statutes concerning proprietary interests. In *Silva v. Silva* (1991), 1 OR (3d) 436, for example, the Ontario Court of Appeal considered the relationship between the *Partition Act* and the *Family Law Act*. According to s. 2 of the *Partition Act*, RSO 1990, c. P.4, a co-owner (joint tenant or tenant in common) is entitled to partition on request. However, in *Silva*, the husband resisted the wife's application for partition and sale prior to the determination of their respective net family properties; in addition, the husband indicated his intention to claim an award of more than one-half the difference between their net family properties and the jointly held matrimonial home, the only asset. Thus, if the wife succeeded in her claim for partition and sale, the asset would not necessarily be available to meet the husband's claim pursuant to the *Family Law Act*.

The Ontario Court of Appeal reviewed the history of the *Partition Act*, the conflict in the case law, and the arguments of the spouses, concluding that the *Partition Act* must be interpreted in the light of the *Family Law Act*, but holding (at 444-45) that the wife's claim to partition or sale on the facts in *Silva* should succeed:

> The *FLA* authorizes the court to do whatever is necessary with the collectivity of spousal assets to bring about an equal division of them. It should be the statute of the first resort in matrimonial disputes, but it is not necessarily the only one. I think it is significant that s. 14(a) of the *FLA* states that "the fact that property is held in the names of spouses as joint tenants is *prima facie* proof that the spouses are intended to own the property as joint tenants." This is a recognition of the identical legal title of both spouses to an undivided ownership in the whole of the property. In my opinion, it is wrong to say, as it was said in *Scanlan v. Scanlan*, that the *FLA* ousts the jurisdiction of the *Partition Act* when dealing with jointly owned spousal property. The two statutes are not incompatible, but where sub- stantial rights in relation to jointly owned property are likely to be jeopardized by an order for partition and sale, an application under the *Partition Act* should be deferred until the matter is decided under the *FLA*. Putting it more broadly, an application under s. 2 should not proceed where it can be shown that it would prejudice the rights of either spouse under the *FLA*.

In the case on appeal, the contemplated partition and sale does not prejudice either spouse's claim with respect to the home under the *FLA*. The wife does not want the home at all and the husband wants the right only to bid on it once it is up for sale. He is entitled to do so under rule 55.06(5). While he wants an unequal division of family assets, any later determination of this claim is irrelevant to the sale of the home as such. His stated concern with respect to an immediate sale is that there will be no longer any security upon which to realize his *FLA* award. Such a sale also means that the husband will have to finance the purchase by raising one-half of the net purchase price, instead of some lesser sum. I can think of no reason why the husband should hold the house hostage until his claim has been adjudicated. The wife needs the money now and I do not think that his concern about collecting a subsequent award, in the circumstances of the case, amounts to prejudice within the meaning of the case law.

For other examples, see *Webster v. Webster* (1997), 32 OR (3d) 679 (Gen. Div.) and *Pastway v. Pastway* (1999), 49 RFL (4th) 375 (Ont. Sup. Ct. J).

Bankruptcy Proceedings

The relationship between the *Family Law Act* and bankruptcy legislation has been particularly complex: for an overview, see Robert A. Klotz, "Bankruptcy and Family Law: Problems and Solutions," in Law Society of Upper Canada, *Special Lectures of the Law Society of Upper Canada, 1993—Family Law: Roles, Fairness and Equality* (Scarborough, ON: Carswell, 1994), 253 and A. Merchant and J. Vogel, "The Bankruptcy Dodge" (1992-93), 9 *Canadian Family Law Quarterly* 161. As the OLRC's *Report on Family Property Law* indicated (at 46-49), there are complicated issues concerning the relationship of bankruptcy procedures and the remedial constructive trust. In addition, the relationship between bankruptcy proceedings and the equalization process may present challenges. For example, in *Malboeuf v. Malboeuf* (1994), 7 RFL (4th) 133 (Ont. Ct. J (Gen. Div.)), the husband declared bankruptcy and was then discharged one month after the parties separated. The wife made a claim for equalization of the net family properties; her husband moved to stay her claim because, as an undischarged bankrupt at the valuation date, his wife's claim was unliquidated and unsecured at that time. The court held that the wife's claim was not provable in the husband's bankruptcy, and because s. 178(2) of the *Bankruptcy Act* released the husband from only those claims provable in bankruptcy, the wife's motion for an equalization of net family properties should be granted. By contrast, in *MacPherson v. MacPherson* (1994), 4 RFL (4th) 214 (Ont. Ct. J (Gen. Div.)), the court held that a separation agreement entered into two weeks before the husband declared bankruptcy was void against the trustee in bankruptcy. How should priorities be determined in relation to family property, as between former spouses and third-party creditors?

SELECTED REFERENCES

A.F. Goldwater, "Bankruptcy and Family Law" (1998), 15 *Canadian Family Law Quarterly* 139.

Robert A. Klotz, "Wrestling with Pensions, Bankruptcy, and Family Law" (1994), 9 *Canadian Family Law Quarterly* 189.

Z.B. Wiseman, "Women in Bankruptcy and Beyond" (1989), 65 *Indiana Law Journal* 107.

IV. EQUITY FOR COHABITING COUPLES: THE USE OF TRUST DOCTRINES

> The constructive trust idea stirs the judicial imagination in ways that *assumpsit*, *quantum meruit* and other terms associated with quasi-contract have never quite succeeded in duplicating.
>
> G.E. Palmer, *The Law of Restitution*, vol. 1
> (Boston: Little, Brown, 1978), 16

As noted at the beginning of this chapter, Mrs. Murdoch's claim for a declaration of trust in the Supreme Court of Canada in the early 1970s was an important catalyst for the creation of provincial statutory regimes for the equal sharing of assets at the dissolution of marriage. Recall that in *Murdoch v. Murdoch*, [1975] 1 SCR 423; 13 RFL 185 a majority of the court held that Mrs. Murdoch had not established the elements necessary for a declaration of resulting trust; by contrast, the dissenting judgment suggested that her contribution to the acquisition of land (title to which was in her husband's name) was sufficient to warrant a declaration of constructive trust, based on principles of unjust enrichment.

At the time *Murdoch* was decided, there was an ongoing debate in English courts about the appropriateness of using constructive trusts in family matters. As the OLRC pointed out (at 21-24), Lord Denning in the English Court of Appeal frequently used trust principles "as a tool to reallocate ownership rights between spouses to reflect their joint efforts and expectations regarding their matrimonial home"; however, the House of Lords rejected this approach, overturning some of the decisions of the Court of Appeal and emphasizing the need to apply legal principles in the same way in both commercial and family settings.

To some extent, the divergence between the majority and dissenting judgments in *Murdoch* reflected the differences between the two levels of courts in England. Some years later, however, the Supreme Court of Canada appeared to concede the validity of the constructive trust in family law matters in its decision in *Rathwell v. Rathwell*, [1978] 2 SCR 436. By that time, however, provincial statutes were creating entitlement for married spouses to equal sharing of marital property (or its value) at separation or divorce; thus, the Supreme Court's decision in *Rathwell* had a less practical impact on divorcing couples than its earlier decision in *Murdoch*. However, in 1980, the Supreme Court considered an appeal from the Ontario Court of Appeal, which involved the dissolution of a cohabiting opposite-sex relationship in which Wilson JA had awarded the woman a one-half interest in land owned by her cohabiting partner. In examining the reasoning in the Supreme Court of Canada, consider the nature of the principles and the evidentiary basis for their application.

Pettkus v. Becker
(1980), 19 RFL (2d) 165; [1980] 2 SCR 834

DICKSON J (Laskin CJC and Estey, McIntyre, Chouinard, and Lamer JJ concurring):
The appellant Lothar Pettkus, through toil and thrift, developed over the years a
successful bee-keeping business. He now owns two rural Ontario properties, where
the business is conducted, and he has the proceeds from the sale, in 1974, of a third
property located in the province of Quebec. It is not to his efforts alone, however, that
success can be attributed. The respondent Rosa Becker, through her labour and earnings, contributed substantially to the good fortune of the common enterprise. She
lived with Mr. Pettkus from 1955 to 1974, save for a separation in 1972. They were
never married. When the relationship sundered in late 1974 Miss Becker commenced
this action, in which she sought a declaration of entitlement to a one-half interest in
the lands and a share in the bee-keeping business.

The Facts

Mr. Pettkus and Miss Becker came to Canada from central Europe separately, as immigrants, in 1954. He had $17 upon arrival. They met in Montreal in 1955. Shortly
thereafter, Mr. Pettkus moved in with Miss Becker, on her invitation. She was 30
years old and he was 25. He was earning $75 per week; she was earning $25-28 per
week, later increased to $67 per week.

A short time after they began living together, Miss Becker expressed the desire
that they be married. Mr. Pettkus replied that he might consider marriage after they
knew each other better. Thereafter, the question of marriage was not raised, though
within a few years Mr. Pettkus began to introduce Miss Becker as his wife and to
claim her as such for income tax purposes.

From 1955 to 1960 both parties worked for others. Mr. Pettkus supplemented his
income by repairing and restoring motor vehicles. Throughout the period Miss Becker
paid the rent. She bought the food and clothing and looked after other living expenses. This enabled Mr. Pettkus to save his entire income, which he regularly deposited in a bank account in his name. There was no agreement at any time to share
either moneys or property placed in his name. The parties lived frugally. Due to their
husbandry and parsimonious life-style, $12,000 had been saved by 1960 and depos-
ited in Mr. Pettkus' bank account.

The two travelled to western Canada in June 1960. Expenses were shared. One of
the reasons for the trip was to locate a suitable farm at which to start a bee-keeping
business.

They returned to Montreal, however, in the early autumn of 1960. Miss Becker
continued to pay the apartment rent out of her income until October 1960. From then
until May 1961 Mr. Pettkus paid rent and household expenses, Miss Becker being
jobless. In April 1961 she fell sick and required hospitalization.

In April 1961 they decided to buy a farm at Franklin Centre, Quebec for $5,000.
The purchase money came out of the bank account of Mr. Pettkus. Title was taken in
his name. The floor and roof of the farmhouse were in need of repair. Miss Becker

used her money to purchase flooring materials and she assisted in laying the floor and installing a bathroom.

For about six months during 1961 Miss Becker received unemployment insurance cheques, the proceeds of which were used to defray household expenses. Through two successive winters she lived in Montreal and earned approximately $100 per month as a baby-sitter. These earnings also went toward household expenses.

After purchasing the farm at Franklin Centre the parties established a bee-keeping business. Both worked in the business, making frames for the hives, moving the bees to the orchards of neighbouring farmers in the spring, checking the hives during the summer, bringing in the frames for honey extraction during July and August and the bees for winter storage in autumn. Receipts from sales of honey were handled by Mr. Pettkus; payments for the purchases of beehives and equipment were made from his bank account.

The physical participation by Miss Becker in the bee operation continued over a period of about 14 years. She ran the extracting process. She also, for a time, raised a few chickens, pheasants and geese. In 1968, and later, the parties hired others to assist in moving the bees and bringing in the honey. Most of the honey was sold to wholesalers, though Miss Becker sold some door to door.

In August 1971, with a view to expanding the business, a vacant property was purchased in East Hawkesbury, Ontario at a price of $1,300. The purchase moneys were derived from the Franklin Centre honey operation. Funds to complete the purchase were withdrawn from the bank account of Mr. Pettkus. Title to the newly acquired property was taken into his name.

In 1973 a further property was purchased, in West Hawkesbury, Ontario, in the name of Mr. Pettkus. The price was $5,500. The purchase moneys came from the Franklin Centre operation, together with a $1,900 contribution made by Miss Becker, to which I will again later refer. 1973 was a prosperous year, yielding some 65,000 pounds of honey, producing net revenue in excess of $30,000.

In the early 1970s the relationship between the parties began to deteriorate. In 1972 Miss Becker left Mr. Pettkus, allegedly because of mistreatment. She was away for three months. At her departure Mr. Pettkus threw $3,000 on the floor; he told her to take the money, a 1966 Volkswagen, 40 beehives containing bees, and "get lost." The beehives represented less than ten per cent of the total number of hives then in the business.

Soon thereafter Mr. Pettkus asked Miss Becker to return. In January 1973 she agreed, on condition he see a marriage counselor, make a will in her favor and provide her with $500 per year so long as she stayed with him. It was also agreed that Mr. Pettkus would establish a joint bank account for household expenses, in which receipts from retail sales of honey would be deposited. Miss Becker returned; she brought back the car and $1,900 remaining out of the $3,000 she had earlier received. The $1,900 was deposited in Mr. Pettkus' account. She also brought the 40 beehives, but the bees had died in the interim.

In February 1974 the parties moved into a house on the West Hawkesbury property, built in part by them and in part by contractors. The money needed for construction came from the honey business, with minimal purchases of materials by Miss Becker.

The relationship continued to deteriorate and on 4th October 1974 Miss Becker again left, this time permanently, after an incident in which she alleged that she had been beaten and otherwise abused. She took the car and approximately $2,600 in cash from honey sales. Shortly thereafter the present action was launched.

At trial Miss Becker was awarded 40 beehives, without bees, together with $1,500, representing earnings from those hives for 1973 and 1974.

The Ontario Court of Appeal varied the judgment at trial by awarding Miss Becker a one-half interest in the lands owned by Mr. Pettkus and in the bee-keeping business.

II

[Dickson J first considered the doctrine of resulting trust, suggesting (at 174) that this case offered "an opportunity to clarify the equivocal state in which the law of matrimonial property was left, following *Rathwell.*" After reviewing the cases in which these principles had been developed and some of the academic literature pointing out the artificiality of the idea of common intention (especially, express intention) in marriage-like relationships, Dickson J noted that the trial judge, somewhat ungallantly, had found as a fact that there had been no common intention between Mr. Pettkus and Ms Becker because Mr. Pettkus so testified at the trial. He concluded (at 179):]

In the view of the Ontario Court of Appeal, speaking through Wilson JA, the trial judge vastly underrated the contribution made by Miss Becker over the years. She had made possible the acquisition of the Franklin Centre property and she had worked side by side with him for 14 years, building up the bee-keeping operation.

The trial judge held there was no common intention, either express or implied. It is important to note that the Ontario Court of Appeal did not overrule that finding.

I am not prepared to infer, or presume, common intention when the trial judge has made an explicit finding to the contrary and the appellate court has not disturbed the finding. Accordingly, I am of the view that Miss Becker's claim grounded upon resulting trust must fail. If she is to succeed at all, constructive trust emerges as the sole juridical foundation for her claim.

III

Constructive Trust

The principle of unjust enrichment lies at the heart of the constructive trust. "Unjust enrichment" has played a role in Anglo-American legal writing for centuries. Lord Mansfield, in the case of *Moses v. MacFerlan* (1760), 2 Burr. 1005, 97 ER 676, put the matter in these words: "[T]he gist of this kind of action is that the defendant, upon the circumstances of the case, is obliged by the ties of natural justice and equity to refund the money." It would be undesirable, and indeed impossible, to attempt to define all the circumstances in which an unjust enrichment might arise. (See A.W. Scott, "Constructive Trusts" (1955), 71 LQR 39; Leonard Pollock, "Matrimonial Property and Trusts: The Situation from Murdoch to Rathwell" (1978), 16 *Alta. Law Rev.* 357.) The great advantage of ancient principles of equity is their flexibility: the judiciary is thus able to shape these malleable principles so as to accommodate the changing needs and mores of society, in order to achieve justice. The constructive trust has proven to be a useful tool in the judicial armoury. See *Babrociak v. Babrociak* (1978), 1 RFL (2d) 95 (Ont. CA); *Re Spears* (1975), 52 DLR (3d) 146 (NSCA); *Douglas v. Guar. Trust Co.* (1978), 8 RFL (2d) 98 (Ont. HC); *Armstrong v. Armstrong* (1978), 22 OR (2d) 223, 93 DLR (3d) 128 (Ont. HC).

How then does one approach the question of unjust enrichment in matrimonial causes? In *Rathwell* I ventured to suggest there are three requirements to be satisfied before an unjust enrichment can be said to exist: an enrichment, a corresponding deprivation and absence of any juristic reason for the enrichment. This approach, it seems to me, is supported by general principles of equity that have been fashioned by the courts for centuries, though, admittedly, not in the context of matrimonial property controversies.

The common law has never been willing to compensate a plaintiff on the sole basis that his actions have benefited another. Lord Halsbury scotched this heresy in the case of *Ruabon SS. Co. Ltd. v. London Assce.*, [1900] AC 6 (HL) with these words, at p. 10: "I cannot understand how it can be asserted that it is part of the common law that where one person gets some advantage from the act of another a right of contribution towards the expense from that act arises on behalf of the person who has done it." Lord Macnaughten, in the same case, put it this way, at p. 15: "There is no principle of law that a person should contribute to an outlay merely because he has derived a benefit from it." It is not enough for the court simply to determine that one spouse has benefited at the hands of another and then to require restitution. It must, in addition, be evident that the retention of the benefit would be "unjust" in the circumstances of the case.

Miss Becker supported Mr. Pettkus for five years. She then worked on the farm for about 14 years. The compelling inference from the facts is that she believed she had some interest in the farm and that that expectation was reasonable in the circumstances. Mr. Pettkus would seem to have recognized in Miss Becker some property interest, through the payment to her of compensation, however modest. There is no evidence to indicate that he ever informed her that all her work performed over the 19 years was being performed on a gratuitous basis. He freely accepted the benefits conferred upon him through her financial support and her labour.

On these facts, the first two requirements laid down in *Rathwell* have clearly been satisfied: Mr. Pettkus has had the benefit of 19 years of unpaid labour, while Miss Becker has received little or nothing in return. As for the third requirement, I hold that where one person in a relationship tantamount to spousal prejudices herself in the reasonable expectation of receiving an interest in property and the other person in the relationship freely accepts benefits conferred by the first person in circumstances where he knows or ought to have known of that reasonable expectation, it would be unjust to allow the recipient of the benefit to retain it.

I conclude, consonant with the judgment of the Court of Appeal, that this is a case for the application of constructive trust. As Wilson JA noted [at RFL 348]: "The parties lived together as husband and wife, although unmarried, for almost 20 years, during which period she not only made possible the acquisition of their first property in Franklin Centre by supporting them both exclusively from her income during 'the lean years,' but worked side by side with him for 14 years building up the bee-keeping operation which was their main source of livelihood."

Wilson JA had no difficulty in finding that a constructive trust arose in favour of the respondent by virtue of "joint effort" and "team work," as a result of which Mr. Pettkus was able to acquire the Franklin Centre property, and subsequently the East Hawkesbury and West Hawkesbury properties. The Ontario Court of Appeal imposed the constructive trust in the interests of justice and, with respect, I would do the same.

IV

The Common Law Relationship

One question which must be addressed is whether a constructive trust can be established having regard to what is frequently, and euphemistically, referred to as a "common law" relationship. The purpose of constructive trust is to redress situations which would otherwise denote unjust enrichment. In principle, there is no reason not to apply the doctrine to common law relationships. It is worth noting that counsel for Mr. Pettkus, and I think correctly, did not, in this court, raise the common law relationship in defence of the claim of Miss Becker, otherwise than by reference to the *Family Law Reform Act, 1978* (Ont.), c. 2.

Courts in other jurisdictions have not regarded the absence of a marital bond as any problem. See *Cooke v. Head*, [1972] 1 WLR 518, [1972] All ER 38; *Eves v. Eves*, [1975] 1 WLR 1338, [1975] 3 All ER 768; *Re Spears, supra*; and, in the United States, *Marvin v. Marvin* (1976), 557 P. (2d) 106 and a comment thereon (1977), 90 Harv. LR 1708. In *Marvin* the Supreme Court of California stated that constructive trust was available to give effect to the reasonable expectations of the parties, and to the notion that unmarried cohabitants intend to deal fairly with each other.

I see no basis for any distinction, in dividing property and assets, between marital relationships and those more informal relationships which subsist for a lengthy period. This was not an economic partnership, nor a mere business relationship, nor a casual encounter. Mr. Pettkus and Miss Becker lived as man and wife for almost 20 years. Their lives and their economic well-being were fully integrated. The equitable principle on which the remedy of constructive trust rests is broad and general; its purpose is to prevent unjust enrichment in whatever circumstances it occurs.

In recent years, there has been much statutory reform in the area of family law and matrimonial property. Counsel for Mr. Pettkus correctly points out that the *Family Law Reform Act* of Ontario, enacted after the present litigation was initiated, does not extend the presumption of equal sharing, which now applies between married persons, to common law spouses. The argument is made that the courts should not develop equitable remedies that are "contrary to current legislative intent." The rejoinder is that legislation was unnecessary to cover these facts, for a remedy was always available in equity for property division between unmarried individuals contributing to the acquisition of assets. The effect of the legislation is to divide "family assets" equally, regardless of contribution, as a matter of course. The court is not here creating a presumption of equal shares. There is a great difference between directing that there be equal shares for common law spouses and awarding Miss Becker a share equivalent to the money or money's worth she contributed over some 19 years. The fact there is no statutory regime directing equal division of assets acquired by common law spouses is no bar to the availability of an equitable remedy in the present circumstances.

V

Settlement or Estoppel

Another question argued is whether acceptance by Miss Becker of $3,000, 40 beehives and a car, upon temporary separation, and the imposition of terms on her return, estopped further claim. The trial judge answered this question in the affirmative. With respect, I think that he was wrong in so holding. A person is not estopped by accepting a sum of money, the amount of which is not negotiated, thrown at one's feet. There was no agreement by Miss Becker as to her interest in what I would regard as joint assets, nor can the conditions exacted by Miss Becker upon resumption of cohabitation be any bar to her claim. The filing by Mrs. Rathwell in *Rathwell, supra,* of a caveat claiming a one-tenth interest was held to be no basis for rejecting her claim to share equally in assets accumulated by her and her husband.

VI

Causal Connection

The matter of "causal connection" was also raised in defence of Miss Becker's claim, but does not present any great difficulty. There is a clear link between the contribution and the disputed assets. The contribution of Miss Becker was such as enabled, or assisted in enabling Mr. Pettkus to acquire the assets in contention. For the unjust enrichment principle to apply it is obvious that some connection must be shown between the acquisition of property and corresponding deprivation. On the facts of this case, that test was met. The indirect contribution of money and the direct contribution of labour is clearly linked to the acquisition of property, the beneficial ownership of which is in dispute. Miss Becker indirectly contributed to the acquisition of the Franklin Centre farm by making possible an accelerated rate of saving by Mr. Pettkus. The question is really an issue of fact: Was her contribution sufficiently substantial and direct as to entitle her to a portion of the profits realized upon sale of the Franklin Centre property and to an interest in the Hawkesbury properties and the bee-keeping business? The Ontario Court of Appeal answered this question in the affirmative, and I would agree.

VII

Respective Proportions

Although equity is said to favour equality, as stated in *Rathwell*, it is not every contribution which will entitle a spouse to a one-half interest in the property. The extent of the interest must be proportionate to the contribution, direct or indirect, of the claimant. Where the contributions are unequal, the shares will be unequal.

It could be argued that Mr. Pettkus contributed somewhat more to the material fortunes of the joint enterprise than Miss Becker but it must be recognized that each started with nothing: each worked continuously, unremittingly and sedulously in the joint effort. Physically, Miss Becker pulled her fair share of the load: weighing only 87 pounds, she assisted in moving hives weighing 80 pounds. Any difference in quality or quantum of contribution was small. The Ontario Court of Appeal in its discretion favoured an even division and I would not alter that disposition, other than to note that in any accounting regard should be had to the $2,600 and the car, which Miss Becker received on separation in 1974.

[Dickson J also noted the conflict of laws question "lurking in the background" in this case. The parties were domiciled in Quebec from 1955 to August 1971, so that it was arguable that laws of the province of Quebec were applicable. However, this issue was not pleaded and the court concluded that it was appropriate to proceed without taking judicial notice of the statutory laws of another province that had been ignored in the pleadings. Thus, Dickson J concluded (at 184):]

I would dismiss the appeal with costs to the respondent.

Discussion Notes

Resulting and Constructive Trusts

Ritchie, Maitland, and Beetz JJ agreed with Dickson J's conclusion, but for "substantially different" reasons. Ritchie J reviewed the cases concerning resulting trusts and the Court of Appeal's reasons and concluded (at 185 RFL) that

> the advances made by [Becker] throughout the period of the relationship between the parties [were] such as to support the existence of a resulting trust which is governed by the legal principles adopted by the majority of this court in [*Murdoch* and *Rathwell*].

Thus, Ritchie J expressly held that Becker had made a financial contribution and that there was a common intention that it be used for the benefit of both parties. Maitland J (Beetz J concurring) similarly concluded that the case could be resolved using the doctrine of resulting trust. After reviewing the idea of constructing trust in Anglo-Canadian law, moreover, he concluded (at 193 RFL) that

> the adoption of this concept [of constructive trust] involves an extension of the law as so far determined in this court. Such an extension is, in my view, undesirable. It would clothe judges with a very wide power to apply what has been described as "palm tree justice" without the benefit of any guidelines. By what test is a judge to determine what constitutes unjust enrichment? The only test would be his individual perception of what he considered to be unjust.

As is apparent, some judges in *Pettkus v. Becker* were not comfortable with discretionary decision making necessary to apply concepts of unjust enrichment in a family dissolution context.

In this case, the parties had been together for a lengthy period of time and they had both done a good deal of work in relation to the disputed property. Thus, while there may have been some difficulties in applying the test set out by Dickson J, the case was reasonably clear. Considering the approach in *Pettkus*, how significant was it that the parties were both without assets at the outset or that the work done by Ms Becker involved "more than just housework"? If the statutory regime in Ontario had been applicable to Ms Becker, even though she was just a cohabitee, what would she have been entitled to receive at separation? In this case, did the court want to achieve equity or equality between the spouses? Which goal requires more discretionary decision making? For an exploration of some of these principles, see Susan Westerberg Prager, "Shifting Perspectives on Marital Property Law," in Barrie Thorne, with Marilyn Yalom, eds., *Rethinking the Family: Some Feminist Questions* (New York: Longman, 1982), 111.

Enforcing the Court's Decision

In *Pettkus v. Becker*, Ms Becker "won." The court declared a constructive trust that entitled her to a one-half interest in property owned by Mr. Pettkus. However, as subsequent news reports explained, Mr. Pettkus resisted legal efforts to realize Ms Becker's entitlement. In November 1986, the *Globe and Mail* reported that she had committed suicide, leaving several letters in which she described her death as a protest against a legal system that prevented her from receiving a penny of the award, worth $150,000 at the time of the Supreme Court's decision: see Oakland Ross, "Ontario Fee System Cited in Woman's Legal Woe," *Globe and Mail*, November 13, 1986. Although the report indicated that Mr. Pettkus had been ordered to sell some property to comply with the court's decision, the sale had realized only $68,000, all of which was used to pay the legal fees of Ms Becker's counsel. In May 1989, the *Globe and Mail* reported that Ms Becker's total estate was $13,000 (she had been working as a housekeeper just prior to her death).

Although there are problems of enforcing court orders in many situations, it is possible that the problems are particularly acute in family law matters, especially in the context of the dissolution of a relationship. How should these problems be addressed? For example, should legislatures design property-sharing regimes for cohabiting couples that permit the transfer of assets (as is possible in some provincial regimes for married couples) rather than sharing in the value of property only? Would that result be preferable to an order making a recalcitrant cohabitee the trustee for the other cohabitee?

Sorochan v. Sorochan
[1986] 2 SCR 38; 2 RFL (3d) 225

[In *Sorochan v. Sorochan*, a cohabiting opposite-sex relationship of more than 40 years ended and the woman sought an interest in land owned by the man. However, he had owned almost all this land at the time when they began to cohabit. Why was this fact a problem in the context of the test enunciated by Dickson J in *Pettkus v. Becker*? Recognizing that the woman in *Sorochan* also contributed significant work over many years, how should this claim have been resolved?]

DICKSON CJC: Mary and Alex Sorochan lived together for 42 years, between 1940 and 1982, on a farm in the Two Hills district of Alberta. During this time, they jointly worked a mixed farming operation and had six children. They never married. Mary Sorochan did all of the domestic labour associated with running the household and caring for the children. In addition, she worked long hours on the farm. The family lived in modest circumstances.

At the time the parties began living together, Alex Sorochan was the owner, along with his brother, of six one-quarter sections of farmland. In 1951, the land was divided between the two brothers and the respondent became the registered owner of three one-quarter sections. From 1942 to 1945, and from 1968 to 1982, the respondent worked as a travelling salesperson. During these periods, Mary Sorochan often assumed responsibility for doing all of the farm chores on her own. In 1982, due to the failing health of the appellant and the deteriorating relationship between the couple, Mary Sorochan moved to a senior citizen's home. She subsequently commenced this legal action for an interest in the farm upon which she had worked for 42 years. ...

[Dickson CJC reviewed the trial judge's application of the test in *Pettkus v. Becker*; the trial judge had ordered the transfer of one of the three-quarter sections of land into the name of Mary Sorochan upon her undertaking to transfer title forthwith to her six children. He also ordered Alex Sorochan to pay her $20,000 within one year (reduced to $15,000 if paid within six months). However, the Court of Appeal allowed an appeal, holding that there was "no link between the acquisition of the property in question and the plaintiff's labour," in accordance with the principles stated in *Pettkus v. Becker*: (1984), 44 RFL (2d) 144, at 149 (Ont. CA). On the facts in *Sorochan*, Mary Sorochan's contribution of labour was directed only to the maintenance, not the acquisition, of property to which Alex Sorochan held title.

In the Supreme Court of Canada, however, Dickson CJC held that the principles of *Pettkus v. Becker* were applicable in that there had been (1) an enrichment, (2) a corresponding deprivation, and (3) the absence of any juristic reason for the enrichment. The court then reviewed the applicability of the constructive trust as a remedy for unjust enrichment in the context of the facts and a number of other cases, including *Murray v. Roty* (1983), 41 OR (2d) 705; 34 RFL (2d) 404 (CA), and held (at 239):]

These cases reveal the need to retain flexibility in applying the constructive trust. In my view, the constructive trust remedy should not be confined to cases involving property acquisition. While it is important to require that some nexus exist between the claimant's deprivation and the property in question, the link need not always take the form of a contribution to the actual acquisition of the property. A contribution relating to the preservation, maintenance or improvement of property may also suffice. What remains primary is whether or not the services rendered have a "clear proprietary relationship" [at 156], to use Professor McLeod's phrase. When such a connection is present, proprietary relief may be appropriate. Such an approach will help to ensure equitable and fair relief in the myriad of familial circumstances and situations where unjust enrichment occurs. ...

In the present case, Mary Sorochan worked on the farm for 42 years. Her labour directly and substantially contributed to the maintenance and preservation of the farm, preventing asset deterioration or divestment. There is, therefore, a "clear link" between the contribution and the disputed assets. ...

[After reviewing the order of the trial judge, Dickson CJC concluded that the monetary judgment was appropriate, but disagreed with the order concerning the land. In allowing the appeal, the court ordered a deletion of the requirement that Mary Sorochan transfer title of the quarter section to her children, stating (at 242):]

Mary Sorochan is the one who suffered the deprivation and it is she who is entitled to the remedy—not her children. She may well decide to transfer title to the land to her children, but this will be her decision alone to make.

Discussion Notes

The Nexus Requirement

Although the court in *Sorochan* concluded that the test for unjust enrichment was met in this case, even though Mary Sorochan's work did not contribute to the *acquisition* of property, the court's decision made clear the requirement of a nexus, or connection, between the work done and the property itself. To what extent is the existence of a nexus between the property claimed and the work done capable of evidence? Does this factor increase or limit the discretion to be exercised by a court in assessing such a claim?

In a number of cases, courts denied claims based on unjust enrichment because there was no sufficient nexus between the work and the property claimed. For example, in *Verson v. Rich* (1988), 16 RFL (3d) 337, the Saskatchewan Court of Appeal denied a declaration of constructive trust because there was no sufficient nexus between the provision of the woman's household services and the acquisition of the property. Why is this case different from the facts in *Pettkus v. Becker* and in *Sorochan*? Note that in both the earlier cases, the claimant had performed *both* household services and extraordinary work outside the home.

By contrast, in *Kutt v. Sam* (1990), 26 RFL (3d) 268, the Ontario High Court held that a woman applicant was entitled to a 25 percent interest in the matrimonial home because she had worked outside the home and provided household services over many years, including entertaining her cohabitant's family for lengthy stays.

Unjust Enrichment: Stanish Parasz

In some cases, courts have denied claims because the traditional division of labour (with the woman doing household work and the man working at paid labour) meant that there was no enrichment or deprivation: for example, see *Stewart v. Whitley* (1992), 41 RFL (3d) 362 (Ont. Ct. J (Gen. Div.)), where the court denied a constructive trust claim on the basis that neither party had been enriched or deprived as a result of their respective contributions.

Similarly, in *Stanish v. Parasz* (1989), 23 RFL (3d) 207 (Man. QB (Fam. Div.)), where the parties agreed that the woman would remain at home to perform household duties and care for a child, she claimed a monetary sum (rather than an interest in the home owned by the man) when the parties separated. Ms Stanish was in receipt of welfare, a factor that the court noted as one basis for her action against Mr. Parasz. In assessing the situation, the court stated (at 210-11):

> Dealing first with the issue of unjust enrichment. ... [Ms Stanish] was employed, in 1972, at a rate of $6 or $7 per hour. She has been out of the work force 15 years, is currently 48 years of age, and can now only earn minimum wage, or approximately $4.70 per hour. She has virtually no assets or security. She alleges there is a corresponding deprivation to her. ...
>
> The evidence falls far short of proving a case of unjust enrichment. Ms. Stanish admits that there was never a discussion of marriage, except on one occasion when she was pregnant, and Mr. Parasz made it known that he was not prepared to get married. The matter was never discussed again. She admits that she did not come to any conclusions about the permanence of their relationship, and in fact she did not give the matter much thought. She admits that no promises were made by either of them, to the other, of any kind, concerning their relationship. She admits that no promises were made by Mr. Parasz, relative to the ownership of the home at 1352 Manitoba Avenue, which he purchased in 1979, and he did nothing to lead her to believe that she would own any part of the home. She does not even allege that she had a reasonable expectation of receiving any interest in the home, or any other form of recompense, for her efforts in their years together.
>
> The parties kept their finances totally separate, had separate bank accounts, and did not even discuss their financial affairs with one another.
>
> While the relationship was clearly "marriage-like," that, of itself, is not enough to found a claim of unjust enrichment. The parties entered into a relationship which was mutually beneficial. Ms. Stanish clearly provided valuable services to Mr. Parasz, but he also provided valuable services to her. Although she had supported herself for 15 to 17 years before she began to live with Mr. Parasz, she preferred to stay home to be with her children. Mr. Parasz was prepared to voluntarily take on a financial obligation not only to her, but to her son, Cory, and to provide total support for them for 15 years.
>
> In looking at the three requirements for unjust enrichment, namely, (a) an enrichment, (b) a corresponding deprivation, and (c) the absence of a juristic reason for the enrichment, the court must look at the reasonableness of the bargain—the *quid pro quo*. Perhaps, to some degree, it can always be said that there is an enrichment to the person receiving the household services, and a deprivation to the person that remains out of the work force for a period of time to provide the services, but there is not the absence of a juristic reason, if the party supplying the services is sufficiently compensated in return. The enrichment must be *unjust*. It must be against the conscience that the recipient should be allowed to retain the benefits without compensation. This requirement will be met where one party prejudices himself/herself with the reasonable expectation of receiving something in return, and the other person accepts that when he/she knows or ought to know of that expectation.
>
> To say that Ms. Stanish is entitled to compensation on the basis of unjust enrichment would be to say that these results flow from common law relationships, on a virtually automatic basis. The legislation has not been extended to provide such benefits to non-married persons, and the doctrine of unjust enrichment should not be so extended.

Having denied Ms Stanish's claim for unjust enrichment, the court considered her entitlement to maintenance, and awarded short-term spousal maintenance. Mr. Parasz also accepted full responsibility for the child who was still under 18; Mr. Parasz was then 61 years of age and without a pension plan.

In denying Ms Stanish's claim, was the court concerned about establishing a precedent for cohabiting couples where there was no evidence of "extraordinary" work on the part of the claimant in relation to the property acquired by the cohabiting partner? Note that in the context of dissolution of cohabiting relationships, many cases are likely to resemble the facts in *Stanish v. Parasz*, with few assets and income. Does this suggest that the principles of constructive trust will generally apply only where there is significant property (other than a matrimonial home) and where the claimant has done work beyond household labour? In thinking about these issues, recall the statistics in chapter 1 about the financial circumstances of families in Canada and the analysis in the previous chapter about the "feminization of poverty" at the breakdown of marriage and cohabiting relationships—to what extent are the principles of constructive trust responsive to the needs of a majority of cohabiting couples at the dissolution of their relationships?

The Constructive Trust Remedy: Georg v. Hassanali

In *Sorochan*, the court also explained that the principles of *Pettkus v. Becker* required both a finding of unjust enrichment as well as a determination that the appropriate remedy was a declaration of constructive trust. That is, the finding of unjust enrichment did not automatically lead to the declaration of constructive trust; instead, the trust would be imposed only if a monetary award were not sufficient. In *Georg v. Hassanali* (1989), 18 RFL (3d) 225 (Ont. SC (HCJ)), an Ontario court similarly assessed the appropriate remedy after a finding of unjust enrichment.

The plaintiff and defendant met in 1969 at an East African resort where the plaintiff (a divorcée) was a manager and the defendant a guest. Within days, they entered into an intimate relationship; the plaintiff was then 28 and the defendant 63 and separated from his wife. They lived together for 15 years in Africa, Europe, and Canada, during which time the defendant proposed marriage repeatedly. According to Walsh J (at 229), "it was this promise and her expectations of their future together that caused the plaintiff to perform the many valuable services she rendered over the years to the defendant, both personally and to his property." However, when the defendant's wife died in 1986, after a lengthy period of separation from her husband, the defendant (an Ismaili Muslim) quickly chose to marry a Muslim woman.

During the early years of his cohabitation with the plaintiff, her services to the defendant were "spousal." When they moved to Canada, the defendant purchased (for $3,300,000) a 183-suite apartment building in Scarborough (where the couple lived in an apartment). The plaintiff spent the next 10 years caring for the building. The defendant always referred to the building as "ours"; he gave her sums of money from time to time, which funds were declared as salary for tax purposes, although the plaintiff claimed these sums were only "pocket money." According to Walsh J (at 230), the plaintiff was actively involved in work in relation to the apartment building as well as in doing household labour for the defendant:

> The plaintiff described in great detail and at considerable length the variety of services and all the duties she performed over this period. She detailed for the court her daily activities, during a rather long period when the building had no superintendent, as commencing with her checking at 5 a.m. for illegal parking, then washing down walls and floors and checking all the garbage chutes on the 15 floors, returning to their apartment by 6:30 in order to

prepare the defendant's breakfast, to polish his shoes, lay out his wardrobe and run his bath. At about 8 a.m. she would go to the office to receive the service requests, which she would then proceed to fulfil. These requests, it would appear from the voluminous material filed, were complaints by tenants as to various problems in their apartments, such as toilets that would not work, broken electrical appliances, doors, windows and locks that were broken, the presence of insects, and other such items requiring repair. She had trained herself to perform these tasks in order to save the costs of plumbers, electricians and carpenters.

She then returned to their apartment and prepared a hot lunch for the defendant, as this was their main meal of the day, following which she would then herself perform any maintenance matters which required attention.

At 6 p.m. she had appointments to show prospective tenants vacant apartments. At 7 p.m. she would accompany the defendant to the garage, as he drove off each night to his Mosque for prayers, and, on his return, would prepare a light meal for their supper.

While the defendant now seeks to belittle and minimize the extent and value of the services the plaintiff performed, it is clear that at the time they were rendered this was certainly not the case.

In a will dated 8th February 1983—the terms of which the plaintiff was totally un-aware—the defendant left her a legacy of $50,000 which he stated to be for "her loyalty and sincerity in maintaining my apartment building as if it were her own property."

There can be no doubt whatsoever that the facts here clearly establish a case of unjust enrichment, and I so find.

Once a finding of unjust enrichment is made, the court must next determine the most appropriate remedy to rectify such enrichment.

It is urged on behalf of the plaintiff that this can best be accomplished by the imposition of a constructive trust.

It is the defendant's submission, however, that the circumstances here do not justify the imposition of a constructive trust and the making of a proprietary award, as sought by the plaintiff.

In the defendant's submission, the relief should be granted *in persona*, either by making a monetary award to the plaintiff on a *quantum meruit* basis or by way of equitable compensation. ...

On the evidence, the plaintiff here has clearly met all three tests formulated by Chief Justice Dickson. However, notwithstanding this finding, given the nature of the property—a 15-story, 183-suite apartment building—the awarding of a proprietary interest therein, with all that entails, is, in my view, in the particular circumstances of this case, neither appropriate nor desirable.

An examination of the equities and circumstances of the parties reveals that he values this building at $8 million and derives rental income therefrom of over $363,000 per year and declares his net worth—after deducting a commitment of some $500,000 to charity—[at] almost $7 million.

By contrast, the plaintiff's financial statement discloses her only assets to be two fur coats given her by the defendant, furniture worth $500 and jewellery having a value of some $2,500. The only income she now receives are welfare payments.

After a most careful and anxious consideration of all the circumstances, I feel that an award of $725,000 is both a fair and realistic amount to require the defendant to pay to the plaintiff to redress her deprivation herein.

I impose a trust or proprietary interest to the extent necessary that such shall be and constitute a proprietary interest or charge against this building—known for municipal purposes as 720 Kennedy Road, Scarborough—until such sum as I have awarded is paid in full. And, in addition, the plaintiff shall retain the exclusive right to occupy Suite 1412 therein, without payment of any kind, for a like period.

How would you characterize the award to the plaintiff in this case? If the court had declared a constructive trust, how would it have differed from the court's order here? To what extent is it possible that the court was mindful of the problems of enforcement in *Pettkus v. Becker*? Note that both the plaintiff here and in *Stanish v. Parasz* were in receipt of welfare—why did the plaintiff here succeed, by contrast with Ms Stanish? Which factors were more important: the amount or nature of work done—that is, non-traditional women's work, by contrast with household labour; or the difference in the assets of the defendants in both cases? To what extent are issues about expectations especially relevant? Consider these issues in relation to the Supreme Court's reasoning in the judgments of McLachlin and Cory JJ in *Peter v. Beblow*, below:

Peter v. Beblow
(1993), 150 NR 1; [1993] 1 SCR 980

[Ms Peter and Mr. Beblow lived in a cohabiting relationship for about 12 years. During their time together, Ms Peter cared for the children and looked after their home and garden; Mr. Beblow owned the home and, prior to his relationship with Ms Peter, he had paid a housekeeper to perform these tasks. Ms Peter also worked on a part-time basis outside the home, while Mr. Beblow did seasonal work. At the end of their relationships, Mr. Beblow had paid off the mortgage on the home; he also owned a car and a boat. Ms Peter owned a vacation property that she had purchased during the relationship.

When their relationship ended, Ms Peter brought an action claiming unjust enrichment, seeking a constructive trust in her favour respecting the home in which they lived or, alternatively, monetary damages as compensation for the labour and services she provided. The BC Supreme Court allowed the action and awarded Ms Peter the full interest in the home on the basis that there was an enrichment, a corresponding deprivation, and the lack of any juristic reason for the enrichment: [1988] BCJ no. 887 (SC). The court also stated that there was a clear causal connection between the contribution founding the unjust enrichment and the property to be subject to the constructive trust. The BC Court of Appeal allowed Mr. Beblow's appeal: (1990), 29 RFL (3d) 268 (BCCA). In the Supreme Court of Canada, the court restored the order of the trial judge so that Ms Peter received the entire interest in the home.]

McLACHLIN J (for La Forest, Sopinka, and Iacobucci JJ): [1] I have had the advantage of reading the reasons of Justice Cory. While I agree with his conclusion, and with much of his analysis, my reasons differ in some respects on two matters critical to this appeal: the issues raised by the requirement of the absence of juristic reason for an enrichment and the nature of application of the remedy of constructive trust. ...

[4] There is a tendency on the part of some to view the action for unjust enrichment as a device for doing whatever may seem fair between the parties. In the rush to
substantive justice, the principles are sometimes forgotten. Policy issues often assume a large role, infusing such straightforward discussions as whether there was a
"benefit" to the defendant or a "detriment" to the plaintiff. On the remedies side, the
requirements of the special proprietary remedy of constructive trust are sometimes
minimized. As Professor Palmer has said: "The constructive trust idea stirs the judicial imagination in ways that *assumpsi, quantum meruit* and other terms associated
with quasi-contract have never quite succeeded in duplicating" (G.E. Palmer, *The
Law of Restitution*, vol. 1, at p. 16). Occasionally the remedial notion of constructive
trust is even conflated with unjust enrichment itself, as though where one is found the
other must follow.

[5] Such difficulties have to some degree complicated the case at bar. At the doctrinal level, the simple questions of "benefit" and "detriment" became infused with
moral and policy questions of when the provision of domestic services in a quasi-
matrimonial situation can give rise to a legal obligation. At the stage of remedy, the trial
judge proceeded as if he were making a monetary award, and then, without fully explaining how, awarded the appellant the entire interest in the matrimonial home on the
basis of a constructive trust. It is only by a return to the fundamental principles laid out
in cases like *Becker v. Pettkus* and *Lac Minerals* that one can cut through the conflicting findings and submissions on these issues and evaluate whether in fact the appellant has made out a claim for unjust enrichment, and if so what her remedy should be.

1. Is the Appellant's Claim for Unjust Enrichment Made Out?

[6] I share the view of Cory J that the three elements necessary to establish a
claim for unjust enrichment—an enrichment, a corresponding deprivation, and the
absence of any juristic reason for the enrichment—are made out in this case. The
appellant's housekeeping and child-care services constituted a benefit to the respondent (1st element), in that he received household services without compensation,
which in turn enhanced his ability to pay off his mortgage and other assets. These
services also constituted a corresponding detriment to the appellant (2nd element), in
that she provided services without compensation. Finally, since there was no obligation existing between the parties which would justify the unjust enrichment and no
other arguments under this broad heading were met, there is no juristic reason for the
enrichment (3rd element). Having met the three criteria, the plaintiff has established
an unjust enrichment giving rise to restitution.

[7] The main arguments on this appeal centred on whether the law should recognize the services which the appellant provided as being capable of founding an action
for unjust enrichment. It was argued, for example, that the services cannot give rise
to a remedy based on unjust enrichment because the appellant had voluntarily assumed the role of wife and stepmother. It was also said that the law of unjust enrichment should not recognize such services because they arise from natural love and
affection. These arguments raise moral and policy questions and require the court to
make value judgments.

[8] The first question is: where do these arguments belong? Are they part of the benefit–detriment analysis, or should they be considered under the third head—the absence of juristic reason for the unjust enrichment? The Court of Appeal, for example, held that there was no "detriment" on these grounds. I hold the view that these factors may most conveniently be considered under the third head of absence of juristic reason. This court has consistently taken a straightforward economic approach to the first two elements of the test for unjust enrichment: *Becker v. Pettkus, supra*; *Sorochan v. Sorochan*, [1986] 2 SCR 38; 69 NR 81; 74 AR 67; [1986] 5 WWR 289; 2 RFL (2d) 225; 46 Alta. LR (2d) 97; *Peel (Regional Municipality) v. Ontario*, [1992] 3 SCR 762; 144 NR 1, 59 OAC 81 (hereinafter "*Peel*"). It is in connection with the third element—absence of juristic reason for the enrichment—that such considerations may more properly find their place. It is at this stage that the court must consider whether the enrichment and detriment, morally neutral in themselves, are "unjust."

[9] What matters should be considered in determining whether there is an absence of juristic reason for the enrichment? The test is flexible, and the factors to be considered may vary with the situation before the court. For example, different factors may be more relevant in a case like *Peel, supra*, at p. 803, a claim for unjust enrichment between different levels of government, than in a family case.

[10] In every case, the fundamental concern is the legitimate expectation of the parties: *Becker v. Pettkus, supra*. In family cases, this concern may raise the following subsidiary questions:

  (i) Did the plaintiff confer the benefit as a valid gift or in pursuance of a valid common law, equitable or statutory obligation which he or she owed to the defendant?

 (ii) Did the plaintiff submit to, or compromise, the defendant's honest claim?

(iii) Does public policy support the enrichment?

[11] In the case at bar, the first and third of these factors were argued. It was argued first that the appellant's services were rendered pursuant to a common law or equitable obligation which she had assumed. Her services were part of the bargain she made when she came to live with the respondent, it was said. He would give her and her children a home and other husbandly services, and in turn she would look after the home and family.

[12] This court has held that a common law spouse generally owes no duty at common law, in equity or by statute to perform work or services for her partner. As Dickson CJ speaking for the court put it in *Sorochan v. Sorochan, supra*, at p. 46, the common law wife "was under no obligation, contractual or otherwise, to perform the work and services in the home or on the land." So there is no general duty presumed by the law on a common law spouse to perform work and services for her partner.

[13] Nor, in the case at bar was there any obligation arising from the circumstances of the parties. The trial judge held that the appellant was "under no obligation to perform the work and assist in the home without some reasonable expectation of receiving something in return other than the drunken physical abuse which she received at the hands of the respondent." This puts an end to the argument that the

services in question were performed pursuant to obligation. It also puts an end to the argument that the appellant's services to her partner were a "gift" from her to him. The central element of a gift at law—intentional giving to another without expectation of remuneration—is simply not present.

[14] The third factor mentioned above raises directly the issue of public policy. While it may be stated in different ways, the argument at base is simply that some types of services in some types of relationships should not be recognized as supporting legal claims for policy reasons. More particularly, homemaking and childcare services should not, in a marital or quasi-marital relationship, be viewed as giving rise to equitable claims against the other spouse.

[15] I concede at the outset that there is some judicial precedent for this argument. Professor M. Neave has observed generally that "[a]nalysis of the principles applied in English, Australian and Canadian courts sometimes fails to confront this question directly ... Courts which deny or grant remedies usually conceal their value judgments within statements relating to doctrinal requirements." (M. Neave, "Three Approaches to Family Property Disputes: Intention/Belief, Unjust Enrichment, and Unconscionability," in T.G. Youdan, ed., *Equity, Fiduciaries and Trusts*, at p. 251.) More pointedly, Professor Farquhar has observed that many courts have strayed from the framework of *Sorochan* for public policy reasons: "the courts ... have, after *Sorochan*, put up warning signs that there are aspects of relationships that are not to be analyzed in the light of unjust enrichment and constructive trust." (Keith B. Farquhar, "Causal Connection in Constructive Trust After Sorochan v. Sorochan" (1989), 7 *Can. J of Family Law* 337, at p. 343.) The public policy issue has been summed up as follows by Professor Neave, *supra*, at p. 251: "whether a remedy, either personal or proprietary, should be provided to a person who has made contributions to family resources." On the judicial side, the view of the respondent is pointedly stated in *Grant v. Edwards*, [1986] 2 All ER 426, at p. 439, per Browne-Wilkinson VC:

> Setting up house together, having a baby and making payments to general house-keeping expenses ... may all be referable to the mutual love and affection of the parties and not specifically referable to the claimant's belief that she has an interest in the house.

Proponents of this view, Professor Neave, *supra*, at p. 253 argues, "regard it as distasteful to put a price upon services provided out of a sense of love and commitment to the relationship. They suggest it is unfair for a recipient of indirect or nonfinancial contributions to be forced to provide recompense for those contributions." To support this position, the respondent cites several cases. ...

[16] It is my view that this argument is no longer tenable in Canada, either from the point of view of logic or authority. I share the view of Professors Hovius and Youdan that "there is no logical reason to distinguish domestic services from other contributions" (*supra*, at p. 146). The notion that household and childcare services are not worthy of recognition by the court fails to recognize the fact that these services are of great value, not only to the family, but to the other spouse. As Lord Simon observed nearly 30 years ago: "The cock-bird can feather his nest precisely because he is not required to spend most of his time sitting on it" (*With All My Worldly Goods*, Holdsworth Lecture, University of Birmingham, 20th March 1964, at p. 32).

The notion, moreover, is a pernicious one that systematically devalues the contributions which women tend to make to the family economy. It has contributed to the phenomenon of the feminization of poverty which this court identified in *Moge v. Moge*, [1992] 3 SCR 813 … per L'Heureux-Dubé J, at pp. 853-854.

[17] Moreover, the argument cannot stand with the jurisprudence which this and other courts have laid down. Today courts regularly recognize the value of domestic services. This becomes clear with the court's holding in *Sorochan*, leading one author to comment that "[t]he Canadian Supreme Court has finally recognized that domestic contribution is of equal value as financial contribution in trusts of property in the familial context" (Mary Welstead, "Domestic Contribution and Constructive Trusts: The Canadian Perspective," [1987] *Denning LJ* 151, at p. 161). If there could be any doubt about the need for the law to honestly recognize the value of domestic services, it must be considered to have been banished by *Moge v. Moge*, *supra*. While that case arose under the *Divorce Act*, RSC 1985 (2d Supp.), c. 3, the value of the services does not change with the legal remedy invoked.

[18] I cannot give credence to the argument that legal recognition of the value of domestic services will do violence to the law and social structure of our society. It has been recognized for some time that such services are entitled to recognition and compensation under the *Divorce Act* and the provincial Acts governing the distribution of matrimonial property. Yet society has not been visibly harmed. I do not think that similar recognition in the equitable doctrine of unjust enrichment will have any different effect.

[19] Finally, I come to the argument that, because the legislature has chosen to exclude unmarried couples from the right to claim an interest in the matrimonial assets on the basis of contribution to the relationship, the court should not use the equitable doctrine of unjust enrichment to remedy the situation. Again, the argument seems flawed. It is precisely where an injustice arises without a legal remedy that equity finds a role. This case is much stronger than *Rawluk v. Rawluk*, [1990] 1 SCR 70 … , where I dissented on the ground that the statute expressly pronounced on the very matter with respect to which equity was invoked.

[20] Accordingly, I would agree with Cory J that there are no juristic arguments which would justify the unjust enrichment, and the third element is made out. Like him, I conclude that the plaintiff was enriched, to the benefit of the defendant, and that no justification existed to vitiate the unjust enrichment claim. The claim for unjust enrichment is accordingly made out and it remains only to determine the appropriate remedy.

2. Remedy: Monetary Judgment or Constructive Trust

[21] The other difficult aspect of this case is the question of whether the remedy which the trial judge awarded—title to the matrimonial home—is justified on the principles governing the action for unjust enrichment. Two remedies are possible: an award of money on the basis of the value of the services rendered, i.e. *quantum meruit*; and the one the trial judge awarded, title to the house based on a constructive trust.

[22] In Canada the concept of the constructive trust has been used as a vehicle for compensating for unjust enrichment in appropriate cases. The constructive trust, based

on analogy to the formal trust of traditional equity, is a proprietary concept. The plaintiff is found to have an interest in the property. A finding that a plaintiff is entitled to a remedy for unjust enrichment does not imply that there is a constructive trust. As I wrote in *Rawluk, supra,* for a constructive trust to arise, the plaintiff must establish a direct link to the property which is the subject of the trust by reason of the plaintiff's contribution. This is the notion underlying the constructive trust in *Becker v. Pettkus, supra,* and *Sorochan v. Sorochan, supra,* as I understand those cases. It was also affirmed by La Forest J in *LAC Minerals, supra.*

[23] My colleague Cory J suggests that, while a link between the contribution and the property is essential in commercial cases for a constructive trust to arise, it may not be required in family cases. ...

[24] I doubt the wisdom of dividing unjust enrichment cases into two categories—commercial and family—for the purpose of determining whether a constructive trust lies. A special rule for family cases finds no support in the jurisprudence. Neither *Pettkus,* nor *Rathwell,* nor *Sorochan* suggest such a departure. Moreover, the notion that one can dispense with a link between the services rendered and the property which is claimed to be subject to the trust is inconsistent with the proprietary nature of the notion of constructive trust. Finally, the creation of special rules for special situations might have an adverse effect on the development of this emerging area of equity. The same general principles should apply for all contexts, subject only to the demonstrated need for alternation. Wilson J in *Syncrude Canada Ltd. et al. v. Hunter Engineering Co. and Allis-Chamber Canada Ltd. et al.,* [1989] 1 SCR 426; 92 NR 1, at p. 519 (adopted by La Forest J in *LAC Minerals, supra,* at p. 675), warns against confining constructive trust remedies to family law cases stating that "to do so would be to impede the growth and impair the flexibility crucial to the development of equitable principles." The same result, I fear, may flow from developing special rules for finding constructive trusts in family cases. In short, the concern for clarity and doctrinal integrity with which this court has long been preoccupied in this area mandates that the basic principles governing the rights and remedies for unjust enrichment remain the same for all cases.

[25] Nor does the distinction between commercial cases and family cases on the remedy of constructive trust appear to be necessary. Where a monetary award is sufficient, there is no need for a constructive trust. Where a monetary award is insufficient in a family situation, this is usually related to the fact the claimant's efforts have given her a special link to the property, in which case a constructive trust arises.

[26] For these reasons, I hold the view that in order for a constructive trust to be found, in a family case as in other cases, monetary compensation must be inadequate and there must be a link between the services rendered and the property in which the trust is claimed. Having said this, I echo the comments of Cory J at para. 99 that the courts should exercise flexibility and common sense when applying equitable principles to family law issues with due sensitivity to the special circumstances that can arise in such cases.

[27] The next question is the extent of the contribution required to give rise to a constructive trust. A minor or indirect contribution is insufficient. The question, to quote Dickson CJ in *Becker v. Pettkus, supra,* at p. 852, is whether "[the plaintiff's]

contribution [was] sufficiently substantial and direct as to entitle her to a portion of the profits realized upon sale of the ... property." Once this threshold is met, the amount of the contribution governs the extent of the constructive trust. As Dickson CJ wrote in *Becker v. Pettkus, supra*, at pp. 852-853:

> Although equity is said to favour equality, as stated in *Rathwell*, it is not every contribution which will entitle a spouse to a one-half interest in the property. *The extent of the interest must be proportionate to the contribution, direct or indirect, of the claimant. Where the contributions are unequal, the shares will be unequal.* (Emphasis added.)

Cory J advocates a flexible approach to determining whether a constructive trust is appropriate; an approach "based on common sense and a desire to achieve a fair result for both parties" (at para. 99). While agreeing that courts should avoid becoming overly technical on matters which may not be susceptible of precise monetary valuation, the principle remains that the extent of the trust must reflect the extent of the contribution.

[28] Before leaving the principles governing the remedy of constructive trust, I turn to the manner in which the extent of the trust is determined. The debate centres on whether it is sufficient to look at the value of the services which the claimant has rendered (the "value received" approach). Cory J expresses a preference for a "value survived" approach. However, he also suggests, at para. 103, that "there is no reason why *quantum meruit* or the value received approach could not be utilized to quantify the value of the constructive trust." With respect, I cannot agree. It seems to me that there are very good reasons, both doctrinal and practical, for referring to the "value survived" when assessing the value of a constructive trust.

[29] From the point of view of doctrine, "[t]he extent of the interest must be proportionate to the contribution" to the property: *Becker v. Pettkus, supra*, at p. 852. How is the contribution to the property to be determined? One starts, of necessity, by defining the property. One goes on to determine what portion of that property is attributable to the claimant's efforts. This is the "value survived" approach. For a monetary award, the "value received" approach is appropriate; the value conferred on the property is irrelevant. But where the claim is for an interest in the property one must of necessity, it seems to me, determine what portion of the value of the property claimed is attributable to the claimant's services.

[30] I note, as does my colleague, that there may also be practical reasons for favouring a "value survived" approach. Cory J alludes to the practical problems with balancing benefits and detriments as required by the "value received" approach, leading some to question whether it is the least attractive approach in most family property cases (see *Davidson v. Worthing* (1986), 9 BCLR (2d) 202; 6 RFL (3d) 113, McEachern CJSC; Hovius & Youdan, *supra*, at 136ff.). Moreover, a "value survived" approach arguably accords best with the expectations of most parties; it is more likely that a couple expects to share in the wealth generated from their partnership, rather than to receive compensation for the services performed during the relationship.

[31] To summarize, it seems to me that the first step in determining the proper remedy for unjust enrichment is to determine whether a monetary award is insufficient and whether the nexus between the contribution and the property described in

Becker v. Pettkus has been made out. If these questions are answered in the affirmative the plaintiff is entitled to the proprietary remedy of constructive trust. In looking at whether a monetary award is insufficient the court may take into account the probability of the award's being paid as well as the special interest in the property acquired by the contributions: per La Forest J in *LAC Minerals*. The value of that trust is to be determined on the basis of the actual value of the matrimonial property—the "value survived" approach. It reflects the court's best estimate of what is fair having regard to the contribution which the claimant's services have made to the value surviving, bearing in mind the practical difficulty of calculating with mathematical precision the value of particular contributions to the family property.

[32] I turn now to application of these principles to the case at bar. The trial judge began by assessing the value received by the respondent (the *quantum meruit*). He went on to conclude that a monetary judgment would be inadequate. The respondent had few assets other than his houseboat and van, and no income save for a War Veteran's Allowance. The judge concluded, as I understand his reasons, that there was a sufficiently direct connection between the services rendered and the property to support a constructive trust, stating that "[the appellant] has shown that there was a positive proprietary benefit conferred by her upon the Sicamous property." Accordingly, he held that the remedy of constructive trust was made out. This approach accords with principles discussed above. In effect, the trial judge found the monetary award to be inadequate on the grounds that it would not be paid and on the ground of a special contribution to the property. These findings support the remedy of constructive trust in the property.

[33] The remaining question is the quantification of the trust. The trial judge calculated the *quantum meruit* for her housekeeping for 12 years at $350 per month and reduced that figure by 50% "for the benefits she received." The final amount was $25,200. He then reasoned that, since the services rendered amounted to $25,200 after appropriate deductions, it follows that the appellant should receive title to the respondent's property, valued at $23,200. The missing step in this analysis is the failure to link the value received with the value surviving. As discussed above, a constructive trust cannot be quantified by simply adding up the services rendered; the court must determine the extent of the contribution which the services have made to the parties' property.

[34] Notwithstanding the trial judge's failure to make this link, his conclusion that the appellant has established a constructive trust entitling her to title to the family home can be maintained if a trust of this magnitude is supported on the evidence. This brings me to a departure from the methods used below. The parties and the Court of Appeal appear to have treated the house as a single asset rather than as part of a family enterprise. This led to the argument that the appellant could not be entitled to full ownership in the house because the respondent had contributed to its value as well. The approach I would take—and the approach I believe the trial judge implicitly to have taken—is to consider the appellant's proper share of all the family assets. This joint family venture, in effect, was no different from the farm which was the subject of the trust in *Becker v. Pettkus*.

[35] With this in mind, I turn to the evidence on the extent of the contribution. The appellant provided extensive household services, over a period of 12 years,

including care for the children while they were living at the house and maintenance of the property. The testimony of the plaintiff's son provides a general idea of her contribution to the family enterprise:

> Q. What sort of things did she do?
>
> A. She did all the motherly duties for all of us.
>
> A. When [the defendant's] two sons and my brother and I were there still, even when my sisters were there, that was quite a long time ago, I was quite young, so there was nothing really bad then, but after the sisters left, she took care of all the duties, cooking and stuff like that, cleaning, laundry. She had her ringer washer, she would do the laundry, she'd worked in the garden, things like that. She took care of all things around the house, when he was gone especially. ...
>
> Q. Do you remember what work your mother did in the yard outside?
>
> A. M'hm, they both got together doing the garden, he would do the roto-tilling, they would both take care of the planting and stuff; when he was gone, she would do all the weeding and keeping up. They would share the watering of the garden. She put together three or four flower gardens all herself, except for the hard heavy work, like lifting rocks, when she first started, that was shared by all of us, including the kids.

Of all the chores performed around the property, the son states that the various siblings had minor chores, such as chopping wood and making beds. "Everything else, the major stuff, she would take care of." Other evidence, including testimony from Catherine Peter and William Beblow, supports this picture of the appellant's contribution. The trial judge held that while the respondent worked in the construction business,

> ... he would be away from home during the week and would return on the weekend whenever possible. While he was absent, the plaintiff would care for the property in the home and care for the children while he was away.
>
> In effect, the plaintiff by moving into the respondent's home became his house-keeper on a full-time basis without remuneration except for the food and shelter that she and the children received until the children left home.

[36] The respondent also contributed to the value of the family enterprise surviving at the time of breakup; he generated most of the family income and helped with the maintenance of the property.

[37] Clearly, the appellant's contribution—the "value received" by the respondent—was considerable. But what then of the "value surviving"? It seems clear that the maintenance of the family enterprise through work in cooking, cleaning, and landscaping helped preserve the property and saved the respondent large sums of money [with] which he was able to pay off his mortgage and to purchase a houseboat and a van. The appellant, for her part, had purchased a lot with her outside earnings. All these assets may be viewed as assets of the family enterprise to which the appellant contributed substantially.

[38] The question is whether, taking the parties' respective contributions to the family assets and the value of the assets into account, the trial judge erred in awarding the appellant a full interest in the house. In my view, the evidence is capable of supporting the conclusion that the house reflects a fair approximation of the value of

the appellant's efforts as reflected in the family assets. Accordingly, I would not disturb the award.

[39] I would allow the appeal with costs.

CORY J (for L'Heureux-Dubé and Gonthier JJ): ...

[74] Business relationships concerned with commercial affairs may, as a result of the conduct of one of the corporations involved, result in a court's granting a constructive trust remedy. The constructive trust has been appropriately used to redress a gain made through a breach of trust in a commercial or business relationship (see for example: *Canadian Aero Service Ltd. v. O'Malley*, [1974] SCR 592; 40 DLR (3d) 371). Yet how much closer and trusting must be a long term common law relationship. In marriages or marriage-like relationships commercial matters and a great deal more will be involved. Clearly, parties to a family relationship will, in a commercial sense, share funds and financial goals. More importantly, couples such as the parties to this case will strive to make a home. By that I mean a place that provides safety, security and love and which is as well frequently the place where children may be cared for and nurtured. In a relationship that involves living and sleeping together, couples will share their worst fears and frustrations and their fondest dreams and aspirations. They will plan and work together to achieve their goals. Just as much as parties to a formal marriage, the partners in a long term common law relationship will base their actions on mutual love and trust. They too are entitled, in appropriate circumstances, to the relief provided by the remedy of constructive trust.

[75] This remedy should be granted despite the fact that [a] family will seldom keep the same careful financial records as business associates. Nonetheless, fairness requires that the constructive trust remedy be available to them and applied on an equitable basis without a minute scrutiny of their respective financial contributions. Indeed, in a situation such as the one presented in this case, it may be very difficult to assess the value of making a house a home and of sharing the struggle to raise children to become responsible adults.

[76] In the present case, although there was no formal marriage, the couple lived and worked together in the most intimate of relationships. They shared work and the monies which they earned. The amount of the contributions may have been varied and unequal. Yet the very fact that in addition to her household work the appellant contributed something of the income from her outside employment indicates that there was a real sharing of income. As a result of the relationship, the Sicamous property was looked after and maintained. None of this could have been achieved without the efforts of the appellant.

[77] Certainly, it cannot be said that the relationship was so short lived that it should not give rise to mutual rights and obligations. Twelve years is not an insignificant period of time to live in a relationship based on mutual trust and confidence. In those circumstances, there is a strong presumption that the services provided by one party will not be used solely to enrich the other. Both the reasonable expectations of the parties and equity will require that upon the termination of the relationship, the parties will receive an appropriate compensation based on the contribution each has made to the relationship.

[78] The respondent asserts that because the appellant loved him she could not have expected to receive compensation or an interest in the property in return for the contributions she made to the home and family. However, in today's society it is unreasonable to assume that the presence of love automatically implies a gift of one party's services to another. Nor is it unreasonable for the party providing the domestic labour required to create a home to expect to share in the property of the parties when the relationship is terminated. Women no longer are expected to work exclusively in the home. It must be recognized that when they do so, women forgo outside employment to provide domestic services and child care. The granting of relief in the form of a personal judgment or a property interest to the provider of domestic services should adequately reflect the fact that the income earning capacity and the ability to acquire assets by one party has been enhanced by the unpaid domestic services of the other. M. Neave in "Three Approaches to Family Property Disputes: Intention/Belief, Unjust Enrichment and Unconscionability," in T.G. Youdan, ed., *Equity, Fiduciaries and Trusts* (1989), lucidly sets out the position in this way at p. 254:

> The characterization of domestic services as gifts reflects a view of family relationships which is now outdated and has a differential impact on women, since they are the main providers of such services. Women no longer work exclusively in the home. Those who do so sacrifice income that could otherwise be earned in paid work. Couples who decide that one partner, usually the woman, will forgo paid employment to provide domestic services and provide child care, presumably believe that this arrangement will maximize their economic resources. Grant of relief, whether personal or proprietary, to the provider of domestic services would recognize that the income-earning capacity of one partner and his ability to acquire assets have been enhanced by the unpaid services of the other and that those services were only provided free because it was believed that the relationship would continue.

[79] This same reasoning has been recently applied in the context of divorce in *Moge v. Moge*, [1992] 3 SCR 813. ... It is appropriate to recognize that the same principle be applied to long term common law relationships. ...

[98] I agree with my colleague that there is a need to limit the use of the constructive trust remedy in a commercial context. Yet I do not think the same proposition should be rigorously applied in a family relationship. In a marital or quasi-marital relationship, the expectations the parties will have regarding their contributions and interest in the assets acquired are, I expect, very different from the expectation of the parties engaged in a commercial transaction. As I have said, it is unlikely that couples will ever turn their minds to the issue of their expectations about their legal entitlement at the outset of their marriage or common law relationship. If they were specifically asked about their expectations, I would think that most couples would probably state that they did not expect to be compensated for their contribution. Rather, they would say, if the relationship were ever to be dissolved, then they would expect that both parties would share in the assets or wealth that they had helped to create. Thus, rather than expecting to receive a fee for their services based on their market value, they would expect to receive, on a dissolution of their relationship, a fair share of the property or wealth which their contributions had helped the parties to acquire,

improve, or to maintain. The remedy provided by the constructive trust seems to best accord with the reasonable expectations of the parties in a marriage or quasi-marital relationship. Nevertheless, in situations where the rights of bona fide third parties would be affected as a result of granting the constructive trust remedy it may well be inappropriate to do so. (See: Berend Hovius and Timothy G. Youdan, *The Law of Family Property, supra*, at p. 146.)

[99] It follows that in a quasi-marital relationship in those situations where the rights of third parties are not involved, the choice between a monetary award and a constructive trust will be discretionary and should be exercised flexibly. Ordinarily both partners will have an interest in the property acquired, improved or maintained during the course of the relationship. The decision as to which property, if there is more than one, should be made the subject of a constructive trust is also a discretionary one. It too should be based on common sense and a desire to achieve a fair result for both parties.

Appeal allowed.

Discussion Notes

Rethinking Family Property and Cohabitees

After reviewing the decision in *Peter v. Beblow*, the OLRC's *Report on Family Property Law* expressed the view (at 39) that there are inevitable problems with the application of the doctrine of unjust enrichment in domestic cases:

> The application of an analysis that rests on evidence of the expectation of the parties concerning property sharing or compensation, and of the respective economic contributions of spouses or others in intimate relationships, is bound to be difficult. Yet in spousal claims, courts experience tremendous pressure to ensure that each spouse receives a fair share of family property.

In this context, the report suggested that these problems may explain why the House of Lords in the United Kingdom adopted a restrictive approach to trust claims, leaving the matter to be addressed by Parliamentary reform. As was explained in the discussion notes following the Supreme Court of Canada decision in *Nova Scotia v. Walsh*, above, there have been numerous recommendations for the extension of legislative property-sharing regimes to cohabiting couples. Is it possible that the majority decision in *Nova Scotia v. Walsh* agreed with the House of Lords that this is a matter for legislative, not judicial, intervention? Interestingly, the majority judgment also expressly identified the existence of trusts as an alternative for cohabiting couples, thereby negating the assertion that discrimination existed between married and cohabiting couples.

After considering the cases in this section, reflect again on the extent to which trusts provide an alternative remedy for cohabiting couples. For example, do you agree with the assessment of the OLRC's *Report on Family Property Law* (at 39-40)?

> The doctrine of unjust enrichment has serious limitations as a tool for the fair allocation of property between spouses, or others who have integrated their economic lives as part of an

intimate relationship. The doctrine rests on a transfer of wealth, typically in the form of services, from one spouse to another, combined with an expectation of compensation, or an interest in an asset in return. In many cases, the expectation will not arise or the transfer of wealth may not be easily demonstrated on the evidence. Yet reasons of social policy may provide a sound basis for a sharing of property at the end of such a relationship. ... The uncertainties that have appeared in the application of the doctrine of unjust enrichment may reflect a poor fit between its requirements and the realities of domestic relationships.

Recall that the OLRC recommended that the legislative regime apply to cohabiting couples (opposite-sex and same-sex): see OLRC, *Report on the Rights and Responsibilities of Cohabitants Under the Family Law Act* (Toronto: OLRC, 1993), recommendation no. 1, and that all spouses (married and cohabiting) be precluded from applying for resulting and constructive trusts: see *Report on Family Property Law*, recommendation no. 30. Do you agree that these proposals are appropriate in terms of overall goals for a family property regime? Why, or why not?

Marriage and Cohabitation: Matta v. Smith

In assessing the contributions of a woman in a cohabiting relationship of 28 years in *Matta v. Smith* (2002), 28 RFL (5th) 395 (Ont. Sup. Ct. J), the court referred to the fact that *Nova Scotia v. Walsh* was about to be considered by the Supreme Court of Canada, and then stated (at para. 75):

> It seems so unfair that a wife in a married relationship, who hypothetically contributes fewer benefits to a marriage than Muriel did to her common-law relationship, results in the wife sharing equally in the family property while Muriel has no statutory right to share equally in the family assets.

Although the court indicated that the woman had made a strong case for an equal division of family property in this case, it seemed that the man had made a more substantial financial contribution. As a result, the court ordered an award of $400,000, and denied a claim for additional spousal support.

Do you agree that it is appropriate to apply the same legislative regime to married couples and cohabitees? If legislative action is required (as seems evident after *Nova Scotia v. Walsh*), what policy issues need to be addressed to decide whether there should be a specific legislative regime for cohabitees or whether the regime applicable to married couples should be automatically extended to them?

To what extent does your assessment of these issues depend on issues about choice in forming such relationships? Do you agree with the OLRC and others that the remedies available to cohabiting couples when their relationships end are not satisfactory? For example, where a woman expressly agreed at the beginning of an eight-year cohabiting relationship to limit her claim if the parties separated, how should a court assess her choice to do so? In *MacFarlane v. Smith* (2003), 35 RFL (5th) 112 (NBCA), the woman changed her mind at the end of the relationship and requested a monetary award of $100,000. In awarding her $65,100, the court expressly noted that the majority judgment in *Nova Scotia v. Walsh* had identified the appropriateness of alternative remedies for cohabiting couples.

Quasi-Spousal Relationships: Nowell v. Town Estate

In considering appropriate legislative responses to property-sharing regimes for cohabitees, consider *Nowell v. Town Estate* (1997), 30 RFL (4th) 107 (Ont. CA); leave to appeal to the Supreme Court of Canada granted (1998), 35 OR (3d) 415; discontinued September 8, 1998. In this case, a woman (Nowell) had a relationship with a married man (Town) for 24 years. During these years, Town was married and both his marriage and his family responsibilities continued. Throughout their relationship, Town and Nowell never cohabited, although Town bought a farm 13 years after the relationship began, and the two spent most weekends there. Nowell made various contributions to the farm, including cooking, cleaning, gardening, and organizing social events that the two attended or hosted together. During the course of their relationship, Town became a famous artist and gave Nowell many works of art as gifts, some of which she later sold for over $120,000.

After the relationship ended, Nowell demanded a settlement of $100,000 from Town on the basis of his previous assurances that he "would look after her." Town delivered certain works of art to Nowell, which she sold. At the time of Town's death, he had assets worth between $20 and $50 million. Nowell brought an action for a declaration that he had been unjustly enriched as a result of the services that she had performed during their relationship. Nowell sought a constructive trust remedy in relation to Town's estate or damages in the alternative.

The trial judge dismissed the action, finding that although Nowell had made many contributions to Town's life, Town, in turn, had enriched her. The court held that Nowell had received gifts of substantial value from Town and had benefited both personally and professionally from having had the opportunity to participate in Town's social and artistic life. Finally, the court also ruled that there was no basis for a finding that Nowell and Town's relationship had been quasi-marital.

Nowell appealed the decision to the Ontario Court of Appeal, claiming a 20 percent entitlement to Town's estate. The appellate court revised the trial decision, and held that although Nowell was not entitled to 20 percent of the estate, she was entitled to a money payment of $300,000. In reaching its decision, the court ruled that the relationship had not been a casual one and that, at least for the last 13 years, it had resembled a quasi-spousal relationship. The court also took note of the many verbal assurances Town had made to Nowell to "look after her," demonstrated in part by his gifts of art to her. With respect to whether Town had been unjustly enriched by Nowell, the court held that Nowell had so demonstrated—the court noted that Nowell made Town the focal point of her life and there was clear evidence of an enrichment to him and a corresponding financial deprivation to her.

It appears that the Court of Appeal viewed the relationship between Nowell and Town as similar to that of cohabitees, although the existence of Town's wife complicated the legal situation for Nowell. Moreover, although the relationship ended before Town's death, Nowell's claim was pursued against his estate—that is, against his widow. Do the principles of *Peter v. Beblow* apply to these facts?

In reflecting on this question, consider the comments of James McLeod, "Annotation of Nowell v. Town Estate" (1997), 30 RFL (4th) 107, at 109:

> While Nowell and Town may have been a "couple," they did not cohabit in any traditional
> sense of the word. Town made clear to Nowell that he would not marry her or leave his

wife. The couple maintained separate bank accounts and separate residences. There is no case law to support the conclusion that people who spend weekends together while one is married and living with his or her spouse are "cohabiting." ... The trial judge held that the case was not like *Peter v. Beblow*. By this he meant that there was no merging of the parties' economic, social and emotional lives. ... The couple formed a symbiotic relationship which met each of their needs and interests. Nowell received an entry to a world and lifestyle that she might not have been able to achieve on her own. She also received valuable gifts throughout the relationship. The legislators created matrimonial property rights for married couples. The Supreme Court of Canada extended similar rights to unmarried couples. The reasons in *Nowell v. Town Estate* come close to asserting an almost automatic right to relief to long-time lovers.

By contrast with the appellate decision in *Nowell v. Town Estate*, the petitioner and deceased in *Pelechaty v. Martyniuk Estate* (1999), 48 RFL (4th) 193 (Sask. QB) had a relationship for 17 years. The deceased had purchased a house for the petitioner to live in, but he charged her rent and he lived in his own residence. The petitioner cooked dinner for the deceased regularly at her house and cleaned and maintained the deceased's house. The petitioner claimed that the deceased had stated that she "would never have to worry" about the house in which she lived. When he died, however, his will left all his property to his nephews and nieces. (The will had been prepared with the help of the family of the deceased's wife, who had died before him; these family members asserted that the relationship between the deceased and the petitioner was that they were just dating.)

The court held that the elements of unjust enrichment had been satisfied and that a monetary award was insufficient. The court also held that the petitioner was entitled to a 20 percent interest and awarded her the home in which she lived (which corresponded to the 20 percent value). Is this case consistent with *Nowell v. Town Estate*? Does *Pelechaty* suggest that unjust enrichment and constructive trusts are available to couples who are not cohabiting? Are there differences between the cases that justify these differing outcomes?

Compare *Pelechaty* to *Knoll v. Knoll Estate*, [2001] 5 WWR 374 (Sask. QB), where a wife claimed unjust enrichment against her husband's estate in relation to her increased financial and caregiving services after her husband fell ill. Before their marriage, the parties had made a prenuptial agreement in which the wife had agreed not to make a claim against her husband's estate (both had grown children from their first marriages when they decided to marry). In denying her claim, the court relied on the agreement between the parties, but also stated (at 379) that "the extra responsibility that goes along with an ill spouse goes hand in hand with marriage" and that the wife had not provided her services for reward, but "out of love and affection for her husband." Is this reasoning consistent with *Peter v. Beblow*? For other examples, see *Tracey v. Tracey* (1998), 41 RFL (4th) 278 (Ont. Ct. J (Gen. Div.) and *Ferrera v. Ouellet* (1999), 48 RFL (4th) 75 (BCSC).

Unjust Enrichment and Same-Sex Relationships

Issues about unjust enrichment and the availability of constructive trusts have also been considered in a number of cases involving same-sex relationships at separation. In *Forrest v. Price* (1992), 48 ETR 72 (BCSC), for example, the court assessed the relationship between the cohabiting same-sex partners and stated (at para. 37):

[T]his was by all accounts a spousal relationship. The parties lived in a lengthy, sexually faithful relationship for 13 years. They fulfilled their traditional roles as homemaker and breadwinner. They intermingled their possessions and finances, with no attempt to keep any track of their respective contributions or the benefits received by either. They impressed all those around them as a couple and discussed "their" homes and projects. They instructed solicitors on two different occasions to prepare mutual wills—that is wills in which each designated the other as beneficiary. ... In light of these facts, I do not accept the defendant's evidence that he repeatedly told the plaintiff he had no proprietary interest in the successive properties. ... Accordingly, I find that, given the history of this relationship and the defendant's assurances throughout, the plaintiff reasonably expected to receive an actual interest in the various properties and that the defendant either was or ought to have been cognizant of that expectation.

In assessing the plaintiff's entitlement to a remedial constructive trust, the court took into account (at 82-85) the defendant's debts, the increase in the value of the property since separation, and a process for selling the contents of the property. Similarly, other courts have held that unjust enrichment has occurred and ordered *quantum meruit* awards or a declaration of constructive trust in same-sex cohabiting relationships: for example, see *Anderson v. Luoma* (1984), 14 DLR (4th) 749 (BCSC).

However, in *Buist v. Greaves*, [1997] OJ no. 2646 (Gen. Div.), the court concluded that there was no unjust enrichment when a lesbian couple separated after a 10-year relationship. At trial Buist claimed that her contributions to the relationship unjustly enriched Greaves and that she was, therefore, entitled to restitution. Buist substantiated her claim by filing volumes of documentation itemizing expenses that she paid for during their relationship and cohabitation. These expenses included living expenses, purchase of assets, and renovations done to Greaves' property. She also sought compensation for the domestic services she performed, such as cutting the grass, helping to build the deck, and doing the gardening. In rejecting this claim, the court held that no unjust enrichment had occurred—there was no evidence that Buist's contributions contributed to the increase in value of any of the assets; Buist did not enhance the earning potential of Greaves; the parties shared equally in the division of household duties; and there was no evidence that Buist was financially worse off personally or professionally because of the relationship.

Rethinking Family Property: Marriage and Cohabitation

As will be clear from this overview of the statutory regimes for property sharing by married couples, by contrast with the trust remedies available to cohabiting couples, property entitlements at family breakdown differ, sometimes in quite significant ways, depending on whether a couple (opposite-sex or same-sex) chose marriage or cohabitation. To what extent do you agree with the majority of the Supreme Court of Canada in *Walsh v. Bona* that these two separate categories of relationships should be preserved, at least in terms of property sharing at the end of a relationship? You may want to reconsider this question after exploring other legal principles concerning corollary relief at divorce (spousal and child support as well as custody arrangements), which do not generally distinguish between married couples and cohabiting couples. Is property entitlement qualitatively distinct from these other aspects of corollary relief?

In reflecting on these issues, note that a number of academic commentators have recommended abolishing the distinctions between marriage and cohabitation at family breakdown. As well, the OLRC's report on cohabitation in 1993 recommended that parts I and II of the *Family Law Act* be extended to cohabiting opposite-sex couples and to cohabiting same-sex couples who registered their relationship as a domestic partnership. Nova Scotia adopted a different model that permits two persons to register their partnership and thereby gain access to all the provisions of the *Matrimonial Property Act*. In this way, the statute applies to all married couples unless they take steps to opt out, but it also provides for other adults to opt in by registering their relationships. Does this legislation achieve an appropriate balance between opting out and opting in? See OLRC, *Report on the Rights and Responsibilities of Cohabitants Under the Family Law Act* (Toronto: OLRC, 1993); Law Reform Commission of Nova Scotia, *Final Report: Reform of the Law Dealing with Matrimonial Property in Nova Scotia* (Halifax: Nova Scotia Law Reform Commission, 1996); and *Law Reform (2000) Act*, SNS 2000, c. 29, *Justice Administration Amendment (2001) Act*, SNS 2001, c. 5, and *Vital Statistics Act*, SNS 2001, c. 45.

In thinking about reform proposals, you may also want to consider how current conceptions of family property do not fully address the ways in which families constitute economic units within society. In a report prepared in the United Kingdom some years ago, the authors recommended a new approach to family property, taking into account relationships to other areas of law—tax, social security, bankruptcy, and pension rights. In addition, the report recommended more empirical study of arrangements for sharing *within* intact families. Is it useful to approach reform of family property entitlements more broadly? Why, or why not? See Judith Freedman, Elizabeth Hammond, Judith Masson, and Nick Morris, *Property and Marriage: An Integrated Approach* (London: Institute for Fiscal Studies, 1988).

SELECTED REFERENCES

Nicholas Bala and Marlène Cano, "Unmarried Cohabitation in Canada: Common Law and Civilian Approaches to Living Together" (1989), 4 *Canadian Family Law Quarterly* 147.

B. Hovius and T.G. Youdan, *The Law of Family Property* (Toronto: Carswell, 1991).

Mary Ann Glendon, *The New Family and the New Property* (Toronto: Butterworths, 1983).

John McCamus, "Restitution on Dissolution of Marital and Other Intimate Relationships: Constructive Trust or Quantum Meruit?" in J. Neyers, M. McInnes, and S. Pitel, eds., *Understanding Unjust Enrichment* (Oxford: Hart Publishing, 2004), 359.

Marcia Neave, "Three Approaches to Family Property Disputes: Intention/Belief, Unjust Enrichment, and Unconscionability," in T.G. Youdan, ed., *Equity, Fiduciaries, and Trusts* (Scarborough, ON: Carswell, 1989), 247.

D.A. Rollie Thompson, "Annotation of Walsh v. Bona" (2003), 32 RFL (5th) 87.

PROBLEM

Roseneck v. Gowling (2002), 62 OR (3d) 789 (CA)

In *Roseneck v. Gowling*, the parties cohabited for approximately one year and then married. Their marriage lasted about four years. Both the husband and the wife had been married previously. At the time of trial, the husband was 40 years old and the wife 46 years old; the husband had one daughter from his first marriage who was 24 years old. Although there appeared to be no issues regarding their wishes to be divorced, the wife made a number of claims with respect to property sharing pursuant to the *Family Law Act*. Consider these claims, and the appropriateness of the court's conclusions, both at trial and on appeal. What is the fundamental problem for the wife in this situation? Is it a problem that should be resolved by legal reform? To what extent would this problem be ameliorated by the adoption of proposals recommended by the OLRC's *Report on Family Property Law*? Were there other solutions available here?

The parties initially cohabited in 1994-95 in a home that Roseneck (the wife) had inherited from her mother. They separated briefly in 1995, during which time Gowling (the husband) purchased a home for $214,000, for which he made a small down payment and then secured a mortgage for $190,000. Gowling also undertook some renovations to this home, paying an additional $59,865. In early 1996, Roseneck sold her home for $106,000 and moved into the home owned by Gowling. To assist with the renovation costs in relation to this home, Roseneck contributed about $89,000 from the proceeds of sale of her own home. The parties married in June 1996 and title to this home was transferred to Roseneck and Gowling as joint tenants in June 1997. The mortgage, however, remained in Gowling's name, and with the exception of the mortgage payment for one month, Gowling paid the monthly mortgage payments as well as the taxes and utilities throughout the marriage. Roseneck, who ceased to work outside the home during the marriage, paid some hydro bills and also did the painting and decorating as well as the landscaping and gardening; she also used some of her RRSP funds to pay for the installation of a deck. Following the parties' separation, the court fixed the value of the matrimonial home and Gowling purchased it for $282,000. The matrimonial home was the main asset of the marriage. During the marriage, both parties had cashed in some RRSPs (Gowling cashed $80,000, while Roseneck cashed $28,600). In February 2000, four months before the parties separated, Gowling received an inheritance from his mother in the amount of $165,000. He did not disclose this inheritance to Roseneck. After gifting some of these funds to his daughter, Gowling retained $133,000 of the inheritance funds at the time of the trial—Gowling was entitled to exclude these funds pursuant to s. 4(2) of the *Family Law Act*. By contrast, Roseneck's inheritance funds had been substantially contributed to the renovations to the matrimonial home—thus, her pre-marriage property value could not be deducted pursuant to s. 4(1).

According to the appeal decision, the trial judge held that, as of the date of the marriage, Gowling was unjustly enriched by Roseneck's pre-marital contribution to the renovations of Gowling's home. Therefore, Wallace J ordered monetary compensation in the amount of $88,779.44 be paid to Roseneck and included in her pre-marriage property, thus enabling her to deduct this amount in calculating her net family property. Wallace J specifically concluded that a monetary amount was preferable to a constructive trust remedy. In addition, she included the total value of the matrimonial home in Gowling's net family property calculation on the basis that the marriage was a short one. In this context, the trial judge rejected Roseneck's claim for an unequal division of matrimonial property pursuant to s. 5(6); however, she also stated that, in the absence of a finding of unjust enrichment, she would have made such an unequal division by awarding an additional payment to Roseneck in the amount of $25,000. In the result, the equalization payment to Roseneck amounted to $31,130.68.

The Ontario Court of Appeal allowed Gowling's appeal. First, the court held that the matrimonial home was held, at the end of the marriage, in joint tenancy, thus creating an entitlement to an equal one-half value for each spouse. As a result, each spouse was entitled to a beneficial joint interest in the property in the absence of any finding that this presumption was rebutted. Moreover, as a result of Roseneck's one-half interest as a joint tenant, she had received an interest equal to Gowling's so that she did not suffer any deprivation *at the end of the relationship*. The appellate court also held that her expectation that she was contributing to the couple's future home was realized, so that there was an absence of juristic reason. Finally, the court concluded that, assuming that Roseneck had succeeded in establishing the basis for her claim of unjust enrichment, it was not appropriate to award monetary compensation in this case, stating (at 799):

> Roseneck's contribution to the matrimonial home was substantial and direct. She expected that the house would be "our home." No doubt she expected that the improvements made to the matrimonial home would be reflected in its value. A constructive trust with respect to one-half the property best accorded with the expectations of the parties.
>
> One of the reasons why the trial judge was moved to adopt the approach she did was undoubtedly the fact that Roseneck had in effect contributed her inheritance to the matrimonial home and would not be excluded, whereas Gowling's inheritance, which had not been so contributed, was. No doubt the trial judge felt it was unfair for Roseneck to be substantially worse off at the end of the short relationship when, at the beginning of the relationship, she was in a slightly stronger financial position compared to Gowling. The fact that the trial judge was of the opinion that the result was unfair cannot ground recovery on the basis of unjust enrichment when the legal test for recovery is not met.

The trial judge also reviewed the provisions of s. 5(6), concluding that there was no basis for awarding an unequal division pursuant to any provisions, with the possible exception of ss. 5(6)(e) and (h). As the appellate court stated (at 802):

> In relation to these two factors, the trial judge concluded that with the amount awarded for unjust enrichment, the result of equalizing the net family properties was not unconscionable. If, however, the amount awarded for unjust enrichment was excluded, the trial judge was of the opinion that, "... it would create an unconscionable situation that should be remedied." Her reasons reflect the fact that both parties received an inheritance but the wife "lost" hers because she contributed it to the matrimonial home. The trial judge also noted that the wife contributed work during the marriage that substantially improved the property. She observed that without an unequal division Roseneck would be leaving the marriage with far less assets than Gowling. Roseneck would have holdings of approximately $115,000 and Gowling $250,000.

By contrast, the Ontario Court of Appeal disallowed the alternative claim for unequal division of family property on the grounds that the parties were required to share the problem that the matrimonial home did not increase in value commensurate with the value of renovations and that the reason for Gowling's better position primarily reflected the fact that his inheritance was more valuable than Roseneck's. The appellate court also declined to interfere with the trial judge's conclusion that Roseneck was not entitled to receive spousal support. In the result, Roseneck's equalization payment was $2,356.43.

Consider these arguments in relation to the different approaches identified at the beginning of this chapter—do you think that a more discretionary approach, such as that provided by the BC *Family Relations Act*, would achieve more fairness? How does the result in *Roseneck v. Gowling* compare with the facts and reasoning in the BC case of *Martin v. Martin*? To what extent is there a need for fundamental rethinking about family property in Canada?

CHAPTER REFERENCES

American Law Institute. *Principles of the Law of Family Dissolution: Analysis and Recommendations* (Washington, DC: Matthew Bender, 2002).

Basch, Norma. *In the Eyes of the Law: Women, Marriage and Property in Nineteenth-Century New York* (Ithaca, NY: Cornell University Press, 1982).

Burrows, G. Edmond and Penny E. Hebert. "The Supreme Court of Canada and Best v. Best" (2000), 17 *Canadian Family Law Quarterly* 263.

Chambers, Lori. *Married Women and Property Law in Victorian Ontario* (Toronto: Osgoode Society for Canadian Legal History, 1997).

Cole, Stephen and Andrew Freedman. "Recent Financial Issues in Family Law" (1990), 6 *Canadian Family Law Quarterly* 101.

Cullity, Maurice. "Ethical Issues in Estate Practice," in *Special Lectures of the Law Society of Upper Canada* (Scarborough, ON: Carswell, 1996).

Fineman, Martha. *The Illusion of Equality* (Chicago: University of Chicago Press, 1991).

_____. "Implementing Equality: Ideology, Contradiction, and Social Change: A Study of Rhetoric and Results in the Regulation of the Consequences of Divorce," [1983] *Wisconsin Law Review* 789.

Freedman, Judith, Elizabeth Hammond, Judith Mason, and Nick Morris. *Property and Marriage: An Integrated Approach* (London: Institute for Fiscal Studies, 1988).

Grant, Stephen. "Deductions Under the Family Law Act: The Sequel" (1990), 6 *Canadian Family Law Quarterly* 257.

Gray, Kevin J. *Reallocation of Property on Divorce* (Oxford: Professional Books, 1977).

Holcombe, Lee. *Wives and Property* (Toronto: University of Toronto Press, 1983).

Hovius, Berend and Timothy G. Youdan. *The Law of Family Property* (Scarborough, ON: Carswell, 1991).

Johnston, J. Jr. "Sex and Property: The Common Law Tradition, the Law School Curriculum, and Developments Toward Equality" (1972), 47 *New York University Law Review* 1033.

Kary, Joseph. "Farmland, Free Markets and Marital Breakdown" (1992), 11 *Canadian Journal of Family Law* 41.

Klotz, Robert A. "Bankruptcy and Family Law: Problems and Solutions," in Law Society of Upper Canada, *Special Lectures of the Law Society of Upper Canada, 1993—Family Law: Roles, Fairness and Equality* (Scarborough, ON: Carswell, 1994).

Knetsch, Jack. "Some Economic Implications of Matrimonial Property Rules" (1984), 34 *University of Toronto Law Journal* 263.

Law Reform Commission of British Columbia. *Report on the Property Rights on Marriage Breakdown* (Victoria: Queen's Printer for British Columbia, 1990).

_____. *Working Paper on Property Rights on Marriage Breakdown* (Victoria: Queen's Printer for British Columbia, 1989).

Law Reform Commission of Canada. *Studies on Family Property Law* (Ottawa: Information Canada, 1975).

Law Reform Commission of Nova Scotia. *Discussion Paper on Matrimonial Property in Nova Scotia: Suggestions for a New Family Law Act* (Halifax: Law Reform Commission of Nova Scotia, 1996).

Manchee, Melanie. "Family Law Update," Canadian Bar Association Ontario, September 1994.

McCallum, Margaret. "Caratun v. Caratun: It Seems That We Are Not All Realists Yet" (1994), 7 *Canadian Journal of Women and the Law* 197.

_____. "Prairie Women and the Struggle for a Dower Law, 1905-1920," in Tina Loo and Lorna McLean, eds., *Historical Perspectives on Law and Society in Canada* (Toronto: Copp Clark Longman, 1994), 306.

McLeod, James. "Annotation of Futia v. Futia" (1990), 27 RFL (3d) 81.

_____. "Annotation of Hines v. Hines" (1988), 23 RFL (3d) 261.

_____. "Annotation of Nowell v. Town Estate" (1997), 30 RFL (4th) 107.

_____. "Annotation of Shute v. Premier Trust Co." (1993), 50 RFL (3d) 441.

Merchant, A. and J. Vogel. "The Bankruptcy Dodge" (1992-93), 9 *Canadian Family Law Quarterly* 161.

Morrison, William, ed. *Blackstone's Commentaries on the Laws of England*, vol. 1 (London: Cavendish, 2001).

Mossman, M.J. "Developments in Property Law: The 1985-86 Term" (1987), 9 *Supreme Court Law Reporter* 419.

Neave, Marcia. "Three Approaches to Family Property Disputes—Intention/Belief, Unjust Enrichment and Unconscionability," in T.G. Youdan, ed., *Equity, Fiduciaries and Trusts* (Scarborough, ON: Carswell, 1989), 247.

Ontario Law Reform Commission. *Report on Family Law: Part IV: Family Property Law* (Toronto: OLRC, 1974).

_____. *Report on Family Property Law* (Toronto: OLRC, 1993).

_____. *Report on Pensions as Family Property: Valuation and Division* (Toronto: OLRC, 1995).

_____. *Report on the Rights and Responsibilities of Cohabitants Under the Family Law Act* (Toronto: OLRC, 1993).

Orlando, Alva. "Exclusive Possession of the Matrimonial Home: The Plight of Battered Cohabitees" (1987), 45 *University of Toronto Faculty of Law Review* 153.

Palmer, G.E. *The Law of Restitution*, vol. 1 (Boston: Little, Brown, 1978).

Patterson, J.B. "Confusion Created in Pension Valuation for Family Breakdown Case Law by the Use of the Expressions 'Termination Method' and 'Retirement Method'" (1998-99), 16 *Canadian Family Law Quarterly* 249.

Pearlston, Karen. "Book Review of Married Women and Property in Victorian Ontario by Lori Chambers" (2000), 12 *Canadian Journal of Women and the Law* 246.

Poirier, Donald. "Les Femmes Collaboratrices et la Loi sur les Biens Matrimoniaux du Nouveau-Brunswick" (1990), 39 *University of New Brunswick Law Journal* 23.

Poirier, Donald and M. Boudreau. "Formal Versus Real Equality in Separation Agreements in New Brunswick" (1992), 10 *Canadian Journal of Family Law* 239.

Poirier, Donald and Lynne Castonguay. "Formal Versus Real Equality in Property Division on Marriage Breakdown of Business Couples: An Empirical Study" (1994), 11 *Canadian Family Law Quarterly* 71.

Prager, Susan Westerberg. "Shifting Perspectives on Marital Property Law," in Barrie Thorne, with Marilyn Yalom, eds., *Rethinking the Family: Some Feminist Questions* (New York: Longman, 1982).

Ross, Oakland. "Ontario Fee System Cited in Woman's Legal Woe," *The Globe and Mail*, November 13, 1986, A10.

Royal Commission on the Status of Women in Canada. *Report of the Royal Commission on the Status of Women in Canada* (Ottawa: Queen's Printer, 1970).

Sheppard, Andrew. "Rawluk v. Rawluk: What Are the Limits of the Remedial Constructive Trust?" (1990), 9 *Canadian Journal of Family Law* 152.

Thompson, D.A. Rollie. "Annotation of Walsh v. Bona" (2003), 32 RFL (5th) 87.

Turpel, Mary Ellen. "Home/Land" (1991), 10 *Canadian Journal of Family Law* 17.

Walker, Thomas J. "Double-Dipping: Can a Pension Be Both Property and Income?" (1994), 10 *Canadian Family Law Quarterly* 315.

Wu, Zheng. *Cohabitation: An Alternative Form of Family Living* (Oxford: Oxford University Press, 2000).

CHAPTER SEVEN

Spousal Support and Post-Separation Dependency: Legislative Objectives, Judicial Orders, and Private Agreements

I. INTRODUCTION

Critics of divorce reform have long argued that a central problem arises from treating the issue as simply divorce, when in fact the issue is marriage and men's and women's roles within it. We believe that in fact the issue is still broader. It implicates fundamental understandings of private relationships and public responsibilities.

> Deborah Rhode and Martha Minow, "Reforming the Questions: Questioning the Reforms," in S.D. Sugarman and H.H. Kay, *Divorce Reform at the Crossroads* (New Haven, CT: Yale University Press, 1990), 191, at 209

Clearly, the way in which the state orders the allocation of resources through its welfare and economic policies and through its regulation of the economic rights and obligations of marital and cohabiting partners privileges certain lifestyles and disadvantages others. So does the ideological approval or disapproval of particular lifestyles that state legislation implicitly or explicitly conveys.

> F. Elliott, "The Family: Private Arena or Adjunct of the State?" (1989), 16 *Journal of Law and Society* 443, at 450

Issues about spousal support must be understood within the broader context of post-separation economic adjustment, including property sharing. As is evident from the materials in chapter 6, there are sometimes important connections between legal issues about property sharing and issues about entitlement to or quantum of spousal support. For example, questions about whether assets should be characterized as property pursuant to provincial legislative regimes require determinations about whether these assets constitute capital or income—recall the cases about whether professional degrees were property for purposes of the *Family Law Act*, discussed in chapter 6. In the end, the Ontario Court of Appeal held that professional degrees were not property, but that the former wife in *Caratun v. Caratun* (1992), 42 RFL (3d) 113 was entitled to a lump-sum amount of spousal support. In this way, the former spouse received compensation for her contribution to the marriage, even though the court declined to recognize that she had a property interest in her former husband's professional degree. Similarly, the Supreme Court of Canada reviewed the relationship between property entitlement and spousal support in an appeal from British Columbia in *Hartshorne v. Hartshorne* (2004), 236 DLR (4th) 193; 2004 SCC 22: see chapter 5.

Yet, it is not appropriate to regard property sharing and spousal support as just similar methods of achieving post-separation economic adjustment for all former spouses. First, because only married spouses have access to property-sharing principles in most provincial regimes (see *Walsh v. Bona*, [2002] 4 SCR 325; 2002 SCC 83, discussed in chapter 6), principles about spousal support interact with trust doctrines for cohabiting spouses, as well as with property-sharing principles for married couples in provincial statutes. Second, property-sharing principles in provincial statutes usually provide for a determination of entitlement at one point in time, a once-and-for-all decision. That is, once the property settlement has been defined in a negotiated agreement or court order, there is generally no opportunity for recalculation of entitlement at a later date. In this way, property-sharing principles appear consistent with ideas of a clean break within the no-fault divorce regime. By contrast, spousal support may often (although not in all circumstances) be varied at a later date, having regard to changes, either positive or negative, in the economic circumstances of the former spouses. As a result, spousal support may appear to encourage ongoing connections between former spouses and thus deflect clean-break objectives. Although the circumstances in which such variations of spousal support are legally available remains a highly contested issue, the basic difference between the finality of property decisions and the potential for variation of spousal support agreements or orders remains.

Third, because some property regimes, such as Ontario's *Family Law Act*, are based on fixed rules (particularly with respect to the elimination of some pre-marriage property from the calculation), it is possible that some assets will not be taken into account in property sharing; courts may thus conclude that there are reasons to exercise discretion to achieve a fair economic adjustment by means of orders for lump-sum or ongoing spousal support. In this way, spousal support may appear to be based on more discretionary decision making than determinations about property. By contrast with Ontario, BC's property regime under the *Family Relations Act* and its definition of property to include all property owned at separation (whether acquired before or after marriage) may arguably diminish the extent of this distinction between decisions about property and support, but it does not entirely eliminate it. As will be seen, issues have arisen in practice in the context of pensions—to what extent does the determination of a spouse's entitlement to share in the value of the other spouse's pension (property sharing) affect the first spouse's right to receive ongoing spousal support payable out of pension income?

Finally, connections between decisions about property sharing and spousal support also need to be examined in the context of the economic circumstances of families at separation. For families that have few, if any, assets at the end of marriage or cohabitation, the property-sharing principles are simply not applicable. In these cases, there may be a greater need for ongoing spousal support, but there may also be few, if any, resources available to meet this need. Of course, there may be some cases in which a former spouse has no assets, but may have significant (actual or potential) income—for example, Dr. Caratun had no assets but he did have an expectation of a substantial income in the future. In this way, economic circumstances in a family may influence the way that principles concerning property sharing and support entitlement at separation or divorce are applied. In addition, entitlement to spousal support is linked to child support, to be discussed in the next chapter. In this context, it is important to note the express direction in the *Divorce Act*, s. 15.3, which provides that, when determining applications for spousal and child support, courts must give priority to child support. Therefore, in the context of limited financial resources, it is possible that there may be neither property sharing nor spousal support award; all available family resources on separation may be directed to child support. In these situations of separation or divorce, principles of property sharing and/or spousal support operate only theoretically.

In this context, moreover, there are continuing debates about the responsibility of families to respond to the economic dependency of former family members. In enforcing such familial obligations, legal principles have created the post-divorce family unit—that is, an economic unit with defined responsibilities for financial support that continues to exist even after the spouses have separated permanently and/or divorced. As the American Law Institute stated, however, such responsibilities have been allocated to former spouses by legislative provisions and judicial decisions without "any satisfactory explanation for placing the obligation to support needy individuals on their former spouses rather than on their parents, their children, their friends or society in general": see American Law Institute, *Principles of the Law of Family Dissolution: Analysis and Recommendations* (Washington, DC: Matthew Bender, 2002), at 789.

In Canada, the issue has focused primarily on the relationship between governmental income security programs and family-based obligations for relieving dependency. Thus, in *Bracklow v. Bracklow*, [1999] 1 SCR 420 (at para. 31), the Supreme Court of Canada held that it was preferable for a needy former spouse to receive support from her former husband, "recognizing the potential injustice of foisting a helpless former partner onto the public assistance role." Although Canadian policies, like those in the United States, currently place primary duties on families rather than the state for dependent family members (including post-separation and divorce), other alternatives have been advocated. Consider, for example, the following recommendations:

> [Our recommendations] imply an expanded concept of responsibility not only for divorcing spouses and parents but also for the state. ... We need both special programs for divorced parties and changes in broader welfare and employment policies that affect family life. ... Expanded child-care and parental leave provisions, flexible workplace schedules, wider health and pension coverage, counselling services for single parents and children, retraining programs for displaced homemakers, and further social initiatives targeting minority and low-income groups are also crucial to any effective reform strategy.

(Rhode and Minow, at 210.)

All these issues about spousal support also need to take into account the extension of spousal status pursuant to judicial decisions and provincial statutes. Clearly, the principles of spousal support in the *Divorce Act*, s. 15.2 apply only to married couples who have applied for divorce: see s. 2(1). As noted in chapter 5, of course, the current definition of spouse in the *Divorce Act* refers only to opposite-sex couples, but it is likely that this section would not survive a challenge as a result of the constitutional challenges to marriage that succeeded in Ontario, British Columbia, and Quebec: see chapter 2. By contrast with the federal *Divorce Act*, the definition of "spouse" in provincial statutes includes large numbers of cohabitees, usually on the basis of a period of cohabitation or shared parenthood; entitlement to such support has generally been extended under provincial statutes to same-sex couples as well. Moreover, with few exceptions, judicial interpretation of spousal support principles under the *Divorce Act* has been applied to provincial statutory provisions; thus, spousal support principles applicable at the end of marriage are virtually the same as those applicable to cohabitees at separation.

This chapter begins by examining the legal definition of spouse for purposes of spousal support. It then explores the development of current legal principles concerning entitlement to spousal support, having regard to responsibilities of families and the state with respect to economic dependency post-separation. Moreover, because issues about spousal support have become particularly entwined with principles concerning variation of agreements and orders, these issues are also examined. In addition, the chapter briefly examines some proposals for reforming principles of spousal support.

SELECTED REFERENCES

Mavis Maclean and John Eekelaar, "Child Support, Wife Support, or Family Support," in Lenore Weitzman and Mavis Maclean, eds., *The Economic Consequences of Divorce* (Oxford: Clarendon Press, 1992), 239.

Janet Mosher, "The Harms of Dichotomy: Access to Welfare Benefits as a Case on Point" (1991), 9 *Canadian Journal of Family Law* 97.

M.J. Mossman, " 'Running Hard To Stand Still': The Paradox of Family Law Reform" (1994), 17 *Dalhousie Law Journal* 5.

Diane Pask, "Family Law and Policy in Canada: Economic Implications for Single Custodial Mothers and Their Children," in J. Hudson and B. Galloway, eds., *Single Parent Families* (Scarborough, ON: Thompson Educational Publishing, 1993), 185.

II. WHO IS A SPOUSE?

A. The Constitutional Context

As explained in chapter 5, spousal support may be provided in accordance with the provisions of the *Divorce Act, 1985* or pursuant to provincial statutes. The federal Parliament has authority to legislate with respect to marriage and divorce under s. 91(26) of the constitution; its authority to legislate corollary relief *in relation to a divorce decree* was recognized in a number of cases after the enactment of divorce legislation in 1968: for example, see *Zacks v. Zacks* (1973), 10 RFL 53 (SCC).

Provincial legislatures have enacted statutes providing for spousal support based on provincial authority for property and civil rights under s. 92(13) of the constitution. In the absence of an application for divorce by married spouses or in relation to the separation of cohabiting couples, provincial legislation applies. As was noted earlier, however, there are some situations in which jurisdictional arguments may delay family law proceedings.

Thus, if one spouse has commenced an action for spousal support pursuant to provincial legislation, and the other spouse then applies for divorce, the provisions of the federal statute will apply according to the doctrine of paramountcy; in addition, after the granting of a divorce in which no claim for support was presented, any subsequent application for spousal support must be made pursuant to the federal statute: for example, see *Richards v. Richards* (1972), 7 RFL 101 (Ont. CA). There are also provisions in some provincial statutes that provide for the staying of an action pursuant to provincial authority in such cases: for example, see Ontario's *Family Law Act*, s. 36. For further information, see Peter Hogg, *Constitutional Law of Canada* (Toronto: Carswell) (looseleaf), 26:5-8.

B. Legislative Definitions of Spouse

1. Spouses Under the Divorce Act, 1985

Section 15.2(1) of the *Divorce Act, 1985* provides that either or both spouses may make an application for an order for spousal support—support may be either a lump-sum or periodic payment; a court may also make an order to secure payment of support. Section 2(1) provides that "spouse" means "either of a man or woman who are married to each other." As noted above, it is likely that a challenge to the opposite-sex requirement of s. 2(1) would be successful, but the divorce legislation has not been amended to permit same-sex applicants (married in Ontario, British Columbia, or Quebec) to make such applications: see also chapter 2.

2. Spouses Under Provincial Legislation

By contrast with the restriction of the *Divorce Act* provisions to married couples, provincial legislation has expanded the definition of spouse for purposes of support to include some cohabitees. For example, provincial statutes may define cohabitees as spouses for purposes of spousal support if they have cohabited for a period of time. The length of time varies—for example, it is three years in Ontario, two years in British Columbia and the Northwest Territories, and one year in Nova Scotia: see *Family Law Act*, RSO 1990, c. F.3, s. 29(a), as am.; *Family Relations Act*, SBC 1996, c. 128, s. 57 as am. by SBC 1997, c. 20; by *Definition of Spousal Amendment Act, 1999*, SBC 1999, c. 29; and by *Definition of Spouse Amendment Act*, 2000, SBC 2000, c. 24; *Family Law Act*, SNWT 1997, c. 18, s. 16(2); and *Family Maintenance Act*, RSNS 1989, c. 160, s. 2(m), as am. by *Law Reform (2000) Act*, SNS 2000, c. 29. Most of these statutes also define cohabitation as a conjugal relationship: for example, see Ontario's *Family Law Act*, s. 1(1). This requirement has been the subject of criticism, as examined below.

In addition, most provincial statutes include in the definition of spouses those cohabitees who are the biological or adoptive parents of a child. For example, Newfoundland's *Family Law Act*, RSN 1990, c. F-2, s. 35(c) defines as a spouse a person who has cohabited with another person for more than one year and who has custody of a child born of the relationship: see also SN 2000, c. 29. Ontario's *Family Law Act*, s. 29(b) defines as spouses persons who are the natural or adoptive parents of a child and "in a relationship of some permanence."

Although these provincial definitions were originally adopted for opposite-sex cohabitees, they have generally been extended to now include same-sex cohabitees. In examining these definitions, this section first explores some interpretive issues arising from the expanded definition of spouse in the context of opposite-sex spouses and then examines developments in courts and legislatures with respect to spousal status for same-sex cohabitees at separation. In addition, the section includes recent criticisms of legislative and judicial approaches to the definition of spouse for purposes of support.

C. Interpreting the Definition of Spouse: Opposite-Sex Cohabitees

Because the wording of the expanded definition of spouse differs from province to province, this review of cases that have interpreted legislative provisions focuses on Ontario's *Family Law Act*, s. 29. One part of the expanded definition of spouse in that section requires cohabitation "continuously for a period of not less than three years." (Note that the same language was used in the former Ontario statute, the *Family Law Reform Act* (s. 14), which was repealed and replaced by the *Family Law Act* in 1986; under the previous statute, the requisite period of cohabitation was five years.) In addition, the definition of "cohabit" in s. 1(1) means "to live together in a conjugal relationship whether within or outside marriage."

In the context of this definition, courts have had to interpret the meaning of cohabitation as a conjugal relationship, as well as the requirement of continuous cohabitation. Examine the reasoning in the cases that follow: how would you characterize the courts' approach to the expanded definition of "spouse"? Do these cases suggest that courts use a narrow or a broad approach? What are the consequences of this approach for families and the state? Is this reasoning consistent with the underlying purposes of the legislation?

Molodowich v. Penttinen

In *Molodowich v. Penttinen* (1980), 17 RFL (2d) 376 (Ont. Dist. Ct.), the court held that there were seven components involved in cohabitation—arrangements for shelter; arrangements for sexual and personal behaviour; arrangements for domestic services; social activities; the attitude and conduct of the community toward the couple; financial arrangements; and the attitude and conduct of the couple toward children. Kurisko DCJ formulated (at 381) the following questions as a basis for determining whether a couple was cohabiting within a conjugal relationship:

1. Shelter

   a. Did the parties live under the same roof?

   b. What were the sleeping arrangements?

   c. Did anyone else occupy or share the available accommodations?

2. Sexual and Personal Behaviour

   a. Did the parties have sexual relations? If not, why not?

b. Did they maintain an attitude of fidelity to each other?

c. What were their feelings toward each other?

d. Did they communicate on a personal level?

e. Did they eat their meals together?

f. What, if anything, did they do to assist each other with problems or during illness?

g. Did they buy gifts for each other on special occasions?

3. Services

What was the conduct and habit of the parties in relation to

a. preparation of meals;

b. washing and mending clothes;

c. shopping;

d. household maintenance; and

e. any other domestic services?

4. Social

a. Did the parties participate together or separately in neighbourhood and community activities?

b. What was the relationship and conduct of each of them toward members of their respective families and how did such families behave toward the parties?

5. Societal

What was the attitude and conduct of the community toward each of them and as a couple?

6. Support (economic)

a. What were the financial arrangements between the parties regarding the provision of or contribution toward the necessaries of life—for example, food, clothing, shelter, and recreation?

b. What were the arrangements concerning the acquisition of ownership of property?

c. Was there any special financial arrangement between them that both agreed would be determinant of their overall relationship?

7. Children

What was the attitude and conduct of the parties concerning children?

Sullivan v. Letnik
(1994), 5 RFL (4th) 313 (Ont. UFC)

BECKETT J: This was the trial of an issue—i.e., whether the applicant is a spouse of the respondent within the meaning of section 29 of the *Family Law Act, 1986*. The applicant claims support and an interest in the respondent's property. The parties are not married, and if the applicant is found not to be a spouse within the meaning of the Act, the Unified Family Court has no jurisdiction in this case. The applicant says that she and the respondent have had both a business and an intimate personal relationship for almost 22 years, of which at least 7 years were as common law spouses. The respondent's position is that, although they had a business relationship as well as an intimate personal relationship, they did not live together continuously so that they could be defined as spouses either under the *Family Law Act, 1986* or its predecessor, the *Family Law Reform Act*.

The Facts

The applicant's evidence is quite different from that of the respondent. Accordingly, I shall review the evidence in some detail, as the credibility of the parties becomes the main issue before me.

The respondent is the owner of a company called Captain Normac's Riverboat Inn Ltd., which operated the vessel "Normac" converted to a restaurant called "Captain John's." The "Normac" was moored at Queen's Quay in Toronto. He had opened this business some time around 1971. With her background in accounting in the hotel industry, the applicant was hired by the respondent in August of 1971. At that time, both parties were married to others. On October 29th, 1972, the business relationship between the parties became intimate, and that date was subsequently remembered by both parties as "their anniversary." There was a period of time in 1972 and 1973 that the applicant was employed elsewhere but continued as a consultant to Mr. Letnik and continued their personal relationship. About 1975, Mr. Letnik found another ship, the "Jadrin," and brought it to Toronto to operate alongside the "Normac." In 1976, the applicant entered into a five-year employment contract with the respondent's company.

On the 2nd of June 1981, the "Normac" was struck at its mooring by the Toronto ferry "Trillium," causing extensive damage, as a result of which the "Normac" sank several days later. On hearing of the accident, Mrs. Sullivan drove to the ship, accompanied by her husband and her daughter.

At this point, I should say something about the relationship between Mrs. Sullivan and her husband. They had married in 1966, but after about 1967, there was no further intimacy between them, and from the evidence, it appears that they had accommodated themselves to a lifestyle that allowed Mrs. Sullivan a great deal of freedom. They have a daughter, who was born in 1971, but she is not the biological child of Mr. Sullivan.

On June 21, 1981, Mrs. Sullivan did not return to her home in Unionville with her husband and child. Instead, she remained on the ship to carry out her administrative duties. At first she slept on the couch in her office but soon after, Mr. Letnik asked her to move into his personal quarters and from that time on, she not only worked for Mr. Letnik but lived with him in a conjugal relationship.

The following spring, on April 29th, 1982, Mr. Letnik asked Mrs. Sullivan to marry him and marked the occasion by giving her an engagement ring, which she displayed in court. He had divorced in 1977, but Mrs. Sullivan was still married. However, they were both Catholics and apparently felt that it was necessary to go through annulment proceedings with the church, which they ultimately did, to which I will refer later.

Up to June 2nd, 1981, Mrs. Sullivan and her husband and daughter had resided at 21 Cullen Street in Carlisle, Ontario, but after that date, she says she spent 85% to 90% of her time on the vessel with Mr. Letnik, and the balance of her time visiting with her daughter at the home in Carlisle, which she owned.

In 1984, the respondent refurbished the "Jadrin" and created a large apartment for himself and for Mrs. Sullivan. She testified that she was responsible for the decorating of this apartment. On completion, they both moved into it and continued to share the apartment, to all intents and purposes as husband and wife.

On January 2nd, 1985, Mr. and Mrs. Sullivan had a conversation in which they decided that the time had come to formally part, and in May of 1985, Mr. Sullivan moved out of the Carlisle house with their daughter. As it was owned by Mrs. Sullivan, she "took over" the house and brought in a housekeeper to look after it. She continued to live on the vessel with the respondent full time from and after January 1985.

In about 1989, the "Normac" was towed to Cleveland, Ohio and, in June of that year, Mr. Letnik opened a "Captain John's" in Cleveland's harbour. Mrs. Sullivan was an important element in Mr. Letnik's business, which required both of them to be in Cleveland a considerable amount of time. As a result, they bought a house in their joint names in a suburb of Cleveland. At this time, the parties were either living on the "Jadrin" or in the Cleveland house or, from time to time, at the house she owned in Carlisle. In 1987, they purchased two farms; in 1988, a building in Strathroy; and in 1989, a third farm. One of the farms was in the corporate name of a company owned by the applicant, another farm in the names of the applicant and respondent, and the third farm in the names of the applicant's company and a company owned by Mr. Letnik's sister and brother.

After the start-up of the Cleveland business, Mrs. Sullivan spent some time there, but mostly spent her time looking after the Toronto operation while Mr. Letnik continued to look after the Cleveland operation. She testified that on weekends, he would return and they would stay together, mostly on the "Jadrin."

Mrs. Sullivan's annulment proceeding in the church was final on the 20th of December 1990 and Mr. Letnik's in 1990 or 1991. It appears to me that the parties had gone through the church annulment procedure in order to marry within the church.

In 1990, trouble developed in the working relationship between Mrs. Sullivan and Mr. Letnik. In January of that year, they had serious arguments about business, as a result of which she claims he physically abused her in Cleveland. She later had Mr. Letnik's corporate lawyer write to him on her behalf to the effect that their working relationship would terminate on May 1st, 1990. Although this saw the end of their working relationship at that time, her testimony, which I accept, was that their personal relationship continued. She went away for a couple of weeks in May and did some work in Cleveland, but did not sleep on the "Jadrin" between May of 1990 and the end of the year for fear of his violence. However, their personal relationship continued off the ship, including at her home in Carlisle.

At the urging of the company's auditor, she agreed to go back to work in January of 1991, and she thereupon committed to stay on the ship full time. Mr. Letnik continued to spend most of the time in Cleveland looking after the business there until that business closed near the end of 1991. They continued, throughout this period, however, to be with each other when he was in Toronto or she was in Cleveland. By January of 1992 and after the Cleveland business had closed, both were on the "Jadrin" living together, and continued to do so until the 1st of March 1992.

The story told by Mr. Letnik varies from that of Mrs. Sullivan: he claims that at no time did they have a "common law" relationship. He maintains that she only stayed from time to time on the "Jadrin" or in the Cleveland house. He painted a picture of an intimate relationship but one that had no degree of continuity or commitment, falling short of what we would understand to be a common law relationship. He denied that he had ever promised to marry her. He denied that she had stayed *most* of the time on the vessel after June of 1981. In his examination and cross-examination, he attempted to paint their relationship as being a business relationship with a personal relationship that was only slightly above casual. His version of the relationship cannot be resolved with hers by allowing for differences only in minor details. I have no hesitation in concluding that the applicant's description of the relationship is credible, while Mr. Letnik's is not.

Mrs. Sullivan is one of those people who rarely throws away a greeting card; she put into evidence over 60 such cards (of which 29 were undated) sent or given to her during the course of their relationship by Mr. Letnik. The majority were sentimental cards with messages of love and affection. Most significantly, many were "To My Wife" or "What is Marriage?," "To my Wonderful Wife on her Birthday" or "My Wonderful Wife on Mother's Day." There were cards for Easter, cards for her birthday, cards for no reason at all, and many for their "anniversary" on the 29th of October. The last dated card was "To my Wife" at Christmas 1991. In cross-examination, Mr. Letnik claimed that he had never referred to Mrs. Sullivan as his wife, but when confronted with the cards, was unable to give any rational explanation. When asked about the anniversary cards, all he had to say was that she had "all kinds of anniversaries." He said he sent her the cards to keep her "cool." He denied that he had promised to marry the applicant. Mrs. Sullivan testified that her parents treated him like their son-in-law, and, in fact, she produced two birthday cards from her parents to Mr. Letnik, referring to him as "son." He seemed to shrug that off. He admitted that he referred to them as "Daddy" and "Mom," but said that this was simply the custom in his culture.

Mr. Letnik and Mrs. Sullivan appeared to hold themselves out to others as husband and wife; as an example, a photograph in the *Cleveland News Herald* showed the parties beside their ship, and referred to Jeannine Sullivan and "her husband," John Letnik. There were portraits of the applicant and the respondent, and pictures at her family Christmas parties and in her garden at Carlisle. Mrs. Sullivan produced a plaque that had hung in their suite on the "Jadrin," "The Marriage Prayer."

Tracey Ostapa, who had worked as a bookkeeper on the ship from November of 1981 to April of 1992, testified that the parties lived together on the boat. She confirmed that it was Mrs. Sullivan who did the interior decorating on the suite that he had constructed on the ship, although Mr. Letnik denies this. She said they were always together, either on the boat or in Carlisle or in Cleveland. Another witness, David Clegg, who knew them both as a friend, testified that, as far as he was concerned, they were engaged and after learning that she had her annulment, expected them to get married. He worked for the company for awhile, and lived in the house in Cleveland. He confirmed that the parties, when they were there, stayed in the master bedroom. Mr. Clegg also testified that at a Christmas staff party in 1989 when Mrs. Sullivan was not present, Mr. Letnik apologized to the assembled guests for "his wife not being there."

Mr. Letnik called, in support of his position, one witness, his friend, William Meleta, a retired fireman. He was a frequent visitor on the "Jadrin." Although he attempted to support Mr. Letnik's evidence that the parties did not live together, I found nothing essentially inconsistent between his evidence and that of Mrs. Sullivan. Although he tried to help Mr. Letnik, I do not accept his evidence when it conflicts with that of the applicant.

In summary, Mr. Letnik and Mrs. Sullivan had an intimate relationship starting in 1972 that continued until she moved on to the "Jadrin" with Mr. Letnik almost full time, in June of 1981. She had an estranged husband and a daughter whom she continued to visit from time to time. By 1984, she was living full time on the "Jadrin" with Mr. Letnik in an open conjugal relationship, apparent to friends and relatives alike. They behaved like any other married couple and times that they were away from each other were times necessitated by business in Cleveland, or the occasional overnights when she returned to her home, or during a period in 1990 when she did not go on the ship for fear of his violence. But even during that period of time in 1990, their personal relationship continued off the ship.

I found Mr. Letnik to be less than frank. He was evasive, hesitant, and his testimony was totally inconsistent with their documented behaviour over the course of their relationship. On the other hand, I found Mrs. Sullivan to be credible, straightforward, and believable. I prefer and accept her evidence over that of Mr. Letnik.

I am of the opinion that the parties cohabited in a conjugal relationship after June 2nd, 1981, and certainly since January 2nd of 1985, when the applicant and her husband formally separated. The relationship was continuous from that time until March of 1992. There was a time when she would not go on the "Jadrin" in 1990 but that was because of the business turmoil between them and her fear of violence, but that did not mean that the relationship had terminated.

It was argued on behalf of the respondent that the cohabitation, if it existed, was not continuous, that the very brief stays at the Carlisle house from time to time interrupted the continuity of the cohabitation. He also argued that the period when she was off the ship from May until December 1990 broke the continuity. With respect, I cannot accept those arguments. Whether couples are separated is a question of intent, not geography; at least one of the parties must intend to permanently sever the relationship.

The Law

Section 29 of the *Family Law Act, 1986* defines "spouse" as follows:

> 29. In this Part.
>
> • • •
>
> "spouse" means a spouse as defined in subsection 1(1), and in addition includes either of a man and woman who are not married to each other and have cohabited,
>
> (a) continuously for a period of not less than three years. ...

In *Harris v. Godkewitsch* (1983), 41 OR (2d) 779 (Fam. Ct.), Nasmith Prof. J, in addressing the requirement of continuous cohabitation under the *Family Law Reform Act*, gives a good review of the case law. He pointed out that there may be interruptions by temporary separations. Their effect depends upon the intentions of the parties.

He relied on *Feehan v. Attwells* (1979), 24 OR (2d) 248 (Co. Ct.), as authority for the proposition that temporary separations do not preclude a finding that the parties have cohabited continuously. In that case, there had been some short periods of separation which the trial judge had considered to be periods of reflection or reassessment, but found no withdrawal from the relationship—no termination of the consortium.

In *Sanderson v. Russell* (1979), 24 OR (2d) 429, 99 DLR (3d) 713, 9 RFL (2d) 81 (CA), Morden JA stated at pp. 87-88 RFL:

> Without in any way attempting to be detailed or comprehensive, it could be said that such a relationship has come to an end when either party regards it as being at an end and, by his or her conduct, has demonstrated in a convincing manner that this particular state of mind is a settled one. While the physical separation of parties following "a fight" might, in some cases, appear to amount to an ending of cohabitation, the test should be realistic and flexible enough to recognize that a brief cooling off period does not bring the relationship to an end. Such conduct does not convincingly demonstrate a settled state of mind that the relationship is at an end.

For the above reasons, I find as a fact that the parties lived continuously in a conjugal relationship, probably from the 2nd of June 1981 but certainly from the 2nd of January 1985 until March 1st, 1992.

The parties are therefore found to be spouses within the meaning of the *Family Law Act, 1986*. The result of this finding is that a trial must now be scheduled in the Unified Family Court for the balance of the issues. Counsel may speak to me concerning this and the question of costs for this portion of the trial.

Order accordingly.

An appeal from this decision was dismissed: (1997), 27 RFL (4th) 79 (Ont. CA).

Discussion Notes

Intentions and Credibility

Examine the factors in *Molodowich v. Penttinen*—to what extent are they objective or subjective? Does the reasoning in *Sullivan v. Letnik* focus on objective or subjective factors? How important was the credibility of Mrs. Sullivan and Mr. Letnik to the outcome? For other examples, see *Ringler v. Dodds*, [2002] OJ no. 949 (Sup. Ct. J) (QL), where cohabitation was held to exist in spite of two short separations; *Wandich v. Viele* (2002), 24 RFL (5th) 427 (Ont. Sup. Ct. J), where cohabitation was also held to exist; and *Cradock v. Glover Estate* (2000), 32 ETR (2d) 52 (Ont. Sup. Ct. J), where the court held that cohabitation existed while the parties lived together, even though the man had not declared a commitment to the woman. See also *Zegil v. Opie* (1994), 8 RFL (4th) 91 (Ont. Ct. J (Gen. Div.)); rev'd. in part (1997), 28 RFL (4th) 405 (Ont. CA) and *Baird v. Iaci* (1997), 32 RFL (4th) 109 (BCSC); in both these cases, the court concluded that women claimants were not spouses pursuant to provincial legislation. Clearly, in many of these cases, courts are required to determine the facts of cohabiting relationships in circumstances where the parties, after their relationships have ended, present differing versions in their evidence, just as in *Sullivan v. Letnik*. Is there any way to avoid issues of credibility in such cases? What policy arguments support restrictive or, alternatively, more generous, interpretations of the statutory definitions of spouse?

Cohabitation and Economic Relationships

Examine the list of factors in *Molodowich* and the reasoning in *Sullivan*—to what extent is the sharing of economic resources relevant to the determination that the parties are spouses? What goal is achieved by focusing on the intimacy of the parties, by contrast with their economic interdependency? If spousal support is intended to relieve economic dependency, why should intimacy be taken into account at all?

In an early case in Ontario, a court held that it was appropriate to interpret the expanded definition of spouse narrowly and thus held that there was no cohabitation within the meaning of the *Family Law Act* when a woman on social assistance had an intimate relationship with a man with whom she shared an apartment; she also did cooking and washing for him. However, she contributed rent each month in relation to the apartment. In *Stoikiewicz and Filas* (1978), 7 RFL (2d) 366 (Ont. UFC), the court concluded that the man and woman were not cohabiting, stating (at 369):

> It is my view that unmarried persons cannot be found to be cohabiting within the meaning of [s. 29] unless it can be determined that their relationship is such that they have each assumed an obligation to support and provide for the other in the same manner that married spouses are obliged to do so.

As a result, the woman in this case was not entitled to support from the man and thus remained eligible for social assistance. Interestingly, it appears unlikely that a similar decision would result for a social assistance recipient now; the relationship between entitle-ment to spousal support and to social assistance is examined later in this chapter. However, subsequent cases have tended to reject the degree of priority accorded to the economic relationship in *Stoikiewicz*: for example, see *Armstrong v. Thompson* (1979), 23 OR (2d) 421 (Sup. Ct. J).

In this context, consider *Brunette v. Quebec*, [2000] RJQ 2664 (CS). A 64-year-old permanently disabled woman, who needed assistance with many aspects of daily living, invited a 54-year-old mentally disabled man to share her accommodation and expenses; they provided each other with care and support and were clearly interdependent, but they did not have a sexual relationship. The welfare authorities ceased paying benefits to the woman, having concluded that the relationship between the parties was marriage-like. Although the decision to terminate her benefits was confirmed before the welfare tribunal, the appeal court held that it was not a spousal relationship because it was non-sexual. As Brenda Cossman and Bruce Ryder argued, the decision raises a number of questions about the emphasis on sex as *the* distinction between conjugal and non-conjugal relationships: see Brenda Cossman and Bruce Ryder, "What Is Marriage-Like Like? The Irrelevance of Conjugality" (2001), 18 *Canadian Family Law Journal* 271, at 306 (discussed further below).

The Charter and the Definition of Common Law Spouse

In *Rossu v. Taylor* (1998), 161 DLR (4th) 266; 39 RFL (4th) 242 (Alta. CA), a woman claimed spousal support under the *Domestic Relations Act*, RSA 1980, c. D-37. Although she had lived with a man for more than 30 years, the parties had not married. Unfortunately, the statute provided spousal support only for married spouses. Both the lower court and the Alberta Court of Appeal held that the exclusion of common law spouses contravened s. 15 of the Charter and was not saved by s. 1; although the trial judge read common law spouses into the legislation, the Court of Appeal decided to declare an infringement of the Charter but to suspend the effect of the declaration for 12 months to permit the provincial legislature to amend the legislation: see now SA 1999, c. 20, s. 2.

In *Brebric v. Niksic* (2002), 60 OR (3d) 630 (CA), the plaintiff cohabited with a man for about 18 months and they bought a home together. The parties shared expenses, including expenses for the plaintiff's two sons from an earlier relationship, and planned to marry in February 1994. Unfortunately, the man was killed in December 1993 in a collision between the vehicle in which he was riding and a train. The plaintiff wished to sue the driver of the vehicle for damages, but her right to do so depended on whether she could demonstrate that she was a spouse pursuant to the *Family Law Act*. She had not cohabited for the requisite three-year period and the parties had not had a child, so the plaintiff challenged the constitutionality of the three-year cohabitation requirement. The Ontario Court of Appeal held that there was no infringement of s. 15, commenting (at 640):

> Although the three-year minimum period of cohabitation may not correspond precisely with the characteristics of all common law relationships, any deleterious effects of the definition of spouse are outweighed by the advantages of having an objective standard by which individuals and the courts can determine when state-imposed support obligations and rights of action arise.

Do you agree with this view? Why, or why not?

Marriage and Spouses

In *Debora v. Debora* (1997), 32 RFL (4th) 48 (Ont. Ct. J (Gen. Div.)); aff'd. (1999), 43 RFL (4th) 179 (Ont. CA), the parties entered into a religious marriage that they knew did not meet the formal requirements of a valid marriage in Ontario and subsequently cohabited. Were they spouses pursuant to s. 29? In *De Souza v. De Souza* (1999), 48 RFL (4th) 63 (Ont. Ct. J (Prov. Div.)), the parties were married, had two children, and then divorced. They subsequently reconciled, lived together for six months, and then separated permanently. The wife sought spousal support; the court held that the six-month period constituted some permanence within the meaning of s. 29(b); because there were children of the relationship, it was not relevant that they were born before the period of cohabitation. Do you agree with this result? Why, or why not?

In *Mahoney v. King* (1998), 39 RFL (4th) 361 (Ont. Ct. J (Gen. Div.)), the court considered an application for interim support claimed by a woman who had had a five- or six-year relationship with a man who was married to a woman with whom he cohabited; the woman applicant had maintained her own separate residence. Although the court did not award interim support, the judge stated that it was possible for the woman to be a spouse even though she lived in a separate residence and even though the man was married to another woman with whom he cohabited. James McLeod criticized the court's decision that the woman was a spouse in these circumstances, preferring the approach of the Ontario Court of Appeal in *Nowell v. Towne Estate* (1997), 30 RFL (4th) 107; 35 OR (3d) 415 (Ont. CA) (discussed in chapter 6) that such relationships were merely quasi-spousal. In his "Annotation" (1998), 38 RFL (4th) 361, at 363, McLeod suggested:

> [Maybe] finding that an affair is cohabitation will strengthen the institution of marriage. It will encourage fidelity. On the other hand, it comes perilously close to institutionalizing the notion of concubinage in 1998 Ontario. ... If these people cohabited, many dating couples and engaged couples are cohabiting. Just how far should the law insinuate itself into private personal relationships?

Do you agree with these views? Which factors are most relevant to the underlying rationale(s) for spousal support—conjugality, economic dependence or interdependence, co-residence, the appearance of marriage, or others? This issue is discussed further after examining the approach to spousal status for same-sex couples.

D. Spousal Support and Same-Sex Relationships

M. v. H.
[1999] 2 SCR 3; (1999), 171 DLR (4th) 577

[Before the decision in *M. v. H.*, provincial statutes that expanded the definition of spouse excluded same-sex couples from making applications for support. For example, Ontario's *Family Law Act*, s. 29, provided that the expanded definition applied to a man and a woman who cohabited continuously or were the parents of a child. In *M. v. H.*, the plaintiff successfully challenged the constitutionality of this opposite-sex requirement.

Two women, M. and H., cohabited in a same-sex relationship from 1982 until they separated in 1992. They lived in H.'s home, started a successful advertising business, and jointly bought business property and a vacation property. H. was more involved in the business. In 1992, M. left the home and applied for support under the *Family Law Act*. She sought a declaration that the opposite-sex definition of spouse in s. 29 of the *Family Law Act* was invalid because it violated s. 15 of the Charter, and was not saved by s. 1. The motions judge granted the declaration and read in words inclusive of same-sex relationships. On appeal by H. and the Ontario Attorney General, the Ontario Court of Appeal upheld the decision of the motions judge, but suspended the decision for one year to allow Ontario time to amend the *Family Law Act*. The Attorney General appealed to the Supreme Court of Canada.

In the Supreme Court of Canada, the appeal was dismissed, Gonthier J dissenting. Both Major and Bastarache JJ wrote opinions concurring with the majority judgment of Cory and Iacobucci JJ (on behalf of Lamer CJ and L'Heureux-Dubé, McLachlin, and Binnie JJ). All the judges stated that they were following the decision in *Law v. Canada*, [1999] 1 SCR 497, in which the court reviewed its approach to s. 15 of the Charter in relation to a claim of age discrimination for a surviving spouse pursuant to the *Canada Pension Plan*. In *Law*, the court held that there was no infringement of s. 15 in that case.

Examine the excerpts from *M. v. H.* below in relation to comments about spousal relationships, both opposite- and same-sex. What differences can be identified in the judicial approaches to the issues in *M. v. H.*? Note also that members of the court expressly stated that this case was confined to issues about spousal support; it was not concerned with same-sex marriage—to what extent is the analysis in *M. v. H.* relevant nonetheless to the marriage reference forwarded to the Supreme Court by the federal government?]

CORY and IACOBUCCI JJ ... The principal issue raised in this appeal is whether the definition of "spouse" in s. 29 of the *Family Law Act*, RSO 1990, c. F3 (*FLA*) infringes s. 15(1) of the *Canadian Charter of Rights and Freedoms*, and, if so, whether the legislation is nevertheless saved by s. 1 of the *Charter*. In addition, M. was granted leave to cross-appeal on the issue of the appropriate remedy to be granted and also as to costs.

Our view on this principal issue may be summarized as follows. Section 15(1) of the *Charter* is infringed by the definition of "spouse" in s. 29 of the *FLA*. This definition, which only applies to Part III of the *FLA*, draws a distinction between individuals in conjugal, opposite-sex relationships of a specific degree of duration and individuals in conjugal, same-sex relationships of a specific degree of duration. We emphasize that the definition of "spouse" found in s. 1(1) of the *FLA*, and which applies to other parts of the *FLA*, includes only married persons and is not at issue in this appeal. Essentially, the definition of "spouse" in s. 29 of the *FLA* extends the obligation to provide spousal support, found in Part III of the *FLA*, beyond married persons to include individuals in conjugal opposite-sex relationships of some permanence. Same-sex relationships are capable of being both conjugal and lengthy, but individuals in such relationships are nonetheless denied access to the court-enforced system of support provided by the *FLA*. This differential treatment is on the basis of a personal characteristic, namely sexual orientation, that, in previous jurisprudence, has been found to be analogous to those characteristics specifically enumerated in s. 15(1).

The crux of the issue is that this differential treatment discriminates in a substantive sense by violating the human dignity of individuals in same-sex relationships. As *Law v. Canada (Minister of Employment and Immigration)*, [1999] SCJ No. 12 (QL) established, the inquiry into substantive discrimination is to be undertaken in a purposive and contextual manner. In the present appeal, several factors are important to consider. First, individuals in same-sex relationships face significant pre-existing disadvantage and vulnerability, which is exacerbated by the impugned legislation. Second, the legislation at issue fails to take into account the claimant's actual situation. Third, there is no compelling argument that the ameliorative purpose of the legislation does anything to lessen the charge of discrimination in this case. Fourth, the nature of the interest affected is fundamental, namely the ability to meet basic financial needs following the breakdown of a relationship characterized by intimacy and economic dependence. The exclusion of same-sex partners from the benefits of the spousal support scheme implies that they are judged to be incapable of forming intimate relationships of economic interdependence, without regard to their actual circumstances. Taking these factors into account, it is clear that the human dignity of individuals in same-sex relationships is violated by the definition of "spouse" in s. 29 of the *FLA*.

This infringement is not justified under s. 1 of the *Charter* because there is no rational connection between the objectives of the spousal support provisions and the means chosen to further this objective. The objectives were accurately identified by Charron JA, in the court below, as providing for the equitable resolution of economic disputes when intimate relationships between financially interdependent individuals break down, and alleviating the burden on the public purse to provide for dependent spouses. Neither of these objectives is furthered by the exclusion of individuals in same-sex couples from the spousal support regime. If anything, these goals are undermined by this exclusion.

In this case, the remedy of reading in is inappropriate, as it would unduly recast the legislation, and striking down the *FLA* as a whole is excessive. Therefore the appropriate remedy is to declare s. 29 of no force and effect and to suspend the application of the declaration for a period of six months. ...

[Cory J set out the factual background and the provisions of the *Family Law Act* and the *Divorce Act*, as well as a resumé of the decisions of the motions judge and the Ontario Court of Appeal. The court decided that the issue was not moot because even though M. and H. had settled their dispute, "the social cost of leaving this matter undecided would be significant." Cory J then considered the application of *Law* to the interpretation of s. 15 and reviewed the structure of the *Family Law Act* in terms of differential treatment.]

In *Law*, Iacobucci J reviewed various articulations of the proper approach to be taken in analyzing a s. 15(1) claim, as expressed in the jurisprudence of this Court. At para. 39, he summarized the basic elements of this Court's approach as involving three broad inquiries, in the following terms:

In my view, the proper approach to analyzing a claim of discrimination under s. 15(1) of the *Charter* involves a synthesis of these various articulations. Following upon the analysis in *Andrews* ... [[1989] 1 SCR 143] and the two-step framework set out in *Egan* ... [[1995] 2 SCR 513] and *Miron* ... [[1995] 2 SCR 418], among other cases, a court that is called upon to determine a discrimination claim under s. 15(1) should make the following three broad inquiries. First, does the impugned law (a) draw a formal distinction between the claimant and others on the basis of one or more personal characteristics, or (b) fail to take into account the claimant's already disadvantaged position within Canadian society resulting in substantively differential treatment between the claimant and others on the basis of one or more personal characteristics? If so, there is differential treatment for the purpose of s. 15(1). Second, was the claimant subject to differential treatment on the basis of one or more of the enumerated and analogous grounds? And third, does the differential treatment discriminate in a substantive sense, bringing into play the *purpose* of s. 15(1) of the Charter in remedying such ills as prejudice, stereotyping, and historical disadvantage? [Emphasis in original.] ...

The definition [in s. 29] clearly indicates that the legislature decided to extend the obligation to provide spousal support *beyond* married persons. Obligations to provide support were no longer dependent upon marriage. The obligation was extended to include those relationships which:

 (i) exist between a man and a woman;

 (ii) have a specific degree of permanence;

 (iii) are conjugal.

Only individuals in relationships which meet these minimum criteria may apply for a support order under Part III of the *FLA*.

Same-sex relationships are capable of meeting the last two requirements. Certainly same-sex couples will often form long, lasting, loving and intimate relationships. The choices they make in the context of those relationships may give rise to the financial dependence of one partner on the other. Though it might be argued that same-sex couples do not live together in "conjugal" relationships, in the sense that they cannot "hold themselves out" as husband and wife, on this issue I am in agreement with the reasoning and conclusions of the majority of the Court of Appeal.

Molodowich v. Penttinen (1980), 17 RFL (2d) 376 (Ont. Dist. Ct.) sets out the generally accepted characteristics of a conjugal relationship. They include shared shelter, sexual and personal behaviour, services, social activities, economic support and children, as well as the societal perception of the couple. However, it was recognized that these elements may be present in varying degrees and not all are necessary for the relationship to be found to be conjugal. While it is true that there may not be any consensus as to the societal perception of same-sex couples, there is agreement that same-sex couples share many other "conjugal" characteristics. In order to come within the definition, neither opposite-sex couples nor same-sex couples are required to fit precisely the traditional marital model to demonstrate that the relationship is "conjugal."

Certainly an opposite-sex couple may, after many years together, be considered to be in a conjugal relationship although they have neither children nor sexual relations.

Obviously the weight to be accorded the various elements or factors to be considered in determining whether an opposite-sex couple is in a conjugal relationship will vary widely and almost infinitely. The same must hold true of same-sex couples. Courts have wisely determined that the approach to determining whether a relationship is conjugal must be flexible. This must be so, for the relationships of all couples will vary widely. In these circumstances, the Court of Appeal correctly concluded that there is nothing to suggest that same-sex couples do not meet the legal definition of "conjugal."

Since gay and lesbian individuals are capable of being involved in conjugal relationships, and since their relationships are capable of meeting the *FLA*'s temporal requirements, the distinction of relevance to this appeal is between persons in an opposite-sex, conjugal relationship of some permanence and persons in the same-sex, conjugal relationship of some permanence. In this regard, I must disagree with the dissenting opinion in the court below, which characterized the distinction arising in s. 29 as being between opposite-sex and same-sex *couples*. This conclusion would require that the section be scrutinized for any discriminatory impact it may have on same-sex couples, and not on the individual members of that couple. Section 29 defines "spouse" as "*either* of a man and a woman" who meet the other requirements of the section. It follows that the definition could not have been meant to define a couple. Rather it explicitly refers to the *individual* members of the couple. Thus the distinction of relevance must be between individual persons in a same-sex, conjugal relationship of some permanence and individual persons in an opposite-sex, conjugal relationship of some permanence. ...

[Cory J determined that sexual orientation was an analogous ground for s. 15 and then considered how there was discrimination here "in a purposive sense."]

In *Law*, Iacobucci J explained that there are a variety of contextual factors that may be referred to by a s. 15(1) claimant in order to demonstrate that legislation demeans his or her dignity. The list of factors is not closed, and there is no specific formula that must be considered in every case. In *Law* itself, Iacobucci J listed four important contextual factors in particular which may influence the determination of whether s. 15(1) has been infringed. He emphasized, at paras. 59-61, that in examining these contextual factors, a court must adopt the point of view of a reasonable person, in circumstances similar to those of the claimant, who takes into account the contextual factors relevant to the claim.

One factor which may demonstrate that legislation that treats the claimant differently has the effect of demeaning the claimant's dignity is the existence of pre-existing disadvantage, stereotyping, prejudice, or vulnerability experienced by the individual or group at issue. As stated by Iacobucci J in *Law*, *supra*, at para. 63:

> As has been consistently recognized throughout this Court's jurisprudence, probably the most compelling factor favouring a conclusion that differential treatment imposed by legislation is truly discriminatory will be, where it exists, pre-existing disadvantage, vulnerability, stereotyping or prejudice experienced by the individual or group [citations omitted]. These factors are relevant because, to the extent that the claimant is already subject to unfair circumstances or treatment in society by virtue of personal

characteristics or circumstances, persons like him or her have often not been given equal concern, respect, and consideration. It is logical to conclude that, in most cases, further differential treatment will contribute to the perpetuation or promotion of their unfair social characterization, and will have a more severe impact upon them, since they are already vulnerable.

In this case, there is significant pre-existing disadvantage and vulnerability, and these circumstances are exacerbated by the impugned legislation. The legislative provision in question draws a distinction that prevents persons in a same-sex relationship from gaining access to the court-enforced and -protected support system. This system clearly provides a benefit to unmarried heterosexual persons who come within the definition set out in s. 29, and thereby provides a measure of protection for their economic interests. This protection is denied to persons in a same-sex relationship who would otherwise meet the statute's requirements, and as a result, a person in the position of the claimant is denied a benefit regarding an important aspect of life in today's society. Neither common law nor equity provides the remedy of maintenance that is made available by the *FLA*. The denial of that potential benefit, which may impose a financial burden on persons in the position of the claimant, contributes to the general vulnerability experienced by individuals in same-sex relationships. ...

[Cory J also examined the other contextual factors—the correspondence (or lack of it) between the ground of the claim and the actual need, capacity, or circumstances of the claimant; whether the impugned legislation has an ameliorative purpose or effect for a group historically disadvantaged in the context of the legislation; and the nature of the interest affected by the impugned legislation; whether the distinction restricts access to a fundamental social institution, affects a basic aspect of full membership in Canadian society, or constitutes a complete non-recognition of a particular group. He continued:]

The societal significance of the benefit conferred by the statute cannot be overemphasized. The exclusion of same-sex partners from the benefits of s. 29 of the *FLA* promotes the view that M., and individuals in same-sex relationships generally, are less worthy of recognition and protection. It implies that they are judged to be incapable of forming intimate relationships of economic interdependence as compared to opposite-sex couples, without regard to their actual circumstances. As the intervener EGALE submitted, such exclusion perpetuates the disadvantages suffered by individuals in same-sex relationships and contributes to the erasure of their existence. ...

[Accordingly, Cory J concluded that the definition of spouse in s. 29 violated s. 15(1) of the Charter. In reviewing the application of s. 1, Iacobucci J then identified the "redefinition of our democracy" brought about by the Charter (as stated in *Vriend*) and considered the "pressing and substantial objective" test in the context of the Preamble of the *Family Law Act*, reports of the Ontario Law Reform Commission (OLRC), and cases such as *Moge v. Moge* and continued:]

My colleague, Bastarache J, argues that the Court of Appeal had no basis for determining that "intimacy" is part of the purpose of s. 29 of the *FLA* (at para. 347).

With respect, I disagree. Section 29 refers to individuals who have "cohabited." Section 1(1), as noted by Cory J at para. 56, defines "cohabit" as "to live together in a conjugal relationship, whether within or outside marriage." The accepted characteristics of a conjugal relationship, as outlined by Cory J at para. 59, go to the core of what we would generally refer to as "intimacy." ...

[Iacobucci J specifically addressed the arguments of the appellant:]

[The appellant's] argument is that a proper consideration of the exclusion of same-sex couples from the definition of "spouse" in s. 29 of the *FLA* reduces the apparent scope of the objective furthered by that provision. The appellant made two arguments in this regard. First, the appellant argued that the *FLA* is a remedial statute designed to address the power imbalance that continues to exist in many opposite-sex relationships. Thus, it was submitted that the inclusion of same-sex couples in a scheme established to deal with problems that are not typical of their relationships is inappropriate. Further, the appellant asserted that where persons fall outside the rationale for which a benefit was established, the legislature is justified in withholding it from those persons.

With respect, I disagree with these submissions. ...

I endorse the description of the objectives of the impugned provisions provided by Charron JA in the court below. These objectives are consonant with the overall scheme of the *FLA* and are not plausibly reinterpreted through examining the omission of same-sex spouses. Providing for the equitable resolution of economic disputes when intimate relationships between financially interdependent individuals break down and alleviating the burden on the public purse to provide for dependent spouses are to my mind pressing and substantial objectives. These objectives promote both social justice and the dignity of individuals—values Dickson CJ identified in *Oakes* ... [[1986] 1 SCR 103], at p. 136, as values underlying a free and democratic society. ...

[Iacobucci J then considered the proportionality test:]

Even if I were to accept that Part III of the Act is meant to address the systemic sexual inequality associated with opposite-sex relationships, the required nexus between this objective and the chosen measures is absent in this case. In my view, it defies logic to suggest that a gender-neutral support system is rationally connected to the goal of improving the economic circumstances of heterosexual women upon relationship breakdown. In addition, I can find no evidence to demonstrate that the exclusion of same-sex couples from the spousal support regime of the *FLA* in any way furthers the objective of assisting heterosexual women. ... [It] is important to recall that the ability to make a claim for spousal support does not automatically translate into a support order. To the extent that *any* relationship is characterized by more or less economic dependence, this will affect the amount and duration, if any, of an award under s. 33(9) of the *FLA*. Thus, it is no answer to say that same-sex couples should not have access to the spousal support scheme because their relationships are typically more egalitarian. In the case at bar, the respondent does not seek a support order, but rather only access to the support structure provided by the Act. ...

No evidence has been supplied to support the notion that the exclusion of same-sex couples from the spousal support regime furthers the objective of providing for the equitable resolution of economic disputes that arise upon the breakdown of financially interdependent relationships. Similarly, it is nonsensical to suggest that the goal of reducing the burden on the public purse is advanced by limiting the right to make private claims for support to heterosexuals. The impugned legislation has the deleterious effect of driving a member of a same-sex couple who is in need of maintenance to the welfare system and it thereby imposes additional costs on the general taxpaying public.

If anything, the goals of the legislation are undermined by the impugned exclusion. Indeed, the *inclusion* of same-sex couples in s. 29 of the *FLA* would better achieve the objectives of the legislation while respecting the Charter rights of individuals in same-sex relationships. ...

[Thus, Iacobucci J concluded that there was no rational connection between the exclusion of same-sex couples from s. 29 and the objectives of the spousal support provisions of the statute. In addition, he concluded that the legislation failed the test of minimal impairment, and thus could not be saved pursuant to s. 1 of the Charter. Iacobucci J thus concluded that s. 29 of the *Family Law Act* should be severed from the statute and declared of no force or effect; he suspended the remedy for six months.]

GONTHIER J [dissenting]: ... The disagreement in this appeal arises from differing views on the purpose of the legislation. Cory and Iacobucci JJ ascribe a purpose to s. 29 of the *FLA* that centres on the interdependency of "intimate" relationships which they refer to as "conjugal" relationships of a specific degree of duration. In contrast, Bastarache J believes that this legislation deals with individuals in "permanent and serious" relationships which cause or enhance economic disparity between the partners. In my opinion, this legislation seeks to recognize the specific social function of opposite-sex couples in society, and to address a *dynamic* of dependence unique to both men and women in opposite-sex couples that flows from three basic realities. First, this dynamic of dependence relates to the biological reality of the opposite-sex relationship and its unique potential for giving birth to children and its being the primary forum for raising them. Second, this dynamic relates to a unique form of dependence that is unrelated to children but is specific to heterosexual relationships. And third, this dynamic of dependence is particularly acute for women in opposite-sex relationships, who suffer from pre-existing economic disadvantage as compared with men. Providing a benefit (and concomitantly imposing a burden) on a group that uniquely possesses this social function, biological reality and economic disadvantage, in my opinion, is not discriminatory. Although the legislature is free to extend this benefit to others who do not possess these characteristics, the Constitution does not impose such a duty on that sovereign body. ...

[Gonthier J provided a detailed analysis of s. 29 of the *Family Law Act* in relation to s. 15 and concluded that there was no infringement of M.'s equality rights.]

Although in most cases, the woman in an opposite-sex relationship will be the one to suffer from the systemic dynamic of dependence, this will not always be the case.

As I discussed above, as women's economic situation improves, more claims will likely be brought by men in the future. However, I emphasize that while women are the *primary* group who suffer from this dynamic of dependence, they are not the *exclusive* group. The evidence before this Court demonstrates that when the female partner is not suffering from this dynamic of dependence, the male partner often is. In 1992, for example, 25.2 percent of all married couples were characterized by the wife being the full-time wage-earner, and the husband either working part-time or not at all: Statistics Canada, *Family Expenditure in Canada 1992*, at p. 160. ... Other evidence submitted to this Court demonstrates other forms of dependency that are similarly unique to individuals in opposite-sex relationships: J.M. Lynch and M.E. Reilly, "Role Relationships: Lesbian Perspectives," *Journal of Homosexuality*, 12(2) (Winter 1985/86), 53-69, at p. 53. Although the dynamic of dependence unique to opposite-sex relationships plays out differently for men, it flows from similar facts: in essence, the dynamic of dependence reduces autonomy and increases attachment in heterosexual relationships: *ibid*, at p. 56.

These realities are captured in the status of "spouse." It is both legitimate and reasonable for the Legislative Assembly to extend special treatment to an important social institution. ...

It is *this* dynamic of dependence that the legislature has sought to address by way of Part III of the *FLA*. The question before this Court is whether the Charter compels the extension of the legislature's efforts to address this problem to long-term same-sex couples. In arguing that the Charter does just that, the respondent M. and several of the interveners contend that long-term same-sex relationships manifest many of the features of long-term opposite-sex relationships. This may well be true. But to my mind, this argument is inadequate. It fails to demonstrate that the specific feature of long-term opposite-sex relationships that the legislature has sought to address by way of Part III of the *FLA*, what I have called the dynamic of dependence, is also present in long-term same-sex relationships. Indeed, it is almost certain that it could not be, because the dependency of women in long-term opposite-sex relationships arises precisely because they are opposite-sex relationships. There is simply no evidence that same-sex couples in long-term relationships exhibit this type of dependency in any significant numbers.

Indeed, the evidence before us is to the contrary. That evidence indicates that lesbian relationships are characterized by a more even distribution of labour, a rejection of stereotypical gender roles, and a lower degree of financial interdependence than is prevalent in opposite-sex relationships: Schneider, *supra*, at p. 237. Same-sex couples are much less likely to adopt traditional sex roles than are opposite-sex couples: M. Cardell, S. Finn, and J. Marecek, "Sex-Role Identity, Sex-Role Behavior, and Satisfaction in Heterosexual, Lesbian, and Gay Male Couples," *Psychology of Women Quarterly*, 5 (Spring 1981), 488-94, at pp. 492-93. Indeed, "research shows that most lesbians and gay men actively reject traditional husband-wife or masculine-feminine roles as a model for enduring relationships": L.A. Peplau, "Lesbian and Gay Relationships," in J.C. Gonsiorek and J.D. Weinrich, eds., *Homosexuality: Research Implications for Public Policy* (1991), 177, at p. 183.

The evidence before us also indicates that partners in a lesbian couple are more likely to each pursue a career and to work outside the home than are partners in an opposite-sex couple: *ibid.*, at pp. 183-84; N.S. Eldridge and L.A. Gilbert, "Correlates of Relationship Satisfaction in Lesbian Couples," *Psychology of Women Quarterly*, 14 (1990), 43-62, at p. 44. As members of same-sex couples are, obviously, of the same sex, they are more likely than members of opposite-sex couples to earn similar incomes, because no male-female income differential is present. For the same reason, the gendered division of domestic and child-care responsibilities that continues to characterize opposite-sex relationships simply has no purchase in same-sex relationships. ...

[No] *pattern* of dependence emerges. Put another way, dependence in same-sex relationships is not systemic: it does not exhibit the gendered dependency characteristic of many cohabiting opposite-sex relationships. ...

[Major J agreed with the result proposed by Cory and Iacobucci JJ, but preferred to do so on a narrower ground:]

The purpose of s. 29 of the *Family Law Act*, RSO 1990, c. F.3 ... is to allow persons who become financially dependent on one another in the course of a lengthy "conjugal" relationship some relief from financial hardship resulting from the breakdown of that relationship. ... The exclusion of same-sex couples from the scheme to determine and redress this dependence on the basis of their sexual orientation denies them equal benefit of the law contrary to s. 15(1) of the *Charter*.

In order to dispose of this appeal it is unnecessary to consider whether other types of long-term relationships may also give rise to dependency and relief. ...

BASTARACHE J: ...

[The judgment of Bastarache J focused on the contextual factors to be considered in determining the degree of deference owed to the legislature in the s. 1 analysis. He also reviewed the social science evidence and the 1993 *Report of the Ontario Law Reform Commission*, stating:]

The preponderance of this social science evidence indicates that same-sex, particularly lesbian, relationships do not generally share the imbalance in power that is characteristic of opposite-sex couples and which causes economic dependency in the course of an intimate relationship. Moreover, the likelihood of household responsibilities becoming a strong source of interdependence and division of labour is lessened with the smaller number of children in same-sex households. Although this is not determinative on its own, it does indicate that a catalyst for dependence and division of labour within the relationship is significantly more common in opposite-sex couples than in same-sex relationships, particularly gay male relationships.

The legislative structure at issue in this case involves mandatory ascription of status, obligations and entitlements. This case is not about the right to choose to be bound by support obligations—that choice already exists within the law of contract. The cost of imposing the s. 29 regime is the reduction of the autonomy of individuals affected. It is argued that while the imposition of such a regime makes sense in the context of a situation of social inequality which itself interferes with the exercise of autonomy, the situation of gay and lesbian couples generally does not suggest that their autonomy is impaired.

On the other hand, it is important to consider that same-sex couples do not have the benefit of consensual access to the family law regime through marriage and that the obligations incurred through the importation of the regime will impose no actual costs on those same-sex partners who are in a situation of equality. The *FLA*'s support provisions affect only those relationships in which there is actual economic dependence of one partner on the other. The issue is whether relationships of dependence in one category can be differentiated from relationships of dependence in the others. ...

Society has an interest in the traditional family. The vast majority of children born in our society are born and raised in this environment, notwithstanding the development of reproductive technologies which arguably make this family form biologically unnecessary. In truth, this opposite-sex family form is a product of socialization. In recognition of the significance of the procreative and socializing role of the opposite-sex family, the modern state has created a host of inducements for this family form, in addition to the obligations between the parties which are intended to mitigate the insecurities created by traditional patterns of gender inequality and specialization.

Both the inducements, and the rights and obligations within the couple, confer an objective benefit to society by creating a regime in which opposite-sex partners will suffer the least harm by virtue of engaging in the sometimes risky enterprise of a family. Even though the institution of marriage is imbued with moral significance for many people, which is the source of their objection to the extension of any marital or quasi-marital status to same-sex couples, there is a social function performed by that legal status which grants a benefit on society, and which is typically applicable to male–female unions, given the current social context of gender inequality. To the extent that moral factors play a role in supporting an important social institution, I do not believe it is wrong for the Court to be aware of the special sensitivities of those judgments in society. Like all factors, they must necessarily be assessed in light of *Charter* values.

I am satisfied, however, that the government's legitimate interest in setting social policies designed to encourage family formation can be met without imposing through exclusion a hardship on non-traditional families. There is no evidence that the social purpose of s. 29 would be endangered by the extension in its application. In fact, the extension sought is consistent with the legislative purpose of ensuring a greater degree of autonomy and equality within the family unit. ...

[After reviewing the legislative history, Bastarache J continued:]

A scrupulous examination of the provisions of the *FLA*, including s. 29, and of the legislative debates surrounding its passage, does not suggest that there was any specific purpose behind defining the category so as to exclude same-sex couples. Rather, those debates and the text of the law indicate that the general purpose of the legislator was to confine the non-voluntarily assumed support obligations as narrowly as possible to those who actually needed the intervention of a mandatory scheme. In particular, the legislative debates focus on the disadvantaged economic position of women relative to men, the household division of labour as between women and men, and the hardships that women frequently suffer upon the breakdown of non-marital relationships of significant interdependence. I would define the legislative purpose of the definition in Part III of the *FLA* as follows: to impose support obligations upon partners in relationships in which they have consciously signalled a desire to be so bound (i.e. through marriage); and upon those partners in relationships of sufficient duration to indicate permanence and seriousness, and which involve the assumption of household responsibilities, or other career or financial sacrifices, by one partner for the common benefit of the couple, and which cause or enhance an economic disparity between the partners. I would add that there is nothing upon which, in coming to this purpose, one can rely to determine that "intimacy" is in part, or substantially, related to the purpose in question. I cannot understand why, on one hand, the Court of Appeal would extract "intimacy" as the sole criterion on which the government relied for its definition of the eligible category while, on the other, excluding the glaring reality of gender inequality which the legislative history establishes was clearly uppermost in the legislator's mind in extending benefits into the non-consensual domain. ...

[Bastarache J examined the legislative history of s. 29, particularly the rejection of the *Equality Rights Statute Law Amendment Act* by the Ontario legislature in 1994, in relation to legislative purpose, concluding:]

It can therefore be inferred that the legislature's purpose was also to exclude all types of relationships not typically characterized by the state of economic dependency apparent in traditional family relationships. ...

The appellant Attorney General insists that the exclusion is serving a valid purpose by not imposing on same-sex couples a reduction in freedom and autonomy that is mandated by economic imperatives largely irrelevant to same-sex couples. Even if one were to accept that the government's true purpose in adopting the limitation is justified for the above-mentioned reasons, there would be no rational connection between that purpose (excluding classes not generally experiencing economic imbalance because there is no need of special protection in their case and because there is no justification for limiting their freedom and autonomy) and the total exclusion dictated by s. 29. Can it be said that this exclusion assists in achieving the objective of eradicating economic dependency within families? No. The gravamen of the respondent M.'s case is that her relationship was one of dependency resulting in serious economic detriment, and that her situation falls four square within the purposes of the legislation defined by the government. In essence, the respondent M. is claiming that her equality rights have been impaired because of an underinclusive marker to define dependent family relationships, which is the government's purpose. Even though most same-sex couples do not experience economic imbalance, some do. What is the purpose in excluding them?

This exclusion is not a valid means of achieving the positive purpose of s. 29, economic equality within the family. By defining restrictively the scope of the family concept, s. 29 in effect is restricting the reach of equality. When, as here, the exclusion specifically detracts from the general legislative purpose, the objective of the restriction cannot be considered pressing and substantial. ...

Even if the primary purpose of s. 29 was simply to recognize and promote the traditional family, and not to secure economic equality within the couple, which could be considered simply a means to an end, the exclusion of same-sex partners could not be demonstrably justified. Denial of status and benefits to same-sex partners does not *a priori* enhance respect for the traditional family, nor does it reinforce the commitment of the legislature to the values in the Charter. ... As for the protection of the freedom and autonomy of persons engaged in same-sex relationships, s. 29 will only affect those who are in fact in situations of economic imbalance analogous to that which more commonly occurs in the case of heterosexual relationships. The entitlement resulting from a wider definition of "spouse" does not create an absolute right to support. The justification for interference with personal autonomy is therefore the same for same-sex partners and opposite-sex partners.

Discussion Notes

Legislative Responses to M. v. H.

Following the Supreme Court's decision in *M. v. H.*, the Ontario legislature enacted the *Amendments Because of the Supreme Court of Canada Decision in M. v. H. Act*, SO 1999, c. 6 in October 1999. The amendments affected 67 Ontario statutes, including s. 29 of the *Family Law Act*. Essentially, the amendments to the *Family Law Act* provided a definition of same-sex partner (analogous to the definition of spouse) and extended spousal entitlements to same-sex partners. Counsel for M. in *M. v. H.* suggested that the provincial legislation did not comply with the Supreme Court's decision—see the letter to the Ontario Attorney General, identifying the creation of a category of same-sex partner in the *Family Law Act* as a separate-but-equal status for gays and lesbians, a status inferior to opposite-sex relationships: see Egale Canada, Press Release, "Ontario's 'Separate and Unequal' Regime To Be Challenged in Supreme Court of Canada" (November 25, 1999), online at http://www.egale.ca/index.asp?lang.

As Cossman and Ryder reported, provincial legislative schemes differ in their recognition of same-sex relationships, with British Columbia, Ontario, Saskatchewan, and Quebec generally extending all the rights and obligations of unmarried opposite-sex cohabitees to same-sex cohabitees: see Brenda Cossman and Bruce Ryder, "What Is Marriage-Like Like? The Irrelevance of Conjugality" (2001), 18 *Canadian Journal of Family Law* 271, at 279-80. The other provinces and the three territories also recognize same-sex cohabitees, but for somewhat more limited purposes: see *Definition of Spouse Amendment Act*, SBC 2000, c. 24; SO 1999, c. 6; SS 2001, c. 50, as am. by SS 2001, c. 51, and *An Act To Amend Various Legislative Provisions Concerning de Facto Spouses*, SQ 1999, c. 14. Significantly, New Brunswick's legislation provides for spousal support obligations when two persons have lived together "in a family relationship in which one person has been substantially dependent upon the other for support," thus extending financial entitlement and responsibility beyond conjugal relationships: see *Family Services Act*, SNB 1983, c. 16, s. 112(3), as am. by SNB 2000, c. 59. Nova Scotia's legislation creates opportunities for two individuals who are cohabiting or intending to cohabit in a conjugal relationship to register as domestic partners; by doing so, the domestic partners attain access to the rights and obligations previously available only to married couples: see *Law Reform (2000) Act*, SNS 2000, c. 29, s. 45. Quebec has similarly enacted civil union legislation: see chapter 2.

In April 2000, the federal House of Commons enacted the *Modernization of Benefits and Obligations Act*, SC 2000, c. 12. This statute altered the definition of spouse in federal statutes to confer the same benefits available to opposite-sex couples to same-sex couples. The interpretation section of the statute expressly declared (in s. 1.1):

> For greater certainty, the amendments made by this Act do not affect the meaning of the word "marriage," that is, the lawful union of one man and one woman to the exclusion of all others.

Recall the discussion of this provision in the *Halpern* decision in Ontario concerning same-sex marriage. To what extent do you agree that this section simply represents a declaratory statement of the common law principle in *Hyde v. Hyde*? What arguments may support the view that this provision represents Parliamentary action with respect to the definition of marriage? How should this section be characterized by the Supreme Court in the marriage reference?

In *S.(R.) v. H.(R.)* (2000), 49 OR (3d) 451 (Sup. Ct. J), the applicant's claim for spousal support at the end of a same-sex relationship was held in abeyance pending the decision in *M. v. H.* and the enactment of the amendments in 1999. Following the decision in *M. v. H.* and the amendments, the parties litigated a number of procedural issues: see also (2000), 52 OR (3d) 152 (CA).

Other Approaches: Recommendations of the Ontario Law Reform Commission

Under the *Family Law Act*, the extended definition of spouse in s. 29 includes heterosexual cohabitees for purposes of spousal support in part III only and, after *M. v. H.*, it includes same-sex partners for these same purposes. Cohabitees, whether opposite-sex or same-sex, have no right to claim equalization (part I) or a right to the matrimonial home (part II), because the definition of spouse for these parts of the *Family Law Act* is confined to married (presumably both opposite-sex and same-sex) spouses: see s. 1(1) and chapter 6. However, cohabitees may make contracts about these matters: see *Family Law Act*, part IV.

A decade ago, the OLRC's *Report on the Rights and Responsibilities of Cohabitees* (Toronto: Ministry of the Attorney General, 1993) recommended the extension of the definition of spouse in s. 1(1) to include all heterosexual cohabitees and those same-sex couples who chose to register as domestic partners. Pursuant to these recommendations, all spouses would be entitled to the benefits and obligations of parts I and II of the statute. As a result, opposite-sex spouses would automatically be entitled to access parts I and II, a situation that may now be less compelling as a result of the Supreme Court of Canada decision in *Walsh v. Bona*, [2002] 4 SCR 325 (discussed in chapter 6). However, the OLRC recommendations distinguished same-sex couples so that the benefits and obligations of parts I and II would apply *only* to those couples who registered their intention to be considered spouses. In particular, the OLRC recommendations included (at 68-69) a revised preamble to the *Family Law Act*:

> Whereas it is desirable to *recognize and accommodate the diversity of family forms*; and whereas for that purpose it is necessary to recognize the equal position of spouses as individuals within *family relationships* and to recognize *family relationships as equal partnerships*; and whereas in support of such recognition it is necessary to provide in law for the orderly and equitable settlement of the affairs of the spouses upon the breakdown of the partnership and to provide for other mutual obligations in family relationships, including the equitable sharing by parents of responsibility for their children.

Consider this language in terms of the underlying rationales for extending s. 29 to same-sex couples, as discussed in *M. v. H.* Which approach is preferable—the court's decision in *M. v. H.* or the OLRC recommendations? What kinds of underlying assumptions support these differing approaches? Recall the discussion in *Walsh v. Bona* about the importance of choice for opposite-sex partners—note that the decision in *M. v. H.* extends access on the part of same-sex couples only to part III (spousal support) of the *Family Law Act*. Are these decisions consistent? Is it possible that the decision in *M. v. H.* constrained the Supreme Court of Canada in its consideration of *Walsh v. Bona*? What is the likely impact of these decisions about spousal status in the marriage reference?

Privatization of Economic Dependency

In relation to the issues in *M. v. H.*, Susan Boyd argued that such cases represent a trend to privatizing responsibilities for economic dependency. As she indicated:

> For some individuals, however, this option of turning to family is simply not possible—if they have no family or are alienated from family members, as lesbians and gay men all too often are. Moreover, some families do not have the economic capacity to meet the needs of their impoverished members even if they are willing.

See Susan Boyd, "Best Friends or Spouses? Privatization and the Recognition of Lesbian Relationships in M. v. H." (1996), 13 *Canadian Journal of Family Law* 321, at 336. According to Brenda Cossman, such privatization tendencies represent a convergence of neo-liberalism and neo-conservatism: see Brenda Cossman, "Family Feuds: Neo-Liberal and Neo-Conservative Visions of the Reprivatization Project," in B. Cossman and J. Fudge, eds., *Privatization, Law, and the Challenge to Feminism* (Toronto: University of Toronto Press, 2002), 169.

Rethinking the Rationale for Defining Spousal Relationships

As was evident in the judgments in *M. v. H.*, there was some disagreement about the underlying rationale for ascribing spousal status, particularly the meaning of a conjugal relationship. Thus, according to Cossman and Ryder (at 296-97):

> In *M. v. H.*, the Supreme Court has once again simply set out a wide-ranging list of factors that will have to be balanced by trial courts. The Court has given very little guidance on the question of what, if anything, makes a spousal relationship unique. Many of the seven

Molodowich factors will be met to varying degrees by most adult domestic relationships. If none is essential, what makes a spouse a spouse? What distinguishes spouses from other interdependent domestic relationships between adults? How many of the factors must co-residents meet before they are considered spouses? Are any of the seven *Molodowich* factors more important than others? The Court gives little guidance, other than to emphasize discretion, flexibility and diversity.

In this context, the authors argued that conjugality was no longer a relevant factor for defining spousal status for purposes of provincial family law statutes. Recall the recommendations of the Law Commission of Canada, *Beyond Conjugality*, discussed in chapter 2, which suggested a need to examine adult personal relationships in terms of specific legal purposes. To what extent do you agree with the conclusions of Cossman and Ryder (at 326):

> We have argued that the question of whether a relationship has a sexual component bears no connection to legitimate state objectives. Once this is recognized, and sex is removed from the scope of relational inquiries, the distinction between conjugal and non-conjugal relationships collapses. And then we need to develop better ways to determine when and how the existence of an adult personal relationship is relevant and should be recognized in law. ... To redirect inquiries to the right questions, it is necessary to reformulate relational definitions to focus more precisely on the facts relevant to the objectives of particular legislative schemes.

What are the facts relevant to the objectives of spousal support in provincial family law statutes? In thinking about this question, you may want to consider the principles of spousal support, defined by legislatures and courts in Canada—what are the connections between judicial definitions of spouse and the basic purposes of spousal support?

SELECTED REFERENCES

N. Bala and R. Jaremko Bromwich, "Context and Inclusivity in Canada's Evolving Definition of the Family" (2002), 16 *International Journal of Law, Policy, and the Family* 145.

Tamara Barclay, "Peering into the Bedrooms of the Province: An Examination of the Different Definitions of 'Spouse' in the Family Law Act and the Ontario Works Act, 1997" (2000), 15 *Journal of Law and Social Policy* 1.

Martha Fineman, *The Neutered Mother, the Sexual Family, and Other Twentieth Century Tragedies* (New York: Routledge, 1995).

Shelley A.M. Gavigan, "Legal Forms, Family Forms, Gendered Norms: What Is a Spouse?" (1999), 14:1 *Canadian Journal of Law and Society* 127.

Patricia Lefebour, "Same-Sex Spousal Recognition in Ontario: Declarations and Denials—A Class Perspective" (1993), 9 *Journal of Law and Social Policy* 272.

III. PRINCIPLES OF SPOUSAL SUPPORT

Social forces have brought about significant change in family law in Canada since 1968. The law of support consequently faces two very challenging and potentially irreconcilable tasks. First and foremost, it must strive to do justice between individual parties before it in a way that is responsive to the dynamic underlying each unique relationship. To this end, it must demonstrate sensitivity to context. Second, it must prove itself capable of evolving with, yet imparting stability to, the very institution it professes to regulate. In this sense, it must be responsive to greater social change, while nonetheless adhering to a reasonably identifiable underlying philosophy. These two divergent mandates, sensitivity to context versus consistency of principle, pose a considerable challenge to lawmakers and judges.

> Claire L'Heureux-Dubé, "Equality and the Economic Consequences of Spousal Support: A Canadian Perspective" (1994), 7 *Journal of Law and Public Policy* 1, at 38

Spousal support rights and obligations ... do not exist in a social or economic vacuum. Statutory support provisions and their judicial interpretation reflect fundamental aspects of social policy, such as the respective obligations of the individual and the State to provide financial security for economic victims of family breakdown and divorce.

> Julien D. Payne, "An Overview of Theory and Reality in the Judicial Disposition of Spousal Support Claims Under the Canadian Divorce Act" (2000), 63 *Saskatchewan Law Review* 403, at 404

As both these comments suggest, spousal support awards must meet a number of different and challenging objectives—doing justice in individual cases, providing certainty and predictability in family law principles, and balancing family and state responsibilities for post-divorce family units.

Before examining current principles for determining entitlement to spousal support, it is important to understand the historical context in which entitlement to ongoing financial support reflected the relative absence of accessible divorce, the use of fault-based grounds for granting divorce decrees, and more widespread acceptance of a gendered division of household labour. Understanding the significance of legal changes introduced in Canada by the *Divorce Act* in 1968, which made divorce widely accessible and introduced the first no-fault grounds, as well as the impact of patterns of economic activity by married women helps to explain current challenges in defining the basis for awarding spousal support.

A. Historical Perspectives on Spousal Support

American Law Institute, *Principles of the Law of Family Dissolution:*
Analysis and Recommendations
(Washington, DC: Matthew Bender, 2002), at 23-25

Alimony was originally a remedy of the English ecclesiastical courts developed at a time when complete divorce was available only by special legislative action, and gender roles in marriage were rigid and unquestioned. The husband had a legal and customary duty to support his wife. This duty continued after divorce because there was no divorce in the modern sense, but only legal separation. When judicial divorce became available in the 18th and 19th centuries, alimony remained a remedy even though its initial justification—the duty of the husband to support his wife—no longer applied. One explanation was that the duty to support his wife could not be extinguished by the husband's own misconduct. Following that rationale, some jurisdictions allowed alimony claims only by "innocent" wives divorcing "guilty" husbands. Other jurisdictions, focusing on women's financial dependency, in theory allowed claims by guilty wives as well. This view was eventually adopted by the English ecclesiastical courts from their concern that the wife might otherwise "be turned out destitute on the streets or led into temptation," the assumption being that women were limited to domestic skills and could not support themselves by employment. The traditional explanation for alimony was weakened considerably once absolute divorce was allowed, and was undermined completely by modern reforms removing fault from divorce and rejecting gender roles. Yet the financial dependency of wives continued in most marriages. On a practical level a doctrine such as alimony was believed necessary even though the law had no theory to explain it.

Unease over the continuing validity of the traditional rationale for alimony affected decisions early in the modern regime of no-fault divorce. These decisions granted only limited-duration alimony to women who had been homemakers in long-term marriages, and expressed the view that alimony's principal purpose was to provide short-term transitional assistance to such women. The inability to articulate any basis for an indefinite continuation of the husband's support obligation, and the conviction that where possible divorce should effect a "clean break" between the marital partners, combined to push the courts in this direction. The result was buttressed by the expectation that the homemaker would develop marketable skills sufficient to afford her an acceptable living standard, at least when combined with her share in the equitable distribution of their accumulated property, an entitlement which was then relatively new in many common-law states.

But these expectations were often frustrated, and this vision of alimony does not describe the law that one finds today in most appellate opinions. At least in long-term marriages one instead finds a widespread view that marital dissolution should not dissolve all financial ties between the former spouses if the result would be a significant disparity in the spouses' post-dissolution financial standing. However this apparent consensus exists only in very general terms, and has produced no dominant theory to explain the alimony award. The prevailing statutory formulation allows the court to grant alimony (now usually called "spousal support" or "maintenance") to the spouse who is in need. Neither the statutes nor the cases, however, explain why a needy person's former spouse should be liable for his or her support rather than the needy person's parents, children, or society as a whole. The result is that the meaning of "need"—the most fundamental issue created by such statutes—is hopelessly confused. Some opinions find an alimony claimant in "need" only if unable to provide for her basic necessities; others find need if the claimant is unable to support himself at a moderate middle-class level; and still others find need when the claimant is unable to sustain the living standard enjoyed during the marriage even if it was lavish.

There can be no principled basis for choosing among these definitions of need without an explanation for imposing the obligation to meet it. In fact, "need" is often used in the law as a conclusory term whose only meaning is that a court has found the spouse entitled to an award of alimony.

Carol J. Rogerson, "The Causal Connection Test in Spousal Support Law" (1989), 8 *Canadian Journal of Family Law* 95, at 105ff.

[In the Canadian context, Rogerson identified a traditional model of spousal support—the "pension for life."]

The traditional model of support law which prevailed pre-family law reform was conceptually clear and coherent. It was rooted in an understanding of marriage as an institution providing economic security for women in a society where women's labour force participation was limited. Marriage was understood as imposing an obligation on a husband to support his wife according to his means. There was no obligation on a wife to work; her obligation was to be a good wife, to remain chaste and to perform household services and child care. In the specific context of marriage breakdown, the law imposed on husbands who had committed a matrimonial fault or wished to abandon the marriage an obligation to support their blameless wives, that is wives who were innocent of any matrimonial fault at the marital standard of living for the rest of their lives (or until they remarried). The metaphor commonly attached to this model of support is the "pension for life."

The substance of the model is familiar. In order to place modern theories of spousal support in context, it is important at this point to focus on the conceptual underpinnings of the traditional model. There were two. The first was the concept of status: traditional support obligations were derived from the status of being married, and more specifically from the status of being a wife. The second relevant concept was that of contract or promise, which includes the concept of fault. Marriage was understood as a social bargain in which a woman was promised economic security for her entire life if she performed her end of the bargain. If her husband breached the contract by committing a matrimonial offense or abandoning the marriage while she remained innocent, and thus not in breach, she was entitled, under general contract principles, to her expectation interest in the form of a pension for life.

Rogerson also identified trends in the "project of reconceptualizing" the role of spousal support at marriage breakdown. As she suggested in the early 1990s, there was no clear consensus as to what should be the basis for spousal support, in part because there are many different kinds of marriages and differing views (both traditional and modern) about the nature of a marriage relationship. Rogerson also suggested that this lack of consensus is well-reflected in the provisions concerning spousal support in both provincial statutes and in the *Divorce Act*, where a number of different objectives and factors to be considered are included, not all of which are complementary and consistent with each other. In this way, the statutes provide a range of rationales for the awarding of support and the courts, not surprisingly, have responded by using those aspects that seem appropriate in a particular fact situation. However, the result is highly discretionary and there are differing views among judges in different courts about how to approach such applications.

In examining these legislative provisions, Rogerson identified (at 106-18) three models or "ways of thinking about and justifying" modern spousal support, although she also noted that they are not "pure models" and that they all interact and modify each other.

1. "Needs and means"—spousal support as an income security scheme:

   According to this model, the basic rationale for spousal support is economic need: "It is the fact of being married, combined with the existence of an economic need, which gives one an entitlement to draw on the resources of the other spouse." In this model, it is irrelevant whether or not the marriage caused the financial need. This model also assumes that it is "the primary responsibility of the family to provide a cushion of income security to those citizens who are unable to meet their own needs and this is one of the obligations which is undertaken in marriage."

   Although the needs-and-means approach does not require any particular level of support, there is some statutory authority to support the idea of spousal support being available in this model at the level of the standard of living during the marriage. Although this model is most similar to the traditional model of marriage and support, it requires an element of financial need, in addition to marriage, to bring it into consideration.

2. "Economic advantages and disadvantages of marriage"—the compensatory/loss-of-opportunity model of spousal support:

   The compensatory model of spousal support is based on the idea of compensating a spouse for "economic disadvantages which they have suffered as a result of the marriage and the economic advantages which they have conferred on the other spouse during the course of the marriage." In this model, the marriage and economic need *per se* do not justify spousal support, but rather the economic consequences that flow from the particular relationship between the spouses. As Rogerson stated: "Spousal support does not redress all needs—it only redresses needs created as a result of the marriage." This model is thus rooted in a concept of "causal connection," although Rogerson prefers the terminology of "compensatory support."

   Under this model, claims for spousal support are often based on the need to compensate a spouse (usually the wife) who has "sacrificed labour force participation in order to perform family responsibilities" for the loss of economic opportunity suffered. This model may also be used to compensate for economic disadvantage flowing from primary child-care responsibilities after divorce. As Rogerson also suggested, this model may also need to take account of the length of a marriage in quantifying the disadvantages experienced.

3. "Self-sufficiency, spousal independence, and the 'clean break' model of spousal support":

The basic idea of this model is that the law of spousal support should recognize that the marriage has ended and should encourage economic disengagement of the parties and the assumption of responsibility for their own support. This model of support may be joined with either of the other two models, but it may also exist on its own. According to Rogerson, where it exists alone, this model encourages the termination of economic ties between the spouses as quickly as possible. In this way, spousal support is seen to be for only a limited time period, as a matter of principle, and spouses are held accountable for their own support regardless of, for example, any negative consequences flowing from the marriage.

According to Rogerson in 1990, the self-sufficiency model (the idea of a clean break) was the least evident model in the legislative provisions, but it was quite frequently used in the cases. Consider what kinds of fact patterns might attract each of these models of spousal support. To what extent do they overlap with each other? You may want to reconsider these models after reviewing the cases that follow.

B. Interpreting Legislative Guidelines: Spousal Support in Court Orders and in Negotiated Agreements

1. Legislative Frameworks

The legislative framework concerning spousal support includes provisions in the federal *Divorce Act, 1985* as well as in provincial statutory regimes. In addition, the legislative language of the earlier *Divorce Act* of 1968 was substantially altered in the federal legislation of the mid-1980s, a situation that created uncertainty about the relevance of cases decided pursuant to the earlier divorce statute. Thus, under the 1968 *Divorce Act*, s. 11(1) authorized a court to make an order for lump-sum or periodic maintenance of the wife and/or children of the marriage "if it thinks it fit and just to do so having regard to the conduct of the parties and the condition, means and other circumstances of each of them." In addition, s. 11(2) provided for the variation of any such order on the same basis. As is apparent, this statutory language created wide scope for judicial discretion; in the context of fault-based divorce under the 1968 Act, conduct remained a relevant consideration for the awarding of spousal support.

By contrast, the *Divorce Act, 1985* (now s. 15.2) provided that a court may make an order for support (s. 15.2(1)), including "terms, conditions or restrictions" as it thinks fit and just (s. 15.2(3)). Section 15.2(4) provides that the court "shall take into consideration the condition, means, needs and other circumstances" of each spouse, including the length of their cohabitation, the functions each performed during cohabitation, and "any order, agreement or arrangement relating to support" of either spouse. Although the scope for judicial discretion remains broad, s. 15.2(4) expressly identifies some factors that must be taken into account. Significantly, s. 15.2(5) provides that the court "shall not take into consideration any misconduct of a spouse in relation to the marriage." Consider the differences in the language of the 1968 statute and the *Divorce Act, 1985*—to what extent are the same factors relevant? Is there any difference in the weight to be accorded to these factors?

In considering these questions, it is also important to take account of s. 15.2(6), which identifies four goals to be achieved by an order for spousal support:

- recognizing economic advantages or disadvantages arising from the marriage or its breakdown;
- apportioning financial consequences arising from child care (over and above child-support obligations);
- relieving economic hardship arising from marriage breakdown; and
- "in so far as practicable," promoting economic self-sufficiency "within a reasonable period of time."

Examine the specific language of s. 15.2(6), as paraphrased above—to what extent is there any inconsistency in these goals, as stated? What kinds of fact situations may attract goals of, for example, "relieving economic hardship" or "promoting self-sufficiency"? As will be evident from the cases that follow, courts have encountered difficulty in applying the legislative requirements of the *Divorce Act, 1985*—is the formulation of the legislative requirements for spousal support in s. 15.2 more or less discretionary than the language in s. 11 of the 1968 statute?

In addition to the statutory language in the *Divorce Act, 1985*, provincial statutes also define principles for awarding spousal support—recall that provincial statutes will apply when the parties are unmarried (either opposite-sex or same-sex) or when married part-ners have separated but neither of them has filed an application for divorce. For example, s. 33 of Ontario's *Family Law Act* identifies the purposes to be achieved by an order for support (s. 33(8)), and the factors to be considered in determining the amount and duration of any order for support (s. 33(9)). In addition, s. 33(10) provides that the obligation to provide support exists "without regard to the conduct" of the spouses; however, in determining the amount of support to be ordered, a court may "have regard to a course of conduct that is so unconscionable as to constitute an obvious and gross repudiation of the relationship." Consider this language in relation to the language of s. 15.2(5) of the *Divorce Act, 1985*—are the requirements of s. 33(10) of the *Family Law Act* the same as those of s. 15.2(5) of the *Divorce Act, 1985*?

In comparing the provisions of federal and provincial legislation, it is also important to note the language relating to variation of support orders. Thus, s. 37(2) of Ontario's *Family Law Act* authorizes a court to "discharge, vary or suspend" a term of an order; relieve a payor from payment of arrears; or make any other appropriate order "if the court is satisfied that there has been a material change" in the circumstances of the payor or payee, or if there is new evidence available. Section 17(4.1) of the *Divorce Act, 1985* also provides that before making a variation of a spousal support order, a court shall satisfy itself that "a change in the condition, means, needs or other circumstances" has occurred since the making of the order and take the change into consideration in making a variation order. Consider the language of these provisions—to what extent does the difference in the language suggest the need for different tests for variation applications pursuant to the federal or Ontario provincial statutes? These questions are considered further in the context of cases interpreting spousal support obligations.

2. Principles of Spousal Support: The Divorce Act, 1968

Orders and Agreements

In addition to different models for spousal support at separation or divorce, the application of principles in practice may be affected by the property entitlements of each spouse, by the priority granted to child support under s. 15.3(1) of the *Divorce Act, 1985*, and by ideas about whether former family members or the state should have responsibility for economic vulnerability in the post-divorce family unit. In addition, of course, an award of spousal support depends on the practical availability of resources.

Canadian jurisprudence on spousal support is further complicated as a result of cases that have distinguished

- spousal support *agreed upon by the parties in a domestic contract*; and
- spousal support *awarded by a court* pursuant to provincial statutes or the *Divorce Act, 1985*.

In cases where parties have agreed on spousal support, courts have tended to respect these private agreements and encouraged parties to settle their own affairs. Thus, as will be seen in the next section, the test for setting aside such a contract to vary entitlement to spousal support is often quite strict. As well, the test of a change in circumstances, which justifies a court in making a variation of an earlier order, often appears to be stricter if the parties negotiated an initial agreement, by contrast with cases where a court has made an order for spousal support. As a result, it is important to note the *context* of spousal support awards, in addition to the complexity of goals.

Messier v. Delage

In *Messier v. Delage*, [1983] 2 SCR 401, the Supreme Court of Canada reviewed the principles of support under the *Divorce Act, 1968*. The parties were married in 1962, and separated in 1974. The wife was awarded custody of the three children, as well as child and spousal support. At that time, the wife, who had not worked outside the home during the marriage, was enrolled in a master's degree program. In 1979, the husband applied to vary the spousal support order on the ground that, although she had not yet secured employment, the wife had completed her studies and had had five years to become self-sufficient. At trial, the amount of support was reduced and a termination date was provided for payment of spousal support. The Court of Appeal reversed the decision with respect to the termination date. In the Supreme Court of Canada, Chouinard J, writing for the majority, held that the trial court had erred in disregarding the actual circumstances of the parties and that the Court of Appeal had intervened appropriately.

Lamer J (as he then was) (MacIntyre and Wilson JJ concurring) wrote a dissenting opinion, stating (at 419-21):

> In my opinion, the purpose of maintenance is to reduce in material terms the consequences resulting from breaking the marriage bond. Maintenance will be awarded to a spouse who cannot provide for her own needs. The division of functions in traditional society has meant that it is nearly always the wife who is in this position. It was almost impossible for her,

without proper training after several years of not earning her living, to find employment and so be able to provide for her own needs.

The evolution of society and the status of women both require us to re-examine what the nature of maintenance should be. Formerly, the ex-wife would, more often than not, remain a burden to her former husband indefinitely. ...

Women cannot on the one hand claim equal status without at the same time accepting responsibility for their own upkeep.

Lamer J endorsed the principles set out by the Law Reform Commission of Canada in *Maintenance on Divorce* (1975), emphasizing that support ought to be rehabilitative in nature, and that each spouse had an obligation to become self-sufficient. He then considered the facts of the case, particularly the wife's ability to work, notwithstanding that she had not secured employment. He concluded (at 426):

> In my view the evolution of society requires that one more step be taken in favour of the final emancipation of former spouses. To me, aside from rare exceptions the ability to work leads to "the end of the divorce" and the beginning of truly single status for each of the former spouses. I also consider that the "ability" to work should be determined intrinsically and should not in any way be determined in light of factors extrinsic to the individual, such as the labour market and the economic situation.
>
> As maintenance is only granted for so long as it takes to acquire sufficient independence, once that independence has been acquired it follows that maintenance ceases to be necessary. A divorced spouse who is "employable" but unemployed is in the same position as other citizens, men or women, who are unemployed. The problem is a social one and it is therefore the responsibility of the government rather than the former husband. Once the spouse has been retrained, I do not see why the fact of having been married should give the now single individual any special status by comparison with any other unemployed single person. In my view, the duty of a former spouse is limited in the case of retrainable persons to the retraining period and the discretion conferred on the judge in s. 11(2) to determine what is fit and just is not a bar to this conclusion, which the evolution of society has now made necessary. The rule is not absolute and remedy under s. 11(2) is never completely excluded to compensate for the financial negative effects of the marriage, but I would only make exception to it in, to use the words of Bergeron J, "very special circumstances." That is not the case here.

The Trilogy: Pelech, Richardson, and Caron

In 1987, the Supreme Court of Canada considered the issue of courts' discretion to vary separation agreements and order an increase in spousal support under the *Divorce Act, 1968* in a trilogy of cases: *Pelech v. Pelech*, [1987] 1 SCR 801 (on appeal from British Columbia); *Richardson v. Richardson*, [1987] 1 SCR 857 (on appeal from Ontario); and *Caron v. Caron*, [1987] 1 SCR 892 (on appeal from Yukon Territory). In all three cases, the Supreme Court of Canada was considering the interpretation of s. 11 of the 1968 *Divorce Act*, even though the new Act (*Divorce Act, 1985*) was in effect by the time these cases were decided. And while the question of spousal support arose within each of these three cases as part of a more specific issue about the scope for varying separation agreements, the causal-connection test articulated by the Supreme Court of Canada has had much broader implications for the law of spousal support.

In *Pelech v. Pelech*, the parties were married for 15 years and had two children. During the marriage, Mr. Pelech ran a general contracting business (which expanded during the course of the marriage), while Mrs. Pelech worked as a bookkeeper and receptionist for the first 10 years or so of the couple's marriage. At the time of separation, the parties, having each obtained independent legal advice, signed a settlement agreement. Under the agreement, Mrs. Pelech received a lump sum, payable over 13 months, in full satisfaction of her maintenance. She also transferred to Mr. Pelech one share that she held in his business. The settlement agreement was incorporated into the divorce decree and the husband paid the money as agreed. At the time of the divorce, Mrs. Pelech was 37 years old and Mr. Pelech was 44.

During the years following the divorce, Mrs. Pelech's physical and mental state deteriorated to the point that she was unable to work full-time and she was forced to draw on her settlement fund in order to survive; by 1982, the fund was completely depleted and Mrs. Pelech was on welfare. Mr. Pelech's position, on the other hand, had improved significantly—at the time of the divorce, his net worth was $128,000; in the 15 years since the divorce, his net worth had grown to $1,800,000. Mrs. Pelech applied under s. 11(2) of the *Divorce Act* (1968) to vary the terms of the parties' separation agreement.

The trial judge allowed the application and ordered Mr. Pelech to pay $2,000 per month to Mrs. Pelech, having regard to Mr. Pelech's resources and the need to avoid having Mrs. Pelech become a burden on the "public purse." Mr. Pelech appealed the decision to the BC Court of Appeal, which overturned the trial decision and held that the parties should be bound by their agreement. Mrs. Pelech appealed to the Supreme Court of Canada, which dismissed her appeal, upholding the decision of the Court of Appeal.

Madam Justice Wilson, writing for the majority of the court (La Forest J wrote a separate, concurring decision), reviewed the authority for an appellate court's review and concluded that a broad jurisdiction existed. Wilson J then focused on the court's jurisdiction to vary a maintenance order under s. 11(2) of the 1968 *Divorce Act*. Within this analysis, she identified three major approaches:

1. The first, the private-choice approach, was used in the Ontario Court of Appeal decision in *Farquar v. Farquar* (1983), 35 RFL (2d) 287. There, the court emphasized individual responsibility and freedom of contract and held that it is preferable for parties to settle their own affairs, specifically, for three distinct reasons. The first is that the parties are more likely to accept and live with an arrangement they have made themselves, as opposed to one imposed on them. Second, by respecting the parties' freedom of contact, the administrative burden of the courts is relieved. And finally, treating the agreement reached by the parties as final allows them to plan their separate futures with relative peace of mind.

2. The second approach identified by Justice Wilson was that of the court's overriding power. This approach was used by the Manitoba Court of Appeal in a number of family law cases, including *Newman v. Newman* (1980), 19 RFL (2d) 122 (Man. CA). With this approach, the court asserts its supervisory role with respect to fairness, and is not constrained by the presence of a binding agreement. In

discussing this approach, Justice Wilson noted that the court often acknowledges that the existence of an agreement is an important circumstance to be considered and that finality in the ordering of post-marital obligations is a laudable objective; however, if the court finds that the agreement does not meet the court's standard of fairness or reasonableness, then the court is justified to exercise its s. 11(2) power under the *Divorce Act*.

3. The final approach that Justice Wilson identified was the compromise. This middle ground was used in *Webb v. Webb* (1984), 39 RFL (2d) 113 at the Ontario Court of Appeal; it holds that where there is an antecedent agreement, the s. 11(2) criterion of change can only be satisfied by a change of considerable magnitude.

In concluding her reasons for decision, Wilson J stated (at 849):

The need to compensate for systematic gender-based inequality advanced by Matas JA in *Ross* [(1984), 39 RFL (2d) 51] forms a counterpoint to the need for finality ... approved by Zuber JA in *Farquar* and Lambert JA in the present appeal. The Alberta Court of Appeal in *Jull* describes the tension in terms of the competing values of fairness and freedom. While I am in sympathy with Matas JA's concern, I believe that the case by case approach and the continuing surveillance by the courts over the consensual arrangements of former spouses which he advocates will ultimately reinforce the very bias he seeks to counteract. In addition, I believe that every encouragement should be given to ex-spouses to settle their financial affairs in a final way so that they can put their mistakes behind them and get on with their lives. I would, with all due respect, reject the Manitoba Court of Appeal's broad and unrestricted interpretation of the court's jurisdiction in maintenance matters. It seems to me that it goes against the main stream of recent authority, both legislative and judicial, which emphasizes mediation, conciliation and negotiation as the appropriate means of settling the affairs of the spouses when the marriage relationship dissolves.

However, as I stated at the outset, the *Hyman* principle [[1929] AC 601] that parties cannot by contract oust the jurisdiction of the court in matters of spousal maintenance is an established tenet of Canadian law. The question thus becomes the nature and extent of the constraint imposed on the courts by the presence of an agreement which was intended by the parties to settle their affairs in a final and conclusive manner. The *Webb* standard of catastrophic change (by which is meant, I believe, that the change must be "dramatic" or "radical" or "gross," not that it must be the result of a catastrophe) is one attempt to reconcile the competing values represented by *Farquar* and *Ross* and still remain within the ambit of the *Hyman* principle and the language of the statute. However, although I agree that radical change should be an important factor in a court's decision to interfere with freely negotiated minutes of settlement, by itself it provides too imprecise a standard. It fails to relate the change in any way to the fact of the marriage so as to justify attributing responsibility for it to the former spouse. Moreover, the legitimation offered in *Webb* and by Wong LJSC in the present appeal in terms of a change which negates a fundamental premise of the contract provides no guidance whatsoever in cases of totally unexpected and unanticipated misfortunes.

The approach taken by Zuber JA in *Farquar* also falls short of articulating a workable criterion by failing to identify the requisites of the "narrow range of cases." I do, however, agree with Zuber JA's emphasis on the importance of finality in the financial affairs of former spouses and that considerable deference should be paid to the right and responsibility of individuals to make their own decisions.

It seems to me that where the parties have negotiated their own agreement, freely and on the advice of independent legal counsel, as to how their financial affairs should be settled on the breakdown of their marriage, and the agreement is not unconscionable in the substantive law sense, it should be respected. People should be encouraged to take responsibility for their own lives and their own decisions. This should be the overriding policy consideration.

The test of radical change in *Webb* is an attempt to carve a fairly narrow exception to the general policy of restraint. It fails, however, in my opinion in one important particular. It makes the mere magnitude of the change the justification for the court's intervention and takes no account of whether or not the change is in any way related to the fact of the marriage. In order to impose responsibility for changed circumstances on a former spouse it seems to me essential that there must be some relationship between the change and the marriage. Matas JA hinted at this in *Ross*. In the case of a wife who has devoted herself exclusively to home and children and has acquired no working skills outside the home, this relationship is readily established. The former spouse in these circumstances should have a responsibility for a radical change in his ex-wife's circumstances generated as a consequence of her total dependency during the period of the marriage. By way of contrast, a former spouse who simply falls upon hard times through unwise investment, business adversity, or a lifestyle beyond his or her means should not be able to fall back on the former spouse, no matter how radical the change may be, simply because they once were husband and wife.

Absent some causal connection between the changed circumstances and the marriage, it seems to me that parties who have declared their relationship at an end should be taken at their word. They made the decision to marry and they made the decision to terminate their marriage. Their decisions should be respected. They should thereafter be free to make new lives for themselves without an ongoing contingent liability for future misfortunes which may befall the other. It is only, in my view, where the future misfortune has its genesis in the fact of the marriage that the court should be able to override the settlement of their affairs made by the parties themselves. Each marriage relationship creates its own economic pattern from which the self-sufficiency or dependency of the partners flows. The assessment of the extent of that pattern's post-marital impact is essentially a matter for the judge of first instance. The causal connection between the severe hardship being experienced by the former spouse and the marriage provides, in my view, the necessary legal criterion for determining when a case falls within the "narrow range of cases" referred to by Zuber JA in *Farquar*. It is this element which is missing in *Webb*. Accordingly, where an applicant seeking maintenance or an increase in the existing level of maintenance establishes that he or she has suffered a radical change in circumstances flowing from an economic pattern of dependency engendered by the marriage, the court may exercise its relieving power. Otherwise, the obligation to support the former spouse should be, as in the case of any other citizen, the communal responsibility of the state. ...

The dependency of the appellant Mrs. Pelech on social assistance is evidence of the extremity of her need. In addition, there are the observations of Wong LJSC at trial that her impoverishment is dire and her future prospects limited if not non-existent. However, although I agree with him that her present state evidences "a gross change in circumstances" since the time of the original order incorporating the minutes of settlement in 1969, no link is found by the trial judge between the change of circumstances and her former marriage to Mr. Pelech. Indeed, quite the contrary. Wong LJSC found that the psychological problems which have resulted in her inability to care for herself pre-dated the marriage and contributed to its failure. He specifically rejected the submission that they stemmed from the marriage or from the behaviour of the respondent during it.

Wong LJSC also rejected the submission that the agreement was improvident and unconscionable. He found that it was entered into freely by Mrs. Pelech on the advice of counsel and was perfectly fair at the time it was made. He found, however, that the basic premise on which it was entered into, namely that Mrs. Pelech would be able to work and support herself, had not materialized.

While I realize that Mrs. Pelech's present hardship is great, to burden the respondent with her care 15 years after their marriage has ended for no other reason than that they were once husband and wife seems to me to create a fiction of marital responsibility at the expense of individual responsibility. I believe that the courts must recognize the right of the individual to end a relationship as well as to begin one and should not, when all other aspects of the relationship have long since ceased, treat the financial responsibility as continuing indefinitely into the future. Where parties, instead of resorting to litigation, have acted in a mature and responsible fashion to settle their financial affairs in a final way and their settlement is not vulnerable to attack on any other basis, it should not, in my view, be undermined by courts concluding with the benefit of hindsight that they should have done it differently.

In *Richardson v. Richardson*, the parties separated in 1979 after 12 years of marriage. During the marriage, Mr. Richardson was a member of the Ottawa city police force; up until the birth of the couple's second child in 1974, Mrs. Richardson worked as a clerk-typist. Following the separation, Mrs. Richardson moved to North Bay to live with her parents; she was unemployed and 46-years-old. At the time of separation, Mr. Richardson was a sergeant with the police force in Ottawa and was 43 years old.

At the pre-trial conference a settlement agreement was reached. The settlement stipulated that Mrs. Richardson was to have custody of one of the children and Mr. Richardson the other. Mr. Richardson agreed to pay child support for an unlimited period and spousal support of $175 per month for one year. The parties further agreed to share responsibility of a $20,000 loan owed to Mrs. Richardson's parents; Mrs. Richardson released her share of the equity in the matrimonial home (the total was approximately $20,000); and Mr. Richardson agreed to assume responsibility for debts of the marriage (approximately $9,500). In the final version of the agreement, which both parties signed, a clause was inserted by the husband's lawyer that the settlement was final and conclusive.

Mrs. Richardson later commenced divorce proceedings. By that time, the one-year period of spousal support had expired, she had been unable to find work, and was receiving welfare. In the light of these factors, the trial judge imposed a further obligation of spousal support on Mr. Richardson. The Ontario Court of Appeal overturned the trial judge's order and held that there had been no change in circumstances to justify the order for additional spousal support.

Mrs. Richardson appealed the decision to the Supreme Court of Canada. Madam Justice Wilson, writing for the majority of the court, noted that *Richardson* differed from *Pelech* because *Richardson* required an examination of s. 11(1) of the *Divorce Act*. However, she asserted that the underlying rationale for both was the same; the only difference was that the change would have taken place earlier. On this basis, the court held that there had been no change of circumstances; the same conditions existed at the time of separation and at the time of the divorce (at both times, Mr. Richardson was a police officer earning about $40,000 and Mrs. Richardson was unemployed). The court also stated (at 868) that it was "questionable whether Mrs. Richardson's position at the time could be attributed to a pattern of economic dependency developed during the marriage" because she had worked full-time as a clerk-typist from marriage until the birth of her second child. She then worked one month in 1974 and for three months in 1976. According to the court (at 868), therefore, she was "employed more often than not during the marriage. ... In this sense, it cannot be said that the marriage atrophied her skills or impaired their marketability."

The court also rejected the appellant's argument that Mrs. Richardson's inability to obtain employment should be taken into account because, according to the court (at 872), it was not "completely outside the reasonable contemplation of the parties." Mr. Justice La Forest gave a dissenting opinion, arguing that s. 11 of the *Divorce Act* gave the court a broader discretion to revise the parties' agreement.

See also *Caron v. Caron*, the third case in the trilogy, where the court applied these same principles.

Discussion Notes

Interpreting Section 11 of the Divorce Act, 1968

Examine the wording of s. 11 of the *Divorce Act, 1968*, especially the stated criteria of "condition, means, needs and other circumstances" for purposes of awarding spousal support. Is the reasoning in *Messier* or in the *Pelech* trilogy more consistent with this language? What factors influenced Wilson J's formulation of the (narrow) test adopted in *Pelech*? What are the advantages of a clean-break approach to divorce? To the extent that Wilson J's reasoning in *Pelech* is consistent with her agreement with the dissent in *Messier*, how would you characterize her views with respect to family versus state responsibility for dependency at the end of marriage? Interestingly, Wilson J recommended state intervention to preserve a basic level of economic well-being for dependent family members in 1983: see B. Wilson, "The Variation of Support Orders," in R. Abella and C. L'Heureux-Dubé, eds., *Family Law: Dimensions of Justice* (Toronto: Butterworths, 1983).

The Clean-Break Approach and Spousal-Equality Goals

The reasoning in the *Pelech* trilogy was criticized by a number of commentators. For example, Martha Bailey argued that the clean-break philosophy failed to acknowledge substantive inequality between former wives and husbands:

> The clean break philosophy relieves men, who are almost always the payors, from continuing support obligations, and enables them to form (and abandon) new relationships without on-going financial burdens. Women are disadvantaged by the emphasis on self-sufficiency and a clean break insofar as their true condition of continuing economic inequality is not addressed.

See Martha Bailey, "Pelech, Caron, and Richardson" (1989-90), 3 *Canadian Journal of Women and the Law* 615, at 626. According to Bailey (at 629), women often experienced relative poverty at the time of execution of a separation agreement. What factors might inhibit women's ability to attain a comfortable level of self-sufficiency post-divorce?

Consider the situation of the wife in *Richardson*, for example. In his dissenting judgment in *Richardson*, La Forest J concluded that her dependency was connected to the marriage because she had worked part-time rather than full-time for a number of years and because she had been out of the workforce to care for her children. Were there other factors that also limited her employability? To what extent were they connected, if at all, to the economic pattern of the marriage?

In 1990, the Department of Justice published an analysis of divorce files for a five-year period. According to this report, women requested support in only 16 percent of applications for divorce and received an award of support in only 6 percent of cases in 1988, in spite of figures that showed that women earned 60 percent of men's earnings in 1988: see Department of Justice, *Evaluation of the Divorce Act, Phase II: Monitoring and Evaluation* (Ottawa: Department of Justice, 1990), and C. Schmitz, "Women, Kids Driven into Poverty by Low Awards Under Divorce Act," *The Lawyers Weekly*, August 31, 1990, 1 and 23. Another assessment of the *Pelech* trilogy concluded:

> Thus, in the family law reform context, it seems clear that the equality concept adopted is one of formal, not substantive equality. The idea of formal equality treats husbands and wives as similarly situated with respect to financial self-sufficiency at marriage breakdown, and does not take account of actual differences in employability (because of years out of the workforce for child care responsibilities), differences in earning capacity (especially where skills may have atrophied by time out of the paid workforce), or future problems of balancing child-raising with full time employment (especially for wives who have more frequent custody of children). Moreover, it is striking that the Supreme Court of Canada adopted a concept of formal equality for spouses at marriage breakdown in the trilogy only two years before its major equality decision in *Andrews v. The Law Society of British Columbia*, a 1989 decision that recognized the limits of the "similarly situated" test and incorporated the idea of comparative "disadvantage" into the idea of equality.

(M.J. Mossman, " 'Running Hard To Stand Still': The Paradox of Family Law Reform" (1994), 17 *Dalhousie Law Journal* 5, at 24.)

Do you agree with this assessment? Why or why not?

The Impact of the Pelech Trilogy

According to Carol Rogerson, who conducted a review of cases concerning spousal support after the trilogy cases in the Supreme Court of Canada, there was a high level of diversity among lower court decisions, both in relation to the principles applied and with respect to the levels of support awarded: Carol J. Rogerson, "Judicial Interpretation of the Spousal and Child Support Provisions of the Divorce Act, 1985 (Part I)" (1992), 7 *Canadian Family Law Quarterly* 155. Rogerson suggested (at 161) that the level of diversity reflected "the absence of clear normative standards in the legislation"; this problem itself reflected "the absence of a strong social consensus on the appropriate principles of support after marriage breakdown." She further noted (at 161):

> Principles of support are ultimately rooted in social understandings of the meaning of marriage and parenthood. Those understandings are currently in a state of confusion as a result of significant social changes during the past two decades, in particular the increasing acceptance of divorce and the changing social roles of women.

Rogerson expressed concern about the unfairness of awards that could vary so greatly. As well, she reported (at 162) that her review of the cases suggested that "courts now operate under a model of support which sees the primary goal of support law as promoting the self-sufficiency of the spouses after divorce. ... This is the [objective] most frequently discussed in the reported cases." According to her analysis (at 163), older women leaving long marriages were not expected to become self-sufficient, by contrast with younger women or those in shorter marriages:

> It would appear that those suffering even more under the legislation, however, are younger women whose marriages break down when they are in their 30s and 40s, who had reduced or ceased their participation in the labour force during the marriage, and who are often left with the post-divorce responsibility for the care of the children. In these cases concepts of self-sufficiency are being given more weight, resulting in either time-limited orders or, as is more often the case, an eventual variation application by the husband to terminate what was originally an indefinite order for support. In these cases it is generally accepted that the support obligation must be brought to an end. ...
>
> The real problem in these cases is the level at which self-sufficiency is being set. One court stated it quite explicitly: self-sufficiency means full-time employment or earning $20,000 per year. A striking aspect of the case law in this area is the relatively low income levels women have achieved at the point at which they are deemed to be self-sufficient and the disparity between their income-earning positions and those of their former husbands. Courts on the whole fail to understand that while the attainment of such income levels may be understood, for social security purposes, as the achievement of self-sufficiency, it does not constitute adequate compensation for the economic losses suffered by these women who have spent the first half of their adult lives giving priority to marriage and children rather than paid employment. Furthermore, in those cases where children remain in the mother's custody, the termination of spousal support results in the indirect deprivation of children, thus undermining the objectives of child support.
>
> A final problem with respect to spousal support concerns the role of contracts. Courts have generally adopted a position of strict enforcement of contractual provisions dealing with spousal support. Admittedly in some cases women receive more generous spousal support in a negotiated settlement than they would if support had been court-ordered. However, with respect to those contracts which are the subject of subsequent dispute and which thus find their way into the law reports, there are indications of a disturbing pattern of contracts in which women have agreed to support much less generous than that which they would have been awarded by the courts. In particular, some women contractually agree to time-limited support, which, as indicated above, many courts are unwilling to impose. This suggests that lawyers negotiating contracts on behalf of wives may assume a model of

spousal support in which spousal self-sufficiency plays an even greater role than is actually accepted by the courts.

Rogerson's analysis of cases after the *Pelech* trilogy suggested that the clean-break approach, as set out in Wilson J's test for judicial intervention in privately negotiated agreements, had become the overriding goal in relation to spousal support. That is, the clean-break approach and self-sufficiency goals became the norm. Yet, at the same time, governmental income security programs were being reduced or eliminated in many parts of Canada, so that former wives and their children had little access to economic support, either from the state or from their former husbands. Not surprisingly, many became poor. As a 1992 report indicated, the breakdown of a marriage or cohabiting relationship increased substantially the risk of poverty—"for those who were married and had children, the risk of poverty rose from 3.1 per cent to 37.6 per cent after divorce or separation": see T. Lemprière, "A New Look at Poverty" (1992), 16 *Perceptions* 18, at 19-20. Consider how these circumstances were reflected in the Supreme Court's decision in *Moge v. Moge* and their influence on the court's reasoning.

SELECTED REFERENCES

Brenda Cossman, "A Matter of Difference: Domestic Contracts and Gender Equality" (1990), 28 *Osgoode Hall Law Journal* 303.

M. McCall, J. Hornick, and J. Wallace, *The Process and Economic Consequences of Marriage Breakdown* (Calgary: Canadian Research Institute for Law and the Family, 1988).

M.J. Mossman, "Family Law and Social Welfare in Canada," in J. Bernier and A. Lajoie, eds., *Family Law and Social Welfare Legislation in Canada* (Toronto: University of Toronto Press, 1986), 43.

Carol Smart, "Feminism and Law: Some Problems of Analysis and Strategy" (1986), 14 *International Journal of Sociology of Law* 109.

3. Reconsidering Principles of Spousal Support: The Divorce Act, 1985

Moge v. Moge
(1992), 145 NR 1; [1992] 3 SCR 813

[The parties were married in Poland in the mid-1950s and decided to emigrate to Canada, moving to Manitoba in 1960. There were three children. The wife had a grade 7 education and had worked briefly in Poland as a sales clerk. During the marriage, she was responsible for child care, laundry, housework, shopping, cooking, etc. She was also employed in the evenings as a cleaner from 5 to 11 p.m. The husband worked as a welder; although he claimed to be equally involved in household chores, the Manitoba Court of Appeal found that the husband did not undertake any chores at home to balance his wife's part-time work and financial contribution to the family.

The parties separated in 1973 and the wife obtained an order for custody of the children. Her husband was ordered to pay $150 per month spousal and child support.

Mrs. Moge continued to work as a cleaner and also took care of the home and the children; the older children babysat during her hours of work. In 1980, Mr. Moge filed a divorce petition and continued after the divorce to pay the same amount of spousal and child support. He remarried in 1984. Mrs. Moge was eventually laid off in 1987, when she was earning about $795 per month; she received unemployment insurance benefits of about $593. She continued to actively seek employment. At this point, Mr. Moge earned about $2,000 per month (gross) and also had some money from investments; he and his second wife had purchased a home and his second wife was also employed.

Mrs. Moge applied to vary the amount of child and spousal support. The Manitoba Court of Queen's Bench ordered a variation in the amount of $200 per month spousal and $200 per month child support, for a total of $400 per month. During the period 1987 to 1989, Mrs. Moge also worked part-time when she was able to get work. In 1989, Mr. Moge applied to vary both orders for support; the court ordered the cessation of child support and ordered that spousal support would also cease on December 1, 1989. On appeal, the Manitoba Court of Appeal allowed Mrs. Moge's appeal in part and ordered spousal support of $150 for an indefinite period. Mr. Moge appealed to the Supreme Court of Canada, citing the *Pelech* trilogy. According to his argument, his ex-wife should have become self-sufficient by now; if not, no link existed between that lack of self-sufficiency and the marriage.

In the Supreme Court of Canada, L'Heureux-Dubé J expressly rejected the broad view of the applicability of the trilogy. She continued (at para. 26):]

A careful reading of the trilogy in general and *Pelech* in particular indicates that the court has not espoused a new model of support under the Act. Rather, the court has shown respect for the wishes of persons who, in the presence of the statutory safeguards, decided to forgo litigation and settled their affairs by agreement under the 1968 *Divorce Act*. In other words, the court is paying deference to the freedom of individuals to contract. ...

[28] Professor J.D. Payne in my view best identifies the flaws of the early interpretation of the trilogy in "Further Reflections on Spousal and Child Support After Pelech, Caron and Richardson" (1989), 20 RGD 477, when he states at p. 487:

> Professor McLeod's proposed extension of *Pelech*, *Caron* and *Richardson* to nonconsensual situations and to provincial statutes as well as the new *Divorce Act, 1985*, virtually eliminates the significance of statutory criteria, whatever their form and substance, and at the same time closes the door to the wise exercise of judicial discretion that can accommodate a diverse range of economic variables on marriage breakdown or divorce.
>
> Notwithstanding the common law's recognition of a spousal agency of necessity, it must not be forgotten that current spousal support laws are of statutory origin. Furthermore, subject to overriding constitutional doctrines, the sovereignty of Parliament ... remains paramount. Judge-made law may explain, but cannot override, statute law.

In addition, there are diverse appellate rulings in Canada that endorse the view that the principles articulated in the trilogy should not be applied to nonconsensual situations. ...

[29] In light of my reading of *Pelech*, I decline to accede to Mr. Moge's argument that this court has already determined the basis on which entitlement, or continuing entitlement, to spousal support rests in the absence of a settlement agreement intended by the parties to be final under the Act.

[30] Since this case is not one which involves a final agreement entered into between the parties in order to settle the economic consequences of their divorce, I leave for another day the question of causal connection under the Act which was discussed in the trilogy in the particular context of a final settlement under the [1968] *Divorce Act*.

[31] The present appeal not only does not involve a final settlement agreement but deals specifically with a variation application following a support order at the time of divorce, a question to which I will now turn. ...

[L'Heureux-Dubé J made several preliminary observations, including rejecting Mr. Moge's argument that the *Divorce Act, 1985* espoused a self-sufficiency model as the only basis for spousal support:]

[35] The self-sufficiency model advanced by Mr. Moge has generally been predicated on the dichotomy between "traditional" and "modern" marriage. Often, in order to draw the line after which no more support will be ordered, courts have distinguished between "traditional" marriages in which the wife remains at home and takes responsibility for the domestic aspects of marital life, and "modern" ones where employment outside the home is pursued. Perhaps in recognition that, as Judge Rosalie S. Abella (now JA) wrote in "Economic Adjustment On Marriage Breakdown: Support" (1981), 4 *Fam. L Rev.* 1, at p. 4, "[i]t is hard to be an independent equal when one is not equally able to become independent," courts have frequently been more amenable to finding that "traditional" marriages survive the so-called "causal connection" test than "modern" ones. ...

[38] There are, however, many cases which do not fall easily into either category. These cases pose difficulties for courts which attempt to make assessments based on two clear stereotypes, especially when determining the question of self-sufficiency. ...

[41] Given the concerns I harbour about making a spouse's entitlement to support contingent upon the degree to which he or she is able to fit within a mythological stereotype, ... the distinction between "traditional" and "modern" marriages does not seem to me to be as useful as perhaps courts have indicated so far. While it may reflect flexibility on the part of courts and constitute an attempt to achieve fairness, I am of the view that there are much more sophisticated means which may be resorted to in order to achieve the objectives set out in the Act, a matter which I will deal with later in these reasons.

[42] The second observation I wish to make is that, in determining spousal support it is important not to lose sight of the fact that the support provisions of the Act are intended to deal with the *economic* consequences, for both parties, of the marriage or its breakdown. Marriage may unquestionably be a source of benefit to both parties that is not easily quantified in economic terms. Many believe that marriage and the family provide for the emotional, economic, and social well-being of its members. It

may be the location of safety and comfort, and may be the place where its members have their most intimate human contact. Marriage and the family act as an emotional and economic support system as well as a forum for intimacy. In this regard, it serves vital personal interests, and may be linked to building a "comprehensive sense of personhood." Marriage and the family are a superb environment for raising and nurturing the young of our society by providing the initial environment for the development of social skills. These institutions also provide a means to pass on the values that we deem to be central to our sense of community.

[43] Conversely, marriage and the family often require the sacrifice of personal priorities by both parties in the interests of shared goals. All of these elements are of undeniable importance in shaping the overall character of a marriage. Spousal support in the context of divorce, however, is not about the emotional and social benefits of marriage. Rather, the purpose of spousal support is to relieve *economic* hardship that results from "marriage or its breakdown." Whatever the respective advantages to the parties of marriage in other areas, the focus of the inquiry when assessing spousal support after the marriage has ended must be the effect of the marriage in either impairing or improving each party's economic prospects.

[44] This approach is consistent with both modern and traditional conceptions of marriage inasmuch as marriage is, among other things, an economic unit which generates financial benefits (see M.A. Glendon, *The New Family and The New Property* (1981)). The Act reflects the fact that in today's marital relationships, partners should expect and are entitled to share those financial benefits.

[45] Equitable distribution can be achieved in many ways: by spousal and child support, by the division of property and assets or by a combination of property and support entitlements. But in many if not most cases, the absence of accumulated assets may require that one spouse pay support to the other in order to effect an equitable distribution of resources. This is precisely the case here, as the parties are not wealthy; for the most part, all they appear to possess are their respective incomes. ...

[47] A third point worthy of emphasis is that this analysis applies equally to both spouses, depending on how the division of labour is exercised in a particular marriage. What the Act requires is a fair and equitable distribution of resources to alleviate the economic consequences of marriage or marriage breakdown for both spouses, regardless of gender. The reality, however, is that in many if not most marriages, the wife still remains the economically disadvantaged partner. There may be times where the reverse is true and the Act is equally able to accommodate this eventuality.

[48] These caveats having been made, the question of spousal support which lies at the heart of this appeal must be dealt with first by examining the objectives of the Act. ...

[L'Heureux-Dubé J recognized that the interpretation of ss. 15 (now 15.2) and 17 of the *Divorce Act, 1985* required a different analysis than the interpretation of sections of the previous divorce legislation, and continued:]

[51] I fully agree with Professor Payne who has commented on these objectives in *Payne on Divorce* (2nd ed. 1988), at p. 101, that:

Judicial implementation of the newly defined policy objectives should, to some degree, result *in a shift from the narrow perspective of a "needs" and "capacity to pay" approach*, particularly in cases where one of the spouses has substantial means. ... In this context, it should be observed that the four policy objectives defined in the *Divorce Act, 1985* are not necessarily independent of each other. They may overlap or they may operate independently, depending upon the circumstances of the particular case. *Legislative endorsement of four policy objectives manifests the realization that the economic variables of marriage breakdown and divorce do not lend themselves to the application of any single objective.* Long-term marriages that ultimately break down often leave in their wake a condition of financial dependence, because the wives have assumed the role of full-time home-makers. The legitimate objective(s) of spousal support in such a case will rarely coincide with the objectives that should be pursued with respect to short-term marriages. Childless marriages cannot be treated in the same way as marriages with dependent children. The two-income family cannot be equated with the one-income family. A "clean break" accommodated by an order for a lump sum in lieu of periodic spousal support can often provide a workable and desirable solution for the wealthy, for the two-income family and for the childless marriages of short duration. Rehabilitative support orders by way of periodic spousal support for a fixed term may be appropriate where there is a present incapacity to pay a lump sum and the dependent spouse can reasonably be expected to enter or re-enter the labour force within the foreseeable future. *Continuing periodic spousal support orders may provide the only practical solution for dependent spouses who cannot be reasonably expected to achieve economic self-sufficiency. There can be no fixed rules*, however, whereby particular types of orders are tied to the specific objective(s) sought to be achieved. In the final analysis, the court must determine the most appropriate kind(s) of order, having regard to the attendant circumstances of the case, including the present and prospective financial well-being of both the spouses and their dependent children. ... [Emphasis added.]

[52] All four of the objectives defined in the Act must be taken into account when spousal support is claimed or an order for spousal support is sought to be varied. No single objective is paramount. The fact that one of the objectives, such as economic self-sufficiency, has been attained does not necessarily dispose of the matter. ... "Section 17(7) of the Act recognizes that each former spouse shall attain economic self-sufficiency, insofar as practicable, within a reasonable period of time, but it does not say that such economic self-sufficiency is the dominant consideration." ...

[53] Many proponents of the deemed self-sufficiency model effectively elevate it to the pre-eminent objective in determining the right to quantum and duration of spousal support. In my opinion, this approach is not consonant with proper principles of statutory interpretation. The objective of self-sufficiency is only one of several objectives enumerated in the section and, given the manner in which Parliament has set out those objectives, I see no indication that any one is to be given priority. Parliament, in my opinion, intended that support reflect the diverse dynamics of many unique marital relationships. ...

[54] It is also imperative to realize that the objective of self-sufficiency is tempered by the caveat that it is to be made a goal only "insofar as is practicable." This

qualification militates against the kind of "sink or swim" stance upon which the deemed self-sufficiency model is premised.

[55] That Parliament could not have meant to institutionalize the ethos of deemed self-sufficiency is also apparent from an examination of the social context in which support orders are made. In Canada, the feminization of poverty is an entrenched social phenomenon. Between 1971 and 1986 the percentage of poor women found among all women in this country more than doubled. During the same period the percentage of poor among all men climbed by 24 percent. The results were such that by 1986, 16 percent of all women in this country were considered poor: M. Gunderson, L. Muszynski, and J. Keck, *Women and Labour Market Poverty* (1990), at p. 8.

[56] Given the multiplicity of economic barriers women face in society, decline into poverty cannot be attributed entirely to the financial burdens arising from the dissolution of marriage: J.D. Payne, "The Dichotomy Between Family Law and Family Crises on Marriage Breakdown" (1989), 20 RGD 109, at pp. 116-117. However, there is no doubt that divorce and its economic effects are playing a role. ...

[L'Heureux-Dubé J referred to the research of Lenore Weitzman in the United States and continued:]

[57] The picture in Canada seems to follow a similar pattern. In the federal Department of Justice (Bureau of Review), *Evaluation of the Divorce Act—Phase II: Monitoring and Evaluation*, it was found, based on client interviews that, following divorce, 59 percent of women and children surveyed fell below the poverty line, a figure that dropped to 46 percent when support was included in the calculation of their incomes (see pp. 92-93). However, a more realistic picture, as it is not restricted to the more affluent segment of the divorcing public, is probably revealed by an analysis of court files, which determined that in 1988, overall two-thirds of divorced women had total incomes which placed them below the poverty line. When support was excluded, 74 percent of divorced women fell below the poverty line (see pp. 94-95). It is apparent that support payments, even assuming they are paid, are making only a marginal contribution to reducing economic hardship among women following divorce. In contrast, a previous study released in 1986, *Evaluation of the Divorce Act—Phase I: Monitoring and Evaluation*, found that only 10 percent of men were below the poverty line after paying support, and the average income was $13,500 above the poverty line in such one-person households after the payment of support.

[58] Other studies confirm the trend. According to Statistics Canada, "Alimony and child support," in *Perspectives on Labour and Income* (Summer 1992), 8, at p. 18, the per capita income of those paying support in 1988 was $25,800 while the per capita income of those receiving it in the same year was $10,500. ...

[62] As Lamer CJ stated in *Multiform Manufacturing Co. Ltd. et al. v. R et al.*, [1990] 2 SCR 624; 113 NR 373; 32 QAC 241, at p. 630 SCR, "[w]hen the courts are called upon to interpret a statute, their task is to discover the intention of Parliament." ...

[63] It would be perverse in the extreme to assume that Parliament's intention to enacting the Act was to financially penalize women in this country. And, while it would undeniably be simplistic to identify the deemed self-sufficiency model of spousal

support as the sole cause of the female decline into poverty, based on the review of the jurisprudence and statistical data set out in these reasons, it is clear that the model has disenfranchised many women in the courtroom and countless others who may simply have decided not to request support in anticipation of their remote chances of success. The theory, therefore, at a minimum, is contributing to the problem. ...

[64] In the result, I am respectfully of the view that the support model of self-sufficiency which Mr. Moge urges the court to apply, cannot be supported as a matter of statutory interpretation, considering in particular the diversity of objectives set out in the Act. ...

[65] A burgeoning body of doctrine and, to some extent, jurisprudence is developing both abroad as well as in Canada which expresses dissatisfaction with the current norms along which entitlement to spousal support is assessed. This body of doctrine in particular proposes instead a scheme based on principles of compensation. ...

[67] The theory, however, is not new, as is evident from the Law Reform Commission Working Papers and Report, 1972-1976. Antecedents of the compensatory spousal support model may be found in portions of the Law Reform Commission of Canada's Working Paper 12, *Maintenance on Divorce* (1975). The Commission recommended, inter alia, that the mere fact of marriage not create a right of maintenance and that the economic disabilities incurred due to marriage and the eventuality of children be compensated. ...

[68] Legislative support for the principles of compensation may be found in ss. 15(7)(a)-(c) and 17(7)(a)-(c) which are extremely broad in scope and which direct the court, in making or varying a support order, to recognize any economic advantages or disadvantages arising from the marriage or its breakdown, to apportion between the spouses any financial consequences arising from the care of children over and above those consequences which have already been made the subject of child support and to relieve economic hardships arising from the marriage. As a matter of statutory interpretation, it is precisely the manner in which compensatory spousal support is able to respond to the diversity of objectives the Act contains that makes it superior to the strict self-sufficiency model.

[69] Although the promotion of self-sufficiency remains relevant under this view of spousal support, it does not deserve unwarranted pre-eminence. After divorce, spouses would still have an obligation to contribute to their own support in a manner commensurate with their abilities. (Rogerson, *Judicial Interpretation of the Spousal and Child Support Provisions of the Divorce Act, 1985 (Part I)*, supra, at p. 171.) In cases where relatively few advantages have been conferred or disadvantages incurred, transitional support allowing for full and unimpaired reintegration back into the labour force might be all that is required to afford sufficient compensation. However, in many cases a former spouse will continue to suffer the economic disadvantages of the marriage and its dissolution while the other spouse reaps its economic advantages. In such cases compensatory spousal support would require long-term support or an alternative settlement which provides an equivalent degree of assistance in light of all of the objectives of the Act. ...

[70] Women have tended to suffer economic disadvantages and hardships from marriage or its breakdown because of the traditional division of labour within that institution. Historically, or at least in recent history, the contributions made by women

to the marital partnership were nonmonetary and came in the form of work at home, such as taking care of the household, raising children, and so on. Today, though more and more women are working outside the home, such employment continues to play a secondary role and sacrifices continue to be made for the sake of domestic considerations. These sacrifices often impair the ability of the partner who makes them (usually the wife) to maximize her earning potential because she may tend to forego educational and career advancement opportunities. These same sacrifices may also enhance the earning potential of the other spouse (usually the husband) who, because his wife is tending to such matters, is free to pursue economic goals. This eventually may result in inequities. ...

[71] The curtailment of outside employment obviously has a significant impact on future earning capacity. According to some studies, the earning capacity of a woman who stays at home atrophies by 1.5 percent for each year she is out of the labour force. ... Labour force interruptions are common and this accentuates the need for compensation. One Statistics Canada report, *Family History Survey: Preliminary Findings* (1985), notes that 64 percent of Canadian women report suffering work interruptions because of parenting or domestic responsibilities. The figure for men was less than one percent (p. 26). The studies, while remaining untested, do illustrate the problems faced by women who re-enter the labour force after a period during which they stay at home to care for the family.

[72] Often difficulties are exacerbated by the enduring responsibility for children of the marriage. The spouse who has made economic sacrifices in the marriage also generally becomes the custodial parent, as custody is awarded to the wife 75 percent of the time, to both parents jointly in 13 percent of cases, and to the husband alone in less than eight percent of divorces (see *Evaluation of the Divorce Act—Phase II: Monitoring and Evaluation*, supra, at p. 101). The diminished earning capacity with which an ex-wife enters the labour force after years of reduced or nonparticipation will be even more difficult to overcome when economic choice is reduced, unlike that of her ex-husband, due to the necessity of remaining within proximity to schools, not working late, remaining at home when the child is ill, etc. The other spouse encounters none of these impediments and is generally free to live virtually wherever he wants and work whenever he wants.

[73] The doctrine of equitable sharing of the economic consequences of marriage or marriage breakdown upon its dissolution which, in my view, the Act promotes, seeks to recognize and account for both the economic disadvantages incurred by the spouse who makes such sacrifices and the economic advantages conferred upon the other spouse. Significantly, it recognizes that work within the home has undeniable value and transforms the notion of equality from the rhetorical status to which it was relegated under a deemed self-sufficiency model, to a substantive imperative. Insofar as economic circumstances permit, the Act seeks to put the remainder of the family in as close a position as possible to the household before the marriage breakdown. As Judge Abella wrote in *Economic Adjustment On Marriage Breakdown: Support*, supra, at p. 3:

> To recognize that each spouse is an equal economic and social partner in marriage, regardless of function, is a monumental revision of assumptions. It means, among other

things, that caring for children is just as valuable as paying for their food and clothing. It means that organizing a household is just as important as the career that subsidizes this domestic enterprise. It means that the economics of marriage must be viewed qualitatively rather than quantitatively.

[74] The equitable sharing of the economic consequences of marriage or marriage breakdown, however, is not a general tool of redistribution which is activated by the mere fact of marriage. Nor ought it to be. It is now uncontentious in our law and accepted by both the majority and the minority in *Messier v. Delage*, supra, at pp. 416-417 SCR, that marriage per se does not automatically entitle a spouse to support. ...

[75] The Act refers to economic advantages and disadvantages flowing from marriage *or its breakdown*. Sections 15(7)(a) and 17(7)(c) may not be characterized as exclusively compensatory. These latter paragraphs may embrace the notion that the primary burden of spousal support should fall on family members, *not* the state. In my view, an equitable sharing of the economic consequences of divorce does not exclude other considerations, particularly when dealing with sick or disabled spouses. While the losses or disadvantages flowing from the marriage in such cases may seem minimal in the view of some, the effect of its breakdown will not, and support will still be in order in most cases. We must recognize, however, as do Payne and Eichler, that family law can play only a limited role in alleviating the economic consequences of marriage breakdown. ...

[76] As economic consequences have to be shared in an equitable manner by both partners, it is my view that the Act, while envisaging compensation for the economic advantages and disadvantages of marriage or marriage breakdown, does not necessarily put the entire burden of such compensation on the shoulders of only one party. I stress here that in the discussion of spousal support one must not lose sight of the fact that the real dilemma in most cases relates to the ability to pay of the debtor spouse and the limits of support orders in achieving fair compensation and alleviating the economic burdens of the disadvantaged spouse. While the disadvantages of the kind I mention hereunder are compensable, though not necessarily automatically or fully compensated in every case, the ultimate goal is to alleviate the disadvantaged spouse's economic losses as completely as possible, taking into account all the circumstances of the parties, including the advantages conferred on the other spouse during the marriage.

[77] The four objectives set out in the Act can be viewed as an attempt to achieve an equitable sharing of the economic consequences of marriage or marriage breakdown. At the end of the day however, courts have an overriding discretion and the exercise of such discretion will depend on the particular facts of each case, having regard to the factors and objectives designated in the Act. ...

[L'Heureux-Dubé J then examined the issue of judicial discretion in ordering spousal support and concluded that it required an examination of all four objectives set out in the Act. She also identified a need to examine the financial consequences of the end of a marriage in broad terms, including issues of loss of seniority, missed promotions, and lack of access to fringe benefits such as pension entitlements and job training programs. In addition, she expressly recognized that the most significant economic consequence of marriage or marriage breakdown arises from the birth of children and it may be necessary to compensate for care of children, both during marriage and after marriage breakdown.

Quoting from *Brockie v. Brockie* (1987), 5 RFL (3d) 440 (Man. QB (Fam. Div.)); aff'd. (1987), 8 RFL (3d) 302 (Man. CA), she stated:]

> To be a custodial parent involves adoption of a lifestyle which, in ensuring the welfare and development of the child, places many limitations and burdens upon that parent. A single person can live in any part of the city, can frequently share accommodation with relatives or friends, can live in a high-rise downtown or a house in the suburbs, can do shift work, can devote spare time as well as normal work days to the development of a career, can attend night school, and in general can live as and where he or she finds convenient. A custodial parent, on the other hand, seldom finds friends or relatives who are anxious to share accommodation, must search long and carefully for accommodation suited to the needs of the young child, including play space, closeness to day care, schools and recreational facilities, if finances do not permit ownership of a motor vehicle, then closeness to public transportation and shopping facilities is important. A custodial parent is seldom free to accept shift work, is restricted in any overtime work by the day care arrangements available, and must be prepared to give priority to the needs of a sick child over the demands of an employer. After a full day's work, the custodial parent faces a full range of homemaking responsibilities including cooking, cleaning and laundry, as well as the demands of the child himself for the parent's attention. Few indeed are the custodial parents with strength and endurance to meet all of these demands and still find time for night courses, career improvement or even a modest social life. The financial consequences of all of these limitations and demands arising from the custody of the child are in addition to the direct costs of raising the child, and are, I believe, the factors to which the court is to give consideration. ...

[84] Although the doctrine of spousal support which focuses on equitable sharing does not guarantee to either party the standard of living enjoyed during the marriage, this standard is far from irrelevant to support entitlement. ... Furthermore, great disparities in the standard of living that would be experienced by spouses in the absence of support are often a revealing indication of the economic disadvantages inherent in the role assumed by one party. As marriage should be regarded as a joint endeavour, the longer the relationship endures, the closer the economic union, the greater will be the presumptive claim to equal standards of living upon its dissolution. ...

[85] In short, in the proper exercise of their discretion, courts must be alert to a wide variety of factors and decisions made in the family interest during the marriage which have the effect of disadvantaging one spouse or benefitting the other upon its dissolution. In my view, this is what the Act mandates, no more, no less.

[86] Such determination demands a complex and, in many cases, a difficult analysis. The same, of course, might be said of the evaluation of damages in contract or in tort. However, this complexity does not excuse judges from hearing relevant evidence nor from fully applying the law. ...

[87] Given the principles outlined above, spousal support orders remain essentially a function of the evidence led in each particular case. In some cases, such evidence might come in the form of highly specific expert evidence which enables parties to present an accurate picture of the economic consequences of marriage breakdown in their particular circumstances. ... Although of great assistance in assessing the economic consequences of marriage breakdown in a particular marriage, such evidence will not be required nor will it be possible in most cases. For most divorcing couples, both the cost of obtaining such evidence and the amount of assets involved are practical considerations which would prohibit or at least discourage its use. Therefore, to require expert evidence as a sine qua non to the recovery of compensation would not be practical for many parties, not to mention the use of court time which might be involved. It would be my hope, therefore, that different alternatives be examined. ...

[L'Heureux-Dubé J considered a number of possibilities, legislative guidelines, and the use of judicial notice. In commenting on the latter possibility, she noted:]

[90] The doctrine [of judicial notice] itself grew from a need to promote efficiency in the litigation process and may very well be applicable to spousal support. ...
[91] Based upon the studies which I have cited earlier in these reasons, the general economic impact of divorce on women is a phenomenon the existence of which cannot reasonably be questioned and should be amenable to judicial notice. More extensive social science data are also appearing. Such studies are beginning to provide reasonable assessments of some of the disadvantages incurred and advantages conferred post-divorce. ... While quantification will remain difficult and fact-related in each particular case, judicial notice should be taken of such studies, subject to other expert evidence which may bear on them, as background information at the very least. ...
[92] In all events, whether judicial notice of the circumstances generally encountered by spouses at the dissolution of a marriage is to be a formal part of the trial process or whether such circumstances merely provide the necessary background information, it is important that judges be aware of the social reality in which support decisions are experienced when engaging in the examination of the objectives of the Act. ...

[L'Heureux-Dubé J then applied these principles to the facts in *Moge*:]

[94] Since this appeal involves an application for a variation order, here an order for the termination of support by Mr. Moge to Mrs. Moge, s. 17(4) of the Act applies.
[95] As a necessary preliminary condition to making such an order, s. 17(4) of the Act requires that the court be satisfied that "there has been a change in the condition, means, needs or other circumstances for either former spouse ... for whom support is or was sought occurring since the making of the support order or the last variation order or the last variation order made in respect of that order."
[96] That there has been a change in the circumstances of the parties since the last support order was not seriously contested and I agree with both the trial judge and the Court of Appeal that the threshold requirements of s. 17(4) of the Act are satisfied.

[97] The sole remaining consideration is whether the application of Mr. Moge to terminate support ought to have been granted in this case. In my view, it should not have, and the majority of the Court of Appeal was right in finding an error of principle on the part of the trial judge. ...

[98] The four objectives of spousal support orders under s. 17(7) of the Act, as explicated above and applied by the Court of Appeal, are met in this case. For this reason, the following specific findings are in order based on the evidence in the record:

1. Mrs. Moge has sustained a substantial economic disadvantage "from the marriage or its breakdown" within the meaning of s. 17(7)(a) of the Act.

2. Mrs. Moge's long-term responsibility for the upbringing of the children of the marriage after the spousal separation in 1973 has had an impact on her ability to earn an income so as to trigger the application of s. 17(7)(b) of the Act.

3. Mrs. Moge continues to suffer economic hardship as a result of the "breakdown of the marriage" within the meaning of s. 17(7)(c) of the Act.

4. Mrs. Moge has failed to become economically self-sufficient notwithstanding her conscientious efforts.

[99] These findings are irrefutable even in the absence of expert evidence relating to the appropriate quantification of spousal support. It follows that in view of all of the objectives of spousal support orders set out in s. 17(7) of the Act, continuing support is in order in this case. Accordingly, there was no error in the Court of Appeal. ...

[McLachlin J agreed with L'Heureux-Dubé J as to the outcome of the appeal, but commented in some detail on the statutory provisions, emphasizing that the case was "first and last a case of statutory interpretation." Thus, she stated (at 879):]

[107] Considering the factors together, the judge's task under s. 17(7) of the statute is to make an order which provides compensation for marital contributions and sacrifices, which takes into account financial consequences of looking after children of the marriage, which relieves against need induced by the separation, and, to the extent it may be "practicable," promotes the economic self-sufficiency of each spouse. Neither a "compensation model" nor a "self-sufficiency model" captures the full content of the second, though both may be relevant to the judge's decision. The judge must base her decision on a number of factors: compensation; child-care; post-separation need; and the goal, insofar as practicable, of promoting self-sufficiency.

[108] The need to consider all four factors set out in s. 17(7) rules out the strict self-sufficiency model which Mr. Moge urged upon this court. The trial judge erred, in my respectful opinion, in giving no weight to the first three factors of s. 17(7) and in imposing a categorical requirement of self-sufficiency.

Appeal dismissed.

Colleen Sheppard, "Uncomfortable Victories and Unanswered Questions:
Lessons from Moge"
(1995), 12 *Canadian Journal of Family Law* 284, at 328

The *Moge* case represents an important victory for women to the extent that it acknowledges the actual economic disadvantages created by the gendered division of labour within the family. Rather than applying an abstract notion of formal equality, the Court recognized the need to redress substantive inequalities through long term spousal support. In a number of recent cases, *Moge* has been relied upon to justify continued and/or more generous spousal support. To the extent that *Moge* symbolizes recognition by the Supreme Court of Canada of the way in which the unequal division of labour within the family contributes to the feminization of poverty, its impact has extended beyond the domain of spousal support law.

Furthermore, L'Heureux-Dubé J, by challenging the traditional versus modern categorical approach, has demonstrated a willingness to reject the confines of dichotomous thinking so as to ensure a more inclusive approach to women who do not fit readily into the existing categories. In the case of spousal support, those women constitute a majority of women, including Zofia Moge.

And yet, while responding to some concerns, the Court's analysis generates others. An approach based on an assessment of marriage-generated disadvantages and advantages contains the same uncertainty and risk of biased application as the trilogy's causal connection test. L'Heureux-Dubé J does provide some guidance for courts in assessing the economic disadvantages related to marriage. She also leaves open other justifications for spousal support. But as the post-*Moge* cases confirm, there remains considerable uncertainty about how to assess fair compensation for the economic consequences of marriage. The dilemma of discretion and malleable legal standards also persists in the legal regulation of spousal support. In addition, *Moge* risks reinforcing the tradition of privatization as the norm of familial economic well-being rather than moving us toward a more public and collective approach to individual economic security.

More troubling than the perhaps inevitable persistence of legal uncertainty, is the silence on the larger context of women's economic vulnerability. The *Moge* case does not address social factors beyond marriage that help to account for Zofia Moge's current economic needs. It does not deal with gender, race, ethnic origin, or language discrimination in the labour force. It does not mention patterns of familial dependence reinforced by immigration law and policy. Nor does it touch upon the absence of affordable and accessible child care or social assistance programs. The litigation model often overlooks the larger systemic dimensions of the issues being adjudicated. But these dimensions matter deeply to anyone concerned about the feminization of poverty and the importance of ensuring that women are provided with fairness, justice, and access to economic security that is not dependent on the resources of individual male spouses. Thus, despite the lengthy discussion of the underlying philosophy of spousal support by L'Heureux-Dubé J, the larger questions of the social context of Zofia Moge's economic insecurity remain beyond the realm of the court debate. Relegated beyond the margins, they should be occupying the centre of public debate about economic rights and family roles.

Carol Rogerson, "Spousal Support After Moge"
(1997), 14 *Canadian Family Law Quarterly* 281, at 385ff.

The landscape of spousal support post-*Moge* is both radically transformed and strikingly familiar. *Moge* has clearly reversed the trend toward minimalist spousal support awards that took hold with the first wave of modern family law reform. Spousal support awards post-*Moge* are more generous than they were in the past: more spouses are entitled to support and awards are, in general, for longer periods of time and higher amounts. Women who have remained out of the labour force for significant periods of time during marriage can now expect judicial recognition of the long-term economic consequences they will carry with them after marriage breakdown.

Yet from another perspective the current landscape of spousal support is a familiar one. Despite the gloss of a compensatory analysis, the expanded role of spousal support post-*Moge* appears to be driven, in large part, by a concern with responding to post-divorce need and preventing post-divorce poverty, rather than by principles of providing fair compensation to women for their unpaid labour in the home and providing for the equitable sharing between the spouses of the economic consequences of the marriage. Although there are exceptions, many lawyers and judges continue to feel more comfortable with a traditional understanding of spousal support as a private scheme of income security rather than with a compensatory model, and continue to rely upon the conventional concept of need (and its corollary, self-sufficiency) to structure and give content to the compensatory principle. As a result, it is those spouses who demonstrate the greatest economic need and who will experience the greatest economic hardship after marriage breakdown—whether by reason of age, illness, lack of skills, or a poor economy—who are viewed as the most sympathetic candidates for spousal support, while those who have youth, good health, and employability in their favour are seen as self-sufficient economic actors, despite their past and on-going responsibilities for the care of children.

While there may be more spousal support post-*Moge* and somewhat less post-divorce poverty, I fear that in the course of things the radical message of *Moge* with respect to the value of women's work in the home and their entitlement to compensation from their husbands has been diluted. While *Moge* has undoubtedly wrought some very positive developments in terms of how we treat those members of our society—mainly women—who assume primary responsibility for the care of children, much remains to be done. The current political climate is, unfortunately, not one that will render that an easy task.

From a broad political perspective, it is no surprise that the compensatory message of *Moge* is being subtly reshaped into a message of the obligation of the family members to provide for each other's economic needs. In a period of diminishing public resources and a recessionary economy, the family has re-emerged as a central economic institution and a locus of economic security for vulnerable citizens. Our political language of rights and entitlements is being replaced with the language of obligations and responsibilities, with particular emphasis on the obligations of family members to care for each other. The fact that many citizens in need have no family resources to draw upon is lost from sight, as is the fact that it is women who will assume responsibility for many of the caring functions being delegated to the family, but whose claims of entitlement to compensation for their work are being delegitimated.

Discussion Notes

The Impact of Moge

According to one family lawyer,

> *Moge* confirms what clients have been telling counsel for years: women remain the more economically disadvantaged partner after marriage breakdown. It thoroughly and accurately discusses the economic impact of marriage and divorce, and why women are plagued by financial difficulties after a separation or divorce.
>
> It would be "perverse in the extreme" to think that seven members of the Supreme Court of Canada would spend eight months writing a unanimous ... decision about a $150 per month support case from Winnipeg if they did not intend to set a new standard of spousal support for the profession and the courts.

See Ronald S. Foster, "Moge v. Moge: What It Means to Family Law Lawyers" (1993), 43 RFL (3d) 465, at 465.

James McLeod also commented on the decision: see James G. McLeod, "Case Comment: Moge v. Moge" (1993), 43 RFL (3d) 455, at 459:

> The legal rulings in *Moge* are not surprising. The result was predictable. ...
>
> L'Heureux-Dubé J's attempt to distance herself from the "causal connection" and the "new support model" labels may have led her to disagree with them while agreeing with the substance of "compensatory" causal connection. Alternatively, she, like many others, may be mistakenly equating "clean break" with "causal connection." The distinction between the two is clear in Professor Rogerson's writing, to which the reasons refer. Professor Rogerson advocates a compensatory causal connection model with limited readjustment to support where the loss experienced is that of access to spousal funds. Socially, she would make an exception for sick or disabled spouses. Given the general confusion and paranoia about the "c" words, they might best be abandoned. Unfortunately, not everyone will appreciate that what has been said may not be exactly what was meant.
>
> The legal analysis in *Moge* will have limited impact on current practice. If full effect is given to the political or philosophical statements, the courts may be close to equalizing incomes as well as family property.

Do you agree with these assessments of the decision in *Moge*? For an analysis of these issues, see *Trewin v. Jones* (1997), 26 RFL (4th) 418 (Ont. CA) and James G. McLeod, "Annotation of Trewin v. Jones" (1997), 26 RFL (4th) 419.

In 1995, the Supreme Court of Canada considered an appeal from Quebec: *G.(L.) v. B.(G.)* (1995), 15 RFL (4th) 201. The majority opinion declined to consider the continued applicability of the *Pelech* trilogy; concurring views of L'Heureux-Dubé, Gonthier, and La Forest JJ reviewed the trilogy in relation to the legislative objectives of the *Divorce Act, 1985* and concluded that the *Pelech* trilogy should not continue to be applied. These differing approaches in the Supreme Court of Canada with respect to the continuing applicability of the *Pelech* trilogy were also reflected in differing views across Canada. For example, in *Wilkinson v. Wilkinson* (1998), 43 RFL (4th) 258 (Alta. QB), the wife's failure to obtain full-time employment as a teacher, as a result of education cutbacks in Alberta, did not warrant a variation of a separation agreement that had limited the duration of spousal support to four years. See also *Allen v. Allen* (1999), 2 RFL (5th) 1 (Alta. QB).

By contrast, an Ontario court considered the same issue and concluded, for purposes of awarding interim spousal support, that *G.(L.) v. B.(G.)*, decided by the Supreme Court of Canada after *Moge*, should be interpreted as altering the applicability of the *Pelech* trilogy, thus expressly disagreeing with *Wilkinson*: see *Bailey v. Plaxton* (2000), 6 RFL (5th) 29 (Ont. Sup. Ct. J).

In *Bailey v. Plaxton*, the parties married in 1965, had three children, and separated in 1985. They signed a separation agreement that required the husband to pay spousal support of $2,000 per month until 1990. The agreement expressly stated that these payments were not to be varied under any circumstances. The husband paid support pursuant to this agreement. The parties divorced, but the separation agreement was not incorporated in the decree. In 1999, the wife commenced an application for lump-sum spousal support and periodic support in the amount of $5,000 per month.

Kiteley J stated that the proceedings constituted an application for corollary relief. (Because no order had been made, there was no jurisdiction to order variation.) She considered the language of s. 11 of the *Divorce Act*, at issue in the *Pelech* trilogy, in relation to s. 15.2 of the *Divorce Act, 1985*, at issue in *Moge*, and ordered interim spousal support in the amount of $5,000 per month and an expedited process for trial. Kiteley J stated (at para. 15):

> [15] In 1985, Parliament fundamentally changed the approach to spousal support. Specifically, the legislature emphasized the criterion of need, and eliminated factors anchored in ideas of fault and blame. In my view, Parliament intended the regime of spousal support to provide fair compensation to spouses for the consequences that flow from the roles they assumed in the marriage, to provide for the reasonable needs of the dependent spouse, and at the same time to factor in the important principles of self-sufficiency and freedom of contract. Unlike the Act at play in the trilogy, which was largely informed by ideas of formal equality and self-sufficiency, the new legislation aims to balance three competing and often conflicting ideas of need, compensation, and independence. Because of the substantial amendments to the law of spousal support, one ought to be cautious about applying the principles established in *Pelech*, *Richardson*, and *Caron*. If courts continue to require that a "radical change" be demonstrated before an order that incorporated a settlement agreement can be varied, the result, in effect, will be a regime which subordinates the "new" principles of need and compensation to the "old" ideas of self-sufficiency, the "clean break" and pure freedom of contract. Similarly, if courts give too much weight to agreements when making orders in the first instance, this same situation will result. In order to be consistent with the rationales in the 1985 legislation, agreements should be given substantial weight, but must also be situated in terms of the other factors articulated in s. 15.2(4) and assessed in terms of their ability to promote all of the objectives listed in s. 15.2(6).
>
> [16] Notwithstanding what I view to be fundamental differences and substantial amendments, the trilogy cases have been applied in countless cases initiated pursuant to the 1985 amendments. They have been applied in corollary relief applications and variations.
>
> [17] In *Wilkinson v. Wilkinson* (1998), 43 RFL (4th) 258 (Alta. QB), the court considered *Pelech*, *Moge*, *Willick v. Willick*, [1994] 3 SCR 670, 119 DLR (4th) 405, and

G.(L.) v. B.(G.), [1995] 3 SCR 370, 15 RFL (4th) 201. *Willick* and *G.(L.) v. B.(G.)* were also variation cases. *Wilkinson* was framed as a variation, but was actually an application for support in the first instance. The Alberta court considered the application of the "radical change" test to the parties' agreement, and concluded that the trilogy test still applied under the new *Divorce Act*. I disagree with that conclusion for several reasons. The reasons for decision begin and end on the basis that this was a "contract case." When the court approaches a spousal support analysis from a contract law perspective, there is a risk that the interests of the dependent spouse will not be properly addressed. Even with independent legal counsel, dependent spouses may not be able to bargain equally with their partners, either as a result of family dynamics, or because they may not have a realistic idea of their own needs and means. As the Supreme Court of Canada repeated in *Bracklow v. Bracklow*, [1999] 1 SCR 420, 169 DLR (4th) 577 at p. 599: "... support agreements are important (although not necessarily decisive) ... . Where need is established that is not met on a compensatory or contractual basis, the fundamental marital obligation may play a vital role." In the family law context, while separation agreements are obviously important factors, the weight given to an agreement should depend on the extent to which the terms of that agreement continue to reflect all the principles and objectives informing the spousal support provisions. It appears that the court in *Wilkinson* afforded greater importance to the contract than the Supreme Court of Canada envisaged. And, for reasons which follow, I do not agree with Sullivan J's interpretation of *G.(L.) v. B.(G.)*, *supra*. With all due respect to my colleague in Alberta, I disagree with both his reasoning and his result.

To what extent do you agree with the interpretation of Kiteley J? What are the underlying rationales of this decision? How should these principles be formulated to accomplish the goals of the *Divorce Act, 1985*?

Gender and Spousal Support

The provisions for awarding spousal support may also require former wives to pay spousal support to former husbands in some circumstances. In *Hough v. Hough* (1996), 25 RFL (4th) 319 (Ont. Ct. J (Gen. Div.)), the parties married in 1974, each for the second time. At the time of the marriage, Mr. Hough was president of Canadian Sports Network and a vice-president for McLaren Advertising. He was prominent in the sports broadcasting industry and had associations with many prominent and wealthy people. At the time of the separation, Mr. Hough was retired from the Molson Group of Companies, where he had been employed as a vice-president. His retirement income from all sources was approximately $81,000 a year. Mrs. Hough was a stockbroker at the time of the marriage and, at separation, she was a commissioned salesperson and a director and vice-president of Scotia McLeod. Although she was over 65 at the time of the trial, she did not intend to retire and hoped to work at least two more years. Her commission income from her employment was approximated at $510,000, and she received an additional $780 per month in Canada Pension Plan (CPP) and old age security (OAS).

Mr. Hough claimed that it was through his contacts with wealthy individuals that Mrs. Hough was able to be so successful and have such a broad clientele. However, Mrs. Hough disputed this, and it was not accepted by the court.

It was uncontroverted that during their 21 years of marriage the parties pooled their resources and that, during the last decade, Mrs. Hough earned substantially more income than Mr. Hough (Mrs. Hough gave evidence that she was in charge of earning income and Mr. Hough was in charge of spending it).

At the time of trial, the parties' net family property had been equalized; each had received assets valued at approximately $1.3 million. The only remaining issue to be resolved was spousal support.

Mr. Hough claimed monthly support from Mrs. Hough so that he could meet his proposed budget of $120,000 per year. Mr. Hough asserted that his proposed budget would approximate the standard of living that he experienced before separation and that it would be an economic hardship if he was forced to live on his existing income without receiving support from Mrs. Hough. Mrs. Hough argued that no spousal support should be paid and that the parties should go their separate ways in every respect.

At the time of the trial, Mr. Hough was sharing his home with his 24-year-old grandson who was employed, but did not pay rent. Mr. Hough stated that his grandson lived with him in order to provide him with companionship and to help care for a pet.

In deciding to award Mr. Hough time-limited spousal support, Justice E. MacDonald stated (at 325):

> I was urged during argument to follow *Moge v. Moge* (1992), 99 DLR (4th) 456 (SCC) ("*Moge*"). One of the results of this decision is that courts have moved away from the clean break model of support which was popular prior to the 1985 amendments to the *Divorce Act*. After *Moge*, support is viewed as essentially compensatory in nature which is awarded to compensate a spouse for economic disadvantage flowing from the roles adopted in the marriage or the breakdown of the marriage. Beyond that, *Moge* is of little assistance to me because the background and circumstances of Mr. and Mrs. Moge are so vastly different from those of Mr. and Mrs. Hough. It is for this reason that the other cases, to which I was referred, are also of little assistance. ...
>
> It is clear that Mr. Hough suffered no economic disadvantage as a result of the marriage. Now that the marriage is over, the court must look at whether the court should relieve against the economic disadvantage that Mr. Hough faces by reason of the fact that he is now separated from and about to be divorced from Mrs. Hough who earns unusually high income.
>
> Ms. DeMarco referred me to the following extract from *Moge* which appears at p. 490:

> The equitable sharing of the economic consequences of marriage or marriage breakdown, however, is not a general tool of redistribution which is activated by the mere fact of marriage. Nor ought it to be. It is now uncontentious in our law and accepted by both the majority and the minority in *Messier v. Delage*, supra, at pp. 13-14, that marriage *per se* does not automatically entitle a spouse to support. Presumably, there will be the occasional marriage where both spouses maximize their earning potential by working outside the home, pursuing economic and educational opportunities in a similar manner, dividing up the domestic labour identically, and either making no economic sacrifices for the other or, more likely, making them equally. *In such a Utopian scenario there might be no apparent call for compensation. The spouses are able to make a clean break and continue on with their respective lives. Such cases would appear to be rare.* [Emphasis added.]

Ms. DeMarco focused on the emphasized portion above and urged me to consider that while such cases are rare, they are not *non-existent* and that *this case* is one of those rare cases. On this analysis, Ms. DeMarco urged me not to award support to Mr. Hough. ...

Section 15(7)(d) directs the court to promote the economic self-sufficiency of each spouse within a *reasonable* period of time *insofar as is practicable*. In my view, it is not reasonable for Mr. Hough, given his age, to adhere to the notion that he will not sell his condominium given its large equity. He is, however, at liberty to make these choices but it is not reasonable for him to visit the consequences of these choices upon Mrs. Hough. Similarly, it is not reasonable for him to say that one of the reasons for his investment strategy is that he wishes to preserve an estate for his children from his first marriage. This is, of course, a natural objective of a parent but Mr. Hough cannot visit the consequences of this objective upon Mrs. Hough who is legally entitled to expect that Mr. Hough will maximize his own resources to support himself.

Having made these findings, I return to the lifestyle issue. Although not explicitly expressed in the statute, it is in my view implied in s. 15(5) by the words the condition means, and needs "and other circumstances of each spouse." These words give the court a wide discretion under s. 15 of the Act. ...

I am fixing support at $5,000 per month for 2 years; the first payment is to be made on November 1, 1996; thereafter Mrs. Hough's support obligation will be $2,500 for another twelve month period. I consider that the applicable objectives of s. 15(7) can be met within the 3 year period. At the end of the 3 year period, Mrs. Hough will not have a support obligation.

Is *Hough* consistent with the reasoning in *Moge*, having regard to the differences based on the gender of the payor spouse and the relative wealth of the parties? Why, or why not?

Compare *Hough* to *Nock v. Nock* (1998), 43 RFL (4th) 110 (Ont. Ct. J (Gen. Div.)). In *Nock*, the parties separated after 28 years of marriage. Both had been employed during marriage, but the husband lost his full-time employment after separation. Although he then obtained part-time work, he was not likely to obtain full-time work without retraining. However, he suffered from learning disabilities that made retraining difficult. The court awarded spousal support of $400 per month for 18 months, citing the decision in *Moge* (at para. 12):

Madam Justice L'Heureux-Dubé at page 387 of the *Moge* case states:

> [T]he four objectives set out in the Act can be viewed as an attempt to achieve an equitable sharing of the economic consequences of marriage or marriage breakdown. At the end of the day, however, courts have an overriding discretion and the exercise of such discretion will depend on the particular facts of each case, having regard to the factors and objectives designated in the Act.

> It is clear that the court's discretion must be in relation to both the factors and the objectives of section 15.2. It is also clear that the court must be ultimately satisfied that, but for the breakdown of the marriage, the ensuing consequence faced by the claimant spouse would not have occurred. Applying the factors of that section to this case, Mr. and Mrs. Nock were married for twenty eight years, were both fully employed, and performed similar functions within the marriage in respect to both employment and family obligations. Within the context of the objectives of section 15.2, Mr. Nock had a significant disability while he

was married, the effects of which caused him no disadvantage as long as he was fully employed. However, it should have been apparent to both parties that should Mr. Nock lose his employment the significant impairment of his learning skills in the job market would present him with a formidable disadvantage in the job market. Had Mr. Nock lost his employment during his marriage he would have been able to rely on the income stream of his spouse for his living expenses until he was able to achieve employability with the tutorial assistance that he required. Because he cannot access that financial resource due to his separation from Mrs. Nock, I find that he has sustained an economic hardship which flows directly from the breakdown of the marriage.

Is this decision consistent with *Moge*?

Applying Section 15.2(6) in Practice

According to Julien Payne, "An Overview of Theory and Reality in the Judicial Disposition of Spousal Support Claims Under the Canadian Divorce Act" (2000), 63 *Saskatchewan Law Review* 403, at 419-20, lawyers and judges should ask 16 questions in every application for an original order for spousal support or in an application to vary an existing order:

    (i) What economic advantages, if any, did the wife obtain from the marriage?

    (ii) What economic advantages, if any, did the husband obtain from the marriage?

    (iii) What economic advantages, if any, did the wife obtain from the marriage breakdown?

    (iv) What economic advantages, if any, did the husband obtain from the marriage breakdown?

    (v) What economic disadvantages, if any, did the wife sustain in consequence of the marriage?

    (vi) What economic disadvantages, if any, did the husband sustain in consequence of the marriage?

    (vii) What economic disadvantages, if any, did the wife sustain in consequence of the marriage breakdown?

    (viii) What economic disadvantages, if any, did the husband sustain in consequence of the marriage breakdown?

    (ix) What are the financial consequences, if any, to the wife resulting from her parenting responsibilities before the marriage breakdown?

    (x) What are the financial consequences, if any, to the husband resulting from his parenting responsibilities before the marriage breakdown?

    (xi) What are the financial consequences, if any, to the wife resulting from her parenting responsibilities after the marriage breakdown?

    (xii) What are the financial consequences, if any, to the husband resulting from his parenting responsibilities after the marriage breakdown?

    (xiii) What economic hardship, if any, has been sustained by the wife in consequence of the marriage breakdown?

    (xiv) What economic hardship, if any, has been sustained by the husband in consequence of the marriage breakdown?

(xv) What is practicable, if anything, to promote the economic self-sufficiency of the wife within a reasonable time?

(xvi) What is practicable, if anything, to promote the economic self-sufficiency of the husband within a reasonable time?

The above questions are intended to ensure that lawyers and courts canvass all the objectives of spousal support orders specifically defined in the *Divorce Act*. The list does not imply that it is possible or desirable to undertake an exact accounting or quantification of the diverse economic implications of the marriage or its breakdown under each of the questions. It is imperative, however, that an answer be given to each question. Only then will it be possible to determine whether spousal support is necessary in order to achieve an equitable sharing of the economic consequences of marriage or marriage breakdown as stipulated by L'Heureux-Dubé J in *Moge*.

Do you agree with Payne's assessment, after *Moge*? Why, or why not?

Compensatory Support and Provincial Legislation: Keast v. Keast

As was evident in chapter 6, the dilemma of professional degrees was resolved in some cases by means of the concept of compensatory support, particularly in accordance with s. 33(9)(j) of Ontario's *Family Law Act*. In an early case, *Keast v. Keast* (1986), 1 RFL (3d) 401 (Ont. Dist. Ct.), the wife had worked as a nurse to support her husband when he decided to forgo his job as a secondary school teacher to train as a physician. She had also maintained their family home in London while he attended medical school in Kingston, looking after their two children as well. A few years later, the couple separated and Mrs. Keast was unemployed and then on welfare by reason of a breakdown in her physical and mental health. By the time of the trial, the judge concluded that Mrs. Keast would be able to work, but probably only on a reduced-hours basis and in a less stressful environment than a public hospital. Killeen J held that:

> I am persuaded that Mrs. Keast should have a support order and one which not only embraces her basic needs, based on her accustomed standard of living before her husband's career change in 1981, but one which recognizes her very real physical, psychological and financial sacrifices and contributions to the realization by her husband of his dream and efforts to become a doctor.

Having regard to the likelihood that Mrs. Keast would not obtain employment as a nurse for at least a year or so, the fact that she would continue to experience uncertain health, her substantial financial contribution to her husband's career change (during a period of deteriorating health), and the potential for substantial increases in earnings for Dr. Keast, Killeen J ordered support (at 410) as follows: $600 monthly in permanent support for life; and "a quasi-restitutionary or compensatory support sum ... [for] her contributions to Dr. Keast's career potential, fixed at $1,000 monthly but commencing in 1990 and continuing for ten years thereafter."

Note that Killeen J also decided the case of *Linton v. Linton* (1988), 11 RFL (3d) 444 (Ont. SC (HCJ)); his approach to professional degrees (using compensatory support rather than property provisions) was subsequently confirmed by the Ontario Court of

Appeal in *Linton* and in *Caratun v. Caratun* (1992), 42 RFL (3d) 113, discussed in chapter 6. For an excellent overview of the issue of compensatory support (and some analysis of American approaches), see N. Bala, "Recognizing Spousal Contributions to the Acquisition of Degrees, Licences, and Other Career Assets: Toward Compensatory Support" (1989), 8 *Canadian Journal of Family Law* 23.

SELECTED REFERENCES

Alison Diduck and Helena Orton, "Equality and Support for Spouses" (1994), 57 *Modern Law Review* 681.

Susan G. Drummond, "Judicial Notice: The Very Texture of Legal Reasoning" (2000), 15:1 *Canadian Journal of Law and Society* 1.

Miriam Grassby, "Spousal Support—Assumptions and Myths Versus Case Law" (1994-95), 12 *Canadian Family Law Quarterly* 187.

Claire L'Heureux-Dubé, "Re-Examining the Doctrine of Judicial Notice in the Family Law Context" (1994), 26 *Ottawa Law Review* 551.

Carol J. Rogerson, "Spousal Support After Moge" (1996-97), 14 *Canadian Family Law Quarterly* 289.

4. Rediscovering Need in Spousal Support?

Bracklow v. Bracklow
[1999] 1 SCR 420; 44 RFL (4th) 1

[The parties were married in December 1989 after living together for four years. During the first two years of their relationship, the appellant paid two-thirds of the household expenses because she was earning more money than the respondent and because her two children from a previous marriage were living with them. After 1987, they shared the household expenses equally. This continued while the appellant was working. When she became unemployed, the respondent kept the family going. The appellant had had various health problems from the beginning of the relationship and, in 1991, she was admitted to hospital suffering from psychiatric problems. She had not worked since then and it seemed unlikely that she would ever work again. Except for periods when the appellant was too ill, the parties divided household chores. They separated in 1992 and were divorced in 1995. The respondent remarried and his new wife was employed. The appellant obtained an interim spousal support order of $275 per month, increasing to $400 per month on May 15, 1994. She also received $787 monthly in disability benefits.

The trial judge found that no economic hardship befell the appellant as a consequence of the marriage or its breakdown. Nor were her health problems due to the marriage. He also found that there was no express or implied agreement between the parties that they were responsible for each other's support. The trial judge concluded that the appellant was not entitled to support from the respondent. However, he ordered the $400 per month payments to continue until September 1996, "a decision based upon the [respondent's] proposal not upon the necessity of law." The Court of Appeal affirmed the decision.

In the Supreme Court of Canada, the court allowed the appeal and remitted to the trial judge the issue of the amount and duration of support for the wife on the basis that she was legally eligible for post-marital support.]

[1] McLACHLIN J (for the court): What duty does a healthy spouse owe a sick one when the marriage collapses? It is now well-settled law that spouses must compensate each other for forgone careers and missed opportunities during the marriage upon the breakdown of their union. But what happens when a divorce—through no consequence of sacrifices, but simply through economic hardship—leaves one former spouse self-sufficient and the other, perhaps due to the onset of a debilitating illness, incapable of self-support? Must the healthy spouse continue to support the sick spouse? Or can he or she move on, free of obligation? That is the question posed by this appeal. It is a difficult issue. It is also an important issue, given the trend in our society toward shorter marriages and successive relationships. ...

[McLachlin J reviewed the facts in the case and set out the relevant sections of the BC legislation and ss. 15.2(1), (4), and (6) of the federal *Divorce Act*. She then reported the decisions of the trial judge and the BC Court of Appeal, confirming that Mr. Bracklow "owed his wife no obligation of support." The Court of Appeal had also confirmed the trial judge's conclusion that there was no "causal connection" between the economic disadvantage and the marriage breakdown and his finding of fact that the parties had no express or implied agreement that one would be responsible for the other's support. The trial judge also expressly decided that the marriage vow to support one another in sickness or in health carried no legal significance.

McLachlin J stated that the issue was whether a spouse has an obligation to support a former spouse over and above compensation for loss incurred as a result of the marriage and its breakdown (or to fulfill contractual support obligations); she answered "yes" to this question:]

[15] The lower courts implicitly assumed that, absent a contractual agreement for post-marital assistance, entitlement to support could only be founded on compensatory principles, i.e., reimbursement of the spouse for opportunities forgone or hardships accrued as a result of the marriage. I conclude, however, that the law recognizes three conceptual grounds for entitlement to spousal support: (1) compensatory; (2) contractual; and (3) non-compensatory. These three bases of support flow from the controlling statutory provisions and the relevant case law, and are more broadly animated by differing philosophies and theories of marriage and marital breakdown. ...

[McLachlin J reviewed the history of spousal support obligations in Canada, including the trend to equality in marriage obligations, now reflected in both provincial and federal legislation; however, she concluded (at para. 18) that the new legislation "did not entirely supplant the traditional obligations to support."]

[18] Legal equality did not translate into actual or substantive equality, and in its absence, one spouse might still be obliged to support the other. Accordingly, the *Divorce Acts* of 1968 and 1986 and provincial family support and property legisla-

tion recognized that in many circumstances one spouse might still be required to provide support for the other upon marriage breakup. The new philosophy of spousal equality brought to the fore the idea that parties' agreements on support should influence their rights and obligations during the marriage and upon its breakup, as well as the idea that to compensate a spouse for his or her contributions to the marriage or for sacrifices made or hardships suffered as a result of the marriage. Contractual support obligations, while not new, were given new emphasis by statutory stipulations that the courts take into account support agreements, express or implied, between the parties. The propriety of compensatory support was recognized by this Court in *Moge*, supra, as flowing from the 1986 *Divorce Act*. While a few cases prior to *Moge* had acknowledged that support criteria extended beyond needs and capacity to pay, the reasons of L'Heureux-Dubé J in *Moge* offered the first comprehensive articulation of the view that when a marriage ends, spouses are entitled to be compensated for contributions to the marriage and for losses sustained as a consequence of the marriage. The same reasons, however, made it clear that compensatory considerations were not the only basis for support. Judges must exercise their discretion in light of the objectives of spousal orders as set out in s. 15.2(6), and after having considered all the factors set out in s. 15.2(4) of the *Divorce Act*. By directing that the judge consider factors like need and ability to pay (as explored below), the new *Divorce Act* left in place the possibility of non-compensatory, non-contractual support. ...

[19] In analysing the respective obligations of husbands and wives, it is critical to distinguish between the roles of the spouses during marriage and the different roles that are assumed upon marriage breakdown.

[20] To begin, when two spouses are married, they owe each other a mutual duty of support: 1986 *Divorce Act*. Marriage, as this Court has said, is a joint endeavour: *Moge*, supra, at p. 870. The default presumption of this socio-economic partnership is mutuality and interdependence. This comports with the statutes and with the reasonable expectations of Canadian society. Thus the *Family Relations Act* states: "A spouse is responsible and liable for the support and maintenance of the other spouse ..." (s. 89(1)). Parties, of course (subject to the Act), may alter this expectation, either through explicit contracting (usually before the union is made with a prenuptial agreement), or through the unequivocal structuring of their daily affairs, to show disavowal of financial interweaving. The starting presumption, however, is of mutual support. We need not elevate to contractual status the marital vows of support "in sickness and health, till death do us part" to conclude that, absent indications to the contrary, marriages are generally premised on obligations and expectations of mutual and co-equal support.

[21] When a marriage breaks down, however, the situation changes. The presumption of mutual support that existed during the marriage no longer applies. Such a presumption would be incompatible with the diverse post-marital scenarios that may arise in modern society and the liberty many claim to start their lives anew after marriage breakdown. This is reflected in the *Divorce Act* and the provincial support statutes, which require the court to determine issues of support by reference to a variety of objectives and factors.

[22] The reason that a general presumption of post-marital support would be inappropriate is the presence in the latter half of our century of two "competing" theories of marriage and post-marital obligation: Carol J. Rogerson, "Spousal Support After Moge"

(1996-97), 14 *CFLQ* 289; Carol J. Rogerson, "Judicial Interpretation of the Spousal and Child Support Provisions of the Divorce Act, 1985 (Part I)" (1991), 7 *CFLQ* 155.

[23] The first theory of marriage and post-marital obligation is the "basic social obligation" model, in which primary responsibility falls on the former spouse to provide for his or her ex-partner, rather than on the government. This model is founded on the historical notion that marriage is a potentially permanent obligation (although it revises the archaic concept of the wife's loss of identity with the voluntary secession of autonomy of two, co-equal actors as the basis for the ongoing duty). The payment corollary of this theory has been referred to as the "income replacement model," because the primary purpose of alimony payments, under the basic social obligation model, is to replace lost income that the spouse used to enjoy as a partner to the marriage union. The advocates of this theory vary in degree of fidelity. For example, some espouse permanent and indefinite support under this model. Others argue that the goal should be not just to meet the dependent spouse's post-marital needs, but to elevate him or her as closely as possible to the standard of living enjoyed during the marriage. Yet others, like Rogerson, contend that the social obligation entitlement to spousal support need not translate into a permanent obligation.

[24] At the other end of the spectrum lies what may be termed the "independent" model of marriage. This model sees each party to a marriage as an autonomous actor who retains his or her economic independence throughout marriage. The parties, while they "formally" commit to each other for life at the time of their vows, regard themselves as free agents in an enterprise that can terminate on the unilateral action of either party. The theory of spousal support that complements this model is the "clean-break" theory, in which a former spouse, having compensated in a restitutionary sense any economic costs of the marriage on the other spouse, moves on with his or her life, possibly to enter into more such relationships. Again, the proponents vary in their degree of allegiance. Some prefer to characterize the clean-break model as encompassing "transitional support," in addition to straight restitution, due to the general dislocation costs of unwinding the partnership.

[25] The independent, clean-break model of marriage provides the theoretical basis for compensatory spousal support. The basic social obligation model equally undergirds what may be called "non-compensatory" support. Both models of marriage and their corresponding theories of spousal support permit individual variation by contract, and hence provide a third basis for a legal entitlement to support.

[26] These two theories (and I recognize that I paint with broad strokes, creating these two anchors for sake of simplicity) represent markedly divergent philosophies, values, and legal principles.

[27] The mutual obligation model of marriage stresses the interdependence that marriage creates. The clean-break model stresses the independence of each party to the union. The problem with applying either model exclusively and stringently is that marriages may fit neither model (or both models). Many modern marriages are a complex mix of interdependence and independence, and the myriad of legislative provisions and objectives discussed below speak varyingly to both models. As *Payne on Divorce* (4th ed. 1996), at pp. 269-70, puts it, "The economic variables of marriage breakdown and divorce do not lend themselves to the application of any single objective."

[28] The independent, clean-break model of marriage and marriage breakdown reflects a number of important policies. First, it is based on the widely accepted modern value of the equality and independence of both spouses. Second, it encourages rehabilitation and self-maximization of dependent spouses. Third, through its acceptance of a clean break terminating support obligations, it recognizes the social reality of shorter marriages and successive relationships.

[29] These values and policies support the compensatory theory of support (and, to some extent, the contractual theory as well). The basic premise of contractual and compensatory support is that the parties are equal. As such, when the relationship ends, the parties are entitled to what they would receive in the commercial world— what the individuals contracted for and what they have lost due to the marriage, and its breakdown. Insofar as marriage may have created dependencies, it is the duty of dependent spouses to strive to free themselves from their dependencies and to assume full self-sufficiency, thereby mitigating the need for continued compensation.

[30] The mutual obligation theory of marriage and divorce, by contrast, posits marriage as a union that creates interdependencies that cannot be easily unravelled. These interdependencies in turn create expectations and obligations that the law recognizes and enforces. While historically rooted in a concept of marriage that saw one spouse as powerful and the other as dependent, in its modern version the mutual obligation theory of marriage acknowledges the theoretical and legal independence of each spouse, but equally the interdependence of two co-equals. It postulates each of the parties to the marriage agreeing, as independent individuals, to marriage and all that it entails—including the potential obligation of mutual support. The resultant loss of individual autonomy does not violate the premise of equality, because the autonomy is voluntarily ceded. At the same time, the mutual obligation model recognizes that actual independence may be a different thing from theoretical independence, and that a mutual obligation of support may arise and continue absent contractual or compensatory indicators.

[31] The mutual obligation view of marriage also serves certain policy ends and social values. First, it recognizes the reality that when people cohabit over a period of time in a family relationship, their affairs may become intermingled and impossible to disentangle neatly. When this happens, it is not unfair to ask the partners to continue to support each other (although perhaps not indefinitely). Second, it recognizes the artificiality of assuming that all separating couples can move cleanly from the mutual support status of marriage to the absolute independence status of single life, indicating the potential necessity to continue the primary burden of support for a needy partner who cannot attain post-marital self-sufficiency on the partners to the relationship, rather than on the state, recognizing the potential injustice of foisting a helpless former partner onto the public assistance rolls.

[32] Both the mutual obligation model and the independent, clean-break model represent important realities and address significant policy concerns and social values. The federal and provincial legislatures, through their respective statutes, have acknowledged both models. Neither theory alone is capable of achieving a just law of spousal support. The importance of the policy objectives served by both models is beyond dispute. It is critical to recognize and encourage the self-sufficiency and independence of each spouse. It is equally vital to recognize that divorced people may

move on to other relationships and acquire new obligations which they may not be able to meet if they are obliged to maintain full financial burdens from previous relationships. On the other hand, it is also important to recognize that sometimes the goals of actual independence are impeded by patterns of marital dependence, that too often self-sufficiency at the time of marriage termination is an impossible aspiration, and that marriage is an economic partnership that is built upon a premise (albeit rebuttable) of mutual support. The real question in such cases is whether the state should automatically bear the costs of these realities, or whether the family, including former spouses, should be asked to contribute to the need, means permitting. Some suggest it would be better if the state automatically picked up the costs of such cases: Rogerson, "Judicial Interpretation of the Spousal and Child Support Provisions of the *Divorce Act, 1985* (Part I)," supra, at p. 234, n. 172. However, as will be seen, Parliament and the legislatures have decreed otherwise by requiring courts to consider not only compensatory factors, but the "needs" and "means" of the parties. It is not a question of either one model or the other. It is rather a matter of applying the relevant factors and striking the balance that best achieves justice in the particular case before the court.

[33] With these theories and policy concerns of marriage and marriage breakdown in mind, I turn to the pertinent statutes. They reveal the joint operation, in different provisions, of both legal paradigms, and hence the compensatory, non-compensatory, and contractual foundations for an entitlement to post-marital spousal support. ...

[McLachlin J then turned to an examination of the BC *Family Relations Act* and the federal *Divorce Act*; she indicated that *Moge* demonstrated the approach to interpreting these provisions. McLachlin J concluded (at para. 37) that the legislative provisions "accommodate both models of marriage and marriage breakdown outlined above." She identified the provisions supporting both the compensatory and contractual bases for spousal support and concluded (at para. 40) that "they do not confine the obligation to these grounds." She examined the provisions of the FRA and then considered the *Divorce Act*:]

[41] Section 15.2(6) of the *Divorce Act*, which sets out the objectives of support orders, also speaks to these non-compensatory factors. The first two objectives—to recognize the economic consequences of the marriage or its breakdown and to apportion between the spouses financial consequences of child care over and above child support payments—are primarily related to compensation. But the third and fourth objectives are difficult to confine to that goal. "[E]conomic hardship ... arising from the breakdown of the marriage" is capable of encompassing not only health or career disadvantages arising from the marriage breakdown properly the subject of compensation (perhaps more directly covered in s. 15.2(6)(a): see *Payne on Divorce*, supra, at pp. 251-53), but the mere fact that a person who formerly enjoyed intra-spousal entitlement to support now finds herself or himself without it. Looking only at compensation, one merely asks what loss the marriage or marriage breakup caused that would not have been suffered but for the marriage. But even where loss in this sense cannot be established, the breakup may cause economic hardship in a larger, non-compensatory sense. Such an interpretation supports the independent inclusion of

s. 15.2(6)(c) as a separate consideration from s. 15.2(6)(a). Thus, Rogerson sees s. 15.2(6)(c), "the principle of compensation for the economic disadvantages of the *marriage breakdown* as distinct from the disadvantages of the marriage" as an explicit recognition of "non-compensatory" support ("Spousal Support After Moge," supra, at pp. 371-72 (emphasis in original)).

[42] Similarly, the fourth objective of s. 15.2(6) of the *Divorce Act*—to promote economic self-sufficiency—may or may not be tied to compensation for disadvantages caused by the marriage or its breakup. A spouse's lack of self-sufficiency may be related to forgoing career and educational opportunities because of the marriage. But it may also arise from completely different sources, like the disappearance of the kind of work the spouse was trained to do (a career shift having nothing to do with the marriage or its breakdown) or, as in this case, ill-health.

[43] In summary, nothing in the *Family Relations Act* or the *Divorce Act* suggests that the only foundations for spousal support are compensatory. Indeed, I find it difficult to confine the words of the statutes to this model. It is true that in 1986 the *Divorce Act* was amended to place greater emphasis on compensation. This represented a shift away "to some degree" from the "means and needs" approach of the 1968 Act: *Payne on Divorce*, supra, at p. 267. But while the focus of the Act may have shifted or broadened, it retains the older idea that spouses may have an obligation to meet or contribute to the needs of their former partners where they have the capacity to pay, even in the absence of a contractual or compensatory foundation for the obligation. Need alone may be enough. More broadly, the legislation can be seen as a sensitive compromise of the two competing philosophies of marriage, marriage breakdown, and spousal support. ...

[McLachlin J then considered the jurisprudence, including *Moge* and the cases decided after it, quoting Carol Rogerson (at para. 47):]

> The current approach is typically justified by reference, first, to *Moge*'s rejection of the applicability of the causal connection test, and second, to the fact that the spouse who is ill suffers disadvantage from the breakdown of the marriage and the loss of financial support from the other spouse.

[McLachlin J also referred (at para. 48) to the report of the Scottish Law Commission, and then concluded:]

[48] Divorce ends the marriage. Yet in some circumstances the law may require that a healthy party continue to support a disabled party, absent contractual or compensatory entitlement. Justice and considerations of fairness may demand no less.

[49] In summary, the statutes and the case law suggest three conceptual bases for entitlement to spousal support: (1) compensatory, (2) contractual, and (3) non-compensatory. Marriage, as the Court held in *Moge* (at p. 870), is a "joint endeavour," a socio-economic partnership. That is the starting position. Support agreements are important (although not necessarily decisive), and so is the idea that spouses should be compensated on marriage breakdown for losses and hardships caused by the marriage. Indeed, a review of cases suggests that in most circumstances compensation

now serves as the main reason for support. However, contract and compensation are not the only sources of a support obligation. The obligation may alternatively arise out of the marriage relationship itself. Where a spouse achieves economic self-sufficiency on the basis of his or her own efforts, or on an award of compensatory support, the obligation founded on the marriage relationship itself lies dormant. But where need is established that is not met on a compensatory or contractual basis, the fundamental marital obligation may play a vital role. Absent negating factors, it is available, in appropriate circumstances, to provide just support. ...

[In considering the issue of quantum of entitlement, McLachlin J suggested (at para. 50) that the issues of eligibility and quantum were connected, in the sense that "the same factors that go to entitlement have an impact on quantum." In this case, Mrs. Bracklow asserted that the court should assess her "needs" to determine quantum and that the only issue was "duration" of the payments. Mr. Bracklow argued that the length of the marital relationship was the only factor relevant to the amount of support (suggesting the length of the marriage as a "proxy" for the extent of interdependency). McLachlin J rejected both approaches:]

[53] Both these arguments miss the mark in that they fix on one factor to the exclusion of others. The short answer to Mrs. Bracklow's argument is that need is but one of a number of factors that the judge must consider. Similarly, the short answer to Mr. Bracklow's contention is that the length of the marital relationship is only one of a number of factors that may be relevant. While some factors may be more important than others in particular cases, the judge cannot proceed at the outset by fixing on only one variable. The quantum awarded, in the sense of both amount and duration, will vary with the circumstances and the practical and policy considerations affecting particular cases. Limited means of the supporting spouse may dictate a reduction. So may obligations arising from new relationships insofar as they have an impact on means. Factors within the marriage itself may affect the quantum of a non-compensatory support obligation. For example, it may be difficult to make a case for a full obligation and expectation of mutual support in a very short marriage. (Section 15.2(4)(a) of the *Divorce Act* requires the court to consider the length of time the parties cohabited.) Finally, subject to judicial discretion, the parties by contract or conduct may enhance, diminish or negate the obligation of mutual support. To repeat, it is not the act of saying "I do," but the marital relationship between the parties that may generate the obligation of non-compensatory support pursuant to the Act. It follows that diverse aspects of that marital relationship may be relevant to the quantum of such support. As stated in *Moge*, "[a]t the end of the day ... , courts have an overriding discretion and the exercise of such discretion will depend on the particular facts of each case, having regard to the factors and objectives designated in the Act" (p. 866).

[54] Fixing on one factor to the exclusion of others leads Mrs. Bracklow to an artificial distinction between amount and duration. The two interrelate: a modest support order of indefinite duration could be collapsed into a more substantial lump-sum payment. It also leads her to the false premise that if need is the basis of the entitlement to the support award, then the quantum of the award must meet the total amount

of the need. It does not follow from the fact that need serves as the predicate for support that the quantum of the support must always equal the amount of the need. Nothing in either the *Family Relations Act* or the *Divorce Act* forecloses an order for support of a portion of the claimant's need, whether viewed in terms of periodic amount or duration. Need is but one factor to be considered. This is consistent with the modern recognition, captured by the statutes, of the variety of marital relationships in modern society. A spouse who becomes disabled toward the end of a very short marriage may well be entitled to support by virtue of her need, but it may be unfair, under the circumstances, to order the full payment of that need by the supporting spouse for the indefinite future.

[55] Mr. Bracklow's fixation on the length of the marital relationship leads to other difficulties. He elevates this Court's observation in *Moge* about general expectations in long-term marriages to an immutable rule constraining the factors applicable to determining quantum of support. And he introduces "morality" into the calculation of quantum. This is unnecessary, because the statutes already state what the judge should consider. It is also unhelpful, because it does not in the end explain why the length of the marital relationship should serve as the sole "moral" determinant of support, to the exclusion of need and other factors. The flexible mandate of the statutes belies such rigidity.

[56] Mr. Bracklow makes a final policy argument. In an age of multiple marriages, he asserts, the law should permit closure on relationships so parties can move on. Why, he asks, should a young person whose marriage lasts less than a year be fixed with a lifelong obligation of support? When can a former spouse finally move on, knowing that he or she cannot be drawn back into the past by an unexpected application for support?

[57] Again the answer is that under the statutes, the desirability of freedom to move on to new relationships is merely one of several objectives that might guide the judge. Since all the objectives must be balanced, it often will not be possible to satisfy one absolutely. The respondent in effect seeks a judicially created "statute of limitations" on marriage. The Court has no power to impose such a limitation, nor should it. It would inject a rigidity into the system that Parliament and the legislatures have rejected. Marriage, while it may not prove to be "till death do us part," is a serious commitment not to be undertaken lightly. It involves the potential for lifelong obligation. There are no magical cut-off dates. ...

[58] The trial judge found that this was a modern marriage of two independent people; that the parties did not confirm expressly or by conduct that they owed each other an obligation of support; and that Mrs. Bracklow had suffered no disadvantage as a result of the marriage or its breakdown. There are two ways of interpreting these findings. The first is that the judge held that Mrs. Bracklow was entitled to neither contractual nor compensatory post-marital support. This fails to address the possibility of non-compensatory entitlement to support. Alternatively, the trial judge may be read as holding that because Mr. and Mrs. Bracklow had no express or implied agreement for intra-marital support, no hardship of any kind was experienced by Mrs. Bracklow on divorce, as she would have been no better off had they stayed married. To say this, however, is to deny the presumption of intra-marital support that may

fairly be imputed to married couples, absent contrary indications. The trial judge—
by holding that absent affirmative, proactive indications, the Bracklows shared no
mutual support expectation during their marriage—turned the presumption on its
head. This belies the reality that it is artificial to expect spousal couples to expressly
"confirm" their mutual obligations and expectations.

[59] Refocusing the facts of this case through the correct juridical lens suggests
that while the early years of the Bracklows' union might indicate the atypical partnership of strict independence (rebutting the presumption of intra-marital mutual interdependency), by the end the Bracklows had established a more interdependent
relationship. In addition to adjusting their expenses to a more even ratio, it is evident
that Mr. Bracklow covered Mrs. Bracklow's needs in the early stages of her illness.
Accordingly, it follows that divorce did in fact render Mrs. Bracklow in a state of
economic hardship, as contemplated by s. 15.2(6)(c) of the *Divorce Act*.

[60] Bearing in mind the statutory objectives of support and balancing the relevant factors, I conclude that Mrs. Bracklow is eligible for support based on the length
of cohabitation, the hardship marriage breakdown imposed on her, her palpable need,
and Mr. Bracklow's financial ability to pay. While the combined cohabitation and
marriage of seven years were not long, neither were they (by today's standards) very
short. Mrs. Bracklow contributed, when possible, as a self-sufficient member of the
family, at times shouldering the brunt of the financial obligations. These factors establish that it would be unjust and contrary to the objectives of the statutes for Mrs.
Bracklow to be cast aside as ineligible for support, and for Mr. Bracklow to assume
none of the state's burden to care for his ex-wife.

[61] I leave the determination of the quantum of support to the trial judge, who is
in a better position to address the facts of this case than our appellate tribunal. My
only comment on the issue is to reiterate that all the relevant statutory factors, including the length of the marital relationship and the relative independence of the parties
throughout that marital relationship, must be considered, together with the amount of
support Mr. Bracklow has already paid to Mrs. Bracklow. I therefore do not exclude
the possibility that no further support will be required, i.e., that Mr. Bracklow's contributions to date have discharged the just and appropriate quantum. Absent settlement between the parties, these issues are for the trial judge to resolve.

Carol Rogerson, "Spousal Support Post-Bracklow: The Pendulum Swings Again?"
(2001), 19 *Canadian Family Law Quarterly* 185, at 187ff.

In 1983 there was *Messier v. Delage*, which directed judges to make awards that
were "fit and just" on the facts before the court, a test that was generally understood
as providing a fairly generous basis for spousal support, and in particular one that
precluded the kind of crystal-ball gazing about future potential for self-sufficiency
involved in time-limited orders. Then in 1987 there was the *Pelech* trilogy with its
test of "causal connection," which narrowed the basis for spousal support and led to
an increased emphasis on clean breaks and the widespread use of time-limited support

orders. In 1992 the pendulum swung back in the direction of a broader basis for spousal support with the release of *Moge* and its re-conceptualization of spousal support around the idea of compensation. And now, most recently, we have *Bracklow*, with its talk of spousal support as a "basic social obligation." In terms of swings of the spousal support pendulum, *Bracklow* is generally regarded as further broadening the basis of spousal support even beyond what was accomplished by *Moge*, although as I shall argue below, I think it also carries with it some narrowing potential.

Some of these shifts in spousal support are probably inevitable and come with the territory. Spousal support raises a difficult set of issues. An enormous amount of academic ink has been spilled trying to come up with an explanation of spousal support that fits with the basic principles and values of modern family law. There are fundamental disagreements, at the level of values and policies, about what the role of spousal support should be given ... contemporary understandings of marriage and conjugal relationships more generally. One of the interesting aspects of the *Bracklow* decision, to my mind, is Justice McLachlin's recognition that there are no simple answers to the question of the appropriate model of spousal support because there are competing and often conflicting policy pulls in this area that have to be balanced, both by the legislature and by individual judges deciding spousal support cases. As her judgment recognizes, on the one hand, marriage is no longer a life-long union; we allow people to divorce fairly easily and to form new relationships and commitments, suggesting that we should place some value on disentangling the spouses and promoting spousal independence after relationship breakdown. As well, we no longer subscribe to the assumption that women are inherently dependent on men for their support. On the other hand, we also know that marriage and cohabitation can create complex interdependencies that are hard to unravel; not every former spouse is going to be able to become economically self-sufficient—and certainly not easily or quickly. How to achieve an appropriate balance of these values is the issue with which the law of spousal support has been struggling for the past several decades. ...

While on the surface *Bracklow* appears to have clarified the bases for spousal support, in practice it has tended to confuse rather than clarify. The recognition of multiple bases for support and the emphasis on the absence of any over-arching philosophy has reinforced a decidedly anti-conceptual, anti-philosophical tendency in spousal support law that discourages clear thinking about the reasons why spousal support is being awarded. In many cases mixed or alternate bases for spousal support are being found; in others, rather than grappling with the compensatory principle, judges simply fall back on the conventional concepts of needs and means and self-sufficiency in a search for results that appear fair and just. ...

To my mind, the most significant impact of *Bracklow*, as evidenced by the subsequent case law, is the Supreme Court of Canada's message that there is no one model or philosophy of spousal support and there are no fixed rules or guidelines for determining spousal support. Put simply, the message is "it's all discretion." Spousal support awards are simply the result of the trial judge exercising his or her discretion in determining the appropriate balance between different support objectives and factors in response to the facts of particular cases. This is a message that has been taken to heart by trial judges and reiterated constantly in the post-*Bracklow* case law. There is no doubt that spousal support was a highly discretionary area of law even prior to *Bracklow*. But *Moge* was a noble attempt to achieve some conceptual clarity and coherence in the face of legislation that simply offers a checklist of factors and objectives. What was needed post-*Moge* were more attempts to find patterns in the evolving case law and to work out guidelines for the implementation of amorphous concepts such as compensation and need. *Bracklow*, I fear, may impede these much-needed efforts. ...

What gets lost when all support claims are lumped together as based on need and dependency is the sense of compensatory support as an earned entitlement, like a share of matrimonial property, based on the economic contributions that women have made to the family through their assumption of responsibility for child rearing, contributions that can be valued not only in terms of wives' foregone opportunities, but also in terms of the economic advantage conferred on husbands who have been able to devote themselves to their employment, while enjoying the benefits of children and family life. When spousal support is conceptualized as grounded only in need and in obligations arising from the fact of marriage, the legitimacy and strength of the support claim is weakened. Although there is a common tendency to see need as offering a broader basis for spousal support than compensation, needs-based support is very vulnerable to limitation. Need is an easily manipulated concept; it is very easy to find that someone who is able to cover their basic necessities or is employed has no need and is self-sufficient. As well, in *Bracklow* the Supreme Court of Canada introduced many potential limitations on the extent of needs based support claims, most obviously the concept that need alone does not determine the support award, and that an award may meet only a portion of the claimant's need. As shown in the redetermination of support by the trial judge in *Bracklow*, for example, non-compensatory support may be time-limited despite on-going need. As well, needs-based support is subject to reduction or termination in light of the payor's re-partnering and assumption of new support obligations, and as well, the recipient's re-partnering.

Admittedly, these fears of a reduction in overall support amounts as a result of *Bracklow* would appear to be unfounded, at least in Ontario at the current time, where, as I will discuss further below, spousal support awards appear to be at an all-time high. However, the same is not true across the country, and the highly discretionary nature of spousal support determinations, reinforced by the rulings in *Bracklow*, may render the situation in Ontario vulnerable to change.

Even if the regressive potential of the "needs and means" analysis does not appear to be an immediate cause of concern, at least in Ontario, I would argue that *Bracklow* has still had an overall negative impact on the general law of spousal support as it deals with the vast majority of typical spousal support cases involving marriages with children in which the primary caregiver has a compromised earning capacity. This negative impact is due to the extreme emphasis in *Bracklow* on discretion and the absence of rules in determining spousal support, which deflects attention away from the important and necessary goal of trying to develop guidelines and rules to bring predictability and consistency to this area of law. ...

There has been some speculation that *Bracklow* may have increased the willingness of courts to order time-limited support. This view is based upon the fact that the Supreme Court of Canada indicated that a support award may only meet a portion of the claimant's need and its suggestion that Mr. Bracklow might have satisfied his obligation through the support previously paid. And on the re-determination of support by the trial judge, a time-limited order was in fact imposed. ...

Spousal support post-*Bracklow* is not too different a world from that of spousal support post-*Moge*. The *Bracklow* decision added very little of a concrete nature to the existing structure of spousal support law. The only clear ruling in the case was that spousal support is not exclusively compensatory in nature—a conclusion that seemed obvious and merely endorsed the dominant practice post-*Moge*. The difficult issues in spousal support are those of quantum rather than entitlement—determining the amount and duration of support—both in the atypical cases that raise pure non-compensatory claims, as well as the vast majority of ordinary spousal support cases where the compensatory aspects of spousal support loom large. *Bracklow* offered no specific guidance on these issues, with the Court even refusing to make a ruling on the appropriate quantum on the facts of *Bracklow*, and instead sending the issue back to the trial court for re-determination. The difficult issues that surfaced as the law of spousal support developed post-*Moge* remain largely the same, with *Bracklow* having provided no answers or guidance.

Discussion Note

Individual Need and Patterns of Dependency in Marriage

In examining the reasoning in *Bracklow* and Rogerson's analysis, consider also the following discussion about comments made by family law solicitors in the United Kingdom: see Carol Smart, *The Ties That Bind: Law, Marriage, and the Reproduction of Patriarchal Relations* (London: Routledge & Kegan Paul, 1984), at 190-91.

> This tendency to individualise and decontextualise domestic disputes tended to lead solicitors to individualistic solutions to the problems posed by divorce. The following solicitor expresses this thinking quite clearly.

> > It's a funny business our matrimonial law. He's more or less supposed to have taken her on for life, for better or for worse, despite the divorce law, and theoretically the only thing that lets him off the hook is when she remarries. And so I always advise men clients who are in the position to pay more money to the wife ... as a joke I don't mean it seriously because if you give her too much she may think she's on to a good thing and hang on to it. But I always say send her expensive perfumes, offer to babysit for her and get her, you know, send her out to dances, you know send a car for her to take her because the *sooner she's off your hands and into somebody else's the better*. You know I say the last thing you want to do is to be upsetting her all the time so that she is perpetually going around weeping and looking [so] awful that nobody else will look at her. You know you've got to strike a nice balance so that she's happy and attractive and then somebody else will take her because theoretically she's on his back until she remarries. (My emphasis.)

> This final quote is an excellent example of a process of depoliticisation. Basically, structural events are interpreted solely as conflicts between individuals where, given enough

cunning, one party can rid himself of an unfortunate problem. In this solicitor's account your sympathy is drawn to the poor husband who has this awful problem and the wife is reduced to a burden. Attention is not drawn to her poverty and her inability to survive financially but to the desirability of offloading her (suitably happy and attractive) on to someone else. And then of course the cycle can repeat itself. Whilst she is happily remarried she can repay her keep in kind (i.e. domestic labour and sex), but should this marriage fail as well she becomes a burden again, hopefully to be passed on to another man although she may well be too old to be considered attractive by then.

What is so noticeably absent in the accounts of most of these solicitors is a recognition that the problems of divorce stem from the problems of marriage. Of course these problems are exacerbated by a drop in living standards as well as a great deal of emotional misery, but the issues of conflict that solicitors deal with do not arise on divorce, they arise from the nature of marriage. There is a continuity from marriage to divorce because the sexual division of labour which is celebrated as natural and desirable during marriage is precisely the basis of the main conflict on divorce.

To what extent do the principles of spousal support in Canada address Smart's concerns? In reflecting on this question, consider again the role of private bargaining with respect to spousal support in the section that follows.

5. Rethinking Orders and Agreements

Miglin v. Miglin
[2003] 1 SCR 303; (2003), 34 RFL (5th) 255

[The parties were married in 1979; five years later, they purchased a lodge in Northern Ontario as equal shareholders and then proceeded to run it as a family business. In this context, they each drew a salary of approximately $80,000 per annum. They had four children and divided their time together between the lodge and the matrimonial home in Toronto. The parties separated in 1993, when the four children were between 2 and 8 years of age. Both the husband and the wife were then in their early 40s. Eventually, after more than a year of negotiations, they executed a separation agreement in which it was agreed that the children would reside primarily with the wife and the husband would pay $60,000 annually in child support. He also agreed to pay the mortgage on the matrimonial home and transferred his one-half interest in the home (valued at $250,000) to the wife. In return, the wife released her interest in the lodge (also valued at $250,000) to the husband. The wife released any interest in an unvalued outfitting business owned by the husband as well. In addition, the parties entered into a consulting agreement in which the wife was entitled to receive an annual salary of $15,000 from the lodge for a period of five years; the agreement was renewable on consent of the parties. Overall, the parties agreed that the wife would fully and finally release any entitlement to spousal support.

After the divorce, relations between the parties became acrimonious; just before the expiry of the consulting agreement, the wife applied for sole custody, child support, and spousal support under s. 15.2 of the *Divorce Act*. The trial judge awarded the wife spousal support in an amount of $4,400 per month for a period of five years, and the Court of Appeal upheld the award of support and removed the five-year limit. On appeal to the Supreme Court of Canada, a majority of seven justices concluded that the appeal should be allowed, LeBel and Deschamps JJ dissenting.]

BASTARACHE and ARBOUR JJ: [1] This appeal concerns the proper approach to determining an application for spousal support pursuant to s. 15.2(1) of the *Divorce Act*, … where the spouses have executed a final agreement that addresses all matters respecting their separation, including a release of any future claim for spousal support. Accordingly, this appeal presents the Court with an opportunity to address directly the question of the continued application of the *Pelech* trilogy … in light of the significant legislative and jurisprudential changes that have taken place since its facts arose and since its release.

[2] In broader terms, the appeal raises the question of the proper weight to be given to any type of spousal support agreement that one of the parties subsequently wishes to have modified through an initial application in court for such support. In that sense, the matter is not restricted to spousal support agreements that contain a time-limited support arrangement or to agreements which contain a full and final release from support obligations by one or both parties.

[3] The parties to this appeal, now divorced, entered into a final agreement that sought to settle all of their financial and personal affairs surrounding the breakdown of their marriage. In addition to property equalization, custody, access and support of their children, and a commercial contract between the respondent and the appellant's company, the parties agreed to release one another from any claims to spousal support. This Court must determine the proper weight to be accorded that agreement where one party subsequently makes an application for spousal support under the *Divorce Act*.

[4] As we explain below, we believe that a fairly negotiated agreement that represents the intentions and expectations of the parties and that complies substantially with the objectives of the *Divorce Act* as a whole should receive considerable weight. In an originating application for spousal support, where the parties have executed a pre-existing agreement, the court should look first to the circumstances of negotiation and execution to determine whether the applicant has established a reason to discount the agreement. The court would inquire whether one party was vulnerable and the other party took advantage of that vulnerability. The court also examines whether the substance of the agreement, at formation, complied substantially with the general objectives of the Act. As we elaborate later, these general objectives include not only an equitable sharing of the consequences of the marriage breakdown under s. 15.2, but also certainty, finality and autonomy. Second, the court would ask whether, viewed from the time the application is made, the applicant has established that the agreement no longer reflects the original intention of the parties and whether the agreement is still in substantial compliance with the objectives of the Act. In contrast, the trial judge's and the Court of Appeal's approaches failed to value a determination by the parties as to what is mutually acceptable to them. We would thus allow this appeal. …

[28] As mentioned earlier in these reasons, this appeal is concerned with the continued application of the *Pelech* trilogy. The three cases making up this trilogy were

decided immediately after the promulgation of the 1985 Act, but deal with situations governed by the 1968 Act. Those cases establish a change-based test under which a court is permitted to override a final agreement on spousal support only where there has been a significant change in circumstances since the making of the agreement. The test establishes a threshold that is defined as a radical and unforeseen change that is causally connected to the marriage. It does not deal with the fairness of the agreement or its attention to the objectives of the *Divorce Act*. It is designed to promote certainty and to facilitate a clean break in the relationship of the parties, focussing on individual autonomy and respect for contracts. Since the release of the trilogy, the law of spousal support has evolved. A compensatory approach was adopted in *Moge v. Moge*, [1992] 3 SCR 813. A more nuanced approach was developed in *Bracklow v. Bracklow*, [1999] 1 SCR 420. Self-sufficiency, autonomy and finality remain relevant factors in our case law, but many question whether the emphasis put on them by the trilogy remains. The question posed is whether agreements concluded with the intent that they be final can, under the 1985 Act, be overridden on grounds other than those defined in the trilogy. ...

[29] The issues in the present appeal resemble those facing this Court in the *Pelech* trilogy. Despite significant changes in the intervening years, the basic question remains: What role should a pre-existing agreement play in determining an application for spousal support? ...

[31] The facts and reasoning of the three cases constituting the trilogy have attracted substantial scholarly and judicial commentary. We do not propose to review those decisions in detail again here. Suffice it to say that the *Pelech* trilogy has come to stand for the proposition that a court will not interfere with a pre-existing agreement that attempts fully and finally to settle the matter of spousal support as between the parties unless the applicant can establish that there has been a radical and unforeseen change in circumstances that is causally connected to the marriage. The trilogy represents an approach to spousal support that has been described as a "clean break," emphasizing finality and the severing of ties between former spouses. ...

[32] With the coming into force of the 1985 Act and the release of the trilogy the following year, confusion ensued as to whether the trilogy had any continued application. The confusion may stem from two main factors. On the one hand, the 1968 Act, while providing less direction on the issue of support, could be interpreted as not inconsistent with the new, more detailed statute. ...

[33] On the other hand, some members of the judiciary and several scholars recognized the potential difficulties in applying the *Pelech* trilogy in the new statutory context. ...

[34] In addition to generating some confusion, the trilogy received no small degree of criticism, from both legal scholars and family law practitioners. The main thrust of the criticism levied at the trilogy was summarized by McLachlin J (as she then was) in a speech delivered to the National Family Law Program over a decade ago. McLachlin J suggested that the "joint venture model" of marriage, which viewed married persons as autonomous individuals entering into equal partnerships who should and do take responsibility for themselves, informed the economic self-sufficiency or "clean break" theory of spousal support endorsed by this Court in

Pelech. Although McLachlin J fully endorsed the model of equality on which the trilogy was based, she cautioned that that model did not necessarily conform to everyone's reality. This disjuncture, in her view0explained much of the criticism to which the trilogy has been subjected (the Honourable Madame Justice B. McLachlin, "Spousal Support: Is It Fair To Apply New-Style Rules to Old-Style Marriages?" (1990), 9 *Can. J. Fam. L.* 131).

[35] Since the trilogy, decisions from this Court have recognized a shift in the normative standards informing spousal support orders. In *Moge, supra*, at p. 849 L'Heureux-Dubé J held for the majority that the underlying theme of the 1985 Act is the "fair and equitable distribution of resources to alleviate the economic consequences of marriage or marriage breakdown." In making an order for support, she noted that the court must have regard to *all four* of the objectives of spousal support, none of which is paramount. Self-sufficiency is only one of those objectives and an attenuated one at that (to be promoted "insofar as practicable" (p. 852)). L'Heureux-Dubé J concluded that Parliament appears to have adopted a compensatory model of support, one which attempts to ensure the equitable sharing of the economic consequences of marriage and its breakdown.

[36] Regarding the trilogy specifically, L'Heureux-Dubé J held that it had no application to the circumstances of that case, where there had been no final agreement between the parties. In her view, the trilogy did not address issues of entitlement to support in the absence of an agreement. Nevertheless, her reasoning with respect to the "compensatory model" of support only served to fuel debate as to whether the *Pelech* trilogy still governed at all. ...

[37] This Court's decision in *G.(L.) v. B.(G.)*, [1995] 3 SCR 370, further illustrated the questions relating to the trilogy's continued relevance. ... Sopinka J held that the trial judge applied the correct test of material change, enunciated by this Court in *Willick v. Willick*, [1994] 3 SCR 670. He further held that there was no basis to interfere with the trial judge's findings of fact and, accordingly, that the threshold of material change had not been met. He noted, finally, that the Court of Appeal had erred in applying a presumption of self-sufficiency to the recipient wife and, accordingly, in granting the husband's application for a reduction in the quantum of his support obligation. ...

[38] In contrast, L'Heureux-Dubé J, writing for a three-member minority, addressed the trilogy directly. She concluded that it is no longer good law. In language cited and relied on extensively by Abella JA in the present appeal, L'Heureux-Dubé J explained that the new 1985 Act adopted "as its underlying philosophy a partnership in marriage and, at the time of a divorce, an equitable division of its economic consequences between the spouses" (*G.(L.)* at para. 41). ...

[39] Whereas the 1968 Act refers only to the "conduct of the parties and the condition, means, and other circumstances of each of them" (s. 11(1)), the 1985 Act abandons the reference to the conduct of the parties and makes explicit both the objectives of spousal support and the factors to be considered in making an order. That these objectives can and do often conflict and compete suggests an intention on the part of Parliament to vest in trial judges a significant discretion to assess the weight to be given each objective against the very particular backdrop of the parties' circumstances. Moreover, we agree that the importance given to self-sufficiency and a "clean break" in the

jurisprudence relying on the trilogy is not only incompatible with the new Act, but too often fails to accord with the realities faced by many divorcing couples. Indeed, in *Bracklow*, *supra*, this Court recognized how these different realities also mirror competing normative standards justifying entitlement to spousal support. ...

[40] In light of these developments in the understanding of spousal support, the question "Does the trilogy apply or not?" is perhaps too mechanical, and the answer does not turn solely on the existence of a new Act. Parliament's recognition of competing objectives of spousal support renders the trilogy's privileging of "clean break" principles inappropriate, but this is not to suggest that the policy concerns that drove the trilogy are wholly irrelevant to the new legislative context. On the contrary, the objectives of autonomy and finality, as well as the recognition that the parties may go on to undertake new family obligations, continue to inform the current *Divorce Act* and remain significant today. What has changed is the singular emphasis on self-sufficiency as a policy goal to the virtual exclusion of other objectives that may or may not be equally pressing according to the specific circumstances of the parties. Such an emphasis on self-sufficiency is inconsistent with both the compensatory model of support developed in *Moge*, and the non-compensatory model of support developed in *Bracklow*. It is also inconsistent with the interpretive point made in both cases that no single objective in s. 15.2(6) is paramount: *Bracklow*, at para. 35; *Moge*, at p. 852. Nevertheless, promoting self-sufficiency remains an explicit legislative objective.

[41] In addition to these competing policy goals, we also note that the current statutory language does not support direct incorporation of the trilogy test. ...

[42] The current statutory context, however, is quite different in that Parliament has explicitly directed the court to consider a change in circumstances only where the application is for variation. ...

[43] Section 15.2 provides no such similar direction. Rather, the court is explicitly directed to take into account certain non-exhaustive factors, and instructed that a support order should advance certain specified objectives. On a plain reading of the statute, then, there is simply no basis for importing a change threshold, radical, material or otherwise, into the provision. Indeed, on an initial application for support, the very concept of "change of circumstances" has no relevance, except to the limited extent that there might have been a pre-existing order or agreement that needs to be considered.

[44] How, then, should trial judges exercise the discretion vested in them by virtue of the Act where a party who makes an initial application for support has previously entered into an agreement that purports to have settled all matters between the spouses? How should trial judges assess the appropriate weight to be given such an agreement where s. 15.2 of the 1985 Act appears to accord it no greater priority than other factors?

[45] It is helpful initially to identify several inappropriate approaches. In our view, the answer to these questions does not lie in adopting a near-impermeable standard such that a court will endorse any agreement, regardless of the inequities it reveals. Neither, however, does the solution lie in unduly interfering with agreements freely entered into and on which the parties reasonably expected to rely. It is also not helpful to read between the lines in s. 15.2 so as to identify a single implicit overriding legislative objective overshadowing the factors specifically set out. The fact that judicial and societal understandings of spousal support have changed since the release of

Pelech and the adoption of admittedly competing factors in s. 15.2(6) does not lead to an unfettered discretion on the part of trial judges to substitute their own view of what is required for what the parties considered mutually acceptable. ...

[46] Nevertheless, the language and purpose of the 1985 Act militate in favour of a contextual assessment of all the circumstances. This includes the content of the agreement; in order to determine the proper weight it should be accorded in a s. 15.2 application. In exercising their discretion, trial judges must balance Parliament's objective of equitable sharing of the consequences of marriage and its breakdown with the parties' freedom to arrange their affairs as they see fit. Accordingly, a court should be loathe to interfere with a pre-existing agreement unless it is convinced that the agreement does not comply substantially with the overall objectives of the *Divorce Act*. This is particularly so when the pre-existing spousal support agreement is part of a comprehensive settlement of all issues related to the termination of the marriage. Since the issues, as well as their settlement, are likely interrelated, the support part of the agreement would at times be difficult to modify without putting into question the entire arrangements.

[47] Having determined that the narrow test enunciated in the *Pelech* trilogy for interfering with a pre-existing agreement is not appropriate in the current statutory context, we now consider the approaches taken by the courts below in this appeal. ...

[The court considered the fairness test applied by the trial judge and the material-change test applied in the Court of Appeal. The court then considered the proper approach to applications under s. 15.2:]

[64] An initial application for spousal support inconsistent with a pre-existing agreement requires an investigation into all the circumstances surrounding that agreement, first, at the time of its formation, and second, at the time of the application. In our view, this two-stage analysis provides the court with a principled way of balancing the competing objectives underlying the *Divorce Act* and of locating the potentially problematic aspects of spousal support arrangements in their appropriate temporal context. Before doing so, however, it is necessary to discuss some of the interpretive difficulties affecting spousal support.

[65] As a starting point, we endorse the reasoning of this Court in *Moge, supra*, where L'Heureux-Dubé J held that the spousal support objectives of the *Divorce Act* are designed to achieve an equitable sharing of the economic consequences of marriage and marriage breakdown. By explicitly directing the court to consider the objectives listed in s. 15.2(6), the 1985 Act departs significantly from the exclusive "means and needs" approach of the former statute. We note, however, that there is a potential tension between recognizing any economic advantages or disadvantages to the spouses arising from the marriage or its breakdown and promoting, even if only to the extent practicable, the economic self-sufficiency of each spouse (ss. 15.2(6)(a), and (d)). The way to reconcile these competing objectives is to recognize that the meaning of the term "equitable sharing" is not fixed in the Act and will, rather, vary according to the facts of a particular marriage. Parliament, aware of the many ways in which parties structure a marriage and particularly its economic aspects, drafted legislation broad enough that

one cannot say that the spousal support provisions have a narrow fixed content. Contrasted with the former Act, then, these objectives expressly direct the court to consider different criteria on which to base entitlement to spousal support, while retaining the objective of fostering the parties' ability to get on with their lives.

[66] The role that these objectives was intended to play, however, must be understood in the proper statutory context. Whether by way of an initial application or an application to vary, the criteria listed in s. 15.2(6) and s. 17(7) pertain to spousal support orders imposed by the court. Nowhere in the *Divorce Act* is it expressed that parties *must* adhere strictly, or at all, to these objectives in reaching a mutually acceptable agreement. Rather, the listed objectives relate only to orders for spousal support, that is, to circumstances where the parties have been unable to reach an agreement. Moreover, the positive obligation that the Act places on counsel to advise their clients of alternatives to litigation, noted above, indicates Parliament's clear conception of the new divorce regime as one that places a high premium on private settlement. Parliament's preference appears to be that parties settle their dispute, without asking a court to apply s. 15.2(6) to make an order. This is not to suggest that the objectives are irrelevant in the context of a negotiated agreement. The parties, or at least their counsel, will be conscious of the likely outcome of litigation in the event that negotiation fails. Consideration of the statutory entitlements will undoubtedly influence negotiations. But the mutually acceptable agreement negotiated by the parties will not necessarily mirror the spousal support that a judge would have awarded. Holding that any agreement that deviates from the objectives listed in s. 15.2(6) be given little or no weight would seriously undermine the significant policy goal of negotiated settlement. It would also undermine the parties' autonomy and freedom to structure their post-divorce lives in a manner that reflects their own objectives and concerns. Such a position would leave little room to recognize the terms that the parties determined were mutually acceptable to them and in substantial compliance with the objectives of the *Divorce Act*.

[67] Having said this, we are of the view that there is nevertheless a significant public interest in ensuring that the goal of negotiated settlements not be pursued, through judicial approbation of agreements, with such a vengeance that individual autonomy becomes a straitjacket. Therefore, assessment of the appropriate weight to be accorded a pre-existing agreement requires a balancing of the parties' interest in determining their own affairs with an appreciation of the peculiar aspects of separation agreements generally and spousal support in particular. ...

[As the court noted, each of the parties suggested a model for the exercise of judicial discretion in the context of a s. 15.2 application. The appellant submitted that the proper test for determining how much weight should be accorded to a pre-existing agreement should be similar to that adopted by provincial legislatures, such as s. 33(4) of the Ontario *Family Law Act*. This test is one of "unconscionable circumstances." By contrast, the respondent proposed a more searching standard of review to examine the prior agreement as a whole, and having regard to the factors and objectives listed in s. 15.2 of the *Divorce Act*. According to the court, both positions had merit, but neither was entirely satisfactory.]

[73] In our view, there is merit to each of these positions. Nevertheless, we believe that the approach that will provide both negotiating spouses and, failing agreement, courts with a principled and consistent framework is not that proposed by either party. The test should ultimately recognize the particular ways in which separation agreements generally and spousal support arrangements specifically are vulnerable to a risk of inequitable sharing at the time of negotiation and in the future. At the same time, the test must not undermine the parties' right to decide for themselves what constitutes for them, in the circumstances of their marriage, mutually acceptable equitable sharing. Our approach, for example, takes greater account of the parties' subjective sense of equitable sharing than the objective "unconscionable circumstances" standard proposed by counsel for the appellant.

[74] Negotiations in the family law context of separation or divorce are conducted in a unique environment. Both academics and practitioners have acknowledged that this is a time of intense personal and emotional turmoil, in which one or both of the parties may be particularly vulnerable. Unlike emotionally neutral economic actors negotiating in the commercial context, divorcing couples inevitably bring to the table a host of emotions and concerns that do not obviously accord with the making of rational economic decisions. ...

[75] Add to this mix the intimate nature of the marital relationship that makes it difficult to overcome potential power imbalances and modes of influence. ...

[76] We also note that, depending on the circumstances of the parties, a wide array of interrelated elements may make up a global separation agreement. Such a separation agreement may comprise division or equalization of marital property, provision for custody and support of any children, as well as provisions for spousal support, be it in the form of lump sum, periodic payment, time-limited payment or a waiver and release. These matters, with the exception of the property division, are primarily prospective in nature, although compensatory spousal support is retrospective. ...

[77] In our view, Parliament's recognition of the potential complications in the process of contracting spousal support is reflected in the *Divorce Act* itself. We see this in the direction to the court to consider an agreement as only one factor among others, rather than to treat it as binding, subject merely to remedies in contract law. Accordingly, contract law principles are not only better suited to the commercial context, but it is implicit in s. 15 of the 1985 Act that they were not intended to govern the applicability of private contractual arrangements for spousal support.

[78] Therefore, in searching for a proper balance between consensus and finality on the one hand, and sensitivity to the unique concerns that arise in the post-divorce context on the other, a court should be guided by the objectives of spousal support listed in the Act. In doing so, however, the court should treat the parties' reasonable best efforts to meet those objectives as presumptively dispositive of the spousal support issue. The court should set aside the wishes of the parties as expressed in a pre-existing agreement only where the applicant shows that the agreement fails to be in substantial compliance with the overall objectives of the Act. These include not only those apparent in s. 15.2 but also, as noted above, certainty, finality and autonomy.

[79] With these broad concerns in mind, we now turn to the specifics of the two-stage approach to the exercise of the court's discretion.

(a) Stage One

[80] In an originating application for spousal support, where the parties have executed a pre-existing agreement, the court should first look to the circumstances in
which the agreement was negotiated and executed to determine whether there is any
reason to discount it.

(i) The Circumstances of Execution

[81] It is difficult to provide a definitive list of factors to consider in assessing the
circumstances of negotiation and execution of an agreement. We simply state that the
court should be alive to the conditions of the parties, including whether there were
any circumstances of oppression, pressure, or other vulnerabilities, taking into account
all of the circumstances, including those set out in s. 15.2(4)(a) and (b) and the conditions under which the negotiations were held, such as their duration and whether
there was professional assistance.

[82] We pause here to note three important points. First, we are not suggesting
that courts must necessarily look for "unconscionability" as it is understood in the
common law of contract. There is a danger in borrowing terminology rooted in other
branches of the law and transposing it into what all agree is a unique legal context.
There may be persuasive evidence brought before the court that one party took advantage of the vulnerability of the other party in separation or divorce negotiations that
would fall short of evidence of the power imbalance necessary to demonstrate unconscionability in a commercial context between, say, a consumer and a large financial
institution. Next, the court should not presume an imbalance of power in the relationship or a vulnerability on the part of one party, nor should it presume that the apparently stronger party took advantage of any vulnerability on the part of the other.
Rather, there must be evidence to warrant the court's finding that the agreement should
not stand on the basis of a fundamental flaw in the negotiation process. Recognition
of the emotional stress of separation or divorce should not be taken as giving rise to a
presumption that parties in such circumstances are incapable of assenting to a binding
agreement. If separating or divorcing parties were generally incapable of making
agreements it would be fair to enforce, it would be difficult to see why Parliament
included "agreement or arrangement" in s. 15.2(4)(c). Finally, we stress that the mere
presence of vulnerabilities will not, in and of itself, justify the court's intervention.
The degree of professional assistance received by the parties will often overcome
any systemic imbalances between the parties.

[83] Where vulnerabilities are not present, or are effectively compensated by the
presence of counsel or other professionals or both, or have not been taken advantage
of, the court should consider the agreement as a genuine mutual desire to finalize the
terms of the parties' separation and as indicative of their substantive intentions.
Accordingly, the court should be loathe to interfere. In contrast, where the power
imbalance did vitiate the bargaining process, the agreement should not be read as
expressing the parties' notion of equitable sharing in their circumstances and the agreement will merit little weight.

(ii) The Substance of the Agreement

[84] Where the court is satisfied that the conditions under which the agreement was negotiated are satisfactory, it must then turn its attention to the substance of the agreement. The court must determine the extent to which the agreement takes into account the factors and objectives listed in the Act, thereby reflecting an equitable sharing of the economic consequences of marriage and its breakdown. Only a significant departure from the general objectives of the Act will warrant the court's intervention on the basis that there is not substantial compliance with the Act. The court must not view spousal support arrangements in a vacuum, however; it must look at the agreement or arrangement in its totality, bearing in mind that all aspects of the agreement are inextricably linked and that the parties have a large discretion in establishing priorities and goals for themselves.

[85] When examining the substance of the agreement, the court should ask itself whether the agreement is in substantial compliance with the *Divorce Act*. As just noted, this "substantial compliance" should be determined by considering whether the agreement represents a significant departure from the general objectives of the Act, which necessarily include, as well as the spousal support considerations in s. 15.2, finality, certainty, and the invitation in the Act for parties to determine their own affairs. The greater the vulnerabilities present at the time of formation, the more searching the court's review at this stage.

[86] Two comments are necessary here. First, assessment of an agreement's substantial compliance with the entire Act will necessarily permit a broader gamut of arrangements than would be the case if testing agreements narrowly against the support order objectives in s. 15.2(6). Second, a determination that an agreement fails to comply substantially with the Act does not necessarily mean that the entire agreement must be set aside and ignored. Provided that demonstrated vulnerability and exploitation did not vitiate negotiation, even a negotiated agreement that it would be wrong to enforce in its totality may nevertheless indicate the parties' understanding of their marriage and, at least in a general sense, their intentions for the future. Consideration of such an agreement would continue to be mandatory under s. 15.2(4). For example, if it appeared inappropriate to enforce a time limit in a support agreement, the quantum of support agreed upon might still be appropriate, and the agreement might then simply be extended, indefinitely or for a different fixed term.

(b) Stage Two

[87] Where negotiation of the agreement is not impugned on the basis set out above and the agreement was in substantial compliance with the general objectives of the Act at its time of creation, the court should defer to the wishes of the parties and afford the agreement great weight. Nevertheless, the vicissitudes of life mean that, in some circumstances, parties may find themselves down the road of their post-divorce life in circumstances not contemplated. Accordingly, on the bringing of an application under s. 15.2, the court should assess the extent to which enforcement of the agreement still reflects the original intention of the parties and the extent to which it is still in substantial compliance with the objectives of the Act.

[88] The parties' intentions, as reflected by the agreement, are the backdrop against which the court must consider whether the situation of the parties at the time of the application makes it no longer appropriate to accord the agreement conclusive weight. We note that it is unlikely that the court will be persuaded to disregard the agreement in its entirety but for a significant change in the parties' circumstances from what could reasonably be anticipated at the time of negotiation. Although the change need not be "radically unforeseen," and the applicant need not demonstrate a causal connection to the marriage, the applicant must nevertheless clearly show that, in light of the new circumstances, the terms of the agreement no longer reflect the parties' intentions at the time of execution and the objectives of the Act. Accordingly, it will be necessary to show that these new circumstances were not reasonably anticipated by the parties, and have led to a situation that cannot be condoned.

[89] We stress that a certain degree of change is foreseeable most of the time. The prospective nature of these agreements cannot be lost on the parties and they must be presumed to be aware that the future is, to a greater or lesser extent, uncertain. It will be unconvincing, for example, to tell a judge that an agreement never contemplated that the job market might change, or that parenting responsibilities under an agreement might be somewhat more onerous than imagined, or that a transition into the workforce might be challenging. Negotiating parties should know that each person's health cannot be guaranteed as a constant. An agreement must also contemplate, for example, that the relative values of assets in a property division will not necessarily remain the same. Housing prices may rise or fall. A business may take a downturn or become more profitable. Moreover, some changes may be caused or provoked by the parties themselves. A party may remarry or decide not to work. Where the parties have demonstrated their intention to release one another from all claims to spousal support, changes of this nature are unlikely to be considered sufficient to justify dispensing with that declared intention. That said, we repeat that a judge is not bound by the strict *Pelech* standard to intervene only once a change is shown to be "radical." Likewise, it is unnecessary for the party seeking court-ordered support to demonstrate that the circumstances rendering enforcement of the agreement inappropriate are causally connected to the marriage or its breakdown. The test here is not strict foreseeability; a thorough review of case law leaves virtually no change entirely unforeseeable. The question, rather, is the extent to which the unimpeachably negotiated agreement can be said to have contemplated the situation before the court at the time of the application.

[90] The court's focus should be on the agreement's continued correspondence to the parties' original intentions as to their relative positions and the overall objectives of the Act, not on whether a change occurred *per se*. That is to say, we do not consider "change" of any particular nature to be a threshold requirement which, once established, entitles the court to jettison the agreement entirely. Rather, the court should be persuaded that both the intervention and the degree of intervention are warranted. That is, at this stage, even if unbending enforcement of the agreement is inappropriate, that agreement may still indicate to a trial judge the parties' understanding of their relationship and their intentions. Even an agreement that is not determinative as a result of the parties' circumstances at the time of the application warrants compulsory consideration under s. 15.2(4).

[91] Although we recognize the unique nature of separation agreements and their differences from commercial contracts, they are contracts nonetheless. Parties must take responsibility for the contract they execute as well as for their own lives. It is only where the current circumstances represent a significant departure from the range of reasonable outcomes anticipated by the parties, in a manner that puts them at odds with the objectives of the Act, that the court may be persuaded to give the agreement little weight. As we noted above, it would be inconsistent if a different test applied to change an agreement in the form of an initial order under s. 15.2 and to variation of an agreement incorporated into an order under s. 17. In our view, the Act does not create such inconsistency. We do not agree with the Ontario Court of Appeal when it suggests at para. 71, that once a material change has been found, a court has "a wide discretion" to determine what amount of support, if any, should be ordered, based solely on the factors set out in s. 17(7). As La Forest J said in his dissent in *Richardson*, *supra*, at p. 881, an order made under the Act has already been judicially determined to be fit and just. The objectives of finality and certainty noted above caution against too broad a discretion in varying an order that the parties have been relying on in arranging their affairs. Consideration of the overall objectives of the Act is consistent with the non-exhaustive direction in s. 17(7) that a variation order "should" consider the four objectives listed there. More generally, a contextual approach to interpretation, reading the entire Act, would indicate that the court would apply those objectives in light of the entire statute. Where the order at issue incorporated the mutually acceptable agreement of the parties, that order reflected the parties' understanding of what constituted an equitable sharing of the economic consequences of the marriage. In our view, whether acting under s. 15.2 or under s. 17, the Court should take that into consideration. ...

[92] In the circumstances of this appeal, we are of the view that the global Separation Agreement should be accorded significant and determinative weight. Looking to the Separation Agreement at the time of its formation, we find nothing to indicate that circumstances surrounding the negotiation and execution of the agreement were fraught with vulnerabilities. On the contrary, the record reveals that these parties underwent extensive negotiation over a substantial time period and engaged the services of several professionals, including experienced and expert counsel. Negotiation of the Separation Agreement lasted some 15 months. Ms. Miglin, in addition to legal advice, received detailed financial advice, both in terms of tax planning and income projections, throughout the negotiation process.

[93] At the trial, Ms. Miglin suggested that she was not content with the Separation Agreement and felt pressured by her husband to agree to the spousal support release. As she phrased it, it was a confusing and emotional time for her. We do not doubt that marital separation is almost inevitably a time of emotional upheaval and confusion. Regardless, in this case there is ample evidence to conclude that any vulnerability experienced by Ms. Miglin was more than adequately compensated by the independent and competent legal counsel representing her interests over a prolonged period, not to mention the services provided to her by other professionals. It is unnecessary, therefore, for us to determine whether Ms. Miglin's evidence relating to her personal feelings would have been sufficient to demonstrate a vulnerability in this case and, if so, whether that vulnerability was exploited. The extent of Ms. Miglin's

professional assistance obviously comes at the upper end of the range, and we would not wish to suggest that hers was the minimum required to assure fair negotiation.

[94] Turning to the substance of the Separation Agreement, we also find nothing to demonstrate a significant departure from the overall objectives of the *Divorce Act*. At the time of separation both the Lodge and the matrimonial home had net values of approximately $500,000. The Separation Agreement provided for Ms. Miglin to transfer to Mr. Miglin her one-half interest in the Lodge in exchange for the transfer to her of his one-half interest in the matrimonial home. Mr. Miglin agreed to assume sole responsibility for the mortgage on the house. We cannot agree with the trial judge's characterization of this arrangement as "not an equal split." He made this assessment on the basis that the business was income-producing and the house was not. Valuation of an asset necessarily takes into account its characteristics, including its potential income, capital appreciation and risks. In the same way that a single asset should not be counted twice (*Boston v. Boston*, [2001] 2 SCR 413, 2001 SCC 43), the factors that went into an asset's valuation should not be considered a second time. Presumably, viewed subjectively, in light of Mr. Miglin's and Ms. Miglin's respective abilities, interests and needs, the business was of greater interest to him and the matrimonial home more attractive to her. That is why they divided the assets as they did. There was no basis for the trial judge to conclude that one asset was worth more than another of identical value. In our view, the division in the Separation Agreement reflects the parties' needs and wishes and fairly distributed the assets acquired and created by them over the course of their marriage.

[95] The Separation Agreement also provided that Ms. Miglin would receive child support in the amount of $1,250 per month, per child, for an annual total of approximately $60,000, taxable in her hands and tax-deductible to Mr. Miglin. The child support arrangement was subject to both an annual cost of living increase and the caveat that it would be revisited, if necessary, once reasons for judgment were released from this Court in *Thibaudeau* ... [[1995] 2 SCR 627], or Parliament enacted legislation that altered the child support tax scheme. The record reveals that the quantum of child support was arrived at in full contemplation of Ms. Miglin's spousal support release. We also note that correspondence between counsel suggests that it was Ms. Miglin's preference to release Mr. Miglin from spousal support on condition that her economic needs were addressed through child support.

[96] The Consulting Agreement, executed between the Lodge and Ms. Miglin, was for a term of five years, with an option to renew on the consent of both parties. Both the trial judge and the Court of Appeal found this arrangement to be "thinly veiled spousal support." If it was, there should be no pejorative sense to the term. If the commercial contract is construed as a form of spousal support, it simply means that the agreement contains a time-limited spousal support agreement with a renewal option, rather than a total waiver of spousal support. Either way, neither is intrinsically unfair nor contrary to the objectives of the Act. There is nothing inherently sinister about a release or a waiver any more than there is about a time-limited arrangement. Any support clause has to be assessed in the full context of the broader agreement, the overall circumstances of the parties, and the degree of compliance with the objectives of the Act. In our view, the Consulting Agreement reflects the parties' intentions to provide Ms. Miglin with a source of employment income for a limited time. That the

parties chose such a method to provide the income to Ms. Miglin does not detract from the commercial nature of the contract. Moreover, the vehicle chosen is appropriate to the manner in which the parties structured their economic lives during the marriage.

[97] It is true that Ms. Miglin stopped receiving her salary of $80,500 from the Lodge. The obvious reason, though, is that she had also stopped working more or less full-time for the Lodge. During the marriage she had hired babysitters to permit her to work at the Lodge. After the separation she could hire babysitters so she could work for a new employer. Or, as in fact she chose, she was free not to seek other employment and to support herself and her children, during the five years of the Consulting Agreement, on the combined income of roughly $75,000 consisting of $60,000 in child support and $15,000 from the Consulting Agreement. Her own financial analyst's tables indicated her choice not to work. Recall too that, since Mr. Miglin had assumed sole responsibility for the mortgage on the matrimonial home, Ms. Miglin's expenses included no rent or mortgage payments.

[98] It is in the context of these arrangements that the final release and waiver of spousal support must be assessed. Overall, the Separation Agreement provided for a certain level of revenue to the wife, in the form of ongoing child support and the consulting fees for a five-year period, with a possibility of renewal. In this way, the Agreement sought to redress any disadvantages arising from the marriage and its breakup in part through the vehicle of the business which was, as it had been throughout the marriage, the parties' major source of income. At the same time, the Separation Agreement sought to facilitate the disentanglement of the parties' economic lives and promote their self-sufficiency. The Separation Agreement advances the 1985 Act's goals of finality and autonomy. During the marriage, Ms. Miglin continued her education (obtaining her BA), earned a salary and obtained work experience; a case was therefore not made out for compensatory support. It is unnecessary, therefore, to determine whether the Separation Agreement would still have complied substantially with the objectives of the Act on facts closer, say, to those in *Moge*.

[99] Accordingly, we find the Separation Agreement at the time of its formation to have been in substantial compliance with the *Divorce Act*.

[100] The Court of Appeal found that, at the time of the support application, the non-renewal of the Consulting Agreement and changes in the child-care arrangements constituted a material change sufficient to justify overriding the spousal support release. As we noted earlier, we do not accept the Court of Appeal's "material change" test as the appropriate basis for dispensing with an otherwise enforceable agreement. Still, with respect to the findings, we believe them to be in error.

[101] With respect to the Consulting Agreement, we note that Ms. Miglin brought her application for corollary relief in June of 1998—prior to the expiry of the five-year term of the contract. Moreover, the parties agree that Ms. Miglin performed the terms of her contract for a period but performed no work for the Lodge, contrary to the Consulting Agreement, for the last two years of the contract. She did, however, continue to receive payment under that contract until its expiry in December 1998. Needless to say, Mr. Miglin opted not to renew the Consulting Agreement at the end of its term. We fail to see how, at the time of application, the ongoing receipt of payment for services not being performed can constitute a change of any kind.

[102] Regarding the purported changes to the child-care arrangements, the *ad hoc* parenting arrangements that developed during the period of amicable relations between the parties no doubt reflected the changing needs of the growing children. These changes are an ordinary fact of life. We note too that by the time of the trial, the eldest child was residing primarily with Mr. Miglin.

[103] Moreover, even if we accept that the expiry of the Consulting Agreement can be construed as occurring at the time of Ms. Miglin's application, we do not consider its non-renewal to be sufficient to render continued reliance on the original agreement inappropriate. First, the contract stipulated that renewal required the consent of both parties. Second, the income projections and tax planning advice provided by Ms. Miglin's accountant at the time of negotiation carried that assumption and thus made her fully aware that she would be without that income in five years. Third, there is no evidence of any damaging long-term impact of the marriage on Ms. Miglin's employability or that at the time of negotiation she underestimated how long it would take to become self-sufficient. Ms. Miglin is an educated woman with employable skills who worked in the business throughout the marriage. Although she is no doubt responsible for the day-to-day care of the three children residing with her, she has previously demonstrated her willingness to engage child-care services. The parties dispute whether Ms. Miglin attempted to pursue any employment. What is clear from the correspondence between counsel during negotiation of the agreement, however, is that Ms. Miglin had no intention of working.

[104] The only real changes we see are the variation of the child support award in accordance with the Guidelines and the fact that the eldest child is now residing primarily with Mr. Miglin. The quantum of child support established in the Agreement provided Ms. Miglin with a minimum amount of income in contemplation of her not working. Her lawyer, in a letter to Mr. Miglin's counsel, states: "She is clearly not going to be working. Taking care of the children is a full time job at this time. It does not change the nature of the spousal support release anyway. ..." Furthermore, the correspondence makes it clear that Ms. Miglin contemplated a reduction in income when the Consulting Agreement ended and was advised by her accountant to plan ahead for this drop in income. In our view, the change to the obligations regarding child care did not take Ms. Miglin's current position outside the reasonable range of circumstances that the parties contemplated in making the Separation Agreement.

[105] At the Court of Appeal, counsel for Ms. Miglin suggested that her financial position deteriorated after the breakdown of the marriage. The record demonstrates (and she concedes), however, that her net worth in fact increased by at least 20 percent. At the time of her support application, a financial statement dated June 2, 1998, filed as part of the record, valued her net worth at $750,000 with essentially no debt. The statement shows that she held $246,000 in RRSPs, $83,000 in cash, and an unencumbered five-bedroom home valued at $395,000. The only debt listed on the statement was an unsubstantial debt for a credit card. By the time of trial, one year later, she valued her home at $400,000. There was no evidence that the terms of the agreement resulted in conditions under which Ms. Miglin could not assure her family's livelihood and had to deplete her assets, thus bringing her outside the range of circumstances in which she pictured herself at the time of executing the Separation Agreement.

[106] The respondent's evidence and argument regarding her circumstances at the time of her support application fail to demonstrate that the agreement fairly negotiated and substantially compliant with the objectives of the 1985 Act at its formation should not continue to govern the parties' post-divorce obligations towards each other. ...

[For the dissenting judges, there was agreement that the *Pelech* trilogy was no longer applicable. LeBel J then reviewed a number of lower court decisions.]

[173] In my view, the lower court cases of particular interest in this context are those in which the court either purports to apply the trilogy but in fact applies a standard that is less stringent, or applies the trilogy standard only reluctantly. These types of cases, and the commentary that they have generated, provide an indication of what makes courts wary of applying the trilogy and thus what is truly at stake in the debate over whether the trilogy should be rejected or reaffirmed.

[174] Two cases are instructive here by way of example. First is the much discussed decision of the Ontario Divisional Court in *Santosuosso* ... [(1997), 32 OR (3d) 143 (Div. Ct.)]. In *Santosuosso*, the parties had entered into a Separation Agreement after a 23-year traditional marriage, in which spousal support was to terminate after two years. The Agreement contained a full waiver and release of all further support even in the face of a catastrophic change in circumstances. After the time-limited support terminated under the Agreement, the wife applied for spousal support pursuant to s. 15 of the Act. She argued that, at the time the Agreement was negotiated, the parties had expected that she would become economically self-sufficient, but that these expectations were not realized. At the time she applied for corollary relief, she had not successfully completed upgrading courses or secured full-time employment. She was working 60 hours a week at low-paying jobs, earning $1,700 monthly. The Divisional Court found that Ms. Santosuosso had suffered a radical, unforeseen change in circumstances that was related to a pattern of economic dependency created in the marriage, concluding, at p. 156, that:

> It was not within the contemplation or expectation or reasonable anticipation of *both parties* to the agreement that the applicant would be working almost 60 hours a week at low-level wages to earn $1,700 a month in 1996. Further, an underpinning of the agreement was that the wife would achieve what can be fairly characterized as a modest and realistic goal for financial independence having regard to her circumstances. [Emphasis in original.]

[175] Critics of the decision have suggested that the court in *Santosuosso*, although paying lip service to the trilogy, applied a considerably less stringent threshold for variation: see, for example, S.M. Grant, "The End of Finality" (1997), 27 RFL (4th) 252. ...

[176] The tension identified here between finality and fairness also surfaces, albeit in a different manner, in *Leopold v. Leopold* (2000), 51 OR (3d) 275. In *Leopold*, the Ontario Superior Court of Justice refused to vary a time-limited support agreement containing a full and final release where the husband sought renewed support. The parties had been married for seven years and had two surviving children. At the time of the marriage, the husband was earning $20,000 per year and had a small net worth of $1,400, while the wife was the beneficiary of a significant family trust. At separation,

the wife's various interests were valued in excess of $4 million. The husband's employability was circumscribed throughout the marriage by health problems which continued after separation. When the parties separated, they entered into agreements whereby the husband received an equalization payment of $205,000 and spousal support in the amount of $1,700 per month for 42 months. After the time-limited support had expired, the husband applied for spousal support under s. 15.2 of the 1985 Act. He cited two factors that in his view should trigger renewed support: the fact that his business plans had not been successful and that the parties' eldest child, who had behavioural and health problems, had begun to live with him. Wilson J applied *Pelech* and denied support, finding that these events did not constitute a radical, unforeseen change in circumstances causally connected to the marriage.

[177] Although she applied *Pelech*, Wilson J also sought to strike a balance between the "important competing objectives of certainty and fairness" (*Leopold*, *supra*, at para. 98). To this end, she devoted considerable effort in her reasons to outlining a less restrictive definition of common-law unconscionability that would fit the unique dynamics of family law, although she ultimately concluded that the agreement in question did not meet even this more relaxed standard. From Wilson J's perspective, an unconscionable agreement in the family law context is an agreement that is outside of the range of what is objectively fair at the time it is entered into. As she outlined at paras. 141 and 143-44:

> [I]n the family law context, the parameters of a strict test of unconscionability begin to blur. *I conclude that the traditional dual test defining what is unconscionable requiring both inequality and improvidence rooted in the common law ignores the special nature of marital relationships.* A rigid application of the inequality requirement ignores the reality that these are not commercial contracts negotiated for commercial gain in emotionally neutral circumstances. ...
>
> I agree with the suggestion of McLeod in his annotation to *B.(G.)*, *supra*, at p. 216 that a court should only intervene if the terms of the settlement are outside the generous ambit within which reasonable disagreement is possible.
>
> I conclude, therefore, that *an unconscionable agreement is one that is clearly outside the range of what is objectively fair when it was made, taking into account the facts and circumstances of the parties. If it is clearly outside the range within which rational people may disagree, then inevitably the statutory objectives of the 1985 Divorce Act will not have been met.* [Emphasis added.]

[178] Although she rejected the routine imposition of "judicial concepts of fairness" in the face of existing agreements, Wilson J suggested that this revised and more flexible notion of unconscionability should serve as a caveat to the trilogy's strict threshold test (paras. 142 and 146(4)). In her view, this is appropriate in part because, in the trilogy itself, the threshold test for judicial intervention in a final agreement was subject to the reservation that the agreement not be "unconscionable in the substantive law sense" (see *Richardson*, *supra*, at p. 872).

[179] The role that Wilson J crafts for unconscionability in *Leopold* in fact represents a significant shift from the role accorded to the stricter common law doctrine by Wilson J in the trilogy. ...

[181] [This approach] is in keeping with a broader and more realistic understanding of the operation of contractual relationships that has emerged in both academic literature and case law in recent years, discrediting earlier, more abstract or formalistic notions of contract law. ...

[182] It is thus important to recognize that, while separation agreements are indeed unique as I will discuss in more detail below, even in commercial law settings contracts are not designed to be, nor are they understood as, unalterable. We must resist the temptation to reify or mythologize the "sanctity" or "finality" of contract, particularly in the field of family law, which primarily concerns the management of human relationships at some of their most sensitive points. That Parliament has resisted this temptation in the family law context is evident in the fact that, in the 1985 Act, separation agreements are recognized as but one of the factors to be taken into account in applications for corollary relief under s. 15.2. It is to a discussion of this statutory framework, as well as the contemporary spousal support jurisprudence of this Court, that I now turn. ...

[LeBel J then reviewed the statutory provisions and spousal support cases, including *Moge* and *Bracklow*, and continued:]

[203] McLachlin J's contextual approach to the marital relationship in *Bracklow* stands in vivid contrast to Wilson J's more narrow approach in the trilogy. By way of example, McLachlin J's conclusion that in certain circumstances a potentially lifelong support obligation—there are, as she says, "no magical cut-off dates" (para. 57)—may arise out of the marriage relationship conflicts with Wilson J's view in *Pelech* that "to burden the respondent with [Mrs. Pelech's] care fifteen years after their marriage has ended for no other reason than that they were once husband and wife seems to me to create a fiction of marital responsibility at the expense of individual responsibility" (*Pelech, supra*, at p. 852). Similar discord flows from McLachlin J's finding that the former spouse, rather than the state, is in many circumstances the appropriate ultimate provider of non-compensatory support where a needy partner cannot attain post-marital self-sufficiency. By contrast, Wilson J held that where a former spouse seeking corollary relief in the face of an existing agreement cannot establish that he or she has "suffered a radical change in circumstances flowing from an economic pattern of dependency engendered by the marriage ... the obligation to support the former spouse should be, as in the case of any other citizen, the communal responsibility of the state" (*Pelech*, at p. 851-52). For McLachlin J, the approach is broad and contextual: "the desirability of freedom to move on to new relationships is merely one of several objectives that might guide the judge" (*Bracklow, supra*, at para. 57). For Wilson J, the clean break is paramount: "[The parties] made the decision to marry and they made the decision to terminate their marriage. Their decisions should be respected. They should thereafter be free to make new lives for themselves without an ongoing contingent liability for future misfortunes which may befall the other" (*Pelech*, at p. 851).

[204] *Bracklow*, like *Moge*, thus emphasizes a more holistic and fact-based approach to spousal support, in keeping with the diversity of factors and objectives in

the 1985 Act. The recognition in *Moge* and *Bracklow* that the relationship of marriage often creates complicated and gender-based interdependencies that cannot adequately be addressed by stressing formal equality or deemed self-sufficiency is incompatible with the mantra of individualism that underscores the trilogy: individual choice, individual responsibility, and individual autonomy. *Moge* and *Bracklow* provide compelling support for the proposition that it is inappropriate to defer to a support agreement based on unrealistic assumptions about the absolute autonomy or deemed self-sufficiency of the parties. The paradigm shift evident in this Court's jurisprudence on the rationales for spousal support bolsters the conclusion that I reached above based on a plain reading of the statute: the trilogy's radical change and causal connection threshold test for judicial intervention in "final" agreements can no longer stand.

[205] To be consistent with the developments in this Court's jurisprudence, the threshold test that replaces it must be one that insists on the substantive equality of the parties during the marriage and at the time of separation, by ensuring that the agreement equitably apportions the economic consequences of the marriage and its breakdown. Before turning to a discussion of the contours of such a test, I think it appropriate to make some prefatory comments about the nature of separation and support agreements themselves. ...

[206] Separation and support agreements aim to disentangle complex relationships and interdependencies. As Bala and Chapman ... ["Separation Agreements & Contract Law: From the Trilogy to Miglin," in *Child & Spousal Support Revisited*, tab 1 (Toronto: Law Society of Upper Canada, 2002], comment, separation agreements are "uniquely significant" contracts that have a "profound and personal effect" on the individuals who enter into them (p. 1-2). Nevertheless, some commentators suggest that contract law principles would provide an adequate means of redressing any injustices that may arise between parties to such agreements (see M. Menear, "*Miglin v. Miglin*—Judicial Assault on Individual Liberty" (2002), 20 *Can. Fam. LQ* 119). I disagree.

[207] As I outlined above, in *Moge* and *Bracklow*, this Court emphasized the importance of a contextual approach to spousal support, which not only respects the diversity of marital relationships, but also recognizes the social and socio-economic realities that shape parties' roles within these relationships and upon marital breakdown. The private contractual model is blind to these realities and is therefore fundamentally incompatible both with the contextual approach to spousal support propounded by this Court and with the language of the 1985 Act.

[208] Under the private contractual model, contracts may only be set aside if they are unconscionable in that they shock the conscience of the court. For a contract to be deemed unconscionable, there must be both a substantial inequality of bargaining power between the parties that is exploited by the stronger party who preys upon the weaker and substantial unfairness or improvidence in the terms of the agreement. ... The stringency of the test for unconscionability reflects the strong presumption that individuals act rationally, autonomously and in their own best interests when they form private agreements. Non-enforcement of the parties' bargain is only justified where the transaction is so distorted by unequal bargaining power that this presumption is displaced. It is inherently problematic to apply this strict standard, which is

more appropriate to arm's-length commercial transactions, in the polar opposite negotiating context of family separation and divorce.

[209] The effect of the private contractual model generally, and the doctrine of unconscionability more specifically, is to preclude any recognition of the unique context in which separation agreements are made and the special circumstances that they are intended to govern. Separation agreements are often negotiated in situations that are emotionally charged. Their negotiation may be further complicated by what are typically gender-based inequities in bargaining positions between the parties. In addition, separation agreements are inherently prospective in nature and, as family law experts stress, the parties may have difficulty accurately forecasting how the economic consequences of their marriage and its breakdown will play out over time. ...

[210] In cases of marriage breakdown, it is not appropriate to require that circumstances rise to the level of unconscionability before parties' agreements will be reopened. Settlement agreements are formed in an environment where the assumptions underpinning the enforceability of freely chosen bargains do not apply to the same extent as in the commercial context. This was Wilson J's concern in *Leopold*, where she stressed that settlement agreements are negotiated in a unique emotional climate, involving much more subtle bargaining inequalities than are at play in a commercial context. ...

[211] In my view, one does not need to entertain a heavy-handed or paternalistic view of the propriety of judicial intervention to "save people from themselves" in order to express scepticism about the background negotiating conditions for separation agreements and about whether, in light of these conditions, waivers of support can always be taken at face value. As La Forest J observed in dissent in *Richardson*, *supra*, in the stressful circumstances of divorce "many people ... do very unwise things, things that are anything but mature and sensible, even when they consult legal counsel" (p. 883). ...

[214] [It is important to recognize] the degree to which social and economic factors may constrain individuals' choices at the bargaining table (see Neave ... ["Resolving the Dilemma of Difference: A Critique of 'The Role of Private Ordering in Family Law' " (1994), 44 *UTLJ* 97], at p. 122). The inequalities in bargaining power at play in the settlement process are not gender neutral. As this Court stressed in *Moge* at p. 850, in many (if not most) marriages, the wife remains the economically disadvantaged partner. Though marriage relationships are, in general, becoming more egalitarian, there continues to be a disjunction between the principle of equality and the lived economic and personal reality of many married women, and the law needs to be able to recognize and to accommodate the situations where this disjunction exists.

[215] We should also recognize that it is typically women who come to the bargaining table as the financially dependent spouse, and hence the more vulnerable party in the negotiating process. Where this is the case, their freedom to negotiate may be significantly constrained by pressure to reach a timely settlement in light of financial need and other stresses, such as the inability to marshal other sources of support during the negotiations, and the fear of losing custody of, or access to, the children. ...

[218] Given these realities, the private contractual model—and similarly any model based on the assumptions that underlie it—has limited value in the spousal

support context. Even where an agreement is not strictly speaking unconscionable, it may nonetheless be inappropriate for the court to uphold it. While it is important to respect the will of the parties, courts cannot assume that the parties' spousal support agreements necessarily provide a clear and transparent guide to their intentions, which, as in any area of the law, are often difficult to ascertain. In the family law context, the parties' "freedom" to contract may be significantly constrained by social and economic factors, and may be decidedly unequal. An agreement may be a product of many implicit, as well as explicit, compromises. It may reflect fundamentally flawed assumptions about how the consequences of the marriage and its breakdown will affect the parties' post-divorce lives. In light of these factors, I question the desirability of a policy of excessive deference that puts the courts in the position of enforcing support agreements because they are presumed to represent the objective expression of the parties' free will. While representation by competent counsel is advisable, even necessary, in this context and while professional advisors should certainly seek a proper settlement and most do, the presence of counsel will not always be sufficient to redress these problems. ...

[After reviewing the change-based test in the Ontario Court of Appeal, LeBel J set out principles for applications pursuant to s. 15.2:]

[227] The appropriate threshold for overriding a support agreement in an application for corollary relief under s. 15.2 is whether the agreement is objectively fair at the time of the application. This test is based on the language of the statute, which gives the court a broad jurisdiction and a duty to ensure that matrimonial agreements prove to be consistent with the objectives of the law. It is also grounded in sound policy reasons which reflect the context in which these agreements are made and the complexities of the breakup of the marriage as they evolve in the parties' lives over time. ...

[228] This threshold allows the reviewing court to intervene regardless of whether the unfairness at the time of the application stems from the unfairness of the initial agreement, the parties' failure at the time the agreement was negotiated to accurately predict how the economic consequences of the marriage or its breakdown would play out over time, or changes in the parties' circumstances. ... It places the emphasis on whether the support agreement has *in fact* brought about an equitable distribution of the economic consequences of the marriage and its breakdown, the ultimate goal of spousal support embodied in the statute and affirmed by this Court. In contrast, the majority's two-part test creates an artificial distinction between an assessment of the agreement at the time it was signed and an assessment of the agreement at the time of the application. Where an agreement is not voidable for reasons relating to the circumstances of execution and is found to be in substantial compliance with the Act at the first stage, it will be subject to a very stringent test for variation at the second stage. As I noted above, this approach is inadequate to deal with the problems that family law experts identify flowing from the inherently prospective nature of spousal support agreements. Its effect is to penalize parties who do not accurately predict the future by subjecting agreements that may have appeared fair at the outset, but that result in unfair circumstances, to a stricter standard for judicial intervention. In addition, the

majority's approach fails to accord appropriate weight to a consideration of whether the agreement is in fact meeting the objectives in s. 15.2(6) at the time of the application. In my view, a single standard is preferable. Courts should not be in the business of enforcing unfair agreements irrespective of whether the unfairness is inherent in the provisions of the initial agreement or manifests itself only as the economic consequences of the marriage and its breakdown play out in the parties' lives over time. ...

[230] ... [T]his approach reflects what Parliament has determined to be the driving consideration in support awards: achieving an *equitable* disentangling of the parties' economic relationship upon marital breakdown. It is inappropriate to allow parties, by way of private agreements, to subvert this statutory policy ... and to require courts to sanction this subversion by mandating deference to unfair agreements.

[231] The process of determining whether an agreement is fair will of necessity be fact and context specific. The issue is whether, in light of all of the parties' circumstances at the time of the application, the agreement adequately meets the spousal support objectives in s. 15.2(6). This will require trial judges to make case-by-case determinations based on the whole picture of the parties' relationship, including their respective functions during the marriage, their allocation of capital and income upon the breakup, their childcare responsibilities, their employment prospects, and a range of other factors. Because parties may attempt to achieve economic equity in a variety of ways (i.e., through property division and spousal support), the *entirety* of the parties' financial arrangement upon marital dissolution and not merely the spousal support provisions in their agreement must be considered. This is precisely the kind of comprehensive inquiry called for under s. 15.2. The inquiry must consider all aspects of the parties' relationship, addressing pure need as well as compensation. ...

[238] I must take issue with Mr. Miglin's argument, reflected in the majority's reasons, that focussing on the degree to which the terms of a support agreement realize the objectives set out in s. 15.2(6) is inconsistent with one of the broader policy goals of the 1985 Act, found in s. 9(2), the promotion of settlement. Section 9(2) requires lawyers acting on behalf of a party to a divorce proceeding to discuss the possibility of a negotiated settlement with their client and to inform their client of any mediation facilities of which they are aware. This provision reflects a broader ethical duty that binds lawyers in the conduct of all litigation as members of the Bar and officers of the court (see, for example, Rules 2.02(2) and 2.02(3) of the *Rules of Professional Conduct* of the Law Society of Upper Canada). However, while as s. 9(2) recognizes, settlement is clearly to be encouraged, I do not think that the 1985 Act may properly be understood to privilege settlement *per se*. A general provision such as s. 9(2) cannot be read independently from the very specific legislative objectives for spousal support outlined in s. 15.2(6). Parties, while encouraged by s. 9(2) to settle their affairs privately, are not permitted to contract out of the Act. The 1985 Act requires courts to make spousal support orders that aim as much as possible to comply with the objectives codified in s. 15.2(6). Given this statutory framework, what the 1985 Act may be said to encourage is not settlement in itself but rather settlements that accord with the legislative objectives for spousal support articulated in s. 15.2(6). To conclude otherwise is to fail to conceive of the 1985 Act as an integrated whole. It is also potentially to put courts in the position of enforcing unfair agreements that

contradict the objectives of the very Act that empowers them to hear support applications in the first place.

[239] In the spousal support context, then, the legislated policy goal is not negotiated settlement but rather the negotiation of fair settlements, with fairness evaluated according to the objectives of the 1985 Act. ...

[LeBel J therefore concluded that it was not appropriate to defer to the spousal support waiver in the separation agreement. As he suggested (at para. 245), the separation agreement and the consulting agreement "failed to realize reasonably the objectives of s. 15.2(6) at the time they were negotiated and ... this continued to be the case at the time of Ms. Miglin's application for corollary relief." In particular, he concluded that Ms. Miglin's disposition of the business resulted in significant disadvantages to her, particularly because the exchange of the business and the matrimonial home, while equally valued, did not create equality—Ms Miglin exchanged an income-producing asset for a non-income-producing asset. She also lost her employment income of approximately $80,000 per annum. Clearly, the fact that the consulting agreement had an open-ended renewal clause also recognized the possibility that she would continue to have need of an income stream. According to LeBel J (at para. 246), "the resulting inequity was compounded when Mr. Miglin failed to renew the consulting agreement." In addition to these economic disadvantages arising from the breakdown of the marriage, she also suffered disadvantages from the roles adopted by the parties during their marriage and in the organization of their domestic lives.]

[253] For the reasons that I have identified, the parties' financial arrangements manifestly failed to address the fact that Ms. Miglin disproportionately suffered economic disadvantages flowing both from the roles that the parties adopted during their 14-year marriage (and in terms of childcare, after the marriage as well) and from the breakdown of the marriage. This was not a situation in which the parties' financial arrangements upon separation provided for an income stream for the dependent spouse that, although somewhat lower than what a court might have awarded, was nonetheless reasonable in the circumstances. The Separation Agreement provided no spousal support or income stream whatsoever to Ms. Miglin, while the Consulting Agreement allowed for only $15,000 annually, which Mr. Miglin terminated after five years despite Ms. Miglin's ongoing need. While the majority suggests that Ms. Miglin's net worth has increased since the parties' separation, the reality is that Ms. Miglin will have no income stream, other than the support that she receives for her children, for the foreseeable future unless she sells her home or divests herself of her RRSPs, which she requires for her future security.

[254] Considered as a whole, then, the parties' financial arrangements were insufficient to fall within the generous ambit within which reasonable disagreement is possible in terms of realizing the spousal support objectives in s. 15.2(6) at the time of Ms. Miglin's application. It was thus appropriate for the trial judge to intervene and award her corollary relief. As the question of quantum of support was not pleaded before this Court, I assume without deciding that the amount awarded by the trial judge, and upheld by the Court of Appeal, was appropriate.

Discussion Notes

Contracts, Orders, and Variation

The *Miglin* case required the Supreme Court of Canada to assess the content of a separation agreement (which provided for a final settlement between the spouses) in relation to an application for spousal support by Ms Miglin. This fact situation clearly constituted a separation agreement and then "an (initial) application for spousal support." By contrast, s. 17 of the *Divorce Act, 1985* and similar provincial statutes in Canada identify a fact pattern concerning "an application to vary an existing order for support." The judgment of the Ontario Court of Appeal appeared to use the change requirement of s. 17 in assessing Ms Miglin's request for an initial order of spousal support. To what extent is such a request appropriate? Is there a fundamental distinction between an initial order for spousal support, granted by a court, and an agreement by the parties to such a payment? In reflecting on this question, consider the comments of an academic lawyer, following the decision of the Ontario Court of Appeal in *Miglin*, but before the Supreme Court decision: see Christine Davies, "The Ever-Changing Picture of Support and Other Developments" (2002-3), 20 *Canadian Family Law Quarterly* 213, at 233-35.

> In *Bracklow v. Bracklow* McLachlin J said that there were three conceptual bases for entitlement to spousal support: (1) compensatory; (2) contractual; and (3) non-compensatory (needs/hardship). The Supreme Court of Canada in *Moge v. Moge* discussed the first type of support (compensatory). In *Bracklow*, the Supreme Court of Canada discussed the third type (non-compensatory—needs/hardship based). The second type of support (contractual) has not been thoroughly dealt with by the Supreme Court of Canada since it decided the trilogy in 1987. Madame Justice Claire L'Heureux-Dubé has made it clear that she believes the trilogy to be out of step with the philosophy of the 1985 *Divorce Act*.
>
> On October 4, 2001 the Supreme Court of Canada granted leave to appeal to it the Ontario Court of Appeal decision of *Miglin*. In *Miglin*, Abella JA (speaking for the Court) took a very similar approach to that taken some five years before by L'Heureux-Dubé J in *L.B. v. G.B.* Let me briefly outline the decision of Abella JA:
>
> 1. The wording of the 1968 *Divorce Act* (under which the trilogy was decided) is very different from the wording of the 1985 *Divorce Act*. Section 11 of the old Act was minimalistic. It did not set out support objectives. The new Act, on the other hand, sets out a comprehensive scheme for support. Economic equity appears to be the overriding objective of the new Act.
> 2. The Supreme Court of Canada jurisprudence on spousal support under the 1985 Act (*Moge*; *Bracklow*) confirms that the new Act represents a profound difference in approach from the old Act. The approach taken in the trilogy reflects the prevailing philosophy—that the clean-break theory was the ultimate support objective and the state was the ultimate provider. The current approach is economic equity with the family (rather than the state) being the ultimate provider.
> 3. It is clear that a court cannot disregard an agreement. Section 15.2(4) of the *Divorce Act* provides that in making a spousal support order the court shall take into consideration (*inter alia*): "Any order, agreement or arrangement relating to support of either spouse." It seems that in coupling prior orders with agreements the legislature may have intended

that they be subject to the same threshold for variation; *i.e.*, like a previous order under the *Divorce Act*, the court cannot vary an agreement unless the applicant for variation has established a material change in circumstances since the agreement was made.

4. The existence of a valid separation or settlement agreement under the 1985 Act results in a two-stage inquiry. The first and threshold stage is to determine if there has been a material change in circumstances. If the threshold has been met, the second stage is to determine what amount of spousal support, if any, is justified under the Act. Some of the factors to be considered at the second stage include:

   (i)   the extent, source and impact of the change in circumstances;
   (ii) whether the agreement reflects a clear and unequivocal intention to insulate it from review or variation;
   (iii) the extent to which the agreement satisfies the objectives of the Act; and
   (iv) where there is an agreement to waive support or limit its duration to a fixed event or time, how lengthy a period has elapsed since the waiver, event or expiration of the time limit.

5. Abella JA left open the question of whether the higher threshold for varying expired spousal support orders found in section 17(10) of the *Divorce Act* should also apply to expired agreements. She did say, however, that in her opinion, the legislature had highlighted an intention in section 17(10) that expired responsibilities should be significantly more difficult to reinstate.

It is unclear how closely the Supreme Court of Canada will endorse Abella JA's reasons. It is highly probable, however, that the Supreme Court of Canada will confirm her view that the trilogy is out of step with the new philosophy of spousal support and will take the opportunity to explain the third limb of its conceptual basis for spousal support—contractual support. Abella JA's judgment is in accord with those given in *Moge* and *Bracklow* and, I submit, the Supreme Court of Canada views will not deviate in any extreme fashion from it.

In the light of this assessment, what influenced the majority decision of the Supreme Court of Canada? Was it a question of weight in relation to the factors; or did the Supreme Court adopt different factors in overturning the decision of the Ontario Court of Appeal? What are the implications of the Supreme Court's approach for couples who wish to negotiate a separation agreement?

As noted in James C. MacDonald and Lee K. Ferrier, *Canadian Divorce Law and Practice*, 2d ed. (Scarborough, ON: Carswell, 1986), at 15:147, the power to override an agreement is different from the power to vary such an agreement. Their discussion of *Miglin* includes an excellent overview (described as of "historical interest only") of cases in which the test of the *Pelech* trilogy was (1) applied and satisfied; (2) applied and not satisfied; and (3) not applied.

Miglin and Gender Issues

According to Julien Payne, "First Impressions of Miglin in the Supreme Court of Canada" (PPFL/2003-001):

The principles formulated by the majority in *Miglin* are conceptually gender neutral and apply equally to payors and payees. In practice, men will fare better than women under *Miglin* because men are typically payors and women are typically payees and finality usually favours the former group. In addition, the principles set out in *Miglin* are inevitably subject to the practicability of the payor's retention of an ability to pay.

To what extent do you agree with this assessment? How were issues about gender disparities conceptualized in the reasoning of the majority and dissenting judgments? To what extent is there a need to continue to take account of gender disparities in marriage, and at marriage breakdown?

Separation Agreements and Marriage Contracts

Recall the discussion in chapter 6 of the Supreme Court's decision in *Hartshorne v. Hartshorne*, 2004 SCC 22. Is there a fundamental distinction between the negotiation of marriage contracts and separation agreements? To what extent are the views of the majority in *Miglin* similar to those expressed (subsequently) in *Hartshorne*? See also two earlier cases: *Charles v. Charles* (1991), 32 RFL (3d) 316 (BCSC) and *Andrews v. Andrews* (1992), 42 RFL (3d) 454 (NSTD) and Payne's suggestion that "a marriage contract might … carry less weight than a separation agreement." Do you agree with this assessment? What, if any, differences were identified in the reasoning of the Supreme Court in relation to the marriage contract in *Hartshorne* and the separation agreement in *Miglin*? For another analysis, see Kirk Makin, "Divorce Deals Stand Till Death Do You Part," *Globe and Mail*, April 18, 2003: "Marriage may not be forever—but a separation agreement cannot easily be rent asunder."

Responses to Miglin: Practice and Theory

The principles in *Miglin* were applied to a comprehensive property and support waiver in a cohabitation agreement signed by a man and woman who lived together for seven years and then married. After the husband committed suicide, the woman wished to claim "dependant's relief" under the *Succession Law Reform Act* because her husband had died intestate. The widow had signed the agreement after receiving "legal information" about it, but not "independent legal advice." In rejecting her claim, the court applied the principles in *Miglin*: see Cristin Schmitz, "Citing Miglin, Court Denies Support to Impoverished Widow," *The Lawyers Weekly*, August 15, 2003.

In a review of the Ontario Court of Appeal decision in *Miglin*, Martha Shaffer and Carol Rogerson concluded that there were compelling reasons to abandon the *Pelech* test in relation to spousal support agreements, but that the appropriate test in such cases remained elusive:

> We believe the arguments for abandoning the trilogy standard for overriding spousal support agreements are compelling and that many of the *Miglin* critics are in fact challenging the legitimacy of the prevailing norms of spousal support rather than defending the practice of settlement. Even accepting, as we do, that the *Pelech* standard is not an appropriate one,

[our] review has shown the challenge of crafting an alternative standard. We gravitate to standards that emphasize fairness rather than change because we believe that agreements should reflect the norms of fairness articulated in the *Divorce Act* and because we recognize that change standards are often manipulated to deal with what are essentially fairness concerns. We acknowledge, however, that crafting an appropriate threshold for intervention on the grounds of fairness is a difficult task, given the uncertainty that currently pervades the law of spousal support. We also recognize that abandoning a change requirement runs counter to the words of the *Divorce Act* where agreements have been incorporated into court orders. Nonetheless, we are optimistic that neither of these problems is intractable. We believe the uncertainty surrounding spousal support will work itself over time, providing clearer norms by which to judge the fairness of agreements. It may be that a legislative response is required to deal with the problem of consistency created by section 17, one that might involve creating a separate regime specific to agreements.

(Martha Shaffer and Carol Rogerson, "Contracting Spousal Support: Thinking Through Miglin" (2003-4), 21 *Canadian Family Law Quarterly* 49, at 100.)

To what extent are their conclusions and recommendations reflected in the Supreme Court decision in *Miglin*? You may want to reconsider these comments in relation to the reform proposals concerning spousal support that are reviewed at the end of the chapter.

SELECTED REFERENCES

Michael Fitz-James, "Methods To 'Bulletproof' a Spousal Support Waiver," *Law Times*, February 10, 2003.

Simon Fodden, *Family Law* (Toronto: Irwin Law, 1999), chapters 3 and 13.

Robert Leckey, "Relational Contract and Other Models of Marriage" (2002), 40 *Osgoode Hall Law Journal* 1.

James G. McLeod and Alfred A. Mamo, *McLeod and Mamo: Annual Review of Family Law 2002* (Toronto: Carswell, 2002).

Mary Morton, "Dividing the Wealth, Sharing the Poverty: The Re(Formation) of 'Family' in Law in Ontario" (1988), 25 *Canadian Review of Sociology and Anthropology* 254.

D.A. Rollie Thompson, "When Is a Family Law Contract Not Invalid, Unenforceable, Overridden, or Varied?" (2001-2), 19 *Canadian Family Law Quarterly* 399.

Carol Rose, "Bargaining and Gender" (1995), 18 *Harvard Journal of Law and Public Policy* 547.

C. Other Issues Concerning Spousal Support

1. Conduct and No-Fault Divorce

Before the enactment of the *Divorce Act, 1968* and provincial legislation of the 1970s, the conduct of spouses was relevant to a common law action for alimony and an application for divorce under the *Matrimonial Causes Act*, 20 & 221 Vict., c. 85. A marital offence such as adultery by the wife could disentitle her from receiving maintenance or alimony from her husband. As noted earlier, the *Divorce Act* of 1968 included "the conduct of the parties" as one factor for judicial consideration under s. 11. However, while conduct remained a relevant consideration, marital misconduct was no longer an automatic bar to maintenance.

Pursuant to the *Divorce Act, 1985*, fault grounds for divorce were eliminated. Thus, the only ground for divorce in Canada now is marriage breakdown: see chapter 5. Consistent with the objectives of no-fault divorce, s. 15.2(5) of the Act provides that a court shall not take into consideration, in making an order for support, "any misconduct of a spouse in relation to the marriage." Similarly, provincial legislation generally makes conduct irrelevant in applications for spousal support, although some statutes permit a court to consider conduct that is especially egregious. For example, s. 33(10) of Ontario's *Family Law Act* provides that the obligation to provide support exists "without regard to the conduct of either spouse," but, in determining the amount of support to be ordered, a court may take account of "a course of conduct that is so unconscionable as to constitute an obvious and gross repudiation of the relationship." Is the test in the Ontario Act more or less stringent than that in the *Divorce Act, 1985*? Is there any reason to have different tests for the relevance of conduct in federal and provincial statutes with respect to entitlement to spousal support?

Recall the discussion in chapter 5 about client experiences with no-fault divorce, including their frustration with the exclusion of fault issues in some circumstances. How might the determination of entitlement to spousal support be influenced by clients' perceptions of fault in relation to marriage breakdown?

Spousal Support and the Divorce Act, 1985

Ungerer v. Ungerer
(1998), 158 DLR (4th) 47; 37 RFL (4th) 41 (BCCA)

[The parties divorced in 1993 after a marriage of 23 years. They had three daughters—one was independent and married, one lived with her father, and the youngest lived with her mother. At the time of the divorce decree, the court ordered the father to pay child support for the youngest child in addition to spousal support in the amount of $1,200 per month. There was also an order that the father have generous access to the child living with the mother; however, the mother refused to cooperate to permit access, so that the father had no access to the youngest child for about five years. In 1996, after being found in contempt in relation to the access order, the mother was imprisoned for 21 days; upon her release, she continued to thwart the father's access to the youngest child.

In 1995, the father successfully applied to reduce the amount of spousal support to $800 per month; he later applied to terminate spousal maintenance altogether on the basis of the mother's conduct since the divorce, but this application was dismissed. Both parties appealed from these two orders. The Court of Appeal reviewed in detail the findings of the trial judge with respect to the circumstances of Mrs. Ungerer, particularly in relation to her ability to become self-sufficient—she had been out of the workforce since 1980, had few marketable skills, and argued that her daughter's condition of juvenile rheumatoid arthritis meant that she was fully engaged in caring for her daughter. However, as a result of assistance from her parents with respect to the purchase of a home, the mother's expenses had been reduced; the father gave evidence about a possible reduction in his income as a result of the impending closure of the plant where he had been employed for 24 years. In assessing all these factors, the court concluded (at para. 29) that "[u]nlike Mrs. Moge who made conscientious efforts to become self-sufficient, Mrs. Ungerer has done absolutely nothing." In the result, the court suggested (at para. 31) that spousal support should have been terminated somewhere between December of 1997 and December of 1999.

The court then proceeded to consider Mr. Ungerer's appeal to terminate spousal support based on Mrs. Ungerer's misconduct post-divorce. Referring to ss. 15.2(5) (with respect to an original order) and 17(6) (with respect to an order for variation), the court stated (at para. 34):]

Mr. Ungerer's argument is that, read together, these sections prohibit consideration of spousal misconduct during the marriage, but that they do not prevent the court from considering spousal misconduct which occurs after the marriage has been dissolved. He says that Mrs. Ungerer's post-divorce misconduct in this case has been so reprehensible as to make continuation of spousal support "repugnant to any one's sense of justice" (per Denning MR in *Wachtel v. Wachtel*, [1973] 1 All ER 829 (Eng. CA) at 835). Counsel points to Mrs. Ungerer's refusal to obey the access order after her time in jail, the judge's conclusion that she had poisoned [the daughter's] mind against her father and completely alienated her affections for him, and the resulting frustration of the court's powers. Counsel also pointed to evidence that Mrs. Ungerer had put [the daughter] up to saying falsely that her father had molested her, and had told others that Mr. Ungerer was suffering from the onset of Alzheimer's disease.

[The court referred to *Day v. Day* (1995), Doc Smithers 6500 (BCSC), where the judge held that there was "outrageous" conduct under the *Family Relations Act* because the wife had attempted to murder the husband by shooting him four times. The court also referred to *McGregor v. McGregor* (1994), 3 RFL (4th) 343 (NBCA), where the appeal court confirmed that the mother's actions in frustrating access to two children constituted sufficient reason to terminate spousal support for the future. The court continued (at para. 40):]

In my view, s. 17(6) of the *Divorce Act* is no bar to considering misconduct in such a case as this, because it is misconduct which has occurred outside the marriage and after its termination, and could not be considered misconduct "in relation to the marriage" in the language of s. 15(6) [now s. 15.2(5)].

As to the nature of Mrs. Ungerer's misconduct, it is true that it does not equate with that of Mrs. Day because her conduct was not violent, and it was not criminal, as was Mrs. Day's. However, I think the question to be asked where misconduct is alleged as a reason to terminate post-divorce spousal support is whether that misconduct is of such a morally repugnant nature as would cause right-thinking persons to say that the spouse is no longer entitled to the support of her former husband, or to the assistance of the court in compelling the husband to pay.

Although the reasons on this issue in *McGregor supra* are brief, they support the view that conduct which has the effect of frustrating a court order can be sufficient to deprive a former spouse of her right to continue to receive support. In this case, I think Mrs. Ungerer's conduct is sufficiently egregious to disentitle her to continued support. To turn a child against her father is reprehensible in the extreme, and that together with her other misconduct summarized earlier … would be more than sufficient to warrant termination of support in the eyes of right-thinking citizens. Most people would be offended by the prospect of a court compelling a husband [sic] to continue paying spousal support in such circumstances, and would consider it unjust to do so.

[The court thus ordered termination of spousal support as of June 30, 1999, six years after the date of the divorce.]

Spousal Support and Provincial Legislation

Smith v. Smith
[2002] Ont. Sup. Ct. J LEXIS 1126 (Lexis)

[The parties cohabited from 1974, along with the woman's son from an earlier marriage. They also had two children and married in 1981. According to the court (at para. 12), the evidence established that the family was a "very dysfunctional one"; the court found (at para. 15) that the husband could have been more assertive, but most of the blame for the dysfunctional family rested with the wife. By the 1990s, the marriage was deteriorating and the wife unilaterally decided to move into the basement of their home; she installed a lock on the basement door and she alone had a key. There was also evidence of physical abuse, sexual infidelities, and abuse of alcohol; the children gave evidence that the wife was also physically abusive to her husband. The court considered the evidence with respect to the separation of the parties for purposes of establishing marriage breakdown pursuant to s. 8 of the *Divorce Act, 1985*, adopting the criteria of *Cooper v. Cooper* (1972), 10 RFL 184 (Ont. Sup. Ct. J) (see chapter 5), and concluded that the appropriate date of separation (for purposes of equalization of the family property) was the date when the wife moved to the basement in 1997. After dealing with the parties' equalization claims, the court considered (at paras. 55ff.) the wife's application for spousal support—her record of gainful employment during the marriage and after separation; her evidence of a medical condition that inhibited employment (but without corroborating medical evidence); and her denial of alcoholism. In response to the husband's claim that the wife was not entitled to spousal support pursuant to s. 33(10) of the *Family Law Act*, the court stated (at paras. 66ff.):]

[T]he law is clear that there is a high threshold to be met before the court will exercise its discretion under this subsection in light of the overall purposes of the Act and the provisions of s. 30 which establishes an obligation on every spouse to provide for the support of the other in accordance with need to the extent that he or she is capable of so doing. …

[The court reviewed the objectives of an award of spousal support under s. 33(8) and the test for applying s. 33(10). In addition, the court cited *Melanson v. Melanson* (1991), 34 RFL (3d) 323 (Ont. Gen. Div.), where there were frequent assaults by the husband in the course of a marriage of 22 years; the assaults constituted punches and slaps that did not result in the wife requiring medical treatment. The court also held that the "wife's challenging attitude" played a role in the husband's behaviour, and thus concluded that the husband's actions did not constitute a repudiation of the relationship within s. 33(10). The court also reviewed *Morey v. Morey* (1979), 24 OR (2d) 124 (Prov. Ct. (Fam. Div.)), a case decided pursuant to earlier legislation in the same terms, which set out the test for s. 33(10) as follows:]

a) the conduct must be exceptionally bad;

b) the conduct must be such as could reasonably be expected to destroy the marriage;

c) the conduct must have persisted in the face of innocence and virtual blamelessness on the part of the other spouse … ;

d) The commission of a so-called matrimonial offence is not necessarily sufficient … ;

e) The party raising the issue of relevant conduct should be prepared to undertake that there is a *bona fide* belief that the test … can be satisfied [with risks of punitive costs if the court finds that the issue is frivolous]; and

f) the pleadings … should set out a summary of the conduct relied on to meet the test. …

In my opinion, the Plaintiff's [wife's] conduct comes very close to an obvious and gross repudiation of the relationship to be such as to justify the court awarding a lower amount of support and a shorter term of support than that to which the Plaintiff would otherwise be entitled.

The Plaintiff, during her evidence, demonstrated a lack of candour on many of the contentious issues in this case while the Defendant, several times, admitted to facts that were clearly contrary to his financial interest.

I have, somewhat reluctantly, reached a decision not to apply the provisions of s. 33(10) of the *Family Law Act* to reduce the quantum or term of support. Notwithstanding that this subsection should be applied only in extreme cases, this case … comes close to being so extreme as to cause the court to apply this section. Every breakdown of marriage, to some extent, involves a repudiation by one or both parties of the relationship. In the result, therefore, I exercise my discretion in favour of the Plaintiff.

[In assessing the quantum of support, the court took into account the wife's ability to earn income in an amount of approximately $20,000 per year, and reduced some of her expenses. In the end, the husband was required to pay spousal support in an amount of $450 per month for three years, but arrears of support payable pursuant to an interim order were rescinded.]

Discussion Notes

Conduct and Spousal Support: Preserving Fault?

Examine the reasoning in the above cases in the context of the wording of the provisions of the federal and provincial statutes. To what extent do you agree with the interpretation in *Ungerer* that s. 15.2(5) does not prevent consideration of *post-divorce* conduct in determining entitlement to spousal support? Consider also *Stewart v. Stewart* (2000), 12 RFL (5th) 218 (NSSC), where the court denied the husband's application for support based on the absence of need. In doing so, the court also considered *post-separation* misconduct on the part of the husband, characterizing it as calculated to influence the negotiation of terms terminating the marriage. Is it appropriate to take account of post-separation conduct pursuant to s. 15.2(5)? Do these cases serve to allow consideration of fault issues within a no-fault divorce regime? Why, or why not?

Do you agree with the result in *Smith*? What policies favour acceptance of a high threshold for the application of s. 33(10). In this context, consider *B.(S.) v. B.(L.)* (1999), 2 RFL (5th) 32 (Ont. Sup. Ct. J), where the court concluded that the test in s. 33(10) was not met, in part because both parties engaged in behaviour that constituted repudiation of the marriage relationship; the wife engaged in a number of affairs, but with the husband's knowledge and sometimes his encouragement. Is this an appropriate interpretation of s. 33(10)? Why, or why not?

In these cases, courts must consider the principles for awarding spousal support pursuant to federal and provincial legislation, described earlier in this chapter, in addition to taking account of conduct. Thus, for example, in *Belleville v. White* (2002), 35 RFL (5th) 1 (Ont. Sup. Ct. J), the court examined the wife's failure to improve her education or to seek employment, as well as her efforts to thwart court orders and to defeat the orderly resolution of the issues in the divorce proceedings, and concluded that she was not entitled to support. In addition, however, the court suggested (at para. 46) that if the decision to deny support was an error, the wife's conduct was so unconscionable that it met the test in s. 33(10); as a result, the wife's application for spousal support was denied on this basis as well. Similarly, in *A.(T.) v. A.(J.)*, [2000] WDFL 298 (Ont. Sup. Ct. J), the level of spousal support payable to a wife was reduced from $800 to $600 per month as a result of hardship the husband experienced in providing for his former wife and children in the context of the parties' accumulated debts. In addition, however, the court expressly relied on s. 33(10) as the ground for this reduction in the amount of support as a result of the wife's extramarital relationships and sexual promiscuity that she claimed were the symptoms of a psychiatric disorder.

What is the overall effect of these statutory provisions concerning conduct in relation to the principles for awarding spousal support? If they operate to widen the scope for discretionary decision making, is this result appropriate? Why, or why not? To what extent does the preservation of any role for conduct in relation to spousal support undermine the objectives of no-fault divorce legislation? In this context, for example, Karen Selick argued that if parties enter marriage with a common understanding about their mutual expectations, it is "perfectly just to say that the spouse who breaches the agreement should compensate the one who abided by it": see Karen Selick, "Spousal Support—Time To Consider Misconduct" (January 1998), 22 *Canadian Lawyer* 46. What are the consequences of this approach for clients; for divorce processes?

Conduct and New Relationships

Issues about spousal conduct may also arise when an application for spousal support is presented by a spouse who has formed a new relationship—to what extent does the existence of a new relationship, which may include some financial support, affect entitlement to support from a former spouse? These issues may be addressed, of course, in relation to the principles for awarding spousal support—for example, a spouse may be entitled to compensatory support with respect to a former marriage or cohabiting relationship, but may not be entitled to non-compensatory support (based on need) by reason of the support available in a new relationship. Because of the history of alimony being available only to "innocent" wives, these issues sometimes arise pursuant to legislative provisions about conduct. However, they are frequently interconnected with the court's analysis of basic principles of support as well: for examples, see *Fisher v. Fisher* (2000), 12 RFL (5th) 348 (NSCA) and *Boddington v. Boddington*, [2003] WL 22300371 (Ont. Sup. Ct. J). In *Mills v. Mills* (1992), 42 RFL (3d) 180 (Ont. Ct. J (Gen. Div.)), the court held that a woman who had formed a new relationship after marriage breakdown (and whose credibility was impugned) was engaged in conduct that met the test of s. 33(10) of the *Family Law Act* and thus the amount of spousal support awarded should reflect this fact; the court stated (at para. 19) that "the economic implications of such relationship should be reflected in any support order."

Credibility was also at issue in *Krigstin v. Krigstin* (1992), 43 RFL (3d) 334 (Ont. Ct. J (Gen. Div.)). The parties separated after a marriage of 26 years; there were three children, two of whom were grown up while the third lived with her mother. The wife moved out of the matrimonial home (as did the husband) and rented it to a male friend until its sale. The husband alleged that the wife was living with the male renter. The wife denied that she was living with her friend, claiming that he did accounting work for her; however, the court found that he was not an accountant and had not billed her for any work. After the matrimonial home was sold, the man moved close to the wife and admitted going out with her socially but refused to provide any information about the economic nature of their relationship. The court reviewed an interim order for spousal support payable to the wife and concluded that it was appropriate to draw a negative inference concerning the financial aspects of the wife's relationship with the man as a result of their refusal to provide information. Relying on s. 33(10), the court reduced the amount of the spousal support award.

In *McNutt v. McNutt* (2000), 5 RFL (5th) 90 (Ont. Sup. Ct. J), the court awarded spousal support of $700 per month to a wife who was cohabiting in a new relationship. In an annotation, James McLeod examined the principles of compensatory and non-compensatory support, suggesting that

> [b]y forming a new relationship, the dependent/payee has made a conscious decision to move on from one relationship to another instead of seeking economic independence. The payee has chosen his or her lifestyle level and changed dependence upon one person to dependence upon another. Whatever support objective the dependence support was meant to address is no longer present on the facts of the case and there is no further justification for support.

See James McLeod, "Annotation of McNutt v. McNutt" (2000), 5 RFL (5th) 90, at 92. Do you agree with this assessment? Why, or why not? For a similar case, see *Waldick v. Waldick* (2002), 22 RFL (5th) 448 (Ont. Sup. Ct. J).

2. Spousal Support and Property

The ideal of marital partnerships has obvious implications for property divisions after divorce. Under partnership principles, the past and future labour-force earnings, benefits, and governmental entitlements of each spouse should be treated as shared family resources, potentially subject to distribution on divorce. Distributive decisions should depend on the parties' domestic as well as economic contributions to the relationship and on their future needs and earning potential. ... [Some approaches to economic adjustment at divorce], which present property as if it were a tangible object rather than a legal construct, mask normative judgments even as they are exercised. "Traditional" features of ownership have always been open to redefinition, and spouses' expectations are in part a function of what courts and legislatures provide.

Rhode and Minow, at 199 and 200

Rhode and Minow recommended a partnership model for economic readjustment at divorce or separation. As is evident, such a model includes all aspects of family wealth for purposes of distribution in accordance with equitable principles. Although many couples who separate or divorce may similarly think of the distribution of their accumulated wealth in these terms, Canadian legislative principles do not enshrine such a partnership model. Instead, provincial statutes define entitlement to property sharing for married couples and courts have applied trust principles with respect to property entitlement for cohabiting couples. By contrast, orders for spousal support do not employ equality principles, but rather define relevant factors and take account of legislative goals for such awards. In this way, the legal regime operates with respect to property using a set of principles quite different from those used for determining entitlement and quantum of spousal support.

In such a context, there have been numerous challenges to the definition of property for purposes of equalization under provincial statutes: see chapter 6. In other words, because the principles applicable to property sharing are different from those concerning spousal support, it is often necessary to determine whether a particular aspect of family wealth should be considered property, and, if not, whether it is relevant to an assessment of the ability to pay spousal support. In addition, if an asset has been included for purposes of property sharing, some payor spouses have argued that income from the asset should not be available to provide spousal support. These issues are often complex with respect to definitions of property and support; they also challenge fundamental policy issues about economic adjustment at divorce or separation. More specifically, in the absence of clear legislative directions, it is necessary for courts to examine statutory language about property and support and their differing goals.

Boston v. Boston

One example of these tensions was illustrated in *Boston v. Boston*, [2001] 2 SCR 413. At the time of the divorce, the husband's pension was included in the equalization calculation, although he had not yet retired and was not receiving any pension benefits. As a result of including the value of the pension in his net family property, the husband was required to pay an amount to his wife, which he accomplished by transferring assets, including the matrimonial home, to her. He was also obliged to pay her spousal support. In due course, the husband retired and began to receive his pension payments. He then argued that, because the value of the pension had been included in the equalization calculation, it was not appropriate for the wife to receive spousal support payable from the same asset—he characterized the issue as "double dipping." The husband also claimed that the wife, who had been out of the workforce for many years, should have become self-sufficient by the time that he retired and began to receive his pension benefits. The motions judge reduced the amount of spousal support payable to the wife, but the Ontario Court of Appeal allowed an appeal.

However, the Supreme Court of Canada allowed an appeal from this decision, Justices L'Heureux-Dubé and LeBel dissenting. The court restored the order of the motions judge, but ordered that the amount payable to the wife should be indexed. In general terms, the majority of the court concluded that the retired former spouse was entitled to reduce his support obligation to his former wife because the pension he was then receiving had been included in the equalization process, stating (at 435):

> When a pension is dealt with by the lump-sum method, the pension-holding spouse (here the husband) must transfer real assets to the payee spouse (here the wife) in order to equalize matrimonial property. The wife can use these real assets immediately. Under a compensatory spousal support order or agreement, the wife has an obligation to use these assets in an income-producing way. She need not dedicate the equalization assets to investment immediately on receiving them; however, she must use them to generate income when the pension-holding spouse retires. The ideal would be if the payee spouse generated sufficient income or savings from her capital assets to equal the payor spouse's pension income. In any event, the payee spouse must use the assets received on equalization to create a "pension" to provide for her future support.
>
> This requirement is based on the principle that, as far as it is reasonable, the payee spouse should attempt to generate economic self-sufficiency. Self-sufficiency is only one factor of many that is weighed. It is obvious that in most cases of long-term marriage, the goal of self-sufficiency is decidedly difficult to attain, particularly for spouses who remained at home during the marriage. Self-sufficiency will often not be practicable largely due to the residual effects of being outside the labour market for a protracted period of time. In addition, there are factors to consider such as age, education and parenting responsibilities. Consequently, it is often unreasonable to expect the payee spouse to earn an income from employment after separation or divorce.
>
> However, where the payee spouse receives assets on equalization in exchange for a part of her former spouse's pension entitlement, she must use those assets in a reasonable attempt to generate income at least by the time the pension starts to pay out. The reason for this requirement is clear. The payee spouse cannot save the assets that she receives upon equalization and choose instead to live on the liquidation of the payor spouse's pension when he retires. If she were permitted to do so, the payee spouse would accumulate an estate while the payor spouse's estate is liquidating.

The dissenting judges focused on both the legislative objectives of spousal support and the facts of the case. For them (at 445), the case represented "a straight-forward matter of assessment of the needs and means of the former spouses in the context of the dynamic relationship that arise from the marriage and its breakdown." They characterized the issues as relating to spousal support principles and concluded (at 458) that "it was fair in the process of support determination for the courts to consider the assets of both parties and the income that could be generated from them if they were used efficiently." However, on the facts of the case, they concurred with the decision of the Ontario Court of Appeal, acknowledging the lack of independence flowing from the wife's married life and its breakdown, factoring in her lifestyle during the marriage, their living standards, and her need to acquire financial security. Particularly because the husband continued to enjoy a comfortable lifestyle, the dissenting judges concluded (at 458) that "the wife is entitled to a reasonable standard of living without having to engage in a massive programme of liquidation of assets."

In considering this case, recall the discussion in chapter 6 concerning whether professional degrees constituted property for purpose of Ontario's *Family Law Act*—to what extent is this case reflective of the same issues concerning access to family resources, regardless of their characterization? Do you agree that a partnership model might better accomplish these objectives? What is the rationale for defining entitlement to property and spousal support according to different criteria?

3. Spousal Support: Families and the State

The state's policy of privatizing the costs of social reproduction wherever possible arises not only with respect to the provision of social benefits to unwed mothers, but also with respect to the economic consequences of marital breakdown when children are involved. As Mary Morton has demonstrated, the effect of establishing a mechanism for enforcing support orders (which includes, among other techniques, criminalizing default) is to lower welfare costs, which is achieved by shifting the burden of social reproduction from the public to the private sphere.

> Judy Fudge, "The Privatization of the Costs of Social Reproduction:
> Some Recent Charter Cases" (1989), 3 *Canadian Journal of Women
> and the Law* 246, at 251

Spousal Support and Social Assistance

The determination of an obligation to pay spousal support occurs in a private law context—that is, it is the two parties whose means and needs are assessed. However, in circumstances where the decision is that no spousal support is owed by the payor spouse, the payee spouse may not in fact be self-sufficient. Thus, the result of a decision denying spousal support is that the dependent spouse (and often children) become applicants for social assistance. In this way, the private law decision has consequences for public policy and community resources.

Yet, except in those cases where a spouse is already receiving welfare, the state is neither part of the process of negotiation between the parties nor represented in their submissions prior to an order by a court. Traditionally, family law has paid little or no attention to the relationship between family law principles about entitlement to spousal support and social assistance principles about entitlement to welfare. For a dependent spouse, of course, it would be helpful if the principles of these two disparate systems for providing financial security meshed. The materials that follow try to show how these two sets of legal principles intersect and reveal some of the problems that currently exist.

M.J. Mossman and M. MacLean, "Family Law and Social Assistance Programs: Rethinking Equality"
in P.M. Evans and G.R. Wekerle, eds., *Women and the Canadian Welfare State: Challenges and Change*
(Toronto: University of Toronto Press, 1997), 117, at 117-19

> With increasing numbers of sequential marriages, solutions to the financial crisis of marriage breakdown must be sought not only within the parameters of family law but also in social and economic policies that promote the financial viability of all persons in need, including the economic victims of marriage breakdown. The war on the feminization of poverty must be won by innovative and coherent socioeconomic policies.
>
> Payne, 1994: 27

Payne's comment usefully highlights increasing recognition in Canada that marriage breakdown is no longer simply a "private" dispute. Instead, the end of a marriage shatters the economic interdependence of family members in an ongoing family unit, leaving some of them less able to assume economic independence post-divorce than others. In general, women and children experience economic disadvantage disproportionately to men at marriage breakdown, thereby contributing to the feminization of poverty. In this way, most of the costs of Canada's policy of accessible divorce are unfairly borne by individual women and children in post-divorce families and relatively less by their husbands and fathers—or by society as a whole.

A decade ago we explored this phenomenon (Mossman and MacLean, 1986) by examining the first decade of statistics on divorce following the enactment of federal divorce reform legislation in 1968: the *Divorce Act*. We concluded that there was an emerging pattern of gender difference in post-divorce economic circumstances in Canada and that family law principles (that emphasized the formal equality of the spouses at marriage breakdown) did not adequately address the differing economic realities experienced by men and women, either in relation to their workforce opportunities or to the burdens more often assumed by mothers for primary care of children after divorce. We also tried to show how social assistance (welfare) programs had adopted principles of entitlement based on familial relationships, principles that were frequently not at all congruent with those emerging in family law based on the formal equality of spouses. Thus, women were frequently assumed to be equal (and economically independent) by family law principles applicable at divorce and thus were not always entitled to spousal support. At the same time, however, they were often viewed by social assistance programs as having a continuing entitlement to familial support and were thus considered ineligible for welfare. In this way, their disentitlement to either familial support or welfare assistance contributed to economic insecurity, and often poverty, for many women and children after divorce. Moreover, even those women who received spousal support or welfare assistance after marriage breakdown often lived in poverty because their post-divorce resources were diminished, especially by contrast with the resources of their former husbands.

Our assessment led us to rethink ideas about dependency and independence in the family law context and to assess the consequences of using "the individual" or "the family" as the basis of entitlement to income security programs in the context of marriage breakdown. We concluded that accessible divorce policies should be augmented by family law and social assistance principles which can ensure fairer distributions of economic burdens and advantages for individual family members at divorce. We made tentative recommendations for reform in light of the data from this first decade after divorce reform.

In the intervening decade there have been numerous legislative changes in family law and some interesting court decisions, with some confirming and others challenging, at least to some extent, our earlier analysis. There have also been some changes in policies in federal and provincial income security programs and significant court challenges by same-sex families claiming entitlement to employment and governmental benefits on the basis of "family status." Yet, most of the changes have not altered legal principles in fundamental ways. And, most importantly, women and children remain significantly disadvantaged, in contrast to men, in terms of their relative post-divorce economic circumstances (Lemprière, 1992; Dooley, 1993). Thus, the work of rethinking policies about family law and social assistance to promote goals of substantive gender equality in Canada remains an important task. This reassessment focuses on the issues identified in our work a decade ago and the extent to which more recent changes in common law provinces in Canada (all provinces except Quebec) have contributed to greater gender equality for post-divorce family members.

The Charter and Social Assistance

As explained in earlier chapters, it is important to examine connections between families and the state, particularly with respect to definitions of responsibility for economic dependency—that is, if there are no obligations of (former) family members, a dependent individual must seek support from the state. In *Bracklow* (at para. 31), for example, the Supreme Court of Canada consciously adverted to "the potential injustice of foisting a helpless former partner onto the public assistance rolls" and thus held that there was a continuing obligation on former spouses to provide for needy former partners. In the context of cuts to social assistance entitlement and levels of payments, such decisions may seem appropriate. At the same time, they raise fundamental questions about responsibility for individual dependency and the respective roles of families and the state.

Issues about entitlement to social assistance have been raised in a number of recent cases, particularly focusing on ss. 7 and 15 of the Charter. In *Gosselin v. Quebec (Attorney General)*, [2002] 4 SCR 429, for example, a class action was dismissed by a majority of the Supreme Court of Canada (5:4) in relation to a denial of the same level of benefits to welfare recipients under the age of 30. In supporting this legislation, the government argued (see para. 246) that persons under 30 were more likely to live with their parents; thus, it appears that the legislation was based on an expectation of family, rather than state, support for such welfare recipients.

By contrast, the Ontario Court of Appeal concluded that a single mother on welfare should remain entitled to benefits even if she established a new relationship with a man, at least for an initial period of time: see *Falkiner v. Ontario* (2002), 59 OR (3d) 481;

leave to appeal to the Supreme Court of Canada granted March 20, 2003. The reasoning of the decision focused on the definition of spouse.

Children's Support for Parents

Some claims concerning spousal support have invoked the assistance of children. For example, in *Ontario (Dir. of Family Support Plan) v. Burgess* (1994), 5 RFL (4th) 451 (Ont. Ct. J (Prov. Div.)), a former husband sought to vary an obligation to pay spousal support that was contained in a separation agreement, based on his reduced income. In his application, the former husband sought to have his now-grown son contribute to his former wife's support; the former wife did not make this request. The husband's application was dismissed. In *Smeland v. Smeland* (1997), 29 RFL (4th) 360 (BCSC), a similar application was also dismissed.

Beyond the context of statutes concerning divorce and separation, however, provincial legislation generally creates some obligations for children who are no longer minors to provide support to their parents if they are in need. For example, s. 32 of Ontario's *Family Law Act* creates such obligations on the part of adult children who have the ability to provide support for a needy parent if the parent "cared for or provided support for the child." In a number of recent cases, courts have considered this provision: for example, see *Godwin v. Bolcso* (1993), 45 RFL (3d) 310 (Ont. Ct. J (Prov. Div.)); affirmed (1996), 20 RFL (4th) 66 (Ont. CA). In British Columbia, similar legislation was reviewed in *Newson v. Newson* (1998), 43 RFL (4th) 221 (BCCA); *Nevill v. Nevill*, [1998] BCJ no. 2802 (QL); and *Anderson v. Anderson*, [2001] BCJ no. 418 (QL).

Dragulin v. Dragulin
(1999), 43 RFL (4th) 55 (Ont. Ct. J (Gen. Div.))

[Octavian Dragulin applied for support from his daughter Helen pursuant to s. 32 of the *Family Law Act*. Mr. Dragulin was 73 years old and recently unemployed. He was divorced from Helen's mother and had remarried (his second wife was 59 and had emigrated from Romania to Canada in 1997; she had no assets and only a small pension). Mr. Dragulin came to Canada as a refugee in 1951. Helen was 45, a clerk with Canada Post, and lived in a home she co-owned with her mother; her sister also lived in the home and paid rent. Helen won a lottery worth $1 million in late 1996, but she continued to live modestly.

The court held that Helen should pay her father $400 per month. Examine the reasoning in the decision (at 57):]

There are three issues to determine in applying s. 32 of the *Family Law Act*: the need of the parent, whether the parent provided care or support for the child, and the capacity of the child to support the parent.

Capacity To Give Support

There is no issue in this case about Helen Dragulin's capacity to support her father. In fact, she provided him with support in the past, when he was in financial difficulties during the period when her parents were in the process of separation and divorce and at a time when her assets were significantly less.

She is employed full time with Canada Post as a clerk, and she still has substantial amounts of her lottery winnings. Her Financial Statement indicates that she has $4,547.24 per month surplus after paying her expenses.

None of the other children were joined in this application. However, the evidence indicates that Helen is the only one with the capacity to provide parental support.

Care and Support from the Parent

The second issue is whether care or support were provided by the plaintiff to the defendant when she was a child. The defendant argued strenuously that she was not cared for by her father as a child, and that her childhood was unhappy, because her father was verbally abusive. She and her sister Anna expressed great bitterness about their treatment by their father. In Helen's view, she received no emotional support from him, and he called her insulting names while she was growing up. Both also described Mr. Dragulin's beatings of his son, Michael.

It was Helen's evidence that she began to support the family from the time she was ten years old, doing cooking and laundry, while her mother was out at work. As a teenager, she also worked part-time to earn money for necessary personal expenses. However, both in examination for discovery and her testimony at trial, she admitted that her father had provided financial support for the family when she was growing up. He was the primary source of financial support for the family until she was ten years old, when her mother began to work outside the home.

There has been minimal contact between the children and their father since the 1984 divorce, and contact ceased following a letter he wrote, addressed "To whom it may concern," in August, 1994, in which he demanded reconciliation or an explanation of the family's past treatment of him within 30 days. It ended with a curse if they did not respond.

The language of s. 32 of the *Family Law Act* is clear: a parent must have "cared for *or* provided support for the child" (emphasis added). The terms are not conjunctive, and the parent need not show both support *and* care. Moreover, the Act includes no defence of fault or misconduct in the award of parental support (see *Godwin v. Bolcso* (1993), 45 RFL (3d) 310 (Ont. Prov. Div.); affirmed (1996), 20 RFL (4th) 66 (Ont. CA)), nor does it take into consideration the nature and quality of the current interaction between parent and child. In contrast, a child is not entitled to parental support if he or she is sixteen years of age or older and has withdrawn from parental control (s. 31(2)).

The evidence is clear in this case that the plaintiff provided financial support for his family when the defendant was a child, and she conceded that. The standard of living was not a high one, but this was a family in which the parents arrived in Canada

in 1951 and had to struggle to establish themselves, learning English, acquiring educational qualifications, and pursuing various employment and business opportunities, some of which proved very poor investments. The children were required to
work hard in the home and contribute financially, but this does not detract from the
fact that they were provided with financial support by their father when they were
children within the meaning of s. 32 of the Act. The family's subsequent estrange-
ment from Mr. Dragulin following the parents' divorce does not undermine the fact
that support was received within the meaning of s. 32. ...

Need of the Parent

The central issue in this case is the need of the plaintiff. Decided cases provide little
guidance with respect to this issue, as the few cases reported have focused on whether
there has been past support by the parent or on the relationship between spousal and
parental support, concluding that spousal support is the primary obligation (see, for
example, *Skrzypacz v. Skrzypacz* (1996), 22 RFL (4th) 450 (Ont. Prov. Div.); *Whiteley
v. Brodie* (May 13, 1994), Doc. Kingston 160/93 (Ont. Prov. Div.)). In *Blum v. Blum*
(1982), 132 DLR (3d) 69 (Ont. Fam. Ct.), a son was ordered to pay his mother $270.00
per month, after taking into account her need and the son's obligations to support his
wife and children, as well as his father. In *Godwin*, supra, support of $1,000.00 per
month was awarded on an interim basis, shared among the four children. ...

While both Mr. Dragulin and Mrs. Dragulin have improved their standard of living
over time, they have continued to live modestly. His proposed budget indicates that
he wishes to improve his standard of living now that his daughter has won the lottery.
However, ss. 32 and 33(9) of the Act provide that his claim must be based on need,
not wants, and he can not seek an increase in his standard of living just because of his
daughter's good fortune. These needs must also be his personal needs, not those of
his second wife, to whom his daughter Helen owes no support obligation.

In determining his needs, I have not considered his claims for vacation, gifts, the
portion of food and expenses for Maria Dragulin, and telephone costs, which include
many calls to Rumania. In addition, his claims for drug expenses are excessive, as
they take no account of public subsidies for senior citizens.

As well, Helen Dragulin has no obligation to fund the taxes for the Lake Simcoe
property. That property could be sold if Mr. Dragulin wished to do so, to pay for
vacations or other expenses. If he does not choose to sell the lot, he must bear its
carrying costs.

The issue of the condominium is more difficult. While Mr. Dragulin does have an
asset here that theoretically could be sold, were he to do so, his living expenses for an
equivalent rental apartment would significantly exceed the $371.41 he now pays.

After subtracting items from his current budget which are not necessities for him
personally, the plaintiff's personal needs still significantly exceed his income of approximately $1,000.00 per month. Therefore, there will be judgment for the plaintiff,
with support of $400.00 per month ordered payable by the defendant, Helen Dragulin,
to Octavian Dragulin, commencing October 1, 1998.

Compare this case with *Skrzypacz v. Skrzypacz* (1996), 22 RFL (4th) 450 (Ont. Ct. J (Prov. Div.)), where an applicant mother sought interim support from her son who had sponsored her to come to Canada from Poland. The son filed evidence supporting his claim that his mother was never his primary caregiver and had never provided support for him. The applicant failed to file any documentation in support of her claim to entitlement under an immigration sponsorship agreement, nor did she file any evidence to counter her son's allegations. Therefore, the court found that she failed to meet the criteria for entitlement under s. 32 of the *Family Law Act*.

To what extent do these cases reveal underlying assumptions about familial obliga- tions for economic support? Is it appropriate that Mr. Dragulin share in his daughter's good fortune in winning the lottery? To what extent do these cases appear consistent with the Supreme Court's emphasis on individual autonomy in *Miglin*? Could the daughter in *Dragulin* have entered into a contract with her father with respect to limitations on his entitlement to support?

SELECTED REFERENCES

Christa Bracci, "Ties That Bind: Ontario's Filial Responsibility Law" (2000), 17 *Cana- dian Journal of Family Law* 455.

Tonya L. Brito, "The Welfarization of Family Law" (2000), 48 *University of Kansas Law Review* 229.

Brenda Cossman and Judy Fudge, eds., *Privatization, Law, and the Challenge to Femi- nism* (Toronto: University of Toronto Press, 2002).

Shelley A.M. Gavigan, "Paradise Lost, Paradox Revisited: The Implications of Familial Ideology for Feminist, Lesbian, and Gay Engagement to Law" (1993), 31 *Osgoode Hall Law Journal* 589.

M.J. Mossman, "Conversations About Families in Canadian Courts and Legislatures: Are There 'Lessons for the United States'?" (2003), 32:1 *Hofstra Law Review* 171.

Jane E. Ursel, *Private Lives and Public Policy* (Toronto: Women's Press, 1992).

IV. REFORMING SPOUSAL SUPPORT

[T]here exists little or no sense of a social obligation of support between formerly married people. ... The obligation arises mainly through the exercise of the discretionary adjustive jurisdiction of the courts, and the courts have found it difficult to draw on any background social obligation to underpin their orders, and the search for an underlying rationale for them remains illusive.

> John Eekelaar, "Uncovering Social Obligations: Family Law and the
> Responsible Citizen," in Mavis Maclean, ed., *Making Law for*
> *Families* (Oxford and Portland, OR: Hart Publishing, 2000), 9, at 19

This assertion, based on experiences with spousal support in the United Kingdom, is similar to the conclusions of the American Law Institute, examined at the beginning of this chapter—there are few consistent rationales for legal principles concerning spousal support at divorce or separation. These concerns have been articulated frequently since the adoption of accessible divorce in the last decades of the 20th century, rendering traditional principles (based on fault and "innocent wives") unworkable—that is, in a context of serial monogamy, what principles justify the imposition of continuing obligations on a former spouse to meet the financial needs of their former partner? As Rogerson's critiques demonstrated earlier in this chapter, the search for legal principles concerning spousal support has clearly become more elusive in the context of no-fault and accessible divorce procedures.

Several decades ago, these concerns were addressed by two UK scholars. In "The Principles of Maintenance" (1977), 7 *Family Law* 229, at 232, Ruth Deech argued:

> The economic position of married and single women in society is well known to be weak but it does not follow from this that the ex-husband, alone in the community, must atone for the deficiencies of the system.

Responding to arguments like these, Katherine O'Donovan argued:

> The arguments for the abolition of maintenance after divorce are compelling. They include arguments based on liberty, justice and equality. Most of those involved in the debate would agree that in the good society the dead marriage should be buried. Let us assume, then, that in the ideal society no person would be under an obligation to support a former spouse after legal termination of the marriage.
>
> Achieving this ideal depends on the necessary material conditions being present in society. What are these material conditions? I think they would be as follows:
>
> a) Equality of partners during marriage including financial equality.
> b) Equal participation by both partners in wage earning activities.
> c) Wages geared to persons as individuals and not as heads of families.
> d) Treatment of persons as individuals and not as dependents by state agencies, such as social security and tax departments.
> e) Provisions for children by both parents, including financial support, child care, love, attention and stimulation.

See Katherine O'Donovan, "Should All Maintenance of Spouses Be Abolished?" (1982), 45 *Modern Law Review* 424, at 427-28. See also O'Donovan, "Principles of Maintenance: An Alternative View" (1978-79), 8-9 *Family Law* 180.

Obviously, O'Donovan's argument is dependent on major reforms, both legal and social. In the absence of such reforms, Canadian courts have focused on developing principles for spousal support in an effort to overcome some of the inequalities within family relationships. Nonetheless, in thinking about these issues, it may be important to revisit fundamental assumptions about family, rather than state, support for individual dependency. What are the advantages and disadvantages of relying on former family members to meet the needs of dependency? To what extent does the choice to rely on family, rather than state, support encourage disparities among the children of divorce— those whose parents are wealthy may benefit from payments of spousal support while others receive nothing? Clearly, these disparities will also be exacerbated by differential amounts of child support, considered in chapter 8. Recall the priority granted by s. 15.3(1) of the *Divorce Act, 1985* for child support, rather than spousal support—for poor families, this requirement will mean payment of minimal child support and perhaps no spousal support at all. By contrast, in more wealthy families, children will receive higher levels of child support and also the benefits of spousal support. Does s. 15.3 exacerbate these disparities? What should be the relationship between spousal and child support? You may wish to reconsider these questions after reviewing chapter 8.

Notwithstanding these arguments in favour of the abolition of spousal support, Canadian courts have been actively developing principles for expanding obligations of former family members at divorce or separation: see especially *Moge* and *Bracklow*. By contrast, spouses who negotiate separation agreements may be able to constrain their ongoing responsibilities: see *Miglin*. All the same, there may be a need to develop more principled and less discretionary bases for awarding spousal support. In this context, the federal government conducted a study in 2003 concerning the feasibility of developing spousal support guidelines. According to a press report, the proposed guidelines might be based on the length of a marriage in relation to the difference in the partners' earnings for determining quantum; they would also include measures for determining duration of the payment of support: see Cristin Schmitz, "Ottawa Secretly Developing Spousal Support Guidelines," *The Lawyers Weekly*, May 9, 2003.

The press report referred to a paper prepared by Carol Rogerson for the Department of Justice. Examine the excerpts from the paper, which follows—to what extent do you agree that this approach is preferable to the current state of spousal support in Canada?

Carol Rogerson, "Developing Spousal Support Guidelines in Canada:
Beginning the Discussion (Background Paper)"
(Ottawa: Department of Justice, 2002), at 33-34 and 65

[The author reviewed the current law of spousal support in Canada, as well as theories of spousal support, and continued:]

Where does this review of theory take us in terms of the project at hand? Several important themes emerge from the review of theory:

- First, that theory is important. Some understandings of spousal support are inconsistent with the basic premises of modern family law, in particular the removal of fault as a relevant factor in the determination of spousal support. Conceptions of spousal support based on expectations or promises flowing from the fact of marriage are theoretically on shaky ground.
- Second, that compensatory theories have a tendency, in practice, to merge with income-sharing theories because of the need to develop proxy measures of loss. While there is a tension between compensatory and income-sharing theories, there is also a fair amount of overlap. Particularly in cases of longer marriages, compensatory and non-compensatory theories may generate similar results.
- Third, that there are many "income-sharing" theories that offer theoretically defensible possibilities for structuring *Bracklow*-style non-compensatory support, the basis for which is now extremely confused. Particularly promising is the "merger over time" theory. These income-sharing theories are not uncontentious; some see them as bringing too much of an element of "status" back into spousal support. But this does seem to be the direction in which our law has moved, so it seems best to accept this and try to structure income-sharing in theoretically appropriate ways.
- Fourth, that the "parental partnership" theories, the "second wave" of income-sharing theories, may offer a way of understanding the developments in our law represented by decisions such as *Andrews*, where one finds extensive spousal support obligations being imposed in cases where there are minor children. But this theory, as well, is not uncontentious. There is some tension between "first wave" and "second wave" theories of income-sharing, which hangs on the significance to be given to children, and in particular the ongoing responsibility for the care of children after dissolution, as a crucial determinant of the extent of the spousal support obligation. ...

[The author reviewed a number of different spousal-support guideline initiatives in the United States, as well as the proposals of the American Law Institute. She also examined empirical evidence concerning awards of spousal support in Canada, noting that the percentage of such orders was quite low. Although there may be a number of different explanations for this low rate of spousal support awards, Rogerson suggested that one possible explanation might be the uncertainty with respect to such claims. She concluded by recognizing the tensions in the project to develop spousal support guidelines:]

The project is put forward as one that builds on current practice. Yet, current practice is diverse. In order to bring more structure and certainty into the law choices have to be made as to what are "emerging trends" or "best practices" and the law will thus be "re-structured" along those lines. The project thus contemplates a certain degree of change, but change that is consistent with the current legislative structure and basic framework that comes from decisions of the Supreme Court of Canada interpreting those provisions. One way to see the project is as facilitating or "speeding up" the normal common law process for the development of the law whereby the best understandings or interpretations of the current law eventually rise to the surface. The normal process of legal development has fallen apart in this area of law because of an excessive emphasis on discretion and individualized decision-making and a failure to focus on underlying principles and structure.

Do you agree with this assessment of the need for reform in relation to spousal support? Is there a need for discussion of more fundamental issues before considering spousal support guidelines, or is more fundamental reform impractical? What advice would you give to the minister of justice with respect to spousal support at divorce or separation?

SELECTED REFERENCES

Alberta Law Reform Institute, *Spousal Support (Family Law Project)* (Edmonton: Alberta Law Reform Institute, 1998).

American Law Institute, *Principles of the Law of Family Dissolution: Analysis and Recommendations* (Washington, DC: Matthew Bender, 2002).

Grace Ganz Blumberg, "The Financial Incidents of Family Dissolution," in Sanford N. Katz, John Eekelaar, and Mavis Maclean, eds., *Cross Currents: Family Law and Policy in the United States and England* (Oxford: Oxford University Press, 2000).

Canadian Centre for Justice Statistics, *Child and Spousal Support: Introduction to the Maintenance Enforcement Survey* (Ottawa: Statistics Canada, 2002).

June Carbone, "The Futility of Coherence: The ALI's Principles of the Law of Family Dissolution, Compensatory Spousal Payments" (2002), 4 *Journal of Law and Family Studies* 43.

Linda Silver Dranoff, "Suggested Formula for Determining Spousal Support" (Toronto: Ontario Bar Association Institute of Continuing Legal Education, 2000).

Marsha Garrison, "The Economic Principles of Divorce: Would Adoption of the ALI Principles Improve Current Outcomes?" (2001), 8 *Duke Journal of Gender, Law and Policy* 119.

Craig Martin, "Unequal Shadows: Negotiation Theory and Spousal Support Under the Canadian Divorce Act" (1998), 56 *University of Toronto Faculty of Law Review* 135.

Jana Singer, "Divorce Reform and Gender Justice" (1989), 67 *North Carolina Law Review* 1103.

Joan Williams, "Is Coverture Dead? Beyond a New Theory of Alimony" (1994), 82 *Georgetown Law Journal* 2227.

PROBLEM

In reflecting on the underlying values in the cases decided in the Supreme Court (*Messier*, the *Pelech* trilogy, *Moge*, *Bracklow*, *Miglin*, and *Hartshorne*), consider the merits of legislated spousal support guidelines and the comments of Carol Rogerson—to what extent can you identify the primary factors relevant to spousal support claims? As will be discussed in chapter 8, child support guidelines include both "rules" and "discretion"— what mixture is appropriate with respect to spousal support? To what extent is it possible to assess spousal support following family breakdown as a matter of general social policy, not just as a matter of a private family concern?

CHAPTER REFERENCES

American Law Institute. *Principles of the Law of Family Dissolution: Analysis and Recommendations* (Washington, DC: Matthew Bender, 2002).

Bailey, Martha. "Pelech, Caron, and Richardson" (1989-90), 3 *Canadian Journal of Women and the Law* 615.

Bala, N. "Recognizing Spousal Contributions to the Acquisition of Degrees, Licences, and Other Career Assets: Toward Compensatory Support" (1989), 8 *Canadian Journal of Family Law* 23.

Boyd, Susan. "Best Friends or Spouses? Privatization and the Recognition of Lesbian Relationships in M. v. H." (1996), 13 *Canadian Journal of Family Law* 321.

Cossman, Brenda. "Family Feuds: Neo-Liberal and Neo-Conservative Visions of the Reprivatization Project," in B. Cossman and J. Fudge, eds., *Privatization, Law, and the Challenge to Feminism* (Toronto: University of Toronto Press, 2002), 169.

Cossman, Brenda and Bruce Ryder. "What Is Marriage-Like Like? The Irrelevance of Conjugality" (2001), 18 *Canadian Family Law Journal* 271.

Davies, Christine. "The Ever-Changing Picture of Support and Other Developments" (2002-3), 20 *Canadian Family Law Quarterly* 213.

Deech, Ruth. "The Principles of Maintenance" (1977), 7 *Family Law* 229.

Department of Justice. *Evaluation of the Divorce Act, Phase II: Monitoring and Evaluation* (Ottawa: Department of Justice, 1990).

Eekelaar, John. "Uncovering Social Obligations: Family Law and the Responsible Citizen," in Mavis Maclean, ed., *Making Law for Families* (Oxford and Portland, OR: Hart Publishing, 2000), 9.

Egale Canada. Press release. "Ontario's 'Separate and Unequal' Regime To Be Challenged in Supreme Court of Canada" (November 25, 1999), available online at http://www.egale.ca/index.asp?lang.

Elliott, F. "The Family: Private Arena or Adjunct of the State?" (1989), 16 *Journal of Law and Society* 443.

Foster, Ronald S. "Moge v. Moge: What It Means to Family Law Lawyers" (1993), 43 RFL (3d) 465.

Fudge, Judy. "The Privatization of the Costs of Social Reproduction: Some Recent Charter Cases" (1989), 3 *Canadian Journal of Women and the Law* 246.

Hogg, Peter. *Constitutional Law of Canada* (Toronto: Carswell) (looseleaf).

L'Heureux-Dubé, Claire. "Equality and the Economic Consequences of Spousal Support: A Canadian Perspective" (1994), 7 *Journal of Law and Public Policy* 1.

Lempriere, T. "A New Look at Poverty"(1992), 16 *Perceptions* 18.

MacDonald, James C. and Lee K. Ferrier. *Canadian Divorce Law and Practice*, 2d ed. (Scarborough, ON: Carswell, 1986).

Makin, Kirk. "Divorce Deals Stand Till Death Do You Part," *Globe and Mail*, April 18, 2003.

McLeod, James G. "Annotation" (2000), 5 RFL (5th) 90.

_____. "Annotation of Nowell v. Towne Estate" (1998), 38 RFL (4th) 361.

_____. "Case Comment: Moge v. Moge" (1993), 43 RFL (3d) 455.

Mossman, M.J. " 'Running Hard To Stand Still': The Paradox of Family Law Reform" (1994), 17 *Dalhousie Law Journal* 5.

Mossman, M.J. and M. MacLean. "Family Law and Social Assistance Programs: Rethinking Equality," in P.M. Evans and G.R. Wekerle, eds., *Women and the Canadian Welfare State: Challenges and Change* (Toronto: University of Toronto Press, 1997).

O'Donovan, Katherine. "Principles of Maintenance: An Alternative View" (1978-79), 8-9 *Family Law* 180.

_____. "Should All Maintenance of Spouses Be Abolished?" (1982), 45 *Modern Law Review* 424.

OLRC. *Report on the Rights and Responsibilities of Cohabitees* (Toronto: Ministry of the Attorney General, 1993).

Payne, Julien D. "An Overview of Theory and Reality in the Judicial Disposition of Spousal Support Claims Under the Canadian Divorce Act" (2000), 63 *Saskatchewan Law Review* 403.

_____. "First Impressions of Miglin in the Supreme Court of Canada" (PPFL/2003-001).

Rhode, Deborah and Martha Minow. "Reforming the Questions: Questioning the Reforms," in S.D. Sugarman and H.H. Kay, eds., *Divorce Reform at the Crossroads* (New Haven, CT: Yale University Press, 1990), 191.

Rogerson, Carol J. "The Causal Connection Test in Spousal Support Law" (1989), 8 *Canadian Journal of Family Law* 95.

_____. "Developing Spousal Support Guidelines in Canada: Beginning the Discussion (Background Paper)" (Ottawa: Department of Justice, 2002).

_____. "Judicial Interpretation of the Spousal and Child Support Provisions of the Divorce Act, 1985 (Part I)" (1992), 7 *Canadian Family Law Quarterly* 155.

_____. "Spousal Support After Moge" (1997), 14 *Canadian Family Law Quarterly* 281.

_____. "Spousal Support Post-Bracklow: The Pendulum Swings Again?" (2001), 19 *Canadian Family Law Quarterly* 185.

Schmitz, Cristin. "Citing Miglin, Court Denies Support to Impoverished Widow," *The Lawyers Weekly*, August 15, 2003.

_____. "Ottawa Secretly Developing Spousal Support Guidelines," *The Lawyers Weekly*, May 9, 2003.

_____. "Women, Kids Driven into Poverty by Low Awards Under Divorce Act," *The Lawyers Weekly*, August 31, 2003.

Selick, Karen. "Spousal Support—Time To Consider Misconduct" (January 1998), 22 *Canadian Lawyer* 46.

Shaffer, Martha and Carol Rogerson. "Contracting Spousal Support: Thinking Through Miglin" (2003-4), 21 *Canadian Family Law Quarterly* 49.

Sheppard, Colleen. "Uncomfortable Victories and Unanswered Questions: Lessons from Moge" (1995), 12 *Canadian Journal of Family Law* 284.

Smart, Carol. *The Ties That Bind: Law, Marriage, and the Reproduction of Patriarchal Relations* (London: Routledge & Kegan Paul, 1984).

Wilson, B. "The Variation of Support Orders," in R. Abella and C. L'Heureux-Dubé, eds., *Family Law: Dimensions of Justice* (Toronto: Butterworths, 1983), 35.

CHAPTER EIGHT

Children of Divorce: Rights, Relationships, and Support

I. INTRODUCTION

The ways in which separation is managed by children can differ widely and are affected by such things as the quality of relationships; the nature, length or frequency of the separation; its causes and predictability; the sense that children make of it; and the resources they have for responding to it. We found that children with unreliable contact with a parent who seemed to make little emotional or practical investment in them could feel extremely unhappy. Yet even children with reliable contact could speak of "missing" the parent from whom they were apart. This could be a matter of sadness even though both parents were fully involved in their lives. At the other end of the spectrum, children with an oppressive or abusive parent could find relief in never having to see that parent again.

> Carol Smart, Bren Neale, and Amanda Wade, *The Changing*
> *Experience of Childhood: Families and Divorce*
> (Cambridge: Polity Press, 2001), 69

In child custody law, women, and those men who provide caregiving labour themselves or understand its demands, must continue to point out the day-to-day demands of caring for children in a society that is structured on the privatization of caring labour. Simultaneously, we must struggle for the structural changes that will be more likely to produce a society that will encourage more collective responsibility for children and those who attend to their needs and their welfare. There is no shortage of research, writing, and activism that imagines what such societies might look like; but there does appear to be a shortage of political will or ability to work towards them.

> Susan B. Boyd, *Child Custody, Law, and Women's Work*
> (Toronto: Oxford University Press, 2003), 226-27

Legal regulation relating to the children of divorce involves complex, often controversial, issues. Viewed from the perspective of individual children who have experienced parental separation or divorce, responses vary in relation to a number of different kinds of factors, including parent–child relationships within the family before breakdown. Thus, as Smart, Neale, and Wade cautioned (at 41), it is important to be wary of research that focuses on the consequences of divorce for children from the perspective of a " 'narrative of harm' ... which suffuses contemporary public debates about divorce."

633

They argued that it was necessary to examine children's own experiences, rather than making research assumptions about outcomes and harms. Significantly, the most obvious finding from their research was that it was not appropriate to assume that "all children are alike or want the same things" (at 167):

> We found some brothers were happy with arrangements while their sisters were not, or that a younger sibling might be content with contact while an older sibling was not. It was not uncommon for two children in the same family to have different parenting arrangements in place, depending on how they each got on with their parents. We cannot therefore assume that all children will benefit from the same processes or solutions. The idea of the welfare of "the child" may be unhelpful simply because it implies that general principles can be devised that can be applied in a blanket fashion—a kind of "one size fits all" approach. A more flexible approach which takes into account the individuality of each child in a family might embrace more elements of citizenship, while also attending rather more to the well-being of each child.

As this conclusion suggests, decisions concerning the children of divorce may require attentiveness to their individual needs. Moreover, in addition to being attentive to the ways in which children's needs may differ within the same family, legal principles must also take account of how children's needs may change over time.

Yet, as Boyd's comment illustrates, it is also necessary to examine how social policies that assume the primacy of parental care for children may exacerbate the impact of separation or divorce, both for children and their adult caregivers. That is, while it may be important to take account of the needs of children as individuals, the scope for meeting children's needs may be significantly constrained by reason of social and legal policies that emphasize extensive *parental* responsibility for their children. If parents are the persons with full legal responsibility for children, concerns tend to focus on the relative strengths and weaknesses of parents as caregivers; however, such analyses all too often fail to examine the role of extended families and communities, as well as public policies that shape the contexts in which children live. Although this problem is particularly relevant with respect to issues of financial support for children, especially post-separation or divorce, it also has an impact on decisions about responsibilities for caregiving. In this way, issues about the children of divorce need to take account of both *private* family relationships as well as *public* policies that provide (or sometimes fail to provide) support for families and children when adult relationships break down. Some of these issues were addressed earlier in chapter 4.

Moreover, these issues are particularly controversial at present. Although the current *Divorce Act, 1985* and provincial legislation concerning children's care and financial support at family breakdown still refer to custody and access, the federal government initiated two major reviews in the 1990s to redefine these legal arrangements: see Canada, Department of Justice, *Custody and Access: Public Discussion Paper* (Ottawa: Supply and Services Canada, 1993) and Special Joint Committee on Child Custody and Access, *For the Sake of the Children* (Ottawa: Parliament of Canada, 1998). Bill C-22, which was introduced into Parliament in December 2002, reflected recommendations of the Report of the Special Joint Committee on Child Custody and Access, *For the Sake of the Children*. The report recommended eliminating the legal categories of custody and access and replacing them with obligations for parents to negotiate parenting plans, with the help of mediation, if necessary; the underlying principle was that just as parents must negotiate about their children's well-being during an intact relationship, they should continue to exercise the same responsibility at post-separation or divorce. In this way, the proposed legislation reinforced the view that, while marriage may end, parenthood lasts forever. Even though spouses may choose to separate because they are no longer compatible, their roles as parents and their obligations to support and to cooperate in parenting their children remain firmly in place. Although this legislation has not been enacted to date, it is clear that such legal principles about custody, access, and child support confirm the existence of the post-divorce family unit.

This chapter provides an overview of these legal issues concerning children at divorce or separation and a brief examination of some of the critiques and recommendations for reform in this area. The introductory material is designed to explore some of the contextual issues, both social and legal, concerning custody, access, and support. The chapter then provides some examples of the implementation in practice of the legal principle that custody and access determinations must be guided by the best interests of the child. In addition, the chapter examines different kinds of custody and access arrangements in relation to reform proposals, especially those set out in Bill C-22. The chapter also focuses on issues concerning child support and the interpretation of national child-support guidelines, introduced across Canada in the late 1990s. Although legal principles concerning custody and access were traditionally distinct from those regarding obligations to pay child support, these principles have recently become more intertwined politically and, at least to some extent, legally. In examining the materials in this chapter, you may wish to consider whether children's best interests are encouraged by these developments.

A. The History of Child Custody and Access

Susan B. Boyd, *Child Custody, Law, and Women's Work*
(Toronto: Oxford University Press, 2003), 2

This book unravels and challenges the dominant images and rationales for change to child custody laws, by tracing historical shifts in legal and social discourses on custody and access in the Canadian context. A framework is developed for analyzing such shifts that reveals a hierarchy of discourses surrounding parenting in different historical periods. The objective is to understand the complex dynamics of the relationship between custody and access law, familial ideologies, and gender relations. ...

The transformation of child custody laws in Canada and most Western countries over the past two centuries has been striking. The broad outline of legal history of child custody laws reveals a more or less complete reversal, and a half-turn again by the 1980s. At the beginning of the nineteenth century, laws in countries such as England and the United States affirmed an almost absolute paternal right to custody of children born within wedlock, reflecting the elevated legal status of the husband/ father within the institution of marriage. By the beginning of the twentieth century, this absolute paternal right had begun to wane and to give way to an emphasis on the welfare of children. By the mid-twentieth century, mothers were said to have a presumption in their favour when seeking custody of children "of tender years." By the 1980s, child custody law was pronounced to be a neutral domain, where the "best interests" of children came first, and where mothers and fathers, and potentially other parties connected to the children, had an equal right to legal custody. By the 1990s, reforms of child custody laws in many jurisdictions purported to embody these changes and to deepen them by emphasizing shared parenting.

Discussion Notes

The Evolution of Legal Principles

Boyd undertook a detailed analysis of the evolution of legal principles of custody and access (and some related issues of child support), demonstrating how legal principles changed in the context of political, economic, and social developments during the past two centuries. According to her analysis, legal principles enshrined in legislation were not always interpreted consistently in judicial decisions and (especially in the 19th century) they were applied more often to middle- and upper-class parents than to poor or disadvantaged families. All the same, the general features of the law of child custody reveal some patterns.

Early 19th-century recognition of paternal rights to custody and guardianship of "legitimate" children, both during marriage and after separation, were well established in Canadian jurisprudence. Then, in 1839, *Lord Talfourd's Act* (*An Act To Amend the Law Relating to the Custody of Infants*, 2 & 3 Vict., c. 54), enacted as a result of the lobbying efforts of Lady Caroline Norton, empowered the English Court of Chancery to grant access to, and sometimes physical custody of, a child who was less than seven years old to a mother. As Boyd noted, however (at 27):

> The limitations of the Act are clear when one realizes that a mother's custody rights were to physical custody only, not legal; that they lasted only until the child reached age seven; and that they were contingent on her not engaging in conduct viewed as sexually "immoral." In contrast, the father's rights remained paramount and subject to few conditions.

Boyd traced developments in Canadian provinces, including Quebec, in the 19th century, concluding (at 30) that mothers obtained some "special rights" pursuant to legislative amendments, but that these amendments always "operated against an assumption that overriding paternal authority over children and their mothers remained the default position."

The early 20th century reveals uneven patterns in legal principles concerning child custody. On the one hand, some provincial legislation and judicial decisions increasingly recognized the tender-years doctrine (which awarded maternal custody for young children), while others failed to do so. In addition, some courts began to focus on the welfare of the child. As Boyd noted (at 71):

> Overall, the doctrine of tender years that emerged in Canadian custody law for a period of time in the twentieth century was not a real maternal presumption during the early 1900s, if ever, and its beginnings were tentative. ... Even at its strongest point during the mid-1900s

to the late 1960s, the doctrine contained significant qualifiers: a mother was to be preferred as the custodial parent of young children only (especially girls), but only provided that all other things were "equal," including her fitness as a parent. Any notion that mothers were favoured in custody cases under this doctrine must be read in light of the intense scrutiny of maternal and wifely conduct that preceded a finding of all things being equal between the parents. Proper conduct was required of the mother before application of the "presumption." As well, there appeared to be a clear preference by gender for paternal custody of older children. In other words, despite the fact that mainly women, not men, were caregivers for children, the tender years doctrine only gave mothers the opportunity to gain custody of children in specific circumstances.

The 1970s and '80s witnessed a significant increase in rates of divorce, after the enactment of the first federal divorce legislation in 1968, creating pressures on the substance of legal principles concerning child custody as well as on processes for resolving family breakdown. The Charter also influenced ideas about parental equality and shared parenting arrangements, and mothers increasingly participated in the paid workforce. In spite of all these changes, Boyd noted (at 101) that:

> For many mothers, however, the liberal spirit of the time was not evident when they went to court to seek custody of their children. Their sexual conduct, their lack of fidelity to marriage and to the sexual division of labour, and their economic viability could all generate difficulties for their claims for custody. ... [T]he equality rights discourse that emerged during the 1980s accelerated the trends towards enhancing the status of fathers in custody and access claims. However, the rising emphasis on equality did not always diminish the scrutiny of women's behaviour when assessing their suitability as custodial mothers.

This overview shows how legal principles concerning child custody changed from the early 19th to the late 20th centuries. Following enactment of the *Divorce Act, 1985* and revised provincial legislation in recent decades, the principle for defining custody entitlement is now the best interests of the child. Yet, older ideas about child custody principles may continue to influence the choice of factors that are, or are not, relevant to interpreting what arrangement accords with a child's best interests. In this way, the historical development of legal principles about child custody may have a continuing impact on current legislation, judicial decision making, and law reform proposals.

Caregiving and Custody: Norms and Ideology

Recall the material in chapter 4 concerning child care and protection. Issues about the appropriate relationship between caring for children during an intact relationship or after its breakdown and custody entitlement remain controversial. As Boyd argued (at 218):

> [T]he ideology of motherhood reproduced in custody and access law relies on a notion that mothers will assume responsibility for children, that they will put aside their own interests, and often their participation in the so-called "public" sphere, in order to do so, and that they can expect to be paid nothing for this labour of love ... . Mothers whose behaviour or choices depart from these assumptions and expectations can expect to be treated more suspiciously, even negatively, in the legal system as well as in society.

Such comments reveal how societal norms about how mothers and fathers behave may affect the interpretation of legal principles. These concerns may have an impact as well on individuals who are outside the norms of the traditional family—lesbian and gay parents, aboriginal parents, or poor parents. Such issues also require a re-examination of the state's role in relation to child care and protection.

SELECTED REFERENCES

Constance B. Backhouse, "Shifting Patterns in Nineteenth Century Canadian Custody Law," in David H. Flaherty, ed., *Essays in the History of Canadian Law*, vol. 1 (Toronto: The Osgoode Society, 1981), 212.

Martha J. Bailey, "England's First Custody of Infants Act" (1995), 20:2 *Queen's Law Journal* 391.

Dorothy E. Chunn, *From Punishment to Doing Good* (Toronto: University of Toronto Press, 1992).

Michael Grossberg, *Governing the Hearth: Law and the Family in Nineteenth-Century America* (Chapel Hill, NC: University of North Carolina Press, 1985).

Mary Ann Mason, *From Father's Property to Children's Rights: The History of Child Custody in the United States* (New York: Columbia University Press, 1994).

M.J. Mossman, "Child Support or Support for Children? Rethinking 'Public' and 'Private' in Family Law" (1997), 46 *University of New Brunswick Law Journal* 63.

Carol Smart and Selma Sevenhuijsen, eds., *Child Custody and the Politics of Gender* (London: Routledge, 1989).

B. The Context for Decision Making About Custody and Access

Jane Gordon, "Multiple Meanings of Equality: A Case Study in Custody Litigation"
(1989), 3 *Canadian Journal of Women and the Law* 256

In this paper, I use my experience of a divorce and custody fight to examine the ways in which judges in the province of Nova Scotia have interpreted the concept of equality. I look at the ways in which both the mother herself and the father had made assumptions about equality, how these were argued or presumed by each party in court, and how they were interpreted in the decisions of the judges. ...

My husband left to take a short-term job halfway across Canada when I was seven and a half months pregnant with our second child. This was in August 1979. Our first child (Jeremy) was just a bit over three years old. I was not consulted about his decision to take that job, and at the time he did not define the separation as permanent. I was left pregnant with Rachel, with a pre-schooler, and three months of maternity leave from a job which I saw as essential to the economic survival of the family. Eventually we agreed on a separation agreement which I thought would keep me safe from any unpleasant surprises and would protect both the children's and my interests.

I eventually filed for divorce in August 1983. My ex-husband contested the application on virtually every issue. The case was heard in September 1984. As in all the subsequent legal proceedings, he argued his case himself. After a two and a half day trial, I was awarded a divorce, custody, token child support, the distribution of matrimonial property as outlined in our separation agreement, and costs of $5000 (my lawyer estimated the bill would be $7500). He received regular access of approximately one and a half days each week.

He appealed the trial court decision *in toto*, including my lawyer's behaviour. He also wrote to the judge objecting to the decree nisi. The appeal was heard in March 1985. The original decision was upheld on every issue except costs, which were reduced by about $2000. He then applied for leave to appeal to the Supreme Court of Canada; that leave to appeal was denied in July, 1985.

The Supreme Court decision was not the end of the legal proceedings, however. From August 1985 until January 1986 I was in court at least once a month on alleged violations of the access order and related matters. None of these alleged violations were upheld. He also challenged the final divorce decree. The hearing of that challenge was the last time I was represented by a lawyer; deeply in debt for legal fees, I represented myself from August 1985 on. The final decree was revoked, although another one was later granted. In July 1986, after the proclamation of the *Divorce Act* of 1985, I received notice to go to court again. He was again asking for joint custody or increased access. The July hearing was adjourned until September because there were too many issues to hear in one day. By September he had retained a lawyer and modified his request to increased access. After another two and a half day trial, this was awarded. ...

Although a variety of legal issues were examined at each level, each new decision tended to reinforce previous decisions. Implicit in most of these decisions was a concept of "equality" which sustains the status quo. This happened by omission as well as by commission; many areas into which the notion of equality should have been introduced were ignored, and an effective double standard arose. In the remainder of this comment, I discuss in detail some of these areas: (1) responsibility for the children during the marriage and the division of domestic and wage-earner responsibilities; (2) domestic and financial responsibility for the children from the end of the marriage until the time of the divorce hearing; (3) legal responsibility for the children; (4) financial responsibility for the children; (5) the allocation of the children's time; (6) the ordinary care and responsibility for the children; and (7) the responsibility to obey court orders. In each of these areas, I found that implicit concepts of equality operated to make my contributions and work invisible at the same time that they helped overvalue his. ...

Financial Responsibility

At the initial divorce hearing I asked for and received $25 a month child support. My lawyer said there was not much chance of getting anything more than symbolic maintenance because I had an adequate income and he was unemployed. At the appeal, when my former husband continued his arguments for joint custody, I pointed out that he had not even been paying the $25 because he claimed he could not afford it—and so how could he afford to provide for half their expenses, something he argued should and would follow from a joint custody arrangement. He dismissed his arrears by saying that it was merely a cash-flow problem. Later in Family Court he continued to plead poverty and debts, and his maintenance was reduced to $1 a month. He still refused to make those payments. ...

Allocation of Children's Time

The division of children's time is, I think, problematic and complex. The notion that time should be evenly divided between parents seems to me to turn children into commodities, treating them as just another piece of matrimonial property to be evenly divided. It reflects the assumption that children have no particular interest in or choices about the way in which their time is allocated; that the interest of children and their parents are identical; and that no matter what the relative involvement of each parent with the child prior to marital breakup, the children's time should be evenly split between adversarial parents.

Fathers like my ex-husband have argued that equal division of children's time between parents is fair and reflects the [principle] of equality. This simply is not the case. This superficial notion reduces time spent parenting to only one dimension: time spent with children. There are other dimensions to parenting. Time spent "with" children can include a number of hours the child spent with the parent, inclusive or exclusive of the activities of the child which do not involve active interaction with the parent—sleeping, voluntary activities of various sorts such as dancing or swimming lessons, nondiscretionary activities such as medical and dental appointments, school, time spent on homework and other school-related tasks, normal recreational time (regular Cub meetings), and special recreational time (Cub camping trips). Time spent *on* children includes shopping for their clothes and shoes; doing laundry; planning special events; arranging for activities, appointments, babysitters, and so on.

If the issue of access to children's time is to be one of true equality, then all dimensions of responsibility for children should be considered. On the one hand, noncustodial parents have often reported they felt like visitors in the lives of their children. On the other, custodial parents have said they felt like drudges and disciplinarians in comparison. If equality is to be an issue in the allocation of parental time with children, then dimensions other than the bare amount of time "with" the children must be considered. ...

Conclusion

Judges have shown a quite flexible attitude toward the meaning of equality when it came to the allocation of the children's time and the costs of raising the children. In those areas they appeared to consider the father's interests and situation to be of paramount importance. His expressed interest in having more time with the children, and the extent to which he was willing to make a nuisance of himself in the legal system, have had a powerful effect on the amount of time he was awarded. In addition, his willingness to use the media and to go public with the circumstances of the lives of his children was effective in mobilizing support among the general public and in creating a provincial lobby group so that his concerns were not seen as isolated ones. Even though I felt it the most appropriate course of action to follow, my unwillingness to comment in public made my contribution to the children's upbringing invisible. And, of course, this silence contributed to the effectiveness of the special interest group because there was no "public debate" on the appropriateness of the concerns of the father's group.

Under the rhetoric of equality and fairness, so commonly argued by my former husband and other fathers' rights activists, the work of parenting has been presented in a way which downplays or hides the amount of work and nurturing women contribute to raising children. Debate has tended to focus on issues of fairness around content which is highly visible and can be dramatically presented.

Carol Smart, Bren Neale, and Amanda Wade, *The Changing Experience of Childhood: Families and Divorce*
(Cambridge: Polity Press, 2001), at 19 and 173

[In this study, the authors analyzed changes in sociological and psychological research about children over several decades and suggested that it is important to investigate the ways in which children experience family relationships, particularly in the context of separation or divorce. As they explained (at 19):]

We wanted to explore how transformations in family life in Britain might be reshaping children's lives and thereby changing the nature of childhood at the turn of the century. More specifically, we wanted to see how children themselves might shape their own childhoods in the face of family change and what this might mean for the way they practised their family lives. In a policy context, too, we wanted to explore how new ideas about childhood might transform how we "see" and respond to children whose parents have separated or divorced. ...

[The authors interviewed children about their experiences in families involved in separation or divorce. They identified ways in which children participated in family decision making, and the ways in which their participation represented a democratization of the family. As they concluded (at 173):]

It has been a major argument in this book that there is more than one story to be told about children's experiences of their parents' divorce. Not all the stories are happy ones but many are about resilience, transformations, growing self-reflexiveness, and the development of a new set of perspectives on parenting and family practices. The growth in the divorce rate in the second half of the twentieth century dramatically changed children's experiences of childhood. Even those children whose parents stay together will know children whose parents are divorced. This does not make divorce easy for children, but it changes the landscape of childhood into one in which these personal transformations become highly probable. In this context children need to acquire new skills (both practical and emotional) to navigate this new moral terrain.

Discussion Notes

Seeing Separation or Divorce: Differing Perspectives

The two excerpts above offer different perspectives on separation and divorce—what factors shape the perspectives of different family members in such a context? To what extent should legal principles take all these perspectives into account? In reflecting on these questions, consider the following psychological description of divorce.

R. Emery, *Renegotiating Family Relationships: Divorce, Child Custody, and Mediation*
(New York: Guilford Press, 1994), 12-13

His and Her Children

As with other emotional conflicts, a couple's disparity in the experience of grief can lead to fights about a variety of issues, including the children and custody. Because of their own, conflicting experiences of grief, Sheila and John are likely to have very different views on how their children are experiencing the separation. Sheila is likely to see the children as she sees herself: as accepting the separation and coping with it relatively well. John also is likely to see the children as he sees himself: as hating the separation and feeling devastated by it.

Each parent projects his or her own feelings onto the children. If no problems are apparent, John may argue that the children are hiding their feelings, protecting their mother, and defending against their terrible pain. Sheila may counter that the children's lack of reaction proves that they are doing fine. In fact, she may see them as happier than they were when they had been exposed to the daily tension, fighting, and unhappiness of the marriage. If the children do show obvious difficulties, this may demonstrate the need for a reconciliation to John, even if only for the sake of the children. To Sheila, the children's problems are proof of their need for stability and the paramount importance of having a clear and stable custody arrangement as soon as possible.

As with other emotional aspects of separation and divorce, a couple's conflicting experience and projection of grief means that custody disputes often involve conflicts about the children that reflect much more than the children. Some of the parents' conflicting interpretations of their children's feelings and needs certainly are due to legitimate differences of opinion. Even impartial mental health professionals have difficulty discerning how children feel and what they want following their parents' marital separation. Still, intentionally or unintentionally, parents in a custody dispute also are likely to project their own experiences onto their children, and thus adopt a somewhat self-serving and inaccurate view of their children's adjustment and needs.

To what extent do these views about the psychological experiences of divorce make assumptions that are different from those identified in the other excerpts above? What are the implications for *legal* processes of divorce in relation to these differing views?

The Impact of Separation and Divorce on Children

Many studies have addressed the outcomes of separation or divorce for children. In an assessment in 1993, for example, Barbara Dafoe Whitehead suggested:

> According to a growing body of social-scientific evidence, children in families disrupted by divorce and out-of-wedlock birth do worse than children in intact families on several measures of well-being [including poverty]. ... Contrary to popular belief, many children do not "bounce back" after divorce or remarriage. Difficulties that are associated with family breakup often persist into adulthood.

(Barbara Dafoe Whitehead, "Dan Quayle Was Right," *The Atlantic Monthly*, April 1993, 47.)

Whitehead's conclusions were later challenged: see Leah McLaren, "The Kids (of Divorce) Are All Right," *Globe and Mail*, September 11, 1999. According to Dr. Robert Glossop, who was quoted in this newspaper article, it is possible that it is not divorce *per se*, but rather the economic consequences of family breakdown that create problems for children. That is, because a large majority of single female parents are among the poorest families in Canada, many children may live in poverty (with their custodial mothers) for some period of time after the separation or divorce of their parents. Recall the data in chapter 5 concerning the economic consequences of separation or divorce—how should these problems of poverty be addressed in legal and social policies?

According to Rhonda Freeman, a number of factors assist children's adjustment to family breakdown—protecting them from conflict and violence; ensuring adequate economic support; developing the adults' capacity for parenting after family breakdown and the creation of clear roles for parents and children; preserving parents' functions in their children's lives; and developing a positive environment (including responding to children's questions and fears and recognizing their culture and heritage): see Rhonda Freeman, "Parenting After Divorce: Using Research To Inform Decision-Making About Children" (1998), 15 *Canadian Journal of Family Law* 79. Like a number of other researchers, Freeman expressed support for the creation of post-divorce parenting plans; she also identified three kinds of circumstances that may require different approaches—situations involving abuse, parental alienation, and high conflict. These issues are discussed later in this chapter in greater detail.

At this point, it is important to consider whether or to what extent research about the impact of separation or divorce on children reflects the (highly variable) experiences of children. It is also important to examine how definitions of the problems of divorce may lead to particular kinds of legal solutions.

Hearing Children's Voices

Changing views about children in the context of divorce or separation have resulted in recommendations for children to be more actively involved in legal processes. For example, some children may be asked to give evidence before or to participate in an interview with a judge. Children may also be the subject of an interview with an expert assessor or required to undergo counselling. In some cases, children may require independent legal representation, a situation that may require special skill and knowledge: for one overview of these issues, see Carol Mahood Huddart and Jeanne Charlotte Ensminger, "Hearing the Voice of Children" (1992), 8 *Canadian Family Law Quarterly* 95.

Some research suggests, however, that children may want to be heard *within their families* rather than in legal proceedings. While not rejecting a possible need for legal rights and independent legal representation for children in divorce proceedings, for example, Smart, Neale, and Wade suggest (at 121-22) that different approaches may be needed:

> Very few of the children and young people we interviewed were interested in having a voice in legal proceedings unless they felt that they had no voice in their family. Very few wanted the privacy of their families opened up to professional intervention and none spoke in terms of legal rights. But many did want to be able to participate in decisions, they wanted fair and caring arrangements and relationships, they wanted respect and dignity too. ...
>
> [W]e suggest that [separate representation for children] is too narrow an approach to achieve the rounded complexity of the enlarged notion of citizenship-in-context that the children we interviewed were implicitly articulating. Very often what the children wanted was flexibility in contact arrangements, a degree of autonomy and control in their lives, ways of resolving differences without extinguishing love and affection, ways of maintaining relationships without losing their sense of selfhood. ... These important ingredients do not add up to legal rights, yet for many children they were the essence of good family life.

You may need to consider these issues in relation to legal principles and proposed reforms—what is the role for law in relation to family breakdown?

SELECTED REFERENCES

Brenda Cossman and Roxanne Mykitiuk, "Reforming Child Custody and Access Law in Canada: A Discussion Paper" (1998), 15 *Canadian Journal of Family Law* 13.

R. Freeman, "Divorce and Children: A Transition Experience" (1995), 19 *Transition* 8.

Renée Joyal and Anne Quéniart, "Enhancing the Child's Point of View in Custody and Access Cases in Quebec: Preliminary Results of a Study Conducted in Québec" (2002), 19 *Canadian Journal of Family Law* 173.

Michael E. Lamb, Kathleen J. Sternberg, and Ross A. Thompson, "The Effects of Divorce on Children's Behavior, Development and Adjustment," in Michael E. Lamb, ed., *Parenting and Child Development in "Nontraditional" Families* (Mahwah, NJ: Lawrence Erlbaum Associates, 1999), 125.

Hon. Claire L'Heureux-Dubé, "A Response to Remarks by Dr. Judith Wallerstein on the Long-Term Impact of Divorce on Children" (1998), 36:3 *Family and Conciliation Courts Review* 384.

Judge A.P. Nasmith, "The Inchoate Voice" (1992), 8 *Canadian Family Law Quarterly* 43.

Sally E. Palmer, "Custody and Access Decisions: Minimizing the Damage to Families" (1980), 12 RFL (2d) 232.

Caroline Sawyer, "Conflicting Rights for Children: Implementing Welfare, Autonomy and Justice Within Family Proceedings" (1999), 21:2 *Journal of Social Welfare and Family Law* 99.

C. The Legal Context: Current Principles and Reform Proposals

Section 16 of the *Divorce Act, 1985* sets out principles for determining applications for custody and access. The basic principle is "the best interests of the child," determined by reference to the condition, means, needs, and other circumstances of the child: s. 16(8). The statute contains few additional provisions for guidance, except that s. 16(9) makes conduct irrelevant unless it affects the ability of a person to act as a parent; and s. 16(10) requires courts to give effect to the principle that a child should have as much contact with each spouse as is consistent with the best interests principle and thus "take into consideration the willingness of each person for whom custody is sought to facilitate such contact" (the friendly-parent obligation). These principles apply to custody and access decisions for which a party has filed an application for divorce.

Similarly, s. 15.1 of the *Divorce Act, 1985* authorizes a court to make an order for payment of child support and requires the court to do so in accordance with applicable guidelines: s. 15.1(3). In specified circumstances, a court may depart from the guidelines, but must provide written reasons for any such decision: see ss. 15.1(5) and (6). The child-support guidelines are set out in regulations: see SOR/97-175, as amended.

These provisions of the federal divorce legislation do not apply to married spouses who have not filed for divorce, nor to cohabiting couples who separate. Provincial legislation that applies in these cases varies to some extent in its language regarding custody and access, but there is substantial uniformity in the child-support guidelines that were adopted after extensive federal, provincial, and territorial negotiations. As discussed in earlier chapters, however, some issues concerning the constitutional division of powers may arise in relation to custody, access, and child support: see Peter W. Hogg, *Constitutional Law of Canada* (Toronto: Carswell) (looseleaf), 26:5-7.

Currently, it is possible to seek orders for custody (including sole custody and joint custody) and for access. Although the content of these orders may depend, at least to some extent, on statutory language, it is important at the outset to grasp the features of these concepts in general terms. Moreover, it is especially important to distinguish between legal authority and physical care with respect to children. For example, where one parent is granted custody of a child, it means that the custodial parent has legal authority to make decisions concerning the child with respect to health, education, and religious faith; a parent who is granted access has the right to spend time with the child, usually in accordance with the terms of the access order or agreement.

However, even where one parent is awarded custody, while the other is awarded access, it is possible for both parents to share equal amounts of time in providing care for children—that is, joint physical custody. By contrast with this arrangement, an award of joint custody means that both former spouses have legal authority to make decisions for children. As a result, it is usually important to determine whether parties who seek joint custody are interested in exercising joint legal authority or in providing joint physical care for children: for an overview, see Sheila Holmes, "Imposed Joint Legal Custody: Children's Interests or Parental Rights?" (1987), 45 *University of Toronto Faculty of Law Review* 300.

Although these legal categories of custody and access remain current law in Canada, a succession of federal reform proposals in the past decade have recommended alternative legal arrangements. Indeed, Bill C-22, introduced into Parliament in December 2002, proposed that custody and access orders be abolished. Instead, it was proposed that the separation or divorce of parents would create no change at all with respect to their joint legal authority for their children; parents would be required to file a parenting plan as part of an application for divorce, detailing their agreed-upon arrangements for their children. Similar proposals have already been implemented in other jurisdictions, including the United Kingdom and Australia, although not with complete success. Since Bill C-22 was not enacted before the federal election in 2004, its provisions are examined in more detail in the discussion of reform issues later in this chapter. At the same time, as you examine the cases in this section, it is important to keep in mind these proposals to reform arrangements for children at divorce and separation.

SELECTED REFERENCES

Nicholas Bala, "A Report from Canada's 'Gender War Zone': Reforming the Child-Related Provisions of the Divorce Act" (1999), 16 *Canadian Journal of Family Law* 163.

Dawn M. Bourque, " 'Reconstructing' the Patriarchal Nuclear Family: Recent Developments in Child Custody and Access in Canada" (1995), 10:1 *Canadian Journal of Law and Society* 1.

Susan B. Boyd, "W(h)ither Feminism? The Department of Justice Public Discussion Paper on Custody and Access" (1995), 12:2 *Canadian Journal of Family Law* 331.

Ross A. Thompson and Paul R. Amato, eds., *The Postdivorce Family: Children, Parenting and Society* (Thousand Oaks, CA: Sage Publications, 1999).

II. POST-DIVORCE PARENTING: RIGHTS AND RELATIONSHIPS FOR PARENTS AND CHILDREN

[All the countries whose law we have examined] are engaged in trying to work out an understanding of sexual equality that takes account of women's roles in procreation and child raising without perpetuating their subordination. ... [T]he principal unresolved problems for family law and policy remain those relating to the situation of women who are raising children, performing the bulk of other homemaking and caretaking roles, and working [in the paid labour force].

> Mary Ann Glendon, *The Transformation of Family Law:*
> *State, Law, and Family in the United States and Western Europe*
> (Chicago and London: University of Chicago Press, 1989), 307

A. Decision Making About Custody and Access: An Example

This section focuses on the principle of best interests in decision making about custody and access of children post-separation or divorce. In this context, recall that the vast majority of such cases are negotiated and settled, rather than litigated before the courts, so that a divorce decree and corollary relief are often granted on consent. As a result, it may be difficult to assess precisely how the best-interests principle is implemented in practice. However, when cases are litigated, courts must assess evidence to determine what arrangement is in a child's best interests. In doing so, the best-interests principle often becomes intertwined with, for example, issues about whether it is more appropriate to order sole custody to one parent with access for the other, to order joint legal custody, or to specify precise periods of access. Perhaps, to a lesser extent, the best-interests principle may be influenced by issues about child support—that is, even though principles concerning custody and access are legally distinct from those affecting child-support obligations, concerns about continuing financial support may often appear linked to decisions about access.

In reflecting on these issues, consider the following case, a lower court decision that illustrates some of the evidentiary and other challenges in such disputes. To what extent can you identify the factors relevant to the child's best interests in this case? Are they the same factors that resulted in the rejection of the father's application for joint custody? Is this a case in which the parties should have been compelled, pursuant to the reform proposals in Bill C-22, to negotiate a parenting plan? Why, or why not?

Carton v. Watts
(1998), 42 RFL (4th) 149 (Alta. Prov. Ct.)

JORDAN PROV. J: This is an application by Byron Carton for custody of his son, Teague Carton. Debbie Watts, Teague's mother, opposes the application. Mr. Carton is one of Teague's legal guardians, Miss Watts having consented to a guardianship order being granted by this Court.

Mr. Carton has applied for sole custody of the child and has offered liberal and generous access to Miss Watts. If he cannot have sole custody, he asks for a joint custody order providing that he is to have day to day care and control of the child, again with liberal and generous access to Miss Watts.

Mr. Carton believes that Miss Watts has a drinking problem and that because she has had difficulties raising a son from a previous relationship, it would be in Teague's best interests for his father to have sole custody, or failing that, day to day care and control of the child in a joint custody regime.

Mr. Carton expressed his concern about Miss Watts' drinking problem on his first day in court on this matter on March 29, 1996. He reiterated that concern during his testimony in the trial of this action in the spring of this year. He offered as proof of his allegations descriptions of a few incidents concerning alcohol use and one incident of alleged illicit drug use. He described Miss Watts "instability" by referring to her inability to raise her son by a previous relationship. He testified that this young man, Frankie, has been in the care of the Director of Child Welfare for several years. He went on to describe how difficult Frankie had been even when Mr. Carton and Miss Watts took him into their home in an ill-fated attempt to turn him around.

Following Mr. Carton's evidence about Frankie, I required Frankie's Child Welfare worker to attend to give evidence the next day. Her name was Patricia Dennis. Miss Dennis did not paint a glowing picture of this young man, but she certainly did not lay blame at Miss Watts' feet. Frankie is a difficult adolescent. He endured his parents' difficulties, he spent an extremely tumultuous 4½ years with his father but was required by this father to leave. He lived for a time with Mr. Carton and Miss Watts but this too was unsuccessful.

At the time she testified, Miss Dennis planned to transition Frankie to Supported Independent Living (a program offered by Alberta Family and Social Services wherein teenagers between the ages of sixteen and eighteen live independently of group homes or foster settings, but with the continued involvement of their social workers. The children must attend to their own room and board or rent, food, clothing and recreation.

They are given a monthly allowance to pay for these things. It is not an overly generous stipend and many young people in the programme have difficulty making ends meet. In part this is because they do not have adequate budgeting skills, or are impulsive in their spending habits. It is also because the amount of money they receive is not sufficient to allow them to have an adequate standard of living in a city such as Calgary where accommodation is at a premium and consequently very expensive.)

Miss Dennis testified that Frankie would have a difficult time adjusting to the financial constraints of the program and that there are difficulties in finding a placement for him. He has an unhealthy need for the finer things of life. Miss Dennis was not describing a young man who merely needed Hilfiger shirts and Docker pants to fit in with the crowd. Instead she described him as an adolescent whose precarious identity was tied to his ability to present himself in such expensive attire. He is a young man with significant problems.

In addition to his own evidence Mr. Carton called three witnesses. Their evidence provides no substantial assistance to the court.

When Miss Watts testified she described her relationship with Teague and her young daughter (Teague's nine year old half sister), her relationship with Mr. Carton, Teague's relationship with his father, and her problems with Frankie. She described the incident at a family get together which deteriorated into a physical altercation.

Miss Watts was nervous but thoughtful and deliberate as she gave her evidence. She perceives Mr. Carton to be a very controlling individual and she believes that he has emotionally abused her. Emotional abuse can, of course, only be measured by a subjective analysis. I am satisfied that Miss Watts was telling me the truth about the abuse she believes she has been subjected to. The subjective test is met. Mr. Carton's demeanour in court is corroborative of her description of him as domineering and controlling. When Miss Watts tells me that he controlled her particularly in financial matters and that he called her names, I believe her and find that he continued until recently to try to control her financially. This is apparent from his begging off from child care responsibilities so that he could do such things as go golfing. He required her to pay for the baby sitting on these not infrequent occasions—something she could not afford to do and for which she could not even plan.

Miss Watts testified that it is Mr. Carton's controlling nature which compels her to ask for sole custody. She believes that she must have the sole right to make the major decisions for Teague because nothing else would be tolerable for her. She is convinced that if Mr. Carton has sole custody of Teague he will use this to continue to control her in the same fashion that he has in the past. She is equally clear that a joint custody order cannot work for the same reason. She is eager, however, for Teague to maintain his relationship with his father.

Miss Watts also testified about her use of magic mushrooms, a substance then prohibited under the *Narcotic Control Act*. I am satisfied that she did not know exactly what it was that she was taking, but that she knew that she was doing something improper, if not illegal. I am further satisfied that the use of this illicit drug was the only thing that Miss Watts was not frank about. She was embarrassed and obviously worried about the impact of this information in this proceeding. I am not overly alarmed by either her evidence to the court or her one time use of an illicit substance. As for the unfortunate altercation at the family gathering, I note that no one was hurt and I am satisfied that it was an isolated incident of the sort which happens from time to time when there are large family gatherings and alcohol is consumed.

Lastly, Miss Watts feels that Mr. Carton should not have sole custody or day to day care and control of the child because he is too emotionally rigid in his parenting style, and he is somewhat laissez-faire in the amount of attention he devotes to Teague while the child is in his care.

Mr. Carton's counsel asked me to draw an inference from Miss Watts' slow and deliberate demeanour that she was taking her time so as to be able to formulate deceptive answers, if not outright falsehoods. I totally reject that suggestion. While there was no expert evidence before me to explain the type of demeanour and behaviour one could expect to observe in a person who has been subjected to controlling behaviour from a partner, I do not believe such evidence is necessary to enable me to draw the conclusion that she is such a woman. Expert evidence is only admissible in a jury trial if it is necessary to explain something outside the range of the ordinary man's experience. The behaviour I am commenting on is well within the experience and observation of most adults in our society. Miss Watts' demeanour on the witness stand was that of a person who found the experience very difficult to cope with. She was facing a man who having controlled her for years, was now seeking to control her in an even more dramatic fashion—he was asking the court for sole custody of their child. There was nothing devious or deceptive about her evidence save for the one matter I have already commented on.

As for Mr. Carton, it is very clear to me that his is a very one-sided description of what went on in this relationship. I find Mr. Carton to be a very controlling individual and find that his evidence is as coloured as one might expect from such an individual. I do not accuse him of lying.

Conclusions

It seemed self-evident at first that I could not deny Mr. Carton's application for custody. How can it be in a child's best interests to stay in the care of a parent who has demonstrated her inability to successfully raise a child? By the end of the evidence I had been reminded of how wrong first impressions can be. Miss Dennis did not testify or even attempt to convince me that Miss Watts was an inappropriate parent. She was not able to substantiate Frankie's complaints that his mother drank too much.

I was satisfied at the end of her evidence that many of Frankie's problems were well beyond her control and certainly not caused by her. I am satisfied that Miss Watts' failures with Frankie do not disentitle her to the opportunity to raise her second son. She is a warm and loving parent. No one has offered any criticism of her parenting of her daughter, now age nine. She is undoubtedly high-strung, and may even on occasion drink too much. But I do not find that her lifestyle interferes with her ability to raise Teague.

Yet, we are not dealing with the question of Miss Watts' "fitness" as a parent. The question in a custody case in 1998 is, what is in the child's best interests? I find that it would not be in Teague's best interest to grant sole or even joint custody to Mr. Carton. He would be subjected to a life with a very controlling, rigid individual. I am satisfied that he would observe his father continue and to some extent succeed in controlling Miss Watts. It is not in a child's best interests [to] be raised in such an environment when there is a suitable alternative available.

I am further satisfied that it is [in] Teague's best interest that his mother have sole custody because I am convinced it is Miss Watts who will ensure and facilitate access. I have no such confidence about Mr. Carton's ability to do the same without attaching strings which will perpetuate the emotional abuse she has endured.

Mr. Carton's application for sole custody is denied as is his application for joint custody.

Miss Watts shall have sole custody of the child. Access is to be spoken to at a later date.

Application dismissed.

Discussion Notes

Best-Interests Decision Making

What factors were relied on to determine custody in *Carton v. Watts*? What kinds of evidence were relied on by the court? To what extent did the court focus on the concrete needs and interests of Teague, the child at the centre of this dispute? Why was it necessary to focus on another child, Frankie, who was not involved in this dispute? What was the relationship between Teague's best interests and the issue of sole or joint custody? To what extent does this judgment reflect discretionary or individualized justice?

Consider the analysis presented by the American Law Institute (ALI), which suggested that there were a number of unavoidable tensions in the law's objectives for the allocation of responsibility for children at family breakdown, including a tension between predictability and individualized decision making:

> The predictability of outcomes helps to reduce litigation, as well as strategic and manipulative behaviour by parents. Predictable outcomes are insufficient, however, unless they are also sound. And it is difficult to imagine sound outcomes in custody cases unless the diverse range of circumstances in which family breakdown occurs are taken into account. In short, predictability is important, but so is the customization of a result to the individual, sometimes unique, facts of a case.

(See American Law Institute, *Principles of the Law of Family Dissolution: Analysis and Recommendations* (Washington, DC: Matthew Bender, 2002), 1.)

The ALI identified other tensions in custody law and recommended (at 2) principles designed to improve planning for children's needs on family breakdown, including parental responsibility for creating a parenting plan—"an individualized and customized set of custodial and decision-making arrangements for a child." Consider this recommendation in the context of *Carton v. Watts*—would it have been preferable for these parents to negotiate a parenting plan? Why, or why not?

Lower Court Decisions and Appellate Review

Carton v. Watts is an example of a trial court decision concerning custody. In *Haider v. Malach* (1999), 48 RFL (4th) 314 (Sask. CA), the appellate court engaged in an extensive analysis of evidence considered by the trial court in a custody and access dispute. As the appeal court noted, however, there is a well-established reluctance on the part of appellate courts to intervene in decisions concerning custody and access—in general, the appeal court will not alter a decision of a lower court in such cases in the absence of an error in principle or a clear factual error in a matter of significance. What is the rationale for such restraint on the part of appellate courts in relation to decisions about the custody of children? You may wish to reconsider this question after reviewing the cases illustrating the best-interests principle in practice. See also Rachel Birnbaum, Elizabeth L. McCarty, and Willson A. McTavish, "Haider v. Malach: Child Custody Guidelines Gone Awry?" (2000-1), 18 *Canadian Family Law Quarterly* 357.

B. Defining the Best-Interests Principle

Clearly, there is an inherent indeterminacy and elasticity to the "best interests" test which makes it more useful as legal aspiration than as legal analysis. It can be no more than an informed opinion made at a moment in the life of a child about what seems likely to prove to be in that child's best interests. Deciding what is in a child's best interests means deciding what, objectively, appears most likely in the circumstances to be conducive to the kind of environment in which a particular child has the best opportunity for receiving the needed care and attention. Because there are stages to childhood, what is in a child's best interests may vary from child to child, from year to year, and possibly from month to month. This unavoidable fluidity makes it important to attempt to minimize the prospects for stress and instability.

Abella JA, in *MacGyver v. Richards*

(1995), 11 RFL (4th) 432, at 443 (Ont. CA)

Nicholas Bala, "The Best Interests of the Child in the Post-Modern Era: A Central but Paradoxical Concept"
in Harold Niman and Gerald P. Sadvari, eds., *Special Lectures of the Law Society of Upper Canada 2000—Family Law: "Best Interests of the Child"* (Toronto: Law Society of Upper Canada, 2001), 1, at 1-5

There are few legal doctrines that have come to so completely dominate an area of law as the rule that governs disputes related to children—the best interests of the child principle. Leading Canadian precedents, federal and provincial statutes and international treaties are all premised on the principle that decisions about children should be based on an assessment of their best interests. This is a central concept for those who are involved in making decisions about children, not only for judges and lawyers, but also for assessors and mediators. Even politicians and parents frequently cite the best interests of the child as the touchstone that guides their actions and decisions.

Interestingly when children themselves make claims, either in the courts or social contexts, they are much less likely to use a best interests approach, which from a child's perspective is paternalistic. Rather, children tend to make claims based on their own rights. Sometimes children argue that it is in their own best interests to be able to exercise their rights, or at least to be able to express their views about decisions that affect them.

The popularity of the best interests principle is scarcely surprising. This principle now has great intuitive appeal, though this was not always the case, and in some other countries the best interests principle plays a much smaller role than in Canada. Although the best interests of the child principle has become the dominant principle for dealing with most child related disputes, it is also important to be aware of its limitations. The best interests principle has a paradoxical nature. While focusing *substantive* decision-making on the best interests of the particular child, it encourages a decision-making *process* that is often harmful to children.

In some of the discussions about the determination of a child's best interests, there are suggestions that this can be an objective and almost scientific inquiry. While the knowledge of child psychologists and other mental health professions can have an important role in best interests decisions, it is also clear that the values, biases, beliefs and experiences of the person making a best interests decision will inevitably affect the decision.

Some academic critics argue that the best interests principle is so vague as to be meaningless, charging: "This standard provides no clues as to how it is to be satisfied. Judges could just as easily have no standard at all." Judges themselves may be less critical, but Justice Southin of the British Columbia Court of Appeal [in *Rockwell v. Rockwell* (1998), 43 RFL (4th) 450, at 460] acknowledged that when making best interests determination "judges are tied by the invisible threads of their own convictions." The noted American legal scholar, Robert Mnookin, observed:

> Deciding what is best for a child poses a question no less ultimate than the purposes and values of life itself. Should the judge be primarily concerned with the child's happiness? Or with the child's spiritual and religious training? Should the judge be concerned with the economic "productivity" of the child when he grows up? Are the primary values in life in warm interpersonal relationships, or in discipline and self-sacrifice? Is stability and security for a child more desirable than intellectual stimulation? These questions could be elaborated endlessly. And yet where is the judge to look for the set of values that should inform the degree of what is best for the child? Normally the custody statutes do not themselves give content or relative weights to the pertinent values. And if the judge looks to society at large he finds neither a clear consensus as to the best child rearing strategies nor an appropriate hierarchy of ultimate values.

[See Robert Mnookin, "Child Custody Adjudication: Judicial Functions in the Face of Indeterminacy" (1975), 39 *Law & Contemporary Problems* 226, at 260-61.]

The recognition that the values and attitudes of decision-makers play a crucial role in determining outcomes has almost become trite in the postmodern world, whether the decisions are made (or influenced) by judges, lawyers, assessors, mediators, parents, politicians or academics. From an increasingly broad range of critical perspectives come charges that judges making best interests decisions are biased. The best interests principle is a virtual Rorschach inkblot test for critics.

Feminists were among the first critics, arguing that the best interests principle allows judges to hide their biases against women who fail to adopt traditional roles and that the use of the best interests test often masks decisions that are harmful to women. More recently fathers groups have been challenging the family law system for its alleged bias against men, claiming that the Canadian judiciary applies the best interests test in a way that discriminates against fathers. It has also been argued that Canadian judges may sometimes give too little or too much weight to issues of race when making best interests decisions. Gays and lesbians have claimed that best interests decisions have reflected a bias against homosexuals, while more recently some "pro-family" scholars have argued that best interests decisions have failed to give sufficient recognition to the importance of heterosexual marriage.

Beyond concerns about bias are charges that the best interests approach promotes litigation and is therefore harmful to children. The best interests principle requires decision-makers to focus on the individual needs and circumstances of the particular child. This type of factually specific decision-making makes it difficult to predict the outcome of cases, and thus encourages litigation rather than settlement. Almost anything might be relevant to [a] child's best interests, so cases can be complex and costly to litigate. Because the test is vague, the outcome of litigation may seem unpredictable, which may encourage exploitative threats by one parent to litigate about children if the other parent does not offer a favourable settlement on other (usually monetary) claims.

While the best interests test is the dominant test in judicial decision-making, it is clear that individuals and agencies who care for children are not motivated solely by the promotion of a child's best interests when making decisions about them. Resource and institutional constraints play a significant role when state agencies are involved in making decisions about children. In intact families, parents frequently make decisions that take account of their own welfare as adults, as well as the welfare of their children.

Although the welfare of children is sometimes increased if their parents separate, the decision to separate is usually made in the interests of one or both adults, and in some cases the children's best interests might be better served if the parents [did] not separate. However, often it is only after separation that parents start to think about the best interests of their children. A tragic irony is that in cases of high-conflict parental separation, the process of litigation and determination of the child's best interests is itself harmful to the child, despite the claim of each parent to be seeking to promote the child's best interests.

Discussion Notes

The Convention on the Rights of the Child

The United Nations General Assembly approved the Convention on the Rights of the Child in 1989, and it has been ratified by a large number of countries, including Canada (in 1991); significantly, however, the United States has not yet ratified the Convention. The Convention creates obligations for states parties to respect and ensure defined rights for children. Article 3 provides that the best interests of the child "shall be *a* primary consideration in all actions concerning children." Although the Convention is not part of Canada's domestic law, courts may use its provisions to interpret domestic laws.

In assessing the scope of the Convention, Martha Bailey and Nicholas Bala suggested that the best-interests principle of the Convention reflects the same indeterminacy as the principle in domestic law:

> As well as affecting Canada's domestic laws, ratification means that Canada is now under an ongoing obligation to report to the UN Committee on the Rights of the Child on its compliance with the Convention. ...
>
> Assessing compliance with the Convention is not a simple matter, because the document does not reflect a unified philosophy of children's rights, and the rights and obligations contained in it are not clearly defined. One of the most important provisions of the Convention is in article 3(1), an "umbrella" provision, which states that "[i]n all actions concerning children, whether undertaken by public or private social welfare institutions, courts of law, administrative authorities or legislative bodies, the best interest of the child shall be a primary consideration." The best interests of the child principle in article 3(1) can be used as an aid to construction in implementing Convention rights and also as the standard to apply in areas that are not covered by express rights. Other articles that require consideration of the best interests of the child are article 9 (separation from parents), article 21 (adoption) (note that Canada has deposited a reservation to allow for customary adoptions among aboriginal peoples), article 37(c) (separation from adults in detention) (note that Canada has deposited a reservation on this article), and article 40(2)(b)(iii) (presence of parents at court hearing of penal matters involving a juvenile). The degree to which the best interests of the child must be considered varies. The "umbrella" provision, article 3(1) requires that the best interests of the child be *a* primary consideration, so other factors may be considered and may be determinative in some circumstances, whereas under article 9 the best interests principle must govern the result—it provides that a child *shall not* be separated from his or her parents *unless it is necessary for the best interests of the child.*
>
> There is difficulty in interpreting and applying the best interests principle because of its indeterminacy. The best interests principle (and the Convention in general) is linked to the cultural context in which it is invoked, and therefore a report on compliance can do no more than express an opinion on whether the law and practices of the state accord with Convention principles as interpreted through the lens of local values and understandings. Even within communities there will be disagreements as to Convention principles. It is important to emphasize that generally the Convention does not offer particular solutions to problems, only vaguely worded principles that should guide resolution of problems. These principles are subject to widely varying interpretations, and compliance assessments will be likewise debatable.

See Martha Bailey and Nicholas Bala, "Assessing Compliance with the UN Convention on the Rights of the Child" (Ottawa: June 4, 1988) (unpublished presentation to Canadian Association of Law Teachers [CALT] Family Section). See also Martha Bailey, "Does Ontario and Federal Legislation Comply with the UN Convention on the Rights of the Child?" in *Canada's Children* (Ottawa: Child Welfare League of Canada, Summer 1999), 15.

Recall the discussion in chapter 1 concerning the decision of the Supreme Court of Canada in *Baker v. Minister of Citizenship and Immigration* (1999), 174 DLR (4th) 193, where some members of the court concluded that the principles of the Convention might be used as interpretive guides in litigation pursuant to domestic legislation. In considering the materials that follow, try to assess how, if at all, the Convention principles may be helpful in custody and access claims.

Structuring Best Interests

The ALI's recommendations concerning custody arrangements after family breakdown were consciously designed to clarify and refine the best-interests principle, rather than to eliminate it. That is, in spite of its indeterminacy, the ALI concluded that it was preferable to retain the best-interests principle. At the same time, the ALI attempted to concretize the content of the best-interests test; specifically, it recommended (at 95-96) that "best interests" be defined as follows:

Best Interests of the Child Defined

1) The primary objective ... is to serve the child's best interests, by facilitating all of the following:

a) parental planning and agreement about the child's custodial arrangements and upbringing;

b) continuity of existing parent–child attachments;

c) meaningful contact between the child and each parent;

d) caretaking relationships by adults who love the child, know how to provide for the child's needs, and place a high priority on doing so;

e) security from exposure to conflict and violence;

f) expeditious, predictable decision making and the avoidance of prolonged uncertainty respecting arrangements for the child's care and control.

2) A secondary objective ... is to achieve fairness between the parents.

To what extent do you find this structuring of the best-interests principle helpful in identifying priorities for decision making about child custody? Is the ALI formulation consistent with the Convention (which has not been signed by the United States)? You may want to reconsider the ALI's recommendations after examining the interpretation of the best-interests test in Canadian cases, as well as the federal reform proposals, later in this chapter. See also Stephen Parker, "The Best Interests of the Child—Principles and Problems" (1994), 8 *International Journal of Law and the Family* 26.

C. Applying the Best-Interests Principle

As noted above, Canadian statutes generally provide for the use of the best-interests principle in decision making about both custody and access. In assessing how the principle works in practice, this section examines some of the cases and critiques in a variety of different contexts. In considering this material, try to identify the factors considered in different contexts and the ways in which priority was assigned to them to achieve a child's best interests.

1. Tender Years and Working Mothers

As explained in the historical overview at the beginning of this chapter, the common law's traditional recognition of fathers' rights to the custody and control of their legitimate children was somewhat modified with the enactment of *Lord Talfourd's Act* in 1839 and recognition of mothers' entitlement to physical custody of children of "tender years" (under age seven). As Boyd's work indicated above, however, there were always significant limitations in relation to this doctrine: see Boyd, at 63-72. In addition, its preference that mothers should provide care for young children (in their best interests) implicitly reflected gendered expectations about the primary responsibilities of mothers for caregiving. Thus, when increasing numbers of mothers began to enter the paid workforce in the 1960s and '70s, "abandonment" of their children sometimes affected the best-interests principle at separation or divorce. This section briefly examines the current status of the tender-years doctrine and some of the cases about working mothers.

a. Tender Years: Talsky v. Talsky

In 1976, the Supreme Court of Canada considered the tender-years doctrine in the case of *Talsky v. Talsky* (1976), 21 RFL 27. De Grandpre J (Laskin CJC and Judson J concurring) held (at 39-41):

> There are several additional matters which are most relevant in considering the welfare of the children. Firstly, there is a well-established tendency that the custody of children of a tender age should be given to the mother. Sometimes that tendency has been put in most graphic terms. In *Bell v. Bell*, [1955] OWN 341 (CA), Roach JA, giving judgment for the Court, said at p. 344:
>
>> There is another circumstance which in my very respectful opinion the learned judge has overlooked, or if it was present to his mind he has not given due weight to it, namely that this infant is a little girl of very tender years. No father, no matter how well-intentioned or how solicitous for the welfare of such a child, can take the full place of the mother. Instinctively, a little child, particularly a little girl, turns to her mother in her troubles, her doubts and her fears. In that respect nature seems to assert itself. The feminine touch means so much to a little girl; the frills and the flounces and the ribbons in the matter of dress; the whispered consultations and confidences on matters which to the child's mind should only be discussed with Mother; the tender care, the soothing voice; all these things have a tremendous effect on the

emotions of the child. This is nothing new; it is as old as human nature and has been recognized time after time in the decisions of our Courts.

Jessup JA, in the Court of Appeal, quoted the learned trial Judge as follows [at 229]:

In order for a Court to deprive a mother of children of tender age, the case must be very strong: *Weeks v. Weeks*, 14 WWR 529, [1955] 3 DLR 704 (BCCA); *Bell v. Bell* [supra]; *Re Doucette* (1970), 3 RFL 115, 3 NSR (2d) 578. Rather than this being so, I believe the evidence is very strong that Mrs. Talsky is in all respects an excellent mother,

and continued [at 229]:

In my view, the rule that children of tender years belong with their mother is a rule of human sense rather than a rule of law as it is erroneously treated by the learned trial Judge: cf., *Re Pittman*, 5 RFL 376, [1972] 1 OR 347, 23 DLR (3d) 131. It is only one factor to be considered with all the circumstances.

I am of the opinion that that criticism is not deserved. The learned trial Judge did not regard the view that children of tender years should be given to the custody of their mother as any rule of law. As Roach JA put it, it is as old as human nature, and, as learned counsel for the appellant put it in this Court, it is a principle of common sense. It is simply one of the more important factors which must be considered in the granting of custody. In the view of the learned trial Judge in the present appeal, it was such a strong factor as to be well nigh conclusive. In the view of the Court of Appeal, it was outweighed by the other matters to which I have referred. Under all the circumstances in the present case and particularly in view of what I have already outlined as the careful plans of the husband for the care and upbringing of the children in his immediate presence, I am of the opinion that the learned trial Judge gave too great a weight to that factor.

In the context of these reasons, how would you describe the current status of the tender-years doctrine? According to Boyd, judicial comments about Mrs. Talsky's conduct in leaving the marriage very nearly undermined her custody claim—although she succeeded in gaining custody, the judgments also revealed a deeply divided court: see Boyd at 86-89.

b. Working Mothers and Children's Best Interests

In a number of cases after *Talsky*, the issue of the continuing application of the tender-years doctrine was considered, particularly in the context of custody claims on the part of mothers who were involved in the paid workforce. Consider the reasoning in the two examples that follow—to what extent do they reflect continuing assumptions about gendered responsibilities for child care?

i. R. v. R.

In *R. v. R.* (1983), 34 RFL (2d) 277, the Alberta Court of Appeal dismissed a mother's appeal from a decision granting custody of a daughter, aged four-and-a-half, to the father, notwithstanding that the mother had had interim custody and that the judge at trial had found her to be a fit parent. The husband was a rancher, working a property with his father; the parties had a homestead near the husband's parents. When the marriage broke down, the wife moved with the daughter to Lethbridge, 50 miles away, and closer to the mother's family. She worked in Lethbridge. At the trial, both parents were held to be fit parents, but the father had plans to remarry while the wife did not. The judge found that the husband was preferable as the custodial parent because he could have the child with him during the day, while he did the farm chores, while the wife would have to put the child in care during her hours of work. The father's mother was also readily available for babysitting. The mother was given liberal access on weekends. On appeal, the court considered whether there were any "errors of law," and reviewed the tender-years doctrine.

In rejecting the appeal, the majority concluded (at 286) that the view expressed by Roach JA in *Bell* no longer applied:

> This view confuses cultural traditions with human nature; it also traps women in a social role not necessarily of their choosing, while at the same time freeing men: if only a mother can nurture a child of tender years, then it is the clear duty of the mother to do so: because the father *cannot* do it, he is neither obliged nor entitled even to try. Also, it is seen by some as self-perpetuating: by putting the female child in the custody of somebody who accepts the maternal role model so described, the rule ordains that she will have just such a role model at close hand during her most impressionable years. Thus, the "tender years prin-ciple," which at first glance seems only innocently sentimental, is seen by many as part of a subtle, systemic sexual subordination.
>
> In my view, it is no part of the law of Canada that a judge is bound to say that human nature dictates that only females can perform that parental role labelled as "maternal." I do not agree with Roach JA; I do not agree with the appellant mother.
>
> Judicial comments about the "tender years" issue must be considered in an historical context. The fact is that there have been substantial changes over the past century in the attitude in our society about the ideal family situation. Once, it was accepted that the husband and father was the decision-maker for the family, even about child-rearing questions and even after a marriage breakdown. ... In its origins, the "tender years" concept was a way to undermine the traditional model and recognize a new model. The new, "modern" marriage model involved not only the idea of the nuclear family, but also of the marital partnership, where all major decision-making is shared. The partnership model has only just recently been accepted fully into the law by the enactment of the *Matrimonial Property Act*, RSA 1980, c. M-9 and similar statutes. The modern marriage model does not concede any special status to the father and therefore requires a new standard to decide custody cases. The courts adopted the "best interests" approach.
>
> Some divergence in the roles of male and female was accepted in this newer model however. The husband could continue to be the bread-winner and the wife could have a special responsibility as a professional homemaker. This was not to say that she alone was to carry the burden of child-rearing. But there were and are, in this model, a measure of acceptably different parental roles based upon gender. To those who prefer this mode, the views of Roach JA are simply inadequate.
>
> To others, however, his views are anathema. In what might be called the supra-modern marriage, strenuous efforts are made to avoid *any* role distinction based upon sex. The many

tasks of homemaking and child-rearing—indeed, child-bearing—are shared as completely as possible, and not on any gender basis. It follows, of course, that both fathers and mothers must, if this model is to work, acquire the skills and make the commitment which is required for effective parenting.

Taken in this context, the remarks made by judges in the past about "tender years principle" do not come to much. All that can be said in this age of changing attitudes is that judges must decide each case on its own merits, with due regard to the capacities *and* attitudes of each parent. We should take care not to assign to this idea or that (all actually of recent origin and unique to our society) the august status of being the only one consistent with human nature or common sense. And we must continue to recognize that the attitude toward child-rearing of the parties to the marriage which the judge is being asked to dissolve could reflect traditional, modern or supra-modern ideals or, more likely, some confused and contradictory spot on the spectrum between these extremes. For example, there is no point giving a father the custody of a child of tender years if that father believes child-rearing to be "women's work." That would not be in the best interests of the child. And we must remember that our role is not to reform society; our role is to make the best of a bad deal for the child who comes before us for help.

The majority concluded that there was no error in the trial judge's conclusion that the child would be better off with the father than in professional daycare (with the mother).

Dissenting from this decision, McGillivray CJA found that the trial judge had given insufficient consideration to the principle that "a girl of tender years is best with her mother," a factor that he asserted should be regarded as one of the most important factors (citing *Talsky*). He also commented that the husband's ability to spend time with the child should not be determinative because "there must be tens of thousands of children doing very well in daycare centres across the country."

ii. Klachefsky v. Brown

In *Klachefsky v. Brown* (1988), 12 RFL (3d) 280, the Manitoba Court of Appeal allowed an appeal by a mother who was denied custody of two children, a girl of eight and a boy of five-and-a-half. At trial, the judge found that the couple had established an excellent arrangement with respect to the children, with each of them spending equal amounts of time with the children; each parent set up a household in Winnipeg in which the children were nurtured. A few years later, after the father had remarried (a woman with whom the children felt very comfortable), the former wife (the children's mother) was required to move to Vancouver for purposes of her work. The trial judge found that both parents were fit, but that "on balance, if this were a contest between Mr. Klachefsky and Ms. Brown, I would choose Ms. Brown." Nonetheless, the judge decided that it was in the best interests of the children to stay with their father during the school term with generous access to their mother during holidays.

According to the appeal court, the trial judge seemed to have given undue weight to the fact that there would be less (or no) need for child care in Winnipeg because the new Mrs. Klachefsky would be available to them 24 hours a day, as well as extended family support. The majority decision (Philp JA dissenting) stated (at 282):

In my opinion, the trial judge committed a palpable error in placing undue emphasis on the fact that the mother in Vancouver will require paid assistance to provide care for her children. The younger child is now enrolled in kindergarten where he spends part of the day. Another portion of the day will be spent in a daycare facility, until he graduates to Grade I in six months' time. Both children will be returning home from school around 3:30 p.m. but the mother does not arrive home from work until around 5:30 p.m. She has made arrangements for a competent person to be at the home from 3:00 o'clock on until the mother's arrival. Daycare and home care arrangements of this kind are a fact of life which many parents and children face, and there was no evidence before the judge that the children would suffer the least harm from being exposed to a few hours when they are neither at school nor with their mother. Whether an alternate caregiver is paid or unpaid cannot be decisive of what is in the best interests of the children.

Further, the judge appears to have overlooked the testimony that, in the future, the mother's parents will probably spend their winter holiday time in Vancouver rather than Florida, and the evidence that there is available to the mother extended family in Vancouver.

The learned judge also, in my opinion, committed error in this case by failing to take into account the relative stability of the parents' way of life. Since the separation, the mother has maintained a stable family unit consisting of herself and her two children with help from her mother and other people with whom she has had good rapport. There is every indication that she could maintain that stable home in Vancouver.

On the other hand, the evidence shows that the home provided by the father, however excellent it has been as found by the learned trial judge, has not been a stable one. ...

The evidence was that he introduced the first woman to his children as a possible stepmother and, when that did not work out, he introduced them to Cathy, the mother of five children. He had a relationship with Cathy for some ten months before discontinuing it. Then he met Elizabeth, his present wife, and he says the children's mother objected to the children becoming attached to Elizabeth, saying in his words:

> She really didn't want to see someone else, referring to the two previous women, previous few years, she didn't want to see someone else pop into the children's lives and then pop out.

The relationship with Elizabeth began in the summer of 1985, but it was not entirely a smooth one. Elizabeth moved into the father's home in December 1985, but she moved out on 1st December 1986, a year later. At that time Elizabeth was uncertain whether the father was firm in his intentions to marry her. She moved out of the household but the relationship between them continued and she became pregnant in early 1987. They had a quarrel in February 1987 just before he left for a vacation with the children to visit his parents in the United States. They reconciled upon his return at the end of the holiday, and they were married in April 1987. At the time of trial Elizabeth was expecting a child in November 1987. They expected the new baby would be treated as a sibling of the two children whose physical custody is in dispute before us.

The judge found that the children are fond of the new Mrs. Klachefsky and he said he was satisfied that, "she has been for the past two years and will continue to be a good caretaker for the children." In making this finding, the learned judge misapprehended the evidence that Mrs. Klachefsky, while she did spend a year in the father's home up to 1st

December 1986, then left the household and ceased to be caretaker for the children for a number of months.

In my opinion, given the judge's conclusions that as between the parents he would prefer Ms. Brown, a preference with which I agree, the judge fell into error in failing to take account [of] the father's record of instability in his home life compared with her stability, and in giving far too much weight to the fact that the mother might have to rely on paid daycare for two hours a day while she looks after the children in Vancouver.

In my opinion, the mother's undoubted right to appeal from the decision appealed from must be given effect to, notwithstanding our concern at interfering with a decision of a trial judge.

Discussion Notes

Tender Years and Ideas About Mothering

In *S.(B.A.) v. S.(M.S.)* (1991), 35 RFL (3d) 400, the Ontario Court of Appeal ordered a new trial. The parties were married in 1986; five months after their child was born in January 1987, the couple separated. In custody proceedings, the expert evidence suggested that the mother was overly protective, but that it did not pose a risk to the child; the Official Guardian's representative recommended custody to the mother. The trial judge, however, interpreted the expert evidence as establishing a risk to the child if she remained in the mother's care and awarded custody to the father. The Court of Appeal concluded that there was an error of magnitude in the trial judge's decision because the judge had concluded that the expert evidence established a danger to the child from the mother. In addition, the Court of Appeal suggested that the trial judge had overlooked the tender-years doctrine and that the mother had cared for the child since the separation quite adequately. The Court concluded that the cumulative effect of these errors was sufficient to have affected the outcome of the case and accordingly ordered a new trial. To what extent does this case reflect continuing problems with the use of the tender-years doctrine? Is there a need for legislative action? How should this issue be resolved? For another example, see *Williams v. Williams* (1989), 24 RFL (3d) 86 (BCCA).

Custody Claims and Working Mothers

Boyd examined the 1994 custody case in British Columbia in which Judy Tyabji, a member of the BC legislature, unsuccessfully sought custody of her three children after she left her husband and became involved with another male politician, Gordon Wilson, then leader of the BC Liberal Party. Although Tyabji had been granted interim custody of the children and two court-appointed experts had recommended that she have primary responsibility for the children because she was the "historical emotional caregiver" for them, the trial judge concluded that her "aggressive, career-oriented lifestyle" made her less attractive than the children's father in terms of custody. The father lived in a more rural setting and worked in a grocery store. Even though Tyabji had frequently made arrangements to stay involved with her children as well as her political activities, the court expressed concern that the children's needs would be sidetracked by her career: see *Tyabji v. Sandana* (1994), 2 RFL (4th) 265 (BCSC).

The decision in this case was controversial. For example, one critique referred to the fact that Prime Minister Trudeau had received custody of his sons while holding high political office, suggesting a different standard for politicians who were fathers, by contrast with those who were mothers: see "Was Pierre Trudeau a Busy Guy?" *Globe and Mail*, March 5, 1994.

SELECTED REFERENCES

Pat Armstrong, *The Double Ghetto: Canadian Women and Their Segregated Work* (Toronto: McClelland & Stewart, 1994).

Susan B. Boyd, "Child Custody and Working Mothers," in Sheilah L. Martin and Kathleen E. Mahoney, eds., *Equality and Judicial Neutrality* (Toronto: Carswell, 1987), 168.

_____, "Looking Beyond Tyabji: Employed Mothers, Lifestyles and Child Custody Law," in Susan B. Boyd, ed., *Challenging the Public/Private Divide: Feminism, Law, and Public Policy* (Toronto: University of Toronto Press, 1997), 253.

Meg Luxton and Harriet Rosenberg, *Through the Kitchen Window: The Politics of Home and Family* (Toronto: Garamond Press, 1986).

Paul Millar, "Explaining Child Custody Determinations in Canada" (1998), 13:2 *Canadian Journal of Law and Society* 209.

2. Conduct, Best Interests, and the Ability To Parent

At one time, the commission of a marital offence such as adultery was sufficient to deny custody to a parent: see *Nicholson v. Nicholson*, [1952] OWN 507 (CA). More recently, there has been a general shift away from the relevance of marital offences in relation to both divorce and custody and access. Recall that s. 16(9) of the *Divorce Act* provides that past conduct of a person is not to be taken into account in relation to custody and access decisions, unless the conduct is relevant to the ability of the person to act as a parent. There are similar provisions in some provincial statutes: for example, see Ontario's *Children's Law Reform Act*, RSO 1990, c. C.12, as amended, s. 24(3).

Consider the reasoning in *Fishback v. Fishback*—to what extent is it possible to distinguish conduct relating to the ability to parent and other kinds of conduct?

Fishback v. Fishback
(1985), 46 RFL (2d) 44 (Ont. Dist. Ct.)

[In *Fishback v. Fishback*, the court considered a custody dispute between a mother and father; as part of the proceedings, there was evidence that the mother was found to have abandoned her marriage because she was "bored" by her husband. She established a new relationship with a man whom the court found to be somewhat unreliable (although perhaps more exciting), while her husband started a new relationship with another woman who impressed the court with her good judgment and fondness for the children. In granting custody to Mr. Fishback, Misener DCJ stated in part (at 48):]

My concern in deciding who should have custody is confined entirely to the best interests of the children. One conclusion I draw from the facts that I have so far related is simply that Mrs. Fishback was quite prepared—and I think that she consciously thought about it—to deprive the children of the benefit of the constant presence of a good father, of at least a good husband, if not a totally satisfactory one, and of a reasonably harmonious family relationship for no other reason than to find more excitement in life. I am not suggesting that she does not now genuinely love Mr. Yeoman; perhaps she does. Perhaps she is totally dedicated to him. The fact remains that she deliberately sought that state of affairs, knowing full well that the children could never derive a benefit anything close to the loss that they would suffer from it. This factor is not of great significance in determining what is in the present and future best interests of the children, but it certainly is a factor that is entitled to some weight in determining custody because it indicates, at least to some degree, the importance that each parent attaches to the best interests of the children in determining their own future conduct. ...

I think that Mr. Fishback's proposal for the care of the children, should he receive custody, is somewhat better than the present arrangements that Mrs. Fishback supplies. Mr. Fishback has become acquainted with Lucinda Tye. She is a married woman, without children, and separated from her husband. Mrs. Tye and Mr. Fishback have been keeping company. There is at least the probability that in due course they will marry, and I hope they do. Mrs. Tye testified. I was most impressed with her. She has become well acquainted with the children. She has for some time helped Mr. Fishback almost continuously in their weekend care. The children like her. Mrs. Tye does not stay overnight. Doubtless, Mr. Fishback would consider that immoral and wrong in the absence of marriage, and I am not able to say that he is wrong in that judgment, or, for that matter, that he is right in that judgment. Regardless, he proposes to have Mrs. Tye look after the children in their home at all times when he is unable to be there because of his employment. Mrs. Tye has undertaken in her testimony to do so, even at the expense of forgoing other employment opportunities. I am satisfied that that arrangement will be put in place immediately.

That is not to say that Mrs. Fishback has not so far fully and properly cared for the children in the last nine months. She has, and I am sure that she has cared for them well. But that care has been built around her relationship with Mr. Yeoman. Mr. Yeoman testified. While I do not wish to be at all unfair, I am obliged to say that neither his past performance nor his demeanour as a witness left me fully confident that his present relationship with Mrs. Fishback will last. They both say that they intend to marry. Needless to say, I hope they do and that it remains a happy one throughout. But I am not as confident of the stability of Mrs. Fishback's life from here on in as I am of the stability of Mr. Fishback's. And I think that Mrs. Tye has more to contribute to the total upbringing of the children in non-economic terms than does Mr. Yeoman.

What factors were relied on in *Fishback* to determine custody? What aspects of Mrs. Fishback's conduct were considered in assessing her ability to parent? What was the relationship between her conduct and the children's best interests? Did the court adhere to the statutory requirement that only conduct relating to parenting ability is relevant: see *Divorce Act, 1985*, s. 16(9)?

Violence in Relation to Conduct and Best Interests

In *Renaud v. Renaud* (1989), 22 RFL (3d) 366, the Ontario District Court held that a spouse's violent conduct was a relevant factor in a custody dispute. According to the court, the husband had been "abusive, uncooperative and meanspirited," and the court held that it was in the best interests of the children to remain with their mother, who had been the primary caregiver. This case marked a departure from earlier cases, which did not generally consider physical abuse between spouses to be relevant to determining ability to parent.

However, it seems that courts may require substantial evidence of violence and its impact. For example, in *Li Santi v. Li Santi* (1990), 24 RFL (3d) 174 (Ont. Prov. Ct. (Fam. Div.)), the wife left the matrimonial home and went with her children (a boy of four and a girl of nine months) to a transition house in London. At the hearing concerning interim custody, there were disputes about the evidence and the extent to which certain exhibits, not in the form of affidavits, were persuasive to justify the wife's allegations. Vogelsang Prov. J stated (at 177):

> The production of these statements in their present form is improper, greatly prejudicial and scandalous. It cannot be salvaged by resort to a plea concerning urgency or the demands of time. I will give them no consideration whatever in deciding this motion.
>
> As to the merits of the motion as it was argued before me, it is enough to say that the matter was hotly contested. Mr. Winninger pressed his position that the fact that the mother was the primary caretaker of the children in the past should determine the issue. He says that I should make an inference, from that fact, that there exists a closer emotional bond between her and the children. With great respect to Mr. Winninger, I am unable to do so. There is nothing in the affidavit material which would satisfy me that either the mother or the father is unable to look after these two children in a perfectly acceptable, loving and caring manner in the short time between now and trial; nor is there any undisputed and cogent evidence of a more substantial bond with either parent.
>
> The family lived together in the former matrimonial home until the sudden departure of the mother with the children. She now lives in a transition state and her future accommodation is not assured. However one may characterize the vicious squabbles between the husband and the wife, there is no doubt that their substance is absolutely disputed by the parties. The wife alleges that she was "abused" and Mr. Winninger asserts that she must not be "forced back" to the matrimonial home. It follows, in his argument, that the children must therefore remain in the shelter to avoid a separation from their mother. He says that her position as their mother has created a status quo which should not now be upset.
>
> This is a question of interim custody. There is no reason why, even with extensive discovery, the trial of this action cannot be heard within 12 or 14 weeks. It is not my place to decide the ultimate issue. That is for the trial judge. The only question before me is where the best interests of these children will be assured between now and the trial.
>
> Mr. Mamo argues that the existing status quo for the children is their residence with the father in their accustomed home. The father says in his affidavit that his religious associates

of the Jehovah's Witness faith have arranged to assist him with child care while he is at work. Although Mr. Winninger thought that arrangement less than desirable, there is not a tittle of evidence that the father, with this available assistance, could not look after the children completely adequately in their usual surroundings. I agree that the mother unilaterally deprived the children of their accustomed home and the life that they had by removing them when she took her dispute with their father into her own hands. There was no evidence before me of any attempt by the mother to reach an agreement about custody with the father, or to bring an application either for exclusive possession of the matrimonial home or for interim custody of the children prior to her abrupt departure.

Mr. Mamo stresses that the actions of the wife were in contravention of the legislated equal custodial rights of a mother and father set out in s. 20(1) of the *Children's Law Reform Act*. I agree that the departure of the wife and the taking of the children, on substantially disputed grounds, was a complete denial of the husband's custodial rights which cannot stand to her credit on this motion. The best interests of the children, were they ever first considered by her, would have militated against such a result. ...

In the result there is no clear and cogent evidence which would justify the mother's removal of the children from their accustomed environment. Their best interests, it seems clear to me, can be safeguarded by their father in the former matrimonial home and an interim order will go granting him their custody. The mother should have generous access to the children. If counsel cannot agree to an appropriate schedule, I may be spoken to. The trial of this action will be expedited and the necessity of a pre-trial waived. Costs are reserved to the trial judge.

Interim custody to father.

The approach in *Li Santi* was reviewed in *Howard v. Howard* (1999), 1 RFL (5th) 375 (Ont. Sup. Ct. J). In *Howard*, the mother left the matrimonial home, taking the children. The court in *Howard* concluded that it was in the children's best interest to return to the matrimonial home (their familiar surroundings), but granted interim custody to the mother. The court also made an order for interim exclusive possession of the matrimonial home to the mother. In relation to *Li Santi*, Aston J stated (at 376):

I agree wholeheartedly that one of the principles that the court must sustain in these matters is to discourage self-help and, rather, encourage parties to put the matter before a judge if they cannot resolve custody and access issues between themselves. The fact that the children have been in London with their mother for a little more than a month is not to be considered a factor in her favour in the decision now to be made. The only "*status quo*" that counts for anything is the "*status quo*" that existed up to [the mother's departure from the matrimonial home].

To what extent do these cases suggest that violent conduct is not relevant to an ability to parent? Or are these cases concerned with the process of disputes, rather than substantive issues? On the basis of these decisions, what legal advice should be given to a woman who claims that her partner is abusing her? Recall the discussion of family violence in chapter 4—how should the family law system respond to issues of violence, especially in relation to custody disputes?

SELECTED REFERENCES

Hilary Astor, "The Weight of Silence: Talking About Violence in Family Mediation," in Margaret Thornton, ed., *Public and Private: Feminist Legal Debates* (Melbourne: Oxford University Press, 1995), 174.

Nicholas Bala, "Spousal Abuse and Children of Divorce: A Differentiated Approach" (1996), 13 *Canadian Journal of Family Law* 215.

Nicholas Bala, Lorne D. Bertrand, Joanne J. Paetsch, Bartha Maria Knoppers, Joseph P. Hornick, Jean-François Noel, Lorraine Boudreau, and Susan W. Miklas, *Spousal Violence in Custody and Access Disputes: Recommendations for Reform* (Ottawa: Status of Women in Canada, 1998).

S. Grace Kerr and Peter G. Jaffe, "Legal and Clinical Issues in Child Custody Disputes Involving Domestic Violence" (1999), 17:1 *Canadian Family Law Quarterly* 1.

Linda C. Neilson, *Spousal Abuse, Children and the Legal System* (Fredericton, NB: Muriel McQueen Fergusson Centre for Family Violence Research, UNB, 2001).

Melanie Rosnes, "The Invisibility of Male Violence in Canadian Child Custody and Access Decision-Making" (1997), 14 *Canadian Journal of Family Law* 31.

Eleanor M. Schnall, "Custody and Access and the Impact of Domestic Violence" (2000), 18 *Canadian Family Law Quarterly* 130.

3. Gay and Lesbian Parents: Best Interests

The extent to which a parent's sexual orientation may affect a claim to custody has been considered in a number of reported decisions. Consider the approach of the judge in *Barkley v. Barkley*, a decision from the 1980s, which follows—what factors were considered relevant to the child's best interests in this and other cases in the 1970s and 1980s? To what extent are these factors no longer relevant, particularly as a result of the changes in family status for gays and lesbians? Is there a need for greater definition of the best-interests test in this context?

Re Barkley and Barkley
(1980), 28 OR (2d) 136; 16 RFL (2d) 7 (Prov. Ct. (Fam. Div.))

[In *Re Barkley and Barkley*, Nasmith Prov. Ct. J reviewed several cases (at 139) in the context of a claim to custody of a daughter by her lesbian mother:]

Three Canadian cases have been cited by counsel and, from my own research, these would seem to be the only Canadian cases reported.

In *Case v. Case* (1974), 18 RFL 132 (Sask. QB), MacPherson J stipulated that homosexuality was *not a bar* to an award of custody and that it was simply a factor to be considered along with others. On the facts as he found them, custody of a 10-year-old daughter and a 4-year-old son [was] granted to the father as against the homosexual mother. The court was influenced by what it saw as unfair and exaggerated charges by the mother as to the father's conduct and I think he was concerned about the fact that the mother slept in the same bed with her homosexual partner and that he had not had the benefit of having the partner as a witness. Reference was made to the mother's hiding her partner from the Court. The extent to which the homosexuality weighed against the mother may have been given away by the closing comments at p. 138:

> ... I greatly fear that if these children are raised by the mother, they will be too much in contact with people of abnormal tastes and proclivities.

In the subsequent case of *K. v. K.* (1975), 23 RFL 58, [1976] 2 WWR 462, Rowe J, of the Alberta Provincial Court, distinguished the *Case* decision.

His Honour agreed with the Saskatchewan Court as to homosexuality being one factor to be considered along with all the others. In awarding custody to a homosexual mother, who also slept in the same bed as her partner, and did not engage in any sexual contact in the presence of the children, the trial Judge was supported by strong evidence from a psychologist who testified that the mother and the child had a close relationship which was one of the best mother–child interactions she had seen in her professional practice. The psychologist noted that the child was happy, well adjusted and doing very well in school, and concluded [at 61] that "the manner in which one fulfills one's sexual needs does not relate to the abilities of being a good parent."

The trial Judge also accepted the evidence of a psychiatrist as to the mother's being an alert, pleasant and healthy person with no major problems who was vitally concerned for the welfare of her daughter. The psychiatrist testified that homosexuality "could be a factor" and it depended mostly on the manner in which it was handled. The trial Judge noted that he was satisfied that the relationship would be discreet and would not be "flaunted to the children or the community at large." It was pointed out by the trial Judge that, unlike the *Case* situation, the homosexual partner was called as a witness and was quite impressive. In the face of the overwhelming support of the mother in the evidence, it is difficult to know how much weight was attached to the mother's homosexuality.

In *D. v. D.* (1978), 20 OR (2d) 722, 88 DLR (3d) 578, 3 RFL (2d) 327, Smith Co. Ct. J dealt with an application to vary a decree *nisi*. The decree had been silent as to custody and the father later sought custody of 13- and 8-year-old children who had been in his *de facto* custody since the separation. It was clear that the father was bisexual but that he was involved in a continuing homosexual relationship. The trial Judge [at 726 OR; 583 DLR] treated his homosexuality as:

> [a] problem which may damage the children's psychological, moral, intellectual or physical well-being and their orderly development and adaptation to society ... . The Court's concern ought to be the children's position in their peer group, the children's sexual orientation and the manner in which the relationship of children to parent is or can be affected by the deviation from the norm in the latter's sexual preferences.

In awarding custody of the children to the father, which confirmed the *status quo*, the trial Judge's concerns about the "problem" of homosexuality were apparently modified by the following findings:

(a) the father was bisexual;

(b) the father was discreet;

(c) he was not an exhibitionist;

(d) the public did not know about his sexual orientations;

(e) he did not flaunt his homosexual activities;

(f) he was not a militant homosexual;

(g) the Court felt that he could "cope with" the problems;

(h) there was no evidence that the children would become homosexual;

(i) the main homosexual partner made a favourable impression on him.

It would appear that the *net* result of the analysis of the homosexual question was the placing of very little weight on the homosexuality of the father.

In the present case, a focus on the quality of the parent–child relationship here produces a good case for the mother as the more appropriate person to have custody of Lynn.

As in *D. v. D.* any possible ill effects for Lynn from the mother's sexual orientation have been minimized by the following circumstances:

(1) she is not militant;

(2) she does not flaunt her homosexuality;

(3) she does not seem to be biased about Lynn's orientation and seems to assume that Lynn will be heterosexual;

(4) there is no overt sexual contact apart from sleeping in the same bed;

(5) the sexual partner has a reasonably good relationship with the child.

Whatever significant risks remain in the area of Lynn's necessary adjustments to our "homophobic" society, they are too esoteric and speculative for me to attach much weight to. I think they must give way here to the more concrete *indicia* of "best interests."

An order will go granting custody of the child to the respondent with reasonable access to the applicant. The details of access are to be worked out through further consultations with Mr. Gardner at the Family Court Clinic, if necessary, or by a further application under s. 35 of the *Family Law Reform Act, 1978.*

Order accordingly.

Bezaire v. Bezaire (1980), 20 RFL (2d) 358

Susan Crean, *In the Name of the Fathers: The Story Behind Child Custody*
(Toronto: Amanita Publications, 1988), at 31-34

Gail Bezaire left her violent and physically abusive husband in 1974, taking her children, then two and three, with her. During her four-year marriage, she testified later, she was battered and sexually brutalized (at her trial she told the court she was raped by her husband a few days after the birth of her son) and her husband had once pleaded guilty and been convicted of assault. Upon Gail's return to her home in Windsor, Ontario, from the hospital following an operation for uterine cancer, he had pushed her downstairs, leaving her with a burst incision to fend for herself. Three-year-old Lisa had called emergency for help. Subsequently the police escorted Gail and her children to Windsor's newly opened shelter for battered women. At a hearing a few weeks later, Gail was awarded custody of the children and her husband George was ordered to pay $15 a month support for each child.

For the next five years Gail raised her son Sean and daughter Lisa on her own; her husband had access which he exercised erratically, and it was not until he sued for divorce in 1978 that custody was contested. Gail had, in the meantime, come out as a lesbian and her husband sued for divorce on the grounds that her sexual preference had caused the breakdown of the marriage. He also claimed it disqualified her as a fit parent. In a bitter court battle which focused on Gail's lesbianism, played for every sensational juicy bit it was worth by Windsor's news media, George Bezaire was granted his divorce, but he did not get custody of the children. In an unexpected departure from tradition, Gail became the first openly lesbian mother to win custody of her children. There were conditions attached to the order, however: that she maintain a stable residence and refrain from engaging in any homosexual relationships. Lesbianism, according to the judge, did not fit the values of Canadians.

Both parents appealed immediately—George the custody decision and Gail the conditions. Three months later, the judge reversed the custody order, stating that because Gail had moved without notifying the court and was involved in a lesbian relationship, the two conditions had been "flagrantly disregarded." Gail had one hour to prepare her children to leave her and go to live with their father. They were, she says, "literally torn from my arms and I could hear their screaming as they drove away." Over the next several months, during visits with her children, Gail became increasingly fearful that they were being physically and sexually abused. She went back to court and asked for the children to be represented by the Official Guardian of the provincial Attorney General's Office, and also requested that a psychiatric assessment be done of the whole family. Yet even when the court-appointed psychiatrist Dr. Elaine Borins corroborated the allegations of sexual abuse and recommended that custody of both children be immediately returned to the mother, even when this recommendation was echoed by the Official Guardian, the appeal court found in the father's favour. The only ray of light was Judge Bertha Wilson's dissenting opinion, in which she stated that she did not feel lesbianism should be a deciding factor in a child custody hearing—cold comfort to Gail Bezaire.

Having appealed for help to all the services available, including Children's Aid, Gail concluded that the justice system (the "injustice system" as she tends to call it) actually considered the presence of a lesbian relationship between consenting adults a greater danger to her children than physical and sexual abuse. Convinced she had no option and would not be able to protect them otherwise, she took her children in 1980 and fled the country. In 1985, after George Bezaire discovered the whereabouts of Lisa in the United States, Gail surrendered to police in Windsor. She was hand-cuffed and shackled and kept in solitary confinement for two weeks, during which time a custody hearing was held and both children were formally returned to their father. At this point in such cases criminal charges are usually dropped. But in Gail's case they weren't, because of her ex-husband's determination to see them pressed. He himself swore out the original information, not the police as is customary in such criminal proceedings. And no doubt the notoriety of the case, in part due to his public campaign through Child Find, made it difficult for the authorities to ignore it.

Gail Bezaire's trial took place in Toronto in May 1987. Rebecca Shamai, the Toronto lawyer who defended her, recognized it as a groundbreaking case. Not only was Gail the first Canadian woman hauled into court for abducting her children, but the case also touched two highly controversial issues which suffuse the debate around child custody: the rights of lesbian mothers and the credibility of women in Canadian courts, especially concerning allegations of sexual abuse raised in the context of a custody dispute. Predictably, the case turned into a high-profile but difficult court battle. Says Shamai: "We honestly thought we would achieve an acquittal once we'd assembled the evidence about what had gone on before and once we'd looked at the law. Without doubt, lesbianism was an inflammatory factor on both sides in 1980. But Gail felt it was an improper basis for a custody order, and she was right; today under the Charter of Rights, it wouldn't go."

The jury listened to the evidence, including testimony from Elaine Borins, and convicted Gail anyway, in effect discounting the allegations of sexual abuse and accepting Lisa's recantation and her father's denial. To Borins, it was an unsettling example of how far off-topic courts can go in pursuit of irrelevant issues. Instead of addressing the matter of the children's welfare, the proceedings focused on Gail Bezaire's sex life. Parental behaviour is a factor which should definitely be taken into consideration by anyone making decisions about custody, and feminists would be the first to insist on it—though with precaution. Rulings in the past have prohibited courts from holding a woman's admitted adultery against her in a custody suit, but the same rule has encouraged many judges to ignore a man's aggressive behaviour towards his wife as bearing any relation to his qualities as a parent. The point is that abusive behaviour does have relevance to parenting; one's sexual orientation does not. To Borins, it was a tragedy. "In 1980 lesbianism was as hysterical an issue from the court's point of view as pot-smoking was in the sixties, and that became the focus rather than what was happening to the children. In the meantime, kidnapping has become a contemporary equivalent of lesbianism, and once again, Gail has been scape-goated." Borins was equally perturbed that so little attention and credibility had been given to the psychiatrist's evidence. "From my point of view it was a very simple assessment. In a situation where there are two equally fit parents, or equally poor ones, the recommendation can be very difficult to make. But where one parent is off-the-wall and the other, while not perfect, certainly is not disturbed, the recommendation is simple. And in this case one parent was grossly unfit to parent. There is no doubt in my mind that the girl had been sexually abused, and I will not be at all surprised to be called in ten years from now when she decides to sue her father. She denies it now which is not hard to understand and very common. But why do courts find it so hard? I don't think to this day the husband has ever been charged with abuse."

In June, Judge Sidney Dymond sentenced Gail Bezaire. On the charge of abduction she granted her an absolute discharge, giving her a three-year suspended sentence for the charges of harbouring, three years probation, and an order to get counselling and to do 300 hours of community work. Judge Dymond noted that the guilty verdict meant the jury had concluded the sexual abuse allegations were not true, but that Gail Bezaire nevertheless truly believed her children were in danger and had acted accordingly. She stated that she was taking Gail's suffering into account, including the five years on the run with the children, which was its own kind of imprisonment and a "living hell" for all concerned. Finally, she drew a distinction between the actions of parents who abduct their children to protect them and those who do it out of spite. Sentencing Gail Bezaire to jail, she rationalized, would have no deterrent effect on other parents in similar distress.

Outside the courtroom, George Bezaire erupted. "I've had it with these lesbians," he exclaimed to a crowd of reporters. "Where's the justice?" The *Globe and Mail*'s Heather Mallick described the scene that then followed. "When his mother began complaining to reporters about the sentence, Mr. Bezaire shoved her away and told her to shut up. Pulling his [present] wife toward him, he said, 'Tell them.'" "There is no abuse at our house," Sue Bezaire said. "The only abuse was when I got married [to Gail]," he said. "I went through 15 years of hell." His mother interrupted, "And I did too." With television cameras rolling, Mr. Bezaire hit his mother on the chest with the back of his hand to silence her so he could tell the story himself.

In *Bezaire v. Bezaire* in the Ontario Court of Appeal, both judges who wrote opinions commented on the impact of lesbian sexual orientation on issues about custody. According to Arnup JA (at 365):

> I would make one comment upon an aspect of the case which gave Judge McMahon a great deal of concern and which has been canvassed at some length before us. That is the question of the effect of and the weight to be given to evidence that the mother not only exhibited homosexual tendencies but clearly lived at various relevant times in a homosexual relationship. ... In my view homosexuality, either as a tendency, a proclivity or a practised way of life, is not in itself alone a ground for refusing custody to the parent with respect to whom such evidence is given. The question is and must always be what effect upon the welfare of the children that aspect of the parent's make-up and life-style has, and it will therefore be a question of evidence in that very case as to whether what has been shown to exist has or may tend to have effects adverse to the welfare of the children.

In her reasons (dissenting on other issues), Wilson JA also stated (at 367):

I would like to add as an addendum to these reasons that in my view homosexuality is a neutral and not a negative factor as far as parenting skills are concerned. To the extent the learned trial judge proceeded on a different view I would respectfully disagree with him.

Discussion Notes

The Impact of Environmental Issues

In a critique of the appellate court decision in *Bezaire*, Katherine Arnup argued that the fair-mindedness of the judges may not be sufficient to overcome prejudice against lesbian mothers:

> The appellate judges argued, then, that each case must be judged on the basis of its evidence. Even such a fair-minded approach, however, contains within it a pitfall for the lesbian mother. Because of the "rampant heterosexism" of our society, the child of a lesbian might well be the object of abuse and ridicule by neighbourhood children if the mother's lesbianism were discovered or even suspected. Such an experience would, of course, be an unpleasant one for the child. Anticipating such derision, judges in Canada, as in the United States, Britain and elsewhere have opted primarily for paternal custody rights, thereby reflecting and reinforcing the prevailing attitudes toward lesbianism.

(See Katherine Arnup, "'Mothers Just Like Others': Lesbians, Divorce, and Child Custody in Canada" (1989), 3 *Canadian Journal of Women and the Law* 18, at 28.)

In reflecting on Arnup's critique, consider *Saunders v. Saunders* (1989), 20 RFL (3d) 368 (BC Co. Ct.), in which a gay father in British Columbia was denied access to his child on the basis of his homosexual relationship. According to Wetmore Co. Ct. J (at 370):

> The child has a normal, stable home in which there are only the normal environmental circumstances for maturity to develop. Surely it cannot be argued the exposure of a child to unnatural relationships is in the best interests of that child of tender years. While it is an impossibility to protect a child from many undesirable situations, even when they are very young, the prudent parent does not voluntarily and deliberately expose a child to any environmental influence which might affect normal development. ...
>
> There can be no doubt that consenting adults may enter into whatever sexual arrangements they wish, for better or worse. I am not convinced ... that the exposure of a child of tender years to an unnatural relationship of a parent to any degree is in the best interests of the development and natural attainment of maturity of that child. That is the issue, not the rights of homosexuals. The courts have on occasion found, in given circumstances, the best interests of the child are served by placing custody with a homosexual father or lesbian mother. In those cases, however, the children have usually been older, but more importantly the parent has exercised great restraint in minimizing the sexual choice of that parent as a role model for the child.

How should these environmental issues be considered, if at all, in custody litigation? Are they at all relevant to the best-interests test? Why, or why not?

Research Studies About Lesbian Parenting

In "Legal, Psychological, and Medical Considerations in Lesbian Parenting" (1992), 2 *Law and Sexuality* 237, Cheryl L. Meyer reported (at 239-41):

> Research investigating the differences between children raised by lesbian versus heterosexual mothers has consistently demonstrated that no significant differences exist. Stability of the home seems to be a more important indicator of adjustment than the sexual orientation of the mother. Researchers generally match divorced heterosexual and homosexual custodial mothers on various demographic characteristics and then compare their children on numerous attributes. Children raised by lesbian mothers have not differed from children raised by heterosexual mothers on measures of popularity, social adjustment, gender role behavior, gender identity, intelligence, self-concept, emotional problems, interest in marriage and parenting, locus of control, moral development, independence, ego functions, object relations, or self esteem. There were also no significant differences between the two groups in teachers' and parents' evaluations of emotional and social behavior, fears, sleep disturbances, hyperactivity, and conduct differences.
>
> A few differences have been noted. One study found children raised by the heterosexual mothers had higher rates of psychiatric disorders and higher rates of psychiatric referrals than the children raised by homosexual mothers. Another reported difference indicated children raised by heterosexual mothers were more self-assertive, more domineering and more often engaged in power struggles than children of homosexual mothers. Children of homosexual mothers evinced more tolerance for diversity.
>
> Additionally, Green noted that daughters of lesbians engaged in more play acting, role playing and rough and tumble play than did daughters of heterosexual mothers. Daughters of lesbians also chose to play with opposite sex partners more often than daughters of heterosexual mothers. Finally, daughters raised by lesbian mothers showed more interest in traditional male occupations than did daughters raised by heterosexual mothers.
>
> In a recent study, adult children of lesbian versus heterosexual divorced mothers were compared. The study found no significant differences between the groups on leadership ability, self-reliance, social adjustment, self-confidence, gender identity, gender role, scores on masculinity or femininity, sexual orientation, self-acceptance, dominance, or interpersonal flexibility. In fact, daughters of lesbians scored higher on feelings of security in the world and relationships than daughters of heterosexual mothers. Stability of the environment was found to be a critical factor in the latter measure. Since lesbian women and heterosexual women have been found to be more similar than dissimilar, and their children test comparably on scales for psychological and social attributes, it is not surprising to find that parenting styles of the two groups of mothers are also comparable.
>
> Bonnie M. Mucklow and Gladys K. Phelan note a major theme in research on parents and children: child-rearing style is a "product of the mother's attitudes, values and personality characteristics," not necessarily her sexual orientation. Lesbian mothers did make more substantial efforts to provide their children with a variety of social contacts and demonstrated greater concern for providing male figures for their children than their heterosexual counterparts. In fact, lesbian mothers repeatedly attempted to strengthen their children's relationships with their fathers, a trend not found among their heterosexual counterparts. Sons of heterosexual women were more likely to have had more than one period of

separation from their fathers, whereas sons of lesbian mothers generally only experienced one period of separation from their fathers. These findings may be due to the greater bitterness heterosexual women harbor toward the failed marriage and men. Lesbian mothers also tend to be "more tolerant of cross-gender play and more supportive of girls developing independence and boys [developing] nurturant interests."

How should courts take into account such research studies about lesbian parenting? To what extent can courts use empirical data to determine what is in a child's best interests? Is this question only an empirical question? Why, or why not?

SELECTED REFERENCES

Katherine Arnup, ed., *Lesbian Parenting* (Charlottetown, PEI: Gynergy Books, 1995).

Susan B. Boyd, "Lesbian (and Gay) Custody Claims: What Difference Does Difference Make?" (1998), 15 *Canadian Journal of Family Law* 131.

Shelley A.M. Gavigan, "Mothers, Other Mothers, and Others," in Dorothy Chunn and Dany Lacombe, eds., *Law as a Gendering Practice* (Toronto: Oxford University Press, 2000), 100.

Jenni Millbank, "Lesbians, Child Custody, and the Long Lingering Gaze of the Law," in Susan B. Boyd, ed., *Challenging the Public/Private Divide: Feminism, Law, and Public Policy* (Toronto: University of Toronto Press, 1997), 280.

Nancy Polikoff, "Lesbian Mothers, Lesbian Families" (1989), 14 *New York University Review of Law and Social Change* 907.

4. Blood Ties and Best Interests

According to some provincial legislation, the existence of blood ties between a child and another person is just one factor to be considered in determining what is in the best interests of a child—it is not accorded priority. In this context, how should courts assess a child's best interests in relation to blood ties?

K.K. v. G.L. and B.J.L.

In *K.K. v. G.L. and B.J.L.* (1984), 44 RFL (2d) 113, the Supreme Court of Canada dismissed an appeal in relation to a decision of a NWT court to award custody of a child to prospective adoptive parents, rather than have a child returned to its biological mother (who had consented to the adoption and then changed her mind). According to the court, the best interest of the child "is the paramount consideration when the court addresses [a custody decision]." The Supreme Court of Canada also reviewed a decision of the Ontario Court of Appeal in which custody of a child was granted to foster parents rather than to the child's biological mother, in accordance with the court's determination as to the child's best interests: see *Re Moores and Feldstein*, [1973] 3 OR 921 (CA). In addition, the Supreme Court referred to *Racine v. Woods* (discussed in chapter 3) and *Beson v. Dir. of Child Welfare for Nfld.*, [1982] 2 SCR 716. In the end, the court in *K.K. v. G.L. and B.J.L.* concluded that the child's best interests mandated custody for the prospective adoptive parents. In part, the court stated (at 126):

This conclusion is consistent with modern authority in this court and others: see *Racine*, *Beson* and *Re Moores and Feldstein*. I would therefore hold that in the case at bar the dominant consideration to which all other considerations must remain subordinate must be the welfare of the child. This is not to say that the question of custody will be determined by weighing the economic circumstances of the contending parties. The matter will not be determined solely on the basis of the physical comfort and material advantages that may be available in the home of one contender or the other. The welfare of the child must be decided on a consideration of these and all other relevant factors, including the general psychological, spiritual and emotional welfare of the child. It must be the aim of the court, when resolving disputes between rival claimants for the custody of a child, to choose the course which will best provide for the healthy growth, development and education of the child so that he will be equipped to face the problems of life as a mature adult. Parental claims must not be lightly set aside, and they are entitled to serious consideration in reaching any conclusion. Where it is clear that the welfare of the child requires it, however, they must be set aside.

Discussion Notes

Crocker v. Sipus: A Different View?

In *Crocker v. Sipus* (1992), 41 RFL (3d) 5 (Ont. Ct. J (Gen. Div.)), a case complicated by a number of procedural issues, a new trial was ordered in relation to claims to custody by the biological father on the one hand and the sister and brother-in-law of the deceased biological mother on the other. In ordering a new trial, the court stated that if the natural parent is able to care for the child, he should be entitled to custody. Is this decision consistent with *K.K. v. G.L. and B.J.L.*? Why, or why not?

Blood Ties Among Siblings

A number of cases have considered the importance of keeping siblings together: for example, see *White v. White* (1994), 7 RFL (4th) 414 (NBQB). For a decision regarding the significance of bonding in these contexts, see *R.(M.) v. H.(S.)* (1997), 32 RFL (4th) 127 (Ont. Ct. J (Prov. Div.)); see also *Poole v. Poole* (1999), 45 RFL (4th) 56 (BCCA).

5. Race and Best Interests

Van de Perre v. Edwards
[2001] 2 SCR 1014; 19 RFL (5th) 396

[In this case, the Supreme Court of Canada considered a custody dispute about a son born to a single Caucasian Canadian woman after her 18-month sexual affair with an African-American professional basketball player. The father was married and had twin daughters; his family was based in North Carolina. The child's mother brought an action for custody and child support when the son was three months old; after a lengthy trial, the trial judge awarded sole custody to the mother and granted access to the father: *K.V. v. T.E.*, [1999] BCJ no. 434 (SC) (QL). The father appealed the trial decision; the father's wife applied for status as a party at the invitation of the BC Court of Appeal, requesting joint custody with the father. Joint custody was awarded, but the judgment was stayed pending the appeal to the Supreme Court of Canada: *V.(K.) v. E.(T.)* (2000), 4 RFL (5th) 436; 184 DLR (4th) 486; 7 RFL (5th) 186 (BCCA). The mother's appeal to the Supreme Court of Canada was allowed and the trial decision restored.

In part, the Supreme Court of Canada was concerned about whether the correct standard of review had been applied by the Court of Appeal. The Supreme Court of Canada concluded that the Court of Appeal had usurped its function in reconsidering the evidence submitted at trial, stating (at paras. 36ff.):]

The Court of Appeal found that the trial judge gave "no consideration" to issues of race and interracial problems that Elijah might face. In fact, the trial judge noted that there had been some testimony at trial related to the race of Elijah and the importance of being exposed to his heritage and culture as the son of an African-American father. Rather than discussing the child's race in detail, however, the trial judge noted that this child is of mixed race and, as such, his Caucasian Canadian heritage must also be considered.

The interveners, the African Canadian Legal Clinic, the Association of Black Social Workers and the Jamaican Canadian Association, submit that race is a critical factor in custody and access cases. In my view, the importance of this factor will depend greatly on many factual considerations. The interveners state that there are key tools a Canadian biracial child will need in order to foster racial identity and pride: the need to develop a means to deal with racism and the need to develop a positive racial identity. The corollary to these needs is the parental ability to meet them. The interveners do not state that the minority parent should necessarily be granted custody; rather, the question is which parent will best be able to contribute to a healthy racial socialization and overall healthy development of the child. This question is one of fact to be determined by the courts on a case-by-case basis and weighed by the trial judge with other relevant factors.

The interveners submit that, although some studies show that Black parents are more likely to be aware of the need to prepare their children to cope with racism, the main issue is which parent will facilitate contact and the development of racial identity in a manner that avoids conflict, discord and disharmony. But again, this is only one factor to be considered by the trial judge. I would also add that evidence of race relations in the relevant communities may be important to define the context in which the child and his parents will function. It is not always possible to address these sensitive issues by judicial notice, even though some notice of racial facts can be taken; see *R v. Williams*, [1998] 1 SCR 1128 (SCC). The weight to be given to all relevant factors is a matter of discretion, but discretion must be exercised with regard to the evidence. In essence, the interveners argue that race is always a crucial factor and that it should never be ignored, even if not addressed by the parties. They favour forced judicial consideration of race because it is essential in deciding which parent is best able to cope with difficulties biracial children may face. This approach is based on the conclusions reached concerning the present state of race relations in Canada.

As I have said, racial identity is but one factor that may be considered in determining personal identity; the relevancy of this factor depends on the context. Other factors are more directly related to primary needs and must be considered in priority (see R.G. McRoy and C.C. Lijima Hall, "Transracial Adoptions: In Whose Best Interest?" in Maria P.P. Root, ed., *The Multicultural Experience* (1996), at pp. 71-73). All factors must be considered pragmatically. Different situations and different philosophies require an individual analysis on the basis of reliable evidence. ...

Race can be a factor in determining the best interests of the child because it is connected to the culture, identity and emotional well-being of the child. New Brunswick, for example, has adopted legislation prescribing mandatory consideration of "cultural and religious heritage" for all custody determinations (*Family Services Act*, SNB 1980, c. F-2.2, ss. 1 and 129(2)). British Columbia has included similar language in its provisions regarding adoption, but not in those found in the *Family Relations Act* applicable in this case. (*Adoption Act*, RSBC 1996, c. 5, s. 3.) The adoption and custody contexts may differ because the adopted child will generally cease to have contact with the biological parent while custody will generally favour contact with both parents. Nevertheless, it is generally understood that biracial children should be encouraged to positively identify with both racial heritage[s]. This suggests the possibility of a biracial identity (i.e. "forming an identity that incorporates multiple racial heritages," see Pollack ... ["The Role of Race in Child Custody Decisions Between Natural Parents Over Biracial Children" (1997), 23 *NYU Rev. L & Soc. Change* 603], at p. 619). It is important that the custodial parent recognize the child's need of cultural identity and foster its development accordingly. I would therefore agree that evidence regarding the so-called "cultural dilemma" of biracial children (i.e. the conflict that arises from belonging to two races where one may be dominant for one reason or another) is relevant and should always be accepted. But the significance of evidence relating to race in any given custody case must be carefully considered by the trial judge. Although general public information is useful, it appears to be often contradictory (T.L. Perry, "The Transracial Adoption Controversy: An Analysis of Discourse and Subordination" (1993-94), 21 *NYU Rev. L & Soc. Change* 33, at p. 59), and may not be sufficient to inform the judge about the current status of race relations in a particular community or the ability of either applicant to deal with these issues.

For the Court of Appeal to intervene, it would have to find a material error. Although Warren J did not discuss in detail the role that race plays in determining the best interests of the child, he did state that there is an overarching need for the child to be in a stable and loving environment. The limited findings of the trial judge on this issue reflected the minimal weight that the parties themselves placed on the issue at trial. Therefore, notwithstanding the role that race may play in custody determinations, it appears that the trial judge noted that this issue was not determinative and that, in this case, Elijah would be in a more stable and loving environment if custody was granted to the appellant. He clearly considered the mixed race of Elijah and implied that race may impact s. 24(1)(a) in some cases; however, the trial judge obviously was of the view that, even if the biological father provided some benefits as regards fostering a positive racial identity, these benefits did not outweigh the negative findings related to him. By intervening in the consideration of race by the trial judge, the

Court of Appeal failed to apply the correct standard of review. It should not have intervened; this issue was given disproportionate emphasis at the initiative of the Court of Appeal.

Discussion Note

The Race Factor in Custody Determinations

According to Boyd (at 180), the Supreme Court clearly rejected the intervenors' argument that race should be a crucial factor in custody determinations, reducing the "question of race to only one of many factors that may be relevant in a given case." As a result, the court's decision provided little guidance on *how much* priority to assign to the issue of race in determining a child's best interests.

In some lower court decisions, however, some courts appear to have been attentive to a child's need to connect to racial heritage, with varying results. For example, in *Ffrench v. Ffrench* (1994), 118 DLR (4th) 571 (NSSC), the court awarded custody to a Caucasian mother, rather than to the children's African-Canadian father, partly on the grounds of the mother's awareness of the children's need for continuing contact with their African-Canadian heritage. By contrast, an African-Canadian mother was awarded custody because she was more attentive to the father's French-Canadian heritage than he was to her cultural background: see *Camba v. Sparks* (1993), 345 APR 321 (NSFC).

As Boyd noted (at 179), however, some custody disputes involving mixed-race children may employ a rather simplistic analysis. For example, in *Kassel v. Louie* (2000), 11 RFL (5th) 144 (BSSC), custody was awarded to a Chinese-Canadian father, rather than to a Caucasian mother, in part because the judge concluded that the child resembled his father in his looks, and in spite of the fact that the child had lived mainly with his mother. According to Boyd, the judge appeared to place emphasis on the fact that, as the only male heir in the family, the boy was important to the life of the father's extended family.

In the context of these cases, identify the priority that should be accorded to race as a factor in determining a child's best interests in custody cases. Recall the discussion in chapter 3 about race in the context of adoption. Are the same considerations appropriate in custody determinations as in the adoption context? Why, or why not?

SELECTED REFERENCES

Emily Carasco, "Race and Child Custody in Canada: Its Relevance and Role" (1999), 16 *Canadian Journal of Family Law* 11.

Marlee Kline, "Child Welfare Law, 'Best Interests of the Child' Ideology, and First Nations" (1992), 30:2 *Osgoode Hall Law Journal* 375.

Beryl Tsang, *Child Custody and Access: The Experiences of Abused Immigrant and Refugee Women* (Ottawa: Education Wife Assault, 2001).

Tammy Wing-Yun Law, "The Race Issue in Custody Law: Is Van de Perre Right?" (2002), 21 *Canadian Family Law Quarterly* 153.

6. Best Interests and Access Determinations

As demonstrated by the examples above, courts determine parental custody on the basis
of what is in a child's best interests. However, access for the other parent is not automatic—parental access must also be determined having regard to the principle of a
child's best interests. In examining the case that follows, identify the factors that the
court considered relevant to deciding the father's claim to access—are these factors the
same as those used in claims for custody? Should they be the same? Why, or why not?

Craig v. Antone

(1987), 7 RFL (3d) 409 (Ont. Prov. Ct. (Fam. Div.))

Although the facts are clear and the evidence reasonably brief at trial, the law to be
applied is of some difficulty and interest. Briefly put, counsel for the respondent supported the view that access is a definitive right which may be lost by a parent only
where the evidence discloses some real apprehension of emotional or physical harm
to the child. Counsel for Ms. Craig urged upon me that that traditional view has been
displaced by a test based on the best interests of the child.

Mr. Davies conceded during argument that the onus was on his client to satisfy me
that access to the respondent would not be in the best interests of the child. It is not so
obvious, however, where the evidentiary burden lies. In *Trudell v. Doolittle*, [1984]
WDFL 933 [(Ont. Prov. Ct., Abbey Prov. J) (May 9, 1984) (unreported)], it was argued
that the provisions of s. 20(4) [of the *Children's Law Reform Act*], particularly the
absence of a statutory suspension of access to a non-custodial parent, implies a presumption in favour of access. Section 20(4) is formulated in the following words:

> (4) Where the parents of a child live separate and apart and the child lives with one of
> them with the consent, implied consent or acquiescence of the other of them, the right of the
> other to exercise the entitlement to custody and the incidents of custody, but not the entitle-
> ment to access, is suspended until a separation agreement or order otherwise provides.

In a judgement that is most persuasive on more than this one point, Abbey Prov. J
said at pp. 13-14:

> Counsel for the applicant invites me to find that by virtue of the provisions, in particu-
> lar, of s. 20(4) there is a presumption in favour of a right of access provided by statute
> and that the onus rests upon the respondent in this proceeding if it is to be denied to
> establish that access is not in the best interests of the child. The position of counsel, in
> essence, is that s. 20(4), by providing that the right to custody but not the right to access
> is suspended, has recognized a prima facie right to access, thereby placing the onus
> upon the party resisting access to establish that the granting of access would not be in
> the best interests of the child.
>
> I am not prepared to take the meaning of s. 20(4) that far. The provision, in my view,
> although it provides that in the circumstances where parents live separately the entitle-
> ment to access, as opposed to the entitlement to custody, is not suspended, does not go so
> far as to create by statute a presumption in favour of access such that, in the determination

of that access by application under the Act, the onus is cast upon the parent resisting the right of the other to access.

With respect to the second point—namely, whether or not a denial of access must be based on apprehended danger to the child—I cannot improve upon the analysis of the trial judge in *Trudell v. Doolittle* in a lengthy passage from his reasons commencing at p. 14 as follows:

> It therefore may be said, I believe, that even prior to the passage of the present s. 24 of the *Children's Law Reform Act*, the paramount principle applicable in the determination of the right of access was the best interests of the child. Although certain other guidelines came to be generally accepted as helpful in the determination of the best interests of the child, those guidelines were secondary to the paramount principle.
>
> As examples of the application of certain of the guidelines and the overriding principle together, the following statements may assist:
>
> (a) Although it may be generally considered as a sound general guideline that access should be granted except where a danger to the child might be apprehended, nevertheless, if upon consideration of the evidence as a whole the granting of access could not be said to be in the child's best interests, it should not be granted even though there be no evidence of apprehended danger.
>
> (b) Although it may be generally presumed that it is in a child's best interests to come to know its biological father, nevertheless, if upon consideration of the evidence as a whole applicable to a particular case it cannot be said that access would be in the best interests of a child, it should not be granted. ...

In my view, the decisions in *Trudell v. Doolittle* and *Boileau v. Boileau* reflect the law of Ontario on this point, although there have been judgments which appear to differ: see *Erlich v. Litwiller* (1984), 7 FLRR 41.

On the facts before me, there is no evidence of more than a chance, and perhaps reluctant, acquaintance between the respondent and the child. The conduct, generally, of the respondent has been disreputable and his relationship with the applicant even less than tenuous. Although the respondent appeared contrite for his past transgressions, his expressed wishes were purely speculative. I conclude that the lack of real motivation which has been a continuing factor through his unproductive attempts at rehabilitation in the past will, unfortunately, probably continue, and to impose his sudden presence on this child in any form would be completely contrary to her best interests.

The words of the respondent in the witness box convince me of his yearning for an illusory relationship of some importance to him, different from the other liaisons in his life. I cannot ignore the fact, however, that his opportunity to form a substantial bond with the applicant and his child was thrown aside by his commitment to an aberrant lifestyle and his opportunistic and callous behaviour towards the applicant. Although he is now apparently repentant, the evidence is that he threatened to kidnap the child only to cause emotional harm to the applicant. In my view of the law, there is no justification for the father having even supervised access to the child and, accordingly, the relief he seeks is denied and his claim dismissed. ...

Order accordingly.

Discussion Notes

Denial/Suspension of Access

As is evident, the court denied the father's claim to access to his child in *Craig v. Antone*; indeed, the court was not even prepared to grant supervised access—that is, access visits that are supervised by a third party. Although somewhat unusual, there are other cases in which parents (usually, but not always, fathers) have been denied access to children, or where existing access arrangements have been suspended or terminated.

For example, in *Lidkea v. Jarrell* (1999), 49 RFL (4th) 324 (Ont. CA), the court dismissed an appeal by the father from a decision suspending access to his daughter. According to the court, there was ample evidence to support the view that suspension of access was in the child's best interests. Similarly, the Saskatchewan Court of Appeal confirmed an order denying a father's access to his son where there was evidence that the son did not wish to have contact with his father after the father acted improperly: see *Gorgichuk v. Gorgichuk* (1999), 50 RFL (4th) 395. Moreover, in *S. v. S.* (1998), 43 RFL (4th) 373, the BC Court of Appeal ordered that a father be prohibited from bringing further suits to compel access to two children, after he had failed in a number of such attempts. The children were the result of an incestuous relationship with his daughter, for which he had been convicted and imprisoned. For another case denying access, see *Abdo v. Abdo* (1993), 50 RFL (3d) 171 (NSCA).

Access Claims by Grandparents and Others

In *D.(G.) v. M.(G.)* (1999), 47 RFL (4th) 16 (NWTSC), the NWT court upheld an access claim for a step-mother after her relationship with the child's father had ended, concluding that such access was in the child's best interests. Somewhat more controversial have been claims for access presented by grandparents. In *T. v. P.* (1999), 45 RFL (4th) 91, the Alberta Court of Appeal denied an access claim presented by grandparents on the ground that their persistent efforts to pursue their claim in the media over a five-year period were not in the children's best interests. In *F. v. S.* (1999), 49 RFL (4th) 250, a grandmother's request for an access order, which was objected to by the child's mother, was denied by the BC Court of Appeal.

Such claims by persons other than parents are often permitted by provincial statutes. In addition, the current *Divorce Act, 1985* permits persons other than parents to apply for standing in proceedings about custody or access of children, but any such application requires leave of the court: see ss. 16(2) and (3). In *Arnink v. Arnink* (1999), 2 RFL (5th) 24 (BCSC), the court reviewed the applicable principles and held that the grandparents were appropriate parties (for purposes of custody and access claims only) in divorce proceedings between their son-in-law and daughter. In this case, the grandparents had been primary caregivers of the two children. The children's father, who was the petitioner in the divorce action, opposed their application. In granting the grandparents' application, the court stated (at 27):

> I am satisfied that the "not frivolous or vexatious" test used by Cummings J is the appropri-
> ate test to use. It should be noted that the sole consideration in a custody dispute is the best

interests of the child: s. 16(8) of the *Divorce Act* and s. 24 of the *Family Relations Act*. In order that the best interests of the child or the children can be determined, any individuals who can bring themselves within the definition of "persons" as set out in the *Family Relations Act* (s. 35(1.1) of the Act) would qualify as persons who should be granted leave to apply for custody. I am satisfied that the onus of showing that the application for leave is frivolous or vexatious lies with the party opposing the application. In the case at bar, the plaintiff has not shown that the request of the Andersens to be at liberty to apply for custody is frivolous and vexatious. The mere fact of them joining with their daughter to add further weight to the application of the defendant for custody and to diminish the ability of the plaintiff to obtain custody can hardly be said to make their application frivolous and vexatious.

The plaintiff relies on the decision in *Fisher v. Fisher* (1985), 166 APR 206 (NSTD) where the court refused to allow grandparents to be joined as parties in divorce proceedings where they were not seeking custody for themselves but wanted to support the application by their son. In rejecting the grandparents' claim, Nathanson J stated at para. 11:

> It does not follow from the mere existence of doting grandparents that their participa-
> tion is necessary to ensure full and effectual adjudication. No doubt there are thousands
> of cases involving grandparents which are adjudicated without their participation.
> The facts of this case are not much different from many others. The grandparents can
> be called to give evidence, but it cannot be said that their participation is necessary to
> ensure a full and effectual adjudication of the matter of custody. That is particularly
> so where they do not claim custody for themselves.

In Nova Scotia at the time, the *Infants' Custody Act* limited the jurisdiction of the Trial Division of the Supreme Court by permitting custody to be granted only to the natural parents of an infant. This jurisdiction must be contrasted with the power available to this court under ss. 35(1) and 35(1.1) of the *Family Relations Act*. Accordingly, I am satisfied that the decision must be limited in its scope by the specific provision of the Nova Scotia *Infants' Custody Act*. In any event, I am satisfied that the later decision of the Newfound-land trial division in *M.(R.) v. B.(G.)* ... [(1987), 6 RFL (3d) 441 (Nfld. TD)] should be preferred.

There is nothing before me which would suggest that the application of Mr. and Mrs. Andersen is anything but a genuine attempt to apply for custody of their two grandchildren along with their daughter. Whether or not that application will ultimately be granted, I am satisfied that leave should be granted pursuant to s. 16(3) of the *Divorce Act*.

The issue of grandparents' access was reviewed extensively in the context of the parliamentary committee's recommendations for divorce reform. Details of the recommendations are included in the discussion of reform proposals at the end of this section.

7. Access, Best Interests, and Religion

Martha J. Bailey, "Custody, Access, and Religion: A Comment on Young v. Young and D.P. v. C.S."
(1994), 11 *Canadian Family Law Quarterly* 317

Introduction

Canada's Department of Justice is currently reviewing the provisions on custody and access in the federal *Divorce Act*. Central to this review is the question of the authority of the custodial parent and the relative position of the access parent. The Department defines part of its task as the resolution of the uncertainty about the legal rights of the custodial parent and which, if any, incidents of custody are limited, restricted or subject to the rights of the access parent. It was essentially this issue that divided the Supreme Court of Canada in two access cases decided on 21 October 1993.

Both cases raised the question of whether the father could share without restriction his Jehovah's Witness faith with his children during access visits over the objections of the custodial mother. In *Young v. Young*, a case emanating from British Columbia and involving the federal *Divorce Act*, this question was decided in favour of the father. Madam Justice McLachlin, who was appointed from British Columbia, wrote the majority decision and L'Heureux-Dubé J the main dissenting opinion. The *D.P. v. C.S.* case, an appeal from the Quebec Superior Court under the Civil Code of Lower Canada, was decided in favour of the mother. Here L'Heureux-Dubé J, who is from Quebec, wrote the majority judgment and McLachlin J the main dissent. Justices McLachlin and L'Heureux-Dubé each rested her decision on the "best interests of the child," but revealed different analyses of the meaning of that standard.

The court was split on the access issue between three francophone justices, two of whom are appointments from Quebec, who voted in favour of access restrictions, and two anglophone common law justices, who voted against restrictions. The swing votes were provided by Justices Cory and Iacobucci, both appointed from the Central Canada province of Ontario, who voted with McLachlin J on the BC case and L'Heureux-Dubé J on the Quebec case, apparently on the basis of distinctive facts.

The reasons for judgment in the two cases, with all the concurring and dissenting reasons, were long and confusing, so much so that the lawyers of the parties in *Young* were not sure of the outcome. This comment aims to clarify the main points of the cases and to offer a critical assessment of the judgments, particularly with regard to issues germane to the current project of reformulating custody and access law. ...

The Constitutional Questions

The fathers in both cases challenged the relevant statutes on several constitutional grounds, but the Court mainly addressed their arguments that the "best interests of the child" test violated the guarantee of freedom of religion and expression in the *Canadian Charter of Rights and Freedoms*.

In ruling on the constitutional challenge, the first question was whether the *Charter* applied to an action for access between two parents. The extent to which the *Charter* will apply in "private" actions has been the subject of much discussion, particularly since the Supreme Court of Canada 1986 ruling on the issue that the *Charter* is available only to protect individuals from "government" action. The issue of whether the *Charter* applies in "private" access actions includes three distinct questions: whether the *Charter* applies to the legislative test for determining access; whether the *Charter* applies to judicial orders made in access proceedings; and, if the *Charter* is not formally applicable to orders made in access proceedings, to what extent should the values of the *Charter* affect the interpretation of the "best interests of the child" test.

Clearly the *Charter* applies to the legislative test for determining access, and there was no disagreement on that issue among the members of the court. Nor was there any disagreement on whether the legislative test in question, the "best interests of the child" test, did in fact violate the *Charter*. All members of the Court agreed that the test, if properly interpreted, did not (although they disagreed on the proper interpretation).

The issue of the application of the *Charter* to court orders in custody and access actions was left unsettled, L'Heureux-Dubé J, with La Forest and Gonthier JJ concurring, said clearly not. McLachlin J said that it was unnecessary to decide, because valid orders made on the "best interests of the child" test could not violate the *Charter*. ...

The Justices agreed that the interpretation of the "best interests of the child test" must take into account the values of the *Charter*, but disagreed on the extent to which *Charter* values should affect the interpretation. L'Heureux-Dubé J, with La Forest and Gonthier JJ concurring, said "[c]ourts must strive to uphold *Charter* values, and preference should be given to such values in the interpretation of legislation over those which run contrary to them. She said that if the order had been based on the sole fact that the father adhered to the Jehovah's Witness faith, it would not be valid, regardless of the *Charter*. ...

On the issue of the applicable standard for imposing conditions on the access parent's religious rights, L'Heureux-Dubé J said that the standard is not one of "harm" but must always be in the "best interests of the child."

McLachlin J interpreted the "best interests of the child" test in light of *Charter* values, but she also offered a distinct, and less broad, interpretation of *Charter* values in cases involving the interests of children, explicitly preferring to err in favour of children's interests rather than the rights of parents, even if those rights are protected by the *Charter*. ...

While L'Heureux-Dubé and McLachlin JJ seem at first to have adopted a similar approach, both ruling that freedom of religion does not protect conduct that violates the best interests of the child, only McLachlin J found it necessary to interpret deprivation of the best interests of the child to mean "harm," thereby fitting into [the] limit on religious freedom established in *Big M. Drug Mart*. More importantly, McLachlin J's expansion of deprivation of the best interests of the child to mean "harm" may be more apparent than real—she also ruled that under the "best interests of the child" test it may be necessary to prove harm or risk of harm before limitations on what a parent may say or do during access visits will be imposed. So rather than expanding the *Big M. Drug Mart* test to further limit religious freedom, she may have diminished "the best interests of the child" test to an absence of harm test for cases like *Young*. ...

The Children's Rights

The approach taken by Sopinka J to the constitutional question was problematic because it would privilege the rights of the parent over the interests of a child in a proceeding in which the child was not a party, was not represented, and had no opportunity to invoke his or her own rights. Sopinka J justified his approach by linking the parent's rights to the child's right and interest in knowing the parent fully, but this is not satisfactory. The child may not want to invoke the right to know the parent fully and may want to invoke other rights that are more important to the child.

As L'Heureux-Dubé J observed, the rights of freedom of expression and religion "are shaped and formed both by the particular context in which they are exercised and the rights of others." The judge considered that

> there are other powerful competing interests which must be recognized, not the least of which, in addition to the best interests of the children are the freedoms of expression and religion of the children themselves. There is cogent, persuasive evidence, found credible by the trial judge, that the children themselves do not want to discuss religion with their father or be subject to his comments about beliefs which are at odds with their own religious upbringing, whether they take the form of indoctrination, instruction or mere observation. Indeed, the letters written to the trial judge disclose that, not only do they not want it, but also that the prospect of such discussions has so profoundly disturbed the children and coloured the periods of access that they no longer wish to continue to see the respondent according to a schedule.

The difficulty with taking into account the rights of children, however, is that children are not parties to the proceeding, and generally are not represented in custody and access hearings. The "rights" of children, particularly a child's right to access, are regularly deployed by judges in their reasons for judgment and by parties in support of their own claims, but children are not given an opportunity to define their interests for themselves.

Even if the parent's rights are not privileged over the interests of the child, it is problematic that a child is not represented in contested proceedings of this kind, but perhaps justifiable within the logic of a welfarist framework, where the child's interests are defined by others but given priority. When the project of protecting the best interests of the child is displaced by that of protecting the *Charter* rights of the parent, however, the child should be permitted representation. Further, as we develop the notion of children as rights-bearing individuals, able, or potentially able, to define their interests for themselves, the opportunities for children to have representation in legal proceedings that profoundly affect their lives must necessarily be expanded. ...

Authority of the Custodial Parent and the Right to Maximum Access

McLachlin J interpreted the best interests of the child test in light of the policy of favouring extensive access and of allowing the child to know fully both parents, and noted that the policy has been legislatively enshrined in s. 16(10) of the *Divorce Act*. Her Ladyship said, "Parliament has expressed its opinion that contact with each parent is valuable, and that the judge should ensure that this contact is maximized. ... To the extent that contact conflicts with the best interests of the child, it may be restricted. But only to that extent." Sopinka J made the additional point that the *Charter* rights of the access parent also support an interpretation of the best interests of the child test in light of the policy of extensive access.

Taking the strong policy favouring access as a starting point, McLachlin J said that "the proposition, put to us in argument, that the custodial parent should have the right to forbid certain types of contact between the access parent and the child, must fail." ...

McLachlin J's introduction of harm as a factor to consider when determining the best interests of the child shows the power of s. 16(10) of the *Divorce Act*. Though stating that the best interests of the child is the only test, the *Divorce Act*, s. 16(10) apparently privileges one factor, the value of contact with the non-custodial parent, despite the fact that the value of contact is only one of many factors to consider and will not always be the most important or decisive consideration. Section 16(10) led McLachlin J to interpret the best interests of the child in light of a presumptive benefit of unrestricted access, and to reason that in some cases the presumption may not be displaced unless there is evidence of harm or a risk of harm. This is incorrect. The general value of unrestricted access is widely recognized, but, despite s. 16(10), it has not yet been promoted to a presumptive benefit that should displace the best interests test, and in my view it should not be. If unrestricted access truly is beneficial to a child, then the best interests test will support it. If it is not in the best interests of the child, taking into account the benefits of access and all other factors, but does not reach the harm threshold proposed by McLachlin J, the best interests should govern the outcome.

L'Heureux-Dubé J disagreed with McLachlin J's approach, objecting to the introduction of a harm test to the interpretation of the best interests of the child. She said, "[t]he best interests of the child is not simply the right to be free of demonstrable harm, it is the positive right to the best possible arrangements in the circumstances of the parties." She stressed the obligation of the legal system to minimize the adverse effects of divorce on children, and said that this "requires a vision of the best interests of the child that is more than neutral to the conditions under which custody and access occur. The harm test clearly cannot meet this objective." Furthermore, she said, the harm test purports to further the best interests of the child by promoting unfettered contact with the non-custodial parent, but "in reality the test subordinates the best interests of children to a presumptive right of the non-custodial parent to unrestricted access."

Also on the issue of the interest of the child in knowing the access parent, L'Heureux-Dubé J stated that restrictions on access do not necessarily prevent children from knowing the access parent in a meaningful way, and that unrestricted access may lead to the deterioration or even the ultimate destruction of the relationship.

While L'Heureux-Dubé J agreed that "maximum contact between the child and the non-custodial parent is a worthwhile goal," she did not stress this factor in her interpretation of the best interests of the child, as did McLachlin J. Rather L'Heureux-Dubé J emphasized the importance of minimizing conflict between parents that adversely affects the child, on the grounds that such conflict "is the single factor which has consistently proven to be severely detrimental to children upon separation or divorce." ...

L'Heureux-Dubé J argued against the trend of increasing the authority of the access parent, pointing out that the *Divorce Act* "neither suggests nor requires the division of parental responsibilities between the custodial parent and the access parent." She linked such an increase in authority with joint custody:

> The arguments in favour of increased authority over the child by the access parent are closely related to those which support a presumption in favour of joint custody. ... They rest on the premise that the relationship of authority and obligation that existed between each of the parents and the child during the marriage should and can continue despite the fact that the parents may no longer be willing or able to cooperate on its exercise.

She argued against joint custody orders on the grounds that in the few custody cases that end up in court, parents generally do not have the requisite willingness to cooperate in child-rearing. Further, she noted that in considering joint custody or access orders, courts should be mindful of that gap between the ideals of shared parenting and the reality that "men as a group have not yet embraced responsibility for childcare," and that women most often bear that responsibility before and after divorce, even if joint custody is ordered. This responsibility includes "increased social, economic and emotional burdens that far exceed those of the intact family." ...

Even more problematic is the fact that a "vast number of non-custodial parents are in default of their most serious obligations to their children, as is [Mr. Young]: the responsibility to provide economic support." Her Ladyship concluded: "There is a certain irony in the claim to greater contact and control on the part of access parents in the face of such widespread neglect of children's basic needs."

L'Heureux-Dubé J argued against greater authority for the access parent on the basis of specific problems faced by custodial mothers and their children. It is not clear, however, that maintaining an authoritative role for the custodial parent and a relatively powerless role for the access parent will address the problems identified or lead to more equitable results. The problem of "deadbeat dads" who default on their child support obligations can probably best be solved by better support enforcement. The problem of "disappearing dads" who do not remain emotionally involved with their children is not likely to be changed by maintaining a restricted definition of access, and may be attenuated by a reformulation of the access role. In reformulating Canada's custody and access law, the trend towards providing for continuing equal parental responsibility for both parents following divorce or separation will have to be seriously considered.

Should disappearing and deadbeat dads be wooed with an enhanced legal role when they have not demonstrated commitment to their children? There is certainly an irony here, and it does seem unfair to diminish the authority of the mother who bears the burden of childcare in order to enhance the role of the father who has contributed relatively little. As L'Heureux-Dubé J pointed out, however, it is not only some access fathers who are seeking a more significant role: many custodial mothers want fathers to be more involved. Rather than massaging the irony of enhancing the role of the access parent, then, it may be more helpful to consider the evidence as to whether an enhanced role for the access parent would alleviate the disappearing dad syndrome without exacerbating other problems. ...

Regardless of the respective roles of custodial and access parent addressed so extensively by L'Heureux-Dubé J, the current law does allow for challenges by the access parent to decisions taken by the custodial parent, and it allows custodial parents to seek restrictions on access. In both cases, the best interests of the child is the relevant criterion, and the authority of the custodial parent is not the issue. There is a relationship between the child's interests and the custodial parent's authority, because the parent's ability to function effectively may be diminished if the authority of the role is reduced and the access parent is permitted to challenge child-rearing decisions. But this is only one factor to consider in coming to a determination of what is in the best interests of the child. In her consideration of this issue, L'Heureux-Dubé J perhaps went too far in identifying the best interests of the child with maintenance of the custodial parent's authority. ...

McLachlin J interpreted the best interests of the child test in light of a presumptive benefit of unrestricted access; L'Heureux-Dubé J in light of a presumptive deference to the custodial parent. The presumptive benefit of access, the more ascendant view, is problematic when it displaces the best interests of the child with a harm test and leads some courts to give insufficient consideration to detrimental aspects of access. The presumptive deference to the custodial parent is problematic because it gives too little weight to concerns of the access parent that may be valid and may inhibit involvement by the access parent. The best interests of the child is the sole test and should be addressed directly, taking into consideration all relevant factors, including the benefits of access and the value of supporting the custodial parent.

Conflicting Beliefs Not Necessarily Harmful

Significantly, no member of the Supreme Court of Canada took [the] view that conflicting religious beliefs between parents are necessarily harmful to children or grounds for restricting access. The fact that the parents have differing views and that each is teaching the child about his or her religion is not necessarily contrary to the best interests of the child. The Justices varied, however, in their views on the level of conflict required to justify imposing restrictions on the access parent. Sopinka J, on one end of the continuum, asserted "conflict between parents on many matters including religion is not uncommon, but in itself cannot be assumed to be harmful unless it produces a prolonged acrimonious atmosphere." McLachlin J did not go so far, and correctly pointed out [that] "[c]onflict between parents is, in and of itself, not a sufficient basis for assuming that the child's interests will not be served." Cory and Iacobucci JJ did not refer to "conflict," but said, "[n]either differences of opinions of parents regarding religious questions nor the frank discussion of their differing religious perceptions by both parents with the children will be automatically harmful. Indeed it may often be beneficial."

Discussion Note

Custody, Access, and Religion

In *S. v. S.*, [1997] 3 SCR 1003; 37 RFL (4th) 344, the Supreme Court of Canada allowed in part a mother's appeal regarding restrictions relating to custody of her child. The trial judge in the Quebec court had granted custody to the mother, but ordered her not to bring the child to religious ceremonies, demonstrations, or other reunions of a similar nature. She was also not allowed to bring the child with her for the door-to-door preachings and was prohibited from indoctrinating the child with the precepts of her faith (Seventh-day Adventist). The Quebec Court of Appeal dismissed the appeal by the mother: [1997] RDF 215. The Supreme Court of Canada held (at 345), "we are not satisfied that the best interest of the child has been compromised by the practices of the custodial parent," and allowed the appeal to the extent of "removing the restrictions imposed upon the appellant as regards the activities which she is entitled to do with or in the presence of her child."

In this context, consider *Fruitman v. Fruitman* (1998), 37 RFL (4th) 416 (Ont. Ct. J (Gen. Div.)), where the court refused to restrict the father's authority regarding the religious upbringing of two children in the orthodox Jewish faith. Both parents were orthodox, but the father had begun to live with a non-Jewish woman who had only recently converted to the Jewish faith. The mother of the children was concerned that the father and his new wife might depart from the restrictions applicable to an orthodox Jew (such as travel by automobile on the Sabbath), but the court held that no such restrictions should be ordered. For earlier cases, see *Britton v. Britton* (1991), 37 RFL (3d) 253 (Ont. Ct. J (Gen. Div.)) and *Avitan v. Avitan* (1992), 38 RFL (3d) 382 (Ont. Ct. J (Gen. Div.)).

SELECTED REFERENCES

J. Mucci, "The Effect of Religious Disputes in Child Custody Disputes" (1986), 5 *Canadian Journal of Family Law* 353.

Shauna Van Praagh, "Religion, Custody, and a Child's Identity" (1997), 35:2 *Osgoode Hall Law Journal* 309.

8. Best Interests and Relocation: Balancing the Interests of Custodial and Access Parents

Gordon v. Goertz, [1996] 2 SCR 27

In 1996, the Supreme Court released its decision in *Gordon v. Goertz*, which focused on the best-interests test in the context of a custodial parent's wish to relocate; in this case, the custodial mother wanted to relocate to Australia to pursue educational goals, while the child's father (who had been granted access) remained in western Canada. Writing for the majority, McLachlin J held that it was in the best interest of the child to move to

Australia with her mother, but the Supreme Court removed a lower court requirement that the father's access be exercised only in Australia, thus permitting the father to exercise access in Canada as well: for lower court decisions, see (1993), 111 Sask. R 1 (UFC) and (1995), 128 Sask. R 156 (CA). In its ruling in *Gordon v. Goertz*, the Supreme Court of Canada provided guidelines concerning the principles applicable to relocation by custodial parents in circumstances where such relocation may affect the access parent's contact with the child.

The decision in *Gordon v. Goertz* attempted to provide principles applicable to the relocation of custodial parents in the context of earlier, and somewhat different, approaches in two cases decided by the Ontario Court of Appeal. In *Carter v. Brooks* (1990), 2 OR (3d) 321, the Ontario Court of Appeal became the first appellate court to decisively rule that the custodial parent did not have an inherent "right to move." In *Carter*, the parties had separated shortly after their son's birth, and the child had remained with the mother with the father's approval. Some years later, the mother informed the father that she planned to move from Ontario to British Columbia with her new partner. The father opposed the move and applied to the court for joint custody and an order restraining the mother from removing the child from his current geographic jurisdiction. The trial judge awarded custody to the mother, but held that it was in the child's best interests to live in close proximity to the father and thus restrained the mother from removing the child. The decision was upheld on appeal. Speaking for the court, Morden JA indicated that the sole matter to be considered was the best interests of the child. Morden JA stated that while he was inclined to the view that a "reasonable measure of respect" should be paid to the custodial parent's interests, he was not prepared to formulate a steadfast rule that placed the onus on the non-custodial parent to prove that the move was not in the child's best interests. Therefore, each parent bore an "evidential burden" to demonstrate to the court what was in the child's best interests; in *Carter*, the court held that the mother had not demonstrated that the child's best interests were better served by the move.

Five years later, a different panel of appellate judges took a different approach. In *MacGyver v. Richards* (1995), 22 OR (3d) 481 (CA), Abella JA, writing for the majority of the court, held that courts *must* have deference to the custodial parent's decision to move in all but the most exceptional cases. Here, the mother wished to move with the parties' child to Washington State for four years while her new fiancé, a master corporal in the armed forces, served a four-year service commitment there. The father opposed the move and applied for joint custody and an order preventing the child's relocation.

At trial, the mother was awarded custody but with the stipulation that the child remain in North Bay, Ontario. On appeal, the custody order was upheld but the restriction was lifted—the mother was free to move with the child.

In dismissing the father's appeal from this decision, Abella JA departed from the court's earlier decision in *Carter v. Brooks* in several ways. Significantly, Abella JA noted that the child's relationship with the custodial parent was generally more important to the child than his or her relationship with the non-custodial parent and that courts should "forcefully acknowledge" that the child's best interests and the custodial parent's interests are "inextricably tied" together. Abella JA also stated that courts had wrongly been passing judgment on the "necessity" of the custodial parent's move, and that so long as the parent was acting "responsibly" the reason for the move should not be further questioned. In *MacGyver*, no evidence was presented that the mother was maliciously trying to keep the child from the father and, because the mother was acting responsibly, Abella JA ruled that impairment of the father's relationship with the child was not a sufficient reason to prevent the move.

Thus, in *Gordon v. Goertz*, the Supreme Court was required to review these and other cases involving relocation of a custodial parent. In doing so, the Supreme Court held that a parent who applies to the court to change a custody or access order under the *Divorce Act* must first establish a material change in circumstances affecting the child. Only when this threshold is met should the judge embark on a fresh inquiry into the best interests of the child having regard to all of the relevant circumstances of the case. The focus of the inquiry must be the child's interests and not the interests or rights of the parents involved. McLachlin J rejected the approach of Abella JA in *MacGyver* and instead adopted the approach taken by Morden JA in *Carter*—while the custodial parent's views are entitled to "great respect," the examination of both the initial ruling and any new evidence cannot begin with a presumption in favour of the custodial parent. Instead, both parents bear an evidentiary burden in establishing the child's best interests.

Justice McLachlin also noted that the maximum contact principle in ss. 16(10) and 17(9) of the *Divorce Act* is not absolute and is subject always to the child's best interests. She then set out (at para. 49) seven factors that, *inter alia*, a judge should consider when assessing the best interests of the child:

(a) the existing custody relationship and relationship between the child and custodial parent;

(b) the existing access arrangement and the relationship between the child and the access parent;

(c) the desirability of maximizing contact between the child and both parents;

(d) the views of the child;

(e) the custodial parent's reason for moving *only* in the exceptional case where it is relevant to that parent's ability to meet the child's needs;

(f) disruption to the child of a change in custody; and

(g) disruption to the child consequent on removal from family, schools and community.

Applying the test to the facts in *Gordon v. Goertz*, the court found that the move to Australia amounted to a material change in circumstances as contemplated by s. 17 of the *Divorce Act*—the mother's proposed move to Australia would seriously curtail the frequent and meaningful contact that the father enjoyed with his daughter; and, as the terms of the prior order were premised on the child remaining within a reasonable distance of the father, the move would breach a previous order. However, the court held that although the trial judge failed to give sufficient weight to these factors, when all the factors were now considered together, the judge was correct in continuing custody with the mother despite the mother's intended move. However, the court found that there was nothing to justify the lower court's order restricting Goertz's access to be exercised only in Australia, and instead ordered that the access order be varied to allow access to be exercised in Canada also.

Although agreeing with the majority justices' result, L'Heureux-Dubé J disagreed with the court's stance on the rights of a custodial parent. In her opinion, any restriction on the rights of custodial parents should be the exception, not the rule, and should not be inferred from generous or specified access provisions—instead, specific stipulations must have been included in the court's initial order. According to L'Heureux-Dubé J, an assessment of the whole situation is warranted only where the alleged change is of such a nature or magnitude as to make the original order irrelevant or no longer appropriate. In this situation, the non-custodial parent should bear the onus of showing that the proposed change of residence is not in the child's best interests and that the custody should be varied or that the child should remain in his or her current jurisdiction.

L'Heureux-Dubé J argued that only where there is an agreement or court order that restricts changing the child's residence should the onus shift to the custodial parent to establish that the decision to relocate is not made to undermine access and that he or she is willing to restructure access. She went on to note that the proposed change of residence by a custodial parent will not normally justify a variation in custody. Indeed, a variation of custody should be considered only where the non-custodial parent demonstrates that the best interests of the child will be detrimentally affected by the move *and* that the quality of the non-custodial parent's relationship with the child is of such importance to the child's best interests that prohibiting the change in residence will not cause detriment to the child that is comparable to or greater than that caused by an order to vary custody.

Discussion Notes

The Impact of Gordon v. Goertz

As Boyd noted (at 152), the decision in *Gordon v. Goertz* "reasserted a wide power of judicial decision-making in the custody realm, despite the abundant evidence that judicial discretion often leads to contradictory and sometimes highly problematic results because of the indeterminacy of the best interests test." Commenting on research undertaken by Rollie Thompson on cases concerning relocation decided after *Gordon v. Goertz*, Boyd also noted the impact of the Supreme Court's decision (at 154-55):

> Some commentators have pointed out that the practical effect of the Supreme Court of Canada's ruling is unclear. ... It may well be that deference to some custodial parents will occur, at least where they appear to have carried out their responsibilities properly. ... A few judges have also been able to appreciate that in some instances, such as where a father has abused a mother, frequent contact between father and child is less of a priority. Thompson found that some judges approved moves in cases where the emotional and financial well-being of the caregiver mother would be enhanced in the new location. ... In practice, it appears that in approximately 60 per cent of cases decided since *Goertz*, the move is permitted, returning to the situation after the indeterminate decision in *Carter v. Brooks* and before the deference decision in *MacGyver v. Richards*. However, the moving parent is often required to pick up a proportion of the increased costs of access expenses, either sharing them equally or paying them all; alternatively, the quantum of child or spousal support paid to the custodial parent may be reduced. ... As well, moves are more likely to be denied in cases involving some form of shared custody. ... Moreover, it seems likely that custodial mothers who are able to obtain good legal advice and representation and who propose a clear plan for contact between children and fathers are more likely to be permitted to move. ...

If "reasonable" custodial parents are more likely to be permitted to relocate, a potential problem still arises in the ways that reasonableness and responsibility will be interpreted. ...

Cases decided since *Gordon v. Goertz* also suggest that economic issues and class may influence judicial decision-making. The parties in *Gordon v. Goertz* had sufficient funds to enable contact between father and child despite the considerable geographical distance. The harder question arises when lack of economic resources will inhibit frequent contact with a non-custodial parent. ... Also worrisome is that many cases where relocation is disputed likely never make their way to court, particularly if finances are limited.

For further details of Thompson's analysis of the impact of *Gordon v. Goertz*, see D.A. Rollie Thompson, "Relocation and Relitigation: After Gordon v. Goertz" (1999), 16:3 *Canadian Family Law Quarterly* 461 and "An Addendum: Twenty Months Later," in Harold Niman and Gerald P. Sadvari, eds., *Special Lectures of the Law Society of Upper Canada 2000— Family Law:"Best Interests of the Child"* (Toronto: Law Society of Upper Canada, 2001), 352.

In considering these issues, examine two post-*Gordon v. Goertz* decisions. In *Woodhouse v. Woodhouse* (1996), 29 OR (3d) 417, for example, the Ontario Court of Appeal refused to allow the mother to relocate to her new husband's native Scotland with the parties' children. At trial, the court accepted an independent assessor's findings that while the best interests of the mother and her new husband would be to live in Scotland, it was not in the children's best interests because the move would make it impossible for the children to maintain a meaningful relationship with their father. Although the mother proposed a schedule of five yearly visits, including a month in the summer, in Canada, the court held that the scheme did not provide for reasonable, frequent access and could only be implemented at great financial expense to the father.

In applying the test in *Gordon v. Goertz*, the Court of Appeal found that the trial judge's findings represented no error to justify overturning the lower court's decision—in keeping with the Supreme Court's decision, the custodial parent's interests were not given an automatic preference; the proposed move represented a material change in circumstance; and there was no indication that the children's best interests would be better served by moving to Scotland rather than staying in Ontario. In considering the facts of the case, the court also examined the financial and economic results of the family moving to Scotland versus staying in Ontario and concluded that the family income would be about the same regardless of residence. With respect to the effect of the move on the children, the court found that to move the children would be more disruptive for them than to remain in Ontario. In coming to its decision, the court also expressed concern about whether the mother would comply with an Ontario order for access, given her previous decision to stay in Scotland with the children beyond an agreed period.

Osbourne JA, dissenting, took the view that the trial judge focused too heavily on the assessor's report and had proceeded on a general assumption that there was a positive correlation between the frequency of access and the best interests of the children in all cases. By doing so, the best interests of the children in *this* case were not fully considered. The Supreme Court of Canada, L'Heureux-Dubé J dissenting, refused leave to appeal: (1997), 99 OAC 80; 209 NR 80 (SCC).

Luckhurst v. Luckhurst (1996), 20 RFL (4th) 373 was released concurrently with *Woodhouse*, and the Ontario Court of Appeal again applied *Gordon v. Goertz*; this time, however, the Court of Appeal upheld the trial judge's decision allowing the mother to move with the children. Upon the parties' separation they had agreed that they would share joint custody of their two children although the children's primary residence was with their mother. The mother entered into a new relationship and began cohabiting with her new partner. They later had a child together. The new partner, unable to obtain secure employment in London, found a job in Cobourg, and the mother applied for an order allowing her to move with her children to Cobourg. In her application for relocation, she stated that she was willing to drive the children to a halfway point in order to assist the father's access. In response, the father brought a cross-application for custody. The Court of Appeal upheld the trial judge's decision to award custody to the mother without a limitation on the children's residence. In reaching its decision, the court followed the decision in *Gordon v. Goertz*, noting that the children would still be able to see their father regularly and, while access would be exercised at some inconvenience to the father, the mother was willing to make reasonable arrangements to assist in the preservation of the quality of the relationship between the father and the children.

In the context of these two decisions, do you agree with the assessment of Thompson and Boyd with respect to the impact of *Gordon v. Goertz*? To what extent is there a need for legislative reform? You may want to reconsider these issues after reviewing the reform proposals at the end of this section.

Reassessing the Principles of Gordon v. Goertz

In assessing the principles adopted by the Supreme Court of Canada in *Gordon v. Goertz*, consider the conclusions of two academic researchers: M. Bailey and M. Giroux, *Relocation of Custodial Parents* (Ottawa: Status of Women Canada, 1998). According to their executive summary (at iii-iv):

> Attention to the issues that arise when a custodial parent plans to relocate with his or her child(ren) has increased in recent years. This is because high divorce rates and increased mobility have generated a significant number of these cases, patterns of post-divorce parenting have changed, and conflicting policy goals have left uncertainty as to the correct emphasis in relocation disputes. In the case of proposed relocations that will hinder access, a conflict arises between the goal of maintaining frequent and continuing contact with both parents and that of maintaining stability in the child's relationship with the custodial parent.
>
> Some countries have abandoned the traditional custody/access model which has been maintained in all the Canadian provinces (except Quebec). They favour instead a continuing shared parental responsibility model, under which both parents remain involved in decision-making after separation. A similar model has also been adopted in Quebec. In jurisdictions where a continuing shared parental responsibility model has been adopted, however, debate on the issue of relocation has been similar to that in Canada. Neither the traditional custody/access model maintained in Canada, nor any form of the continuing shared parental responsibility model adopted in Quebec or elsewhere, eliminates problems relating to relocation, or even provides obvious answers to them.
>
> Relocation disputes are governed by the best interests of the child test. Some have argued in favour of adopting a presumption that the custodial parent's relocation plans are

in the best interests of the child. Any such presumption would undermine the best interests of the child standard and should not be adopted. In determining the best interests of the child, however, careful attention should be given to the potential negative effect on the child should the custodial parent be restricted from relocating. The relative importance of maintaining frequent and continuing contact with both parents should also not be over-emphasized in relocation disputes. Social science evidence indicates that other factors—specifically, a well-functioning custodial parent and avoidance of parental conflict—are also linked with positive outcomes for children. There is no evidence to support giving priority to maintaining frequent and continuing contact with both parents in cases of conflict.

Canada's law on relocation is set out in the *Divorce Act* as interpreted by the Supreme Court of Canada's decision in *Gordon v. Goertz*. The basic rule that relocation disputes should be governed by the best interests of the child should be maintained. Aspects of the current law that should be maintained or emphasized, and recommendations for amendments that would clarify or improve the operation of the law, are outlined below.

Summary of Recommendations

1. Although the term "mobility rights" has been used widely in Canada, it is preferable to use the term "relocation" to refer to the issues that arise when custodial parents wish to relocate with their children. The mobility rights of each parent and the child are protected by the *Canadian Charter of Rights and Freedoms* and by international conventions. These rights, however, are subject to the best interests of the child. The term "relocation" better captures the broader issues at stake, including the rights and interests of the child, the custodial parent and the access parent.
2. Relocation disputes should continue to be governed by the best interests of the child; there should be no legal presumption either for or against relocations.
3. The wishes of the child should be given careful attention in determining the child's best interests, provided the child is old enough to express those wishes. The weight given to the wishes of the child should increase with the maturity of the child. It will normally be in the best interests of the child to give effect to the wishes of a mature adolescent.
4. In determining the best interests of the child, the following should be considered: the particular economic challenges faced by custodial parents, most of whom are women; the advantages to the child of supporting the decisions of the custodial parent; and the negative impact on the child of restricting relocation.
5. Subsections 16(10) and 17(9) of the *Divorce Act* should be amended to reflect the fact that continuing contact with each parent is only one factor associated with positive outcomes for children. Other factors—specifically, a well-functioning custodial parent and avoidance of parental conflict—are also associated with positive outcomes for children. No one factor should be given primacy in the legislation.
6. Social scientists should be supported in continuing research on the effect of various post-separation arrangements on children. Social science evidence that identifies factors generally associated with positive outcomes for children is helpful in determining the best interests of the child. It should not be used selectively, however, to support presumptions or "sub-rules" in determining the best interests of the child.
7. The rules governing which parent must commence proceedings should be clarified, specifically, whether the custodial parent should be obliged to obtain a variation of the

terms of access prior to moving in the absence of a non-removal order. If there is no general requirement to this effect, Canada's law should be amended to require custodial parents to give notice of a proposed move to the other parent or to the court. The custodial parent should also be required to propose new arrangements for access. The notice requirement should provide for exceptions in cases where it would create a risk of domestic violence.

8. Courts have the option of a) allowing a custodial parent to move; b) transferring custody to the access parent; or c) issuing a non-removal order to preserve the *status quo*. Non-removal orders have a particularly negative impact on the rights and freedoms of the custodial parent. Such orders should not be granted lightly, but should remain an option for the exceptional cases where such an order will serve the best interests of the child.

9. The Supreme Court of Canada has said that the custodial parent's reasons for moving are a relevant consideration only in exceptional cases where the reasons go to the parent's ability to meet the needs of the child. In most cases, however, the reasons for the move will be relevant to the best interests of the child determination (e.g., when the move is to take a better job or to join a new spouse). While custodial parents should not be subject to a special onus to prove that a move is necessary, the reasons behind the move should be considered as they affect the best interests of the child.

10. Education programs on the effects of parental divorce and separation and alternative dispute resolution mechanisms (particularly mediation) on children should be made available and encouraged in order to promote responsible agreements on child custody and access.

SELECTED REFERENCES

Susan B. Boyd, "Child Custody, Relocation, and the Post-Divorce Family Unit: Gordon v. Goertz at the Supreme Court of Canada" (1997), 9:2 *Canadian Journal of Women and the Law* 447.

Carol S. Bruch and Janet M. Bowermaster, "The Relocation of Children and Custodial Parents: Public Policy, Past and Present" (1996), 30:2 *Family Law Quarterly* 245.

Christine Davies, "Mobility Rights and Child Custody: A Contradiction in Terms?" (1997), 15 *Canadian Family Law Quarterly* 115.

D.A. Rollie Thompson, "'Beam Us Up Scotty': Parents and Children on the Trek" (1995-96), 13 *Canadian Family Law Quarterly* 219.

Judith S. Wallerstein and Tony J. Tanke, "Psychological and Legal Considerations in the Relocation of Children Following Divorce" (1996), 30:2 *Family Law Quarterly* 305.

Convention on the Civil Aspects of International Child Abduction (The Hague Convention)

The Convention on the Civil Aspects of International Child Abduction attempts to provide a systematic procedure for dealing with children when their parents separate and one parent (without judicial authorization) removes them from their ordinary jurisdiction of residence, commencing custody proceedings in another jurisdiction. In *Parsons v. Styger* (1989), 67 OR (2d) 1 (SC), for example, the court examined provisions of the Convention (often included as a schedule to provincial statutes such as Ontario's *Children's Law Reform Act*) to decide upon the rights to custody of a 21-month-old boy, where the father resided in California and the mother had moved with the child to Ontario. In this case, the court concluded that the child (and the child's mother) should return to California.

In *Thomson v. Thomson* (1994), 6 RFL (4th) 290, the Supreme Court of Canada reviewed a complex matter of custody pursuant to the Convention and ordered that the mother return the child (from her home in Manitoba) to Scotland, where the father had (before the child's removal to Manitoba) obtained a custody order. The Alberta Court of Appeal also reviewed the application of the Hague Convention in *Hoge v. Hoge* (1995), 10 RFL (4th) 1: see also Vaughan Black and Christopher Jones, "Case Comment on Thomson v. Thomson" (1994-95), 9 *Canadian Family Law Quarterly* 321.

In *Kinnersley-Turner v. Kinnersley-Turner* (1997), 24 RFL (4th) 252 (Ont. CA), the court dismissed the mother's appeal from the trial decision ordering her to return her child to England. Following the mother's and father's divorce, the mother was granted custody and the father was awarded access. The custody order permitted the mother to move to Canada, but it contained an undertaking by the mother to return the child to England if called upon to do so. The mother and child lived off and on between Canada and England for a few years, but during a time in England, the father decided that the mother was unfit and applied for custody. Without notice to the father or to the court, the mother returned to Canada, with the child, stating to her solicitor that she did not wish the father to have further access to the child. Upon the father's application to have the child returned, pursuant to the Hague Convention, the English court so ordered. The Ontario court agreed that the mother, pursuant to the Convention, was obliged to return the child to England. See also *Medhurst v. Markle* (1996), 17 RFL (4th) 428 (Ont. Ct. J (Gen. Div.)); *Morris v. Nevins* (1997), 24 RFL (4th) 275 (Ont. Ct. J (Gen. Div.)); and *F.(P.) v. F.(S.)* (1997), 29 RFL (4th) 59 (Ont. Ct. J (Gen. Div.)). For a comprehensive recent examination of the Hague Convention, see *Rechsteiner v. Kendall* (1998), 39 RFL (4th) 127 (Ont. Ct. J (Gen. Div.)) and the appeal, at (1999), 1 RFL (5th) 101 (Ont. CA).

In a number of recent cases, however, the interpretation of the Convention has been complicated by issues about violence, usually raised by mothers as a justification for removal of children from their usual jurisdiction of residence. Examine the court's reasoning in the following appellate decision—to what extent does the Convention permit an examination of issues of violence or abuse in its implementation? How are these principles different from those enunciated in *Gordon v. Goertz*? What difference does it make whether a parent seeks an order for relocation or simply departs the jurisdiction with a child? How should these legal issues be resolved?

Finizio v. Scoppio-Finizio
(1999), 1 RFL (5th) 222; 46 OR (3d) 226 (CA)

[The parties married and resided in Italy with their two children. The husband was an Italian national with landed immigrant status in Canada. The wife was born in Italy and emigrated to Canada, but later worked in Italy. The children held dual citizenship and were fully bilingual. After the parties separated in 1998, the wife claimed that her husband physically assaulted her. She left Italy with the two children and came to Toronto, the home of her parents. The husband brought an application in Ontario under the Convention. The trial judge held that the removal of the children was wrongful, but that it was not appropriate to make an order for their return because to do so "would place them in an inherently intolerable situation" and expose them to "grave risk of psychological harm."

In the Court of Appeal, there were competing submissions as to the requirements of the law of custody of separated, but not divorced, spouses. The appellate court agreed with the trial judge, in the light of evidence submitted by the central authority charged with the administration of the Convention in Italy, that the father had standing to challenge the wife's removal of the children. Thus, according to s. 12 of the Convention, the Ontario court was mandated to return the children to Italy. However, s. 12 is subject to the exceptions set out in s. 13. The Court of Appeal reviewed the trial judge's analysis of s. 13 (at 227):]

Article 12 does not provide an absolute rule of return. There are some circumstances in which a court can refuse to make a return order. These circumstances are set out in Article 13 which provides in relevant parts:

Article 13

Despite the provisions of the preceding Article, the judicial or administrative authority of the requested State is not bound to order the return of the child if the person, institution or other body which opposed its return establishes that: ...

(b) there is a grave risk that his or her return would expose the child to physical or psychological harm or otherwise place the child in an intolerable situation.

Before Paisley J the wife contended that Article 13(b) governed her situation. Paisley J agreed with her submission. He reasoned, at pp. 4-5:

I am satisfied that there is credible evidence that the wife has been subjected to an assault causing her bodily harm, that the assault took place within the home where the children were residing with their mother, that no safeguard was put in place for the protection of the mother by the judicial system of Italy prior to her departure, although she had reported her complaint to the police and supported that complaint with medical records, and that she has a well founded and credible fear for the safety of herself and the well-being of her children as a result. The children are infants, and it would be intolerable for them to be forced to return to Italy without their mother. It is a matter of common sense that returning these children to a violent environment would place them in an inherently intolerable situation as well as exposing them to a grave risk of psychological harm. The respondent has satisfied the onus of establishing that the children should not be ordered to return to Italy pursuant to Article 13(b) of the Convention.

The assault to which Paisley J refers in this passage is one which the wife alleges took place at her parents' summer home in Italy on November 17, 1998. The wife states that her husband punched her in the face. Her claim is supported by her mother, Michelina Luzopone, who was present at the summer home on that date. In her affidavit Ms. Luzopone states:

4. I was present on November 17, 1998, when my son-in-law Giampiero came over to my summer home to pick up some more of his belongings. He went to the garage with my daughter Grazia. I could hear Giampiero's raised voice from the house. When I went to investigate, I saw Grazia on the floor with her hand on the side of her face. It was apparent to me that Giampiero struck Grazia. I told Giampiero to leave. I immediately took Grazia to the hospital in Bitonto. She was extremely upset and was crying. Subsequently there were bruises on the side of her face.

The husband denies that the assault took place. The wife did not file any medical report to support her claim. She did file a copy of a report she made to the police on November 17, 1998. However, it is a standard police report; it simply records what the wife says happened.

In spite of the sparse record, I see no reason to question Paisley J's conclusion that there is "credible evidence" that an assault took place. The question which flows from this factual finding is whether it was sufficient to justify Paisley J's invocation of Article 13(b) of the Convention as the basis for an order refusing the return of the children to Italy.

It seems to me that this question must be addressed in light of what the Supreme Court of Canada said in *Thomson v. Thomson, supra.* In that case a Scottish court made an interim order for custody in favour of the mother. However, the court also ordered that the child was to remain in Scotland until further court order. The mother disobeyed the order and took the child to Manitoba.

In arriving at its decision to order the return of the child to Scotland, the Supreme Court conducted an extensive study of the Convention and set out the general principles governing its interpretation by Canadian courts. With respect to Article 13(b) La Forest J stated, at pp. 596-97:

> It has been generally accepted that the Convention mandates a more stringent test than that advanced by the appellant. In brief, although the word "grave" modifies "risk" and not "harm," this must be read in conjunction with the clause "*or otherwise* place the child in an intolerable situation." The use of the word "otherwise" points inescapably to the conclusion that the physical or psychological harm contemplated by the first clause of art. 13(b) is harm to a degree that also amounts to an intolerable situation … .
> In *Re A. (A Minor) (Abduction)* … [[1988] 1 FLR 365 (Eng. CA)], Nourse LJ, in my view correctly, expressed the approach that should be taken, at p. 372:
>
> > … [T]he risk has to be more than an ordinary risk, or something greater than would normally be expected on taking a child away from one parent and passing him to another. I agree … that not only must the risk be a weighty one, but that it must be one of substantial, and not trivial, psychological harm. That, as it seems to me, is the effect of the words "or otherwise place the child in an intolerable situation."

Does the situation faced by the wife in Italy in the late fall of 1998 come within this description of Article 13(b) of the Convention? In my view, it does not. I reach this conclusion for several reasons.

First, there is no evidence that the husband has ever done anything to harm the children. The wife makes no allegation that he has ever struck the children or otherwise abused them in any way. On this point, the fact that the father continued to visit the children after the alleged assault on November 17, 1998 indicates that the wife does not fear that contact between the husband and children will be detrimental to the children.

Second, the alleged single incident of assault at the summer home in Italy is, even on the wife's evidence, the only incident of a physical altercation between the spouses in their eight-year marriage.

I think there is no question that in certain circumstances a physical attack on a mother could cause psychological harm to children. Indeed, this court said as much recently in *Pollastro v. Pollastro* (1999), 43 OR (3d) 485 (Ont. CA). However, the situation in the Finizio/Scoppio-Finizio family is far removed from the terrifying situation chronicled by Abella JA in *Pollastro*.

In his reasons Paisley J said that "no safeguard was put in place for the protection of the mother by the judicial system of Italy prior to her departure" (Reasons, at p. 4). With respect, I do not think that this is a fair criticism of the Italian judicial system. With respect, to the courts, it needs to be emphasized that the wife took *no* steps to raise issues of support or custody in the Italian courts before removing the children to Canada. Accordingly, there was simply no role the Italian courts could play.

Third, there is simply no basis for suggesting that the Italian courts are not well-suited to deal with matrimonial issues, including support, custody and access. I agree with Jennings J who said in *Medhurst v. Markle* (1995), 17 RFL (4th) 428 (Ont. Gen. Div.), at 432:

> It is to be presumed that the courts of another Contracting State are equipped to make, and will make, suitable arrangements for the child's welfare.

The English courts have taken a similar position on this issue. In *C. v. C.*, [1987] 1 WLR 654 (Australia CA), at 664, Lord Donaldson of Lymington MR said:

> It will be the concern of the court of the State to which the child is to be returned to minimize or eliminate this harm and, in the absence of compelling evidence to the contrary or evidence that it is beyond the powers of those courts in the circumstances of the case, the courts of this country should assume that this will be done. Save in an exceptional case, our concern, i.e. the concern of these courts, should be limited to giving the child the maximum possible protection until the courts of the other country— Australia in this case—can resume their normal role in relation to the child.

Fourth, in *Thomson v. Thomson, supra*, the Supreme Court of Canada indicated that Canadian courts can impose undertakings on parties to deal with the transition period between the time when a Canadian court makes a return order and the time at which the children are placed before the courts in the country of their habitual residence. As expressed by La Forest J at p. 599:

> Through the use of undertakings, the requirement in Article 12 of the convention that "the authority concerned shall order the return of the child forthwith" can be complied with, the wrongful actions of the removing party are not condoned, the long-term best interests of the child are left for a determination by the court of the child's habitual residence, and any short-term harm to the child is ameliorated.

It does not appear that the parties addressed the question of undertakings before Paisley J. In my view, this is an important factor which counsel should place squarely before a judge hearing a Convention application. The strong language of the Convention, coupled with what I view as the height of the bar set by the Supreme Court in *Thomson v. Thomson*, will inevitably result in many children being returned to the country from which they have been wrongfully removed. Given that prospect, both counsel should be prepared to deal fully with the issue of *how* the children are to be returned, and to do so before the judge hearing the initial Convention application.

In this case, the wife raised this issue on the appeal and it was addressed by both counsel in their oral submissions. The wife made this submission in her factum:

> 51. ... [T]he Respondent mother requests that this court order the husband to undertake to provide the following:
>
> (1) the husband should provide airline tickets for the wife and children,
> (2) the husband should provide suitable housing that approximates the accommodation the parties enjoyed prior to separation for the wife and children exclusively,
> (3) the husband should pay a lump sum of $35,000 Cdn. as prepaid support for six months,
> (4) the husband should be ordered to refrain from annoying, harassing or molesting the wife, despite the limits of the jurisdiction of the Ontario Court.

Before this court, the husband agreed to the first and second undertakings. He also agreed to the fourth undertaking, with the caveat that he was not admitting that he had engaged in such conduct in Italy. With respect to the third undertaking, the husband pointed out that on May 5, 1999 he filed a Petition/Claim for Judicial Separation in the court in Bari, Italy. This petition places the issue of the custody of the children before the Italian court. The matter will come before the court on October 20, 1999. In light of this schedule, the husband undertook to pay the wife $5,000 immediately to assist her and the children upon their return to Italy and to pay a further $5,000 on October 20, 1999 if for some reason the Italian court has not heard his application. Bearing in mind that when the wife returned to Canada she brought with her approximately $200,000 which had been designated for the purchase of a new home, the husband's undertaking to provide $10,000 as interim support strikes me as fair.

For these reasons, it has not been established that the return of the children to Italy would constitute a "weighty risk of substantial harm" to the children.

I conclude with a final observation. In *Droit de la famille—1763* ... [[1996] 2 SCR 108]], L'Heureux-Dubé J engaged in an extensive analysis of the Convention and of the Quebec statute implementing the Convention in that jurisdiction. She stated, at pp. 135-36:

> The automatic return procedure implemented by the Act is ultimately intended to deter the abduction of children by depriving fugitive parents of any possibility of having their custody of the children recognized in the country and thereby legitimizing the situation for which they are responsible. To that end, the Act favours the restoration of the *status quo* as soon as possible after the removal of the child by enabling one party to force the other to submit to the jurisdiction of the court of the child's habitual place of

residence for the purpose of arguing the merits of any custody issue. The Act, like the Convention, presumes that the interests of children who have been wrongfully removed are ordinarily better served by immediately repatriating them to their original jurisdiction, where the merits of custody should have been determined before their removal.

In my view, this is a clear and powerful articulation of the philosophy and implications of *The Hague Convention on the Civil Aspects of International Child Abduction*. In the present appeal, a proper reading of the Convention, and of the decisions of the Supreme Court of Canada in *Thomson v. Thomson* and *Droit de la famille— 1763*, requires that the Finizio children return almost immediately to Italy, the country of their birth and of their habitual residence until they were wrongfully removed.

SELECTED REFERENCES

Martha Bailey, "The Right of a Non-Custodial Parent to an Order for Return of a Child Under the Hague Convention" (1996), 13 *Canadian Journal of Family Law* 287.

V. Black, "Statutory Confusion in International Child Custody Disputes" (1992-93), 10 *Canadian Family Law Quarterly* 279.

C. Davies, "The Enforcement of Custody Orders: Current Developments," in Katherine Connell-Thouez and Bartha Maria Knoppers, eds., *Contemporary Trends in Family Law: A National Perspective* (Scarborough, ON: Carswell, 1984), 125.

Andrea Himel, "Parents Stealing Kids: Part I—A Canadian Perspective on the Legal and Social Problem of Child Abduction" (2000), 18 *Canadian Family Law Quarterly* 225.

George Steward, "Interpreting the Child's Right to Identity in the UN Convention" (1992-93), 26 *Family Law Quarterly* 221.

9. Best Interests, Access, and Allegations of Abuse

The issue of parental access in the context of allegations of child abuse presents difficult issues of proof and judgment for courts. In 1992, the Ontario Court of Appeal dismissed an appeal (with one dissent) by a father from a trial decision cancelling access to the father, even though the court also found that the mother had not proved her allegations of sex abuse in relation to their daughter. In part, the majority (Abella and Tarnopolsky JJA) reached their conclusion on the ground that there should be a variation of an order only where there has been a material change in circumstances. They concluded that "in the absence of any benefit to the child from continued contact with the father, and based on solid evidence of years of harassment by the father, the judge made no error in terminating the access. ... The father's biological relationship should not be allowed to override the child's welfare": *M.(B.P.) v. M.(B.L.D.E.)* (1992), 42 RFL (3d) 349 (Ont. CA); leave to appeal to the SCC refused (1993), 48 RFL (3d) 232 (SCC).

In *Dinelle v. Sametz* (1994), 7 RFL (4th) 277, the Ontario Court of Justice (General Division) awarded a mother supervised access to her children on condition that she maintain ongoing psychiatric treatment. In *Fullarton v. Fullarton* (1994), 7 RFL (4th) 272 (NBQB), the mother unilaterally terminated the father's access to children (in contempt of an order) where the children had witnessed the father assaulting his wife on many occasions. In these circumstances, the court imposed no sanction on the wife. The relevance of clinical literature about abuse, especially sex abuse, was also addressed in *Young v. Young* (1989), 19 RFL (3rd) 227 (Ont. HCJ).

In *Armstrong v. Kahn* (1998), 33 RFL (4th) 438 (Ont. Ct. J (Gen. Div.)), the parties had joint custody of their one child. The child resided with his mother, and his father had unsupervised access to him. Shortly after this custody agreement was reached, the child began complaining that his father was abusing him; specifically, he complained that his father called him "bad names" and hit him. The boy began to react violently whenever he was scheduled to see his father and his school performance deteriorated. The father had also threatened the mother's life in the child's presence and the child had begun to talk about his own death on a daily basis. The mother applied for sole custody with no access to the father and a restraining order.

Both of the mother's requests were granted. The court found that the father physically, verbally, and emotionally abused the child, who was suffering from post-traumatic stress syndrome as a result of the abuse. The court found that the child's behaviour would further deteriorate if even supervised access was allowed to continue. For another case, in which the court criticized the investigation of allegations of sex abuse, see *T.(M.) v. T.(J.)* (1998), 33 RFL (4th) 430 (Ont. Ct. J (Gen. Div.)).

Discussion Notes

Access to Records

In *Smith v. Smith* (1987), 32 RFL (4th) 361 (Sask. QB), the mother applied for sole custody of the parties' children, claiming that the father was abusive and controlling toward them. The father, in turn, contended that the mother was mentally unstable and had suicidal tendencies. The father applied to the court seeking full disclosure of all clinical notes, results of meetings and attendances, diagnostic services, and consultation and treatment received from all the professionals who had provided counselling to the mother and the parties' children. In his application for the disclosure, the father contended that the disclosure was relevant and necessary for his trial preparations. Specifically, the father claimed that the mother never mentioned abuse to her therapist following separation, that she had sought counselling to improve her own relationship with the parties' children, and that the mother had fabricated the allegations of abuse. The father further contended that he was entitled to be advised of any parenting concerns discussed by the mother with her therapist, and finally that he was also entitled to the information because the therapist was listed as a source of information in the custody and access report. With respect to his request for disclosure from the children's counsellor, the father contended that he was entitled to the information as a joint custodial parent and because the counsellor was listed as a source of information in the custody and access report.

The court relied on the decisions in *M.(A.) v. Ryan*, [1997] 1 SCR 157; 143 DLR (4th) 1 and *Hill v. Church of Scientology of Toronto*, [1995] 2 SCR 1130; 24 OR (3d) 865 in the Supreme Court of Canada to grant the father's application in part. Specifically, the court ordered that the mother's therapist and the Catholic Family Services disclose all clinical notes and/or a typewritten summary of such notes pertaining to the mother. The disclosure was to include the results of all meetings, attendances, diagnostic services, consultations, and treatments received by the mother, including the findings of tests, if any, and any reports prepared or received in relation to the mother. The order, however, was subject to the following four conditions: (1) that the inspection be confined to the father's lawyers and expert witnesses and that the father himself not see them; (2) that any person entitled to see the documents not disclose their contents to anyone not entitled to inspect them; (3) that the documents be used only for the purposes of the custody litigation; and (4) that only one copy be made by the father's lawyers, which could then be passed on to the father's expert witnesses.

With respect to the children's counselling sessions, the court denied the father's request for disclosure, ruling that disclosure would not be in the best interests of the children. The court held that the only record of the children's counselling sessions was to be the summary prepared by the children's therapist (which the therapist advised the court she would prepare and which would be available to both parents) of her findings and recommendations as to what were the best interests of the children. In dismissing the father's application, the court stated that a child is not well-situated to rationalize and comprehend the need for intrusion upon her thoughts and feelings, and that to urge upon children the virtues of counselling only to compel them to divulge their confidences at a later point was a hypocrisy in which the court would not participate.

Access Enforcement

Amendments to the *Children's Law Reform Act* in Ontario were enacted by the provincial legislature several years ago, but they have not been proclaimed in force: see SO 1989, c. 22. The amendments were designed to expedite applications to the courts where parents (mainly fathers) wished to complain about access difficulties.

There have also been some cases in which custodial parents, usually mothers, have been found in contempt and jailed for failing to abide by the terms of access orders. For example, in *L.B. v. R.D.*, [1998] OJ no. 858 (Prov. Div.) (QL), Dunn Prov. J held a mother in contempt for failing to abide by arrangements for court-ordered access and ordered her to be imprisoned for 60 days. On appeal, the term was reduced to 9 days (already served): see (1998), 40 RFL (4th) 134 (Ont. Ct. J (Gen. Div.)).

In *McMillan v. McMillan* (1999), 47 RFL (4th) 173 (Ont. Ct. J (Gen. Div.)), the court reviewed the circumstances of a mother's ongoing actions interfering with the father's access to two children, aged 12 and 14. The mother had been found in contempt previously; on this occasion, the court held that imprisonment for five days was appropriate. The mother was also ordered to pay costs of $2,000. The court stated (at 180):

> I am aware that there is a period of time immediately following the separation of spouses when emotions run high and otherwise sensible people are prone to act like vengeful lunatics. A court order deliberately breached during that delicate time frame may attract the compassion of the court. However, a court order which is wilfully, deliberately and repeatedly breached many years after such compassion can reasonably be expected to extend is an entirely different matter. Such is the situation facing this court. I also note that this case is not an instance where the breach of the court order was well motivated; neither is it an example of an isolated or non-continuing contempt.

> Our system of justice cannot and should not tolerate the deliberate disobedience or defiance of a court order. The protection of the administration of justice requires that such conduct be dealt with appropriately.

Abuse and Assessments

The context of allegations of abuse in child custody proceedings appears to be quite fraught. As Boyd reported (at 126-27), a study conducted by Paula Caplan, a Canadian psychologist, and Jeffery Wilson, a lawyer, for the Law Society of Upper Canada in 1990 revealed some disturbing findings. According to their report, 13 percent of professional assessors who prepared reports for judges neglected to report allegations of sexual abuse by parents. As Boyd concluded (at 126):

> Given that judges accept the recommendations of assessors around 92 per cent of the time, this information was alarming, as was the finding that only 75 per cent of assessors regularly obtained information about the children and their parents from third parties. In other words, assessors may rely as much on personal impressions of the parents as judges do. Indeed, 10.5 per cent of assessors said that their recommendation was "no more reliable than a wager based on the toss of a coin."

Courts have attempted to define the criteria for requesting an assessment and the role of such assessments in decision making about custody and access: for example, see *Linton v. Clarke* (1993), 50 RFL (3d) 8 (Ont. Ct. J (Gen. Div.)), appeal dismissed (1995), 10 RFL (4th) 92 (Ont. Ct. J (Gen. Div.)). In *Levine v. Levine* (1993), 50 RFL (3d) 414 (Ont. Ct. J (Prov. Div.)), the court confirmed that assessments would not be ordered in every case and that, even if an assessment is ordered, it remains the responsibility of the court to decide what is in a child's best interests. In *Delisle v. Delisle* (1998), 43 RFL (4th) 186 (Ont. Ct. J (Prov. Div.)), the court reviewed the role of an assessor, holding that it was beyond the scope of the assessor's role to attempt to mediate disputes between the parties.

In *Marko-Laschowski v. Laschowski* (1999), 44 RFL (4th) 433 (Alta. QB), an Alberta court reviewed the applicable legal principles in relation to an order for an assessment and concluded (at 440):

> While the majority of cases that were cited by counsel are fact-driven, the following principles emerge:
>
> 1. The court has a discretion to order a custody/access assessment where it appears that one would be materially helpful;
> 2. There must be some evidence upon which to base the exercise of such a discretion. The sole consideration is the best interest of the child;
> 3. The custody/assessment is a factor to be considered together with all of the evidence in making that determination; and
> 4. The court must determine what is in the best interests of the child.

In considering the facts in this case, the court confirmed that an assessment should not be ordered automatically and that the applicant has the onus of justifying such a request. In considering the factual situation, however, the court concluded (at paras. 25-26) that it was appropriate to order an assessment in this situation:

Mr. St. Jacques and Mrs. Marko-Laschowski have been separated for almost three years. Mr. St. Jacques has remarried and his wife has a child a few years older than Brodie. Mr. St. Jacques and Mrs. Marko-Laschowski are involved in a highly conflicted situation. Her father was placed on a peace bond after threatening to shoot Mr. St. Jacques. Access has been a problem and continues to be a problem. The police have in the past been involved in enforcing access. The child is dropped off and picked up at a neutral location such as a restaurant or the police station. Each of the parties has accused the other of physically abusing Brodie and each is convinced that they are the better parent. Mr. St. Jacques alleges that Mrs. Marko-Laschowski's father has verbally and physically abused the child. Each alleges that the other is mentally unstable. In the past Mrs. Marko-Laschowski has questioned the child concerning physical injuries that he has sustained while in the care of his father. The child is being drawn into the acrimonious situation that exists between his parents. There have been incidents of violence in front of Brodie. The situation does not appear to have resolved or become less incendiary during the three years since these parties have separated. Custody and access are still hotly disputed. There is significant conflict in the affidavits.

The purpose of an assessment is to identify the needs of the child and to provide information as to which parent is best able to meet those needs. I am satisfied that a home study is required to allow the parties to understand the needs of the child and the need for cooperation.

Hearing Children's Voices: A Need for Legal Representation?

The issue of children's independent representation in custody and access disputes remains problematic. In *Bazinet v. Bazinet* (1998), 42 RFL (4th) 140 (Ont. Ct. J (Gen. Div.)), for example, an Ontario court dismissed the husband's application to appoint the Children's Lawyer to act for the infant children. The court concluded (at 142) that such representation would not assist the court, citing Fleury J in *Reynolds v. Reynolds* (1996), 7 OTC 389 (Gen. Div.):

> This remedy should not be available only for the asking. Inasmuch as it implicates the children very directly in the entire litigation, it is a very blunt instrument indeed. It can cause untold harm to impressionable children who may feel suddenly inappropriately empowered against their parents in a context where the children should be protected as much as possible from the contest being waged over their future care and custody. All actions involving custody and access over children should be governed by one paramount consideration: no one should be allowed to act in a way that might endanger their well-being. The test of "the best interests of the children" as insipid and fluid as it might be still remains the benchmark against which any person wishing to interfere in their lives should be measured.

By contrast, in a lengthy analysis of applicable principles, the court in *H. v. H.* (1999), 48 RFL (4th) 305 (Nfld. UFC) agreed to exercise its *parens patriae* jurisdiction to appoint an *amicus curiae* to be paid for by the Department of Justice. For a classic case on the role of child's counsel, see *Strobridge v. Strobridge* (1994), 4 RFL (4th) 169 (Ont. CA).

In this context, what recommendations are appropriate for reform of issues of custody and access? You may also wish to reconsider these questions in the context of the discussion of Canadian reform proposals at the end of this section.

SELECTED REFERENCES

Nicholas Bala and John Schuman, "Allegations of Sexual Abuse When Parents Have Separated" (1999), 17 *Canadian Family Law Quarterly* 191.

Linda Elrod, "Counsel for the Child in Custody Disputes: The Time Is Now" (1992-93), 26 *Family Law Quarterly* 53.

M.S. Fahn, "Allegations of Child Sexual Abuse in Custody Disputes: Getting to the Truth of the Matter" (1991), 25 *Family Law Quarterly* 193.

J. Melbourne McGraw and Holly A. Smith, "Child Sexual Abuse Allegations Amidst Divorce and Custody Proceedings: Refining the Validation Process" (1992), 1:1 *Journal of Child Sexual Abuse* 49.

Jeffery Wilson, "The Ripple Effect of the Sexual Abuse Allegation and Representation of the Protecting Parent" (1986-87), 1 *Canadian Family Law Quarterly* 159.

L. Zarb, "Allegations of Childhood Sexual Abuse in Custody and Access Disputes" (1994), 12 *Canadian Journal of Family Law* 91.

D. Custody and Care of Children: Joint Custody and Other Options

As noted earlier, traditional legal principles required courts to make orders for custody and access, in accordance with children's best interests. The federal *Divorce Act, 1985* and most provincial statutes reflect these traditional legal categories. However, as Boyd explained (at 120), the federal legislation adopted in the mid-1980s also permitted courts to make orders for joint custody; joint custody awards then began to increase:

> The rising appeal of joint custody during the 1980s is not difficult to understand. Judges became more conscious of the arbitrariness of the adversarial system in divorce ... . At the same time professionals in social work and mediation were redefining divorce as an emotional or therapeutic process rather than a legal one ... . Judges and lawyers, who find custody cases difficult ... , were more than happy to accept guidance from non-legal professionals and to delegate authority to the psy-professions where possible.

Although Canada's divorce legislation did not create a presumption in favour of joint (legal) custody, some judges increasingly regarded it as appropriate unless there were very good reasons for not awarding it, even though the Ontario Court of Appeal had concluded in two cases in 1979 that it was not appropriate to *order* joint custody; it was an arrangement requiring a mutual agreement of the parties: see *Baker v. Baker* (1979), 8 RFL (2d) 236 (Ont. SC (CA)) and *Kruger v. Kruger* (1979), 11 RFL (2d) 52 (Ont. SC (CA)). By the 1980s, however, Boyd reported (at 121) that "joint custody seemed to lend itself to social engineering efforts by judges." Coupled with increasing reliance on mediation and counselling, therefore, joint custody became more frequent, although, as Boyd reported (at 123-24), there is evidence that mothers have continued to have primary responsibility for day-to-day child care.

This section examines some aspects of joint custody and other efforts to define arrangements and responsibilities for children post-divorce or separation.

1. A Clinical Perspective

A. Leonoff, "Joint Custody and Beyond"
(1995), 29(1) *Law Society Gazette* 29, at 35-37

The Choice of Joint Custody

My experience in working with joint custody as an option in divorce is that it works well when one motive in particular dictates its choice—a deep underlying commitment to children and especially the nurturing of children. Those successful joint custody families have parents who uphold co-parenting as a key value. They will intrinsically and automatically show a respect for the worth and contribution of the other parent even if they disagree with certain aspects of their approach or personality. The right of each parent to parent in their allotted time will never be questioned no matter how hurt or upset they are with each other. Typically, examination of the family history will reveal close, genuine relationships to children before and after the separation.

We can conceive of a joint custody continuum beginning with joint legal custody with standard access provisions and ending with joint physical custody including 50/50 sharing. In the latter case, the utmost in co-parenting, parents should reveal the above characteristics to a maximum degree. They should gravitate to shared parenting for the right reason and they should reveal a conspicuous recognition of the other's paren-tal value no matter what the specific fate of their own personal relationship. Commu-nication will be a usual occurrence as compared to being just possible and the parents will reveal some history of problem solving even after the separation occurred.

At the entry level of the joint custody scale, parents should reveal some core aspects of the above but may have certain discordant factors such as lifestyle differences, financial limitations, or parenting conflicts that would not permit a more elaborate shared arrangement. They should still be able to communicate and problem solve when necessary and it should be a choice of the parents or a recommendation that is readily acceptable to both parties.

Amongst these cases of joint legal custody without greatly enhanced access, I would specifically include those parents who assume a non-residential role but whose history of involvement has been substantial. Hence, when joint custody recognizes or acknowledge[s] a non-residential parent's past and ongoing involvement with the children as a primary focus, it is an appropriate option. Some fathers, for example, may well have had major roles in their children's lives while in divorce financial limitations may limit the extent of care they can provide. Joint custody is a way of recognizing that parent's role while not insisting on equal sharing of time and resources. Again, though, this assumes that the other positive factors are also present as well.

As a rule of thumb, I would add that joint custody should always be a specific option in the parents' mind even if they are guided by others towards adopting it. It should not be a choice born of mediation to stave off the worst aspects of divorce or used as a bargaining chip to insure cooperation in settling other issues. We must also guard against promoting joint custody as a palliative against the pain of divorce or the injury of being the NCP [non-custodial parent]. These represent erroneous reasons for selecting this option and they will likely put the family at greater risk of difficulties in the future.

Perhaps it may be helpful, at this juncture, to outline the major contraindications to any form of shared care and control. The presence of any one of these should eliminate the prospect of recommending such an option:

1. When one of the parents, usually the one most likely designated as the primary caretaker, resists or rejects it out of hand;

2. When one or both of the ex-spouses employ to a major degree a psychology of blame. By blaming, I do not include finding fault with the other, for this is natural, but instead, relate to those circumstances where the parent disavows, denies and avoids any sense of personal responsibility and makes the incredible leap to viewing the other in almost intentionally evil terms;

3. When the child rearing premises of both parents are so discordant that the children are unlikely to be able to integrate them. This implicates attitude and character more than it does specific rules or procedures. Children can synthesize differences such as in the case where one home is more rigidly structured by curfews and rules as compared to another that is not so rigorous in applying them. Children would find it harder, however, to negotiate a shared custody if one home valued education while the other did not;

4. When one or both parents exhibit a sense of ownership over the children and negate the importance of the other parent. These are parents who have a tendency to defy the other and act with a haughty indifference to the other's legitimate claims. They are most likely parents who confuse their own needs with those of their children and they insist on an exclusive right to interpret the children's needs and best interests;

5. When parents tend to argue through their children and use child rearing as a field of combat. For example, a parent clashes with the other parent through the child by berating his school performance and blaming it on the mother's lacklustre supervision. Or, when the mother disciplines the son for rudeness while complaining that he is turning out like his father who thinks nothing of denigrating her. These parents seem to interpret their children's negative behaviours always as a result of the negative influence of the other parent;

6. When neither adult is adequate enough as a parent to assume the custodial role on their own. This may seem paradoxical for would not two halves make a whole? Unfortunately what in fact often happens is that both parents flounder while blaming the other. It is preferable to support one of the parents over the other and arrange supplementary and support services to ease the load;

7. When there is evidence of mental illness, personality disorder or severe addiction in one or both parents;

8. When there is hotly contested litigation over custody, shared parenting is most often not an option. Here, I am not referring to those unresolved cases where

the parents, although reasonable, cannot determine what is truly best for their children. These are people who are aware of the complex interactions of their family and are prepared to work matters out with the assistance of a family assessment. When disputes assume an irrational and escalating bent, however, ... joint custody, in any form, will not likely work.

Compare the factors identified by Leonoff to those reflected in the differing judicial approaches in the following cases—what kinds of assumptions underlie judicial approaches to joint custody?

2. Legal Perspectives on Joint Custody

Biamonte v. Biamonte

As noted, courts have expressed different views about whether joint custody should be imposed on reluctant parents or whether it should be available only for parents who choose such an option. A recent example of the latter is *Biamonte v. Biamonte* (1998), 36 RFL (4th) 349 (Ont. Ct. J (Gen. Div.)), where the court examined the ongoing acrimony on the part of the husband toward his former wife. In relation to custody, Fleury J stated (at 359):

> The central issue in these proceedings was the mother's claim for custody and the father's request for an order for joint custody or in the alternative for sole custody. It is obvious that this couple would never survive any order for joint custody. Because the parties are not in agreement as to joint custody, there is no choice on my part but to dismiss the claim for joint custody. (*Kruger v. Kruger* (1979), 25 OR (2d) 673 (Ont. CA).) In mid-trial, Mr. Biamonte asked for permission to amend his pleadings to claim sole custody of the two children, notwithstanding that he had just signed an agreement whereby he had granted sole custody to his wife. Which leads me to examine which of these two parties would be the best parent. There is no doubt in my mind that the wife is a much more concerned and appropriate parent. This is even though she may have associated with Mr. Vattovaz whose past performances leave this court with a somewhat acrid taste in its mouth. But as indicated above, there is no claim by Mr. Vattovaz for custody of the children and his past behaviour should not be looked at with a fine-tooth comb especially where there is no allegation that he might ever be a danger to the children themselves. Mr. Biamonte's main concerns for his children's welfare appeared to be centered on his wife's boyfriend. These concerns, I am satisfied, have more to do with Mr. Biamonte's obsession at trying to control his ex-wife than at a genuine concern for the welfare of his children. Therefore, there will be an order that custody of the children be entrusted to Mrs. Biamonte with access to the children as laid out in the minutes of settlement filed at the start of the proceedings.

By contrast, in the following case, joint custody was awarded—to what extent do you think that the outcomes reflect different factual circumstances or different legal approaches, or both? What are the advantages and disadvantages, to the parties and to the court, in these cases? To what extent do they achieve fairness or encourage litigation?

Mudie v. Post
(1998), 40 RFL (4th) 151; 72 OTC 29 (Gen. Div.)

[In *Mudie v. Post*, Salhany J awarded joint custody in circumstances where an un-married couple were the parents of two young boys; the mother was seeking sole custody. The court stated (at 159):]

Historically, custody battles have been an all or nothing proposition. Sole custody orders have been the norm with access to the non-custodial parent through visitation rights. Such orders have granted legal responsibility and physical control to a single custodial parent to the exclusion of the other. A sole custodial order has given the custodial parent the right to decide where the child will live, how the child will be educated, what religion, if any, the child will adopt and what medical and dental care will be provided. The result has been that the voice of the non-custodial parent in the upbringing of his or her child has been essentially unheard. Any voice of the non-custodial parent in such important decisions affecting the life of "their" child has only been heard where the custodial parent has cared to listen.

I pause to stress the word "their" in reference to the child. It is often forgotten that the child, whatever result the court reaches, is the product of both parents. No decision of the court, no matter how limiting in the access granted to the non-custodial parent, can ever take away the fact that the non-custodial parent is still the parent of that child. It is for that reason that where a sole custody order has been made, the losing parent leaves the courtroom, feeling not only alienated from "their" child, but also alienated from the justice system which has adopted the winner-take-all approach to a custody dispute.

... One of the main arguments advanced by those who believe that legal custody should not be separated from physical custody is that it does not work. My experience, after trying custody cases for almost 20 years, is that it does work and works far better to reduce post-trial applications than a sole custody order. Indeed, the frequent applications that are brought in this Court in this jurisdiction after a sole custody order has been made to enforce an access order has led me to the conclusion that joint custody orders are less subject to ongoing litigation than sole custody orders.

I found that the most insidious impediment to the cooperation of equally competent parents is the question of "who should be in control." Far too often parents are prepared to "battle to the end" and to endure the strain and expense of a custody battle, without recognizing the harmful effects on the child, so that they can have the "last word." This attitude has prevailed even where one parent has recognized that the other parent has a valuable contribution to make to the life of the child. It has been my experience that an order for joint legal custody, with clearly defined times for physical custody, has proved to be more effective in settling the dust of battle. Clearly defined periods of legal and physical custody declare the limits of control which each parent will have over the child. More importantly, they ensure that the child will have unimpeded access to the parent who has legal custody during that defined period. ...

I have come to the conclusion that it is in the best interests of the children in this case that there be a joint custody order. I say that because I am convinced that if sole custody were granted to the respondent, she would continue to obstruct the applicant's attempts to develop a relationship with the children. As I said earlier, it was my distinct impression from her evidence that she would prefer that the applicant be entirely out of her life and the life of the children. I am satisfied that if I were to grant her sole custody, she would make every effort to limit the applicant's contact with the children. In my view, the only practical solution to prevent this is to ensure that she is not given absolute control of the children. Indeed, this is a case where neither should be in absolute control.

For similar decisions of Salhany J, see *Lewis v. Lewis* (1989), 18 RFL (3d) 97 (Ont. Dist. Ct.); *Alfoldi v. Bard* (1989), 20 RFL (3d) 290 (Ont. Dist. Ct.); *Kaemmle v. Jewson* (1993), 50 RFL (3d) 70 (Ont. Ct. J (Gen. Div.)); and *Crawford v. Crawford* (1991), 36 RFL (3d) 337 (Ont. Ct. J (Gen. Div.)). See also *Tacit v. Drost* (1998), 43 RFL (4th) 242 (Ont. Ct. J (Gen. Div.)), where the parties' separation agreement provided for joint custody; the mother's request for sole custody was refused even though the parents' relationship remained acrimonious.

Discussion Notes

The Primary Caregiver Presumption

In considering whether sole custody or joint custody orders are appropriate, some courts in the United States have adopted presumptions as to what arrangement is in a child's best interests. For example, California adopted a joint-custody presumption, while West Virginia adopted a primary-caregiver presumption. In relation to the primary-caregiver presumption, courts were required to determine which parent had primary responsibility for caregiving in the intact family, using a number of defined factors; in most cases, the legal presumption would then require an order for custody for the caregiving parent. In thinking about the role of legal presumptions for deciding child custody arrangements, consider the comments in the following excerpts—to what extent do you agree with the concerns expressed? Is it appropriate to make primary caregiving a legal presumption? Or, should it be an important factor, but not a presumption, in applying the best-interests test?

Susan B. Boyd, "From Gender Specificity to Gender Neutrality? Ideologies in Canadian Child Custody Law"
in Carol Smart and Selma Sevenhuijsen, eds., *Child Custody and the Politics of Gender* (London: Routledge, 1989), 126, at 149-52

In West Virginia, USA, a new means of legally recognizing women's child caring responsibilities has arisen through judicial development of a "primary caretaker presumption." In *Garska v. McCoy* [278 SE 2d 357] (1981), the West Virginia Supreme

Court of Appeals developed the primary caregiver presumption when considering the interaction between new custody legislation which eliminated any gender-based presumption, and a previously binding custody case which established a strong maternal presumption. A lower court had awarded custody to a father based on his better education, greater intelligence, ability to offer a better social and economic environment, and his better command of the English language. The appellate court found that as there was no evidence that the mother as primary caregiver had been an unfit parent, the lower court was not justified in removing custody from her and vesting "it in a parent who had had no previous emotional interaction with the child" (p. 360). The court's enunciation of a primary caregiver presumption may eliminate some problematic aspects of both the "tender years doctrine" and more modern legislation based on the "best interests of the child" which, as we have seen, takes insufficient account of gender.

The *Garska v. McCoy* case rightly stressed the terrifying spectre to primary caregiver parents, usually mothers but sometimes fathers, of losing their children. Also recognized was the link between custody and financial issues such as support, and the tendency for non-primary caregiver parents, normally in the superior financial position, to trade custody for lower alimony and child support payments in negotiation or mediation. In the court's view, the private ordering of family affairs currently encouraged by the legal system, for instance through mediation, has not been accompanied by a reliable legal framework within which to bargain intelligently. In order to protect each spouse during out-of-court bargaining, in particular the primary caregiver parent who suffers most from uncertainty because of her/his willingness to sacrifice everything in order to retain the children, the court held that there was a presumption in favour of the primary caregiver parent obtaining custody if a minimum objective standard of fit parenting was met. Primary parenting was defined as including many activities often overlooked by courts:

1. preparing and planning of meals;

2. bathing, grooming, and dressing;

3. purchasing, cleaning, and care of clothes;

4. medical care, including nursing and trips to physicians;

5. arranging for social interaction among peers after school;

6. arranging alternative care such as day-care;

7. putting child to bed at night, attending to child in middle of the night, waking the child in the morning;

8. disciplining, such as teaching manners and toilet training;

9. educating in religious, cultural, and social sphere;

10. teaching elementary skills such as reading (p. 363).

If these tasks were shared entirely equally, no presumption would arise and a court would have to inquire into relative degrees of parental competence. But if one parent were clearly the primary caregiver, then if fit, she or he should be given custody if the

child were of tender years (under 6 years). Older children would be given the opportunity to give their own opinions as to which parent they would prefer to stay with. In
West Virginia court-ordered joint custody is not encouraged, although parents can
agree to it voluntarily. ...

Efforts by Canadian feminists to "socialize" the judiciary into an appreciation of
the significance of primary caregiving, and an awareness of the pitfalls for women of
the equality principle and the ideology of equality accompanying it, have been instructive of the difficulties of arguing that social and economic differences between men
and women should be taken into account in legal determinations. ... One judge's
opinion was probably typical and was indicative of the problem: he mistakenly felt
that in emphasizing any criteria such as primary caregiving feminists were asking for
a favouring of mothers' claims in child custody determinations which discriminated
against fathers. A related danger is that if judges are asked to pay further attention to
primary caregiving by mothers, they may resuscitate traditional criteria such as maternal chastity, with possible detrimental consequences for women. We do not want
to encourage, in gender neutral form, a set of expectations attached to primary
caregiving which would operate in a differential fashion depending on whether female
or male primary caregiving was being examined.

Neither do we wish to devalue work which some men are putting into caring for
children, but only to emphasize that at present, contrary to public opinion, these men
constitute only a small minority and the basic sexual division of labour remains intact.
The advantage of a primary caregiver presumption, in contrast to a maternal presumption, is its ability to recognize paternal primary care where it exists, and thereby
to encourage it. It also gives a fairer basis upon which women (and men) can choose
whether to ask for custody or not, with greater certainty as to the likelihood of success.

Susan B. Boyd, "Potentialities and Perils of the Primary Caregiver Presumption"
(1990-91), 7 *Canadian Family Law Quarterly* 1, at 28-29

We must also realize that a primary caregiver presumption cannot solve all problematic issues in the field of custody. Even when sole custody is "won" by a primary
caregiver mother, limitations on her mobility, among other novel restraints on her
autonomy, can make sole custody seem like joint custody. We must also keep our
eyes on developments *within* phenomena such as joint custody as well as considering
its pros and cons. Some judges have recognized the wisdom of giving a joint custody
parent with primary physical custody the ultimate decision-making power. This development may acknowledge the primary caregiver even within a legal arrangement
labelled joint custody. One American author has argued for a reconciliation of joint
custody and a sensitivity for primary caregiving. He recommends that where parents
cannot agree, and one parent establishes that she or he is the primary caregiver, both
parents should have joint physical custody, with the child spending most time with
the primary caregiver parent, who would have decision-making authority over those
areas not affecting the physical custody arrangement. These types of configurations

challenge us to think through the implications and practicalities of changing roles before and after family breakdown, while retaining some sensitivity to the role of women as primary caregivers.

Child custody law on its own cannot answer all of these questions arising from the gendered division of labour in childcare and continuing power relations in the family. Hochschild notes at the end of her book that "it is time for a whole generation of men to make a second historic shift—into work at home" (the first having been women's historic shift into the economy). However, she also notes that we need a meaningful and progressive "pro-family" policy in order to do so. Canadian feminists have made similar suggestions. Compressed time options and flexible working hours have been found inadequate as strategies to ease the ability of workers to reconcile the demands of parenting and labour force participation. Reducing the actual hours of work per week may be the appropriate point on which to lobby. Part-time work accompanied by pay and benefits proportional to those of full-time work would also improve the ability of fathers and mothers to manage labour force involvement. Legal provision of paternity leave *in addition* to maternity leave settlements would enhance the already existing trend for fathers to attend the birthing process and to engage in some early childcare of children. The struggle for adequate national childcare geared to various types of parental jobs, including shiftwork, is intimately connected with all of these proposals.

Without more structural changes to enhance the ability of parents to participate meaningfully in the labour force and in parenting, we will not achieve real changes to the sexual division of labour in both spheres.

The No-Order Alternative: Waugh v. Waugh

In *Waugh v. Waugh* (1998), 42 RFL (4th) 415 (Ont. Ct. J (Gen. Div.)), the father requested an order for interim joint custody of the couple's only child, while the wife asked for interim sole custody. The father claimed a need for joint custody in order to maximize his bonding with the child (a one-year-old) and to allow him to demonstrate his ability to care for the child pending determination of the custody issue. (There was also an issue about whether the husband should have the child every weekend, or only every second weekend.) In assessing the alternatives, the court concluded (at para. 6):

> The issues then are relatively narrow. The first being whether or not the father will have "joint custody" with the mother pending the trial; and secondly, whether the father will have the child for the entire weekend each weekend or simply on alternate weekends.
>
> The parties have separated. Since then while one can anticipate, given the pleadings filed and affidavits delivered, there is going to be antagonism between them, the fact is that they seem to have worked out between themselves, with the assistance of their counsel, a fairly reasonable sharing of child care obligations. The mother is entitled to some time for herself without having to worry about the child. It is only right that the father assist her in that regard by assuming child care responsibilities. He, for his part, is willing to do this and indeed is willing to do this even more than the mother is requesting.
>
> With respect to the issue of the so called "joint custody" of the child, the fact is that at law at the present time the two parents are equally entitled to share the responsibilities and

the benefits of custody. In other words, at law they in fact each have coextensive custody of the child at the present time.

I do not anticipate any major decisions that must be decided between now and the trial. In the pleadings each raises serious allegations about the ability of the other to care for the child over a long period of time.

Quite frankly, I am inclined simply to make no order as to custody thereby leaving the general rule in place. There will be, in the circumstances, an order in the nature of a residential order directing where the child will live but making no other provision with respect to custody.

The court held that the child would reside with her mother and, on alternate weekends, with the father. Although the no-order option in *Waugh* was made in the context of an interim decision only, such an order appears similar to the proposals of Bill C-22, in which all orders for custody and access would be eliminated and replaced by parenting plans. To what extent is this no-order option similar to joint custody? If it is similar, are the concerns identified by Leonoff relevant to this arrangement too? These issues are addressed later in this chapter in connection with reform proposals.

3. Custody and Access: A Case Study

Buist v. Greaves
[1997] OJ no. 2646 (Gen. Div.) (QL)

[In reading the decision in *Buist v. Greaves*, consider the assessment of issues about custody and access and the interrelationship of these issues to other claims—sole or joint custody, relocation, the definition of mother, the use of experts, unjust enrichment, and same-sex relationships. Do you agree that the court reached the appropriate result? Why, or why not?]

BENOTTO J: The plaintiff, Ms. Buist, and the defendant, Ms. Greaves, are very intelligent, successful women who lived together in a same sex relationship in London, Ontario between 1988 and 1995. They are both high profile feminists. While together, Ms. Greaves bore a child Simon who is now 4½ years old. Ms. Buist claims sole or joint custody of Simon and an order that he not be removed from London. This is a significant request because Ms. Greaves has been offered a job in Vancouver and wishes to move there with Simon. Ms. Buist also claims a declaration that she is a "mother" of Simon and compensation for the unjust enrichment she says Ms. Greaves enjoyed as a result of her contributions during their relationship. Ms. Greaves counterclaims for child support.

Ms. Buist is a lawyer. She works primarily in the area of family law with an emphasis in women's issues. She is a politically active feminist. Ms. Greaves is a doctor of sociology, a writer, researcher and consultant. She is widely renowned in feminist circles and the past vice-president of the National Action Committee on the Status of Women. She was, until recently, the director of the Centre for Research on Violence Against Women and Children and a faculty member at Fanshawe College.

Ms. Buist and Ms. Greaves began dating in 1985 when Ms. Buist was at the beginning of her legal career. Ms. Greaves, nine years her senior, was more established in her profession. Ms. Greaves had been previously married to Harry Panjer, a professor at Guelph University. They had a son Lucas who lived with Ms. Greaves.

In 1988 Ms. Buist moved into a home owned by Ms. Greaves on Wellington Street. It had been the matrimonial home of Ms. Greaves and Dr. Panjer and she had recently acquired title to it. Lucas was then 8. Ms. Greaves also had a country property in Elora. In 1988 it was owned by Dr. Panjer. Ms. Greaves would acquire title to it from Dr. Panjer four years later, in 1992. Ms. Buist had no assets of significance.

Ms. Greaves had wanted for some time to have another child. She unsuccessfully attempted conception through heterosexual intercourse. She and Ms. Buist then went to Boston together to a fertility clinic known to be accepting of lesbians. They planned and discussed the conception. For a while, sperm was delivered by courier from Boston to Toronto. This did not result in a pregnancy. Ms. Greaves requested and received a referral to a fertility clinic in a hospital in Toronto where she attended by herself because she did not wish to disclose that she was in a lesbian relationship. She got pregnant but suffered a miscarriage. After the miscarriage, her relationship with Ms. Buist ran into difficulty because Ms. Buist had an affair with a female law student she had hired. Ms. Greaves still wanted a child and returned to a clinic in London. Ultimately, Simon was conceived.

Ms. Buist and Ms. Greaves planned for Simon's birth together. They retained the services of a mid-wife. Friends had a baby shower for them. Ms. Buist carried a beeper around with her so she would know when Ms. Greaves went into labour. Ms. Buist was with her in the delivery room when Simon was born on December 16, 1992. Together they had a "Mad Hatter" party for Simon to celebrate his birth. Two women friends, also in a same sex relationship, were Simon's "goddess mothers."

Simon was a very loved baby. He lived with his mother, Ms. Greaves, Ms. Buist who also cared for him, and his brother Lucas. Ms. Greaves and Ms. Buist shared in all aspects of his life. They divided their time between the Wellington Street home and the property in Elora. They went on trips together and became close friends with Simon's goddess mothers who had a child of their own a few months later. This child, Avery, became Simon's friend. Although Ms. Buist was publicly recognized as a lesbian, Ms. Greaves did not open her private life to the public to the same degree. It is clear, however, that Ms. Greaves and Ms. Buist were, and considered themselves to be, a family.

Ms. Buist shared greatly in Simon's care. She got up in the night and early in the morning to feed him. She was involved in the choice of nannies, of doctors and of schools. Many of the friends that they shared at the time gave evidence about Ms. Buist's involvement in Simon's life. Clearly she was very involved. She was not however, the primary care giver. I accept the evidence of Ms. Greaves and find that Ms. Greaves was the primary care giver. This became more clear as the years went by as the events unfolded which will be described below.

Simon is a lovely child. Unfortunately, he has a learning disability which requires therapy. He is slow in his speech. He also has behaviour problems. He attends speech therapy, currently three times a week. He has also attended special behavioural and developmental therapy. He has been given an enormous amount of loving care and intense attention by Ms. Greaves. Thus, the prognosis for him looks good. One of his doctors, Dr. Rosenbaum, said in November 1996, that his "long-term outlook is probably much better than was originally thought, and that the more Simon shows us what he knows and can do, the more comfortable [Ms. Greaves] will feel about his long-term future."

In October 1994, when Simon was not quite two, Ms. Buist began having a sexual affair with another law student employed by her named Leslie Reaume. Ms. Reaume was then married to a man. Ms. Greaves suspected something was wrong but Ms. Buist denied the sexual aspect of the relationship. In the spring of 1995, on the 10th anniversary of their relationship, Ms. Buist told Ms. Greaves that she was in love with Ms. Reaume.

Ms. Greaves did not want the relationship to end and was willing to do whatever was necessary to keep the relationship together. She offered to put Ms. Buist on title to her property; they even discussed Ms. Buist adopting Simon. Ms. Greaves was upset by the prospect of separation. She was concerned about the effect of a separation on Simon and also on Lucas who by then was 15. Ms. Buist had developed a close relationship with Lucas. Although Ms. Buist would later give evidence that the worst possible thing for Simon is change, she chose to leave the relationship. She moved out in September 1995. This was the greatest change in Simon's life to that date. He was 2½ years old.

Within eleven days of the separation, Ms. Buist had her counsel write a letter to Ms. Greaves about access to Simon. While the letter itself was written in conciliatory terms, Ms. Greaves did not know that. She was too upset to even open it. It was a letter from a lawyer and she perceived that as a threat.

Access to Simon became a source of great conflict between the parties. Ms. Greaves was busy trying to put her life back together and provide stability for Simon. Ms. Buist wanted to spend as much time with him as she could. Ms. Greaves thought access was disruptive, Ms. Buist wanted as much access as possible. The conflict escalated. In March 1996 this action was started. In May 1996 Madam Justice Chapnick made an interim order for access. It provided more access than Ms. Greaves wanted but she felt relieved that at least there would be some order in her life and Simon's. The order did not provide as much access as Ms. Buist wanted and within a short time she was asking for more and the conflict resumed. When she wanted to keep Simon for a long weekend, Ms. Greaves refused. At one point Ms. Greaves threatened to call the police if Simon was not returned in accordance with the order. Justice Chapnick had made no order as to custody.

In the fall of 1996 Ms. Greaves was recruited by the British Columbia Women's Hospital and Health Centre to be its Executive Director. She was offered the job in December. The job is a significant step up for her both financially and career wise. It represents the chance for Ms. Greaves to move to a larger funding base and out of a very focused area of violence to women's health issues generally. She would be the leader of a major initiative, enjoying a broader scope and larger networks. In many ways, this is the position that her entire career has been directed to. It is clearly a major step up.

It is a credit to Ms. Greaves that Dr. Penny Bellem, a physician and vice-president of the hospital, came to Toronto to give evidence about the position and about how they hope to have her in Vancouver. The job was to start on May 1, but that was postponed because of this litigation to July 15.

The facilities available for Simon in Vancouver are superb. Ms. Greaves will be part of a network of hospitals that will provide for him excellent therapy and care. A letter was filed in evidence from Dr. Robert Armstrong, the head of Developmental Paediatrics at the University of British Columbia. He spoke about the facilities available in British Columbia. Dr. Alexander, who was in Ontario for eleven years, and is a colleague of Dr. Rosenbaum (one of Simon's doctors), said "with full confidence" that the services available to Simon would "equal if not exceed" those in Ontario. Counsel for Ms. Buist initially objected to the admission of Dr. Alexander's letter into evidence. Counsel for Ms. Greaves then undertook to call him as a witness. Ms. Greaves also signed a direction authorizing Ms. Buist and her counsel to speak to Dr. Alexander about his evidence in the expectation that his attendance would not be necessary. I was then advised that Dr. Alexander would not be called. Ms. Buist's counsel told the court that he need not be called on her account. She then, however, took the position that his letter could not be referred to for the truth of its contents. That was the reason that Ms. Greaves' counsel undertook to call him and to thereby have him available for cross-examination. Ms. Buist's counsel said it was not necessary to call him. The implication was that she did not need to cross-examine him. I therefore allow the letter to stand as evidence of its contents. I add, however, that even without the evidence in the letter, my decision would not change. I am satisfied on the evidence of Ms. Greaves and of Dr. Bellem, that Simon, being Ms. Greaves' first priority, will receive the same high level of care in British Columbia as he has received in Ontario.

Ms. Greaves told Ms. Buist of her wish to move to the Vancouver job in January 1997. "Over my dead body," Ms. Buist replied. She threatened to take Simon away from her. Her claim was amended to seek sole custody of him. In submissions, her counsel said this was only to afford the court an option should Ms. Greaves decide to move to Vancouver without Simon. Ms. Greaves, however, stated that she would not move without Simon.

Custody and Relocation

At the heart of the very emotional issues in this case is four year old Simon. I must determine what is in his best interest. The focus of my determination is Simon's interests, not the interests and rights of Ms. Greaves and Ms. Buist.

Ms. Greaves is Simon's biological mother and has been his primary care giver since his birth. When the parties were together, they shared in the decision making process. However, Ms. Greaves was still the primary decision maker and care giver. In April 1994, when Simon was 16 months old, Ms. Buist prepared and commissioned a Statutory Declaration sworn by Ms. Greaves which included the sentence: "There is no other parent of [Simon] who is known to me or who has any legal claim for parental rights including custody."

Ms. Buist and the witnesses called by her agree that Ms. Greaves is an excellent mother. I have no doubt that this is true. Moreover, Ms. Greaves is the centre of Simon's world, and thus of his security. When he was away from her last summer for the court ordered access, Ms Buist brought him home early because he missed his mother so much. When he is with his nanny during the day, he speaks of his mother, not of Ms. Buist. There is absolutely no doubt that Simon must remain with his mother. This is generally acknowledged by Ms. Buist. She states that she does not want to take Simon away from his mother and that her claim for sole custody was simply to provide the court with an option if Ms. Greaves chose to leave for Vancouver without him. As Simon must remain in the care of Ms. Greaves, the issue becomes whether joint custody sought by Ms. Buist is in his best interest.

Dr. Goldstein, a well recognized assessor, conducted an assessment pursuant to the order of Mr. Justice Ferrier. The assessment was ordered only a few weeks before trial. The focus of his assessment was "whether the move [to Vancouver] is in the best interest of Simon." Despite the stated objective of his assessment, and the very short time available to him to complete it, he ventured an opinion on joint custody. He felt that it is the optimum situation for a child where the parents have the child's best interest at heart, are reasonable enough to communicate, and intelligent and sensitive enough to deal properly with other people in the lives of the children. He would recommend joint custody for Simon and would like to see a mechanism (such as mediation) that would allow for it.

While I agree with Dr. Goldstein's general views on joint custody, I do not accept his recommendation. In my view, Dr. Goldstein, in the short time available to him, could not have done the investigation necessary to make a determination on custody. A joint custody order, here, would invite disaster. The level of conflict is simply too high. While Ms. Buist held Ms. Greaves responsible for the animosity that exists between them, I find that, as in most cases, the responsibility is divided. I believe that Ms. Greaves felt hurt and abandoned after the separation. She then felt very threatened by the involvement of a lawyer. Ms. Buist, on the other hand, was intent on pursuing her relationship with Simon. She believes that Simon is her son and that she is unfairly being kept from him. I had the distinct impression that her pursuit of her claims had more to do with her perception of her own rights than they did with the best interests of Simon.

This is not an exceptional case where joint custody should be imposed against the parties' wishes. The parties can scarcely speak to each other. The litigation has driven the parties even farther apart. Moreover, I do not find that both parents are equally suitable to the custodial parent. Ms. Greaves is the sole person who should have custody. Simon cannot be separated from his mother. Even Ms. Buist recognizes that.

The fact that Simon has special needs and requires therapeutic intervention increases the need for the parties to be able to work cooperatively. Even during trial there were problems between the parties in relation to Simon's speech therapy. Ms. Buist went to Thames Valley Centre where he was supposed to be receiving therapy. Instead, she found Simon being looked after by a care giver. The therapist was meeting with Ms. Greaves. She assumed that a clandestine meeting was taking place and that this was further proof of Ms. Greaves' wish to exclude her from Simon's life. In fact, the triggering even for the meeting was a letter written by Ms. Buist's counsel to the Centre wherein she insisted that Ms. Buist be treated the same as Ms. Greaves. Although leave was granted during trial for Ms. Buist to be recalled to give this evidence, she did not mention the letter until cross-examination. As it became clear, the people at the Centre were seeking clarification about, and trying to comply with, her letter. This is but one example of the level of suspicion, misunderstanding and difficulty that permeates the current relationship of Ms. Greaves and Ms. Buist. It is so pervasive that, in my view, it would not be in Simon's best interest to be placed in the midst of it. I have no doubt that Ms. Greaves will make informed, reasoned, careful and correct decisions for Simon if she is granted sole custody. Furthermore, I believe that she will keep Ms. Buist informed of all matters relating to him. I therefore find that it is in Simon's best interest to be in the sole custody of Ms. Greaves.

The next issue is whether it is in his best interests to move. I am guided by the summary of the law in *Gordon v. Goertz* (1996), 19 RFL (4th) 177. The importance of Simon remaining with Ms. Greaves must be weighed against the continuance of full contact with Ms. Buist, his community in London, and his extended family. The ultimate question is his best interests. In considering Simon's best interest, I have regard to the following factors:

1. The existing custody arrangement and the relationship between Simon and Ms. Greaves: As already stated, I view Simon's continued close relationship with his mother to be crucial to his well being. There is no doubt in my mind that to remove him from Ms. Greaves' care would be disastrous.

2. The existing access arrangement and the relationship between Simon and Ms. Buist: Simon sees Ms. Buist on alternate weekends and one evening during the week. It is clear that he loves Ms. Buist and considers her part of his family. This is not disputed by Ms. Greaves.

3. The desirability of maximizing contact between the child and both Ms. Greaves and Ms. Buist: Maximum contact between Simon and Ms. Buist can only be achieved if they remain in the same city. Simon's difficulty with the language would make it difficult, if not impossible, for him to maintain regular contact with Ms. Buist. She fears that he will be unable to express his feelings about losing her and this will cause him harm. Dr. Goldstein said that it is not in Simon's best interest to be moved. Simon has limited flexibility and limited vocabulary. He worried about a lack of further development or a regression as a consequence of the loss he would suffer.

4. Ms. Greaves' reason for moving is only to be looked at in the exceptional circumstance where it is relevant to her ability to meet Simon's needs: I have no doubts about Ms. Greaves' ability to meet Simon's needs. She is intimately involved in the details of his speech therapy and schooling. She has done an extraordinary amount of research on the therapy and care available to him in Vancouver.

5. Disruption to the child of a change in custody: A change of custody would be devastating to Simon.

6. Disruption to the child consequent on removal from family, schools and the community he has come to know: A move for Simon would involve a change in therapists and schools, friends, and a change in the pattern of contact with people close to him, most importantly, Ms. Buist. Lucas is going to move and Simon would have him as a constant. Ms. Greaves' parents plan to spend time in Vancouver with him. His close friend David Currah is hoping to move to Vancouver. He has changed schools and nannies in the past. While the transition was not easy, it was done carefully and sensitively and he did adjust. Ms. Buist saw no difficulty in introducing him to her new partner Leslie Reaume, who she says "Simon loves." Simon adjusted to that change as he did to the separation.

Dr. Goldstein was concerned about the many changes Simon would have to face if he moves: a new school, new home, new therapists and, most importantly, a loss of regular contact with Ms. Buist. He said that it would be in Simon's best interest not to have these changes take place and not to experience this loss "if it could be arranged for all of this to take place in an atmosphere of cooperation, and devoid of undue struggle." This assumption that he makes is not consistent with the evidence that I have heard. The ongoing conflict between the parties makes undue struggle a necessary consideration.

Dr. Goldstein was wisely motivated by the desire to eliminate any risk for Simon and viewed the move as a risk. He sought to avoid change without adequate consideration to the fact that this change may be beneficial. He did not have, in my view, the information necessary to adequately weigh the alternatives of life in Vancouver versus life in London. By not speaking to Dr. Penny Bellem, he did not know of the extent of the vast resources available to Simon, or of the policy of Ms. Greaves' prospective employer that encourages mothers in their child raising duties. In Vancouver, Ms. Greaves will have a job which significantly advances her career, Simon will have the advantage of her higher income and the facilities available to him at vastly reduced costs. He will have his brother Lucas with him. In London, Simon will have to move anyway because the Wellington property has been sold, primarily so that his mother could pay her legal fees. His care giver, Jennifer Guay, has gone back to school. His mother, in London, has resigned from her job. Some of Ms. Greaves' previous support network in London has dissipated because many of her former friends gave evidence in the proceedings. (Many of them, who gave evidence at trial, seemed surprised that the effect of their involvement in the case would be to end their relationship with Ms. Greaves. This, notwithstanding the fact that some of the evidence given related to private talks they had with Ms. Greaves when she was in the midst of despair as a result of the separation.) If Ms. Greaves were required to remain in London, she would have an inferior job and a different home. This is not in Simon's best interest.

Dr. Goldstein did not contact any of Simon's doctors or therapists although the basis of his recommendation turns on Simon's special needs. He did not seem to appreciate the unworkable nature of the joint custody agreement he hoped for. He said that moves were always difficult but acknowledged that the main thing for a successful move is that the primary parent will take the child's needs into account. As I have already stated, I have no concerns about Ms. Greaves in this regard.

In weighing all of the pros and cons of a move to Vancouver, I come to the inescapable conclusion that Simon must move with his mother. The losses that will inevitably flow from a less regular schedule of contact with Ms. Buist are more than offset by the benefits of moving with his mother and brother.

Ms. Buist takes the position that it is in Simon's best interest that he not be moved because change is not good for him. She thinks the mother should put her needs secondary to him. I note that, when she made the decision to leave Ms. Greaves, she chose what was best for her, not for Simon. In making her choice, she precipitated the most significant change in his life. I also note that Simon adjusted to that change, as I believe he will to the move.

The sexual orientation of the parties is not relevant to my decision. Families exist in a variety of forms. What is important is the love, nurturing and security in which Simon can continue to grow and prosper. Whenever families separate, upset for the child is inevitable. From the child's perspective, the best solution is an intact family. One of the unhappy by-products of a separation is that all choices, from the child's point of view, are thus second best. Where the courts are called upon to resolve these issues, the choice is often to pick amongst these second best choices. It is somewhat unrealistic for parties to assume a lack of change after separation.

I believe that Simon's best interest is served by being with his mother in Vancouver and by maintaining regular contact with Ms. Buist. I believe Ms. Greaves when she says that she will ensure an ongoing relationship with Ms. Buist. This is demonstrated by the parenting plan she put forth as part of her opening trial statement. It sets out extensive times, including three weeks in the summer, for Ms. Buist to have time with Simon. The proposal and her demeanour in the witness box when she confirmed it, convince me that the ongoing relationship with Ms. Buist will continue. The parenting plan as put forth by Ms. Greaves will form part of the order. As Ms. Buist may not have complied with the May 1 notice requirement for August vacation, I may be spoken to if there are difficulties with this summer or the time for commencement of the parenting plan.

Declaration that Ms. Buist Is a Mother.

Ms. Buist asks for a declaration that she is a "mother" of Simon pursuant to section 4 of the *Children's Law Reform Act* which provides that:

> Any person having an interest may apply to a court for a declaration that a male person is recognized in law to be the father of a child or that a female person is the mother of a child. ...

Ms. Buist has made it clear that she wants to be named mother in addition to, not in substitution for, Ms. Greaves. She says the declaration would crystallize her relationship with Simon. She also points out that there is precedent for a child having two mothers in the case of a same-sex adoption.

The authority for the declaration she seeks must be found in section 4 above. The use of the definite article "the" indicates that the drafters of the legislation did not consider that more than one person be the mother of a child. Furthermore, even if such a declaration were possible, the test for making such determination as set out in section 4(3) must be met. That section provides that, in order to make the declaration, there must be a finding on balance of probabilities that the "relationship of mother and child has been established." There is no doubt that the relationship between Simon and Ms. Buist is very close; however, Simon does not consider her his mother. Ms. Greaves is his mother. He calls her "mama" while he calls Ms. Buist "gaga" which is short for "Peggy." He was given Ms. Greaves' last name at birth. I accept Ms. Greaves' evidence that Ms. Buist did not start referring to him as her son until after the separation. (She learned about it when she read a magazine article quoting Ms. Buist.) Most significantly, when with Ms. Buist and away from Ms. Greaves for an extended time, he is distraught. Ms. Buist lived with Simon's mother in a relationship that was not committed. She began her second affair of the relationship when Simon was less than 2. She left her home when Simon was 2½. She drafted and commissioned an affidavit confirming that Ms. Greaves (not she) was Simon's parent. Most significantly, from Simon's perspective, Ms. Greaves, not Ms. Buist, is his mother. Thus, even if I had the jurisdiction to declare that a child could have two mothers under section 4, I would not, on the facts of this case, exercise my discretion to do so. Ms. Buist has not, on balance of probabilities established the relationship of mother and child.

[Benotto J also considered and rejected Ms Buist's claim that Ms Greaves had been unjustly enriched, and that Ms Buist was therefore entitled to restitution. Ms Buist substantiated her claim by filing volumes of documentation itemizing expenses which she paid for during their relationship and cohabitation. Among other things, these expenses included: living expenses; purchase of assets; and renovations done to Ms Greaves's property. Ms Buist also sought compensation for the domestic services she performed, such as cutting the grass, helping to build the deck, and doing the gardening.

In rejecting the claim, Benotto J held that no unjust enrichment had occurred: there was no evidence that Ms Buist's contributions contributed to the increase in value of any of the assets; Ms Buist did not enhance the earning potential of Ms Greaves; the parties shared equally in the division of household duties; and there was no evidence that Ms Buist was financially worse off personally or professionally because of the relationship.

In relation to child support, Benotto J also ordered that Ms Buist pay Ms Greaves $450 per month in child support for Simon retroactive to the date that the claim for child support was advanced by Ms Greaves. In ordering that child-support payments be paid Benotto J took note of the evidence that indicated that at one point Ms Buist agreed to a child-support payment of approximately $900 per month. However, the judge also noted that Simon's special expenses were expected to decrease in Vancouver while Ms Buist's costs of seeing Simon would rise substantially. She thus found that half of the initial amount claimed was appropriate.]

SELECTED REFERENCES

Nicholas Bala and Susan Miklas, *Rethinking Decisions About Children: Is the "Best Interests of the Child" Approach Really in the Best Interests of Children?* (Toronto: Policy Research Centre on Children, Youth, and Families, 1993).

Brenda Cossman and Roxanne Mykitiuk, "Child Custody and Access—Discussion Paper" (1998), 15:1 *Canadian Journal of Family Law* 13.

Elizabeth J. Hughes, "Mother's Vicarious Hand: Primary Caregiving Reconceived as Relationship and Responsibility" (2002), 20 *Canadian Family Law Quarterly* 467.

Nancy Mandell, "The Child Question: Links Between Women and Children in the Family," in Nancy Mandell and Ann Duffy, eds., *Reconstructing the Canadian Family: Feminist Perspectives* (Toronto: Butterworths, 1988), 49.

Karen M. Munro, "The Inapplicability of Rights Analysis in Post-Divorce Child Custody Decision Making" (1992), 30 *Alberta Law Review* 852.

Carol Smart, "The Legal and Moral Ordering of Child Custody" (1991), 18:4 *Journal of Law and Society* 485.

_____, "Power and the Politics of Child Custody," in Carol Smart and Selma Sevenhuijsen, eds., *Child Custody and the Politics of Gender* (London: Routledge, 1989), 1.

E. Reform Proposals

As in a number of other jurisdictions, there have been several proposals in Canada for reforming legal arrangements for children post-separation and divorce. As noted at the beginning of this chapter, the federal government initiated two reviews in the 1990s and introduced Bill C-22 in December 2002. In addition, there have been numerous private members' bills presented to the House of Commons, particularly in relation to issues of custody and access by grandparents and others. Consider the following excerpts from the parliamentary report *For the Sake of the Children*, some of which are reflected in the provisions of Bill C-22. To what extent do you agree that these proposals will enhance legal decision making in relation to caring for the children of divorce?

Special Joint Committee on Child Custody and Access, *For the Sake of the Children*
(Ottawa: Parliament of Canada, 1998)

[The committee received input from a large number of groups and individuals and made 48 recommendations for change to the *Divorce Act* and provincial legislation regarding children in post-divorce family units. For example, they recommended that children be heard in relation to parenting decisions affecting them, that the language of custody and access be eliminated in favour of parenting orders, that a list of factors be included to define best interests, and that parenting responsibilities and child-support legislation be connected. In part, the report stated (at 31-34):]

Shared parenting arrangements involving substantially equal time sharing, when agreed to by the parents through the assistance of a counsellor or mediator, are often spelled out in detail in parenting plans. More elaborate than the traditional separation agreement or court order upon which many couples rely, these agreements specify where the child is to reside throughout the year, how decision-making responsibilities are to be shared by the parents, and the mechanism parents will use to deal with any disputes that arise between them. Parenting plans, while not enshrined in any Canadian custody and access legislation, are used routinely in therapeutic or negotiation settings, to help parents make decisions about parenting arrangements.

Lawyers, therapists and mediators described the benefits of this tool to the Committee. Parenting plans shift parents' focus away from labels ("I have custody, you just have access") to the schedule, activities and real needs of the child. The Committee recognizes the usefulness of parenting plans as a decision-making tool, commends them to divorcing parents and to professionals working with them, and concludes that all shared parenting orders should take the form of parenting plans. Cognizant of the disadvantages of long mandatory parenting plans (such as those that have to be filed in the state of Washington), the Committee cautions the Minister of Justice, in implementing these recommendations, to ensure that forms are brief and straightforward enough to be accessible and useful to parents and the professionals assisting them.

Parenting plans, especially if negotiated directly between parents or with the help of a mediator, are customized to meet the needs of a particular child and family and have the additional advantage of flexibility. Such plans can account for children's specific needs, in terms of activities and schedules, but can also provide for much-needed review as the child develops and his or her needs and interests change. Other people important to the child can be accommodated in a parenting plan, such as by scheduling time with grandparents or other extended family members, or by specifying that such contact is important and that the parents will facilitate such contact. Of course, such provisions would not apply in a case where such contact was considered contrary to the best interests of the children involved. In addition to establishing a dispute resolution mechanism to which the parents will have recourse should they be unable to settle a disagreement, parenting plans should specify the timing and process by which parents will revisit the plan as necessary as the child matures.

In some cases, of course, parents will be unable to agree on a parenting plan either on their own or in mediation. In that event, the parents will be able to make application under the *Divorce Act* for a shared parenting determination. Judges making such determinations will be able to give consideration to proposed parenting plans filed with the court by each parent, and, guided by the "best interests of the child" test, make a court order in the form of a parenting plan. Such a plan, although judicially imposed, will retain the benefits of being focused on the child's needs and interests, as well as the advantages of flexibility and adaptability.

Recommendations

11. This Committee recommends that divorcing parents be encouraged to develop, on their own or with the help of a trained mediator or through some form of alternative dispute resolution, a parenting plan setting out details about each parent's responsibilities for residence, care, decision making and financial security for the children, together with the dispute resolution process to be used by the parties. Parenting plans must also require the sharing between parents of health, educational and other information related to the child's development and social activities. All parenting orders should be in the form of parenting plans. ...

13. This Committee recommends that the Minister of Justice seek to amend the *Divorce Act* to require that parties applying to a court for a parenting order must file a proposed parenting plan with the court.

· · ·

Non-Adversarial Dispute Resolution

The Committee heard a great deal about the effectiveness of mediation and other forms of alternative dispute resolution in helping parents make arrangements for their children following divorce. Experts in mediation from across Canada testified about the importance of promoting this non-adversarial method of helping families restructure themselves after divorce. The benefits of mediation and other alternative dispute resolution mechanisms include reducing rather than escalating tension and conflict between divorcing parents and reducing expenses; they also have the capacity to include children and other interested parties more easily than would be the case with litigation. The growth of mediation as a forum for making parenting decisions after separation or divorce is a widespread international phenomenon. Indeed, in Australia, the 1995 *Family Law Reform Act* refers to mediation and arbitration as "primary dispute resolution," intending to signal that it is litigation that should be seen as "alternative."

Legislation in Quebec requires that divorcing parents attend at least one information session about the benefits of mediation. If they decide to continue with mediation, they are entitled to up to six sessions paid for by the provincial government. The Quebec legislation permits parties in appropriate cases, such as those with a risk or history of domestic violence, to opt out (including from the information session) by signing a release filed with the court.

Women's advocates and some mediators expressed concern about mediation in situations where there has been abuse. They believe that the abusive partner would use mediation as a forum in which to harass or overpower the other partner. These groups also testified that since violence is a common occurrence in Canadian families, mandated mediation would put many women and children at risk.

Mediation is usually inappropriate in situations of violence. Mediation is usually inappropriate in such cases because of the inequality of bargaining power in abusive relationships and because of the ongoing risk of additional abuse during the mediation process. (Martha Bailey, Queen's University, Faculty of Law, Meeting #11)

Mediators who appeared as witnesses argued that there needs to be a shift away from adversarial thinking in divorce situations. Howard Irving stated:

In the past decade, the adversarial system, especially as it pertains to family law, has increasingly been brought into question. The primary thrust of this criticism has been that the communication and compliance behaviours that are necessary if individuals are to work together as parents after they cease to be spouses are more difficult to maintain [in an adversarial forum]. In other words, a major difficulty of family law is that the problems brought by clients are frequently not legal problems: they are deep, human problems in which the law is involved. While legal problems must be resolved, their resolution does not alleviate the human problems, and, more important for the lawyer, frequently the legal problem cannot be handled properly unless the human problem is dealt with. ... (Howard Irving, University of Toronto, Faculty of Social Work, Meeting #11)

Recommendation

14. This Committee recommends that divorcing parents be encouraged to attend at least one mediation session to help them develop a parenting plan for their children. Recognizing the impact of family violence on children, mediation and other non-litigation methods of decision making should be structured to screen for and identify family violence. Where there is a proven history of violence by one parent toward the other or toward the children, alternative forms of dispute resolution should be used to develop parenting plans only when the safety of the person who has been the victim of violence is assured and where the risk of violence has passed. The resulting parenting plan must focus on parental responsibilities for the children and contain measures to ensure safety and security for parents and children.

Widening the Circle: Involving Others with the Children of Divorce

Children whose parents are separating often feel isolated and powerless. A number of witnesses, including mental health professionals, children, grandparents and other extended family members, discussed means of including other people in the divorce process, as support or resource persons, advocates or intermediaries, on behalf of children. Some families, of course, seek professional therapeutic assistance for their children, and some may have no need for it, but many are unaware of the potential helpfulness of counsellors experienced in the dynamics of parental separation and its impact on children.

The Committee listened with interest to the evidence of supports for children already present in our society, often in the form of grandparents or other extended family members. The Committee recognized the value of this type of support in Recommendation 3, where we recommended that judges have the power to appoint interested family members or others to support children through the divorce process. Such interested third parties could be valuable sounding boards for children experiencing difficulties related to their parents' separation or divorce and could perhaps in some cases even speak on behalf of the children in court. ...

Grandparents from across Canada testified before the Committee and asked that their relationship with their grandchildren be respected in law after parents divorce.

The Committee heard many painful examples of how divorce had severed a caring and loving relationship between grandparents and grandchildren. These witnesses also pointed out that grandparents often provide a child's continuing involvement with his or her heritage and that this should be honoured in law. ...

Recommendation

[12. This Committee recommends that the relationships of grandparents, siblings and other extended family members with children be recognized as significant and that provisions for maintaining and fostering such relationships, where they are in the best interests of those children, be included in parenting plans.]

[In addition, the report considered the best-interests test and recommended the addition of criteria defining best interests (at 45):]

Recommendation

16. The Committee recommends that decision makers, including parents and judges, consider a list of criteria in determining the best interests of the child, and that list shall include

16.1 The relative strength, nature and stability of the relationship between the child and each person entitled to or claiming a parenting order in relation to the child;

16.2 The relative strength, nature and stability of the relationship between the child and other members of the child's family who reside with the child, and persons involved in the care and upbringing of the child;

16.3 The views of the child, where such views can reasonably be ascertained;

16.4 The ability and willingness of each applicant to provide the child with guidance and education, the necessaries of life and any special needs of the child;

16.5 The child's cultural ties and religious affiliation;

16.6 The importance and benefit to the child of shared parenting, ensuring both parents' active involvement in his or her life after separation;

16.7 The importance of relationships between the child and the child's siblings, grandparents and other extended family members;

16.8 The parenting plans proposed by the parents;

16.9 The ability of the child to adjust to the proposed parenting plans;

16.10 The willingness and ability of each of the parties to facilitate and encourage a close and continuing relationship between the child and the other parent;

16.11 Any proven history of family violence perpetrated by any party applying for a parenting order;

16.12   There shall be no preference in favour of either parent solely on the basis of that parent's gender;

16.13   The willingness shown by each parent to attend the required education session; and

16.14   Any other factor considered by the court to be relevant to a particular shared parenting dispute.

Discussion Notes

The Efficacy of Law Reform

In reflecting on these proposals, it is important not to overstate the extent to which law reform is effective in accomplishing fundamental change. In the context of similar reforms in the United States, for example, researchers examined their impact on parental practices post-separation and divorce and the extent to which significant changes occurred: see Eleanor Maccoby and Robert Mnookin, *Dividing the Child* (Cambridge, MA: Harvard University Press, 1992). As the authors noted (at 266):

> In California, as elsewhere, reformers sought to eliminate gender stereotypes, to encourage divorced fathers to remain more involved in their children's lives, and to create greater gender equity for mothers and fathers alike. Various substantive and procedural changes were adopted in the hope of dampening legal conflict and diminishing the adversarial nature of divorce. California sought to encourage "frequent and continuing contact with both parents," and to authorize explicitly joint physical custody and joint legal custody so that parents might choose to share responsibility more equally. Cooperative co-parenting, not conflict, was the goal. ...
>
> **The Impact of the Law and Legal Change**
>
> ... [T]he reforms enacted in California divorce law, explicitly authorizing joint custody and encouraging frequent and continuing contact with both parents, have had something to do with our finding of relatively high frequencies of joint physical custody awards and sustained visitation. Once again, however, we cannot be sure, and we find it plausible that the California legal reforms may reflect social change more than create it. ... When it comes to the broader aspirations underlying the California reforms, however—to foster greater gender equity and support cooperative co-parenting—our findings suggest a mixed picture. First, and most fundamentally, the gender roles of divorced parents remain substantially differentiated. While there is apparently little legal conflict, and legal conflict usually does not require formal adversarial proceedings in court for resolution, most divorcing parents are unable to develop cooperative co-parental relations, despite the policy changes.
>
> These basic findings clearly point to limits in how far the reach of the law can extend when it comes to creating fundamental change in gender roles or influencing co-parental relations. ... For women, roles within the household—especially with regard to parenting—and opportunities in the [labour] market are closely connected. Long before our study, it was well known that mothers typically cared for children both before and after divorce and were often at a substantial economic disadvantage compared to fathers.

Using family law to modify gender role differentiation may be a worthy aspiration, but is it realistic to believe that law can have a substantial impact in this regard? We have argued that the gender differentiation that follows divorce rests largely on the differential roles that parents occupied before the separation. Unless family law can modify the pre-divorce roles, then, it is doubtful that it can have a much greater impact on the post-divorce division of parental responsibilities; most divorcing couples would still typically end up allocating primary child-rearing responsibility to mothers. ...

Law can be used to create enforceable support obligations and to divide property. We very much applaud efforts to improve support schedules and enforcement mechanisms in order to require non-custodial fathers to pay more for the support of their children. Even though law may have limited impact on which parent the children live with, this does not mean that it is unimportant at the time of divorce. It can also make an important difference in stabilizing the residential arrangements of the custodial parent and protecting them from interference by the secondary parent. Moreover, as we have noted, it can provide important visitation rights to the secondary parent. But we doubt that changing divorce custody standards alone is likely to have significant effects on the way most parents allocate basic responsibility for day-to-day care, either before or after separation.

We are not suggesting that gender roles are fixed now and forever. Indeed, our study suggests some modest social change. Instead, we are expressing skepticism about the power of family law. The function of law as an agent of [behavioural] change is a complex issue. ... As we see it, family law may reflect and reinforce some tendencies, but its effects will be mainly at the margins, affecting mainly those cases in which the pre-existing parental roles are unclear or in which parents are ambivalent about what they want. It can hardly bring about fundamental change in gender roles. Deeper forces—cultural, economic, and, some would claim, biological—limit the power of law in this domain.

Although these American researchers were examining the impact of presumptions of joint legal and joint physical custody for children, their comments may also be relevant to the Canadian recommendations and Bill C-22—to what extent will the use of parenting plans and mediation accomplish fundamental change? What kinds of resources will be required to make these recommendations effective in practice?

Reform Experiences in Other Jurisdictions

As noted earlier in this chapter, the ALI was also involved in reform proposals in relation to custody and access. As well, other common law jurisdictions, including the United Kingdom and Australia, have adopted new arrangements for the children of divorce. Significantly, these reforms have generally eliminated orders for custody and access in favour of shared-parenting proposals. However, as Helen Rhoades suggests, these legal changes have not always succeeded: see Helen Rhoades, "The Rise and Rise of Shared Parenting Laws: A Critical Reflection" (2002), 19 *Canadian Journal of Family Law* 75. Assessing the results of three empirical studies of the impact of these legal reforms in Australia, Rhoades states (at 90-91):

The findings of the three studies show that the intended results of the reforms have largely failed to materialize. Parents continue to organise their arrangements around a custody and access division of labour, the new terminology remains alien to the bulk of the population (including separated couples), litigation has increased, and judges and practitioners approach final hearings about residence much as they did before.

A range of reasons were given for this failure by respondents to the studies, including the inherent logistical difficulties of co-parenting across two households, and the perceptions of many practitioners that the reforms were no more than "old wine in new bottles." But a dominant theme of the responses was that the separation process is simply not conducive to co-operation between former spouses, particularly among those who use the legal system to resolve their disputes. As one registrar of the Court put it:

> The shared parenting concept is totally at odds with the types of parents who litigate.

Rhoades's study focused particularly on the relationship between the goals of increased contact with both parents, on the one hand, and protection from violence on the other, concluding that these messages were contradictory. Although there were a number of problems with the reforms, Rhoades suggested (at 107) that the basic vision was flawed:

> The shared parenting reforms were based on a vision of the ideal post-separation family. This is not just a matter of marginalising women's (tentatively raised) concerns about violence. It also ignores the diverse reality of families generally. For one thing, it takes no account of the inherent fluidity of family life which affects parenting before and after separation. The reforms created a paradox by encouraging ongoing collaboration while at the same time imposing an enforceable right of contact that assumes a static arrangement. ... [M]ore dangerously, the shared parenting regime treats all children alike, as a monolithic group with the same needs. In doing so it marginalises children from violent homes, whose perspective of family is very different to that of children who have not shared their experience. And collaboration between these children's parents is not uppermost in their list of needs. ...
>
> Perhaps more fundamentally there is a sense that these reforms were a cynical exercise, a sympathetic (empathetic?) response to the complaints of a particular constituency, with little genuine commitment to bringing about cultural change.

In reflecting on these comments, consider the extent to which legal reforms can succeed in achieving fundamental cultural change. What is the role for law with respect to arrangements for the children of divorce?

SELECTED REFERENCES

American Law Institute, *Principles of the Law of Family Dissolution: Analysis and Recommendations* (Washington, DC: Matthew Bender, 2002).

Nicholas Bala, "A Report from Canada's 'Gender War Zone': Reforming the Child-Related Provisions of the Divorce Act" (1999), 16 *Canadian Journal of Family Law* 163.

Susan B. Boyd, *Child Custody, Law, and Women's Work* (Toronto: Oxford University Press, 2003).

_____, "W(h)ither Feminism? The Department of Justice Public Discussion Paper on Custody and Access" (1995), 12 *Canadian Journal of Family Law* 331.

Jonathan Cohen and Nikki Gershbain, "For the Sake of the Fathers? Child Custody Reform and the Perils of Maximum Contact" (2001), 19 *Canadian Family Law Quarterly* 121.

Christine Davies, "Report of the Special Joint Committee on Custody and Access and the Concept of Shared Parenting" (2001), 19 *Canadian Family Law Quarterly* 363.

John Dewar, "The Family Law Reform Act 1995 (Cth) and the Children Act 1989 (UK) Compared—Twins or Distant Cousins?" (1996), 10 *Australian Journal of Family Law* 19.

Elizabeth J. Hughes, "The Language and Ideology of Shared Parenting in Family Law Reform: A Critical Analysis" (2003), 21 *Canadian Family Law Quarterly* 1.

Bren Neale and Carol Smart, " 'Good' and 'Bad' Lawyers? Struggling in the Shadow of the New Law" (1997), 19:4 *Journal of Social Welfare and Family Law* 377.

Helen Reece, *Divorcing Responsibly* (Oxford and Portland, OR: Hart Publishing, 2003).

Helen Rhoades, "Posing as Reform: The Case of the Family Law Reform Act" (2000), 14 *Australian Journal of Family Law* 142.

Helen Rhoades, Reg Graycar, and Margaret Harrison, *The Family Law Reform Act 1995: Can Changing Legislation Change Legal Culture, Legal Practice and Community Expectations? Interim Report* (Sydney: University of Sydney and the Family Court of Australia, 1999).

Carol Smart, Bren Neale, and Amanda Wade, *The Changing Experience of Childhood: Families and Divorce* (Cambridge: Polity Press, 2001).

Bruce Smyth, ed., *Parent–Child Contact and Post-Separation Parenting Arrangements* (Melbourne: Australian Institute of Family Studies, 2004).

III. CHILD SUPPORT

A. Introduction

Child support enforcement is part of a wholesale shift in the legal regulation of the family and the balance of relationships between mothers and fathers. Child support starts from the need to insure that a larger percentage of the nation's resources are linked to children, but ... child support in itself is unlikely to solve the problem of child poverty. Rather, its greatest impact is likely to be on the middle class and on the conduct of relationships that never become the subject of court orders. Like many exercises in setting norms, the most visible aspects of the process may well be the sanctions against those who fail to comply. The success of the endeavour, however, is more likely to lie with the creation of a new ethic of parenthood.

> June Carbone, "Child Support Comes of Age: An Introduction to the Law of Child Support," in J. Thomas Oldham and Marygold S. Melli, eds., *Child Support: The Next Frontier* (Ann Arbor, MI: University of Michigan Press, 2000), 3, at 11

As June Carbone's comment suggests, legal obligations of child support reflect a societal commitment to the economic well-being of children. However, just as the principles of spousal support discussed in chapter 7 revealed an emphasis on privatized family support for dependency, so the legal obligations of child support reinforce the family's responsibility for the well-being of children. According to Carbone, concerns about child poverty as a result of rising divorce rates and single-parent families became intertwined in the

1990s with broader fiscal policies that emphasized the need to conserve governmental resources. Thus, in a number of jurisdictions, including Canada, there were major efforts to reform legal obligations of child support, both to increase the levels of support for children and also to ensure better enforcement of these obligations. As Carbone explained (at 3), legal principles concerning child-support obligations have become more significant: "Once the stepchild of family law, child support has moved onto centre stage in the modern effort to define and enforce family obligation."

As these comments suggest, child-support obligations need to be examined within the larger context of public policies about responsibility for dependency. In addition, however, Carbone argued (at 3) that child-support obligations represent "a critical element in a larger shift from the husband–wife relationship to parent–child ties as the defining element of family obligation." Moreover, she suggested that this change has been accomplished without addressing a number of fundamental questions:

> This legal shift is problematic at least in part because it proceeds from a public-policy consensus on the need for greater financial contributions to children without clearly addressing the relationship between fathers and mothers necessary to bring about such contributions. Reform supporters, an otherwise unlikely alliance of women's groups committed to greater equality and conservatives eager to protect the public fisc, agree only on a starting point—the principle that all parents should support their children. The almost universal support for the governing principle, however, begs the difficult questions of implementation: How does "natural" obligation translate into dollar amounts? Is it independent of the parents' relationship to each other? Of the circumstances of the child's conception and birth? Of obligation toward other children? Of ideas of equality and fairness between the parents?

Some of these questions continue to be addressed in Canada with respect to national child-support guidelines adopted in 1997, following a series of negotiations among the federal, provincial, and territorial governments. Although the guidelines were intended to provide greater certainty with respect to child-support obligations, judicial discretion has also been required to interpret their application in individual circumstances. This section begins by examining the legal definitions of "parent" and "child" for purposes of child-support obligations, and then provides an overview of the basic principles of the guidelines. In doing so, the materials briefly address experiences in other jurisdictions and critical commentary about child support.

SELECTED REFERENCES

Vicky Barham, Rose Anne Devlin, and Chantale LaCasse, "Are the New Child-Support Guidelines 'Adequate' or 'Reasonable'?" (2000), 26:1 *Canadian Public Policy* 1.

Christine Davies, "The Ever-Changing Picture of Support and Other Developments" (2002), 20 *Canadian Family Law Quarterly* 213.

Ross Finnie, "The Government's Child Support Package" (1997), 15 *Canadian Family Law Quarterly* 79.

Tina Maisonneuve, "Child Support Under the Federal and Quebec Guidelines: A Step Forward or Behind?" (1999), 16 *Canadian Family Law Journal* 284.

Paul Miller and Anne H. Gauthier, "What Were They Thinking? The Development of Child Support Guidelines in Canada" (2002), 17 *Canadian Journal of Law and Society* 139.

Laura W. Morgan, "Family Law at 2000: Private and Public Support of the Family—From Welfare State to Poor Law" (1999), 33:3 *Family Law Quarterly* 705.

M.J. Mossman, "Child Support or Support for Children?: Re-Thinking the 'Public' and 'Private' in Family Law" (1997), 46 *University of New Brunswick Law Journal* 63.

J. Thomas Oldham and Marygold S. Melli, eds., *Child Support: The Next Frontier* (Ann Arbor, MI: University of Michigan Press, 2000).

B. Defining a Parent–Child Relationship

1. Legislative Definitions

The definition in s. 2(1) of the *Divorce Act, 1985* of "child of the marriage" includes minor children who have "not withdrawn from [parental] charge," as well as children who have reached the age of majority or older and are under parental charge, but who are unable "by reason of illness, disability or other cause" to withdraw from parental charge or obtain the necessaries of life. Provincial legislation defines child and/or parent in different ways: for example, see Ontario's *Family Law Act*, s. 31. (Child-support guidelines also contain definitions of child, but they generally incorporate those in the *Divorce Act, 1985* and in provincial statutes: for example, see O Reg. 391/97, as amended, s. 2(1).) Arguably, it is possible that a child might meet the requirements of one definition, but not the other. In practice, however, it seems that judicial interpretation of the definitions has tended to be expansive and inclusive.

For example, in *Sullivan v. Sullivan* (1999), 50 RFL (4th) 326 (Ont. Div. Ct.), a 22-year-old woman was awarded interim child support payable by her father, pursuant to s. 31 of the Ontario statute, even though the daughter attended school, because of illness, only part-time. In commenting on this and other cases, James McLeod explained (at 327):

> Over the past few years, it has become increasingly clear that courts are not particularly troubled by the words of the relevant legislation in child-support cases. However, this appears to be the first time that an appeal court has simply ignored the words of the legislation and the existing case law to reach what it considers a fair result.
>
> An adult child has a more limited right to support under the *Family Law Act* than under the *Divorce Act*. Under the *Divorce Act*, s. 2(1) "child of the marriage," a spouse must pay child support for his or her adult children who are under parental charge and unable to withdraw from parental charge or maintain themselves for a legally acceptable reason: see *Welsh v. Welsh* (November 3, 1998), Doc. St. Catharines 35,110/95 (Ont. Gen. Div.), where Quinn J reviewed in detail the circumstances when an adult child was entitled to support under the *Divorce Act*. According to the definition of "child of the marriage" in s. 2(1) of the *Divorce Act*, a court cannot order child support for an adult child who has withdrawn from parental charge. In many cases, courts ignore the requirement that an adult child is entitled to support only if he or she is still under parental charge and extend support to any child who is unable to maintain himself or herself for a legally acceptable reason. This interpretation ignores that, grammatically, the statutory requirement that an adult child must

be under parental charge applies to both children who are unable to withdraw from parental charge and children who are unable to obtain necessaries for themselves. The courts have extended child support under the *Divorce Act* to adult children in school who no longer live with a parent at any point in the school year. One of the more extreme examples of the current overinterpretation of s. 2(1) of the *Divorce Act* is *Colonval v. Munson* (May 5, 1998), Doc. Victoria 5939/26455 (BCSC), where Cowan J held that an adult child continued to be entitled to support as long as he remained in school, notwithstanding the fact that he cohabited with his girlfriend; see also *Collins v. Collins* (1998), 221 AR 111 (QB) (no need for child to live at home to receive support).

The court had less discretion as to whether to award child support under the *Family Law Act* in *Sullivan* than if the claim had been brought under the *Divorce Act*. Pursuant to s. 31 of the *Family Law Act*, an adult child is entitled to support only if he or she has not voluntarily withdrawn from parental control and is enrolled in a full-time program of education. The onus is on a person claiming child support to prove that an adult child is entitled to support: *Keighley v. Keighley* (December 30, 1997), Doc. New Westminster DO 16392 (BCSC), except that a court will not presume voluntary withdrawal from parental control under s. 31(2) of the *Family Law Act*: *Giess v. Upper* (1996), 28 RFL (4th) 460 (Ont. Gen. Div.); *Zedner v. Zedner* (1989), 22 RFL (3d) 207 (Ont. Prov. Ct.). In *Sullivan*, the mother alleged that the child still lived at home and was under her control. At least at an interim stage, this should be sufficient to overcome the proviso in s. 31(2) of the *Family Law Act* (voluntary withdrawal from parental control). ...

The problem in *Sullivan* is that even if the adult daughter is under parental control, she is not enrolled in a full-time educational program. The undisputed evidence is that the daughter attended university only part time. It is interesting to note that s. 31(1) of the *Family Law Act* does not state that the child must attend school full time, just that she must be enrolled in a full-time program of education. Arguably, if a child is enrolled full time but attends school only part time, she may still be entitled to support: *Copeland v. Copeland* (December 9, 1992), Doc. Newmarket 24698/92 (Ont. Gen. Div.), [1993] WDFL 122, TLW 1236-023 (court not to impose a standard of devotion, priority and effort on a child as a condition of continuing a claim for support). However, in *Geiss v. Upper* ... [(1996), 28 RFL (4th) 460 (Ont. Gen. Div.)], the court held that a child's participation in an educational program must be meaningful and of such a nature and quality as to be consistent with the program's purposes and objectives. ...

Although courts tend to grant support to children in need, especially children making a reasonable effort to pursue an education within their limitations, a court cannot grant support to a child who is not entitled to support under the relevant legislation. It is submitted that Walsh J erred in granting support under the *Family Law Act* to an adult child who was not enrolled in a full-time program of education and the Divisional Court erred in upholding the daughter's support entitlement, albeit in a reduced amount. The court's refusal to award the daughter any of her costs of the proceedings suggests that the court recognized that its conclusion was questionable, to say the least. The father had more resources than the daughter, did not succeed in extinguishing support and could better afford the costs of the litigation. In most cases, it is submitted that the daughter would have received at least part of her costs.

(James McLeod, "Annotation of Sullivan v. Sullivan" (1999), 50 RFL (4th) 326.)

What is the explanation for the court's expansive interpretation in *Sullivan*? To what extent do you agree with McLeod's critique that the decision was not in accordance with the statutory definition in s. 31 of the *Family Law Act*? Is it relevant that governmental support for students has declined in recent years? Does this case reflect a shift in responsibility for dependency to families? As noted later in relation to the *Child Support Guidelines*, there has been some criticism about the fact that separated or divorced parents may have obligations to support adult children to pursue educational programs, by contrast with the absence of any legal obligations to do so for parents in intact families. If parents in intact families do not have such legal obligations, does this fact change your view of the court's expansive interpretation of s. 31 in *Sullivan*? Why, or why not?

In this context, consider *Hyde v. Lange* (1996), 22 RFL (4th) 317 (Ont. Ct. J (Gen. Div.)). Following separation, the parents made an agreement, which was sanctioned by the court, whereby the father would not see the couple's child and he would not pay support. The mother supported the child financially and emotionally and neither the parents nor the child attempted to re-establish the father's relationship with the child. Upon completing her first year of college, however, the child applied for support under the *Family Law Act*; pursuant to the agreement, the father alleged that the child was not entitled to support. The court, however, held that she was so entitled because she was attending school full-time as required under s. 31. Stating that the *Family Law Act* is rooted in dependency, the court held that the child's right to support should not be affected by the fact that the parent did not exercise access, or from any arrangement by her parents that compromised her right to support. Is this case consistent with the outcome in *Sullivan*? What are the implications of this expansive approach to the interpretation of the legislative definitions of child? See Terry W. Hainsworth, "Support for Adult Children" (1999), 17 *Canadian Family Law Quarterly* 39.

Discussion Notes

Legislative Definitions: Presumptions and Social Parents

As explained in the following sections, federal and provincial statutes contain other definitions for "child" and "parent," including presumptions of paternity and situations of *in loco parentis* (literally, a person standing in place of a parent). In this way, a child may have social as well as biological parents, all of whom may have child-support obligations. Issues about the allocation of responsibilities where several parents have such obligations are considered later in relation to the *Child Support Guidelines*.

Child-Support Obligations and Parent–Child Relationships

Consider the language of the definition in the *Divorce Act, 1985*. Should a parent be obliged to pay child support in the absence of contact with a child? In *Parsons v. Parsons* (1996), 17 RFL (4th) 267 (Ont. Ct. J (Gen. Div.)), the husband was ordered to pay child support to his wife for his 24-year-old daughter, a medical student, of $400 per month for one year. The court ordered payment of this support even though the daughter had no ongoing relationship with her father. In doing so, however, the court did not rule that child support should always be required for an adult child who had deliberately ended the parent–child relationship; nonetheless, the court held that the daughter in this case was a "child of the marriage," and that she had not disentitled herself from assistance. At the same time, the court declared that the husband could apply for a review of the support after one year if no parent–child relationship had been re-established by that time. In the context of *Parsons*, how would you characterize the relationship between child-support obligations and parent–child relationships? For a compelling critique, see Jeffery Wilson, "The Forgotten Child: Children Who Have Withdrawn from Parental Control" (Presentation to the Continuing Education Program of LSUC-OBA (Family Law Section), Toronto, May 2 and 3, 2002).

Biological Parents and Fiduciary Obligations

In *Louis v. Lastman (No. 1)* (2002), 61 OR (3d) 449, the Ontario Court of Appeal dismissed an appeal by two brothers, born in 1958 and 1962 respectively, who claimed that their biological father, known to them in their childhood simply as a friend of their mother, had a fiduciary obligation to make adequate provision for their support. The brothers had been raised by their mother and her husband, until the parents separated in 1969; thereafter, they received social assistance and small monthly payments from their biological father. However, in 1974, their mother executed a release of all claims against him, in return for which she received a lump sum of $25,000 and legal fees. The biological father was a wealthy merchant and later mayor of Toronto. In concluding that the brothers' claims should be dismissed, the court held (at 454):

> No matter how the appellants attempt to frame their action, in the end it is nothing more than a claim for retroactive child support and, as such, it cannot succeed. I would not foreclose the possibility of a fiduciary claim for child support outside the legislative scheme where the child is in need and there is a gap in the legislative scheme. That, however, is not this case. The appellants concede that had their mother made a claim for child support under the legislation in force while they were children, the court could have made an order for support. It is not open to the appellants to come forward and make a support claim decades after they are no longer dependent.

According to newspaper accounts of this case, the two brothers wished to establish the fiduciary claim because they had been raised in poverty, while two other sons of their biological father grew up "with wealth and privilege": see Jack Lakey and Moira Walsh, "Lastman's Secret Affair Shocks City," *The Toronto Star*, December 1, 2000. To what extent is this case concerned with legislative definitions of parent–child relationships?

Consider also *S.(L.) v. P.(E.)* (1999), 175 DLR (4th) 423 (BCCA). In this case, a young woman had become pregnant by the same man three times in the 1970s; each time, she had obtained an abortion. However, she eventually decided that she wished to have a child with him, and without disclosing to him that she was no longer using birth control pills, she became pregnant and bore a child. When she wished to have the child baptized, it was necessary for her to identify the father; by that time, the father was married to another woman and denied his paternity. However, after a hearing on the issue, he was declared the father of the child. At the time, the child's mother made no claim of financial support for the child as she was able to support her son and wished to do so herself. In 1995, however, the mother sought and was granted an order for support of the child. In addition, she sought retroactive child support based on a claim of unjust enrichment.

The trial judge concluded that the mother had suffered a detriment, while the father had enjoyed a benefit as a result of making no contribution to the child's support. However, the court held that there was no unjust enrichment because the arrangement was agreed upon by the parties and confirmed in a nominal order only at the time of the paternity proceedings. The BC Court of Appeal also concluded that retroactive child support should not be ordered, but noted (at para. 86):

> It is disturbing that the order made in the Provincial Court in 1984 failed to reflect the fact that the obligation to support a child falls on both parents. If today's jurisprudence respecting child support obligations were applied, I have no doubt that such an order would not be regarded as supportable. Nevertheless, the order was made and there is no indication that the foundation for the award was the result of some blameworthy conduct on the part of the [father].

Why is there hesitancy on the part of courts to order child support retroactively? To what extent is there scope for the use of equitable doctrines in such cases?

2. Determining Paternity

a. Presumptions of Paternity: Low v. Low

Provincial legislation, such as Ontario's *Children's Law Reform Act*, contains presumptions of paternity: see s. 8. In addition, the statute includes provisions for judicial declarations of paternity. Recall the discussion of these provisions in chapter 3 in relation to applications for such declarations; in this section, the decision in *Low v. Low* illustrates the application of these provisions at separation or divorce. Consider the reasoning in *Low*—to what extent is the divorce context relevant to the judge's approach to these issues here?

Low v. Low

(1994), 4 RFL (4th) 103; 114 DLR (4th) 709 (Ont. Ct. J (Gen. Div.))

[In *Low v. Low*, a married couple decided, because of the husband's low sperm count and inability to conceive, to arrange for artificial insemination of the wife by an anonymous donor. The child Karen was born and the husband certified the child's birth as her father under the *Vital Statistics Act*, RSO 1990, c. V.4. By the time of the child's birth, however, the parties' relationship had so deteriorated that the wife demanded that the husband leave the home. He did so 10 days later. Eventually the husband sought and obtained a divorce.

The wife sought a declaration that the husband was not the father of the child; the husband sought a declaration that he was the father. In reviewing the applications, the court stated (at 111):]

Paternity Declarations

As indicated, the husband seeks a declaration under ss. 5(1) and (3) of the *Children's Law Reform Act*, RSO 1990, c. C.12 ("CLRA"), that he is Karen's father. The wife seeks a declaration pursuant to the CLRA that he is not Karen's father. ...

[Ferrier J considered ss. 1, 4, 5, and 8 of the CLRA and continued (at 113):]

The words "natural," "natural parent," "parent," "father," and "natural father," appearing in these sections, are not defined in the legislation. In s. 1(1), the word "natural" appears before the word "parents." In s. 8(1)3, the word "natural" appears before the word "father." The omission of the word "natural" as an adjective in describing "father" in other sections suggests the intention of a meaning broader than mere "biological" father, in those sections.

I note also that the declaration authorized in s.4(1) is *not* that a male person is the "natural father," rather that he is "recognized in law" to be the "father" of the child. This also suggests an intention of a meaning broader than merely the "biological" father.

As well, where a presumption does not arise under s. 8, a person may apply under s. 5(1) for a declaration that a person is his "child" (not "his natural child" or his "biological" child). The declaration is permitted when "the relationship of father and child has been established" (s. 5(3)). This subsection does not use the expression "natural father."

Section 4 provides the remedy of a declaration to those who are able to rely on the presumptions in s. 8. In the case at bar, the presumption has been raised by s. 8(1) and 8(1)5. Is such presumption rebutted by the fact of artificial insemination? It is not necessary to decide this question, because, in my view, a declaration can be made under s. 5.

Nowhere in s. 5 is there any suggestion that "the relationship of father and child" must have a biological or genetic character. As above noted, this section does not use the word "natural" in describing "father" or "relationship." Why was the expression "relationship of father and child" used in s. 5(3)? I conclude that this expression must mean something broader than a mere biological relationship.

In coming to this conclusion, I am guided by s. 10 of the *Interpretation Act*, RSO 1990, c. I.11:

> 10. Every Act shall be deemed to be remedial, whether its immediate purport is to direct the doing of anything that the Legislature deems to be for the public good or to prevent or punish the doing of any thing that it deems to be contrary to the public good, and shall accordingly receive such fair, large and liberal construction and interpretation as will best ensure the attainment of the object of the Act according to its true intent, meaning and spirit.

In *Bagaric v. Juric* (1984), 44 OR (2d) 638, the Court of Appeal made the following observations about the CLRA, at p. 647:

> The Act, being solely concerned with the status of children, does not deal with the consequences which might flow from the declaration of that status as a result of other legislation. The importance and significance of a declaration of parentage by itself is emphasized in that: "any person having an interest" may apply under s. 4(1) for such a

declaration where s. 8(1) is applicable; the child may apply for a declaration that a female person is the mother; the child may apply for a declaration of paternity where no presumption under s. 8(1) applies; a male person may apply to have a child declared to be his child. There is no time limitation on these applications except that under a s. 5 application both persons to the relationship must be living. Finally, there is no necessity for corroboration, although the Act introduces the right to secure blood tests, the results of which might, under particular circumstances, be considered to be corroborative of the mother's evidence.

At p. 648, it was further stated:

> The fact that the Legislature severed from the declaration of parentage any issue as to expenses and maintenance, placing them in new and different statutes, is of significance. It is also of significance that the right was greatly widened involving all children and both mothers and fathers. The Legislature recognized by this legislation present social conditions and attitudes as well as recognizing that such declarations have significance beyond material ones. It must be remembered that the Act itself is entitled "*Children's Law Reform Act*." (Emphasis added.) [Emphasis in original.]

Apparently there is no previous decision interpreting this legislation where a declaration is sought in a case of artificial insemination by an anonymous donor. Counsel were unable to refer me to any Canadian case involving similar legislation, but courts in the United States have dealt with similar issues. While recognizing that the legislation being considered was, in each case, different from that being considered here, I note that in most cases the United States courts have found "the husband" to be the lawful father of the child for virtually all purposes. Although not binding on this court, the American case law is instructive, and of assistance. I make particular reference to two US decisions.

In *S. v. S.*, 440 A2d 64 (1981), the Superior Court of New Jersey held that a husband in Mr. Low's position is the lawful father of a child conceived via artificial insemination. At p. 68 of that decision, the court looks at the issue in the context of public policy:

> Insofar as this is the case, the best interests of the child, the mother, the family unit and society are served by recognizing that the law surrounding AID insemination *deals with the creation of a family unit and more particularly with the creation of parent–child relationships*. Thus viewed, the public policy objectives served by legitimacy laws should similarly and consistently be applied in dealing with closely related problems presented by the use of AID techniques. [Emphasis added.]

In *Brooks v. Fair*, 532 NE 2d 208 (1988), the mother of the child asked the court to determine the non-existence of the parent–child relationship between her child, who was conceived via artificial insemination, and the man who was her husband at the time of the birth. The Court of Appeals of Ohio agreed with the lower court's determination that there existed a parent–child relationship.

Considering the language of the CLRA, the *Interpretation Act* and the observations of the Court of Appeal in *Bagaric v. Juric*, I conclude that Mr. Low is entitled to the declaration he seeks under s. 5 of the *Children's Law Reform Act*. Accordingly, a declaration shall issue that Timothy David Low is the father of Karen Elizabeth Low, born April 10, 1990.

[The court ordered custody to the mother, with liberal access to the father.]

Recall *A.A. v. B.B. and C.C.*, discussed in chapter 3, and the court's conclusion in that case that the lesbian partner of a child's mother was not entitled to a declaration of parentage pursuant to the *Children's Law Reform Act*. The lesbian partner in that case had no biological relationship to the child, just as the father in this case was not related biologically to Karen. What factors resulted in the differing outcomes in these two cases? Which factor(s) appeared most significant? Note that in both cases, the claims were made to attain legal recognition of the parent–child relationship, rather than in a dispute about child support—what are the consequences of both cases in terms of obligations for payment of child support? You may wish to reconsider this question after reviewing the material about the *Child Support Guidelines* later in this section.

b. Proving Paternity

Provincial legislation generally permits the use of blood tests to determine paternity: for example, see Ontario's *Children's Law Reform Act*, s. 10. Note that the section permits a court to grant leave for blood tests, but there is no legal requirement for a person to undergo such tests. However, s. 10(3) appears to create some risk for a person who chooses not to take blood tests after leave has been given. What factors should be considered by a court in granting leave for blood tests pursuant to s. 10? In reflecting on this question, examine the reasoning in the case that follows—to what extent do you think that these factors remain appropriate now? Would this case be decided differently today, or not?

Re Rhan and Pinsonneault
(1979), 27 OR (2d) 210 (Co. Ct.)

[In *Re Rhan and Pinsonneault*, Clements Co. Ct. J reviewed the law concerning the exercise of judicial discretion to permit blood tests in determining paternity. The mother brought an application for child support 22 months after the birth of the child and apparently only because she was requested to do so by welfare authorities. The court dismissed the application in this case, stating (at 212):]

The novel issue arising in this particular case, however, is whether this Court should exercise its discretion and give the applicant leave to obtain a blood test of the respondent. In other words, what criteria or standard should be applied in exercising the discretion. It is clearly recognized that the discretion to be exercised by the trial Judge depends on the facts of each case and it is trite to say that such discretion must be exercised judicially. ...

Under our legislation, of course, the Court merely grants leave in its discretion to the applicant but does not compel the respondent to submit to blood tests. It should be borne in mind, however, that a person so named who refuses to submit to the blood test subjects himself to the Court drawing such inferences as it thinks appropriate from such refusal.

In this case the applicant has set out in her affidavit that she and her girl-friend on or about May 20, 1977, were "picked up" by the respondent and another man. The two couples went to the Kent Motel and arrived there at approximately three or four in the morning. The said motel is located on Highway 2 East near Thamesville, Ontario. Apparently, Marcel Pinsonneault and the applicant occupied room 11 and had sexual intercourse for a period of approximately two hours. The other couple occupied room 12. The applicant deposes that she commenced her period on May 6th and made a note of it on her calendar.

Subsequent to the evening or morning in question the applicant never saw the respondent again.

When the applicant did not have her period in the month of June she was concerned but decided to wait until July to attend on her doctor. The applicant did so in July and she was advised that she was pregnant. The applicant says that at no time did she have sexual intercourse with any man other than Marcel Pinsonneault since her period of May 6, 1977, down to the date of swearing her affidavit.

The reason given by the applicant for failing to bring an application between the birth of the child on February 16, 1978, and the taking of her affidavit on April 10, 1979, was that due to advice from her lawyer she was concerned that if she applied for support the respondent could seek visiting rights. This advice was sought in October or November of 1978. Since the applicant did not want the respondent to have visits with the child she did not bother pursuing the question of support.

Shortly thereafter the applicant went on welfare and near the end of February, 1979, the Welfare Bureau in Chatham advised her that unless an application for support was brought against the respondent she would be cut off welfare. At the time of swearing the affidavit the applicant was no longer on welfare but employed at Wheels Motor Inn in the City of Chatham as a dishwasher.

The respondent admits meeting the applicant in the early morning hours in May of 1977. In his affidavit he states that he was riding down a street in the City of Chatham at 4 o'clock in the morning with his friend. The parties spoke and according to the respondent, went for a few drinks and that was the end of the evening. He denies intercourse and denies, therefore, being the father of the child.

In determining the criteria or standards to be applied in the exercise of the discretion under s. 10 of the *Children's Law Reform Act, 1977* the following would be of assistance to the Court:

1. Were the applicant and respondent married at the time the child or children were born? This is the situation in *Re H. and H.* referred to above, where the husband was seeking divorce on grounds of living separate and apart from his wife since 1958 and the wife alleged that five children of the marriage resulted from the husband's access during separation. Here, clearly, there is a presumption

that the husband is the father of the children born during marriage and the order was granted.

2. Did the parties cohabit in a common law relationship of some duration during which time or shortly thereafter a child was born?

3. Did the respondent admit sexual intercourse with the applicant at or near the time calculated to be the point of conception but now denies that he is the actual father of the child but alleges another is? That would appear to be the position in the *Evans and Martin v. Hammond* case.

4. Although there was not a common law union, did the respondent admit to an extramarital relationship with the applicant wherein sexual intercourse occurred from time to time thus making it possible that he is the putative father?

5. Was the applicant able, through affidavit and other evidence, to establish a *prima facie* case of putative fatherhood notwithstanding the denial of the respondent as to fatherhood and/or ever having sexual intercourse with the applicant?

In this particular case none of the criteria are reached. There is the bald statement by the applicant that as a result of a chance meeting and a one-night stand at a motel the respondent must be the father of the child. Although this incident occurred in May of 1977, an application for support is not brought into Court until the applicant is advised by the welfare authorities that her support will cease unless such application is brought. Her affidavit in support is sworn April 10, 1979, and the respondent was served on April 23, 1979, with the application for support and custody. ...

This Court, however, does have a discretion clearly set out under the relevant section and while the Court has a duty to see that the interests of the child are not neglected, the Court also has an obligation to see that the personal rights of the respondent are not infringed.

On the facts of this case, to make such an order bearing in mind that approximately 22 months went by before notice was given to the respondent of his alleged fatherhood, on the basis of an accusation stale with age arising out of an alleged experience of two-hour duration between parties who had no previous or subsequent relationship, platonic or otherwise, and brought into Court on the heels of the demands of the welfare officials for action would not be in keeping with the spirit of the section and the spirit of justice as this Court understands it.

Accordingly, the application will be denied and the question of costs will be reserved to the trial judge.

Discussion Notes

Judicial Discretion and Proving Paternity

What factors were most important in the exercise of discretion in *Rhan*? How important were issues of credibility to the court's reasoning? In reflecting on the evidentiary issues, consider *S.(E.A.) v. B.(K.M.)* (1989), 24 RFL (3d) 220 (Ont. Dist. Ct.). In this case, a court reviewed a man's request for blood tests under s. 10 to assist in determining whether he was the father of a child born to a woman with whom he had engaged in sexual relations. At the time of their relationship, the woman was in the process of divorcing her husband (who was the father of her two older children); after her divorce, however, she married a man other than the applicant. The woman also gave evidence that she was engaging in sexual relations with another man (who was married), as well as the applicant, at the time she conceived the child who was the subject of the application for blood tests. When the woman refused the request for blood tests for the child, the court considered s. 10(3) and drew the inference that the applicant was the father of the child. What factors may have influenced the court to infer that the applicant was the father of the child in this case?

Who has the burden of proof in an application for a declaration of paternity? Consider *M. v. S.* (1999), 48 RFL (4th) 145, in which the Nova Scotia Family Court denied a mother's application for a declaration of paternity. The alleged father denied paternity, and neither party could afford blood tests. Thus, the court held that there was insufficient evidence to meet the burden of proof of paternity. Is this case consistent with the reasoning in *Rhan*? For a case in which an application for blood tests was denied, see *L.(F.A.) v. B.(A.B.)* (1995), 15 RFL (4th) 107 (Man. CA).

Constitutional Challenges

There have been a number of challenges to the constitutionality of provisions such as s. 10. For example, in *P.(K.) v. N.(P.)* (1988), 15 RFL (3d) 110 (Ont. SC (HCJ)), the applicant challenged the validity of this section pursuant to s. 7 of the Charter, but the court held that there was no constitutional infringement, stating (at 111):

> I do not find that the impugned provision interferes with the physical or mental integrity of the individual. It does not authorize the forcible taking of blood. The impugned provision requires that the party seeking a blood test must apply to court for leave to obtain the tests and to then submit the results in evidence. If the court grants leave to obtain blood tests, the individual is nonetheless entitled to refuse to submit to the tests pursuant to s. 10(3) of the Act. The result of such a refusal is to provide the court with the power to "draw such inferences as it thinks appropriate."
>
> The drawing of an inference against a party who does not provide relevant evidence in a court proceeding, when that evidence is within the exclusive control of that party, does not constitute compulsion or coercion. It is an evidentiary matter to be considered in the context of a civil proceeding in which paternity is an issue.
>
> If there is no compulsion or coercion involved in an order made under s. 10 of the Act, the provision constitutes neither a denial nor an infringement of the rights guaranteed by s. 7 of the Charter.
>
> Although it is unnecessary for me to address the issue of whether or not the defendant's s. 7 rights were deprived in a manner contrary to the principles of fundamental justice in light of my findings, I will nevertheless briefly comment on this point. The power of the court, under s. 10 of the Act, to order leave to obtain blood tests encompasses the authority

to grant leave upon the terms and conditions which it thinks proper. If the terms and conditions to be ordered by a court to regulate the procedure of a blood test are thought to be inadequate or if exemplary procedures are not followed, an individual is open to challenge these matters in our adversarial court setting. Such procedural safeguards which provide the individual with the opportunity to challenge the terms of the blood test order demonstrate the consistency of s. 10 of the Act with the principles of fundamental justice.

In that I have found no breach of s. 7 of the Charter, there will be no need for me to address the s. 1 argument put forward by counsel in their factums.

The constitutionality of s. 10 of the Ontario statute was reviewed and upheld again in *Silber v. Fenske* (1995), 11 RFL (4th) 145 (Ont. Ct. J (Gen. Div. Fam. Ct.)). See also *Rath v. Kemp* (1997), 26 RFL (4th) 152 (Alta. CA).

DNA Testing

Section 10 of the *Children's Law Reform Act* in Ontario, like some other provincial statutes, refers expressly to leave for blood tests; there is no general authority for other kinds of testing for biological relationships. However, some cases have permitted the use of DNA testing: for example, see *S.(C.) v. L.(V.)* (1992), 39 RFL (3d) 294 (Ont. Ct. J (Prov. Div.)). In this case, Wilkins Prov. J considered an application for child support where the respondent denied paternity. The blood test was inconclusive and the mother requested DNA tests. The court held that it was appropriate to order DNA tests in such cases and that expenses and inconvenience could be dealt with in costs.

The Ontario Court of Justice (General Division) dismissed an appeal from this decision, holding that the DNA test would not be a "second test" but merely a continuation of the first one. Because the point was a novel one, no costs of the appeal were ordered; the mother was obliged to pay for the DNA tests, subject to being accounted for in the costs of the action: see (1992), 39 RFL (3d) 298 (Ont. Ct. J (Gen. Div.)) and Brad Daisley, "DNA Evidence: It Makes Headlines in Criminal Trials, but Lawyers Use It in Custody and Immigration Cases, Too," *The Lawyers Weekly*, February 26, 1993. For another successful application for DNA testing, see *D.(J.S.) v. V.(W.L.)* (1995), 11 RFL (4th) 409 (BCCA).

3. In Loco Parentis and Settled-Intent Children

According to s. 2(2) of the *Divorce Act, 1985*, a "child of the marriage" includes children for whom one or both of the spouses stand in the place of a parent. Similarly, provincial legislation generally includes (within the definition of "child") some relationships between children and non-biologically related adults. For example, s. 1 of Ontario's *Family Law Act* includes persons who have demonstrated a "settled intention" to treat a child as "a child of his or her family." In the context of the breakdown of adult relationships through divorce or separation and the repartnering of parents in new relationships, there is considerable scope for adults who are not biologically related to a child to "stand in the place of a parent." Moreover, because there is little legislative guidance as to the factors that are relevant to such parent–child relationships, judges have been required to exercise discretion to determine whether such relationships have been established.

Thus, children may have both biological parents and social parents, and problems may arise if adult relationships that include a social parent break down. Can a social parent terminate a parent–child relationship when the relationship with the child's biological parent has ended? This issue has been addressed by a number of different appellate courts in Canada: for example, see *Carignan v. Carignan* (1989), 22 RFL (3d) 376 (Man. CA); *Theriault v. Theriault* (1994), 149 AR 210 (Alta. CA); *Andrews v. Andrews* (1992), 38 RFL (3d) 200 (Sask. CA); and *A. v. A.* (1999), 48 RFL (4th) 205 (BCCA). See also *Siddall v. Siddall* (1994), 11 RFL (4th) 325 (Ont. Ct. J (Gen. Div.)).

Chartier v. Chartier
(1999), 43 RFL (4th) 1; [1999] 1 SCR 242

[The Supreme Court of Canada addressed this issue in *Chartier v. Chartier* (1999), 43 RFL (4th) 1. In *Chartier*, the parties were married for one year and had one biological child. However, the wife had a child from a previous relationship, for whom the husband stood "in place of a parent" in accordance with s. 2(2) of the *Divorce Act, 1985*. When the marriage ended, the wife applied for support for both children. The trial judge held that the husband had terminated the relationship with the wife's child and so ordered no support for her: see (1996), 111 Man. R (2d) 27 (QB (Fam. Div.)). Relying on its earlier decision in *Carignan v. Carignan*, the Manitoba Court of Appeal dismissed the appeal: see (1997), 29 RFL (4th) 96; 118 Man. R (2d) 152 (CA). On appeal to the Supreme Court of Canada, the wife's appeal was allowed. In part, Bastarache J stated (at para. 17):]

There is one body of case law, exemplified by *Carignan, supra*, that states that a person standing in the place of a parent is entitled to make a unilateral withdrawal from the parental relationship. The other body of case law is typified by *Theriault v. Theriault* (1994), 149 AR 210 (Alta. CA); it states that a person cannot unilaterally withdraw from a relationship in which he or she stands in the place of a parent and that the court must look to the nature of the relationship to determine if a person in fact does stand in the place of a parent to a child.

Before considering these two lines of authority, I would note that in both cases the courts have engaged upon a historical review of the doctrine of *loco parentis* and taken the view that the words "in the place of a parent" used in the *Divorce Act* were intended to have the same meaning. The doctrine of *loco parentis* was developed in diverse contexts, trust law, tort law, master–apprentice relationships, schoolmaster–pupil relationships, wills and gifts … , at another time. Alison Diduck, in "*Carignan v. Carignan*: When Is a Father Not a Father? Another Historical Perspective" (1990), 19 *Man. LJ* 580, explains how this common law doctrine was applied in family matters, over the years, in various jurisdictions. She concludes, at pp. 601-602, by saying:

> The *in loco parentis* doctrine is a creature of 19th century patriarchy. It evolved during a time when it was a morally offensive notion for a man to be held responsible for another man's child. As Mendes de Costa UFJ stated in a 1987 decision, it has "its roots deep in history" and "carries with it connotations of times past" (*Re Spring and Spring* (1987), 61 OR (2d) 743 at 748). Notwithstanding Parliament's choice of similar wording in the *Divorce Act, 1985*, it is arguably open to counsel (or to courts) to suggest

that Parliament deliberately chose to reject the common law notion of *in loco parentis*, and that the current statute should be interpreted "free from the shadow of earlier authorities." (*Ibid.*, at 749.)

I agree that the policies and values reflected in the *Divorce Act* must relate to contemporary Canadian society and that the general principles of statutory interpretation support a modern understanding of the words "stands in the place of a parent." ...

This being said, it is my opinion that the decision in *Theriault, supra*, provides the proper approach to this issue as it recognizes that the provisions of the *Divorce Act* dealing with children focus on what is in the best interests of the children of the marriage, not on biological parenthood or legal status of children. *Theriault* was an appeal from an interim maintenance award made to the mother and primary caregiver of two children made against the husband in a pending divorce suit. The children were not the husband's biological children. The husband gave advice and supervision to the two children from infancy but, at the hearing for interim support, he argued that his commitment to the children arose from the marriage and was conditional on the continuation of that relationship.

Kerans JA rejected the approach in *Carignan, supra*, and held, at p. 213, that once someone "has made at least a permanent or indefinite unconditional commitment to stand in the place of a parent," the jurisdiction of the courts to award support under the *Divorce Act* is triggered and that jurisdiction is not lost by a subsequent disavowal of the child by the parent. Underlying Kerans JA's decision is the best interests of the child. At p. 213, Kerans JA held:

> Our society values parenthood as a vital adjunct to the upbringing of children. Adequate performance of that office is a duty imposed by law whenever our society judges that it is fair to impose it. In the case of the natural parent, the biological contribution towards the new life warrants the imposition of the duty. In the case of a step-parent, it is the voluntary assumption of that role. It is not in the best interests of children that step-parents or natural parents be permitted to abandon their children, and it is their best interests that should govern. Financial responsibility is simply one of the many aspects of the office of parent. A parent, or step-parent, who refuses or avoids this obligation neglects or abandons the child. The abandonment or neglect is as real as would be a refusal of medical care, or affection, or comfort, or any other need of a child.

... Whether a person stands in the place of a parent must take into account all factors relevant to that determination, viewed objectively. What must be determined is the nature of the relationship. The *Divorce Act* makes no mention of formal expressions of intent. The focus on voluntariness and intention in *Carignan, supra*, was dependent on the common law approach discussed earlier. It was wrong. The Court must determine the nature of the relationship by looking at a number of factors, among which is intention. Intention will not only be expressed formally. The court must also infer intention from actions, and take into consideration that even expressed intentions may sometimes change. The actual fact of forming a new family is a key factor in drawing an inference that the step-parent treats the child as a member of his or her family, i.e., a child of the marriage. The relevant factors in defining the parental relationship include, but are not limited to, whether the child participates in the extended family in the same way as would a biological child; whether the person provides financially for the child (depending on ability to pay); whether the person disciplines the child as a parent; whether the person represents to the child, the family, the world, either explicitly or implicitly, that he or she is responsible as a parent to the child; the nature or existence of the child's relationship with the absent biological parent. The manifestation of the intention of the step-parent cannot be qualified as to duration, or be otherwise made conditional or qualified, even if this intention is manifested expressly. Once it is shown that the child is to be considered, in fact, a "child of the marriage," the obligations of the step-parent towards him or her are the same as those relative to a child born of the marriage with regard to the application of the *Divorce Act*. The step-parent, at this point, does not only incur obligations. He or she also acquires certain rights, such as the right to apply eventually for custody or access under s. 16(1) of the *Divorce Act*.

Nevertheless, not every adult–child relationship will be determined to be one where the adult stands in the place of a parent. Every case must be determined on its own facts and it must be established from the evidence that the adult acted so as to stand in the place of a parent to the child.

Huband JA, in *Carignan, supra*, expressed the concern that individuals may be reluctant to be generous toward children for fear that their generosity will give rise to parental obligations. I do not share those concerns. The nature of a parental relationship is complex and includes more than financial support. People do not enter into parental relationships with the view that they will be terminated.

Discussion Notes

The Impact of Chartier on Adult Relationships

Consider the reasoning in *Chartier*—to what extent does the case present barriers for adults who wish to form new relationships? In reflecting on this issue, consider the comments of James McLeod (at 3):

> Bastarache J's reasons are consistent with the weight of recent authority. An adult should not be allowed to terminate his or her relationship with a child. It is not in a child's best interests to have parent figures passing through his or her life. With respect, holding that a step-parent incurs a long-term child-support obligation does not prevent that from happening. The Supreme Court of Canada seems to assume that a person will continue his or her relationship with a child if he or she has to pay support. The court ignores the fact that, in many cases, denying or terminating support merely makes the law reflect the reality of the post-separation relationship between step-parent and child.
>
> The fact that adults live together does not amount to a commitment that they will remain together. Many relationships are of short duration. Many people are not inclined to make the accommodations necessary to ensure that their relationship will continue. In light of this, should the courts impose a long-term financial commitment on a person who was pleasant to a partner's child for a short time? The Supreme Court of Canada apparently believes that

it should. It is surprising that a short-term spousal relationship that is insufficient to give rise to a spousal support claim may be sufficient to give rise to a child-support claim where the adult–child relationship was incidental to the spousal relationship.

The Supreme Court of Canada rejected the suggestion that a person may not be as inclined to interact with a child if he or she will incur a long-term financial relationship. Bastarache J does not explain how he decided what effect his decision would have on peoples' actions. With respect, people are more aware of the legal consequences of their actions in a family law context than they were a few years ago. The increase in the use of the remedial constructive trust to share property and the extension of rights to less traditional family units has led to a greater awareness that personal relations carry legal consequences. It will not be surprising if men, in particular, seek contractual protection from child support or attempt to minimize their interaction with a partner's child. While it may not speak well of many men, it also would not be surprising if women with children had an even more difficult time forming family relationships after *Chartier*.

In *Chartier*, the parties cohabited, married, separated, reconciled and separated again, all within three years. As a result, Mr. Chartier acquires a long-term child-support obligation. Whether that is reasonable is not the question. The Supreme Court of Canada has decided that it is the law. The task facing many lawyers will be to advise their clients on how to prevent that from happening to them. It appears that the only way to prevent a long-term child-support commitment is never to establish a parent–child relationship with a partner's child. Social scientists will have to decide whether that is a good way to force people to interact.

(James McLeod, "Annotation of Chartier v. Chartier" (1999), 43 RFL (4th) 2.)

Marriage, Cohabitation, and "in Loco Parentis" Parents

In *Chartier*, the Supreme Court of Canada decided that a married spouse stood in the place of a parent to the other spouse's child. To what extent should the *Chartier* principles apply in situations involving cohabitation only? Recall the Supreme Court's decision in *Walsh v. Bona*, discussed in chapter 6, and the extent to which the court held that marriage constitutes a choice about rights and responsibilities that do not necessarily apply to cohabiting couples—should this same argument apply with respect to the issue of whether a person who cohabits with a parent becomes a social parent to his or her child?

In *Monkman v. Beaulieu*, 2003 MBCA 17, a majority of the Manitoba Court of Appeal held that the *Chartier* principles apply to cohabiting couples as well as to those who are married. In this case, the parties began to cohabit in August 1988 and separated in January 1992. They had one child together, but the mother had four other children, one of whom was the focus of this case. She was one month old when the adults' relationship began and had called the respondent "Dad" from about the age of two. The affidavit evidence demonstrated that the respondent had accepted her as his stepchild; the child had no connections with her biological father. Thus, according to Steel JA, the evidence supported an inference that the respondent stood in the place of a parent to this child.

The court then considered the provisions of the *Family Maintenance Act*, RSM 1987, c. F20, and the requirement in s. 2(1) that the best interests of a child "shall be the paramount consideration of the court." In exploring this requirement, Steel JA stated (at paras. 30-31):

Unilateral severance focuses on the interests of the adult who assumed the *in loco parentis* relationship. A court should instead give the provisions an interpretation which protects the interests of the dependent child. The interpretation that best serves children is one that recognizes that when adults intentionally take on the role and responsibilities of a parent, then the children can depend on the continuation of that role.

An interpretation that adopts unilateral severance disregards any notions of bonding and attachment between the child and a psychological parent. Family law affecting children has moved from preserving parental rights over children to decisions identifying the best interests of children and promoting children's welfare. Those, I believe, are the objectives of the Acts, and *in loco parentis* should be interpreted harmoniously with those objectives.

In addition, Steel JA considered the relevance of the fact that the parties in *Monkman* had cohabited, rather than married, noting the rising numbers of cohabiting relationships in Canada and the trend in family law to extend legal obligations to children regardless of the legal status of adult relationships. She also examined the wording of s. 36 of the statute, and concluded (at paras. 46 and 48) that

> in situations dealing with children, where the best interests test prevails, there should be no distinction in the application of the *in loco parentis* test between children living in a relationship where the parties are married and children living in a relationship where the parties are not married. This general conclusion does not preclude the possibility that in a particular case, the evidence may be that the parties did not marry specifically because of a hesitancy on the part of the non-parent in assuming the role of a parent towards a child. Such evidence might tend to negate the existence of a deliberate intention to enter into a parental role and would be relevant to the factual determination of whether an alternative parenting relationship had been established in that particular case. ...
>
> In summary, the crucial element in all of this should be the relationship between the child and the adult and not the relationship between the adults.

In reaching this conclusion, Steel JA acknowledged (at para. 47) that her approach created uniformity between the federal and provincial statutes, a result that she approved for family law matters. By contrast with this approach, Huband JA dissented, in part relying on the present tense in s. 36(4). For him, there were clear distinctions between the purposes of the divorce legislation, by contrast with the *Family Maintenance Act*. In addition, however, Huband JA expressed concern that the motions judge had only affidavit evidence on which to base a conclusion that the respondent stood *in loco parentis*.

What are the implications of the majority decision in *Monkman*? To what extent does the majority approach tend to further expand the potential for identifying parents to whom child-support obligations may attach? What policies are thereby furthered? In this context, consider *N.B. v. Hodnett* (1995), 14 RFL (4th) 138 (NBCA), where a father claimed (unsuccessfully) that he had been "set up" when his partner claimed to be using birth control pills. In addition, in *Cheng v. Cheng* (1996), 21 RFL (4th) 58 (Ont. CA), a mother brought a motion to amend her statement of claim to proceed against her father-in-law and mother-in-law to claim support for herself and her children. The claim for child support was said to be based on the provisions of the *Family Law Act*, particularly asserting that the grandparents had "demonstrated a settled intention" to treat the children as children of their family. The Ontario Court of Appeal allowed the mother's appeal from the trial decision dismissing her motion. The appellate court held that the Act did not exclude grandparents as persons who might be responsible for the support of children.

By contrast with these expansive approaches to defining *in loco parentis* parents, a few cases have concluded that a parent's partner does not meet the requirements of standing in the place of a parent. For example, an Ontario court held in *Do Carmo v. Etzkorn* (1995), 16 RFL (4th) 341 (Ont. Ct. J (Gen. Div.)) that cohabitation was an essential requirement for "settled intention" pursuant to s. 1 of the *Family Law Act*; thus, the existence of an ongoing relationship, but without cohabitation, did not create a settled-intention parent.

In *Gardiner v. Gardiner* (2001), 194 NSR (2d) 233; 606 APR 231, the Nova Scotia Supreme Court (Fam. Div.) considered a father's application for a declaration that his wife stood *in loco parentis* to his two sons (from a previous relationship). The parties had cohabited for two years and been married for three. There was evidence that the children's biological mother had remained in contact with the children, that their father and a nanny had provided most of their day-to-day care, and that the wife had not expended money to support the children nor had she provided primary care for them because she worked outside the home. In addition, however, the evidence established that the two sons were experiencing difficulties—the older son had behaviour problems while the younger one, Nicky, had cerebral palsy. The court stated (at 244):

> Therefore, should Cheryl Gardiner be found to be in loco parentis to Nicky, she will carry with her the financial obligation to contribute to the support of that child for so long as he continues to be dependent, which will be for the rest of his natural life.
>
> Does a relationship of five years with Nicky's father warrant this life-long responsibility to her husband's son? According to *Chartier*, it does. *Chartier* stands for the proposition that once in loco parentis is established, the child must be treated in the same manner as one's biological or adopted child.

In the end, although the court found (at 247) that the wife had taken on some responsibilities as a parent or caregiver, the relationship did not establish the foundation for the long-term implications attached to a finding of *in loco parentis*. To what extent should this case be regarded as exceptional? See also *A.(V.) v. F.(S.)* (2000), 197 DLR (4th), in which a majority of the Quebec Court of Appeal applied the principles of *Chartier*, but concluded that the non-biological parent did not stand in place of a parent pursuant to the *Divorce Act, 1985*. According to Brossard JA (at 506), the factors relied on by the motions judge were

> just as consistent with an intent ... to please the [child's mother] and to lay the basis of a family relationship of excellent quality with her. ... The fact that [the appellant] wanted to be a friend of the son of his new spouse does not necessarily mean ... that there was intent to act *in loco parentis* with respect to the child, and to assume all the consequences which arise therefrom.

Apportioning Responsibilities for Child Support

Because it is clear that there may be both social and biological parents with child-support obligations, the question of apportioning such responsibilities may arise. This issue is addressed later in this section in relation to the *Child Support Guidelines*.

SELECTED REFERENCES

Alison Diduck, "Carignan v. Carignan: When Is a Father Not a Father? Another Historical Perspective" (1990), 19 *Manitoba Law Journal* 580.

Keith B. Farquhar, "Termination of the in Loco Parentis Obligation of Child Support" (1990), 9 *Canadian Journal of Family Law* 99.

Alison Harvison Young, "This Child Does Have Two (or More) Fathers ... : Step-Parents and Support Obligations" (2000), 45 *McGill Law Journal* 107.

C. Child Support: The Social and Legal Context

1. The Costs of Raising Children

In examining the principles of child support and the *Child Support Guidelines*, it is important to take account of economic data about the costs of raising children. Some data about children were included in chapter 1, while chapter 5 included materials about the economic consequences of divorce and separation. In addition, however, it may be useful to examine some data about the costs of raising children. For example, the Canadian Council on Social Development reported in 1998:

> The costs of raising children in Canadian society are high, and they are increasing at a time when incomes are declining for many families. In 1998, the cost of raising a child from birth to age 18 was estimated to be $160,000—up by $4000 from 1995 (constant 1998$). The largest portion of this cost—33 per cent—was attributed to child care, and shelter was the next largest expenditure, at 23 per cent.

(Canadian Council on Social Development, *The Progress of Canada's Children 1998* (Ottawa: Canadian Council on Social Development, 1998), 19.)

The same report also noted (at 19) that "about one-quarter of young Canadians under age 25 live in poverty," although the proportions were higher for children and youth who were immigrants or aboriginal persons. You may wish to reflect on these figures in relation to the discussion of levels and obligations of child support in the materials that follow.

2. Child-Support Principles: Background to the 1997 Child Support Guidelines

> Canada has long had a discretionary child support law, with individualized determinations based on an assessment of the "reasonable" amount of support. Thus, inconsistent orders were being made, though the courts tended to rely on highly discretionary, judicially developed, rules to establish the amount of child support.
>
> Martha Bailey and Nicholas Bala, "Child Support Guidelines,
> Parental Mobility, and Redefining Familial Relationships," in
> A. Bainham, ed., *The International Survey of Family Law 1996*
> (The Netherlands: International Society of Family Law, 1998), 69

Judicial principles for determining child-support awards reflect this highly discretionary approach. In Ontario, for example, the decision in *Paras v. Paras* (1970), 2 RFL 328; 14

DLR 546 (Ont. CA) established that child support should be set at a level that would maintain the child at the pre-divorce standard of living and that the costs of achieving that standard be apportioned between the parents in proportion to their respective incomes.

As is apparent, the *Paras* principle requires considerable discretion to determine the amount payable in each particular case. As well, the principle assumes the continued existence of sufficient resources to enable children to have the same standard of living post-divorce (in spite of the need to support two households) as they had enjoyed in the intact family. Clearly, there are many situations in which family resources are insufficient to meet this standard. Moreover, the variability of child-support awards, partly as a result of the wide scope for discretionary decision making by judges, increasingly creates concerns about fairness and consistency. In one assessment, for example, Carol Rogerson concludes:

> Problems begin to appear ... when one examines more closely the way in which the costs associated with children are calculated, the way in which they are apportioned between the parents, and finally, the quantum of child support awarded. As in the spousal support cases ... , there is often an obvious disjuncture between the principles articulated and the actual outcomes in terms of quantum of support. The end result is that in the majority of child support cases awards are not set at levels which will meet the *Paras* standard or even at levels which would guarantee an equal standard of living between the children's house-hold and that of the non-custodial parent. Typically the household of the custodial parent (usually the mother) and children is left with an income between 40 and 80 per cent of that enjoyed by the non-custodial parent. Thus what is typically a three-person household subsists on less than what is typically, until the husband remarries, a one-person household.

(Carol Rogerson, "Judicial Interpretation of the Spousal and Child Support Provisions of the Divorce Act, 1985 (Part II)" (1991), 7 *Canadian Family Law Quarterly* 271, at 274.)

Rogerson's assessment is similar to other studies of child support in Canada; some studies also address the problem of uneven enforcement: see further the references in chapter 5. In addition, there are related recommendations for changes in tax laws to improve the financial well-being of Canadian children. For example, it has been suggested that the financial circumstances for children post-divorce could be promoted by legal principles that recognize (1) the need to identify financial support, post-separation, as a joint responsibility of the parents; (2) the need for the legal system to take account of the comprehensive financial circumstances of the parents; and (3) the need to define "ability to pay" as a *primary responsibility*, not a matter of the availability of residual income: see N. Blown and S. Milliken, "The Failure of the Legal System to Protect the Economic Rights of Children" (1989), 7 *Canadian Journal of Family Law* 366.

In two cases in the 1990s, moreover, courts tried to define more precisely how to determine the obligations of parents for child support. In *Levesque v. Levesque* (1994), 4 RFL (4th) 375, the Alberta Court of Appeal set out a list of factors to be considered in determining the amount of child support; this analysis was substantially accepted by the Supreme Court of Canada in *Willick v. Willick* (1994), 6 RFL (4th) 161: see Christine Davies, "The Emergence of Judicial Child Support Guidelines" (1995), 13 *Canadian Family Law Quarterly* 89. In the context of these developments, however, the Supreme Court of Canada considered an appeal from Quebec concerning the treatment of child support in relation to income tax. In particular, Suzanne Thibaudeau argued (in part) that the inclusion/deduction provisions of s. 56 of the *Income Tax Act*, RSC 1985, c. 1 (5th Supp.), pursuant to which her former husband (the payor) could deduct the amount of his child support payments, while she (as the payee custodial parent) had to include them in the calculation of her income, violated the equality guarantee in s. 15 of the Charter. In *Thibaudeau v. Queen* (1995), 12 RFL (4th) 92, a majority of the Supreme Court of Canada concluded that the inclusion/deduction provisions did not infringe the equality rights guaranteed by s. 15(1) of the Charter. Two justices, the only two women members of the court, dissented, adding to the controversy about the need for reform of child support in Canada. In this context, national child-support guidelines were enacted by the federal, provincial, and territorial governments in Canada.

SELECTED REFERENCES

Nicholas Bala, "Ottawa's New Child-Support Regime: A Guide to the Guidelines" (1999), 21 RFL (4th) 301.

Lisa Philipps and Margot Young, "Sex, Tax and the Charter: A Review of Thibaudeau v. Canada" (1995), 2 *Review of Constitutional Studies* 221.

Dianne Pothier, "M'Aider, Mayday: Section 15 of the Charter in Distress" (1996), 6 *National Journal of Constitutional Law* 295.

Lorne Wolfson, "Reflections on R v. Thibaudeau" (1996), 13 *Canadian Family Law Quarterly* 163.

Faye Woodman, "The Charter and the Taxation of Women" (1990), 22 *Ottawa Law Review* 625.

3. The Child Support Guidelines

a. The Scope of the Guidelines

Federal, provincial and territorial governments in Canada are currently examining the feasibility and desirability of implementing child support guidelines that will provide fixed amounts of child support rather than leave the amount of support to the discretion of the individual trial Judge. Fixed schedules or formulae for the determination of child support could promote (i) simple and inexpensive administrative procedures for assessing the amount of child support; (ii) consistency of amounts in comparable family situations; and (iii) higher child support payments that more realistically reflect the actual costs of raising children. They are unlikely, however, to resolve the economic crisis of separation and divorce for women and children. The war on poverty requires more than piecemeal reform of child support.

> Julien Payne, "Spousal and Child Support After Moge, Willick and
> Levesque" (1995), 12 *Canadian Family Law Quarterly* 261, at 298

Child Support Guidelines were promulgated, effective May 1, 1997, as regulations pursuant to amendments to the federal *Divorce Act, 1985*: see SC 1997, c. 1 and SOR/97-175, as amended. Although these provisions are directly applicable only in divorce proceedings, most provinces and territories adopted identical or similar guidelines applicable to child-support applications in situations that do not involve divorce; according to

Bailey and Bala (at 71), the Quebec guidelines constitute a slightly different model. Along with the guidelines, the tax inclusion/deduction system was abolished and enforcement measures were strengthened. Overall, the previous discretionary approach has been replaced by a new model of legislative guidelines for child support across Canada.

b. An Overview of the Guidelines

i. The Basic Provisions

The basic principles of the *Child Support Guidelines* were developed as part of the consultation process among the federal, provincial, and territorial governments: see Federal/Provincial/Territorial Family Law Committee, *Child Support: Public Discussion Paper* (Ottawa: Department of Justice, 1991) and Canada, Department of Justice, *Federal Child Support Guidelines Reference Manual* (Ottawa: Supply and Services Canada, 1998).
　　In general terms, the guidelines include:

- a list of objectives (s. 1);
- a presumptive rule that child support is to be paid according to tables for each province and having regard to the number(s) of children (s. 3), or in accordance with special rules
  — for payors whose income exceeds $150,000 (s. 4); and
  — for determining income, including imputed income (ss. 17-19);
- a list of "special or extraordinary expenses" (s. 7), the cost of which may be added to the table amounts; and
- adjustments based on sharing of child expenses by biological and other parents (s. 5), split custody (s. 8), shared custody (s. 9), and undue hardship (s. 10 and schedule II).

As will be evident, the existence of table amounts for child support appears to provide more certainty in determining child-support awards, but some provisions of the guidelines clearly continue to require discretionary decision making by judges. For an early example of the application of the guidelines and the need for ongoing judicial discretion, see *Middleton v. MacPherson* (1997), 29 RFL (4th) 334 (Alta. QB).
　　This section provides some examples of the interpretation of the *Child Support Guidelines* in relation to these key provisions.

ii. The Objectives: Section 1

Examine the objectives of the *Child Support Guidelines* in s. 1. Consider whether it is possible to achieve all four objectives in every case—for example, are goals of fairness always consistent with improved efficiency? Which of these objectives is more likely to be achieved by clear rules; by the exercise of judicial discretion? In reflecting on these questions, consider the assessment of the guidelines four years after they were promulgated—you may wish to keep these comments in mind as you review examples of judicial decisions concerning the guidelines in this section.

**D.A. Rollie Thompson, "Who Wants To Avoid the Guidelines?
Contracting Out and Around"**
(2001), 19 *Canadian Family Law Quarterly* 1, at 2-3

My early impression of the Guidelines has been the alacrity, the cheerful willingness, with which lawyers and judges have embraced only two of the objectives of the Guidelines, clauses (b) and (d) of section 1—"certainty" and "consistency." As contestants, most of us have narrowed the answers to just (b) and (d), to improve our chances of getting the right answer. Lost in the shuffle have been "adequacy" and "efficiency": "a fair standard of support" in clause (a) and improving efficiency of the process by giving guidance and encouraging settlement in clause (c).

Let us call these two approaches the "BD" and "AC" approaches.

A large number of BD lawyers and judges are just happy to have tables and formulas, whatever the consequences. The majority of the Nova Scotia Court of Appeal in *Raftus* [(1998), 37 RFL (4th) 59 (NSCA)] leaps to mind here. Another segment of the BD camp believes that certainty and consistency will lead to adequacy and efficiency, or at least that the losses in individual cases are outweighed by the systemic gains.

To date, the AC camp have appeared to be traditionalists, those lawyers and judges unwilling to give up their old individualistic ways, a minority resisting the rules of the new regime. Another growing segment have been hard-headed practical types, who see the impact of the Guidelines and tax changes in individual cases, like the BC Court of Appeal in *Wang v. Wang* [(1998), 39 RFL (4th) 426 (BCCA)].

In the Supreme Court of Canada's only decision on the Guidelines *Francis v. Baker* [(1999), 50 RFL (4th) 228 (SCC)], there are some broad remarks that lend support to the AC camp, or at least suggest that there must be some softening of the BD approach. ...

[Thompson's comments were made in the context of an examination of the scope for agreements by parents, "contracting around" the *Child Support Guidelines*. After reviewing a number of appellate court decisions in different provinces, particularly with respect to the requirement to apply the *Child Support Guidelines* to applications for variation, Thompson suggested (at 19):]

The *Child Support Guidelines* constitute a clear statement of public policy, prescribing in minute detail the determination of child support amounts. To be effective public policy, there must be limits upon the parties' ability to "contract out," otherwise the benefits of certainty and consistency will be lost. Inevitably, to make that policy effective, the courts now play an expanded role in approving and monitoring agreements and orders.

The more intrusive judicial role flows from three characteristics of the Guidelines. First, the tables provide a clear "floor" or minimum against which child support can be tested. Under the "old" system, there was no "objective" minimum, only a subjective, individualized, flexible minimum. Second, the Guidelines provide formulas and rules for many variations up, down and around the table amounts. Formulas and rules reduce the range of "reasonable arrangements" and force explanations, from lawyers and from courts. Third, more detailed financial disclosure is required by the Guidelines and related provincial rules, allowing judges to better assess the adequacy and Guidelines compliance of child support. ...

[Thompson provided an analysis of a number of cases in which parties attempted to make agreements that reflected their needs and circumstances and the extent to which courts accepted departures from the guidelines. Noting that courts are unlikely to recognize the appropriateness of child support amounts that are lower than the guidelines amount, he also explored the relationship between child support and the disposition of property, tax implications, spousal support awards, and social assistance. He concluded (at 51):]

[T]here must be regular, ongoing dialogue between local Bench and Bar over their respective views on the balance between judicial scrutiny and parental autonomy, between the Guidelines policy of disclosure and the realities of available information, and between enforcing Guidelines compliance and encouraging individualized settlements.

iii. Applying the Table Amount: Determining the Payor's Income

Because the table amounts are applied to the payor's income, it is necessary to obtain disclosure of all information relevant to income. In many cases, this issue will not be complicated—income tax and pay statements will provide financial information on which to calculate the projected income for the next year. Nonetheless, the determination of a party's income for purposes of applying the *Child Support Guidelines* may well involve some discretionary decision making. For example, consider the brief excerpt from *Middleton v. MacPherson*, in which the court attempted to determine the wife's income—to what extent is judicial discretion involved in the determination of income for purposes of applying the table?

Middleton v. MacPherson
(1997), 29 RFL (4th) 334, at 337; 204 AR 37 (QB)

In the case of the wife, she testified that if she was permitted to complete her internship in Calgary while finishing her Masters degree, she would expect to earn approximately $200 per week. This could result in the wife's earnings dropping from her earnings in 1996. I prefer to base the wife's present income on the total income reflected in her 1996 income tax return, as urged upon me by her counsel. Although the wife worked part-time as a teacher while taking course work to permit her to obtain a massage therapist's license, then worked as a massage therapist for a period of time, I am of the view that to impute income to her, as urged by counsel for the husband, equal to that of the husband would not be equitable. As a result of taking up a course of study, the wife was able to take on more daytime weekday child care responsibilities. I accept her testimony that her course work will be heavy until she completes her degree [in] the spring of 1998. Her internship should be concurrently undertaken so that she can start to build up a private practice. I therefore find that her income for purpose of the table calculation is $14,563 per year (based on her 1996 tax return). This figure should of course change when the wife receives her Masters degree in the spring of 1998 and is eligible for fulltime employment as the child will be in grade one.

Judicial Discretion To Determine Income

The guidelines expressly permit a court to determine income in some defined situations: see ss. 17-19. Where, for example, a payor's income has fluctuated in recent years, the guidelines permit the court to find that the amount of the payor's income is the average amount: for example, see *Adams v. Adams* (2001), 15 RFL (5th) 1 (CA), where the court relied on s. 17(1)(b) to apply a three-year average to determine the payor's income. In *Arnold v. Washburn* (2001), 57 OR (3d) 287 (CA), the court reviewed the wording of the former s. 17(1)(c) and the revised wording in s. 17(1), effective as of November 1, 2000, and concluded (at 291) that both sections permitted the exercise of judicial discretion with respect to the trial judge's determination that stock options paid to the payor spouse in 1999, valued at more than $3 million, did not form part of the payor's income for that year.

Section 19 also permits the exercise of judicial discretion with respect to imputing income to a payor of child support, in accordance with a range of defined circumstances. For example, where a parent is "intentionally under-employed or unemployed," s. 19(1)(a) permits a court to impute an appropriate income to the parent. In *Drygala v. Pauli* (2002), 61 OR (3d) 711 (CA), the court reviewed two lines of cases that had interpreted the intention requirement in s. 19(1)(a)—one line of cases required evidence of a bad-faith intention to undermine or avoid a child-support obligation, while the other group of cases held that there was no need to find a specific intent to evade child-support obligations before finding such an intention. According to the court (at 718):

> Read in context and given its ordinary meaning, "intentionally" means a voluntary act. The parent required to pay is intentionally under-employed if that parent chooses to earn less than he or she is capable of earning. That parent is intentionally unemployed when he or she chooses not to work when capable of earning an income. The word "intentionally" makes it clear that the section does not apply to situations in which, through no fault or act of their own, spouses are laid off, terminated or given reduced hours of work.
>
> I note that there is no requirement of bad faith in the provision itself, nor is there language suggestive of such a requirement.

In *Drygala*, the court imputed part-time income to the payor spouse who was attending university. In *Moffatt v. Moffatt* (2003), 67 OR (3d) 239, the Superior Court of Justice (Family Court) considered *Drygala* in its reasoning, concluding that a payor's decision to take early retirement did not affect the level of his child-support obligations. In addition, the Ontario Court of Appeal applied *Drygala* in *Riel v. Holland* (2003), 67 OR (3d) 417, when a payor chose to cease working as an independent electrical contractor and take a salaried position instead; although his income was significantly reduced, the appeal court confirmed the trial judge's determination to impute the previous higher income to him for purposes of determining his child-support obligation.

Similarly, courts have exercised discretion to impute income in a variety of other circumstances. Where the payor won $1 million in the lottery and ceased to work and earn income, an Alberta court imputed both employment and investment income to him: *A. v. A.* (1999), 45 RFL (4th) 5 (Alta. QB). Where the payor had ceased working overtime at separation, an Ontario court imputed shiftwork income to him in determining the table amount: *Odendahl v. Burle* (1999), 45 RFL (4th) 37 (Ont. Ct. J (Gen. Div.)). Where a payor was dismissed from his employment for cause, a BC court imputed his employment income to him: *Baldini v. Baldini* (1999), 46 RFL (4th) 407 (BCSC). Similarly, where an architect payor earned less than the court found to be possible, the Alberta court imputed additional income: *Lobo v. Lobo* (1999), 45 RFL (4th) 366 (Alta. QB).

To what extent do these examples support the following assessment?

> Courts have been given broad discretion when it comes to determining income. A review of the case law has confirmed that the court will impute income if doing so is reasonable in the circumstances and would benefit the children. ...
>
> Numerous cases illustrate that the court will not tolerate parents who arrange their affairs so as to avoid paying child support. Neither will they trust a parent who has not presented adequate financial information. It is a lawyer's job to advise clients accordingly.

(Nathalet Boutet and Christine Kish, "Income Determinations Under the Child Support Guidelines: A Case Law Review" (2000-1), 19 *Canadian Family Law Quarterly* 283, at 302.)

Payors and Income over $150,000

The *Child Support Guidelines* tables are applicable to payors' incomes up to $150,000. For incomes over that amount, s. 4 of the guidelines authorizes a court to determine the appropriate amount payable if the table amount is considered inappropriate. In a number of cases involving extremely high income-earning payors, courts have struggled to identify the factors to be considered in determining the appropriateness of child-support awards. Obviously, these cases have little bearing on the vast majority of payors of child support. At the same time, they reveal some important insights about underlying assumptions with respect to child-support obligations.

For example, in *Francis v. Baker*, [1999] 3 SCR 250; 50 RFL (4th) 228, the custodial mother of two girls requested child support in accordance with the *Child Support Guidelines*. In 1997, she was earning $63,000 per year and receiving $30,000 in child support; the payor had left her five days after their second daughter was born in 1985. The father earned $945,538 in 1997 and his net worth was $78 million. The trial judge awarded the mother child support based on the table and the payor's income: (1997), 150 DLR (4th) 547 (Ont. Ct. J (Gen. Div.)); the Ontario Court of Appeal dismissed the appeal: (1998), 38 OR (3d) 481. In the appellate court, Abella JA held that the word "inappropriate" in s. 4(b) should be interpreted as "inadequate" so that no downward variation was permissible; she also held that, even if incorrect in relation to this interpretation, there had been no abuse of discretion on the part of the trial judge in her award in this case.

On appeal to the Supreme Court of Canada, Bastarache J stated (at paras. 39-41):

Based on the wording of s. 1 and the legislative history, a fair description of the purpose of the Guidelines is to establish fair levels of support for children from both parents upon marriage breakdown, in a predictable and consistent manner. They are designed to ensure, as I said in a different context in *Chartier*, supra, at p. 257, "that a divorce will affect the children as little as possible," or as the Minister said, "to put children first." Indeed, s. 4(b)(ii) itself emphasizes the centrality of the actual situation of the children by expressly requiring that the "condition, means, needs and other circumstances of the children" be considered in the assessment of an appropriate amount of support payable in respect of income over $150,000. In my opinion, it is not at all clear from the statute or the words of the Minister that any single element of this general legislative purpose is to be given more weight than any other, and certainly not more weight than the actual circumstances in which the children find themselves. While Abella JA is correct to point out that predictability, consistency and efficiency are among the Guidelines' objectives, these are not the only considerations. I thus respectfully disagree with the Court of Appeal's suggestion that these legislative objectives dictate that child support awards can never be reduced under s. 4.

A proper construction of s. 4 requires that the objectives of predictability, consistency and efficiency on the one hand, be balanced with those of fairness, flexibility and recognition of the actual "condition, means, needs and other circumstances of the children" on the other. Furthermore, this balancing must take into account the ordinary meaning of the word "inappropriate," as well as its use elsewhere in the statute. In my opinion, the plain language of s. 4 is consistent with such an interpretation. Accordingly, the word "inappropriate" in this section must be broadly defined to mean "unsuitable" rather than merely "inadequate." Courts thus have the discretion to both increase and reduce the amount of child support prescribed by the strict application of the Guidelines in cases where the paying parent has an annual income exceeding $150,000. I would note that the respondent did not take issue with this interpretation in either her written or oral submissions.

I add one final comment. As noted above, Abella JA was concerned with the differential treatment of children. In my respectful opinion, a broad interpretation of the word "inappropriate" in s. 4 does not deny children of high income parents any of the intended benefits of the Guidelines. ... In my opinion, child support undeniably involves some form of wealth transfer to the children and will often produce an indirect benefit to the custodial parent. However, even though the Guidelines have their own stated objectives, they have not displaced the *Divorce Act*, which clearly dictates that maintenance of the children, rather than household equalization or spousal support, is the objective of child support payments.

In the result in *Francis v. Baker*, the Supreme Court of Canada rejected the Ontario Court of Appeal's approach and held that downward variation of the guidelines figure was permissible under s. 4. However, the court also held that the appellant had failed to demonstrate that the trial judge erred in failing to exercise her discretion and, accordingly, the appeal was dismissed. Thus, the trial judge's award of $10,034 per month for two children was upheld.

In reviewing *Francis v. Baker*, Brenda Cossman noted a number of other cases involving payors with high incomes: *Simon v. Simon* (1999), 46 OR (3d) 349 (CA); *Tauber v. Tauber* (2000), 48 OR (3d) 577 (CA); and *Metzner v. Metzner*, [2000] BCJ no. 1693 (CA) (QL). She concluded:

Each of these child support cases involves payor parents with extraordinarily high incomes. *Francis v. Baker* has established that the Federal *Child Support Guidelines* presumptively apply to these high income earners, subject to their ability to rebut the Guideline amount as inappropriate. The ensuing cases have had to interrogate whether the payor could rebut this presumption [and concluding that no such rebuttal was established in *Simon* and *Metzner*]. The Ontario Court of Appeal's ruling in *Tauber*, however, suggested that at some point, that Guideline amount is just too much; there are limits to how much child support children of very rich parents will receive. ...

[However,] the ruling [in *Francis v. Baker*] has rather fewer implications for more modest income earners, who represent the vast majority of Canadian families.

(Brenda Cossman, "Developments in Family Law: The 1999-2000 Term" (2000), 13 *Supreme Court Law Review* (2d) 307, at 315-16.)

Consider this comment in relation to recent decisions involving high-income payors. For example, in *R. v. R.* (2002), 58 OR (3d) 656, the Ontario Court of Appeal confirmed that the trial judge was correct to take account of the modest lifestyle of a family, where the payor's annual income was $1.4 million, but that the trial judge had erred in not giving weight to the increased income of $4.1 million of the payor after separation, particularly having regard to the increased expenses after separation. The trial judge had awarded $16,000 per month for four children. As Laskin JA stated (at 664), this amount represented errors in two respects:

First, [the trial judge] based his order entirely on the parties' lifestyle and pattern of expenditure while they lived together. By doing so, the trial judge failed to adequately take into account the large increase in Mr. R.'s income after he and his wife separated. Second, the trial judge erred in failing to consider whether the options proposed by Mrs. R. in her April 2000 budget were reasonable in the light of the increase in Mr. R.'s income.

Significantly, the Ontario Court of Appeal decided that it was appropriate to assess the amount of child support rather than to order a new trial and reassessment. After reviewing the budget submitted by Mrs. R., the court decided that it was appropriate to award discretionary expenses of $20,000 monthly as well as the basic expenses of $12,000 monthly and $4,000 under s. 7 for a total monthly amount of $36,000.

In 2001, a BC court awarded a monthly support payment of $59,500 in circumstances where the payor's income for 2000 was $6.5 million: see Cristin Schmitz, "BC Children Awarded Record $59,000 Monthly Support," *The Lawyers Weekly*, June 22, 2001, at 3. In 2002, an Ontario court reviewed the obligations of high-income payors in *Pakka v. Nygard* (2002), 61 OR (3d) 328 (Sup. Ct. J) (publication of decision deferred: [2002] OJ no. 3859 (Sup. Ct. J) (QL)). In this case, the payor gave evidence of his financial support for seven children (born to four different women) in Canada and the United States—he explained that he provided Cdn.$3,000 monthly to the Canadian children and US$3,000 to the American children and that he also paid school fees, as required. According to his evidence, he paid $216,000 in 2000 for the support of six children; he argued that he had treated his children fairly and equally. Kiteley J rejected this argument, stating (at 342):

I reject the "fairness and equality" argument. It is predicated on the ability of a parent to decide what in his/her mind is a "fair and equal" treatment of the children. That has not been the law for decades. I do not reject the defendant's assertion that he is acting in what he considers to be good faith and that, as a result of having children in different relationships, he has tried to ensure that he has treated them all similarly. That may be a sound approach morally. But it has nothing to do with the state of the law in Ontario today. One need only look at the consequences of applying such a position in our society today: it would allow payors to be virtually uninhibited in imposing what they consider to be a sound moral approach; it would victimize payees who would be subjected to the application of a subjective standard by the payor; and it would make a mockery of the *Child Support Guidelines* and in particular the first objective. ... It would be inconsistent with the principles adopted by the Supreme Court of Canada and the Ontario Court of Appeal that the emphasis must be on the actual situation of the child, not the wishes and subjective perspective of the payor. ... It would allow the payor to make the rules.

In the result, the court considered (at 348-50) the principles articulated in *Francis v. Baker* and other decisions of the Ontario Court of Appeal and concluded that the payor had not provided "clear and compelling evidence" that the table amount was inappropriate or unsuitable; in addition, the court awarded (at 352) arrears to July 2001. The court also established June 27, 2002 as the date for a settlement conference. However, according to press reports, the parties reached an undisclosed settlement on March 19, 2004: see Gay Abbate, "Nygard Support Case Ends with Settlement," *Globe and Mail*, March 19, 2004, A11.

iv. Section 7: Special or Extraordinary Expenses

In addition to the basic table amount, s. 3 of the *Child Support Guidelines* provides for the addition of amounts determined pursuant to s. 7, entitled "special or extraordinary" expenses. Section 7 permits additional amounts of child support for identified expenses, taking account of the "necessity of the expense in relation to the child's best interests" as well as "the reasonableness of the expense in relation to the means of the spouses and those of the child and to the family's spending pattern prior to the separation." Thus, by contrast with the table amounts in s. 3, there are a number of discretionary factors to be considered in relation to the additional amounts in s. 7.

Appellate courts in Canada have reached different conclusions about whether an objective or subjective approach should be applied in considering whether an expense is special or extraordinary. Initially, the Courts of Appeal for Saskatchewan, British Columbia, and Alberta adopted the subjective approach: see *Koefoed v. Fichter* (1998), 39 RFL (4th) 348 (Sask. CA); *McLaughlin v. McLaughlin* (1998), 44 RFL (4th) 148 (BCCA); and *Sanders v. Sanders*, [1998] AJ no. 565 (CA) (QL). In *Andries v. Andries* (1998), 36 RFL (4th) 175 (Man. CA), the Manitoba Court of Appeal favoured an objective approach. In *Andrews v. Andrews* (1999), 50 RFL (4th) 1, the Ontario Court of Appeal considered s. 7 in the context of a trial judge's order for payment of child and spousal support that resulted in 60 percent of the party's net disposable income being allocated to the wife and three children. Mr. Andrews appealed the award pursuant to s. 7. (Based on his annual income of $200,000, he had been ordered to pay the table amount of $2,953 per month and also $1,200 per month pursuant to s. 7; the amount of $1,200 represented Mr. Andrews' contribution to total additional educational costs for the children of $1,578.75, so that Mrs. Andrews was responsible for the difference.) The appellate court noted (at 12) that the trial judge had not specifically addressed the wording of s. 7, but nonetheless confirmed the trial judge's order:

> Mr. Andrews concedes that the private school fees for Adam and Mark and the expenses for Melina's home schooling are extraordinary expenses. Because of Mr. Andrews' concession, I need not address the debate over the proper approach to determining "extraordinary expenses" reflected in the thorough and thoughtful judgment of Prowse JA in *McLaughlin v. McLaughlin*. I do, however, agree with Prowse JA that in adopting an "add on" approach under s. 7, the drafters of the Guidelines "recognized the importance of addressing the needs of a particular family with particular expenses." The Andrews family has particular educational needs and expenses associated with those needs. These expenses are not covered by the basic table amount Mr. Andrews must pay for child support under the Guidelines.
>
> The evidence shows that the expenses for each of the three children are necessary in relation to their best interests. The expenses for Melina most obviously satisfy the necessity criterion, and also meet her particular need to be schooled at home. For her home schooling she requires the assistance of various therapeutic, computer and other programs. The cost of these programs is not disputed.
>
> The private school expenses for Adam and Mark also satisfy the necessity criterion. When Mr. and Mrs. Andrews cohabited, Adam and Mark went to private elementary schools. Adam, after finishing grade 8 at a private school, enrolled in a local high school in a special education program. However, he was harassed and bullied and found he could not cope in the public school environment. Midway through the year, Mrs. Andrews arranged for his transfer to a private school. Mark was attending a private school with the concurrence of Mr. Andrews. However, unprofessional behaviour by Mark's classroom teacher caused several parents, including Mrs. Andrews, to withdraw their children from the school. Mrs. Andrews placed Mark in another private school at an additional cost of about $240 per month. Mrs. Andrews arranged these transfers for Adam and Mark in their best interest and to address their special needs. Mr. Andrews agreed that Mrs. Andrews' decisions were well thought out and in the children's best interests.
>
> His main argument focussed on the reasonableness criterion. I agree with him that the necessity of an extraordinary expense must be weighed against its reasonableness. However, considering the parties' and especially Mr. Andrews' means, and considering that Mr. and Mrs. Andrews sent the children to private schools during cohabitation, I am satisfied that the expenses for all three children meet the reasonableness criterion.
>
> Under the Guidelines, child support payments are not tax deductible. Mr. Andrews' marginal tax rate is 50% and an order of $1,200 per month must be paid in after-tax dollars. He says that he cannot afford it. But it seems to me that he can on an income of $200,000. The trial judge implicitly found that he could reasonably afford these expenses in her discussion of his lifestyle and of what he has been able to pay for since separation. Moreover, as Mrs. Andrews points out, the extraordinary expenses for Mark—$605 per month—will likely end after he finishes grade 8 in the year 2000. Then he will either go to the local public school or he will go to the private school Adam attends, in which case he will pay no additional fees as long as Adam is in the school. I would therefore not give effect to Mr. Andrews' submission on extraordinary expenses for his children's education. If

there is to be any reduction in the amount of support ordered by the trial judge, it should be a reduction in spousal support, not child support.

In relation to the reasoning in *Andrews*, it is important to note the results of a pilot study of child-support awards in 1999. In examining s. 7 awards, the report stated:

> The most commonly awarded type of expense was medical or dental insurance premiums (9.7 percent of total cases). This was followed by extracurricular activities at 9.3 percent, and child care or day care at 8.5 percent. The least frequently awarded expenses were primary/secondary education (4.7 percent) and post-secondary education (6.9 percent). ... [In addition, the report indicated that there] was a consistent increase in the proportion of cases with special or extraordinary expenses awarded as income level increased. At the lowest income level, only 11.5 percent of cases had special expenses awarded; this proportion increased to 59.5 percent at the highest income level.

(Joseph P. Hornick, Lorne D. Bertrand, and Nicholas M.C. Bala, *The Survey of Child Support Awards: Final Analysis of Pilot Data and Recommendations for Continued Data Collection* (Ottawa: Minister of Justice, 1999), at 28-29.)

Does the reasoning in *Andrews* appear consistent with the empirical data about s. 7 awards? What does this data suggest in terms of the use of s. 7 in child-support awards? If lower-income earners are generally restricted to table amounts, what are the consequences for equality among children of divorce or separation?

v. Adjustments and Discretion

This section focuses on four sections of the *Child Support Guidelines* that may require adjustments of the amounts determined in accordance with ss. 3 (in relation to the sections defining income) and 7. Some of them also offer opportunities for discretionary decision making, thus making the overall determination of child support a combination of rules and discretion. In examining s. 5 (additional parents with child-support obligations), s. 8 (split custody), s. 9 (shared custody), and s. 10 (undue hardship), you may want to agree with Thompson, who argued:

> Contrary to popular impressions, the Guidelines lack any real intellectual coherence. The Guidelines can't quite make up their minds what they really want to be, partaking a little bit of every conceivable child support model: percentage-of-income (the tables), *Paras*-style cost-sharing (section 7 expenses), household income equalization (undue hardship), and individualized budgets (a variety of departures).

(Thompson, at 20.)

A. *Section 5*

Section 5 authorizes a court to determine an "appropriate" amount of child support payable by a spouse who stands in the place of a parent, and permits the court to take account of a parent's obligation to pay child support in determining an appropriate amount. Clearly, this section may affect the quantum of child support payable by *Chartier* parents. In a recent Ontario case, however, the Court of Appeal clearly confirmed that s. 5 is not applicable to the determination of an order for support against a biological parent where another person is also paying support.

In *Wright v. Zaver* (2002), 59 OR (3d) 26; [2002] OJ no. 1098 (CA), all five judges confirmed the trial judge's award of support payable by a child's biological father. Ms Wright and Mr. Zaver were unmarried parents of a son born in 1985; they had engaged in an intimate relationship for about three years, but it deteriorated shortly after the child's birth. The parties signed minutes of settlement a few months later, granting custody to Ms Wright, denying access to Mr. Zaver, and providing that he would provide a lump-sum child-support payment of $4,000. In 1990, Ms Wright married; she and her husband had a child together. Throughout the marriage, Ms Wright's husband treated her son as his own; when the Wrights separated in 1999, Mr. Wright was ordered to pay child support for both children.

In the context of some financial hardship, Ms Wright filed an application for child support against Mr. Zaver with respect to his son. Although Mr. Zaver argued that there should be apportionment of child support payable for his son in accordance with s. 5, the trial judge held that neither a natural nor an adoptive parent can rely on s. 5: see *Wright v. Zaver* (2000), 49 OR (3d) 629 (Sup. Ct. J), at 638. More specifically, the court stated (at 639):

> [T]he unique circumstances of this case do not fit into any exceptions to the presumptive rule that the biological father should pay child support at the Table amount specified in the Guidelines. That result is perhaps troubling from the perspective that it might seem unfair now to require a father who has been shut out of his child's life for 15 years to commence paying support. The apparent unfairness stems, I think, from the expectation by an access parent that he is entitled to exercise a parental role in exchange for support payments. That, however, has never been the law. The obligation for support is entirely independent of the rights of access. In any event, who is to say that the father might not be able to establish a relationship with the child. It may not be too late and court sanctioned support may very well be a catalyst for such a relationship.
>
> With respect to the issue of double dipping, I can see no authority in the Act to order anything other than Table support for the child. If that means that the mother is able to provide her son with a standard of living that is slightly better than their basic needs require, so be it. The biological father is extremely well off. It will not be a hardship for him to share some of his wealth with his child. One of the objectives of the Guidelines was to ensure that children "benefit from the financial means of their parents." One might even suggest that the biological father has had a 15-year holiday from support obligations and it is now proper that he honour his moral and legal obligation to his child.

What kinds of assumptions underlie the trial court's reasoning in this case? In an assessment of 120 cases about step-parent support between 1997 and 2000, Carol Rogerson concluded that there were many unanswered questions about the obligations of step-parents. In reflecting on her comments, consider whether there were aspects of the factual circumstances in *Wright v. Zaver* that were given too little weight.

> What has struck me most forcefully after reviewing this entire body of law is that we do not have a very clear idea of why we are imposing support obligations on step-parents. Our

current approach ... has been adopted in the absence of a clear articulation of the basis on which such support obligations are being imposed—is the law primarily concerned with psychological attachment, intention to assume the role and responsibilities of a parent, or the protection of reliance (and if so what sorts of reliance—economic or also psychological)? The law has also developed without reference to the social science literature on the nature and functioning of step-families. That literature, which shows the complexity, diversity and potential instability of step-family relationships, raises both questions about the reasonable social expectations that attach to these relationships and concerns about the appropriateness of imposing long-term support obligations when these relationships break down after a relatively short period of time.

(Carol Rogerson, "The Child Support Obligations of Step-Parents" (2001), 18:1 *Canadian Journal of Family Law* 9, at 152-53.)

The Ontario Court of Appeal confirmed the trial judgment in *Wright v. Zaver*. Two of the five appellate judges wrote opinions, but they mainly focused on the nagging issue about whether the coming into force of the *Child Support Guidelines* constituted (automatically) a change in circumstances entitling an applicant to a variation of a pre-existing order or not. As Simmons JA noted (at para. 35), courts have taken different views, with the appellate courts in British Columbia (*Wang v. Wang* (1998), 58 BCLR (3d) 159; 164 DLR (4th) 146 (CA)), New Brunswick (*Parent v. Pelletier* (1999), 219 NBR (2d) 102; 1 RFL (5th) 22 (CA)), and Alberta (*Laird v. Laird* (2000), 182 DLR (4th) 357; 3 RFL (5th) 241 (Alta. CA)) all deciding that courts have a residual discretion with respect to such applications for variation; by contrast, appellate courts in Saskatchewan (*Dergousoff v. Dergousoff*, [1999] 10 WWR 633; 48 RFL (4th) 1 (Sask. CA)) and Nova Scotia (*MacKay v. Bucher* (2001), 196 NSR (2d) 293; 208 DLR (4th) 472 (CA)) concluded that the enactment of the guidelines created a right to variation.

In Ontario, the Court of Appeal initially decided that the enactment of the guidelines did not create a right to variation (*Sherman v. Sherman* (1999), 44 OR (3d) 411; 45 RFL (4th) 424 (CA)), but the same court subsequently stated in obiter comments that *Sherman* was wrongly decided and that the enactment of the guidelines creates a right to vary a prior order: see the judgment of Laskin JA in *Bates v. Bates* (2000), 49 OR (3d) 1; 188 DLR (4th) 642 (CA). In *Wright v. Zaver*, the Ontario Court of Appeal followed the views expressed in *Bates*, thus deciding that the guidelines constituted a need for variation. The appellate court upheld the trial judge's reasoning with respect to the order for child support payable by Mr. Zaver.

How should s. 5 be interpreted in a situation where a spouse has stood in the place of a parent unknowingly—that is, in a situation in which a spouse believes himself to be a biological father but is not? In *Peters v. Graham* (2001), 198 NSR (2d) 175; 210 DLR (4th) 753 (SC), a father of twin boys born in 1990 later learned that he was not the biological father, his wife having deceived him about the boys' parentage; the lack of biological connection was established by DNA testing. Relying on the comments in *Chartier* about the test for standing in place of a parent, the court in *Peters v. Graham* referred to the Saskatchewan decision in *M.(K.F.) v. M.(M.J.)* (1999), 2 RFL (5th) 113 (Sask. QB), in which the court held that the common law emphasis on intention and voluntariness was no longer the basis for recognizing an *in loco parentis* status; rather, the focus of the inquiry now is on the best interests of the child. On this basis, the Nova Scotia court held that Mr. Peters stood in place of a parent to the two boys; the court ordered payment of child support in an amount based on one-third of the table amount he would otherwise be required to pay. In doing so, the court noted that the biological father might be unaware of the fact that the boys were his children; the mother had been cohabiting with the brother of the biological father, a successful fisherman who was supporting the boys, since separation from Mr. Peters.

For other cases relating to the interpretation of s. 5, see *Kobe v. Kobe* (2002), 30 RFL (5th) 135 (Ont. Sup. Ct. J); *Nelson v. Nelson* (1999), 44 RFL (4th) 365 (Alta. QB); and *C.(K.) v. B.(S.)* (2003), 36 RFL (5th) 22 (Ont. Sup. Ct. J)—all these cases appear to assume that it is "appropriate" pursuant to s. 5 for children to receive child support from different payor parents in an amount that exceeds the table amount. Is this discretion appropriate pursuant to the objectives of child support in s. 1 and the language of s. 5?

B. Split Custody: Section 8

Section 8 of the *Child Support Guidelines* appears to offer little opportunity for the exercise of discretion, and it has not created significant problems in practice: for a review of some of the cases concerning s. 8, see Carol Rogerson, "Child Support Under the Guidelines in Cases of Split and Shared Custody" (1998), 15 *Canadian Journal of Family Law* 11. As she concluded (at 15):

> The cases involving split custody are relatively straightforward, and any complexity is the result of the complexity built into the Guidelines calculations themselves. Because two support obligations are being calculated rather than one, that complexity is potentially doubled. In the simplest cases there is simply an offset of the two table amounts, subject of course to any issues regarding the determination of income. In other cases the calculation of the two child support obligations is complicated by additional factors built into the Guide-lines calculation such as s. 7 add-ons claimed by one or both parents; the fact that one or more of the children is over the age of majority allowing a departure from the table amount; the fact that one or more of the children for whom support is claimed are step-children to whom other persons also owe support obligations; or the combination of split and shared custody arrangements with respect to different children in the family.

As is evident, s. 8 provides for a calculation, based on the income of each parent or spouse, with respect to the child-support obligations that they would have if custody of children were not split between them. However, the apparent ease of calculation for split custody arrangements must be contrasted with shared custody situations in s. 9; more-over, the s. 8 calculation may sometimes be invoked with respect to s. 9. Thus, s. 8 provides both a contrast and an analogy to s. 9 decisions.

C. Shared Custody: Section 9

Particularly as a result of increasing interest in joint physical custody arrangements and shared parenting, s. 9 of the *Child Support Guidelines* has been the subject of consider-able litigation. In practice, s. 9 involves two distinct issues:

1. has the 40 percent threshold been met; and if so

2. how should support obligations be determined?

Regarding the 40 percent threshold, some courts have accepted the approach adopted in *Meloche v. Kales* (1997), 35 RFL (4th) 297 (Ont. Ct. J (Gen. Div.)) that the calculation of time proceeds from the assumption that the custodial time is initially 100 percent of the child's time (including school time) and the non-custodial parent's access or physical custody of the child must amount to at least 40 percent of that time over a year. (For other cases, see *Cross v. Cross* (1998), 40 RFL (4th) 242 (BCSC) and *Billark v. Billark* (1998), 36 RFL (4th) 361 (Ont. Ct. J (Gen. Div.)) for discussion of the possibility of excluding school and sleep time from the calculation.) Most courts have approached the 40 percent threshold as a fairly strict mathematical calculation, though a few cases suggest a preference for considering the nature and quality of the time spent by each parent with the child (see, for example, *Rosati v. Dellapenta* (1997), 35 RFL (4th) 102 (Ont. Ct. J (Gen. Div.)) and *Dennett v. Dennett* (1998), 225 AR 50 (QB)).

In assessing quantum of support, courts have adopted a variety of methods. In some cases, a set-off approach (like that established in s. 8 for split custody cases) has been applied, so that each parent's obligation under the guidelines tables is calculated, with the higher-earning parent owing the difference between those two amounts to the lower-earning parent (see, for example, *Middleton v. MacPherson*, discussed earlier in this section). In *Hunter v. Hunter* (1998), 37 RFL (4th) 260 (Ont. Ct. J (Gen. Div.)), Justice Brockenshire, in considering the increased costs of shared custody pursuant to s. 9(b) of the guidelines, accepted the "Colorado method" of assuming roughly 50 percent of a custodial parent's costs are fixed costs. As a result, the court grossed up the set-off amount by 50 percent to reflect the increased costs of shared custody. Other courts, such as the Ontario Court of Justice (General Division) in *Burns v. Burns* (1998), 40 RFL (4th) 32, have declined to assume the appropriateness of a 50 percent gross-up absent parties' submission of evidence of their actual increased costs. Finally, some courts have simply calculated the paying parent's obligation as a proportion of the guidelines table amount that reflects the amount of time the child is in the care of the custodial parent: for example, see *Spanier v. Spanier* (1998), 40 RFL (4th) 329 (BCSC), where the father, who met the 40 percent threshold, was required to pay the mother 60 percent of the guidelines table amount applicable to his income level. See also *Penner v. Penner* (1999), 44 RFL (4th) 294 (Man. CA).

Clearly, s. 9 may require complicated, and changing, calculations with respect to child-support obligations. Indeed, in a recent decision of the Ontario Court of Appeal in *Contino v. Leonelli-Contino* (2003), 67 OR (3d) 703, the complexity of such calculations was clearly evident. In *Contino*, the father applied to reduce his child-support obligations because the amount of time that his son was in his physical custody had increased to 50 percent. The motions judge granted the father's motion, reducing the amount of monthly child support using the formula of s. 8 and setting off the father's and mother's table amounts. As a result, the father's child-support payments were reduced from $550 per month to $100 per month. The mother appealed to the Divisional Court, which held that the table amount is in the best interest of a child (relying on *Francis v. Baker*) and that unless the father could provide clear and convincing evidence to rebut the presumptive table amount, he was obliged to pay it; as a result, the Divisional Court ordered that the father pay the table amount of $688, subject to annual adjustments according to his income. The father then appealed to the Ontario Court of Appeal, which held that both the motions judge and the Divisional Court had proceeded on the basis of inappropriate principles for calculating child support in these circumstances.

The Court of Appeal commenced its analysis by noting (at para. 5) that the motions judge had essentially adopted a "formulaic approach," which had merit in terms of predictability, but which failed to take into account the s. 9 language concerning "the condition, means, needs and other circumstances of each spouse and of any child for whom support is sought." By contrast, the appellate court characterized the approach of the Divisional Court as a "discretionary approach" and suggested that while it reflected the language of s. 9, it suffered from a lack of predictability. Thus, the court suggested (at para. 7):

> For the reasons that follow, we generally prefer the more discretionary approach. We are, however, of the view that it is possible to structure that discretion to provide some predictability and objectivity and that formulae, when used in appropriate cases, can assist the court in achieving a result that is fair and in the best interests of the child.

Although the court expressed concern about the lack of detailed information before the motions judge, the appellate court concluded that the father's appeal should be allowed, decreasing the amount of child support to $399.61 monthly.

The Court of Appeal began by reviewing the factual circumstances and the decisions of the motions judge and the Divisional Court. Then, in considering the application of s. 9, the court identified the need for an interpretation that promotes the guidelines' objectives of consistency and reducing conflict, as well as establishing a fair standard of support. Turning to s. 9(a) and the table amounts, the court suggested (at para. 54) that "the set-off approach in s. 8 can be useful as a starting point because it brings some consistency and objectivity to the determination." However, the court also identified the need to retain judicial discretion. The court also expressly noted (at para. 57) how a formula "that has the effect of dramatically reducing support can create financial incentives on the part of a custodial parent to limit access, and on the part of the access parent to seek increased time with the child or children solely to reduce the quantum of the child support obligation." Indeed, in this case, which resulted from the mother's request to the father to provide child care for one additional evening per week while she attended a course, the potential reduction in child support was from $688 to $100 monthly. As the court noted, the "cliff effect" (where a modest increase in access results in a dramatic reduction in support) must be avoided.

The court then considered a number of alternative approaches, including the principles adopted in *Moran v. Cook* (2000), 9 RFL (5th) 352 (Ont. Sup. Ct. J) (based on a formula that took into account the *increased* amount of time with the child beyond 39 percent); *Harrison v. Harrison* (2001), 14 RFL (5th) 321 (Ont. Sup. Ct. J) (which took into account the mother's table amount); and the set-off provision of s. 8. However, the court concluded (at para. 66) that none of these approaches was entirely satisfactory. Thus, after reviewing the words of ss. 9(a) and (b), the use of a "multiplier" to avoid the need for evidence of actual increased costs of shared custody arrangements, the increased costs of the applicant parent, the need for detailed evidence, and the guidelines' requirement to consider undue hardship, the court concluded (at para. 85):

To summarize, the Guidelines are based on the principle that spouses have a joint obligation towards their children in accordance with their financial means. The objectives of the Guidelines are to achieve a fair, objective, consistent measure of support. To reach these objectives, judicial discretion is limited to five specific situations. ...

On application by the payor parent, s. 9 requires the court to make a determination, "by taking into account" the three factors that follow. ...

We would adopt the following approach in this case. First, we see no reason not to start with the simple set-off. We would then adopt an appropriate multiplier to reflect the mother's fixed costs. [The court explained why, on the facts in this case, a multiplier of 50 percent was not appropriate, choosing instead a multiplier of 67.6 percent.]

Accordingly, we begin in this case with the simple set-off amount of $128. To that we would add $86.62, reflecting the use of a 67.6 per cent multiplier. This produces a figure of $215 (rounding off). ...

It is then necessary to consider the factors in subsection (c) by looking at the actual spending patterns of the parents. [The court then examined evidence of actual expenses, concluding that the difference between the mother's variable expenses and those of the father was $133.41; it then calculated these expenses on the basis of the ratio of the two parents' incomes. This resulted in an additional sum payable to the mother of $100.] When $100 is added to the $215 figure, it produces a total of approximately $315 regular support to be paid. Factoring in the expense for the mother's contribution to an RESP of $153.84 as a special expense in the same proportion, we would add $84.61 to the $315 for a total of $399.61 in support to be paid by the father to the mother based on the 2001 financial information.

Leave to appeal to the Supreme Court of Canada in this case was granted: see [2003] SCCA no. 557.

Clearly, the use of judicial discretion was significant in *Contino*. Although it is possible to argue that this decision is unusual, it demonstrates the difficulty of achieving both consistency and fairness, as well as promoting goals of efficiency and private settlement pursuant to the *Child Support Guidelines*. Moreover, it is important to assess this decision in the context of the recommendations for shared parenting, discussed in relation to issues of custody and access—to what extent is it likely that the introduction of shared parenting will avoid difficult decisions concerning custody and access, only to face even more complex principles and decision making about child support? What is the solution to this dilemma?

In her earlier analysis of s. 9 cases, for example, Rogerson suggested (at 94):

I would favour an approach that allowed a degree of judicial discretion to adjust the Guideline amounts to recognize the financial realities of the parties—the parties' actual expenditures on the children and any significant income disparities between the parties which reflected on their respective abilities to bear the costs of a shared custody arrangement. While I believe it is helpful to see what the Guideline amounts on each parent's income are—in part to provide a comparison point for the numbers which are generated in a *Paras*, budget-based analysis—some discretion to depart from a strict offset of the amounts is necessary in order to ensure that one of the parents is not being deprived of adequate support to meet the children's needs. One must recall that what is often (although not always) at issue in these cases is a reduction from the basic table amount to be paid by the higher income parent. One of the stated objectives of the Guidelines, after all, is to establish a fair standard of support for children.

How would you assess this approach, especially in the context of recommendations for shared parenting? Is it appropriate to conclude that the idea of fixed rules is unworkable and that only judicial discretion can achieve fairness?

D. Undue Hardship: Section 10

Section 10 of the *Child Support Guidelines* permits some variation up or down with respect to the amount of a support obligation, based on undue hardship; however, any such variation will be denied if the household claiming undue hardship would have a higher standard of living than the other household. According to the language of s. 10, it is the relative *standard of living in each household*, not the *incomes of individual payors or recipients* of child support, that must be compared. Schedule II provides guidance with respect to the comparison of household standards of living. In addition, s. 10 uses permissive language, thus preserving judicial discretion with respect to such claims.

In providing an overall assessment of the meaning of the statutory language in s. 10, D.A. Rollie Thompson focused on the words in the section:

> What takes a circumstance of "potential hardship" into the sphere of "undue hardship" has sent judges to the dictionary and the thesaurus: "excessive, extreme, improper, unreasonable, unjustified," "hard to bear ... and ... inappropriate, unwarranted and excessive," or "excessively hard living conditions." Section 10 creates "a tough threshold to meet," requiring "cogent evidence." In the words of Julien Payne, repeated in various cases, "the hardship must be exceptional or excessive, rather than the inevitable consequence of dividing limited resources between two households."

(D.A. Rollie Thompson, "The Second Family Conundrum in Child Support" (2001), 18 *Canadian Journal of Family Law* 227, at 230, citing J.D. Payne, "Child Support Under the Federal Child Support Guidelines" (QL DB PDCS), at G.10.)

As Thompson noted, a claimant has the burden of proof and must also provide the information required to assess the claim under s. 10; however, even if the claimant has provided all the necessary data, Thompson argued (at 231) that the court retains discretion with respect to the amount to be ordered and that this residual judicial discretion has proved to be "a critical and unpredictable step in the hardship analysis."

To illustrate the use of s. 10, consider *Schmid v. Smith* (1999), 1 RFL (5th) 447 (Ont. Sup. Ct. J). In assessing the claim, the court held (at para. 34):

> Under the provisions of section 10 of the *Guidelines* counsel for the husband asks the court to award an amount of child support that is different from the amount determined under section 4 on the basis that the husband would otherwise suffer undue hardship. Clause 10(2)(b) sets out a number of circumstances that may cause undue hardship. It is not an exhaustive list. The husband claims that there are three circumstances that cause him undue hardship.
>
> First, the husband claims that he has unusually high expenses in relation to exercising access to the children, a circumstance of potential undue hardship set out in clause 10(2)(b). This relates to the husband's cost of travelling between Canada and the UK to see the

children. I understand that the cost is approximately $6,000 per year. I accept the cost as accurate. I find that this is a circumstance of undue hardship.

Secondly, the husband claims that his legal duty to support Alison is a circumstance that causes undue hardship. Clause 10(2)(d) of the *Guidelines* provides that a circumstance that may cause undue hardship is the legal duty to support a child, other than a child of the marriage. Since Alison is a child of the marriage the duty to support her is not an undue hardship.

Thirdly, the husband claims that the higher cost of living in the UK compared with that in Canada is an undue hardship. He deposed his own experience, that the cost of goods and services in the UK is approximately 50% greater. He appended to his affidavit OECD data for February 1999 showing that the same "basket of goods and services" costs approximately 45% more in the UK than in Canada. This data is of little assistance. Expert evidence would be required to interpret it. In any event, to succeed in proving that he suffers undue hardship because of an increased cost of living, it is incumbent on the husband to identify and quantify how he personally has been affected. He has failed to do so.

I have found that the husband's unusually high access costs are an undue hardship. Subsection 10(3) of the *Guidelines* requires me to compare the standard of living of the husband's household with the standard of living of the wife's household. Subsection 10(4) provides that to do so I may use the comparison of household standards of living test set out in Schedule II of the *Guidelines*. I have done this. I have found that after taking support and the husband's access costs into account his household income ratio is approximately 1.25 higher than the wife's household income ratio. In using this comparison I am aware that it is based on "low-income measures amounts for households" based on Canadian economic studies. The husband's household is in the UK and the wife's is in Canada. However there is no other way in which I can make an objective comparison on the evidence before me. Subjectively, the husband is left with approximately $8,500.00 more in net income (after support and access costs) to support himself and one child, than the wife will have to support herself and two children. In addition, the husband has a vehicle supplied to him by his employer, which was not included in his income. Consequently, I find that the standard of living of the husband's household exceeds the standard of living of the wife's household. As a result, I am compelled to dismiss the husband's request under subsection 10(3).

As Thompson noted, claims of undue hardship will often arise in the context of second families. As a result, issues about undue hardship often appear alongside issues about support obligations on the part of persons who are standing in the place of a parent pursuant to s. 5. In these cases of blended families, Thompson argued (at 265) that the policy approach should not favour either first or second families, but should provide for "equal treatment of all children." In reflecting on this analysis, identify the ways in which ss. 5 and 10 should be interpreted—do you agree that such an approach is appropriate in terms of "subordinating parental 'rights' to children's needs and best interests"? To what extent does such an approach assume the existence of adequate levels of income to support all children equally? Does this approach confirm or challenge child support as a private family matter?

Discussion Note

The Enforcement of Child-Support Obligations

The problem of enforcement of child-support obligations has been consistently identified as serious and widespread. For example, a study of support orders at the Family Court in Toronto in 1986 found that 82 percent of the orders were in some degree of default. Such statistics have repeatedly fuelled waves of legislative initiatives, by the federal government as well as provincial legislatures, to ensure that orders are enforced. Such statutes have provided for increasingly serious sanctions—for example, Ontario's *Family Responsibility and Support Arrears Enforcement Act, 1996*, SO 1996, c. 31 provides that where no support payments have been received for a period of three months and the arrears are more than $300, the payor will be reported to credit bureaus. There are also provisions in several statutes that permit the denial of licences, including drivers' licences, where child-support obligations have been ignored: for example, see *Mainwaring v. Alberta* (1998), 48 RFL (4th) 171 (Alta. QB). Overall, it appears that governments have determined that the financial well-being of children is the responsibility of the post-divorce family and that the role of the state is to enforce these obligations. See also *Interjurisdictional Support Orders Act, 2002*, SO 2002, c. 13.

SELECTED REFERENCES

Justice David R. Aston, "An Update of Case Law Under the Child Support Guidelines" (1998), 16 *Canadian Family Law Quarterly* 261.

Martha Bailey and Nicholas Bala, "Child Support Guidelines, Parental Mobility, and Redefining Familial Relationships," in A. Bainham, ed., *The International Survey of Family Law 1996* (The Netherlands: International Society of Family Law, 1998), 69.

Nicholas Bala, "Ottawa's New Child-Support Regime: A Guide to the Guidelines" (1999), 21 RFL (4th) 301.

Barbara R. Bergmann and Sherry Wetchler, "Child Support Awards: State Guidelines versus Public Opinion" (1995), 29:3 *Family Law Quarterly* 483.

G. Feltham and A. Macnaughton, "Predicting the Popularity of Child Support Strategies" (1997), 30 RFL (4th) 428.

Ross Finnie, "The Government's Child Support Package" (1997), 15 *Canadian Family Law Quarterly* 79.

Laura Morgan, "Child Support and the Anomalous Cases of the High-Income and Low-Income Parent" (1996), 13 *Canadian Journal of Family Law* 161.

Barry M. Tobin, "Enforcement of Support Orders in Ontario" (1998), 15 *Canadian Family Law Quarterly* 317.

D. Critiquing the Guidelines: Child Support or Support for Children?

Recall the discussion about the objectives of the *Child Support Guidelines* at the beginning of this section—to what extent do these goals appear consistent? Is it possible in practice to achieve both fairness in relation to individual family circumstances and overall consistency? Do the guidelines promote efficiency and reduce conflict? To what extent are the principles for enforcing child-support obligations consistent with the principles for determining custodial arrangements post-separation and divorce? Assuming that parents remain financially responsible for the children of divorce, how are their responsibilities to be shared in relation to children of subsequent families?

Special Joint Committee on Child Custody and Access,
For the Sake of the Children
(Ottawa: Parliament of Canada, 1998)

[It is interesting that, although legal principles concerning child support have usually been treated as quite distinct from principles about custody and access, the parliamentary committee report *For the Sake of the Children* (discussed earlier in this chapter) focused expressly on concerns about the impact of the *Child Support Guidelines* on the process of parental negotiations about the children of divorce. In reflecting on their critique of the guidelines (at 47-51), consider the extent to which the recommendations for reforming custody and access are consistent with the goals of the *Child Support Guidelines*:]

One of the most frequently mentioned sources of dissatisfaction with the legal mechanism for dividing financial and other responsibilities between parents after separation and divorce was the Federal Child Support Guidelines. ... The guidelines came into force at the same time as the tax treatment of child support was changed so that child support payments are no longer taxable in the hands of the recipient, usually the custodial parent, or deductible by the payor, usually the non-custodial parent.

The guidelines have created conflict in many cases where there had been none: cases long settled were reopened by virtue of the provision that made the existence of the guidelines sufficient to entitle a support recipient to apply to vary the amount of child support being paid. For newly separated parents, the guidelines seem unfair in their exclusive focus on the income of the payor parent. ...

The Federal Child Support Guidelines are generally recognized as having contributed in a positive way to improving predictability with regard to the amount (or "quantum") of child support and to reducing the incentive to argue or litigate over the issue of quantum. However, this was seen as inadequate justification for the extent to which they have increased the conflict between divorcing couples in a number of ways. One of the contentious issues (which was not the direct result of changes stemming from Bill C-41, but was nevertheless part of the controversy around that bill and remains unchanged) relates to the definition of "child of the marriage" in the *Divorce Act*, which has been interpreted judicially to include children over the age of majority (sometimes into their 20s) if they are engaged in post-secondary education. The effect of this judicially established rule has often been to compel non-custodial parents to pay for their children to attend post-secondary institutions, even though parents in intact families obviously are not required to do so. ...

Many presenters asked that the *Divorce Act* be amended to provide that the definition of "the child of the marriage" not include children above the age of majority who are engaged in post-secondary education, save and except those with disabilities or identified as having "special needs." Alternatively, it was suggested by a number of witnesses that the guidelines should allow support payments for such children to be paid directly to the student or to the educational institution. The opposing argument is that children whose parents have divorced often suffer a disadvantage with respect to the financing of post-secondary education. Without a full-scale examination of the topic, given that it was outside the strict mandate of the Committee, Members wish to highlight the issue and raise it for further discussion, but also to emphasize the counter-argument—that children whose parents have divorced will be less likely to be able to continue their education if the definition of "child of the marriage" is changed. As Professor Bala argued:

> Children of divorce find it extremely difficult to pursue post-secondary education. I think having a legal regime there is extremely important. If you would like to amend it so that the money can go directly to the adult child, I think there would be much to be said for that. Indeed, how some judges interpret the legislation has seen them make orders that way already. If you want to clarify the law for people and put that in it, I think that might well be appropriate. I would very strongly urge you not to eliminate that obligation, however, but to simply redefine it. (Meeting #6)

Another of the concerns raised with respect to the Federal Child Support Guidelines is the so-called 40% rule: the section of the Guidelines that provides that where the payor exercises rights of access to, or has custody of, the child for at least 40% of the time in a given year, the quantum of child support is not determined solely on the basis of the amount set out in the table. In such cases, the court will have regard to the table amount, the increased costs associated with the shared custody arrangement, and the conditions, means and other circumstances of the parents and the child. This very contentious provision was intended to give legal recognition to the increased costs borne by a non-residential parent who spends a large amount of time caring for the child. As a number of witnesses said, the rule has had the unfortunate effect of encouraging parents, who might otherwise have agreed, to fight over the residential schedule for the child. ...

Another aspect of this problem is that the guidelines continue to ignore the expenses of the non-custodial parent who provides for and cares for the child during access visits. Non-custodial parents, even those who spend less than 40% of the time with their child, can incur significant expenses. Indeed, arguably they should be encouraged to do so as part of their role as responsible parents. ...

Many witnesses agreed that the 40% figure was too arbitrary, citing cases where fathers spending as much as 38% of the time with children were still required to pay the full amount under the guidelines. Most of these witnesses argued that recognition of non-residential parents' expenses should be based on a range of 20 to 40% of the time, provided there are proven significant expenses. The expenses of these parents when living a significant distance from their children can be particularly burdensome and should not be ignored. For reasons of fairness, the Committee is concerned about the 40% rule and the guidelines' failure to take into account significant parenting expenses. Members are even more disconcerted by the negative impact of the 40% rule on parenting negotiation and decision making. Witnesses asked the Committee to recommend that the Government investigate further how these aspects of the guidelines should be altered.

This Committee, along with the Senate Social Affairs Committee, heard a number of witnesses object strongly to the perceived unfairness of basing child support solely on the income of the payor, without taking the recipient parent's income into account. The pre-guidelines test for the amount of child support to be paid by the non-custodial parent—the apportionment of the costs of raising the child between the parents according to their relative ability to pay—seems to many to be intuitively more reasonable and palatable. Similarly, the guidelines' financial disclosure provisions, which require regular disclosure by the payor to the recipient, apply only to the payor. This apparent inequity rankles non-residential parents, who feel that the concerns of custodial or primary residential parents are being attended to without any government action on non-custodial parents' access enforcement problems. ...

Two other related matters came to the attention of the Committee. One is the mandatory, non-discretionary nature of the guidelines. Even if they wish to, parents are not free to agree to opt out of the support tables or other provisions. Judges will sign child support orders or judgements only if they are satisfied that the requirements of the guidelines have been met. This limit on parents' freedom to settle their affairs by agreement was seen by some as an unreasonable restriction on their ability to make post-separation arrangements for their family as they see fit.

The Committee is also concerned about the impact of the guidelines on parties receiving public assistance. The concern, Members were told, is that in some parts of Canada a recipient parent could be deemed to be in receipt of the amount of child support that had been ordered under the guidelines, even if the support order was in default. The result would be that the support amount would automatically be deducted from that parent's public assistance benefits, potentially leaving the family without adequate funds in the event of non-payment of support. Although the administration of public assistance programs is not within federal legislative jurisdiction, Members of the Committee thought it important that the impact of the guidelines on that type of income be examined carefully.

As consideration of the Federal Child Support Guidelines did not fall strictly within the Committee's mandate, and as the Committee had not actively sought evidence on this topic, most Members of the Committee felt that it would not be appropriate to recommend to the Minister of Justice just how the problems with the guidelines should be corrected. A number of witnesses did not address issues related to the guidelines, or child support more generally, and the Committee expects that many would have if they had been asked to do so. However, given the volume of evidence dealing with concerns related to the guidelines, the Committee felt that our witnesses' objections should be reviewed by the Minister of Justice.

**Faye L. Woodman, "Tax Aspects of the New Child Support Guidelines:
One Year Later"**
(1998), 15 *Canadian Journal of Family Law* 221, at 226-29

[In addition to concerns about the relationship between the *Child Support Guidelines*
and principles concerning custody and access decisions, other criticisms have been
directed to inequities in relation to tax obligations. For example, Faye Woodman
argued that the *Child Support Guidelines* create a number of anomalies in the tax
consequences of child support.]

While the new rules vindicate women's equality concerns and alleviate custodial
spouses from the burden of taxation, they also raise some conventional tax policy/tax
unit questions. Now custodial parents who do not receive child support are even more
disadvantaged. To add insult to injury, not only do they not receive child support, but
they must pay higher taxes than similarly situated single parents who do receive child
support. The anomaly, if there is one, is further exaggerated by the intersection of
child support, the child benefit and social welfare. Since child support is no longer
included in income, it does not reduce the custodial parents' entitlement to the child
tax benefit. (Benefits decrease after family income, defined to include only the custodial parent and children, exceeds approximately $25,000.) On the other hand, child
support most certainly does reduce the amount of social assistance. In most, if not all
provinces, child support replaces social assistance dollar for dollar.

The differing treatments of child support, child tax benefits and social assistance
in the hands of the custodial parent may support a future examination of the new tax
rules. If the economic well-being of children can be measured (directly or indirectly)
for the purposes of some (but not all) social benefits by the income of the custodial
parent, should not child support be included in income? In other words, if we think of
the old system not in terms of subsidy but in terms of measurement of economic
well-being—or ability to pay—it appears somewhat more justifiable and rational.

But then what about the children? Should not children of separated or divorced
parents be treated for tax purposes the same as children of two-partner families? This
similar treatment was, after all, the basis for the constitutional challenge [in *Thibaudeau*]. Surely the unfair burden that the old rules imposed on custodial parents/
women, hence intensifying their already considerable economic disadvantage, could
not be ignored. Nevertheless, alternatives, including adjustments to the old system,
seemed to have been given rather short shrift.

From a more academic perspective, the emphasis of traditional tax policy on ability to pay and horizontal and vertical equity may to some degree be incongruent with
evolving theories of equality under the Charter. In the tax area, some feminist commentators have posited an approach which emphasizes group equality rights over or
in addition to tax equity. Under that approach, fairness in the tax system also requires
an examination of the impact of the taxation system on groups taking into account
gender, sexual orientation, race, disability, and other characteristics. Thus the inclu-
sion/deduction system would be examined critically with the understanding that

ninety-eight per cent of the deductions for child support are claimed by men and ninety-eight per cent of the inclusions were made by women.

The reasoning in *Thibaudeau* still stands. *Thibaudeau* with *Symes* are the two cases decided by the Supreme Court concerning "women and taxation." In both cases, the women "lost." In neither case was the majority prepared to address directly the concept of women's inequality under the tax system. While *Thibaudeau*, unlike *Symes*, generated a legislative response, the legislation itself presents concerns and contradictions which are not easily resolved.

In this context, moreover, a number of criticisms have been directed to the *Child Support Guidelines* in relation to their impact on child poverty. Clearly, the implementation of the guidelines was intended to assure that children of divorce receive ongoing support from their parents. Yet, as with the situation for spousal support, discussed in chapter 7, the result is that children whose payor parent is of only modest means or unemployed, ill, or disabled will be entitled to much less support than children whose payor parent is a high-income hockey player or lawyer. Thus, the inequities in the financial well-being of intact families are reproduced for the children of divorce, undoubtedly exacerbated by the need to provide for two households, not just one. In these circumstances, a number of critiques have focused on the ways in which the *Child Support Guidelines* have reprivatized economic support for families and children. For example, consider the following critique—what are the appropriate responses?

Paul Millar and Anne H. Gauthier, "What Were They Thinking? The Development of Child Support Guidelines in Canada"
(2002), 17:1 *Canadian Journal of Law and Society* 139, at 157-58

Although child poverty is a major social problem, it is unlikely that child support will play a major role in the solution to that problem. Child poverty exists among poor families. Fathers of the children of poor never-married mothers are also likely to be from a similar social background. When a poor family breaks up, there are extra costs because of the existence of two households instead of one. This is especially true when both parents want to remain active in their children's lives and need accommodation for themselves and their children. Thus the reliance on child support to reduce child poverty puts a large amount of financial strain on one of two poor parents. So while child and spousal support is useful to share financial difficulties pursuant to divorce, it is unlikely to bring a large proportion of divorced custodial parents out of poverty. ...

Child support collected may not even benefit the other parent, but may instead go to replace social benefits that have been accessed by the recipient parent. In this way, child support represents a major initiative to privatize social benefits. This is likely to increase economic stratification, not reduce it. To put it another way, this is a method of circumventing the progressive taxation system by taxing those who can least afford it. Child support, appropriately implemented, may be useful for reducing inequities after divorce among middle and upper class families, where the children are not poor, but unreasonably large amounts and severe enforcement measures may be detrimental to economic stratification for the poor and working classes. One study of low income non-custodial parents who were behind in their support payments found that while these low income parents were desperately looking for opportunities to work, they suffered from feelings of powerlessness and social and economic isolation. The vast majority had extremely tenuous living arrangements. ...

[See E.S. Johnson and F. Doolittle, "Low-Income Parents and the Parent's Fair Share Program," in I. Garfinkel et al., eds., *Fathers Under Fire: The Revolution in Child Support Enforcement* (New York: Russell Sage, 1998), 253, at 274-75.]

Child support regimes must be carefully implemented in light of these limitations, or the results may be harmful, rather than beneficial to children of poor parents. Child poverty needs a predominantly public approach to be effective—heavy reliance on private support will not produce the desired results.

The insidious aspect of using child support to deal with child poverty is that government and society are now off the hook, since the cause of poverty no longer appears to lie with government or social policy. Rather, a parent's poverty is the fault of a former spouse, someone he or she is no doubt already disposed to blame. Claiming lack of child support as the cause, and increased child support as the cure, of child poverty in Canada will most likely increase hostility between divorced spouses, while removing the impetus for society to assist with the problem. Poor families, by themselves, are not likely to pull themselves out of poverty. To insist otherwise only makes poverty increase.

See also Richard Shillington, "Child Poverty and the Benefit of an Illusion" (Summer 1999), *Canadian Perspectives* 14.

PROBLEM

Children ... need the cultural capital that will help them to manage the personal and social transformations associated with family change. We have argued that in seeking to create family policies more suited to the 2000s than the 1950s, we need to import different ethical guidelines, as well as starting to attend more closely to what children say.

> Carol Smart, Bren Neale, and Amanda Wade, *The Changing Experience of Childhood: Families and Divorce* (Cambridge, Polity Press, 2001), 173

Civil society must be built and re-built everyday around the nation's kitchen tables. Neither individuals nor the larger society can hope to survive, much less thrive, without the many gifts and benefits that family members give each other.

> Robert Glossop, "Families as Architects of a Civil Society" (Spring 2004), *Transition* (Vanier Institute of the Family), 3, at 3

In thinking about the views excerpted above, identify the problems and possibilities in current legal principles concerning the children of divorce. Consider how these principles about caregiving and financial support could be better integrated and the extent to which these issues require public, as well as private, support. Assume that you are asked to provide advice to the federal minister of justice about Bill C-22. What would be the key elements of your advice?

CHAPTER REFERENCES

Abbate, Gay. "Nygard Support Case Ends with Settlement," *Globe and Mail*, March 19, 2004, A11.

American Law Institute. *Principles of the Law of Family Dissolution: Analysis and Recommendations* (Washington, DC: Matthew Bender, 2002).

Arnup, Katherine. " 'Mothers Just Like Others': Lesbians, Divorce, and Child Custody in Canada" (1989), 3 *Canadian Journal of Women and the Law* 18.

Bailey, M. and M. Giroux. *Relocation of Custodial Parents* (Ottawa: Status of Women Canada, 1998).

Bailey, Martha J. "Custody, Access, and Religion: A Comment on Young v. Young and D.P. v. C.S." (1994), 11 *Canadian Family Law Quarterly* 317.

Bailey, Martha and Nicholas Bala. "Assessing Compliance with the UN Convention on the Rights of the Child" (Ottawa: June 4, 1998) (unpublished presentation to Canadian Association of Law Teachers [CALT] Family Section).

_____. "Canada and the UN Convention on the Rights of the Child: How Do We Measure Up?" in *Canada's Children* (Child Welfare League of Canada, Summer 1999).

_____. "Child Support Guidelines, Parental Mobility, and Redefining Familial Relationships," in A. Bainham, ed., *The International Survey of Family Law 1996* (The Netherlands: International Society of Family Law, 1998).

Bala, Nicholas. "The Best Interests of the Child in the Post-Modern Era: A Central but Paradoxical Concept," in Harold Niman and Gerald P. Sadvari, eds., *Special Lectures of the Law Society of Upper Canada 2000—Family Law: "Best Interests of the Child"* (Toronto: Law Society of Upper Canada, 2001), 1.

Birnbaum, Rachel, Elizabeth L. McCarty, and Wilson A. McTavish. "Haider v. Malach: Child Custody Guidelines Gone Awry?" (2000-1), 18 *Canadian Family Law Quarterly* 357.

Black, Vaughan and Christopher Jones. "Case Comment on Thomson v. Thomson" (1994-95), 12 *Canadian Family Law Quarterly* 321.

Blown, N. and S. Milliken. "The Failure of the Legal System To Protect the Economic Rights of Children" (1989), 7 *Canadian Journal of Family Law* 366.

Boutet, Nathalet and Christine Kish. "Income Determinations Under the Child Support Guidelines: A Case Law Review" (2000-1), 19 *Canadian Family Law Quarterly* 283.

Boyd, Susan B. *Child Custody, Law, and Women's Work* (Toronto: Oxford University Press, 2003).

_____. "From Gender Specificity to Gender Neutrality? Ideologies in Canadian Child Custody Law," in Carol Smart and Selma Sevenhuijsen, eds., *Child Custody and the Politics of Gender* (London: Routledge, 1989), 126.

_____. "Potentialities and Perils of the Primary Caregiver Presumption" (1990-91), 7 *Canadian Family Law Quarterly* 1.

Canada, Department of Justice. *Federal Child Support Guidelines Reference Manual* (Ottawa: Supply and Services Canada, 1998).

_____. *Custody and Access: Public Discussion Paper* (Ottawa: Supply and Services Canada, 1993).

Canadian Council on Social Development. *The Progress of Canada's Children 1998* (Ottawa: Canadian Council on Social Development, 1998).

Carbone, June. "Child Support Comes of Age: An Introduction to the Law of Child Support," in J. Thomas Oldham and Marygold S. Melli, eds., *Child Support: The Next Frontier* (Ann Arbor, MI: University of Michigan Press, 2000).

Cossman, Brenda. "Developments in Family Law: The 1999-2000 Term" (2000), 13 *Supreme Court Law Review* (2d) 307.

Crean, Susan. *In the Name of the Fathers: The Story Behind Child Custody* (Toronto: Amanita Publications, 1988).

Daisley, Brad. "DNA Evidence: It Makes Headlines in Criminal Trials, but Lawyers Use It in Custody and Immigration Cases Too," *The Lawyers Weekly*, February 26, 1993.

Davies, Christine. "The Emergence of Judicial Child Support Guidelines" (1995), 13 *Canadian Family Law Quarterly* 89.

Emery, R. *Renegotiating Family Relationships: Divorce, Child Custody, and Mediation* (New York: Guilford Press, 1994).

Federal/Provincial/Territorial Family Law Committee. *Child Support: Public Discussion Paper* (Ottawa: Department of Justice, 1991).

Freeman, Rhonda. "Parenting After Divorce: Using Research To Inform Decision-Making About Children" (1998), 15 *Canadian Journal of Family Law* 79.

Glendon, Mary Ann. *The Transformation of Family Law: State, Law, and Family in the United States and Western Europe* (Chicago and London: University of Chicago Press, 1989).

Glossop, Robert. "Families as Architects of a Civil Society" (Spring 2004), *Transition* (Vanier Institute of the Family) 3.

Gordon, Jane. "Multiple Meanings of Equality: A Case Study in Custody Litigation" (1989), 3 *Canadian Journal of Women and the Law* 256

Hainsworth, Terry W. "Support for Adult Children" (1997), 17 *Canadian Family Law Quarterly* 39.

Hogg, Peter W. *Constitutional Law of Canada* (Toronto: Carswell) (looseleaf).

Holmes, Sheila. "Imposed Joint Legal Custody: Children's Interests or Parental Rights?" (1987), 45 *University of Toronto Faculty of Law Review* 300.

Hornick, Joseph P., Lorne D. Bertrand, and Nicholas M.C. Bala. *The Survey of Child Support Awards: Final Analysis of Pilot Data and Recommendations for Continued Data Collection* (Ottawa: Minister of Justice, 1999).

Huddart, Carol Mahood and Jeanne Charlotte Ensminger. "Hearing the Voice of Children" (1992), 8 *Canadian Family Law Quarterly* 95.

Lakey, Jack and Moira Walsh. "Lastman's Secret Affair Shocks City," *The Toronto Star*, December 1, 2000, A1 and A10.

Leonoff, A. "Joint Custody and Beyond" (1995), 29:1 *Law Society Gazette* 29.

Maccoby, Eleanor and Robert Mnookin. *Dividing the Child* (Cambridge, MA: Harvard University Press, 1992).

McLaren, Leah. "The Kids (of Divorce) Are All Right," *Globe and Mail*, September 11, 1999, D1 and D6.

McLeod, James. "Annotation of Chartier v. Chartier" (1999), 43 RFL (4th) 2.

_____. "Annotation of Sullivan v. Sullivan" (1999), 50 RFL (4th) 326.

Meyer, Cheryl L. "Legal, Psychological, and Medical Considerations in Lesbian Parenting" (1992), 2 *Law and Sexuality* 237.

Millar, Paul and Anne H. Gauthier. "What Were They Thinking? The Development of Child Support Guidelines in Canada" (2002), 17:1 *Canadian Journal of Law and Society* 139.

Parker, Stephen. "The Best Interests of the Child—Principles and Problems" (1994), 8 *International Journal of Law and the Family* 26.

Payne, J.D. "Child Support Under the Federal Child Support Guidelines" (QL DB PDCS).

_____. "Spousal and Child Support After Moge, Willick and Levesque" (1995), 12 *Canadian Family Law Quarterly* 261.

Rhoades, Helen. "The Rise and Rise of Shared Parenting Laws: A Critical Reflection" (2002), 19 *Canadian Journal of Family Law* 75.

Rogerson, Carol. "The Child Support Obligations of Step-Parents" (2001), 18:1 *Canadian Journal of Family Law* 9.

_____. "Child Support Under the Guidelines in Cases of Split and Shared Custody" (1998), 15 *Canadian Journal of Family Law* 11.

_____. "Judicial Interpretation of the Spousal and Child Support Provisions of the Divorce Act, 1985 (Part II)" (1991), 7 *Canadian Family Law Quarterly* 271.

Schmitz, Cristin. "BC Children Awarded Record $59,000 Monthly Support," *The Lawyers Weekly*, June 22, 2001, 3.

Shillington, Richard. "Child Poverty and the Benefit of an Illusion" (Summer 1999), *Canadian Perspectives* 14.

Smart, Carol, Bren Neale, and Amanda Wade. *The Changing Experience of Childhood: Families and Divorce* (Cambridge: Polity Press, 2001).

Special Joint Committee on Child Custody and Access. *For the Sake of the Children* (Ottawa: Parliament of Canada, 1998).

Thompson, D.A. Rollie. "An Addendum: Twenty Months Later," in Harold Niman and Gerald P. Sadvari, eds., *Special Lectures of the Law Society of Upper Canada 2000—Family Law: "Best Interests of the Child"* (Toronto: Law Society of Upper Canada, 2001), 352.

_____. "Relocation and Relitigation: After Gordon v. Goertz" (1999), 16:3 *Canadian Family Law Quarterly* 461.

_____. "The Second Family Conundrum in Child Support" (2001), 18 *Canadian Journal of Family Law* 227.

_____. "Who Wants To Avoid the Guidelines? Contracting Out and Around" (2001), 19 *Canadian Family Law Quarterly* 1.

"Was Pierre Trudeau a Busy Guy?" *Globe and Mail*, March 5, 1994.

Whitehead, Barbara Dafoe. "Dan Quayle Was Right," *The Atlantic Monthly*, April 1993, 47.

Wilson, Jeffery. "The Forgotten Child: Children Who Have Withdrawn from Parental Control" (presentation to the Continuing Education Program of LSUC—OBA (Family Law Section), Toronto, May 2 and 3, 2002).

Woodman, Faye L. "Tax Aspects of the New Child Support Guidelines: One Year Later" (1998), 15 *Canadian Journal of Family Law* 221.

Epilogue

Susan B. Boyd, "Legal Regulation of Families in Changing Societies"
in Austin Sarat, ed., *The Blackwell Companion to Law and Society*
(London: Blackwell, 2004), 255, at 265

Precisely because laws on the family have changed so radically since the 1970s, and because the ways in which law regulates family transcend disciplinary boundaries within law itself, family law offers a perfect terrain for sociolegal studies. ...

Studies on family law show that law's impact within society in any particular instance is difficult to predict and there is no necessary causal relationship between legislative change and social, or even legal, outcomes. Sending positive messages by encouraging processes such as mediation or using new legal terminology such as "joint custody" or "parental responsibility" has not succeeded in changing [behaviour] or making parents share responsibilities. Despite the intent of parenting law reformers to reduce conflict and enhance shared parental responsibilities, conflict and litigation have increased and most children still reside primarily with their mothers. ... Drawing on this lesson, Dewar and Parker* suggest that legislative messages regarding parental responsibilities are heard differently by different audiences. ...

A related important insight, at a more systemic level, is that family law's capacity to deal with deeply rooted social problems such as the sexual division of [labour], or child poverty (which is usually closely related to parental poverty) is limited unless it is integrated with accompanying social policy changes. Studies suggest that male participation in childcare would be encouraged more effectively by adequate public policy on and support for familial responsibilities outside a patriarchal framework than by legally enacting shared parenting norms in relation to postseparation parenting. There is a growing sense that family law has been asked to solve too many deeply rooted economic and social problems, when it is only a microcosm of a much more complex social system that influences familial relations.

Another lesson gleaned from examination of legal regulation of family issues is that withdrawal of law from a social field may require the study of effects or constraints

---

* J. Dewar and S. Parker, "The Impact of the New Part VII Family Law Act 1975" (1999), 13 *Australian Journal of Family Law* 96.

as they emerge in other areas. For instance, the trends in some jurisdictions to decriminalize abortion and protect women's reproductive choice from veto by male partners did not eliminate the difficulties that women experience in exercising meaningful choice concerning abortion. ... These obstacles point to the need for researchers to attend to material and ideological constraints on individual autonomy as well as the limits of law in resolving social problems.

The best law and society scholarship places law and law reform in a context that explores its contradictions, limits, and possibilities, as well as its relationship to power. As we have seen, numerous contradictions arise within modern family law, for example, between the new emphasis on biological parenthood, especially paternity, for the purposes of assigning child support obligations, and the new emphasis on social parenting evidenced, for instance, in the so-called "second mother" adoptions. Such contradictions raise the question of whether one family law can accommodate the variety of familial forms now existing, both within and outside the traditional, heterosexual, nuclear definition of family. ... These trends challenge sociolegal scholars to confront fragmentation and contradiction in family law, while keeping in mind the social relations of power. ... The challenge for twenty-first century scholars is to assess what the role of family law can be within a less clearly status-based system, but one that rests on various social hierarchies still related to persistent, if shifting, power relations of gender, race, class, and sexuality.